66Jay Warner takes us through singing group history from the '30s all the way to the '90s with a wealth of information that has never before appeared all in one place. I am proud to be included among so many of my favorite performers. This book will be enjoyed by all music history fans like myself.**99**

TONY ORLANDO, TONY ORLANDO AND DAWN

66Reading this book was like taking a journey back into my musical past greeting old friends.**99**

PATTI LaBELLE, PATTI LaBELLE AND THE BLUE BELLES

66This archival and entertaining book by Jay Warner supplies the missing link that was needed to complete the fascinating history and evolution of singing groups. A massive gathering of information that was nearly lost through the passage of time. An invaluable 'bible' for ourselves and for many generations to come. Obviously a labor of love. Congratulations.**99**

JOHN PHILLIPS, THE MAMAS AND THE PAPAS

66This book is an overdue tribute to vocal groups. I was amazed to discover just how much influence singing groups have had on the origin and development of today's musical styles, from R&B and soul to rock and roll to pop, not to mention the impressive list of solo artists who spent their early years in a group.**99**

DONNY OSMOND, THE OSMONDS

66Jay, I'm impressed! Thanks for caring enough to dig in deep and bring out so many interesting and entertaining facts about so many of the artists we all love and want to know more about. This book is a treasure for all who love American vocal groups—and a must-have for all of us who sing.**99**

SHIRLEY ALSTON REEVES, THE SHIRELLES

66All I can say is, thank God! I'm thrilled to see that the rich history of singing groups will not fade away.**99**

MELVIN FRANKLIN, THE TEMPTATIONS

66Congratulations! You have done what should have been done long ago. Your stories on the formation and careers of our classic vocal groups are concise, exciting, and accurate. Great history, great reading.**99**

TIM HAUSER, THE MANHATTAN TRANSFER

66It's about time somebody told the true story of America's singing groups. These are some of the most in-depth and well-researched biographies we have ever read.**99**

LEN BARRY, JERRY GROSS, MARK STEVENS, THE DOVELLS

66*Billboard* magazine, known for its awareness of the music scene, has again lived up to its rep by reaching out to the qualified and competent. This time they selected Jay Warner. He did his homework, y'all. Warner's research brings to life the human drama that had such a profound effect on the lives of the singers that made up the groups. I especially applaud Warner's attempt to sift through the rubble of rumors and hearsay, separating facts from fiction.**99**

EZEKIEL "ZEKE" CAREY, THE FLAMINGOS

66You always hear about new books on music history, but they rarely fulfill your hopes. This one is head and shoulders above the rest. A monumental achievement. As a pretty good historian myself, I have to admit that nobody has done it quite as well as Jay.**99**

JERRY BUTLER, JERRY BUTLER AND THE IMPRESSIONS

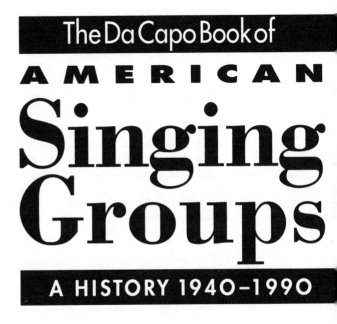

The Da Capo Book of

AMERICAN

Singing Groups

A HISTORY 1940–1990

JAY WARNER

DA CAPO PRESS

To my Dad and Mom,
Robert Wayne Warner and
Ray Lillian Blackstein

First published 1992 as *The Billboard Book of American Singing Groups*, by Billboard Books, an imprint of Watson-Guptill Publications, a division of BPI Communications, Inc., 1515 Broadway, New York, NY 10036

Library of Congress Cataloging in Publication Data

Warner, Jay.
  [Billboard book of American singing groups]
  The Da Capo book of American singing groups : a history, 1940–1990 / Jay Warner.—
1st Da Capo Press ed.
    p. cm.
  Originally published: The Billboard book of American singing groups. New York :
Billboard Books, 1992.
  ISBN 0-306-80923-0 (pbk.)
    1. Popular music—United States—Bio-bibliography. I. Title.
ML106.U3 W2 2000
782.42164'0973—dc21

                                    00–020606

First Da Capo Press Edition 2000

Published by Da Capo Press
A Member of the Perseus Books Group
http://www.dacapopress.com

1 2 3 4 5 6 7 8 9 10——04 03 02 01 00

Contents

THE 1940s 1

THE 1950s 63

THE 1960s   321

THE **1970s** 477

THE **1980s** 519

Foreword

When I was asked to write a foreword for this book it set in motion a time machine of memories. Many of the vocal groups Jay Warner has written about are old friends, and I've crossed paths with hundreds of these acts at various times in their careers. Of course, vocal groups hold a special place in my heart, but I believe that anyone who's ever sung with a friend or two, or just enjoyed listening to an act that happened to be a singing group, can appreciate the unique feeling that harmony brings to all forms of music. Barbershop, pop, gospel, blues, jazz, rock and roll, country, rhythm and blues, soul, folk, hip-hop, and any combination of styles you can think of, all benefited from and grew popular because of attempts by trios, quartets, quintets, and sextets to find that perfect wave, their own perfect harmony and style.

Behind all those harmonies and styles are stories of human interest. Each and every group had something to contribute to music history, even if many didn't become the successes the Ink Spots, the Beach Boys, the Supremes, and the Bangles were. Maybe that's what makes vocal groups fascinating. The big acts are always interesting, but lesser-known groups (who often contributed future solo stars) made their mark as well. What has kept all of these groups confined to a place in history based only on the type of music they sang or how successful they were is the fact that there has been no reference work that put them all together in one place, where the big and small, the hits and the misses, could be seen side by side for what they did and how they did it. I remember the struggles and fears, the one-nighters and grueling tours, the frustration and exhilaration of recording sessions, the elation of hitting the charts, the good and bad performance venues, the TV show turmoils, the extremely hard work and rehearsals, the light moments and the good times, the ironies, the coincidences, and the transient nature of vocal groups that often required one to have a score card. I remember these things, not only about my own group but about all the groups we met, performed with, grew up with, or watched retire before us.

So does Jay Warner. He's captured it all here, but most importantly he's given a sense of independence, importance, and dignity to an area of music never before addressed as an entity unto itself in book form. In a positive light, he's summarized their contributions and detailed their struggles in a comprehensive, accurate, up-to-date history. It's gratifying to see the groups getting some long-overdue recognition. Having come from a vocal quartet I can appreciate what Jay has done by virtue of creating this momentous encyclopedia: by finally setting down, between these covers, the full history of American vocal groups, he has provided historians with a platform on which to build and chronicle the groups of the future. I've never been so thoroughly entertained while being informed. My only real complaint is: Jay—what took you so long?

Frankie Valli
The Four Seasons

Preface

Being a teenager in Brooklyn, New York, during the dawning of the 1960s was an exciting time. I divided my days between getting an education my parents' way (high school, college, and that looming-on-the-horizon career decision) and getting an education *my* way (which girl to date, how to put the ball into left field, and which record to buy). Well, girls came and went and base hits became numbers in a composition book, but all of a sudden I was consumed by an interest in music—both the listening and the buying of it. The more I listened, the more I bought, and the more I bought, the more I wanted to find more to buy. I started collecting records on June 15, 1960 (true collectors keep track of such things), buying my first 45 rpm single, "The Mule Skinner Blues" by the Fendermen, in a little record shop on Nostrand Avenue in Brooklyn. Those seven-inch discs of plastic and paper labels not only held magic sounds, but even felt exciting to the touch. Grabbing a pile and rummaging through the variety of colored labels became a passion. The royal blue of Apollo, the jet black of Onyx, the bright red of Ember, the stark black and silver of Argo, and the smooth blue and silver of Chess provided a rainbow of colors that I escaped into after days in school and afternoons in the outfield. I kept track of every record I bought and the date I bought it, even numbering the records until it became too time-consuming to do so (after about 2,500 singles). I bought country, rock and roll, blues, sound effects, classical, jazz, R&B, themes, doo wop, film soundtracks, female vocals, groups—in short, if I liked it and it was for sale, I bought it.

Eventually I developed a preference for group records. Not groups as we think of them today, with high-tech electronic keyboards, stick guitars, and wireless mikes, but vocal groups—four or five guys standing around a stationary microphone or in an echoed hall hitting harmony that tingles your skin. Floating falsettos, simple and complex "blow" harmonies or "doo-wah" midrange, a two- or three-part background, and a solid bass vocal pattern, all served to bring the lead singer's sound to life. If music in general was a passion for me, vocal groups became an obsession. Listening was no longer enough. By the end of the '60s I had amassed hundreds of magazines, books, photos, and 15,000 records, most all of which were associated with or recorded by vocal groups. Apart from collecting, listening to, and analyzing the music, I began to read all I could find that related to it, just for enjoyment. Going to vocal group shows and singing in my own group covered the participation phase, and I eventually founded the Rock N Roll Music Association (RRMA), which helped support the hobby. But the next logical step had to wait until 1988.

I would like to say this book came out of a premeditated and specific plan, but it didn't. It grew out of necessity and frustration, for while I was continuing to collect all kinds of vocal group recordings and information, as time went on I found it harder and harder to come by such things. As you'll see in this book, the '40s, '50s, and '60s were considered the glory days of vocal groups. The '70s were dismal, but I was too busy catching up on what I'd missed from the earlier decades to notice how slim the pickings were. And even though they were an improvement from the '70s, the '80s still left much to be desired.

Books on the subject were even harder to find than records. In a country where someone has written something on just about everything, there was nothing devoted strictly to vocal groups. Encyclopedias of rock and roll abound. Histories of the blues, jazz, and country are numerous. Biographies of individual musicians and bands are published in volume after overlapping volume. But in a world that is more music-conscious than ever, there has never been a history of vocal groups.

I set out to fill the gap by writing *The Billboard Book of American Singing Groups*.

Deciding on the scope of the book presented a challenge right at the outset, since without restrictions it could easily spill over into multiple editions. To keep it a manageable size, and to make it a reference work that would also entertain, I've aimed for a balance of well-known groups and obscure-but-interesting ones, while not attempting to list every group in history. The period covered is from the early 1940s (when most music historians acknowledge the vocal group sound came into its own) through 1990. Only American singing groups are listed (except for a few nearby Canadians) since the vocal group sound is mainly of U.S. origin. In terms of musical style I have kept the focus on pop, R&B, doo wop, gospel, jazz, rock and roll, and soul, with an occasional foray into folk and country groups who I felt may have spent more time practicing a vocal modulation than tuning their guitar strings. (My definition of a vocal group, by the way, is three or more people singing in harmony—in other words, more than a duet and less than a chorus.) A further requirement for inclusion in this book is that the group recorded one or more released 45 rpm records or at least one LP.

Since the entries are arranged alphabetically within separate decades, the decision for listing a group in a particular decade was usually based on the year the performing or recording career began. However, certain acts that covered several decades and began in the later part of one (for example, the Impressions started in 1958) are listed in the first decade of their greatest activity (and for the Impressions that was the 1960s).

The *Billboard* charts played an important part in the history of vocal groups. Founded in 1894, *Billboard* published an ever-evolving popularity survey that included lists of best-selling sheet music and the "Best-Selling Retail Records" chart (starting in 1940). Other charts included "Most Played in Juke Boxes" (ending in 1957), "Best Sellers in Stores" (up until 1958), and "Most Played by Jockeys" (through July 1958). *Billboard*'s "Top 100" chart debuted in 1955 and changed to the all-encompassing "Hot 100" in August 1958. Many of these differently titled listings are cited throughout this book in discussions of particular songs.

Other charts mentioned in the following vocal group histories include the "Bubbling Under" list (covering records that charted below the top 100) and the chart for rhythm and blues music. The latter has gone by such different names as "Hot R&B Sides," "Best-Selling Rhythm & Blues Singles," and "Hot Black Singles," but is referred to in this book simply as "R&B." England and Australia have their own pop charts, and they are cited where applicable.

Singing groups are cross-referenced throughout this book. When an entry cites a group that has its own separate entry, that group's name is printed in capital letters the first time it appears.

As with any undertaking of this size, mistakes can creep in. If any knowledgeable person has corrections or additions, I invite them to address them to me in care of the publisher.

The vocal group sound is an American art form that is becoming a forgotten part of our heritage. If this book helps in any way to pass the enjoyment and knowledge of the pop harmony tradition from one generation to another, then it will have been worth every ounce of the effort and every minute of the time it took to compile it.

Acknowledgments

A very special thank you to the following groups, vocalists, and their associates who provided information and corroboration that distinguished the facts from the myths: Bob Alcivar (the Signatures), Sean Altman (Rockapella), Linda Amato (the Chaperones), Gilda Maiken Anderson (the Skylarks), Maxene Andrews (the Andrews Sisters), H.B. Barnum (the Dootones), Sir Norman Bergen (the Tokens), Mickey Borack (Tico and the Triumphs), Eddie Brian (the Ducanes), Bob Burmeister (Déjà Vu), Norman Burnett (the Tymes), Tony Butala (the Lettermen), Jerry Butler (the Impressions), Nick Caldwell (the Whispers), Stephen Caldwell (the Orlons), Zeke Carey (the Flamingos), Les Cauchi (the Del-Satins), George Chacona (the Saints), Pete Chacona (the Exquisites), Herbie Cox (the Cleftones), Dom D'Elia (the Sparrows Quartette), Lenny Dell (the Demensions), Kenny Demmo (the Paramounts), Joe DiBenidetto (the Four-Evers), Henry Farag (Stormy Weather), Bob Flanigan (the Four Freshmen), Harvey Fuqua (the Moonglows), Bob Gaudio (the Four Seasons), Ron Gitman (the Magnificent Men), Zack Glickman (the Mighty Clouds of Joy), Bruce Goldie (the Dreamers), "Little Anthony" Gourdine (the Imperials), Dobie Gray (Pollution), Ken Greengrass (the Highwaymen), Dickie Harman (the Del-Vikings), Wilbur Hart (the Delfonics), Tim Hauser (the Manhattan Transfer, the Criterions), Bobby Hepburn (Memory), Renee Hinton (the Capris), Frank Iovine (the Five Boroughs), "Big D" Irwin (the Pastels), Adam Jackson (the Jesters), Claude Johnson (the Genies), David Johnson (Little Caesar and the Romans), Marty Kaniger (Big Daddy), Dee Dee Kennibrew (the Crystals), Ben E. King (the Drifters), John Kuse (the Excellents), Richie LeCausi (the Imaginations), Jerry Gross and Len Barry (the Dovells), Mike Lewis (the Concords), Ginny Mancini (the Meltones), Phil and Mitch Margo (the Tokens), Lee Maye (the Crowns), Reparata Mazzola (Lady Flash, Reparata and the Delrons), Gene McDaniels (the Admirals), Phyllis McGuire (the McGuire Sisters), Carolyn McMichael (the Merry Macs), Donny Osmond (the Osmonds), Olive Osmond (the Osmonds), Richard Perry (the Escorts), Vito Picone (the Elegants), Jerry Pilgrim (B.Q.E.), Val Poliuto (the Jaguars), Gene Puerling (the Hi-Los), Teddy Randazzo (the Three Chuckles), Mike Regan (the Camelots), L.J. Reynolds (the Dramatics), Earnestine Rundless (the Meditation Singers), Nick Santa Maria (the Capris), Jack Scandura (the Blendairs, Ricky and the Hallmarks), Jay Siegel (the Tokens), Scott Simon (Sha Na Na), Jo Stafford (the Pied Pipers), Jack Strong (the Lytations), Glenny T (Fourteen Karat Soul), Spencer Taylor, Jr. (the Highway QCs), Joe Terry (Danny and the Juniors), Robert Therier (Norman Fox and the Rob-Roys), Freddy Toscano (the Ribitones), Bill Tracy (the Modernaires), Frankie Valli (the Four Seasons), Michael Wendroff (the Holidays), Maurice Williams (the Zodiacs, the Gladiolas), J.B. Willingham (the Pastels), and Jim Woods (Mixed Company).

Additionally, this book could not have been written without the help of the following industry people, organizations, record collectors, and dealers: Paul Adler (ASCAP), Pete Antell, Dr. Dave Antrell, Sam Atchley, David Babcock (Motown Records), Carolyn Baker (Warner Brothers Records), John Bauer and Peter Bennett (The Four Seasons Partnership), Shelly Berger (Star Directions Inc.), Steve Blitenthal (Whirlin' Disc Records), Todd Brabeck (ASCAP), Nathaniel Brewster (Sony Records), Don Butler (Gospel Music Society), Tony Camillo (T.C. Records), Nancy Carroll, Al Cattabiani (Avenue D Records), Geary Chansley (MCA Records), Michelle Cooper (Shakeji Inc.), Walter DeVenne, Mark Edmunds (Baytown Records), Leigh Ann Ericson, Henry Farag (Canterbury Records), Donn Fileti (Relic Records), Marilyn Freeman (Liaison II Music), John Goddard (Village Music), Jamie Goldberg (East-West Records), Eddie Gries (Relic Records), Phil Groia (Phillie Dee Productions), Arthur Hamilton (ASCAP), Tony Hart (KGFJ Radio), Martha Hertzberg (Ken Fritz Management), Terri Hinte (Fantasy Records), Julie Horowitz, Joe Isgro (Private I Records), Ronnie "I" Italiano (The United in Group Harmony Association), Michele Johnson (Warner Brothers Records), Fred Kaplan (Memory Lane Records), Joel S. Katz, Ken and Joe (Rhythm Records), Morty Kraft (Warwick Records), Bob Kretzschmar (Starlight Records), Julie Larson (Richard Perry Productions), Floyd Lieberman (SAS Inc.), Kenya Love (Shakeji Inc.), Carolyn

Marrujo (Warner Brothers Records), David Mc-Cullough (Grafixation), Andy McKaie (MCA Records), Charles McMillan, John Mistler (Sister Sledge), Bernadette Moore (RCA Records), John Moore (Middle Room Records), Julie Moss (Motown Records), Richard Nader (Richard Nader Enterprises), Bill O'Conner (The Topps Company, Inc.), Sid Ordower, Bruce Patch (Classic Artists Records), Nancy Portner (Stiefel Phillips Entertainment), Kevin "Computer" Quinn, Vince Ravine, Ray Regalado, Larry Richard (Legends Gallery), Rick Ricobono (BMI), Alan Rubens, Rick Sanjek (BMI), Vickie Scarborough, Jay Schwartz (Ken Fritz Management), Sid Seidenberg (SAS Inc.), Ron Shapiro (MCA Records), Billy Shibilski (Mellomood Records), Val Shively (R&B Records), Dr. John Stalberg, Wayne Thompson, Bob Tucker, Veda's Magical Typing, Hy Weiss (Old Town Records), Linda Wells (Bugle Boy Productions), Paul Wexler (Atlantic Records), Thad Whyte (Sister Sledge), Frank Williams (Malaco Records), Sandy Woolbright, and Jerry Zidel (Starlight Records).

Also, my sincerest appreciation to *Billboard* magazine and to John Babcock, Jr., Tad Lathrop, and Fred Weiler for believing in the project. Lastly, my everlasting love and appreciation to my wife, Jackie, for her patience and encouragement over the three years it took me to make this dream come true.

I would also like to express my appreciation for the myriad of historians, authors, and columnists who have contributed to the subject matter and have kept interest in vocal groups alive long before I thought to write about them. Just some of those are: Roy Adams, Frank Aita, Jason Amal, Will Anderson, Guy Aoki, John Apostle, Steve Applebaum, John Apugliese, Sr., Chris Beachley, Jeff Beckman, Bob Belniak, Sandy Benjamin, Stephen Bennett, Ken Berger, Jeff Bleiel, Robert Bosco, Jane Bradley, Larry Cedilnik, Phil Chaney, Ken Cohen, Phil Craig, Lisa Anne Culp, Tony D'Ambrosio, Bill Dahl, Hank Davis, Jim Davis, Jim Dawson, Jack Day, Tony DeLura, Nick DeMeo, Bob Diskins, Richard W. Dunn, Ed Engel, Hank Feigenbaum, Richard Ferlingere, Donn Fileti, Steve Flam, Ray Funk, Maxim Furek, Rick Gagnon, Bob Galgano, R. Anthony Galgano, Dennis Garvey, Bob Getreuer, Dave Gnerre, Marv Goldberg, Walter Gollender, Ferdy Gonzalez, Peter Grendysa, Spider Harrison, Paul Heller, Donna Hennings, Lee Hildebrand, Randal C. Hill, Dave Hinckley, Emory Holmes, Charlie Horner, James Hunt, Ronnie "I" Italiano, Wayne Jancik, Carl and Nancy Janusek, Bjorn Jentoft, Wayne Jones, Mark Kearney, Curt Krafft, Arlene Kramer, Jeff Kreiter, Joseph F. Laredo, Alan Lee, Mark Linder, Tom Luciano, Jean Charles Marion, Don Mennie, Greg Milewski, Bill Millar, Sal Mondrone, George Moonoogian, Jim Muskewitz, Nay Nasser, Ralph M. Newman, Dan Nooger, Debbie Papio, Mike Piazza, Marvin Podd, J. Poet, Herman Pruitt, Robert Pruter, John Pugh, Mike Rascio, Randy Ray, Mike Redmond, Tony Russo, Ed Salamon, Sal Salzano, Jack Sbarbori, Bill Schwartz, Phil Schwartz, Scott Shea, Joseph T. Sicurella, Phil Silverman, Wayne Stierle, Brian Stillwell, Ralph Surley, Jeff Tamarkin, Carl Tancredi, Kevin Tong, Freddy Toscano, Art Turco, Neal Umphred, Marcia Vance, Billy Vera, Bob Volturno, Steve Wasserman, Joel Whitburn, Cliff White, Rick Whitesell, and Drew Williamson.

Record Label Abbreviations

The following is a list of record labels referenced in this book's singing group discographies for which abbreviations were used due to limited space. The abbreviations and corresponding labels are as follows:

CODE	RECORD LABEL
A	
ABC P	ABC Paramount
Abnr	Abner
Acad	Academy
AftrH	After Hours
Aldn	Aladdin
Al Plt	All Platinum
AmArts	American Arts
AmbiS	Ambient Sound
Am Int	American International
	Artists
Ardl	Aardell
AREA	A.R.E. American
Astro	Astro-Scope
Atln	Atlantic
Avco	Avco Embassy
B	
BBB	Bim Bam Boom
BbyGr	Baby Grand
Bcn	Beacon
BdSty	Bed-Sty
BgDl	Big Deal
BgTr	Big Tree
BgWl	Big Wheel
BklynBrdg	Brooklyn Bridge
Blbd	Bluebird
Bl Ct	Blue Cat
Bl Rk	Blue Rock
Bl Thm	Blue Thumb
Bltn	Beltone
Blvd	Boulevard
Brns	Brunswick
Brthr	Brother
BTP	B.T. Puppy
C	
CanAm	Canadian American
Cant	Canterbury
Cap	Capitol
Casa	Casablanca
CasaG	Casa Grande
Cata	Catamount
Cdnc	Cadence

CODE	RECORD LABEL
Chim	Chimneyville
Chi S	Chi-Sound
ChkMt	Check-Mate
Chkr	Checker
Chlng	Challenge
Chmp	Champagne
Chnc	Chancellor
Chnl	Channel
Chrtr	Charter
Cit	Citation
Cliftn	Clifton
Clndr	Calendar
ClsArt	Classic Artists
Clst	Celeste
Cndlt	Candlelight
Col	Columbia
Colo	Colossus
Comp	Companion
Const	Constellation
Cot	Cotillion
CPrkr	Charlie Parker
Crbu	Caribou
Crmsn	Crimson
Crna	Corona
Crnt	Coronet
Crnvl	Carnival
Crtq	Critique
CrysB	Crystal Ball
Csns	Cousins
Cycln	Cyclone
D	
Dca	Decca
Dcatr	Decatur
DDsc	Duo Disc
DfJm	DefJam
DkHrs	Dark Horse
Dltn	Deltone
DLx	DeLuxe
Dnhl	Dunhill
Dvs	Davis
Dwnst	Downstairs
E	
Eld	Eldorado
Elek	Elektra
Ever	Everlast

CODE	RECORD LABEL
Evrst	Everest
Excl	Exclusive
Exelo	Excello
F	
Fdlty	Fidelity
Fed	Federal
1stCh	1st Choice
Flstd	Felsted
Fntna	Fontana
Frbrd	Firebird
Frtn	Fortune
G	
Gall	Galliant
GenAm	Gen'l American
Gmbl	Gamble
Grdy	Gordy
Grmcy	Gramercy
GrSea	Green Sea
Grv	Groove
Gtwy	Gateway
H-I	
Hlywd	Hollywood
Hmltn	Hamilton
HOTB	Home of the Blues
Hrmny	Harmony
Hrtg	Heritage
HtWx	Hot Wax
Imprl	Imperial
Inf	Inferno
Invcts	Invictus
ItsN	It's a Natural
J-K	
Jnita	Juanita
Jubi	Jubilee
KamaS	Kama Sutra
Kirsh	Kirshner
KngT	King Tut
K-Ron	Kay-Ron
Kystn	Keystone
L	
Lbrty	Liberty
Lndmk	Landmark

CODE	RECORD LABEL
Lndn	London
LstNt	Lost Nite
LStr	Little Star
Lumtn	Lummtone
Luni	Luniverse
LuPn	Lu Pine
M	
MamaS	Mama Sadie
Mchl	Michelle
Md Int	Midland Int'l
Mdl Tn	Middle Tone
Merc	Mercury
MgcMo	Magic Moment
MiaSd	Mia Sound
Mill	Millenium
MjrLg	Major League
Mjstc	Majestic
Mlmd	Mellomood
Mlotn	Melotone
Mlstn	Milestone
Mndla	Mandala
Mnln	Mainline
Moon	Moon Shot
MPcok	Mr. Peacock
Mrcl	Miracle
MrPk	Mr. Peeke
Mrwd	Mirwood
MsClf	Music Clef
MscNt	Music Note
Mscr	Musicor
Mscrft	Musicraft
Msctn	Musictone
MsMkr	Music Makers
Mtwn	Motown
Myhw	Mayhew
N-O	
Nat'l	National
Nctwn	Nicetown
NoAmr	North American
Nptn	Neptune
NtTrn	Night Train
Ntwrk	Network
Nwtm	Newtime
Nwtwn	Newtown
Octva	Octavia

CODE	RECORD LABEL	CODE	RECORD LABEL	CODE	RECORD LABEL	CODE	RECORD LABEL
OldTn	Old Town	RdBrd	Red Bird	Sl Cty	Soul City	Tort	Tortoise
OrigS	Original Sound	RdLbl	Red Label	Sl Jm	Soul Jam	Tri	Tri-Phi
OTW	Off the Wall	RdRbn	Red Robin	Sl Trn	Soul Train	Trmrs	Trommers
		Rich	Richcraft	Snglr	Singular	Trntb	Turntable
P-Q		RIH	Recorded in	SnSt	Sun State	TrplX	Triple X
Pay-4	Pay-4 Play		Hollywood	Spec	Specialty	20th	20th Century
Pclo	Piccolo	Rnbw	Rainbow	Sphr	Sphere Sound		
Pcok	Peacock	Rndvs	Rendezvous	Spkn	Spokane	**U-V**	
Phila	Philadelphia	Rnwd	Rainwood	SPrk	South Park	UA	United Artists
	International	Roul	Roulette	SprM	Super M	UGHA	United in Group
Phlps	Philips	Rprs	Reprise	StClr	St. Clair		Harmony
PhlyG	Philly Groove	RrBd	Rare Bird	Stir	Stirling		Association
Plnt	Planet	Rvra	Riviera	Stltn	Steeltown	Vctr	Victor
PnWld	Pan World	Rvrsd	Riverside	Stndrd	Standard	Vctry	Victory
Poly	Polydor	RylRst	Royal Roost	Stntn	Stenton	Verv	Verve
Prds	Paradise	RZan	Ro-Zan	Straw	Strawberry	Visct	Viscount
Prfct	Perfect			Strlt	Starlight	Vlnt	Valiant
Prkwy	Parkway	**S**		Strm	Streamline	Vocln	Vocalion
Prmnt	Paramount	Scptr	Scepter	Strmy	Stormy Weather		
Prvt I	Private I	Sebr	Sebring	Strtws	Streetwise	**W-Z**	
PSpec	Phil Spector	SeHrn	Sea-Horn			Whpt	Whippet
	International	S4E	Seasons 4 Ever	**T**		Win	Winchester
Psprt	Passport	SgWy	Seg-Way	Taur	Taurus	WldArt	World Artists
QnBee	Queen Bee	Shrwd	Sherwood	Teen	Teenage	Wldct	Wildcat
		Shwbt	Showboat	Titnc	Titanic	WrlnD	Whirlin' Disc
R		Silh	Silhouette	TmMch	Time Machine	Wrnr	Warner Brothers
RbnHd	Robin Hood	Sl Clk	Soul Clock	TmsSq	Times Square	Wrwk	Warwick
RCA	RCA Victor	Slctv	Selective	T-Nk	T-Neck	W-Spec	Warner-Spector

Vocal Group Record Labels

Throughout the vocal group era, certain record labels have by choice issued mostly vocal group recordings. In the '50s, they included Jubilee, Josie, Gone, End, Rama, Red Robin, Old Town, Rainbow, Fury, Apollo, Aladdin, Chance, Checker, Chess, Deluxe, Federal, King, Ember, Gee, Herald, and many others.

In the '60s, a number of vocal group labels also helped to set new trends in pop music: Gordy, Tamla, and Motown created the Motown sound; Laurie Records pioneered the white teen doo wop sound; Philles presented Phil Spector's "wall of sound"; and Red Bird promoted the girl-group sound.

During the '70s and '80s, despite the paucity of traditionally styled new vocal groups, a number of labels sprang up across the country catering almost exclusively to vocal group artists. They not only provided outlets for new groups but also helped to keep the traditions of the past alive by reissuing old and often obscure collectors' items and sometimes distributing previously unreleased singles.

Labels of the '70s and '80s like Bab, Arcade, Blue Sky, Crystal Ball, Greco, Relic, Monogram, Owl, Robin Hood, King Tut, Popular Request, Pyramid, and Roadhouse had sporadic releases, but the most consistent flow came from Bruce Patch's Classic Artists Records of Oxnard, California; Ronnie "I" Italiano's Clifton and U.G.H.A labels of Clifton, New Jersey; Jerry Zidel and Bob Kretzschmer's Starlight Records of Queens, New York; and Al Cattabiani's Avenue D Records based in East Islip, Long Island, New York.

THE 1940s

THE MODERNAIRES

THE ANDREWS SISTERS

THE DELTA RHYTHM BOYS

The 1940s are generally regarded as the era in which vocal groups—harmony singers who kept the focus on the group sound rather than on an individual—first achieved widespread popularity. But the vocal harmony sound, as applied to popular song, had antecedents that can be traced to preceding decades and back into the 19th century. Before the revolutionary war, for example, William Billings organized singing schools in New England, teaching the basics of group singing.

The first famous vocal quartet was the Hutchinson family of New Hampshire. Consisting of three brothers (John, Judson, and Asa) and one sister (Abby), the family originally called themselves the Aeolian Vocalists and gave their first public performance in 1842, singing sentimental songs and popular ballads. They became so popular that they toured both America and England.

Minstrel shows—music and comedy revues that later evolved into vaudeville—became popular during this period, and the first popular vocal group to emerge from them were the Virginia Minstrels, a quartet formed in 1843. The Minstrels included Dick Pelham, Bill Whitlock, Frank Bower, and Daniel Emmett. Lead singer Dan Emmett was also an accomplished songwriter, having penned the immortal "Dixie."

By the 1870s vocal quartets were a featured part of minstrel shows. Minstrel groups of the time included the Harmoniums, the Sable Harmonizers, the White Serenaders, and the Nightingale Serenaders. Musical families like the Hutchinsons and minstrel singers such as the Continental Vocalists introduced the public to new songs like "Oh! Susannah" and "Blue Tail Fly" ("Jimmie Crack Corn"). Though minstrel shows performed mostly in large cities and towns, groups like the Continental Vocalists traveled to even the most remote places to perform starting in the 1850s.

Interest in group singing was growing, as indicated by the publication in 1855 of the *Continental Vocalists Glee Book* of songs. Five years later (one year before the Civil War started) the first successful spiritual group arrived on the scene in the form of the Fisk Jubilee singers. And by the 1870s barbershop quartets were springing up, though they were not actually called that until 1911, when a song titled "Mr. Jefferson Lord, Play that Barbershop Chord" started making the rounds. Among these first quartets were the Continental Four, the original American Four (1878), and the original Big Four. One of the first, if not *the* first of the black barbershop foursomes were the Hamtown Students (1873).

Other outlets for group singing were known as the "traveling chautauquas," which were really tent shows which grew out of an 1874 Forum called the Lake Chautauqua Assembly. They consisted of readings and lectures punctuated by the vocalizing of barbershop quartets.

By the 1890s the musical structure of barbershop harmony was set. The lead, a second tenor, would sing the melody line; the first tenor sang above the lead and the baritone sang below; the bass would sing the root of the chord.

As vaudeville developed, many quartets diversified into four-man comedy groups called "four acts." At least one member of each of these acts (such as the Four Shamrocks) would imitate and/or exaggerate the characteristics of various ethnic minorities, sandwiched in between the group's slapstick routines and its barbershop songs. The most famous of these, formed in 1900, was the Avon Comedy Four. Others from the early 1900s included the Casion Four (which included Al Jolson for a time), the Monarch Comedy Four, and the American Comedy Four. Barbershop quarteting attracted a variety of interesting variations, from the Thousand Pounds of Harmony to the Chung Hue Chinese Four.

Vocal group harmonizing switched from the "see and hear" mode to the "hear only" medium with the advent of recordings in the early 1890s. The Manhasset Quartet recorded in September 1891 for the North American Records label.

The first black foursome to record was the Dinwiddie Colored Quartet. They did six single-sided discs for Monarch in 1902 starting with "Down the Old Camp Ground." Among the early recording groups were the Criterion Quartet and the Imperial Quartet.

Many of the top barbershop groups became the most successful recording artists of the day due to Thomas Edison's invention. Acts like the American Quartet (recording for Edison and Victor with 66 charted records from 1910 to 1925), the Hayden Quartet (Berliner and Victor, 62 chart hits from 1898 to 1914), and the Peerless Quartet (Columbia and Victor, 108 charters, 1904 to 1926) paved the way for such talent as the Revelers (the '20s' most famous group), the Columbia Stellar Quartet (1912–1922), the Imperial Quartet of Chicago (1916), and the Orpheus Quartet (1914–1919).

One of the first female groups to record was the That Girl Quartet for Victor in 1911, and one of the first mixed groups was Columbia's Mixed Quartet (two guys and two girls) in 1912.

The burlesque stage was another avenue of expression for vocal groups, and among the foursomes that chose this route, one of the most popular was the Empire City Quartet.

The advent of radio changed harmony. Barbershop quartets started disappearing from the recording and performing scene and were replaced by big bands, jazz musicians, and torch-song vocalists. Minor seventh chords of 1930 songs became difficult to harmonize, and a new style of vocal group would soon emerge to perform the more challenging material.

Acts like the Boswell Sisters began singing jazz-flavored songs mixed in with their New Orleans blues and spirituals. For three white sisters this was unusual music, but the public loved them to the tune of 20 chart records between 1931 and 1938. Jazz and blues had an affect on both black and white groups, but in the 1930s it seemed that the black groups were the ones making the greater strides (creatively, not financially). One of the pioneering jazz-styled vocal ensembles was the Norfolk Jazz Quartet, from Norfolk, Virginia, in 1921. On the spiritual side, there were acts like the Mobile Four (Columbia, 1928). The Southernaires Quartet, who performed on the Blue Network (black radio's version of syndicated radio) for over eight years starting in the late '20s, were among the forerunners of blues and spiritual radio performers.

The Southern Negro Quartet recorded for Columbia in the early '20s with a style that could pass for early rhythm and blues. The Silver Leaf Quartet of Norfolk in 1929 performed in a way that suggested combinations of spiritual, blues, and the remnants of barbershop; it was a style that would later be classified as "pop."

White vocal groups were emerging, like the Westinghouse Quartet (an exceptional barbershop group) of Wilkensburg, Pennsylvania, the Carolon Quartet, and the Hoboken Four (featuring a young Frank Sinatra). There were lesser known foursomes (sometimes integrated) that were more interested in carrying on tradition and enjoying singing than trying for a career; these included the East Liberty Four (featuring three white members and the black bass singer Wilbur Gray). For the most part, however, white vocalists were going solo, joining bands, or forming trios as part of big-band America.

Quartets and quintets were developing more from such 1930s black combos as the Four Southern Singers (1931), the Mississippi Mudmashers (1935), the Four Blue Birds (1934), the Five Jones Boys, the Five Jinx (Bluebird, 1927), the Five Breezes, including Willie Dixon, (Bluebird, 1939), and the Golden Gate Quartet (from the mid-'30s). These acts were among the first to sing strictly secular music based on spiritual or blues roots. Before the 1930s black aggregations had sung mixed repertoires of sacred and secular songs that included blues and jazz compositions.

The act that changed the vocal group scene forever was the Mills Brothers (1931) of Piqua, Ohio. They were four brothers who were inspired not just by previous vocal groups but by the orchestral arrangements and jazz instrumental work of Duke Ellington and Louis Armstrong. Their style of rhythm and blues with touches of jazz was so popular that they were the inspiration for more vocal groups than any other (with the possible exception of the Ink Spots). Their new style of singing combined the vocal imitation of wind instruments with a smooth harmony sound that attracted both white and black audiences, making them the first truly popular vocal group in the nation. Right behind them were the Ink Spots, who made their first recordings in 1935. Starting as a vocal jive-styled quartet, they became the kings of rhythm and blues balladeers in the '40s, introducing the "talking bass" and formulating the "ooh" and "ah" backup sounds that became a staple of '40s and '50s groups.

A musical trend that was on a collision course with the Mills Brothers/Ink Spots pop and early R&B style was the development of modern gospel music from the spiritual tradition. In the '30s, spiritual music was often interpreted as a deliberate refinement and softening of the original jubilee enthusiasm, so that the music would be more widely accepted. The '40s and '50s saw a resurgence of the earlier unbridled gospel music, now sung by young black vocal groups with a new rhythmic drive and often with raw but emotionally honest vocals. Many of these groups spawned the next generation of vocal groups and solo stars that would serve as the foundation of rhythm and blues, rock and roll, and soul music. Some included the Soul Stirrers (Sam Cooke and Little Johnny Taylor), the Pilgrim Travelers (Lou Rawls), the Thrasher Wonders (Gerhart and Andrew Thrasher of the Drifters), the Drinkard Singers (Dionne Warwick), and the Jerusalem Stars (Brook Benton).

Many black acts of the '40s contributed to the growth of interest in vocal group music. They included the Charioteers (Columbia), the Deep River Boys (RCA), the Four Vagabonds (Bluebird), the Delta Rhythm Boys (Decca), the Basin Street Boys (Exclusive), and the Five Red Caps (Beacon), and in the late '40s, the fathers of rhythm and blues the Orioles (Jubilee) and the Ravens (National).

The white groups, fewer in number, were led by the Ames Brothers (Decca) and the Andrew Sisters (Decca).

Obviously, World War II had a pronounced effect on the number of performing groups, since so many young men were called into the service from 1941 to 1945. But the ones that were around contributed greatly to a changing and developing music scene. ∎

The Ames Brothers

One of the most popular groups of the late '40s and '50s, the Ames Brothers were actually the four Urick brothers from Malden, Massachusetts: Ed (lead), Vic (first tenor), Gene (second tenor), and Joe (bass). They were a tight-knit singing quartet, starting as far back as their grammar school days in the 1930s, in spite of diverse interests: Gene wanted to be a baseball player, and made it to the semi-pro circuit in New England. Vic seemed on his way to becoming a serious actor until one of his high school performances had the crowd in stitches, paving the way for a later role as the Ames Brothers' resident comedian. Ed became a ping-pong perfectionist and won his way into interstate tournament play. Joe had operatic aspirations and turned down several scholarships to continue his music studies.

Cajoling by his mother changed Joe from Pagliacci to pop; she wanted to see her firstborn sons sing together (the four boys were the first of nine children). She got her wish: after winning several Boston area amateur contests the group earned their first one-week professional job at the Foxes and Hounds; it stretched out to three months. In 1948 the Ames Brothers (ages 21 through 24) signed with Signature Records vocalist Monica Lewis for their initial chart record, "A Tree in the Meadow" (#21). The group next emerged on Coral Records and had solo chart success in February 1949 with an adaptation of an old German song, "You, You, You Are the One" (#23).

The Ames Brothers' first release of the '50s became their first number one record and million seller, "Ragmop." Their very next single, "Sentimental Me," also went to number one. The boys scored 15 more chart records for Coral between June 1950 and March 1953, including "Can Anyone Explain" (#5, 1950) and "Undecided" (#2 in 1951).

The Brothers then signed with RCA, and their first release became their biggest all-time hit: "You, You, You" reached number one in mid-1953, staying there for eight weeks and remaining on the charts for nearly eight months. Their biggest international record was "The Naughty Lady of Shady Lane." It hit the charts in November of 1954, skyrocketing to number three in America and number six in England, selling over one-and-a-quarter million singles.

The Ames Brothers performed in every major club in America, from Ciro's in Hollywood to the Roxy Theatre in New York, and they appeared regularly as TV guests of Milton Berle, Perry Como, Jackie Gleason, and Ed Sullivan.

Billboard magazine voted them Best Vocal Group of the Year in 1958. In 1956 the group charted eight songs (one almost every seven weeks), and did it again in 1958.

Their last *Billboard* best seller came in February of 1960 with "China Doll" (#38).

Ed Ames later ventured out as a solo artist, earning seven chart singles between 1965 and 1969 including "My Cup Runneth Over" (#8, 1967) from the Broadway musical *I Do, I Do*. He won an acting part on the "Daniel Boone" TV series playing Mingo, the Indian, a role made especially memorable by a hilarious guest appearance on "The Tonight Show" in which Ames pitched a tomahawk at a man-shaped target and hit it in the crotch.

The Ames Brothers' music, always smooth and clean, brought a refreshing variety to pop music. They delighted in singing and recording a wide range of material, from pre-World-War-I college songs ("The Sweetheart of Sigma Chi") and folk songs ("Goodnight Irene"), to R&B ("I Love You for Sentimental Reasons") and Western ballads ("Cool Water"). They also created LPs with themes like *The Ames Brothers Sing Famous Hits of Famous Quartets* (1959) and *Destination Moon* (1958), in which each song related to the stars, the sun, the moon, or the sky. The Ames Brothers left a legacy of 50 chart singles attesting to their popularity.

THE AMES BROTHERS

A SIDE/B SIDE	LABEL/CAT NO	DATE
Bye Bye Blackbird / I'm Looking Over A Four Leaf Clover	Coral 24319	2/48
If You Had All The World / Tell Me A Story	Coral 24329	2/48
On The Street Of Regret / A Tree In The Meadow	Coral 24411	4/48
Where The Apple Blossoms Fall / If I Live To Be A Hundred	Coral 24447	1948
More Beer / You, You, You Are The One	Coral 60015	11/48
Far Away Places / Lorelei	Coral 60016	11/48
Good Fellow Medley, Etc. / I'm Just Wild About Harry	Coral 60017	1/49
Oh, You Sweet One / St. Bernard Waltz	Coral 60065	4/49
Barroom Polka / We'll Still Be Honey-Mooning	Coral 60052	5/49
Lingering Down The Lane / Still Waters And Green Pasture	Coral 60091	7/49
Noah's Ark / Tears Of Happiness	Coral 60092	8/49
White Christmas / Winter Wonderland	Coral 60113	9/49

A SIDE/B SIDE	LABEL/CAT NO	DATE
Good Fellow Medley Etc. / Good Fellow Medley Etc.	Coral 60114	8/49
I Love Her Oh! Oh! Oh! / Music! Music! Music!	Coral 60153	1/50
Clancy Lowered The Boom / I Didn't Kiss The Blarney Stone	Coral 60154	1/50
Bring Her Out Again (Fifi) / Sing Until The Cows Come Home	Coral 60164	2/50
Blue Prelude / Sentimental Me	Coral 60173	4/50
Hoop-De-Doo / Stars Are The Windows Of Heaven	Coral 60209	4/50
Dorm! Dorm! (Sleep, Sleep) / Marianna	Coral 60185	5/50
Can Anyone Explain? (No, No) / Sittin' 'N Starin' 'N Rockin'	Coral 60253	7/50
Twelve Days Of Christmas / Wassail Song	Coral 60267	7/50
Adeste Fideles / Silent Night	Coral 60268	7/50
Hark The Herald Angels / It Came Upon The Midnight Hour	Coral 60269	7/50
God Rest Ye Merry Gentlemen / Oh Little Town Of Bethlehem	Coral 60270	7/50
I Don't Mind Being All Alone / Thirsty For Your Kisses	Coral 60300	10/50
Oh! Babe / To Think You've Chosen Me	Coral 60327	11/50
Music By The Angels / The Thing	Coral 60333	1/51
In The Evening By the Moonlight / Just A Dream Of You Dear	Coral 60336	1/51
Till We Meet Again / You Tell Me Your Dream I'll Tell You Mine	Coral 60337	1/51
Because / Love's Old Sweet Song	Coral 60339	1/51
More Than I Care To Remember / Three Dollars & Ninety Nine Cents	Coral 60363	2/51
I Love You Much Too Much / My Love Serenade	Coral 60404	3/51
Hoop-De-Doo / Rag Mop	Coral 60397	4/51
Marianna / Sing Until The Cows Come Home	Coral 60398	4/51
Clancy Lowered The Boom / More Beer	Coral 60399	4/51
Barroom Polka / Noah's Ark	Coral 60400	4/51
Somewhere There Must Be Happiness / Too Many Women	Coral 60452	5/51
Wang Wang Blues / Who'll Take My Place	Coral 60489	6/51
Everything's Gonna Be Alright / Only, Only You	Coral 60549	8/51
I Wanna Love You / I'll Still Love You	Coral 60617	1/52
Lovely Lady Dressed In Blue / Mother, At Your Feet Is Kneeling	Coral 60628	1/52
Deep River / Dry Bones	Coral 60633	3/52
Shadrack / Swing Low Sweet Chariot	Coral 60634	3/52
Go Down Moses / Joshua Fit De Battle Of Jericho	Coral 60635	3/52
Blind Barnabas / Who Built The Ark	Coral 60636	3/52
And So I Waited Around / The Sheik Of Araby	Coral 60680	4/52
Crazy Cause I Love You / Star Dust	Coral 60751	5/52
Aufwiederseh'n Sweetheart / Break The Bands That Bind Me	Coral 60773	7/52
Absence Makes The Heart Grow / String Along	Coral 60804	8/52
Al-Lee-O', Al-Lee-Ay! / A Favorite Song	Coral 60846	10/52
Sing A Song Of Santa Claus / Winter's Here Again	Coral 60861	11/52
Do Nothin' Till You Hear From Me / No Moon At All*	Coral 60870	11/52
Can't I / Lonely Wine	Coral 60926	2/53
At The End Of The Rainbow / Candy Bar Boogie	Coral 60967	4/53
You You You / Once Upon A Time	RCA 5325	5/53
Always In My Dreams / This Is Fiesta	Coral 61005	6/53
My Love, My Life, My Happiness / If You Want My Heart	RCA 5404	7/53
Lazy River / Star Dust	Coral 61060	10/53
I Can't Believe That You're In Love With Me / Boogie Woogie Maxixe	RCA 5530	10/53
The Man With The Banjo / Man, Man, Is For The Woman Made	Coral 5644	1/54
Don't Believe A Word They Say / Don't Lie To Me	Coral 61145	3/54
Leave It To Your Heart / Let's Walk and Talk	RCA 5764	5/54
Don't Believe A Word They Say / Helen Polka	Coral 61127	5/54
One More Time / Hopelessly	RCA 5840	8/54
Addio / The Naughty Lady Of Shady Lane	Coral 5897	10/54
I Got A Cold For Xmas / There'll Always Be A Xmas	Coral 5929	11/54
Sweet Brown-Eyed Baby / Sympathetic Eyes	Coral 6044	2/55
Southern Cross / Gotta Be This Or That	Coral 6117	5/55
Wrong Again / Merci Beaucoup	Coral 6156	1955
My Bonnie Lassie / So Will I	Coral 6208A	8/55
The Next Time It Happens / My Love, Your Love	Coral 6323	1955
Forever Darling / I'm Gonna Love You	Coral 6400	1/56
If You Wanna See Mamie Tonight / It Only Hurts For A Little While	Coral 6481	5/56
49 Shades Of Green / Summer Sweetheart	Coral 6608	8/56
I Saw Esau / The Game Of Love	Coral 6720	10/56
Did You Ever Get The Roses / I Only Know One Way To Love You	Coral 6821	1957

A SIDE/B SIDE	LABEL/CAT NO	DATE
Yeah, Yeah, Yeah (It's So Good) / Man On Fire	Coral 6851	1957
Tammy / Rockin' Shoes	Coral 6930	4/57
Melodie D'Amour / So Little Time	Coral 7046	9/57
In Love / Little Gypsy	Coral 7142	1/58
A Very Precous Love / Don't Leave Me Now	Coral 7167	2/58
Stay / Little Serenade	Coral 7268	7/58
No One But You (In My Heart) / Pussy Cat	Coral 7315	8/58
When The Summer Comes Again / Red River Rose	Coral 7413	11/58
(Yes I Need) Only Your Love / Dancin' In The Streets	Coral 7474	1959
Someone To Come Home To / Mason Dixon Line	Coral 7526	4/59
Not It's Me / Now Hear This	Coral 7567	1959
Take Me Along / What Do I Hear	Coral 7604	1959
China Doll / Christopher Sunday	Coral 7566	1/60

* with Les Brown

The Andrews Sisters

The Andrews Sisters were by far the most successful female vocal group of the pre-rock era. Patty (1920), Maxene (1917), and LaVerne (1915) grew up in Minneapolis, Minnesota. Patty was only 11 when the trio caught the show business bug following a nervous first performance in a 1931 singing contest. LaVerne was especially hooked and convinced her sisters to leave school and travel the vaudeville circuit. Inspired by the harmonies and sound of the Boswell Sisters, the Andrews girls began as imitators but eventually developed their own clean, fresh, and unique vocal sound.

In the fall of 1933, while performing in a Minneapolis kiddie revue, the trio came to the attention of bandleader Larry Rich, who took them on the road to perform in a vaudeville show. Though none of the sisters could read music, their collective ears were so well tuned they could pick up a song just by hearing one or two plays. This expertise earned them a dollar a day from Rich (for all three girls). The group stayed with Rich for 18 months before moving on to Joey Howard's troupe for seven months. Then, in rapid succession, they played with Ted Mack's band, Murray Sherman's orchestra (who paid them the enormous sum of $35 a week), and Leon Blasco's band in 1936. That tour ended when the Mayfair Club in Kansas City burned to the ground, sending their arrangements and costumes up in smoke. Blasco went to New York for new charts and costumes; he returned with Vic

Schoen, who would become the trio's orchestra leader and arranger for decades to come. The band continued to tour, returning to New York in 1937, where it played the New Yorker Hotel until Blasco disbanded the outfit.

Returning to Minneapolis, the sisters had barely unpacked when the desire hit them again to make a go of it in New York. But this time their parents disapproved, so a bargain was struck in which the girls could go on the condition that if they didn't make it by the end of the summer they'd return home to stay.

Once back in New York they met a music publisher named Bernie Pollack of Mills Music at the New Yorker Hotel, who let them use his office to rehearse their act. (The New Yorker was one of numerous hotels where music publishers plied their trade, trying to interest bands in the publisher's latest songs. If a bandleader liked a tune and played it on one of the many radio shows broadcast from hotels like the New Yorker, the song could earn vast sums of money in airplay performance and subsequent sheet music sales.)

Along with Mama Andrews' blessings came a 15¢-a-day allowance for food, which was almost always spent at Hector's Cafeteria. That king's ransom bought the girls a sandwich and coffee that they split three ways.

The summer deadline was approaching, and work opportunities were scarce. One day, while the girls were rehearsing at Pollack's office, Vic Schoen arrived with the news that he was now working with the Billy Swanson Band at the Edison Hotel. He convinced Swanson to listen to the girls, but after one chorus of "Sleepytime Down South" Swanson told them he wasn't interested. Dismayed and upset, the girls began to leave the Edison Hotel through the dining room when a woman sitting in a booth noticed their distress and asked what happened. The lady was one Maria Cramer, and after hearing the girls' story she confronted Swanson, asking why he wouldn't give the girls a chance to sing on his radio show. Swanson said he couldn't afford them, but Miss Cramer pressed on, asking, "Well what *can* you afford?" The beleaguered bandleader said $15, $5 each, to which Maxene responded, "We'll take it!" Swanson was stuck. After all, Maria Cramer was the owner of the Edison Hotel.

When the trio showed up that Saturday to perform, they found that their staunch ally, Mrs. Cramer, had been called back to Brazil to be with her ailing husband. Left in the hands of Billy Swanson, they were lucky to get to sing the one song they performed on radio that night ("Sleepytime Down South" once again) before being un-ceremoniously canned. Meanwhile across town, Decca Records president Dave Kapp was riding home in a cab, listening with interest to the Andrews clan's radio debut.

On Sunday the girls returned to the Edison to bid farewell to Vic Schoen; the Cinderella sisters' carriage of dreams was to turn into a pumpkin the next day, the deadline for the return home. Suddenly a young man burst into the soda fountain area where the girls and Vic were perched on stools. He asked Vic if he knew the names of those girls who sang on the radio the previous night, because Decca's Dave Kapp wanted to audition them. The trio whirled around on their stools as if in a Busby Berkeley musical and announced "We're the girls!"

At nine a.m. Monday they auditioned with seven songs (including, yet again, "Sleepytime Down South") and won Dave Kapp over. Now, instead of returning home, they were signed to Decca for $50 a record. (The young man Kapp had sent to find the sisters was theatrical agent Lou Levy, whose keen ear for hit songs would play an important part in the trio's development.)

The Andrews' first single was "Why Talk About Love" (1937), which received little public attention. Then Lou dug up a song from the 1933 Yiddish musical *I Would If I Could*. The song went by the unlikely title of "Bei Mir Bist Du Schon," and its January 1938 Decca release proved Levy to be a crafty song plugger: it went to number one on the Best Seller charts. And if that weren't enough to make Lou and the girls a team, his marriage to Maxene certainly was.

Their next single, "Nice Work If You Can Get It" (#12) from *A Damsel in Distress*, hit the charts on January 8th, just one week after "Bei Mir," and it was the first of their many releases associated with films. In all, they had nine chart singles in 1938. As if their hits weren't keeping them busy enough, they performed on WBBM radio in Chicago five days a week and then flew to New York to record each weekend.

By the end of 1938 the sisters were earning $1,000 a week at the New York Paramount doing seven shows a day. In 1939 they had six chart records, including "Hold Tight Hold Tight" (#2). Their hits ran the gamut of international melodies in those first recording years, including Yiddish ("Joseph Joseph," #18, 1938), Latin American ("Say Si Si," #4, 1940), Italian ("The Woodpecker Song," #6, 1940), Russian ("Pross-Tchai Good-bye," #15, 1939), and even Czechoslovakian ("Beer Barrel Polka," #4, 1939).

Late in that year they began an association that became a career within a career: the girls had the first of 23 singles credited to Bing Crosby and the Andrews Sisters.

In 1940 they racked up seven more hits under their own name, including their second number one record, "Ferryboat Serenade."

When war broke out the Andrews Sisters joined the star-laden victory caravan traveling via special train to entertain the soldiers. The three "jive bombers," as they were affectionately described by servicemen, played more army, navy, marine, and air force bases than any other vocal group. They also sang on a variety of Armed Forces Radio shows and made many special recordings sent directly to U.S. forces overseas. Signed to Universal Film Studios, the girls performed in a number of wartime musicals including *Follow the Boys*, *Private Buckaroo*, *Buck Privates in the Navy*, and *Swing Time Johnny*. They also appeared in the film *Hollywood Canteen*, singing their 1944 hit "Don't Fence Me In" with Bing Crosby (which followed "A Hot Time in the Town of Berlin," also with Bing and also a number one record). During the war years the Andrews racked up an incredible 38 *Billboard* best-sellers, including nine with Crosby.

Though not their biggest hit, the singers' best remembered work is the frantically paced 1941 pop-jazz classic "Boogie Woogie Bugle Boy" (#6), its fame due in part to an excellent hit remake (#8) by Bette Midler some 32 years later.

By the end of the war, the Andrews trio had sold over 30 million records and were back playing the New York Paramount, only this time around they were earning $20,000 a week. They continued to record for six more years, issuing head-turning titles such as "Strip Poker" (#6), "Is You or Is You Ain't My Baby" (#2), "Get Your Kicks on Route 66" (#14), "Beat Me Daddy, Eight to the Bar" (#2), and "Scrub Me Mama with a Boogie Beat" (#10). The postwar years were good to the Andrews Sisters: they hit the *Billboard* Best Seller list with 51 additional 78s between 1946 and 1951, including 12 more Crosby collaborations. Bing, however, wasn't the only vocalist the girls supported on record. They also backed up Danny Kaye ("Civilization," #3), Dick Haymes ("Theresa," #21), Burl Ives ("Blue Tail Fly," #24), Carmen Miranda ("Cuanto La Gusta," #12), Ernest Tubb ("I'm Bitin' My Fingernails and Thinkin' of You," #30), and others.

Even the musicians' union problems of the mid-to late '40s didn't put a halt to Andrews Sisters recordings. When they couldn't get the musicians they needed, the girls recorded the "Sabre Dance" in the spring of 1948 with the Harmoni-Cats (harmonica players weren't considered serious musicians, at least until the girls circumvented the union by using them).

By the time they called it quits as a trio in 1951 the Andrews Sisters had amassed a phenomenal 113 chart singles, sold 75 million records, and recorded more than 1800 songs earning them 19 gold records and eight number ones. By the 1950s, they had appeared in 22 films. Their last number one was "I Want to Be Loved" in the summer of 1950, and the Decca label read just Patty Andrews, although Maxene and LaVerne backed her up.

When the trio disbanded, Maxene taught theatre at a college in Lake Tahoe and formed an organization to help wayward children and drug addicts.

In the mid-'60s the trio began performing again on television, but activity halted in 1967 when LaVerne died. In 1974 Patty and Maxene appeared before audiences in the nostalgia-packed Broadway hit *Over There*. Maxene did her first and only solo album in 1985 on Bainbridge Records simply titled *Maxene of the Andrews Sisters*.

For their professionalism, sound quality, and success, the Andrews Sisters ruled pop music of the '30s and '40s.

THE ANDREWS SISTERS

A SIDE/B SIDE	LABEL/CAT NO.	DATE
Just A Simple Melody /		
Why Talk About Love	Decca 1496	11/37
Bei Mir Bist Du Schon /		
Nice Work If You Can Get It	Decca 1562	12/37
It's Easier Said Than Done /		
Joseph! Joseph!	Decca 1691	3/38
Ti-Pi-Tin / Where Have		
We Met Before	Decca 1703	3/38
Ooooo-Oh Boom /		
Shortenin' Bread	Decca 1744	3/38
Oh! Ma-Ma (The Butcher Boy) /		
Pagan Love Song	Decca 1859	6/38
Oh! Faithless Maid / Says My Heart	Decca 1875	7/38
From The Land Of The Sky Blue /		
I Married An Angel	Decca 1912	8/38
Sha-Sha* / Tu-Li-Tulip Time*	Decca 1974	8/38
Love Is Where You Find It /		
When A Prince Of A Fella	Decca 2016	1938
Lullaby To A Little Jitterbug /		
Pross Tchai (Goodbye Goodbye)	Decca 2082	4/39
Billy Boy* / Hold Tight*	Decca 2214	12/38
Begin The Beguine /		
Long Time To See	Decca 2290	1/39
Rock Rock-A-Bye Baby /		
You Don't Know How Much You	Decca 2414	4/39
Beer Barrel Polka / Well, All Right	Decca 2462	5/39

A SIDE/B SIDE	LABEL/CAT NO	DATE
Chico's Love Song / The Jumpin'		
Jive (Jim Jam Jump)	Decca 2756	10/39
Ciribiribin** / Yodelin' Jive**	Decca 2800	11/39
Oh Johnny, Oh Johnny, Oh! /		
South American Way	Decca 2840	1/40
Let's Have Another One /		
Say "Si Si"	Decca 3013	2/40
Down By The Ohio /		
The Woodpecker Song	Decca 3065	3/40
Rhumboogie / Tuxedo Junction	Decca 3097	4/40
The Crookeyed Mayor Of		
Kaunakak / Let's Pack		
Our Things	Decca 3245	5/40
I Want My Mama /		
Oh He Loves Me	Decca 3310	8/40
Ferryboat Serenade /		
Hit The Road	Decca 3328	9/40
Beat Me Daddy / Pennsylvania		
6-5000	Decca 3375	10/40
Mean To Me / Sweet Molly Malone	Decca 3440	11/40
Johnny Peddler / Scrub Me Mama		
With A Boogie Beat	Decca 3553	12/40
Boogie Woogie Bugle Boy /		
Bounce Me Brother	Decca 3598	1/41
Yes, My Darling Daughter /		
You're A Luck Fellow	Decca 3599	2/41
I, Yi, Yi, Yi, Yi / I'll Be With You		
In Apple Blossom	Decca 3622	3/41
Aurora / Music Makers	Decca 3732	4/41
Daddy / Sleepy Serenade	Decca 3821	6/41
Sonny Boy / Gimme Some Skin,		
My Friend	Decca 3871	7/41
The Booglie Wooglie Piggy /		
The Nickel Serenade	Decca 3960	8/41
Why Don't We Do This More Often	Decca 3966	9/41
Elmer's Tune / Honey	Decca 4008	10/41
Jealous / Rancho Pillow	Decca 4019	10/41
Any Bonds Today?	Decca 4044	11/41
Chattanooga Choo Choo /		
For All We Know	Decca 4094	12/41
Jack Of All Trades /		
The Shrine Of Saint Cecilia	Decca 4097	12/41
He Said-She Said /		
I'll Pray For You	Decca 4153	2/42
What To Do / A Zoot Suit (For My		
Sunday Gal)	Decca 4182	3/42
Don't Sit Under The Apple Tree /		
At Sonya's Cafe	Decca 18312	4/42
(Toy Balloon) Boolee Boolee Boo /		
Three Little Sisters	Decca 18319	4/42
Pennsylvania Polka / That's The		
Moon, My Son	Decca 18398	7/42
The Humming Bird / I've Got A Gal		
In Kalamazoo	Decca 18464	8/42
Mister Five By Five / Strip Polka	Decca 18470	8/42
Here Comes The Navy /		
Massachusetts	Decca 18497	9/42
East Of The Rockies / When		
Johnny Comes Marching	Decca 18533	4/43

A SIDE/B SIDE	LABEL/CAT NO	DATE
Ehelena / I Love You		
Much Too Much	Decca 18563	9/43
Pistol Packin' Mama** /		
Vic'try Polka**	Decca 23277	10/43
Jingle Bells** / Santa Claus Is		
Coming To Town**	Decca 23281	11/43
Sing A Tropical Song /		
There'll Be A Jubilee	Decca 18581	4/44
Straighten Up And Fly Right /		
Tico Toco	Decca 18606	5/44
Hot Time In The Town Of Berlin** /		
Is You Is Or Is You Ain't**	Decca 23350	8/44
Don't Fence Me In** /		
The Three Caballeros**	Decca 23364	11/44
Corns For My Country /		
I'm In A Jam (With Baby)	Decca 18628	11/44
Rum and Coca Cola /		
One Meat Ball	Decca 18636	12/44
Ac-Cent-Tchu-Ate The Positive** /		
There's A Fellow Waiting**	Decca 23379	1/45
Great Day / Pack Up Your Troubles	Decca 23412	4/45
Along The Navajo Trail** /		
Good, Good, Good**	Decca 23437	8/45
The Blond Sailor /		
Lily Belle	Decca 18700	8/45
Put The Ring On My Fingers /		
The Welcome Song	Decca 18726	11/45
Johnny Fedora And Alice Blue† /		
Money Is The Root Of All Evil†	Decca 23474	12/45
Patience And Fortitude /		
Red River Valley	Decca 18780	2/46
Don't Fence Me In** /		
Pistol Packin' Mama**	Decca 23484	3/46
Atlanta G.A. / Coax Me A Little Bit	Decca 18833	4/46
Avocado / Her Bathing Suit	Decca 18840	4/46
Azusa / I Don't Know Why		
(I Just Do)	Decca 18899	6/46
Get Your Kicks On Route 66 /		
South America Take It Away	Decca 23569	7/46
Bei Mir Bist Du Schon (Means) /		
Joseph! Joseph!	Decca 23605	8/46
Hold Tight* / Well, All Right*	Decca 23606	8/46
Beat Me Daddy (Eight To The Bar) /		
Scrub Me Mama With A		
Boogie Beat	Decca 23607	9/46
The House Of Blue Lights /		
A Man Is A Brother	Decca 23641	9/46
Rumors Are Flying /		
Them That Has Gets	Decca 23656	9/46
Christmas Island† /		
Winter Wonderland†	MCA 65020	11/46
The Coffee Song /		
A Rainy Night in Rio	Decca 23740	11/46
Lullably Of Broadway /		
My Dearest Uncle Sam	Decca 23824	2/47
His Feet Too Big For De Bed /		
Jack, Jack, Jack	Decca 23860	4/47
Go West, Young Man** /		
Tallahassee**	Decca 23885	6/47
Red River Valley	Decca 25149	6/47
The Lady From 29 Palms /		
The Turntable Song	Decca 23976	7/47
Anything You Can Do** /		
There's No Business Like		
Show Business**	Decca 40039	7/47
On The Avenue / Sweet Marie	Decca 24102	8/47
The Freedom Train**	Decca 23999	9/47
How Lucky You Are / Near You	Decca 24171	9/47
Sing A Tropical Song /		
South American Way	Decca 25095	9/47
Aurora / Rum and Coca Cola	Decca 25096	9/47
Begin The Beguine /		
Ti-Pi-Tin	Decca 25097	9/47
Tico Tico	Decca 25098	9/47
Bread And Butter Woman§ /		
Civilization§	Decca 23940	9/47
Too Fat Polka / Your Red Wagon	Decca 24268	12/47
Alpalachicola, Fla.** /		
You Don't Have To Know**	Decca 24282	1/48
My Sin§§ / Teresa§	Decca 24320	2/48
Big Brass Band From Brazil /		
It's A Quiet Town§	Decca 24361	3/48
I Hate To Lose You /		
Toolie Oolitie Dollie	Decca 24380	3/48
The Bride And Groom Polka /		
We Just Couldn't Say Good-Bye	Decca 24406	4/48
Don't Blame Me / Run, Run, Run	Decca 23827	5/48
Alexander's Ragtime Band /		
I Want To Go Back To Michigan	Decca 24424	5/48
Heat Wave / When The Midnight		
Choo Choo	Decca 24425	5/48
How Many Times /		
Some Sunny Day	Decca 24426	5/48
Jealous / Mean To Me	Decca 25303	5/48
Put 'Em In A Box Tie 'Em With§ /		
The Woody Woodpecker§	Decca 24462	7/48
Blue Tail Fly◊ / I'm Going Down		
The Road◊	Decca 24463	7/48
Cuanto La Gusta# /		
The Matador#	Decca 24479	8/48
At The Flying "W"** / A Hundred		
And Sixty Acres**	Decca 24481	8/48
Underneath The Arches /		
You Call Everybody Darling	Decca 24490	8/48
Bella Bella Marie /		
The Money Song	Decca 24499	9/48
I'd Love To Call You My Sweet§§ /		
What Did I Do§§	Decca 24504	10/48
Amelia Cordelia McHugh§ /		
Beatin', Bangin' 'N Scratchin'§	Decca 24536	1/49
Let A Smile Be Your Umbrella /		
More Beer!	Decca 24548	1/49
Underneath The Linden Tree	Decca 24560	2/49
Don't Rob Another Man's		
Castle## / I'm Bitin' My		
Finger Nails##	Decca 24592	3/49
In The Good Old Summertime /		
Take Me Out To The Ball Game	Decca 24605	4/49

A SIDE/B SIDE	LABEL/CAT NO	DATE
Hurry! Hurry! Hurry! / I Didn't		
Know The Gun Was Loaded	Decca 24613	4/49
Hohokus, N.J. / Malaguena	Decca 24645	5/49
Homework / Only For Americans	Decca 24660	6/49
Now! Now! Now! Is The Time*** /		
Oh, You Sweet One***	Decca 24664	6/49
I Can Dream, Can't I††† /		
The Wedding Of Lili Marlene†††	Decca 24705	8/49
Lovely Night◇◇ /		
Whispering Hope◇◇	Decca 24717	9/49
Betsy** / Weddin' Day**	Decca 24718	9/49
Christmas Candles† /		
Merry Christmas Polka†	Decca 24748	10/49
He Rides The Range§§§	Decca 24809	12/49
Charley My Boy*** / She Wore A		
Yellow Ribbon***	Decca 24812	12/49
The Blossoms On The Bough /		
Open Door, Open Arms	Decca 24822	1/50
Have I Told You Lately That** /		
Quicksilver**	Decca 24827	1/50
I See, I See (Asi, Asi)# /		
The Wedding Samba#	Decca 24841	1/50
Count Your Blessings /		
The Wedding Samba	Decca 14502	3/50
Ask Me No Questions** /		
Lock, Stock And Barrel**	Decca 24942	3/50
I Love To Tell The Story† /		
Softly and Tenderly†	Decca 14509	4/50
Jolly Fella Tarantella / Stars Are		
The Windows of Heaven	Decca 24965	4/50
Ca-Room' Pa Pa# / Yipsee-I-D#	Decca 24979	4/50
Muskrat Ramble /		
Walk With A Wiggle	Decca 24981	4/50
Choo'N Gum / I'm Gonna Paper		
All My Walls	Decca 24998	5/50
I Wanna Be Loved††† / I've Just		
Got To Get Out Of†††	Decca 27007	5/50
'Way Down Yonder In New		
Orleans§ / The Old Piano		
Roll Blues§	Decca 27024	5/50
The Ninety And Nine /		
Shall We Gather At The River	Decca 14521	7/50
Can't We Talk It Over /		
There Will Never Be Another	Decca 27115	8/50
High On The List** /		
Life Is So Peculiar**	Decca 27173	9/50
The Glory Of Love† /		
A Rainy Day Refrain†	Decca 27202	9/50
Here Comes Santa Claus** /		
Twelve Days Of Christmas**	Decca 24658	10/50
Mele Kalikimaka** / Poppa		
Santa Claus**	Decca 27228	10/50
A Merry Christmas At		
Grandmother's . . .§	Decca 24769	10/50
Jing-A-Ling Jing-A-Ling / Parade		
Of The Wooden Soldiers	Decca 27242	10/50
The Christmas Tree Angel /		
I'd Like To Hitch A Ride . . .	Decca 27251	10/50

A SIDE/B SIDE	LABEL/CAT NO	DATE
A Bushel And A Peck /		
Guys and Dolls	Decca 27252	10/50
Ching-Ara-Sa§ / Songs From		
Mr. Music§	Decca 27261	10/50
Sleigh Ride / The Telephone Song	Decca 27310	11/50
A Penny A Kiss-A Penny A Hug /		
Zing Zing-Zoom Zoom	Decca 27414	1/51
Between Two Trees /		
I Wish I Knew	Decca 27421	2/51
I'm In A Jam / Three O'Clock In		
The Morning	Decca 27432	2/51
Forsaking All Others** /		
Sparrow In The Treetop**	Decca 27477	3/51
I Remember Mama / My Mom	Decca 27537	4/51
Brighten The Corner / Let The		
Lower Lights Be Burning	Decca 14539	5/51
I Want To Be With You Always◇◇ /		
Satins And Lace◇◇	Decca 27609	6/51
Black Ball Ferry Line** /		
The Yodelling Ghost**	Decca 27631	7/51
He Bought My Soul At Calvary	Decca 14566	7/51
I'm In Love Again††† / It Never		
Entered My Mind†††	Decca 27635	7/51
Betsy** / Weddin' Day**	Decca 27555	7/51
Dimples And Cherry Cheeks /		
There Was A Night	Decca 27652	7/51
I Used To Love You	Decca 27700	7/51
Carioca / Daddy	Decca 27757	9/51
Love Is Such A Cheat /		
Lying In The Hay	Decca 27760	9/51
Goodbye Darling, Hello Friend /		
Nobody's Darling But Mine	Decca 27834	11/51
The Three Bells /		
The Windmill Song	Decca 27858	11/51
All The World To Me /		
The Blond Sailor	Decca 27878	11/51
Down In The Valley /		
Red River Valley	Decca 27894	12/51
I'm On A Seesaw Of Love /		
Play Me A Hurtin' Tune	Decca 27910	1/52
Poor-Whip-Poor-Will / Wondering	Decca 27979	2/52
It's Fun Learning Music /		
That Ever Lovin' Rag	Decca 28042	3/52
Dreams Come Tumbling Down /		
Music Lessons	Decca 28116	5/52
Linger Awhile*** /		
Wabash Blues***	Decca 28143	5/52
Here In My Heart§§ / I'm Sorry§§	Decca 28213	5/52
Idle Chatter / One For The Wonder	Decca 28276	6/52
I'll Si-Si Ya In Bahia** /		
The Live Oak Tree**	Decca 28256	7/52
Adios / Carmen's Boogie	Decca 28342	8/52
My Isle Of Golden Dreams△ /		
Naiani△	Decca 28294	8/52
The Cockeyed Mayer Of		
Kaunakak / King's Serenade	Decca 28295	8/52
Good Night Aloha△ /		
Malihini Mele△	Decca 28297	8/52

A SIDE/B SIDE	LABEL/CAT NO	DATE
Cool Water** / South Rampart		
Street Parade**	Decca 28419	10/52
No Deposit No Return	Decca 28492	12/52
Don't Be That WayΔΔ /		
Sing Sing SingΔΔ	Decca 28480	2/53
If I Had A Boy Like You /		
Piccolo Pete	Decca 28481	2/53
East Of The Sun / In The Mood	Decca 28482	2/53
The Mambo Man	Decca 28483	2/53
Fugue For Tin Horns /		
Now That I'm In Love	Decca 28680	4/53
Tegucigalpa / You Too, You Too?	Decca 28773	7/53
Love Sends A Little Gift§§ /		
This Little Piggie§§	Decca 28929	12/53
My Love, The Blues And Me /		
There's A Rainbow	Decca 29149	6/54
Bury Me Beneath The Willow◊◊ /		
She'll Never Know◊◊	Decca 29222	9/54

*	with Jimmy Dorsey	***	with Russ Morgan
**	with Bing Crosby	†††	with Gordon Jenkins
†	with Guy Lombardo	§§§	with Jerry Gray
§	with Danny Kaye	◊	with Burl Ives
§§	with Dick Haymes	◊◊	with Red Foley
#	with Carmen Miranda	Δ	with Alfred Apaka
##	with Ernest Tubb	ΔΔ	with Skip Martin

The Bachelors

The little-known recordings by the Bachelors are of special interest because most of the act's members eventually went on to well-known groups.

Formed in 1947 at Garner Patterson High School in Washington, D.C., the group first called themselves the Cavaliers, then the Jets. Their neighborhood would eventually spawn groups like THE CLOVERS, THE HEARTBREAKERS, the Parakeets, and the Serenaders, but the Jets were one of the first of the Washington street-corner quintets. Their membership included Waverly "Buck" Mason (lead), James "Toy" Walton (first tenor), Walter Taylor (second tenor), Herbert Fisher (baritone), and John Bowie (bass). Also participating was part-time second baritone and guitarist Charles Booker.

They played clubs and parties for four years, pulling their act together wherever they could earn and learn. Some places, like the Club Cavern, would garner the boys as much as $6 a week each plus food and tips. They were discovered in 1952 by Earthaline Lee at Washington's Cotton Club, and by the fall of 1952 she had them recording for Rainbow Records of New York.

By the time their first single, "The Lovers," was released in the summer of 1953, Buck Mason was army bound and Robert Russell had replaced him on lead. "Lovers" was a pretty R&B ballad, more than competently performed by the quintet and slightly reminiscent of THE SWALLOWS' 1951 recording of "Dearest." (It's probably no coincidence that Buck Mason's smooth lead vocal sounded similar to Swallows lead Eddie Rich: the Swallows were well-known in the Washington area, based just across the Maryland border in Baltimore.) One unusual (and pleasant) element of "The Lovers" is that it seems to be one of the first R&B vocal group ballads to have a sax solo backed by vocal harmony at equal volume for the entire section. But this uniqueness didn't earn the record sufficient promotion, and "The Lovers" was soon one more obscure single.

Later in 1953, an appearance at Turner's Arena brought the Jets to the attention of recording artist Amos Milburn. Amos was signed to West-Coast-based Aladdin Records, and he arranged a New York recording session for the group. Since Aladdin prexy Ed Meisner let it be known he already had an act called the Jets (actually THE HOLLYWOOD FLAMES cutting under one of their numerous aliases), the Washington Jets quickly became (for no apparent reason other than the fact that all five actually were) the Bachelors.

Their New York session—and the resulting single, "Can't Help Loving You"—came and went almost as quickly as the group had changed names.

More than two years passed before the group's next recording opportunity: a member of THE SOLITAIRES directed the Bachelors to New-York-based Royal Roost Records. A fateful recording session for Royal Roost in 1956 almost turned the group's fortunes around. Songwriter Otis Blackwell played the guys two songs prior to their recording of three they had already entitled "You've Lied," "Raining in My Heart," and "Baby." The group chose one of the two, "I Found Love," as their fourth side. Had they picked the other song they might have had a big hit and robbed Elvis Presley of his third number one record. The song was "Don't Be Cruel." "You've Lied" became their single and arguably their best release, but it never got off the ground.

The quintet began to search for a new label as well as some new faces. Walter Taylor and Herb Fisher left. Don Covey (formerly of the Rainbows) spent a minute with the act, and finally second tenor/baritone James Taylor (definitely not the "Fire and Rain" troubador) settled in.

In 1957 the group—now a quartet—had joined Poplar Records, also the new home of their Washington neighbors the Clovers. "After" was their only release. After it was over, the group realized that four singles on four labels in five years was no smooth road to success, so they broke up. In 1958, however, Walton and Fisher pulled together a group that included bass John Terry (formerly of the Dominoes), Joe Woodly, and Wilbert Dobson (both baritones).

Sporting three natural baritones, the group recorded for Teenage Records as the Links with "She's the One." One more interim group as the Knickerbockers (no recordings) and the Jets/Bachelors/Links began filtering into name groups.

By 1959 John Bowie had joined the original MOONGLOWS, taking Harvey Fuqua's place. He soon after became a member, with Harvey, of the new Moonglows, another Washington, D.C., group originally called the Marquees. John Terry joined THE DRIFTERS in 1962. Walton and Roosevelt Hubbard (of the Knickerbockers) joined the Clovers along with former Bachelors lead Robert Russell. By the early '60s, three fourths of Harold Lucas's Clovers were actually the Bachelors/Links/Knickerbockers, and by 1969 John Bowie had become a member following Robert Russell's death.

Keeping the tradition of the great groups alive via post-peak membership was probably the Bachelors' greatest legacy, although they did leave behind some fine R&B vocal group recordings. Collectors today seem to share that feeling: an authentic R&B vocal group sound combined with scarcity have made "You've Lied" valued at over $200 and "Can't Help Loving You" worth as much as $750.

The Barrett Sisters

One of the nation's top female gospel trios, the Barrett Sisters spent a good part of their youth singing solo before they became a long-term family group. The three sisters, Delois, Billie, and Rodessa began singing in the Morning Star Baptist Church at 3991 South Park Boulevard in Chicago around 1940. Rodessa (first soprano) was six, Delois (second soprano) was 10, and Billie (contralto) was eight when the trio, directed by their aunt Mattie Dacus, became first the Barrett and Hudson Singers (as they sang briefly with cou-

sin Johnnie Mae Hudson) and then simply the Barrett Sisters.

The girls attended Englewood High School, and while in her senior year, Delois was recruited by the famed Roberta Martin Singers. She returned to graduate and then spent the next 18 years as a member of Martin's group. Meanwhile, Rodessa moved to Gary, Indiana, and became the choir director of the Galileo Baptist Church. Billie studied voice training at the American Music Conservatory and became a church soloist.

In 1962 the three sisters drifted back together and re-formed the Barrett Sisters. Roberta Martin took the talented trio to Fred Mendelsohn at Savoy Records and in September of 1963 they issued their first LP *Jesus Loves Me*. The Barrett Sisters' fame began to spread, and their vocal blend earned them the name "The Sweet Sisters of Zion."

Over the years their status as consummate messengers of gospel music has enabled them to tour much of the world. In the U.S., they've performed all over, from Ford's Theatre in Washington and the Civic Opera House in Chicago to the Cow Palace in San Francisco. Their TV exposure has included Oprah Winfrey's show and "The Tonight Show." Today Billie Barrett Greenbey, Rodessa Barrett Porter, and Delois Barrett Campbell are still performing and touring the country.

The Basin Street Boys

Many vocal groups racked their collective brains to come up with an interesting name, only to find out later that another group had already used the same moniker (*i.e.*, THE DRIFTERS on Atlantic in 1953 preceded by the Drifters on Choral in 1950; THE ANGELS on Caprice in 1961 preceded by the Angels on Grand Records in 1954; THE DIAMONDS on Mercury in 1957 preceded by the Diamonds on Atlantic in 1951, and so on).

The Basin Street Boys of the late '40s, however, knew what they were doing when their lead singer named them after a popular Lynchburg, Virginia, act fronted in the '30s by the legendary Steve Gibson (see THE FIVE REDCAPS). The original "Boys" had moved to Los Angeles in 1937 and a young Belmont High student named Ormand Wilson had come to know the members. Influenced by the group, Wilson began his own singing career with Ben Cartens' Plantation Boys singing on the radio and doing movies. Several members of the Plantation Boys, including Ormand on lead, formed a group called the Dreamers in the early '40s.

By 1945 Ormand saw fit to form a new act, and with warm regards for his roots (Steve Gibson had even taught Ormand how to play guitar) he brought together Gene Price, Reuben Saunders, and Arthur Rainwater (a.k.a. Artie Waters) as the Basin Street Boys. Their sound suggested the best aspects of THE INK SPOTS while leaning toward the developing rhythm and blues style. They signed with Leon Rene's Los Angeles-based Exclusive Records and began recording in late 1945. (Rene later owned the Class record label and had written the 1941 standard "When the Swallows Come Back to Capistrano.")

The quartet's first release had them backing up then unknown (and still unknown) Judy Carroll on the Modernaires-styled shuffle "I Want to Love and Be Loved."

Their second shellac single, "Jumpin' at the Jubilee," got local attention, but it wasn't until the summer of 1946 that the group reached its peak popularity with the release of Leon and Otis Rene's "I Sold My Heart to the Junkman." "Junkman" never made the national pop or R&B charts, although the song was a beautiful ballad, with Ormand's crooning style very much in evidence and a solid backing by the group. But it *was* successful in performance and on radio, giving the group the opportunity to tour the country in the fall of 1947 with a stopover in New York. There they played the Apollo Theater and began doing the local New York/New Jersey club circuit, starting with the Twin Bass in Gloucester, New Jersey.

By now Exclusive had released five more Basin Street Boys singles. None had the magic of "Junkman," though "I'll Get Along Somehow," a very pretty ballad, deserved greater recognition. So did "Junkman," for that matter. But the song remained obscure until THE STARLETS made it a number 13 hit in 1962 under the name the Bluebells (see PATTI LABELLE AND THE BLUE BELLES).

By September of 1948, while the group was performing in the Cleveland area, Mercury Records had bought eight sides that the group had cut in Philadelphia. The labels now read "Ormand Wilson and the Basin Street Boys," and the first Mercury release coincidentally (or not) was "If I Can't Have You," the same song that the Five Redcaps (with Steve Gibson) had just released on MGM. (Completing the circle, it's rumored that

Ormand joined the Redcaps to perform at Chubby's Club in Collingswood, New Jersey in 1949.)

None of their records, as good as they were, got much attention beyond the club and theater circuits. The group earned its bread and butter as a performing unit (they were reported to have been a favorite of the Miami Mafia set) and this kept them going for the six years of their existence.

The group had split up by 1951 and melted into musical obscurity. Ormand Wilson hasn't been seen or heard from since 1969. Nonetheless, their 12 singles had an impact on the music that would soon become 1950s rhythm and blues.

THE BASIN STREET BOYS

A SIDE/B SIDE	LABEL/CAT NO	DATE
Judy Carol and the Basin Street Boys		
Changes / I Want To Love And Be Loved	Excl 215	1945
The Basin Street Boys		
Jumpin' At The Jubilee / Nothin' Ever Happens To Me	Exlc 220	1946
I Sold My Heart To the Junk Man / Voot Nay On The Vot Nay	Exlc 225	1946
This Is The End Of A Dream / I Need A Knife, Fork And A Spoon	Excl 229	1946
I'm Gonna Write A Letter To My Baby / Josephine	Excl 239	1947
I'll Get Along Somehow / Exactly Like You	Excl 247	1947
Summertime Gal / Satchel Mouth Baby	Excl 19x	1947
You're Mine Forever / Near You	Excl 21x	1947
Ormond Wilson and the Basin Street Boys		
If I Can't Have You / Come To Me	Merc 8106	10/48
Please Give My Heart A Break / To Make A Mistake Is Human	Merc 8120	12/48

The Beavers

In the 1940s and '50s many groups were formed by would-be singers in junior high schools, high schools, and colleges, but only a handful were put together by *teachers* for the express purpose of recording and performing. The Dominoes, a New York group, were formed by teacher Billy Ward; the Velvets from Odessa, Texas, were assembled by music instructor Virgil Johnson. One of the more obscure groups to come together in this manner was the Beavers. Voice teacher Joe Thomas put his dream group together in 1949 using students at his New York music school. They included leads Fred Hamilton (tenor) and John Wilson (baritone), Raymond Johnson (bass), and Dick Palmer (tenor and brother of THE JIVE BOMBERS lead singer, Clarence "Bad Boy" Palmer).

Their recording opportunity came later in 1949 when Joe Thomas got them a contract with Coral Records. Neither of their two releases charted, but the group became a vehicle for the songwriting of Thomas and Howard Biggs, the group's arranger (and former arranger for THE RAVENS). Two outstanding songs were "I'd Rather Be Wrong than Blue" and "If You See Tears in My Eyes." The former was later recorded by the Shadows on Lee Records and the latter was done beautifully by THE DELTA RHYTHM BOYS on Atlantic in 1950. The Beavers had greater success when their name wasn't on the label: Lionel Hampton and the Hamptones covered the AMES BROTHERS hit "Ragmop" in February of 1950, which went top five on the R&B charts and rose to number seven on the pop charts. You guessed it—the Hamptones *were* the Beavers. They were also the unsung background heroes on Herb Lance's 1949 R&B top 10 hit, "That Lucky Old Son" on Sittin' In Records. The group broke up in 1950 when Palmer and Johnson left to join THE BLENDERS, and by 1951 Johnson had moved on again, this time to join the Marshall Brothers on Savoy.

THE BEAVERS

A SIDE/B SIDE	LABEL/CAT NO	DATE
If You See Tears In My Eyes / I Gotta Do It	Coral 65018	10/49
I'd Rather Be Wrong Than Blue / Big Mouth Mama	Coral 65026	3/50
That Lucky Old Son	Sittin In	1949
Rag Mop†	Decca 24885	1950

† as the Hamptones

The Blenders

When one member of a group gets in on the flip of a coin, a second is okayed by a singer from another group, and a third joins when he is replaced in his previous group by a new lead singer, you tend to conclude that their collaboration was an

accident. That's how the Blenders came together, and though they were not a big success, they were one of those important interim groups that served as a link between late '40s gospel and pop and early '50s R&B.

Their story began in 1949 in New York City. Ollie Jones, a second tenor, was the replaced vocalist who decided to start his own group. His original quartet was none other than the legendary RAVENS. Pressed by group leader and bass Jimmy Ricks to move up, Ollie became the act's tenor lead on their first recordings for the Hub label in 1946. Soon after, however, his position became jeopardized when the amazing Maithe Marshall signed on. By 1948, Ollie and baritone Tommy Adams were touring as part of another group called the Four Notes. By 1949, Jones felt it was time to act. He found bass singer James DeLoach, and took him to Jimmy Ricks to see what Ricks thought. Auditioning for someone not in the group he was trying to join seemed a little strange to James, but when Ricks said he sounded fine, DeLoach quickly jumped on the bandwagon. Ollie and James then began interviewing tenors, and when they found two of apparently equal caliber, they made the decision by flipping a coin; Abel DeCosta was added to the roster. Tommy Adams of the Four Notes joined as a baritone and the quartet was on its way. Proud of their smooth harmonies, they named themselves the Blenders.

The group's Ravens-like arrangements were no accident; Jimmy Ricks was actively working with the group as an unofficial manager. It was through him that the Blenders met National Records exec Lee Magid (the Ravens were on National from 1947 to 1951). The Blenders cut only one single for National in the fall of 1949: "I Can Dream Can't I" with Tommy Adams on lead. In early 1950, Magid went to work for Decca and took the Blenders with him.

Their first Decca release came in May of 1950, with an excellent ballad entitled "Gone." Its blues sound and background vocal "oh's" were exemplary of R&B at the time. Groups like the Blenders were taking what they learned from gospel groups, blues artists, and THE INK SPOTS and translating it into a more acceptable pop sound in the early '50s. Later, young groups would emulate their harmonies while adding a rock beat and rhythm. Both sides of the Blenders single had a tenor lead by Ollie Jones, as Lee Magid was not convinced that the world needed another bass lead group like the Ravens. But when "Gone" failed, he gave the Ravens approach a shot in June of 1950 with the DeLoach lead "Count

Every Star" (actually a cover of the Ravens' far superior version released two months earlier). For the next single, the Blenders released a version of "I'm So Crazy for Love," recorded in October 1950 and released the following month. Returning the earlier favor, the Ravens recorded the same song in November and released their version in December. It was not uncommon in the '50s for two or more acts to cut the same song when word got around that someone had a hot song. In this case, however, the competition managed to kill off both versions.

The quartet's first record of 1951 was a beautiful version of the classic "The Masquerade Is Over," also cut at the October session. By this time membership changes were having an effect on the group's stability. Dick Palmer replaced ailing baritone Tommy Adams. Dick had been a member of the Palmer Brothers with brothers Clarence and Earnest. (Six years later Clarence would become lead of the JIVE BOMBERS on the classic "Bad Boy.") James DeLoach also succumbed to illness, and Ray Johnson joined the act. Now half of the Blenders (Palmer and Johnson) on Decca were formerly half of the BEAVERS on Coral, who had just split up due to their exit. By the summer of 1951, DeLoach was back and Johnson was on baritone; then both he and Palmer left and baritone Napoleon "Snaggs" Allen came in the revolving door.

Throughout 1951 and 1952, the group released singles on Decca and toured extensively on the club circuit. In March of 1952, the group played a week at the Apollo Theatre even though their score card at the time read "seven singles out, no success." That same week a riot broke out at a show in Cleveland hosted by up-and-coming disc jockey Alan Freed, forcing the cancellation of that event.

They turned out two more singles for Decca in April and June 1952, neither of which helped their stalled recording career. But the group kept moving forward. Dropped by Decca after eight singles, they were signed by new manager Rita Don to MGM for two well-crafted but unpromoted releases. When MGM exec Joe Davis left to set up his own Jay Dee label, the group found themselves a new recording home for the fourth time in four years. The result was the Ollie Jones-led "Don't Play Around with Love," which became a popular East Coast record and by far their most successful recording. Joe Davis had the group revise the lyrics slightly on one tape and sent tape copies of "Don't F--- Around with Love" to various deejays. This recording became the group's last release under their own name while still together. In January of 1956, Davis released "Somebody's Lying" (under

the name the Millionaires) from the group's original session with him in 1953. Decca put out two previously unreleased cuts in July of 1961, and collectors everywhere cheered when Kelway Records, an obscure Staten Island label, put out "Don't F--- Around with Love" on a single in 1971. The group, however, had long since disbanded in 1954, as founder Ollie Jones took Abel DeCosta from the transitional Blenders to form one of the premier background groups of the mid- to late '50s, THE CUES.

THE BLENDERS

A SIDE/B SIDE	LABEL/CAT NO	DATE
I Can Dream Can't I /		
Come Back Baby Blues	Nat'l 9092	11/49
Gone / Honeysuckle Rose	Decca 48156	5/50
Count Every Star / Would I Still Be		
The One In Your Heart	Decca 48158	6/50
I'm So Crazy For Love /		
What About Tonight	Decca 48183	10/50
I'm Afraid The Masquerade Is		
Over / Little Small Town Girl	Decca 27403	1/51
All I Gotta Do Is Think		
Of You / Busiest Corner In		
My Hometown	Decca 27587	1951
My Heart Will Never Forget /		
You Do The Dreamin'	Decca 48244	10/51
I'd Be A Fool Again /		
Just A Little Walk With Me	Decca 28092	4/52
Never In A Million Years /		
Memories Of You	Decca 28241	6/52
I Don't Miss You Anymore /		
If That's The Way You Want		
It Baby	MGM 11488	5/53
Please Take Me Back /		
Isn't It A Shame	MGM 11531	7/53
You'll Never Be Mine Again /		
Don't Play Around With Love	Jay-Dee 780	9/53
Somebody's Lying* /		
Kansas Kapers*	Davis 441	1/56
Tell Me What's On Your Mind /		
When I'm Walkin' With My Baby	Dvs 31284	1961
Don't F— Around With Love /		
I'm Gonna Do That Woman In	Kelway 101	1971

* as the Millionaires

The Brown Dots

The Brown Dots came together in New York City in 1944, and were actually the first spin-off group of THE INK SPOTS. Deek Watson, tenor and an original member of the Spots from 1931, departed after a dispute with the group and formed another Ink Spots with Jimmy Gordon (bass), Joe King (tenor), and Pat Best (baritone). Jimmy Nabbie, a singer with a beautiful operatic voice and a founder of the pop group the Orange Blossom Singers (1940–41), auditioned for the group and became a member, soon replacing Joe King. Meanwhile, the original Ink Spots filed a lawsuit to stop Watson's group from using the name. Deek, not wanting to lose the association with his past success, changed the name, just barely, from the Ink Spots to the Brown Dots.

They signed to record for the Newark-based Manor label in 1946 and turned out some excellent pop harmony records over the next four years. A versatile group, all but Gordon sang lead on one or more of their 18 single releases. Several of the members became accomplished songwriters as well: Watson and Best wrote the classic "I Love You for Sentimental Reasons." The song became the B side of their second single. In 1946, it was released again, this time as the A side, but it never charted nationally. The writers did, however, see the song become a number one record in 1946 by Nat King Cole and then a top 20 hit in 1957 for Sam Cooke. It was also covered by the Riviliers on Baton in 1954 and then again by THE CLEFTONES on Gee in the fall of 1961.

In the late 1940s and after 13 single releases, friction developed between the group and Deek Watson. Gordon, Nabbie, and Best brought in Danny Owens of the spiritual group the Colemanaires and changed their name to the Sentimentalists, while Watson formed a new Brown Dots aggregation.

No sooner had the Sentimentalists logged a few releases than they were requested by bandleader Tommy Dorsey to change their name. It turned out that Dorsey had a vocal group with the same name, and even though his group had disbanded, he still had the name first, and he owned it.

The group, taking stock of the songs they had not yet recorded under the name the Sentimentalists, realized the collection added up to only four tunes. Naturally the group therefore took the name THE FOUR TUNES.

Meanwhile, Deek Watson closed out the Brown Dots history in 1949 with four competent but unsuccessful singles, including "If I Could Be with You," featuring a female lead sung by Gwen Bell. Unlike Deek's original Brown Dots assemblage, which recorded new compositions, his later group recorded several standards like "Dark Town Strutters' Ball" and "My Bonnie Lies Over the Ocean."

THE BROWN DOTS

A SIDE/B SIDE	LABEL/CAT NO	DATE
Let's Give Love Another Chance / Thirty-One Miles For A Nickel (Subway Serenade)	Manor 1005	1945
For Sentimental Reasons / You're Heaven Sent	Manor 1009	1945
Just In Case You Change Your Mind / You're A Heartache To Me	Manor 1015	1945
That's What She Gets / Escuchame	Manor 1016	1945
It Is Right / Patience And Fortitude	Manor 1017	1945
Surrender / Satchemouth Baby	Manor 1026	1946
If I Can't Have You / I'm Loving You For You	Manor 1027	1946
Please Give A Broken Heart A Break / Well Natch	Manor 1032	1946
Rumors Are Flying / You Took All My Love	Manor 1040	1946
It's A Pity To Say Goodnight / For Sentimental Reasons	Manor 1041	1946
How Can You Say I Don't Care / Long Legged Lizzie	Manor 1044	1947
I Don't Know From Nothing Baby / Shout Brother Shout	Manor 1057	1948
That's What She Gets / Why You Know Knock	Manor 1075	1948
Let's Give Love Another Chance / Just In Case You Change Your Mind	Manor 1163	1949

The Sentimentalists		
Silent Night / O Come All Ye Faithful	Manor 8002	1948
Ave Maria / White Christmas	Manor 8003	
I Want To Be Loved / Foolishly Yours	Manor 1046	1948
I'll Close My Eyes / Save Me A Dream	Manor 1047	1948
I'd Rather Be Safe Than Sorry / I'll Be Waiting For You	Manor 1049	1948

Deek Watson's Second Brown Dots Group on Manor		
Darktown Strutters' Ball / As Tho' You Don't Know	Manor 1166	1948
At Our Fireplace / Bow-Wow-Wow	Manor 1170	1948
If I Could Be With You / After Awhile	Manor 1171	1948
My Bonnie Lies Over The Ocean / You Better Think Twice	Manor 1179	1948

The Cats and the Fiddle

"**A** group that was ahead of its time" best describes the '40s vocal/instrumental combo the Cats and the Fiddle. Formed in Chicago in 1937, Jimmy Henderson, first tenor, Ernie Price, second tenor, and Chuck Barksdale, bass, were searching for a lead singer when they met Austin Powell. Austin had been the featured vocalist for a local high school quartet known as the Harlem Harmony Hounds. The new quartet christened itself the Cats and the Fiddle from an old nursery rhyme. The fact that the term "cats" came from jazz slang and "fiddle" related to Barksdale's stand-up bass made for a satisfying choice of name.

From the beginning their harmony was a blend of jazz and gospel with a touch of MILLS BROTHERS. Their recording career began in 1939 when Victor Records representative Lester Melrose spotted the boys at one of their numerous live performances in Chicago. Signed to Victor's Bluebird affiliate, the group issued its first release in August with the unlikely title of "Nuts to You." Though racial barriers of the period kept the "Cats" sound confined mostly to black audiences, they did appear in a few films with white stars, most notably *Goin' Places* with Dick Powell and Anita Louise. Playing stable boys, they were featured singing "Jeepers Creepers" in the 1939 flick.

After four more single releases the group hit with the Jimmy Henderson-penned ballad "I Miss You So." The mid-tempo shuffle (the label said "fox trot"), with high tenor harmonies carried through the entire recording, included a tipple-led instrumental (a tipple is a long-forgotten 10-stringed instrument that looks like a small acoustic guitar and sounds like a ukulele). The song, later slowed down and recorded by THE ORIOLES, is now a standard, but in early 1940 it was just another excellent black vocal-group recording unknown to the mass market. Still, it was popular in black communities and enabled Austin and company to continue their whirlwind schedule of national one-nighters, from the Apollo Theatre to elegant supper clubs.

Tragically, Henderson contracted meningitis during "I Miss You So's" climb to popularity, and he died before 1940 was over. A former member of the Harlem Harmony Hounds, Herbie Miles, took over the first tenor slot in July until Lloyd "Tiny" Grimes replaced him in January 1941 starting with the single "If I Dream of You." The quartet's trage-

dies continued when Barksdale died in 1941 and was supplanted by George Steinback. The first tenor spot rotated again as Tiny left in 1942 to be replaced by Mifflin "Pee Wee" Branford.

The group recorded the last of its 21 singles for Bluebird on October 17th, just 50 days before Pearl Harbor. The record, ironically titled "Life's Too Short (To Worry 'Bout That)," was issued in February of 1942, and between the war, the shortage of shellac (used to make records), and the recording industry strike of that year, there was little further opportunity for the act to wax their performances. The group continued to appear, but without Austin Powell, who had been drafted in 1943. His position was temporarily covered by Hank Haslett and later by the returning Herbie Miles.

In late 1944 the Cats and the Fiddle signed with the Regis/Manor group of labels, rerecording "I Miss You So" with Ernie Price up front. Austin Powell returned in 1946 just in time to lead the group on the Loveday-Kreska standard "That's My Desire," 11 years before THE CHANNELS' magnificent version borrowed from the Cats creativity.

Several personnel changes occurred in the mid-to-late '40s, including the addition of Shirley Moore singing lead on their next-to-last Manor single "Honey Honey Honey."

By 1950 they were on Gotham Records of Philadelphia, achieving local success with "I'll Never Let You Go"; they ended their recording career that year with one single for Decca.

In 1951 Powell formed a new act consisting of Doris Knighton, Johnny Davis (tenor), Stanley Gaines (bass), Beryl Booker (formerly of the Toppers), and Dottie Smith (formerly of the Harlemaires on Atlantic). He called the act the Austin Powell Quintet, and they recorded one Decca single, "All This Can't Be True," in 1951. The group soon fell apart as both Austin and Dottie moved over to Louis Jordan's group.

The Cats legacy of 36 releases only partially tells their story. Of course they had to be good to get that many chances, but beyond that the group pioneered their style of vocal harmony many years before it was popular to do so.

The Charioteers

One of the tightest and most popular harmony groups of the 1940s, the Charioteers were another of the handful of aggregations put together in school by a teacher. Their mentor and vocalist was professor Howard Daniel, and their school was Wilberforce University in Ohio. Professor Daniel built his group around the brilliant lead voice of tenor Billy Williams; the other members were Ira Williams and Ed Jackson. Forming in 1930, they originally called themselves the Harmony Four. Later they changed it to the Charioteers, from the song "Swing Low, Sweet Chariot," a favorite from the group's repertoire. Starting out with spirituals, the group expanded its collection to include a greater number of popular tunes. Their first break came after winning the Ohio State Quartet contest in 1931, and soon after, they were brought in to perform on a Cincinnati radio show at station WLW. They ended up staying with the station for over two years, until another radio series brought them to New York.

They signed their first recording contract with Decca Records in 1935. Between 1935 and 1939 they recorded for V-Disc, Vocalion, Brunswick, and Decca without having a hit, yet their popularity grew through radio and live performances. Unlike most of the popular black vocal groups of the time (like THE INK SPOTS and THE DELTA RHYTHM BOYS) who did little backup work, or rarely received credit on records when they did back up major vocalists, the Charioteers had the good fortune to record with three major singers over a 10-year span (1935–1945): Pearl Bailey, Frank Sinatra, and Bing Crosby. Their long run as guests on the Bing Crosby radio show seems to have justified label credit alongside the stars.

In 1938, they signed with Columbia (and its Okeh affiliate), where they would stay for over 10 years. Ironically, in all that time they only had one R&B chart record, a beautiful ballad "A Kiss and a Rose," in the summer of 1949. The song, which the Charioteers copied from the Ink Spots' original rendition of the same year, went to number eight on the R&B charts. Ironically, Billy Williams, a recording member for 14 years, left the Charioteers only five months after their first and only hit. He then formed a new group in early 1950. The rest of the Charioteers also left Columbia in 1950 and drifted through five labels over the next seven years, never quite regaining the popularity they had with Billy.

Given the Charioteers' lack of hits, it was pure talent, performance popularity, and relatively stable membership that kept them together for 26 years, recording 75 single releases over 22 of those years. Their last single release was "The Candles" on MGM records in 1957.

THE CHARIOTEERS

A SIDE/ B SIDE	LABEL/CAT NO	DATE
Along Tobacco Road / Ridin' Around In The Rain	Decca 420	1935
Little David Play On Your Harp / Snowball	Decca 421	1935
Cancel The Flowers / The Train Song	V-Disc 431	
One More Dream*	V-Disc 673	
My Lord, What A Mornin / I've Got A Home In That Rock Medley From "The Fleet's In"*	V-Disc 729	
Ooh, Look-a There, Ain't She Pretty	V-Disc 839	
Who**	V-Disc 865	
Words That Are Breaking My Heart	V-Disc 893	
Sing A Song Of Six Pence / Way Down Yonder In New Orleans	Vocln 3923	1/38
Song Of The Volga Boatmen / Dark Eyes†	Vocln 4015	4/38
A Brown Bird Singing†	Vocln 4068	5/38
Laughing Boy Blues / Sing You Sinners††	Vocln 4125	5/38
Let's Have Harmony / The Man Who Cares (Penny Wise)	Bms 8237	10/38
My Gal Sal / Forget If You Can	Vocln 5025	8/39
Don't Dally With The Devil§ / Sometimes I Feel Like A Motherless Child§	Okeh 5209	1939
Steal Away To Jesus / Water Boy	Brns 8459	9/39
Swing Low, Sweet Chariot / All God's Chillun Got Shoes	Brns 8468	10/39
I'm Gettin' Sentimental Over You / Why Should I Complain	Col 35229	10/39
Don't Dally With The Devil§ / Sometimes I Feel Like A Motherless Child§	Vocln 5209	11/39
So Long / The Gaucho Serenade	Col 35424	4/40
Water Boy / Swing Low, Sweet Chariot	Col 35693	9/40
Go Down Moses / Were You There	Col 35718	9/40
Darling, Je Vous Aime Beacoup / Calling Romance	Col 35736	10/40
I'm In His Care / All God's Chillun Got Shoes	Col 35741	10/40
Love's Old Sweet Song / Silver Threads Among The Gold	Col 35749	10/40
I Don't Want To Cry Anymore / Only Forever	Col 35765	10/40
Calliope Jane / I Should Have Known You Years Ago	Col 35779	11/40
Steal Away To Jesus / Jesus Is A Rock In A Weary Land	Col 35787	11/40
The Call Of The Canyon / We'll Meet Again	Col 35811	11/40

A SIDE/ B SIDE	LABEL/CAT NO	DATE
Goodnight, Mother My Heart's On Ice	Col 35851	12/40
Old Folks At Home / Carry Me Back To Old Virginny	Col 35887	1/41
May I Never Love Again / Why Is A Good Gal So Hard To Find	Col 35942	2/41
Between Friends / I'll Forget	Col 35981	2/41
Braggin' / You Walk By	Col 36027	3/41
I Understand / A Dream For Sale	Col 36094	5/41
Song Of The Volga Boatmen / Dark Eyes†	Okeh 4015	1941
Speak To Me Of Love / A Brown Bird Singing†	Okeh 4068	1941
Laughing Boy Blues / Sing You Sinners††	Okeh 4125	1941
Forget If You Can / My Gal Sal	Okeh 5025	1941
All Alone And Lonely / Careless Love	Okeh 6220	6/41
Daddy / Down, Down, Down	Okeh 6247	6/41
Wrap Up Your Troubles In Dreams / I Heard Of A City Called Heaven	Okeh 6292	7/41
The Cowboy Serenade / Yes Indeed	Okeh 6310	7/41
I Don't Want To Set The World On Fire / One Two Three O'Lairy	Okeh 6332	8/41
Elmer's Tune / Hawaiian Sunset	Okeh 6390	9/41
Nothin' / Call It Anything It's Love	Okeh 6424	10/41
I Got It Bad And That Ain't Good / Cancel The Flowers	Okeh 6509	12/41
Tica-Tee Tica-Ta / The Train Song	Okeh 6589	2/42
Sylvia / This Side Of Heaven	Col 36730	8/44
Don't You Notice Anything New / It Doesn't Cost You Anything	Col 36792	4/45
Lily Belle§§ / Don't Forget Tonight Tomorrow§§	Col 36854	9/45
No Soup / One More Dream	Col 36903	1/46
On The Boardwalk / You Make Me Feel Young	Col 37074	8/46
Bagel And Lox / Rogue River Valley	Col 37195	12/46
Open The Door, Richard / You Can't See The Sun When You're Crying	Col 37240	2/47
Say No More / Chi-Baba Chi-Baba	Col 37384	5/47
So Long / Ride Red Ride	Col 37399	6/47
Sylvia / I'm Gettin' Sentimental Over You	Col 37518	6/47
The Gaucho Serenade / We'll Meet Again	Col 37519	6/47
I Miss You So / You're Breaking In A New Heart	Col 37546	6/47
I've Got A Home In That Rock / Jesus Is A Rock In A Weary Land	Col 37853	9/47
I'm In The Mood For Love / Sweet Lorraine	Col 37912	11/47

A SIDE/ B SIDE	LABEL/CAT NO	DATE
Sleepy Time Gal / My Fate Is In Your Hands	Col 37913	11/47
If I Could Be With You / On The Sunny Side Of The Street	Col 37914	11/47
I Can't Get Started / Sweet Marie	Col 37915	11/47
What Did He Say / Oooh! Look-A There Ain't She Pretty	Col 38065	12/47
Now Is The Hour# / Peculiar#	Col 38115	2/48
When I Grow Too Old To Dream / The Last Thing I Want Is Your Pity	Col 38187	4/48
Run, Run, Run / The Tourist Trade	Col 38261	7/48
It's Too Soon To Know / Until	Col 38329	9/48
A Kiss And A Rose / A Cottage In Old Donegal	Col 38438	3/49
Who** / Don't Ever Leave Me**	Hrmny 1059	10/49
This Side Of Heaven / Hawaiian Sunset	Col 38602	
S'Posin' / I'm The World's Biggest Fool	Kystn 1416	1952
I've Got My Heart On My Sleeve / Don't Play No Mambo	Josie 787	1955
Easy Does It / Tremble, Tremble, Tremble	RCA 47-6098	4/55
Thanks For Yesterday / I'm A Stranger	Tuxedo 891	1955
Forget If You Can / Sleepy River Moon	Tuxedo 892	1955
The Candles / I Didn't Mean To Be Mean To You	MGM 12569	1957

*	with Bing Crosby	§	with Mildred Bailey
**	with Pearl Bailey	§§	with Frank Sinatra
†	with Maxine Sullivan	#	with Buddy Clark
††	with Fletcher Henderson		

The Coleman Brothers

During the '40s and '50s, various publications and radio stations began issuing charts to indicate the most popular records. Whether it was pop, R&B, country, or some crossover combination, charts covered everything from jukebox plays to record sales. One area of music that was not directly affected by the hits list was spiritual music.

Performers doing spirituals earned their success the long hard way, through performances and radio activity, but not in a competitive mode. A group's greatness was judged mainly on its artistic ability and longevity. Among those with both were the

Coleman Brothers, nearly three generations of them, encompassing 10 family members in three Coleman groups.

The first Coleman Brothers formed in Montclair, New Jersey, in 1917 after various family members moved from Kenbridge, Virginia. There were almost as many ministers in the family as there were singers, and the church was the center of Coleman family life. The members were David, Lewis, Matthew, and Levi Coleman. Known as the Coleman Brothers Quartet, they spent years building a reputation as a stirring and emotive group.

In 1925 younger cousin Everette Coleman and his family arrived in New Jersey and quickly formed the second Coleman family group, consisting of Everette (lead), Lander (tenor), Wallace (tenor), Jack (bass), and non-family members Howard Harris and Robert Tippins, both baritones. A year after that, New Jersey became Coleman country as a third and even younger group emerged, including Lander (moonlighting in both groups), Octavius, Melvin, and Robert Bright, ranging in age from 12 to 16. They christened themselves the Jubilee Four and performed under that name until 1932 when they merged with the second Coleman Brothers.

The first group had retired in 1926 without ever recording. The new combination evolved by 1933 to include Russell, 17 (first tenor), Lander, 20 (second tenor), Wallace, 19 (baritone), and Melvin, 21 (bass). Everette also stayed with the Colemans but mostly played guitar. Rounding out the group with Danny Owens, the Brothers-plus-one jumped from radio shows to national tours without skipping a beat.

In 1943 manager Milton Lesnick took charge of the Coleman Brothers and eventually brought them to Decca Records to record. Their first 78, in November of 1944, was "Low Down the Chariot," which would become one of their most popular and memorable performances.

They began singing on WABC radio every day and became the house group at CBS radio with their own morning show in New York. They were now performing a wider variety of music; the show included everything from spirituals to country and western. They became one of the first black groups to do television commercials for major products when in 1945 they advertised Chase & Sanborn coffee on NBC.

The brothers were so popular and successful that they set up their own business empire encompassing a record label (Coleman Records), a lodge, a hotel in Newark, and a collection of barbeque restaurants in the Newark area. Melvin became the record company president, Lander was vice president, and Russell operated as secretary. Soon after, A. J. Eldridge replaced Melvin so the latter could work full time on the Brothers' lucrative business enterprises.

By 1946 they'd moved on to Cincinnati to work on WLW, the same station that launched the Mills Brothers.

They sporadically issued 78s like "Get Away Mr. Satin, Get Away" on Decca, and in 1945 made four records for the Manor label. In 1947 Coleman Brothers records came out on both Decca and Manor, indicating that one of the labels had extra sides in the can or the Brothers were recording unethically for one of the companies.

By the end of 1948, the Coleman Brothers had done numerous commercials, TV shows, radio shows, national tours, and even had a hit on their own record label with the Ray-O-Vacs, "I'll Always Be in Love with You," an R&B best seller reaching number eight in January of 1949. The group toured so much they traveled the equivalent of 16 times across the country each year from 1948 to 1951. They appeared with every spiritual great of the times, from Mahalia Jackson to Sister Rosetta Thorpe, on a variety of occasions. In 1950, having pretty much done it all, the group recorded three secular singles for Regal Records and then retired in 1951.

Lander became manager of a supper club in northern Newark. The boys sold Coleman Records to Savoy a year after Melvin died in 1959. Russell became a minister, as did two other brothers, James and William.

Lander, however, still had a desire to sing and perform, so a new Coleman Brothers Quartet was created with John Bryant, Fred Perry, and A. J. Eldridge in 1964. It was his first time with a group outside the family since he did a stint in 1934–35 with the Chain Gang Quartet, a spiritual group that performed in prison costumes in a vaudeville show featuring Georgia-chain-gang-fugitive-turned-author Robert E. Burns. A bizarre enterprise for a religious boy, to say the least.

The Coleman Brothers Quartet did an LP for Savoy titled *Milky White Way* after Lander's most successful song, having been recorded by Elvis Presley. The Quartet's career ended abruptly in 1978 when Bryant and Perry were shot down by robbers in New York. They both recovered, but the group didn't. For many years after, Lander performed as a solo artist in the United States and Europe.

THE COLEMAN BROTHERS

A SIDE/B SIDE	LABEL/CAT NO	DATE
Low Down The Chariot / His Eye Is On The Sparrow	Decca 8662	11/44
It's My Desire / The End Of My Journey	Manor 100	1945
We'll Understand / New Milky White Way	Manor 101	1945
Plenty Of Room In The Kingdom / I Can See Everybody's Mother But Mine	Manor 102	1945
Plenty Of Room In The Kingdom / I Can See Everybody's Mother But Mine	Manor 1003	1945
Get Away Mr. Satan, Get Away / Raise A Ruckus Tonight	Decca 8673	1/46
New What A Time / When The Saints Go Marching In	Manor 1055	1947
Noah / My Eye Is On The Sparrow	Manor 1065	1947
Sending Up My Timber / Where Shall I Be	Decca 48041	6/47
See / We're Living Humble	Decca 48051	10/47
His Eye Is On The Sparrow / Low Down The Chariot	Coral 65003	1/49
Ooh La La / Goodnight Irene	Regal 3281	1950

The Colemans

You Know I Love You, Baby / I Don't Mind Being All Alone	Regal 3297	1950
I Ain't Got Nobody / If You Should Care For Me	Regal 3308	1950

The Deep River Boys

The Deep River Boys were another 1940s group whose success was predominantly in the live performance medium and not in the recording field, though they had ample opportunity to reach the shellac and vinyl buyers via 39 singles and 11 albums over a 25-year period.

As did so many other black groups of the '30s and '40s, the future River Boys met at college, in this case Virginia's Hampton Institute. Each grade had a different name for its quartet group: the sophomores were in the Armstrong Quartet (named after the school's founder, General Armstrong); the juniors, the Junior Quartet; and the seniors, the Senior Quartet. Vernon Gardner (first tenor) and George Lawson (second tenor) were in the Junior aggregation while Harry Douglas (baritone) and Edward Ware (bass) were members of the Armstrong group.

In 1936 Lawson and Gardner saw Douglas and Ware perform and asked the sophs if they'd like to try a few songs as a foursome. The blend was a good one and, encouraged by Lawson, the group set off for New York.

Their first performing competition was on the "Major Bowes' Amateur Hour" radio show; they won and carved up the $100 prize. Their next break was a dressing room audition at the Suffern Summer Theatre for producer Josh Logan; he hired them to sing prior to the main show, *Emperor Jones*. The Hampton Institute Junior Quartet (as they christened themselves) were now earning the astronomical sum of $40 per man a week.

When the show closed Ingram invited them on a promotional trip for his new film, *Green Pastures*, and renamed them after their theme song, "Deep River."

Unlike most groups that left school for an entertainment career, come September the boys actually returned, staying there for almost two months until Ingram contacted them with a job in Eddie Dowling's Caravan, a political/entertainment road show for the New York State Democratic Party. The campaign was short-lived, and the boys all too quickly found themselves with no money and their only asset: a repertoire of spirituals. When the disappointment of a CBS radio turndown set in during late 1936 (not because they weren't good, but because they had no pop songs), the quartet set out to put together a trove of songs while taking whatever work they could get.

By the spring of 1937 the group had about 20 songs and a spot in the very short-lived Broadway play *How Come Law'd*, starring Rex Ingram. The play was harpooned by the critics but the Boys got positive reviews. They caught the attention of CBS, and one day after *Law'd* closed, the Law'd of radio called. CBS was a great exposure medium for vocal groups in the '40s, often providing a launching pad for successful careers. The Deep River Boys replaced the Oleanders, whose lead, Billy Williams, left to recruit THE CHARIOTEERS. The Boys were later replaced by THE GOLDEN GATE QUARTET, who in turn were replaced by THE DELTA RHYTHM BOYS.

The Boys had to learn 20 to 30 songs a week to meet the demands of the show.

In 1940 the group signed to Bluebird Records. Their first 78, "Nothing But You," came out in March, about the same time they moved over to NBC's Blue Radio Network.

They began touring with famous toe tapper Bill "Bojangles" Robinson and did *The Ed Sullivan Variety Show* at the Loew's State. (That's right, *that*

Ed Sullivan, eight years before he hit TV.) Speaking of TV, the Deep River Boys had a historic performance on an experimental closed-circuit TV broadcast with Betty Furness overseen by David Sarnoff in July of 1940, some six years before network series television hit the market.

When the U.S. went to war in 1941 the Boys joined forces with the USO. By now the group had released seven 78s, including the Classics' "By the Light of the Silvery Moon" with Fats Waller (originally a number one record in 1910 by the Haydn Quartet), a riveting version of Billie Holiday's "God Bless the Child" (released about the same time), and a smooth jump-shuffle pop jazz-tinged single titled "I Wish I Had Died in My Cradle." Leroy Wayman replaced Douglas, who was now organizing vocal groups for the troops. The army would ferry Douglas and his groups out to incoming ships full of wounded troops to perform and lighten the load on the injured. One of the many famous entertainers working alongside Harry was Red Skelton.

As the war dragged on, the shortage of oil for shellac became critical and few records were made. The group had to depend on performing, which was back in high gear after they acquired former Fats Waller manager Wallace T. "Ed" Kirkeby (Waller died in 1943). He brought in Rhett Butler (no relation to the *Gone with the Wind* character) to take over baritone for Wayman. Douglas returned in 1946.

The mid- and late '40s were an active period for the River Boys, with appearances on Milton Berle's, Morton Downey's and Kate Smith's shows and tours with Bojangles. In 1946 they signed with RCA Victor and released some of their finest work: "I Left Myself Wide Open," "Heads You Win, Tails I Lose," and "Don't Ask Me Why," black pop ballads all with rich, soothing harmonies. None could dent the popularity chart, however, and it wasn't until 1948 that the group finally put their 23rd 78, "Recess in Heaven," on the pop charts at number 18. (The B side, "It's Too Soon to Know," was recorded at about the same time as THE ORIOLES' hit version.)

As the new wave of young black groups captured the public's imagination in the late '40s, the Deep River Boys followed the route of another great '40s group, the Delta Rhythm Boys, and went off to Europe to work. In England they recorded for HMV and became the only black group ever to play the Palladium for five consecutive years. The group became so popular that they would tour Europe six months of the year and record half a year's worth of

15-minute shows for Radio Luxembourg to play while they were back in the States.

By 1950, George had decided to retire from singing and went to work for the postal service; Jimmy Lundy and Carter Wilson (1951) took his spot. Ed Ware retired in 1956 and died soon after; the new bass was Al Bishop. Vernon also left that year and the group continued as a trio. A later version, into the '80s, consisted of original member Harry Douglas and newcomers Bill Jones (tenor) and Richard Sparks (bass).

A truly fine vocal quartet, The Deep River Boys appeared at the special request of President Dwight Eisenhower at the White House in 1955.

THE DEEP RIVER BOYS

A SIDE/B SIDE	LABEL/CAT NO	DATE
Nothing But You / Ev'ry Sunday Afternoon	VI 26533	3/40
I Was A Fool To Let You Go / Bullfrog And The Toad	BB 10676	4/40
A Bird In The Hand / You Don't Know Nothin'	BB 10847	8/40
My Heart At Thy Sweet Voice / Cherokee	BB 11178	6/41
I Wish I Had Died In My Cradle / Utt-Da-Zay	BB 11217	7/41
God Bless The Child / Sometimes I Feel Like A Motherless Child	VI 27579	8/41
By The Light Of The Silvery Moon / Swing Out To Victory	BB 11569	7/42
My Guy's Come Back / These Foolish Things	Mjstc 1017	1945
Just A-Sittin' And A-Rockin' / Hurry Home	Mjstc 1023	1945
That Chick's Too Young To Fry / Story Of Ee Bobba Lee Bob	VI 10-1863	4/46
Foolishly Yours / William Didn't Tell	VI 20-1990	10/46
Necessity / Old Devil Moon	VI 45-0013	1947
Jealous / Charge It To Daddy	VI 20-2157	2/47
Live Humble / Tween Four And Twenty Elders	VI 20-2265	5/47
Dream Street / Get Up Those Stairs	VI 20-2305	6/47
Bloop Bleep / I Left Myself Wide Open	VI 20-2397	8/47
By The Light Of The Silvery Moon / Come And Get It	VI 20-2448	9/47
It Had To Be You / Heads Up Win, Tails I Lose	VI 20-2517	10/47
I'm Sorry I Didn't Say I'm Sorry (The Mumble Song) / What Did He Say	VI 20-2610	12/47
Purgatory / Swing Low Sweet Clarinet	VI 20-2622	1/48

A SIDE/ B SIDE	LABEL/CAT NO	DATE
Two Blocks Down, Turn To The		
Left / I Wanna Sleep	VI 20-2808	4/48
Ain't Misbehaving / That's What		
You Need To Succeed	VI 20-2998	7/48
Recess In Heaven /		
It's Too Soon To Know	VI 20-3203	10/48
Wrapped Up In A Dream /		
Don't Ask Me Why	VI 22-0003	2/49
Cry And You Cry Alone /		
No One Sweeter Than You	VI 22-0013	3/49
Solid As A Rock / Mine Too	VI 20-3699	2/50
If You Love God, Serve Him /		
Free Grace	VI 22-0078	5/50
Tuxedo Junction /		
Opportunity	VI 20-3825	1950
Truthfully / Doesn't Make Sense		
To Me	Beacon 9143	3/52
All I Need Is You /		
Sleepy Little Cowboy	Beacon 9146	1952
The Biggest Fool /		
Oo-Shoo-Be-Do-Be	VI 20-5268	4/53
Sleepy Little Cowboy	Beacon 104	1954
Truthfully / No One Else Will Do	Jay-Dee 788	1954
Whole Wide World / All My Love		
Belongs To You	Vik 0205	4/56
You're Not Too Old / (Home) How		
Dear Can It Be	Vik 0224	8/56
Nola / Kissin'	Gallant 101	1959
I Don't Know Why /		
Timber's Gotta Roll	Gallant 2001	1959
Are You Certain /		
The Vanishing American	Wand 117	11/61
More 'N' More Amour /		
The Clouds Before The Storm	Mchl 1001	1965

The Delta Rhythm Boys

Quick: Which singers performed in more motion pictures than any other group in history? The Beatles? Wrong. THE MILLS BROTHERS? Wrong again. The Delta Rhythm Boys appeared in 15 films from the early '40s to 1956. But this was only one of the many achievements of the pioneering rhythm and blues group. If their name doesn't have the same familiar ring as THE INK SPOTS or Mills Brothers it's because their 50-year career yielded only one chart hit. But in terms of singing, they were a hit every time out and became popular through the media of radio, live performances, films, and even Broadway shows.

Their story begins at Langston University in Oklahoma. Second-year student Lee Gaines had been chosen by school president Dr. Isaac Young to form a university quartet. Lee, a sousaphone player who had led his freshman vocal quartet to a first prize in class competition, recruited first tenor Elmaurice Miller, second tenor Traverse Crawford, and baritone Essie Atkins while keeping himself on bass. The group arranged to transfer to Dillard University of New Orleans after meeting Dr. Horace Mann Bond (father of politician Julian Bond), who got the boys excited about the new music program he was assembling at Dillard as its new dean. In their haste, the group arrived at Dillard a week before classes and had to move furniture and clean floors in order to settle in at the dorm ahead of time.

During the school year, the tutelage of Professor Frederick Hall and the various concerts at the college and in New Orleans sharpened the group's harmonies on their repertoire of folk songs, spirituals, and Mills Brothers pop.

On a tour of Southern universities, the group was so well received that when they returned to school they were informed that their tuition fees and costs had been absorbed by the college, in effect granting them full scholarships.

They would never get to use those scholarships fully, however: they met a radio personality from Buenos Aires who was in New Orleans for Mardi Gras to find an act for Argentine radio. When he came to the college and heard the Frederick Hall Quartet (they had named themselves after their musical mentor), Señor Adolpho Avaliz asked Dr. Hall if the group's services could be acquired for several months. The Doctor agreed they could go when school ended and kept the secret until the quartet's last appearance of the school year.

In the summer of 1936 the Quartet made their first professional appearance a continent away from home, performing in Buenos Aires and singing weekdays on Argentina Radio Splendid. A three-month stay turned into seven months of radio work, musical theatre, and performances in Peru and Chile. Having already missed half the school year, the group decided to take their career further by moving to New York. They took up residence on 138th Street and 7th Avenue in Harlem in the house where composer Eubie Blake was living. Blake heard the group rehearsing and tipped the boys to an audition for the Broadway show *Sing Out the News*, an integrated play requiring a black vocal group. The quartet won the audition over such luminaries as the DEEP RIVER BOYS and THE CHARIOTEERS.

By now they were calling themselves the Delta Rhythm Boys. For the next few years their reputations grew through their 15-minutes-a-day radio show on CBS and other Broadway shows such as *Hellzapoppin'* and Mike Todd's *The Hot Mikado* starring Bill "Bojangles" Robinson.

In 1939 the group met Paul Kapp (brother of Decca Records exec Dave Kapp), and their lengthy recording career began with the recording on December 16, 1940, of four songs for that label. The first two songs, "Chilly and Cold"/"Gimme Some Skin," were released in March 1940. Meanwhile, they kept up a whirlwind of performance activity, which culminated in a film contract with Universal Pictures.

The early '40s saw a new look for the Delta Rhythm Boys: Clinton Holland took over first tenor and was replaced shortly thereafter by Carl Jones; Essie Atkins was replaced by Kelsey Pharr on baritone.

Their multifaceted career continued. In 1942, they began playing Las Vegas (when it only had two hotels). They spent two years singing on the "Amos and Andy" radio show. By the beginning of 1945 they'd already recorded 20 singles (including five with Mildred Bailey and two with Fred Astaire) and appeared in 11 Universal films and shorts including *Weekend Pass* and *Follow the Boys*.

In June of 1945 Decca released the first of their sides done with Ella Fitzgerald, "It's Only a Paper Moon"/"Cry You Out of My Heart." "Paper Moon" was a particularly fine shuffle-beat smoothie that had Ella and the boys trading leads.

In December of 1945 the Delta Rhythm Boys' 23rd 78 hit the market. "Just A-Sittin and A-Rockin" rose to number 17 on the pop charts—their first (and only) chart success.

In 1947, they signed with RCA Records, and among the many classic sides released on the label was the spiritual "Dry Bones" (done with the half-step modulations that the group had used in auditions as far back as 1937) and an arrangement of Duke Ellington's "Take the 'A' Train." If you wonder when the vocalese style (that groups like Manhattan Transfer used) started, it was most likely with this recording. Another nifty RCA release was the bouncy bass-led "Ain't Gonna Worry 'Bout a Soul." The group's success and diversified career can be attributed not just to their talent but also to their training, since the members could both write arrangements and read music.

In March of 1949 the Deltas recorded under the name the Four Sharps for Atlantic. Victor began reissuing several of their 78s on 45 rpm in April 1949, and Decca continued to record and release Rhythm Boys product. Still, they managed to back Ruth Brown on "I'll Come Back Someday" in 1950 on Atlantic and even recorded under their own name for that label in late 1949 with another bass-led ballad, "Sweetheart of Mine." Possibly their best Atlantic effort was the jazz-tinged "If You See Tears in My Eyes" of March 1950.

In 1949, the Deltas made their first trip to Europe, performing in Stockholm and then London. They went on to record numerous Swedish folk songs in Swedish (for Metronome Records in Stockholm) and Finnish folk tunes in Finnish.

During a 1956 trip to Montreal, the group had an impromptu backstage visit from Albert Tavel of the French agency Tavel and Marouani. He managed to lure the group to Paris for a New Year's Eve show at the Moulin Rouge; it turned into a nine-month engagement. The "vedettes Americaines" (American stars) became so popular that they signed to record with the French Barclay Records in 1957 and Vega Records in 1958.

In 1960, Kelsey Pharr died in Honolulu after a trip to Japan. Soon after, Carl Jones left to have more time with his family and was replaced by first tenor Herb Coleman. Hugh Bryant replaced Kelsey.

With the American music scene changing rapidly, the Deltas found their appeal diminishing. Overseas they were royally received, however, so in the early 1960s the group made Paris their home base for years of European performances.

In 1974, Herb Coleman was shot in Paris and died in the arms of Lee Gaines. Original Delta member Traverse Crawford died in the following year. By 1979, the lineup was Gaines, Bryant, Walter Trammell on first tenor, and Ray Beatty on second tenor.

The group had been together more than 50 years when founder Lee Gaines died on July 15th, 1987, in his home of only one year, Helsinki, Finland. In a bizarre scenario that brought the group more attention in America than it had received in more than 30 years, Hugh Bryant sang at Lee Gaines' funeral and upon completing the song died on the spot.

Though not as well-known as some other groups in America, the Rhythm Boys' musical impact is undeniable. Jimmy Ricks, the legendary bass of THE RAVENS, chose a singing career due to his being enamored with Lee Gaines' singing. The Mills Brothers readily acknowledged them as their favorite group.

THE DELTA RHYTHM BOYS

A SIDE/B SIDE	LABEL/CAT NO	DATE
Gimmie Some Skin / Chilly 'N Cold	Decca 8514	3/41
Dry Bones / Joshua Fit De Battle		
Of Jericho	Decca 8522	1941
Star Dust / Would It Be Asking		
Too Much	Decca 8530	1941
My Imaginary Love /		
My Blue Heaven	Decca 8542	1941
When That Man Is Dead And		
Gone* / Jenny*	Decca 3661	4/41
Georgia On My Mind* /		
I'm Afraid Of Myself*	Decca 3691	1941
I Do, Do You (Believe In Love) /		
The Things I Love	Decca 8554	1941
She Believed A Gypsy /		
Do You Care	Decca 8561	1941
Rockin' Chair* /		
Sometimes I'm Happy*	Decca 3755	5/41
Everything Depends On You* /		
All Too Soon* (no group)	Decca 3888	7/41
It's So Peaceful In The Country* /		
Lover Come Back To Me*		
(no group)	Decca 3953	8/41
Take The "A" Train /		
Let Me Off Uptown	Decca 8578	9/41
Playing The Game /		
Down On The Delta Shore	Decca 8584	11/41
Since I Kissed My Baby G'Bye** /		
So Near And Yet So Far**		
(no group)	Decca 18187	1941
The Wedding Cake Walk** /		
Dream Dancing**	Decca 18188	1941
When I'm Gone You'll Soon		
Forget, When You're Gone I		
Won't Forget	Decca 4128	1/42
Mad About Her, Sad Without Her,		
How Can I Be Glad Without Her		
Blues / Keep Smilin', Keep		
Laughin', Be Happy	Decca 4266	6/42
Dry Bones / Praise The Lord And		
Pass The Ammunition	Decca 4406	11/42
Do Nothin' Til You Hear From Me /		
Travelin' Light	Decca 4440	4/44
Gee, Ain't I Good To You? /		
Is There Somebody Else	Decca 18650	2/45
It's Only A Paper Moon† /		
Cry You Out Of My Heart†	Decca 23425	6/45
Baby, Are You Kiddin' /		
Honeydripper	Decca 23451	9/45
Just A-Sittin' and A-Rockin' /		
Don't Knock It	Decca 18739	12/45
Just A-Sittin' And A-Rockin' /		
No Pad To Be Had	Decca 23541	4/46
But She's My Buddy's Chick /		
Walk It Off	Decca 18911	7/46
For Sentimental Reasons† /		
It's A Pity To Say Goodnight†	Decca 23670	10/46
Georgia On My Mind* /		
Rockin' Chair*	Decca 11083	1946
Hello, Goodbye, Forget It /		
Just Squeeze Me (But Don't		
Tease Me)	Decca 23771	12/46
Bye Bye Alibi Baby /		
Jenny Kissed Me	Vctr 202183	3/47
Hey John (Put Your Glasses On) /		
I'm Awfully Strong For You	Vctr 202271	5/47
Every So Often / Come In Out Of		
The Rain	Vctr 202365	7/47
My Future Just Passed /		
I'm In Love With A Gal	Vctr 202436	9/47
A One-Sided Affair§§ /		
What Would It Take§§	Decca 24193	10/47
Dry Bones / September Song	Vctr 202460	11/47
Take The 'A' Train/ East Of The		
Sun, West Of The Moon	Vctr 202461	11/47
St. Louis Blues / Everytime We		
Say Goodbye	Vctr 202462	11/47
One O'Clock Jump / If You Are But		
A Dream	Vctr 202463	11/47
Little Small Town Girl / Ain't Gonna		
Worry 'Bout A Soul	Vctr 202588	12/47
Never Underestimate The Power		
Of A Woman / You're Mine, You	Vctr 202855	4/48
I Can't Tell A Lie To Myself /		
My Blue Heaven	Vctr 203007	7/48
Don't Ask Me Why / Fantastic	Mscrft 597	3/49
Don't Ask Me Why†† /		
I Can Hardly Wait††	Atlantic 875	3/49
(45 rpm reissue of Victor 202460)	Vctr 472826	4/49
(45 rpm reissue of Victor 202461)	Vctr 472827	4/49
(45 rpm reissue of Victor 202462)	Vctr 472828	4/49
(45 rpm reissue of Victor 202463)	Vctr 472829	4/49
Sweetheart Of Mine / The Laugh's		
On Me	Atlantic 889	11/49
(I'll Come Back) Someday*** /		
Why ***	Atlantic 899	2/50
You Go To Your Church, I'll Go To		
Mine Beyond The Sunset /		
Should You Go First	Decca 48138	2/50
Nobody Knows / If You See Tears		
In My Eyes	Atlantic 900	3/50
I'd Rather Be Wrong Than Blue /		
You Are Closer To My Heart	Decca 48140	3/50
It's All In Your Mind /		
Fan Tan Fannie	Decca 48148	4/50
Sentimental Journey*** / I Can		
Dream, Can't I*** (no group)	Atlantic 905	5/50
All The Things You Are /		
Blow Out The Candle	London 1145	1/52
Gypsy In My Soul /		
I've Got You Under My Skin	Merc 1407	8/52
On The Sunny Side Of The		
Street / They Didn't Believe Me	Merc 1408	8/52
Lover Come Back To Me /		
All The Things You Are	Merc 1409	8/52
I'll Never Get Out Of This World		
Alive / I'm Used To You	Vctr 475094	12/52

A SIDE/ B SIDE	LABEL/CAT NO	DATE
Dancing With Someone /		
Long Gone Baby	Vctr 475217	2/53
It's All In Your Mind*** /		
Sentimental Journey***	Atln 1023	3/54
It's Only A Paper Moon*** /		
For Sentimental Reasons†	Decca 29136	5/54
Have A Hope, Have A Wish, Have		
A Prayer / Mood Indigo	Decca 29273	9/54
Shoes / Kiss Crazy Baby	Decca 29329	11/54
Headin' For The Bottom / Babylon	Decca 29528	5/55
Don't Even Change A Picture On		
The Wall / That's Just The Way		
I Feel	Decca 29582	10/55
(Reissue of Decca 25019)	Decca 30466	1957
My Own True Love / Work Song	Phlps 40023	7/62

*	with Mildred Bailey	†† as the Four Sharps
**	with Fred Astaire	§§ with Les Paul
†	with Ella Fitzgerald	*** with Ruth Brown

The Dixie Hummingbirds

The Dixie Hummingbirds are probably the best-known of the black gospel quartets, having performed for over 50 years throughout America and Europe. They became the inspiration for countless R&B and soul singers, from Jackie Wilson and Clyde McPhatter to Bobby "Blue" Bland and THE TEMPTATIONS.

The group was formed in Greenville, South Carolina, by James Davis in 1928, a year before the Great Depression. The members were Barney Gipson (lead), Davis (tenor), Barney Parks (baritone), and J. B. Matterson (bass). In their early teens they sang in the Bethel Church of God in the junior chorus. Soon Fred Owens became the bass and the group became the Sterling High School Quartet. Davis changed the name to the Dixie Hummingbirds.

Following local activity, the group went to the National Baptist Convention in Atlanta where they met such top acts of the day as the Heavenly Gospel Singers, THE SWAN SILVERTONES, and Kings of Harmony. The Hummingbirds' reception there encouraged them to tour.

During the '30s the group went through a succession of bass singers until Jimmy Bryant of the Heavenly Gospel Singers joined in 1939, just as the group signed to Decca Records. Also that same year the group obtained the lead singing services of

Ira Tucker of Spartanburg, South Carolina. Tucker had been singing with his own group the Gospel Carriers. One night the Carriers competed in a battle of the gospel groups against the Dixie Hummingbirds and the Heavenly Gospel Singers. The Birds were the obvious winners and Tucker became a member that same night. Willie Bobo, one of the legendary gospel basses and the Heavenlies' bass that night, also joined the Dixies soon after.

Tucker had been influenced by the Norfolk Jubilee Singers, and his mixture of gospel and blues added a versatility to the Dixies' style that helped make them the leading black Southern quartet. As time went on he developed his showmanship, becoming the first to run up and down the aisles and jump off stages; it's very possible that James Brown learned his moves from Tucker.

The Hummingbirds began on Philadelphia radio at station WCAU as the Jericho Boys and the Swanee Quintet, and performed in packed stadiums without the benefit of a hit record. In 1945 the group recorded for Apollo and then Gotham.

Beachy Thompson of the Five Gospel Singers and the Willing Four joined the group in 1944, and by World War II's end the lineup was Tucker (lead), Davis (tenor), Thompson (baritone), and Bobo (bass).

They hit their stride in 1952 recording gospel standards like "Jesus Walked the Water" and "I Just Can't Help It" for Peacock. In the early '50s James Walker joined and became the group's second lead. Swan Silvertones great Claude Jeter also spent some time with the group in the '50s.

In 1966 the Hummingbirds performed at the Newport Folk Festival and were an instant sensation. Seven years later they backed Paul Simon on his gospel-flavored composition, "Loves Me Like a Rock." The record sold a million copies and reached number two in the late summer. Soon after, the group recorded its own version.

The Hummingbirds continued into the '80s with a number of personnel changes. James Davis retired in 1984 after 56 years on the circuit. Willie Bobo died in 1976. Ira Tucker and James Walker were still featured as of the late '80s.

THE DIXIE HUMMINGBIRDS

A SIDE/B SIDE	LABEL/CAT NO	DATE
I Know I've Been Changed /		
Trouble In My Way	Pcok 1705	1952
Lord If I Go / Eternal Life	Pcok 1713	1953
Let's Go Out To The Programs /		
I'll Keep On Living After I Die	Pcok 1722	1953

A SIDE/ B SIDE	LABEL/CAT NO	DATE
Live Right, Die Right / Prayer Wheel	Pcok 1727	1954
Christian Testimonial / Will The Lord Be With Me?	Pcok 1736	1954
I'm Not Uneasy / Sinner, Sin No More	Pcok 1740	1/55
It Must Have Been The Lord (That Touched Me) / Take Care Of Me	Pcok 1742	1955
Poor Pilgrim Of Sorrow / Devil Can't Harm A Praying Man	Pcok 1757	1955
Troubles Will Be Over / Way Up On High	Pcok 1763	1956
Thank You Lord For One More Day / Get Right Church	Pcok 1764	1956
Loving Hand / Cool Down Yonder	Pcok 1770	1956
Live On Forever / Just Trusting	Pcok 1773	1957
Christian's Automobile / Stop By Here	Pcok 1780	11/57
Walls Of Zion / Just A Little While	Pcok 1783	1958
I Don't Know Why (I Have To Cry Sometime) / Let's Go Out To The Programs No. 2	Pcok 1788	1958
Make One Step / Come On And See About Me	Pcok 1791	1959
Nobody Knows The Trouble I See / The Final Edition	Pcok 1803	1959
I Want To Feel The Holy Spirit / What A Friend	Pcok 1808	1959
Jesus Hold My Hand / Leave Your Burdens There	Pcok 1817	1959
He Cares For Me / God's Goodness	Pcok 1831	1961
Have A Little Talk With Jesus / In The Morning	Pcok 1844	1962
Our Father's Children / Bedside Of A Neighbor	Pcok 1861	1962
Another Day / If You Trust Him	Pcok 1889	1962
Come Ye Disconsolate / Our Prayer For Peace	Pcok 3012	1964
Lord I Come To Thee / If Anybody Asks You	Pcok 3045	1965
Prayer For The Sick / You Don't Have Nothing	Pcok 3073	1965
The Old Time Way / Gabriel	Pcok 3084	1965
Only Jesus / Confidential God	Pcok 3098	1966
Your Good Deeds / What The Lord Is To Me	Pcok 3109	1967
The Inner Man / I'm Going On	Pcok 3148	1968
God Is Going To Get Tired / Don't Let Me Fall	Pcok 3165	1968
Payday / Somebody	Pcok 3179	1968
Somebody Is Lying / Lord, If You Don't Help Us	Pcok 3191	1968
Love Me Like A Rock / I've Been Born Again	Pcok 3198	1968
Come Ye Disconsolate / Our Prayer For Peace	Pcok 3402	1968

The Five Blind Boys of Mississippi

One of the few gospel groups to make the R&B charts, the Five Blind Boys of Mississippi were a powerful aggregation who were known to have influenced Ray Charles, among others.

In the 1930s some blind students of the Piney Woods School near Jackson, Mississippi, formed a singing quartet. They were Archie Brownley (lead), Joseph Ford, Lawrence Abrams, and Lloyd Woodard. The school was one of the pioneer establishments in education for blacks, and it had a separate teaching program for blind children.

The group was first called the Cotton Blossom Singers, with influences ranging from THE MILLS BROTHERS and THE FOUR VAGABONDS to Reebert Harris and his SOUL STIRRERS. They began singing on the school grounds in 1936; in 1937 they recorded for Alan Lomax, who was traveling the South making recordings for the Library of Congress. Later, they traveled and performed to earn money for the school and played for white audiences such as Kiwanis and Lion's Clubs. When the boys graduated they decided to make singing a career and became two groups in one, the Cotton Blossom Singers for secular music and the Jackson Harmoneers for gospel audiences.

The addition of Melvin Henderson on second lead made the group a quintet as they began working out of New Orleans. In the mid '40s, sighted lead singer Percell Perkins took Melvin's place and also became the group's manager. They began calling themselves the Five Blind Boys.

While based in Cleveland during 1946 the group met Leon René, owner of Excelsior Records in Los Angeles, and they went west to record their first 78. They performed all across the country.

In 1948 Joseph Ford left and was replaced by another blind singer, J. T. Clinkscales of South Carolina, previously with the Masters of Harmony. In that same year they recorded for the Coleman label. THE COLEMAN BROTHERS had a convenient setup: they owned a Newark, New Jersey, hotel and kept a recording studio and record company in the basement. When a quality act like the Blind Boys stayed there, they'd run them downstairs to record a few sides.

By 1950 the group was based in Houston and signed with Peacock Records, where they attained their greatest recording success. The song "Our

Father" became a huge gospel success; it also charted R&B on December 30, 1950, reaching number 10 nationally. Around this time another blind gospel group, the Five Blind Boys of Alabama, started appearing with the Mississippi group, and the friendly competition increased the interest in both acts. The Mississippi Blind Boys stayed with Peacock through the '60s, recording 27 singles and five LPs. As one of the premier acts of the '50s, the Blind Boys toured constantly through the United States. Percell Perkins eventually became Reverend Perkins and left for the ministry. He was subsequently replaced by Reverend Samy Lewis, Reverend George Warren, and Tiny Powell.

Archie Brownley's legendary ear-piercing screams were the reference point for many '60s soul singers, and Ray Charles's style owes much to his colorful vocalizing. But by 1959 the constant touring had taken its toll, and Brownley died in New Orleans in 1960. Roscoe Robinson took over his lead spot, backed by second lead Willmer "Little Axe" Broadnax. With new members, the Blind Boys tradition continued through the '70s and '80s. Lloyd Woodard died in the mid-'70s and Lawrence Abrams passed away in 1982. J. T. Clinkscales was still at it in 1986 for short tours.

The Five Red Caps

When the term "vocal group" is mentioned most people envision singers standing around a microphone, but many of the early vocal groups (especially the black groups) were vocalists *and* musicians, like the very popular Five Red Caps. It wasn't until the late '40s and early '50s that a majority of groups were singers only.

The Caps tale began in 1940, when the members of three Los Angeles groups joined together to become the Four Toppers. Steve Gibson (bass vocals and guitar) had been with the Basin Street Boys of Lynchberg, Virginia (not the Excelsior Records Basin Street Boys); Jimmy Springs (lead tenor and drums) had been part of the 5 Jones Boys and toured with the famous cowboy singer Gene Autry (who had discovered him singing with the Dixie Cottonpickers—vocalists on Gene's national "Barn Dance" radio show); both David Patillo (tenor and bass player) and Richard Davis (baritone and piano) had been members of the 4 Blackbirds. Together they called themselves the Four Toppers because they had all performed with the top groups on the L.A. scene.

Unable to sustain a living, the foursome moved to New York, where they met a fifth Topper: second tenor and saxophone player Emmett Mathews. They changed the name of the band to the Five Red Caps.

In 1943, supported by Romaine Brown on second lead and piano, the Caps met record label owner Joe Davis while they appeared at the Enduro Club on Flatbush Avenue in Brooklyn.

Davis had entered the record business by buying a scarce allotment of shellac in 1942 from an inactive company, Gennett Records (Richmond, Indiana), in exchange for financing to upgrade its pressing facilities.

The Five Red Caps recorded 26 singles for Davis's various labels (Davis, Beacon, Joe Davis, and Gennett) from 1943 through 1946, with Springs singing the ballad leads and Brown and Gibson leading on the jump tunes, which were usually written by the multi-talented Davis. The group's biggest hit was "I've Learned a Lesson I'll Never Forget," which peaked at number 14 in 1944 (#3 R&B).

With a stage act that included singing, playing, dancing, and comedy routines, the group toured the Atlantic seaboard supperclub circuit from New York to Miami and performed in Las Vegas and Los Angeles. They also appeared on numerous TV shows, from Jackie Gleason and Ed Sullivan to "American Bandstand."

In 1944 they hit the R&B charts three more times with "Boogie Woogie Ball" (featuring some of the best boogie-woogie piano playing you'll ever hear), "Just for You," and "No One Else Will Do." Each reached number 10.

In 1947 they moved to Mercury Records as Joe Davis's operation became inactive. On Mercury they had a 1948 hit with "Wedding Bells Are Breaking Up That Old Gang of Mine," featuring Earl Plummer on lead. At this point the group became known as Steve Gibson and the Red Caps. Some of their best material was issued on Mercury, including "Blueberry Hill" and "Are You Lonesome Tonight." The Mercury deal ended in 1950, and by November they had signed to RCA, switching Springs back to lead.

In the midst of their recording activity, the group appeared in the 1950 movie *Destination Murder* as well as some film shorts. They had previously exploited their name via an appearance as baggage handlers wearing red caps in the 1949 film *Excess Baggage*.

Their most popular RCA cut was "I Went to Your Wedding," covered by Patti Page (#1) in 1952 and later partially plundered for lyrics for the PENGUINS classic "Earth Angel."

The RCA contingent included Steve Gibson, Jimmy Springs, Earl Plummer, Romaine Brown, Emmett Matthews, Dave Patillo, and newcomer vocalist Damita Jo (actually Damita Jo DuBlanc, later married to Gibson). By 1953 the Red Caps were in transition as Damita, Romaine, and Earl all left. Drummer Bobby Gregg joined for a brief time; he later had an instrumental hit with "The Jam, Part I" (#29, 1962).

A whole new Red Caps emerged around Steve Gibson in 1956 as he signed to ABC Paramount with Emmett Matthews and Bill, Peck, and Joe Furness (three of the four Furness brothers, also known as the Four Keys). The best of their four ABC issues was a nice cover of the Rays' "Silhouettes," but by 1957 the Red Caps style was a bit passé.

But the show went on. In 1959 Gibson, Matthews, Damita Jo, Springs, Brown, and Gregg joined with George Tindley (Dreams, Savoy). But their records for the Rose and Hunt labels couldn't compete. By the early '60s, Gibson's group was gone. Tindley, however, formed his own version, bringing in former CASTELLES lead George Grant (Grand); in 1966 they recorded a fine version of the FLAMINGOS classic "Golden Teardrops" for Swan.

Romaine Brown, who had his own group, the Romaines, when not with the Caps, reportedly died in the late '80s. David Patillo died in the '60s and Jimmy Springs passed away on October 4, 1987, at the age of 76. Steve Gibson had a heart attack in the late '80s. Damita Jo had a few pop chart singles in the early '60s, including an answer song to the DRIFTERS hit "Save the Last Dance for Me" titled "I'll Save the Last Dance for You" (#22, 1960) and "I'll Be There" (#12, 1961). She is still performing as a nightclub singer. Emmet Matthews turned in his red cap for a sky cap and was reported to be working at New York's JFK Airport.

THE FIVE RED CAPS

A SIDE/B SIDE	LABEL/CAT NO	DATE
I'm The One / Tuscaloosa	Bcn 115	9/43
I Made A Great Mistake / There's A Light On The Hill	Bcn 116	9/43
Don't Fool With Me / Mama Put Your Britches On	Bcn 117	10/43
No Fish Today / Grand Central Station	Bcn 118	1943
I'm The One / I Made A Great Mistake	Bcn 7115	1943

A SIDE/ B SIDE	LABEL/CAT NO	DATE
There's A Light On The Hill / Don't Fool With Me	Bcn 7116	1943
Tuscaloosa / Mama Put Your Britches On	Bcn 7117	1943
No Fish Today / Grand Central Station	Bcn 7118	1943
Just For You / I'm Going To Live My Life Alone	Bcn 7119	1943
I've Learned A Lesson I'll Never Forget / Words Can't Explain	Bcn 7120	1/44
Boogie Woogie Ball / Lenox Avenue Jump	Bcn 7121	2/44
Don't You Know / Strictly On The Safety Side	Bcn 7122	1944
Somebody's Lyin' / Was It You	Bcn 7123	5/44
Sugar Lips / Gabriel's Band	Bcn 7124	1944
Don't Say We're Through / Destination Unknown	Bcn 7125	1944/5
The Tables Have Turned On Me / Never Give Up Hope	Bcn 7126	1944/5
Red Caps Ball / I Didn't Mean To Be Mean To You	Bcn 7127	1944/5
If I Can't Have You / After I've Spent My Best Years On You	Bcn 7128	1944/5
It's Good Good Good / Spellbound	Bcn 7129	1944/5
No One Else Will Do / I'm Crazy 'Bout You	Bcn 7130	1944/5
I Was A Fool To Let You Go / Thinking	Bcn 7131	1945
Pleasant Dreams / Mary Had A Little Jar	Bcn 7132	1945
I'm To Blame / Boogie Woogie On A Saturday Night	Bcn 7133	1945
In The Quiet Of The Dawn / Through Thick And Thin	Bcn 7134	1945
You Thrill Me / The Boogie Beat'll Getcha If You Don't Watch Out	Bcn 7135	12/45
My Everlasting Love For You / I'll Remind You	Bcn 7136	1946
Confused / Have A Heart For Someone	Bcn 7141	1946
Words Can't Explain / Strictly On The Safety Side	Bcn 7142	1946
Seems Like Old Times / I'm Glad I Waited For You	Dvs 2101	3/46
I Love An Old Fashioned Song / Atlanta, GA	Dvs 2102	1946
Bless You / You Can't See The Sun When You're Crying	Merc 5011	1/47
Jack! You're Dead / San Antonio Rose	Merc 8038	5/47
I'll Never Love Anyone Else / I Want A Roof Over My Head	Merc 5380	5/47
I Don't Want To Set The World On Fire / You Never Miss The Water Till The Well Runs Dry	Merc 8052	1947
Walkin Through Heaven / You're Driving Me Crazy	Merc 8059	1947

A SIDE/ B SIDE	LABEL/CAT NO	DATE
Wedding Bells Are Breaking Up		
That Old Gang Of Mine / I'd		
Love To Live A Lifetime For You	Merc 8069	1/48
Little White Lies / Turnip Greens	Merc 8085	4/48
Danny Boy / Scratch And You'll		
Find It	Merc 8091	6/48
Money Is Honey / Give Me Time	Merc 8093	6/48
Thru Thick And Thin /		
I'm To Blame	MGM 4001	
Boogie Woogie On A Saturday		
Nite / If I Can't Have You	MGM 10285	1948
Sugar Lips / I Learned A Lesson		
I'll Never Forget	MGM 10330	12/48
You Made Me Love You /		
I Learned A Lesson I'll		
Never Forget	Merc 8109	12/48
Blueberry Hill / I Love You	Merc 8146	7/49
Petunia / I've Been Living For You	Merc 8157	10/49
They Ain't Gonna Tell It Right /		
I Wake Up Every Morning	Merc 8165	1/50
Are You Lonesome Tonight /		
Sentimental Me	Merc 8174	3/50
Steve's Blues / Dirt Dishin' Daisy	Merc 8186	7/50
Am I To Blame / The Thing	RCA 47-3986	12/50
Three Dollars And Ninety-Eight		
Cents / D'Ya Eat Yet, Joe	RCA 47-4076	3/51
I'm To Blame / Sidewalk Shuffle	RCA 50-0127	5/51
Would I Mind / When You Come		
Back To Me	RCA 50-0138	7/51
Shame / Boogie Woogie On A		
Saturday Night	RCA 47-4294	9/51
I May Hate Myself In The		
Morning / Two Little Kisses	RCA 47-4670	4/52
Bobbin' / How Do I Cry	RCA 47-4835	7/52
Truthfully / Why Don't You Love Me	RCA 47-5013	10/52
Big Game Hunter / Do I, Do I, I Do	RCA 47-5130	1/53
Wedding Bells Are Breaking Up		
That Old Gang Of Mine /		
Second Hand Romance	Merc 70389	5/54
My Tzatskele / Win Or Lose	RCA 47-5987	1/55
Feelin' Kinda Happy /		
'Nuff Of That Stuff	RCA 47-6096	4/55
Bobbin' / How Do I Cry	RCA 47-6345	11/55
Ouch / It Hurts Me But I Like It	Jay-Dee 796	1954

Steve Gibson and the Red Caps

A SIDE/ B SIDE	LABEL/CAT NO	DATE
Rock And Roll Stomp /		
Love Me Tenderly	ABC 9702	1956
Write To Me / Gaucho Serenade	ABC 9750	1956
You May Not Love Me /		
You've Got Me Dizzy	ABC 9796	1957
Silhouettes / Flamingo	ABC 9856	1957
I-Bitty-Bitty / I Want To Be Loved	Hi Lo 101	9/58
Forever 'N' A Day / It's Love	Hi Lo 103	1958
I Miss You So / Bless You	Rose 5534	1959
Bless You / Cheryl Lee	Hunt 326	3/59
Where Are You / San Antone Rose	Hunt 330	1959
I Went To Your Wedding / Together	ABC 10105	1960

The Four Knights

Most black gospel groups that sang in the '40s or '50s and then changed their musical direction, changed it to rhythm and blues. The Four Knights, however, were a refined gospel group that became a refined pop blues group.

Actually they started out in 1943 as the Southland Jubilee Singers in Charlotte, North Carolina. The membership included Gene Alford (lead), John Wallace (second tenor and guitar), and Oscar Broadway (bass).

By 1944 Oscar had brought in a baritone he knew, Clarence Dixon, and the lineup was set. Their soft and breezy harmonies drew immediate attention and the group made its debut on NBC's affiliate WSOC-Charlotte radio.

In six months they moved up to CBS's mega power station, the 50,000-watt WBT-Charlotte. The quartet replaced the Southern Sons on the station's "Carolina Hay Ride" show, a popular program that attracted one listener in particular, Cy Langois of Lang-Worth Transcriptions. He signed the group to management.

His first move was for a name change to the Four Knights. He took them to New York and they started appearing on Arthur Godfrey's radio show in 1945. Lang-Worth was a company that made what were called transcriptions, actually early albums containing four to six songs on each side of an eight-inch disc that played at 33-1/3 rpm. These discs were not sold to the public; most all were sent to radio stations, allowing a local disc jockey to give the impression the group was right in the studio. The Knights did a number of these recordings. Between this type of exposure and the Godfrey show the group became fairly well-known.

In 1946 they signed with Decca Records and in April of that year they released their first single, "Just in Case You Change Your Mind." After four singles featuring Gene's mellow lead, Oscar's broad bass, and usually incorporating Gene's whistling over the instrumental section, the group was moved to Decca's Coral affiliate for three more 78s through 1949.

They toured with dancer Bill "Bojangles" Robinson and got a shot as regulars on the Red Skelton radio show in 1948. They spent two years doing Skelton in Los Angeles and performing in clubs across the country. The Knights lost the Skelton job in 1950 when their manager wanted more than the show could pay, and so he pulled the group. They then discharged him for losing what they considered to be a prime exposure medium.

In 1951 they brought their soft harmony to Capitol Records and began with "I Love the Sunshine of Your Smile" (#23). They also began covering R&B and pop artists on songs like "The Glory of Love" (THE 5 KEYS), "Sin" (THE FOUR ACES), which they took to number 14, and their biggest pop cover record at number eight in 1953, "Oh Happy Day" (Don Howard).

The group's biggest hit came in 1954 when "I Get So Lonely When I Think About You (Oh Baby Mine)" reached number two and ran for 24 weeks, even becoming a smash in England at number five, a tough thing for a black American group to do in 1954. The Pat Ballard-penned original was so popular in England that when it fell off the charts it resurfaced the following month (July), reaching number 10.

Toward the end of 1953 George Vereen began subbing on studio work and singing lead at live shows for Gene Alford, whose epilepsy was affecting his ongoing involvement with the group. Vereen was replaced in 1955 by ex-DELTA RHYTHM BOYS member Cliff Holland as Alford retired.

Prior to their 1952 recordings the group sang with only a guitar backup, but Capitol soon had them working with full orchestras.

By 1953, tours for the four were in full swing, and they played clubs from Las Vegas to Rio de Janeiro while appearing on the TV shows of Perry Como, Ed Sullivan, and of course Red Skelton. On August 27, 1954, they headlined at the famed Apollo in New York.

During the mid-'50s the reigning king of Capitol's roster, Nat King Cole, ran into the group and liked their style; he asked Capitol to have the Knights back him on some recordings. Their first collaboration, in early 1955, was titled "A Blossom Fell." Though it didn't chart, Nat and the Knights tried again in January 1956, and by September their "That's All There Is to That" was number 16 on the pop chart and number 14 R&B, the first time the Knights had ever appeared on the black charts. The next time out with Nat was the last: a ballad, "My Personal Possession," released in May 1957 and reaching number 21 (#3 R&B).

The only pop charter of the mid- and late '50s for the group by themselves was "O Falling Star" (#83, 1959) after they'd re-signed with Coral in late 1957. Capitol stayed with them for 39 45s throughout the '50s.

In 1960 Gene Alford died. Clarence left the act in 1963 and the Knights disbanded three years after his departure. John Wallace died in 1978. Dixon and Broadway moved to the suburbs of Los Angeles in retirement.

THE FOUR KNIGHTS

A SIDE/B SIDE	LABEL/CAT NO	DATE
Just In Case You Changed Your Mind / Don't Be Ashamed To Say I Love You	Decca 1103	4/46
Walking With My Shadow / Funny How You Get Along With Me	Decca 48014	11/46
Lead Me That Rock / He'll Understand And Say Well Done	Decca 40018	1/47
So Soon / I'm Falling For You	Decca 24139	8/47
Don't Cry, Cry Baby / Wrapped Up In A Dream	Coral 60046	4/49
Fantastic / Crystal Gazer	Coral 60072	5/49
Sentimental Fool / I Love The Sunshine Of Your Smile	Cptl 1587	6/51
Walkin' And Whistlin' Blues / Who Am I	Cptl 1707	7/51
Got Her Off My Hands (But I Can't Get Her Off Of My Mind) / I Go Crazy	Cptl 1787	9/51
(It's No) Sin / The Glory Of Love	Cptl 1806	9/51
In The Chapel In The Moonlight / I Wanna Say Hello	Cptl 1840	10/51
Charmaine / Cry	Cptl 1875	11/51
Five Feet Two, Eyes Of Blue / Marshmallow Moon	Cptl 1914	12/51
I Wish I Had A Girl / The Way I Feel	Cptl 1930	1/52
There Are Two Sides To Every Heartache / Walkin' In The Sunshine	Cptl 1971	1/52
The More I Go Out With Somebody Else / The Doll With The Sawdust Heart	Cptl 1998	2/52
I'm The World's Biggest Fool / It's A Sin To Tell A Lie	Cptl 2087	4/52
Win Or Loose / Doo Wacka Doo	Cptl 2127	6/52
That's The Way It's Gonna Be / Say No More	Cptl 2195	8/52
Lies / One Way Kisses	Cptl 2234	9/52
Oh, Happy Day / A Million Tears	Cptl 2315	12/52
A Few Kind Words / Anniversary Song	Cptl 2403	3/53
Tennessee Train / Baby Doll	Cptl 2517	6/53
I Couldn't Stay Away From You / (Oh Baby Mine) I Get So Lonely	Cptl 2654	1953
I Was Meant For You / They Tell Me	Cptl 2782	1954
How Wrong Can You Be / Period	Cptl 2847	1954
In The Chapel In the Moonlight / Easy Street	Cptl 2894	1954
Saw Your Eyes / I Don't Wanna See You Cryin'	Cptl 2938	1954
Write Me, Baby / Honey Bunch	Cptl 3024	1/55
Inside Out / Foolishly Yours	Cptl 3093	1/55
A Blossom Fell / If I May*	Cptl 3095	1/55
Me / Gratefully Yours	Cptl 3155	1/55
Believing You / Don't Sit Under The Apple Tree	Cptl 3192	1/55

A SIDE/ B SIDE	LABEL/CAT NO	DATE
Perdido / After	Cptl 3250	1/55
You / Guilty	Cptl 3279	1955
Happy Birthday Baby /		
I Love You Still	Cptl 3339	1956
Bottle Up The Moonlight /		
Mistaken	Cptl 3386	1956
My Dream Sonata / That's All		
There Is To That*	Cptl 3456	6/56
You're A Honey / Don't Depend		
On Me	Cptl 3494	1956
It Doesn't Cost Money / How Can		
You Not Believe Me	Cptl 3689	1957
Walkin' And Whistlin' Blues /		
I Love That Song	Cptl 3730	5/57
My Personal Possession* /		
Send For Me	Cptl 3737	5/57
Four Minute Mile / When Your		
Lover Has Gone	Coral 61936	1/58
Yes I Do / If You Ever Change		
Your Mind	Coral 61981	3/58
Oh Falling Star / Foolish Tears	Coral 62045	1958
Where Is The Love / Things To		
Do Today	Coral 62110	4/59

* with Nat King Cole

The Four Tunes

Probably the only group with a name based on the number of songs in its repertoire, the Four Tunes found the need to use it because their previous moniker, the Sentimentalists, was controlled by bandleader Tommy Dorsey. Before they were the Sentimentalists they were THE BROWN DOTS, and before that they were an offshoot of THE INK SPOTS and used the name until the original group protested.

The Four Tunes consisted of lead Jimmie Nabbie, tenor Danny Owens (formerly of THE COLEMAN BROTHERS), baritone Pat Best, and bass Jimmy Gordon. Having recorded for Manor as the Sentimentalists they were already in place to record as the Four Tunes.

Their first single in December of 1946 under the new name was with Savannah Churchill on lead. Her abilities ran the musical gamut: she started in gospel, switched to blues and jazz, and with the Tunes became an established pop-blues singer. The record was "I Want to Be Loved," and it propelled Savannah and the Tunes to the upper stratosphere of success. The record shot to number one on the R&B chart for eight weeks and stayed on the charts for 25 weeks total in the spring and summer of 1947; it also reached number 21 on the Pop chart. Miss Churchill was from Colfax, Louisiana, and was 26 when she teamed with the Tunes. She had begun singing professionally to support her two children when her husband David Churchill died in a car crash in 1941. By 1945 she had reached number three R&B on Manor with "Daddy Daddy" and had already toured with Nat King Cole.

The Tunes and Savannah issued 25 sides together from the group's 29 original releases on Manor, its affiliate Arco, and Columbia (which purchased four sides from Manor) between 1947 and 1950. In 1948 the group charted twice with Savannah on "Time Out for Tears" (#20 Pop, #10 R&B) and "I Want to Cry" (#14 R&B).

The Tunes' first single featuring the group alone was "I'd Rather Be Safe than Sorry" in December of 1946 with baritone Best on lead. That single was originally issued under the name the Sentimentalists.

By mid-1950 the Four Tunes signed to RCA and issued an Ink Spots song, "Do I Worry." Meanwhile, they toured the country, performing with the likes of Cab Calloway, Sarah Vaughan, and Ruth Brown. On October 10, 1952, they began a week at the Apollo with Bull Moose Jackson and Wini Brown.

They had numerous single shots on RCA (17 in all) between 1950 and the end of '53, most generating regional activity but achieving no real national success. The group moved to Jubilee later that year.

The Four Tunes belatedly got even with Tommy Dorsey for making them change their name: they had a hit with his original "Marie" (#13 Pop, #2 R&B). This was followed by their biggest hit, the Pat Best-penned "I Understand" (#6 Pop, #7 R&B) in 1954.

In 1955 tenor Billy Wells came aboard in the unique capacity of full-time replacement for vacationing members. As the group had been working regularly at Las Vegas's Hacienda Hotel from 1955 to '63, this was a logical way to keep the quartet busy at all times.

Savannah, meanwhile, was singing solo and often recording with the Striders (Apollo). Her career came to a sudden end in a freak accident in 1956: her pelvis was broken when a drunk fell out of a balcony and landed on top of her while she was performing at a club in Brooklyn. She died of cancer in 1974.

The Four Tunes couldn't follow up "I Understand" despite 13 more Jubilee 45s and two on Crosby Records in 1958, but they kept performing until 1963 when Jimmie Nabbie went solo.

In 1965 Nabbie joined the group he had technically been in during the early '40s, the Ink Spots. Danny Owens, meanwhile, joined the Silver Dollars. Best and Gordon formed the Rainbeaus but in 1970 reestablished the Four Tunes with Wells and tenor Frank Dawes. By the late '80s the Four Tunes consisted of Gordon, Best, Lee McKay, and Frank Dawes.

The Four Tunes were a classy pop black act whose 65 singles (not including their Brown Dots sides) rated them as one of the more prolific recording acts of their day.

THE FOUR TUNES

A SIDE/B SIDE	LABEL/CAT NO	DATE
Silent Night / O Come All Ye Faithful*	Manor 8002	1946
Ave Maria / White Christmas*	Manor 8003	1946
I Want To Be Loved / Foolishly Yours*	Manor 1046	1946
I'll Close My Eyes / Save Me A Dream*	Manor 1047	1946
I'd Rather Be Safe Than Sorry / I'll Be Waiting For You*	Manor 1049	1946
Too Many Times / I'll Always Say I Love You	Manor 1050	1946
Darling You Make It So / Du Bist Mein Wiener Tzatzkellah	Manor 1076	1947
Where Is My Love / Sometime Someplace Somehow	Manor 1077	1947
Wrapped Up In A Dream / I Found Love When I Found You	Manor 1083	1947
Dreams / Chillicothe, Ohio (Betty Davis)	Manor 1087	1947
Is It Too Late** / I Understand	Manor 1093	1947
Time Out For Tears** / All My Dreams	Manor 1116	1948
Tell Me So** / Little Jane**	Manor 1123	1948
I Want To Cry** / Someday	Manor 1129	1948
Confess / Don't Know	Manor 1131	1948
How Can I Make You Believe In Me / Don't You Ever Mind	Manor 1141	1948
I'll Never Belong To Anyone Else** / Try To Forget***	Manor 1142	1948
It's Raining Down In Sunshine Lane** / How Could I Know**	Manor 1152	1948
(I Wonder) Where Is My Love / Take My Lonely Heart	Col 30145	11/48
The Best Of Friends** / The Things You Do To Me**	Col 30146	11/48
My Muchacha / I'm Gonna Ride Tillie Tonight	Manor 1154	1949
Would You Hurt Me Now** / All Of Me**	Manor 1168	1949
Mister Sun / The Sheik Of Araby	Manor 1173	1949
Don't Try To Explain** / Savannah Sings The Blues**	Manor 1180	1949

A SIDE/ B SIDE	LABEL/CAT NO	DATE
Someday / Karen Lynn	Manor 1195	1949
Careless Love (Do) / You're Heartless	RCA 50-0008	5/49
I'm The Guy (Do) / My Last Affair**	RCA 50-0016	6/49
I Want To Cry*** / My Baby Kin***	Arco 1220	10/49
I'll Never Be Free** / Get Yourself Another Guy***	Arco 1202	11/49
Daddy Daddy / Why Was I Born***	Arco 1222	11/50
Lonesome Road / I'm Just A Fool In Love	RCA 50-0042	12/49
Don't Try To Explain** / Savannah Sings The Blues**	Arco 1229	1950
Don't Cry Darling** / Don't Take Your Love From Me***	Arco 1236	1950
Am I Blue / There Goes My Heart	RCA 50-0072	3/50
You're My Love / Don't Blame My Dreams	Arco 1246	4/50
Old Fashioned Love / Kentucky Babe	RCA 50-0085	5/50
I Want To Be Loved** / Foolishly Yours**	Arco 1253	1950
Time Out For Tears** / All My Dreams	Arco 1257	1950
The Devil Sat Down And Cried** / Can Anyone Explain**	Arco 1259	8/50
May That Day Never Come / Carry Me Back To The Lone Prairie	RCA 50-0131	6/51
Old Bojangles' Gone / I'm In The Mood For Love†	RCA 47-3149	
Do I Worry / Say When	RCA 47-3881	8/50
Cool Water / How Can You Say That I Don't Care	RCA 47-3967	11/50
Wishing You Were Here Tonight / The Last Round Up	RCA 47-4102	3/51
I Married An Angel / The Prisoner's Song	RCA 47-4241	8/51
(It's No) Sin** / I Don't Believe In Tomorrow**	RCA 47-4280	1951
Early In The Morning / My Buddy	RCA 47-4305	10/51
I'll See You In My Dreams / Tell Me Why	RCA 47-4427	12/51
The Greatest Song I Ever Heard / Come What May	RCA 47-4489	1/52
Can I Say Anymore / I Wonder	RCA 47-4663	4/52
They Don't Understand / Why Do You Do This To Me	RCA 47-4828	6/52
Let's Give Love Another Chance / I Don't Want To Set The World On Fire	RCA 47-4968	10/52
Water Boy / Don't Get Around Much Anymore	RCA 47-5532	11/53
Savannah Sings The Blues** / I Want To Be Loved**	K-Ron 1000	1954
Just In Case You Change Your Mind / I Understand	K-Ron 1005	1954
Marie / I Gambled With Love	Jubi 5128	11/53
I Understand Just How You Feel / Sugar Lump	Jubi 5132	2/54

A SIDE/ B SIDE	LABEL/CAT NO	DATE
My Wild Irish Rose / Do-Do-Do- Do-Do-Do-Do It Again	Jubi 5135	3/54
The Greatest Feeling In The World / Lonesome	Jubi 5152	7/54
L'Amour Toujours L'Amour / Don't Cry Darling	Jubi 5165	10/54
Let Me Go Lover / I Sold My Heart To the Junkman	Jubi 5174	1/55
I Hope / I Close My Eyes	Jubi 5183	2/55
Time Out For Tears / Tired of Waiting	Jubi 5200	7/55
Brooklyn Bridge / Three Little Chickens	Jubi 5212	8/55
At The Steamboat River Ball / You Are My Love	Jubi 5218	9/55
Our Love / Rock 'n' Roll Call	Jubi 5232	1/56
I Gotta Go / Hold Me Closer	Jubi 5239	1956
Dancing With Tears In My Eyes / Far Away Places	Jubi 5245	1956

The Ballad Of James Dean /
   Japanese Farewell Song
   (Sayonara)
	Jubi 5255	1956

A Little On The Lonely Side / Cool Water	Jubi 5276	1957
Never Look Down / Don't You Run Away	Crosby 3	1958
Twinkle Eyes / Starved For Love	Crosby 4	

* as the Sentimentalists ***Savannah Churchill
**with Savannah Churchill solo
† with Juanita Hall

The Four Vagabonds

An exceptionally good quartet in the tradition of THE MILLS BROTHERS (especially in their vocal imitations of musical instruments), the Four Vagabonds had a distinctive sound that can be heard as linking THE INK SPOTS' and CHARIOTEERS' styles with that of THE ORIOLES in the late '40s. Unlike those other acts, the Vagabonds earned most of their following through radio exposure rather than record sales, issuing only 16 78s in their career—a fraction of the output of their legendary predecessors.

The Vagabonds began their career at Vashon High School in St. Louis, Missouri, four years into the Great Depression. Baritone Norval Tuborn and lead John Jordan joined with first tenor Robert O'Neal and bass and guitarist Ray Grant, Jr. dur-

ing the school year of 1933. The foursome's natural blend had them graduating from only three weeks of practice to singing on the University of St. Louis's WEW radio station. This opportunity led to a half-hour Sunday show on WIL that netted the teenagers a weekly stipend of $25. The group divided its time over the next two-and-a-half years between the WIL show and a network show on KSD (also in St. Louis).

The Vagabonds started on the professional leg of their odyssey in 1936 when radio luminary Joseph Jones heard them on St. Louis radio and brought them to Chicago. There they starred on Don McNeil's "Breakfast Club" on NBC's Blue Network and performed spiritual and pop songs three times a week. While still doing the "Breakfast Club" in 1938, they sang daily on the "Club Matinee," another Blue Network radio program with Garry Moore and Durward Kirby in 1938. They augmented this exposure with other shows such as a series of performances with Amos and Andy. They also had the historic opportunity to perform on Zenith's experimental TV show when its signal range was only in the 50-mile category during the late '30s.

With the group's name spreading from five years of constant radio activity in the Windy City, the Bluebird Record Company (an RCA subsidiary) started issuing Vagabonds 78s in 1941. Their first single, recorded on December 17, 1941 (only 10 days after the bombing of Pearl Harbor), was the ballad "Slow and Easy" backed with a harmony version of the "Duke of Dubuque."

During the war years the Four Vagabonds included at least one war-related side on each of their next four releases, including the popular "Rosie the Riveter" and "Ten Little Soldiers," which was their second national pop chart record in July 1943 (#20), their first being the A side, "Rose Ann of Charing Cross," which also reached number 20 only four months earlier in April.

Their fourth and last Bluebird single had the unusual distinction of being one of the few records in history to have its A side chart Pop while its flip charted only R&B. The uplifting and bouncy "Comin' in on a Wing and a Prayer" reached number 24 on the pop chart in July 1943, while the flip side, the brilliant jazz-influenced ballad "It Can't Be Wrong," became their biggest hit, reaching number three R&B in July and charting for 11 weeks.

Between 1942 and 1944 the musicians' strike immobilized the recording industry, but it didn't stop the Vagabonds, who could segue from a straightforward harmony to imitations of various instruments (such as muted trumpets and bass fiddles) and back again without missing a beat.

The group's career took them across the country, from McBan's Club in Buffalo, New York, to Billy Bird's in Los Angeles.

When the war ended, RCA issued "G. I. Wish" (June 1945). The group then wound up with Mercury Records and later Apollo, ending their recording career in late 1947.

In 1945 Ray went blind, but the quartet had rehearsed on- and off-stage movements so well that audiences never had a clue.

In 1949 the group appeared on another historic TV show. The date was April Fool's day when Chicago's WENR-TV became the first station in the nation to broadcast an all-black show right down to the all-black studio audience. The show's host was Ray Grant.

The group called it quits in 1952.

THE FOUR VAGABONDS

A SIDE/B SIDE	LABEL/CAT NO	DATE
Duke Of Dubuque / Slow And Easy	Blbd 11519	4/42
Rosie The Riveter / I Had The Craziest Dream	Blbd 200810	2/43
Ten Little Soldiers / Rose Ann Of Charing Cross	Blbd 300811	3/43
Comin' In On A Wing And A Prayer / It Can't Be Wrong	Blbd 300815	6/43
A.G.I. Wish / If I Were You	RCA 20-1677	6/45
Taking My Chance With You / When The Old Gang's Back On The Corner	Merc 2050	2/46
Oh, What A Polka / I Can't Make Up My Mind	Atlas 111	1946
Kentucky Babe / Hoe Cake, Hominy and Sassafras Tea	Apollo 1030	1946
Do You Know What It Means To Miss New Orleans / The Pleasure's All Mine	Apollo 1039	1947
Dreams Are A Dime A Dozen / I Wonder Who's Kissing Her Now	Apollo 1055	1947
The Freckle Song / P.S. I Love You	Apollo 1057	1947
Ask Anyone Who Knows / Oh My Achin' Heart	Apollo 1060	1947
Choo-Choo / Lazy Country Side	Apollo 1075	1947
The Gang That Sang Heart Of My Heart / That Old Gang Of Mine	Apollo 1076	1947
Mighty Hard To Go Thru Life Alone / My Heart Cries	Miracle 141	10/49
P.S. I Love You / Lazy Country Side	Lloyds 102	1953

The Golden Gate Quartet

Jubilee was a secularized form of church music that was acceptable in nightclubs and concerts during the '30s and '40s. The most popular of the Jubilee quartets, the Golden Gate Quartet started singing as the Golden Gate Jubilee Quartet in the mid-'30s when they were students at Booker T. Washington High School in Norfolk, Virginia. The membership included Willie Johnson (baritone and narrator), Henry Owens (first tenor), William Langford (second tenor), and Orlandus Wilson (bass). The singers chose their name for its musical sound, and they were more likely describing the doors to heaven than the bridge over San Francisco Bay. Their harmonies became very sophisticated, laced with a heavy dose of jazz and a MILLS BROTHERS influence right down to their vocal imitation of instruments. In fact, next to the Mills Brothers, they were probably the best at that "sounding like instruments" technique.

They built their reputation through performing on local radio shows and in churches.

In 1937 the Gates signed to Victor's Bluebird affiliate and applied their unique jazz-swing sound to gospel titles like "Go Where I Send Thee," "The Preacher and the Bear," and "When the Saints Go Marchin' In." On August 4, 1937, they recorded an amazing 14 songs in two hours at the Charlotte Hotel in North Carolina. They performed in the same year on NBC Radio's "Magic Key Hour."

By 1939 they were working out of New York, and Clyde Riddick had replaced William Langford.

In June of 1940 they recorded several sides with the legendary folk singer Leadbelly, released in 1941 on Bluebird's parent label, Victor. By now they had dropped the Jubilee portion of their name, presenting themselves strictly as the Golden Gate Quartet.

Though their recorded repertoire from 1937 to 1940 includes mostly gospel and Jubilee songs, they did record two pop-jazz 78s: "Stormy Weather" and "My Prayer." One of the highlights of this period was a performance for President Franklin Roosevelt's inauguration, which led to a number of appearances at the White House at the request of Eleanor Roosevelt.

In 1941 they moved to Columbia's Okeh affiliate, and their entire recorded output during the war years was on that label. The most successful of these records was a version of "Comin' in on a Wing and a Prayer" in 1943. It was also in '43 that Wilson and Johnson joined the war effort at the request of Uncle Sam, and Alton Bradley and Cliff Givens replaced them, respectively. Wilson and Johnson rejoined in 1946 and Givens moved to THE INK SPOTS.

Their biggest record success came in 1947 with the song "Shadrack."

In 1948 the group appeared in the RKO musical *A Song Is Born*, starring Benny Goodman, Danny Kaye, and Louis Armstrong. Willie Johnson soon left to take the lead of the Jubalaires, and Orville Brooks joined the Gates. Later that year they jumped from Columbia to Mercury and, along with the usual Jubilee tunes, cut a few R&B and pop 78s like "Will I Find My Love Today."

By 1957 the foursome, now including Caleb J. C. Ginyard of the Dixiaires, were following the lead of other black American groups, like THE DELTA RHYTHM BOYS, who were finding warmer receptions in Europe. In 1959 the Golden Gate Quartet moved to Paris and landed a two-year deal to perform at the Casino de Paris. While based in Europe they recorded for EMI-UK, Pathe Marconi in France, and EMI-Germany, creating over 50 LPs.

By the late 1970s Orlandus Wilson and Clyde Riddick were the only remaining originals singing with Calvin Williams (second tenor) and Paul Brembly (baritone). Over the years the group amassed a travelogue of 76 countries performed in.

One of the truly great vocal groups, the Gates were cited as an inspiration to many rhythm and blues groups of the '50s.

THE GOLDEN GATE QUARTET

A SIDE/B SIDE	LABEL/CAT NO	DATE
Golden Gate Gospel Train / Gabriel Blows His Horn	Blbd 7126	8/37
Jonah / Behold The Bridegroom Cometh	Blbd 7154	1937
Born Ten Thousand Years Ago / The Preacher And The Bear	Blbd 7205	10/37
Put On Your Old Grey Bonnet / Massa's In The Cold Cold Ground	Blbd 7264	11/37
Bedside Of A Neighbor / Found A Wonderful Savior	Blbd 7278	11/37
Go Where I Send Thee / Won't There Be One Happy Time	Blbd 7340	12/37
Job / Stand In The Test In Judgement	Blbd 7376	1/38
Carolina In The Morning / The Dipsy Doodle	Blbd 7415	2/38
Motherless Child / Travelin' Shoes	Blbd 7463	3/38
I Was Brave / Sampson	Blbd 7513	4/38

A SIDE/ B SIDE	LABEL/CAT NO	DATE
I Was Brave / Samson	Blbd 7564	5/38
Lead Me On And On / Take Your Burdens To God	Blbd 7617	6/38
John The Revelator / See How They Done My Lord	Blbd 7631	6/38
Swanee River / Sweet Adeline	Blbd 7676	7/38
My Lord Is Waiting / Rock My Soul	Blbd 7804	9/38
Let That Liar Alone / To The Rock	Blbd 7835	9/38
God Almighty Said / Bye And Bye Little Children	Blbd 7848	10/38
When The Saints Go Marching In / When They Ring The Golden Bells	Blbd 7897	10/38
I Heard Zion Moan / Noah	Blbd 7962	12/38
What Are They Doing In Heaven Today / Lord, Am I Born To Die	Blbd 7994	1/39
Cheer The Weary Traveler / Packing Up—Getting Ready To Go	Blbd 8019	2/39
Troubles Of The World / Everything Moves By The Grace Of God	Blbd 8087	3/39
Ol' Man Mose / Change Partners	Blbd 10154	3/39
Lis'n To De Lambs / Dese Bones Gonna Rise Again	Blbd 8123	4/39
Noah / This World Is In A Bad Condition	Blbd 8160	1939
Old Man River / Precious Lord	Blbd 8190	7/39
What A Time / Alone	Blbd 8286	11/39
If I Had My Way / Way Down In Egypts Land	Blbd 8036	12/39
He Said He Would Calm The Ocean / Every Time I Feel The Spirit	Blbd 8328	12/39
I Looked Down The Road And I Wondered / You'd Better Mind	Blbd 8348	1/40
My Prayer / What's New	Blbd 10569	1/40
Hide Me In Thy Bosom / I'm A Pilgrim	Blbd 8362	2/40
What Did Jesus Say / Valley Of Time	Blbd 8388	3/40
Darling Nellie Gray / My Walking Stick	Blbd 8565	11/40
Whoa Babe / Stormy Weather	Blbd 8579	12/40
Julius Caesar / The Devil With The Devil	Blbd 8594	12/40
Timber / Jonah In The Whale	Blbd 8620	1/41

The Golden Gate Quartet and Leadbelly

Midnight Special / Ham and Eggs	RCA 27266	2/41
Gray Goose / Stew-Ball	RCA 27267	2/41
Pick A Bale Of Cotton / Alabama Bound	RCA 27268	2/41

The Golden Gate Quartet

Jonah / The Preacher And The Bear	RCA 27322	2/41
Job / Noah	RCA 27323	2/41

A SIDE/ B SIDE	LABEL/CAT NO	DATE
Samson / John The Revelator	RCA 27324	2/41
Jezebel / Daniel Saw The Stone	Okeh 6204	5/41
Anyhow / Time's Winding Up	Okeh 6238	6/41
Blind Barnabus / The Sun Didn't Shine	Okeh 6345	8/41
Didn't It Rain / He Never Said A Mumblin' Word	Okeh 6529	12/41
Stalin Wasn't Stallin' / Dip Your Fingers In The Water	Okeh 6712	5/43
Run On / Comin' In On A Wing And A Prayer	Okeh 6713	6/43
I Will Be Home Again / The General Jumped At Dawn	Okeh 6741	5/45
Bones, Bones, Bones / Moses Smote The Waters	Col 36937	2/46
Jonah / Travelin' Shoes	RCA 20-2073	12/46
Shadrack / Atom And Evil	Col 37236	2/47
Job / Go Where I Send Thee	RCA 20-2134	4/47
Didn't It Rain / He Never Said A Mumblin' Word	Col 37475	5/47
The Sun Didn't Shine / Blind Barnabus	Col 37476	5/47
Time's Winding Up / Anyhow	Col 37477	5/47
Pray For The Lights To Go Out / High, Low And Wide	Col 37499	6/47
No Restricted Signs / I Will Be Home Again	Col 37832	10/47
Wade In The Water / Joshua Fit De Battle Of Jericho	Col 37833	10/47
Swing Down, Chariot / Blind Barnabus	Col 37834	10/47
God's Gonna Cut You Down / Jezebel	Col 37835	10/47
Stand In The Test Of Judgement / When The Saints Go Marching In	RCA 20-2797	2/48
Rock My Soul / Gabriel Blows His Horn	RCA 20-2921	5/48
Didn't It Rain / He Never Said A Mumblin' Word	Col 30042	5/48
The Sun Didn't Shine / Blind Barnabus	Col 30043	5/48
Time's Winding Up / Anyhow	Col 30044	5/48
Broodle-OO, Broodle-OO / Abdullah	Col 30128	6/48
Hush / Do Unto Others	Col 30136	8/48
I Looked Down The Road And I Wondered / This World Is In A Bad Condition	RCA 20-3159	10/48
Behold The Bridegroom Cometh / Bedside Of A Neighbor	RCA 20-3308	12/48
Mene Mene Tekel / Talkin' Jerusalem To Death	Merc 8118	12/48
Look Up / Will I Find My Love Today	Merc 5242	2/49
Didn't That Man Believe / There's A Man Going Round Taking Names	Merc 5385	4/50

A SIDE/ B SIDE	LABEL/CAT NO	DATE
Mary Mary / Jesus Met The Woman At The Well	Merc 8124	3/49
John Saw / Lord I Am Tired And Want To Go Home	Merc 8142	5/49
Toll The Bell Easy / Fare You Well, Fare You Well	Col 30160	5/49
Satisfied / Religion Is Fortune	Merc 8155	10/49
Lord I Want To Walk With Thee / You Ain't Got Religion	Merc 8158	12/49
Same Train / Ride On Moses	Merc 8162	1/50
Blessed Jesus / Lord Have Mercy	Merc 8164	1/50
Seven Angels And Seven Trumpets / Lord I Want To Be A Christian	Merc 8243	7/51
I Just Telephone Upstairs / Rain Is The Teardrops Of Angels	Okeh 6897	7/52
Sittin' In With Mother's Love / On Top Of Old Smokey	Sittin In 2022	1952
Mother's Love / You Better Mind	Sittin In 2024	1952
His Eye Is On The Sparrow / Steal Away And Pray	Sittin In 2025	1952
Bones, Bones, Bones / Round The Great White Throne	Sittin In 2026	1952

The Ink Spots

One of the two granddaddies of vocal groups, the Ink Spots introduced a number of firsts that had a direct impact on the development of rhythm and blues in the '40s and rock and roll in the '50s. Although THE MILLS BROTHERS were successful years before the Ink Spots and turned out many more hits (71 to the Spots' 46), each had a tremendous influence on music, the public, and future vocalists, and chances are that a group or singer influenced by one was also influenced by the other.

Bill Kenny's soaring tenor paved the way for Sonny Til (THE ORIOLES), Maithe Marshall (THE RAVENS), Frankie Lymon (THE TEENAGERS), Curtis Mayfield (THE IMPRESSIONS), Russell Tompkins, Jr. (THE STYLISTICS), and many others to follow. Hoppy Jones's revolutionary talking-bass parts redefined a bass singer's value and role in a group, and his style was emulated by Jimmy Ricks (the Ravens) and almost every rhythm and blues and rock and roll bass since then. More broadly, the Ink Spots were one of the first black groups to cross the racial barrier in radio and live performances.

▲ THE MERRY MACS

▲ THE MILLS BROTHERS

▲ THE INK SPOTS

▼ THE AMES BROTHERS

▲ THE SOUL STIRRERS   ▼ THE SKYLARKS

▼ THE FOUR VAGABONDS

The ballad style for which they gained fame came about by chance and was not part of their original sound. The group met in Indianapolis, Indiana, around 1931. The original members were Ivory "Deek" (Deacon) Watson (lead), formerly of the swing group the Four Riff Brothers (1929) and before that the Percolating Puppies (1928), a vocal band influenced by Duke Ellington and McKinney's Cotton Pickers; Charlie Fuqua (second tenor and baritone), the uncle of MOONGLOWS lead singer Harvey Fuqua; and Jerry Daniels (first tenor), who sang with Charlie in the vaudeville team Charlie and Jerry.

The latter duo had started out harmonizing and playing guitar and ukulele (Jerry) and four-string banjo and guitar (Charlie). Deek Watson met them at Charlie's shoeshine stand in Indianapolis near the old Stutz automobile factory (famous for the Stutz Bearcat cars). They formed a trio called the Swingin' Gate Brothers and later King, Jack and Jester (1931), and launched their career on a 15-minute radio show on WHK in Cleveland.

They moved on to Cincinnati's WLW, doing commercials for CBC (Crosley Broadcasting Company), and were announced by a young Red Barber, later a great sportscaster. At this time, one of the aforementioned Four Riff Brothers, Orville "Hoppy" Jones, joined the group on bass vocals and stand-up bass—actually a re-tuned cello. The resulting group sound drew from vaudeville and jazz band music.

The quartet came to New York in the early '30s and immediately ran into a name conflict with the already famous Paul Whiteman orchestra group, the King's Jesters. The problem was solved by Harlem's Savoy Ballroom owner and new group manager, Moe Gale, who simply sat down and thought up the name the Ink Spots.

They started out with a 15-minute show on New York's WJZ radio. Unlike most black acts of the time, they were being accepted at white performance venues, allowing them to play the Apollo one day and the Waldorf Astoria the next.

The foursome's first encounter with recording happened on January 4, 1935, at RCA Studios, and in the same month RCA issued their first release, "Swingin' on the Strings"/"Your Feet's Too Big." When two 78s went nowhere, the group broadened its popularity by leaving the country, doing transatlantic radio broadcasts over London's BBC in the winter of 1935.

In early 1936 Moe Gale took notice of Bill Kenny, the winner of an amateur contest at the Savoy Ballroom, and brought him into the group.

With the addition of the new member, Jerry Daniels left the Spots and moved to Indianapolis, later singing with local acts like the Deep Swingin' Brothers and the Three Shades.

That same year the Ink Spots signed with Decca and on May 12, 1936, waxed "T'ain't Nobody's Bizness If I Do" and a rerecording of "Your Feet's Too Big," issued as their first two sides. The group began doing package shows with other Gale acts like Ella Fitzgerald and Moms Mabley.

Over the next three years the group, with Deek usually on lead, tried everything from Gershwin ("Let's Call the Whole Thing Off") to vocal versions of big-band tunes like "Stompin' at the Savoy," but by the end of 1938, after 10 singles, nothing had really grabbed the public's interest. About this time, Billy Kenny met 25-year-old Johnny Smith of the Alphabetical Four, a group that sang both gospel and blues. Smith became a swing man filling in on occasion when someone was unavailable.

The group was on the verge of calling it quits as bookings were down and record sales had never been up. Then, on January 12, 1939, the history of popular music took an important turn thanks to a young aspiring songwriter named Jack Lawrence. He brought a composition he'd written to a Spots session that was supposed to be for the recording of a jive song, "Knock-Kneed Sal." The group worked up Lawrence's ballad, "If I Didn't Care," with Kenny doing his now famous quivering tenor lead and Hoppy improvising his talking bass bridge.

A lot of people *did* care, as it turned out. Issued in February of 1939, by April 15 the song had charted in *Billboard* and reached number two within weeks, selling a million copies to a broad spectrum of listeners.

The fate of Lawrence's catalog of compositions is indicative of the potential sentimental and financial value of songs: it was sold more than 30 years later for over half a million dollars. Along with "If I Didn't Care" was a song Jack wrote for his lawyer's daughter in 1938 called "Linda." His lawyer's name was Lee Eastman, and Eastman's offspring later married a man named Paul McCartney. That's right—the Beatles' Paul McCartney. And the buyer of Lawrence's songs? Why, Paul McCartney, of course.

Hit after hit in the style of "If I Didn't Care" came forth from the Ink Spots and Decca, including "Address Unknown" (#1, 1939), "My Prayer" (#3, 1939, later a hit for THE PLATTERS), "When the Swallows Come Back to Capistrano" (#4, 1940), "Maybe" (#2, 1940), "We Three" (#1, 1940), "Do I Worry" (#8, 1941), "I Don't Want to Set the World on Fire" (which was #4 in December 1941), and "Don't Get Around Much Anymore" (#2, 1943).

The group broke attendance records wherever they appeared, performing with Glenn Miller's Orchestra, Lucky Millinder's Band, and countless others, and they even did films like *The Great American Broadcast* in 1941 and Abbott and Costello's romp, *Pardon My Sarong*. A 1944 radio poll voted them the number two favorite singing unit behind Fred Waring's Glee Club and ahead of greats like THE ANDREWS SISTERS.

In mid-1943 Charlie Fuqua joined the service and hand-picked his replacement, Bernie Mackey from Indianapolis.

From August 1942 to September 1943 the musicians' union strike put a halt to any new recordings, but the Spots still placed four singles on the charts (out of only five releases), including "Every Night About This Time" (#17, 1942), "Don't Get Around Much Anymore (#2, 1943), "If I Cared a Little Bit Less" (#20, 1943), and "I'll Never Make the Same Mistake Again" (#19, 1943). The group's arranger during most of the war years was Bill Doggett, who went on to work with Louis Armstrong, Ella Fitzgerald, Louis Jourdan, and his own combo in 1952. In '56 he had hits for King on "Honky Tonk" (#2 Pop, #1 R&B) and "Slow Walk" (#26 Pop, #4 R&B).

In late 1944 Deek Watson, who had been at odds with Bill Kenny for some time, left to form his own Ink Spots but was stopped by a court injunction; he renamed his new group Deek Watson and THE BROWN DOTS. Bill Bowen of McKinney's Cotton Pickers took Deek's place.

On October 18, 1944, Hoppy Jones's booming bass was stilled forever when he died at the age of 39. He was replaced later by former GOLDEN GATE QUARTET member Cliff Givens. There were more transitions: Huey Long took over for Mackey, Herb Kenny (Bill's brother) replaced Givens, and in late 1945 Fuqua returned to replace Long (who never recorded with the group).

Decca wanted to keep the Ink Spots on the charts as often as possible, even if they didn't have enough new material to justify it. Thus from 1945 through '48, they issued 35 78s of which 17 singles contained recordings that were as many as five years old.

In 1949, Herb Kenny moonlighted with a trio for a while. In 1951 Adriel McDonald, the group's valet (and former nonrecording member of the Cabineers) subbed for Herb Kenny when he missed a radio show, and he became the full-time replacement. Herb went on to record for Federal ("Only

You") in 1952 as lead of Herb Kenny and the Comets. The Comets were actually a white group called the Rockets that used to back up Perry Como. Herb recorded with them on MGM for five singles in 1952 and 1953.

As friction grew in 1952, both Bill Bowen and Charlie Fuqua exited. An explosion of groups tried to cash in on the name the Ink Spots. Bowen formed Billy Bowen and the Butterball Four (MGM); Fuqua formed his own Ink Spots, but was taken to court by Bill Kenny. Fuqua won, so his new group, with Harold Jackson, Jimmy Holmes, and Leon Antoine, joined King Records for nine quality singles between late 1953 and 1955. Essix Scott replaced Antoine during the latter sessions.

Bill Kenny, meanwhile, was doing a lot of solo work during the early '50s, while forming yet another Ink Spots, this one including Adriel McDonald, Jimmy Kennedy, and Ernie Brown. The group's demise came in 1953 when they were asked to appear on an Ed Sullivan-sponsored show for returning Korean war vets. Kenny okayed the deal but told the group he was appearing solo and couldn't afford to pay them. The group had had enough and split. Sullivan was so furious that he listed Kenny at the bottom of the bill.

Though the originals sang together no more, Ink Spots groups sprang up like weeds. Kenny was once vacationing in Las Vegas during the mid-'70s and found three groups posing as the Spots at the same time. At the beginning of the 1990s, over 40 groups claimed to be the Ink Spots. Fill-in Johnny Smith supposedly had exclusive authority from Bill Kenny's widow to represent the group. Watson had the rights but sold them to Bill Kenny in the '40s for $20,000.

Such was the value of the name for fans as well as future vocal groups. Many of their recordings were copied and reworked for new generations in later years. The Platters made a career of covering Ink Spots songs. Bobby Day and the Satellites (actually THE HOLLYWOOD FLAMES) did "When the Swallows Come Back to Capistrano"; the Sharps did "We Three"; THE HEARTS "Until the Real Thing Comes Along"; THE ISLEY BROTHERS and THE BELMONTS covered "Don't Get Around Much Anymore"; the Roommates did "A Lovely Way to Spend an Evening"; BILLY WARD AND THE DOMINOES cut "The Gypsy"; the Orioles revived "I Cover the Waterfront"; and James Brown and His Famous Flames covered "Prisoner of Love." There were many more.

Charlie Fuqua died in 1970 at the age of 60. Deek Watson passed away in November of 1969, and Bill Kenny died in 1978.

THE INK SPOTS

A SIDE/B SIDE	LABEL/CAT NO	DATE
Swinging On The Strings / Your Feets Too Big	RCA 24851	1/35
Don't 'Low No Swingin' In Here / Swing, Gate Swing	RCA 24876	3/35
Swinging On The Strings / Your Feets Too Big	Blbd 6530	1936
T'Aint Nobody's Biz-Ness If I Do / Your Feets Too Big	Decca 817	1936
Christopher Columbus / Old Jones Hittin' The Jug	Decca 883	1936
Stompin' At The Savoy / Keep Away From My Door	Decca 1036	1936
Alabama Barbecue / With Plenty Of Money And You	Decca 1154	1937
Swing High, Swing Low / Whoa Babe	Decca 1236	1937
Let's Call The Whole Thing Off / Slap That Bass	Decca 1251	1937
Don't Let Old Age Creep Up On You / Yes-Suh	Decca 1731	1937
Oh Red / That Cat Is High	Decca 1789	1938
I Wish You The Best Of Everything / When The Sun Goes Down	Decca 1870	1938
Brown Gal / Pork Chops And Gravy	Decca 2044	1938
If I Didn't Care / Knock Kneed Sal	Decca 2236	2/39
Its Funny To Everyone But Me / Just For A Thrill	Decca 2507	1939
You Bring Me Down / Address Unknown	Decca 2707	8/39
My Prayer / Give Her My Love	Decca 2790	9/39
Bless You / I Don't Want Sympathy I Want Love	Decca 2841	10/39
Memories Of You / I'm Through	Decca 2966	12/39
I'm Getting Sentimental Over You / Coquette	Decca 3077	3/39
What Can I Do / When The Swallows Come Back To Capistrano	Decca 3195	1940
Whispering Grass / Maybe	Decca 3258	1940
Stop Pretending / You're Breaking My Heart All Over Again	Decca 3288	1940
I'll Never Smile Again / I Could Make You Care	Decca 3346	1940
We Three / My Greatest Mistake	Decca 3379	1940
Do I Worry / Java Jive	Decca 3432	1940
I'm Only Human / Puttin' And Takin'	Decca 3468	1940
Ring, Telephone, Ring / Please Take A Letter, Miss Brown	Decca 3626	1941
We'll Meet Again / You're Looking For Romance	Decca 3656	1941
That's When Your Heartaches Begin / What Good Would It Do	Decca 3720	1941
I'm Still Without A Sweetheart / So Sorry	Decca 3806	1941

A SIDE/ B SIDE	LABEL/CAT NO	DATE
Keep Cool, Fool / Until The Real Thing Comes Along	Decca 3958	1941
I Don't Want To Set The World On Fire / Hey Doc	Decca 3987	8/41
Nothin' / Someone's Rockin' My Dream Boat	Decca 4045	9/41
Is It A Sin / It's A Sin To Tell A Lie	Decca 4112	1/42
It Isn't A Dream Anymore / Shout Brother Shout	Decca 4194	3/42
Don't Leave Now / Foo-Gee	Decca 4303	4/42
Don't Tell A Lie About Me, Dear / Who Wouldn't Love You	Decca 18383	6/42
Ev'ry Night About This Time / I'm Not The Same Old Me	Decca 18461	8/42
This Is Worth Fighting For / Just As Though You Were Here	Decca 19466	8/42
Don't Get Around Much Anymore / Street Of Dreams	Decca 18503	10/42
If I Cared A Little Bit Less / Mine All Mine, My My	Decca 18528	11/42
I Can't Stand Losing You / I'll Never Make The Same Mistake Again	Decca 18542	3/43
I'll Get By / Someday I'll Meet You Again	Decca 18579	4/44
Don't Believe Everything You Dream / A Lovely Way To Spend An Evening	Decca 18583	5/44
Cow-Cow Boogie* / When My Sugar Walks Down The Street**	Decca 18587	2/44
I'm Making Believe* / Into Each Life Some Rain Must Fall*	Decca 23356	10/44
I'm Beginning To See The Light* / That's The Way It Is*	Decca 23399	3/45
I Hope To Die If I Told A Lie / Maybe It's All For The Best	Decca 18657	3/45
I'd Climb The Highest Mountain / Thoughtless	Decca 18711	9/45
I'm Gonna Turn Off The Teardrops / The Sweetest Dream	Decca 18755	1/46
The Gypsy / Everyone Is Saying Hello Again	Decca 18817	4/46
I Cover The Waterfront / Prisoner Of Love	Decca 18864	4/46
I Never Had A Dream Come True / To Each His Own	Decca 23615	8/46
If I Didn't Care / Whispering Grass	Decca 23632	8/46
Do I Worry? / Java Jive	Decca 23633	8/46
We Three / Maybe	Decca 23634	8/46
I'll Never Smile Again / Until The Real Thing Comes Along	Decca 23635	8/46
I Get The Blues When It Rains / Either Its Love Or It Isn't	Decca 23695	10/46
Bless You For Being an Angel / Address Unknown	Decca 23757	12/46
That's Where I Came In / You Can't See The Sun When You're Crying	Decca 23809	1/47

A SIDE/ B SIDE	LABEL/CAT NO	DATE
Cow Cow Boogie* / That's The Way It Is*	Decca 25847	1/47
I Want To Thank Your Folks / I Wasn't Made For Love	Decca 23851	4/47
Ask Anyone Who Knows / Can You Look Me In The Eyes	Decca 23900	6/47
Everyone Is Saying Hello Again / The Gypsy	Decca 23936	6/47
Information Please / Do You Feel That Way Too?	Decca 24111	8/47
Always / White Christmas	Decca 24140	9/47
Just For Me / Just Plain Love	Decca 24173	9/47
We'll Meet Again / My Greatest Mistake	Decca 25237	9/47
I'll Get By / Just For A Thrill	Decca 25238	9/47
I'd Climb The Highest Mountain / I'm Gettin' Sentimental Over You	Decca 25239	9/47
Coquette / When The Swallows Come Back To Capistrano	Decca 25240	9/47
Home Is Where The Heart Is / Sincerely Yours	Decca 24192	10/47
I'll Lose A Friend Tomorrow / When You Come To The End Of The Day	Decca 24261	11/47
I'll Make Up For Everything / It's All Over But The Crying	Decca 24286	1/48
The Best Things In Life Are Free / I Woke Up With A Teardrop In My Eye	Decca 24327	2/48
I'm Gonna Turn Off The Teardrops / I'm Beginning to See The Light*	Decca 25344	2/48
Don't Leave Now / Ring, Telephone, Ring	Decca 25378	5/48
Just For Now / Where Flamingos Fly	Decca 24461	7/48
Aladdin's Lamp / My Baby Didn't Even Say Goodbye	Decca 24496	9/48
Say Something Sweet To Your Sweetheart / You Were Only Fooling	Decca 24507	10/48
Am I Asking Too Much / Recess In Heaven	Decca 24517	11/48
Bewildered / No Orchids for My Lady	Decca 24566	2/49
It Only Happens Once / As You Desire Me	Decca 24585	3/49
Kiss And A Rose / A Knock On The Door	Decca 24611	4/49
If You Had To Hurt Someone / To Remind Me Of You	Decca 24672	7/49
Who Do You Know In Heaven / You're Breaking My Heart	Decca 24693	8/49
Echoes / Land Of Love	Decca 24741	9/49
With My Eyes Wide Open, I'm Dreaming / Lost In A Dream	Decca 24887	2/50
My Reward / You Left Everything But You	Decca 24933	3/50

A SIDE/ B SIDE	LABEL/CAT NO	DATE
I Don't Want To Set The World On Fire / Someone's Rocking My Dream Boat	Decca 25431	6/49
Sometime / I Was Dancing With Someone	Decca 27102	7/50
Right About Now / The Way It Used To Be	Decca 27214	9/50
Time Out For Tears / Dream Awhile	Decca 27259	10/50
A Friend Of Johnny's / If	Decca 27391	1/51
Little Small Town Girl* / I Still Feel The Same About You*	Decca 27419	1951
Castles In The Sand / Tell Me You Love Me	Decca 27464	1951
A Fool Grows Wise / Do Something For Me	Decca 27493	4/51
And Then I Prayed / Somebody Bigger Than You And I	Decca 27494	4/51
What Can You Do / More Of The Same Sweet You	Decca 27632	7/51
I Don't Stand A Ghost Of A Chance With You / I'm Lucky I Have You	Decca 27742	1951
Honest And Truly / All My Life	Decca 27996	3/52
It's A Sin To Tell A Lie / That's When Your Heartaches Begin	Decca 25505	5/52
Sorry You Said Goodbye / A Bundle From Heaven	Decca 23289	7/52
If I Didn't Care / Do I Worry	Decca 11050	9/52
Forgetting You / I Counted On You	Decca 28462	11/52
Memories Of You / It's Funny To Everyone But Me	Decca 29750	1955
Every Night About This Time / Driftwood	Decca 29957	6/56
My Prayer / Bewildered	Decca 29991	7/56
The Best Things In Life Are Free / I Don't Stand A Ghost Of A Chance With You	Decca 30058	9/56
All My Life / You Were Only Fooling	Decca 25533	10/61

Charlie Fuqua's Ink Spots

A SIDE/ B SIDE	LABEL/CAT NO	DATE
Here In My Lonely Room / Flowers, Mister Florist, Please	King 4670	12/53
Ebb Tide / If You Should Say Goodbye	King 1297	12/53
Changing Partners / Stranger In Paradise	King 1304	1/54
Melody Of Love / Am I Too Late	King 1336	4/54
Planting Rice / Yesterdays	King 1378	7/54
Someone's Rocking My Dreamboat / When You Come To The End Of The Day	King 1425	1/55
Melody Of Love / There Is Something Missing	King 1429	1955
Don't Laugh At Me / Keep It Movin'	King 1512	1955

A SIDE/ B SIDE	LABEL/CAT NO	DATE
Command Me / I'll Walk A Country Mile	King 4857	11/55

* with Ella Fitzgerald
**Ella Fitzgerald solo

The Mariners

The forerunners of racially integrated groups, the Mariners were formed in the Coast Guard at Manhattan Beach, New York, in 1942. Each of them had appeared as soloists when one of their officers requested they sing as a group for a Coast Guard function. The quartet's blend was so pleasing that they decided to stay together and become the Coast Guard Quartet.

The members were Thomas Lockard, a music major from UCLA who had sung with the Los Angeles Opera Company; James O. Lewis, a nightclub performer who appeared in *The Hot Mikado* with Bill Robinson; Nathaniel Dickerson of New York's Juilliard School of Music, who had sung in *Porgy and Bess* and *Finian's Rainbow*; and Martin Karl of the Chicago Opera Company.

The two white and two black vocalists performed throughout the New York area and in 1945 did a tour of installations in the Pacific. When they became civilians after World War II they made their professional debut on a radio broadcast on December 22, 1945. They continued doing broadcasts until coming to the attention of Arthur Godfrey and singing on his show for over seven years.

In the late '40s they signed with Columbia Records and began recording pop and spiritual songs like "On the Island of Oahu" (their first single) and "Be the Good Lord Willing." Their sixth single, "Sometime" (1950), was their first chart hit at number 16. Toward the end of 1951 they charted again with "They Call the Wind Mariah" (#30). Their last chart single was their biggest: "I See the Moon," a cross between barbershop harmony and a beer-hall song, reached number 14 in 1953.

The group recorded 31 singles for Columbia and stayed on Godfrey's show long enough to become nationally known. They then switched to the Cadence label, continuing their spiritual and pop/barbershop vocalizing. One particularly good recording was their early 1956 release of "His Gold Will Melt," about which *Billboard's* reviewer stated, "A very attractive ditty with a catchy refrain and a smart set of novelty lyrics gets a very solid performance by the Mariners, likely to get strong exposure."

The Mariners continued with Cadence into the late '50s and then disappeared as more contemporary artists came into prominence.

THE MARINERS

A SIDE/B SIDE	LABEL/CAT NO	DATE
Leprechaun Lullaby / On The Island Of Oahu	Col 38724	1949
Be The Good Lord Willing / Angels Watching O'er Me	Col 38667	1950
Poison Ivy / I Don't Know Whether To Laugh Or Cry Over You	Col 38677	1950
Sometime / Stars	Col 38781	1950
Minnequa / Beyond The Reef	Col 38966	1950
Our Lady Of Fatima / The Rosary	Col 39042	1950
It Is No Secret / How Near To My Heart	Col 39073	1951
My Little Grass Shack / An Old Friend Is The Best Friend	Col 39101	1951
With These Hands / Castles In The Sand	Col 39193	1951
Loving Is Believing / Light In The Window	Col 38219	1951
The Shannon, The Shamrocks And You / And Then I Prayed	Col 39332	1951
Everyone Is Welcome In The House Of The Lord / Only, Only You	Col 39422	1951
Good Luck, Good Health, God Bless You / Hello Sunshine	Col 39445	1951
Mighty Navy Wings / The Mariners' Song	Col 39515	1951
The Tinkle Song / They Call The Wind Maria	Col 39568	1951
The Gentle Carpenter of Bethlehem / I See God	Col 39606	1952
It's All Over But The Memories / Take Me Home	Col 39607	1952
Come To The Casbah / Beautiful Isle Of Somewhere	Col 39655	1952
One Love / Jeannine	Col 39718	1952
I Just Want You / I See The Moon	Col 40047	1952
Sweet Mama, Tree Top Tall / A Red, Red Robin	Col 40104	1953
They Don't Play The Piano Anymore / Sentimental Eyes	Col 40157	1954
Steam Heat / When I Needed You Most	Col 40241	1954
In The Chapel In The Moonlight / Oh Mo'Nah	Col 40271	1954
Jambo / They'll Forget About You	Col 40318	1954
An Old Beer Bottle / Hey, Mabel!	Col 40405	1955
Do As You Would Be Did By / I Didn't Come To Say Hello	Col 40439	1955
Chee Chee-oo Chee / A Rusty Old Halo	Col 40514	1955

The Merry Macs

Back in the early '20s, when America was singing in three parts and barbershop style, a trio of teenaged brothers, Ted, Judd, and Joe McMichael, heard a fourth harmony part usually played only by musical instruments and never before sung. So different was the resulting sound of their smooth four-part blend that only other musicians had an inkling of what they were doing.

Their emphasis on four-part harmony helped stoke the fires of popular demand for vocal groups.

The Merry Macs formed in Minneapolis, Minnesota, in the 1920s and sang harmony with their mom singing the melody. They attended West High School and sang at school proms and college dances, fine-tuning their close-harmony style.

In 1926 they were discovered by organist Eddie Dunsteder, who hired them to sing on his WCCO radio show in Minneapolis. He concocted the name the Mystery Trio for the group and had them wear masks—a little comical considering that no one could see them on radio. After a year of local broadcasting the trio met bandleader Joe Haymes, changed their name to the Personality Boys, discarded their masks, and toured the country.

In 1930 they added a girl, Cheri McKay, to sing the melody line. While searching for a new name (somehow, Cheri didn't qualify as a Personality Boy), they realized all their last names started in "Mc," so they became the Merry Macs.

Influenced by THE MILLS BROTHERS, the close-harmony quartet began with Ted on baritone, Joe and Judd on tenor, and Cheri singing melody. Their blend was so incredibly tight that it was difficult to distinguish one vocalist from another.

In 1932 the group's manager, Harry Norwood, got them signed to Victor Records, source of their historic four-part harmony 78 "The Little White Church on the Hill." This was also the year of their first live performance at the Chicago Theatre and the commencement of their appearances on Don McNeil's "Breakfast Club" program several times a week under an NBC Radio contract.

A number of firsts are attributable to this trend-setting group: they were the first close-harmony quartet to include a female, the first to use purely rhythmic accompaniment, and reportedly the first to wear white tie and tails, thus setting the trend toward formal attire on stage.

In 1936 the Macs performed on NBC's national network show, "The Maxwell House Showboat Program," and soon after, they were in demand for all the important network shows from the "Lucky Strike Hit Parade" to "Fred Allen's Town Hall Tonight," where a single performance blossomed into a three-year contract. During that same year Cheri was replaced by Helen Carroll.

With their 1938 appearance in *Love Thy Neighbor*, starring Jack Benny and Fred Allen, the Merry Macs became the first close-harmony group to show up in a Hollywood film. This supplemented a performing schedule that had them headlining with Glenn Miller, Ray Noble, Glen Gray, Paul Whiteman, and other top orchestras of the era.

In 1938 the foursome signed with Decca Records, recording the single "Pop Goes the Weasel" on August 4, 1938. They also signed a 10-year contract with Universal Studios, leading to appearances in such films as *Ride 'Em Cowboy* with Abbott and Costello and *Mr. Music* with Bing Crosby.

A national hit came in March 1939 with the unlikely title "Ta Ha Wa Nu Wa (Hawaiian War Chant)" (#14). By now Mary Lou Cook had become the obligatory female lead of the group, replacing Helen Carroll.

"The Hut Hut Song" (June 1941) was their initial Decca hit of the '40s. Marjory Garland stepped in for Mary Lou Cook in 1941 and spent the next 22 years with the Macs, eventually marrying one (Judd).

Known for their bouncy pop tunes, the Merry Macs were also polished jazz stylists, as one listen to their 1940 single "Vol Vistu Gaily Star" will prove. They hit the top 10 with the bounce tune "Jingle Jangle Jingle" (#4, 1942), and contributed to the war effort with the 1942 number eight hit, "Praise the Lord and Pass the Ammunition." The Macs' biggest hit came in early 1944 with "Mairzy Doats," which reached number one for five weeks.

Around this time Joe died and was replaced by Clive Erard, who stayed until the War's end and was then replaced by Dick Baldwin.

In 1945 they hit with "Sentimental Journey" (#4) and in 1946 with "Laughing on the Outside" (#9). Their last of 12 chart hits had as strange a title as their first and several in-between: "Ashby De La Zooch" (#21, 1946).

The group continued to perform worldwide. They recorded commercials with Gilda Maiken (Anderson) of THE SKYLARKS singing melody. The group stayed with Decca until 1949, when they moved over to Capitol and later to Era.

In 1954 Vern Rowe took over for Dick Baldwin. The foursome of Judd and Ted McMichael, Marjorie Garland McMichael, and Vern Rowe continued the group's activities until 1964 when the act retired.

Their last American performance was a 1968 reunion at the Hollywood Bowl.

One of Ted's daughters, Geri Benson, became a second-generation lead singer of the Merry Macs, keeping the group's tradition alive. Ted is the only surviving member of the group and lives in Hemet, California, with his wife Carolyn.

THE MERRY MACS

A SIDE/B SIDE	LABEL/CAT NO	*DATE
Pop Goes The Weasel / Stop Beatin' 'Round The Mulberry Bush	Decca 1968	8/38
On The Bumpy Road To Love / There's Honey On The Moon Tonight	Decca 1969	1938
Ferdinand The Bull / I Got Rings On My Fingers	Decca 2238	12/38
Chopsticks / Ta-Hu-Wa-Hu-Wa-I	Decca 2333	2/39
Cuckoo In The Clock / Patty Cake, Patty Cake	Decca 2334	2/39
La Paloma / A Rubel A Rhumba	Decca 2404	3/39
Chinatown, My Chinatown / Hello Frisco	Decca 2471	3/39
Rumpel-Stilts-Kin / Too Tired	Decca 2495	5/39
I'm Forever Blowing Bubbles / Igloo	Decca 2506	5/39
My Cat Fell In The Well / Vol Vistu Gaily Star	Decca 2759	9/39
In The Mood / Shoot The Sherbert To Me Herbert	Decca 2842	11/39
Clap Yo' Hands / I Got Rhythm	Decca 2877	9/39
Breezin' Along With The Breeze / Ma	Decca 3025	2/40
Ho! Sa Bonnie! / Johnson Rag	Decca 3088	1940
I Get The Blues When It Rains / The Way You Look Tonight	Decca 3347	7/40
Dry Bones / Red Wing	Decca 3390	7/40
Do You Know Why / Isn't That Just Like Love	Decca 3483	10/40
It Just Isn't There / You'll Never Get Rich	Decca 3690	1/41
The Hut-Sut Song / Mary Lou	Decca 3810	5/41
Honk Honk / Kiss The Boys Goodbye	Decca 3930	7/41
By-By-O (The Louisiana Lullaby) / Rose O'Day	Decca 4023	9/41
Annabella / The Little Guppy	Decca 4074	9/41
Deep In The Heart Of Texas / Kimaneero Down To Cairo	Decca 4136	12/41
Breathless / Hey Mabel	Decca 4265	2/42
Idaho / Olivia	Decca 4313	2/42
Cheatin' On The Sandman / Jingle Jangle Jingle	Decca 18361	2/42
Put On The Old Grey Bonnet / Rolled Rolling Along	Decca 18436	1942
Pass The Biscuits Mirandy / Under A Strawberry Moon	Decca 18478	6/42

A SIDE/ B SIDE	LABEL/CAT NO	DATE
Praise The Lord And Pass The Ammunition / Tweedle O'Twill	Decca 18498	7/42
I Wanna Go Back To West Virginia / Sunday	Decca 18527	7/42
I Got Ten Bucks And Twenty Fo / Mairzy Doats	Decca 18588	2/44
Pretty Kitty Blue Eyes / Sing Me A Song Of Texas	Decca 18610	6/44
Let's Sing A Song About Susie / Up Up Up	Decca 18622	9/44
Ten Days With Baby / Thank Dixie For Me	Decca 18630	11/44
If I Has You / On The Atchison, Topeka And T	Decca 23436	8/45
Just A Blue Serge Suit / Looking At The World Through Rose-Colored Glasses	Decca 18715	10/45
Laughing On The Outside	Decca 18811	3/46
Pop Goes The Weasel / Ta-Hu-Wa-Hu-Wa-I	Decca 25191	7/47
I Love My Love / It's Easy To Say You're Sorry	Decca 24262	11/47
You Made Me Love You (I Didn't)	Decca 25424	4/49
The Forties / Jingle Jangle Jingle	DL-4007	10/60

* Dates through 7/42 are recording dates; dates from 2/44 to 10/60 are release dates.

The Mills Brothers

The Mills Brothers were not only the first black vocal group to have wide appeal among whites, they were the most successful American male group of all time, with 71 chart singles (THE ANDREWS SISTERS had 113) spanning four decades.

Born in Piqua, Ohio, Herbert (1912), Donald (1915), Harry (1913), and John Mills, Jr. (1911) began practicing in their father's barbershop. John, Sr. himself was an excellent light-opera stylist and sang with a group called the Four Kings of Harmony. Barbershop harmony was the Mills boys' forte, and they never did bring much spiritual or gospel flavor into their sound (although they did ultimately do a few sides for Decca's Faith series).

The brothers began performing at the local opera house (and even on street corners) while imitating instruments with kazoos. In one performance during the 1920s the teens forgot their kazoos and began improvising the sound of musical instruments with their voices while cupping their hands over their mouths. (This became a musical breakthrough for them.) John mastered the bass trumpet and tuba; Harry mimicked trumpet and sang baritone; Herbert did sax, trombone, and trumpet; and Donald was the tenor lead vocal. John, Jr. played the guitar—the only actual instrument the group used.

In the late '20s the quartet was signed to perform in a variety of shows, on WLW-Cincinnati. In order to make it seem as if more than one group was doing all that singing, each sponsor of each show gave the act a different name. Hence they sang as the Steamboat Four, the Tasty East Jesters, and Will, Willie, Wilbur and William, among other names. They finally worked on a show (ironically unsponsored) under the name the Mills Brothers.

The group's fame spread to New York. Agent Tommy Rockwell got the drift and brought the brothers east, where they wound up on the CBS radio network.

By 1931 they were recording for Brunswick Records. The brothers would go on to have five number one records of which the first was "Tiger Rag," issued in December of 1931. The amazing brothers were still youngsters when they sat atop the musical world in 1931, ranging in age from 16 to 20. Brunswick then released their "Gems from George White's Scandals" with Bing Crosby and the Boswell Sisters. It reached number three while "Tiger Rag's" flip side, "Nobody's Sweetheart," held the number four spot. Their second chart topper came shortly after their first: "Dinah," again with Bing Crosby, charted on January 9, 1932, and spent two weeks at number one.

Perhaps trying to draw attention to the Brothers' talent, Brunswick had its labels all read, "No musical instruments or mechanical devices used on this recording other than one guitar."

Film now became a big part of the group's across-the-board exposure, as they performed in *The Big Broadcast* (1932), *Operator 133* (1933), and *Twenty Million Sweethearts* (1934).

Not only were the Mills Brothers destined to be emulated by hundreds of vocal groups, but many of their recordings would later be covered by other groups in the style that came to be called rhythm and blues. THE RAVENS took their recording of "Loveless Love" and reworked it into "Careless Love." The Mills's recording of "Gloria" (1948) became THE CADILLACS' classic in 1954 and THE PASSIONS' mini-classic in 1960. The Brothers' 1934 version of "Nagasaki" was done by the Five Chances in 1954, and 1932's "Sweet Sue" later became a great recording for THE CROWS in 1954.

"Rockin' Chair" (#4), issued in May of 1932, had what some historians consider to be the first talking-bass part in a black group record.

In 1934 the group went to Decca Records and to England. While Decca released new sides and reworked versions of old sides, Brunswick recordings were being reissued on the Melotone and Perfect labels as budget line issues. Since British tastes differed, Mills Brothers releases on British Decca (not all of which made it to the States) were generally more jazz and blues oriented than their domestic product.

After a royal command performance at the London Palladium in 1935, John, Jr. became ill. He died in January of 1936 at the age of 25. John, Sr. then took over for his son.

Hits like "Chinatown, My Chinatown" (#10, 1932), "Sweet Sue" (#8, 1932), "It Don't Mean a Thing (If It Ain't Got that Swing)" (#6, 1932), "Sweet Sister" (#2, 1934), "Sleepyhead" (#2, 1934), and "Sixty Seconds Get-Together" (#8, 1938) kept the group touring the world from Europe to Australia.

The Brothers' biggest hit came smack in the middle of World War II. Recorded February 18, 1942, and released in May, "Paper Doll" took more than a year to chart. When it did so on July 17, 1943, it reached number one and stayed there for a full 12 weeks, ultimately selling more than six million copies. Their fourth number one came in the summer of 1944 with "You Always Hurt the One You Love," and its flip, "Till Then," made it to number eight. "Till Then" was also their biggest R&B charter, going to number one. As the available listings only started in the early '40s, the Mills Brothers racked up only 11 recordings on the R&B hit lists between 1943 and 1949, indicating they may have been going over better with whites than blacks.

By 1950 the quartet had 50 chart hits. Their last number one was 1952's "Glow Worm," adapted from the German operetta *Lysistrata*. It also became their only hit in England, ranking number 10 at the beginning of 1953.

Up to 1950 almost every Mills Brothers recording featured only a guitar behind their voices in harmony and/or imitating instruments. It was a gutsy move to imitate trumpets behind Louis Armstrong and his real trumpet ("Marie" and "The Old Folks at Home," among others), and on one cut, "Caravan" (1938), they didn't sing at all, just parodied their instruments. The group dropped their instrumental mimicking in the early '50s, opting instead for backing bands and orchestras. To keep in step with the time the Brothers occasionally found themselves doing renditions of songs by groups who had learned from Mills Brothers' own records of the '30s and '40s. They covered THE CHARMS' "Gumdrop" in 1955, THE CLOVERS' "Smack Dab in the Middle," and a cover of THE SILHOUETTES' rocker "Get a Job" in early 1958, though by now their pop barbershop sound was becoming passé.

John, Sr. retired in the mid-'50s, but the brothers stayed on the performing scene as a trio and continued to record for Dot. In 1959 "Yellow Bird" peaked at number 70, and it looked like the record buyers had moved on to other sounds. But nine years later the group, now in their mid-to late 50s, hit the charts three times in the midst of the soul and psychedelic era. "Cab Driver" (#23, 1968) was followed by "My Shy Violet" (#73) and "The Ol' Race Track" (#83), their last charter ever.

Unfortunately, John, Sr. never got to see the comeback: he died in 1967. Harry died in 1982 at the age of 68 while Herbert passed away in 1989 at the age of 77. In the early '90s, Donald and his son John III continued on as a duo.

The Mills Brothers' influence was pervasive: they made black music acceptable to a wide audience and encouraged other black vocalists to carry on what they had started. And lest we forget, they did it with dignity and grace in difficult racial times, carried forward by their warmth of character and mellow sound.

THE MILLS BROTHERS

A SIDE/B SIDE	LABEL/CAT NO	DATE
Tiger Rag / Nobody's Sweetheart	Brns 6197	12/31
George White's Scandals / George White's Scandals	Brns 20102	12/31
You Rascal, You / Baby, Won't You Please Come Home	Brns 6225	1/32
Dinah* / Can't We Talk It Over*	Brns 6240	2/32
I Heard / How Am I Doing Hey, Hey	Brns 6269	4/32
Shine* / Shadows On The Window*	Brns 6276	4/32
Rockin' Chair / Good-Bye Blues	Brns 6278	5/32
Chinatown, My Chinatown / Loveless Love	Brns 6305	5/32
Sweet Sue, Just You / St. Louis Blues	Brns 6330	6/32
Bugle Call Rag / The Old Man Of The Mountains	Brns 6357	8/32
OK America Part 1 / OK America Part 2	Brns 20112	8/32
It Don't Mean A Thing / Coney Island Washboard	Brns 6377	9/32
Dirty Dishing Daisy / Git Along	Brns 6340	12/32
Dinah / Shine	Brns 6485	2/33
Fiddlin' Joe / Anytime, Any Day, Anywhere	Brns 6490	2/33

A SIDE/ B SIDE	LABEL/CAT NO	DATE
Doin' The New Low-Down / I Can't Give You Anything But Love	Brns 6517	3/33
Diga Diga Doo / I Can't Give You Anything But Love	Brns 6519	3/33
Smoke Rings / My Honey's Lovin' Arms	Brns 6525	3/33
Jungle Fever / I've Found A New Baby	Brns 6785	3/34
Swing It Sister / Honey In My Pockets	Brns 6894	6/34
Put On Your Old Grey Bonnet / Sleepy Head	Brns 6913	6/34
Jungle Fever / Sleepy Head	Mlatn 13177	1934
Coney Island Washboard / St. Louis Blues	Mlatn 13178	1934
How Am I Doin', Hey Hey / Good-Bye Blues	Mlatn 13179	1934
I Heard / Loveless Love	Mlatn 13180	1934
Sweet Sue, Just You / Rockin' Chair	Mlatn 13181	1934
Chinatown, My Chinatown / Bugle Call Rag	Mlatn 13182	1934
St. Louis Blues / Coney Island Washboard	Oriole 3006	1934
I've Found A New Baby / Baby Won't You Please Come Home	Oriole 3034	1934
St. Louis Blues / Coney Island Washboard	Prfct 13057	1934
Good-Bye Blues / How Am I Doin', Hey Hey	Prfct 13058	1934
I Heard / Loveless Love	Prfct 13059	1934
Rockin' Chair / Sweet Sue, Just You	Prfct 13060	1934
Chinatown, My Chinatown / Bugle Call Rag	Prfct 13061	1934
Baby Won't You Please Come Home / I've Found A New Baby	Prfct 13081	1934
Dirty Dishin' Daisy / Fiddlin' Joe	Prfct 13082	1934
"Ida" Sweet As Apple Cider / My Gal Sal	Decca 165	1934
Miss Otis Regrets / Old Fashioned Love	Decca 166	1934
Rockin' Chair / Tiger Rag	Decca 167	1934
Lazybones / Nagasaki	Decca 176	1934
I've Found A New Baby / Some Of These Days	Decca 228	1934
Limehouse Blues / Sweeter Than Sugar	Decca 267	1934
Sweet Georgia Brown / There Goes My Heartache	Decca 380	1934
Don't Be Afraid To Tell Your Mother / What's The Reason	Decca 402	1935
Moanin' For You / Sweet Lucky Brown	Decca 497	1935
Rhythm Saved The World / Shoe Shine Boy	Decca 961	1936
London Rhythm / Solitude	Decca 1082	1936

A SIDE/ B SIDE	LABEL/CAT NO	DATE
Pennies From Heaven /		
Swing For Sale	Decca 1147	1937
Big Boy Blue** /		
Dedictated To You**	Decca 1148	1937
Love Bug Will Bite You /		
Rockin' Chair Swing	Decca 1227	1937
Carry Me Back To Old Virginny† /		
Darling Nellie Gray†	Decca 1245	1937
Long About Midnight /		
Old Folks At Home	Decca 1360	1937
Since We Fell Out Of Love / In The		
Shade Of The Old Apple Tree	Decca 1495	1937
Caravan / Flat Foot Floogee	Decca 1876	1938
The Walking Stick† / The Song		
Is Ended†	Decca 1892	1938
Julius Caesar / Sixty Seconds		
Got Together	Decca 1964	1938
Lambeth Walk / The Yam	Decca 2008	1938
Funiculi Funicula / Just A Kid		
Named Joe	Decca 2029	1938
Sweet Adeline / Just Tell Me Your		
Dreams, I'll Tell You Mine	Decca 2285	1939
Good-Bye Blues / Sweet Sue,		
Just You	Decca 2441	1939
Side Kick Joe / Way Down Home	Decca 2599	1939
Asleep In The Deep / Meet Me		
Tonight In Dreamland	Decca 2804	1939
It Don't Mean A Thing / Put On		
Your Old Grey Bonnet	Decca 2982	1939
Old Black Joe / Swanee River	Decca 3132	1940
Marie† / W.P.A.†	Decca 3151	1940
Cherry† / Boog It†	Decca 3180	1940
Just A Dream Of You Dear /		
My Gal Sal	Decca 3225	1940
Sleepy Time Gal / Marie	Decca 3291	1940
Moonlight Bay / On The		
Banks Of The Wabash	Decca 3331	1940
Once Upon A Dream / When You		
Were Sweet Sixteen	Decca 3381	1940
Love's Old Sweet Song / Can't You		
Heah Me Callin' Caroline	Decca 3455	1940
Bird In The Hand / When You		
Said Goodbye	Decca 3486	1940
By The Watermelon Vine, Lindy		
Lou / I've Been In Love Before	Decca 3545	1940
Did Anyone Call / How Did		
She Look	Decca 3567	1940
Georgia On My Mind / S-H-I-N-E	Decca 3688	1940
Break The News To My Mother /		
Darling Nellie Gray	Decca 3705	1941
Down, Down, Down / Rig A Jig Jig	Decca 3763	1941
Brazilian Nuts / I Yi Yi Yi Amigo	Decca 3789	1941
If It's True / The Very Thought		
Of You	Decca 3901	1941
The Bells Of San Raquel /		
I Guess I'll Be On My Way	Decca 4070	11/41
Window Washer Man / Delilah	Decca 4108	12/41
Lazy River / 627 Stomp	Decca 4187	2/42

A SIDE/ B SIDE	LABEL/CAT NO	DATE
Dreamsville, Ohio /		
Beyond The Stars	Decca 4251	3/42
Way Down Home / When You		
Were Sweet	Decca 4348	7/42
Paper Doll / I'll Be Around	Decca 18318	5/42
I Met Her On Monday /		
In Old Champlain	Decca 18473	8/42
Tiger Rag / Paper Doll	Decca 11051	9/52
Till Then / You Always Hurt The		
One You Love	Decca 18599	5/44
My Honey's Lovin' Arms* / Please*	Col 4304	10/44
Shine* / Some Of These Days*	Col 4305	10/44
I Wish / Put Another Chair At		
The Table	Decca 18663	4/45
Don't Be A Baby, Baby / Never		
Make A Promise In Vain	Decca 18753	1/46
There's No One But You / I Don't		
Know Enough About You	Decca 18834	4/46
You Tell Me Your Dreams, I'll Tell		
You Mine / Sweet Adeline	Decca 23623	7/46
My Gal Sal / Just A Dream		
Of You, Dear	Decca 23624	7/46
Meet Me Tonight In Dreamland /		
Can't You Hear Me Callin'		
Caroline	Decca 23625	7/46
Moonlight Bay / On The Banks Of		
The Wabash	Decca 23626	7/46
Way Down Home / When You		
Were Sweet Sixteen	Decca 23627	7/46
Too Many Irons In The Fire /		
I Guess I'll Get The Papers	Decca 23638	8/46
I'm Afraid To Love You / You Broke		
The Only Heart That Ever		
Loved You	Decca 25713	11/46
Lazy River / Cielito Lindo	Decca 25046	1/47
Dream, Dream, Dream / Across		
The Alley From The Alamo	Decca 23863	4/47
Shine*/Some Of These Days*	Col 4421-M	4/47
You Always Hurt The One You		
Love / Till Then	Decca 23930	6/47
Oh! My Aching Heart / What You		
Don't Know Won't Hurt You	Decca 23979	7/47
You Never Miss The Water		
Till The Well Runs Dry /		
After You	Decca 24180	9/47
If It's True / The Very		
Thought Of You	Decca 25284	10/47
George White's Scandals Part 1 /		
George White's Scandals Part 2	Brns 85001	10/47
I'm Sorry I Didn't Say I'm Sorry /		
I'll Never Make The Same		
Mistake Again	Decca 24252	11/47
I Wish I Knew The Name /		
Mañana	Decca 24333	2/48
S-H-I-N-E / Love Is Fun	Decca 24382	3/48
Someone Cares / Confess	Decca 24409	5/48
Baby, Don't Be Mad At Me /		
I Couldn't Call My Baby	Decca 24441	5/48

A SIDE/ B SIDE	LABEL/CAT NO	DATE
Two Blocks Down, Turn To The Left / I'll Never Be Without My Dream	Decca 24472	7/48
Gloria / I Want To Be The Only One	Decca 24509	10/48
Dedicated To You** / Big Boy Blue**	Decca 25361	1948
Don't Be A Baby Baby / Across The Alley From The Alamo	Decca 25516	1948
Down Among The Sheltering Palms†† / Is It True What They Say About Dixie††	Decca 24534	1/49
I've Got My Love To Keep Me Warm / Love You So Much It Hurts	Decca 24550	1/49
Cherry† / Marie†	Decca 25536	1948
Words / I'm Happy Being Me	Decca 24621	4/49
Single Saddle / Gather Your Dreams	Decca 24656	6/49
St. Louis Blues / Anytime, Any Day, Anywhere	Hrmny 1001	6/49
Smoke Rings / Put On Your Old Grey Bonnet	Hrmny 1002	6/49
Lora-Belle Lee / Out Of Love	Decca 24679	7/49
Someday / On A Chinese Honeymoon	Decca 24694	8/49
I Want You To Want Me / Who'll Be The Next One	Decca 24749	9/49
If I Had My Way / Sweet Genevieve	Decca 24756	11/49
On This Christmas Eve / My Christmas Song For You	Decca 24768	10/49
Till We Meet Again / Honey, Dat I Love So Well	Decca 24757	11/49
Love's Old Sweet Song / Long Long Ago	Decca 24758	11/49
On The Banks Of The Wabash / Moonlight Bay	Decca 24759	11/49
You Tell Me Your Dream, I'll Tell You Mine / Sweet Adeline	Decca 24761	1/50
My Gal Sal / Just A Dream Of You Dear	Decca 24762	1/50
Meet Me Tonight In Dreamland / Can't You Hear Me Callin', Caroline	Decca 24763	1/50
Way Down Home / When You Were Sweet Sixteen	Decca 24764	1/50
I Gotta Have My Baby Back** / Fairy Tales**	Decca 24813	12/49
Daddy's Little Girl / If I Lived To Be A Hundred	Decca 24872	2/50
The Old Rugged Cross / In The Sweet By And By	Decca 14503	3/50
Open The Gates Of Dreamland / I've Shed A Hundred Tears	Decca 24994	5/50
The Tunnel Of Love / Why Fight The Feeling	Decca 27104	7/50
Paper Doll / I'll Be Around	Decca 27157	7/50

A SIDE/ B SIDE	LABEL/CAT NO	DATE
Jesus, Savior, Pilot Me / When The Roll Is Called Up Yonder	Decca 14525	8/50
A Star For Everyone To Love / I'm Afraid To Love	Decca 27184	9/50
I Still Love You / Daddy's Little Boy	Decca 27236	10/50
Nevertheless / Thirsty For Your Kisses	Decca 27253	10/50
Wonderful Words Of Love / I Need Thee Every Hour	Decca 14536	11/50
Funny Feelin' / I Don't Mind Being All Alone	Decca 27267	11/50
Around The World / You Don't Have To Drop A Heart To Break It	Decca 27400	1/51
Now The Day Is Over / Will There Be Any Stars	Decca 14550	3/51
Mister And Mississippi / Wonderful Wasn't It	Decca 27579	5/51
Love Me / Who Knows Love	Decca 27615	6/51
Lord Ups And Downs / A Cottage With A Prayer	Decca 27683	8/51
I Ran All The Way Home / Got Her Off My Hands	Decca 27762	9/51
Love Lies / Be My Life's Companion	Decca 27889	12/51
You're Not Worth My Tears / High And Dry	Decca 28021	3/52
Pretty As A Picture / When You Come Back To Me	Decca 28180	6/52
Just When We're Falling In Love / Blue And Sentimental	Decca 28309	8/52
The Glow-Worm / After All	Decca 28384	9/52
Lazy River / Wish Me Good Luck Amigo	Decca 28458	11/52
A Shoulder To Weep On / Someone Loved Someone	Decca 28459	10/52
Shine* / My Honey's Lovin' Arms*	Hrmny 51226,7	10/52
I Want Someone To Care For / Twice As Much	Decca 28586	2/53
I'm With You / Say Si Si	Decca 28670	5/53
Don't Let Me Dream / Pretty Butterfly	Decca 28736	6/53
Beware / Who Put The Devil In Evelyn's Eyes	Decca 28818	9/53
The Jones' Boy / She Was Five And He Was Ten	Decca 28945	11/53
Marie† / My Walking Stick†	Decca 28984	12/53
I Had To Call You Up To Say I'm Sorry / You Didn't Want Me When You Had Me	Decca 29019	2/54
Go In And Out Of The Window / Carnival In Venice	Decca 29115	5/54
How Blue / Why Do I Keep Lovin' You	Decca 29185	7/54
You're Nobody Till Somebody Loves You / Every Second Of	Decca 29276	10/54
It Must Be So§ / Straight Ahead§	Decca 29359	12/54
Paper Valentine / The Urge	Decca 29382	1/55

A SIDE/ B SIDE	LABEL/CAT NO	DATE
Opus One / Yes You Are	Decca 29496	4/55
Smack Dab In The Middle / Kiss Me And Kill Me With Love	Decca 29511	5/55
Daddy's Little Girl / Daddy's Little Boy	Decca 29564	6/55
That's All I Ask Of You / Mi Muchacha	Decca 26921	8/55
Suddenly There's A Valley / Gum Drop	Decca 29686	9/55
You Don't Have To Be A Santa Claus / I Believe In Santa Claus	Decca 29754	12/55
I've Changed My Mind A Thousand Times / All The Way 'Round The World	Decca 29781	12/55
Dream Of You / In A Mellow Tone	Decca 29853	3/56
Standing On The Corner / King Porter Stomp	Decca 29897	4/56
I'm The Guy / Ninety-Eight Cents	Decca 29977	6/56
That's Right / Don't Get Caught	Decca 30024	9/56
That's All I Need / Tell Me More	Decca 30136	11/56
The Knocked Out Nightingale / In De Banana Tree	Decca 30224	2/57
Queen Of The Senior Prom / My Troubled Mind	Decca 30299	4/57
Change For A Penny / Two Minute Tango	Decca 30430	9/57
The Barbershop Quartet / You Only Told Me Half The Story	Decca 30546	1/58
Get A Job / I Found A Million Dollar Baby In A Five And Ten Cent Store	Dot 15695	1/58
Music Maestro, Please! / Me and My Shadow	Dot 15827	1958
Yellow Bird / Baby Clementine	Dot 15858	10/58
Beaver / You Can't Be True Dear	Dot 15909	2/59
Lullabye In Ragtime / Te Quiero	Dot 15950	4/59
Take Me Along / You Always Hurt The One You Love	Dot 15987	1959
Glow Worm / Paper Doll	Dot 16037	12/59
I Miss You So / Oh! Ma-Ma	Dot 16049	1/60
I Got You / Highways Are Happy Ways	Dot 16091	1960
Baby Clementine / Yellow Bird	Dot 16234	1961
Ballerina / I'll Take Care Of Your Cares	Dot 16258	1961
I Found The Only Girl For Me / Queen Of The Senior Prom	Dot 16360	4/62
Big City / End Of The World	Dot 16451	1963
Don't Blame Me / It Hurts Me More Than It Hurts You	Dot 16579	1/64
Welcome Home / You're Making The Wrong Guy Happy	Dot 16705	1/65
By Bye Blackbird / Chum Chum Chittilum Chum	Dot 16733	4/65
Smack Dab In The Middle / Honeysuckle Rose Blues Bossa Nova	Dot 16972	1966

A SIDE/ B SIDE	LABEL/CAT NO	DATE
Cab Driver / Fourtuosity	Dot 17041	9/67
My Shy Violet / The Flower Road	Dot 17096	1968
But For Love / The O' Race Track	Dot 17162	1968
The Jimtown Road / Dream	Dot 17198	1969
Buy On The Go / What Have I Done For Her Lately	Dot 17235	1969
Up To Maggie Jones / I'll Never Forgive Myself	Dot 17285	1969
It Ain't No Big Thing / Help Yourself To Some	Dot 17321	1969
Smile Away Each Rainy Day / Between Winston-Salem And Nashville, Tennessee	Prmnt 0046	1970
I'm Sorry I Answered The Phone / Happy Songs Of Love	Prmnt 0095	1971
Strollin' / L-O-V-E	Prmnt 0117	1971
Come Summer / Sally Sunshine	Prmnt 0147	1972
A Donut And A Dream / There's No Life On The Moon	Prmnt 0181	1972
Cab Driver / Truck Stop	Rnwd 961	1973
Opus 1 / Till Then	Rnwd 105	3/74
You Always Hurt The One You Love / You're Nobody Till Somebody Loves You	Rnwd 106	3/74
Glow Worm / Paper Doll	Rnwd 107	3/74
He Gives Me Love / I'm Afraid To Love You	Rnwd 974	4/74
On A Chinese Honeymoon / Tiger Rag	Rnwd 1003	9/74
You Are My Sunshine / Between Winson-Salem And Nashville, Tennessee	Rnwd 1020	3/75
El Paso / Till Then	Rnwd 1040	4/75
Daisies Never Tell / Sawdust Heart	Rnwd 1042	12/75
Coney Island Washboard / Nevertheless	Rnwd 1054	4/76

*   Bing Crosby and the Mills Brothers
**   Ella Fitzgerald and the Mills Brothers
†   Louis Armstrong and the Mills Brothers
††   Al Jolson and the Mills Brothers
§   Peggy Lee and the Mills Brothers

The Modernaires

A very popular '40s group, the Modernaires had their biggest success as part of Glenn Miller's Orchestra. The original members were a trio of Hal Dickinson (lead and second tenor), Bill Conway (baritone), and Chuck Goldstein (first tenor). The 17- and 18-year-olds began harmonizing at Lafayette High School in Buffalo, New York, during 1935. They called themselves Three Weary Willies, and their early influences included Paul

Whiteman and the Rhythm Boys with Bing Crosby. The Willies became popular on Buffalo radio WGR, earning the enormous sum of $10 a month.

The group headed for New York in the mid-'30s after one member hocked his watch to finance the trip. Performing as Don Juan and Two and Three, they managed to land a 26-week stint on CBS radio. First tenor Ralph Brewster joined the group; Chuck shifted to baritone while Bill moved to bass. The new quartet joined up with Ray Noble's band but left in 1939 to sing with a new organization formed by a young trombonist named Glenn Miller, who had also been with Noble.

Hal spotted a billboard that advertised a new cleaning process called modernizing; the Modernaires became the name of the group.

Meanwhile, a singer named Paula Kelly was singing with Artie Shaw's and Dick Stabile's bands before joining Glenn Miller in 1940 as a soloist. Though she had never recorded with Shaw on Columbia's Bluebird label, Paula wound up there anyway with Miller.

The Modernaires had performed with Miller for two years before they and Paula issued their first record, "Perfidia" (the group's personal favorite) with Dorothy Claire. "Perfidia" charted on April 19, 1941, moving up to number 11. It was the first of an incredible string of 10 chart records in 1941, including "The Booglie Wooglie Piggy" (#7) with Tex Beneke, "I Guess I'll Have to Dream the Rest" (#4) and "Elmer's Tune" (#1) (both with Ray Eberle), "I Know Why" (#18), and "Jingle Bells" (#5), with Tex and Ernie Caceras. The biggest record they issued with Miller in 1941 (the productive bandleader had 14 charting singles *without* the Modernaires) was "Chattanooga Choo Choo," the first record officially certified as a million seller.

1942 was another smash year (Miller and company had now moved over to Victor Records), yielding a number of hits like "Serenade in Blue" (#2) from the film *Orchestra Wives*, "Sweet Eloise" (#7), and three number one records, "Don't Sit Under the Apple Tree" from the film *Private Buccaroo*, and "(I've Got A Gal in) Kalamazoo" (both with Marion Hutton), and Miller's second biggest hit of all time, "Moonlight Cocktails" (10 weeks at number one; only "In the Mood" stayed longer at the top spot—12 weeks). Though not their biggest hit, one of their most memorable records was "Jukebox Saturday Night" (#7, with Marion Hutton). NINO AND THE EBB TIDES updated it some 19 years later.

By September of 1942 Miller had enlisted in the air force. The shortage of materials to make records slowed the whole market system during the war years, so that only the group's early recordings

were released. Still, the Modernaires, with Miller's Orchestra, managed a number one hit in 1943, "That Old Black Magic" (with Skip Nelson) from the film *Star Spangled Rhythm*.

Miller's plane was lost on a trip from England to the Continent on December 15, 1944. The band never recovered, although Jerry Gray and Ray McKinley took over to keep Glenn's memory alive.

After World War II, the Modernaires moved over to Columbia for their first recordings without an orchestra. Their initial charter was "There! I've Said It Again" (#11, 1945). One of their first singles was "Salute to Glenn Miller," featuring a medley of "Elmer's Tune" and "Chattanooga Choo Choo" (#18) in July 1946. The group's most popular records were the ballad "To Each His Own" (#3, 1946) and "Zip-A-Dee-Doo-Dah" (#11, January, 1947) from the Disney film *Song of the South*.

During the '40s, Paula and Hal Dickinson were married, and a few personnel changes occurred, including the addition of Alan Copeland, Vernon Polk, and Tommy Traynor (the latter formerly a vocalist with the Jerry Grey Orchestra). In early 1950 Paula and the boys backed up Frank Sinatra on two releases, "The Old Master Painter" (#13) and "Sorry" (#28).

In 1953 the group, now on Coral, charted with their own updating of "Jukebox Saturday Night" (#23). Their last charting single was "April in Paris" (#97) on March 31, 1956. The group released over 20 singles on Coral from 1951 to '58.

Paula and Hal's three daughters sang for a spell as the Kelly Girls. By the early '60s Paula Kelly, Jr. had become the newest female member of the Modernaires, eventually replacing her mother.

In 1967 they were joined by former Ray Charles Singers and Fred Waring Chorale member Rich Maxwell. Paula Kelly, Jr. left the Modernaires in 1970 to marry TV actor Michael Polster ("The Mod Squad") but returned later. Steve Johnson joined in 1973; he was replaced in 1975 by Bill Tracy, once half of the Curtis and Tracy comedy team.

Today the only living original member is Paula Kelly, who lives in Laguna Beach, California.

More than 35 years after the Modernaires' last chart record, their tradition of big-band vocal styling is carried on by a second generation of Modernaires (Traynor, Maxwell, Tracy, and Paula Kelly, Jr.) in clubs around the world.

THE MODERNAIRES

A SIDE/B SIDE	LABEL/CAT NO	DATE
There I've Said It Again	Col 36800	7/45
Salute To Glenn Miller	Col 36922	7/46

A SIDE/ B SIDE	LABEL/CAT NO	DATE
To Each His Own	Col 37063	8/46

The Modernaires with Frank Sinatra

A SIDE/ B SIDE	LABEL/CAT NO	DATE
The Old Master Painter	Col 38650	12/49
Why Remind Me	Col 38662	1/50
Sorry	Col 38662	1/50
Kisses And Tears*	Col 38790	4/50
When The Sun Goes Down	Col 38790	4/50

The Modernaires

A SIDE/ B SIDE	LABEL/CAT NO	DATE
Lovely Is The Evening / Wishing You Were Here Tonight	Col 60408	4/51
Alice In Wonderland / I'm Late	Col 60439	5/51
Never Again / Why Did I Tell You I Was Goin'	Col 60521	7/51
Out Of Breath / Please Don't Cry	Col 60522	7/51
Whoo-loo-ee-siana / You'll Always Be The Sweetheart	Col 60525	7/51
October 2nd, 1992 / Stompin' At The Savoy	Col 60609	11/51
The Dipsy Doodle / I'll Always Be Following You	Col 60658	3/52
Bugle Call Rag / Goody Goody	Col 60726	5/52
Four Or Five Times / When My Love Comes Back To Me	Col 60824	9/52
Gotta Be This Or That / Wildflower	Col 60881	11/52
New Juke Box Saturday Night	Col 60899	2/53
He Who Has Love / Say You're Mine Again	Col 60982	†3/53
Put Some Money In The Juke Box / Rock-A-Bye Boogie	Col 61037	8/53
Honeymoon / The One Rose	Col EC81031	9/53
I Want A Girl / Let The Rest Of The World Go / Oh, How I Miss You Tonight	Col 81032	9/53
You'll Never Be Mine / You'll Never Be Mine	Col 61086	11/53
Salute To Glenn Miller (New Medley)	Col 61110	1/54
I Know Why / That's You, That's Me	Col 61199	6/54
Mood Indigo / Teach Me Tonight	Col 61265	10/54
Birds and Puppies and Tropical Fish / Mine! Mine! Mine!	Col 61348	†11/53
Close Your Eyes / How Important Can It Be / I Wanna Hug You Kiss You Squeeze / I'm Always Hearing Wedding Bells / It May Sound Silly / Pledging My Love	Col 61378	3/55
Slewfoot / Wine, Women and Gold	Col 61412	†4/55
Just Like You Used To Do / La Festa	Col 61449	7/55
The Milkman's Matinee / Wake Up The Place	Col 61490	9/55
Alright, Okay, You Win / At My Front Door	Col 61513	9/55

A SIDE/ B SIDE	LABEL/CAT NO	DATE
Santa's Little Sleigh Bells / Sleepy Little Space Cadet	Col 61547	12/55
Ain't She Sweet / Go On With The Wedding	Col 61555	1/56
April In Paris / Hi-Diddlee-I-Di	Col 61599	3/56
The Milkman's Matinee / Wake Up The Place / (Open House)	Col CRL57051	
(Rock 'n' Roll Dance Party) / The Great Pretender / Only You (And You Alone)	Col 57063	8/56
Ask For Joe / Ninety-Eight Cents	Col 61674	†6/56
I'm Ready To Love Again / Noah	Col 61764	12/56
Harmony Is The Thing / Let The Rest Of The World Go	Col 57141	1/57
Calypso Melody / Cinderella Baby	Col 61837	5/57
Here Come The Modernaires / April In Paris	Col 57140	8/57
A Foggy Day / Makin' Whoopee	Col 61873	8/57
Harmony Is The Thing / Dear Old Girl	Col 59141	1/58
Act Your Age / As Long As I Have You	Col 61949	2/58

† date recorded
* with Jane Russell

The Pied Pipers

Notable for distinctive modern harmony and phrasing, the Pied Pipers began in Hollywood in 1938 as a merging of eight members of three different groups. While waiting on the 20th Century-Fox lot to get a shot at working in the musical *Alexander's Ragtime Band*, hopefuls the Four Esquires, the Stafford Sisters, and the Three Rhythm Kings whiled away the waiting time by harmonizing together. Jo Stafford of the sisters began singing with the Esquires' and Kings' seven male members, and soon after, when sister Pauline's marriage ended the Stafford Sisters' career, the Pied Pipers were born.

Besides Stafford, the original members were John Huddleston, Hal Hooper, Chuck Lowry, Bud Hervey, George Tait, Woody Newbury, and Dick Whittinghill.

Through two of the King sisters, Alyce and Yvonne, the Pipers came to the attention of Paul Weston and Axel Stordahl, who were arrangers for the Tommy Dorsey band. According to Joseph Laredo's liner notes on the Pied Pipers' 1991 CD, Paul Weston stated, "The Pipers were ahead of their time. Their vocal arrangements were like those for a sax section and a brass section, and they would interweave, singing unison or sometimes sing against each other's parts. It was revolutionary and we'd never heard anything like it." Weston made that assessment at a jam session he was having at his house, and one guest, a visiting ad executive, was so impressed he hired the group to sing with Tommy Dorsey's band on the Raleigh-Kool cigarettes program.

The group drove to New York and lasted about six weeks before being canned by a pompous British sponsor who came to the studio and was aghast at their overly (to him) off-color repertoire, which included "Hold Tight (Want Some Seafood Mama)." But before leaving New York to return to Hollywood they managed to record two 78s for RCA Victor, "Polly Wolly Doodle" and "What Is This Thing Called Love."

Back in Los Angeles, the octet was now a quartet of Jo Stafford, her husband John Huddleston, Billy Wilson, and Chuck Lowry. Things were going so poorly they unofficially rechristened the group Poverty Inc. At the bleakest of moments Stafford received a call from Dorsey in Chicago saying he couldn't afford eight Pipers but he'd like it if she would pare them down to a quartet and join him. With only four members and one unemployment check left, this was an easy request to accommodate.

The group moved to Chicago in 1939; Billy Wilson left to be replaced by Clark Yocum, a Dorsey guitarist and vocalist. Paul Weston left Dorsey to work as Dinah Shore's musical director, but he would have an important involvement with the group at a later date.

In early 1940 Dorsey hired another vocalist who had sung with Harry James's band in 1939 and with a vocal group, the Hoboken Four, in 1935. The vocalist—whose influences were Billie Holiday, Bing Crosby, and Dorsey himself—had a hit right off the bat with "Polka Dots and Moonbeams" (#18, April 1940) backed by Dorsey's orchestra. Two months later the Pipers put a notch in their musical holster by hitting with "My My" from the film *Buck Benny Rides Again* (#13, June 1940).

On June 29, 1940, an historic pairing of that vocalist, Frank Sinatra, and the Pied Pipers resulted in one of the biggest hits of the pre-rock era, "I'll Never Smile Again," which was number one for 12 weeks, spending 20 weeks on the charts.

In August the five hit again with "The One I Love Belongs to Somebody Else" (#11).

The group went on to have 11 more chart hits with Dorsey, nine of those singing with Sinatra, including "Stardust" (#7, January 1941), "Do I Worry" (#4, April 1941), and "Just As You Thought

You Were Here" (#6, July 1942). Without Ol' Blue Eyes, the Pipers hit with "You've Got Me This Way" (#14, January 1941) and "Let's Get Away from It All" (#7, May 1941). Even Jo Stafford found some recognition, charting as a solo vocalist on "Yes Indeed" (#4, July 1941).

A burst of group loyalty around Thanksgiving 1942 changed the Pipers' future when Dorsey, who was prone to fits of temper, fired one of the members at a Portland, Oregon, train station for inadvertently sending him in the wrong direction. In a display of one-for-all and all-for-one comradeship, the remaining Pipers picked up their pickled peppers and left the train, heading immediately for Hollywood. The number one record in the country around that time was "There Are Such Things" by Frank Sinatra and the Pied Pipers. It was their last Victor release with Dorsey.

In Los Angeles they signed with Capitol Records, while John Huddleston joined the war effort and was replaced by one of the original octet, Hal Hooper. Working at Capitol was none other than Paul Weston, and he became the arranger and orchestra leader for most of the Pipers' recordings. Jo became a soloist, scoring a hit ahead of her group with "How Sweet You Are" (#14, February 1944).

The group charted in April with "Mairzy Doats" (#8) though THE MERRY MACS had scored the number one hit version two months earlier.

By June Jo's solo career was off and running, so June Hutton of the Stardusters took over the Pipers' lead. Her first hit with the boys was their biggest hit, "Dream" (#1, March 1945), originally used as the closing theme on Johnny Mercer's radio show. Mercer, one of America's most prolific lyricists, was the founder of Capitol Records and had the Pipers sing with him on such hits as "Candy" (#1, February 1945) and "Zip-A-Dee-Doo-Dah" (#8, December 1946).

The Pied Pipers had 12 chart singles for Capitol, their last being "My Happiness" (#3, June 1948).

From 1945 through '46 the quartet took part in a series of National Theatre tours with Frank Sinatra while still doing radio programs in Los Angeles. They became the resident vocal group on Frank's own weekly CBS radio show from September 1945 through mid-1947.

The Pipers were voted the Top Vocal Group in *down beat* magazine's annual poll for six straight years from 1944 to 1949.

In 1950 June Hutton left and was replaced by Sue Allen and later Virginia Marcy. Jo Stafford (who was divorced from Huddleston in 1943) married Paul Weston in 1952 and went on to have one of the most successful solo careers of all time, charting 75 times between 1944 and 1954, including "You Belong to Me" (#1, 1952) and "Make Love to Me" (#1, 1954).

June, who married the other half of Dorsey's early arranging team, Axel Stordahl, had several solo releases for Capitol in the early '50s, including "Say You're Mine Again" (#21, 1953), in which Axel was the orchestra leader. She died on May 2, 1973, at the age of 53.

At the start of the 1990s, a touring Pied Pipers carried on the tradition of vocal expertise.

THE PIED PIPERS

A SIDE/B SIDE	LABEL/CAT NO	DATE
Sugar Foot Stomp / Polly Wolly Doodle	Vctr 26320	1938
In A Little Spanish Town / What Is This Thing Called Love?	Vctr 26364	1938
My! My!	Vctr 26535	6/40
I'll Never Smile Again*	Vctr 26628	6/40
The One I Love Belongs To Somebody Else*	Vctr 26660	8/40
Star Dust*	Vctr 27233	1/41
You've Got Me This Way	Vctr 26770	1/41
Oh, Look At Me Now	Vctr 27274	3/41
You Might Have Belonged To Another*	Vctr 27274	3/41
Dolores	Vctr 27317	4/41
Do I Worry?*	Vctr 27338	4/41
Let's Get Away From It All	Vctr 27377	5/41
I Guess I'll Have To Dream The Rest*	Vctr 27526	10/41
The Last Call For Love*	Vctr 27849	5/42
Just As Though You Were Here* / Street Of Dreams*	Vctr 27903	7/42
I'll Take Tallulah*	Vctr 27869	8/42
There Are Such Things*	Vctr 27974	11/42
It Started All Over Again*	Vctr 1522	2/43
Mairzy Doats	Capitol 148	4/44
The Trolley Song	Capitol 168	10/44
Candy**	Capitol 183	2/45
I'm Gonna See My Baby**	Capitol 183	3/45
Dream	Capitol 185	3/45
On The Atchison, Topeka, And The Santa Fe**	Capitol 195	7/45
Lily Belle / We'll Be Together Again	Capitol 207	9/45
Surprise Party	Capitol 217	1/45
Aren't You Glad You're You?	Capitol 225	12/45
In The Middle Of May	Capitol 225	1/46
Personality**	Capitol 230	1/46
In The Moon Mist	Capitol 243	4/46
Remember Me? / Walk It Off	Capitol 264	7/46
My Sugar Is So Refined**	Capitol 268	8/46
Ugly Chile (You're Some Pretty Doll)**	Capitol 268	9/46
Either It's Love Or It Isn't / Walkin' Away With My Heart	Capitol 306	11/46
Zip-A-Dee-Doo-Dah**	Capitol 323	12/46

A SIDE/ B SIDE	LABEL/CAT NO	DATE
A Gal In Calico**	Capitol 316	12/46
Winter Wonderland**	Capitol 316	1/47
Open The Door, Richard	Capitol 369	3/47
Mam'selle / It's The Same Old Dream	Capitol 396	5/47
Penny	Capitol 478	12/47
Ok'l Baby Dok'l / I'll See You In My Dreams	Capitol 495	3/48
My Happiness	Cap 15094	6/48

* Frank Sinatra
** Johnny Mercer

The Pilgrim Travelers

One of the champion '40s and '50s gospel groups, the Pilgrim Travelers were the singers "school" from which Lou Rawls graduated to become a top soul artist in the 1960s.

Formed in 1936 in Houston, Texas, the quartet consisted of founder Joe Johnson, leads Kylo Turner and Keith Barber (Turner's cousin), and Rayfield Taylor (bass). All were members of the Pleasant-grove Baptist Church. An opportunity to spread their colorful harmony beyond the Houston area came when they won a talent show in 1944. The prize was a national tour with THE SOUL STIRRERS, another Houston group of world renown. The experience helped them polish their smooth sound: both Turner and Barber gained from exposure to Soul Stirrers' lead Rebert (R. H.) Harris, with his ability to make dramatic transitions in vocal tone and register.

In 1947 the group moved to Los Angeles and added J. W. Alexander of Coffeyville, Kansas (a former Negro league ball player and member of the Southern Gospel Singers) on tenor and Jessie Whitaker of the Golden Harps of Oakland on baritone.

The group began recording in 1948 for small Los Angeles labels Big Town, Greenwood, and Swing Time before hooking up with Art Rupe's Specialty Records. They proceeded to record regularly for Specialty from the late '40s to the mid-'50s. The group's performance profile was high, including shows with THE FIVE BLIND BOYS OF MISSISSIPPI, THE DIXIE HUMMINGBIRDS, the Fairfield Four, and the Clara Ward Singers. Some of the Travelers' most significant recordings included the tender "Mother Bowed," the great old-time hymn "The Old Rugged Cross," the powerful "Satisfied with

Jesus," their very first release "Standing on the Highway," and their most famous, "Jesus Met the Woman at the Well."

In the mid-'50s, Rayfield Taylor was replaced by George McCurn of Chicago, a member of the Golden Harps (with Whitaker) and the Kings of Harmony. In 1957 Kylo Turner and later Keith Barber completed their "tours of duty" with the Pilgrims and departed. Ernest Booker of the Alpha and Omega Singers of Houston joined, with 21-year-old Chicagoan Lou Rawls. Lou had started with the Teenage Kings of Harmony and the Holy Wonders, though there are rumors he hit occasional harmony with Chicago's secular sensations THE FLAMINGOS. In the early '50s, Lou had been brought into the Chosen Gospel Singers, labelmates of the Pilgrim Travelers, by Joe Johnson. After Rawls finished his military commitment as a paratrooper for the 82nd Airborne he became a Traveler.

The group found itself on the Andex label in the late '50s. Lou shared leads with Jessie and Ernest and occasionally with George. Sam Cooke even slipped in for one session when they needed a tenor. They issued their last LP in 1957 on Andex, but Ernest Booker was already gone; the group carried on as a pop quartet known as the Travelers ("I'll Be Home for Christmas," "I Go for You," Andex, 1958).

A near fatal car crash in Arkansas hospitalized both Rawls and Sam Cooke; Cooke was touring with the Travelers at the time, having left the Soul Stirrers to become a solo pop artist.

Commercial success remained elusive and the Travelers disbanded in 1959. J. W. Alexander partnered with Cooke to form Sar Records, catering to former gospel artists like Kylo Turner, Johnny Taylor (the man who replaced Sam in the Soul Stirrers), the Valentinos (actually the Womack brothers), and Sam's brother L. C. Cooke of the Magnificents. Lou went on to tremendous popularity as the consummate deep-voiced soul singer, issuing 28 R&B hits from 1961 through 1987, including "Love Is a Hurting Thing" (#1, 1966), "Dead End Street" (#3, 1967), and "You'll Never Find Another Love Like Mine" (#1, 1976).

The Ravens

The Ravens have stood the test of time as one of the best of all pioneering rhythm and blues groups. They were the first to make continuous use of a bass vocalist (Jimmy Ricks) and a falsetto tenor (Maithe Marshall) on lead. They were also the first to incorporate dance steps into an R&B act.

Though there had been black groups before, like THE MILLS BROTHERS, THE CHARIOTEERS, THE INK SPOTS, and the DELTA RHYTHM BOYS, they tended to sing popular songs for white audiences in a soft, smooth, inoffensive style. The Ravens (and a bit later THE ORIOLES) used bits of jazz, blues, gospel, and rhythm to make music that appealed to both races. In fact, record industry personnel and the media dubbed their music "race music."

The Ravens were the brainchild of Jimmy Ricks and baritone Warren "Birdland" Suttles, two Harlem waiters. They decided to go to the Evans Booking Agency and recruit two more singers to form a group in 1945. That visit brought them in contact with first tenor Ollie Jones and second tenor Leonard Puzey.

The foursome decided to call themselves the Ravens, thus setting in motion what would become the first group-name craze, this one centered around birds.

The members were fans of acts like the Delta Rhythm Boys and began practicing tunes like "Darktown Strutters' Ball." They met up with Howard Biggs, who became their musical arranger and wrote many of their original songs.

The Ravens' first performance was in 1946 at the Club Baron on West 132nd Street and Lenox Avenue in Harlem.

In the spring of 1946 the group joined Hub Records, and their first 78, "Honey," was issued on July 1. It was immediately followed by two more R&B singles, the better of which was a Dee Lippman-penned jump tune, "My Sugar Is So Refined." They opened with this song when they appeared at a benefit show with Nat King Cole and Stan Kenton at the legendary Apollo Theatre. Puzey sang lead, but when Ricks took over, his booming bass brought the house down.

Ollie Jones then left, and a key addition came when Jimmy Ricks found falsetto tenor supreme Maithe Marshall tending bar and asked him to join. The group then rerecorded their Hub sides for King in 1946, who reissued them usually with an instrumental B side by the Three Chords.

In 1947 they signed with National Records (owned by Albert Green) and began a series of releases that usually featured Ricks on a jump tune while Maithe Marshall and his crystal-clear falsetto led the group on the flip-side ballads. Marshall, consequently, labeled himself a B-side singer. He would be gratified to know that in the '60s, '70s, and '80s collectors literally fought to obtain Ravens records containing his B sides.

The National recordings started with the Howard Biggs-penned "Write Me a Letter." On December 13, 1947, it became the first R&B record to hit the national top 25, charting at number 24. As "Write Me" didn't hit the R&B charts until January 10, 1948, the Ravens, the world's first successful rhythm and blues group, actually charted Pop before they charted R&B, where "Write Me" reached number five Juke Box and number 10 Best Seller.

But it was their second National single, a rhythmic version of the standard "Old Man River," full of Ricks's cavernous bass, that established the group and its sound internationally. It supposedly sold over two million copies though it only reached number 10 R&B.

The years 1947 through '49 saw a number of beautiful ballads and bouncy pre-rock Ravens records on National, including standards like "Summertime," "September Song," "Once in a While," "Until the Real Thing Comes Along," "Deep Purple," and "Count Every Star." Their sixth National single, "Send for Me If You Need Me," charted R&B on July 3rd, reaching number five Best Seller and number seven Juke Box. In August one of the King recordings, "Bye Bye Baby Blues," reached number eight Best Seller and number 13 Juke Box.

In September of 1948 they covered a new group's first release, the Orioles' "It's Too Soon to Know," but the rookie Orioles reached number one while the Ravens' single, a fine bluesy version, only reached number 11.

The group began touring on what would become the legendary chitlin circuit, a series of theatre venues on the East Coast and in the Midwest in which thousands of rhythm and blues groups would perform. From the Uptown and Earl Theatres in Philadelphia, the Howard in Washington, the Royal in Baltimore, the Regal in Chicago, the Syria Mosque in Pittsburgh, and the State in Hartford to the crown jewel of theatres, the Apollo in New York, the Ravens blazed a trail for thousands of vocal groups.

In November 1948 National issued the group's incredible rhythm version of "White Christmas" (#9 Juke Box, #14 Best Seller), setting the standard for the 1954 version by THE DRIFTERS (an almost note-for-note copy) that became the rock and roll standard. "White Christmas's" flip was an equally thrilling ballad version of "Silent Night."

In 1949 "Ricky's Blues" reached number eight on the Juke Box R&B lists on June 11th as well as number 13 Best Seller. In February of 1950, "I Don't Have to Ride No More" became their last National charter at number nine Best Seller, number 13 Juke Box.

During 1950 Louis Heyward took the baritone part as Suttles took one of his frequent sabbaticals

(previously replaced by Joe Medlin—later a national promo exec for Atlantic Records—and Bubba Ritchie for short periods). Their last National single was "Lilacs in the Rain" featuring Marshall's magical natural falsetto.

In late 1950 the Ravens signed with Columbia, recording fine sides like the Ricks-led blues tune "Time Takes Care of Everything" and the Marshall-featured "I'm So Crazy for Love." After a few sides for Columbia's Okeh affiliate, the Ravens moved to Mercury in late 1951. This was a relatively new Ravens incarnation, however, with Jimmy Stewart taking over for Puzey on tenor, Louis Frazier in for Heyward, and a young falsetto lead named Joe Van Loan from a Philadelphia gospel group known as the Canaanites. Though Maithe Marshall's sound was unique and much imitated in years to come, the man who came closest to his sound was his incredible replacement Joe Van Loan.

The Ravens became a top-drawer attraction. As an indication of their popularity, in a February 1951 performance at Middlebury College in Vermont, they received $2,000, a hefty sum in those days for one night's work.

Mercury issued some softer jump sides like "Begin the Beguine" and charted for the first time in two-and-a-half years with "Rock Me All Night Long" (#4 Juke Box, #8 Best Seller, 1952). The best-loved Mercury sides were ballads such as "Who'll Be the Fool" and "September Song." *Billboard*'s February review of "September Song" described it as a "moody rendition of the evergreen, with the high voice of the lead singer soaring slickly overall, a very strong entry." Perhaps the best ballad ever recorded by a Ravens group was the Joe Van Loan-led "Don't Mention My Name" (December 1952), a nearly overlooked jazz, blues, and pop classic that had Van Loan's glass-breaking falsetto weaving on top of a mellow sax.

Despite the fact that three-fourths of the group were new additions, the Mercury quartet sounded as good as the National label originals. In 1953 Suttles returned to replace Frazier and Tommy Evans spent some time performing with the group, while Ricks soloed for a while.

In early 1955 the Ravens of Ricks, Van Loan, Stewart, and Frazier (back again) signed with Jubilee. By the spring of 1956 Ricks had decided on a full-time solo career; Van Loan, however, wasn't ready to give up the name, and he recruited his brothers Paul (second tenor) and James (baritone) along with David "Boots" Bowers (bass) as a new Ravens. The quartet maintained the vocal sound of the original when they signed to Argo Records in the fall of 1956.

Their first single was the powerful "Kneel and Pray," with outstanding harmony and Van Loan at his stratospheric best. Though not a national hit, it received enough sales and airplay to prompt the release of a similar powerhouse, "A Simple Prayer," which included another stirring performance and earth-shattering final notes from Van Loan.

Their last great effort was a remake of the Scarlets' 1954 "Dear One" in the summer of 1957.

The group's road manager, Nat Margo, bought the Ravens name from Ricks, and a variety of Ravens showed up on the tour circuit through the '60s and '70s.

In the 1970s Ricks, Van Loan, Stewart, and Frazier re-formed to tour Europe with Benny Goodman. In 1971 Ricks and Suttles performed as the Ravens with Gregory Carroll of the Four Buddies and Jimmy Breedlove of THE CUES.

All the original Ravens went on to sing with other groups, sometimes moonlighting with two at a time. The first time Suttles left in 1950 he formed THE DREAMERS with Harriet Calender, Freddie Francis, and Perry Green recording for Mercury and Jubilee. He remained in New York City and became manager of a restaurant and bar.

Leonard Puzey had introduced the "applejack" to group choreography. Ironically, the Ravens themselves didn't like the dance step ideas, but the audiences loved them so Ricks and company kept them in. Puzey's moves became a part of vocal group performances from the Orioles and THE CADILLACS to THE TEMPTATIONS and THE MIRACLES for decades to come. After the Ravens, Puzey joined the Hi Hatters and after the service sang with both Orville Brooks and Deek Watson's Ink Spots. He retired to live in Minnesota.

Louis Heyward sang with the Chestnuts and became a disc jockey in Philadelphia and New Orleans. Maithe Marshall joined the Hi Hatters with Puzey and Heyward in 1951 (no recordings). He then joined the Marshall Brothers (Savoy) and in the '60s had an all-star group of Orville Brooks (Ink Spots), Bob Kornegay (THE DU DROPPERS), and David Bowers (Argo, Ravens) called the Buccaneers (no recordings). In 1963 Maithe joined Brooks's Ink Spots (later joined by Puzey) and he too moved to Minnesota.

Ollie Jones joined the Cues (Capitol) and became a songwriting success with tunes like "Send for Me" (Nat King Cole). Joe Van Loan sang with the Dixieaires (Harlem), the Bells (Rama), and the Dreamers (Mercury) with Suttles throughout the Ravens years. After their demise he joined the Du Droppers (Groove) and in the early '70s sang with Charles Fuqua's Ink Spots.

In 1950 Jimmy Ricks left the Ravens to appear and record with Benny Goodman and had a hit (#25) duetting with Nancy Reed on "Oh Babe!" (Columbia, 1950). After his final recording stint with the Ravens in 1956 Ricks went on to record solo for more labels than there were Ravens members, including Atco, Atlantic, Jubilee, Josie, Decca, Fury, Felsted, Baton, Pilgrim, Peacock, Signature, and Mainstream, but he never charted as a solo artist. He moved to Florida, performed with Count Basie, and stayed active on the club scene until his death on July 2, 1974, at the age of 50.

The Skylarks

The Skylarks were formed in the unlikely surroundings of the Panama Canal zone during World War II. The four army servicemen included Bob Sprague (first tenor), Harry Gedicke (second tenor), Harry Shuman (baritone), and arranger/leader George Becker. They toured bases throughout Panama starting in 1942 while starring in a weekly program on the area's Armed Forces Radio Network.

After their discharge they reorganized in Detroit and added lead singer Gilda Maiken, whom they had heard on WJR radio. The group rehearsed at the YMCA in Highland Park, Michigan, practicing songs like "Night and Day" and "I Don't Stand a Ghost of a Chance." Through Gilda's connections the group appeared with the Don Large Chorus on a coast-to-coast radio show. Bandleader Woody Herman heard them and engaged the group to perform with his orchestra.

The quartet originally called themselves the Velvetones, but upon joining Herman they became known as the Blue Moods, since Woody's orchestra was billed as "the band that plays the blues." They recorded "Stars Fell on Alabama" in August 1946 in Los Angeles and then set off with Herman for the National Theatre tour circuit.

In 1947 Herman's band broke up while the Blue Moods were in New York, but they eventually had the good fortune to meet and record with Bing Crosby. He changed their name to the Skylarks and they recorded two sides with him, "Ko Ko Mo Indiana" and "Chaperone."

In 1948 they joined Jimmy Dorsey's Orchestra and made several MGM recordings before Dorsey's band broke up.

Music publisher Rocky Carr became their manager and wired them to come to California where work might be easier to find. The smooth-sounding quintet's reputation preceded them and without so much as an audition they were hired by Harry James. They recorded on Decca with trombonist Russ Morgan in February 1949 and had a million seller in the number one hit "Cruisin' Down the River." Its follow-up, "Forever and Ever," charted for 26 weeks and also reached number one.

The group performed with such stars as Dinah Shore, Eddie Fisher, Danny Kaye, Betty Hutton, Dean Martin, Jerry Lewis, and Frank Sinatra.

By the '50s the group included originals Gilda Maiken and George Becker with Joe Hamilton, Earl Brown, and Jackie Gershwin. They signed to RCA Records in the early '50s and had one chart single, "I Had the Craziest Dream" from the film *Springtime in the Rockies* (#28, April 1953). The group also appeared in the TV musical game show "Judge for Yourself" with Fred Allen in 1953.

Jackie Gershwin was later replaced by Carol Lombard, and the group kept performing. Included in their travels were four years of tours with Dinah Shore and the last tour with Dean Martin and Jerry Lewis. The Skylarks were staples of variety-show TV ranging from the Danny Kaye and Dinah Shore shows in the '50s to Carol Burnett's and Sonny and Cher's shows in the '60s.

In 1979 the Skylarks made their last public appearance at the Hollywood Palladium, 37 years after they were formed.

The individual members kept quite busy in show business after their group retirement. George Becker became production coordinator for "The Tim Conway Show" and worked on Carol Burnett's shows for 15 years. Earl Brown became a material writer for TV and nightclub acts including THE OSMONDS, Steve Martin, Suzanne Somers, and the New Smothers Brothers. Joe Hamilton produced Carol Burnett's long-running TV show. Jackie Gershwin and Carol Lombard went on to work as backup singers as did Donna Manners and Peggy Clark, who had also spent some time with the group. Lively and charismatic Gilda Maiken (Anderson), the only lead singer the group ever had, opened her own talent agency and later became chairman of the celebrated Society of Singers.

The Soul Stirrers

The most revolutionary group in gospel music, the Soul Stirrers and their succession of incredible lead singers were largely responsible for the development of modern soul music. The concept for the Soul Stirrers developed in an upper room at 1608 Andrew Street, Houston, Texas, in September 1929. Walter Lee "W. L." La Beaux of Houston wanted to form a quartet. He chose the name the New Pleasant Green Gospel Singers from the New Pleasant Green Church and on September 10th organized the group with himself as tenor and manager, Edward Allen (E. A.) Rundless, Jr. of Walliceville, Texas (second tenor), C. N. Parker (baritone), and W. R. Johnson (bass). After four years, Johnson died and O. W. Thomas took his place. A year later Parker passed on and Senior Roy (S. R.) Crain of Trinity, Texas, joined in his spot. At that time they changed the group's name to the Soul Stirrers of Houston, Texas.

In 1934 W. L. La Beaux chose to preach the gospel and A. L. Johnson joined up. On July 26, 1936, Jessie James (J. J.) Farley of Pennington, Texas, came into the group. That same year, Alan Lomax recorded the Soul Stirrers for the Library of Congress, the group's very first recordings.

By 1937 the group included S. R. Crain (first tenor), Rebert H. (R. H.) Harris (second tenor), A. L. Johnson (baritone), M. L. Franklin of Trinity, Texas (second tenor), and J. J. Farley (bass).

R. H. Harris became the innovator, handling the lead and directing the group away from the old-fashioned Jubilee style toward a modern gospel approach. He created the concept of a second lead singer, turning quartets into quintets and providing for consistent four-part harmony under the alternating lead singers. He also introduced the concept of ad-libbing lyrics, singing in delayed time, and repeating words in the background. When R. H. joined the Stirrers he revered blues artists like Leroy Carr, Blind Lemon Jefferson, and Lil Green.

With all their innovation and talent, the Stirrers weren't going to get rich on gospel singing. One revival they played in a small Oklahoma town earned the whole group $2.65—for a week's worth of singing.

In 1939 the Stirrers began performing on radio alongside the white Stamps Baxter Quartet.

By the 1940s they were one of the superior gospel groups, on a level with THE PILGRIM TRAVELERS, THE GOLDEN GATE QUARTET, THE DIXIE HUMMINGBIRDS, and THE FIVE BLIND BOYS OF MISSISSIPPI.

During World War II they performed on a variety of USO shows and sang for President Roosevelt and Winston Churchill at the White House.

Their first public recordings were made in 1948 for Aladdin and in 1950 for Specialty, where they did the legendary "By and By." Toward the end of that year R. H. Harris decided to retire. Hall Foster became the new second lead in 1949. In 1950 S. R. Crain brought in a 19-year-old from

Chicago who had idolized Harris to the point of imitation. But the youngster, whose name was Sam Cooke, soon developed his own style along with a gospel yodel that first appeared in the 1954 recording of "He'll Make a Way" and later in his own secular 1957 hit "You Send Me."

Sam, however, had an influence before that; his very first recording with the Soul Stirrers on March 1, 1951, "Peace in the Valley," was later recorded not once but twice by Elvis Presley, first for Sun Records and in 1957 for RCA.

With Foster's raspy shouting style and Sam's smooth, sexy sound the Soul Stirrers had one of gospel's great one-two punches. The Stirrers, like almost all gospel groups prior to 1950, sang a cappella but they became among the first to switch to instrumental backup.

During the '40s and '50s many other great gospel voices sang with the Stirrers, including James Medlock, Leroy Taylor, R. B. Robinson (who founded THE HIGHWAY QCs, from which several of the group's lead singers were drawn), Julius Cheeks, and T. L. Brewster.

On March 31, 1956, *Billboard* reviewed the Soul Stirrers' recording of "Wonderful," one of their classics, calling it "A gentle deeply sincere reading of a pretty prayer meeting tune." Later that year, while Sam was still in the group, a single was issued on Specialty called "Lovable" that closely resembled "Wonderful." The artist was Dale Cook, a name Sam adopted to hide his secular pursuits from his gospel followers. This was the actual spelling of his name before he moved into pop music in 1957 for a legendary solo career. Sam went on to place 43 singles on the pop charts including "You Send Me" (#1, 1957), "Chain Gang" (#2, 1960), and "Another Saturday Night" (#10, 1963).

His replacement was Highway QCs alumnus, Johnnie Taylor, who was then singing with the Melodymakers and who patterned his early sound after Sam's, just as Sam had styled himself after R. H. Harris. One of the group's more notable recordings with Taylor was "Stand by My Father," later restyled to become Ben E. King's "Stand by Me." Johnny had already sung with an R&B group in 1954 (the Five Echoes) so it was not surprising when he moved on in 1963 and issued lusty shouting hits like "Who's Makin' Love" (#5 Pop, #1 R&B, 1968), "Take Care of Your Homework" (#20 Pop, #2 R&B, 1968), and "Disco Lady" (#1 Pop and R&B, 1976) among his 39 R&B and 24 pop charters from 1963 to 1987. Jimmy Otler took over lead from Taylor and was succeeded by yet another Q.C.s member, Willy Rogers, in 1967.

Despite numerous changes in the '60s, '70s, and '80s the Soul Stirrers' level of quality remained high. Jessie Farley was the last remaining original Stirrer, continuing with the group until his death in 1990. Sam Cooke died on December 11, 1964, from gunshot wounds in a Los Angeles motel. Paul Foster, as of the '80s, was a vegetable deliveryman in Las Vegas and James Medlock was a doorman in Chicago. Jimmy Otler was killed during a fight in 1967.

R. H. Harris formed the Christland Singers in the '50s with two ex-Stirrers, James Medlock and Leroy Taylor. He later sang with the Paraders, recording for Sam Cooke's Sar Records in the early '60s. He eventually became a florist but always stayed close to the gospel scene.

The Swan Silvertones

An influence on a variety of rhythm and blues and pop acts as diverse as THE TEMPTATIONS and Paul Simon, the Swan Silvertones started out in West Virginia as the Four Harmony Kings in 1938. The four coal miners were Claude Jeter (lead), Leroy Watkins, Eddie Boroughas, and John Myles. Jeter's legendary falsetto led the group through hours of rehearsal, and soon they were working weekends in West Virginia and North Carolina.

During 1942 or 1943 they auditioned and won a spot on a high-powered Knoxville, Tennessee, radio station and then changed their name to the Silvertone Singers so they wouldn't be confused with the Kings of Harmony, another active gospel group. Soon after, the Swan Bakery became their sponsor so they changed again, this time to the Swan Silvertones. The Tones performed every weekday at 12:15 for 15 minutes and worked churches and halls at night.

In about 1946 they went to Cincinnati and recorded their first sessions for King Records. Around this time Henry Brossard, a renowned bass formerly of the Bluejays of Birmingham, joined the Swans. Henry was among a small group of bass singers in gospel who created and developed the vocal "boom boom boom boom" sound that was borrowed and expanded on in rhythm and blues and rock and roll of the '50s and early '60s.

With regular work on radio the group became extremely proficient at their smooth harmony, perfecting it through ceaseless microphone practice on technique.

Soloman Womack joined the Swans as a contrasting lead with a tougher sound than Claude Jeter's. Soloman was the man who had recommended Henry Brossard to the group.

In 1948, after more than five years on radio, the group decided it was time to do more extensive touring. Several contrasting leads entered and left the Swans, including Reverend Percell Perkins, Reverend Robert Crenshaw, and Roosevelt Payne, while Claude Jeter remained the first lead.

In 1951 the former tenor lead of the sensational Nightingales and THE DIXIE HUMMINGBIRDS, Paul Owens, joined the Swans. Owens lent an unusual quality to the Swans: unlike most gospel singers, he was influenced by THE FOUR FRESHMEN and THE HI-LOS.

The Silvertones were well-known performers but far from stars and they faced a problem typical of the R&B world: agents and promoters taking off with the advance money and leaving them shortchanged.

But they kept going. In 1955 William Connor of the Trumpeteers took over for Brossard; the group moved from Specialty to Vee-Jay Records in 1959. Louis Johnson of the Spiritualaires added yet a third lead, this one of the "shouting" school.

The Swans gospel standard "Mary Don't You Weep" became famous beyond their expectations when Blood, Sweat, and Tears member Al Kooper, a fan of the Swans, introduced their music to a young Paul Simon. An inspiration for his hit "Bridge Over Troubled Water" supposedly came from a line in "Mary," "I'll be a bridge over deep water." Simon also borrowed the Swans' "Mary" chord progressions for his "Loves Me Like a Rock" hit with the DIXIE HUMMINGBIRDS.

In 1963 Claude was ordained a minister and left the group, to be replaced in the mid-60s by Carl Davies. Owens and Connor also departed and a myriad of newcomers came aboard, performing with last original member John Miles until he retired in 1978, 40 years after the group began. That same year saw a one-time reunion show in Chicago for most of the former members.

Louis Johnson carried on the Swans' tradition through the '80s. By this time most of the Swans' early members had died, including Connors and Miles. As of the early '90s, Jeter lived in retirement on 118th Street and 7th Avenue in Harlem, just down the block from the Hotel Cecil where THE FLAMINGOS once practiced and many gospel groups stayed.

Sonny Til and the Orioles

Along with THE RAVENS, Sonny Til and the Orioles were the founding fathers of rhythm and blues and the premier love-song balladeers of the late '40s and early '50s. With their smooth style, the Orioles had more of an influence on R&B groups of the next 20 years than almost any other act. While the Ravens brought prominence to black groups by doing white swing material, the Orioles were the first black group to gain national popularity by recording black songs. The Orioles became the innovators of what would later be defined as pure R&B four-part harmony. In his book *They All Sang on the Corner*, Phil Groia described the Orioles as having "a mellow, soft second tenor lead, a blending baritone featured as a 'gravel gertie' second lead, a floating high first tenor and a dominant bass." This description would easily fit some of the great 1940s gospel groups like THE SOUL STIRRERS; it's more than likely these gospel legends inspired Til and company.

The Orioles' flight to fame began in Baltimore in 1946 after Erlington Tilghman returned from military service. Erlington (later Sonny Til) had always aspired to sing and even wrote in his high school yearbook that his aim was "to become one of the greatest singers in show business." His girlfriend persuaded him to perform in a local amateur show; Sonny won first place two nights in a row, and began vocalizing with subsequent winners.

A group evolved that included Sonny (lead and second tenor), Alexander Sharp (first tenor), George Nelson (second lead and baritone), Johnny Reed (bass), and guitarist Tommy Gaither. Sonny named them the Vibranairs. Their harmonizing on Pennsylvania and Pitcher Streets earned them a chance to sing at the bar on that corner. Inside they met songwriter/salesclerk Deborah Chessler, who'd written a ballad, "It's Too Soon to Know."

Chessler became their manager, rehearsing them at her house and arranging for them to appear in New York on "Arthur Godfrey's Talent Scouts" show in 1948. They lost out to George Shearing, but Godfrey was so impressed he brought them back for his morning show. Jerry Blaine, a record distributor, signed them to his It's a Natural label that summer, changing their name to the Orioles.

On the release of "It's Too Soon to Know," a reviewer in the September 4, 1948, issue of *Billboard* remarked, "New label kicks off with a fine quintet effort on a slow race ballad. Lead tenor shows fine lyric quality." The review was historic in its noting of the Orioles' first effort and in its categorization of the single as "race music." The song climbed to number 13 (#1 R&B); never before had a black act singing black music reached the pop top 15.

Blaine's label became Jubilee in August 1948, and the sales of "It's Too Soon to Know" were credited to that company. Their next release, "Lonely Christmas," reached number eight on the R&B chart. Two singles later "Tell Me So" became their second R&B number one. A *Billboard* reviewer described it as "one of those slow easy torch ballads that lend themselves to the group's glistening note-bending style. Could be an important platter in the race mart."

More great ballads followed: "A Kiss and a Rose" (#12), "Forgive and Forget" (#5 R&B, 1949), and "What Are You Doing New Year's Eve" (#9, 1949); the flip side hit number five, a second charting for "Lonely Christmas," now on its way to becoming a Christmas perennial.

Some of the group's best ballads, though selling well, never made the national R&B Top 20. These included "At Night" (that *Billboard* cited on April 8, 1950: "Chalk up another hit for the high-flying group, tune is a standout; group delivers one of their best jobs yet") and "I Wonder When" (reviewed on June 3rd with the observation, "Group does one of their top performances here on a promising torcher"). The latter's flipside, a cherished collectors' item called "Moonlight," was described in *Billboard* as merely an "ordinary ballad side in comparison with the standout flip job."

The Orioles were on top of the world, playing for top dollar on the chitlin circuit and appearing on TV shows like "The Star Night Show" with Perry Como. But at the end of 1950 their success came to a crashing halt: an auto accident killed Tommy Gaither and seriously injured George Nelson, Johnny Reed, and Sonny Woods, Orioles valet and founding member of the Royals (Federal).

Ralph Williams took over guitar (he also occasionally subbed on baritone for the recovered Nelson, who was becoming unreliable). The first of their singles with Williams was "Oh Holy Night."

In April 1951 Jubilee issued "Pal of Mine," the group's tribute to the sorely missed Gaithers. A number of Orioles' subsequent recordings were not up to their usual quality as the group's interest waned. It was reflected in *Billboard* reviews of records like "Bar Fly" ("Orioles are not very exciting on this new weeper ballad. Though the lead does an effective job—side may get spins") and

"You Belong to Me" ("The group works over the pop hit in a schmaltzy style. Not their best effort, though their fans will probably take to it").

But they began to come out of it with "I Miss You So," released in early 1953, and the beautiful "I Cover the Waterfront."

Around this time George Nelson left and Gregory Carroll (Four Buddies, Savoy) joined with Charlie Harris, making the group a quintet. Their next single, "Crying in the Chapel," became the standard they would always be known for. Recorded on June 30, 1953, it prompted a *Billboard* reviewer to write, "The Orioles have here what is undoubtedly the strongest record in the past two years, and one of the strongest R&B discs released in the past few months. The tune is the serious ditty now getting action in the country and pop markets and the boys hand it a powerful rendition, full of feeling and spark by the fine lead singer. This could be a big, big hit!" By summer's end it was at number 11 (#1 R&B). The group followed with "In the Mission of St. Augustine," which reached number seven R&B by October and turned out to be their last national hit. The Orioles disbanded when they found it difficult to earn top dollar in a market flooded with a new generation of groups.

Sonny, however, found a new Orioles complete and intact when he spotted a modern harmony group, the Regals, performing at the Apollo in 1954. Together, they issued a string of Jubilee sides through 1956 including excellent versions of "Runaround" and "Don't Go to Strangers." The new members were Gerald Holeman, Albert Russell, Billy Adams, and Jerry Rodriguez. They signed with Vee Jay Records in 1956 for three singles, the most popular being "Happy Till the Letter."

In 1962 Til formed yet another Orioles with Gerald Gregory (of THE SPANIELS), Delton McCall (from THE DREAMS) and Billy Taylor (THE CASTELLES). They recorded an LP on September 21 for Charlie Parker along with a few nicely done remakes of the group's old hits. The most interesting was an answer record to "Crying in the Chapel" called "Back to the Chapel."

Meanwhile, Jubilee issued a number of oldies LPs in a "battle of the groups" style, and the Orioles' early records were well represented. The LPs were popular sellers from the beginning and became cult classics. In 1971 Til formed a new Orioles with Clarence Young, Mike Robinson, and Bobby Thomas. The latter two, who had idolized the Orioles since their youth, belonged to a group named after Til's original, the Vibranairs (After Hours). They recorded one excellent LP with Sonny for RCA that year.

In 1978 the Orioles did a tribute LP to the original group, *Sonny Til and the Orioles Today* (Dobre), with Pepe Grant (tenor), Larry Reed (baritone), and George Holms (bass). Sonny's last recording was in 1981 on the LP *Sonny Til and the Orioles Visit Manhattan Circa 1950s.*

George Nelson died of an asthma attack around 1959, and Alex Sharp died in the '70s while singing with an Ink Spots group. Johnny Reed retired from singing, and Ralph Williams was seen with a band in St. Louis during the '70s. On December 9, 1981, Sonny Til died at the age of 51.

SONNY TIL AND THE ORIOLES

A SIDE/B SIDE	LABEL/CAT NO	DATE
It's Too Soon To Know / Barbra Lee	ItsN 5000	7/48
It's Too Soon To Know / Barbra Lee	Jubi 5000	8/48
Dare To Dream / To Be With You	Jubi 5001	11/48
Lonely Christmas / To Be With You	Jubi 5001	11/48
Please Give My Heart A Break / It Seems So Long Ago	Jubi 5002	2/49
Tell Me So / Deacon Jones	Jubi 5005	4/49
I Challenge Your Kiss / Donkey Serenade	Jubi 5008	6/49
A Kiss And A Rose / It's A Cold Summer	Jubi 5009	8/49
So Much / Forgive And Forget	Jubi 5016	10/49
Lonely Christmas / What Are You Doing New Year's Eve	Jubi 5017	11/49
Would You Still Be The One In My Heart / Is My Heart Wasting Time	Jubi 5018	1/50
At Night / Every Dog-Gone Time	Jubi 5025	3/50
Moonlight / I Wonder When	Jubi 5026	5/50
You're Gone / Everything They Said Came True	Jubi 5028	7/50
I'd Rather Have You Under The Moon / We're Supposed To Be Through	Jubi 5031	8/50
I Need You So / Goodnight Irene	Jubi 5037	9/50
I Cross My Fingers / Can't Seem To Laugh Anymore	Jubi 5040	10/50
Oh Holy Night / The Lord's Prayer	Jubi 5045	11/50
I Miss You So / You Are My First Love	Jubi 5051	1/51
Pal Of Mine / Happy Go Lucky Local Blues	Jubi 5055	4/51
Would I Love You / When You're A Long, Long Way From Home	Jubi 5057	5/51
I'm Just A Fool In Love / Hold Me, Squeeze Me	Jubi 5061	8/51
Don't Tell Her What's Happened To Me / Baby, Please Don't Go	Jubi 5065	10/51

A SIDE/ B SIDE	LABEL/CAT NO	DATE
When You're Not Around / How Blind Can You Be	Jubi 5071	12/51
Trust In Me / Shrimp Boats	Jubi 5074	2/52
It's Over Because We're Through / Waiting	Jubi 5082	4/52
Barfly / Gettin' Tired, Tired, Tired	Jubi 5084	6/52
Don't Cry Baby / See See Rider	Jubi 5092	8/52
You Belong To Me / I Don't Want To Take A Chance	Jubi 5102	11/52
I Miss You So / Till Then	Jubi 5107	1/53
Teardrops On My Pillow / Hold Me, Thrill Me, Kiss Me	Jubi 5108	3/53
Bad Little Girl / Dem Days	Jubi 5115	3/53
I Cover The Waterfront / One More Time	Jubi 5120	6/53
Crying In The Chapel / Don't You Think I Ought To Know	Jubi 5122	7/53
In The Mission Of St. Augustine / Write And Tell Me Why	Jubi 5127	10/53
There's No One But You / Robe Of Calvary	Jubi 5134	1/54
Secret Love / Don't Go To Strangers	Jubi 5137	2/54
Maybe You'll Be There / Drowning Every Hope I Ever Had	Jubi 5143	5/54
In The Chapel In The Moonlight / Thank The Lord! Thank The Lord!	Jubi 5154	7/54
If You Believe / Longing	Jubi 5161	10/54
Runaround / Count Your Blessings Instead Of Sheep	Jubi 5172	12/54
I Love You Mostly / Fair Exchange	Jubi 5177	1/55
I Need You Baby / That's When The Good Lord Will Smile	Jubi 5189	3/55
Please Sing My Blues Tonight / Moody Over You	Jubi 5221	10/55
Angel / Don't Go To Strangers	Jubi 5231	1/56
Happy Till The Letter / I Just Got Lucky	Vee-Jay 196	1956
For All We Know / Never Leave Me Baby	Vee-Jay 228	1956
Sugar Girl / Didn't I Say	Vee-Jay 244	1957
Sugar Girl / Didn't I Say	Abner 1016	1958
Tell Me So / At Night	Jubi 5363	1959
Crying In The Chapel / Forgive And Forget	Jubi 6001	1959
The First Of Summer / Come On Home	Jubi 5384	1960
Secret Love / The Wobble	CPrkr 211	1962
In The Chapel In The Moonlight / Hey! Little Woman	CPrkr 212	1962
Back To The Chapel Again / Lonely Christmas	CPrkr 213	1962
What Are You Doing New Year's Eve / Don't Mess Around With My Love	CPrkr 214	1962
It's Too Soon To Know / I Miss You So	CPrkr 215	1963
Write And Tell Me Why / Don't Tell Her What Happened To Me	CPrkr 216	1963
I Miss You So / Hey! Little Woman	CPrkr 219	1963

THE 1950s

THE DIAMONDS

THE PLATTERS

THE McGUIRE SISTERS

The 1950s were the golden age of vocal groups. Estimates reveal that over 10,000 different acts recorded during the decade.

With World War II and the 12 years of depression now part of history, the American economy was booming. People were finding the time to pursue leisure activities and enjoy music. Radios, record players, and TVs were selling in record numbers. Adults and their kids were purchasing the records they liked, and they liked a lot of records. Million-selling discs became routine and the record business thrived.

With more radio stations came more diversity in music, Jazz, blues, pop, gospel, country, and eventually rhythm and blues and rock and roll earned their own substantial followings; vocal groups sang music of each style to the delight of growing audiences.

The three basic time frames of musical change in the '50s were almost equal in length. For black groups, 1950 to 1953 followed the merging of gospel and blues as extolled by the Ravens and the Orioles in the 1940s. Groups like the Clovers, the Drifters, and the Dominoes created a synthesis of city blues, country blues, gospel, and jazz that resulted in rhythm and blues during that period. Thousands of groups embraced the sound in the early and middle '50s, including the Four Buddies, the Swallows, the 5 Royales, the Du Droppers, the Coronets, the Vocaleers, the Velvets, the Royals, the Crickets, the Spiders, the Crows, the Checkers, the Robins, the Turbans, the Leaders, the Moroccos, the Jaguars, the Rivileers, the Solitaires, the Bobbettes, the Charts, the Cadets, the Castelles, the Hollywood Flames, the Wheels, the Heartbreakers, the Mastertones, and the Tempo-tones. Some of the best were the Five Keys, the Larks, the Flamingos, the Moonglows, the Cadillacs, the Teenagers, the Cleftones, the Harptones, the Jesters, the Channels, the Cardinals, and the Schoolboys.

Rhythm and blues began to stretch out beyond its original black audience in the South. In 1952 and 1953 record distributors and sales people started noticing that white high school and college students were picking up on R&B, primarily as dance music. Alert disc jockeys who noticed the growing trend switched to R&B music and saw their audiences grow enormously. Groups like the Orioles and the Ravens were not only pioneers of this style of music, they were also the ones who unleashed the flurry of groups named after birds—the Wrens, the Robins, the Crows, the Flamingos, the Hawks, the Swans, the Warblers, the Jayhawks, the Falcons, the Swallows, the Cardinals, the Sparrows, the Five Owls, the Larks, and the Pelicans were a few who followed their flight pattern.

Another group trend in the mid- and late '50s was centered on cars. There were the Cadillacs, the Ramblers, the Corvettes, the Valiants, the El Dorados, the Bonnevilles, and the Edsels.

By the mid-'50s (1954 to 1957) rhythm and blues was growing more popular, picking up a stronger beat, making more use of backup harmonies, and placing those harmonies closer to the lead. Bass lines, borrowed from gospel, started being used under high tenor leads.

After the Crows' 1953 classic "Gee," rhythm and blues began developing into what would become rock and roll.

Certain ancillary styles were also developing and became known by their areas of origin. Among them were "the Philadelphia sound," which included the high tenors of the Dreamers, the Castelles, the Capris, and Lee Andrews and the Hearts; the polished, bluesy "Chicago sound" of the Flamingos, the El Dorados, the Orchids, the Five Thrills, the Shepards, the Dells, and the Magnificents; the "Los Angeles sound," a looser harmony as performed by the Penguins, the Hollywood Flames, the Flairs, the Turks, and the Medallions; and the "New York sound," a tight three- and four-part harmony blend, with bouncing bass and falsetto tenor lead as practiced by the Jesters, the Channels, the Paragons, Anthony and the Imperials, the Charts, the Bop Chords, the Ladders, and the Lovenotes.

Rhythm and blues also had its country influences, like Hank Ballard and the Midnighters. The third basic time frame, 1957 to 1959, saw the emergence of black pop acts like the Platters, the Rivieras, and the Cues alongside R&B groups like the Dubs, the Coasters, the Tuneweavers, the Jive Bombers, the Cellos, the Six Teens, the Olympics, the Students, the Danleers, and groups experimenting with bluesier approaches, like the Falcons and Jerry Butler and the Impressions, whose early recordings were considered the starting point for soul.

White vocal groups in the early third of the decade were for the most part recording folk, pop, and jazz. The Weavers were one of the leading folk groups. Jazz groups like the Four Freshmen and the Hi-Lo's modeled their three-, four-, and five-part harmonies from a combination of jazz bands and the earlier efforts of acts like the Merry Macs and the Pied Pipers.

Pop vocal groups were continuing the style of vocal acts singing with bands in the '30s and '40s, like the Andrews Sisters and the Ames Brothers. Some better known early '50s pop acts included the McGuire Sisters, the Fontane Sisters, the Bonnie Sisters, the Hilltoppers, the Four Aces, the Four Lads, the Four Preps, and the Four Voices.

The early and middle '50s found many white acts emulating the current black groups' and solo artists' recordings, thus "covering" the original rhythm and blues release in what they considered a more palatable form for digestion by white radio and its listeners. Groups like the Diamonds, the Four Coins, the Crew-cuts, the Lancers, the Bop-a-loos, the Cheers, the Hutton Sisters, the DeCastro Sisters, the DeMarco Sisters, the Fontane Sisters, the McGuire Sisters, and even the Mills Brothers cut anywhere from one to a career's worth of covers.

Just as there were transition groups in rhythm and blues acting as conduits between the pop black and gospel acts of the '40s and the R&B and rock and roll acts of the '50s, so were there transitional white groups who many claimed gave greater exposure to the R&B and rock black performers by delivering their music to a white audience. Some R&B purists countered that groups like the Crew-cuts only succeeded because they covered the songs of black artists. The truth combines those arguments. It's quite possible that had white artists not copied black vocal group recordings in the mid-'50s, then, given the country's racial policies, rock and roll and R&B would very likely not have crossed over into mass market radio as rapidly as it did (Elvis Presley was doing the same thing with R&B songs). On the other hand, a good record, black or white, could by 1956 make the charts largely on its merit (and promotion). Otherwise, Frankie Lymon and the Teenagers' "Why Do Fools Fall in Love" would not have beaten out three white cover versions all at the same time.

The black groups that were copied covered the spectrum of rhythm and blues music, and included names like the Drifters, the Flamingos, the Platters, the Orioles, and countless more.

Most of the white male and female groups were in their 20s and 30s. By the late '50s the biggest change in their direction was the development of teen groups who had grown up singing songs recorded by early '50s black groups. They emulated the groups' styles on new compositions, thus creating a rock and roll doo wop style (earlier black groups were singing doo wop before it had a name). Some ground breakers were Danny and the Juniors, the Elegants, the Skyliners, Dion and the Belmonts, the Bay Bops, the Fascinators, and the Passions.

Racially mixed groups also came into view, starting with acts like the Mariners, the Crests, the Jaguars, the Del-Vikings, and the Impalas.

Cover records began to die out with the development of rock and roll and the availability of original black group versions. A vocal group craze similar to the cover record fad was the "answer record," in which an act would have a hit and then the same act or others would create a sequel similar in style and melody and with lyrics that continued the story line. The most notable of these was the "Annie" craze, started by Hank Ballard and the Midnighters with their 1954 hit "Work with Me Annie." It was followed by numerous answers, such as "Annie Had a Baby" (the Midnighters), "Annie Met Henry" (the Cadets), "Annie's Answer" (Hazel McCollum and the El Dorados), "My Name Ain't Annie" (Linda Hayes), "Annie's Aunt Fanny" (the Midnights), and "Annie Kicked the Bucket" (the Nutones).

Gospel music entered the '50s flourishing but went out with its future in doubt. The best lead vocalists were leaving in droves for rhythm and blues and, in the late '50s and early '60s, the newly emerging style called soul. Some defectors were Sam Cooke (the Soul Stirrers), Brooke Benton (the Jerusalem Stars), Wilson Pickett (the Violinaires), Lou Rawls (the Pilgrim Travelers), David Ruffin (the Dixie Nightingales), and Della Reese (the Meditation Singers). Many great gospel groups performed and recorded in the '50s, including the Highway QCs, the Soul Stirrers, the Pilgrim Travelers, the Caravans, the Swan Silvertones, the Dixie Hummingbirds, the Sensational Nightingales, the Golden Gate Quartet, and the Five Blind Boys of Mississippi.

An intriguing aspect of the R&B and rock and roll business of the '50s was the fact that many of the owners of the small and mid-size record labels who were catering to the teen market were men and women from the Jewish community. These were the people who were not only producing, marketing, promoting, and selling the records, but were the ones picking which rhythm and blues and rock and roll songs their groups would record. Just a few of these musical entrepreneurs were George Goldner (End/Gone/Rama/Gee/Goldisc), Morty Craft (Melba/Warwick/Bruce), Irv Spice (Mohawk), Herb Abramson (Atlantic/Jubilee), Hy Weiss (Old Town/Barry/Paradise/Whiz), Bob and Gene Schwartz (Laurie/Rust), Bess Berman (Apollo), Florence Greenberg (Tierra/Scepter), Kal Mann and Bernie Lowe (Cameo/Parkway), Al Silvers (Herald/Ember), Morris Levy (Roulette), Herb Newman (Dore/Era), Irving Berman (Arco/Manor), Johnny Bienstock (Bigtop), Herb Slotkin (Grand), Herman Lubinsky (Savoy), and Sydney Nathan (King/Federal).

Men and women who were mostly unaware that what they were doing would last helped to create a rich history in a decade of musical transformation. ■

The Admirations

If the quality of a vocal group was judged by the number of records released, then the Admirations would have been judged unfairly. One of the best late-'50s white doo wop groups, the Admirations were also one of the few such acts with only two records on a major label. The quintet would have been better off with one of New York's rock and roll independents, who were used to breaking records like theirs, but in 1958, 15-year-old high school students couldn't possibly foresee such things.

The group members were all friends from the same neighborhood in Brooklyn, growing up around Elderts Lane and Liberty Avenue. They consisted of lead Joe (Cookie) Lorello, Fred Mastanduno (first tenor), John Mahlan (second tenor), Ralph Minichino (baritone), and Lou Moshella (bass). They practiced in hallways, on street corners, and at the neighborhood candy store. It was on one such occasion that the group, in search of a name, looked around that candy store and locked their eyes on a large advertisement for Admiration cigars. At that moment the Admirations were born. They began doing dances and record hops, performing songs by their favorite groups like THE FLAMINGOS and BELMONTS. In the fall of 1958, an A&R assistant to Mercury's Clyde Otis named Jerry Maggett saw the group perform and brought them to Otis, who signed them up.

Although their first recording was done in February 1959, for some inexplicable reason "The Bells of Rosa Rita" was not released by Mercury until November of that year. It became one of those classic East-Coast doo wop records that seemed more popular as an "oldie" than it was at the time of its ill-fated initial release. With Mercury's interest on the wane after just one record, the group decided to disband, but in 1960 they reformed with Joe Mertens and Diane Salemme (Joe's wife) replacing John Mahlan (in the army) and Ralph Minichino.

By the summer of 1960, the group got an opportunity and cut four more sides for Mercury, two of which were never released and two ("To the Aisle" and "Hey Senorita") that weren't issued until 1961. Though their record releases were few, the Admirations' powerful five-part chime harmony on "Bells of Rosa Rita" have endeared them to vocal group enthusiasts for almost 30 years. Disappointed with Mercury's disinterest, the group disbanded for a second time later that year as John became a police officer, Joe and Fred joined the sanitation department, and Lou joined a construction company. In 1974, the group was resurrected for a third time doing various revival appearances in the New York City area. The lack of exposure for Admirations records is evident in the rarity of those recordings on the collector's market. Members of the group have acknowledged at one time or another that even they don't have a copy of "To the Aisle."

THE ADMIRATIONS

A SIDE/B SIDE	LABEL/CAT NO	DATE
The Bells Of Rosa Rita / Little Bo-Peep	Merc 71521	1959
To The Aisle / Hey Senorita	Merc 71833	1961

The Altairs

Many vocal groups, good and bad, recorded during the '50s, but few of them ever got the opportunity to perform with almost every rhythm-and-blues luminary that passed through their town. Among the lucky ones were the little-known Altairs.

Formed in the rest rooms of Herron Hill Junior High School in Pittsburgh, the harmonizers were Timothy Johnson (lead), William Herndon (first tenor), Nathaniel Benson (second tenor), Richard Harris (baritone—not the "MacArthur Park" vocalist), and Ralph Terry (bass—definitely not the New York Yankees pitcher).

It was 1958, and the quintet of teens got their performing experience playing assemblies at different schools thanks to the interest of one of their teachers. Soon after forming, Johnson dropped out and Nathaniel's cousin, 14-year-old George Benson (that's right—*that* George Benson) was asked to join. Adding his guitar for rhythm and his voice on lead, the group began performing at local record hops for deejay Sir Walter and legendary Pittsburgh broadcaster Porky Chedwick. They also acquired a manager in the form of Richard Harris's father Raymond and the name the Altairs courtesy of the Birdland Record Shop owner.

Their break came when disc jockey Bill Powell of radio WAMO brought the quintet into the station's studio to do backup vocals for Anne Keith (actually Anna Mae Jackson), who had also recorded some sides with another excellent Pittsburgh group, THE EL VENOS. This was not George Benson's first session, however, as he had recorded in New York for Groove Records (RCA) in the spring of 1954 at the tender age of 10, cutting "It Should Have Been Me" and three other tunes.

The Altairs recorded only one side with Anne, "Lover's Prayer," as the flip was one of her previously unreleased El Veno sides. The July 1959 release on the miniscule Memo label went nowhere, but the group earned valuable experience performing with and without Anne all over Pittsburgh. Their finely tuned harmony made them a top local attraction, and whenever any name act was passing through Pittsburgh (from THE MIRACLES to FRANKIE LYMON) the Altairs were on the bill.

The act's next recording opportunity came when Billie Ford (of Billy and Lillie, "La Dee Dah," #9, 1958) saw the Pittsburgh juveniles perform and helped them get a record deal with New York-based Amy Records late in 1959. The teens recorded several sides including "If You Love Me" and "Groovie Time," both with George on lead. Young George didn't play guitar on the session as the company opted for studio professional Mickey "Guitar" Baker (formerly of Mickey and Sylvia, "Love Is Strange," #11, 1957). "If You Love Me" was a nice shuffle-styled doo wop rocker with George's baritone-to-tenor lead sounding much like Cornelius Harp, lead of THE MARCELS. The group ably assisted but radio did not, and the record never got past the starting gate.

By the end of 1960 George had left the Altairs to join the Four Counts. The Altairs then met songwriter Otis Blackwell through Richard Harris's brother, Ray Harris, Jr. (their current manager), and in 1961 the group cut demos for Otis to place with other artists. Had they taken the demos to a label themselves, the Altairs might have ended up as more than an obscure footnote in music history: one of the songs was "Return to Sender." Elvis Presley cut it with the same vocal arrangement used on the demo, though that was of little consolation to the group.

Rhythm and blues vocalist Dinah Washington became the group's next mentor after seeing their dazzling performance at a Lodi, New Jersey, club she co-owned. She arranged for their signing to Queens Booking Agency, and the Altairs were off on a whirlwind six months of touring playing opposite Dinah and every other hit act from Chubby Checker to THE SHIRELLES. Then Dinah formed a new "supergroup" with the Altairs as the nucleus. The lineup included William Herndon (first tenor), Johnny Carter (first tenor, of THE DELLS), Nat Benson (second tenor), Cornell Gunter (second tenor, of THE COASTERS), Richard Harris (baritone), and Chuck

Barksdale (bass, of the Dells). Renamed Dinah's Gentlemen (later revised to D's Gents), their sound turned from rock and roll doo wop to modern harmony.

When Dinah died in December of 1963, the group separated. Richard went to work as a choreographer for Golden World Records in Pittsburgh and taught dance steps to the Reflections ("Romeo and Juliet," #6, 1964) among others. That same year Harris and Herndon joined with Leroy Grammer (the Enchantments, Alanna) and part-timer Wayne Walker (El Dupreys and the Enchantments) to form These Gents. The group occasionally backed the Marcels at shows. When Marcels bass Fred Johnson revamped his group he added Herndon and Harris, so that from 1964 to 1980 Herndon and Harris sang with both These Gents *and* the Marcels.

In 1973 These Gents cut their only released single, the ballad "Yesterday Standing By (Parts I and II)" for Pittsburgh's Western World label, produced by Marcels member Walt Maddox and with a talking intro by Fred Johnson.

From 1980 onward two of the three actively performing members of the Altairs, Herndon and Harris, sang as full-time members of Johnson's Marcels. The third Altairs alumnus, George Benson, went on to become one of the legends of modern jazz, garnering a 1976 Grammy award for "This Masquerade" as Record of the Year, and scoring 23 R&B chart records and 14 pop charters through 1986. Some of his best-remembered recordings include "On Broadway," "Give Me the Night," and "Turn Your Love Around."

Lee Andrews and the Hearts

One of the finest R&B vocal groups of the '50s, Lee Andrews and the Hearts would have been one of the best pop groups too if white radio had been more open to black vocalists in those days.

Born of a musical family in Goldsboro, North Carolina, Arthur Thompson (his father Beechie Thompson sang with THE DIXIE HUMMINGBIRDS) moved to Philadelphia when he was two. He began singing with four friends from Bertram High School in 1952 and they decided on the Dreamers as their name. Royalston "Roy" Calhoun (first tenor), Thomas "Butch" Curry (second tenor),

James "Jimmy" McCalister (baritone), and John Young (bass) made up the quintet who in their formative days were tutored on spirituals by Butch's aunt. The group was influenced by such acts as THE MOONGLOWS, THE ORIOLES, THE DRIFTERS, THE 5 ROYALES, THE FIVE KEYS, THE MIDNIGHTERS, and THE RAVENS, while Arthur leaned towards soloists like Bing Crosby, Frankie Laine, Frank Sinatra, and someone you could almost hear in his voice, Nat King Cole.

Between 1952 and 1954 they picked up some secular songs and began singing rhythm and blues.

In early 1954 the group went to radio WHAT to audition for on-air personality Kae Williams. Kae allowed teens to dance in the studio next to his while his show was on and often went in to speak to them about their favorite records. When the quintet said they had a great group, Kae told them to wait until his show was over and he'd listen to them. They sang only two songs, the 1948 Gordon Jenkins hit (#3) "Maybe You'll Be There" and the 1920 evergreen by Francis Alda (#7) "The Bells of St. Mary's." Williams was so awed by this unique assemblage that he resolved to manage them on the spot.

In the spring of that year Williams recorded the Dreamers at Reco Arts Studio on "Maybe You'll Be There" and "Baby Come Back." When the session ended so did the group's nominal identity as they learned that there was another group called the Dreamers. Jimmy saw a small heart on the secretary's desk and suggested they call themselves the Hearts. Since Arthur was to be featured on lead and on the labels he began shuffling his names around to come up with something he felt would sound better than Arthur Thompson and the Hearts. His full name was Arthur Lee Andrew Thompson; it's obvious what he settled on. Williams brought the tracks to Eddie and Bobby Heller who owned a club in north Philadelphia. More importantly Eddie also owned Rainbow Records in New York City.

"Maybe You'll Be There" was issued in mid-May 1954 and *Billboard*'s May 15th reviewer commented: "A tender ditty, it's sung with a good deal of warmth by the group. Lee Andrews' tenor carries the lead. Okay wax." The single garnered lots of Philadelphia airplay but the nearly a cappella 45 (accompanied only by piano) couldn't compete with a concurrent version by the polished and established Orioles.

"The White Cliffs of Dover," their second single, was a better overall group performance but saw even less activity. The group went with another standard for their third Rainbow release, "The Bells of St. Mary's" in October. Unfortunately the dual-version syndrome hit them again when the Drifters came out with a better-produced recording and wrapped up most of the sales. (The Hearts might have had a better chance if someone had thought to flip the 45 and play the beautiful Lee Andrews-penned ballad "The Fairest.") Kae Williams obviously thought three tries was enough for Rainbow and pulled the group from the label. As they were signed to him and not Rainbow they had to go where he put them. The trouble was, Williams didn't put them anywhere except into clubs. Still, this maneuver gave the group some worthwhile experience.

By 1955 Jimmy was Navy bound, replaced by another neighbor from the Woodland Avenue and 49th Street section of town, Ted Weems. They continued to rehearse at places like the recreation center on Kingsessing and 49th but as all were now high school grads they had to think of full-time employment. Ted went to work in a lamp factory; Lee and Roy went to work at Gotham Record Distributors hoping to also get an audition with owner Ivan Ballen's label. For quite a while the group hadn't known that their contract with Kae Williams wasn't valid as they had all been minors when they signed without parental authority. Now knowing they were free Lee and Roy reportedly asked Ballen to audition them. Ballen's main interest was gospel music, however, and he kept putting them off until the end of 1955 when he relented and gave them a listen.

On January 3, 1956, the Hearts signed to Gotham and began rehearsing and recording at their 1626 Federal Street studio. Their first single, the Davies-Heyman standard "Bluebird of Happiness," finally made it into Gotham's release schedule in May 1956. *Billboard*'s June 2nd reviewer called it "a sincere, moving vocal interpretation of the sentimental oldie by Lee Andrews and the Hearts." Again local airplay opened the door that was quickly shut everywhere else. The Hearts, who were now recording with more instrumentation than on their Rainbow sides, with drums, bass, piano, and sax (for the up-tempo flips), were also cutting A-side ballads written by Lee. Well, almost. His first A-side composition was a cloning of the Larks' 1952 (Apollo) single "In My Lonely Room," which he retitled "Lonely Room." Still, it was a beautifully performed rendition and garnered the most radio acceptance of their Gotham sides, getting airplay throughout Pennsylvania, Delaware, and New Jersey.

Performances in those days were always an adventure for new acts and if the club owner didn't stiff you, the people representing you often did. One example of unrewarded effort occurred when the Hearts were at Cards Beach, Maryland, in 1956. After performing, they went looking for roadie Bill Scott, who was responsible for collecting their pay. They finally found him, drunk asleep on the toilet in the men's room with a cigar sticking out of his mouth but without a cent of their money. The group's pianist reportedly risked his future livelihood by smacking the wrecked roadie clear off of the seat.

Their last Gotham side, which listed Andrews as writer but was reportedly penned by Rita Sherwood, came out toward the end of 1956. "Just Suppose" had a more complex melody than their previous efforts and was superbly sung by the group, but it quickly and quietly vanished as Gotham's heart was not in promoting R&B records. The Hearts' frustration over their released failures was no greater than what they felt about songs they had recorded that remained unreleased, like "Long Lonely Nights," "Try the Impossible," "Sipping a Cup of Coffee," "Window Eyes," and "Why Do I" to mention just a few. They decided to audition for another disc jockey/manager because, as with Kae, it would guarantee local airplay that might stimulate national action.

They auditioned in early 1957 at Ted Weems's home for Philadelphia (WDAS) and New York (WOV) jock "Jocko" Henderson. They met him while promoting "Just Suppose" and knew how powerful a radio voice he was. Jocko and partner Barry Golder owned Mainline Record Distributors and the Hearts looked like the perfect vehicle to start up their long-planned Mainline label. Before they could record, however, John Young left for New York and a succession of basses took John's place including their piano player Gerald Thompson, Tom Hackett, and finally Roy's brother Wendell.

In June 1957 Mainline issued a new recording of the Hearts doing "Long Lonely Nights." Airplay was expected but sales followed and Jocko smelled a hit. Knowing his distribution potential was limited he contacted both Atlantic and Chess for national distribution, settling on Chess when their deal included Mainline's right to keep the record for their own territory. Not to be outdone, Atlantic recorded the song with their ace Clyde McPhatter, and to further complicate one of the great mid-'50s black cover battles, the Kings on Baton also covered "Long Lonely Nights." The latter version had been the doing of Chess. The Kings were actually

THE RAVENS, who were signed to Chess affiliate Argo. Obviously hedging their bet against losing distribution of the Hearts original to Atlantic (before they had been chosen), Chess covered the song with the Ravens. When they won the original version's rights, rather than be caught with their hands in the cookie jar having two versions competing through their own company, they leased the Ravens to Baton as the Kings. Clyde's version was a given as both he and Lee climbed nationally on the R&B list on August 5th, but Lee's pop styling enabled the group and recording to scale the pop charts concurrently with Clyde, the week of August 12th, just three days after Lee and company appeared on "American Bandstand." The race was a close one, and there's no doubt the Hearts recording could have hit top 10 Pop without the fierce competition. As is, the Hearts reached number 45 Pop to Clyde's number 49, and number 11 R&B to the former Drifters lead's number one showing. The Hearts' consolation is that as great a singer as McPhatter was, their version has become the choice of oldies radio to this day, while Clyde's record is now known only by hard-core collectors.

The credit game on "Long Lonely Nights" and its flip "The Clock" is amusing (but only in retrospect)—another great example of countless fingers in the hit pie. The credits of "Long Lonely Nights" read Uniman, Abbott, Andrews, Henderson. "The Clock" read Curry, Golder, Binnick, Davis. Now the fun begins. Uniman was Mimi Uniman, wife of big-time Philadelphia disc jockey Hy Lit. Abbott was another disc jockey named Larry Brown. Andrews was Lee; and Henderson, the inimitable Jocko. Curry was Butch Curry of the Hearts, the actual writer. Golder was Jocko's partner Barry. Binnick was Bernie Binnick, a co-owner of Swan Records. Davis was Bernice Davis, Philadelphia deejay Georgie Wood's fiancée and later wife. Add up the score and you find two disc jockeys, two disc jockeys' wives or fiancées, one record company owner, one disc jockey partner, and trailing along behind, two members of the Hearts. All were talented enough and had enough time to sit down and write those classics, right? Nevertheless, this was the golden age of the Hearts as they appeared on the Labor Day bill at the Apollo with THE HARPTONES, Fats Domino, Bo Diddley, and emcee (who else?) Jocko Henderson.

They did the traditional East Coast theatre circuit, including the dreaded Royal in Baltimore (shades of THE CLEFTONES). The Royal was known as the Bottle Theatre because the rowdy crowds would throw miniature whiskey bottles at the stage. To counter this the Hearts asked the bandleader to play their opening number very fast so the group could keep moving on stage. The rowdies apparently liked it and the group was spared the bottle barrage. Their billmates weren't as fortunate: both FRANKIE LYMON AND THE TEENAGERS and THE EL DORADOS were bottled.

In November 1957 "Teardrops" was issued by Chess nationally but in Philly on Argo as part of the distribution deal between Chess and Mainline. Another classic beautifully sung by Lee and the guys (the song was written by Roy and their pianist Tommy White—no matter *what* the labels say), Chess pulled out all the stops. With no competing covers, the song charted Pop on November 25, 1957, and R&B January 6, 1958, eventually reaching number 20 Pop (#4 R&B).

After two hits and short-shrifted royalties from Chess, Jocko issued the Hearts' next single on United Artists with the Philadelphia area seeing copies on his locally distributed Casino label (owned by Mickey Golder, Barry's brother—Barry, remember, was Jocko's partner and one of "The Clock's" brilliant "writers"). The song "Try the Impossible" (another Butch Curry beauty), was another re-recording of those terrific sides they did for Gotham. "Try" charted Pop (as the group's sound, consistent ballad quality, and Lee's voice all bent that way) on June 2nd reaching number 33, but they never again charted R&B.

The group spent a lot of 1958 performing with Jackie Wilson, Bobby Day, and LaVern Baker, but touring was still tantamount to being an expeditionary force with Lewis and Clark. The South was the biggest adventure zone as the group traveled in its own white-and-gold station wagon with their name emblazoned on the side. Once, in Birmingham, Alabama, Calhoun and Curry were arrested by police. The cops threw them against a wall while pointing guns at their heads, perhaps an overreaction considering the crime the two terrified singers had committed—jaywalking. Their later tours were more organized; they did "The Dick Clark Travelogue" in buses with large contingents of stars like Fabian, Frankie Avalon, THE MONOTONES, and Bobby Darin. In June 1958 another oldie/newie, "Why Do I," replete with strings and female background, was recorded in New York and released to good though not overwhelming response, failing to chart nationally. The same happened to remakes of "Maybe You'll Be There" in November and "Just Suppose" in early 1959.

By now Weems had joined the service and Lee had gone solo. The group became the Five Hearts

consisting of Tommy White (lead); Roy and Wendell Calhoun and Butch Curry of the Hearts; and Eddie Custus (the Superiors, Mainline) in 1959 doing "It's Unbelievable" for Arcade. The group's third disc jockey/manager, Hy Lit, took a re-formed Hearts to Chancellor Records where the new quartet (Calhoun, Curry, Custus, and Sonny Gordon) re-recorded "It's Unbelievable" and earned it some airplay in New York and Philadelphia. This aggregation tried once more on Guyden in November 1962 with "Aisle of Love" and then separated.

Lee surfaced on Swan for three singles with an uncredited group (later identified by a reissue as the Neons) of Bobby Bell, Richard Mason, Richard Booker, and Lee's first female member, Sandra Mingo. The best of these sides were "A Night Like Tonight" and "P.S. I Love You."

In February 1962 the group reunited for "Together Again" on Gowen with a lineup of Andrews, Curry, the Calhoun brothers, and Custus. Lee then soloed (if you can call a record with backgrounds by the Dreamlovers, Rick and the Masters, and various Hearts a solo) on his favorite recording "I'm Sorry Pillow" in December 1962 on Parkway.

By 1963 the Hearts' recordings had become collectors' dreams, so Grand Records apparently struck a deal with Gotham for some of its old sides. Collectors' demand mushroomed into popular demand prompting Lee to form a new Hearts group of Richard Booker, Robert Howard, Richard Mason, and Victoria McCalister, and by the summer of 1966 they had recorded and issued a splendid ballad, "You're Taking a Long Time Coming Back" on RCA.

Lee and company then signed with Crimson and eventually wound up two singles later on its parent company, Lost Night, recording three original singles (an unusual move for this all-oldies reissue company), the best of these sides being "Cold Gray Dawn" and "Island of Love" in 1968.

By the time they did a live LP for Lost Night at a club in Fairless Hills, Pennsylvania, the Hearts were Lee, Richard Howard, Richard Booker, and Tommy White.

Lee then went into retirement and opened a successful dress shop. In a 1971 interview he stated that he formed a new group called First Born with music teachers Grace Simmons, Georgia Patton, and perennial Richard Booker and they were in the process of going to Columbia. No such record release ever took place, however.

He later reemerged at the urging of producer friend Billy Jackson (THE TYMES), who knew Lee's interests were now leaning in a 5th Dimension direction, so they formed Congress Alley with Booker, Jackie Andrews (Lee's wife), and Karen Brisco.

Two singles and an LP on Avco Embassy went nowhere. In 1981 Collectible Records unearthed the original first studio session tapes from Gotham and issued three singles. Among them were the original "Long Lonely Nights" (lyrically different from the hit), with just a piano accompaniment and crystal-clear harmonies, and the nearly a cappella treatment of "Just Suppose," which weaved between exquisite harmonies and flat notes.

The rock revival of the '70s provided momentum for Lee to form one more Hearts, a family affair with Lee, his wife Jackie, son Ahmir, and daughter Dawn. Life wasn't as good to the other Hearts: Roy Calhoun died in an apartment fire in 1979; Butch Curry became ill with multiple sclerosis; Wendell Calhoun still lives in Philadelphia and Ted Weems joined the Pheasants ("Out of the Mist," Throne) in 1963 and later had a group called Tribute. He now manages a housing development.

LEE ANDREWS AND THE HEARTS

A SIDE/B SIDE	LABEL/CAT NO	DATE
Maybe You'll Be There / Baby Come Back	Rnbw 252	5/54
Maybe You'll Be There / Baby Come Back	Riviera 965	1954
White Cliffs Of Dover / Much Too Much	Rnbw 256	1954
The Fairwest / Bells Of St. Mary's	Rnbw 259	1954
Bluebird Of Happiness / Show Me The Merengue	Gotham 318	5/56
Lonely Room / Leona	Gotham 320	1956
Just Suppose / It's Me	Gotham 321	1956
Long Lonely Nights / The Clock	Mnln 102	6/57
Long Lonely Nights / The Clock	Chess 1665	6/57
Teardrops / The Girl Around The Corner	Argo 1000	11/57
Teardrops / The Girl Around The Corner	Chess 1675	11/57
Try The Impossible / Nobody's Home	Casino 452	1958
Try The Impossible / Nobody's Home	UA 123	1958
Why Do I / Glad To Be Here	UA 136	1958
All I Ask Is Love / Maybe You'll Be There	UA 151	11/58

Lee Andrews (with the Hearts)

Just Suppose / Boom	UA 162	3/59
I Wonder / Baby Come Back	Casino 110	1959

A SIDE/B SIDE	LABEL/CAT NO	DATE
The Five Hearts		
Unbelievable / Aunt Jenny	Arcade 107	1959
The Hearts		
It's Unbelievable / On My Honor	Chnc 1057	1960
Lee Andrews (with the Hearts)		
I've Got A Right To Cry / I Miss You So	Swan 4065	1961
A Night Like Tonight / You Gave Me	Swan 4076	1961
P.S. I Love You / I Cried	Swan 4087	1961
Lee Andrews and the Hearts		
Together Again / My Lonely Room	Gowen 1403	1962
I'm Sorry Pillow / Gee But I'm Lonesome	Prkwy 860	1962
The Famous Hearts		
Aisle Of Love / Momma	Guyden 2073	11/62
Lee Andrews (with the Hearts)		
Looking Back / Operator	Prkwy 866	1963
Lee Andrews and the Hearts		
Teardrops / The Girl Around The Corner	Grand 156	1963
Long Lonely Nights / The Clock	Grand 157	1963
Lee Andrews (with the Hearts)		
You You You / Hug-A-Bee	V.I.P. 1601	1965
Lee Andrews and the Hearts		
You're Taking A Long Time Coming Back / Quiet As It's Kept	RCA 8929	8/66
Island Of Love / Never The Less	Crmsn 1009	1968
I've Had It / Little Bird	Crmsn 1015	1968
Cold Grey Dawn / All You Can Do	LstNt 1001	1968
Oh My Love / Can't Do Without You	LstNt 1004	1968
Quiet As It's Kept / Island Of Love	LstNt 1005	1968
Congress Alley		
God Bless The Children / Congress Alley	Avco 4610	1972
God Save America	Avco 4616	1973
Lee Andrews and the Hearts		
Sipping A Cup Of Coffee / Just Suppose (alternate)	Gotham 323	1981
Window Eyes / Long Lonely Nights (alternate)	Gotham 324	1981
I Miss My Baby / Boom (alternate)	Gotham 325	1981

The Aquatones

One of the best things about local talent shows in the 1950s was that they offered the real possibility that a vocal group could be discovered and thus launch a professional career. It was often a booking agent or manager who was out looking for talent. In the case of the teen group known as the Aquatones, it was a record company executive from a small New York label, Fargo Records, who spotted them at a local show and signed them in 1958.

The group formed in 1957 in Valley Stream, Long Island, and consisted of Larry Vannata, Gene McCarthy, David Goddard, and lead singer Lynn Dixon. Lynn had originally aspired to an opera career and had even taken lessons to that end, but the chance for pop success was apparently a greater lure. It was no accident that her vocal prowess dominated the group's pop harmony sound: all their 45 rpm recordings have her soprano mixed far out in front of the bland accompaniment.

Ironically, the fledgling group's debut on Fargo was also Fargo's debut; record number 1001, entitled "You," was released in the early spring of 1958. As could only happen in the '50s, Lynn's sound coupled with a pleasing, tear-jerking ballad brought Fargo and the Aquatones their one and only hit. Surprisingly, the very pop-sounding group and record did better on the R&B charts (number 11) than it did on the pop chart (number 21). The group got the opportunity to perform on the usual circuit of deejay record-hops hosted by such New York luminaries as "Cousin" Bruce Morrow, Peter Tripp, and Alan Fredricks (the first disc jockey in America to play songs officially considered "oldies" back in 1957, when he played rock and roll records from 1954 to 1956). The group also did a variety of TV shows, including those hosted by Alan Freed, Dick Clark, and Dean Martin.

The Aquatones lasted only until 1960, despite numerous concert appearances with the likes of Bobby Darin, THE SHIRELLES, and DANNY AND THE JUNIORS. In all, they recorded eight single releases between 1958 and 1962, two of which were released by Fargo after the group had disbanded. Most of their 16 recordings, including "You," were written by Vannata and Goddard and occasionally McCarthy, but aside from "You" their best effort was a reworking of THE HEARTBEATS' 1956 ballad "Crazy for You" (it had a nice descending line between verses that was vocally and melodically reminiscent of a riff from THE TEDDY BEARS' hit "To Know Him Is to Love Him"). In the early '70s Vannata built a new Aquatones group that included Russ Nagy of the Bellnotes (of "I've Had It" fame on Time Records in 1958) and new lead singer and wife Barbara Lee.

THE AQUATONES

A SIDE/B SIDE	LABEL/CAT NO	DATE
You / She's The One For Me	Fargo 1001	1958
Say You'll Be Mine / So Fine	Fargo 1002	1958
Our First Kiss / The Drive-In	Fargo 1003	1958
My Treasure / My One Desire	Fargo 1005	1959
Every Time / There's A Long, Long Trail	Fargo 1015	1959
Crazy For You / Wanted	Fargo 1016	1961
Say You'll Be Mine / My Treasure	Fargo 1022	1962
My Darling / For You, For You	Fargo 1111	1962

The Avons

The Avons, like many young singing hopefuls from New Jersey in the mid-'50s, longed for the opportunity to burst out of their hallways and on to the recording scene that beckoned from across the Hudson River. Unlike most of the other hallway hopefuls, however, the Avons really *did* have the talent to succeed, and for a while it looked like they would.

Formed in high school in Englewood, New Jersey, Bob Lea (lead) pulled together a collection of classmates that included his two brothers, Bill (baritone) and Wendel (second tenor), along with Curtis Norris (bass) and Ervin Watson (first tenor).

They called themselves the Robins when they formed in 1954, but soon got wind of a West-Coast aggregation who had been using the same moniker on records since 1949. Bill rectified the situation by coming up with a new name. One evening while he was doing his homework on Shakespeare he read about the river Avon in England and the name just popped off the page. The new name was enthusiastically accepted by the other members (who most likely had never heard of the Avon Lady and her cosmetics). The group's dedicated practice sessions quickly led to several school dances. The quintet became well-known in the Englewood area and in 1955 they acquired the services of a local businessman, Edward Prindle, to be their manager. He took the act to Bea Caslon, owner of Hull Records, and they auditioned right in her office. Liking what she heard, she made the Avons the second group signed to her label, the first being the now-legendary HEARTBEATS. The Avons' first release, "Our Love Will Never End," in the fall of 1956, was met with mild local activity. Years later it became a tri-state favorite getting oldies play on the "Time Capsule Show" and Danny Styles's "Kit Cat Club."

Before they could even get their second record released ("Baby," 1957), bass Curtis Norris joined Uncle Sam and was replaced by Franklin Cole. It became apparent that if you sang bass for the Avons you were destined to wind up in the armed forces: Frank Cole went in after their third release ("You Are So Close to Me," 1957) only to be replaced by bass George Coleman, who went army-bound two records later. By then the group had given up trying to keep a bass, and their last two sides for Hull were as a quartet.

Their local recording activity afforded them the opportunity to perform in the New York, New Jersey, Connecticut, and Pennsylvania area, with a stop at the famed Apollo Theater. By 1962, baritone Bill Lea went—you guessed it—into Uncle Sam's organization and was replaced by one Sunny Harley for their last release, "A Girl to Call My Own." Soon after this song's release and subsequent demise, the group broke up without ever having scored a chart single let alone a hit record.

THE AVONS

A SIDE/B SIDE	LABEL/CAT NO	DATE
Our Love Will Never End / I'm Sending an S.O.S	Hull 717	1956
Baby / Bonnie	Hull 722	1957
You Are So Close To Me / Gonna Catch You Nappin'	Hull 726	1958
What Will I Do / Please Come Back To Me	Hull 728	1958
What Love Can Do / On The Island	Hull 731	1959
Whisper / If I Just	Hull 744	1961
The Grass Is Greener On The Other Side / A Girl To Call My Own	Hull 754	1962

Hank Ballard and the Midnighters

Hank Ballard and the Midnighters were an important early rock and roll group that had one of the more colorful careers on record. The group will mainly be remembered for starting the "Annie"

answer-record craze along with a dance fad that for the first time brought parents onto the dance floor gyrating to the same music their kids were enjoying, thus helping to finally legitimize rock and roll. Henry Booth (lead and tenor), Charles Sutton (lead and tenor), Lawson Smith (baritone), and Sonny Woods (bass), with occasional vocal contributions from guitarist/arranger Alonzo Tucker, made up a group called the Royals in Detroit during 1950. Two other local kids who reportedly sang with Smith and Woods before Booth and Sutton settled in were named Levi Stubbs (later the lead of THE FOUR TOPS) and Jackie Wilson (the one and only).

The boys were from Dunbar High School and like most aspiring rhythm and blues groups of the time worked their way into an amateur contest in early 1952 at the Paradise Theatre. They were spotted by King/Federal Records talent scout Johnny Otis, who liked them enough to recommend them to Federal. He also wrote their first single, "Every Beat of My Heart," released in April of 1952. The smoothly sung ballad was overlooked by radio but became a huge hit for GLADYS KNIGHT AND THE PIPS (#6 Pop, #1 R&B) in 1961 after she and her group learned the song from the Royals' recording. The flip, "All Night Long," included the baritone harmonizing of studio guest Wynonie Harris. Other beautiful ballads, usually led by Sutton, went nowhere, including "Moonrise" and "The Shrine of St. Cecilia."

The group's early influence was THE ORIOLES but in 1953, when Lawson Smith left for the army, a new influence entered the scene and joined the group: 16-year-old Ford assembly line worker Hank Ballard. The youngster had come from Bessemer, Alabama, when he was 13 although he was born in Detroit.

The group had seen five of their ballad sides go by the wayside, so to make some money they began touring under a slightly altered name. They became the Five Royales mainly because the real group of that name was on the charts with "Baby, Don't Do It" on Apollo. A quick Apollo court injunction put a stop to their impersonation, however, and the Royals were back to being their hitless selves.

In the early summer of 1953 that changed as Ballard, who had a gospel tinge to his voice, wrote raunchy songs, and loved country music (his big idol before Clyde McPhatter was Gene Autry), came up with "Get It." The single went to number six R&B.

With Hank now singing lead and writing, the emphasis was upbeat, and three singles later "up-beat" became "legendary."

In March 1954 Federal issued a record that became so big it ended the Royals' 10-record career. "Work with Me Annie" charted R&B on April 24, 1954, and began steadily climbing the charts. Now that the Royals were enjoying some belated success they didn't want there to be any confusion with THE FIVE ROYALES (in moments between ecstasy and paranoia, our heroes might have worried that the Five Royales were out masquerading as *them*), so they changed their name to the Midnighters, which is what the label read by the time it reached number one R&B. "Annie" also reached number 22 Pop.

The original title fell somewhere between "Rock with Me Annie" and "Sock It to Me Mary," depending on which story you hear, but whatever "Annie" originally was, she not only was a hit, she launched a new institution called the answer record. No fewer than 21 "Annie"-related recordings, most with the same melody and different lyrics, were issued over the next few years. The Midnighters added fuel to the fire by throwing in a few of their own, compliments of Ballard's magic pen. "Sexy Ways" (#2 R&B), "Annie Had a Baby" (#23 Pop, #1 R&B), "Annie's Aunt Fanny" (#10 R&B), and "Henry's Got Flat Feet (Can't Dance No More)" (#14 R&B) kept the Midnighters busy through 1955. Johnny Otis jumped in, reworking the song into "The Wallflower" for a half black, half Italian teen named Etta James. The song became better known as "Roll with Me Henry." Though rock and roll was becoming a well-known term in white America through a new generation's music, it had for some time been used in the black community as another name for intercourse.

By the time Georgia Gibbs got her hands on "Annie"/"Henry," it had become watered down to "Dance with Me Henry." Both Gibbs and James had number ones with their shots at Henry—Georgia's went Pop and Etta's went R&B. Some of the other colorful "Annies" were "Annie's Back" (Little Richard), "Annie Get Your Yo-Yo" (Little Junior Parker), "Annie Pulled a Humbug" (The Midnights—you can't get closer than that!), "My Name Ain't Annie" (Linda Hayes and THE PLATTERS), and the unforgettable "Annie Kicked the Bucket" (the Nu-Tones). (How widespread was the Annie craze? Well, it was reported that there was a New York maternity boutique called "Annie Had a Baby"!) It seemed everyone but Dick Clark liked "Annie." He thought the record was dirty (as did many radio stations that banned the record) and wouldn't play it or any other Midnighters records. This situation had an interesting effect on dance record history some years later.

Hank and company wailed through another hit in August 1955 ("It's Love Baby," #10 R&B) but then hit a drought. Some excellent singles were either ignored by radio or not promoted by Federal; recordings like "House on the Hill," "Partners for Life," "Open Up the Back Door," and "In the Doorway Crying" never got a public trial. Years before the term "funky" came into vogue, *Billboard's* reviewer knew how to apply it to the Midnighters in his January 14, 1956, observation of "Sweet Mama Do Right" (the flip of "Partners for Life"): "The boys knock off this blues with lots of heart and style, and the side has a good funky sound."

In 1957 Charles Sutton left and Lawson Smith returned. By 1958 Sonny Woods (who had reportedly been a valet for SONNY TIL AND THE ORIOLES prior to his Royals/Midnighters days) had left and been replaced by Norman Thrasher.

King dropped Hank and company in 1958, so Ballard went label shopping with a new demo of a song he'd written called "The Twist," actually a revision of THE DRIFTERS' 1955 hit "What Cha Gonna Do." But whose revision? Doo wop folklore tells us that a spiritual group called the Nightingales offered "The Twist" to THE SPANIELS (they turned it down) months before Hank wrote the song. (The Nightingales reportedly never put their name to the song because it was taboo in the '50s for gospel acts to write let alone record or sing secular music.) Hank has stated that he saw the Midnighters working up a frantic, twisting dance routine on stage and got the idea for "The Twist." He then wrote the song in about 20 minutes. The dance, then, was invented by the Midnighters, not a certain Ernest Evans (but more on him later). Vee-Jay Records heard "The Twist" and turned it down. King Records then picked up the group's option and recorded "The Twist" as the B side to a pretty ballad called "Teardrops on Your Letter."

The act now became Hank Ballard and the Midnighters, and in February 1959 "Teardrops" came out and charted R&B March 16th.

Sometimes the most obvious reason a record is the A side is overlooked. Henry Glover, A&R man for King, wrote "Teardrops on Your Letter," thus ending any debate. But Hank felt "The Twist" was the hit, and even though "Teardrops" was charting and doing well, he and the group kept promoting "The Twist" at their shows. While Hank and the boys were pounding out "The Twist" King issued the Midnighters' rocking version of Wilbert Harrison's "Kansas City," which reached number 16 R&B and number 72 Pop.

Nothing much happened until the Midnighters performed at the Royal Theatre in Baltimore and some kids took the dance over to the Buddy Dean TV show. Dean called Dick Clark to tell him of the excitement "The Twist" was causing among the teens: "Man, you should see the kids over here. They're onto a record called 'The Twist' by Hank Ballard and the Midnighters. They're dancin' and not even touchin'!" Clark, who vividly remembered that Ballard's records were bawdy, didn't even want to hear the song, but Dean sent him a copy anyway. Convinced it was clean, Clark played it on the show, liked the audience response, and invited Hank and company to come on "American Bandstand" and kick off the dance. For some reason the date never came off, so Clark got someone else to record the new dance tune and perform it on the air—an 18-year-old ex-chicken plucker turned singer/impersonator named Ernest Evans, whom Dick renamed Chubby Checker because his wife thought he was a cute version of Fats Domino. Chubby (probably to his lasting chagrin) was not even the first Clark choice; the song was reportedly offered to Freddy Cannon and DANNY AND THE JUNIORS who for various reasons nixed it.

If you don't know what happened then, you weren't on this planet in 1960. Checker appeared on "Bandstand" and his record on Parkway shot through the roof, reaching number one on September 19th and selling millions, but most people aren't aware that Ballard's own version made it to number 28 Pop and number six R&B. This was especially impressive given that he must have lost sales to people who thought they were buying his version but purchased Checker's near sound-alike. (Ballard himself has stated that when he first heard Checker's copy on the radio, he thought it was his own recording. In a sense that's a tribute to Chubby as well.)

Meanwhile, King Records hadn't been wrong about Ballard's A side, "Teardrops": it rose to number four R&B and number 87 Pop.

When the King original of "The Twist" finally hit the charts, the Midnighters' newest single "Finger Poppin' Time" was already there, and the catchy Ballard-penned rocker hit number two R&B and number seven Pop in the summer of 1960.

By 1961 Mr. Checker had gone to number one with "Pony Time," a song written by Don Covay and John Berry (of the Rainbows, Red Robin) with a note-for-note "Oh baby oo eee" bridge right out of a 1954 song called "Sexy Ways"—by the Midnighters.

To Hank's credit he was never bitter about Chubby's success, realizing that Checker's record took his song to heights his label was never able or willing to reach.

When Hank's newest and favorite creation for the Midnighters, "Let's Go, Let's Go, Let's Go" hit the charts in September 1960 and went into the top 40 before "The Twist" and "Finger Poppin' Time" could drop out, the Midnighters became the first recording artists to have three simultaneous singles in the top 40.

"Let's Go" became their biggest hit (#6 Pop, #1 R&B) and was followed by some more country-rock rhythm and wailing gospel that kept the group charting through "The Hoochi, Coochi, Coo" (#23 Pop, #3 R&B), "The Continental Walk" (#33 Pop, #12 R&B), and "The Switch a Roo" (#26 Pop, #3 R&B).

The Midnighters' last of 13 chart records was "Do You Know How to Twist" (#87, February 1962), which was followed by another twist of sorts, "It's Twistin' Time," which was actually "Finger Poppin' Time" with twistin' lyrics.

You can't blame Hank for trying: Chubby was back up to number one for an unprecedented second time in two years with "The Twist" (winter 1961–62). Still, industry people and artists in the '60s knew the genuine article. Appearing in Miami circa 1965, Hank and the Midnighters found all four Beatles watching their show. Afterwards the mop tops jammed with the group backstage.

The hits stopped coming for the Midnighters after 1961 and by the mid-'60s the group had disbanded. Hank re-formed with Walter Miller, Frank Stadford, and Wesley Hargrove, and after performing with the James Brown Revue recorded a few solo sides produced by Brown. He also recorded for Chess, Silver Fox, Polydor, and Stang among others over the late '60s and '70s, dropping out of the music scene from around 1974 to 1982 when he put his own revue together and toured Europe and the U.S.

The current Midnighters are Eddie Stovall, James Dorsey, Eugene Hudson, and Ony Kaye. As of this writing Henry Bernard Ballard and company are still out there living up to the legacy that began more than 40 years ago.

HANK BALLARD AND THE MIDNIGHTERS

A SIDE/B SIDE	LABEL/CAT NO	DATE
The Royals		
Every Beat Of My Heart /		
All Night Long	Fed 12064	4/52
Starting From Tonight /		
I Know I Love You So	Fed 12077	5/52
Moonrise / Fifth St. Blues	Fed 12088	7/52
A Love In My Heart /		
I'll Never Let Her Go	Fed 12098	9/52
Are You Forgetting / What Did I Do	Fed 12113	12/52

A SIDE/B SIDE	LABEL/CAT NO	DATE
The Shrine Of St. Cecilia /		
I Feel So Blue	Fed 12121	4/53
Get It / No It Ain't	Fed 12133	1953
Hey Miss Fine / I Feel That-A-Way	Fed 12150	1953
That's It / Someone Like You	Fed 12160	1/54
Work With Me Annie / Until I Die	Fed 12169	3/54

The Midnighters

A SIDE/B SIDE	LABEL/CAT NO	DATE
Work With Me Annie /		
Sinner's Prayers	Fed 12169	4/54
That Woman / Give It Up	Fed 12177	4/54
Sexy Ways / Don't Say Your		
Last Goodbye	Fed 12185	1954
Annie Had A Baby /		
She's The One	Fed 12195	1954
Annie's Aunt Fanny / Crazy Loving	Fed 12200	10/54
Tell Them / Stingy Little Thing	Fed 12202	1954
Moonrise / She's The One	Fed 12205	1954
Ashamed Of Myself /		
Ring A-Ling A-Ling	Fed 12210	2/55
Why Are We Apart /		
Switchie Witchie Titchie	Fed 12220	4/55
Henry's Got Flat Feet /		
Whatsonever You Do	Fed 12224	1955
It's Love, Baby / Looka Here	Fed 12227	1955
That Woman / Give It Up	Fed 12230	8/55
Rock And Roll Wedding /		
That House On The Hill	Fed 12240	12/55
Don't Change Your Pretty Ways /		
We'll Never Meet Again	Fed 12243	1/56
Partners For Life / Sweet Mama,		
Do Right	Fed 12251	1956
Rock, Granny, Roll /		
Open Up The Back Door	Fed 12260	1956
Tore Up Over You /		
Early One Morning	Fed 12270	1956
I'll Be Home Someday /		
Come On And Get It	Fed 12285	12/56
Let Me Hold Your Hand /		
Ooh Bah Baby	Fed 12288	1/57
E Basta Cosi / In The		
Doorway Crying	Fed 12293	3/57
Is Your Love So Real /		
Oh So Happy	Fed 12299	1957
Let 'Em Roll / What Made You		
Change Your Mind	Fed 12305	1957
Daddy's Little Baby /		
Stay By My Side	Fed 12317	2/58
Baby Please / Ow-Wow-Oo-Wee	Fed 12339	10/58
The Twist / Teardrops On		
Your Letter	Fed 12345	2/59
The Twist / Teardrops On		
Your Letter	King 5171	2/59
Kansas City / I'll Keep You Happy	King 5195	1959
Sugaree / Rain Down Tears	King 5215	1959
House With No Windows /		
Cute Little Ways	King 5245	1959
Never Knew / I Could Love You	King 5275	1959

A SIDE/B SIDE	LABEL/CAT NO	DATE
Look At Little Sister / I Said I		
Wouldn't Beg You	King 5289	1960
Waiting / The Coffee Grind	King 5312	1960
Finger Poppin' Time / I Love You,		
I Love You So-o-o	King 5341	4/60
Let's Go, Let's Go, Let's Go /		
If You'd Forgive Me	King 5400	1960
The Hootchie Cootchie Coo /		
I'm Thinking Of You	King 5430	1960
Let's Go Again / Deep Blue Sea	King 5459	1/61
The Continental Walk /		
What Is This I See	King 5491	1961
The Switch-A-Roo / The Float	King 5510	1961
Nothing But Good /		
Keep On Dancing	King 5535	1961
Big Red Sunset / Can't You		
See I Need A Friend	King 5550	1961
I'm Gonna Miss You /		
Do You Remember	King 5578	1961
Do You Know How To Twist /		
Broadway	King 5593	1962
It's Twistin' Time / Autumn Breeze	King 5601	1962
Good Twistin' Tonight / I'm Young	King 5635	1962
I Want To Thank You / Excuse Me	King 5655	1962
When I Need You / Dreamworld	King 5677	1962
Shakey Mae / I Love And		
Care For You	King 5693	1962
She's The One / Bring Me		
Your Love	King 5703	1962

The Bay Bops

Rarely had a group formed as spontaneously and in such a moment of tension as the Bay Bops of Sheepshead Bay in Brooklyn. Anticipating a group called the Starlighters, the dance crowd at St. Mark's church got a surprise when Danny Zipfel and Barney Zarzana came on stage to announce their group's demise only days earlier. As is typical of teen crowds, this one wouldn't take no for an answer. When Zipfel and Zarzana declined to become an on-the-spot singing duo, two members of the audience, George Taylor, Jr. and Bobby Serrao, asked if they could sing with the remaining Starlighters. A short rehearsal in the men's room and the four were on stage harmonizing to a wildly enthusiastic reception. Even the quartet was surprised at the hard-edged doo wop sound they had so quickly created. So it was that on a night in September 1957 one more vocal group was born.

It took them longer to find a name than a vocal blend; they tossed around countless ideas before

Barney hit upon the Bay Bops. All the hip guys of the '50s would bop down the street (a term that meant strut), and the members were all from Sheepshead Bay. One of Bobby's bops down Emmons Avenue in the Bay was no doubt the inspiration for the new name.

They practiced numerous rock and roll group songs like "My Heart's Desire" (the Wheels) and "Smoke from Your Cigarette" (THE MELLOWS), but unlike most white groups of the time that were trying to sound black, their sound emerged as unadorned white rock and roll doo wop. Whether by chance or design, that quality proved to be the group's legacy.

In 1957, Danny Zipfel talked the Bay Bops into doing an a cappella demo session in New York City. One subway ride and $60 later ($15 apiece), the Bay Bops emerged with three recorded songs from Bell Sound Studios and not a clue about what to do with them. They didn't have to go far to get a professional opinion, however. While they walked out of the studio with demos in hand, a man asked to hear them. Ushered into a nearby office, the boys waited with sweating palms and surging adrenaline as the first strains of "Joannie" came bursting from the record player. The listener turned out to be veteran manager (and later vice president of Warner Brothers Records) Frank Military. He liked "Joannie" enough to sign the group and promptly lined up a recording contract for them with Coral Records.

In March of 1958 the group recorded "Joannie" and "Follow the Rock" with help from Sam "The Man" Taylor on sax and the Dick Hyman trio. An aspiring recording artist named Neil Sedaka did the vocal arrangements (Sedaka was still nine months away from his own first chart hit "The Diary").

Upon the single's release, airplay was split: "Joannie" emerged as the A side even though New York powerhouse disc jockey Alan Freed was pushing "Follow the Rock." By May it was peaking at 58 .on the *Cashbox* top 60 (it never charted on *Billboard*'s top 100) selling about a quarter of a million singles.

The group's sound on these first recordings, though not exactly sparkling or full, was still innovative for a white group in early 1958, placing them on the line between pop and rock/doo wop. The group's strong suit was Danny Zipfel's semi-polished lead vocal. Danny (who preferred to be called Dino) had a sound reminiscent of Jimmy Gallagher, lead of THE PASSIONS, and Vito Picone, lead of THE ELEGANTS. Although Gallagher and

Picone earned greater success, Dino's recordings predated theirs. In fact, the group managed to predate almost all the white rock/doo wop vocal groups. They were among the first to have a chart record and appear on national TV (Steve Allen, Dick Clark, and a Dean Martin Telethon). And only DANNY AND THE JUNIORS' "At the Hop" and THE MELLO-KINGS' "Tonite Tonite" were earlier recording successes, and the Mello-Kings sound was presumed to be black. Given the group's exposure on TV and live with the likes of THE DRIFTERS, THE DEL-VIKINGS, and THE FLAMINGOS, there can be little doubt about their influence on other white vocal groups in general and Brooklyn groups in particular. Many of these aggregations knew each other and often sang with members of the Bay Bops. Had they not succumbed to internal strife, they might have honed their skills into a sound as polished as other Brooklyn groups like the Passions, THE MYSTICS, or THE EARLS.

Coral Records, knowing nothing of the group's problems, released the second single, "My Darling, My Sweet" (originally called "Refreshing" and later cut by the Holidays on Pam) b/w "To the Party." Both sides were from the group's original master sessions in March.

By June 1958, Coral had sent the boys back to Bell Sound to record eight more sides. When the group emerged from the session fighting over who wrote the songs, the end was in sight. The group split into two factions, and when word got back to the label, all efforts to support the record ceased.

The first faction, Zarzana, Serrao, and Taylor, searched in vain for a new lead. The closest they came was when they found former Raven Lou Frazier working at Lundy's seafood restaurant in Brooklyn, but the group lasted only a month since Frazier's preference was for singing standards while the others wanted to do original songs. Zipfel, meanwhile, formed a group that included Bobby Feldman, who later went on to become a member of the Strangeloves "(I Want Candy," #11, 1965) and a cowriter of the ANGELS hit "My Boyfriend's Back" as part of the successful writing/producing team of Feldman, Goldstein, and Gottehrer. Zipfel's group was also short-lived and never recorded. Danny did, however, get a record deal with MGM as a solo artist in 1964. His longstanding rift with Barney Zarzana must have healed by this time as Barney sang backup on Danny's "Hey, Hey Girl" release.

A Bay Bops group ultimately got another recording deal with Coral affiliate Decca Records. This time Barney Zarzana and his three brothers, Sal,

Vinnie, and Michael, formed a new Bay Bops in late 1958, but uncertainty about the assignment of parts ruined the group's chance to record. 21 years later, the second Bay Bops, calling themselves the Zarzana Brothers, recorded a side for an a cappella compilation LP entitled *They All Sang in Brooklyn* on the Crystal Ball label. Also included on the LP were two unreleased demos by the original Bay Bops.

George Taylor, Jr. went on to become a New York City detective while Bobby Serrao became a mechanic for the Sanitation Department. Barney still sings with vocal groups on occasion, while Danny's whereabouts are unknown.

The Blossoms

The Blossoms were probably the most successful unknown group of the '60s. They made a career out of singing backup for scores of artists from Paul Anka to Elvis Presley with a versatility that allowed them to be a choral group one minute (as on Ed Townsend's hit "For Your Love") and a surf sound doo wop group for Jan and Dean's hits the next.

The group started out not as the Blossoms, but as the Dreamers. They were students at Fremont High School in Los Angeles circa 1954 and were discovered by singer Richard Berry at a school talent show. At that time the group consisted of Fanita James, sisters Annette and Nanette Williams, and Gloria Jones. It wasn't long before their natural blend was put to the test on several Richard Berry singles recorded and released in 1954 and 1955 on Flair Records. Though all three releases got local airplay, only their first single "Bye Bye" sold much, and none of the sides ever made the national R&B charts. By late summer 1956, the quartet had their first chance to record on their own. The results were two beautiful R&B ballads, "Since You've Been Gone" and "Do Not Forget," both written by Richard Berry and loaded with blow harmony and falsetto riffs. "Since You've Been Gone" was particularly dynamic and noteworthy in that it was recorded a year before THE BOBBETTES' "Mr. Lee" and THE CHANTELS' "He's Gone," both recognized as forerunners of the girl-group sound. Only THE HEARTS' "Lonely Nights" from March 1955 preceded the Dreamers. They, like the Chantels and Bobbettes, were East Coast groups. To hear the Dreamers one would have thought they emanated from 125th Street in Harlem. They were

in fact brought up listening to West Coast blues and gospel vocalists.

"Since You've Been Gone" never got the support Tiny Flip Records had to offer; the label had its hands full following the success of the Six Teens' "A Casual Look" (#25) with their new release "Far into the Night." They were also preparing to release a recording by Richard Berry and his new male group, the Pharoahs: a Berry-penned tune called "Louie, Louie"—yes, *that* "Louie, Louie."

Though their recordings weren't hits, the Dreamers stirred interest from numerous corners of the music business, garnering the quartet a great deal of backup work. Their first chart record came as backup vocalists with Jessie Belvin on Etta James's November 1955 hit "Good Rockin' Daddy" (#6 R&B). It was only Etta's second chart record in a career that saw her score 30 charters between 1955 and 1978. Her first hit "The Wall Flower" (a revision of HANK BALLARD AND THE MIDNIGHTERS' 1954 number one R&B hit "Work with Me Annie") was recorded with another Los Angeles vocal group known as the Peaches, along with a male call and response by none other than Richard Berry. Considering the success of "The Wall Flower," the Dreamers were lucky to get a chance with Etta, although their talent and steady reliability assured them an eventual shot recording with any number of artists.

It was through vocal coach Eddie Beale that the quartet was brought to their first major label, Capitol Records. Executive Tom Fransend renamed the group the Blossoms. The blossoming, however, was delayed while the group issued three less-than-exciting singles between 1957 and 1958. But they did have another backup hit, this time with newcomer Ed Townsend on "For Your Love" (#13 Pop, #7 R&B) in April 1958.

That year also brought a lineup change: Fanita James attended a wedding and heard 20-year-old Darlene Wright sing. She knew then and there that the gifted Darlene should become the lead of the Blossoms. By 1960, the Williams twins had left and the group was a trio.

Their first "solo" chart record was for the small Challenge label. The Blossoms just barely cracked *Billboard*'s top 100 with "Son in Law" (#79) in May 1961, but neither that tune nor the immediate followups were enough to make the public aware of them. Still, they kept earning a good living doing backup, as on Sam Cooke's hit "Everybody Loves to Cha-Cha-Cha" (#31, 1959) and as Duane Eddy's Rebelettes on "Dance with the Guitar Man" (#12, 1962).

In the summer of 1962, fate stepped in to make the trio the ultimate uncredited group of the '60s. Producer Phil Spector, fresh from a number 13 hit with THE CRYSTALS ("Uptown"), was back in Los Angeles with his newest discovery, "He's a Rebel." Convinced that he possessed a number one hit, he was mortified to learn that the Crystals were reluctant to come to Los Angeles from Brooklyn because they were afraid of flying. Spector knew he couldn't sit on the song—someone else would certainly record it. His partner Lester Sill (who went on to become a legendary music publisher) calmly extolled the virtues of a hot backup group known as the Blossoms. So on July 13 one of the classic rock and roll songs of the '60s was cut with the Blossoms and with vocalist Bobby Sheen singing high tenor. The Blossoms never imagined the record would be released under the name the Crystals. Nor did they guess that by November it would be the number one record in the U.S. and reach number 19 in England. Coincidentally, their one Okeh release under their name was out at the same time, but received no attention.

A few weeks after the release of "Rebel," Darlene Wright was signed by Spector, but she never knew whose name would be on the released records. For example, on August 24 they recorded a "wall of sound" version of the Disney classic "Zip-A-Dee-Doo-Dah." This time, Bobby Sheen sang lead with the Blossoms on backup. When it came out in November the label read Bob B. Soxx and the Blue Jeans. Though the trio continued backing artists as diverse as Doris Day and Duane Eddy, their main claim to "ghostly" chart fame came from Spector's recordings between 1962 and 1964. They began 1963 with a powerhouse hit "He's Sure the Boy I Love" (#11), which once again was credited to the Crystals. In February it was back up the charts as Bob B. Soxx and the Blue Jeans on "Why Do Lovers Break Each Other's Heart?" (#38).

By April "(Today I Met) the Boy I'm Gonna Marry" hit the airwaves; this time half of Darlene's name made the label copy as Spector created a new star named Darlene Love. Darlene Wright didn't seem to mind when the record went to a modest number 39 (modest for Spector), and she herself adopted the new moniker.

Just when it started to become predictable that Darlene or Bobby would lead the Blossoms through a new Spector recording, Darlene's lead was wiped from what would become another Crystals classic. Lala Brooks, second lead of the Crystals, replaced Darlene's vocal on "Da Doo Ron Ron" while all three Blossoms did their usual backup (that's three

Blossoms *including* Darlene, since they'd already recorded the backup track). It went to number three and became the Blossoms' last uncredited—or credited—top 10 record. They finished out the year for Spector with another Bob B. Soxx and Blue Jeans tune and three more Darlene Love singles.

The first, "Wait Till My Bobby Gets Home" (#26), was lyrically reminiscent of THE ANGELS' "My Boyfriend's Back" though gentler and less threatening to the male ego. The next, "A Fine, Fine Boy" (#53), showed some nice vocal work, but it was apparent by now that Spector was more interested in his new find, THE RONETTES, than in developing his backup vocalists into stars even though they had collectively had more chart hits than most groups at that time (nine in one year for Philles Records alone). The fourth Darlene Love (and the Blossoms) single of 1963 was an all-time "killer," probably the most exciting, emotion wrenching Christmas recording ever made, "Christmas Baby Please Come Home" (written by Ellie Greenwich, Jeff Barry, and Phil Spector). It included not only the Blossoms' vocals, but also the Ronettes, the Crystals, and a rumored performance by Cher. It could have been a number one record, but the untimely death of president John F. Kennedy in November 1963 put a shroud over anything not traditionally Christmas for that season.

In 1964, the group, with Jeannie King now in place of Gloria Jones, was introduced to producer Jack Goode by recording artist Jackie DeShannon. Goode brought the trio to an audition for a new TV show called "Shindig," which lead to two years as regulars. They issued one record under the name the Wildcats ("What Are We Gonna Do" in 1964) on Reprise Records, but it wasn't until 1966 that they returned to the recording scene under their own name (again via Reprise) with "Good Good Lovin'," written by Barry Mann (see THE EDSELS) and Cynthia Weil. They released several noncharting singles, including "Deep in My Heart," while singing backup dates for the likes of Bobby Darin, Paul Anka, and Buck Owens.

In December 1967 an executive at Reprise matched their first single "Good Good Lovin'" with their last single "Deep in My Heart" and put out a new record. It went to number 45 on the R&B chart. From 1967 through 1972, the Blossoms put out 10 records on Ode, MGM, Bell, and Lion, most notably covers of the Righteous Brothers' hits "You've Lost that Lovin' Feeling" and "Soul and Inspiration" in 1969. The early '70s took the group away from the studios and on tour with Elvis Presley. Darlene left the group in the '80s, performing first in Las Vegas and then singing in the Jeff Barry soundtrack for the film *The Idol Maker* while doing backup work for Dionne Warwick in 1982. She did "The Darlene Love Music Special" on cable TV, performing old Crystals, Bob B. Soxx, and Darlene Love songs backed up by her sister Edna (see THE HONEY CONE) and Gloria Jones. In 1985 she appeared in Ellie Greenwich's musical *Leader of the Pack*, for which a cast album was released. Darlene ended the '80s with a budding career in film (*Hairspray* and *Lethal Weapon*) and a Columbia album released in 1988.

Fanita James started doing backup for Tom Jones performances in the early '70s but always had a Blossoms group ready to work, the latest incarnation being Fanita, Angela Lewis, and Cynthia Woodard.

In 1989, a Blossoms group released a single under their own name for the first time in 17 years when Fanita and company recorded "Lonely Friday Night" for Bruce Patch's Classic Artists label. The song was reminiscent of THE CHIFFONS' "One Fine Day" but was even more reminiscent of a time when the Blossoms were the premier West Coast hit vocal group—that the public never knew.

THE BLOSSOMS

A SIDE/B SIDE	LABEL/CAT NO	DATE
The Dreamers		
Bye Bye / At Last	Flair 1052	1955
Daddy Daddy / Baby Darling	Flair 1058	1955
Together / Jelly Roll	Flair 1075	1955
Do Not Forget / Since You've Been Gone	Flip 319	1956
The Blossoms		
Move On / He Promised Me	Cap 3822	1957
Little Louie / Have Faith In Me	Cap 3878	1958
Baby Daddy-O / No Other Love	Cap 4072	1958
Son-In-Law / I'll Wait	Chlng 9109	1961
Hard To Get / Write Me A Letter	Chlng 9122	1961
Big Talking Jim / The Search Is Over	'Chlng 9138	1962
I'm In Love / What Makes Love	Okeh 7162	1962
Good, Good Lovin' / That's When The Tears Start	Rprs 0436	1966
My Love, Come Home / Lover Boy	Rprs 0475	1966
Deep Into My Heart / Let Your Love Shine On Me	Rprs 0522	1966
Good Good Lovin' / Deep Into My Heart	Rprs 0639	1967
Stoney End / Wonderful	Ode 101	1967
Wonderful / Cry Like A Baby	Ode 106	1967
Tweedle Dee / You Got Me Hummin'	MGM 13964	1968

A SIDE/B SIDE	LABEL/CAT NO	DATE
You've Lost That Lovin' Feeling / Something So Wrong	Bell 780	1968
Soul And Inspiration / Stand By	Bell 797	1969
Stoney Love / Wonderful	Ode 125	1969
I Ain't Got To Love Nobody Else	Bell 857	1970
One Step Away	Bell 937	1970
It's All Up To You / Touchdown	Lion 108	1972
Cherish What Is Dear To You / Grandma's Hands	Lion 125	1972

The Bobbettes

In an era dominated by male groups, it took an unlikely quintet of public school teens to show the world a female group could succeed. Via their monster hit "Mr. Lee," the Bobbettes became the first female group to have both a top 10 hit (#6), and a number one R&B record.

It all started as a pastime for eight girls, ranging in age from 9 to 11, in New York's Harlem. The schoolmates began singing in the glee club of P.S. 109 in 1955. Christening themselves the Harlem Queens, they began doing local amateur nights over the next two years while the octet shrank down to five members. They performed at the Apollo Theatre's famed amateur night, and though they didn't win, they did broaden their already growing following. Soon after, the Queens piqued the interest of manager James Dailey, who took on the group but was adamant about a name change. "The Harlem Queens" seemed too raunchy for five girls in their early teens. So it was that in late 1956 Reather Dixon (lead), Emma Pought (second lead), Janice Pought (soprano), Helen Gathers (alto), and Laura Webb (tenor) became the Bobbettes.

Dailey got the group a contract with Atlantic Records and they were in the studio recording by the end of February 1957. All four of their first recordings were group compositions, no mean feat for such young performers (between 11 and 13 years old at the time) and it wasn't a fluke. Group members went on to write 10 of their first 18 recorded songs.

The group had written a few songs up to this point and one was the legendary "Mr. Lee," who was actually a teacher of some of the Bobbettes at P.S. 109. That song was the group's first single, released in June 1957. Although the lyric of "Mr. Lee" spoke glowingly of how their collective hearts "ached for him," the original lyrics were not the least bit flattering. The girls had an immense dislike of the educator and the song was originally written as a put-down. At the request of Atlantic's A&R executives the group had revised the lyric to make it more commercial (or possibly less controversial). Be that as it may, "Mr. Lee" became the best-known public school teacher in America when the record went top 10 in July 1957. The record also spent four weeks at number one on the R&B chart at the same time. Lyrical repetition may have been the hit formula here: "Mr. Lee," their "favorite teacher," was sung by the lead and backup vocalists 69 times in the song.

Their next four singles, between October 1957 and summer 1959, failed to nudge even the top 100, while the girls continued doing the ever-popular "one-dayers"—theater bookings—since they were too young to do club dates or "one-nighters." They also did some uncredited background singing for Clyde McPhatter and Ivory Joe Hunter.

Their last recording session for Atlantic, in February 1959, included the sequel to "Mr. Lee" entitled "I Shot Mr. Lee." This time the girls got to say what they really felt about him, but Atlantic shelved it, opting instead for a release of "You Are My Sweetheart" b/w "Don't Say Goodnight." A nice but undistinguished doo wop ballad, it failed to chart.

The Bobbettes then left Atlantic to sign with Triple X. Their first release? A recording of "I Shot Mr. Lee." It shot up the charts, forcing Atlantic to release their original version. Poetic justice prevailed as the little label's superior recording reached number 52 on the national charts before falling off. This incident more than likely helped to institute the so-called "five-year clause" in recording artist contrasts, in which an artist could not re-record a song for another company for a minimum of five years in order to avoid potential competition.

The quintet's next 45 was a remake of the Billy Ward and THE DOMINOES single "Have Mercy, Baby," with a rip-off of "Dance with Me, Henry" on the B side ("Dance with Me, Georgie"). Both sides made the pop charts, with the former reaching number 66 and the latter peaking at number 95. In the fall of 1960, despite the three Triple X chart singles on just two releases, the group found itself on the Gallant label for one release, a remake of the early '50s Eddie Fisher hit "Oh, My Papa." It was then on to the End label for a reworking of the old standard "Teach Me Tonight."

Their last chart single (as a featured act) came in the form of an answer song to Chris Kenner's "I Like It Like That" titled "I Don't Like It Like That"

(#72). It was issued on Gone Records (like End, a George Goldner label) for some inexplicable reason, beginning an odyssey that found the group on six labels in five years (1961 to 1966). Their manager seems to have been making deals, having the group cut a few sides, and moving on to new and hopefully better deals before the release of the previous label's recordings. Their longest stay in one place following the Atlantic days was on Diamond Records, where they cut six singles. Before the release of their first Diamond single, however, the group sang backup for Johnny Thunder on "Loop De Loop" (#4), thus giving the girls their last chart record and second top 10 hit. Too bad they didn't get credit for it.

Helen Gathers left the group before the Diamond signing, so only the quartet is heard on those 12 sides. One notable exception is the second single, "Close Your Eyes," a beautiful 1963 remake of the Five Keys classic, with backup work by former Epic Records group the Chateaus.

In 1964 the girls recorded "Love that Bomb" for the motion picture *Dr. Strangelove* while continuing their string of unsuccessful releases for Diamond. In the spring of 1966, the group signed with their first major label, RCA, but the results stayed the same.

Five years passed before their next and last recording opportunity, on Mayhew Records (1971–1974). The Bobbettes remained together through the '70s oldies revival, touring both the U.S. and England. If the Bobbettes never released another single, they would still go down in rock and roll history as the first female group to have a top 10 hit. And if history is kind, they will also be remembered as one of the better female groups.

THE BOBBETTES

A SIDE/B SIDE	LABEL/CAT NO	DATE
Mr. Lee / Look At The Stars	Atln 1144	1957
Speedy / Come-A Come-A	Atln 1159	1957
Zoomy / Rock And Ree-Ah-Zole	Atln 1181	1958
The Dream / Um Bow Bow	Atln 1194	1958
Don't Say Goodnight / You Are My Sweetheart	Atln 2027	1959
I Shot Mr. Lee / Untrue Love	Atln 2069	1960
I Shot Mr. Lee / Billy	TrplX 104	1960
Dance With Me Georgie / Have Mercy Baby	TrplX 106	1960
I Cried / Oh My Papa	Gall 1006	1960
Teach Me Tonight / Mr. Johnny Q.	End 1093	1961
I Don't Like It Like That, Part 1 / Part 2	End 1095	1961

A SIDE/B SIDE	LABEL/CAT NO	DATE
I Don't Like It Like That /		
Mr. Johnny Q.	Gone 5112	1961
Oh Mein Papa / Dance With		
Me Georgie	King 5490	1961
Looking For A Lover /		
Are You Satisfied	King 5551	1961
My Dearest / I'm Stepping		
Out Tonight	King 5623	1962
Over There / Loneliness	Jubi 5427	1962
A Broken Heart / Mama Papa	Jubi 5442	1962
Teddy / Row, Row, Row	Diamond 133	1962
Close Your Eyes / Somebody Bad		
Stole De Wedding Bell	Diamond 142	1963
My Mama Said / Sandman	Diamond 156	1964
In Paradise / I'm Climbing		
A Mountain	Diamond 166	1964
You Ain't Seen Nothing Yet /		
I'm Climbing A Mountain	Diamond 181	1965
Teddy / Love Is Blind	Diamond 189	1965
Having Fun / I've Gotta Face		
The World	RCA 8832	1966
It's All Over / Happy Go Lucky	RCA 8983	1966
That's A Bad Thing To Know /		
All In Your Mind	Myhw 712297	1971
Tighten Up Your Own Home /		
Looking For A New Love	Myhw 712237	1972
It Won't Work Out / Good Man	Myhw 712861	1974

The Bonnie Sisters

Many are the singers who, after succeeding or failing, have gone on to different careers. But it has rarely happened the other way around, with groups forming after their members have succeeded at non-music professions. Yet that is precisely how the Bonnie Sisters came together.

All three, Jean, Sylvia, and Pat (reportedly not related) were professional nurses living in New York and working at New York's Bellevue Hospital in the mid-1950s. The mental image of three nurses singing in the operating room may be a bit far-fetched, but the trio did practice in the hospital vicinity, and those rehearsals led to an appearance on Arthur Godfrey's nationally televised talent scout show in the fall of 1955.

When they won the contest the singing nurses came to the attention of Rainbow Records exec Eddie Heller, who signed the group immediately. Rainbow was an R&B label with product by THE CLOVERS, THE FIVE CROWNS, and LEE ANDREWS AND THE HEARTS, but that didn't stop Heller from going the pop route with the Bonnies. Though it was an established practice for white acts to cover black records that looked like they were going to be hits, the Bonnie Sisters went out on a limb and recorded the B side of a black group's current single. The song was "Cry Baby," the flip of the Scarlets' (later THE FIVE SATINS) "True Love" released earlier in 1955. It was also the song they won the Godfrey Show contest with. Mickey "Guitar" Baker (a year away from becoming half of Mickey and Sylvia of "Love Is Strange" fame) and his orchestra backed the girls on the tune.

Rainbow released it in November 1955 with a seasonal flip side, "I Saw Mommy Cha-Cha-Cha with You-Know-Who." Heller probably figured that if the top side failed, he'd at least get some Christmas mileage out of it. He needn't have worried since "Cry Baby" charted on February 18, 1956, rising to number 18.

The three medical missionaries resigned from Bellevue to dedicate their lives to music, but fate intervened when their second release, "Wandering Heart," shipped in April and wandered back just as fast. Following one more 1956 release titled "Confess" and some occasional performances as on Ted Steele's TV show, the Bellevue brunettes were back on the sidelines.

At least Jean, Sylvia, and Pat didn't have to worry about starting a new career.

The Bop Chords

In the mid-1950s, vocal groups formed usually for one (or more) of four reasons: 1) they loved to sing; 2) they wanted to be stars; 3) they wanted to emulate the stars they idolized; or 4) they had nothing better to do. The only group to record out of jealousy is probably the Bop Chords.

Formed in Mrs. Martin's building on 115th Street in Harlem in 1955, the same building that spawned members of the Ladders (Vest), THE CHANNELS (Whirlin Disc), and the Willows (Melba), the Bop Chords were Ernest Harriston (lead), William Dailey (first tenor), Ken "Butch" Hamilton (second tenor), Leon Ivey (bass), and Morris "Mickey" Smarr (baritone). All had sung with others in the neighborhood and Hamilton had even recorded with the Five Wings in early 1955 on their "Tributes to the Late Johnny Ace—'Johnny Has Gone' b/w 'Johnny's Still Singing' " on King Records. He had also sung with an unrecorded group by the name of the Holidays—the first vocal group for then-bass Ben E. King (see THE DRIFTERS).

They were the slickest-looking group in the neighborhood. When the Bop Chords bopped down to the corner of Lenox Avenue and 115th Street to sing, they could do no wrong with the local ladies. That is, until THE WILLOWS one-upped the Chords by recording the hit "Church Bells May Ring" in March 1956 and the females began to fall all over *them*. Only then did the Bop Chords direct themselves toward recording, and it took the help of a rival to make it happen. Freddie Donovan (bass of the Willows) took Harriston and company to Danny Robinson's new label, Holiday Records. One of their own practice songs became their first single: "Castle in the Sky" brought the group instant local fame in late spring 1956 and pulled the heartstrings of the neighborhood ladies once again.

"Castle" was a terrific doo wop mid-tempo rocker replete with an attention-getting chime intro, Harriston's smoky-smooth lead, a wailing sax instrumental, and a bridge made for stereo with a call and response between the basses' "bo pos" and the group's "bop bahs."

A week of performances at the Apollo Theater that summer enhanced the group's image among the female fans, and their second single, "When I Woke Up This Morning," added to the aura with another tri-state charter. In the '50s you did not have to have a national hit to have success in the microcosm of your own local backyard. And New York was one of the biggest backyards around. But the Bop Chords obviously weren't ready for it. The group (which reportedly had sold over 100,000 records each of "Castle" and "When I Woke") saw little of the profits and began allowing their young egos to clash over costumes, rehearsal times, and other trivialities. Soon after the second release, first tenor William Dailey and baritone Mickey Smarr left to be replaced by Skip Boyd (baritone) and the group's first female member, Peggy Jones (first tenor). Their last single was "So Why" in 1957, a strong uptempo rocker that saw little attention. By the end of 1957 the group had split up, though Harriston continued to record as a background vocalist for Shep and the Limelites. He also did a single as Ernie Johnson called "We Need Love" in 1962 on the Asnes Label.

14 years after the breakup, a quartet of Bop Chords reemerged featuring Ernie on lead, Ken on second tenor, Skip on baritone, and Leon on bass, as the oldies revival was in full swing. The group performed at various local venues but never again recorded.

Both "Castle" and "When I Woke Up" are now considered East Coast doo wop standards and are played on oldies radio stations alongside national hits of the time.

Although their career was brief, if the Bop Chords hadn't had such an affinity for the ladies, these fine recordings would never have been made at all.

The Buccaneers

Among R&B vocal groups of the freewheeling '50s, the rules were simple: Find some original songs, find someone who liked you singing those songs, and hope they had a contact to a record label so you could get an audition. In the case of the Buccaneers, however, there were no original songs and no record company. The Buccaneers are probably the only rhythm and blues group that was ever scouted by white college kids for a label that didn't exist.

It happened one night in north Philadelphia in November 1952. The group was performing some cover tunes in a local bar. Two teenagers from Temple University walked in, heard them perform, and felt compelled to sign the group. Trouble was, Jerry Halperin and Ed Krensel had neither a record label nor any experience in the music business. What they did have was a wealth of enthusiasm and what they felt was a working knowledge of early '50s rhythm and blues music, learned from the WHAT and WDAS rhythm and blues radio shows and from hunting for records in downtown Philly.

They somehow convinced the Buccaneers (lead Ernest "Sonny" Smith, tenors Richard Gregory and Julius Robinson, and bass Donald Marshall) that they could have a hit together, and the group soon began rehearsing a song called "Dear Ruth" written by Halperin for his girlfriend.

The song, along with the B side "Fine Brown Frame," was recorded at Reco-Art Studios in downtown Philly with instrumental backing by the Joe Whalen Trio on side A and Matthew Childs' Drifters on side B. Halperin and Krensel still didn't have an office, but that didn't stop them from releasing the Buccaneers single on their newly christened Southern label in January 1953. It was the same week that THE FLAMINGOS joined Chance Records. By the end of February "Dear Ruth" was number 10 in Philadelphia on *Billboard*'s regional chart, and the Temple University entrepreneurs were established in their office on North Broad Street. The

Buccaneers' first recording did well in Philly and received some airplay in Los Angeles, New York, and the Baltimore-Washington area. They sold over 3,000 records. According to a *Billboard* magazine blurb in April 1953, Rainbow Records thought enough of the recording's activity to purchase the master for national distribution. But it turned out that more than local support was needed to succeed on a national level: the amateurish performance and recording relegated the record to instant oblivion. Halperin still believed in the group, however, and decided that since his partner was army-bound anyway he might as well try to get a bigger company interested. That larger entity turned out to be George Goldner's Rama label.

The group was signed in August and recorded four songs in New York, two of which, "You Did Me Wrong" and "Come Back My Love," were written by Halperin and Buccaneers lead Sonny Smith. The quality of production and harmony was markedly better than on the previous efforts.

Although a picture and caption printed in the September 12, 1953, issue of *Cashbox* indicated that "You Did Me Wrong" was to be the A side of a single, "In the Mission of St. Augustine" became the push side. Wrong move: THE ORIOLES released their own highly popular version at approximately the same time, and the Buccaneers record didn't even have a local chance.

"The Stars Will Remember" b/w "Come Back My Love" became the Buccaneers' last release; like its predecessor, it failed to stir any excitement.

Three unsuccessful singles ushered in the group's early retirement, leaving them with the distinction of having recorded Southern Records' one and only release. A further distinction is the fact that their recordings are more sought after now than they were decades ago. The combination of rarity, raw R&B doo wop harmony, and Julius Robinson's floating falsetto has justified high prices on the collectors' market for "In the Mission" and "The Stars Will Remember."

The Cadets

The Cadets had the most intriguing dual careers in rock and roll history. From 1955 to 1957 they recorded and performed as both the Cadets and THE JACKS, each group with its own hits and each with a distinctly different sound and musical direction.

Formed in 1954 in Los Angeles, the group had Aaron Collins (lead and second tenor), Will "Dub"

Jones (lead and bass), Willie Davis (first tenor), Lloyd McCraw (baritone and group manager), and Ted Taylor (first tenor).

A tremendously versatile bunch that could sing jump tunes, rhythm and blues, ballads, calypso songs, and rock and roll, they signed with Modern Records in 1955 under the name the Jacks. Modern's Joe Bihari renamed them the Cadets and made them Modern's house group for the sole purpose of covering other R&B artists' songs. With Modern's strong national distribution, Bihari knew he could record a song that was starting to move in a version by another act on a smaller label and still beat it to most of the marketplace. Possessing a keen ear for local hits that could go national, Bihari had his machine primed and ready.

In April 1955 a cover of Nappy Brown's "Don't Be Angry" became the Cadets' first single and it did well, out-selling Nappy's Savoy recording released three weeks earlier. A calypso-flavored cover of the Marigolds' "Rolling Stone" was next and it, too, outdid its Excello Records competition. At about the same time, the Cadets put out their third single, "I Cried," and they backed vocalist Dolly Cooper on her release of "My Man," but neither attracted much attention.

In the summer of 1955, the Cadets got their most unusual assignment while trying to take advantage of the "Annie" craze that had begun 16 months earlier with HANK BALLARD AND THE MIDNIGHTERS' release of "Work with Me Annie." Bihari must have believed there was still life in the old girl when he had the quintet record "Annie Met Henry." It was the twelfth Annie record in a year, joining some of the more outrageous ones like "Annie Had a Baby" and "Annie's Aunt Fannie" (both by the Midnighters on Federal) and the Nutones' "Annie Kicked the Bucket." Market saturation had apparently set in: the record's rhythm-ballad flip "So Will I" got the higher profile.

The Cadets' next Modern release was an exciting uptempo revision of THE DRIFTERS' 1955 R&B hit (#2) "What'cha Gonna Do" titled "Do You Wanna Rock," with Aaron Collins doing his best Clyde McPhatter impression spiced with a dash of Little Richard. (If you want to hear who else "borrowed" from the Drifters' "What'cha Gonna Do," listen to Hank Ballard or Chubby Checker's "The Twist.") Though the Drifters were considered a sacred cow, the Cadets definitely out-rocked them on this recording. But out-rocking didn't translate into out-selling.

By February 1956 the Cadets had covered both Elvis Presley and THE WILLOWS on one single:

"Heartbreak Hotel" b/w "Church Bells May Ring." The March 31st issue of *Billboard* commented: "The group covers the Willows' version of the tune with a free swinging happy job. The tune is strong and some of the loot should come this way." In reference to "Heartbreak," the reviewer wrote, "The Presley disc will grab most of the interest on the tune, but this Cadets' version stacks up okay in its league with an effective deep down solo." Needless to say, Elvis's record slaughtered the Cadets', but the only R&B version of "Heartbreak" on the market did garner some good sales for the group.

While all this cloning was going on, Aaron Collins brought his two sisters, Rosie and Betty, to Joe Bihari with an original song he and Willie Davis had written. Bihari liked the act and the song, christening the girls the Teen Queens; by the spring Aaron's little sisters had the number two R&B record in America and number 14 on the pop chart. The song was "Eddie My Love."

Now it was the Cadets' turn. Prentice Moreland replaced Ted Taylor (although he only recorded with the group) and Lloyd McCraw left to be replaced by former Flairs baritone Thomas "Pete" Fox after their next single. Their June 1956 cover (what else?) of the Jayhawks' novelty rocker "Stranded in the Jungle" made the trip up the charts that Bihari had envisioned since signing the group seven singles before. "Stranded" went to number four R&B and number 15 on the pop listing. But he couldn't have predicted that it would later be viewed as a rock and roll classic. Though most cover groups and artists were looked upon with disdain by music lovers of the '50s and '60s (especially the white acts that covered the usually superior versions by black acts), the Cadets were so good that their covers were often equal to if not better than the original. In the case of "Stranded," their version was far superior to the Jayhawks' rough and ragged original (as the Jacks, their interpretation of "Why Don't You Write Me" was also preferable to the Feathers' prototype).

In September, two oldies surfaced as the next Cadets single: "Dancin' Dan," which was actually "Sixty-Minute Man" by the Dominoes (Federal, 1951), and "I Got Loaded" by Peppermint Harris (Alladin, 1951). The Dub Jones-led two-sider was a disappointment sales-wise, and the follow-up, "I'll Be Spinning" (originally number 10 in 1957 by Johnnie and Joe—Johnnie was Johnnie Richardson, member of the Jaynettes of "Sally Go Round the Roses" fame in 1963) b/w "Fools Rush In" (from the number one recording by Glenn Miller in 1940), also failed to spur the buying public.

Their last record of 1956, "Love Bandit" elicited the same lackluster response even though it was a rollicking cut reminiscent of "Stranded in the Jungle." Its five-note sax intro later showed up in the DUBS' intro to their classic "Could This Be Magic" a year later. Loaded with lots of rock and roll excitement, "Love Bandit" named half the outlaws and sheriffs of the Old West before the Cadets faded into the sunset and the record faded out of circulation, signalling a diminishing return for Modern's investment. Still, Modern issued their first LP (and one of the first rhythm and blues group LPs) in February 1957 under the title *Rockin' 'n' Reelin'*, which included most of their previous A and B sides. A May 1957 release of "Pretty Evey" listed the Cadets as the artists when in fact it was Aaron singing lead with another obscure house group. Their last Modern single was "Ring Chimes" in December 1957. Davis and Collins formed a new Cadets after Dub Jones left to become the bass of THE COASTERS in 1958, at that time at the peak of their success. The new Cadets were Thomas Miller, baritone, and George Hollis, bass, both of the Flairs (ABC). After two singles in 1960 the Cadets (actually half Cadets, half Flairs) were ready to call it a career, but in name only; with Randolph Jones subbing for Hollis on bass, the quartet became the Peppers in 1961 singing "One More Chance" on Ensign.

In 1961, with Hollis back on bass, the group became the Flares on Felsted and their third single for the label, the energetic dance record "Foot Stomping—Part I," went to number 25 (#20 R&B). The group then switched to Press Records for seven more singles that went nowhere.

In 1962 Davis and ex-cadet McCraw teamed to form the Thor-ables (Titanic), but their two singles were behind-the-times ballads with little chance for play.

Ted Taylor, having gone solo in 1956 on a variety of labels, finally hit the R&B charts in November 1965 with "Stay Away from My Baby" on Okeh. On October 22, 1988, Ted and his wife died in a car accident while touring in Louisiana. As of the early '90s, Aaron had a shoe repair shop in Los Angeles, Willie was running a car upholstery business, and Dub Jones was singing with Billy Guy's Coasters.

The Cadets were put in an unusual position by their producers but they were creatively up to the task. The ultimate tribute to this versatile vocal combo is that a recording act covered by the Cadets was in effect getting a left-handed compliment. If they had something good, the Cadets usually made it better.

THE CADETS

A SIDE/B SIDE	LABEL/CAT NO	DATE
Don't Be Angry / I Cried	Modern 956	4/55
Rollin' Stone /		
Fine Lookin' Woman	Modern 960	6/55
Mary Lou / Don't Think I Will		
(Young Jesse)	Modern 961	7/55
I Cried / Fine Lookin' Woman	Modern 963	7/55
Ay La Ba / My Man		
(Dolly Cooper)	Modern 965	11/55
So Will I / Annie Met Henry	Modern 969	1955
Do You Wanna Rock /		
If It Is Wrong	Modern 971	11/56
Church Bells May Ring /		
Heartbreak Hotel	Modern 985	2/56
Stranded In The Jungle /		
I Want You	Modern 994	6/56
Dancin' Dan / I Got Loaded	Modern 1000	9/56
Fools Rush In / I'll Be Spinning	Modern 1006	1956
Heaven Help Me /		
Love Bandit	Modern 1012	12/56
You Belong To Me /		
Wiggie Wiggie Woo	Modern 1017	1957
Pretty Evey / Rum Jamaica Rum	Modern 1019	5/57
Hands Across The Table /		
Love Can Do Most Anything	Modern 1024	8/57
Ring Chimes / Baby Ya Know	Modern 1026	12/57
I'm Looking For A Job /		
One More Chance	Shrwd 211	1960
Car Crash / Don't	Jan-Lar	1960

The Peppers

A Place In My Heart /		
One More Chance	Ensign 1706	1961

The Thora-bles

Our Love Song / Get That Bread	Titnc 1001	1962
My Reckless Heart /		
Batman And Robin	Titnc 1001	1962

The Flares (The Cadets)

Loving You /		
Hotcha-cha-cha Brown	Felsted 8604	1961
Jump and Bump / What Do You		
Want If You Don't Want Love	Felsted 8607	1961
Foot Stomping Part 1 /		
Foot Stomping Part 2	Felsted 8624	11/61
Rock And Roll Heaven Part 1 /		
Rock And Roll Heaven Part 2	Press 2800	1962
Truck and Trailer /		
Doing The Hully Gully	Press 2802	3/62
Mad House / Make It Be Me	Press 2803	1962
Yon We Go / Do It With Me	Press 2807	1963
Hand Clappin' / Shimmy		
and Stomp	Press 2808	1963
The Monkey Walk /		
Do It If You Wanna	Press 2810	1963
Write A Song About Me / I Didn't		
Lose A Doggone Thing	Press 2814	1964

The Cadillacs

One of the first vocal groups to emphasize choreography, the Cadillacs were a mid-'50s marvel to behold. Born in 1953 on the streets of New York City (7th and 8th Avenues near 131st Street), the rhythm and blues singers originally called themselves the Carnations, and each member wore one in his lapel to bring home the point.

The original quartet consisted of Earl Carroll, Bobby Phillips, Cub Gaining, and LaVerne Drake. Their "battle of the groups" shows at St. Mark's Church readied them for the annual Public School 43 talent show. It was there that FIVE CROWNS member Lover Patterson saw the group and recommended they meet Esther Navarro, a lady who was both a manager of artists and a songwriting secretary for the Shaw Booking Agency. By the time the group arrived for their audition, "creative differences" had eliminated Gaining and added James "Poppa" Clark (also of the Five Crowns) and Johnny "Gus" Willingham. Navarro liked the Carnations but not their name. The inspiration for a new one came from some other musicians. A group of Asbury Park, New Jersey, vocalists called the Vibranaires came to sign with Navarro; she felt that they, too, had an undesirable tag. While looking through books of birds for an idea one of the members saw a pink Cadillac drive by and mentioned it. Soon the room was abuzz with the idea of using that for the name and Navarro instantly liked it. The Vibranaires went home thinking they would now be the Cadillacs. Little did they realize the songwriting secretary had other plans: she christened the Carnations the Cadillacs, took them to Josie Records, and had them on the radio within four weeks with a first single titled "Gloria," in July 1954.

The first of the so-called "car" groups, the Cadillacs were followed by a series of automobile-named vocal acts like THE EDSELS, the Ramblers, THE CAPRIS, the Lincolns, THE EL DORADOS—in total, almost as many as there were bird groups in the early '50s.

A classic New York-style ballad, "Gloria" opens a cappella with lead Earl Carroll's repetition of the name sounding distant then closer until the bass chimes in with four notes leading to the strongest "oohs" this side of THE MOONGLOWS. The vocals are so attention-grabbing that a tinkling piano background isn't really noticed until near the end of the first verse. The Cadillacs never dreamed that this recording would end up being the measure by which every East Coast would-be doo wop group for the next 30 years would judge their harmonizing abilities. It became the favorite practice song of street-corner groups and was probably sung by more people than had ever owned an original copy of its July 1954 single. The label showed Navarro as a writer, but there seems to have been some theft of Leon Rene's 1948 MILLS BROTHERS hit of the same name.

Their second A side, released in November 1954, was a ballad called "Wishing Well." Though not in a class with "Gloria," it was an effective song held together by the group's strong blend and Earl Carroll's distinctive interpretation and warm talking bridge.

Soon after this release the quintet experienced the first of its 18 personnel changes from 1954 to 1970. Earl Wade (formerly of the CRYSTALS) and Charles "Buddy" Brooks replaced Clark and Willingham. These changes made the group stronger: Wade was a terrific lead on both jump tunes and ballads.

Their next single had both. The ballad "Sympathy" was released in January 1955 coupled with the Cadillacs' first uptempo A side, "No Chance." While Earl Carroll warned "If his girl made a fool of him, he'd have to put her down," Jesse Powell smoked with a searing sax solo and the rest of the Cadillacs chanted contagiously.

But the contagion was not yet leading to widespread popularity. As the group approached their fourth single, they knew the road to success could be a long one and decided that, apart from their sound, the more professional they looked and acted the longer they'd last. Giving free reign to their zany personalities, the Cadillacs honed their dance and performance skills in small downtown clubs. They solidified an image as a bunch of hip, tough street guys via "Down the Road," the June 1955 follow-up to "No Chance." By the fall of 1955 "the crazy Cadillacs" (a description justified by their onstage antics) found themselves poised for bigger things thanks to a song whose origin has become blurred through the passing of time. Some say Earl Carroll (known as Speedy to his friends) wrote it about himself. Others claim that Esther Navarro finally wrote one that she didn't lift from someone else. The truth is, neither originated the song ultimately called "Speedoo." In the spring of 1955 the Cadillacs were sitting in the audience at the Apollo Theater while the Regals were rocking onstage with a Russell-Cornelius original, "Got the Water Boiling Baby." Anyone who gets a chance to hear this classic jump tune will know where the melody of

"Speedoo" came from. The Regals were also the first rhythm and blues vocal act to be choreographed by Cholly Atkins.

The Cadillacs' immortal "Speedoo" hit the streets in October 1955 and by December 10th had breached the national charts, rising to number 17 (#3 R&B). So extensive was its appeal that Speedy Carroll found himself changing his nickname permanently to Speedo.

The group's natural dancing talents helped make them highly competitive, but their ace in the hole was the tutelage of Charles Atkinson (Cholly Atkins). Destined to be the man who put the dance step in the Motown machine, from Smokey Robinson and the MIRACLES to the SUPREMES, Cholly was hired shortly before Christmas of 1955 to mold the Cadillacs' dance steps into choreographed routines. The singers were attentive pupils and showed off their freshly tuned skills at Alan Freed's Christmas Show at the Academy of Music in New York, their first big performance. From there it was off across the nation in the legendary barnstorming package tours that included the likes of Ray Charles, Fats Domino, and THE TURBANS. Wearing their matching white jackets, black pants, and white shoes, the group dazzled their audiences, not realizing that they were enjoying the peak of their popularity.

Before "Speedoo" could fall from the charts, Josie released another great rocker, "Zoom," around March 1956. It never even charted.

In May 1956 the group made two changes. First, James (J. R.) Bailey (of THE CRICKETS and Velvetones) joined, replacing Drake. Second, the group released "Woe Is Me," a mid-tempo blues-turned-pop concoction with a big-band horn sound. A more sophisticated style was emerging from the Cadillacs, and their November release, "The Girl I Love," took them further in this direction, no doubt a disappointment for the fans of their raucous jump sides. Even their Christmas recording of "Rudolph the Red-Nosed Reindeer" seemed overly controlled for a group that one year before would have rocked the halls with "Speedoo" energy. "Reindeer" became only the second of nine singles to get national attention (#11 R&B). With the pop sounds not working, the Cadillacs reverted to jump-rock with the Chuck Willis goodie "Sugar Sugar" (*not* the ARCHIES recording). Why it was unsuccessful is beyond comprehension: it was as upbeat a rock and roll rave-up as one could find in the mid-'50s.

In the spring of 1957, a typical music business event was followed by a less typical one. The Cadillacs split up. But then two new groups emerged *both* called the Cadillacs and both recording on Josie. The new Cadillacs consisted of J. R. Bailey, Bobby Spencer (of the HARPTONES on Rama and the Crickets on Jay Dee), Bill Lindsey (of the Starlings on Josie and the Twilighters on MGM) and Champ Rollow. Their first release, "My Girlfriend" (May 1957), was a courageous one. Though the tune was melodic, vibrant, and full of harmony, there was possible madness in the decision to release a rock record that was a cappella except for a semi-audible stand-up bass and hand claps. Only collectors know what the masses missed.

Meanwhile, the remaining Original Cadillacs (according to the label) of Carroll, Wade, Phillips, and Brooks saw their single, the beautiful ballad "Hurry Home" (the very next release on Josie after the new Cadillacs single), take the same route to the doo wop graveyard as "My Girlfriend." The other side, "Lucy," was a COASTERS-styled rocker. One more release (a failed cover of the HOLLYWOOD FLAMES' "Buzz-Buzz-Buzz") and the group returned to near-original form as Carroll, Wade, and Phillips joined with Bailey and new member Caddy Spencer for the appropriately titled "Speedo Is Back" in March 1958.

The Cadillacs then seemingly decided if you can't lick 'em, copy 'em, and from such great thinking hits often emerge. Right out of the Coasters textbook, "Peek-A-Boo" had a light comical lyric and a rollicking rhythm that brought the Cadillacs their last hit, reaching number 28 Pop and number 20 R&B in early 1959.

The rest of 1959 found the group trying to recapture that song's success to no avail. Carroll left when his lead spot began floating between Spencer and Bailey. He joined Howard Guyton's group as Speedo and the Pearls for a June 1959 release "Who You Gonna Kiss?" In 1960 he went out to build a new Caddy with Roland Martinez (of the Vocaleers and the SOLITAIRES), Kirk Davis, and bass Ronnie Bright (of the VALENTINES and bass on the Johnny Cymbal hit "Mr. Bass Man," 1963).

Several singles and transient members later, the new decade's version of the Cadillacs emerged on Mercury Records with Carroll, Spencer, Martinez, and Milton Love and Reggie Barnes of the Solitaires. In effect, Mercury paid for the Cadillacs, and three-fifths of the group were the Solitaires!

By 1961 the revolving-door car company had moved over to Mercury's Smash affiliate with an interesting new lineup of Carroll, Martinez, Curtis Williams and Ray Brewster (both of the PENGUINS and the Hollywood Flames), and Irving Lee Gail (of the original Miracles on Fury and the Vocaltones on

Apollo). To spice the mix further, their late summer 1961 mid-tempo recording, "What You Get," also had the Ray Charles Singers, a Spanish-flavored trumpet solo by Doc Severinson, Clyde McPhatterized vocals, and a bridge suspiciously similar to that of Clyde's 1958 hit "A Lover's Question." With all that, the record made the R&B charts at number 30 and then disappeared.

Soon after, Speedo packed his Cadillac and drove over to sing with the act his group had been borrowing from, the Coasters. To honor his arrival, the Coasters' March 1964 single featured Earl on "Speedo's Back in Town." Josie, meanwhile, had been blissfully continuing to issue unreleased less-than-vintage Cadillac cuts (of both groups) right up to the end of 1963.

The firm of Baily, Spencer, Brewster, and Martinez, all former Cadillacs at one time or another, signed up with Capitol in 1963 for two undistinguished singles. During that same year, Bailey found time to pair up with original Caddies Brooks and Phillips along with Billy Prophet and lead singer Eugene Pitt (both of THE JIVE FIVE) for one magical record as the Jive Five on "Rain," a beautiful ballad worthy of either group. 1964 rang in with an amalgam of Solitaires in Cadillacs clothing as Brewster, Bobby Baylor, Fred Barksdale, and lead singer Milton Love (all late of the Solitaires) released a single of "Fool."

Entering the '70s, the last Cadillacs single came from the contingent of Bailey, Phillips, Spencer, and Leroy Binns of THE CHARTS. Despite the socially relevant title "Deep in the Heart of the Ghetto," it couldn't bring the group deep enough into the heart of the new age. With the addition of Steven Brown and the deletion of Phillips, the half Cadillacs, half Charts continued to perform through the decade. In 1979 THE EARLS (Earl "Speedo" Carroll and Earl Wade, that is) along with Phillips and Johnny Brown (of THE FIVE SATINS and New York City) gathered together for a Subaru commercial. Three fourths of that assemblage (along with Gary K. Lewis) were still together in the early '90s performing with distinction and keeping alive the tradition of a great rock and roll group. A new standard in singing and dancing had been set when the Cadillacs drove into town.

THE CADILLACS

A SIDE/B SIDE	LABEL/CAT NO	DATE
Gloria / I Wonder Why	Josie 765	7/54
Wishing Well / I Want To Know About Love	Josie 769	11/54

A SIDE/B SIDE	LABEL/CAT NO	DATE
Sympathy / No Chance	Josie 773	1/55
Down The Road / Window Lady	Josie 778	6/55
Speedo / Let Me Explain	Josie 785	10/55
Zoom / You Are	Josie 792	3/56
Betty My Love / Woe Is Me	Josie 798	5/56
The Girl I Love / All I Need	Josie 805	10/56
Shock-A-Doo / Rudolph The Red-Nosed Reindeer	Josie 807	11/56
Sugar-Sugar / About That Gal Named Lou	Josie 812	2/57
My Girlfriend / Broken Heart	Josie 820	5/57

The Original Cadillacs

Lucy / Hurry Home	Josie 821	6/57
Buzz-Buzz-Buzz / Yea Yea Baby	Josie 829	11/57

Jessie Powell and the Caddies

Ain't You Gonna / Turnpike	Josie 834	2/58

The Cadillacs

Speedo Is Back / A Looka Here	Josie 836	3/58
I Want To Know / Holy Smoke Baby	Josie 842	7/58
Peek A Boo / Oh, Oh, Lolita	Josie 846	10/58
Jay Walker / Copy Cat	Josie 857	2/59
Please, Mr. Johnson / Cool It Fool	Josie 861	4/59
Romeo / Always My Darling	Josie 866	7/59
Bad Dan McGoon / Dumbell	Josie 870	9/59

Speedo and the Original Cadillacs

It's Love / Tell Me Today	Josie 876	1960
That's Why / The Boogie Man	Josie 883	1960
Thrill Me So / I'm Willing	Merc 71738	11/60
You Are To Blame / What You Bet	Smash 1712	8/61

Bobby Ray and the Cadillacs

Groovy Groovy Love / White Gardenia	Cap 4825	8/62
La Bomba / I Saw You	Cap 4935	2/63
I'll Never Let You Go	Josie 915	11/63

Ray Brewster and the Cadillacs

Fool / The Right Kind Of Lovin'	Arctic 101	1964

The Capris
(NEW YORK)

A music business variation of the old adage "If at first you don't succeed . . ." is "If at first your record doesn't succeed, put it out again." The group to whom that adage most accurately applies is the Capris. Theirs is probably the only record of the rock era to be released over three different years on three different labels before becoming a hit.

The group formed in the Ozone Park section of Queens, New York, and its members included Nick Santa Maria (a.k.a. Nick Santo, lead), Mike Mincelli (first tenor), Vinnie Narcardo (baritone), Frank Reina (second tenor), and John Cassese (bass). Vinnie, Mike, and John all went to John Adams High School, while Nick was a student at Woodrow Wilson and Frank attended Franklin K. Lane. The distance between schools confined the group's practice sessions to street corners in the areas of Lefferts Boulevard and 135th Avenue and John's basement.

They originally called themselves the Supremes but soon changed to the Capris. It is often thought their name came from the island of Capri as the boys were all Italian, but Nick confirms that he named the group after a car model that was out the year the group formed (1957). The Capris were all around 15 years of age at the time and had never heard of the Philadelphia CAPRIS, a 1954 black group on Gotham Records. By coincidence, the first song Nick ever wrote (in 1957) was entitled "God Only Knows," the same title the other Capris had out as their first release. In fact, Nick didn't learn of his group's forebears until 1961 when his mother brought their record home after purchasing what she thought was a recording of her son's group and song.

The quintet was influenced by such songs as "A Thousand Miles Away" (THE HEARTBEATS), "My Juanita" (THE CRESTS), and "One Summer Night" (THE DANLEERS) as well as groups like DION AND THE BELMONTS, THE FLAMINGOS, LITTLE ANTHONY AND THE IMPERIALS, and THE CADILLACS. Nick himself felt a great affinity for Clyde McPhatter (of THE DRIFTERS) and James Sheppard (lead of THE HEARTBEATS) and began writing songs derivative of the black group ballad tradition. The Capris performed songs by these groups at school dances and churches such as St. Fortunatas.

During that time the group performed with other acts who would later go on to varying degrees of success: THE BOB KNIGHT FOUR, THE CHIMES, THE FIVE DISCS, and THE ADMIRATIONS, the latter three all from the Cityline section of Queens.

During the fall of 1958 they ran across an ad by two would-be record producers looking for recording artists. The Capris attended an audition and sang Nick's original ballad "There's a Moon Out Tonight." (Nick remembers another artist auditioning that day as being a likeable but strange fellow with a ukelele named Tiny Tim.)

Shortly thereafter they found themselves in Bell Sound Studios in New York City cutting "Moon" along with a song entitled "Indian Girl." The producers took the two sides to Planet Records and in the fall of 1958 "There's a Moon Out Tonight" was released. To say the record got no response would be an understatement. It became such an instant obscurity that an original copy (of which only a few hundred were pressed) is currently valued at $150. A pity, too, since it was an excellent record with a memorable hook and a distinctive five-part "ooh" following each verse's opening line. And the ending had a unique effect not heard up to that time: instead of chiming from bass to falsetto on a word or two, the Capris reversed it, chiming *down* from falsetto to bass. The group would sing "There's a" in harmony, and Nick would break into falsetto singing "moon out tonight," followed by Mike, Frank, and Vinnie echoing and descending on the same words; then John the bass would sing "There's a" as the whole group closed with one more extended "moon out tonight." This effective ending was further enhanced by each member singing his part just slightly lower than that of the preceding member.

Mike got married, Nick enlisted in the army, and the Capris disbanded. End of story? Normally yes, but fate in the form of an obsessive record collector interceded. Jerry Greene worked at Time Square Records, an oldies shop below ground leading to the midtown New York subway. An indication of Jerry's fanaticism was the fact that he agreed to work at the store in exchange for records (not dollars) at the equivalent of a dollar an hour since the proprietor, Irving "Slim" Rose, couldn't afford to pay him.

In 1960 a customer brought in a copy of "There's a Moon Out Tonight" for credit against more expensive records in the store. This was a unique practice Jerry had devised to get collectors to bring in hard-to-find records so he could resell them. Greene gave the customer 50¢ credit for the Capris single (which he'd never heard before) and brought it to Allen Fredericks' "Night Train" radio show. Fredericks played it, mentioning that Times Square Records would give a dollar credit for a copy of it. Instead of getting copies of the record, Jerry received almost a hundred calls asking to buy the single. Two weeks later a friend of Greene's called to tell him he had just bought 10 copies directly from Planet Records.

The young entrepreneur saw a good thing evolving and with three other collectors chipped in and bought 100 copies from Planet and sold them to Slim Rose for a tidy profit. They sold out in about a

week and Jerry repeated the buy-and-sell formula. When he returned to Planet for a third try the owner told him all the records were gone but he'd sell Jerry's cartel the masters for $200. The investing collectors bought the masters but passed up purchasing the publishing rights for $10 more, because they felt they'd spent all they could. Jerry then formed Lost Nite Records with his pals, pressed 330 copies on red plastic vinyl and gave a few to disc jockeys. Within a week the record was on the air and more orders were coming in than the fledgling label could handle. Not wanting to lose a potential hit, Greene turned the record over to Hy Weiss at Old Town Records for distribution.

In the fall of 1960 (almost two years after the Capris originally recorded it) group members got wind of their new release. Mike, now driving a bus, came home just in time to get a call from John exclaiming that the record was on WINS (a New York radio station) and deejay Murray the K was playing it! Sure enough, Mike tuned in to hear the quintet sounding better on radio than he could imagine. No one believed the song could be a hit on Lost Nite, but when Old Town got involved, the record hit the charts in the first week of 1961 and stayed there for 14 weeks.

It won New Record of the Night on Murray the K's show but lost out in the weekly competition to THE SHIRELLES' new single "Will You Love Me Tomorrow." Strangely, up to this point no one actually owned the recording of "There's a Moon Out Tonight;" the recording studio and musicians were never paid until Hy Weiss coughed up the money upon the record's chart success (three years and three labels after its 1958 recording).

The group now re-formed and Hy Weiss, not wanting to lose track of his budding stars, assigned a manager named Charles Merenstein to work with them. (Actually Merenstein's duties were more like a baby-sitter's; his real profession up to that time had been a job as a pretzel salesman.) By February 27 "Moon" was the number three record in the country, displacing the Shirelles' hold on that same number on the previous week.

For all its airplay, however, the song is reported to have sold only about 160,000 copies during its chart run. Since then it's sold three to four times that.

The group's first major gig was a show at the Regal Theatre in Chicago early in 1961. By April, the five Italian lads from Queens were playing the Apollo with James Brown and Etta James. In March, Old Town released their second single, "Some People Think," before "Moon" was even off the charts. The Capris' first single initially netted the individual members about $265 each. When "Some People Think" stalled at radio, Old Town flipped over the beautiful ballad with its intricate modulation in favor of "Where I Fell in Love," a formula ballad with hints of "There's a Moon Out Tonight." It reached number 74 in April but died off shortly thereafter. Still, two chart records in two shots gave the Capris a chance at the premier performance gig of the '50s and '60s, the Easter Holiday Show at the Brooklyn Paramount Theatre alongside Johnny Mathis, Jackie Wilson, THE MARCELS, the Shirelles, and THE MIRACLES, among others.

The Capris also played Murray the K's and Bruce Morrow's shows and began practicing at Hy Weiss's office for future recordings. A young singer/writer used to hang out there and occasionally chimed in while also trying to interest the group in recording some of his songs. It was too bad for the group that they didn't, because the young songwriter was named Paul Simon.

The group released another original ballad in the late spring ("Tears in My Eyes") that never charted. In September, they tried again with "Girl in My Dreams," a ballad that spent one week nationally at number 92 before failing. The group continued to work, even doing a 1961 behind-the-curtain backup for Dion on a Clay Cole TV appearance.

By 1962, the Queens quintet had signed to Mr. Peeke Records and tried to capitalize on the limbo craze with their first uptempo A side, "Limbo." It lasted one week at number 99 and was the last Capris chart record. It was also their last new record for 20 years; Nick left the group in 1963 to become a New York City policeman working the Midtown Division and then the 32nd Division in Harlem.

Frank took over lead as the group toured with the Clay Cole Revue. By 1965 Vinnie (baritone) and John (bass) were gone, replaced by John Apostle on bass and Tony Dano on baritone. In 1982 Nick came back as lead to do an LP for Ambient Sound Records entitled *There's a Moon Out Again.* Tommy Ferrara (late of THE DEL-SATINS) replaced Apostle, and the Capris recorded a marvelous 1980s album with glowing overtones of their 1960 sound. The highlights included "There's a Moon Out Again" and "Guardian Angel" (originally by the Selections) along with a cross section of songs from THE CADILLACS ("You Are") to John Lennon ("Imagine"). The crown jewel, however, was Nick Santo's original entitled "Morse Code of Love," soon released as a single. (Two years later THE MANHATTAN TRANSFER recorded "Morse Code of Love" under the title "Baby Come Back to Me.") Though Ambient Sound was distributed by Columbia, it never got the big company's support for the record, yet a phenomenal thing happened. Because of the tune's '60s doo wop sound and contagious hook, oldies stations started picking it up thinking it was a hot oldie they'd overlooked; in coming years the record would chart on many major nostalgia stations' yearly lists of favorites, alongside "In the Still of the Night" (THE FIVE SATINS) and "I Only Have Eyes for You" (the Flamingos). Based on the exposure of "Morse Code," the group began performing at more shows in the tri-state area and beyond than they ever had when "Moon" was out. "Morse Code" eventually became the number one requested "oldie" in Pittsburgh, Boston, and Philadelphia—even though it was a new record.

The group continued to perform into the '90s though each member had forged a separate career during preceding decades. Of the original members, first tenor Mike Mincelli still drives a schoolbus, second tenor Frank Reina is a traffic forwarder at Kennedy Airport, baritone Vinnie Narcardo is in the moving business, bass John Cassese owns a company making hair pieces, and lead Nick Santo is retired from the 112th Street Forest Hills Division of the New York City Police Department.

The Capris were one of the better white doo wop East Coast harmony groups of the late '50s/early '60s. A fitting tribute to the group is that their first fan, Jerry Greene, saw fit some 21 years later to take all their Old Town sides and create the Capris' first LP on his Collectibles label. More than 10 years after the LP's release, it's still available and selling.

THE CAPRIS (New York)

A SIDE/B SIDE	LABEL/CAT NO	DATE
There's A Moon Out Tonight / Indian Girl	Plnt 1010,11	1958
There's A Moon Out Tonight / Indian Girl	LstNt 101	1960
There's A Moon Out Tonight / Indian Girl	OldTn 1094	12/60
Where I Fell In Love / Some People Think	OldTn 1099	3/61
Tears In My Eyes / Why Do I Cry	OldTn 1103	1961
Girl In My Dreams / My Island In The Sun	OldTn 1107	9/61
There's A Moon Out Tonight / Indian Girl	Trmrs 101	1961
Morse Code Of Love	AmbiS 02697	1982

The Capris
(PHILADELPHIA)

The Capris were a teen group with raw, untrained street harmony whose records now sound even older than they really are. Not to be confused with the white CAPRIS of "There's a Moon Out Tonight" fame, these Capris were a black quintet from West and South Philadelphia who came together in 1953, well before their New York counterparts.

The 15-to-16-year-olds were Charlie Stroud (lead), Harrison Scott (first tenor), Eddie Warner (second tenor), Ruben Wright (baritone), and Bobby Smart (bass). When Stroud decided to jump ship, the Capris went looking for a new lead. In June 1954 the group was doing a show as a foursome at the Haddington Recreational Center on 57th Street and Vine when they met the lead singer of a local girl group, the Lovettes. Thinking that a female lead would distinguish them from the army of all-male groups on the scene, they asked 14-year-old Renee Hinton to join and she agreed. Ruben Wright wanted a "car" group identity, so he came up with the name the Capris. When it was unanimously accepted, the teen quintet went about the task of rehearsing, mostly at Renee's house on 62nd and Callahill since she had a piano. With Ruben on piano, Bobby playing bass, Harrison on sax, and Eddie on drums, the Capris' rehearsals were rarely a cappella affairs. The group, however, never played on their actual sessions or in live performances.

Heavily influenced by THE CLOVERS (though Renee's favorites were THE PLATTERS), the group developed a widely voiced harmony style in which each part could be identified relatively easily.

Prior to Renee's joining, the boys had met a Mr. Sid Goldstein, who had arranged a record deal with Gotham Records and become their manager. Before the group could record, Stroud had left and Renee found herself joining a group that was to be in a New York studio within two days. They quickly wrote a song titled "God Only Knows" to go with the five they already knew, and recorded six songs that June including "Too Poor to Love," "Let's Linger Awhile," and "That's What You're Doin' to Me" (THE DOMINOES), which became the B side of the August release "God Only Knows."

With only a piano accompaniment, Renee's little-girl voice led the Capris through the pretty ballad while Bobby's bass droned against the group's high-tenor harmonies, all of which made for an unusual, almost primitive sound.

Philadelphia radio began playing "God" and it became a local hit. Outside of Philadelphia, however, it received little attention. The group did only a few live performances though Renee remembers doing a show with LEE ANDREWS AND THE HEARTS and Charlie and Ray (on Broad Street) soon after "God" came out. She was so shy and nervous that she spent the entire time in the dressing room, and the boys had to come backstage and physically take her out to perform.

In the fall of 1954 Eddie, Ruben, and Bobby joined the air force, and Harrison went on the road with a band. Although Renee had offers to sing with other groups she chose instead to wait for the guys to return on leave. They did in late 1954, and the group cut the A side for their second single, "It Was Moonglow," another Philly-styled piano-only ballad that became an almost immediate collector's item. Their last Gotham single, "It's a Miracle," followed "Moonglow's" path to obscurity.

Renee finally went back to sing with the Lovettes (who now called themselves the Laraes), doing shows at roller-skating rinks.

In 1958 the boys returned from the armed forces, picked up Fred Hale to replace the touring Harrison Scott, and with Renee once again on lead, recorded "My Weakness" for Gotham affiliate 20th Century. Their best record production-wise, this 1960 release also showed that they seemed to be maturing musically, even though the harmonies were more conventional than on their earlier efforts. But the record never made a dent in the marketplace; their career was over as most members (except for Eddie and Renee) lost interest. During the early '60s' first oldies revival, the Capris' records had a certain mystique as little was known about the group. The B side of their first single contributed to the mystery since Renee had mistakenly read a lyric sheet intended for a male lead, that included the line "Lord, won't you tell me why I love that woman so." This mistake and the eerie quality of their harmonies helped make Capris singles prized collectors' items.

In 1987, disc jockey Charlie Horner hosted an oldies show at the Black Museum in which Renee sang Capris songs backed by THE CASTELLES.

Eddie died in 1987, Ruben continues to play piano in clubs around Philly, Fred works for the post office, and Renee, the once-shy 14-year-old who wouldn't come out of her dressing room, now sings with three different church choirs in Philadelphia.

THE CAPRIS (Philadelphia)

A SIDE/B SIDE	LABEL/CAT NO	DATE
God Only Knows / That's What You're Doing To Me	Gotham 304	8/54
It Was Moonglow / Too Poor To Love	Gotham 306	1955
It's A Miracle / Let's Linger Awhile	Gotham 308	1955
My Weakness / Yes, My Baby, Please	20th 1201	1960

The Cap-Tans

If patience is a virtue, Harmon Bethea would by all standards be a saint. The young vocalist started performing professionally in 1956, and 10 groups, 10 name changes, and 22 years later finally managed to score a hit.

After World War II Harmon attended Washington Junior College of Music and joined a gospel group known as the Progressive Four, managed by Lillian Claiborne (who is mentioned frequently in this book; she seemed to manage just about everyone who sang in the Washington, D.C., area).

A few years later Miss Claiborne picked up another group from the Danewood area of Washington calling themselves the Buddies. They consisted of Sherman Buckner (lead), Floyd Bennett (first tenor), Alfred Slaughter (second tenor), and Lester Fountain (baritone).

Convincing Bethea that switching to secular material was a good career move, Claiborne turned the Buddies into a quintet with his addition in 1950. They renamed the group the Cap-Tans and recorded their first single for Claiborne's own D.C. label, released in July of that year. Sherman sang lead, doing his best Bill Kenny (THE INK SPOTS) imitation on a pretty ballad called "I'm So Crazy for Love" written by baritone Lester Fountain. The smooth background harmony lay right on the border between MILLS BROTHERS/Ink Spots pop and the R&B stylings of THE ORIOLES and RAVENS. After some local airplay the single was sold to Dot Records, a company with larger distribution capabilities.

Fountain's song was covered by the Ravens in a beautiful version the same year. This became a regular occurrence since Cap-Tans songs fell just short of rhythm and blues as done by the group, leaving the door open for full-fledged R&B readings by others. Their next single, "Chief, Turn the Hose on Me" (December 1950), became an R&B

rocker titled "Call a Doctor" for THE CROWS in 1953, and the Crows got writing credit for it. "Crazy 'Bout My Honey Dip," the flip of their first single, was covered by the Saigons as "Honey Gee" on Dootone in 1955.

Claiborne continued to produce the Cap-Tans and sell their masters to other companies, so the act was never signed to a record label. After two more singles were leased to Gotham Records of Philadelphia in 1951 Fountain departed to fulfill his commitment to the service. Ray Reader came in for their next set of "traveling masters" which went to Coral in New York for a December 1951 release. Both sides were pleasing ballads that saw some sales, but national attention remained out of reach. The group then split up, as Bethea returned to gospel with a new group known first as the Progressivaires and by 1954 as the Octaves.

But in 1958 it was back to rhythm and blues for Bethea and a new collection of Cap-Tans, which he first called the L'Cap-Tans (perhaps hoping to attract the Latin record buyers). The new cast included Lester Britton (lead), Richard Stewart (first tenor), Elmo Anderson (second tenor), and Bethea (bass and lead), with Francis Henry on guitar. Their first and only Hollywood Records release, "The Bells Ring Out," was a strong ballad that would have had a better chance two years earlier. The flip side showed them stealing their own property: it was a new version of "Call a Doctor." In 1959 "Baby Jim" Belt was added to the group, and they recorded "Say Yes," another past-its-prime ballad for D.C. Records, subsequently sold to Savoy. The A side, "Homework," was a ROBINS/COASTERS-styled R&B jump tune with a talking bass that was their most commercial side to date.

From here on the group changed members faster than an auctioneer could speak. By the time they made it to Anna Records as the Cap-Tans in 1960 (four labels after their Savoy release in 1959) the group was Bethea, Belt, "Tippie" Hubbard, and "Toy" Walton, the latter two fated for membership in Harold Lucas's CLOVERS within a year.

In 1968, Bethea's latest collection of Cap-Tans, desperate for industry attention, came up with a promotional idea inspired by the Lone Ranger: Harmon put on a black mask and the group became Masked Man and the Captans. By late 1968, John Hood (tenor), Paul Williams (baritone), Tyrone Gray (bass), and Tonto's sidekick Bethea on lead became Maskman and the Agents signed with Dynamo Records, distributed by New York's Musicor. Their second single in the fall of that same year, "One Eye Open," was the record Bethea had been waiting for those 22 years. It ascended the *Billboard* R&B chart on Pearl Harbor Day (December 7th) and went as high as number 20. A further measure of satisfaction occurred when the single spent a week on the Pop charts. Their next single ("My Wife, My Dog, My Cat") also charted R&B (#22) and Pop (#95) two months before Woodstock (June 1969) and kept the group working well into the '70s.

THE CAP-TANS

A SIDE/B SIDE	LABEL/CAT NO	DATE
The Cap-Tans		
(Paul Chapman featured)		
You'll Always Be My Sweetheart /		
Coo-Coo Jug-Jug	DC 8054	7/50
The Cap-Tans		
I'm So Crazy For Love /		
Crazy 'Bout My Honey Dip	Dot 1009	9/50
With All My Love / Chief Turn The		
Hose On Me	Dot 1018	12/50
My, My, Ain't She Pretty /		
Never Be Lonely	Gotham 233	1951
Yes / Waiting At The Station	Gotham 268	1951
Asking / Who Can I Turn To	Coral 65071	12/51
With All My Love /		
I'm So Crazy For Love	Dot 15114	11/53
L'Cap-Tans		
The Bells Ring Out / Call a Doctor	Hlywd 1092	1958
L'Cap-Tans with the Go Boys		
Homework / Say Yes	DC 0416	1959
L'Cap-Tans		
Homework / Say Yes	Savoy 1567	1959
Bethea and the Cap-Tans		
You Better Mind /		
I Wanna Make Love	Sabu 501	10/63
Whenever I Look At You /		
Round The Rocket	Sabu 103	10/63
Cap-Tans		
I'm Afraid / Tight Skirts	Anna 1122	1960
Bob Marshall's Crystals and		
Jerry Holland with the Cap-Tans		
Big Bite of the Blues / Ain't No Big		
Thing (inst.)	DC 0433	1962
Maskman and the Agents		
There'll Be Some Changes /		
Never Would've Made It	Gamma 674	1968
Maskman and Agents		
There'll Be Some Changes /		
Never Would've Made It	Dynamo 118	1968
One Eye Open / Y'All	Dynamo 125	1968

A SIDE/B SIDE	LABEL/CAT NO	DATE
My Wife, My Dog, My Cat /		
Love Bandito	Dynamo 131	1969
Get Away Dreams /		
I Wouldn't Come Back	Dynamo 136	1969
Stand Up Part 2	Vigor 707	1970
The Maskman		
(featuring Harmon Bethea)		
Prices and Crisis / Prices and		
Crisis (The Maskman's Band)	Jan Jan 804	1974

The Cardinals

In the early to mid-'50s there was a proliferation of rhythm and blues vocal groups. Many had good all-around ability, some were especially good with a slow song, but only a few were considered consummate balladeers. The Cardinals were in that elite class. They would probably be remembered as the best ballad act to come out of Baltimore if that city hadn't also happened to be the home of the legendary ORIOLES.

The Cardinals' career began in 1946 (one year ahead of that other bird group) as Leon Hardy and Merredith Brothers convinced Donald Johnson to join them in harmony on the corner of Gay Street and Forest. Donald drafted his friend Ernie Warren to round out a quartet and the new group on the block became the Mellotones. They did the usual round of Baltimore bars and nightclubs for experience, singing the songs of black and white pop groups like THE FOUR TUNES, THE INK SPOTS, and THE AMES BROTHERS. They picked up a fifth member, Jack Aydelotte, when he and they were separately scheduled to perform on a local TV talent show ("The Major Baumgartner Show"). They never got on the air as the show ran overtime, but thanks to the booking they now had five members including an accompanist (Jack also played guitar).

The years passed and the Mellotones' sound became mellower. A record contract came their way with the help of record store owner Sam Azrael. With group member Donald Johnson working in the store (Super Music Record Shop) for years, Azrael had had plenty of exposure to the crooners. When Herb Abramson, cofounder of Atlantic Records, passed through Baltimore in 1951 on a talent search, Azrael made sure that he gave the act an audition, and it's reported the group left the shop that very night as the newest artists on Atlantic.

In March 1951 the group came to New York, cutting four sides for their first release and simultaneously becoming the Cardinals (Atlantic was apparently aware of another Mellotones group already recording for Columbia since 1950 and decided to rename their own artists). The singing order on this historic first session had Ernie on lead, Merredith and Jack as tenors, Donald on baritone, and Leon as bass. "Shouldn't I Know" was a very pretty ballad not too far afield from "It's Too Soon to Know," the Orioles' 1948 R&B hit (#1) that the Mellotones at one time performed. The Cardinals composition was written by Merredith, but in a maneuver that was typical of the music business at the time, store owner Azrael (now Cardinals manager) wound up listed as a cowriter. It took "Shouldn't" five months from its release to make the *Billboard* Best Seller R&B chart at number seven in October 1951, a success that moved the Baltimore balladeers up to the top notches of the performance ladder. Now they were able to play the Apollo in New York, the Earle Theatre in Philadelphia, and the Palace in New Orleans alongside Lowell Fulsom, Bull Moose Jackson, and Lil Green.

Their next session of five songs, recorded on October 6th, included "Under a Blanket of Blue," "The Wheel of Fortune," and their second single "I'll Always Love You," another ballad that featured Ernie's strong lead ably supported by the warbling Cardinals. The flip was a cover of the Tampa Red (actually Hudson "Woodbridge" Whittaker of Smithville, Georgia) number seven blues outing, "Pretty Baby Blues." The Cardinals' two-sider was issued in November 1951 while Tampa Red's recording charted on October 27th.

The circumstances surrounding the release of the third single showed how a group could take advantage of a cover song battle to sell records in its own market. In February–March 1951, various versions of "The Wheel of Fortune" were pop hits for Kay Starr (#1), Bobby Wayne (#6), the Bell Sisters (#10), and Sunny Gale (#13). (This could only happen in America in the '50s!) Enter Atlantic's foresighted production people who had cut the song in October 1950 with the Cardinals. They released this R&B version—the *only* R&B version—and the outcome was a number six R&B record all to themselves.

Right after the release of "Wheel" in February 1951, Ernie was drafted and replaced by Leander Tarver. The new member led the group through their next single, "The Bump," released the first week of August 1952. An early "We Want to Teach You a Dance" type slow shuffle, it's inconceivable that the writers of THE DIAMONDS' 1958 "The Stroll" (#4) didn't listen to "The Bump" before creating their own dance tune.

Toward the end of 1952 Tarver left and James Brown (no, not *that* one) joined. Ernie returned on leave from the military just in time to record "You Are My Only Love" and three other tunes on January 13, 1953. (With Brown still in the lineup, this session benefited from six very good voices.)

The group had not had a single in five months and it was beginning to appear that Atlantic was either losing interest or waiting for Ernie to return full-time from the army. This is at least one possible explanation for the release of only two singles in two years. They were "You Are My Only Love" (released the fourth week of May 1953) and "Under a Blanket of Blue" (released the third week of April 1954 and recorded nearly two-and-a-half years earlier). Neither ballad succeeded in getting any attention. The failure of "Under a Blanket" was particularly disappointing given its beautiful reworking of the 1933 hit by Florence Case with Don Bestor and his orchestra. Ernie rejoined the group full-time in March 1954, but the septet wasn't brought in to record until January 18, 1955 (two years and five days after their last session). The primary yield of this four-song date was the Chuck Willis-penned "The Door Is Still Open (To My Heart)," which was issued the fourth week of February.

A stunning vocal interpretation of a deceptively simple melody gave the Cardinals their biggest hit as "Door" reached top 10 R&B Best Seller and number seven Jukebox for a total of 13 weeks. *Billboard* R&B charts later listed it as the 43rd best seller of 1955. (The flip side, "Miserlou," a hit for Harry James in 1941, was probably the first R&B vocal group record to use an oboe solo in the instrumental.) The Cardinals found 1955 to be their most productive year as they played such top-flight one-nighters as the second edition of the Rock and Roll Show at the Philadelphia Arena with Bill Haley and the Comets, THE RAVENS, and THE NUTMEGS, on June 24th. They also did the Pop R&B Show tour through the Midwest and the South with Sarah Vaughan, THE MOONGLOWS, Red Prysock, and Muddy Waters, among others; Alan Freed's Labor Day week-long show at the Paramount Theatre in Brooklyn with THE HARPTONES, Chuck Berry, Tony Bennett, Nappy Brown, the Moonglows, and the Nutmegs; and Buddy Johnson's (see THE CHANTERS) big Rock & Roll Show with THE SPANIELS, THE FOUR FELLOWS, and Chuck Berry. They finished up the year in fine style headlining at the Howard Theatre in Washington with Lloyd Price and THE TURBANS on December 30th in the "Happy New Year Review."

The Cardinals' records at this time were some of their best though not their most popular. In July 1955 Atlantic released the group's eighth single and first up-tempo A side, "Come Back My Love," a song issued five months earlier by Rama Records artists the Wrens. Neither charted though both would later become doo wop cult classics. December arrived with "Here Goes My Heart to You," an ultra-smooth ballad that somehow escaped notice. The same happened to their all-time best ballad effort "Offshore" and "The End of the Story," their next-to-last Atlantic single.

The group's last Atlantic single was another tasty ballad titled "One Love," worth mentioning because of the unusual writing team that created it, Tin Pan Alley songsmith Lou Stallman and Brooklyn's own Tilden High School principal Joe Shapiro (the same odd couple who wrote Perry Como's hit "Round and Round"). It was released in January 1957, just around the time the group called it quits. Ernie formed a new group in late 1957 with tenors Sonny Hatchett and Jimmy Ricks (not the Ravens' bass lead), baritone Richard Williams, and Jim Boone on bass. They recorded several sides, including the early-'50s-sounding ballad "Have I Been Gone Too Long." These almost a cappella recordings stayed in the vaults for 17 years until Bim Bam Boom Records (a division of the collectors' magazine of the same name) released an EP of the songs. In 1958, Ernie re-formed the original Cardinals with Johnson, Brothers, and Johnny Douglas (who sat in for their classic "Offshore" session), as well as Jim Boone. After a few months, the group added an all-white backup band, a strange combination for 1958. The members, Jerry Passion (guitar and baritone), Lee Cornell (drums), Jimmy Harrison (piano), and Bob Passion (Fender bass), played with the Cardinals for a year, after which the band left to become a doo wop group called the Trend-Els on Tilt Records recording a nice version of the Students standard "I'm So Young."

The Cardinals performed into the early '60s and then drifted apart for the last time.

Among rhythm and blues record enthusiasts the group is as popular today as they were in the mid-'50s. Their nine Atlantic recording sessions produced 36 sides of which only 24 have ever been released. Perhaps in time they will be heard. It's never too late for a group that sounds as classy as the Cardinals.

THE CARDINALS

A SIDE/B SIDE	LABEL/CAT NO	DATE
Shouldn't I Know /		
Please Don't Leave Me	Atln 938	5/51
I'll Always Love You /		
Pretty Baby Blues	Atln 952	11/51
Wheel Of Fortune / Kiss Me Baby	Atln 958	2/52
The Bump / She Rocks	Atln 972	8/52
You Are My Only Love /		
Lovey Darling	Atln 995	5/53
Under A Blanket Of Blue /		
Please Baby	Atln 1025	4/54
The Door Is Still Open / Miserlou	Atln 1054	2/55
Come Back My Love /		
Two Things I Love	Atln 1067	7/55
Here Goes My Heart To You /		
Lovely Girl	Atln 1079	12/55
Off Shore / Choo Choo	Atln 1090	3/56
The End Of The Story / I Won't		
Make You Cry Anymore	Atln 1103	8/56
One Love / Near You	Atln 1126	1/57
Have I Been Gone Too Long /		
Sure Nuff / Train (Choo Choo) /		
Love Me	BBB EP1000	1974

The Carollons

The Carollons were another of the early racially mixed groups to come out of New York City in the mid-'50s, but unlike the majority of R&B street-corner groups, the Carollons had a versatility that covered pop ("Hold Me Close"), country rock ("It's Love"), doo wop ("My Heart"), and rock and roll ballads ("Chapel of Tears").

The group formed in the Bedford-Stuyvesant section of Brooklyn as the Emeralds with Irving Brodsky, Artie Levy, Jimmy Laffey, Tyler Volks, and Robert Dunson (lead). By the time they became Lonnie and the Carollons the lineup had already changed to Irving Brodsky (lead as "Lonnie," age 16), Richard Jackson (first tenor, age 21), Eric Nathonson (second tenor, age 18), Jimmy Laffey (baritone, age 21), and Artie Levi (bass, age 17). Richie was black; the others were white and mostly Jewish. The new name came from the fact that Eric had stayed at the Carollon Hotel in Florida during summer vacation and Irving just liked the sound of the name Lonnie. Though they loved groups like THE CHANNELS, THE MOONGLOWS, THE DELLS, and THE FLAMINGOS and rehearsed other artists' hits like "That's My Desire," "Sincerely," and "Oh What a Night," the songs they would eventually record were all originals, many of which the group members wrote themselves.

In early 1958 the group wandered through Manhattan's maze of music companies singing for whoever would listen. After a number of turndowns they came upon Mohawk Records at 1674 Broadway, where the proprietor Irv Spice was, in their minds, their last shot before they gave it all up. Spice liked the Carollons, and on March 3, 1958, the group started recording at Dick Charles Studios.

A strong rock-ballad called "Chapel of Tears" was soon issued and became a Northeast regional area success. The group did the promo tour circuit of New York, Connecticut, Boston, and Philadelphia, and appeared on Clay Cole's TV show. "Chapel" was to be the B side of "My Heart" (an outstanding rocker that deserved its own A side) but a last-minute change of heart made "Chapel" the promoted song.

Their second single, "Hold Me Close," made the Carollons sound like the link between the '50s' FOUR COINS and the '60s' VOGUES. A pop ballad with full harmonies and little similarity to the style of their first record, it generated only scattered activity.

With a lack of radio interest in their last single, "You Say," the group was soon another singing statistic.

In 1981, through the efforts of Brooklyn's Sherlock Holmes of white vocal groups, Bob Diskin, the Carollons were reunited and performed at Ronnie I's UGHA show during the summer. After all those years apart, the members found out that they lived within a 10-mile radius of each other.

The Carols

One of the first rhythm and blues groups to appear on a major label in the 1950s, little is known about the short-lived career of the mysterious Carols.

They formed in Detroit in 1949 as a gospel group, the United Baptist Five, made up of Tommy Evans (bass lead), Richard Coleman (first tenor), William Davis (second tenor), Wilbert Tindle (baritone), and James Worthy (piano). Heavily influenced by THE RAVENS, the five auto workers began practicing secular songs and renamed themselves the Carols.

An amateur night contest at the Frolic Show Bar turned into regular weekend work for the group and also provided them with a manager, owner Hymie Gastman. The aggressive innkeeper arranged bookings for his new act in New York at Harlem's

Baby Grand and on TV's "Cavalcade of Bands" show. Toward the end of 1949, he also got them signed to Columbia Records, no easy achievement given Columbia's almost all-pop roster at the time. The Ravens-styled quartet recorded four songs for the label on April 20, 1950. With bass Tommy Evans leading the way, the group's first single, "Please Believe in Me" b/w "Drink Gin," came out in June 1950. The bouncy call-and-response vocals and harmony were meritorious but received little exposure; Columbia was not yet familiar with the promotion of rhythm and blues records.

Their next two-sided 78 (both Carols records were only available on 78 rpm), "If I Could Steal You from Somebody Else" b/w "I Should Have Thought" (August 1950), fared no better and the group settled into three years of Detroit-area performances. Columbia must have liked the Ravens-like sound of the Carols since they recorded the real Ravens in October of that same year.

In 1952 Kenneth Duncan joined the Carols when Richard Coleman left, and Hymie Gastman gave the group another try by getting them signed to Savoy Records. A DOMINOES-styled single, the clever "Fifty Million Women" (May 1953), received little interest and the group was forced out of recording and back to performances only.

In 1954 Tommy Evans made the quantum leap from adoring fan of the Ravens to replacement for his counterpart in that group. Nat Margo, the Ravens' manager, saw the Carols perform at the Frolic Show Bar. Less than a month later he sent Evans a note with the price of a ticket to New York to replace his temporarily departed idol, Jimmy Ricks, on bass lead. The Carols soon fell apart, never to replace their lead or to record again.

THE CAROLS

A SIDE/B SIDE	LABEL/CAT NO	DATE
Please Believe In Me / Drink Gin	Col 30210	6/50
If I Could Steal You From Somebody Else / I Should Have Thought	Col 30217	8/50
I Got A Feelin' / Fifty Million Women	Savoy 896	5/53

The Casanovas

The Casanovas were a spiritual quartet turned rhythm and blues group from High Point, North Carolina. They started out as the Jubilee Kings a few years after World War II, joining Frank and

Willie McWilliams with nephews Chester and L. D. Mayfield. The church was their main musical outlet, and their polished harmonizing was good enough to earn them a regular spot on radio WHPE's Sunday gospel show. The teens sang right up to, through, and past the Korean War (they were all drafted and became paratroopers during the campaign) until they were discovered by 5 ROYALES roadie Bob Woodward in 1954. He introduced them to William Samuels, brother-in-law of Lowman Pauling of the 5 Royales, and Melvin Stowe, both from nearby Winston-Salem.

By 1954 the spiritual quartet became an R&B quintet (with part-timer L. D. Mayfield contributing on occasion). Woodward had contacts at Apollo Records (which was becoming a home to such North Carolina groups as THE LARKS and the 5 Royales) and sent owner Bess Berman one of the group's demo tapes. The result was a trip to New York for the vocalists to record their first songs in November 1954.

"That's All" (April 1955), with Chester singing lead, was their first release on Apollo. (The group sported three lead singers, and each had several chances to front the group on subsequent recordings.) "That's All" was a straightforward R&B ballad with no particular merit other than the appealing harmony and a sincere reading from the lead. Their second single, out in May, was a blues ballad with harmonic turns reminiscent of THE MOONGLOWS' 1953 Chance masterpiece "Baby Please." Plodding ahead, the group recorded and released a third single in July titled "I Don't Want You to Go." Though no more distinguished than its predecessors, this song's Chester-penned melody did serve as the nucleus for Lowman Pauling's "Dedicated to the One I Love," which he and his 5 Royales released in 1957 and which later became a hit for THE SHIRELLES in 1961 (#3) and THE MAMAS AND THE PAPAS in 1967 (#2).

The week before Christmas brought in the Casanovas' next ballad A side (come to think of it, *all* of their A sides were ballads), a nice high-tenor recording by Melvin Stowe called "My Baby's Love." The Carolina quintet didn't record or have a record out in 1956 and worked mostly on a local club basis.

In the summer of 1957 they returned to New York for another shot, recording the beautiful ballad "Please Be Mine," sounding like a '50s forerunner of THE STYLISTICS. Their last 45 came out in 1958 but by this time it was apparent that Apollo was just going through the motions, and the group gave up singing together by the end of the decade.

No, they didn't have any hits, weren't very unique, had no members who went on to solo success, and weren't a pivotal group in pop history. All they did was record six very enjoyable singles that have become rhythm and blues collectors' items. They were good, but they were overlooked.

THE CASANOVAS

A SIDE/B SIDE	LABEL/CAT NO	DATE
That's All / Are You For Real	Apollo 471	4/55
Hush-A-Meca / It's Been A Long Time	Apollo 474	5/55
I Don't Want You To Go / Please Be My Love	Apollo 477	7/55
My Baby's Love / Sleepy Head Mama	Apollo 483	12/55
Please Be Mine / For You And You Alone	Apollo 519	11/57
You Are My Queen / Good Lookin' Baby	Apollo 523	1958

The Castelles

The Castelles (not to be confused with the white pop '60s group spelled CASTELLS, on Era and Warner Bros. Records) were the pioneers of what became known as the Philadelphia or Philly sound in the early to mid-'50s. Different from the '50s vocal group styles of New York, L.A., or the Baltimore-Washington area, it should not be confused with the '60s and '70s Philly sound that was developed by such acts as THE ORLONS, THE BLUE NOTES, DANNY AND THE JUNIORS, and in particular the Cameo and Parkway stable of artists.

The early Philly sound was created accidentally by these West Philadelphia youths. Though difficult to describe it's easy to recognize: a four- or five-member group blending in complex harmony, its high tenor lead singer supported by equally high first and second tenors.

The Castelles' average age was 11 when they started harmonizing near 49th and Brown Streets in 1949. George Grant was the lead, accompanied by Octavius Anthony, first tenor, Frank Vance, second tenor, William Taylor, baritone, and Ronald Everett, bass. They were all neighborhood friends who went to Sulzberger Junior High, and when they weren't playing basketball or hitting the books they were practicing and starting to sing at the school's dances. Though their early idols were groups like the Four Buddies and the ORIOLES, when they opened their own mouths to sing a new, mystical sound came out.

By 1953 the group members were in Overbrook High School except for George Grant, who went to West Philadelphia High. Frank Vance had begun to write songs, and his first finished work was "My Girl Awaits Me," inspired by the Edna McGriff recording "Heavenly Father." The group felt it complemented their ballad vocal style and they immediately went to a penny arcade to record it on one of the quarter slot machines that popped out a paper (sometimes combined with metal) six-inch disc.

The group then stopped at a small appliance (and records) store named Treegoobs and asked the clerk to play the recording since the group was too excited to wait till they got home to hear it. The owner, Herb Slotkin, liked what he heard, and after learning that the Castelles had no management, he decided to team up with his associate, Jerry Rogovoy, to record the group. Wanting to avoid the obstacles of record label rejection or interference, Slotkin formed Grand Records right out of his appliance store.

In November 1953 "My Girl Awaits Me" was the first Grand release on the now legendary shiny blue (later yellow) 45 rpm label. The times dictated that if the A side were a ballad the B side would usually be a jump tune, so the group had written "Sweetness," an up-tempo blues progression with an incessant "wap wah doo wop" backup and Octavius's yodel-like falsetto. Taylor or Anthony sang the jump leads, leaving the ballads to Grant's splendid tenor voice. "My Girl" was an exquisite shuffle ballad. From its chime harmony bass-to-tenor intro to its four-part harmony bridge accompanied by falsetto riffing, it was a whole new sound in rhythm and blues. "My Girl" began to sell all over the East Coast but particularly well in New York, Washington, Baltimore, and the group's Philadelphia home base.

Around this time, George Grant was being considered to replace Clyde McPhatter in THE DOMINOES by Atlantic execs, but the Castelles lead chose to stay with his group. The Dominoes slot was turned over to a young Jackie Wilson.

The Castelles' next single was a Rogovoy composition titled "This Silver Ring" (1954). Since the group wrote almost all of their recorded songs (though they usually chose only one member to get writer credit) "This Silver Ring" turned out to be Rogovoy's only writing contribution for the act. (He later made a name for himself writing songs for Janis Joplin like "Piece of My Heart," "Try," and "Cry Baby.") On some Grand pressings it didn't

matter who wrote the songs since writer credits were usually left off the label. The group put lots of work into meticulously crafting such ballad A sides as "Do You Remember," "Over a Cup of Coffee" (*Billboard*'s August of 1954 review said, "Pretty ballad is sung expressively by the combo, which manages to project an unusual sound in this disking"), and the beautifully melodic "Marcella," but when it came to up-tempo tunes, they would often wait until the actual session to write something, and rumor has it that the final touches for the jump numbers were often created in the studio men's room.

In the fourth week of October 1954, they released "I'm a Fool to Care," a splendid rhythm and blues reworking of the Les Paul and Mary Ford pop hit of a few months before, but it went nowhere and took "Marcella" with it. In 1955, their last single out of Grand's headquarters at 4095 Lancaster Avenue was "Heavenly Father" backed with "My Wedding Day."

Before the group could record again Frank Vance and Ronald Everett left. A Philly friend, Clarence Scott, joined the group in 1956 and the newly revamped quartet was brought to Atlantic by Slotkin to record one single, the Castelles-written "Happy and Gay." *Billboard*'s R&B reviewer for the June 16th issue wrote, "The Castelles, formerly on the Grand label, sing out with style and verve on this bouncy rhythm item, which should pull plenty of spins. The platter is highlighted by an effective scat-ology gimmick at the opening and close." The Castelles were now singing in a new style. Gone was George Grant's pristine lead as Clarence Scott sang up front. Also gone were the treetop tenor harmonies, replaced by up-tempo CLEFTONES-styled doo wop. And gone was the group's career when the record flopped.

Vance landed with THE SPANIELS but never recorded with them. Taylor joined SONNY TIL AND THE ORIOLES for their 1962 releases on Charlie Parker Records. George joined the Modern Redcaps in 1961 (through 1969), sharing leads with old friend George Tindley (of the Dreams on Savoy) recording for Swan, Rowax, and Penntown Records. William Taylor joined the Redcaps for a period. Among their releases was a version of THE FLAMINGOS' 1953 classic, "Golden Teardrops," a daring record for the Beatles era produced by former VALENTINES lead Richard Barrett.

In 1989 George Grant recorded with a Castelles imitation group for Classic Artists Records. "At Christmastime" and "One Little Teardrop" showed he had lost none of his sound and evoked the early days on those Philadelphia streets where the Cast-elles originated their much-imitated style. All the tenor groups that followed—from the Marquees and the CAPRIS to THE DELFONICS and STYLISTICS—owe much to the Castelles.

THE CASTELLES

A SIDE/B SIDE	LABEL/CAT NO	DATE
My Girl Awaits Me / Sweetness	Grand 101	11/53
This Silver Ring / Wonder Why	Grand 103	2/54
If You Were The Only Girl / Do You Remember	Grand 105	5/54
Over A Cup Of Coffee / Baby Can't You See	Grand 109	8/54
Marcella / I'm A Fool To Care	Grand 114	10/54
Heavenly Father / My Wedding Day	Grand 122	1955
Happy And Gay / Hey Baby Baby	Atco 6069	4/56

The Cellos

A New York street-corner group that could really sing, the Cellos chose to make their niche in the oddball world of novelty records. Banding together at Charles Evan Hughes High School in downtown Manhattan were Alton Campbell (lead), Billy Montgomery (first tenor), Clifford Williams (second tenor), Bobby Thomas (baritone), and Alvin Williams (bass).

They formed in 1955 and at first called themselves the Marcals. Influenced by groups ranging from THE COASTERS to THE HARPTONES, the youngsters practiced the hits of the day in the halls of school until Alvin started writing. One of his compositions was a catchy rocker with a wacky lyric about a guy who got all the girls because he was a Japanese sandman. They took that song ("Rang Tang Ding Dong") and several others to Nola Studios in January 1957. $4 later they had such an outrageous demo that engineer Lew Merenstein felt compelled to play it for his uncle Charles Merenstein of Apollo Records. Charles heard the potential, and by January 24th the Cellos were in Mastertone studios cutting the master that would be released in April. From its ear-catching intro and wailing Sam "the Man" Taylor sax solo to the ragged vocal stop where Alvin exclaims, "All you guys say the big things, all *I* get to say is he goes," "Rang Tang" was a happy hit-bound 45.

The song was covered by a 16-year-old named Ray Stevens, who would go on to make a career of

recording novelty records like "Ahab, the Arab" (#5, 1962) and "The Streak" (#1, 1974).

On May 27, 1957, the Cellos' "Rang Tang Ding Dong" slipped onto the *Billboard* Top 100, rising to number 62 by the summer. Surprisingly, the record never made the R&B charts, but the Cellos were too excited and busy to care. With Lew managing the group, they appeared on Alan Freed's Easter show in April at the Brooklyn Paramount alongside THE CLEFTONES and THE SOLITAIRES. A mere four months had passed since their first recording experience, but the group took its fast rise in stride. With confidence and exuberance they created a new novelty marvel, "Juicy Crocodile," about the group's efforts to avoid the creature that's devouring them one at a time. Though not of "Rang Tang" caliber it was still hook-laden rock and roll, deserving greater exposure than it received in the summer of 1957.

Their next single (sounding like a cross between THE CADETS meet THE TEENAGERS), "Be-Bop Mouse" (September 1957), another novelty natural in the "Rang Tang" styling, seemed to be the victim of Apollo's diminishing ability to promote; it garnered little activity beyond the New York area. The Cellos' fourth and last release was "What's the Matter for You," a cross between "Little Bitty Pretty One" (Thurston Harris) and "Jim Dandy (to the Rescue)" (LaVern Baker) with a lead vocal borrowed from an Italian immigrant's dialect. It hit the streets in January 1958 and went the downhill route of the previous two outings.

Despite their novelty-song reputation, the boys could also sing ballads. "I Beg for Your Love," "Under Your Spell," and "You Took My Love" clearly show that had they stayed together longer, they might have done great things for the right label. Instead, Alton and Billy went off to sing with the CHANNELS in 1959, and that was it for the Cellos.

They were a group that deserved more attention, and the Cellos' releases were finally compiled on an LP in the late '80s on Apollo by Relic Records.

THE CELLOS

A SIDE/B SIDE	LABEL/CAT NO	DATE
Rang Tang Ding Dong / You Took My Love	Apollo 510	1957
Under Your Spell / The Juicy Crocodile	Apollo 515	1957
The Be-Bop Mouse / Girlie That I Love	Apollo 516	1957
I Beg For Your Love / What's The Matter For You	Apollo 524	1958

The Channels

On the East Coast in the 1950s there were certain vocal groups that managed to become immensely popular without having national record sales success. The two groups that best fit into that category were the immortal HARPTONES and the incomparable Channels.

Late 1955 New York City was the setting for the latter's formation. Larry Hampden (first tenor), Billy Morris (second tenor), and Edward Doulphin (baritone) started a quintet they called the Channels, from 115th Street and 116th Street, along with two other long-since-forgotten part-timers. When the short-termers made their final exit, the remaining Channels went looking for a lead and bass. It so happened that a talent show was being held in February 1956 at the community center at 101st Street between Columbus and Amsterdam in Harlem, and appearing along with new recording sensation FRANKIE LYMON AND THE TEENAGERS was a group dubbed the Lotharios. By the time of the next talent show, the Channels had absorbed Lotharios' lead and bass, Earl Michael Lewis and Clifton Wright. With only a few days of rehearsal the Channels won that show at P.S. 113 singing THE FLAMINGOS' ballad "I'll Be Home." A week later, they graced the stage of the famed Apollo Theatre and won second place in an amateur night contest with THE PLATTERS' recent hit "The Magic Touch."

THE CADILLACS' classic "Gloria" was the song the Channels chose for their first demo. It would be their last oldie for quite a while as Earl Lewis, who began writing songs at the age of 10 while delivering newspapers, started amassing some beautiful ballads.

In spring 1956, one of three scenarios took place, depending on which bit of folklore you accept: (1) the group was heard by Bobby Robinson (owner of Red Robin Records and his own record store) at their Apollo performance and were asked to audition; (2) the Channels were in a studio doing demos and Robinson heard them, offering the quintet a contract on the spot; or (3) they walked into his store, played him several demos, and set up an audition.

Whichever is the case, they did sign a two-year contract with his new Whirling Disc company. On their first session for Robinson (June 29, 1956) it took them only two run-throughs to produce the beautiful ballad "The Closer You Are," written by the 15-year-old Earl Lewis. To save money, producers like Robinson would often record more than one group at a time, so after the Channels' session

the Brooklyn group the Continentals came in and recorded the rocker "Fine Fine Frame" along with the doo wop classic "Dear Lord," which set a vocal group standard for decades. Unlike the Continentals, who were signed because they had a good salable vocal group sound, Robinson had recorded the Channels because they had a unique style. They were influenced by groups like THE ORIOLES and MELLO-MOODS, yet they didn't sound anything like them.

Up to that time all vocal group arrangements had certain similarities. The lead singer would solo on the verses opening the song, with the remaining members "oohing" or "aahing" in the background. The chorus or bridge might continue that approach or feature the group together in four- or five-part harmony, but for the most part harmony remained separate and in the background. The Channels created a different sound by opening with the verse sung in full five-part harmony, often with the first tenor, second tenor, and baritone slightly louder than the bass and falsetto lead. Then Lewis would take over traditional lead in the bridge. This distinct type of arrangement made the Channels instantly recognizable from the very first notes of their recordings.

"The Closer You Are" became an instant success on the nation's airwaves in August, but since it was Whirling Disc's debut disc, its disjointed airplay and sales never gelled enough to land it on the national charts. It did have wide appeal up and down the East Coast and even in the far West, though it was very much a New York street-corner record.

On August 24, they made the Apollo as pros (as opposed to amateur night) alongside THE FIVE SATINS, THE CLOVERS, THE VALENTINES, and the Schoolboys for Dr. Jive's WWRL Show. A follow-up show had them billed as new rhythm and blues stars of 1956 with the Flamingos, THE DELLS, and THE SOLITAIRES, among others.

Their next single was "The Gleam in Your Eye" (October 1956), a ballad written by Earl Lewis when he was 10 years old. The harmony-laden love song gave new indication of Earl's exceptional vocal ability. The record boosted the group's popularity and they began a career of live performances that would take them through such venues as the Howard Theatre in Washington, the Royal in Baltimore, and of course the Apollo for over 35 years.

Around this time, the group picked up a manager named Floyd Lewis (no relation) who was ineffective. Since Bobby Robinson had been acting as manager before Floyd (without a contract) the sudden nosedive of label support for "The Gleam in

Your Eye" was most likely a reflection of Robinson's disappointment with their move.

"I Really Love You," another choice Channels cut, was their third ballad single in a row. Its wall-of-harmony intro was characteristic of the Channels and a stirring start to a quality recording that garnered fewer sales than its predecessor. Its flip was "What Do You Do." In a rare attempt to improve a B side, Robinson had taken the original up-tempo doo wop version of the song and rerecorded it, adding a more Latin-flavored instrumental track while toning down the falsetto and bass vocals. Robinson was perhaps of the mind to push the flip side for airplay, but it never happened.

It was late spring of 1957 when the Channels' fourth (and last) Whirling Disc single was released. "Flames in My Heart" was another first-rate Earl Lewis ballad that could have been performed better if they'd had more than 20 minutes in which to record it. It saw less activity than any of the others, so it came as no surprise when Robinson told the group he was closing down the label. Robinson's cash flow at the time was such that the group was lucky to have had the chance to immortalize the song on wax at all. But the label's demise was probably in the group's best interest, since Earl was undoubtedly fed up with seeing all of his solely written songs gain a partner in Robinson when they showed up on the record label. It was an unfortunate fact of life in the '50s that writers would find their songs cowritten with strange bedfellows as the price of getting a record deal or airplay. For example, LEE ANDREWS AND THE HEARTS' "Long Lonely Nights" was written by Lee Andrews. The label however, showed the names Henderson (disc jockey "Jocko" Henderson), Abbott (a.k.a. disc jockey Larry Brown), Uniman (Mimi Uniman, wife of disc jockey Hy Lit), and Andrews. With that as a potential fate, Earl Lewis probably got off easy.

More than four months passed before the Channels, armed with new originals by Earl, auditioned for George Goldner's recently formed Gone Records. He liked the group but asked for different material. Their next audition produced several newer songs including "The Girl Next Door" and "All Alone." Still not convinced they had a hit, Goldner recorded them doing bandleader Sammy Kaye's 1947 number two hit "That's My Desire." (One-and-a-half years later, DION AND THE BELMONTS would lift the Channels' beautiful arrangement for their own B side of the number three hit "Where or When.") "That's My Desire" was the Channels' first recording since the unreleased demo song "Gloria" that Lewis didn't write and

arrange, though Earl reportedly felt it was the group's best recording.

Their first single on Gone (both sides arranged by former Valentine and Goldner house A&R man, Richard Barrett) was issued in late summer 1957 and brought the group back into the spotlight with air and jukebox play all over the country. "Altar of Love" was their next single, but its lack of audience response hastened the quintet's departure from Gone. Clifton Wright had already left after "That's My Desire" and only the remaining four were heard on "Altar." Neither the song nor the style were typically of the Channels, and no one (except Goldner) was surprised when it failed.

By early 1959 the Channels, with only two fifths of the original cast, were back with Robinson on his new Fury label. The group had had a falling out about realigning with Robinson and his robberbaron ethics, but Lewis and Wright wanted to keep the act active so they joined forces with three replacements, John Felix, Alton Thomas, and Billy Montgomery (recently of the CELLOS on Apollo). They then recorded two terrific Lewis compositions, "My Love Will Never Die" and "Bye Bye Baby." This time Lewis didn't have to worry about writer credit since Robinson outdid himself by not crediting anyone. "My Love Will Never Die," however, turned out to be one of their more successful records. (It might have done even better had Fury not focused all its efforts on pushing the Wilbert Harrison record, "Kansas City.") Two of the original Channels who had foregone the Fury sessions, Larry Hampden and Billy Morris, relented and rejoined Lewis, Alton Campbell (also of the Cellos), and Billy Montgomery in the fall of 1959 to record two songs that George Goldner had passed on two years earlier, "The Girl Next Door" and "My Heart Is Sad." The group shifted to Fury's Fire subsidiary.

The three replacements on the Fury sessions joined forces with lead singer Jackie Rue and became the Starlites, who in 1960 recorded "Valerie," one of the great lead singer "crying" songs of all time. (Singers would literally cry while talk-singing a bridge or verse.)

Another fine Lewis and company recording, "The Girl Next Door," was notable as the first Channels release that read Earl Lewis and the Channels.

By late 1959 the group had disbanded. Two years later, the Jubilee Records Port subsidiary started releasing the Whirling Disc sides in the same order as originally released, just as if they were new records. By 1961 the East Coast was ablaze with '50s vocal group mania, and the Channels became highly revered.

In January 1963 Hit Records issued the first new Channels record in over three years. Although first tenor Larry Hampden was the only original group member, the sound was vintage Channels (spelled Channells on the label). The other members, Tony Williams (lead—not the Platters vocalist), Gene Williams (second tenor), and Revo Hodge (bass), got into the spirit of things with a striking ballad performance of the group-written effort "You Hurt Me."

Hampden's group reverted to the original spelling for a Channels group's one and only backup performance. In the fall of 1964 Herald Records released a two-sider, "Did I Hear You Right" b/w "Love's Burning Fire" credited as Edie and the Channels. The former, a cha-cha A side, did nothing, and the flip side actually had a girls' chorus backing Edie.

Hampden, though talented, seems to have been a glutton for punishment as he took the group back to Bobby Robinson one more time for a release on the Enjoy label. When that failed, Hampden hooked up with songwriter Edna Lewis, who had connections with RCA. She arranged a record deal with their Groove Records subsidiary and recorded two singles (minus Revo Hodge) written by Hampden. To foster the image of a reunited original Channels, Larry credited Edna Lewis as cowriter so the labels read "E. Lewis—L. Hampden." Hoping this might fool fans into thinking that Earl was back (E. Lewis could have been Earl, after all), it made little difference. Though the recordings were good soul harmony products in the IMPRESSIONS-DELFONICS mold, they saw little exposure, and by 1965 Hampden's act had broken up.

Earl himself kept a low profile until the rock revival days of the late '60s when he formed the Earl Jades. In 1971 after an Academy of Music show as the Channels, the new group (first tenor Henry Fernandez, second tenor Jack Brown, bass Felix, and Earl) signed with another George Goldner associated label, Rarebird Records, and released a single of the Neil Sedaka oldie "Breaking Up Is Hard to Do."

Having had enough of other people's labels, Earl started Channel Records later in 1971, and along with Billy Vera's band began recording new songs and favorite oldies (like "Gloria," "We Belong Together," and "A Thousand Miles Away") as singles for his fans. They recorded six singles and an LP between 1971 and 1974. By the mid-'70s the Channels were actually Earl Lewis and four members of

Dino and the Heartspinners (minus Dino): Joe Odom, Cecil Wiley, Butch Phillips, and Bernard Jones. By the '80s, Jones had joined THE DRIFTERS and Phillips THE DEL-VIKINGS. Wes Neil came aboard in Phillips's place, and that lineup stayed in place into the '90s while the Channels continued to delight East Coast audiences just as Earl had done more than 35 years before. In 1987 Earl Lewis and Channel III came full circle as they recorded "The Closer You Are" in a contemporary vein for Soul Jam Records. This song had been their first recording.

Though never as well-known as the Moonglows, the Teenagers, the Flamingos, or some other great R&B groups of the '50s, the Channels are considered among the period's 10 to 15 most revered groups.

THE CHANNELS

A SIDE/B SIDE	LABEL/CAT NO	DATE
The Closer You Are / Now You Know (I Love You So)	WrlnD 100	8/56
The Gleam In Your Eyes / Stars In The Sky	WrlnD 102	10/56
I Really Love You / What Do You Do (early spring rec.)	WrlnD 107	1957
I Really Love You / What Do You Do (2nd version)	WrlnD 107	1957
Flames In My Heart / My Lovin' Baby	WrlnD 109	1957
That's My Desire / Stay As You Are	Gone 5012	9/57
Altar Of Love / All Alone	Gone 5019	1/58
My Love Will Never Die / Bye Bye Baby	Fury 1021	3/59
The Girl Next Door / My Heart Is Sad	Fire 1001	1959
The Closer You Are / Now You Know	Port 70014	4/61
The Gleam In Your Eye / Stars In The Sky	Port 70017	1961
Flames In My Heart / My Lovin' Baby	Port 70022	1961
I Really Love You / What Do You Do	Port 70023	1961

The Hampden Group of Channels		
You Hurt Me / In My Arms To Stay	Hit 700	1/63
Sad Song / My Love	Enjoy 2001	1963
Did I Hear You Right* / Love's Burning Fire*	Herald 584	1964
I've Got My Eyes On You / Anything You Do	Grv 58-0046	1964
You Can Count On Me / Old Chinatown	Grv 58-0061	1965

A SIDE/B SIDE	LABEL/CAT NO	DATE
The Lewis Group		
of New Channels		
Breaking Up Is Hard To Do /		
She Blew My Mind	RrBd 5017	1971
Gloria / You Said You Loved Me	Chnl 1000	1971
We Belong Together /		
Hey Girl, I'm In Love With You	Chnl 1001	1972
You Got What It Takes /		
Crazy Mixed Up World	Chnl 1002	1972
Close Your Eyes /		
Work With Me Annie	Chnl 1003	1973
(You Hurt Me) Over Again /		
In My Arms To Stay	Chnl 1004	1974
A Thousand Mile Away / Don't Let		
The Green Grass Fool You	Chnl 1006	1974
I'm Sorry You're Gone / Dear Lord	KngT 174	1970s
Yo Te Quiro (I Love You) /		
22 Years From Love	KngT 175	1970s
The Closer You Are / Donna	Sl Jm 712	1987

* Edie and the Channels

The Chantels

One of the first female R&B vocal groups to have nationwide success, the Chantels are also considered by many to have been the best female group of all time. Their choir-like sound and close-knit harmony brought a new dimension to rock and roll and R&B songs.

Arlene Smith (lead), Lois Harris (first tenor), Sonia Goring (second tenor), Jackie Landry (second alto), and Rene Minus (alto/bass) began their musical journey in their preteens while attending choir practice at St. Anthony of Padua school in the Bronx. By 1957 the members, aged 14 through 17, had been singing together more than seven years. A staple of their musical diet had been Gregorian chants taught to such perfection that changing notes and trading parts were second nature.

In contrast to their male counterparts, the girls weren't able to "hang out" on a street corner at all hours practicing; five young Catholic schoolgirls live a more restricted lifestyle. So in 1957 much of their practice took place in the unlikely surroundings of the girls' locker room at St. Anthony's. Being one of the taller girls in school, Arlene Smith became a member of the girls' basketball team and, win or lose, the group would sing after each game. The choir-like quintet began doing talent shows with the Sequins (Red Robin Records) and THE CROWS (Rama Records) at the P.S. 60 Community Center and at St. Augustine's church. That same year their school team went up against the hoopsters of St. Francis de Chantelle. One of the girls (to this day no one remembers which) suggested they end their long search for a group name by calling themselves the Chantelles. It soon became the Chantels.

The girls had a strength apart from their angelic vocal presence: the writing ability of lead singer Arlene Smith. There weren't many girl groups around in the mid-'50s and even fewer that contributed to the recording process with their own lyrics and melodies (although THE BOBBETTES come to mind, but all five of their members pooled their writing resources). Arlene contributed both words and music, and the combination of her classical and gospel background with simple yet poignant lyrics would make her more successful than she could possibly imagine at the tender age of 16. "He's Gone," Arlene's first song, was written with a boyfriend in mind while she was working her way through piano practice.

Legend has it that the five classmates were on the second floor of the Broadway Theatre building on Broadway and 53rd Street in Manhattan when several of THE VALENTINES passed by underneath the window. The girls recognized them from an Allen Freed Show performance and scampered down to hunt for autographs. Amid the chatter it came to Valentines member David Clowney's attention that the girls were a singing group. Producer/writer/arranger and Valentines' lead Richard Barrett entered the conversation. Thinking he was putting the girls on the spot he asked them to sing right there under the Broadway Theatre marquee, and sing they did. He was floored at the sound of the girls singing a hymn, and with his leaning toward rhythm and blues, he perhaps wondered how they would sound singing that kind of music. He took their phone number.

The girls were thrilled at Barrett's interest; they knew he was the right-hand man of record entrepreneur George Goldner, owner of Gee and Roulette Records. Ironically, they had tried to sing for Goldner only weeks before, but he hadn't been in when they showed up for their audition at Gee Records' 42nd Street office.

Several weeks passed after the Broadway Theatre meeting without a call from Barrett. Not being timid, Jackie Landry told a friend of hers in THE TEEN CHORDS of their encounter and he gave her Barrett's address. The entire Chantels cast dropped in on Barrett and reminded him of their meeting. This time the multi-talented producer wasted no time in calling rehearsals, meeting the group's mothers, and arranging the teens' first two songs, the Arlene Smith compositions "The Plea" and "He's Gone."

By the early summer of 1957 the girls were signed to Goldner's End label, which he had just formed after selling off the Roulette/Rama/Gee organization. In fact, the girls' first single was the second release (Malcolm Dodds and the Tunedrops' "It Took a Long Time" was the first) on the label that was to be the future home of such stalwarts as LITTLE ANTHONY AND THE IMPERIALS, THE FLAMINGOS, THE MIRACLES, Little Richard, THE TEENAGERS, the Bobbettes, THE VELOURS, THE DELSATINS, and the one and only Wilt "The Stilt" Chamberlain ("By the Riverside," 1960).

The Chantels' first single was "He's Gone," released in August 1957. From the four-part a cappella chime harmony intro topped by Arlene's floating falsetto to its duplicate ending, "He's Gone" instantly set a new standard of quality for female group recordings. By September 30, the record was on the *Billboard* national Top 100 charts but inexplicably stopped at number 71, spending a mere six weeks in competitive company. Still, it was a major breakthrough. This record charted only seven weeks after the Bobbettes hit the top 100 with their first release, the infamous "Mr. Lee." Ironically, these two trend-setting groups of the '50s lived less than a few miles from each other.

The Chantels' first live performance was at a Jocko show at the Apollo Theatre (Jocko was a legendary New York disc jockey at the time) in which the group was not even on the bill. Richard Barrett brought them backstage and waited for an opportune time for Jocko to present them to the world. For Arlene, her classical recitals at Carnegie Hall must have felt like a far cry from this; the Chantels' wowed the enthusiastic audience with "He's Gone."

Their next recording session, on October 16, 1957, was scheduled not at a regular studio but at a refurbished church in midtown Manhattan, apparently for its acoustics. Richard Barrett played the piano along with supportive bass and drums for this Chantels recording of the Arlene Smith composition "Maybe." The single was released in December; by January 20, 1958, it was heading up the pop charts and a week later was climbing the rhythm and blues charts. "Maybe" reached number 15 Pop by late winter and number two R&B. Interestingly (though not uncustomarily for the time) the original record's writer credits read Casey (whoever he was) and Goldner (we know who he

was). Later issues and reissues had "Arlene Smith and Goldner." As recently as 1987 a Chantels compilation appeared on a Murray Hill three-LP set with "Maybe" listed as being written by R. Barrett.

Two days after "Maybe" hit the pop charts the group was recording again. Barrett was now heavily devoting his attention to the girls, even dropping his own group the Valentines by summer 1957. On January 22, 1958, the most productive recording session of the Chantels career generated five sides, all eventually released on singles or EPs: "Sure of Love," "I Love You So," "Every Night," "Whoever You Are," and "Memories of You" (the old HARPTONES classic). (In the girls' sessions, Barrett would always rehearse the Chantels to perfection, yet when it came to the musicians, on-the-spot arrangements and one or two rundowns would suffice.)

The Chantels' third single for End was "Every Night (I Pray)," another gem that sounded suspiciously like Arlene's writing style although it showed George Goldner's name on the record. "Every Night" hit the pop charts on March 31, 1958, and reached number 39 (#16 R&B).

That spring the Chantels became the first female rhythm and blues aggregation to release an EP; it included "Sure of Love," "Prayee," "I Love You So," and "How Could You Call It Off." The latter two became their fourth single in April. "I Love You So" was the first non-Arlene Smith composition to be released as an A side. It was written by Watkins and Davis, the latter a member of the Crows (it was featured as the B side of their April 1954 hit "Gee"). A further piece of information in the continuing "what's in a name" game has an early '60s 45 rpm pressing listing G. Goldner and Davis as writers, while a 1972 LP containing "I Love You So" as performed by the Crows lists writing credits of M. Levy (the now deceased president of Roulette Records, Morris Levy) and D. Norton (Daniel "Sonny" Norton, lead singer of the Crows).

Regardless of who wrote it, "I Love You So" was another perfect Chantels musical confection (#42 Pop, #14 R&B), but it would turn out to be their last hit on End. After "I Love You So," the label released a second group EP, an unprecedented move for an act that had only released four singles. It was an honor usually reserved for acts like THE CLOVERS or COASTERS who had been having hits for years. End seemed to be trying to capitalize on the group's current visibility (rather than planning on a long-term justification for an EP release). The cuts included "Memories of You" from the January 22 session, along with "Congratulations," "I'll Walk Alone," and "C'est Si Bon," all cut on July 24. "Sure of Love" and a reworked gospel song entitled "Prayee" were released in July and became the first Chantels single to fail. Three more singles followed (and failed) through the end of 1958 and early 1959, including a beautiful recording of "Goodbye to Love," immortalized in 1961 in a powerful arrangement by THE MARCELS.

The success of Little Anthony and the Imperials and the Flamingos kept End Records preoccupied in late 1958 and 1959, meaning less promotional support for the Chantels. (End stood to earn more from a touring group of male vocalists than they could from five high school girls still tied to their parents.) Although the Chantels became one of the first female vocal groups of the rock era to have an LP under their own name (*We Are the Chantels* in September 1958), they were dropped from End by April 1959.

Arlene Smith decided to go it on her own while Lois Harris went on to college. Chantels records were still being issued, except that the lead was one Richard Barrett and the label was Gone, an affiliate of End. In May 1959 "Come Softly to Me" (the former FLEETWOODS hit) came out and quickly failed. In July 1959 a most unusual record hit the marketplace entitled "Summer's Love." The label again read Richard Barrett and the Chantels. Recorded in late 1958, the ballad had all the earmarks of a hit but only went to number 93 Pop (#29 R&B). It has shown up on three different labels over the years, with three distinctly different background vocal arrangements. Each included the Chantels with Richard Barrett on lead, but that's where the similarity ended. The original Gone release had the Chantels holding sustained chords behind Barrett's lead. An End "battle of the groups" EP from the early '60s had a male group doing a call-and-response backup with an occasional "shoo-do" and "shoo-be-do" (similar to THE FIVE SATINS' "In the Still of the Night") while the Chantels held their sustained harmony. A third version on Crackerjack Records in 1963 had the girls without the male backup vocals, but the Chantels were now singing "shoo-do" and "shoo-be-do" along with their sustained harmony.

In 1960 Barrett started his own label and recorded a new girl group similar to the Chantels which he called the Veneers. Their release of "I" b/w "Believe Me (My Angel)" went unnoticed but it helped him solve his Chantels problem by matching Veneers lead singer Annette Smith (no relation to Arlene) with the three remaining Chantels, Sonia,

Jackie, and Rene. In April 1960, still trying to capitalize on the group's name, End released "Whoever You Are," formerly the B side of "Every Night"; it had all the original Chantels magic but still lacked the driving commitment of the label.

In the summer of 1961 George Goldner apparently got wind of Barrett's move to take the revamped Chantels to Carlton Records; running low on Chantels tracks in the can, he decided to pass off a bogus group to the public, issuing the Veneers recording "I" under the name of the Chantels. His move didn't work but Barrett's did. "Look in My Eyes," the first release on Carlton for Annette and company, went all the way to number 14 on the pop charts (#6 R&B). The ballad was reminiscent of the Chantels' early classics though the arrangement was a more modern string-laden affair. Annette's lead, which was very similar to Arlene's, blended well with the group and only the most discerning ear could tell that a switch had taken place.

The group's fortunes were once again on the rise, and everyone connected tried to get a piece of the action. End Records released an LP of canned tracks that including the Veneers' two cuts (as the Chantels, of course), entitled *There's Our Song Again* (End LP 312). By 1962 Carlton had released their own more honest LP entitled *The Chantels on Tour* that contained seven Chantels cuts and songs by Chris Montez, the Imperials, and Gus Backus. Gus Backus was a member of the DEL-VIKINGS, and the Imperials recording was without Little Anthony. The LP included their second Carlton single, an answer to Ray Charles' number one record "Hit the Road Jack" called "Well, I Told You." It was the Chantels' first up-tempo single, and from a creative standpoint would probably have served their reputation better had it never been released. The song had the group confined to unison call-and-response vocals while a Ray Charles imitation sang the lead. Still, it made number 29 Pop by December 1961 and the group wasn't about to argue with success.

They couldn't have known it was to be their last big record. One more single for Carlton, the ethereal jazz-tinged ballad "Summertime," and they were off the recording scene until landing at Luther Dixon's Ludix label.

Meanwhile, Arlene Smith had hooked up with a young hotshot producer named Phil Spector for a Big Top Records one-off of the Clovers hit "Love Love Love" backed by the Paris Sisters song "He Knows I Love Him Too Much."

The Chantels began their Ludix association with the song "Eternally" (#77, March 1963), produced by longtime believer Richard Barrett. It was the third time in six years that their initial release on a label had charted. Still, there were more Chantels records coming out and failing than there were successes. George Goldner released "I'm the Girl" (October 1961) and "Mon Cherie Au Revoir" (February 1963), and Ludix tried again with "Some Tears Fall Dry" (April 1963). Then it was on to 20th Century-Fox, Verve, and finally RCA before the group disbanded in 1970. The charts had become almost oblivious to fine harmonies and melodic ballads, now favoring records with a harder edge.

In 1973 Arlene Smith, who had gone on to the prestigious Juilliard School of Music, reformed the Chantels with newcomers Barbara Murray and Pauline Moore for some oldies revivals shows. By the early '80s Sonia Goring, Lois Harris, Rene Minus, and Jackie Landry were all married and living in the New York area. Arlene went on to become a school teacher in the Bronx and continues to sing with the Chantels group to this day.

THE CHANTELS

A SIDE/B SIDE	LABEL/CAT NO	DATE
He's Gone / The Plea	End 1001	8/57
Maybe / Come My Little Baby	End 1005	12/57
Every Night / Whoever You Are	End 1015	2/58
I Love You So / How Could You Call It Off	End 1020	4/58
Sure Of Love / Prayee	End 1026	7/58
If You Try / Congratulations	End 1030	9/58
I Can't Take It / Never Let Go	End 1037	12/58
Come Softly To Me* / Walking Through Dreamland*	Gone 5056	1959
Goodbye To Love / I'm Confessin'	End 1048	7/59
Summer's Love* / All Is Forgiven*	Gone 5060	1959
Whoever You Are / How Could You Call It Off	End 1069	4/60
I / Believe Me (My Angel)	End 1103	6/61
Look In My Eyes / Glad To Be Back	Carlton 555	9/61
I'm The Girl / There's Our Song Again	End 1105	10/61
Well, I Told You / Still	Carlton 564	11/61
Summertime / Here It Comes Again	Carlton 569	1961
Mon Cherie Au Revoir / To Live My Life Again	End 1120	1962
Eternally / Swamp Water	Ludix 101	1/63
Some Tears Fall Dry / That's Why You're Happy	Ludix 106	1/63
There's No Forgetting You / Take Me As I Am	20th 123	1965
Soul Of A Soldier / You're Welcome To My Heart	Verv 10387	1966
It's Just Me / Indian Giver	Verv 10435	8/66

A SIDE/B SIDE	LABEL/CAT NO	DATE
Maybe / There's No Forgetting You	Roul 7064	1969
I'm Gonna Win Him Back / Love Makes All The Difference In The World	RCA 7A-0347	4/70

* Richard Barrett and the Chantels

The Chanters

The phrase "keeping it in the family" applied to numerous singing groups, from the Boswell Sisters of the 1930s to THE JACKSONS in the '70s. Some families that took it even further than the brother and sister level acts were THE RONETTES (two sisters and a cousin), THE COWSILLS (a mother and seven children), THE STAPLE SINGERS (dad and the four kids), and of course the King Family, which at one time included a near battalion of relatives.

The Chanters are set apart not by the family singers but by the family behind the scenes. The greatest contribution of most teen group parents in the '50s was giving record companies and managers permission to utilize the services of their offspring. Not so for the parents of these Queens, New York, youngsters.

In 1957 Fred Paige (first tenor), Bud Johnson (second tenor) of Andrew Jackson High School, and junior high schooler Bobby Thompson (bass) were passing their free time hitting a few notes when Bud's father Buddy Johnson heard their efforts and encouraged them to form a full five-man group. This was not just the coaxing of a proud parent: Buddy, Sr. was a well-respected singer, pianist, and composer (the standard "Since I Fell For You") who had earned eight top 10 R&B records and 13 charters in all for Decca and Mercury from 1943 to 1957, and apparently he heard some potential in the boys' warblings. The trio thrived on the FRANKIE LYMON AND THE TEENAGERS sound, and when kiddie lead Larry Pendergrass was found along with baritone Elliott Green, they began honing their blend through regimented practice sessions. To round out the family affair, Bud, Jr.'s mother, Bernice, became the group's manager. After picking their name randomly from a dictionary, Buddy, Sr. took the quintet to King Records where they were signed to the Deluxe subsidiary.

Their first single was a bouncy bit of up-tempo bubblegum written by the group entitled "My My Darling" (1958), right out of a TEEN CHORDS teen rocker mold. It received some local airplay but failed to make the charts. Ditto for its equally infectious follow-ups, "Row Your Boat" and "Five Little Kisses."

The group's last single of 1958 was an outstanding two minutes and 14 seconds of rock and roll titled "No No No," co-composed by Bud and Elliot. This teen delight might have been a hit had it been recorded by Frankie Lymon and his group but for the Chanters it was another worthwhile effort wasted on a label with promotional problems. From its bass intro and Latin rock rhythm to Larry's Lymon sound-alike sincerity and the group's solid backing, this should have been a chart icebreaker, but for now it wasn't. Even the flip side, a solid reworking of the Arlen-Harburg classic "Over the Rainbow," merited much more attention than it got. The vocal arrangement and orchestra backing were the work of Buddy, Sr. (as were all the group's arrangements), which helps to explain why the label read Bud Johnson and the Chanters even though Bud, Jr. never sang lead.

By 1959 the group had moved on to Craft Records. Fred Page left for the armed forces to be replaced by another Fred—Bud, Jr.'s cousin Freddie Johnson.

A Johnson finally did get to sing lead on a Chanters cut when cousin Freddie was featured on "For Sentimental Reasons," only now the group had changed its name to Voices Five. This would be the group's last recording but not their last release. Early in 1961 Irving "Slim" Rose, proprietor extraordinaire of the Times Square Record Shop in New York City and self-styled disc jockey, began playing Chanters records on his oldies show. Noting that the record hawks who hovered around his shop seemed especially interested in high-tenor kid leads, he decided to drum up some business by playing records like the Chanters that he could easily obtain in good quantity. Eventually the interest created by buyers prompted Deluxe Records to pursue a full-scale reissue of the Chanters' last single, "No No No," with a new flip side called "I Make This Pledge."

On June 19, 1961, more than two years after they last recorded, the unimaginable happened: "No No No" charted and kept charting up to number 41 Pop and number nine R&B, spending a dazzling three months in a paradise of popularity. Unfortunately, the group had already disbanded and never got to reap any of the benefits of their celebrity status. There were two more reissues between September 1961 and 1963, but the lightning couldn't strike twice, especially without a group to parade in front of the fans.

In 1957 Frankie Lymon's Teenagers had their last chart record. By 1958, the new heir apparent teen group should have been Larry Pendergrass and the Chanters. That they weren't is one more example of the injustices of a business with too many hopefuls and too few opportunities.

THE CHANTERS

A SIDE/B SIDE	LABEL/CAT NO	DATE
My My Darling / I Need Your Tenderness	DLx 6162	1958
Row Your Boat / Stars In The Skies	DLx 6166	1958
Angel Darling / Five Little Kisses	DLx 6172	1958
Bud Johnson and the Chanters		
Over The Rainbow / No, No, No	DLx 6177	1958
Voices Five		
For Sentimental Reasons / All Alone	Craft 116	1959
The Chanters		
No, No, No / I Make This Pledge	DLx 6191	1961
At My Door / My My Darling	DLx 6194	1961
No, No, No / Row Your Boat	DLx 6200	1963

The Charms

The Charms were neither an East Coast group nor a West Coast group, but they *were* one of the most popular rhythm and blues acts of the mid-'50s. They were also considered the top black cover group, eclipsing the popular L.A.-based CADETS, even though they were covered as much as they covered others.

The Cincinnati group included Rolland Bradley (tenor, 19), Donald Peak (tenor, 20), Joseph Penn (baritone, 19), Richard Parker (bass, 18), and lead singer Otis Williams (16). They auditioned for Henry Stone's Rockin Records, and he was sufficiently impressed to release their first self-penned single, "Heaven Only Knows," in January of 1953. An overstated shuffling saxophone dominated the harmony of this nice but undistinguished ballad.

The record did nothing but got a second chance (to do nothing) when Rockin was acquired by Sid Nathan's King Records in August. The Deluxe label was reactivated by King, and the first release in its new 6,000 series was the Charms' "Heaven Only Knows." A year's worth of original singles (five, to be exact) brought the group valuable attention, airplay, and performance opportunities, but their sixth single (released the fourth week of September, 1954), a cover of West Coast group the Jewels' "Hearts of Stone," put them on the map. Released one week after the Jewels' version, theirs entered the charts on November 27, 1954. 14 days later, the Fontane Sisters' version of the Charms' version of the Jewels' version (you get the idea), made the charts and the race was on. By January 1955 the Charms had a number 15 Pop hit (#1 R&B). The Fontanes' homogenized version went all the way to number one Pop, and the Jewels' side went nowhere.

The Charms' next release, led by high school dropout Otis Williams (no relation to the TEMPTATIONS member), was an unusual one in that it wasn't just one release, it was *two* singles, both issued in the second week of December 1954. The first was an original named "Mambo Sha-Mambo," and the second was a cover of THE FIVE KEYS' October release "Ling, Ting, Tong." "Mambo" died quietly but "Ling" raced right alongside the Five Keys' version, finishing at number six on the R&B Best Sellers (to the Five Keys' number five) and beating the Newport News group on the Pop chart 26 to 28. (Interestingly, the Five Keys version is the overwhelming favorite on oldies radio and always has been.) Meanwhile, the Charms flip side ("Bazoom") went to number 15 R&B. It beat out a white trio on Capitol known as the Cheers, featuring Bert Convy of later acting fame.

February 1955 saw the release of another Charms cover, in a five-way fight. "Ko Ko Mo" was originally done by Gene and Eunice (Combo), followed rapidly by the Charms (Deluxe), Marvin and Johnny (Specialty), THE CREWCUTS (Mercury), and Canonsberg, Pennsylvania's favorite barber, Perry Como (RCA), not necessarily in that order. The Charms' unison shouter was lackluster and finished out of the running as Gene and Eunice (#6 R&B), Perry (#2 Pop), and "The Cuts" (#6 Pop) proved to be the winners. The Charms' B side, "Whadaya Want," was better, with a more contagious rock and roll rhythm and a hot sax solo.

Three weeks after "Ko Ko Mo," the Charms released an Otis Williams/Henry Glover (A&R director of King)/Henry Stone original titled "Two Hearts." That same week, Pat Boone (actually Eugene Charles Boone) covered it, reaching number 16 Pop and starting his streak of 60 chart records. The Charms managed a number eight R&B position on a hooky, gimmicky recording (Otis's squeals must have delighted the young girls!) that was one of their better harmony efforts.

After "Two Hearts" the group did two more originals on two singles. With no competition on these sides, the records kept the group visible while they started touring on the "Top Ten R&B Show" with THE MOONGLOWS, THE CLOVERS, Joe Turner, and Bill Doggett and playing the usual venues in New Orleans, St. Louis, Memphis, and Washington, D.C.

At this point the group, feeling underpaid, put in a request for higher wages at Deluxe while Otis asked to be featured on the labels. The result was the firing of the Charms (except for Otis) and the addition of three new and less expensive Charms, Larry Graves, Rollie Willis, and Chuck Barksdale (formerly of THE DELLS). The first single with "Otis Williams And His New Group" (as it read on the label) was "Gum Drop," a Rudy Toombs original (with overtones of THE FIVE SATINS' "The Jones Girl") that was a Charms natural. Once again the Crewcuts (who seemed to be making a career out of sanitizing Charms recordings) beat them to the sales list, registering a top 10 spot on *Billboard*'s Best Sellers chart in September even though their record was released more than a month after Otis's. To confuse matters further, Deluxe released an old Charms master, "It's You You You," in the summer and followed with the new group's "Tell Me Now" single in October.

Enter the original Charms (they had gone off to Miami with Henry Stone and his new Chart label), who filed an injunction to stop Deluxe from releasing any more Otis Williams masters (like "It's You You You") using the Charms name. To get around this, Deluxe issued two singles in December under the name Otis Williams and His Charms ("That's Your Mistake" and "Ivory Tower") just as the original group came out with "Love's Our Inspiration," their first single for Chart.

On October 29, 1955, Otis Williams and His Charms appeared at Carnegie Hall with the Five Keys, Joe Turner, Gene and Eunice, Etta James, Bill Doggett, and Charlie and Ray for the very first rhythm and blues show on that concert stage. In January, *down beat* magazine named the Charms (we can only assume they knew which one they were referring to) the best rhythm and blues group of 1955. Otis and team made *down beat* look good in the spring when "That's Your Mistake" reached number 14 R&B and "Ivory Tower" hit number 12 (#5 R&B), their biggest hit ever. However, Bronx-born Cathy Carr and Texas-bred Josephine Cottle (a.k.a. Gale Storm) beat them to the real money with their versions (#6 and #10 respectively).

Personnel changes once again hit Otis's band of not-so-merry men as Barksdale decided to rejoin the Dells and Graves quit. With the release of the year's first single, "One Night Only," the lineup was Williams and Willis with newcomers Winfred Gerald, Lonnie Carter, and Matt Williams.

In March, the group played the Apollo alongside the CHORDS. Then in May they performed at Olympia Arena in Detroit at the Command Performances Concert, an early Alan Freed show, along with the PENGUINS, Dinah Washington, and the Count Basie Orchestra.

Two more singles followed in 1956, including the particularly nice recording "I'd Like to Thank You Mr. D.J." Somewhere in 1956 the second original Charms release came and went with little fanfare.

Five singles into 1957 and eight releases after their last chart hit, the Charms scored once again with a cover of the Lovenotes doo wop classic, "United" (also from 1957). Similar to the "Ling, Ting, Tong" situation, the Charms had the higher chart credentials (number five Best Seller R&B to the Lovenotes' number 13 D.J. chart listing), but the best-remembered version is by the latter group.

Two more odd records connected with the Charms came out some time in 1957. The first was the last Charms release on Chart, but it was an old unreleased master ("I'll Be True") of the original group with Otis. The second was "Ring Around My Finger" by Tiny Topsy and the Charms on Federal in October 1957, which included Otis and possibly the new Charms.

"United" turned out to be the last hit for Otis and his bunch, but while most groups would have been dropped after a few misses, Williams and company kept churning singles out of 1540 Brewster Avenue (Deluxe/King headquarters) for several years: 11 more Deluxe releases through 1959 and 11 more on King through 1963.

But by then the group was down to a quartet. Lonnie Carter joined the original Charms who became the Escos on Federal in 1960, and their first release—in the "if you can't lick 'em, join 'em" category—was a cover of the Paradons' recording "Diamonds and Pearls."

Meanwhile Otis's Charms managed to scrape the bottom of the Top 100 in 1961 with two of their King releases, "Little Turtle Dove" (#95) and "Panic" (#99).

By the summer of 1965 the group was on Okeh Records faring no better. After Okeh, Otis finally got to do what he had wanted to for years: sing country music. He signed up as a solo artist on Stop Records.

In its various forms, the Charms released 57 singles, three EPs, and one LP from 1953 to 1966 and were by all accounts a stalwart group of musical survivors.

THE CHARMS

A SIDE/B SIDE	LABEL/CAT NO	DATE
Otis Williams and the Charms		
Heaven Only Knows / Loving Baby	Rockin 516	1/53
Heaven Only Knows / Loving Baby	DLx 6000	10/53
Happy Are We / What Do You Know About That	DLx 6014	12/53
Bye-Bye Baby / Please Believe In Me	DLx 6034	1/54
Quiet Please / Fifty-Five Seconds	DLx 6050	4/54
My Baby Dearest Darling / Come To Me Baby	DLx 6056	8/54
Who Knows / Hearts Of Stone	DLx 6062	9/54
Mambo Sh-Mambo / Crazy, Crazy Love	DLx 6072	12/54
Bazoom / Ling, Ting, Tong	DLx 6076	10/54
Ko Ko Mo / Whadaya Want	DLx 6080	2/55
Two Hearts / The First Time We Met	DLx 6065	2/55
Whadaya Want / Crazy, Crazy Love	DLx 6082	3/55
When We Get Married / Let The Happenings Happen	DLx 6087	4/55
Gum Drop / Save Me, Save Me	DLx 6090	6/55
It's You, You, You / One Fine Day	DLx 6089	9/55
Tell Me Now / Miss The Love	DLx 6088	10/55
Rolling Home / Do Be You Love, Love / Love's Our Inspiration	DLx 6092	11/55
Love, Love / Love's Our Inspiration	Chart 608	12/55
That's Your Mistake / Too Late I Learned	DLx 6091	12/55
Ivory Tower / In Paradise	DLx 6093	1956
One Night Only / It's All Over	DLx 6095	1956
I'd Like To Thank You R.M. D.J. / Whirlwind	DLx 6097	1956
Gypsy Lady / I'll Remember You	DLx 6098	1956
I Offer You / Heart Of A Rose	Chart 613	1956
Blues Stay Away From Me / Pardon Me	DLx 6015	1/57
Walkin' After Midnight / I'm Waiting Just For You	DLx 6115	2/57
No Got De Woman / Nowhere On Earth	DLx 6130	4/57
Talking To Myself / One Kind Word From You	DLx 6137	5/57
United / Don't Deny Me	DLx 6138	6/57
Dynamite Darling / Well Oh Well	DLx 6149	1957
Tiny Topsy and the Charms		
Come On, Come On, Come On / Ring Around My Finger	Fed 12309	10/57
Otis Williams and the Charms		
Could This Be Magic / Oh Julie	DLx 6158	11/57
The Charms		
I'll Be True / Boom Diddy Boom Boom	Chart 623	1957
Let Some Love In Your Heart / Baby-I	DLx 6160	1958

A SIDE/B SIDE	LABEL/CAT NO	DATE
Burnin' Lips / Red Hot Love	DLx 6165	1958
Don't Wake Up The Kids /		
You'll Remain Forever	DLx 6174	1958
My Friends / The Secret	DLx 6178	1958
Pretty Little Things Called Girls /		
Welcome Home	DLx 6181	1958
My Prayer Tonight / Watch Dog	DLx 6183	1958
I Knew It All The Time /		
Tears Of Happiness	DLx 6185	1958
In Paradise / Who Knows	DLx 6186	1959
Blues Stay Away From Me /		
Funny What True Love Can Do	DLx 6187	1959
It's A Treat / Chief Um	King 5323	1960
Silver Star / Rickety		
Rickshaw Man	King 5332	1960
Image Of A Girl / Wait A		
Minute Baby	King 5372	1960
The First Sign Of Love / So Be It	King 5389	1960
And Take My Love / Wait	King 5421	1960
Little Turtle Dove / So Can I	King 5455	1/61
Just Forget About Me /		
You Know How Much I Care	King 5497	1961
Panic / Pardon Me	King 5527	1961
Two Hearts / The Secret	King 5558	1961
When We Get Together /		
Only Young Once	King 5682	1962
It'll Never Happen Again /		
It Just Ain't Right	King 5816	1963
Baby You Turn Me On /		
Love Don't Grow On Trees	Okeh 7225	6/65
I Fall To Pieces / Gotta Get		
Myself Together	Okeh 7235	12/65
Welcome Home / I Got Loving	Okeh 7248	5/66
Ain't Gonna Walk Your Dog No		
More / Your Sweet Love	Okeh 7261	10/66

The Charts

A group of Harlem teenagers had a dream. The dream was to make the charts...and they did.

The Charts were probably one of the only groups in America to get booed off the stage at an Apollo Theatre amateur night and still go on to success. One of those New York City street-gang vocal groups (like the Juveniles on Mode and THE BELMONTS on Laurie), the Charts must have seemed like a logical next step when street fighting lost its charm. Originally eight gang members from the 115th Street area, the group had pared itself down to a quintet by late 1956, leaving Joe Grier (lead), Leroy Binns (first tenor), Steven Brown (second tenor), Glenmore Jackson (baritone), and Ross Buford (bass). They practiced on street corners and in hallways until they felt ready for the stairway to stardom that was the Apollo's Tuesday night amateur competition.

Always scanning *Billboard* magazine, the group decided to name themselves after *Billboard's* hits list with the intent of one day seeing themselves on the charts. Joe Grier, the oldest member at 17, wrote a song entitled "Deserie" that fit the group's raw, free-form style perfectly. While the first and second tenor and baritone "wah wah-ed" and the bass "aye yah-ed," Joe alternated between a smokey-voiced lead and a soaring falsetto that reminded many of a yodel. It was this sound coupled with "Deserie's" three slow and seemingly endless verses (with no chorus or bridge) that the Apollo crowd heard on that fateful night, and sure enough the combination was too weird to be taken seriously. The group wah-wahed its way through the boos. Shaken (but not stirred) they barely made it off the stage. Among the onlookers, however, was one Les Cooper, formerly of the Whirlers on Bobby Robinson's Whirling Disc label and a member of the Empires on Harlem, Whirling Disc, and Wing. Cooper felt this unusual sound had potential and immediately introduced himself to the nervous teens. Shortly after the Apollo fiasco, Cooper—now the group's manager—introduced them to Dan Robinson (Bobby's brother), who was starting his own label.

By June 1957, Everlast 5001 was being played all over the tri-state area. By July 15, 1957, it had reached *Billboard's* Pop chart spending four weeks in the rarified air of success and peaking at number 88. "Deserie" became a huge East Coast doo wop cult classic and has been listed among the top 10 oldies of the New York area each year for more than three decades. Such was and is the extent of the record's airplay that in the more than 30 years since its release it's reported to have sold well over a million singles. (Good for the group but not too good for young Joe Grier, who had sold off the writer's share of the song to a photographer of the stars named James Kriegsman.) Meanwhile the B side, "Zoop," an up-tempo, infectious rocker, was getting lots of play on its own. It was a quality cut in an era when B sides were often throwaways.

The group next released "Dance Girl," a "Zoop"-like recording that featured Joe Grier's immediately identifiable nasal rock sound. It saw local activity but neither "Girl" nor its beautiful ballad B side "Why Do You Cry" reached sales levels as high as they deserved. The single "You're the Reason" (arguably their best ballad) closed out 1957 with little fanfare; their Latin-based "All Because of Love" had the same non-effect on the general population during its early 1958 run.

The group's last Everlast single was a "Deserie" sound-alike entitled "My Diane" (spring 1958) which had absolutely no exposure and therefore no chance to chart. Joe Grier joined the service after "My Diane" flopped, and the group disbanded. When Joe returned he hooked up with his old manager to play tenor sax on a composition entitled "Wiggle Wobble." The contagious instrumental became a number 22 hit for Les Cooper and the Soul Rockers. Grier never returned to the Charts, but a revised group (that included holdovers Steven Brown [now on lead] and Leroy Binns [now on bass] along with newcomers Frankie Fears and Tony Harris) recorded an up-tempo powerhouse version of "Deserie" on Wand Records in 1966. It flopped, its follow-up ("Living the Nightlife") failed, and the group once again dispersed, only to be reincarnated in 1976 as the Twelfth of Never. (Before that however, Leroy and Steven surfaced with THE CADILLACS in the late '60s.) By March 1980 the group had reformed as the Charts with Leroy, Steven, Leroy's brother Ray on second tenor, John Trusdale on first tenor, and Jerry Burden on baritone. The new quintet made their first appearance in Symphony Hall with THE CLOVERS, VITO AND THE SALUTATIONS, and the Laddins, but never recorded again.

The Charts had a unique, raw sound, and the quality of Joe Grier's voice alone should have made the group more successful than it was. Collectors still scramble for their original label recordings, evidence of current popularity more than 35 years after their first release.

THE CHARTS

A SIDE/B SIDE	LABEL/CAT NO	DATE
Deserie / Zoop	Ever 5001	10/57
Dance Girl / Why Do You Cry	Ever 5002	1957
You're The Reason / I've Been Wondering	Ever 5006	1957
All Because Of Love / I Told You So	Ever 5008	1958
My Diane / Baby Be Mine	Ever 5010	1958
Deserie / Zoop	Ever 5026	1963
Deserie / Fell In Love With You Baby	Wand 1112	1966
Livin' The Nightlife / Nobody Made You Love Me	Wand 1124	1966

The Chestnuts

A fine vocal group in the mid- to late '50s, the Chestnuts were known for their warm, roasted ballad sound. The members resided in New Haven, Connecticut, and came together in late 1955. The rhythm and blues quintet consisted of Leroy Griffin (lead, but not the lead singer of another New Haven group, THE NUTMEGS), Lymon Hopkins (first tenor), Frank Hopkins (second tenor), Jimmy Curtis (baritone), and Reuben White (bass). The Hopkins boys wrote a pretty ballad called "Love Is True" with White and Griffin and rehearsed it with the intent of getting a recording contract. The paucity of recording opportunities in New Haven forced the group to look for interest in New York, where they met Joe Davis of Jay Dee and Davis Records at his 441 West 49th Street offices. Davis heard their potential but was more interested in finding a group fronted by a female since he had let go of Lillian Leach and the Mellows (see THE MELLOWS) in the fall of 1955. The Chestnuts rolled back to the New Haven streets, found one Ruby Whitaker, and began rehearsing "Love Is True." (When Ruby came in, Leroy went out.) Her soft but powerful voice elegantly complemented the group's blend. Apparently Jimmy Curtis either left the group or was omitted from the session log: the Chestnuts recorded four sides in New York for Davis on April 11, 1956; the members listed for all four ("Love Is True," "It's You I Love," "Forever I Vow," and "Brother Ben") were Ruby, Reuben, Frank, Lymon Hopkins, Jr., and (oddly) Lymon Hopkins, Sr.

Billboard reviewed their first single "Love Is True" and "It's You I Love" (with a male lead, Ruby on falsetto, a wailing sax solo by Sam "The Man" Taylor, and the words "It's You" sung 45 times). Their reviewer picked "It's You I Love" as the hit side, calling it "a happy swinger with a rhythm that gives an energetic kick to the material. Lyrics are cute in that it strings together nursery rhymes and children's verses cleverly into expressions of love. There is a lot of commercial potential here if properly exploited." He called "Love Is True" "a more conventional R&B ballad also skillfully harmonized and adorned with a heartfelt solo by the lead." Ruby's emotional vocal and the group's full falsetto-to-bass harmony made for a beautiful recording with a melody line that the Students must have borrowed for their 1958 hit "I'm So Young." With little promo support the Chestnuts were soon onto their second single, another pretty ballad called "Forever I Vow," which received even less of Joe Davis's time.

By 1957, the group was back in New Haven with one single for the local standard label and one for the New York-based El Dorado Records.

1958 saw no Chestnuts releases. Ruby left the group. Jimmy Curtis joined the Four Haven Knights (Atlas). Bill Baker (former lead of THE FIVE SATINS on "To the Aisle") took Ruby's place and

Jimmy was replaced by a Hopkins brother named Arthur. In 1959 the Chestnuts recorded "Won't You Tell Me My Heart" for Elgin Records, by far the best recording to come out of the offices at 22 Burke Street, Hamden, Connecticut, but like their follow-up "Wonderful Girl" (originally by the Five Satins in 1956) it received little exposure.

The Chestnuts dropped out soon after. Ruby died in the late '60s and Jimmy Curtis went on to sing with the Five Satins of the '60s and '70s. An underrated group (maybe because they had so few recordings), the Chestnuts might have been the Ruby and the Romantics of the '50s if given half a chance.

The Chips

The Chips had only one record in their early career, but a mention of that one release will always bring a smile to the face of a typical vocal group enthusiast. The street-wise teens joined together on the corners of Bergen Street, Classon Avenue, and Clifton Place in the Bedford-Stuyvesant section of Brooklyn in 1956. Membership included lead Charles "Kenrod" Johnson, Sammy Strain on first tenor, Shedwick Lincoln on second tenor, baritone Nathaniel "Little John" Epps, and bass Paul Fulton. The song in question, "Rubber Biscuit," came to life in the unlikely surroundings of the Warwick School for Delinquent Teenagers when Kenrod created an alternative to the army's marching "hup-two-three-four sound off." The hilarious "chou chou huma laga duga laga" verses and talking bridge gave the Chips an offbeat song that Josie Records couldn't resist; on August 3, 1956, the quintet recorded the nonsense novelty song to tape at Belltone Studios in New York City.

Josie released "Rubber Biscuit" in September and although it never became a national hit it did manage to find favor with disc jockeys and listeners for years to come, especially in the east. "Rubber Biscuit" put the Chips on the performance bill of Dr. Jive's Rhythm and Blues Revue with such stars as THE DELLS, Bo Diddley, THE CADILLACS, and the Schoolboys. It also earned them a one-shot at the Apollo. In September 1957 they appeared at the Empire Theatre with THE HEARTBEATS, but with no further recordings (presumably no one felt they could top "Rubber Biscuit") the Chips scattered. Paul Fulton went on to join THE VELOURS (Cub) and the Poets (Sue) in 1958, and Sammy Strain hooked up with the Fantastics (RCA) in 1960 and LITTLE ANTHONY AND THE IMPERIALS in the '60s and '70s.

Lincoln crashed the Invitations and Kenrod spun with THE PLATTERS for a while. 23 years after that fateful Chips record, John Belushi and Dan Aykroyd (the Blues Brothers of TV's "Saturday Night Live") released their own "Rubber Biscuit" that went to number 37 on the Top 100 in the spring of 1979. Renewed interest in the Chips original brought the group back together in 1979 (except for Sammy Strain who had joined THE O'JAYS). With Dave Eason on first tenor, they appeared at Ronnie I's Just for U show.

In April 1980, the Chips had their first release in 24 years with two oldie a cappella cuts on Clifton Records, "Everyone's Laughing" (THE SPANIELS) and "When I'm with You" (THE MOONGLOWS).

When not doing one of their occasional performances, Fulton is a sergeant for a security firm, Lincoln is with a chemical company, Epps is a chauffeur, and Johnson is a free-lance commercial artist.

The Chordettes

The Chordettes were one of the more popular white female groups of the '50s, but unlike most of their counterparts who needed record successes to get into TV and radio, they established themselves over the air and on the small screen years before ever cutting their first record. Formed in Sheboygan, Wisconsin, the quartet of Dorothy Schwartz (lead), Jinny Lockard (tenor), Carol Buschman (baritone), and Janet Ertel (bass) practiced their barbershop-style harmony to perfection in the late '40s.

They joined Arthur Godfrey's "Talent Scouts" show on radio in 1949 and soon graduated to his TV show as regulars. In 1953, both Dorothy and Jinny were replaced by Lynn Evans and Margie Needham, respectively. Early in that year Archie Bleyer, musical director for Godfrey, started his own record company called Cadence (it could have been dubbed Julius LaRosa Records since the first eight releases were all by the Brooklyn-born singer). The tenth single, in April 1954, was by the Chordettes as Bleyer felt there was room on records for another ANDREWS or MC GUIRE SISTERS. The girls' first release, "It's You, It's You I Love," went nowhere, but their second single, a lilting pop lullabye titled "Mister Sandman," took off (helped by its TV exposure) and went all the way to number one in the U.S. and to number 11 in England. With seven weeks at the top and 20 weeks on *Billboard*'s Best Sellers chart, "Mister Sandman" and the Chordettes were on top of the recording world. It was all the more embarrassing when their next two singles failed to chart at all; it wasn't until January 1956 that another Chordettes recording, "The Wedding," hit the Top 100, though it quickly dropped from the list. It was during this drought that the Chordettes decided to take the route of other white pop artists of the early '50s: when all else failed, cover a black artist's song and ride it up the chart. Thus the Teen Queens' "Eddie My Love" became the Chordettes' first top 20 record in two years. (The Teen Queens version fought it to a tie at number 14 Pop in the spring of 1957.) The girls' seventh single became one of their biggest yet, as "Born to Be with You" hit number five in the summer stateside and number eight in the U.K.

The group's most remarkable quality seemed to be its survivability. Every time they were written off as another too-sweet-for-the-times female group, they would emerge with another hit, straddling the fence between the pop world and the emerging rock and roll audience. After "Lay Down Your Arms" (#16, 1956) b/w "Teenage Goodnight" (#45) had a successful run, two more singles failed before the success of another two-sider, "Just Between You and Me" (#8, 1957) b/w "Soft Sands" (#73). Then their next single failed to chart. In fact the only two back-to-back top 20 records in their career were "Born to Be With You" and "Lay Down Your Arms."

In the spring of 1958 they burst onto the scene with a sound that both mature pop audiences and rock teens could like, embodied in "Lollipop." With its chime intro and a verse like a sing-along children's song, it was soon a number two hit from Malibu to Maine (and number six on the U.K. charts). Four of their next five singles were charters, including the theme from the popular TV show "Zorro" (#17, 1958) and the theme from the film *Never on Sunday* (#13, 1961). One that didn't make it but should have was the haunting Glenn Yarbrough folk song "All My Sorrows" in 1962.

By then, however, the group had become passé—not hip enough for the emerging rock and roll set. But the Chordettes' accomplishments were enviable (14 chart records and four top 10s in 22 releases) and their professionalism and attraction were undeniable. Archie Bleyer thought so. He even went so far as to marry one (Janet).

THE CHORDETTES

A SIDE/B SIDE	LABEL/CAT NO	DATE
It's You, It's You I Love / True Love Goes On And On	Cdnc 1239	4/54
Mr. Sandman / I Don't Wanna See You Cry	Cdnc 1247	10/54

A SIDE/B SIDE	LABEL/CAT NO	DATE
Lonely Lips / The Dudelsack Song	Cdnc 1259	4/55
I Told A Lie / Hummingbird	Cdnc 1267	8/55
The Wedding / I Don't Know, I Don't Care	Cdnc 1273	12/55
Eddie My Love / Whispering Willie	Cdnc 1284	2/56
Born To Be With You / Love Never Changes	Cdnc 1291	5/56
Lay Down You Arms / Teenage Goodnight	Cdnc 1299	9/56
Come Home To My Arms / (Fifi's) Walking The Poodle	Cdnc 1307	1/57
Echo Of Love / Like A Baby	Cdnc 1319	4/57
Just Between You And Me / Soft Sands	Cdnc 1330	8/57
Photographs / Baby Of Mine	Cdnc 1341	12/57
Lollipop / Baby Come-A Back-A	Cdnc 1345	2/58
Zorro / Love Is A Two-Way Street	Cdnc 1349	5/58
No Other Arms, No Other Lips / We Should Be Together	Cdnc 1361	3/59
A Girl's Work Is Never Done / Wheels	Cdnc 1366	8/59
All My Sorrows / A Broken Vow	Cdnc 1382	6/60
Never On Sunday / Faraway Star	Cdnc 1402	6/61
The Exodus Song / Theme From Goodbye Again	Cdnc 1412	2/62
Adios / White Rose Of Athens	Cdnc 1417	4/62
In The Deep Blue Sea / All My Sorrows	Cdnc 1425	7/62
True Love Goes On And On / All My Sorrows	Cdnc 1442	9/63

The Chords

In 1954 rhythm and blues was beginning to make inroads as a competitor to pop music, but the battle of the pop charts was still being won by white acts covering black artists' recordings. White-run radio stations would rarely play the original R&B version instead of or in competition with the often bland copy. Black vocal groups didn't have it any better than solo artists: from 1948 to mid-1954 only a handful had broached the pop charts and even fewer had made the top 20 without a white cover version leaving them in the dust, notable exceptions being THE ORIOLES' "It's Too Soon to Know" (#13, 1948), THE DOMINOES' "Sixty-Minute Man" (#17, 1951), and THE CROWS' "Gee" (#14, 1954). (The Crows' success was partially due to the inexplicable fact that no popular white act was competing against them with their own song.)

In fact, no rhythm and blues or rock and roll artist (depending on your definition of those two terms in 1954, and THE MILLS BROTHERS and INK

SPOTS were considered pop) had ever made the magical top 10. The Chords were simply the first.

Teaming up circa 1951, the five members brought a wide range of musical experience to their union. While most street-corner groups were only versed in gospel and blues, this new quintet had singers schooled in jazz, pop, and swing as well as blues and gospel. They were influenced not only by THE RAVENS and Orioles but also by THE FOUR FRESHMEN and MODERNAIRES and other pop and jazz acts. Carl and Claude Feaster (lead and baritone respectively) were from the Tunetoppers, first tenor Jimmy Keyes came from the Four Notes, second tenor Floyd "Buddy" McRae hailed from the Keynotes, and bass Ricky Edwards had been with a group previously dubbed the Chords. They were all from the Bronx and called themselves the Keynotes, but by the time they began rehearsing at Public School 99 the quintet had acquired the name the Chords. Their goal was to create a polished jazz, pop, R&B sound.

Armed with some original songs, the group went to New York to see Red Robin Records owner Bobby Robinson. They arranged to sing for him while he was sick in bed, probably a bad idea as he passed on both their new song "Sh-Boom" and the group itself.

Taking pride in the fact that they had never sung on a street corner, the Chords were nonetheless discovered not far from one. In 1954, they were singing on their way into a subway station when they were overheard by one Joe Glaser of Associated Booking, a major New York talent agency. Glaser gave them a business card. When the group came to audition, his associate, Oscar Cohen, felt impressed enough to bring the group to Atlantic Records. A talented Atlantic exec named Jerry Wexler was looking for a more sophisticated rhythm and blues group to record Patti Page's current piece of pop pabulum "Cross Over the Bridge."

On Monday, March 15, 1954, the Chords recorded a bouncy, swing-styled, call-and-response version of "Cross Over" that Wexler loved. He decided the B side should be the song they auditioned with, a strange, jazzy, swingin' concoction called "Sh-Boom." At that moment, with Atlantic in such a rush to get "Cross Over" on the market, and with B sides usually considered throwaways, it's conceivable they would have let the group sing a rock and roll version of "The National Anthem" if the Chords had it ready to record. And that's just about what "Sh-Boom" became. When word started coming out of California that the Chords record was getting very heavy sales orders, Atlantic was thrilled. Their reaction changed to shock when they

found out the side generating the orders was "Sh-Boom." But they recovered quickly enough to pull "Cross Over" from the record in June, adding a new B side recorded at the "Sh-Boom" session titled "Little Maiden." The strategy was to issue "Cross Over" at a later date. Strangely, Atlantic never did.

"Sh-Boom" was so hot that Atlantic required help from other distributors—including its competitor Mercury—to keep the record flowing to the stores while it was in demand. On July 3, 1954, the Chords' version of "Sh-Boom" hit both the Pop and R&B charts, scaling the heights to number two and an unprecedented number five Pop. It stayed on *Billboard*'s Best Seller list for four months.

The quintet toured from Boston to Los Angeles in July and on July 17, 1954, appeared at the fifth annual Rhythm and Blues Jubilee held at Hollywood's Shrine Auditorium, along with THE ROBINS, THE HOLLYWOOD FOUR FLAMES, and THE FOUR TUNES. In one of the stranger match-ups in musical history they appeared on the "Colgate Comedy Hour" and sang with New York Giants "Hall of Fame" outfielder Willie Mays on "Say Hey Willie."

By August their record had been issued on EMI in England and by October they were appearing on "Jukebox Jury" alongside satirist Stan Freberg, who had cut his own parody version of "Sh-Boom."

It seemed that only a loss of identity could interrupt the group's successful run. Then, of course, that's exactly what happened. In the fall of 1954 the group was forced to change its name due to legal action taken by the representatives of an obscure group called the Chords that had been recording since June 1953 on Gem Records. Carl Feaster's group then became the Chordcats. This bit of bad luck, compounded by the poor chart performance of an earlier release called "Zippity Zum," meant that the Chordcats' November single of the pretty ballad "A Girl to Love" never stood a chance. The Cats began to feel that the only way to regain their recognition was to rename themselves after their hit. The tactic was not destined to help. In October 1955 the Sh-Booms watched their last Atlantic single, "Could It Be," sink into oblivion. Its downward motion was not halted by the fact that their manager, Lou Krefetz, was spending an inordinate amount of time on his other act, THE CLOVERS.

In 1957 the Sh-Booms signed with Vik Records (RCA) for two sides, with baritone Arthur Dix and bass Joe Dias replacing Buddy McRae and Ricky Edwards. The group then broke up but re-formed with McRae and Edwards, the Feaster brothers, and Jimmy Keyes in November 1960 to record again for Atlantic. The song was a "Sh-Boom"-style standard, "Blue Moon," and their interpretation certainly had a degree of originality—not enough, however, to eclipse the MARCELS' version from March 1961.

"Blue Moon" ended up being the Chords' last release. In 1963, Jimmy Keyes joined the Popular Five (Rae-Cox) with Arthur Dix and made another attempt to resurrect "Sh-Boom," but to no avail. Apparently the song was good for only one passage through time and space, though the trip landed it in the history books as one of the signals of rock and roll's birth.

THE CHORDS

A SIDE/B SIDE	LABEL/CAT NO	DATE
Sh-Boom / Cross Over The Bridge	Cat 104	4/54
Sh-Boom / Little Maiden	Cat 104	6/54
Zippity Zum / Bless You	Cat 109	9/54
The Chordcats		
Hold Me Baby / A Girl To Love	Cat 112	11/54
The Sh-Booms		
Pretty Wild / Could It Be	Cat 117	10/55
Lu Lu / I Don't Want To Set		
The World On Fire	Vik 0295	9/57
Blue Moon / Short Skirts	Atln 2074	8/60
Sh-Boom / Little Maiden	Atco 6213	12/61

The Clefs

Arlington, Virginia, is the home of the National Cemetery and the Clefs. Any connection between the Clefs' career and the national burial ground is purely coincidental.

The Clefs became a group in high school in 1951, and included Scotty Mansfield on lead, Pavel Bess on tenor, Frank Newman on second tenor, Fred Council on baritone, and Gerald Bullock on bass. They performed locally for about a year at schools and parties and on radio and TV shows. Though impressed by hit groups like THE CLOVERS, THE ORIOLES, and THE DOMINOES, they tried to develop their own brand of rhythm and blues vocalizing.

In 1952, at the time of their first demo, James Sheppard (not THE HEARTBEATS' lead) was an occasional backup tenor and Leroy Flack (brother of '70s recording artist Roberta Flack) became a replacement for Gerald Bullock on bass.

The demos they made at US Recording somehow fell into the hands of Baltimore-Washington area talent finder and manager Lillian Claiborne. Most

groups of this period were either discovered performing in clubs or when they took their demos into someone's office. The Clefs, however, heard from Mrs. Claiborne without even knowing that she had listened to their tracks. She brought them to Chicago's Chess Records in 1952 where they recorded "We Three" along with "Right On." "We Three" had originally been recorded by THE INK SPOTS (#1, 1940); the Clefs' version was a bluesier interpretation with a surprising jump middle and jazz-flavored saxophone augmenting the fine harmony and Scotty Mansfield's silky lead. The record got enough reaction to keep the group working for a while, but not enough to chart.

In 1955 the quintet became a quartet when Flack dropped out and Bess became the bass. The Clefs then hooked up with Bosko Boyd to improve their recording fortunes. Their first release was an unsuccessful reworking of a past hit, so the group wrote some original songs and sent them to Houston's Peacock Records. Don Robey, Peacock's owner, was impressed enough to send them a contract in the mail. Instead of signing, the Clefs became perhaps the first unknown R&B group to go shopping for a deal after they'd received a contract offer. They auditioned for Vee-Jay Records in Chicago and found themselves with a second offer. Logic would have dictated that their East Coast sound would get more attention and greater exposure with the R&B-oriented Vee-Jay than it would with the Southern gospel and blues-based Peacock label. So naturally the Clefs signed with Robey's company.

Their first release of 1955 was "I'll Be Waiting," and they *kept* waiting, while the song saw little daylight. Willing to try anything to jump start the career machine, the Clefs changed their name to Scotty Mann and the Masters. It didn't help. Their next release, "Just a Little Bit of Loving," gained as little response as its predecessors, and the group began to concentrate on eking out a living from performances.

As a last straw, Robey refused to release the group from the label, even though he was failing to issue any of the numerous sides they had already recorded as the Clefs. They couldn't sign anywhere else even though there was reported interest from Verve Records in the late '50s.

By then, the members were finding the security of day jobs more attractive than the seemingly hopeless struggle for a career in the limelight. With three worthy but barely known efforts, their contribution to early '50s R&B was limited. But as one of the first groups attempting to choose rather than be chosen, they deserve to be remembered.

The Cleftones

The Cleftones were the only group in rock and roll history to get their start in an election campaign. They sang campaign slogans for a school election at Jamaica High School in Jamaica, New York, which pitted the intellectuals, often referred to as the nerds (the Cleftones' party), against the unbeaten jocks. When the singers decided to stay together after the election, rock and roll was the true winner (along with their party).

The group started out as a blending of two school groups: the Clefs, with Herbie Cox (lead and second tenor), Berman Patterson (second tenor and second lead), and Warren Corbin (bass); and Silvertones members Charlie James (first tenor) and William "Buzzy" McClain (baritone).

Herbie has fond memories of Billy Sturgis, an occasional sixth member in the early days who couldn't sing a lick but was a member because his mother would let them sing in her basement.

Herbie wrote a slogan over THE CROWS smash "Gee" in the fall that brought them hero status among their peers, giving them incentive to start playing local gigs.

Renamed the Cleftones (no one really remembers why), they practiced in Saint Albans Park and occasionally did vocal battle with neighbor Gene Pearson's white-leather-jacketed Rivileers (Pearson lived in the same apartment building as Herbie on 159th Street) and James Sheppard's Hearts (later to become the legendary HEARTBEATS). The group practiced in the back room of a beauty parlor owned by Buzzy's parents on 107th Avenue and Merrick Road in what the boys used to call "Bricktown" because of the rows of brick buildings on the block. Though each member had his own favorite groups (Charlie liked THE SWALLOWS and THE DIAMONDS; Buzzy, THE CARDINALS; Warren, Nat "King" Cole; Herbie, THE MOONGLOWS; and Berman, THE PENGUINS), the Cleftones' sound was truly unique, not leaning toward any one of their idols more than another. Though influenced by ballad-oriented groups, the 16- to 18-year-old members preferred and wrote up-tempo songs.

When they went auditioning for record labels in the fall of 1955 with their new manager and schoolmate Dave Rollneck, they sang mostly original songs that Dave had encouraged Berman Patterson and Herbie Cox to write. Rollneck, a super senior (in the '50s that meant someone who had been left back), had tried singing with the group without satisfactory results; out of frustration he one day announced on the handball court, "If I can't sing with you, let me manage you." Herbie remembers the group saying, "Fine, what's there to manage? We're going to play basketball." But Dave did schedule regular practices, encouraged the group, and focused their attention. He arranged the Cleftones' first gig at the Hillcrest Jewish Center in Flushing, where they earned $25 in the spring of 1955 singing MELLOWS tunes like "Smoke from Your Cigarette" and "How Sentimental Can I Be," as well as "Dear Lord" by the Continentals.

The Cleftones auditioned for Apollo, Baton, and Old Town Records and were turned down by each. Unbeknownst to the group (for many years thereafter) Old Town already had an R&B quartet known as the Cleftones ("The Masquerade Is Over," 1955) when Herbie and company auditioned.

Their next stop was 220 West 42nd Street in Manhattan and George Goldner's Rama label. Unlike the other office building record labels, Rama was several flights above a storefront housing PAL (the Police Athletic League), and it looked like anything but a record company. Herbie chuckles at the memory of walking up a flight of stairs and being accosted on the first landing by a man stacking boxes who brusquely inquired, "Whada you guys want?" The guys said, "We're looking for Mr. Goldner." "Well, who wants to see him?" came the response, to which they replied that they were the Cleftones and had set up an audition. Seeming satisfied with their answer, he told them to go to the next floor, knock on the door, and wait. The boys followed his instructions and knocked several times, but no one answered. Finally a voice from inside yelled at them to come in. The group and Dave pushed through two doors. Sitting behind the desk was the same man who had been stacking boxes, only now he was wearing a sports jacket and smoking a stogie. "I'm George Goldner," he announced. "Whada you guys call yourselves?"

After a half an hour of singing four or five original songs like Berman's "You Baby You" (though they opened with the Crows' "Gee" hoping to impress Goldner with a better version of his own group's song), the group left in shock with the knowledge Goldner wanted them in the studio to record on Tuesday.

The session and recording career of the Cleftones almost came to an abrupt end that weekend as the parents of Berman, Warren, and Herbie all objected to terms in Rama's contract; unlike most parents of 1950s teen groups, they called an attorney to suggest changes. When the revised contracts were sent via Rollneck back to Goldner, he was so furious he told Dave, "I never wanna see that group again!" When Dave compromised on certain terms two days later, Goldner agreed to sign the group and left in several key points that the parents' attorney had requested.

Released the third week of December 1955, "You Baby You" had the distinction of being the first release on Goldner's new Gee label (supposedly named after the Crows hit and a recurring good luck word for Herbie and company if ever there was one!).

"You" took a lock on the East Coast airwaves and managed a number 78 position on the *Billboard* Pop chart by February 18, 1956 (one week after FRANKIE LYMON AND THE TEENAGERS' "Why Do Fools Fall in Love" charted on the same label). Initially selling over 150,000 copies, the Cleftones were off and running. From its slow a cappella harmony intro to the sudden up-tempo verse to Jimmy Wright's driving sax, "You" captivated teen listeners.

The B side was a surprising white group-styled ballad that suggested the Cleftones' potential for mass appeal. Few black groups of the time had the ability to sound so pop, and though the song was mediocre you couldn't tell it was a rock and roll group (let alone a black act) until the final doo wop ending. Interestingly, the writer credits for both sides read "Berman-Vastola-Patterson," probably the first time a writer was credited twice on the same song.

The next Cleftones cut to click was the Herbie Cox-penned rocker "Little Girl of Mine," and by late spring of 1956 the whole country was singing "diddle little little little lit, yeah." *Billboard*'s R&B chart hosted its climb to number eight on both the Best Seller and Jukebox listings, and it peaked on the Pop chart at number 57. As usual, Jimmy Wright's sax winged its way through three minutes of the most satisfying vocal group rock of the '50s, and Herbie's voice became a sound that teens identified with. The Cleftones harmony was more noticeable on "Little Girl" than on "You Baby You" and showed them to be a first-rate supporting cast to Herbie's up-front vocals. "Little Girl" sold over 750,000 copies during its heyday and probably close to a million since then.

"Can't We Be Sweethearts" (Herbie's personal favorite), was another up-tempo cut written by Berman and Herbie and was released in June. *Billboard*'s June 23rd review called it "a strong follow-up to 'Little Girl of Mine.' The youngsters have another tricky-beat rhythm ballad right in the current teenage taste groove." It sold nearly 200,000 copies, but by now Gee was devoting its attention to Frankie Lymon's group and anyone else who walked in the door and sounded like they had a hit. Sadly,

most record people of the time had little belief in artist development, possibly thinking that rock and roll was merely a fad; the standard strategy was to find a hot new hit and sound as fast as they could.

The group did benefit from its exposure and used the opportunity to play every venue imaginable from the Murray the K dance parties to the Apollo Theater, where they set a record by appearing 12 times in one year. Their professionalism, stable lineup, and quality records made them favorites of Alan Freed, who used them on nine holiday special shows. (On one such Paramount show in 1957 the group backed up Charlie Gracie on his hit "Butterfly" while singing from the wings. They also backed Roulette label mate Jimmy Rodgers on stage in about 1959.) Through their career the Cleftones performed with such acts as THE PLATTERS, THE DRIFTERS, The Teenagers, and numerous others. Their first big show in 1956 was at Detroit's Fox Theatre with THE CADILLACS, LaVern Baker, Lonnie Donegan, Bobby Lewis, Bob Crewe, and a group Herbie describes as "the best performing vocal group bar none," the Royal Jokers (Atco). Unfortunately the Cleftones showed up for that show with no charts and no idea what a chart was. To bail them out, old pro Bobby Lewis said, "Okay, I'll sing it," and Bob Crewe said, "I'll write up the chart for the musicians." Bobby Lewis, who had been recording for Parrot Records since 1952, became the group's "show business father" as Herbie put it. (Five years later Bobby would have his monster number one record "Tossin' and Turnin'." Bob Crewe would also have his day in the sun as the producer of most of THE FOUR SEASONS' hits.)

The Cleftones' fourth single, "String Around My Heart" (September 1956), was another formula jump tune that sold more on its merit and group reputation than on its label support; it finished up at around 70,000 copies. The Cleffies' last record of 1956 was "Why Do You Do Me Like You Do," their first rocker not containing a searing sax solo, and another fine example of Berman Patterson writing, Cleftones harmonizing, and Gee Records malfunctioning. (The cute nickname was coined by Little Richard, who loved the group and often referred to them as "my little Cleffies.") Indicating an apparent attempt to get the songwriting credits right for a change, "Why" now read "Patterson and Patterson" (Berman is probably still laughing).

Their first release of 1957 was also their first A side ballad, "See You Next Year." By switching to a non-rocker and creating a timely song about school being over, the Cleftones hoped to get back on the charts and put Gee in gear. Neither idea worked. It was back to up-tempo tunes in the fall with a strange twist. "Hey Babe" (and its ballad flip "What Did I Do That Was Wrong?") sounded like the Cleftones had walked into a style changer and come out as the FOUR ACES or THE FOUR FRESH-MEN. These recordings might be best described as sounding like a black group imitating a white group imitating a black group. Neither song was written by the quintet.

A classic Cleftones story took place around this time on what performers called the "grits and gravy circuit"—the Apollo (New York), the Howard (Washington), the Royal (Baltimore), and the Regal (Chicago) theatres, and the Royal Peacock (Atlanta) and the Flame (Detroit) clubs. The group had avoided playing the Royal because of its reputation as the rowdiest theatre on the circuit, with balcony members who hurled miniature bottles at performers. The group finally had no choice and in late 1957 drove their station wagon into the alley of the Royal where they met an assortment of pre-show hang-arounds. One character approached them and promised, for the sum of $10, to calm the balcony rowdies. The Cleffies went for it even though they'd heard Little Richard had recently been bottled on that very stage and they knew that if Richard got nailed the Cleftones would, too. But they paid the man and he quickly disappeared. At showtime the nervous quintet took the stage and performed to cheers from the balcony throughout the show. Afterward they ran into their savior (whom they had nicknamed Slick) and asked what had happened to the balcony malcontents. Apparently Slick had bought them a few cheap bottles of wine "compliments of the Cleftones."

1958 started with the group's best two-sider, the contagious "Lover Boy" and the sensitive ballad "Beginners at Love." The Herbie Cox tunes were perfect for radio, but radio didn't agree, at least not yet. A chance meeting in 1958 with former King A&R exec Henry Glover, now working for Roulette, triggered a move to that label and the release of a "Little Girl of Mine" spin-off entitled "She's So Fine." A far superior effort to the following year's "Cuzin Casanova," both ended up with the same less-than-favorable fate. "Casanova's" B side, "Mish Mash Baby" was even worse, but it had an excuse: it was co-written by Murray the K's mother.

One more release that was not up to true Cleftones standards and the Jamaica High juveniles were ready for a change.

In 1958 Buzzy McClain left and former Rivileers lead and Jamaica neighbor Gene Pearson replaced him. Berman Patterson also jumped ship and Gene's friend Patricia Span came aboard. In 1961, Henry Glover introduced the group to

Drifters manager George Treadwell, who soon assumed that duty for the Cleftones. The Drifters, by the early '60s, were in such disarray that Treadwell actually asked the Cleftones if they would become the new Drifters so he could fire the whole bunch. When they declined, he managed to lure Gene Pearson away to sing second tenor on numerous Drifters charters from 1963 on.

By 1961 Glover had convinced the group that recording standards was the way to go. The quintet wound up back on Gee (now a part of Roulette) doing the Larry Clinton hit "Heart and Soul" (#1, 1938). It became their first chart record in five years, hitting number 18 (#10 R&B). Their August release, a remake of Nat "King" Cole's number one ballad "For Sentimental Reasons," also charted Pop, reaching number 60 in the fall. The Cleftones were vocally in great form and had apparently found a good niche. At the same time, the label execs heard a cut from the group titled "Vacation in the Mountains" that they wanted to issue. Not daring to release a second Cleftones single while "Sentimental Reasons" was clicking, they issued it by Herbie Cox on their Rama subsidiary (the last release ever issued on that label).

The summer of 1961 ushered in the group's first LP, *Heart and Soul*, and by December they had another, *For Sentimental Reasons*.

Of their next four ballad-turned-jump remakes, "Earth Angel" (the Penguins, 1956), "Again" (Doris Day, 1949), "Lover Come Back to Me" (Paul Whiteman, 1929), and "How Deep Is the Ocean?" (Guy Lombardo, Rudy Vallee, and Ethel Merman, all 1932), only "Lover" charted, and its brief appearance at number 95 in December 1962 signaled the end of the remake releases. "Again," by the way, had Sherman Garnes of the Teenagers on bass replacing Warren Corbin. Over the years the Teenagers and the Cleftones remained very close friends. Frankie Lymon looked up to Warren Corbin as a big brother; Herbie and Teenager Joe Negroni got along particularly well; and Charlie and Jimmy Merchant would sit together for hours trying to outsing each other and still do it to this day. The group's personal and professional relationship has lasted over 35 years, and as recently as early 1991 both acts played Carnegie Hall together.

The Cleftones' last original release came in 1964 on a Roulette subsidiary, Ware Records, but "He's Forgotten You" was hardly recognizable as the Cleftones and was forgotten. Surprisingly, while the British were taking America town by town, Pittsburgh's number one record for a time in 1964 was a reissued Cleftones Gee single titled "Lover Boy." The group worked extensively in that area thanks to the local success some six years after the song's original release.

Though never officially breaking up, the group became inactive until 1970 when Berman and Herbie met in a bar and decided to put the act back together, including Herbie's cousin Tony Gaines. A few oldies revival shows later and they were once again doing regular performances. At some point in the '70s several old cuts from the *Sentimental Reasons* LP were issued by collectors on Robin Hood Records.

In December 1990, Classic Artists Recordings (the best of the vocal group labels of the '80s) issued the first new Cleftones single in 24 years, "My Angel Lover" b/w "You Lost the Game of Love," both songs worth the wait. The members on that recording were Herbie Cox on lead, his cousin Tony Gaines on first tenor, Nick Saunders on bass baritone, and Herbie overdubbing second tenor parts. The group later added Charlie James, not available for that record. In April 1991, the Cleftones made it to Europe for the first time, appearing at the Wembley Convention Center in London with THE FIVE KEYS.

The Cleftones were still active in the early '90s, though all were backing up their singing with separate careers. Charlie James became an engineer with IBM, Buzzy McClain retired in 1988 as an automobile salesman, Gene became a New York City transit cop, Berman retired from the police force's Department of Corrections in New York, Warren Corbin died of cancer in the late '70s, Pat sang with Thad Jones's Big Band, and Herbie retired in 1990 as a vice president of Manufacturers Hanover Trust bank, while going on to manage THE CHORDETTES of "Lollipop" fame.

THE CLEFTONES

A SIDE/B SIDE	LABEL/CAT NO	DATE
You Baby You / I Was Dreaming	Gee 1000	1955
Little Girl Of Mine / You're Driving Me Mad	Gee 1011	3/56
Can't We Be Sweethearts / Neki Hokey	Gee 1016	6/56
String Around My Heart / Happy Memories	Gee 1025	9/56
Why Do You Do Me Like You Do / I Like Your Style Of Making Love	Gee 1031	11/56
See You Next Year / Ten Pairs Of Shoes	Gee 1038	6/57
Hey Babe / What Did I Do That Was Wrong	Gee 1041	10/57
Lover Boy / Beginners At Love	Gee 1048	1/58
She's So Fine / Trudy	Roul 4094	1958

A SIDE/B SIDE	LABEL/CAT NO	DATE
Cuzin Casanova / Mish Mash Baby	Roul 4161	8/59
She's Gone / Shadows Of The Very Last Row	Roul 4302	11/60
Heart And Soul / How Do You Feel	Gee 1064	4/61
For Sentimental Reasons	Gee 1067	8/61
Earth Angel / Blues In The Night	Gee 1074	5/62
Again / Do You	Gee 1077	7/62
Lover Come Back To Me / There She Goes	Gee 1079	9/62
How Deep Is The Ocean / Some Kinda Blue	Gee 1080	11/62
He's Forgotten You / Right From The Git Go	Ware 6001	1964
Since We Fell In Love / Heavenly Father	RbnHd 132	1970s
Please Say You Want Me / So You And I Can Climb	RbnHd 133	1970s

The Clovers

Throughout pop music history, record company presidents have gone to great lengths to coax hit records out of their artists, but rarely have they gone to the extreme of writing the hits for the acts themselves. Ahmet Ertegun did that for the Clovers, however. In fact, Ertegun wrote eight A or B sides for that group out of their first nine singles, including their first two number one R&B chart records.

The Clovers story started in Washington, D.C., in 1946. Harold "Hal" Lucas founded the group by choosing schoolmates at Armstrong High School. The original members were tenor Thomas Woods, bass Billy Shelton, and Harold (all were from the area of T Street and 7th in the nation's capital). When John "Buddy" Bailey came on board as lead, Harold moved over to baritone. Hal wanted to give his music career a lucky start so he named the group the Four Clovers. By 1949, second tenor Matthew McQuater had replaced Thomas Woods. The group played clubs and amateur shows, singing songs by THE INK SPOTS, THE ORIOLES, and THE RAVENS. It was at one such show that Harold Winley met the group and wound up replacing Billy Shelton. They officially became the Clovers when guitarist Bill Harris gained membership in 1949.

In 1950 they met record store owner Lou Krefetz at a club they were playing (called the Rose Club) right in the neighborhood they grew up in. Krefetz became their manager and took them to Eddie Heller's Rainbow Records at 767 Tenth Avenue in

New York City, a label so small it shared space with a Hell's Kitchen storefront known as Sonny's Deli. Rainbow signed the Clovers, making them the label's first vocal group. Rainbow would become the launching pad for two more great acts, LEE ANDREWS AND THE HEARTS and THE FIVE CROWNS (who later became THE DRIFTERS).

A recording session produced two sides. One was a remake of the 1925 Gene Austin hit "Yes Sir, That's My Baby" in an Ink Spots style with John Bailey doing an excellent imitation of Spots lead Bill Kenny. Accompanied by a tinkling piano and a standup bass, the group's solid harmony was much in evidence, as were the Ravens and CHARIOTEERS influences. Rainbow Records slipped up on their promotional efforts, however, and "Yes Sir" never had a chance. The record was reviewed by *Cashbox* magazine on January 6, 1951 as a pop release, indicative of the industry's initial perception of the quartet. Krefetz, noting Rainbow's inabilities and still very high on his group's potential, immediately took the Clovers to Ahmet Ertegun's Atlantic Records. Ahmet, a son of the former Turkish ambassador to the United States, had launched Atlantic on an investment of $10,000 from his family's dentist in late 1947.

Ertegun didn't really like Ink Spots-type groups (he didn't even like the Ink Spots) and was reluctant to sign the Clovers, but when "Waxie Maxie" Silverman interceded on his friend Krefetz's behalf, the Atlantic chief began to see how he could mold the group into a successful act. To achieve that end he wrote a song that would forever dictate the style and direction of the Clovers. On February 22, 1951 the Clovers recorded "Don't You Know I Love You," a mid-tempo, choppy-rhythmed shuffle with Buddy Bailey's blues-tinged vocal leading the group. The surprising use of a sax solo (one of the first on a vocal group record) came about when bandleader Frank Culley demanded to be paid even though he and his sax were not supposed to play on the record. Since Ertegun had to pay Frank as a leader anyway, he let him play and Culley winged it from there. The B side was another old song, the ballad "Skylark" written by Johnny Mercer and Hoagy Carmichael and recorded in 1942 by Dinah Shore (a top five pop hit for her).

The songwriting credit for "Don't You Know I Love You" on Atlantic 934 read Nugetre—Ertegun spelled backward. (He may have been trying to avoid embarrassment for his relatives stemming from the notion of a diplomat's son writing R&B songs.) Actually Nugetre wrote "head" melodies since he couldn't play an instrument or write music. He would record his songs in Times Square recording booths, then take the paper discs and give them to his musicians to reproduce.

The single came out in March 1951 to little fanfare; vocal group records with a mid-tempo blues feel had not yet reached the black record buyer's consciousness. Another obstruction was the fact that in 1950 the black charts consisted of only 10 positions, so a record really had to be selling to make it. But by June "Don't You Know" had built up enough momentum to jump on the R&B top 10 at number three. It took the Clovers 13 more weeks to get to number one, finally beating out THE DOMINOES' "Sixty Minute Man" for the coveted spot. All told it lasted 21 weeks in the top 10 and sold a reported quarter-of-a-million copies.

The Clovers' next session was on July 12 at WHOM Studios where they cut "Needless" by guitarist Harris, tenor McQuater, and manager Krefetz (everyone was getting in on the writing act), and another Ertegun tune called "Fool, Fool, Fool." Their Ink Spots styling gone, the Clovers were now a pioneering blues vocal group. The group's sound was rough and unpolished. They sang riffs usually played on a keyboard. Buddy's lead was bluesy, a little like what B. B. King might have sung.

"Fool" became their second number one hit, staying at the top of the *Billboard* R&B chart for six weeks and selling more than half a million platters. Amazingly, with two number one records Atlantic was still recording only two sides at a time. On December 17, they cut yet another Ertegun song, "In the Middle of the Night," with a pounding drum beat and walking bass line woven into a bluesy ballad. The other recording done that day was "One Mint Julep," a witty Rudy Toombs composition about one libation too many. "In the Middle" rose to number three, giving Ertegun his third hit in a row as a writer. "One Mint Julep" went to number two and was only kept out of the top spot because of Rudy Toombs himself: the number one record at the time, "5-10-15 Hours" by Ruth Brown, was also one of Rudy's compositions. In that same month the Clovers cut three sides of which two, "Ting-A-Ling" and "Wonder Where My Baby's Gone," charted in July. "Wonder" went to number seven while "Ting-A-Ling," another Ertegun slice of R&B, went to number one.

The next release was another chart-bound two sider: "Hey Miss Fannie" (cut at an August 7th session) and "I Played the Fool" (from the March session that produced "Ting-A-Ling"). "Fool" was their prettiest and most harmony-oriented ballad since "Skylark," with a weaving falsetto harmony behind Bailey's lead that was ahead of its time by several years. "Fannie" was an out and out rocker with more than a passing similarity to THE MOON-GLOWS' 1954 "Real Gone Mama" and THE PARAGONS' 1957 "Hey Little Schoolgirl." It was a rock and roll cut two years before such recordings were considered to exist. "Fannie" (another Ertegun original) peaked at number two R&B while "I Played the Fool" went to number three.

By the time the Clovers charted with "Crawlin'," their ninth song on six singles, lead John Bailey had been in the army almost four months. "Crawlin'" was Bailey's last lead for two years. While it was reaching the number three spot in March 1953, Bailey's slot was filled by former DOMINOES and Checkers member Charlie White. Their next single had White on lead. Ertegun's "Good Lovin'" reached number two, spending four-and-a-half months on the charts.

In 1954 White made his biggest contribution to the ever-growing Clovers legend when he led the group through two scorching blues rockers, "Little Mama" (#4) and the Ertegun co-penned "Lovey Dovey" (#2). The "Little Mama"/"Lovey Dovey" September 24th session was the first Clovers production matching Ertegun with the now-legendary producer Jerry Wexler.

Ongoing chart recognition enabled the quartet to work the top theaters around the country, from the Apollo to the Howard and the Regal. They also played Alan Freed's first rock and roll show in early 1954 and toured with other Atlantic artists such as Big Joe Turner, the Drifters, and Ruth Brown.

By April 1954 Charlie White had joined the Playboys on Cat (another Atlantic subsidiary) and was replaced by Atlantic vocalist Billy Mitchell. He had previously issued four singles on Atlantic as a solo artist between 1951 and 1952 but had never charted. His stint with the Clovers changed that with "Your Cash Ain't Nothin' But Trash" (#6, 1954). The B side, a holdover from the "Little Mama" session, was written by Harold Winley's brother Paul (Paul would go on to write many of the great recordings of the Paragons and THE JESTERS), and it reached number seven. By the fall of 1954 Bailey had returned; the group decided to retain Mitchell for alternate leads.

"I Confess" (written by Nugetre and featuring Charlie White) and "All Right Oh Sweetie" (Bailey's re-debut) came out in November and failed to chart. Luckily the R&B hit list had expanded allowing a number 14 charting for the classic ballad "Blue Velvet," issued in late 1954 with an exceptional Buddy Bailey lead and harmony background. By early 1955 the R&B market was saturated with vocal groups and record labels, all competing for the top spots on the charts. The

Clovers' new releases weren't up to the competition: "Love Bug" failed and "Nip Sip" spent two weeks getting to number 10. In January 1956 Atlantic released the Clovers' 15th single, a pop-sounding ballad entitled "Devil or Angel" that lifted the group back up to number three while its flip side, the rocking "Hey Doll Baby," went to number eight and became the last of six double-sided charters for the group.

By mid-1957 the Clovers (the most popular R&B vocal group of the first half of the '50s, with 19 hits on 15 singles) had accomplished about everything a group could do except put a record on the pop listings. That changed in June 1956 when "Love, Love, Love" rose to number 30 (#10 R&B). But instead of leading to a greater degree of national popularity, the pop hit had just the opposite effect. Their next six singles failed to chart on either of the Pop or R&B lists. Having taken the Clovers to the masses, Atlantic now found itself losing its original R&B base. In August 1957 the label's dismay led them to release a four-year-old recording, "Down in the Alley," whose chief feature was its "changity-changity-changity-chang-chang" intro and an exit borrowed from the feel of Joe Turner's "TV Mama." The B side was a reworking of "O Solo Mio" (from 1899) (and the Clovers' version quite possibly gave Elvis the idea for his 1960 hit "It's Now or Never").

Though their deal expired with Atlantic in July 1957 Ertegun's company still released two more singles—that went nowhere. Lou Krefetz then decided to start his own Poplar label, releasing two less-than-exciting singles and an LP by Bailey and company. In 1959 they moved to United Artists and continued their slump with nine non-charting records, including an average reading of the oldie "Old Black Magic." In the summer of 1959 the magicians behind the COASTERS hits, Jerry Leiber and Mike Stoller, took hold of the Clovers and wrote a cross between "One Mint Julep" and half the records recorded by the Coasters. Titled "Love Potion No. 9," it was their most successful release ever on the pop listings, peaking at number 23 in October (#23 R&B, December).

Trying to keep the magic going, they remade their old hit "One Mint Julep." It, and the next three U.A. singles, stirred little interest. By November 1961, the Clovers found themselves back on Atlantic for only one release.

The original Clovers disbanded, but Bailey and Hal Winley formed a new Clovers to record for Paul Winley's Winley Records in 1961. In 1962, Harold Lucas formed a second Clovers group with Roosevelt "Tippie" Hubbard on lead, Jerome "Toy" Walton at tenor, and Robert Russell on bass. This group sang for Brunswick, Stenton (as Tippie and the Clovermen), and Tiger Records (as Tippie and the Clovers). Meanwhile, Bailey's Clovers had moved over to Porwin Records for two singles, the best of which, a ballad titled "Stop Pretending," featured background harmonies that were closer to a girl-group sound than the typical Clovers raunchiness. In April 1965 Bailey and Lucas, with Jimmy Taylor on tenor and Robert Russell, recorded "Poor Baby" and "He Sure Could Hypnotize," produced by original Atlantic co-owner Herb Abramson. Soon after, Russell died and Bailey's Winley Clovers never recorded again. It's reported that Lucas, with the addition of Walton, John Bowie (he and Walton were formerly in the Bachelors on Royal Roost), and Tippie, recorded for Josie in 1968 and continued to perform into the '70s. 43 years after he formed the Clovers, Harold Lucas and the current contingent (John Bowie, Steve Charles, and Johnny Mason) recorded "Run Rudolph Run" (formerly by Chuck Berry) and an original song called "The Magic of Christmas Eve." Both were included on the 1989 LP *A Capitol Xmas* (BJM Records).

The Clovers were the most successful rhythm and blues vocal group of the '50s, scoring 21 chart records, far more than any other group. That alone would have secured their place in music history. But their distinctive style is better remembered than many of their hits. Under the guidance of Ahmet Ertegun, Herb Abramson (who coproduced many of their early hits with Ahmet), and Jerry Wexler, they reworked blues and gospel into blues with a beat. In so doing they became one of the first R&B groups to cross the bridge to rock and roll.

THE CLOVERS

A SIDE/B SIDE	LABEL/CAT NO	DATE
Yes Sir That's My Baby / When You Come Back To Me	Rainbow 122	1950
Don't You Know I Love You / Skylark	Atln 934	3/51
Fool Fool Fool / Needless	Atln 944	8/51
One Mint Julep / Middle Of The Night	Atln 963	3/52
Ting-A-Ling / Wonder Where My Baby's Gone	Atln 969	6/52
I Played The Fool / Hey Miss Fannie	Atln 977	10/52
Yes It's You / Crawlin'	Atln 989	2/53
Here Goes A Fool / Good Lovin'	Atln 1000	6/53
Comin' On / The Feeling Is So Good	Atln 1010	11/53
Lovey Dovey / Little Mama	Atln 1022	2/54

A SIDE/B SIDE	LABEL/CAT NO	DATE
I've Got My Eyes On You / Your Cast Ain't Nothin' But Trash	Atln 1035	6/54
I Confess / Alrighty, Oh Sweetie	Atln 1046	10/54
Blue Velvet / If You Love Me	Atln 1052	12/54
Love Bug / In The Morning Time	Atln 1060	4/55
Nip Sip / If I Could Be Loved By You	Atln 1073	8/55
Devil Or Angel / Hey Doll Baby	Atln 1083	1/56
Love Love Love / Your Tender Lips	Atln 1094	5/56
From The Bottom Of My Heart / Bring Me Love	Atln 1107	8/56
Baby Baby Oh My Darling / A Lonely Fool	Atln 1118	11/56
Here Comes Romance / You Good-Looking Woman	Atln 1129	3/57
I'll Love You / So Young	Atln 1139	5/57
Down In The Alley / There's No Tomorrow	Atln 1152	8/57
Wishing For Your Love / All About You	Atln 1175	1/58
The Gossip Wheel / Please Come On To Me	Popular 110	1958
The Good Old Summertime / Idaho	Popular 111	1958
Old Black Magic / Rock And Roll Tango	UA 174	1959
Love Potion #9 / Stay Awhile	UA 180	8/59
One Mint Julep / Lovey	UA 209	1960
Easy Lovin' / I'm Confessin' That I Love You	UA 227	1960
Yes It's You / Burning Fire	UA 263	1960
Have Gun / The Honey Dripper	UA 307	1961
The Bootie Green / Drive It Home	Atln 2129	11/61
Wrapped Up In A Dream* / Let Me Hold You*	Winley 255	6/61
Be My Baby* / They're Rockin' Down The Street*	Winley 265	1961
I Need You Now* / Gotta Quit You*	Winley 265	1961
Bossa Nova Baby** / The Bossa Nova**	Tiger 201	12/62
Please Mr. Sun† / Gimme, Gimme, Gimme†	Stntn 7001	1962
Stop Pretending* / One More Time*	Porwin 1001	6/63
Love Love Love†† / The Kickapoo††	Brns 55249	8/63
It's All In The Game* / That's What I Will Be*	Porwin 1004	1963
Poor Baby / He Sure Could Hypnotize	Port 3004	1965
Too Long Without Some Loving / For Days	Josie 992	1968
Try My Lovin' On You / Sweet Side Of A Soulful Woman	Josie 997	1968

*	The Baily Group
**	Tippie and the Clovers (Lucas Group)
†	Tippie and the Clovermen
††	The Clovers (Lucas Group)

The Coasters

The Coasters were the clown princes of late '50s rock and roll. Formed by the ace songwriting/ producing team of Jerry Leiber and Mike Stoller as an extension of the ROBINS, the Coasters were lead Carl Gardner and bass Bobby Nunn (both formerly of the Robins), along with second tenor Leon Hughes (founder of THE HOLLYWOOD FOUR FLAMES in 1950 and member of THE LAMPLIGHTERS in 1953), and Billy Guy (of Bip and Bob on Alladin in 1955).

The Coasters really came about because of the achievements of the L.A.-based Robins. In 1956 Leiber and Stoller, buoyed by their songwriting success on such records as "Hound Dog" by Big Mama Thornton, started their own Spark label, taking the Robins with them from RCA. Their November 1955 release of "Smokey Joe's Cafe" grabbed the attention of Atlantic Records and a unique pact (for 1956) was arranged. Jerry and Mike would sell their Robins masters to Atlantic's new Atco subsidiary and would act as outside producers on the Robins' new recordings. Since various members of the Robins were opposed to going to the new East Coast label, the two who weren't (Gardner and Nunn) became half of the newly christened Coasters, so named because they were all from the West Coast.

Leiber and Stoller now had a tailor-made group to promulgate their unusual perceptions of real-life scenarios as expressed in semi-comic songs. Instead of dealing with the out-of-the-ordinary, as in the Robins' "Riot in Cell Block #9," the Coasters sang about everyday events, like the trials and tribulations of youth in "Yakety Yak."

The first Coasters single, "Down in Mexico," was set in a dingy bar. *Billboard*'s February 25th review enthusiastically proclaimed, "Here's a new and definitely swinging crew and they deliver a couple of highly commendable sides. 'Down in Mexico' is a fetching ditty which is very close to 'Smokey Joe's Cafe.' This group carries the lead and bass singer from the Robins unit which recorded the 'Smokey' side." The March 17th issue of *Billboard* listed it as a "best buy," stating, "This record is getting excellent R&B and pop reaction. Pittsburgh, Baltimore, Buffalo, Cleveland, Chicago, Nashville, Atlanta, Durham and St. Louis are among the areas in which it has found broad acceptance."

By April it was number eight on the R&B Juke Box listings and number nine on *Billboard*'s R&B

Best Sellers and Disc Jockey chart. From "Down in Mexico," the quartet took its next musical journey to "Brazil," although it was the B side ("One Kiss Led to Another") that made the Coasters' first impression on the pop charts, reaching number 73 in September 1956 (#11 R&B).

The L.A.-based group was now two-for-two on the charts but did not record again for a year due to an increased schedule of touring and resettling in New York. But the wait was worth it. When the Coasters emerged from the studio on February 12, 1957, they had completed two of the finest recordings of their career. "Young Blood" shot to number eight (#2 R&B); the flip side, "Searchin'," passed it at number three (#11 R&B). Their first of four million-sellers was the first two-sider to go top 10 Pop for a black group since THE MILLS BROTHERS did it in 1949 with "I Love You So Much It Hurts" (#8) b/w "I've Got My Love to Keep Me Warm" (#9). Around this same time the Coasters ghosted behind LaVern Baker on "Jim Dandy Got Married" (#7 R&B), giving them three records on the R&B top 10. Both "Jim Dandy Got Married" and "Searchin'" hit the charts the same day (May 13, 1957).

The Coasters were unique in more ways than one. While most '50s groups sang love songs, the Coasters sang about the real lives of teenagers (thanks to Leiber and Stoller), often with a comic touch and a bit of sarcasm, as in "Charlie Brown." Additionally, while most of the other '50s acts were smoothing out their "oohs" and "ahs" behind the lead vocal, the Coasters were often singing in a raunchy unison or backing up the lead with more of a call-and-response than a doo wop or blow harmony accompaniment. With the help of the lyrics, they got away with some pretty primitive blues and R&B under the guise of novelty rock and roll. One such recording was "Idol with the Golden Head," an August 1957 release that had a slowed-down Bo Diddley rhythm and only rose to number 64 Pop in the closing months of the year. The opposite side, "My Baby Comes to Me," should have done better; it was a lyrical forerunner of "example" songs like THE TEMPTATIONS' 1964 hit "The Way You Do the Things You Do" and THE MIRACLES' "I'll Try Something New" from 1962.

A quick January 1958 failure, a draggy, funky, blues rendition of "Sweet Georgia Brown," and the group was set for its first changes. Nunn and Hughes quit for the domestic life, with Hughes replaced by tenor and lead Cornell Gunter of the early PLATTERS on Federal and the Flairs (Flair). Nunn's replacement was Will "Dub" Jones of THE CADETS (Modern). The new Coasters' first recording session, on March 17, 1958, brought forth two more immortal tracks. Today's pop fans young and old know that when they hear that intro of "take out the papers and the trash, or you don't get no spending cash," they're listening to a comical parody of '50s parenthood called "Yakety Yak." By the summer it was number one Pop and R&B and number twelve in England, their second charter in the British Isles ("Searchin'" was the first). The flip of "Yakety" was a departure for the group, an infectious mid-tempo doo wop version of the old Judy Garland tune (#22, 1943) "Zing Went the Strings of My Heart." Though eclipsed by the success of "Yakety Yak" it has since become one of the favorites of Coasters fans.

While "Georgia Brown" bombed in 1957 her brother "Charlie" was an instant success in 1959. By March, "Charlie Brown," with its "why is everybody always pickin' on me" hook, had reached number two Pop (kept from the top spot by Frankie Avalon's "Venus" three weeks running) and number two R&B while becoming their biggest British blockbuster at number six. For teens it was practically the national anthem, honking sax solos and all. Now that the Coasters and company had successfully taken on parenthood and teen angst, they decided to tackle the current craze, TV westerns (seven out of 10 top-rated 1959 shows were shoot 'em ups). The result was the hilarious "Along Came Jones," with the same kind of infectious rhythm, honking sax solo, tongue-in-cheek lyrics, and contagious Coasters chanting that made "Charlie" and "Yakety" immortal. In the spring the kids were singing about "Brown" and in the summer they were singing about "Jones" as he peaked at number nine (#14 R&B). It's a strong possibility that Leiber and Stoller's concept for "Jones" had been influenced by the OLYMPICS summer 1958 hit "Western Movies" (#8), but since the Olympics were self-confessed admirers of the Coasters, any borrowing by L&S was from an extension of their own original creation. The group's July 16, 1959, session yielded the memorable "Poison Ivy," which went to number seven (#1 R&B) while escalating to number 15 in the U.K.

The Coasters' year-end release was "What About Us," a biting social statement that managed to slip by the programming arbiters. With lyrics like "he's got a house made of glass, got his own swimming pool (what a gas), we've got a one-room shack, a pile of sticks by the railroad tracks, what about us, what about us, don't wanna cause no fuss but what about us," it's a wonder 1959 white radio played it at all. Perhaps they were more distressed by its flip "Run Red Run," which depicted a beer-guzzling poker-playing monkey trying to shoot his owner for cheating at cards. Either way, the decision was split: "What About Us" went to number 47 (#17 R&B) while "Run Red Run" reached number 36 (#29 R&B), denying "What About Us" the chance to be recognized as a Coasters classic and a telling commentary on the times.

A throw-away recording of Jimmy Dorsey's "Besame Mucho" reached number 70 in May 1960, and the first Coasters-written charter (Billy Guy) followed in the form of "Wake Me Shake Me," a Leiber-Stoller-style romp through life from a garbageman's perspective (#51 Pop, #14 R&B).

The Coasters had increased their following not only with hit records but with a sizzling stage routine that invited comparison with THE CADILLACS. On one tour the Coasters added a temporary replacement for lead Carl Gardner by the name of Lou Rawls. The young former gospel vocalist (and member of THE PILGRIM TRAVELERS from 1957 to 1959) was still more than five years from his first solo hit, "Love Is a Hurtin' Thing" (#13, 1966).

The Coasters' next four singles ("Shoppin' for Clothes" [#83], "Wait a Minute" [#37], "Little Egypt" [#23], and "Girls, Girls, Girls Part II" [#96]) did more pop charting than R&B. Only "Little Egypt" broached the R&B lists and it's no coincidence that it was the most imaginative and zany of the crop of Coasters cuts spanning 1960 to 1961.

During 1961 Cornell Gunter left the Coasters, and the Cadillacs' Earl "Speedo" Carroll took his spot. Of the singles released between 1962 and 1966, only "T'Ain't Nothin' to Me" charted (#64, 1964). The A side was "Speedo's Back in Town," a belated tribute to Earl that was recorded live at the Apollo Theatre some two years after he joined the group.

In 1964 the Coasters issued "Wild One," which took a gentle jab at the Beatles with "oohs" from "I Saw Her Standing There." The group resorted to cover songs late in their career, but versions of THE CLOVERS' "Lovey Dovey" and THE DRIFTERS' "Money Honey" fell on deaf mid-'60s ears. Will Jones left in 1965, leaving the group with Carroll of the Cadillacs, Guy, Gardner, and Ronnie Bright as bass (formerly of THE VALENTINES). This foursome left Atco in 1966 and subsequently recorded for Lloyd Price's Turntable Records and cut three singles for Date through 1969 with no success.

For the first time in 13 years the quartet was without a label, but they made the most of the touring opportunities six past top 10 hits can provide.

In 1971 several of their Date masters, produced once again by Leiber and Stoller, were acquired by King Records. One of them was a re-recording of the Clovers' biggest pop hit "Love Potion #9" (#23, 1959), though you'd barely recognize it. With a rhythm track that sounded like a merging of Santana and Jethro Tull, the Coasters rode the tune to number 76, their first chart outing in seven years. They continued with two more King singles and a few small label releases until their last record in 1976, a remake of the PETER, PAUL AND MARY 1962 hit, "If I Had a Hammer."

Cornell Gunter started his own Coasters group in 1963, although they were mostly former PENGUINS (Randolph Jones, Dexter Tisby, and Teddy Harper). Along with Cornell's sister Shirley (the Flairs) they recorded "Wishful Thinking" b/w "Key to Your Heart" in 1964 on Challenge under the name Cornell Gunter. His group shifted from a quartet to a trio over the next 25 years until February 26, 1989, when Cornell was tragically shot and killed in his car in north Las Vegas. He and his Coasters were scheduled to perform at the Lady Luck Hotel that night.

Since the Coasters' final recording, the club and concert audience has seen almost as many Coasters groups as they've heard Coasters hits. Bobby Nunn had one until his death of a heart attack in 1986. "Dub" Jones and Billy Guy had one together and Leon Hughes had one.

In the early '80s, Earl Carroll went back to reform his Cadillacs. Carl Gardner, Ronnie Bright, Jimmy Norman, and Curley Palmer continued as yet another of the original-member Coasters acts.

The Coasters were imitated and often covered. Elvis recorded "Girls, Girls, Girls" and "Little Egypt." The Beatles did "Three Cool Cats" (the flip of "Charlie Brown") and "Searchin' " on their demonstration tape for Decca Records. And the Rolling Stones recorded "Poison Ivy" early in their career. Of course, much of the credit goes to Leiber and Stoller, but the Coasters were the best interpreters of Leiber and Stoller songs and were an important part of a talented team. 19 chart records in 38 tries shows just how talented. The Coasters were true rock and roll pioneers.

THE COASTERS

A SIDE/B SIDE	LABEL/CAT NO	DATE
Down In Mexico / Turtle Dovin'	Atco 6064	2/56
Brazil / One Kiss Led To Another	Atco 6073	7/56
Searchin' / Young Blood	Atco 6087	3/57

A SIDE/B SIDE	LABEL/CAT NO	DATE
Idol With Golden Head / My Baby Comes To Me	Atco 6098	8/57
What Is The Secret Of Your Success / Sweet Georgia Brown	Atco 6104	10/57
Gee Golly / Dance!	Atco 6111	1/58
Yakety Yak / Zing Went The Strings Of My Heart	Atco 6116	4/58
The Shadow Knows / Sorry But I'm Gonna Have To Pass	Atco 6126	9/58
Charlie Brown / Three Cool Cats	Atco 6132	1/59
Along Came Jones / That Is Rock and Roll	Atco 6141	5/59
Poison Ivy / I'm A Hog For You	Atco 6146	8/59
What About Us / Run Red Run	Atco 6153	11/59
Besame Mucho Part 1 / Besame Mucho Part 2	Atco 6163	3/60
Wake Me, Shake Me / Stewball	Atco 6168	6/60
The Snake And The Bookworm / Shoppin' For Clothes	Atco 6178	9/60
Wait A Minute / Thumbin' A Ride	Atco 6186	1/61
Little Egypt / Keep On Rolling	Atco 6192	4/61
Girls Girls Girls Part 1 / Girls Girls Girls Part 2	Atco 6204	8/61
Just Like Me / Bad Blood	Atco 6210	11/61
Ridin' Hood / Teach Me How To Shimmy	Atco 6219	2/62
The Climb / The Climb	Atco 6234	1/63
The P.T.A. / Bull Tick Waltz	Atco 6251	1/65
Speedo's Back In Town / T'Aint Nothin' To Me	Atco 6287	2/64
Lovey Dovey / Bad Detective	Atco 6300	5/64
Wild One / I Must Be Dreaming	Atco 6321	10/64
Lady Like / Hungry	Atco 6341	2/65
Money Honey / Let's Go Get Stoned	Atco 6356	5/65
Crazy Baby / Bell Bottom Slacks And A Chinese Kimono	Atco 6379	9/65
She's A Yum Yum / Saturday Night Fish Fry	Atco 6407	3/66
Soul Pad / Down Home Girl	Date 1552	3/67
She Can / Everybody's Woman	Date 1607	5/68
Everybody's Woman / D.W. Washburn	Date 1617	7/68
Act Right / The World Is Changing	Trntb 504	1969
Love Potion Number Nine / D.W. Washburn	King 6385	1971
Cool Jerk / Talkin' Bout A Woman	King 6389	1971
Soul Pad / D.W. Washburn	King 6404	1973
Take It Easy Greasy / You Move Me	Sal Wa 1001	1975

The Coasters Two Plus Two

Searchin' '75 / Young Blood	Chelan 2000	1975
If I Had A Hammer / If I Had A Hammer	Am Int 1122	1976

The Colts

The Colts remained relatively obscure even though they had a hit. Drawn from the church choir in the desert of Bakersfield, California, were Ruben Grundy (lead), his brother Joe, and Carl Moland. Various occasional part-timers rounded the Colts into a foursome that would practice and play around town, even entertaining truckers and travelers at a local drive-in restaurant.

In 1955 the three Coltsmen were attending Los Angeles City College when they met up with former Golden Glove contender Leroy Smith; the New Jersey native became the fourth Colt appendage. The group's ongoing search for a sound brought them to the attention of PLATTERS and PENGUINS manager Buck Ram. Buck, who was one of the few managers in rhythm and blues during the '50s who really *did* write the groups' hits, not just take credit for them (e.g., "Only You" and "The Great Pretender" for the Platters) wrote a song for the Colts titled "Adorable."

Buck signed the quartet to Vita Records of Pasadena and they recorded the tune in August of 1955 along with "Lips Red as Wine." Undoubtedly the best record to come out of Vita's tiny 1486 North Fair Oaks headquarters, "Adorable" was released the third week of September and gained instant popularity across the West and parts of the East. It also came to the attention of Atlantic Records, who were looking for a follow-up to THE DRIFTERS' spring-summer hit, "What 'Cha Gonna Do." "Adorable" seemed to be the answer as Atlantic released a cover by the Drifters in the fourth week of October.

Even though Vita had a five-week lead, they were no match for the Drifters' version or Atlantic's machine. The Colts charted on October 29, 1955, with the Drifters right behind one week later. The Bakersfield boys had enough momentum to reach number 11 R&B, but the Drifters went to number one.

The success of "Adorable" allowed for an appearance at New York's Apollo Theatre and a variety of West Coast gigs like the "Rock and Roll Revue" at the Paramount Theatre in Los Angeles with the Platters, the Penguins, and Dinah Washington on November 2.

In the long run, the Drifters' recording so eclipsed the Colts' that while there may have been room enough in the 1955 marketplace for two hit versions, history recalls only the Drifters recording as the definitive release, relegating the Colts version to a footnote in rock history (except among collectors).

Their next two Vita singles (released in January and April, respectively) saw considerably less activity as Buck Ram directed his attention to the overwhelming success of the Platters' number one hit "The Great Pretender" and their rising April release, "The Magic Touch." *Billboard*, meanwhile, briefly described the Colts' "Never No More" as a "routine ballad, adequately done" (May 26, 1956). Their February 11 review described the Colts' second single, "Sweet Sixteen," in a somewhat better light: "Here's a heavy play to the teenage market, and it's well rendered by the group; purity angle, however, may stretch the imagination."

Buck did pull the group from Vita and put them on his own Antler label in 1957 for two releases, both with an A side of the "Sheik of Araby" and different B sides.

In lieu of true success, the Colts can console themselves with the fact that they were one of the few groups to have their picture printed right on the label of their hit recording.

THE COLTS

A SIDE/B SIDE	LABEL/CAT NO	DATE
Adorable / Lips Red As Wine	Mambo 112	1955
Adorable / Lips Red As Wine	Vita 112	9/55
Sweet Sixteen / Honey Bun	Vita 121	1/56
Never No More / Hey You, Shoobeeboohboo	Vita 130	4/56
Sheik Of Araby / Never No More	Antler 4003	3/57
Sheik Of Araby / Guiding Angel	Antler 4007	10/57
I Never Knew / Oh When You Touch Me	Delco 4002	7/59

The Coronets

Among the most notable groups to come out of Cleveland, Ohio, were the Regals on Atlantic, the Valentinos on Sar, THE PONI-TAILS on Roulette, the Carousels on G.C., the Secrets on Phillips, and the Coronets on Chess. The Coronets, though not the best, were the first of them to hit the charts.

Formed at Thomas Edison High School, the Cleveland quintet consisted of Lester Russaw on first tenor, Sam Griggs on second tenor, George Lewis on baritone, and Bill Griggs (Sam's brother) on bass. Several other singers from the school glee club were in and out on occasion and included Greg Morris, Leonard Parker, and Cullen Maiden. The high school singing days were just for fun, and when school ended the group separated. Sam got married and began a boxing career, but his heart was still in singing so he pulled the old bunch together in 1953. With the addition of Charles Carruthers' soft and gentle lead voice, the Coronets were born. They did a few amateur contests and performed at Cleveland's Ebony Club in June alongside THE ORIOLES, who swiped a Coronets arrangement for "Don't You Think I Ought to Know," the B side of their July 1953 release, "Crying in the Chapel." Recovering from that piece of news, the Coronets changed their emphasis from live performances to recording. At Snyder Studios they made a demo of Carruthers original "Nadine" along with "I'm All Alone" and then barged unannounced into the office of WJW disc jockey Alan Freed to get his reaction. The only thing they got was the door and a promise from Freed's manager Lew Platt that if Freed liked their recording he'd call them.

Within weeks the 30-year-old guru of local radio kept his promise and instructed the boys to contact Chess Records, where he had sent their presentation. One call later and the Coronets were on their way to Chicago to record.

A pretty ballad, "Nadine" featured Charles's easygoing lead with a rough, amateurish harmony by the group. Still, this was Chess's pick for the first single. The label's writer credit read "A. Freed," possibly indicating what the price was for making the group's presentation to Chess.

On September 19, 1953, it jumped onto the R&B chart, climbing to number three and staying chartside for two and a half months. Their next record, "It Would Be Heavenly," was another nice, slow side recorded in October and released in November, but lightning was not meant to strike twice for the Coronets. Over the next months both Lester and Charles were drafted (these were the Korean War days) and Charles Brown took over lead on the last two sides cut for Chess ("Corbella" and "Beggin' and Pleadin'"), which were never issued.

Bobby Ward became their new lead for "Don't Deprive Me" on Stirling Records in 1955 and two singles sold by Stirling to Groove Records (RCA) that same year. With nary a ripple of radio response, the group wisely disbanded until Charles returned from active duty. With Sam and two newcomers (Desious Willie Brooks, first tenor, and Lucky Jordan, bass) the Coronets took another local label shot with Job Records on "Footsteps" in 1960. When this effort stalled the group disbanded.

Several of their part-time members became well-known in other fields. Cullen Maiden went on to fame as a baritone in a professional opera company. He paid for his opera training the same way Sam Griggs used to earn a living: by boxing. Len Parker became an actor and wound up on TV's "Naked City." And Greg Morris will forever be known as Barney, Mr. Phelps' technical genius on the long-running TV hit "Mission Impossible."

The Coronets' full-time members, on the other hand, have long since faded into history.

THE CORONETS

A SIDE/B SIDE	LABEL/CAT NO	DATE
I'm All Alone / Nadine	Chess 1549	8/53
It Would Be Heavenly / Baby's Coming Home	Chess 1553	11/53
Don't Deprive Me / The Little Boy	Stir 903	1955
I Love You More / Crime Doesn't Pay	Groove 0114	7/55
Hush / The Bible Tells Me So	Groove 0116	8/55
Footsteps / Long John Silver	Job 100	1960

The Crests

One of the most popular of the late '50s groups, the Crests were often thought to be an all-black aggregation. In fact, they were about as integrated as a group could get, with four men (two blacks, a Puerto Rican, and an Italian), and one black female. Talmadge (Tommy) Gough (first tenor), Harold Torres (second tenor), and Patricia Van Dross (tenor) were all from the Alfred E. Smith housing projects in Chinatown on the Lower East Side of Manhattan. In 1955, while students at P.S. 160 Junior High, they teamed up with Jay (J. T.) Carter (bass) of Delancey Street to form a singing group. With influences ranging from THE MILLS BROTHERS to THE AMES BROTHERS (with THE HARPTONES, THE CLOVERS, THE 5 ROYALES, THE FIVE KEYS, THE PENGUINS, and THE ORIOLES thrown in for good measure) the unnamed quartet started performing at hospitals and charity functions for experience while learning the craft of harmonizing from an old singer known only as Mr. Morrow.

In 1956, Mulberry Street resident John Mastrangelo met the group at the Henry Street Settlement House. John's previous group had also been integrated, and reportedly included a young Tony Orlando. Mastrangelo's strong voice and natural feel for R&B made him an instant asset to the group and they joined forces. J. T. Carter came up with the name the Crests (a good many years before the toothpaste). The group found the New York subway system to be an excellent place to polish their sound. On one occasion they boarded the Lexington IRT at the Brooklyn Bridge and took the opportunity to practice. To their astonishment, as the train pulled into the next stop, a woman got up, walked over, handed them a business card, and left the train without even mentioning her name. The card read "Al Browne and Orchestra," Mr. Browne being the well-known arranger who backed up THE HEARTBEATS and other acts. The group scrambled to call him, set up an audition, and by June 1957 were recording two original Mastrangelo compositions. The mysterious lady on the train turned out to be Mrs. Al Browne.

The songs "Sweetest One" and "My Juanita" were tremendous first efforts for a new group, especially considering the medieval production work and studio sound. "My Juanita" was an up-tempo rocker with a slow double-chime prelude, a smooth lead from Mastrangelo (now calling himself Johnny Maestro), and a tight background by the Crests. "Sweetest One" was an understated ballad. Its simplicity was classic, but most in the know would have put their money on "Juanita." On July 15, 1957, the tiny Joyce Records (run out of the back room of a Brooklyn record store) bet on "Sweetest One," putting all two minutes and four seconds on the national Top 100 chart peaking at number 86. "My Juanita" subsequently became a standard rehearsal tune for every street-corner group.

The Crests' next single was "No One to Love," a beautiful ballad with an "Earth Angel" intro followed by wondrous harmony and an original arrangement. Lightning didn't strike twice, but Maestro recalls that each member received a $17.50 royalty for the tune. It probably went to buy the checkered sport jackets and thin black ties they wore at their local gigs (with Pat in her gown, the performers looked like four Bo Diddleys and a prom queen).

After almost a year of shows, the Crests got a break in the form of an introduction by songwriter Billy Dawn Smith to music publisher George Paxton, a veteran of the Brill building. Paxton formed Coed Records and signed the group just as they became a quartet. Pat was forced to leave when her mother refused to let her tour with the older guys (in 1958 the members were 18 to 19 years old). Had Patricia's younger brother been old enough to do more than hang out to hear the group sing, he would have been an interesting vocal addition to the Crests. His name was Luther Van Dross.

The Crests' first Coed single was "Pretty Little Angel" b/w "I Thank the Moon," the former written by Maestro, arranger Bert Keyes, and Luther Dixon (writer of several SHIRELLES hits), and the latter by Billy Dawn Smith. "Pretty" did well in New York (for example one Rochester station, WRVM's survey had it at number 25 and moving up on March 31st) but soon fizzled out. The next release was "Beside You," a pretty ballad with loads of harmony and a mid-'50s sound. When deejay Alan Freed and TV's Dick Clark received their copies they both flipped it over and took a liking to a sentimental birthday song called "16 Candles." The record entered the *Billboard* pop charts on November 24, 1958, and the R&B charts almost two months later. The group then played the first of many shows for Alan Freed's Christmas party at the Loew's State Theatre along with three giants of rock who would all be dead within six weeks: Buddy Holly, Ritchie Valens, and the Big Bopper. In the week of January 26, 1959, "16 Candles" was number four nationally and Valens's "Donna" was number three. J. T. Taylor had a friendly bet with Valens that week as to whose record would hit number one first. On February 3, 1959, Valens, Holly, and the Big Bopper (J. P. Richardson) died in a plane crash while on tour. *Billboard's* chart of February 9 had "16 Candles" at number two and "Donna" at number three. Ironically, neither recording ever made it to number one. The record that kept both from that position was Lloyd Price's "Stagger Lee." At its peak, "16 Candles" was selling 25,000 records a day and well on its way to becoming one of the most popular birthday songs since "Happy Birthday." "16 Candles" actually started out as "21 Candles" written by Luther Dixon and Allyson Khent, but since the average age of targeted record buyers was much younger, the number of candles was brought down a few notches.

The Crests were now playing all the major venues from the Apollo to the Paramount along with the prime-time Saturday night radio version of "American Bandstand." (Dick Clark may remember his first encounter with the Crests at the Little Theatre on 47th Street in New York City. The Crests were cavorting in the dressing room when Clark peeked in to say hello. When one of the boys fell against the door Clark got a black eye for his trouble.) The boys appeared on what in those days were called all-star shows—and they really were. On a given night the Crests would appear with the likes of Jackie Wilson, THE MOONGLOWS, Chuck Berry, the Everly Brothers, Bo Diddley, THE FLAMINGOS, DION AND THE BELMONTS, Frankie Avalon, and more saxophone-led orchestras than you could shake a stick at, including those of Sam "the Man" Taylor, King Curtis, Big Al Sears, Red Prysock, Earl Warren, and more. From 1958 to 1960 the group was almost always on the road.

Their first single after "Candles" was a swaying, dreamy stroll-styled ballad called "Six Nights a Week" (#28 Pop, #16 R&B). As was *not* the case with many acts, the charts were a relatively accurate barometer of the quality of the Crests records from this point on. "Flower of Love" was bland in comparison to other Crest cuts and only attained a six-week run up to number 79. But the charting proved that the Crests were out in front with deejays and the public; far superior records of the time (such as "Millionaire Hobo" by the Fantastics, "My Heart" by THE CAROLLONS, and "Lovers Never Say Goodbye" by the Flamingos) had less activity.

Their next single, however, was a catchy love song called "The Angels Listened In" (#22 Pop, #14 R&B). It was the last Crests single to chart R&B. Their fall 1959 release, "A Year Ago Tonight," was an up-tempo take on "16 Candles," and it probably overachieved by reaching number 42. 1960 kicked off with two catchy and danceable tunes, "Step by Step" (#14) and "Trouble in Paradise" (#20). (The latter title was significant, for by now the group was starting to feel growing pressure from Coed for Johnny to go solo.) The last two singles of 1960, "Journey of Love" and "Isn't it Amazing," barely charted (numbers 81 and 100, respectively).

A long overlooked Crests single titled "I Remember" was actually the old FIVE SATINS standard "In the Still of the Night"; done competently by Maestro and company, it was their last Coed single together.

"Little Miracles" was their next single; it showcased new lead James Ancrum and became the first Crests single in 10 tries that didn't make the top 100 (#102). Gough then quit, moving to Detroit to work for auto giant General Motors. Gary Lewis (not Jerry's son) replaced him. Johnny went solo as long predicted, but what was not predicted was that his records would gain absolutely no acceptance. He tried a few one-shots with other groups (THE TYMES' "Over the Weekend" b/w "I'll Be True" in 1963 and "Try Me" b/w "Heartburn" with a studio group calling themselves the Crests in 1966), but they also failed.

The Crests, meanwhile, were caught up in a court dispute with Coed over ownership of the name. The group finally won and signed with Morty Craft's Selma Records (Craft owned more labels than the Crests had singles), recording "Guilty" in

January 1962 and charting only at number 123. The group went back to touring when their 1963 Selma side "Did I Remember" flopped. A 1964 sequel to "16 Candles" leased by Craft to Coral suffered a similar fate; its prescient title was "You Blew Out the Candles."

Kenneth Head filled in for Ancrum on one single for Trans Atlas in 1962, but the songs weren't as good as the ones the Coed Records staff had provided. (George Paxton was a good publisher, with a knack for finding hits for his acts.)

Through the '60s, the Crests toured on their name and signed no further record deals. Maestro went on to form THE BROOKLYN BRIDGE in 1968. By then, Harold Torres had left for upstate New York and become a jeweler. The Crests turned into a lounge act with J.T., Ancrum, and Lewis. In 1978 J.T. joined Charley Thomas's DRIFTERS for a year, then moved to Plainfield, New Jersey, to teach voice and set up his own recording studio. In 1980, J.T. formed a new Crests from over 200 singers he screened at his studio. The final group became Bill Damon (a Maestro sound-alike), Greg Sereck, Dennis Ray, and J.T., and they toured with a five-piece backup that included J.T.'s wife Leona on the keys. In June 1987, Johnny, J.T., Harold, and Tommy, the original Crests, appeared together at a show in Peekskill, New York.

THE CRESTS

A SIDE/B SIDE	LABEL/CAT NO	DATE
My Juanita / Sweetest One	Joyce 103	7/57
No One To Love /		
Wish She Was Mine	Joyce 105	10/57
Pretty Little Angel /		
I Thank The Moon	Coed 501	3/58
Sixteen Candles / Beside You	Coed 506	11/58
Six Nights A Week / I Do	Coed 509	2/59
Flower Of Love / Molly Mae	Coed 511	6/59
The Angels Listened In /		
I Thank The Moon	Coed 515	8/59
A Year Ago Tonight / Paper Crown	Coed 521	11/59
Step By Step / Gee	Coed 525	2/60
Trouble In Paradise / Always You	Coed 531	6/60
Journey Of Love / If My Heart		
Could Write A Letter	Coed 535	9/60
Isn't It Amazing / Molly Mae	Coed 537	10/60
Good Golly Miss Molly /		
I Remember (In The Still		
Of The Night)	Coed 543	12/60
Little Miracles / Baby I Gotta Know	Coed 561	10/61
Guilty / Number One With Me	Selma 311	1/62
The Actor / Three Tears		
In A Bucket	Trans Atlas	7/62
Did I Remember / Tears Will Fall	Selma 4000	1963

A SIDE/B SIDE	LABEL/CAT NO	DATE
Johnny Maestro and the Crests		
My Time / Is It You	Parkway 987	1963
Come See Me / I Care About You	Parkway 999	8/66
My Time / Is It You	Parkway 118	1967

The Crew-cuts

The Crew-cuts were among the first white vocal groups to reap the benefits of covering recordings of black performers and exposing those songs to a wider audience. One of the few successful white groups that resulted from church singing, they got together in 1952 as the Canadaires at the Cathedral Choir School in Toronto.

By early 1954 the quartet consisted of lead John Perkins, Pat Barrett on first tenor, baritone Rudi Maugeri, and John's brother Ray on bass. Around that time they crossed the border from their native Canada to perform on the Gene Carroll TV show in Cleveland for $100. They also performed on Arthur Godfrey's "Talent Scouts" show, but their performance was not up to par and certainly didn't help their career.

The age of the teen group had not yet hit the music business so the Canadaires fit right in: they were 22 and 23 when they met Cleveland disc jockey Bill Randall. The deejay suggested they name themselves after the haircut that was stylish at the time, which they all wore. He also took the quartet under his wing and arranged an audition for them with Mercury Records (the eventual home of the premier cover group THE DIAMONDS). In rapid succession, the act signed a contract and released its first single, the original Barrett/Maugeri composition "Crazy 'Bout Ya Baby" in March 1954; by June it was number eight on the national charts.

It was rare for a white group in the early '50s to have a hit on a composition written by its members. Tin Pan Alley (the New York music publishing community) and record company A&R men usually worked in concert to find songs by professional writers for vocalists and groups. Having gone against the odds and succeeded, Mercury then did an about-face by bringing the group a song that was already getting a lot of exposure on the R&B market via a CHORDS recording released in April. The song was called "Sh-Boom." Unimpressed with the ditty, the group nevertheless cut it and Mercury released it in June, three months after the Chords'

version. When the Chords single charted on July 3, 1954, it looked like the Crew-cuts would soon be back doing original songs, but one week later their "Sh-Boom" charted and didn't stop until it reached number one, where it stayed for nine weeks. From an historic standpoint, the record has been cited by many as the first mass-appeal rock and roll record. The Chords version went to number two on the R&B charts, lending credence to the song's "across-the-board" popularity. Perhaps Mercury felt that covering the Chords tune was fair play. The Chords' original A side was not "Sh-Boom" but their own cover of pop vocalist Patti Page's "Cross Over the Bridge." When it flopped the Chords' "Sh-Boom" was reissued a month later with a different B side. Patti (actually Clara Ann Fowler of Muskogee, Oklahoma) was a Mercury artist who was rarely covered by black vocalists even though she had garnered 84 chart records between 1948 and 1968.

The Crew-cuts were now so popular that even "Sh-Boom's" B side took on a life of its own, reaching number 24 at the same time. The formula was now set: their next single was a cover of Shirley Gunter (sister of Cornell Gunter of THE COASTERS) and the Queens' rhythm and blues rocker "Oop-Shoop"; it went to number 13 in October, while the Queens' version went to number eight R&B in the same month.

By the dawn of 1955, the quartet had become internationally known. "Sh-Boom" had reached number 12 in England, where the only U.S. artists who had charted were solo vocalists such as Bing Crosby, Eddie Fisher, Perry Como, Frankie Laine, and Doris Day. The Crew-cuts were only the second white vocal group to ever hit the British list (the first was THE FOUR COINS some four months earlier.) But the first North American group to place itself among the English elite was THE MILLS BROTHERS with "Glow Worm" in January 1953.

The Perkins brothers *et al* started touring Europe and Japan while their newest cover, a version of THE PENGUINS' classic "Earth Angel," hit the stratospheric U.S. position of number three and spent over five months on the U.K. charts, rising to number four.

Despite detractors who felt (with or without justification) that the group built a career by robbing rhythm and blues songs, the Crew-cuts were talented enough to do their own arrangements, unlike many white vocal groups of the time. And the fact that the arrangements set contemporary rhythm and blues tunes in big-band settings gave the recordings a distinctive feel, made more so by the distinctly "pop" sound of the group's vocal blend.

As a result, the group exposed those often raunchy lyrics and R&B melodies to a wider audience in what many listeners have since called "homogenized" versions.

The Crew-cuts didn't stop trying for hits with original songs, but after group-penned records like "The Barking Dog" and "Dance Mr. Snowman, Dance" went to an early vinyl grave, Mercury dragged the group back to the cover records road.

Their next effort was an old 1953 FLAMINGOS flop entitled "Ko Ko Mo" that charted rhythm and blues in January 1955 by Gene and Eunice. Actually the flip side of "Earth Angel," "Ko Ko Mo" once again proved that the public was hot for anything Crew-cuts, moving to number six in early 1955.

Nappy Brown's "Don't Be Angry" was the Cuts' spring 1955 charter. But this time the R&B artist gave Mercury's stars a good run for their money as the former gospel vocalist with the Selah Singers and Golden Bell Quintet rang the bell at number two R&B and number 25 Pop; the Crew-cuts reached only 11 points higher. The B side of the Cuts' "Angry" was another very good R&B-turned-pop song entitled "Chop Chop Boom," originally by THE DANDELIERS of Chicago on States Records (also covered by the Savoys on Combo). Apparently Mercury's moguls were intent on getting the most out of their Crew-cuts singles by promoting both sides.

The summer of 1955 brought the former Canadaires another hit with the NUTMEGS classic "Story Untold." The number 16 charting of this song was a relief for a group that had just been humiliated in a previous cover race against two different black vocalists. In April, Roy Hamilton of Leesburg, Georgia, formerly of the Searchlight Gospel Singers, and Al Hibbler of Little Rock, Arkansas, a blind vocalist formerly with Duke Ellington, each released a dynamic version of "Unchained Melody" from the film *Unchained*. Hamilton's went to number one R&B and number six Pop; Hibbler's also went to number one R&B, and his label, Decca (Hamilton's was on Epic), pushed the soon-to-be standard all the way to number three Pop. This left no room on the charts for a Crew-cuts version released around the same time. The B side was a version of "Two Hearts" by THE CHARMS of Cincinnati. R&B chartwise at least, the Charms were doing to everyone what the Crew-cuts were doing to blacks; their version of "Two Hearts" reached number eight.

The Cuts kept on hitting; the fall of 1955 arrived to the strains of their top 10 hit "Gumdrop," a cover of another Charms recording. "Gumdrop" turned out to be their last top 10 record and, inexplicably,

the group stopped covering R&B songs. Of their first 22 sides, 11 were covers of black artists, 10 of which were groups. Of their next 13 Mercury issues, none were rhythm and blues songs, and the group only charted five times, including the originals "Angels in the Sky" (#11) b/w "Mostly Martha" (#31) in the winter of 1955–56.

Their last chart record was in January 1957. Ironically, it was a cover of two white vocalists, actor/singer Tab Hunter (a.k.a. Arthur Andrew Kelm) and country vocalist Sonny James (dubbed the Southern Gentleman), who had each recorded a beautiful ballad called "Young Love." The writing must have been on the wall when both Hunter and James reached the brass ring at number one and the Crew-cuts recording stopped at number 17.

Over the years the group had sung a variety of material and had even taken a reasonably good stab at rock with a version of Ronnie Hawkins's "Suzie Q," complete with harmony over a Bill-Haley-and-the-Comets-style guitar instrumental. The Cuts even cut a western swing tune in 1957 entitled "Such a Shame." By mid-1958 they'd signed with RCA, but eight singles later (one of which was a version of the evergreen "That's My Desire") they were label hunting. From 1961 to 1970 they recorded for six labels, including Vee-Jay, Whale, ABC, Chess, Warwick, and Firebird, where they had their last single release, "My Heart Belongs to Only You." In 1982 the group recorded a '50s-style LP for a small label called First American Records.

Aside from issuing cover records, the quintet had a penchant for recording oddball titles like "The Legend of Gunga Din," "Electric Chair," "Hey, You Face," and the ever-popular "Bei Mir Bist Du Schon." Still, the Crew-cuts shouldn't be dismissed as just another pop white '50s group. In their own way they contributed to the ever-growing bridge between rhythm and blues and pop music.

Today the Crew-cuts live diverse lifestyles across the country. Pat lives in New Jersey and works in the auto business, John's a newspaper man in New Orleans, Ray is in real estate in California, and Rudi is a musical director at Radio Arts Syndication in California.

THE CREW-CUTS

A SIDE/B SIDE	LABEL/CAT NO	DATE
Crazy 'Bout Ya Baby / Angela Mia	Merc 70341	3/54
Sh-Boom / I Spoke Too Soon	Merc 70404	6/54
Oop-Shoop / Do Me Good Baby	Merc 70443	8/54
The Barking Dog / All I Wanna Do	Merc 70490	10/54

A SIDE/B SIDE	LABEL/CAT NO	DATE
Twinkle Toes / Dance Mr. Snowman Dance	Merc 70491	10/54
The Whiffenpoof Song / The Varsity Drag	Merc 70494	11/54
Earth Angel / Ko Ko Mo	Merc 70529	1/55
Don't Be Angry / Chop Chop Chop	Merc 70597	4/55
Unchained Melody / Two Hearts, Two Kisses	Merc 70598	5/55
A Story Untold / Carmen's Boogie	Merc 70634	5/55
Gumdrop / Present Arms	Merc 70668	7/55
Gumdrop / Song Of The Fool	Merc 70668	7/55
Slam! Bam! / Are You Havin' Any Fun	Merc 70710	1955
Mostly Martha / Angels In The Sky	Merc 70741	11/55
Seven Days / That's Your Mistake	Merc 70842	12/55
Out Of The Picture / Honey Hair, Sugar Lips, Eyes Of Blue	Merc 70840	3/56
Tell Me Why / Rebel In Town	Merc 70890	5/56
Bei Mir Bist Du Schon / Thirteen Going On Fourteen	Merc 70922	7/56
Love In A Home / Keeper Of The Flame	Merc 70977	9/56
The Varsity Drag / The Halls Of Ivy	Merc 70988	10/56
Young Love / Little By Little	Merc 71022	12/56
The Angelus / Whatever, Wherever, Whoever	Merc 71076	2/57
Susie-Q / Such A Shame	Merc 71125	5/57
I Sit In My Window / Hey, You Face	Merc 71168	7/57
Be My Only Love / I Like It Like Like That	Merc 71223	1957
Hey, Stella! / Forever, My Darling	RCA 47-7320	8/58
That's My Desire / Baby Be Mine	RCA 47-7359	10/58
Can You Hear Me / Fraternity Pin	RCA 47-7446	1/59
Gone, Gone, Gone / Someone In Heaven	RCA 47-7509	4/59
Bermuda / Kin-Ni-Ki-Nic	RCA 47-7577	8/59
It Is No Secret / No, No Nevermore	RCA 47-7667	1/60
American Beauty Rose / The Shrine On The Top Of The Hill	RCA 47-7734	4/60
Going To Church On Sunday / Aura Lee	RCA 47-7759	6/60
Legend Of Gunga Din / Number One With Me	Wrwk 623	2/61
Electric Chair / Twistin' All Around The World	Whale 507	1962
Laura Love / Little Donkey	Whale 508	1962
Hush Little Baby / Ti' Pi' Tum	Whale 509	1962
The Three Bells / Spanish Is A Loving Tongue	Vee-Jay 569	12/63
Hip-Huggers / You're A Star Donna Donna	ABC 10450	8/63
Yea, Yea, She Wants Me / Ain't That Nice	Chess 1892	5/64
My Heart Belongs To Only You / You've Been In	Frbrd 1805	1970

The Crickets

An excellent group of balladeers, the Crickets were actually three different groups strung together by the beautiful lead vocals of one Grover Barlow.

The original quintet didn't think much about names and couldn't even remember what they called themselves (if anything) before they made their first record deal. Formed in the Morrisania section of the Bronx in 1951, the original group included Grover Barlow (lead), Harold Johnson (tenor), Eugene Stapleton (tenor), Leon Carter (baritone,) and Rodney Jackson (bass).

Grover got his start singing in Detroit with a school group that would entertain their fellow students over the school's loudspeakers before classes. Bronx-based Harold Johnson and company paid their practice dues at the Forest House Community Center and added Grover to the quartet soon after he moved from Detroit.

The Bronx boys demonstrated loyalty and commitment when Rodney was hospitalized for a long period. Rather than break in a new bass or do local shows without one, they spent every Sunday at the hospital practicing with Rodney and singing for all the ward's patients.

The group admired the work of THE LARKS, THE RAVENS, the Four Buddies, THE ORIOLES, and THE SWALLOWS, incorporating many of their songs into their act. In 1952, agent Cliff Martinez introduced the group to the producer of THE DEEP RIVER BOYS, Joe Davis, also the owner of Beacon Records from 1943 to 1948.

It was at this time that the five youths from the Bronx (ranging in age from 16 to 21) became the Crickets, more than four years before the formation of Buddy Holly's Crickets.

On December 2, 1952, Davis produced four sides with the Crickets, signing both the group and ownership of the group's name to his company. Davis was probably one of the first producers to own a group's name; it meant that he could replace all or any number of them while keeping the name for his own use. Buck Ram had similar ownership of THE PLATTERS' name a few years later as did manager George Treadwell with THE DRIFTERS.

Davis took the Crickets cuts to MGM and obtained both a deal for them and an A&R job for himself with their masters. The quintet's first release was "You're Mine," a pretty ballad with Grover's satiny-smooth lead predominating. Slowly but surely gaining momentum on the East Coast, it was a top 10 hit in New York by March 1953. On Independence Day, the Crickets really had something to celebrate when "You're Mine" hit number 10 on *Billboard*'s National Jukebox Chart seven months after its release and one day before the group performed at the Apollo Theatre with Ruth Brown. Not bad for a quintet that only a month before had been playing dances at the Bedford Avenue YMCA in Brooklyn.

Their next single, "For You I Have Eyes," is considered by many collectors to be the original group's best. Unfortunately, MGM didn't make it happen and Davis didn't wait around to give them another chance. He left to start Jay-Dee Records (his second label since the '40s), taking the Crickets and THE BLENDERS with him.

Meanwhile, the Crickets were experiencing some of the usual (and not so usual) trials of touring life, such as being left stranded in Virginia when Fats Domino abruptly left due to an altercation with his band, performing in barns in the South, and sleeping on floors of various homes (including George Nelson's of the Orioles) while performing in Baltimore.

In the first week of August 1953, "When I Met You," another Crickets love song, was released with little fanfare and even less success.

Three more singles were released between October 1953 and December 1954, including the magnificent ballad "Be Faithful." It had a flip side by the Deep River Boys; Davis had no more Crickets sides in the can and had no plans for new ones since he wanted Barlow to become a solo act (but didn't release a solo Barlow recording until February 1955). The fact that the "Be Faithful" label read Dean Barlow and the Crickets suggests that Grover was already paving the way for his new role.

The Dean name came at Davis's suggestion (it was his mom's maiden name) since Grover didn't strike him as sounding appropriate for a recording artist. Barlow used the name for the rest of his career.

By mid-1953 several changes took place. While the original group was having records released, Davis disbanded them and had Dean form a second Crickets that included J. R. Bailey (tenor), Bobby Spencer (baritone,) and Fred Barksdale (bass). Davis apparently felt it premature to put "Dean" out as a solo. Each of those three performers went on to success with major acts (Bailey with THE CADILLACS; Spencer with the Cadillacs, THE HARPTONES, and THE CHORDS; and Barksdale, with the Cadillacs and THE SOLITAIRES), though this particular combination didn't hold together beyond a few local performances; the members rarely found the desire to practice. Barlow soon formed a third Crickets with Robert Bynum (first tenor), William Lindsey (second tenor), and Joseph Dias (bass).

The third Crickets group tried to capitalize on the contemporaneous pop success of Patti Page's number three hit "Changing Partners" in January 1954 but garnered few sales; they had similar lack of success with "Just You" and an equally arresting love song "Are You Looking for a Sweetheart." In effect, Davis had five Crickets singles on the market in 1954, two by the original group and three by the third group.

In February 1955, Jay Dee finally released a solo Dean Barlow record with "I'll String Along with You" (a remake of the 1934 Ted Fio Rito hit) followed in May by "Forever" and in July by "True Love," but with no success.

Of the original members of the group, only Harold Johnson continued to record, joining THE MELLOWS in 1954. The third Crickets group became the Bachelors on Earl Records in 1956 (with Robert Bynum replaced by a tenor known only as Rudolph). Their recordings of "Dolores" and "Tell Me Now" were good examples of mid-'50s R&B that earned more attention in later years than when they were initially released.

In 1957, the Crickets-Bachelors became the Montereys on Onyx (minus Joseph Dias who went back to his original group, the Chords, and plus tenor Ed Jordan) for one New York success, "Dearest One," and one failure, "Angel" (it was recorded but never released).

For the next six years, Dean recorded solo for Davis, Warwick, Lescay, Seven Arts, and Rust Records, with only his 1961 Lescay release of "Third Window from the Right" getting much attention.

In 1967 Dean and VOCALEERS member Joe Duncan were in the process of forming an act but gave it up when George Treadwell, the group's mentor, died.

Of the original Crickets, Harold Johnson and Rodney Jackson passed away in the '70s. Joe Dias died in the early '80s. Grover "Dean" Barlow became a director for community relations with Western Union and retired in the mid-'70s.

The Crickets, though never obtaining long-term success, were a fine rhythm and blues vocal quintet in both their incarnations. It's disappointing that neither they nor Grover "Dean" Barlow, one of the best of the '50s vocalists, were able to achieve greater renown.

THE CRICKETS

A SIDE/B SIDE	LABEL/CAT NO	DATE
You're Mine / Milk And Gin	MGM 11428	1/53
For You I Have Eyes /		
I'll Cry No More	MGM 11507	5/53
When I Met You /		
Dreams And Wishes	Jay-Dee 777	8/53
I'm Not The One You Love /		
Fine As Wine	Jay-Dee 781	10/53
Changing Partners / Your Love	Jay-Dee 785	1/54
Never Gonna Give Up Hope / Are		
You Looking For A Sweatheart	Jay-Dee 789	2/54
Just You / My Little Baby's Shoes	Jay-Dee 786	3/54
Man From The Moon / I'm Going		
To Live My Life Alone	Jay-Dee 795	10/54
Dean Barlow and the Crickets		
Be Faithful / Sleepy Little Cowboy	Beacon 104	12/54
The Bachelors		
I Want To Know About Love /		
Delores	Earl 101	1956
Baby / Tell Me Know	Earl 102	1956
The Montereys		
Dearest One / Through The Years	Onyx 513	1957

The Criterions

The Criterions were formed in 1958 and became the forerunner of one of the most popular vocal quartets of the '70s and '80s, THE MANHATTAN TRANSFER. Though the Transfer's repertoire covers jazz, bop, gospel, pop, and R&B, their forebears were basically a pop doo wop group from Belmar, New Jersey.

But their story actually began in Asbury Park, New Jersey in the summer of 1956. 16-year-old SPANIELS-influenced Tim Hauser and several friends went to see FRANKIE LYMON AND THE TEEN-AGERS perform at the Convention Center but instead wound up in a near riot. To avoid the fights, young Tim jumped on the stage and ended up in the wings, where a small black youth asked if Tim knew where the dressing room was. Since he'd performed at the Center for numerous Boy Scout Jamborees, Tim was able to take the youngster (who turned out to be Frankie Lymon) right to the dressing room. In appreciation he was invited in. While kids were trying to beat each other up a scant 50 yards away, Tim Hauser found himself sitting on the floor of the dressing room while the Teenagers stood in a circle around him practicing their newest single, "I Promise to Remember." Tim recalls, "It

was like a lightning bolt from God saying, this is where you're going, this is what you're going to do. It's either this or becoming Mickey Mantle."

Throughout late 1956 and 1957 he tried to organize a neighborhood group. Unfortunately, no one he found could sing in tune. Then in February 1958 a classmate at St. Rose High School named Tommy Picardo, who had heard about the encounter with his idol Frankie Lymon, came over to Tim in the schoolyard. Their budding friendship (and the fact that Tommy could sing) propelled the duo to recruit schoolmates Jimmy Ruff, Steve Casagrande, and Phil Miller into a group. They took their name from the Criterion restaurant on the Boardwalk in Asbury Park and began rehearsing at Tommy's house at 27 Albany Road in Neptune. Tim reminisces it was "around the corner from Jackie Nicholson, as Tommy referred to the now famous actor."

Joe Ernst replaced Phil. The quintet now had Tim on lead, Tommy as top tenor, Jimmy at second tenor, Steve on baritone, and Joe on bass. They began practicing and recording old favorites like "My Juanita" (THE CRESTS) and "So Why" (THE BOP CHORDS) on Tommy's old Wolensak tape recorder. The Criterions also rehearsed in the shower stalls of the boys' locker room in school. They felt they had arrived when applause greeted their vocalizing through the air vents connected to the girls' locker room.

Their first real show took place in the summer of 1958 at the Polish-American Hall in Plainfield. They were opposite THE HEARTBEATS. Tommy played piano for those stars while Tim and company sang their portion of the show a cappella on "I'm So Happy" (THE TEENCHORDS), "Zoom Zoom Zoom" (the Collegians), and their favorite, "My Juanita."

In August 1958 the "stars" of Belmar ventured to New York City to try their luck with End Records prexy George Goldner. The reception area contained LITTLE ANTHONY AND THE IMPERIALS and THE CHANTELS, both waiting to get in for their rehearsals, while THE ISLEY BROTHERS were already in a side room rehearsing with Richard Barrett. As the Criterions waited, the Imperials practiced their next scheduled release ("So Much") in the hall. The wait wasn't worth it as the group was turned down flat, but while riding the elevator down to the lobby of 1697 Broadway, they met producer Al Browne, who invited the quintet out to his Brooklyn digs on Eastern Parkway to audition.

By September, they were in the studio recording "My Juanita" (which Browne revised into "Nita Juanita") and a Tommy Picardo original, "Don't Say Goodbye." When Browne tried to sell the masters and came up empty he brought the group back in a month later to try again on the same songs, hoping a better production would mean a sale. Since Al was not a high-rolling producer, he had an arrangement with the group in which they split the session costs 50-50. When the session whizzed along ahead of schedule, Al asked the Criterions if they minded giving their remaining half hour to a group sitting outside that had no money. The guys obliged and sat through Eddie and the Starlites' classic doo wop recording of "To Make a Long Story Short." The Criterions, however, didn't have as much luck. Browne struck out again when their two sides were rejected by such luminous labels of the times as Central Records. Ironically, the Criterions outlasted Central, which went under that same year after the failure of its last record, "Blue and Lonely" by the Pretenders.

By now, the Criterions' consensus was that perhaps a different lead vocal would change their luck, so Joe Ernst's friend John Mangi from Point Pleasant was brought in. A new tape was made and Arc Records of New Jersey offered the group a contract. They turned it down thinking they could do better. Through a series of associations starting with Tim's father, the sextet (Tim moved to first tenor when John took over lead) met Marty Foglia, sound engineer to disc jockey Alan Freed. Marty owned Cecilia Records (another one-man conglomerate) and signed the group in April 1959.

Their first single was penned by Marty's attorney, Ben Newgaborn, titled "I Remain Truly Yours." Alan Freed started playing it almost immediately. It went top 30 on the local New York distributor survey and the group booked some performances due to its airplay. One memorable show at the Convention Center (the site of Tim's meeting with Frankie Lymon three years earlier) had Tim, Tommy, and Jimmy singing "Where or When" with DION AND THE BELMONTS members Carlo and Freddy. That show was the scene of a fateful encounter: Tim met a member of the Keyport, New Jersey, volunteer fire company named Larry Vecchio. Larry was in a band called the Fabulous Dominoes and asked Tim if he could get Alan Freed to put on a show in Keyport to raise money for the fire department. After Tim followed the usual chain of communication (Tim's dad to engineer Marty to deejay Alan Freed) the response came back positive. The Criterions and others were preparing to play Keyport when the Chamber of Commerce, fearing another rock and roll riot, banned the show.

This might have been the end of things except that Tim and company wanted to record another few sides before going off to college in the fall. Marty Foglia had no money so a deal had to be struck. He'd pay for the studio and the Criterions would bring in a band. None other than the Keyport Volunteer Fire Brigade, a.k.a. the Fabulous Dominoes, agreed to back the group if they could cut a few songs themselves. All was set. Enter, Tim's dad playing A&R executive; he was convinced that an old instrumental favorite of his, a 1953 Herbie Fields recording, could be the basis for a new hit. Tim gave the song to the Dominoes and all converged on the studio mere weeks before the Criterions would head in separate directions for college. The vocalists did a beautiful block harmony arrangement of the standard "Over the Rainbow" along with the original titled "Remember," and the firehouse five (actually Bobby and Joe Spievak, guitar and bass, respectively; Clark Smith, drums; Harry Haller, tenor sax; and Larry Vecchio on organ) recorded a few sides that included Tim's dad's recommendation.

Fall came, Tim and Tommy went off to Villanova University, and Jimmy went to the University of Pennsylvania. Their second Cecilia single (from earlier sessions), another try at "Don't Say Goodbye," came and went with little fanfare, but the Fabulous Dominoes had themselves a hit as Madison Records picked up their masters from Foglia, renamed the group the Viscounts, and pushed "Papa" Hauser's favorite song "Harlem Nocturne" onto the national charts for 16 weeks (#52).

The Criterions' "Over the Rainbow" was never issued, but once again the group found themselves curiously intertwined with someone else's success. In the summer of 1960 the airwaves became filled with the strains of a uniquely beautiful block harmony arrangement of "Over the Rainbow" by THE DEMENSIONS (#16). Later that summer, Vecchio revealed to the Criterions that the Demensions learned the song from their arrangement, having heard the tapes at Broadway Studios (where Foglia had them stored). Since Cecilia was distributed by Laurie and Mohawk (the Demensions' label) was also in the Laurie web, it's a likely scenario.

The Criterions came together in the summer of 1960 to do a few more gigs, and except for an uncredited backup role on female vocalist Jerry Perci's sole Cecilia outing, they never recorded again.

Tommy Picardo became Tommy West of Cashman, Pistilli and West (Capitol) and producer of Jim Croce's early '70s hits. He helped found MTM Records and produced for them in Nashville. Today he lives on a farm in New Jersey and continues to write and record acoustic pop music. Steve is a successful businessman in St. Louis, Joe Ernst lives somewhere in New Jersey, Jim lives in Connecticut and is a securities analyst for Merrill-Lynch, and John Mangi is in Texas reportedly cleaning up as a hair dresser.

Tim went on to become an executive at Nabisco in New York City until the music lure once again found him forming a group, this time called the Manhattan Transfer. That same year (1969), while rummaging through the 45 bins of an oldies record store in Greenwich Village, he came upon a record by the Kents on Relic. The A side was "My Juanita," and when Tim turned it over and saw the flip was "Don't Say Goodbye," he knew Al Browne had finally placed his 11-year-old recordings.

THE CRITERIONS

A SIDE/B SIDE	LABEL/CAT NO	DATE
I Remain Truly Yours /		
You Just You	Cecilia 1208	1959
Don't Say Goodbye /		
Crying The Blues Over Me	Cecilia 1210	1959
I Remain Truly Yours /		
You Just You	Laurie 3305	1964
The Kents		
My Juanita / Don't Say Goodbye	Relic 1012	1966

The Crows

Let's set the record straight: "Sh-Boom" by THE CHORDS or THE CREW-CUTS was not the first rock and roll hit, though both versions were huge mass-appeal records in the summer of 1954. If the definition of early rock and roll is R&B music by black or white artists that crossed over to white audiences via so-called white radio stations, then the honor of being the first rock and roll group with the first rock and roll hit would have to go to the Crows for their song "Gee." Furthermore, if it hadn't been for the angry girlfriend of a Los Angeles disc jockey, American music history would have unfolded differently, and those fans of the Crew-cuts and/or Chords would have been right. But more on that later.

The Crows started out as so many others did, practicing street-corner harmony on the sidewalks of Harlem (142nd Street between 7th Avenue and Lenox Avenue to be exact) around 1951. The neigh-

borhood friends were Daniel "Sonny" Norton (lead), William "Bill" Davis (baritone), Harold Major (tenor), Jerry Wittick (tenor), and Gerald Hamilton (bass). Wanting to emulate their favorites, who were mostly bird-named groups (THE FLAMINGOS, THE RAVENS, and THE CARDINALS), they came up with the name the Crows and turned from sidewalk singers to serious students of the sound when they first heard THE FIVE KEYS singing "The Glory of Love." Starting at the Doniker Center, they broadened their performance base via the usual assortment of community centers, parties, and school dances. When they felt they had it together the Harlem quintet set out for 125th Street and the Apollo Theatre to wait on the Monday lines that eventually led to the Wednesday amateur night contests.

In early 1952 their chance came as the Crows appeared singing Bill and Harold's original "You're Mine" (later reworked and recorded by the Crickets on MGM) and won the coveted contest. Talent agent Cliff Martinez witnessed their triumph and took the Crows under his wing. Their first recording opportunity was not what the group expected: they were confined to background vocals for Frank "Fat Man" Humphries, a Louie Armstrong-style vocalist and trumpeter on Jubilee Records. Their May 1952 recording of "I Can't Get Started with You" b/w "Lu Lu Belle Blues" had them credited as the Four Notes, leaving the group with an identity problem. Undaunted, Martinez paired the group with singer, pianist, and arranger Viola Watkins in a tit-for-tat arrangement: she worked as their pianist and arranger and they in turn sang backup for her.

Around this time in 1952, Wittick joined Uncle Sam and Martinez replaced him with another Apollo amateur night winner, tenor/guitarist Mark Jackson. While most groups seemed to have revolving-door membership policies, the Crows would maintain this lineup without additions or substitutes for its entire career.

Cliff's acquaintance with record mogul George Goldner proved helpful in 1953 when Goldner was cajoled into coming to Viola's house to hear the group, a rare occurrence since Goldner discovered most of his acts via live auditions right in his own office. He liked both the Crows and Viola Watkins and set up a session to record the group, only once again it would be as background, this time for Viola on the song "Seven Lonely Days." But all was not lost: Goldner departed with a comment directing Davis to get some original songs together. Davis sat down in his sister's house and, in the time it takes to cook up a three-minute egg twice, wrote a little ditty called "Gee." He wrote another one called "I

Love You So" while sweeping the floor and using the handle like an old-fashioned floor microphone, drawing laughs from the guys sitting around.

By April 1953, those three songs and a fourth ("No Help Wanted") were recorded at Beltone Studios, and their first Rama Records single, "Seven Lonely Days," debuted the second week of May. It went nowhere. In June 1953, "Gee" b/w "I Love You So" became the first single strictly by the Crows. (In that same week Atlantic released THE CLOVERS' "Good Lovin'" and Imperial released Fats Domino's "Please Don't Leave Me.") Reviewing "Gee," *Billboard* commented, "The boys have a bright rocker here and they hand it a lively reading." The single blanketed the major East Coast cities but by summer's end the flip side, "I Love You So," was the public's favorite. By September, *Cashbox* had "I Love You So" at number 10 R&B in Philadelphia and "Gee" at number nine R&B in Los Angeles, but the two-sider was slowly running out of steam. In July Sonny Norton and company had been back at Beltone recording "Heartbreaker" (originally by THE HEARTBREAKERS on RCA in 1951) and "Call a Doctor" (a revision of THE CAP-TANS' 1950 "Chief, Turn the Hose on Me" on DC Records) for a release that same month. (For unknown reasons, West Coast copies of "Heartbreaker" list the artists as the Jewels, though one could conclude that the shrewd Goldner did not yet believe his "Gee" record was dead, and if it wasn't, he didn't want to hasten its death with another quick Crows release.) "Heartbreaker" became an instant rarity and 1953 ended with no further recordings from the quintet. Then it happened. When "Gee" first came out, Los Angeles disc jockey Huggy Boy (Dick Hugg) had been doing his nighttime remote show from the window of Dolphins of Hollywood Record Store. He promptly trashed the disc only to have it wind up in the hands of his girlfriend, who liked it. Early in 1954 Huggy and his girlfriend had a fight and she stormed out of the studio. Huggy frantically searched for the Crows' "Gee" knowing his girl would be listening in the car on her way home. He played the song three or four times in a row until she called, telling him to stop or he'd risk getting fired. "I'm not taking it off until you come back here" was Huggy's retort. She relented, he relented, and two days later while visiting a record distributor Huggy got a shock when he was told that "Gee" was selling wildly thanks to his repeat play. By February 1954 the Crows' future classic had sold over 50,000 records in Los Angeles alone. The record took off nationally, and by spring of 1954 it had peaked at number 14 Pop, number six R&B Best Seller, and

number two on the nation's jukeboxes. This was a full four months before the chart run of "Sh-Boom" and more than two months before Bill Haley's "Rock Around the Clock."

The Crows jumped on the tour bandwagon to take advantage of "Gee's" success and headed west with the Johnny Otis Show compliments of Associated Booking. Performing from Seattle, San Francisco, and Los Angeles to as far south as Mexico, the group had no idea that "Gee" was the first of the newly minted rock and roll records.

By the time they returned to New York, two sides they'd recorded in February, "Baby" b/w "Untrue," were in release. Over the years, collectors have prized "Untrue" as a raw gem of a blues ballad. Released the same week as "I Smell a Rat" by Young Jessie and "I Wonder, Little Darling" by John Lee Hooker (both on Modern), it went nowhere fast. Ditto for the Crows' next single "I Really Really Love You" (a close reworking of "Gee" with a nice chime ending) and its pretty ballad flip, "Miss You." Not pretty enough—like the front, the flip was a flop.

If having a flop after a hit is deflating to a group, the Crows must have been traumatized by their four losers, in the space of two months. The third one was a mambo novelty take-off of the Manischevitz wine commercial titled "Mambo Shevitz" on the Tico label (another Goldner label only for Latin product) backed by Melino and his orchestra. The B side was an instrumental titled "Mambo Number Five by the Band" (although some swear there is a Crows flip on some releases titled "I Love My Baby"). The fourth single out in April was an earlier 1954 recording in which they backed up Lorraine Ellis on a jazzy, Latin-flavored version of the 1941 big band hit "Perfidia." Their single was issued on Gee Records. That's right, Gee Records, the label Goldner started to honor his million-selling hit song, activating it only weeks after "Gee" hit the pop charts. Perhaps it was "G" for Goldner but then became Gee after the hit. Regardless, the Crows were dismayed. Despite their hit they remained relatively unknown, and the agency that sent them to California wouldn't book them in New York. Ironically, they had been discovered at the Apollo yet never got a chance to play there after turning professional. In July 1954 Rama gave them one more shot and they came up with a blues-swing, boogie-woogie rendition of the 1928 Earl Burnett hit "Sweet Sue," with lead chores going to Bill Davis (all other Crows leads had been handled by Sonny Norton). It deserved accolades and success, yet its lifespan was as short as the

Crows' other overlooked recordings. After "Sue" the group packed it in. Bill went to sing with the Continentals (also on Rama) for their one and only single, "You're an Angel" (December, 1955). In 1963 Davis missed a chance to join the Flamingos; instead he chose to stay with a group called the Honeycoles, whose sides for Columbia were never released. Hopes of any Crows' reunions were dashed as Gerald Hamilton died in the '60s and Daniel Norton passed away in 1972.

The Crows were much more than a one-hit group with an eight-record legacy; they sang rhythm and blues into the hearts of many latter-day listeners. The rapid succession of their releases shows that most of their records were given little chance from the outset, yet the legions of fans that have surfaced over the last 30 years have made their original label releases collectively worth more than the Crows earned on their California tour. The fact that one of their records broke through the R&B mold and lifted the group to immortality in no way diminishes the quality of these other works. The Crows will be remembered, if only for "Gee," as long as there is rhythm and blues or rock and roll. Firsts are always remembered, and they were the first.

THE CROWS

A SIDE/B SIDE	LABEL/CAT NO	DATE
Fat Man Humphries and the Four Notes		
I Can't Get Started With You / Lu Lu Belle Blues	Jubi 5085	5/52
The Crows		
Seven Lonely Days / No Help Wanted	Rama 3	5/53
Gee / I Love You So	Rama 5	6/53
Heartbreaker / Call A Doctor	Rama 10	7/53
Mambo Shevitz / Mambo No. 5	Tico 1082	4/54
Baby / Untrue	Rama 29	5/54
Miss You / I Really Really Love You	Rama 30	5/54
Baby Doll / Sweet Sue	Rama 50	7/54

The Cues

The Cues were the first vocal group formed strictly to do professional backup work on record. The concept was the brainchild of Atlantic Records arranger Jesse Stone. Prior to that time (mid-1954), choruses were put together for a spe-

cific recording or a record company would try to match a solo artist with a vocal group for a one-off, like Ella Fitzgerald and THE INK SPOTS or Little Esther Phillips and THE DOMINOES.

Stone wanted to create an in-house group that had the versatility and skill to back all the solo acts on the label. With this in mind he approached vocalist/songwriter Ollie Jones, a former lead and tenor with THE BLENDERS, to put together this quartet of specialists. They added Robie Kirk (who later wrote under the name of Winfield Scott) on baritone, Eddie Barnes on bass, and former Blenders member Abel DeCosta, tenor. A bit later, Jimmy Breedlove was added.

Actually, the Cues, as Stone called them, didn't start out doing backup work. Jesse had a dual purpose in mind and put the group to work doing demos of his songs so he could play the tapes for other artists to record. The Cues became the first of the demo specialists as a variety of writers and publishers began to use them after hearing their work for Jesse. On May 7, 1954, the quartet went to work for real singing backup on Ruth Brown's "Oh What a Dream." Released the third week of July 1954 it went straight to number one R&B and stayed there for eight weeks. The Cues, however, never got any recognition (except within the industry) as the label always read Ruth Brown and the Rhythm Makers. (In this way, the Cues would eventually record under more names than almost any group in history.) In August, Jesse Stone moved over to Aladdin Records' East Coast operation and gave the Cues their first shot at recording under their own name on Aladdin's Lamp affiliate label for an October release of "Scoochie Scoochie."

Though the Cues' single wasn't much in demand, their services were, and when Jesse moved back to Atlantic every solo act on the label began to get vocal support from the Cues. And it was always under a new name. For example, on Ivory Joe Hunter sides they were his Ivorytones; when they sang with Carmen Taylor they were her Boleros; for Joe Turner, his Blues Kings; with LaVern Baker they became the Gliders, and so on. Most of the time, they received no credit at all on records ranging from those by Ray Charles ("Drown in My Tears") to the early hits of Bobby Darin ("Dream Lover").

The group was kept so busy that at times Jones would enlist a second team of pros to sub as the Cues when sessions conflicted. Yet it was more than a year before the A team was offered a record deal, and it came not from one of the R&B indies but from the pop giant, Capitol.

Their first release on that label, "Burn that Candle," spent one week on the pop chart at number 86 but fell victim to Bill Haley's version (#16) on the Best Sellers. Meanwhile, the group continued its rigorous (and profitable) schedule of demos and backup sessions, now working with artists on other labels: Roy Hamilton ("Don't Let Go" for Epic), Nat Cole (Capitol), and Brook Benton (Mercury), to name just a few.

Occasionally they wound up on both sides of the cover war, as with the song "Tweedle-Dee." They backed LaVern Baker on the original and were asked to do the same thing by Mercury for their Georgia Gibbs cover. In effect, during late winter of 1955, the Cues had two records of the same song in the top 20 (Gibbs's version at number three Best Seller and Baker's at number 14 Jukebox) and nobody knew it.

The group's second Capitol release, "Charlie Brown" (not the COASTERS song but a definite inspiration for Leiber and Stoller's idea and title), was a jazzy jump-pop outing that featured Ollie on lead and went ignored by radio. Such was the fate of their next single, "Destination 2100 + 65" (which would be an interesting number for Manhattan Transfer to try).

Their next Capitol single was a slightly restrained version of "The Girl I Love," a song more associated with THE CADILLACS' side of several months later, though neither was successful. Their last Capitol single with Breedlove on lead had the same fate as their first, spending one week on the pop charts; it reached number 77.

In May 1957 "I Pretend" (from their last session at Capitol) surfaced on the Prep label, a Capitol subsidiary. Meanwhile, the Cues maintained a full-steam schedule, vocalizing on such hits as "C. C. Rider," "Jim Dandy," "Corinna, Corinna," and "Since I Met You Baby," all Atlantic releases.

Ironically, the Cues never got to record for Atlantic under their own name as Jesse probably didn't want to distract them from the work at hand. When all the members weren't available, such notables as Luther Dixon (writer and producer for THE SHIRELLES), Jim Stewart of THE RAVENS, Gregory Carroll and Larry Harrison of the Four Buddies, and even Doris Troy (who went on to have the 1963 hit "Just One Look" [#10]) would fill in.

By 1960, the individuals were all eager to pursue other opportunities, but not before they recorded two more sides ("Old Man River" and "Always Remember") for Herb Abramson in January, with Eddie Barnes singing lead. Some mystery surrounds "Old Man River" since it showed up on a 1985 LP titled *Boss Vocal Groups of the Sixties* with credit going to Jimmy Ricks and the Ravens. Closer scrutiny further confuses as the notes go on to say the recording is by Jimmy Ricks on bass lead with Ollie Jones of the original Ravens and Abel DeCosta and Robin Kirk from the Cues. What happened to Breedlove, let alone Barnes? Anyway, Ollie went on to write hits for THE CRESTS ("Step by Step") and Fabian ("Tiger") and joined the Billy Williams Quartet in 1959. Robie continued writing (he wrote "Tweedle-Dee"), and as late as 1985 Eddie was performing with a New York trio. Jimmy went on to a solo career and Abel sang with several different Ink Spots groups.

Without having a hit, the Cues had a profound effect on rhythm and blues and doo wop music as the first of a new breed of vocal groups. Their behind-the-scenes success paved the way for a new and exciting alternative to the pop-sounding choruses that formerly supported solo artists.

THE CUES

A SIDE/B SIDE	LABEL/CAT NO	DATE
Scoochie Scoochie / Forty 'Leven Dozen Ways	Lamp 8007	10/54
Burn That Candle / Oh My Darlin'	Cap 3245	10/55
Charlie Brown / You're On My Mind	Cap 3310	1/56
Destination 2100 And 65 / Don't Make Believe	Cap 3400	4/56
Girl I Love / Crackerjack	Cap 3483	7/56
Why / Prince Or Pauper	Cap 3582	10/56
I Pretend / Crazy, Crazy Party	Prep 104	5/57
Old Man River / Always Remember (Not To Forget)	Festival	1/60

The Danderliers

If at first you don't succeed, go to the park and sing. Such was the nature of a key event in the career of the Danderliers, a quality Chicago R&B group of the mid-'50s.

The quintet merged their musical talents in early 1955 on Chicago's South Side around Cottage Grove between 60th and 68th Streets. James Campbell (lead on slow sides), Dallas Taylor (lead on fast sides), Bernard Dixon (first tenor), Walter Stephenson (baritone), and Richard Thomas (bass) decided to name themselves the Danderliers, an offshoot of the dandelion flower, hoping to differentiate themselves from all the car and bird groups on the scene.

The Chicago Vocational and Englewood High Schoolers began practicing in earnest upon graduation and on several occasions trudged over to United/States Records to audition. On each occasion they were unceremoniously rejected. After one such letdown they rallied at Washington Park, picking up their spirits with some original riffing that was developing into a song called "Chop Chop Boom." At that very moment Sam Smith of United drove by, heard the group, and hauled them into Al Smith's basement rehearsal hall to polish "Chop" and one other tune, a beautiful ballad, "My Autumn Love," both written by Dallas Taylor.

By the first week of April 1955, "My Autumn Love" (States) was hitting the Chicago airwaves. Many disc jockeys began to flip the record to the rhythm side, "Chop Chop Boom," which tested the tiny Southside label to the breaking point when it hit the *Billboard* Rhythm & Blues chart and rocketed to number 10 on the Disc Jockey lists and number 14 on the Best Seller scorecard.

Appearances in Michigan, Pennsylvania, Texas, Tennessee, and Ohio followed as the group scrambled to build up a performance repertoire of songs like "Glory of Love" (THE FIVE KEYS), "Jump Children" (THE FLAMINGOS), and "Pardon My Tears" by schoolmates and labelmates the Moroccos. Inspiration for their bluesy style came from a cross-section of groups like THE DELLS, THE DU DROPPERS, the Moroccos, and THE DOMINOES. THE CREW-CUTS and their Mercury label thought enough of the Danderliers' single to cover it, taking the song to number 14 as the flip of "Don't Be Angry" in the spring of 1955.

Their next single, released in the third week of July, was a cha-cha rocker in the "Chop Chop" vein that was to be titled "New Way" since it featured Dallas and the group repeating the refrain "Dally's got a new way." When someone in the record company asked, "Dally's got a new way to what?," the answer ran the censorship flag up the pole so fast that the group soon found its song retitled "Shu-Wop." Whether "New Way" or "Shu-Wop," the end result was lots of Chicago airplay and nothing much beyond United's Illinois borders.

The same held true for the gospel doo wop ballad "May God Be with You" and their last single, another fine ballad, "My Love."

A few unreleased demos were done for Mercury later, but with no management direction the group soon disbanded. Dallas did one record in 1961 as a member of a revised Dells ("Swingin' Teens" on Vee-Jay) and the group reunited for one release on "All The Way" (Midas) in 1967.

Dallas passed away in 1986 and former members of the Danderliers sang "May God Be with You" at his funeral.

THE DANDERLIERS

A SIDE/B SIDE	LABEL/CAT NO	DATE
Chop Chop Boom /		
My Autumn Love	States 147	4/55
Shu-Wop / My Loving Partner	States 150	7/55
May God Be With You / Little Man	States 152	1956
My Love / She's Mine	States 160	11/56
All The Way / Walk On		
With Your Nose Up	Midas 9004	1967

The Danleers

The Danleers were one-time winners in the rock and roll sweepstakes, but their one shot became a summertime standard. Formed in Brooklyn, New York, circa 1958, teenagers Jimmy Weston (lead), Johnny Lee (first tenor), Willie Ephraim (second tenor), Nat McCune (baritone), and Roosevelt Mays (bass) made up the original quintet.

After refining their street-corner sound they began searching for some professional assistance. That help came in the form of Danny Webb, a young man with songwriting and management aspirations. Danny rehearsed the Brooklyn boys and called them the Danleers, a mutation of his own first name. He wrote two songs that the boys practiced, "Wheelin' and Dealin'" and "One Summer Night," which the group recorded.

Bill Lasley's small Amp 3 label on 7th Avenue in New York was the first to hear the group, signing them up in the spring of 1958. Some confusion developed when the group's name was given to the record company over the phone for label copy and was spelled D-a-n-d-l-e-e-r-s on the first pressings.

"One Summer Night" was a classic ballad given an elegant reading by Jimmy, with able assistance from the group and reinforcement on the bass in just the right places. Released in May 1958, by June it was already radio's summer song, and Amp 3's distributor, Mercury, was so impressed that they picked up the group's contract and reissued the record on the Mercury label without missing a beat. It climbed *Billboard*'s Pop charts, reaching number seven (#4 R&B Disc Jockey, #11 Best Seller). The eventual million seller would go on to become one of the most popular summer rock and roll recordings ever, but the group's euphoria dissipated when their follow-up release "I Really Love You" (another Webb composition) failed to chart. With a structure almost identical to that of "One Summer Night," "I" opened with an a cappella solo by Weston but otherwise suffered from ordinariness and a paucity of background harmony.

The Danleers' third Mercury single (and third ballad), "Prelude to Love," failed to ignite any radio interest. Its flip side ("A Picture of You") earned four stars in *Billboard*, however. The magazine noted the "strong vocal stint by the lead singer and group on an effective medium tempo rock-a-ballad. This one could bring the boys back." It didn't. Neither Mercury nor radio paid much attention to the tune.

By late fall, manager Webb had placed another group, the Webtones, with MGM for one quick unheralded release, "My Lost Love."

The Danleers' last Mercury single, "I Can't Sleep," never woke up, and the depressed group found themselves dropped by Mercury.

By early 1960 the Danleers had dissolved, but through Jimmy's determination and Danny's desire to continue seeing his songs on 45s, a new Danleers rose from the ashes. Three members of the Webtones joined Jimmy and a Webtones member's brother to become the new Danleers. Besides Jimmy, the "Dan Webs" (Danny could easily have named them that) were Louis Williams (first tenor), Doug Ebron (second tenor), Terry Wilson (baritone), and Frankie Clemens (bass).

In 1960, the group signed with Epic and released "If You Don't Care," a Platters-style ballad cowritten by Webb and someone named Villa. The group toured extensively on the strength of "One Summer Night," but they weren't able to find another hit among the subsequent singles released on Epic, Everest, Smash, or Le Mans.

On July 23, 1988, the original Danleers sang together for the first time in almost twenty years at the Westbury Music Fair on Long Island. By the late '70s, original Danleers Weston and McCune plus Webtone Ebron and Bill Carey of THE FOUR FELLOWS (Tri-boro) had become the regular Danleers lineup, and in 1990 the group was still doing occasional shows, with Weston's lead on "One Summer Night" still thrilling memory lane lovers.

THE DANLEERS

A SIDE/B SIDE	LABEL/CAT NO	DATE
The Dandleers		
One Summer Night /		
Wheelin' And A-Dealin'	Amp 3 2115	5/58

A SIDE/B SIDE	LABEL/CAT NO	DATE
The Danleers		
One Summer Night /		
Wheelin' And A-Dealin'	Merc 71322	6/58
I Really Love You /		
My Flaming Heart	Merc 71356	8/58
A Picture Of You / Prelude To Love	Merc 71401	12/58
I Can't Sleep / Your Love	Merc 71441	3/59
If You Don't Care / Half A Block		
From An Angel	Epic 9367	3/60
I'll Always Believe In You /		
Little Lover	Epic 9421	10/60
Foolish / I'm Looking Around	Evrst 19412	1961
If / Were You There	Smash 1872	1/64
Where Is Love /		
The Angels Sent You	Smash 1895	6/64

Danny and the Juniors

Performers of rock's national anthem, "Rock and Roll Is Here to Stay," Danny and the Juniors are remembered more for their hits than for holding a pivotal place in vocal group history. Not too many groups of the late '50s or early '60s would have cited the Juniors as an early influence. They came along when most white groups, like THE FOUR COINS and THE FOUR LADS, were singing straight pop, but before acts like THE ELEGANTS, THE EARLS, and DION AND THE BELMONTS were on the scene. That made Danny and the Juniors one of the first acts to interpret black music and R&B in the context of white rock and roll.

Dave White was the initial culprit, forming the Juvenairs in John Bartram High School in Philadelphia during 1955.

The members were Danny Rapp (lead), Dave White (Tricker) (first tenor), Frank Maffei (second tenor), and Joe Terry (Terranova) (baritone).

Influenced early on by the likes of FRANKIE LYMON AND THE TEENAGERS, the Four Lads, THE FOUR FRESHMEN, the Schoolboys, THE RAVENS, and Steve Gibson and his RED CAPS, the group practiced in the back of a car (just like the Freshmen).

By 1957 the Juvenairs, like many of Philadelphia's groups, were also practicing on street corners, only they decided to kill two birds with one song by singing on a corner under the window of producer John Madara. After telling them several times, "Get lost—you're waking my kids," he finally went downstairs and was impressed enough to take them to local disc jockey Larry Brown and Larry's partner Artie Singer of Singular Records. The group had a few originals including a ballad called "Sometimes" and a dance tune titled "Do the Bop." Singer took "Do the Bop" to a friend for an opinion. The friend was Dick Clark of "American Bandstand." He liked it, but knowing that the dance the bop was on its way out, he suggested a name change to "At the Hop."

In November 1957 "At the Hop" came out (the group had been renamed Danny and the Juniors by Singer), but it wasn't getting much attention. On December 2, 1957, Dick Clark frantically called Singer saying the group scheduled to appear on his show (reportedly LITTLE ANTHONY AND THE IMPERIALS) couldn't show up and he needed a fill-in act immediately. Artie sent over Danny and company, who lip-synced "At the Hop." The switchboard lit up with hundreds of callers wanting to know what that was and who was singing it.

ABC Paramount quickly became aware of the record, bought the masters, and issued the single. One week (December 9th) after their TV appearance, the record appeared on the *Billboard* charts, and a month later Danny and the Juniors had the number one record in America.

It stayed there for an amazing seven weeks and remained in the Top 100 for three times that. This revolutionary rocker (written by Madara and White) also reached number one on the R&B charts, this time for five weeks. It became an international hit as well, charting in England (#3), Australia (#16), and other countries outside the U.S. The record sold over two and a half million copies and the Juniors soon found themselves in Alan Freed's touring revue.

Next came the song that teens over the next 10 years would sing to their parents whenever they were told to "turn that damn thing down!"—David White's "Rock and Roll Is Here to Stay." It charted on March 3, 1958, and rose to number 19 Pop and number 16 R&B, but radio played it as if it were number one!

"Dottie," with nothing to distinguish it, reached only number 39 as their third release in the summer of 1958, while a beautiful ballad called "A Thief" (their fourth single) never charted at all. Their next three ABC singles had the same radio reception as "A Thief." Their next-to-last ABC disc ("Somehow I Can't Forget") in 1959 had the distinction of being the first stereo 45 RPM single.

In late 1960 the group minus White (who went into indy record production) and plus Billy Carlucci (later of Billy and the Essentials, Mercury) joined Swan Records and issued the quality dance record "Twistin' USA," which charted at number 27. Once again the group's great ballad abilities, demonstrated on their excellent B side interpretation of THE HEARTBEATS' "A Thousand Miles Away," were ignored.

"Pony Express" (which would have been a great record for the Dovells) rose only as high as number 60 in early 1961, indicating that the group was losing its chart grip. As usual, another strong ballad was passed over on the flip side ("Daydreamer").

One of the best sequel records, "Back to the Hop," came out in the late summer of 1961 and managed to climb to number 80 (though it did reach the top 20 in a variety of eastern cities).

Their last Swan charter, "Doin' the Continental Walk," barely made number 93 in the spring of 1962 and the group moved over to another Philly label, Guyden, for their last chart record. "Oo-La-La-Limbo" took advantage of the limbo craze (#99, 1963).

After one Mercury issue in 1964 they broke up, but re-formed in 1968 for a contemporary recording of "Rock and Roll Is Here to Stay" on Capitol. While at Mercury they did one vocal backup assignment for Dean Christie on "Mona."

In the '70s Danny and Joe had their own oldies show on WCAM in Camden, New Jersey, with newest Junior's member Jimmy Testa (the Fabulous Four, Chancellor, and the Four J's, Jamie).

In 1976 "At the Hop" was re-issued in Britain and brought the populace back to those days of yesteryear as it charted up to number 39. Meanwhile the group's sax player, Lenny Baker, carried on the group's strong tradition by cofounding SHA NA NA.

Frank went on to become an optometrist; Dave continued producing, including hits by Chubby Checker ("The Fly") and Len Barry of THE DOVELLS ("One, Two, Three"). Danny became assistant manager in a toy factory and sadly was found dead in Parker, Arizona, of apparent suicide on April 8, 1983, at the age of 41.

In the '90s the legacy of this fine rock vocal group was kept alive with a new Danny and the Juniors (now known as Danny and the Juniors featuring Joe Terry) performing classic rock and roll. Joe's Juniors included original member Frank Maffei and recent addition Bobby Love.

DANNY AND THE JUNIORS

A SIDE/B SIDE	LABEL/CAT NO	DATE
At The Hop / Sometimes	Snglr 711	1957
At The Hop / Sometimes	ABC 9871	12/57

A SIDE/B SIDE	LABEL/CAT NO	DATE
Rock And Roll Is Here To Stay /		
School Boy Romance	ABC 9888	1958
Dottie / In The Meantime	ABC 9926	1958
A Thief / Crazy Cave	ABC 9953	1958
I Feel So Lonely / Sassy Fran	ABC 9978	1958
Do You Love Me / Somehow I		
Can't Forget	ABC 10004	1959
Playing Hard To Get / Of Love	ABC 10052	1959
A Thousand Miles Away /		
Twistin' U.S.A.	Swan 4060	8/60
O Holy Night /		
Candy Cane, Sugary Plum	Swan 4064	11/60
Pony Express / Daydreamer	Swan 4068	2/61
Cha Cha Go Go / Mr. Whisper	Swan 4072	1961
Back To The Hop /		
The Charleston Fish	Swan 4082	8/61
Twistin' All Night Long /		
Some Kind Of Nut	Swan 4092	1961
Mashed Potatoes / Doin' The		
Continental Walk	Swan 4100	2/62
We Got Soul / Funny	Swan 4113	1962

The Billy Dawn Quartette

If you can't imagine what would constitute instant oblivion for a vocal group in the '50s, try this: having four records released under four different names. Though they didn't plan it that way, that's how the cards were dealt to the Billy Dawn Quartette.

The Crown Heights area of Brooklyn was the stomping ground for four youths out to harmonize their time away. Billy Dawn Smith (lead) formed the group with his brother Tommy (baritone), Donnie Myles (tenor), and Sonny Benton (bass). Al Browne (later to become producer of THE CRESTS' "My Juanita" and his own hit "The Madison" [#23, 1960]) filled in on occasion for baritone Tommy Smith and played piano for the Quartette while moonlighting with his own band. When passing time evolved into serious singing the group took their song uptown to a Harlem record store where they could get what they considered to be a professional opinion. The proprietor liked them enough to send them to David Levitt's Decatur Records, and he in turn recorded them in 1952.

"This Is the Real Thing Now" came out on the tiny label under the name of the Billy Dawn Quartette to absolutely no fanfare and just as little success. Undaunted, the boys went looking for

help, which appeared in the form of MELLO-MOODS (Red Robin) manager Joel Turnero. He took the group to Duke Records, who released "Why Can't I Have You" in the late summer of 1952. This time the group's name was the Mighty Dukes, courtesy of the label.

Their next single, an adequate recording of "Crying in the Chapel" (with Donnie doing lead chores) released the first week of September 1953 (six weeks after THE ORIOLES' version) was under yet another name since the label once more felt compelled to eradicate the act's past. Now they were the Four Dukes. Their version did pocket some sales, particularly in the South, and it would seem this would have been the time to build on their name. That became difficult when the group was not picked up for another single by Duke.

It took almost a year to find a new record deal, this time with Al Silver's Herald Records. Al liked two Billy Dawn songs, "Eternal Love" and "Gonna Love You Everyday," and decided to do a single with the group; Silver renamed them the Heralds. When "Eternal Love," a bluesy Billy Dawn-led ballad, struck out in September 1954, the enterprising Billy worked his way into an A&R job at the label. His position with Herald enabled the group to sing backup for numerous Ember and Herald records.

The Heralds performed around town for another year and regularly appeared on the "Spotlight on Harlem" TV show as the Heralds, formerly the Billy Dawn Quartette.

The foursome split up in 1956 as Billy began to spend more time as a writer than as a singer. During 1956, Billy, Bea Caslon (a secretary at Herald), and William Miller (the father of the Miller Sisters on Herald) pooled several hundred dollars and formed Hull Records, the future home of THE HEARTBEATS. Donnie later went on to sing with the Victorians and Billy became a top writer with co-written hits such as "Step by Step," "The Angels Listened In," "Six Nights a Week," and "Trouble in Paradise," all for the Crests; "To the Aisle" by THE FIVE SATINS; and "This Is My Love (Sweeter Than)" by THE PASSIONS.

THE BILLY DAWN QUARTETTE

A SIDE/B SIDE	LABEL/CAT NO	DATE
This Is The Real Now /		
Crying For My Baby	Dcatr 3001	1952
Why Can't I Have You /		
No Other Love	Duke 104	1952
Crying In The Chapel /		
I Done Done It	Duke 116	9/53

A SIDE/B SIDE	LABEL/CAT NO	DATE
Eternal Love / Gonna Love You Every Day	Herald 435	9/54

The Dells

O ne of the most durable acts in vocal group history, the Dells stayed together for over 35 years with only one member change. Starting out as five friends from Thornton Township High School in Harvey, Illinois (about 15 miles from Chicago), the teenaged street singers included Johnny "Junior" Funches (lead), Marvin Junior (first tenor), Verne Allison (second tenor), Mickey McGill (baritone), and Chuck Barksdale (bass), along with Mickey's brother Lucius.

Street corners, schoolyards, and candy stores were their rehearsal halls. They were determined to sing no matter what the setting; even a bucket of water dropped on them by an irate apartment dweller didn't dampen their enthusiasm.

It was 1953 as the new sextet decided on a name Mickey McGill chose from his Spanish textbook: the El-Rays. Translated, it meant the Kings, but the sound of it was more important than the meaning, and no one in Harvey, Illinois, would dare to nit-pick when the El-Rays started to sing. They were raised on MOONGLOWS, DOMINOES, and RAVENS 78s, and when they felt they sounded good enough, the group started writing songs like "Darling I Know" and "Christine."

In the spring of 1954 the boys ventured to Chicago to audition. They found Chess Records' new offices at 4550 Cottage Grove Avenue and proceeded to audition their originals for the owner, Leonard Chess. The audition led to a session, and in the fourth week of May, "Darling I Know" b/w "Christine" came out on Chess affiliate Checker Records. It's a wonder the two very raw recordings came out at all; Leonard Chess reportedly told "Christine" lead Marvin Junior that he should quit singing and go drive a cab.

The SPANIELS-style rhythm ballad "Darling I Know" had three different lead vocalists, with bass Barksdale on the bridge, and showed that the group had a long way to go.

Nevertheless the group gained valuable performing experience from "Darling's" limited exposure. They began working at Boots and Saddles, a small bar and restaurant in Markham, Illinois (where rodeos were held) for $2 a night and a

hamburger dinner. After a month they were rewarded with $2 a night and a barbeque dinner. Realizing they had to improve their sound, the El-Rays began their tutelage with local pros the Moonglows, who actually took the time to rehearse the group and teach them the fine points of vocal blending. The resulting improvement gave them enough confidence to return to Chicago in the early spring of 1955, but this time the quintet (Lucius had departed after the barbeque dinners) went across the street to 4747 Cottage Grove Avenue, the home of Vee-Jay Records. Vivian Carter Bracken (Vee), James Bracken (Jay), and Vivian's brother Calvin Carter liked the El-Rays but felt a name change was necessary. They dropped various possibilities into a hat and out popped the Dells, a moniker possibly inspired by the local resort area, Wisconsin Dells.

In April 1955 "Tell The World" was released, but few outside of Harvey, Illinois, knew about it. (In their enthusiasm, the Dells probably gave away more records of "Tell" and "Darling" than they sold.) "Tell" was a nicely done ballad with an apparent Moonglows influence on a song written by Vern Allison.

"Dreams of Contentment," also written by Allison, was a bluesier ballad and did a little better, setting the stage for a song that Marvin Junior and Johnny Funches wrote after a particularly festive evening with the Five Dells, five girls, and a passel of chicken.

"Oh What a Nite" came out in July 1956, but the Dells were not around to care. They had succumbed to the demoralization of three failed singles. Chuck Barksdale had not even been around for the "Nite" sessions, having jumped ship to join Otis Williams and THE CHARMS in Cincinnati. The others were playing basketball on a fateful late summer day when the Moonglows drove up in their Cadillac and informed the Dells that they had heard their record in New York. At first the group thought they were kidding, but Harvey Fuqua said, "You've got a hit, man."

"Oh What a Nite" was a summer lover's ballad with vibrant harmonies and a beautiful variation on the call-and-response vocals employed by gospel and R&B groups of the time.

Chuck rejoined the Dells and the group began its legendary career by appearing at New York's Apollo. On November 10, 1956, "Nite" hit *Billboard*'s Best Seller list and by year's end had reached number four (#5 Disc Jockey, #5 Jukebox). The Dells continued to put forth some excellent singles in 1957 and 1958, most notably "Why Do You Have to Go" (written by Allison) and

"Pain in My Heart" (penned by Marvin and Johnny), both ballads. But none of these releases had the impact of "Oh What a Nite."

In late 1958 the Dells' career and lives nearly came to an end when their station wagon went out of control en route to a Philadelphia gig. Mickey's broken leg put him in the hospital. Although Chuck had gone through the windshield and the others were badly shaken, the four still performed on schedule at the Uptown Theatre in Philadelphia with THE ISLEY BROTHERS and THE FLAMINGOS. The accident took its toll, however, and the group did not perform for almost two years after that. In the meantime, Vee-Jay continued to release Dells singles, including "Dry Your Eyes" (written by Allison) in 1959 and a reissue of "Oh What a Nite" toward the end of 1959. But radio wasn't biting, even though *Billboard*'s February 1, 1960, reviewers gave "Oh What a Nite" four stars and wrote, "The group turns in a spirited, semi-shouted reading on a medium-paced ballad effort. Satisfying wax."

The members were getting married and doing day jobs to get by. In 1959 the group decided to try for stardom again, but Junior Funches, under his wife's mandate, would not go along.

A fateful meeting in a Chicago bar between long-time Flamingos vocalist Johnny Carter (who was working as a plastering contractor at the time) and the remaining Dells resolved with the quintet striking camp the next day for Philadelphia accompanied by voice specialist Curt Stewart. But they weren't yet able to go back out under their own power; a second career as backup vocalists was about to emerge. Thanks to Stewart's coaching (he managed Sarah Vaughn) the Dells became proficient in modern harmony à la THE FOUR ACES and THE HI-LOS, adding a new dimension to their rhythm and blues, doo wop, and gospel vocalizing. Stewart arranged an audition for the Dells with Dinah Washington, who took them on the road as her background singers and cut four sides with them during 1959 (with no credits) on her *Tears and Laughter* LP. From this auspicious beginning, the Dells would go on to do more backup work on record (mostly with no credit) than any other name group in history.

After the Washington LP, the group separated again due to financial disagreements. Barksdale and Carter stayed with Dinah's new group (D's Gentlemen) that also included Cornel Gunter of THE COASTERS and three members of the Pittsburgh group THE ALTAIRS. This group lasted until her death in 1963. A few of the remaining Dells went back to Vee-Jay for one single in 1961, "Swingin' Teens," along with DANDERLIERS lead, Dallas Taylor.

In 1962 the Dells wound up on Argo Records (a division of Chess) due to a deal between the failing Vee-Jay and the organization that eight years before recorded the El-Rays (Chess). Their first 45 was a nice blues/pop harmony arrangement of "God Bless the Child" that failed to connect with the masses, but their next release became their first national pop charter. Taking advantage of the latest dance crazes that were sweeping the nation (the "bossa nova" and the "bird"), the Dells did a very uncharacteristic "Bossa Nova Bird," which flew to number 97 before being shot down.

Two more undistinguished Argo singles and the group found itself (through no choice of its own) back on Vee-Jay as the Chess/Vee-Jay deal was apparently aborted or terminated. With Carter and Barksdale back from D's Gents, the group turned out 45s like "Oh What a Good Nite" written by Funches, a harmony-laden but lackluster clone of "Oh What a Nite," and a good cover of Tom Jones's hit "It's Not Unusual," which Vee-Jay released the same month Tom's version first charted (April 1965).

Their next-to-last Vee-Jay release, "Stay in My Corner," was a soul/harmony effort that made only *Billboard*'s Bubbling Under list (#122) in June 1965, but it reached number 23 on the R&B charts, their first R&B listing in nine years (since "Oh What a Night"). As if in tribute to the Moonglows, the final refrains were as close to their sound as any group had ever come.

Still, Vee-Jay was dying and the group's last single, "Hey Sugar," saw no promotion at all.

By the summer of 1966 the Dells were back at Chess. This group literally worked both sides of the street. Between 1954 and 1975 they were on Vee-Jay three different times and across the street with the Chess organization three separate times.

Their fourth single on Cadet (another Chess affiliate), "O–O I Love You," marked the beginning of their longest run of chart hits. "O–O" reached number 61 Pop (#22 R&B). The follow-up (which was the flip side of "O–O" released as an A side with a new flip), "There Is," jumped on the R&B lists in February of '68 reaching number 11 and becoming their biggest pop record to date (#20). "There Is" was a FOUR TOPS-style soul/rocker with a contagious shaking rhythm.

The Dells had successfully entered the soul era. They did an extended rerecorded version of "Stay in My Corner" (over six minutes long) that went to number one R&B and number 10 Pop in the summer of 1968. Songs like "Always Together" (#18 Pop, #3 R&B) and "I Can Sing a Rainbow" b/w "Love Is Blue" (#22 Pop, #5 R&B) were further examples of the soul harmony approach that enabled them to successfully bridge the old and the new.

In 1969 they recorded "Oh What a Nite" with a long talking intro and harmonies more reminiscent of the Moonglows than the Dells. The sparkling Bobby Miller production and Charles Stepney arrangement (he of the Rotary Connection) had more upfront harmonies than even the original. It was a refreshing chart break from the year's hard rock and bubblegum music. By September 27, 1969, the Dells had the number 10 single in America (#1 R&B). This led to a series of Dells remakes: "Nadine" (THE CORONETS), "Long Lonely Nights" (LEE ANDREWS AND THE HEARTS), and "Glory of Love" (THE FIVE KEYS) that all charted well for the Harvey, Illinois, alumni.

Throughout the '60s decade, the Dells spent almost as much time recording behind other acts as they did recording for themselves. Jerry Butler, Etta James, Wade Flemons, Joann Garrett, Ted Taylor, and even the Players had the Dells supporting them. Barbara Lewis's number one single "Hello Stranger" (1963) should have read Barbara Lewis and the Dells. At least 60 recordings included Dells backup, and there are probably countless more recordings that no one—(not even the members of the group)—can remember.

In 1973, the Dells had their first RIAA certified million seller with "Give Your Baby a Standing Ovation." One of their most incredible recordings in that era was not a hit at all but was an eerily recorded and brilliantly arranged Charles Stepney version of "Walk on By," originally a hit for singer Dionne Warwick.

In 1975 the Dells made an experimental recording with THE DRAMATICS applying 10 voices to songs like "Love Is Missing from Our Lives."

After 27 charters for Cadet, the Dells moved over to Chicago's major label, Mercury, in late 1975 and then to ABC, 20th Century, and Private I on through the '80s.

Their last charter was "Love On" (#60 R&B, 1984) on Private I, but as of the early '90s the group was still performing with a 35-year-old polished sound (without the usual upheaval associated with membership changes).

All told, the Dells had 43 rhythm and blues chart records along with 24 pop hits and a legacy of ever-evolving quality music.

THE DELLS

A SIDE/B SIDE	LABEL/CAT NO	DATE
The El-Rays		
Darling I Know / Christine	Vee-Jay 794	5/54
The Dells		
Tell The World / Blues At Three	Vee-Jay 134	4/55
Dreams Of Contentment /		
Zing, Zing, Zing	Vee-Jay 166	12/55
Oh What A Nite / Jo-Jo	Vee-Jay 204	7/56
Movin' On / I Wanna Go Home	Vee-Jay 230	12/56
Why Do You Have To Go /		
Dance, Dance, Dance	Vee-Jay 236	3/57
A Distant Love / O-Bop She-Bop	Vee-Jay 251	8/57
Pain In My Heart / Time Makes		
You Change	Vee-Jay 258	11/57
The Springer / What You Say Baby	Vee-Jay 274	4/58
I'm Calling / Jeepers Creepers	Vee-Jay 292	8/58
Wedding Day / My Best Girl	Vee-Jay 300	12/58
Dry Your Eyes / Baby, Open Up		
Your Heart	Vee-Jay 324	9/59
Oh What A Nite / I Wanna		
Go Home	Vee-Jay 338	1959
Swingin' Teens / Hold On To What		
You've Got	Vee-Jay 376	5/61
Shy Girl / What Do We Prove	Vee-Jay 595	5/64
God Bless The Child /		
I'm Going Home	Argo 5415	1962
The Bossa Nova Bird /		
Eternally	Argo 5428	10/62
It It Ain't One Thing Its Another /		
Diddley Dee Dum Dum	Argo 5442	6/63
After You / Goodbye, Mary Ann	Argo 5456	10/63
Oh What A Good Nite /		
Wait Till Tomorrow	Vee-Jay 615	8/64
Stay In My Corner /		
It's Not Unusual	Vee-Jay 674	4/65
Hey Sugar / Poor Little Boy	Vee-Jay 712	12/65
Thinkin' About You / The Change		
We Go Through	Cadet 5538	6/66
Run For Cover / Over Again	Cadet 5551	11/66
Inspiration / You Belong To		
Someone Else	Cadet 5563	1967
O-O, I Love You / There Is	Cadet 5574	8/67
There Is / Show Me	Cadet 5590	1/68
Wear It On Your Face / Please		
Don't Change Me Now	Cadet 5599	3/68
Stay In My Corner /		
Love Is So Simple	Cadet 5612	6/68
Always Together /		
I Want My Momma	Cadet 5621	9/68
Make Sure / Does Anybody Know		
I'm Here	Cadet 5631	12/68
Hallways Of My Mind /		
I Can't Do Enough	Cadet 5636	2/69
I Can Sing A Rainbow / Love Is		
Blue / Hallelujah Baby	Cadet 5641	4/69
Oh, What A Night /		
Believe Me	Cadet 5649	7/69

A SIDE/B SIDE	LABEL/CAT NO	DATE
When I'm In Your Arms / On The Dock Of The Bay	Cadet 5658	10/69
Oh, What A Day / The Change We Go Through	Cadet 5663	12/69
Nadine / Open Up My Heart	Cadet 5667	3/70
Long Lonely Nights / A Little Understanding	Cadet 5672	5/70
The Glory Of Love / A Whiter Shade Of Pale	Cadet 5679	1971
The Love We Had / Freedom Means	Cadet 5683	1971
It's All Up To You / Oh, My Dear	Cadet 5689	1972
Walk On By / This Guy's In Love With You	Cadet 5691	1972
I'd Rather Be With You / Just As Long As We're In Love	Cadet 5694	1973
Give Your Baby A Standing Ovation / Closer	Cadet 5696	1973
My Pretending Days Are Over / Let's Make It Last	Cadet 5698	1973
I Miss You / Don't Make Me A Storyteller	Cadet 5700	1973
I Wish It Was Me You Loved / Two Together Is Better Than One	Cadet 5702	1974
Learning To Love You Was Easy / Bring Back The Love Of Yesterday	Cadet 5703	1974
Learning To Love You Was Easy / Sweeter As the Days Go By	Cadet 5703	1974
The Glory Of Love / You're The Greatest	Cadet 5707	1975
Love Is Missing From Our Lives / I'm In Love	Cadet 5710	1975
We Got To Get Our Things Together / The Power Of Love	Cadet 5711	1975
We Got To Get Our Things Together / Reminiscing	Merc 73723	10/75
Gotta Get Home To My Baby / The Power Of Love	Merc 73759	1975
Slow Motion / Ain't No Black And White In Music	Merc 73807	1976
No Way Back / Too Late For Love	Merc 73842	1976
Our Love	Merc 73909	5/77
Betcha Never Been Loved (Like This Before)	Merc 73901	8/77
Private Property	Merc 73977	1/78
Super Woman	ABC 12386	7/78
(You Bring Out) The Best In Me	ABC 12440	1/79
I Touched A Dream	20th 2463	8/80
Passionate Breezes	20th 2475	12/80
You Just Can't Walk Away / Don't Want Nobody	Prvt I 4343	1984
One Step Closer / Come On Back To Me	Prvt I 4448	1984
Love On / Don't Want Nobody	Prvt I 4540	1984

The Delroys

Singers and street gangs—that was the world of teens in 1956 Long Island City, New York. Vocal group battles were as common as gang battles, but most were amateur sounding and none achieved even local success until the Delroys came along.

They were all from the Queensbridge Housing Projects, and as its name indicated, it overlooked the East River and the 59th Street Bridge leading from Queens to Manhattan. Reggie Walker and Milton Holder belonged to a 12th Street group who found themselves vocally battling it out with the COLEMAN BROTHERS (Robbie and Bobby) 10th Street quintet at the house of one of the Coleman members. Though Reggie's group won that particular battle, his keen ear told him the Colemans really knew harmony, so shortly thereafter Reggie, the Colemans, and John Blount from a third group joined in a new entity along with a lead known only as Snookie.

The Long Island City high schoolers were heavily influenced by THE VELOURS and THE SPANIELS. The name Delroys came from Ronnie, who had witnessed the Five Flying Delroys, an acrobatic team, perform on TV (probably on "The Ed Sullivan Show").

Their break came right in the halls of the housing projects. A lady heard them and contacted manager Ernest Kelly, who came with vocalist Milton Sparks to see the group at Queensbridge. For the audition, Snookie was replaced by John Blount on lead. The group sang "Bermuda Shorts," an up-tempo tune they cowrote with Milton Holder, their 12th Street rival, and Kelly liked it enough to take it to Apollo Records.

The label was having success with THE CELLOS' novelty rocker "Rang Tang Ding Dong (I Am the Japanese Sandman)" at the time. As far as interest in Kelly's presentation was concerned, they were more interested in Kelly's other act, Milton Sparks, than they were in the Delroys. Kelly, apparently driving a hard bargain, parlayed Apollo's desire for Sparks into a deal for the Delroys as well.

Apollo Records had the last laugh in the business sense when they pressed the Delroys' "Bermuda Shorts" on to the B side of a Milton Sparks A side called "Time." ("Bermuda" was cut the same night as the Cellos' song "Juicy Crocodile" and was a "Stranded-in-the-Jungle"-styled novelty rocker with a bass lead and a nice chime harmony ending.) But the Delroys (the group members all of 14 and 15 years old at that time) enjoyed the last laugh creatively when their B side started getting play throughout the New York City area during the summer of 1957.

Though the group saw no royalties, their record apparently made enough noise to justify a few tours, and they appeared with their idols, the Velours, at the Syria Mosque in Pittsburgh along with THE BOBBETTES, THE DEL-VIKINGS, and THE CLOVERS. The Delroys even played the Apollo Theatre with THE DOMINOES, Little Joe and the Thrillers, and a new Decca Records artist named Bobby Darin.

The street-singing battles and neighborhood gang fights were no preparation for the hard reality of the touring wars; when their road manager absconded with the receipts from a Washington appearance at the Howard Theatre, the boys were left high and dry 300 miles from home. The promoters paid their way back, but by that time John Blount had decided this was not the career for him. Bobby Taylor of the Uniques took his place and Junior Talbot came aboard to make it a quintet. The lineup was now Bobby Taylor (lead), Ronnie (first tenor), Junior (second tenor), Bobby Coleman (baritone), and Reggie (bass).

They teamed up once again with Sparks and Kelly, recording on their fledgling Sparkell label (formed in 1959). A release of the Delroys ballad "Wise Old Owl" went nowhere. The group then disbanded, and in 1961 Ronnie formed a new Delroys with neighbors Ray Pain on lead, Norman Boquie on second tenor, and Cliff Davis on baritone. They joined Jerry Love's Carol Records and put out a fine single, "Love Me Tenderly," a rock-a cha-cha affair with a nice baritone lead and lots of strings. The generally overlooked flip side, "Pleasing You," was a rocking doo-wopper with lots of harmony and a fast-paced lead vocal. Radio station WABC played the record to the tune of number 36 on its local chart, but outside New York it remained unknown.

In 1970 the Coleman Brothers and Reggie Walker became the First Three and recorded their fourth single for their fourth label, Deep Records. Bobby Taylor went on to sing with a group that had recorded in the early '70s, We the People. He moved to Chicago in 1974, married, and went on to work for Sears.

The Delroys were re-formed in 1982 out of the Colemans and Reggie. In 1987 they cut a single for their own RSVP label titled "Talk to Me" (the 1958 Little Willie John hit). In between, Reggie became a New York City policeman and Ronnie went to work for the post office.

The Del-Vikings

The Del-Vikings were the first successful racially integrated group in rock and roll and one of the few hit makers organized in the U.S. Air Force. The group was formed by Clarence Quick at the NCO Service Club located at Pittsburgh's airport in 1956. Bass singer Clarence (who had originally sung with his cousin William Blakely in Brooklyn, New York, in a group called the Mellowlarks) joined together with Corinthian "Kripp" Johnson (lead and tenor), Samuel Patterson (lead and tenor), Bernard Robertson (second tenor), and Don Jackson (baritone) to form the Del-Vikings. The Vikings was the name of a basketball-playing social club in Brooklyn that Quick belonged to. When he put Del (meaning "the") in front of Vikings he unintentionally created a redundant moniker—like saying "the The Vikings" (similar to the Dells [the Thes] and the El Rays). Unbeknownst to most, the five original members were all black.

Their participation in (and winning) the base's "Tops in Blue" contests earned them a spot in the All Air Force talent show in New York City, where they won again (beating out over 700 worldwide groups) singing a song by Quick titled "Come Go with Me." One of the groups they beat in the finals that day was the Rocketeers, who went on to become THE PASTELS of "Been So Long" fame.

After one of their Pittsburgh talent shows the Del-Vikings were approached to record by local disc jockey Barry Kaye and producer Joe Averback. Before the sessions, however, Patterson and Robertson were assigned to an air base in Germany and were replaced by Norman Wright (of Philadelphia) and the group's first white member, Dave Lerchey of New Albany, Indiana.

The recordings turned out to be a cappella renditions of nine songs, all recorded in Kaye's tiny basement—so small and ill-equipped, in fact, that several members had to sing from a closet for both space and sound considerations. Averback leased the recordings to Dickie Goodman's Luniverse label (he of the "Flying Saucer" novelty break-in records) where they were to sit a bit. Then Averback decided to sign the group to his own Fee Bee label and added instrumental backing to a few of the a cappella sides at a studio in the Sheraton Hotel in November 1956.

One side was Quick's "Come Go with Me," released as Fee Bee 205 in December and immediately leased to national distributor Dot Records.

On February 16, 1957, the record took off like an air force jet, rising on *Billboard*'s Pop chart to number four (#2 R&B). The simplicity of the song's swinging verse melody and punchy bridge had everyone within radio range singing along for months to come—it lasted an amazing 31 weeks on the charts and became a million seller.

"Come Go with Me" became the first top 10 hit by a racially mixed rock and roll group, but it wasn't something the members had thought of when Lerchey joined. Nor was it on their minds when Don Jackson shipped out to Germany and Donald "Gus" Backus of Southhampton, Long Island, another white serviceman, took his place.

This was the lineup that sang on the Del-Vikings' second session, spawning the Kripp Johnson-led "Whispering Bells." Originally written and rehearsed as a ballad, "Whispering Bells" (another Quick song) became a classic rocker in the studio, filled with the Del-Vikings' best-ever harmonies.

The release of "Bells" was preceded by a less-than-effective, calypso-tinged tune called "Down in Bermuda" that couldn't jump-start itself to interest Dot.

Meanwhile, the group's new manager Al Berman was negotiating behind the scenes, and before you could say "Come Go," most of the Del-Vikings went—to Mercury Records, that is. Apparently they had been underage when they signed with Fee Bee; Kripp Johnson, however, had been over 21 and therefore had to stay at Fee Bee/Dot. Before the others left they recorded numerous sides, including one backing country vocalist Joey Biscoe in what became Fee Bee's next single, "What Made Maggie Run," best described as '50s country rock blended with doo wop. Dot paired it with a "Ka Ding Dong" (G-Clefs) sounding side, "Little Billy Boy," and released it in April 1957. Its prompt demise ushered in the May release of "Whispering Bells" on Fee Bee. Once again Dot kicked into high gear and "Bells" began ringing all over the country to the tune of number nine Pop (#5 R&B) through the spring and summer of 1957.

Meanwhile the Del-Vikings on Mercury Records (Wright, Lerchey, Backus, Quick, and Quick's Brooklyn friend William Blakely) began recording, and they released their first single, "Cool Shake," in May 1957. By mid-July, "Cool" was on the pop charts, one week after "Bells" hit the list.

America's disc jockeys didn't know what was going on but they played both records. The Gus Backus-led Mercury recording held its own, rising to number 12 (#9 R&B). Not to be left out in the cold, Kripp Johnson formed a new Del-Vikings that including Eddie Everette, Arthur Budd, and Chuck Jackson, along with the newly-returned-from-Germany Don Jackson (no relation). Fee Bee put the new group in the studio; the yield was sides like "Willette" and "I Want to Marry You" (Fee Bee 221 in mid-1957) with Chuck singing lead. The young Winston-Salem, North Carolinian had previously sung with the Raspberry Gospel Singers and had been influenced by Jackie Wilson.

Adding to the confusion, Luniverse Records (remember them?) added instruments to their a cappella tracks and in 1957 released eight of them on an LP titled *Come Go with the Del-Vikings*, featuring a picture of the group during the period when "Whispering Bells" was recorded (two whites, three blacks) rather than when their LP's worth of songs were done (one white, four blacks). They also released a magnificent ballad version of "Over the Rainbow," which deserved more radio attention than "Cool Shake" received. Of the more than 50 vocal group versions of the Garland standard, the one by the Del-Vikings was surely in the top five, quality-wise.

To simplify things (they thought) Dot issued Kripp and company's next single "When I Come Home" as the Del*l*-Vikings and Kripp Johnson. The flip "I'm Spinning" was done by the full group, but the label read only "Kripp Johnson, lead singer of 'Whispering Bells.'" But Mercury began legal proceedings against Fee Bee for the use of the group's name; one "l" or two, they wanted it all.

In August, Mercury issued "Come Along with Me," a rocker in the style of "Come Go with Me" that lacked the original's magic. Both Fee Bee and Dot released Del-Vikings singles through the fall of 1957 but Dot dropped out of the picture after "When I Come Home." Over the years the Del/Dell-Vikings confusion would continue when different or rearranged recordings of the *same songs* showed up on two or more of the Vikings' labels: "When I Come Home" came out on both Dot and Mercury; "I'm Spinning" on Fee Bee, Dot, and Mercury; and "Come Go with Me" on Luniverse, Fee Bee, and Dot. And not helping matters was the extensive use of a photo showing the Mercury version of the group as the definitive Del-Vikings even though "Come Go with Me" was cut by the four black, one white aggregation that included Johnson and Don Jackson but never Blakely.

In December of 1957 Mercury gained legal authority over the name, and Fee Bee issued its remaining Del-Vikings sides under the name the

Versatiles (and sometimes under Chuck Jackson's name) after its release of "True Love" at the end of 1957.

Kripp's contract with Fee Bee terminated in 1958 and he rejoined his original Del-Vikings friends at Mercury, thus disbanding the second group. By this time Gus had been sent to Germany, compliments of the air force.

Chuck Jackson went on to a solo career and in early 1961 had a top five R&B hit, "I Don't Want to Cry" (#36 Pop, Wand). He went on to have 23 more charters both R&B and Pop including "Any Day Now" (#2 R&B, #23 Pop, 1962).

Kripp sang on the last two Del-Vikings Mercury singles, "You Cheated" and "How Could You." "You Cheated" was interesting in that it had a racially mixed group from Pittsburgh covering a black group from Los Angeles (the Shields) who had covered a white group from Texas (the Slades). Justice was served this time as the Shields' far superior version beat out both (#12, 1958). In 1959, after the group had done their last singles for Mercury, Kripp recorded two 45s ("Everlasting" and "A Door That Is Open") with an anonymous singing group behind him (possibly the Del-Vikings).

When the group finally received their individual discharges they were able to take advantage of their name recognition and tour the length of the country from Las Vegas to Radio City Music Hall, also doing such TV shows as "The Ed Sullivan Show," "The Tonight Show," and Dick Clark's and Alan Freed's programs. In October 1960, they released a one-shot on Alpine, a harmony-drenched doo wop ballad titled "The Sun." It set much too soon.

They signed with ABC Paramount Records in the spring of 1961. Their first release, a Latin-flavored DRIFTERS-style rocker called "Bring Back Your Heart," looked like just the winner to bring them back when New York radio jumped on it. Unfortunately, the national charts didn't reflect the New York excitement and "Heart" died at number 101, dynamite vocals, kettledrums, Spanish guitars, swirling strings, Chuck Sagle's arrangement, and all. Several more terrific singles followed including "I Hear Bells" and "Face the Music," but ABC was too busy with Ray Charles and THE IMPRESSIONS to care.

On March 3, 1962, one of *Billboard*'s Spotlight Singles picks was "The Big Silence," about which their reviewer intoned, "The boys may have their first big hit in some time with this showmanly side. The plaintive rock-a-ballad is sung with consider-

able feeling and sales savvy by the lead warbler, who also contributes a sock narration bit. Watch it." Del-Vikings fans watched it disappear as ABC let it slip away.

During the early and mid-'60s the group worked the southern college circuit and then disbanded. By 1970 they were back again with Johnson, Lerchey, Blakely, Wright, and Quick as the membership.

In November 1972 the quintet recorded a contemporary version of "Come Go with Me" for Scepter. It became their last new single for almost 20 years.

They went international via the London Palladium and England's "Top of the Pops" TV show, then toured the Far East. In 1979 there once again became two Del-Vikings groups touring the oldies circuit. Johnson's group consisted of himself, Lerchey, John Byas (since 1965), and Ritzy Lee. By 1990, the lineup read those four plus Norman Wright.

On June 22, 1990, 57-seven-year-old Kripp Johnson died of cancer.

The second group, formed by Quick, consisted of Herbert McQueen, Louis Velez, Arthur Martinez, William Blakely, and of course, Clarence Quick. Over the years the Quick contingent had Dickie Harmon ("Windsong" on Clifton) replacing McQueen and Frank Ayers taking over for Blakely. In early 1991 Quick's quintet recorded a terrific two-sider in the '50s style ("My Heart" b/w "Rock and Roll Remembered") on BVM Records, which oldies stations embraced.

That the Del-Vikings epitomized the sound of mid-'50s rock and roll is evident in the uses of their songs and recordings in the '70s and '80s. The film *American Graffiti* (1973) featured their songs as did the 1986 hit *Stand By Me*. That they had more success on their first few records than most acts have in a lifetime is indicative of their talent.

THE DEL-VIKINGS

A SIDE/B SIDE	LABEL/CAT NO	DATE
Come Go With Me / How Can I Find True Love	Fee Bee 205	12/56
Come Go With Me / How Can I Find True Love	Dot 15538	1/57
Down In Bermuda / Maggie	Fee Bee 206	2/57
What Made Maggie Run / Down By The Stream	Fee Bee 210	3/57
What Made Maggie Run / Uh Uh Baby	Fee Bee 210	3/57
What Made Maggie Run / When I Come Home	Fee Bee 210	3/57

A SIDE/B SIDE	LABEL/CAT NO	DATE
What Made Maggie Run /		
Little Billy Boy	Dot 15571	4/57
Whispering Bells / Don't Be A Fool	Fee Bee 214	4/57
Whispering Bells / Don't Be A Fool	Dot 15592	5/57
Cool Shake / Jitterbug Mary	Merc 71132	5/57
I'm Spinning / You Say You		
Love Me	Fee Bee 218	1957
When I Come Home / I'm Spinning	Dot 15636	8/57
Come Along With Me / Whatcha		
Gotta Lose	Merc 71180	8/57
When I Come Home / I'm Spinning	Merc 71198	9/57
Somewhere Over The Rainbow /		
Hey, Senorita	Luni 106	1957
Willette / Woke Up This Morning	Fee Bee 221	1957
Your Book Of Life / Snowbound	Merc 71241	11/57
Willette / Woke Up This Morning	Fee Bee 221	1957
Finger Poppin' Woman / Tell Me	Fee Bee 227	1957
True Love / Baby, Let Me Be	Fee Bee 902	12/57
The Voodoo Man / Can't Wait	Merc 71266	1/58
You Cheated / Pretty Little Things		
Called Girls	Merc 71345	7/58
How Could You / Flat Tire	Merc 71390	10/58
Come Go With Me / How Can I		
Find True Love	Dot 16902	5/60
The Sun / Pistol Packin' Mama	Alpine 66	10/60
I'll Never Stop Crying /		
Bring Back Your Heart	ABC 10208	4/61
I Hear Bells / Don't Get Slick		
On Me	ABC 10248	10/61
Face The Music / Kiss Me	ABC 10278	1/62
The Big Silence / One More		
River To Cross	ABC 10304	2/62
Kilimanjaro / Confession of Love	ABC 10341	6/62
Angel Up In Heaven /		
The Fishing Chant	ABC 10385	1/63
Sorcerer's Apprentice /		
Too Many Miles	ABC 10425	3/63
A Sunday Kind Of Love /		
Come Along With Me	Merc 30112	1963
We Three / I've Got To Know	Gtwy 743	1964
Cold Feet / I Want To Marry You	BBB 111	1972
Watching The Moon / You Say You		
Love Me	BBB 113	1972
Girl Girl / I'm Spinning	BBB 115	1972
Come Go With Me /		
When You're Asleep	Scptr 12367	11/72
My Heart / Rock & Roll		
Remembered	BVM 002	1991

The Desires

The Desires were a doo wop group of the late '50s who brought a high degree of vocal professionalism to the marketplace in their short career. They met at the 118th Street Youth Center in New York

City and originally called themselves the Students. The membership came from three separate area high schools and consisted of Robert "Bootsie" White (lead from Cooper High School), Charles Hurston (tenor, Herrod High), George "Smithy" Smith (baritone, Herrod High), Charles Powell (bass, Franklin High), and Jim Whittier (tenor from Rochester, New York and former member of the Jivetones on Apt). They changed their name upon hearing of the *other* Students ("I'm So Young") and began a rigorous schedule of rehearsals to sharpen their sound. Unlike many street groups of New York, the Desires worked with a vocal coach, Eddie Jones, formerly of the Demens on Teenage and the Emersons on Newport.

In 1959 the group attracted the attention of BOBBETTES manager James Dailey, and it was he who took the youngsters to Hull Records with several demos of songs they'd written.

Their first release was a solid New York-style ballad, "Let It Please Be You," with Bootsie singing his Frankie Lymon-like heart out. Despite its weak national showing, it was a song destined to become an East Coast favorite and a part of almost every '60s doo wop group's repertoire. The uptempo B side, "Hey Lena," also showcased their strong harmonies and a sound reminiscent of the TEENAGERS.

Taking advantage of regional radio reaction to "Let It Please Be You," the Desires played such swank venues as Bellevue Hospital (home of THE BONNIE SISTERS) in New York and Jocko's Rollerskating Rink in New Jersey while traveling up and down the East Coast performing with THE PARAGONS, THE JESTERS, and THE KODAKS, among others.

The group had their very own fan club of which Patricia Bennett, Judy Craig, and Barbara Lee were active members, shouting support at every local Desires performance. Those three girls and Sylvia Peterson later went on to become THE CHIFFONS.

The Desires' second 45, "Rendezvous with You," was released in 1960 and received somewhat less response than their previous effort. Still, its New York play earned them a spot on Murray the K's Brooklyn Fox show. A bad management decision kept the group from making a deal with Scepter, and when their third single went unreleased by Hull, the Desires' recording career was over.

They continued to perform until the jobs ran out and they disbanded in 1961.

Jim went into the Navy and then became a radio station engineer, winding up at the nation's number one oldies station, WCBS-FM in New York. It must be quite a feeling of nostalgia when the disc jockey asks him to cue up that great doo wop ballad by the Desires, "Let It Please Be You."

The Diablos

Nolan Strong and the Diablos were, without knowing it, the forerunners of the Detroit rhythm and blues sound. They merged Latin, blues, and modern rhythms into a style that later on influenced the mighty music machine at Motown.

Formed at Central High School in Detroit during 1950, the quartet included Nolan Strong (lead), Juan Guieterriez (tenor), Willie Hunter (baritone), Quentin Eubanks (bass), and Bob Edwards (guitar). Nolan, born in Scottsboro, Alabama (January 22, 1934), had one of the most sensitive and beautiful falsetto voices ever, and it's no coincidence that his idol was another super tenor, Clyde McPhatter.

The Diablos practiced and performed for four years, inspired by recordings of THE DOMINOES and the Royals (later HANK BALLARD AND THE MIDNIGHTERS).

In April 1954 the group traipsed over to Fortune Studios, a back-room, two-track affair at 11629 Lindwood, to cut a few demos. Their hope was obviously to hook up with one of the period's hot rhythm and blues labels. They never got the chance as Devora Brown, co-owner of the studio and the small Fortune label with her husband Jack, signed them as soon as she heard them.

The rocking rhumba "Adios, My Desert Love" was their first single, written by Devora and released the fourth week of April 1954. A terrific lead by Nolan was backed by weaving harmonies, constant castanets, and piano glisses aplenty. The Diablos managed a harmony that was strong, delicate, and haunting. "Adios" was a success in Detroit but couldn't break through in most of the other major markets. Later that year the group was presented with a Silver Record for "Adios's" popularity in Detroit by Fortune, the Detroit Council of Youth, and Senator Bristoe Bryant at the Madison Ballroom in front of over 10,000 fans.

Their next release was epic. Written by the group, "The Wind" gains stature with every listen and each passing year. The hauntingly beautiful ballad was issued the third week of September 1954 and prompted *Billboard*'s reviewer to write, "The Diablos have some unusual material here that will rate considerable airplay. Sentimental ballad with a recited lyric toward the end is set in a tasty, rather colorful arrangement." The eeriest of '50s vocal group records, "The Wind" had Strong's pristine lead supported by the now-legendary "blow wind" chorus; it also boasted a talking bridge by Strong that set the standard for tenor talking bridges. You could almost hear a breeze accompanying the song even though there were no sound effects on the record. Airplay was initially heavy in New York, Detroit, Chicago, and Cleveland, but Fortune was just too small a company to sustain a record nationally. Still, "The Wind" was a sleeping giant and would rise again.

That same year a 14-year-old Detroiter was so enamored with the mystical sound of Nolan Strong that he formed a vocal group and cut a rough demo on "Adios, My Desert Love," trying to sound as much like Nolan as possible. Come to think of it, Smokey Robinson still does.

No sooner had "The Wind" blown through the record stores than Juan and Quentin left the group to be replaced by Nolan's brother Jim (tenor) and George Scott (bass).

Their next 45 was a good rocker ("Route 16"), but its flip, "Hold Me Until Eternity," was a particularly fine example of Nolan and company rising above a noisy studio production to bring out the best in a ballad.

In the first week of May 1955, "Do You Remember What You Did," a rock and blues tune in a Chuck Berry groove, came and went.

The fifth week of October marked the release of the beautiful Nolan Strong-penned blues ballad with a rock and roll double-time piano: "The Way You Dog Me Around." This time Fortune mustered all its forces when the strength of the record opened up the marketplace; "Dog" spent three months clawing its way to number 12 on the national R&B Disc Jockey chart. The Diablos then toured extensively, playing alongside acts like THE SPANIELS, THE EL DORADOS, and THE DELLS. On December 9 they headlined the Apollo in New York with THE TURBANS, and on December 23 they began a Christmas week party at the Howard in Washington with THE ORIOLES and Sonny Boy Williamson. Their outlandish yellow pants, shirts, and ties with purple satin jackets made them a sight to see as well as a sound to hear.

In April 1956 a double-sided goodie came out that had the reviewer in *Billboard*'s May 5 issue commenting, "The group has a listenable entry in the slow, wailing pleader ["You're the Only Girl Dolores"]. Strong and crew show impressive spots. Jocks may well give it spins." On the rocking flip,

"Strong has a wild and fascinating way of wandering around a note. Impassioned tones with the Diablos in the backup add up to a good selling job." It was the first single to bear the inscription Nolan Strong and the Diablos; previous releases credited the Diablos featuring Nolan Strong.

One more single, in November ("A Teardrop from Heaven"), and Nolan was off to the army. A beautiful ballad called "Can't We Talk This Over" was culled from Nolan's previous sessions and issued in May 1957. The group also did one single in 1958 with Strong on lead ("Harriet"), but it was obvious that while Nolan was away the heart was missing from the Diablos.

His return marked the 1959 release of the Diablos' first cover, "I Am with You" (the Dominoes, 1951). They faithfully continued to record for the mom and pop Fortune company but their records were not being heard, and after 1960 the material wasn't of the highest quality anyway. One exception was a perfect follow-up to "The Wind," the 1960 blues ballad "Since You've Gone." Even the spastic piano player couldn't dim the glow of the Diablos' harmonies.

In the same year the Diablos managed to dent the pop charts with an unexpected entry, a reissue of "The Wind," picking up radio play in May and garnering enough to reach number 114 in late June. Meanwhile Nolan and Jimmy's cousin Barrett Strong had a hit with "Money" (#23 Pop, #2 R&B.)

In 1962 Nolan was given solo status (though the Diablos were right behind him) on "Mind Over Matter," a dance tune that did well in the Midwest and made some worthwhile Top 40 station charts. But it fell short of national status.

By 1963 Jim Strong and George Scott were gone and the lineup had become Nolan (lead), Bob Calhoun (tenor), Cy Iverson (tenor), Willie Hunter (baritone), and J. W. Johnson (bass). This entity made a little bit of musical history after two members met record collector Angelo Pompeo in a Jersey City record store. They told him that their quintet was in town on tour and invited him up to the Madison Hotel, where they were staying. The group had been practicing right in the hotel room and taping their rehearsals on an old home machine. Angelo was so knocked out by their sound on songs like "Blue Moon" and "I'm in Love" he impulsively asked if he could buy a tape. The group sold him the previous night's a cappella rehearsal session (which, since they were under contract to Fortune, they were technically not allowed to do). Angelo played the tape for all his friends and in a flash the single "I'm In Love" turned up on the Medievel label and all the oldies tri-state shows from "Danny Styles" to "Slim's Times Square Show" under the name the Velvet Angels.

Later on, Relic Records acquired the original tape of eight a cappella songs along with an obscure seven-song studio recording and issued a Velvet Angels LP. It sold quite well to the community of collectors that was growing in the early and mid-'60s.

Ironically, as the Diablos' career wound down their music became increasingly desirable. To this day, Fortune Records makes a living from reissuing records rather than creating new ones.

In December 1963 the Diablos had 12 records on Times Square Records' top 125 list, with 10 in the top 70. They released their last single in 1964, titled "Are You Making a Fool Out of Me?" As members came and went, Nolan and company did some shows and club dates when the oldies revival set in.

Nolan died on February 21, 1977, at the age of 43.

The lasting influence of Nolan Strong and the Diablos is undeniable. Nolan was the link between Clyde McPhatter and Smokey Robinson and could not have helped but influence young Frankie Lymon. It's reported that in early 1961 Motown offered the Browns a million dollars for Nolan's contract and the Diablos' past catalog. The Browns, who were certainly making no fortune with the group, turned Motown down. If that isn't belief in a group's talent, what is?

THE DIABLOS

A SIDE/B SIDE	LABEL/CAT NO	DATE
Adios My Desert Love / An Old-Fashioned Girl	Frtn 509,10	4/54
The Wind / Baby Be Mine	Fortune 511	9/54
Route 16 / Hold Me Until Eternity	Fortune 514	3/55
Daddy Rockin' Strong / Do You Remember What You Did	Fortune 516	5/55
The Way You Dog Me Around / Jump, Shake And Move	Fortune 518	10/55
You're The Only Girl, Dolores / You Are	Fortune 519	4/56
A Teardrop From Heaven / Try Me One More Time	Fortune 522	11/56
Can't We Talk This Over / The Mambo Of Love	Fortune 525	5/57
For Old Time's Sake / My Heart Will Always Belong To You	Fortune 529	1958

A SIDE/B SIDE	LABEL/CAT NO	DATE
Harriet / Come Home, Little Girl	Fortune 541	1958
Goodbye Matilda / I Am With You	Fortune 531	2/59
If I Could Be With You / I Wanna Know	Fortune 532	1959
Since You've Gone / Are You Gonna Do	Fortune 536	1960
The Wind / Baby Be Mine	Fortune 511	5/60
The Wind / Baby Be Mine	Fortune 511	2/62
Blue Moon / I Don't Care	Fortune 544	1962
Mind Over Matter / Beside You	Fortune 546	1962
I Really Love You / You're My Love	Fortune 553	1963
If I Oh I / I Wanna Know	Fortune 532	1963
Village Of Love / Real True Love	Fortune 563	1964
Are You Making A Fool Out Of Me / You're My Happiness	Fortune 564	1964
I'm in Love* / Let Me Come Back*	Mdvl 201	1964
Baby I Want to Know* / Since You've Been Gone*	Mdvl 207	1964

* The Velvet Angels

The Diamonds
(NEW YORK)

Long before the "Little Darlin' " DIAMONDS of Canada emerged on the music scene there was a New York City rhythm and blues group that had one of the most beautiful harmony styles around. The group began as a trio from Harlem labeling themselves the Three Aces in 1948. Harold "Sonny" Wright on lead, first tenor Myles Hardy, and bass Daniel Stevens idolized THE RAVENS and THE ORIOLES, singing as many of their tunes as the trio could learn for their performances at 132nd Street's St. Mark's Church on Friday nights (the starting place for THE CADILLACS and many other legendary groups).

It became the Four Aces in 1951 when Ernest Ford joined, but since eight aces already existed (a black foursome on Trilon and an emerging white quartet) these Aces changed suits to the Four Diamonds and then pared down to just the Diamonds. (Some say their name came about when the group signed with Atlantic Records and the company had a contest for the public to name them.)

In 1952 Sonny Wright took a solo shot on the Apollo amateur night contest and won. After several more weeks and wins, theater owner Bobby Schiffman offered him a week on the bill. Sonny told Schiffman of his group and the Apollo entrepreneur ran them through an audition. He was so impressed he not only gave them the week's worth of work but took on the quartet for management.

This brought the Diamonds to the attention of Atlantic, who signed them in September 1952, the same week they signed a young blind R&B singer named Ray Charles.

Their first four sides were recorded on October 29, 1952, and "A Beggar for Your Kisses" became their first single in December. A shuffle-style ballad with exquisite harmony, "A Beggar" went begging for airplay. (The imperfection of early '50s recording techniques [or possibly the rush to get the job done] allowed the listener to pick up two of the Diamonds talking at the end of "Beggar" before the machine was turned off, and the record was pressed that way.)

Their next single, "Two Loves Have I," was a gorgeous ballad derived from a French melody, with Sonny singing his heart out and Myles's constant falsetto nearly establishing a trademark sound for the group. But it seems no one at Atlantic was paying much attention, what with all the success THE CLOVERS were having with their recording "Middle of the Night."

The Diamonds' last single was "Romance in the Dark" b/w "Cherry," the latter an outstanding side that deserved a better fate.

The group broke up in 1955, but not before they had a chance to wow the audience at Philadelphia's Town Hall on June 17, 1955, alongside Dean Barlow (THE CRICKETS on Jay Dee), Ruth Brown, the Dreams (Savoy), Bo Diddley, and Screamin' Jay Hawkins.

Sensing frustration with Atlantic early on, Sonny had already been moonlighting for several years with the Regals, a hot quintet with a modern harmony style. When the Regals (named after a Regal shoestore) agreed to become Sonny Til's new Orioles, Wright went his own way. He formed a new group who auditioned for Archie Blyer's Cadence Records and became the only black vocal group on this predominantly pop label. The members (Al Avant, Bobby Vaughn, John Coleman, and Sonny Wright) were named the Metronomes by Blyer in keeping with the name of his company. Two fine but unsuccessful singles later and the Metronomes, like the Diamonds, were just a footnote in vocal group history.

Only in the '60s, when commercial success was not the only criterion for a good recording, did Diamonds gems gain attention from oldies radio and collectors of R&B records.

▲ THE CRESTS   ▼ THE COASTERS   ▼ THE FIVE SATINS

▲ THE DEL-VIKINGS   ▲ THE CRITERIONS   ▼ THE FLAMINGOS

The Diamonds
(ONTARIO)

The Diamonds were the most successful white pop group of the mid-'50s and the daddy of the cover groups. Their career followed a route similar to that of an earlier cover group, THE CREW-CUTS. Both were from Canada, both got their big break from the same disc jockey, and both wound up on the same label. But unlike the Crew-cuts, whose typical cover was no match for the original and who never put one of their records on the R&B chart, many of the Diamonds' recordings were very good and did sell to the R&B market. Seven of their singles made the black charts, along with their 16 Pop chartings.

The dawn of the Diamonds was in the fall of 1954 in their home of Ontario, Canada. Stan Fisher (lead), Ted Kowalski (tenor), Phil Leavitt (baritone), and Bill Reed (bass) were students at the University of Toronto and formed a pop quartet singing pop, show tunes, barbershop songs (Bill's dad actually owned a barbershop), and even spirituals. They attended a local TV show audition for "Now Is Your Choice," but instead of performing for the TV people, they were invited by a radio technician/would-be singer into an empty studio to harmonize; by the day's end the quartet was now a quintet with the addition of David Somerville.

After weeks of rehearsal they set out for their first job, a performance at St. Aquinas Church. Stan couldn't make the show as he had an exam, so Dave took over lead. En route, Ted came up with a name for the as-yet-unnamed students. His choice: the Diamonds. Of course, they had no knowledge of New York's fine black group on Atlantic in the early '50s with the same name.

By the summer of 1955 the Diamonds had crossed the U.S. border with their new manager Nat Goodman. He arranged for an audition with New York's Coral Records, and by the third week of September "Black Denim Trousers and Motorcycle Boots" was on its way to radio stations. The song, along with its flip, "Nip Sip," had been picked by A&R man Dick Jacobs. "Black Denim" was a cover of the Cheers, a white West Coast group that included soon-to-be-actor Bert Convy. When the Diamonds recorded it, they had no idea that it wasn't an original song. They were massacred by the Cheers' version. Score: Cheers, number six; Diamonds, zip. Adding insult to injury, their "Nip Sip" cover of THE CLOVERS' R&Ber was also soundly

thrashed. Score: Clovers, number 10 R&B; Diamonds, zip again.

Returning home, the group took heart from the success of another Canada quartet, the Crew-cuts, so they set out for Cleveland, home of disc jockey and Crew-cuts discoverer Bill Randall.

An a cappella audition convinced Randall to bring them to Mercury Records, the same place he brought the Cuts one year earlier. When the group auditioned for Mercury execs with spiritual songs, some Einstein thought it was rock and roll and signed the group to the division that handled that style of music instead of pop. (At that time, Mercury's definition of white rock and roll was mass market imitations of black records.)

So it was that the Diamonds recorded their first Mercury single in January 1956, "Why Do Fools Fall in Love" (FRANKIE LYMON AND THE TEENAGERS) backed with "You Baby You" (THE CLEFTONES). *Billboard*'s February 11th reviewer described it as "a nice cover side, with the lead singer showcased well by the arrangement. Could share the loot if the number continues to climb via the Teenagers' original." "Fools" became their first hit, reaching number 16 on the Top 100 and number 12 on the Disc Jockey list. Still, the Teenagers' record broke down all the barriers (#7 Pop, #1 R&B).

Coral, meanwhile, had two Diamonds sides left from their August 1955 session and released them in February 1956 to capitalize on the success of "Fools," but their "Smooch Me" release seemed almost of another generation by comparison.

The Diamonds, courtesy of Mercury's A&R execs, began narrowcasting. They recorded songs that were up-tempo and mostly by black vocal groups from New York. Their March release, "Church Bells May Ring" (THE WILLOWS) b/w "Little Girl of Mine" (the Diamonds were becoming the white Cleftones), reached number 14 Best Seller and number 15 on the Jukebox lists while the Willows' recording scored number 11 R&B and number 62 Pop. The black/white battle continued with "Love Love Love" (the Clovers) going to number 30 Pop, coincidentally the same number the Clovers' original attained, but then history takes a twist. The Clovers record, as expected, became an R&B smash reaching number four, but the Diamonds managed to reach number 14 on the R&B list. Crossing back to the black market with a white cover was a relative impossibility at that time. And the Diamonds started to make a regular practice of it. They may have fooled the black public to some degree, as many of their recordings sounded less like pure pop white covers and more like pop black groups (like the Four Knights) trying to do rock and roll. The musical arrangements were the giveaway, of course, being cleaner and better produced than many R&B cuts.

"Ka-Ding Dong" (the G-Clefs) was a further example of the Diamonds' R&B appeal. The Massachusetts-based G-Clefs scored a solid 24 on the Pop Best Sellers and number nine R&B, while the Diamonds hit 35 Pop and a number eight R&B. The key might have been David Somerville, whose vocal timbre fell somewhere between white pop and black rhythm and blues (ah, in confusion there is profit). What threw a monkey wrench into the group's hit philosophy was the B side of "Ka-Ding Dong." "Soft Summer Breeze" was a non-cover, a pop shuffle ballad that sounded as far afield of "Ka-Ding Dong" as a rock flip side could get from a pop tune on the same 45. And this flip side scored a notch higher than the A at number 34.

In the fall of 1956 Mercury misinterpreted the fluke success of "Soft Summer Breeze" and released an original by the boys titled "My Judge and Jury." Deejays judged it a bomb and the public jury condemned it to failure.

By December it was back to covers, but the oldie they decided to go with was a ballad, THE HEART-BEATS' classic "A Thousand Miles Away," and it was shades of the Coral days as the score read Heartbeats 53 Pop and number five R&B to the Diamonds' zip and zip.

Then, in a fated moment, Diamonds manager Nat Goodman saw a new 45 on Mercury orchestra leader David Carroll's desk. Playing it, he knew this was a smash for his group to cover. He rehearsed the boys all night to learn the song; the group was giddy by morning and decided to exaggerate the falsetto and bass parts on the record. The song was MAURICE WILLIAMS AND THE GLAD-IOLAS' "Little Darlin'," and its release on February 8, 1957, was a key event in vocal group history. With its cowbells, castanets, Spanish rhythm guitar, and exciting piano gliss, this "too fast for a cha-cha" rocker became an instant smash. The vocal exaggerations came off simply as a bit of musical creativity, and the bass talking bridge (on the original Maurice Williams did the bridge in his natural tenor voice) has become one of the most enjoyable examples of '50s rock over the decades. Only TV audiences got an inkling of the group's whimsical approach to the song. The background singers stood behind the lead, and each time the tenor's falsetto "La la la la la" part came up, he would run to Somerville, put his head on Dave's shoulder, and sing the part.

The Gladiolas original, complete with a much raunchier rhythm that had what sounded like one guy banging on garbage cans while another was shaking a box of coffee beans, reached number 41 Pop and number 11 R&B. The Diamonds' superior record shot to number two Disc Jockey and number three Best Seller (only Elvis's "All Shook Up" topped them) and an incredible number two R&B. (Obviously the rhythm and blues buyers liked it, too.) The climb didn't stop there, however. It hit number three in the U.K., spent more than half a year on the U.S. charts, and went on to sell over four million records for the Diamonds.

Frequent TV and tours kept the group busy while Mercury tried to figure where all this was going. The Diamonds followed "Little Darlin'" with Buddy Holly's "Words of Love" done with a deep bass intro, a '50s country rock feel, a talking bass bridge, and a "Love Is Strange" guitar lick; it partially worked, going to number 13 Disc Jockey, but only to 76 on the Top 100.

By September 1957 the Diamonds became the ultimate cover act by copying both sides of THE RAYS' single "Silhouettes" b/w "Daddy Cool" for their new 45. Again, the jukebox listeners were willing to spend a nickel to hear it (#10 DJ), but many buyers weren't ready to plunk down 79¢ to own it (#60 Best Seller), especially when there was a superior Rays record around (#3 Top 100, #5 DJ). Surprisingly, there was a near split decision on the R&B charts as the Rays reached number three while the Diamonds made it to number six.

In December the Diamonds had their only original hit, "The Stroll," which Dick Clark's "American Bandstand" popularized into the number one dance of 1958 and a number four Pop hit (#5 R&B).

Soon after "The Stroll," Ted and Bill departed, replaced by Evan Fisher and John Felton. From this point on the Diamonds' singles were predominantly originals like the title song from the Patty McCormack film *Kathy-O* (#16 Pop), which opened the door to Australia for the group, reaching number 12 there ("The Stroll" had made it to #21) in 1958.

Up until their last 45 in 1962 ("The Horizontal Lieutenant") they released only two more covers. Both charted: "Walking Along" (THE SOLITAIRES) made it to number 29 while continuing their popularity down under at number 13.

Their last chart record was a remake of "One Summer Night" (THE DANLEERS, #7, 1958), which rose to number 22 in the summer of 1961.

Felton then took the lead as Somerville became David Troy, folk singer, for more than six years.

During the late '50s, a close relationship developed between the Diamonds and another group on the tour circuit, THE FOUR PREPS. When the bass of the Preps departed in 1967, David joined the group. The Preps were history by 1969, so Bruce Belland (Preps lead) and David sang as a duo and later with Danny Cox as a trio on Allen Ludden's "Gallery" TV show. David then joined Keith Barber and Gail Jensen in a group known as W. W. Fancy.

In 1974 the original Diamonds made their first appearance together in 13 years at a New York oldies revival.

Over the years Bill Reed went into record promotion out of Florida, Ted Kowalski went back to Toronto and became an engineer, and David hooked up with a revised Four Preps as recently as 1990.

Although the Diamonds could hold their own with most white pop groups of the '50s, their extra edge was in their ability to sound less "square" than some of their counterparts when doing rock and roll and covering black vocal groups.

THE DIAMONDS (Ontario)

A SIDE/B SIDE	LABEL/CAT NO	DATE
Black Denim Trousers And Motorcycle Boots / Nip Sip	Coral 61502	9/55
Smooch Me / Be My Lovin' Baby	Coral 61577	2/56
You Baby You / Why Do Fools Fall In Love	Merc 70790	1/56
The Church Bells May Ring / Little Girl Of Mine	Merc 70835	3/56
Love, Love, Love / Every Night About This Time	Merc 70889	5/56
Ka-Ding-Ding / Soft Summer Breeze	Merc 70934	7/56
Put Your House In Order / My Judge And Jury	Merc 70983	10/56
A Thousand Miles Away / Every Minute Of The Day	Merc 71021	12/56
Little Darlin' / Faithful And True	Merc 71060	2/57
Words Of Love / Don't Say Goodbye	Merc 71128	5/57
Oh, How I Wish / Zip Zip	Merc 71165	7/57
Daddy Cool / Silhouettes	Merc 71197	9/57
The Stroll / Land Of Beauty	Merc 71242	12/57
Kathy-O / Happy Years	Merc 71330	6/58
Walking Along / Eternal Lovers	Merc 71366	9/58
She Say / From The Bottom Of My Heart	Merc 71404	12/58
Gretchen / A Mother's Love	Merc 71449	3/59
Holding Your Hand / Sneaky Alligator	Merc 71468	5/59
Young In Years / The Twenty-Second Day	Merc 71505	8/59
Batman, Wolfman, Frankenstein or Dracula / Walkin' The Stroll	Merc 71534	10/59
Real True Love / Tell The Truth	Merc 71586	1/60

A SIDE/B SIDE	LABEL/CAT NO	DATE
Pencil Song / Slave Girl	Merc 71633	4/60
The Crumble / You'd Be Mine	Merc 71735	11/60
I Sho' Lawd Will / You Short-Changed Me	Merc 71782	2/61
The Munch / Woomai-Ling	Merc 71818	4/61
One Summer Night / It's A Doggone Shame	Merc 71831	5/61
The Horizontal Lieutenant / Vanishing American	Merc 71956	3/62

The Dootones

The Dootones were an odd combination of the professional and the amateur. On the pro side, H. B. Barnum was a self-taught teen musician from Manual Arts High School in East Los Angeles; he played several instruments, including piano and saxophone. He and his drummer friend Ronald Barrett from Fremont High played in a jazz band together while still in their teens. The amateur side came from Charles Gardner and the much older Marvin Wilkins (H. B. states he must have been over 30), whom H. B. had found snapping his fingers and singing on skid row.

They banded together in 1954, rehearsing at H. B.'s house in the Aliso Housing Projects. The quartet came to the attention of Dootsie Williams and soon found themselves doing backup harmony work for the Meadowlarks and THE PENGUINS.

In April 1955, Dootsie named the boys the Dootones (after himself and his label), recorded them at American Studios, and released their single of the PLATTERS-like ballad "Teller of Fortune." With H. B. teaching style and technique, the Dootones became more than an ordinary rhythm and blues group: much of their vocalizing tended to smack of pop and modern harmony. Even the R&B "Teller" had strong pop overtones in its background vocals. Though H. B. readily acknowledges his favorite groups were THE MOONGLOWS and THE FIVE KEYS, the deep R&B sounds of those acts weren't reflected in "Teller."

Los Angeles airplay allowed the group to perform up and down the coast of California; they appeared with and even sang backup for the likes of Jackie Wilson, Etta James, and Al Hibbler.

In mid-1955 Vernon Green of THE MEDALLIONS was Medallion-less. Dootsie put him together with the Dootones for a tour of Canada and went so far as to paste a picture of Vernon in the lower left-hand corner of the Dootones' publicity photo and call them the Medallions. That entity never recorded together and the Dootones, looking for greener pastures, disbanded.

In 1962 a cut they did in 1955 ("Down the Road") came out as the A side of "Sailor Boy" by an unknown group Dootsie had also dubbed the Dootones. This followed the second Dootones' first single, "Strange Love Affair," from that same year.

Ronnie went on to join the Meadowlarks, Charles became part of Vernon Green's new group, the Medallions, and H. B. teamed up with Chuck Higgins and then became part of THE ROBINS on Whippet.

Today, Charles Gardner is a minister in Pasadena, Ronnie Barrett is a roofer in Los Angeles, and Marvin Wilkins resides in Los Angeles. H. B. Barnum went on to become one of the most versatile and talented arranger/musicians on the coast, working with everyone from Ray Charles to Lou Rawls.

The Drifters
(1953–1957)

Such was the success of the Drifters that even the most casual rock and roll fan has heard of them. The Drifters were famous not only for numerous hit recordings but because at various stages of their career they were trendsetters in rhythm and blues and rock and roll. Part of the reason is that the Drifters were not just one group, they were at least two, with enough members between 1953 and 1971 to make up several quintets. They had 12 different lead singers, 11 from other groups, and even boasted two members named Charlie Thomas who knew each other and were both originally from Virginia.

Before the original hit group formed there were at least three different units going under the name the Drifters. The first, a modern-sounding black pop group, recorded two singles for Coral Records, "I'm the Caring Kind" (September 1950) and "And I Shook" (November 1950).

The next Drifters were on the L.A.-based Excelsior label in June 1951 with an earthy bass-lead blues ballad called "Mobile" written by Otis Rene. The third and most obscure of the early Drifters groups recorded "Three Lies" for Class in 1953.

Six months after the original Drifters formed, another namesake showed up on the Beverly Hills–based Crown Records singing "The World Is Changing" in February 1954. But for popular history's sake, the Drifters' story really all started with Clyde McPhatter, whose innocent-sounding falsetto could merge raunchy blues with gospel to yield an exciting R&B mix.

By early 1953 this underpaid, underbilled lead singer decided to leave BILLY WARD AND HIS DOMINOES (though some say he was fired). As vocal groups were coming into their own, Clyde decided he should build one around himself. That sentiment was echoed by Atlantic Records guru Ahmet Ertegun, who went to see Clyde and the Dominoes perform at the Royal Roost in Manhattan only to be told Clyde was gone from Ward's domain. As fast as you can see dollar signs, Ertegun sought out Clyde and on May 7, 1953, signed him to Atlantic with a mandate to go build his group.

Clyde Lensley McPhatter, who came to New York at age 12 from Durham, North Carolina, sought out his friends in the Mount Lebanon Singers of Harlem's 132nd Street Mount Lebanon Church. He had sung lead for them in the late '40s at the age of 14 and felt it was a natural place to merge his secular singing with his gospel roots. The group thus became Clyde (lead), David "Little David" Baughn (tenor), William Anderson (tenor), David Baldwin (baritone), and James Johnson (bass). Contrary to general opinion the group's name was not chosen because they drifted together from other acts. Each member put a name of his choice on a piece of paper and dropped it in a hat. The one picked was David Baldwin's, a name taken from his father's book of birds that included a "Drifter." The group was actually four-fifths of the old Mount Lebanon gospel group, but not for long. The first session on June 29, 1953 resulted in four less-than-competitive recordings; the group sound didn't work as well with Clyde's voice as it had on gospel tunes. One song, "Lucille," was kept and later issued as the B side of their second single "Such a Night." The other three ("Gone," "Whatcha Gonna Do," and "Let the Boogie-Woogie Roll") were all rerecorded on August 9th by a new aggregation—the one Clyde put together when he realized the Mount Lebanon contingent wasn't working. Sticking with gospel vocalists, he drafted tenor Bill Pinkney from the Jerusalem Stars (of whom Brook Benton was a member), second tenor Andrew "Bubba" Thrasher and baritone Gerhart "Gay" Thrasher (both of the Thrasher Wonders with their sister Bernice), and bass Willie Ferbie.

Though they formed in New York City, all were originally from North or South Carolina. Bill was from Dalzell, S.C., and had originally sung with the Singing Cousins gospel group from 1946 to

1949. Bubba and Gay had been with the Silvertone Gospel Singers of Oxford, North Carolina.

The group recorded "Money Honey," the Drifters' first Atlantic single, released the second week of September 1953. No one could have imagined the huge success awaiting "Money": it turned Clyde and company into overnight R&B sensations. It hit the *Billboard* charts on October 31st and flew to number one, staying there for an amazing 11 weeks and spending over five months on the Best Seller list. Without hitting the Pop list it became a million seller. But already changes were taking place. Willie became ill; Bill dropped down to bass when he departed.

By January 1954 the new stars were touring and appearing with the likes of Ella Fitzgerald (when they performed at the Howard Theatre on January 15th). All was not a star's life, however. During one tour, the group was passing through Fredricksburg, Virginia, on their way to Atlanta when car trouble forced them to wire for money. After repairs and while cruising the town waiting for the wire transfer, they were picked up by the police, who thought they fit the description of a gang who had just robbed a loan company. With guns in their faces and sweat on their brows the Drifters spent anxious hours in police custody until they were finally cleared.

The single of "Such a Night" was recorded on November 12, 1953, and came out the first week of the new year. Clyde's performance on this lyrically suggestive (for the time) mover and shaker earned the group three weeks at number two. Both Bunny Paul and Johnny Ray covered the Lincoln Chase-penned hit, so that by February Clyde felt compelled to issue a press release stating that he would sue anyone who copied his musical arrangement or vocal styling on the song. But by March 13, WXYZ in Detroit had banned all three versions as being too racy (even though the Johnny Ray version was banned in the United Kingdom—the Drifters original never even got a shot there—it still made it to number one). Even the Drifters flip "Lucille" made it to number seven R&B in the U.S., which in effect had a different group on each side (except for Clyde) calling themselves the Drifters. "Lucille's" group could easily have been called Little David Baughn and the Mount Lebanon Singers.

On April 16th Clyde was reunited with his old friend, boxer-turned-singer Sugar Ray Robinson (Clyde and the Dominoes did many shows with Robinson), when the Drifters, Ray, and Ruth Brown began a series of one-nighters at the Regal Theatre in Chicago. So much has been said about the vocal work of the Drifters over the years that few realize what a skilled performing and dance act they were. While Clyde stood off to the left, the group would gyrate through some of the hippest acrobatic and tap routines this side of Motown (and about eight years ahead of Motown). Adding the rapidly flashing lights of the Apollo Theatre you had a cross between an early light show and a silent movie. But all the fun and games were interrupted when on May 7, 1954, a letter came for Clyde from Uncle Sam. He was to be stationed in Buffalo, New York, which meant, fortunately, that he could return for weekend gigs.

In the first week of June, the group's calypso-influenced "Honey Love" rode up the Best Seller chart to number one by mid-summer, and remained there for eight weeks. Another million seller, it held on to the hit list for 23 weeks total. "Honey Love" also became their first pop charter, going to number 21 in October.

In August the group was part of the second annual "Biggest R&B Show" for a five-week tour with Alan Freed, THE SPANIELS, LaVern Baker, Roy Hamilton, Faye Adams, and the Counts. They hit Cincinnati; Flint, Michigan; Detroit; Gary, Indiana; Indianapolis; Chicago; St. Louis; Kansas City; and Dayton, Ohio (where 4,700 people, the largest audience for a non-racing event, saw the show at the Speedway). The tour finished up at the Brooklyn Paramount for the five-day Labor Day weekend show.

"Bip Bam" followed in October going to number seven; the flip "Someday You'll Want Me to Want You" was far and away the best of the group's McPhatter-led ballads. In the second week of November, Atlantic released what would become the most popular vocal group Christmas record of all time, the Drifters' version of "White Christmas." A note-for-note clone of THE RAVENS' brilliant 1949 release (#9 R&B), it nevertheless opened up a wider audience for both versions while becoming the Drifters' second pop chart record at number 80. It made it to number two R&B, with subsequent chartings at number five in December 1956 and number 12 in December 1957. The flip "The Bells of St. Mary's" was also an inspiring reading.

The new year ushered in Alan Freed's first rock and roll ball (January 14th and 15th), an extravaganza held at the St. Nicholas Arena in New York that was sold out a week in advance. These shows were noteworthy in that the performers were all black while more than half the people in the audience were white teens. The bill included Fats Domino, the Clovers, Joe Turner, THE MOONGLOWS, THE

HARPTONES, Red Prysock's Combo, Buddy Johnson's Orchestra, and, of course, the Drifters.

In March, the boogie-woogie rocker "Whatcha Gonna Do" (written by Nugetre—Ertegun spelled backwards; see THE CLOVERS) was let loose and skyrocketed up *Billboard*'s R&B listings, this one carving a niche at number two for two weeks. The flip "Gone" (from the group's August 9th session, their first) was a gem of a ballad with free-flowing falsetto harmony and a surprising modulation that gave Clyde and Company another vocal dimension to wail through. "Whatcha Gonna Do"/"Gone" was technically the last Drifters single with Clyde. Though he had recorded his last four sides with the group on October 24, 1954, "Three Three Three" was not released until used in the Drifters' LP *Their Greatest Recordings, The Early Years* in 1971. "Sugar-coated Kisses" was not issued at all and "Everyone's Laughing" b/w "Hot Ziggetty," listed in Atlantic's discography as record 1070 released in August 1954, never made the charts. The fact that Clyde formally announced in mid-July he was leaving the Drifters could have precipitated a recall of the single and a regrouping (thus explaining why a record could fail that miserably when the group was so hot). Little David (16 at the time and fresh from recording with the Checkers on King) became an interim replacement, but his only lead wasn't released until March 1961 as the B side to a later Drifters recording of "Some Kind of Wonderful." (One of Atlantic's practices was to take old unreleased tracks and put them on the flip of later Drifters A sides. They did this maneuver several times for Clyde's solo A sides as well.)

During this transition period the group was in Cleveland on tour when Bill Pinkney found the Drifters a new lead singer. Johnny Moore was singing by himself in a men's room and Bill was so knocked out he hired this former lead of the Hornets (States) right there and then. Little David, young, undisciplined, and drinking heavily, left to form the Harps ("I Won't Cry," Savoy, 1955) and later sang with Bill Pinkney's *original* Drifters in 1958 that recorded two singles for End ("Am I to Be the One" and "Gee") as the Harmony Grits. Little David died in 1970.

By September 1955, the Drifters had recorded five new sides; two of them, "Adorable" and "Steamboat," began charging up the charts together in November and December respectively. "Adorable," led by Moore, became the group's first and only cover (see THE COLTS) and went to number one R&B while "Steamboat" paddled to number five with Pinkney on lead.

That December, the group fought in a mock "battle of the quartets" to beat THE EL DORADOS at the Magnolia Ballroom in Atlanta. It was shows billed as battles that led to the highly successful "Battle of the Groups" LPs of the middle and late '50s (*The Paragons Meet the Jesters* and others).

The Drifters' February 1956 release was a dynamic two-sider with the early nod going to the ballad side, "Your Promise to Be Mine." *Billboard*'s April 7th review stated: "A gentle ballad builds into an intense exciting production as the lead singer [Gerhart Thrasher in one of his few lead roles] turns in a truly outstanding performance. Could be another big one for the boys." Of the B side, "Ruby Baby," the reviewer said: "The high lead [Johnny Moore] takes over on this pounding 16-bar blues theme taken at a good rock tempo. Less weight than on the flip, though it's an infectious item." In the April 21st issue, *Billboard*'s "Best Buys" reviewer commented, "Preference for side is still sharply divided with both sparking considerable interest." But by May 12th "Ruby" (penned by Leiber and Stoller and produced in Los Angeles by Nesuhi Ertegun, Ahmet's brother) was on its way to becoming a classic, topping off at number 10 R&B. (Had "Promise" been coupled with a lesser side, it too might have been a champion.) Almost seven years later DION and THE DELSATINS would record "Ruby Baby," taking it to number two Pop and garnering R&B approval to the tune of number five.

The next Drifters' single, "I Gotta Get Myself a Woman" (#11), was the last for a couple of the old guard. Pinkney was fired by manager George "Stingy" Treadwell when he asked for a raise for the group. Andrew was shown the door when he defended Bill. Pinkney, not one to brood, immediately put together a group called the Flyers with former CROWNS and SWALLOWS (King) member Bobby Hendricks. They signed to Atlantic's Atco subsidiary for one 45, "My Only Desire."

Bill's spot was covered by former CAROLS (Columbia) and Ravens (Columbia) bass, Tommy Evans.

It seems that the Drifters found a number of their members in various men's rooms. "Carnation" Charlie Hughes, formerly a tenor for THE DIAMONDS (Atlantic) and lead of THE DU DROPPERS, was met by old friend Gerhart Thrasher in the toilet of 1650 Broadway while Treadwell was holding auditions a few doors down for Andrew Thrasher's spot. The minute they heard "Carnation" sing, the other hopefuls were dismissed. While all this was going on, McPhatter was charting with Ruth Brown ("Love

Has Joined Us Together," number eight, December 1955) and his first solo hit "Seven Days" (#2, February 1956).

The Moore, Gerhart Thrasher, Charlie Hughes, and Evans quartet became the first Drifters unit since the "White Christmas" group to register a top 10 R&B record and hit the Pop charts when "Fools Fall in Love" went to number 69 (#10 R&B) in the spring of 1957.

From here on, changes became more rapid and the attitude more laissez-faire, coinciding with less-than-quality releases.

In the summer of 1957 Moore and Hughes were drafted. Bill Pinkney, who'd been in and out for performances but not recording, got in touch with ex-Flyers lead Bobby Hendricks, who jumped at the chance to front the group. Jimmy Millender replaced Hughes on baritone and the last "original" Drifters group was formed in time to record three sides on April 28, 1958, less than five years since the first Drifters group session. One terrific single emerged from that session, the Leiber and Stoller classic "Drip Drop." With a lead sung by a Clyde McPhatter-inspired Bobby Hendricks, "Drip Drop" made it to number 58 Pop but (surprisingly) never charted R&B, possibly signaling that the public wanted a new sound from the Drifters.

These last original Drifters (Hendricks, Thrasher, Millender, and Evans) watched their popularity wane; soon they were forced to do one-nighters posing as both THE COASTERS and the Ravens.

Their fateful night in June of 1958 was approaching, but the Drifters' name and legacy would live on.

Clyde McPhatter went on to solo stardom and recognition as one of the best and most original voices in rhythm and blues history. Between 1955 and 1965 he registered 16 R&B and 21 Pop chart records, including "A Lover's Question" with THE CUES (#6 Pop, #1 R&B, 1958), "Lover Please" (#7 Pop, 1962), "Without Love" (#19 Pop, #4 R&B, 1957), "Since You've Been Gone" with the Cookies and the Cues (#38 Pop, #14 R&B, 1959), "Long Lonely Nights" with the Cues (#49 Pop, #1 R&B, 1957), and his all-time classic "Treasure of Love" (#16 Pop, #1 R&B, 1956). Clyde died on June 13, 1972, not realizing the impact his voice would have on the R&B and rock and roll scene for decades to come.

Through turmoil and changes the Drifters managed to set musical trends and give the public 13 chart hits, most of which are legendary recordings today. (See THE DRIFTERS, 1958–1979, for the remainder of their story.)

The Drifters
(1958–1979)

The average oldies fan who remembers the Drifters is almost always (whether he realizes it or not) talking about the Ben E. King group that had international success with records like "Save the Last Dance for Me." King's aggregation was to the original group as night is to day. Where Clyde McPhatter and company were rhythm and blues trailblazers and perennial R&B chart climbers, Ben E. and the boys built international mass appeal and became perpetual pop chart residents.

They did have two things in common. The new group had as many (and more) lead singers as the old group, and like the original group, which had mostly the Mount Lebanon Singers at first, the new Drifters were an entirely different act before taking up the Drifters banner.

In June 1958 the established Drifters clan of Bobby Hendricks (lead), Gerhart Thrasher (tenor), Jimmy Millender (baritone), and Tommy Evans (bass) were appearing at the Apollo theatre. The quartet hadn't had a hit in more than a year and were reported to be hitting the bottle pretty hard. Manager George Treadwell's shrewd negotiations had wrangled the group a guaranteed 10-year deal with the Apollo's Bobby Schiffman for two appearances each year—that is, *any* group with the name Drifters, since Treadwell owned the moniker. The opening act that night was a young Harlem group calling themselves the Crowns, formerly part of THE FIVE CROWNS. They had had a terrific single out for a few months, "Kiss and Make Up" on R&B Records, when the opportunity to appear at the Apollo arrived. A great rhythm and blues rocker, "Kiss" was the only single ever released on the label owned by writing legend Doc Pomus. The 115th Street teens impressed Treadwell so much that he asked them to become the Drifters. When they jumped at the chance for instant name recognition, Treadwell waited out the show, then went backstage and fired the old group on the spot.

Bobby Hendricks immediately launched a solo career and by September 15th, he placed on the charts with "Itchy Twitchy Feeling" (#25 Pop, #5 R&B, Sue Records), though his solo career wasn't in reality so solo because there was a backup group named THE COASTERS featured prominently on his hit.

Thrasher went home to Florida and Tommy Evans reportedly joined Charlie Fuqua's INK SPOTS.

The new Drifters boasted three tenor leads in Charlie Thomas (the Five Crowns), James "Poppa" Clark (the Five Crowns, THE CADILLACS), Benjamin Earl Nelson (the Holidays and the Millionaires), along with Dock Green (the Harmonaires, the Five Crowns) on baritone and Elsbeary Hobbs (the Five Crowns) on bass. Clark was not interested in becoming a Drifter, however, so the remaining foursome hit the road for almost 10 months to satisfy the old group's touring commitments and get some on-the-job training. Thus these Drifters, newly christened in June 1958, didn't record until March 1959.

When the time came, the pairing of innovative producer/writers Leiber and Stoller with the young Drifters became the catalyst for a whole new approach to pop and rhythm and blues.

The March 6, 1959, session centered on four songs including one by Benjamin Nelson called "There Goes My Baby," on which he would sing lead. But where was Ben E. King at this stage? He emerged after the Drifters had been touring a few months. This same Ben Nelson, who had originally sung bass for a Harlem group, the Holidays, took the last name of his uncle Jimmy King and became . . . Ben E. King.

In May 1959 Atlantic released the mesmerizing "There Goes My Baby" replete with pounding kettle drums (a first on an R&B record), out-of-tune timpani, a slow Latin rhythm (the Drifters originally performed it fast when on the road in 1958), and Ben E. King singing way over his baritone range. The song sounded as if you were tuned to two stations on your car radio, each receiving a different song yet each somehow working together.

The most innovative aspect of the record was the haunting use of strings, alternating between a classical sound (you could hear arranger Stan Applebaum's classical training and the similarity of his staccato string lines to those in the prelude to the cannon firing in Tchaikovsky's *1812 Overture*) and the thrust of gypsy violins. Though the recording is touted as the first R&B record with strings, it is more appropriate to label it the first R&B *hit* with strings, since THE ORIOLES used violins as far back as July 1950 on their recording of "Everything They Said Came True."

But "There Goes My Baby" almost didn't come out at all; everyone agreed that the musical collage sounded out of whack. Jerry Wexler, Atlantic A&R man and a gifted ear, hated the song while Leiber, Stoller, and Ertegun found something captivating about it and almost apologetically felt that they should at least try it on the public.

By June 1st it had hit the *Billboard* Top 100 and by August 17, 1959, it was number two (#1 R&B). The first record by the Crowns/Drifters and the fourteenth under the Drifters name, it was the biggest success to date. On July 29th, Ben E. and the boys recorded a follow-up with King singing lead on the samba-influenced "Dance with Me." This was the beginning of a Latin influence on Drifters recordings and the impact of the Drifters on such later groups as JAY AND THE AMERICANS and Tony Orlando and DAWN.

Working strings, more prevalent harmonies from the group, and a top-notch King lead made "Dance with Me" number 15 (#2 R&B) by Christmas of 1959. It also opened the door to Europe as the Drifters' first U.K. chart hit, reaching number 17 in January 1960. The flip, "True Love, True Love" (#33 Pop, #5 R&B), featuring newcomer Johnny Lee Williams, helped the Drifters have their first two-sided charter since "Such a Night"/"Lucille" in 1954. With syncopated chimes and strings, the Doc Pomus/Mort Shuman song set the stage for one of the new Drifters' best, "This Magic Moment." Another Pomus/Shuman opus, "Magic" was a King showcase, although when the Drifters were allowed to harmonize, their solid baritone-dominated sound accented a great arrangement. The rising and falling string arpeggios were adventurous for a black group, but Drifters records were becoming less and less black-sounding as each release became more popular. The public wasn't the only audience studying Drifters records at this point. A young Phil Spector couldn't have helped but hear the string lines of "Magic" since they appeared in Spector's brilliant production of "Every Breath I Take" by Gene Pitney and the Halos in 1961 (#42 Pop). "This Magic Moment" soared to number 16 (#4 R&B) in the spring of 1960.

By May, a combination of King's solo desires and road manager Lover Patterson's arguments with Drifters manager George Treadwell brought the King-Drifters short-lived dynasty to an end. On May 19th King and company recorded their last four sides together, "Sometimes I Wonder," "Nobody But Me," "I Count the Tears," and another Pomus/Shuman Latin-rhythmed mini-epic, "Save the Last Dance for Me." Since Patterson held the contract on King (from the Crowns days), he refused to let him perform with the Treadwell-controlled Drifters. Consequently, by the time "Save" came out in August 1960, Ben was not even in the Drifters.

"Save the Last Dance for Me" lifted the group to international star status. By October 17th it was number one (#1 R&B), and it became one of a very few records in history to drop out of the number one spot (on October 24th "I Want to Be Wanted" by Brenda Lee took over first place) only to regain its position a week later (October 31st for two weeks). In England it reached number two about the same time and went to number one in Australia and New Zealand. To further confuse the public, the original group's "White Christmas" hit the pop charts for the second time in five years (#96) in December 1960.

At the peak of their success the Drifters began a series of personnel changes that made the early years look like the model of solidarity. On a trip into the South, Johnny Lee Williams decided to jump ship when the group toured through his hometown of Mobile, Alabama.

Between the time the group recorded in May 1960 and again in February 1961 there had been five roster moves. The group that sang "Some Kind of Wonderful," "Please Stay," "Room Full of Tears," and "Sweets for My Sweet" on February 1, 1961, included Rudy Lewis (lead), Charlie Thomas (first tenor), Dock Green (baritone), and Tommy Evans (he of the 1957 "fired" Drifters on bass). While that very productive session was going on (all four sides would be future Drifters A-side singles and chart hits), Ben E. King's last lead, "I Count the Tears," was chugging up the charts, entering *Billboard*'s Hot 100 on January 23rd and eventually landing at number 17 Pop (#6 R&B) while reaching number 28 in England. Coincidentally that's the same date King's solo standard-to-be, "Spanish Harlem" (written by Phil Spector and Jerry Leiber, their only writing collaboration), hit the charts, ending up at number 10 (#15 R&B).

Part of the reason for the group's consistent success during those years has to go to Treadwell and Leiber and Stoller. No matter what member was inserted, the objective was always clear: create pop R&B, Latin-flavored, mid-tempo songs for the masses. And having such a hot act helped get the best songs from the professional songwriting community. "Some Kind of Wonderful" with Rudy Lewis (formerly of the Clara Ward Singers) on lead, written by Carole King and Gerry Goffin and with a dramatic vocal intro, was a good example of the formula. It was also the first of a series of releases over the next two years that would include the voices of an unnamed female foursome who would go on to their own individual success. The quartet consisted of Doris Troy ("Just One Look," #10 Pop, 1963), Cissy Houston ("Be My Baby," #31 R&B, 1971, and mother of Whitney Houston), Dee Dee

Warwick ("I Want to Be with You," #9 R&B, 1966), and Dionne Warwick (1963 to 1988, 54 chart records). The latter three were all originally in the Drinkard Singers, then the Gospelaires, and Cissy was Dionne and Dee Dee's aunt.

The B side of "Wonderful" was the David Baughn-led original Drifters' six-year-old track of "Honeybee." (In those days, when you bought a Drifters single odds were you got a variety of Drifters.)

But over the next year the lineup remained stable and the group had four sparkling singles, "Please Stay," an early co-write by Burt Bacharach (with Rudy on lead, #14 Pop, #13 R&B), "Sweets for My Sweet" (Charlie Thomas on lead, #16 Pop, #10 R&B), "Room Full of Tears" (Thomas lead, #72 Pop), and "When My Little Girl Is Smiling" (Thomas on lead, #28 Pop).

Before "Please Stay" peaked at number 13 R&B, the Drifters had run an incredible streak of eight straight top 10 records.

In June 1962 Atlantic issued "Sometimes I Wonder," a terrific record that evoked the Ben E. King "There Goes My Baby" period, and well it should have as it was recorded by King and company on the May 19, 1960, "Save the Last Dance for Me" session and released in hopes that it would bring the group a top 10 pop hit, something they hadn't had for seven singles. When it failed to speak to radio, a new Goffin-King song was tried called "Up on the Roof." In November 1962 "Roof" (with Lewis on lead) gave the Drifters another charter, finishing up at number five (#4 R&B).

Dock Green left soon after, and Gene Pearson, fresh from THE CLEFTONES, took his place.

And guess what showed up on the pop charts once again in December? Right—"White Christmas" (#88).

The next biggie was an all-star writing collaboration: Leiber, Stoller, Mann, and Weil, all working to create "On Broadway." And who was in the studio learning his craft and watching Leiber and Stoller pour forth their production secrets? Why, Phil Spector, but this time he was also a hired hand, playing guitar in the instrumental break. "On Broadway" (#9 Pop, #7 R&B, #9 in Australia, curiously not charting in the U.K.) became an anthem for those with hopes of success back in 1963 and is to this day one of the most performed songs on radio each year.

Tommy Evans soon left the Drifters, this time of his own accord, and was replaced by Johnny Terry of THE DOMINOES and James Brown's Famous Flames.

By late summer of 1963 Leiber and Stoller had decided to direct all their attention toward a new label they were forming called Red Bird Records, and the Drifters began working with producer/writer Bert Berns.

Johnny Moore rejoined in time for the April 12, 1963, session which was distinguished by the fact that the group had recorded a Leiber/Stoller song that all felt was a hit. Nothing unusual about that except that it was never released by the Drifters and their vocals disappeared from the track. The song was "Only in America," and considering the racial tensions of the time it seemed risky to put out a song with a black group singing about "the land of opportunity," so Leiber and Stoller and company lifted the Drifters vocals, substituted Jay and the Americans, and took the whole track over to United Artists.

The Drifters' next few singles varied from marginal successes like "I'll Take You Home" (#25 Pop, 1963) to "Rat Race" (#71 Pop, 1964).

In 1964 Rudy Lewis suddenly died; ironically, his last lead single was "Via Con Dios" (#43 Pop, February 1964).

Johnny Moore took over the majority of the group's leads from this point until their last recording for Atlantic in 1971. In the summer of 1964 the Drifters were Moore, Thomas, Pearson, and Evans, which added up to a Drifters group made up of members of the Hornets, the Five Crowns, the Cleftones, and THE CAROLS. Still, the formula worked with a slight variation as the group was now singing pop-soul on the Artie Resnick/Kenny Young-penned "Under the Boardwalk," a perfect radio summertime soother that reached number four in the U.S. and number 45 in the U.K. It probably would have done better in the British Isles if it had hit their shores earlier than its September 24th chart debut. By then England's six-week summer was long since gone.

At this time, Lover Patterson formed another Drifters group that included "Carnation" Charlie Hughes, Dock Green, and Tommy Evans. Meanwhile, Bill Pinkney of the original group had formed his own "Original Drifters" after the Flyers broke up. Little David sang and sounded like Clyde McPhatter on lead along with Pinkney and the Thrasher brothers through the early '60s. They performed but had no singles until 1964 when Bobby Lee Hollis of the Sunbeams (Herald) took over lead and the group recorded "Do the Jerk" (Fontana).

Over the next six years, Pinkney's Drifters had almost as many members as the other group, not including people like Little David and Bobby Hendricks who kept coming and going. In 1971 Pinkney, Clarence Walker, Bruce Caesar, and Duke Richardson recorded "Old Man River" for the Game label as the original Drifters.

Later in the '70s those Drifters were Pinkney, Walker, Chuck Cochran, and Russell Henry.

Back in the '60s, the "new" Drifters followed the success of "Boardwalk" with a sequel called "I've Got Sand in My Shoes," another Resnick/Young ode to the beach (#33 Pop), and "Saturday Night at the Movies" by Mann and Weil (#18). It seemed the new lyrical direction was to take teen life and put it in various settings; the logical next step after "Boardwalk" and "Movies" was "At the Club," their January 1965 release. Though it only reached number 43 domestically, it lived three lives on the U.K. charts (#35 in April 1965, #39 in March 1972, and #3 coupled with "Saturday Night at the Movies" in April 1972).

From this point on only one of 12 Drifters releases made the top 50 (#48, 1966, "Memories Are Made of This," the old Dean Martin song). The only constant was Johnny Moore, who weathered 10 member changes after taking over for Rudy Lewis in 1964, including Charles Baskerville of Shep and the Limelites, Milton Turner and Bill Fredericks of the Packards ("Ding Dong" on Paradise, 1956), and Charlie Thomas (the second one!), who joined in 1969, two years after the original Charlie Thomas left. To eliminate confusion (as if that were possible), the second Thomas became Don Thomas.

In March 1970 the Johnny Moore version of the group broke up, but Drifters splinter groups were all over the music scene. In 1971, for example, Dock Green, Charlie Thomas (the first), Elsbeary Hobbs, and Al Gardner re-formed at an Academy of Music show in New York, and for a while even Turbans lead Al Banks sang with them.

In June 1974 Green, Thomas, Hobbs, and Bobby Ruffin (the Royal Jokers on Atco) released a single on Musicor titled "On a Midsummer Night in Harlem." That same quartet recorded a live LP at Harvard University on December 2, 1972 (A&D Records) that included an a cappella version of "Bells of St. Mary's" along with the hits. In 1977 the group represented the U.S. for a bicentennial tour of Russia and even appeared at the White House for President Ford.

By the 1980s, Charlie and Charlie (Don) Thomas were finally singing together (it was inevitable) along with Hobbs and Terry King, a part-timer with THE TEMPTATIONS in 1978. In 1979, Dock formed the Dock Green Drifters with Bernard Jones

(THE CHANNELS in 1975), Matthew Stevenson (the Coasters in the '70s), and Lloyd Phillips.

In August 1972 fate made sure the Drifters' name would continue for some time to come. Atlantic Records in England reissued a seven-year-old single, "Come on Over to My Place," with Johnny Moore on lead. It shot to number nine and convinced Moore to form a newer Drifters with Bill Fredericks, Grant Kitchings, and Butch Leaks. They signed directly to a British company, Bell Records, a seemingly unorthodox move until one remembers that the Drifters had already achieved 13 chart 45s in 12 years in England. Such records as their Bell U.K. debut, "Like Sister and Brother" (#7, 1973), "Kissin' in the Back Row of the Movies" (#2, 1974), "Down on the Beach Tonight" (#7, 1974), "There Goes My First Love" (#3, 1975), and "You're More than a Number in My Little Red Book" (#5, 1979), all have added to a Drifters legacy that includes over 20 million singles sold and eight million LPs in the U.S. alone.

During the '80s, Ben E. King joined the group for appearances until his 1986 reissued hit "Stand by Me" (bolstered by the success of the film of the same name) reached number nine in the U.S.

Throughout the Drifters' history, Clyde McPhatter and Ben E. King have been the most visible lead singers, producing some of the Drifters' best recordings. But the group(s) could not have maintained such a legendary status for so many years without strong leads during the act's anonymous periods. Johnny Moore sang lead on 51 A- or B-side American singles including "Adorable," "Under the Boardwalk," and many other of the group's biggest hits. Clyde, in comparison, sang on only 14 and Ben on only nine. Even Rudy Lewis, whose premature death robbed the music-loving public of a terrific voice, sang on more singles (15) than either Clyde or King.

This degree of success had to be based on quantity as well as quality. From Gerhart Thrasher's magnificent lead on "Your Promise to Be Mine" to Charlie Thomas's "When My Little Girl Is Smiling," the Drifters' secret was simply that they had a large quantity of quality.

THE DRIFTERS

A SIDE/B SIDE	LABEL/CAT NO	DATE
Money Honey / The Way I Feel	Atln 1006	9/53
Lucille / Such A Night	Atln 1019	1954
Honey Love / Warm Your Heart	Atln 1029	5/54
Someday You'll Want Me To Want You / Bip Bam	Atln 1043	10/54

A SIDE/B SIDE	LABEL/CAT NO	DATE
White Christmas / The Bells Of St. Mary's	Atln 1048	11/54
Gone / Whatcha Gonna Do	Atln 1055	2/55
Everyone's Laughing / Hot Ziggety	Atln 1070	8/55
Adorable / Steamboat	Atln 1078	10/55
Your Promise To Be Mine / Ruby Ruby	Atln 1089	3/56
Soldier Of Fortune / I Gotta Get Myself A Woman	Atln 1101	8/56
It Was A Tear / Fools Fall In Love	Atln 1123	1/57
Hyptonized / Drifting Away From You	Atln 1141	5/57
I Know / Yodee Yakee	Atln 1161	10/57
Drip Drop / Moonlight Bay	Atln 1187	5/58
There Goes My Baby / Oh My Love	Atln 2025	5/59
Since You've Been Gone / Try Try Baby*	Atln 2028	6/59
There You Go* / You Went Back On Your Word	Atln 2038	10/59
(If You Cry) True Love True Love / Dance With Me	Atln 2040	10/59

The Harmony Grits (the original Drifters minus Clyde McPhatter)

A SIDE/B SIDE	LABEL/CAT NO	DATE
Am I To Be The One / I Could Have Told You	End 1051	1959
Gee / Santa Claus Is Coming	End 1063	1959

The Drifters (Ben E. King)

A SIDE/B SIDE	LABEL/CAT NO	DATE
Don't Dog Me* / Just Give Me A Ring	Atln 2049	2/60
This Magic Moment / Baltimore	Atln 2050	2/60
Let The Boogie Woogie Roll* / Deep Sea Ball	Atln 2060	5/60
Lonely Winds / Hey Senorita	Atln 2062	5/60
Save The Last Dance For Me / Nobody But Me	Atln 2071	8/60
Go! Yes Go!* / If I Didn't Love You Like I Do	Atln 2082	11/60
I Count The Tears / Suddenly There's A Valley	Atln 2087	12/60
Some Kind Of Wonderful / Honey Bee	Atln 2096	3/61
Please Stay / No Sweet Lovin'	Atln 2105	5/61
Sweets For My Sweet / Loneliness Or Happiness	Atln 2117	9/61
Room Full Of Tears / Somebody New Dancin' With You	Atln 2127	12/61
When My Little Girl Is Smiling / Mexican Divorce	Atln 2134	2/62
What To Do / Stranger On The Shore	Atln 2143	4/62
Sometimes I Wonder / Jackpot	Atln 2151	6/62
Up On The Roof / Another Night With The Boys	Atln 2162	10/62
On Broadway / Let The Music Play	Atln 2182	3/63

A SIDE/B SIDE	LABEL/CAT NO	DATE
Rat Race / If You Don't Come Back	Atln 2191	5/63
It'll Take You Home / I Feel Good All Over	Atln 2201	8/63
In The Land Of Make Believe / Vaya Con Dios	Atln 2216	1/64
One-Way Love / Didn't It	Atln 2225	4/64
Under The Boardwalk / I Don't Want To Go On Without You	Atln 2237	6/64
I've Got Sand In My Shoes / He's Just A Playboy	Atln 2253	9/64
Don't Call Me** / Do The Jerk	Fntna 1956	1964
Saturday Night At The Movies / Spanish Lace	Atln 2260	11/64
The Christmas Song / I Remember Christmas	Atln 2261	12/64
At The Club / Answer The Phone	Atln 2268	1/65
Come On Over To My Place / Chains Of Love	Atln 2285	4/65
Follow Me / The Outside World	Atln 2292	6/65
Far From The Maddening Crowd / I'll Take You Where The Music's Playing	Atln 2298	7/65
We Gotta Sing / Nylon Stockings	Atln 2310	11/65
Memories Are Made Of This / My Islands In The Sun	Atln 2325	3/66
Up In The Streets Of Harlem / You Can't Love Them All	Atln 2336	5/66
The Masquerade Is Over** / I Found Some Lovin'	Veep 1264	1966
Aretha / Baby What I Mean	Atln 2366	11/66
Ain't It The Truth / Up Jumped The Devil	Atln 2426	7/67
Still Burning In My Heart / I Need You Now	Atln 2471	1/68
Your Best Friend / Steal Away	Atln 2624	4/69
Black Silk / You Got To Pay Your Dues	Atln 2746	8/70
A Rose By Any Other Name / Be My Lady	Atln 2786	3/71
Old Man River** / Millionaire	Game 394	1971
Every Night† / Something Tells Me	Bell 1269	1972
You've Got Your Troubles† / I'm Feeling Sad (And Oh So Lonely)	Bell 45320	1973
Like Sister And Brother† / The Songs We Used To Sing	Bell 45387	1973
Peace Of Mind†† / The Struggler	Stltn 671	1973
Say Goodbye To Angelina† / I'm Free (For The Rest Of Your Life)	Bell 1339	1974
Kissin' In The Back Row Of The Movies†	Bell 1358	6/74
Down On The Beach Tonight†	Bell 1381	10/74
Love Games†	Bell 1396	2/75
There Goes My First Love†	Bell 1433	9/75
Can I Take You Home Little Girl†	Bell 1462	11/75
Hello Happiness†	Bell 1469	3/76
Every Night's A Saturday Night With You†	Bell 1491	9/76

A SIDE/B SIDE	LABEL/CAT NO	DATE
You're More Than A Number In My Little Red Book†	Arista 78	12/76

*   credited to Clyde McPhatter only, but includes the Drifters
** the original Drifters
†   the Johnny Moore group
†† the Charlie Thomas group

The Dubs

The Dubs were the outgrowth of two fine but short-lived mid-'50s rhythm and blues vocal groups, the 5 Wings and the Scale-Tones. The 5 Wings were from Seventh Avenue and 129th Street in New York's Harlem and included Jackie Rue (lead), Frank Edwards (first tenor), Billy Carlisle (second tenor), Melvin Flood (baritone), and Tommy Grate (bass).

Originally called the 5 Stars in its 1954 infancy, the group found itself in the studio, thanks to their manager Hiram Johnson (brother of famed musician and bandleader Buddy Johnson), recording two posthumous tributes to Johnny Ace (celebrated R&B vocalist and hard-luck Russian roulette player) titled "Johnny's Still Singing" b/w "Johnny Has Gone" for King Records. Two ill-fated singles later and three of the 5 Wings (Edwards, Flood, and Rue, the latter going on to become the lead of Jackie and the Starlites of "Valerie" fame) flew the coop. Kenny "Butch" Hamilton (the Sonics on Groove, 1955) joined in time for the 5 Wings (now a trio) to back vocalist Billy Nelson on a great blues harmony ballad, "Walk Along."

Soon after that November 1955 session, Billy Carlisle's cousin Richard Blandon landed in the Wings courtesy of the U.S. Air Force, who no longer required his services. The Nelson/Wings single was released in February 1956, one month after the Scale-Tones, who were also from Harlem, recorded their first and only single, "Everlasting Love" b/w "Dreamin' and Dreamin'," for Joe Davis's Jay Dee label on January 6th. That group consisted of Cleveland Still (lead), James Montgomery (tenor), James "Jake" Miller (baritone), and Thomas Gardner (bass). Coincidentally, their record also came out in February and had the same less-than-desirable results.

The two going-nowhere groups seemed on the brink of extinction when Blandon met Still at a Scale-Tones rehearsal and a new group emerged.

This lineup read Blandon (lead) and Carlisle (second tenor) of the 5 Wings along with Still (first tenor), Miller (baritone), and Gardner (bass) of the Scale-Tones. They even inherited 5 Wings manager Hiram Johnson, and while he was signing the group, newly christened the Marvels, to ABC Paramount Records late in 1956, ex-Wings Grate had already joined the Vocaltones (Apollo) while Hamilton boarded THE BOP CHORDS (Holiday). The Marvels did a (really) marvelous single for ABC, "I Won't Have You Breaking My Heart," that was released in November. Though it got little radio attention the Blandon-led ballad, with strong support from the full-sounding Marvels, showed the group's promise. It also showed the influence that groups like THE HARPTONES, THE WANDERERS, and THE SPANIELS had on the Marvels.

Johnson decided not to wait around for ABC to lose another record and formed his own label called Johnson Records. Early in 1957 the Marvels decided to change their name to the Dubs (music business terminology for a demo or demonstration record) and recorded the Richard Blandon-penned "Don't Ask Me to Be Lonely." (In a 1970 interview Blandon claimed he was the sole writer of the song even though the record credited both him and Johnson.)

Radio acceptance of the March release was almost immediate, and Johnson found himself with a local hit that required a national distributor. In stepped George Goldner, and the Dubs soon found themselves on his Gone label. It took five months, but on July 15th "Don't Ask Me" finally slipped on to the national charts and peaked at number 74, though it was top 10 on many local East Coast radio station surveys.

Before the quintet returned to the studio in August, Gardner left and opened the door for 5 Wings alumnus Tommy Grate. The Dubs were now three-fifths of the old 5 Wings. Though the group had recorded six sides on the earlier "Don't Ask Me" session (including a new version of "I Won't Have You Breaking My Heart"), Johnson and Gone flipped when they heard Blandon's newest songwriting effort, "Could This Be Magic," so the August session produced that and its B side, "Such Lovin.'"

By November 4th the Dubs had scored their second national pop charter of the year and their biggest hit, rising to number 23. The winter of 1957 seemed a little warmer whenever this outstanding ballad floated out over America's airwaves, and despite its relatively low chart number it is recognized today as a rock and roll standard.

Surprisingly, neither "Magic" nor any of the other Dubs releases ever made the R&B charts; they were fine examples of late-'50s rhythm and blues and doo wop vocalizing with cross-over mass appeal. A beautiful ballad called "Beside My Love" followed in February 1958, and this Blandon-scribed single should also have seen more than occasional radio play.

The first non-Blandon-penned single, "Be Sure My Love," quickly came and went in May 1958 though it was sung to perfection by the Dubs. It got another shot in 1960 on the smaller Mark-X label but with the same results. The group toured extensively in the U.S. and Canada during this period and appeared on shows for Alan Freed, Dick Clark, Jocko, and Tommy Smalls, among others. On October 20, 1958, their best single, "Chapel of Dreams," was recorded along with "Is There a Love for Me." Its November debut received little reaction and the Dubs, disappointed over the meager earnings in their chosen career, disbanded.

It sometimes happens that a record company's belief in a record allows for a second chance. So it was that in July 1959, eight months after its initial release, "Chapel of Dreams" came out again. Cleveland Still was already working as a shipping clerk when "Chapel" jumped into the Top 100 on August 24th, rising to number 74 after six weeks, the Dubs' last entry on the national hit list. The group came together again, replacing Still with Cordell Brown and signing with ABC Paramount, the same label they were with three years before as the Marvels. Though all five of their ABC singles were fine recordings (with "If I Only Had Magic" and "For the First Time" as standouts), their November 1959 to November 1961 run at ABC yielded no successes. *Billboard* reviewed their second ABC 45, describing "Don't Laugh at Me" as a "fervid vocal plea by lead singer and group on a moving rock-a-ballad." About the B side, "You'll Never Belong to Me," the reviewer wrote, "Plaintive rock-a-ballad is sung with heart and sincerity by lead warbler and group. Dual market appeal."

Still returned for the last ABC single, "Down Down Down I Go" (which is exactly where the single went), and by early 1962 it was back to Goldner for one End release, one Gone release, and a pretty single on Wilshire, "Your Very First Love." *Billboard*'s reviewer liked "Now That We Broke Up" on End, calling it "a soulful, emotional chanting job by the lead as he asks what happened to his love. Side is done to a moderate tempo with fiddle and a woo-wooing support from the group. Could grab spins."

In 1963 Cordell was back for Still as the Dubs signed with Josie for half an LP, in the tradition of "The Paragons meet the Jesters" called *The Dubs Meet the Shells*. The August 1963 issue contained such excellent reworkings of group oldies as "Wisdom of a Fool" (THE FIVE KEYS), "This I Swear" (THE SKYLINERS), "Blue Velvet" (THE CLOVERS), and re-recordings of "Don't" and "Magic" that wound up on the Lana label in 1964 as singles.

By the '70s the group was a trio of Blandon, Still, and Kirk Harris (tenor), though Still had almost joined a new group with Willie Winfield of the Harptones and Bill Brown of the Dominoes. The new trio recorded an LP of past Dubs songs for the Candlelite label. David Shelly (baritone) joined in 1973 for two singles, but the Dubs' chart recording years were behind them. In 1973 four unreleased sides from the early 1957 Johnson session showed up on Johnson Records (see discography) and were more than likely issued by collectors.

In the '80s Cleveland Still returned to the scene with his own Dubs made up of Bernard Jones (of Dock Green's Drifters), Steve Brown and John Truesdale (THE CHARTS), and Leslie Anderson.

On September 13, 1985, the Dubs appeared at a Frankie Lymon memorial benefit at the "United in Group Harmony" show, appearing with THE CHANNELS, THE IMPALAS, and THE SHELLS. Another live UGHA show in New Jersey during May 1986 saw the Cleveland Still Dubs with Leslie Anderson on lead performing an a cappella version of the Dubs' 1958 record "Beside My Love," which was captured live and released on the UGHA label in the winter of 1986.

The Dubs' superior handling of fine ballads merited them greater success than they actually earned. In 1988 a portion of their recorded legacy was compiled on a Murray Hill LP in tribute to this talented quintet.

THE DUBS

A SIDE/B SIDE	LABEL/CAT NO	DATE
Don't Ask Me To Be Lonely / Darling	Johnson 102	1957
Don't Ask Me To Be Lonely / Darling	Gone 5002	6/57
Could This Be Magic / Such Lovin'	Gone 5011	10/57
Beside My Love / Gonna Make A Change	Gone 5020	2/58
Be Sure My Love / Song In My Heart	Gone 5034	5/58
Chapel Of Dreams / Is There A Love For Me	Gone 5046	11/58

A SIDE/B SIDE	LABEL/CAT NO	DATE
Chapel Of Dreams / Is There A Love For Me	Gone 5069	7/59
No One / Early In The Morning	ABC 10056	11/59
Don't Laugh At Me / You'll Never Belong To Me	ABC 10010	4/60
For The First Time / Ain't That So	ABC 10150	10/60
Be Sure My Love / Song In My Heart	Mark-X 8008	1960
If I Only Had Magic / Joogie Boogie	ABC 10198	3/61
Down, Down, Down I Go / Lullaby	ABC 10269	11/61
Now That We Broke Up / This To Me Is Love	End 1108	2/62
You're Free To Go / Is There A Love For Me	Gone 5138	9/62
Your Very First Love / Just You	Wlshr 201	3/63
Wisdom Of A Fool / This I Swear	Josie 911	8/63
Blue Velvet / Could This Be Magic	Lana 115	1964
Don't Ask Me To Be Lonely / Your Very First Love	Lana 116	1964
I'm Downtown / Lost In The Wilderness	Vicki 229	1971
I Only Have Eyes For You / Where Do We Go From Here	Clifton 2	1973
Connie / Home Under My Hat	Johnson 097	1973
I Won't Have You Breaking My Heart / Somebody Goofed	Johnson 098	1973
Heartaches / You're Welcome	Clifton 5	1975
Beside My Love / If I Didn't Care	UGHA	1986

The Du Droppers

The Du Droppers were one of the oldest recording vocal groups on the scene in the early '50s, with their ages averaging over 40. But in no way were they late starters; each was a pro with years of experience, mostly in the gospel field.

The group assembled in Harlem in 1952 and included J. C. "Junior" Caleb Ginyard (lead), Willie Ray (tenor/baritone), Harvey Ray (tenor/baritone), and Eddie Hashew (bass). J. C. had sung with the Royal Harmony Singers in Florida in 1936, becoming the Jubalaires (Decca). In 1948 he joined the Dixieaires (Continental, Sunrise, and Sittin' In With), and when they disbanded in 1950 he came to New York. The Ray brothers had sung with the Southwest Jubilee Singers. The new group began practicing secular songs in a basement at 149th Street and Seventh Avenue in the apartment building where J. C. lived.

Paul Kapp (manager of THE DELTA RHYTHM BOYS) got wind of the Du Droppers and became their manager. In late 1952 an audition for Bobby Robinson's Harlem-based Red Robin Records resulted in their first release, an answer to THE DOMINOES' "Sixty Minute Man" entitled "Can't Do Sixty No More." The Dominoes must have liked the answer record since they recorded it two years later for a single that didn't end up doing much better than the Du Droppers' release. Rather than hang on with what they perceived as a small-time operation like Red Robin, the quartet went on to audition at record giant RCA, which at that time was deciding whether or not to remain in the rhythm and blues field.

Hashew was then replaced by Brooklyn native Bob Kornegay (formerly a solo act on the Sittin' In With label), and the new combination rang the bell with their first RCA release, the raunchy rhythm single "I Want to Know (What You Do When You Go Round There)."

Released the fourth week of March 1953, by April 18th it was on the R&B charts scaling the heights to number three. That hit by four middle-aged Harlem residents put a whole slew of RCA employees back to work in the R&B department. "I Want to Know" turned out to be *Billboard's* lucky number 13 R&B "Record of the Year," and made the group the sixth most popular act (so said *R&B* magazine).

Not wanting to miss an opportunity, Red Robin released a single from the vaults, "Come On and Love Me Baby," while the group was touring the U.S. and Canada. The record received very little attention, unlike their RCA follow-up, an answer to "I Want to Know" titled "I Found Out (What You Do When You Go Round There)." This second RCA release took the blues rockin' Du Droppers back up the charts soon after its late May issuance. By July it too had reached number three. Extending the "I Want to Know" story into a trilogy, Atlantic's Eve Foster released "You'll Never Know" in that same month.

Though most of their recordings were rockers (and racy ones at that), they released the ballad "Don't Pass Me By" as their fourth RCA 45, which displayed the gospel roots of J. C. on lead but was largely ignored by radio. A distinguishing feature of the B side ("Get Lost") was the last line of the lyric telling that woman, "Baby drop dead."

Another Du Droppers ballad they released was the haunting "Laughing Blues," the flip of "I Want to Know."

RCA took notice of their softer side and paired them with luscious blonde pop vocalist Sunny Gale for "The Note in the Bottle" in November.

To differentiate its R&B releases from the pop side, RCA formed the Groove subsidiary in February 1954, and the debut disk was a two-sided blues rocker from the Du Droppers with the quality edge going to "Dead Broke."

In early 1954 the group added young Prentice Moreland to the Droppers lineup for their next Groove single, the FIVE KEYS-styled "How Much Longer." A worthy track, it couldn't crack the hit charts—as had been the case with every record since "I Found Out." Even so, most of their records sold enough to keep them working regularly. They were one of the few R&B acts in the early '50s to work in Hawaii, performing at Lau Lee Chai's club in Honolulu.

Moreland soon went off to join the Dominoes, the Chanteclairs, and THE CADETS, but by August 1954 the group was once again a quartet with the addition of Joe Van Loan, who was still singing with THE RAVENS. Harvey Ray left in September as the group prepared to sign with Herald Records. The only problem was, RCA picked up their option for another year and the group had to stay. This created a conflict for newcomer Van Loan who was signed to Jack Angel's Jubilee label (he also owned Herald). In an apparent "tit for tat," Jubilee refused RCA the services of Van Loan.

To contribute to the growing confusion, Van Loan continued to perform with the Droppers while new lead singer Charlie Hughes (later of THE DRIFTERS) only sang on recordings and was never considered a full-time member of the group. He is first heard on the 45 released the third week of April 1955 titled "Give Me Some Consideration."

As the group was about to embark on another Canadian tour, Van Loan bolted back to the Ravens and Harvey Ray re-enlisted for the group's last session, which produced the early September single "You're Mine Already."

At this point Ginyard heard his gospel roots calling and joined THE GOLDEN GATE QUARTET. Roger Bowers took J. C.'s place, but by then the group was disintegrating. The Ray brothers formed a new group with 19-year-old Edna McGriff ("Heavenly Father," #4, Jubilee, 1952), Bill Brown (the Dominoes), and Little David Baughn (the Drifters), but they never got to record. Bob Kornegay went back to solo work, this time for Herald and King.

In 1959 Van Loan, Orville Brooks, and Kornegay formed the Valiants for one Joy release, "Let Me Go Lover." J. C. left the Golden Gaters in 1971 to go solo. He took up residence in Switzerland where he died on August 11, 1978.

THE DU DROPPERS

A SIDE/B SIDE	LABEL/CAT NO	DATE
Can't Do Sixty No More / Chain Me Baby	RdRbn 108	1952
Come On And Love Me Baby / Go Back	RdRbn 116	1953
I Wanna Know / Laughing Blues	RCA 47-5229	3/53
I Found Out / Little Girl. Little Girl	RCA 47-5321	5/53
Whatever You're Doin' / Somebody Work On My Baby's Mind	RCA 47-5425	8/53
Don't Pass Me By / Get Lost	RCA 47-5504	10/53
The Note In The Bottle / Mama's Gone, Goodbye	RCA 47-5543	11/53
Speed King / Dead Broke	Groove 0001	2/54
How Much Longer / Just Whisper	Groove 0013	4/54
Boot 'Em Up / Let Nature Take Its Course	Groove 0036	9/54
Talk That Talk / Give Me Some Consideration	Groove 0104	4/55
You're Mine Already / I Wanna Love You	Groove 0120	8/55

The Edsels

"If you don't succeed now, pray somebody plays your record later," is a bit of advice that would have been prescient for the Edsels. The quintet was from Campbell, Ohio, near Youngstown, forming in 1957. George Jones, Jr. (lead), Larry Green (first tenor), James Reynolds (second tenor), Harry Green (baritone and Larry's brother), and Marshall Sewell (bass) were the Essos (named after a brand of gasoline at a nearby service station). They switched their name from gas to a car when Ford's Edsel came out. In order to avoid the pitfalls of lackadaisical attitudes held by group members the guys had sung with before, they set up a strict schedule of rehearsals that had them starting every morning at nine A.M. at Marshall's house. Since all had afternoon or evening jobs, the four to five hours they practiced each morning was the most opportune time to get together. Heavy effort was expended on a song George wrote while in the air force titled "Rama Lama Ding Dong."

The group soon moved out of Marshall's house and on to the local variety show circuit. The owner of a local music store arranged an audition with music publisher Jim Manderitz right in the instrument shop, and Manderitz was so impressed he whipped out a contract (music publishers carried contracts like cops carried guns) and signed them on the spot.

They recorded at Snyder Studios in Cleveland and Jim began searching out every label he could find, but alas, there were no takers. Finally, he came upon Foster Johnson and his new Dub label in Little Rock, Arkansas.

The record came out in the summer of 1958, only Foster Johnson had changed the title on the label to "Lama Rama Ding Dong." Regardless, the record never got a notice except for some initial activity in Baltimore.

The Campbell quartet then met producer Tony Marsh, who obtained their release from publisher Manderitz and recorded a solid harmony-laden R&B ballad by Tony and the group called "Do You Love Me." (Those whose only acquaintance with the Edsels is through "Rama Lama" would be most impressed with this fine example of their ballad singing.)

Roulette Records of New York picked up "Do You Love Me" (unique chime ending and all) and in the spring of 1959 issued it with no real support.

In the fall of 1960 another ballad, "What Brought Us Together," came out on the local Tammy label distributed by Ember. Produced by Marsh (who had recently done "My Guardian Angel" with the Monorays for that label) the slow, strolling love song took off locally and spread enough for the group to get its first taste of the road at the Howard Theatre in Washington, the Regal in Chicago, the Apollo in New York, and on Dick Clark's "American Bandstand."

Before the Edsels could record a follow-up, their follow-up was chosen for them. When THE MARCELS hit the airwaves like a stuttering juggernaut in February and March 1961 with "Blue Moon," resourceful disc jockeys across American began wracking their brains to come up with a record that could follow the novel rocker. One disc jockey in New York remembered a record from a few years before that was in the same style, had a similarly wacko intro, and would segue beautifully out of "Blue Moon." The record? "Lama Rama Ding Dong."

He started playing it and the phones lit up like a Christmas tree. When Jim Manderitz heard all the commotion about his record, he licensed it to Hy and Sam Weiss's Old Town conglomerate and they issued it on their Twin affiliate.

By May 1, 1961, it charted and began selling all over the U.S., reaching number 21. Meanwhile, Arkansas entrepreneur Foster Johnson had moved to California and, not to be left out, issued his recording, only he did two things that drive buyers crazy and collectors into fantasyland. He corrected the Dub label from "Lama Rama" to "Rama Lama" and he issued an alternate take of the recording with a weaker production and a different sax solo from the original. Manderitz wasn't finished with the Edsels, however, as he had two sides left in the can that he now sold to Dot Records. Tammy licensed two more sides to Ember and Edsel masters were suddenly selling in larger quantities than Edsel cars.

Neither of these singles, "Three Precious Words" (Ember) or "My Whispering Heart" (Dot) did much, but the Edsels were too busy to notice as Tony had marched the group to Capitol Records for three more unsuccessful singles, the best of which was a rousing Jeff Barry-penned rocker, "Shake Shake Sherry," that sounded like a contemporary extension of "Rama Lama Ding Dong" and boasted one of the wildest sax instrumental sections on 45 vinyl. It did get some New York airplay but unfortunately didn't catch on.

The highlight of the group's performing career was their appearance at the Apollo with "The Bobby Show" featuring Bobby Bland, Bobby Freeman, and Bobby Marchan along with THE ANGELS.

The group lasted into the early Beatles era. Two more Tammy issues followed, but with little money earned, the group decided to call it quits.

Marshall became a detective in Cleveland, Larry joined Discount Records, Harry became a security guard, and James became a minister, all in Youngstown. George continued to sing, joining the Winston Wall Trio and then the New Affair.

THE EDSELS

A SIDE/B SIDE	LABEL/CAT NO	DATE
Lama Rama Ding Dong / Bells	Dub 2843	7/58
Do You Love Me /		
Rink-A-Din-Ki-Do	Roul 4151	5/59
What Brought Us Together /		
Don't Know What To Do	Tammy 1010	4/60
Rama Lama Ding Dong / Bells	Twin 700	4/61
Rama Lama Ding Dong / Bells	Dub 2843	5/61
My Jealous One /		
Bone Shaker Joe	Cap 4588	9/61
Three Precious Words / Let's Go	Tammy 1014	9/61
Three Precious Words / Let's Go	Ember 1078	9/61
Shake, Shake, Sherry / If Your		
Pillow Could Talk	Cap 4675	1/62
My Whispering Heart / Could It Be	Dot 16311	1/62
Shaddy Daddy Dip Dip /		
Don't You Feel	Cap 4836	9/62
Got To Find Out About Love /		
The Girl I Love	Tammy 1023	1963
Count The Tears /		
Twenty-Four Hours	Tammy 1027	1963

The El Dorados

Any group that can call themselves the Five Stars even though they have six members must have an interesting history, and the El Dorados do. Actually the original group *did* have five members when they formed in the Englewood section of Chicago's south side in 1952 while attending Englewood High School (the same school the Morroccos went to). The roster included Pirkle Lee Moses, Jr. (lead), Louis Bradley (tenor), Jewel Jones (second tenor and baritone), James Maddox (baritone and bass), and Robert Glasper (bass).

In one of the unusual twists of their career, they were so well liked by the school's custodian, Johnny Moore, that he became their manager. In 1954 Moses and Glasper took advantage of the air force's 90-day active duty program, but while Moses returned Glasper stayed in. By then Arthur Bassett (tenor) had temporarily replaced Moses, and Richard Nickens came in for Glasper. The Five Stars were now six, and a name change was inevitable. They were about to become the Cardinals (with no knowledge of New York's Atlantic group) when the car-group craze hit. Since they couldn't call themselves the Cadillacs, why not its hottest model, the luxurious El Dorado?

Though never truly a gospel group, they sang many songs by THE PILGRIM TRAVELERS and THE SOUL STIRRERS along with songs by THE ORIOLES, THE DRIFTERS, and THE DOMINOES, among others. Their exciting harmony blend made them a hot local act, and at one particular talent show at the Club De Lisa (where they won first prize) they came to the attention of Chicago disc jockey Al Benson. He arranged for an audition of sorts at a contest Vee-Jay Records was holding at the Park City Skating Rink in which groups were challenged to compete against Vee-Jay's own SPANIELS. The El Dorados rose to the occasion, winning the contest and a recording contract with Vivian Carter's label.

Their first release came in September 1954. While nothing out of the ordinary, the blues ballad "My Lovin' Baby" introduced the public to Pirkle's voice and was a regional seller.

The El Dorados' next effort had them backing up Hazel McCollum on Vee-Jay's contribution to the ongoing "Annie" saga begun by the Midnighters in early 1954 and that eventually included "Work with Me Annie" (February 1954), "Sexy Ways" (June 1954), and "Annie Had a Baby" (August 1954). So it was that in the third week of October, "Annie's Answer" opened the floodgates for such additional responses as "My Name Ain't Annie" (Linda Hayes), "Annie's Aunt Fannie" (with the Midnighters still at it), and the unforgettable "Annie Kicked the Bucket" (the Nutones).

Billboard's December review stated, "They all have been telling a bunch of lies, shouts Annie, in this case Hazel McCollum supported by the El Dorados" and gave it a rather excellent rating. But the "Annies" killed each other off, and it was back to an unspectacular ballad, "One More Chance" (released the first week of March 1955), that went nowhere.

Arthur Bassett soon left for the call of the wild blue yonder (less romantically known as the air force), and the sextet became a quintet. Despite the less-than-successful singles, their airplay and performance reputation was spreading.

On December 3, 1954, the El Dorados had drawn 6,700 people to the Sixth Annual WDIA Radio Goodwill Review in Memphis along with the Five Cs (United), Gatemouth Brown (Peacock), and Eddie Boyd (Chess). In February 1955 they had spent a week at the Apollo Theatre in New York with Willie Mae Thornton, Charlie and Ray, and Danny Overbea.

In the third week of September 1955, Vee-Jay released "At My Front Door." It had an intro that seemed to sneak up, leading into Al Duncan's pounding drum rhythm and El Dorados harmonies. Before one could catch a breath the group kicked in with "wop, wop, doodley wop, wop wop doodley, wop, wop, wop" followed by a rousing sax solo. The "baby talk" pre-finale by Pirkle made the record soar even further, and the story of that "crazy little mama" became as legendary as "Annie." "At My Front Door" stormed the *Billboard* R&B chart on September 24th and the Top 100 on October 15th. By the end of the year it was number 17 as a Pop Best Seller and number one R&B, hanging on for 18 weeks. All this despite more people walking into record stores asking for "Crazy Little Mama" (the first line of the song) than for "At My Front Door" and despite the fact that the Pied Piper of pasteurized pop, Pat Boone, covered it, bringing his version to number seven Pop. The El Dorados' legendary status was now established, although the group itself could not foresee the song's future as a rock and roll standard.

The group toured the country and performed with many of the hottest acts of the day. One particularly spectacular show was on September 30, 1955, at the Howard Theatre where they appeared with THE HEARTS, LaVern Baker, Al Hibbler, and Red Prysock's Rockin' Combo.

Their follow-up to "Door," in the second week of December, was just slightly more restrained but every bit as good as "Crazy Little Mama." "I'll Be Forever Lovin' You" was a polished pop R&B panacea. The rocker exuded jazz, pop, and R&B overtones that should have clinched the group's hold on stardom, but although it made it to number eight R&B in February 1956 it never charted Pop. In fact, "Forever" (which was originally recorded by the Rip Chords and never released) was the last chart record the group would ever have. To heap on disappointment, the group's best-ever ballad, a HARPTONES-styled weeper ("I Began to Realize"), was lost because it was "Forever's" flip and received split airplay, with neither song getting enough promotion to go all the way.

The group then became a quartet when Richard Nickens left after "Forever." Of their next few releases the best shots were "A Fallen Tear" in a Marvin and Johnny styling that did well in a few cities, and an "At My Front Door" sequel titled "Bim Bam Boom," which should have been called "At My Back Door." Its name inspired the legendary oldies publication formed in August 1971 through August 1973 by vocal group enthusiasts Sal Mondrone, Bob Galgano, and Steve Flam.

The group was often better than its songs, as indicated in a *Billboard* April 14, 1956, review of "Now That You've Gone" that read: "Tender and expressive chanting, again the group comes through with a performance that outdistances the material they have to work with. Good listening."

"Tears on My Pillow" (not Little Anthony's record) was the last 45 of the original El Dorados; the group and Pirkle separated over a disagreement on new management. In 1957 Jones, Bradley, and Maddox left Vee-Jay and joined Academy Records of Chicago with new lead Marvin Smith. Their 1958 issue of "A Lonely Boy," a modest ballad that sounded older than it was, had smooth harmonies but an obtrusive and unnecessary flute. To avoid legal problems with Vee-Jay, the group's name was changed to Those Four El Dorados and Jewel Jones's name on the label was spelled "J-u-e-l-l" (each member's name was listed).

Feeling the need for a change the group went west, hooked up with Don Barksdale (former NBA basketball star) and his Rhythm Record Company of Oakland, California, and did one single as the Tempos, a tough ballad titled "Promise Me." The flip, "Never Let Me Go," was an El Dorados-styled rocker that couldn't be hidden behind the Tempos' name. When Rhythm Records couldn't make it a success, the group returned to Chicago and split up in 1961. Marvin Smith went on to join the Artistics on Okeh and Brunswick Records as the lead for such R&B charters as "I'm Gonna Miss You" (#55 Top 100, #9 R&B, 1966) and "Girl I Need You" (#69 Top 100, #26 R&B, 1967).

Following the separation back in 1957, Pirkle had been left with no group; another Vee-Jay act, THE KOOL GENTS, had been left without a singer when their front man, Dee Clark, departed for a solo career. Presto! John McCall (tenor), Douglas Brown (second tenor), Teddy Long (second tenor and baritone), and Johnny Carter (bass) of the Kool Gents joined with Pirkle Lee Moses, Jr., to become the New El Dorados. They released two singles in 1958 for Vee-Jay, the best of which was an excellent shuffle ballad, "Lights Are Low," but when neither sold, Vee-Jay released the group.

By 1959 Pirkle's group was no more. Johnny Carter kept the name alive by forming a new El Dorados with John McCall, Danny Edwards, and Eugene Huff (the latter formerly of the Valquins on Gaily in 1959 with "Falling Star") lasting until 1965.

Carter tried again in 1971, hooking up with Huff, Spence Goulsby, Jr., and Lee Toussaint on lead for two sides on Paula. That group was gone by the early '80s.

Pirkle recorded with an unknown group as the Squires in 1963 on Boss ("It's Time") and then did a solo effort titled "The Docks." In 1965 Pirkle, Melvin Morrow, and George Prager (the latter two late of the Morroccos) came together as the Major Minors.

In 1969 they once again became the El Dorados, doing a single for Torrid Records called "In Over My Head." Pirkle then quit for almost a decade but returned with another El Dorados with Norman Palm tenor (from THE PASTELS on United), Billy Henderson (second tenor), George Prayer (baritone), and Anthony Charles (bass).

Circa 1985 Henderson left and Charles died. Gene Huff (of Carter's El Dorados) and Larry Johnson (Morroccos) took their places and the group recorded a ballad, "Ease the Pain," for Delano Records in 1987. In effect, that last El Dorados recording group contained members of four Chicago groups: the Palms, the Morroccos, the Kool Gents, and the El Dorados.

In 1988, original El Dorado Richard Nickens took over for Prayer and the group continued doing oldies shows in the Chicago area through the early '90s. One of the most exciting vocal acts to come out of the Windy City, the El Dorados were an R&B class act that created a rock and roll classic.

THE EL DORADOS

A SIDE/B SIDE	LABEL/CAT NO	DATE
My Loving Baby / Baby I Need You	Vee-Jay 115	9/54
Annie's Answer / Living With Vivian	Vee-Jay 118	1/54
One More Chance / Little Miss Love	Vee-Jay 127	3/55
At My Front Door / What's Buggin' You Baby	Vee-Jay 147	9/55
I'll Be Forever Loving You / I Began To Realize	Vee-Jay 165	12/55
Now That You've Gone / Rock 'n' Roll's For Me	Vee-Jay 180	3/56
A Fallen Tear / Chop Ling Soon	Vee-Jay 197	1956
There In The Night / Bim Bam Boom	Vee-Jay 211	10/56
Tears On My Pillow / A Rose For My Darling	Vee-Jay 250	1956
Three Reasons Why / Boom Diddle Boom	Vee-Jay 263	1958
Lights Are Low / Oh What A Girl	Vee-Jay 302	1958

Those Four El Dorados		
A Lonely Boy / Go Little Susie	Acad 8138	1958

The Tempos		
Promise Me / Never Let Me Go	Rhythm 121	1958

The Squires		
It's Time / Girls	Boss 2120	1964

The El Dorados		
In Over My Head / You Make My Heart Sing	Torrid 100	1970
Since You Came Into My Life / Looking In From The Outside	Paula 347	1971
Loose Bootie / Loose Bootie (inst.)	Paula 369	1971

The Fabulous El Dorados		
Ease The Pain / Remember Sherrie	Delano 1099	1987

The Elegants

Wolfgang Amadeus Mozart hit upon the melody that would become "Twinkle Twinkle Little Star" in 1764. The eight-year-old boy wonder's lullabye would be an inspiration 194 years later to five singing teenagers in Staten Island, New York, in 1958.

The Elegants' story began a few years earlier on Staten Island's boardwalk, where 15-year-old Vito Picone sang with fellow New Dorp High Schoolers Carman Romano, Ronnie Jones, and Pat Croccitto, their female lead. They were performing for amusement at local dances when a friend recommended them to Carl Edelson's Club Records in New York.

In November 1956 their Picone-penned rocker "Darling Come Back" came out under the name Pat Cordel (Croccitto) and the Crescents. Sounding like a cross between a white FRANKIE LYMON AND THE TEENAGERS and Kathy Young (who didn't release a record till four years later), Pat and the guys stirred enough local attention to warrant dream-like tours with the likes of THE FIVE SATINS, THE VALENTINES, and THE CADILLACS.

Mr. Croccitto probably had heart palpitations about his 15-year-old daughter traipsing around the U.S. with four adolescents; the history of the Crescents became a short one.

But Vito and Carman were not about to give up; they recruited James Moschella, Frank Tardogno, and Arthur Venosa in 1957. The lineup now was Vito (lead), Artie (first tenor), Frank (second tenor), Carman (baritone), and Jimmy (bass). Looking for a special title they came upon a sign that read, "Schenley, the whiskey of elegance." There, in all its simplicity, was their name.

They started over, once again practicing and playing local talent shows and dances. Along the way they picked up a 19-year-old manager, Kathy Watts, who schooled them choreographically and musically.

One particular talent show at the Cromwell Center in Staten Island garnered them a $50 first prize and a recording contract with Aladdin Records. When Aladdin, a major "indy" label in the R&B field, didn't record them, they kept playing shows and auditioning for other companies like Ivy Records. Vito and Artie then wrote a song titled "Little Star" that maestro Mozart would have been proud of. They began using it in their performances until they learned that another Staten Island group on Decca, the Secrets ("See You Next Year" [Decca], a cover of THE CLEFTONES' song, 1957) had heard it and were planning to record it. The Elegants feverishly set about the task of finding a record deal. As they were fans of THE HEARTBEATS (Hull Records) it's likely this inspired them to call upon Bea Caslon, owner of Hull. She liked "Little Star" immediately and in April 1958 recorded it along with another Elegants original, "Gettin' Dizzy," a rocker that one could imagine as the soundtrack to Ann-Margret swinging her hair and dancing wildly in a '60s teen beach movie.

"Gettin' Dizzy" collared its own share of interest, especially among the kind of teenagers that would study records for interesting lyrical passages to bring up in school. "Gettin' Dizzy" had a reputation for raunchiness based on a line that was so slurred it seemed to be about an action occasionally practiced by consenting adults. The actual phrase, according to Vito Picone, is "The doctor said it can't be fixed, it's just because two wrong hearts mixed."

Bea Caslon knew from past experience that she couldn't bring a hit home on her own small label, so she licensed the sides and the group to ABC-Paramount without ever issuing it on Hull. She tried it in October 1957 on her Mascot affiliate with THE PASTELS' "Been So Long," and soon after had to license it to Argo to keep it going.

In June 1958 ABC released "Little Star" on their new Apt affiliate and it took off like a SAM missile. On July 21st it entered Billboard's Pop charts and by August 25th it was number one. (To put it in perspective, that was the same week Michael Jackson was born.) This was a tremendous accomplishment not only because it was the Elegants' first record, but also because they were only the second white doo wop group in history to have a number one hit (DANNY AND THE JUNIORS' "At the Hop" was the first in 1957).

The two million-plus seller for Vito and company didn't stop even at the U.S. borders. In England it went to number 25, in Australia number nine, and in Italy number one. The tours and TV shots began almost instantly, and the Elegants weren't completely prepared for the whirlwind. (Once at the Brooklyn Fox the group had to borrow jackets from the oversized DANLEERS in order to have a picture taken.) DION AND THE BELMONTS, Buddy Holly, Bobby Darin, Chuck Berry, Frankie Avalon, and THE COASTERS, just to name a few, all shared stages with the Elegants that year, and the group got its share of Dick Clark and Alan Freed's TV appearances as well.

The importance of "Little Star" went beyond the record's own success: the sound influenced many young white groups of the late '50s and early '60s such as THE CAPRIS, RANDY AND THE RAINBOWS, Gene Cornish of the Rascals, THE PASSIONS, and THE MYSTICS. In fact the Mystics' hit "Hushabye" came about because Laurie exec Gene Schwartz asked songwriters Doc Pomus and Mort Schuman to write something like "Little Star."

The group's second Apt single was a love song in the tempo of "Little Star." In "Please Believe Me," the Elegants sounded strikingly similar to their onstage buddies Dion and the Belmonts. It's reported that Dion wanted to record "Please Believe Me," but since he was coming off of a hit ("No One Knows," #19) and had a new release in the works

("Don't Pity Me," #40, early 1959), he cut those thoughts short. Apt, meanwhile, was losing the record; although it had widespread initial airplay, "Please" never even touched the Top 100.

One more single in early 1959, an ordinary outing written by Venosa and led by Frank titled "True Love Affair," and the group was dropped by ABC. Hull held onto the quintet for one more release, the nursery rhyme-like "Little Boy Blue." The group's sound and effort was better than the material; "Little Boy" disappeared into the blue.

Billboard had an upbeat view of their second release on United Artists (their first, "Speak Low," had spoken nary a word to radio). About "Spiral," the reviewer wrote: "Attractive rocker about a new dance in the current groove receives a first-rate vocal from the boys here, with the group backing the lead with cute expressions. Side has a lilt that could carry it far. Watch it." United Artists watched it flop. "Ah om boga boga" were the so-called "cute expressions," and the record sounded like Dion and the Belmonts meet the Clovers in the verse. Someone should have given the "Little Star"-styled flip, "Happiness," a shot instead.

In 1961 the group was back with the Apt organization, this time on the parent ABC label for a nice two-sider, "Tiny Cloud" (another celestial attempt), and a rocker, "I've Seen Everything," that saw little promotion.

Around this time Vito was injured in an accident and was laid up for several months. The group decided to go it alone, prompting Vito to pursue a solo career when he recovered. Had he made that decision earlier he might have been a star on Warner Bros. or United Artists, as both companies had made overtures toward him, Warner during the "Little Star" days and UA just prior to his accident. He had turned both down to stay with the Elegants, an especially painful thought considering that UA had approached him to sing the title song for *Town Without Pity* and had given it instead to Gene Pitney (#13, 1961). (Had Vito taken it, the song might have been "Town Without Pitney.")

Vito went solo in 1963 for one single on I.P.G. ("Path in the Wilderness") and two on Admiral ("Song from Moulin Rouge" and "Still Waters Run Deep") in 1964.

The four remaining Elegants did one more single with Frank as lead on Photo Records ("Dressin' Up," with a picture of them on the label) before ending their recording career. But as late as 1971 they were still performing with a lineup of originals Frank Tardogna, Jimmy Moschella, and newcomers Anthony Moscato and Freddie Redman.

In 1965 Vito signed with Laurie Records and was matched with a Bronx group, the Tremonts (Ronnie Lapinsky, Bill Frye, and Dave Romano), who had recorded Vito's composition, "Please Believe Me," as "Believe My Heart" (the Pat Riccio label, 1961).

The group became Vito and the Elegants, releasing "A Letter from Vietnam" as a single (a poor choice of subject matter for a doo wop group). Then, thanks to a subtle change, they were the Elegantes for "Wake Up," an up-tempo side marred by a persistent falsetto alarm clock sound. It worked in "Rockin' in the Jungle" (THE ETERNALS) but not here. The Elegantes then became the Tremonts, while Vito formed a new Elegants with original Jimmy Moschella, Fred Redman, and ex-Majestics Nino Armotto. Their one Laurie release as Vito and the Elegants ("Belinda") was a Swedish hit translated for the U.S. market, but except for some New York airplay the guys might as well have sung the song in Swedish. Their last Laurie recording had them backing up the Barbarians, a band with only a lead singer and a drummer who had a hook for a left hand. Their recording of "Moulty" (the drummer's nickname) had a talking verse, a "Hang On Sloopy" rip-off bass line in the chorus, and a shouting group. It was the Elegants' most bizarre recording, and it made number 90 nationally in early 1966.

During the late '60s Vito toured with his own band, Bo Gest and the Legions, and later formed a group called the Velvet Kite.

Inactive musically during the early '70s, Vito regrouped the Elegants late in that decade with Freddie, Nino, and new member Bruce "Sonny" Copp.

In 1981 they recorded a terrific doo wop LP, *A Knight with the Elegants* (Crystal Ball), that included "Maybe" (THE CHANTELS), their first single in 16 years, "Peace of Mind" (THE SPANIELS), "Out of Sight, Out of Mind" (THE FIVE KEYS), and of course a new rendition of "Little Star."

Today Frank Tardogna is retired from the Department of Sanitation, Jimmy Moschella works for the Manhattan Transit Authority, Artie lives in California and owns a club, and Carman owns a hair salon. Of the Crescents, Ronnie Jones became a commercial artist; Pat (Croccitto) Cordel became a June Taylor dancer and later a sky diver, winding up back in New York as a hair dresser. And Vito? He redirected his music business experience and expertise toward personal management, handling one of the hottest hip-hop vocal groups of the late '80s, THE FORCE M.D.'S.

THE ELEGANTS

A SIDE/B SIDE	LABEL/CAT NO	DATE
Pat Cordel and the Crescents		
Darling Come Back / My Tears	Club 1011	11/56
The Elegants		
Little Star / Getting Dizzy	Apt 25005	6/58
Please Believe Me / Goodnight	Apt 25017	10/58
True Love Affair / Pay Day	Apt 25029	2/59
Darling Come Back / My Tears	Mchl 503	1959
Little Boy Blue / Get Well Soon	Hull 732	1/60
Speak Low / Let My Prayers Be		
With You	UA 230	6/60
Happiness / Spiral	UA 295	12/60
Tiny Cloud / I've Seen Everything	ABC 10219	1961
A Dream Come True / Dressin' Up	Photo 2662	1963
Darling Come Back / My Tears	Vctry 1001	1964
Elegantes		
Wake Up / Bring Back Wendy	Laurie 3298	1965
Vito and the Elegants		
A Letter From Viet Nam /		
Barbara Beware	Laurie 3283	1965
Belinda / Lazy Love	Laurie 3324	1965
Maybe / Woo Woo Train	CrysB 139	1981

The El Venos

One of the best of Pittsburgh's '50s rhythm and blues groups, the El Venos' chances were marred by too little financial and family support.

Formed as a sextet, they stayed that way through the release of their two singles. The members were Leon Daniels (lead), Daniel Jackson (first tenor), Anna Mae Jackson (lead, Daniel's sister), Leon Taylor (second tenor), Joey Daniels (baritone, Leon's brother), and Bernard Palmer (bass).

Raised in the Penn Hills and Duquesne area outside Pittsburgh, the six 16-year-olds started hitting street-corner harmonies during 1955. They came to the attention of WILY radio jock Bill Powell who arranged for a record deal with RCA. In 1956 the group was packed off to New York City to record five songs, issuing the Leon Taylor-penned "Geraldine" on RCA's Groove subsidiary by late fall. "Geraldine" was a rockin', New York-styled doo wopper with an incessant, fun-filled "dooley pady-wah" background and Leon's soft-voiced lead. Its flip, "Now We're Together," was a cha-cha flavored, harmony-filled delight with Leon and Ann trading leads. "Geraldine" got immediate play on Dick Clark's "American Bandstand," but when Bill Powell (now their manager) arranged for a live appearance on that program the boys couldn't raise the money from their parents for the Pittsburgh to Philadelphia trek. With no finances to tour or do anything but local TV, the strong radio play of "Geraldine" (from New England to New Orleans) couldn't keep the record happening. Still, the El Venos performed locally with many hit acts that were passing through Pittsburgh on one-nighters, THE TURBANS and THE HEARTBEATS among them.

Their next single, "You Must Be True" (1957), was issued on another RCA affiliate, Vik Records, but saw even less activity.

Two years passed while the group raised money to audition in New York for Calico Records. Auditioning the same day was another Pittsburgh group, THE SKYLINERS. Doo wop folklore says the El Venos were actually favored by Calico on that fateful day, but the Skyliners' unique sound afforded them the first recording opportunity, subsequently yielding the now standard "Since I Don't Have You." The El Venos did get to do two sides for Calico, but they never saw the light of day.

On yet another New York trip, the group managed to cut two more songs for Mercury's Amp 3 division, but these also remained in the can.

On her return to Pittsburgh, Anna Mae Jackson left the El Venos. Bill Powell, meanwhile, was busy putting the voices of his new group THE ALTAIRS on the El Venos Amp 3 tracks, leaving only Anna's lead vocal. He also dubbed in Altairs lead George Benson's guitar work.

Though Powell pumped the record on his show, Amp 3 wasn't impressed enough to release it. Around this time, Ms. Jackson changed her name to Anne Keith and recorded "Lover's Prayer" backed by the Altairs and released on Memo Records in mid-1959.

They soon went their separate ways: Anne Keith moved to New Jersey, Bernard Palmer stayed in Pittsburgh, Leon Taylor went to New York City, and Joey Daniels became a New York City artist. Daniel Jackson joined the service and Leon Daniels stayed in Pittsburgh to become a meat department manager in a Giant Eagle Supermarket.

The Eternals

The Eternals were a novelty-record vocal act with a Latin styling. Had their manager not overzealously sued a competitor, the group might have made the big time.

Formed during the late '50s, in the Freeman Street neighborhood of the Bronx, the quintet started out singing in junior high school as the Gleamers. Their roll call included Charlie Gerona on lead, Fred Hodge on first tenor, Ernie Sierra on second tenor, Arnie Torres on baritone and Alex Miranda on bass. The members attended several high schools, including Morris, Monroe, and Samuel Gompers, while cutting their teeth on THE FLAMINGOS and SPANIELS. Charlie Gerona, meanwhile, was crafting songs more in the tradition of THE COASTERS, THE CADETS, and THE OLYMPICS than in the smooth harmony style the rest of the Gleamers (now calling themselves the Orbits) were emulating. But when the combination came together, it clicked, and a Charlie original titled "Christmas in the Jungle" became the door-opener to an introduction with local manager Bill Martin. Martin knew WABC disc jockey Bruce Morrow, who turned them on to Melba Records chief Morty Craft.

The group entered Beltone Studios in late spring of 1959 and Craft, not wanting to wait for Christmas, had "Christmas in the Jungle" revised to "Rockin' in the Jungle." The group, feeling the elation that recording for a label can bring, decided a new name was in order and crowned themselves the Eternals, no doubt hoping for everlasting success. Unlike most small-label '50s groups, the members were actually paid $25 a man for their session.

Released in early summer on Craft's new Hollywood Records label, "Rockin' " was an immediate New York airplay favorite, eventually rising to number 11 locally. On July 13th it hit *Billboard*'s national Pop Charts, rising to number 78.

Complete with jungle sounds and bird calls (mostly done by the group's baritone), "Rockin' " had an infectious rhythm, primal screams, and chants that made it a crowd pleaser. In fact it was such a crowd pleaser that the boys soon found themselves performing on the Murray the K and Bruce Morrow shows and at Palisades Amusement Park.

Their second release was "Babalu's Wedding Day" (fall 1959), another novelty number in a call-and-response mode with Charlie's bouncy Latin lead and a hot sax solo by King Curtis. As the record started to break, the Eternals' manager felt compelled to sue some shady booking agents who were apparently attempting a less-than-ethical move on the group. As a result of the court case, "Babalu's" distribution was stopped and the Eternals were denied their shot at stardom.

Making matters more humiliating was a benefit performance in which their lip-synced record was played all the way through at 33-1/3 rpm instead of 45.

In January 1961 their last single, "Blind Date," was issued through Morty Craft's Warwick Records. Meanwhile, "Babalu's Wedding Day" kept the group's image alive for years to come sung by the Eternals as a jingle on WABC disc jockey Bob Lewis's radio show.

The group disbanded in 1962 but by 1972 re-emerged for an oldies show at the Academy of Music; they were one original (Ernie Sierra) and four newcomers (his brother Richie on baritone, Jack Damon lead, George Santiago first tenor, and Hector Garcia bass).

The original members have long since left the recording scene for the work-a-day world. Fred Hodge went to work at Bellevue Hospital, Ernie Sierra (when not singing) became an air conditioner repairman, Alex Miranda died in 1971, Arnie Torres lives somewhere in New Jersey, and Charlie Gerona is in business in California.

THE ETERNALS

A SIDE/B SIDE	LABEL/CAT NO	DATE
Rockin' In The Jungle / Rock 'n' Roll Cha-Cha	Hlywd 68	1959
Babalu's Wedding Day / My Girl	Hlywd 70	1959
Blind Date / Today	Warwick 611	1961

The Falcons

Despite their place in history as one of the first acts to pass from rhythm and blues into soul, the Falcons had considerably less success than their similarly rooted contemporaries Jerry Butler and THE IMPRESSIONS. Like the Impressions, however, the Falcons became a launching pad for solo soul careers.

The Falcons didn't start out as a pure rhythm and blues group, nor did they begin with only black members. The group was racially mixed and sang modern and pop R&B harmonizers with a touch of gospel. Bob Manardo and Eddie Floyd worked together in a Detroit jewelry store and decided to form a vocal group. Bob drafted his friend Tom Shetler and Eddie brought in Arnett Robinson. A local street singer, Willie Schofield, made it a quintet that Arnett dubbed the Falcons. The group had no idea there were previous Falcons groups that recorded for Regent ("How Blind Can You Be," 1951), Savoy ("It's You I Miss," 1953), Flip ("Stay Mine," 1954), and Cash ("I Miss You Darling," 1955).

The lineup read Floyd (lead), Manardo (first tenor), Robinson (second tenor), Shetler (baritone), and Schofield (bass). Manardo and Shetler were white and the others black. This group surfaced years before the same racial combination showed up in THE DEL-VIKINGS and THE MARCELS.

The group rehearsed incessantly and was very serious about their singing. Eddie introduced the Falcons to his uncle, Robert West, owner of the Lupine and Flick labels, who arranged a few bookings and signed them to Chicago's Mercury Records for one solid doo wop rocker in a CLEFTONES (Gee)/MOONLIGHTERS (Checker) style with a sax solo and a driving cha-cha beat, titled "Baby That's It."

By 1957 they'd moved over to Ewart Abner's Falcon label for "Now That It's Over" and the rhythmic, harmony-filled flip "My Only Love."

Changes were now occurring: Manardo was drafted, Shetler volunteered, and Robinson left, all in the space of a month. Baritone Bonny "Mack" Rice (of the Five Scalders, Drummond) replaced Shetler, Lance Finnie took over first tenor, and Joe Stubbs joined as the new lead singer.

The group now began leaning more toward gospel and blues blended with modern R&B. Singles with Kudo and Silhouette went nowhere so West finally decided to put them on his own Flick label. The first issue was a song written by Schofield, Finnie, and West that would initiate some changes in rhythm and blues music.

Released in early 1959, "You're So Fine," with its raw, bouncy, funky, shuffle beat and Joe Stubbs's rough-edged vocal, took the public by storm. Flick made a quick deal with United Artists' Unart label for both the group and the release of the single. *Billboard*'s March 14th review gave it four stars, commenting, "The group comes through with the authentic church sound on this pulsating effort, sung with feeling by the strong lead with help from the group. It could grab coins." It did, charting number two R&B April 6th and number 17 Pop.

Their next charter came from Chess Records, trying to capitalize on the Unart hit by repeating the title melody of "You're So Fine" in the chorus of "Just for Your Love" (#26 R&B, late 1959). The group had a few sides on the Unart parent label, United Artists, making noise only with "The Teacher" (#18 R&B), with another strong Stubbs lead.

Their last UA issue was "Working Man's Song." By now, Stubbs had left (later going on to sing on occasion with his brother Levi's group, THE FOUR TOPS, as well as the Contours and the Originals), replaced by a 19-year-old from Prattville, Alabama, named Wilson Pickett.

He did the lead vocal on their 1962 hit "I Found a Love" (#75 Pop, #6 R&B), but before the year was over the group found West farming them out to another label (Atlantic) to further capitalize on the success he'd built.

None of the three Atlantic sides drew much interest and when Schofield was drafted in 1963, the group disbanded.

Robert West wasn't about to let the golden goose get cooked, however, so he took Carlis "Sonny" Monroe, Johnny Alvin, Frank Holt, and James Gibson, known collectively as the Fabulous Playboys, and made them the Falcons. They sounded pretty good, too, especially on the loose, breezy jazz-blues rhythm ballad, "Standing on Guard" (#107 Pop, #29 R&B, fall 1966). That incarnation of the group died off in the late '60s. Bonny Mack Rice became the new Falcons' road manager and then started his own solo career as Sir Mack Rice, hitting with "Mustang Sally" (#101 Pop, #15 R&B, Blue Rock, 1965). Montgomery, Alabama-born Eddie Floyd went on to his own solo success as a staple of the Stax label scoring with 18 R&B charters (13 of which crossed to Pop) that included "I've Never Found a Girl" (#40 Pop, #2 R&B, 1968), "Bring It on Home to Me" (#17 Pop, #4 R&B, 1968), and his classic "Knock on Wood" (#28 Pop, #1 R&B, 1966). Wilson Pickett became the most famous ex-Falcon with 49 R&B chart singles between 1963 to 1987, 40 of which went Pop (his biggest successes with Atlantic were from 1965 through 1972). He turned out such soul standards as "Funky Broadway" (#8 Pop, #1 R&B, 1967), "I'm a Midnight Mover" (#24 Pop, #6 R&B, 1968), "Don't Let the Green Grass Fool Ya" (#17 Pop, #2 R&B, 1971), and "In the Midnight Hour" (#21 Pop, #1 R&B, 1965). He also did a version of "Mustang Sally" that beat out his old singing partner Rice (#23 Pop, #6 R&B, 1966).

THE FALCONS

A SIDE/B SIDE	LABEL/CAT NO	DATE
Baby That's It / This Day	Merc 70940	8/56
Can This Be Christmas / Sent Up	Silh 521	1957
Now That It's Over / My Only Love	Falcon 1006	12/57
This Heart Of Mine / Romania	Kudo 661	1958

A SIDE/B SIDE	LABEL/CAT NO	DATE
You're So Fine /		
Goddess Of Angels	Flick 001	1959
You're So Fine /		
Goddess Of Angels	Unart 2013	3/59
You Must Know I Love You /		
That's What I Aim To Do	Flick 008	1959
Just For Your Love /		
This Heart Of Mine	Chess 1743	11/59
You're Mine / Country Shack	Unart 2022	1959
The Teacher / Waiting For You	UA 229	1960
I + Love + You / Wonderful Love	UA 255	1960
Workin' Man's Song /		
Pow: You're In Love	UA 289	1960
I Found A Love / Swim	LuPn 1003	1962
Lah-Tee-Lah-Tah / Darling	Atln 2153	6/62
Take This Love I've Got / Let's Kiss		
And Make Up	Atln 2179	2/63
Oh Baby / Fine Fine Girl	Atln 2207	10/63
Lonely Knights / Has It Happened		
To You	LuPn 1020	1964
I Must Love You / Love, Love, Love	BgWl 321,2	1966
Standing On Guard /		
I Can't Help It	BgWl 1967	1966

The Five Crowns

"Unique with a mystique" were the Five Crowns, one of hundreds of Harlem rhythm and blues vocal groups of the '50s. Unlike most of the others, however, they became a rags-to-riches success.

The quintet sang on stoops, street corners, and in the dimly lit schoolyard of Wadleigh Junior High School on 115th Street between Seventh and Eighth Avenues. Formed in 1952, the collection included Wilbur "Yunkie" Paul (lead); the three Clark brothers, James "Poppa," Claudie "Nicky," and John "Sonny Boy"; and baritone/bass Doc Green. All but Doc were tenors, giving them a unique sound; the mystique came from their obscure and now highly prized single records issued starting in late 1952.

Influenced by THE FIVE KEYS, THE ORIOLES, and THE RAVENS, the Five Crowns were a raw, unschooled group when they signed to Rainbow Records in July 1952.

Their first single, the blues-based ballad "You're My Inspiration," was their most successful single. Issued in October it reached number nine R&B in New York and number eight in Philadelphia.

Two more singles in November and December sold poorly (including an R&B version of Joni James's "Why Don't You Believe Me").

Their second single, "Who Can Be True," did so badly it was only issued on 78 RPM. (Singles of the time were issued first on 78 then, if successful, on 45.)

Their fourth Rainbow release, in March 1953, was "Alone Again," a solid ballad that went nowhere.

After a dispute with Rainbow's boss Eddie Heller, the group moved to Hy Weiss's Old Town label while he was still working as a salesman for Cosnat Record Distributing in July 1953. Two unheralded but now expensive collectors' items were issued ("You Could Be My Love" and "Lullabye of the Bells") and the group went back to Rainbow for their best recording as the Five Crowns, "You Came to Me," released in 1955 on Rainbow's Riviera affiliate.

Later in 1955 the group broke up, dissatisfied with its sales. Doc formed a new Five Crowns with Elsbeary Hobbs on bass and did one single for Gee called "Do You Remember."

By the end of 1955 the Five Crowns were Wilbur Paul, James Clark, Jessie Facing, Doc Green, and Elsbeary Hobbs. Benjamin Nelson replaced Clark and they did one single for Transworld which wound up issued on Caravan ("I Can't Pretend") in 1955.

In 1956 Rainbow issued "You Came to Me" under the Five Crowns name and then inexplicably reissued it with the same record number but credited to the Duvals.

By 1958 the Five Crowns had dropped the "Five" and reorganized with Nelson, Green, and Hobbs joined by originals James and Nicky Clark and newcomer Charlie Thomas, making the group a first-time sextet. During the six off-and-on years of the Five Crowns, Doc had also sung with the Five Willows and Poppa Clark with THE CADILLACS while Nicky had done some work with THE HARPTONES. Wilbur Paul would later sing with the Harptones. But in 1958 Nelson, Green, Hobbs, James Clark, and Thomas (Nicky was gone) had a date with destiny. They recorded the one and only record issued on Doc Pomus's R&B label, "Kiss and Make Up," a rhythm and blues rocker that enabled them to perform at the Apollo Theatre one night on the same bill with the Drifters. The group performed so well they inspired Drifters manager George Treadwell to fire his group. For the rest of the story see THE DRIFTERS. Sneak preview: Benjamin Nelson eventually became known as Ben E. King.

THE FIVE CROWNS

A SIDE/B SIDE	LABEL/CAT NO	DATE
You're My Inspiration / A Star	Rnbw 179	10/52
Who Can Be True / $19.50 Bus	Rnbw 184	11/52
Keep It A Secret /		
Why Don't You Believe Me	Rnbw 202	12/52
Alone Again /		
I Don't Have To Hunt No More	Rnbw 206	3/53
You Could Be My Love /		
Good Luck Darlin'	OldTn 790	1953
Lullaby Of The Bells /		
Later, Later Baby	OldTn 792	2/54
You Came To Me / Ooh Wee Baby	Rvra 990	2/55
God Bless You /		
Do You Remember	Gee 1001	11/55
I Can't Pretend / Popcorn Willy	Trswld 717	1956
You Came To Me / Ooh Wee Baby	Rnbw 335	1956

The Crowns

Kiss And Make Up /		
I'll Forget About You	RNB 6901	1958

The Five Discs

One of the East Coast's first integrated groups, the Five Discs had little success during their active days, but when the oldies radio boom hit in the late '60s, they finally became revered for one classic street-corner song and a classic street-corner sound.

The group came together in the Bedford-Stuyvesant section of Brooklyn, New York, in 1954 with Joe Barsalona (baritone), Tony Basile (second tenor), Paul Albano (first tenor), and Joe Brocco (lead). They practiced in front of 138 McDougal Street, called themselves the Flames, and found inspiration in THE PARAGONS (Winley) and the Royaltones (Old Town), two other neighborhood groups.

The Flames began as an all-white Italian group, but two members of the Love Notes, an all-black sextet, came up the block when their group disbanded. The pair of Mario deAndrade and Andrew Jackson were idolized by the Flames, and a quick reshuffling resulted in a new lineup of Mario (lead), Paul (first tenor), Tony (second tenor), Joe (baritone), and Andrew (bass). The group practiced everywhere, from street corners, alleys, and rooftops to subway stations (like Brooklyn's echo-filled Fulton Street stop) and classrooms at Junior High School 73.

Mario taught the others group harmony and helped them develop the sound they would maintain through the coming years and numerous member changes. Their first performance was on Valentine's Day, 1956, at the school. They recorded a few demos at New York City's Bell Sound including the deAndrade-penned "I Remember," a model of street-corner doo wop if there ever was one.

The group canvassed the New York independent labels in the Brill Building at 1650 Broadway including Hull, Gone, and Old Town, but they eventually concluded that, although people seemed to like them, no one wanted an interracial group. No one, that is, until they met songwriter Billy Martin, who brought record men Gene and Bob Schwartz to see the group perform at Junior High School 73. The Flames were signed to the Schwartz brothers' Emge label (their famous Laurie label had not yet come into being) and were put in the studio to record "I Remember."

Unlike most sessions of the time in which the lead and background were cut concurrently, the group did their vocals first and Mario came in a week later to do lead. Right after the session, the group sat on Paul's stoop bouncing around new monikers when Paul's sister suggested they name themselves after the slang word for records. Thus the Five Flames became the Five Discs.

Emge issued "I Remember" in 1958 from its 1674 Broadway stronghold, and the song rapidly became an East Coast radio favorite. It reached number two in Boston and number 28 in New York, but, typically, the Schwartzes had by now launched Laurie Records and DION AND THE BELMONTS and couldn't afford to promote both groups. This, combined with label credits that listed Joe Abarno as a songwriter (Abarno was actually their neighbor/manager whose real profession was an ambulance driver) and the group had ample reason for frustration. The Five Discs, now playing gigs in the Northeast with acts like THE AQUATONES and THE TEDDY BEARS, pressured Emge to lease the record to an interested Vik Records (an affiliate of RCA) who issued it and promptly went broke.

One single for the miniscule Dwain label ("My Chinese Girl" in 1959) and the group was justifiably ready for some changes.

Meanwhile, Rust Records, a Laurie affiliate, issued "I Remember" in 1960 for the song's third release on three labels in two years.

In that same year Mario and Andy left and were replaced by Lenny Hutter (the Chalets, "Fat Fat Mommio," Dart, 1961) on lead and John Russell on bass. The group was once again all white. Billy Martin recorded "Come on Baby" in 1961 on his

Yale label. It went nowhere and Lenny Hutter left soon after.

Enter John Carbone, possibly the best lead they ever had, to record two tremendous deAndrade songs, "Adios" and "My Baby Loves Me."

Al Brown of the Paragons had brought Barsalona and company to Andy Leonetti (who had the Paragons on his Tap label). Leonetti seized the moment and put the Five Discs on wax for his Calo affiliate. "Adios," a rockin' doo wopper with bouncing bass, flying falsetto, and soaring four-part harmony had such a contagious sound that even its tempo mistakes and clashing sax play couldn't mar the record. Its failure to chart can only be chalked up to Calo's lack of promotion.

The Five Discs next moved to Cheer Records, part of the Blast label, with new bass Charlie DiBella taking over for Russell. The raucous "Never Let You Go," with the zaniest intro since THE MARCELS' "Blue Moon," was issued around the time new lead Eddie Parducci (the DeLVons) joined.

Eddie's DeLVons, from Eastern Parkway, included young Vito Balsamo, who would soon stray south to Church Avenue and begin singing with a group that would become VITO AND THE SALUTATIONS.

"Never Let You Go" was Murray the K's "Boss Record of the Week" on WINS, peaking at number 28 in New York soon after.

Trying for a change of luck, the group became the Boyfriends and signed for one single on Kapp titled "Let's Fall in Love."

By 1965, DiBella, Albano, and Basile had seen enough; with replacements the group became Parducci (lead), Donnie LaRuffa (first tenor), Frank Arnone (second tenor), and the ever-present Barsalona (baritone).

In 1968 (two years before Tony Orlando gave up publishing for stardom as Tony Orlando and Dawn) the Five Discs/Boyfriends became Dawn on Rust for a remake of Sam Cooke's "Bring It on Home to Me."

In 1972, a Hunter College doo wop extravaganza brought NORMAN FOX AND THE ROB BOYS, THE BOP CHORDS, NINO AND THE EBBTIDES, Vito and the Salutations, THE BLUE NOTES, and the Schoolboys together with Parducci, Barsalona, Albano, Arnone, and DiBella as the Five Discs rock and rolled for one night before DiBella and Albano deserted again.

Their last recorded single, "Rock & Roll Revival," included the Dawn lineup with Mike Strippoli (bass) added. The quintet went out with the

company they had come in with 14 years before, Laurie Records.

In the early '90s, the original Five Discs were all still in the New York area. Mario deAndrade was in the computer industry and living in Roosevelt, Long Island, Andrew Jackson was in Brooklyn and working for the post office, Paul Albano was living in Lindenhurst, Long Island, and had retired from the New York City police force, Tony Basile was in banking and living on Long Island, and the man with the Five Discs for 37 years, Joe Barsalona, was in Queens working in maintenance.

The most recent group made its first trip to perform in California in the summer of 1991 at the Doo Wop Society Show. They were Eddie Parducci (lead), Paul Albano (first tenor), Jack Scandora (second tenor, Ricky and the Hallmarks, Amy Records, 1961—see THE BLUE STARS), Joe Barsalona (baritone), and Mike Strippoli (bass).

One of Brooklyn's finest, the Five Discs were carrying the legacy of fun rock and roll into the '90s.

THE FIVE DISCS

A SIDE/B SIDE	LABEL/CAT NO	DATE
I Remember / The World Is A Beautiful Place	Emge 1004	1958
I Remember / The World Is A Beautiful Place	Vik 0327	4/58
Roses / My Chinese Girl	Dwain 803	1959
Roses / My Chinese Girl	Dwain 6072	1959
I Remember / The World Is A Beautiful Place	Rust 5027	1960
I Don't Know / Come On Baby	Yale 243,4	1961
Adios / My Baby Loves Me	Calo 202	1961
Never Let You Go / That Was The Time	Cheer 1000	1962
Roses / My Chinese Girl	Mlmd 1002	2/64
The Boyfriends		
Let's Fall In Love / Oh Lana	Kapp 569	1964
Dawn		
Bring It On Home / Baby I Love You	Rust 5128	1968
The Five Discs		
Rock & Roll Revival / Gypsy Woman	Laurie 3601	1972
Mirror Mirror / Most Of All, I Wonder Why	CrysB 114	1978
Unchained Melody / The Shrine Of St. Cecilia	CrysB 120	1978
Playing A Game Of Love / Bells	CrysB 136	1980
This Love Of Ours / To The Fair	CrysB 141	1981

The Five Keys

One of the most popular, influential, and beautiful sounding R&B singing groups of the '50s, the Five Keys were not only a link between the gospel/pop units of the '40s and the later R&B and rock groups, they led by example, having hits in R&B, rock and roll, and pop before the decade was through.

The Keys formed from two sets of brothers, Rudy and Bernard West and Raphael and Ripley Ingram. Calling themselves the Sentimental Four, they practiced in their local church in Newport News, Virginia, and on the streets of Jefferson Avenue and 25th Street. The Huntington High School students originally sang gospel songs but segued into secular material around 1949 when Rudy was 17, Bernie 19, Ripley 19, and Raphael 18. The group did some touring in the late '40s with Miller's Brown-Skinned Models, an all-black revue that played fairs and carnivals. They garnered valuable on-the-job training and returned to Newport News to play talent shows for exposure and prize money.

The foursome won the Wednesday night amateur contest at the Jefferson Theatre three times, qualifying them for a trip to New York to compete in a similar event at the Apollo Theatre. They won that, too, beating over 30 other acts. Word of this superior vocal foursome spread during engagements that followed at the Royal Theatre and the Howard. Eddie Meisner, president of L.A.-based Aladdin Records, signed them in February 1951 but lost Raphael to the army before they could record. He was replaced by Rudy's classmate and member of the Avalons, Maryland Pierce, along with Dickie Smith.

The group now called themselves the Five Keys, three of whom were the most talented lead singers any group ever had. Dickie Smith was a soulful lead, Maryland Pierce had a fantastic blues sound, and Rudy West possessed a smooth, polished, clear-as-a-bell tenor.

On March 22, 1951, the Five Keys recorded five songs. "With a Broken Heart" b/w "Too Late" was released in April as their first single, receiving scattered airplay but setting the stage for their brilliant version of the 1936 Benny Goodman hit (#1), "Glory of Love."

Released in July, "Glory" charted on August 18th and became a number one R&B record by September, spending four weeks on top. The Keys' captivating harmonies helped make "Glory" an eventual million seller and put them on the cross-country tour circuit for years to come. In December, Aladdin issued "It's Christmastime" as a follow-up single. Releasing a Christmas record after a number one hit was like not issuing anything; few Christmas records ever last longer than the month of December and this single was no exception.

The Keys had 10 more single releases between 1952 and 1953, but none cracked the hit lists though many, such as "Red Sails in the Sunset," "My Saddest Hour," "These Foolish Things," and "Serve Another Round," would have with more promotion, and they were all great listening.

By 1953 Rudy and Dickie were army bound, replaced by Ulysses Hicks and Ramon Loper.

The Keys' first release of 1954, "Someday Sweetheart," recorded on October 9, 1952, was a stunning pop/blues ballad that apparently couldn't gain the attention of its own label, let alone radio, although *Billboard* described it as a "pop evergreen sold with taste, with some fine tenor lead work. Best cut by the group in a while."

With their contract at Aladdin coming to an end in 1954, Keys manager Sol Richfield signed the group to RCA's Groove label, cutting four sides that included "I'll Follow You" b/w "Lawdy Miss Mary" in July 1954. He then obtained a better deal with Capitol, but when RCA found out they pulled the DJ copies of "I'll Follow You" off the market, making it one of the rarest of vocal group records (only one copy is known to exist). Richfield then ran into a problem when his new lead, Ulysses Hicks, died after recording their first single "Ling, Ting, Tong" for Capitol (Maryland on lead, Ripley and Ulysses on tenor, Ramon on baritone, and Bernie on bass). The group had to replace him quickly; they reportedly reached out to HARPTONES member Willie Winfield, the young cousin of Dickie Smith, a big fan of Rudy West. When the Harptones' career started to take off, however, Willie returned to that group and sadly never recorded with the Five Keys.

"Ling, Ting, Tong," aided by Capitol's savvy in the pop market, hit *Billboard*'s Top 100 a week before it hit the R&B charts on January 1, 1955. A catchy combination of rock, novelty, and R&B, "Ling, Ting, Tong" and its "Tie-sa-moke-um-boot-a-yay" background (one of the weirdest until the Quinns recorded "Hong Kong" in 1957, which is still undergoing translation 35 years later), became a number five R&B hit and hit number 28 on the Pop 100. That success led to an appearance on the famed Ed Sullivan show.

Rudy West returned in time to be a part of one of their all-time best sellers, the classic "Close Your Eyes." With Maryland on lead, Rudy echoing him, and the other Keys smoothly and elegantly harmonizing, the Chuck Willis-penned "Close Your Eyes" was a ballad that every generation pulls out, dusts off, and redefines for its own time (Peaches and Herb had a number eight hit version in 1967). The Keys' recording went to number five R&B in the spring of 1955 but surprisingly never crossed over to pop. From this point on in their Capitol career the group aimed more toward pop, and records like "The Verdict" (sounding like an updated INK SPOTS ballad) were meant to appeal to the masses. This cut only got the attention of the R&B listeners, however, reaching number 13 in the summer of 1955.

Excellent performances like the doo wop rhythm ballad "I Wish I'd Never Learned to Read" went unnoticed altogether. In January 1956 "You Broke the Rules of Love" came out of Capitol's cupboards and prompted *Billboard*'s January 28th reviewer to write, "The group sells solidly on an appealing ballad with a steady pulsating beat. This has plenty of play potential and could break Pop as well." It didn't, but that same week Aladdin tried to take advantage of the Keys' overall R&B popularity by issuing "Story of Love" b/w "Serve Another Round." "Sentimental hymn of love is sung with feeling by the group," commented *Billboard* on the A side. "They set a fine mood in this one, a waxing out of their former association with Aladdin." About the B side, the reviewer wrote, "The Keys have an interesting side here and it should win plenty of airplay if promoted." Of course, it wasn't, and the quintet had to wait until Capitol's July release of their Ivory Joe Hunter/Clyde Otis-penned ballad "Out of Sight, Out of Mind" for the pop audience to finally take notice. Ironically, what marred this record the most (a syrupy female background chorus almost totally obscuring the Keys' own harmonies) was what legitimized it for the Pat Boone radio fraternity to the tune of number 23 Pop, their biggest hit ever and a million seller.

The follow-up was a Roy Alfred/Abner Silver song, "Wisdom of a Fool," and though the now-obligatory female chorus was still evident, one could more clearly hear the Keys' background behind Rudy's crystal-clear lead. "Wisdom" went to number 35 Pop, but by now their records were predictably losing their R&B base. Except for "Let There Be You" in the spring of 1957 (#69 Pop), the Keys couldn't chart for Capitol any longer.

By 1958 Rudy had lost his desire to tour and retired from the scene. The group then signed with King Records in mid-1959 and now consisted of Rudy's replacement Dickie Threat (lead and tenor),

Maryland (lead and tenor), Ramon Loper (tenor), Dickie Smith (baritone), and Bernie West (bass). They recorded nine singles for the Cincinnati label, the best of which was "I Took Your Love for a Toy." Around the same time Rudy did an excellent version on King of THE PASSIONS' recent single "Just to Be with You," with a strong uncredited white-sounding doo wop vocal group.

In 1962, three-fifths of the Keys (Rudy, Bernie, and Dickie Smith) along with Willie Friday and John Boyd recorded "Out of Sight, Out of Mind" for Segway Records of New York, and this time there was no female syrup to cover up the song and the group.

In 1965 Rudy and a new collection of Keys recorded "No Matter" for Inferno, and various combinations of members toured through the oldies revival of the late '60s and early '70s.

By the mid-'60s Ripley, Bernie, and Dick were gone from the group. Gene Moore became the slow-song lead and Ray Haskiss and Daytill Jones replaced the others.

On March 24, 1973, Rudy and the Keys recorded several sides for Landmark Records including "Goddess of Love." With some time left at the session's end, *Bim Bam Boom*'s editor convinced the group to do their two classics a cappella, and "Close Your Eyes" and "Out of Sight, Out of Mind" became record number 116 in 1973, a beautiful final offering to Five Keys fans.

By the mid-'70s Ramon Loper was a shoe salesman in New York and Maryland Pierce was in the vicinity of Ohio. Bernie West was working in a Virginia shipyard and Rudy went to work for the post office in Hampton, Virginia.

Rudy kept on singing and was with a new Keys combination at New York's Radio City Music Hall on October 3, 1981, when vocal groups of the '50s performed for the first time at the prestigious 50-year-old hall in the Royal New York Doo Wop Show.

In 1989 Rudy and the Keys issued their most recent recordings, "Miracle Moments of Love" and, later that year, "I Want You for Christmas."

Influencing the Harptones, THE CADILLACS, THE SOLITAIRES, THE HEARTBEATS, and countless others including many white groups, the Five Keys were a vocal group for all time.

THE FIVE KEYS

A SIDE/B SIDE	LABEL/CAT	DATE
With A Broken Heart / Too Late	Aldn 3085	4/51
The Glory Of Love /		
Hucklebuck With Jimmy	Aldn 3099	7/51

A SIDE/B SIDE	LABEL/CAT NO	DATE
It's Christmastime /		
Old MacDonald	Aldn 3113	12/51
Yes Sir, That's My Baby /		
Old MacDonald	Aldn 3118	1/52
Darling / Goin' Downtown	Aldn 3119	2/52
Red Sails In The Sunset /		
Be Anything But Be Mine	Aldn 3127	4/52
Mistakes / How Long	Aldn 3131	5/52
I Hadn't Anyone Till You / Hold Me	Aldn 3136	7/52
I Cried For You /		
Serve Another Round	Aldn 3158	11/52
Can't Keep From Crying /		
Come Go My Bail, Louise	Aldn 3167	1/53
There Ought To Be A Law / Mama	Aldn 3175	3/53
I'll Always Be In Love With You /		
Rocking and Crying Blues	Aldn 3182	4/53
These Foolish Things /		
Lonesome Old Story	Aldn 3190	5/53
Teardrops In Your Eyes /		
I'm So High	Aldn 3204	9/53
My Saddest Hour / Oh! Baby!	Aldn 3214	12/53
Someday Sweetheart /		
Love My Loving	Aldn 3228	3/54
Deep In My Heart / How Do		
You Expect Me To Get It	Aldn 3245	5/54
I'll Follow You / Lawdy Miss Mary	Grv 0031	8/54
My Love / Why, Oh Why	Aldn 3263	11/54
Ling, Ting, Tong / I'm Alone	Cap 2945	9/54
Close Your Eyes /		
Doggone It, You Did It	Cap 3032	1/55
The Verdict / We Make		
Um Pow Wow	Cap 3127	5/55
I Wish I'd Never Learned To Read /		
Don't You Know I Love You	Cap 3185	7/55
Gee Whittakers /		
Cause You're My Lover	Cap 3267	11/55
Story Of Love /		
Serve Another Round	Aldn 3312	1/56
What Goes On /		
You Broke The Rules Of Love	Cap 3318	1/56
She's The Most /		
I Dreamt I Dwelt In Heaven	Cap 3392	4/56
Peace And Love /		
My Pigeon's Gone	Cap 3455	6/56
Out Of Sight, Out Of Mind /		
That's Right	Cap 3502	7/56
Wisdom Of A Fool /		
Now Don't That Prove I Love You	Cap 3597	12/56
Let There Be You / Tiger Lily	Cap 3660	3/57
Four Walls / It's A Groove	Cap 3710	5/57
This I Promise /		
The Blues Don't Care	Cap 3738	6/57
The Face Of An Angel /		
Boom-Boom	Cap 3786	8/57
Do Anything / It's A Cryin' Shame	Cap 3830	10/57
Just For A Thrill / The Gypsy	Cap T-828	1957
From Me to You / Whippety Whirl	Cap 3861	12/57
With All My Love / You're For Me	Cap 3948	3/58

A SIDE/B SIDE	LABEL/CAT NO	DATE
Emily Please / Handy Andy	Cap 4009	7/58
One Great Love / Really-O Trul-O	Cap 4092	11/58
I Took Your Love For A Toy /		
Ziggus	King 5251	8/59
Dream On / Dancing Senorita	King 5273	10/59
How Can I Forget You /		
I Burned Your Letter	King 5302	1/60
Gonna Be Too Late / Rosetta	King 5330	3/60
I Didn't Know /		
No Says My Heart	King 5358	6/60
Valley Of Love / Bimbo	King 5398	9/60
You Broke The Only Heart /		
That's What You're Doing To Me	King 5446	1/61
Stop Your Crying /		
Do Something For Me	King 5496	5/61
Out Of Sight, Out Of Mind /		
You're The One	SgWy 1008	1962
I Can't Escape From You /		
I'll Never Stop Loving You	King 5877	6/64

Rudy West and the Five Keys

No Matter / Hey Girl	Inf 4500	1965

The Five Keys

Goddess Of Love / Stop	Lndmk 101	5/73
Close Your Eyes /		
Out Of Sight, Out Of Mind		
(a cappella)	BBB 116	1973
Miracle Moments Of Love /		
When Was The Last Time	ClsArt 112	1989
I Want You For Christmas /		
Express Yourself Back Home	ClsArt 115	1989

The 5 Royales

Southern rhythm and blues was well-represented on the charts in the early and mid-'50s thanks to the 5 Royales. The group had a few similarities to THE LARKS: they both came from North Carolina, both started as gospel groups, and both wound up recording for New York's Apollo Records. Musically, however, the Larks were ballad specialists while the 5 Royales were a raunchy blues group, with risqué *double entendres* like the "Laundromat Blues" lyric that brags, "My baby's got the best washing machine, the best washing machine in town, just relax and take it easy, while her machine goes round and round."

With these as typical Royales lyrics, it's hard to believe the quintet started out as the Royal Sons Gospel Group of Winston-Salem, North Carolina, in the 1940s. The fivesome had Lowman and Clarence Pauling, Otto Jeffries, Johnny Tanner, and William Samuels. Activity centered around guitarist, songwriter, and bass Lowman Pauling, while Johnny Tanner usually sang their power-packed leads.

The Royal Sons delighted southern churchgoers for years until they decided to go north and try to record. They came upon Bess Berman and Carl LeBow's Apollo Records at their 457 West 45th Street digs in New York City and started recording gospel as the Royal Sons Quintet. LeBow became their mentor, renaming them the 5 Royales for the R&B market.

Their first single was "Give Me One More Chance," a spiritual-turned R&B with some word changes. The group then went through personnel adjustment and by the September 1952 release of "You Know, I Know," the members were Johnny Tanner (lead), Jimmy Moore (tenor), Obadiah Carter (tenor), Eugene Tanner (baritone/bass and brother of Johnny), and Lowman Pauling (bass and guitar).

"You Know, I Know" became a local hit, setting the table for their December 1952 single, "Baby Don't Do It." Those beautiful red plastic, blue-labeled 45s sailed right on to black radio; by January 24, 1953, the song was at number one R&B, staying on the charts for 16 weeks.

Combining their gospel vocal styling with great visual flair in performance, the 5 Royales were as influential as THE CLOVERS and THE DOMINOES on the new wave of R&B artists that surfaced in the mid-'50s, from THE ROBINS to James Brown and his Famous Flames.

Their next 45, "Help Me Somebody," went to number one for five weeks in the spring of 1953 and for 15 weeks remained among the nation's most popular R&B records. It also topped the Jukebox chart for five weeks while its flip ("Crazy, Crazy, Crazy") reached number five Jukebox and number seven Best Seller.

The group performed one nighters at a frantic pace and by early 1953 became aware that the Royals of Detroit were impersonating them. On January 7, 1952, Apollo hit the Royals with a $10,000 lawsuit in Columbus, Georgia, enjoining them from using the 5 Royales' name and picture.

Starting on January 16, 1953, the real 5 Royales played the Apollo for the first time, appearing for a full week with Willy Mabon and Gene Ammons. The group did the theatre circuit with such artists as Little Esther, Jimmy Forrest, Sonny Stitt, THE FLAMINGOS, Woody Herman's Orchestra, Lulu Reed, THE PENGUINS, Memphis Slim, Dakota

Staton, and the Tab Smith Combo, with whom they toured regularly through the South.

As it was for most R&B acts, touring was fraught with peril for the 5 Royales. On August 13, 1953, while enroute to Tyler, Texas, there was an accident involving the car that contained Charlie Ferguson and his All-Girl Band (the Royales' accompanists on their charting songs). Their 19-year-old bass player was killed and Charlie was critically injured (though he survived).

In that same month their record "Too Much Lovin'" reached number four on the R&B Best Seller lists and number five on the nation's R&B jukeboxes. The flip, "Laundromat Blues," was one of the group's most popular songs in live performance and seemed for a while to be the A side due to its extensive East Coast play.

The 5 Royales began 1954 with a bang as "I Do" reached number six with the able assistance of Charlie Ferguson's Orchestra.

Further confusion was added to the name game when another group from Detroit was found to be calling themselves the Royals (Venus Records). They quickly changed to the Royal Jokers and signed with Atco.

Carl LeBow had been the group's chief supporter at Apollo. He moved over to King Records in late 1953 and by April 1954 was wooing them with King's Syd Nathan. (That same month the Detroit Royals changed their name to THE MIDNIGHTERS.) The 5 Royales soon signed with King, citing royalty disputes with Berman as the reason for the defection. A lawsuit ensued in which Apollo claimed they had rights to the 5 Royales until 1956. King won, but what they and the 5 Royales actually gained was dubious: the group, still turning out fine R&B records, only charted twice more out of 41 singles issued through 1965. Those singles were "Tears of Joy" (#9, July 15, 1957) and "Think" (#9, September 1957), the latter becoming their first national pop record at number 66.

A January 21, 1956, *Billboard* review of "Right Around the Corner" was typical of the response to the Royales even though record sales were slow: "The boys contribute a bouncy, good-natured vocal interpretation of a catchy rhythm novelty with an infectious beat and slightly suggestive lyrics. The disc should grab off considerable jukebox play and could very well go pop."

Their second and last pop charter was the renowned classic "Dedicated to the One I Love," which reached number 81 Pop in January and February 1961 and later was a hit for THE SHIRELLES

(#83, 1959 and #3, 1961) and THE MAMAS AND THE PAPAS (#2 Pop, 1967).

The Lowman Pauling classic was actually taken from a Chester Mayfield composition called "I Don't Want You to Go." Who's Chester Mayfield? He was the lead singer of a Winston-Salem, North Carolina, group called THE CASANOVAS who were also signed to Apollo in 1954. One of the members of the Casanovas was former Royal Sons member William Samuels, who was also Lowman Pauling's brother-in-law. It doesn't take a long stretch of the imagination to figure out how Lowman heard Chester's song and revised it.

As with the Shirelles' version, the 5 Royales' "Dedicated" was issued twice, once in December 1957 when it did little (although that's how the Shirelles first heard it), and once in January 1961 when it charted.

The group then left King, signing with several labels while looking for that elusive hit. They even rerecorded "Baby Don't Do It" twice (Todd, 1963 and Smash, 1964) but never again charted.

The group broke up in the mid-'60s and returned to Winston-Salem. Clarence Pauling became Clarence Paul, joining Motown Records as a producer and A&R director; he was instrumental in the development of Marvin Gaye and Stevie Wonder. Lowman Pauling died in 1974.

THE 5 ROYALES

A SIDE/B SIDE	LABEL/CAT NO	DATE
Too Much Of A Little Bit / Give Me One More Chance	Apollo 434	1951
You Know I Know / Courage To Love	Apollo 441	9/52
Baby Don't Do It / Take All Of Me	Apollo 443	12/52
Help Me Somebody / Crazy Crazy Crazy	Apollo 446	4/53
Laundromat Blues / Too Much Lovin'	Apollo 448	8/53
I Want To Thank You / All Righty!	Apollo 449	10/53
Good Things / I Do	Apollo 452	1/54
Cry Some More / I Like It Like That	Apollo 454	4/54
Let Me Come Back Home / What's That	Apollo 458	7/54
Behave Yourself / I'm Gonna Run It Down	King 4740	8/54
Monkey Hips And Rice / Devil With The Rest	King 4744	10/54
One Mistake / School Girl	King 4762	12/54
Six O'Clock In The Morning / With All Your Heart	Apollo 467	1/55

A SIDE/B SIDE	LABEL/CAT NO	DATE
You Didn't Learn It Home / Every Dog Has His Day	King 4770	1/55
How I Wonder / Mohawk Squaw	King 4785	3/55
When I Get Like This / I Need Your Lovin' Baby	King 4806	6/55
Women About To Make Me Go Crazy / Do Unto You	King 4819	8/55
Someone Made You For Me / I Ain't Gettin' Caught	King 4830	10/55
Right Around The Corner / When You Walked Thru The Door	King 4869	1/56
My Wants For Love / I Could Love You	King 4901	3/56
Come On And Save Me / Get Something Out Of It	King 4952	7/56
Just As I Am / Mine Forever More	King 4973	10/56
Thirty Second Lover / Tears Of Joy	King 5032	5/57
Think / I'd Better Make A Move	King 5053	1957
Say It / Messin' Up	King 5082	10/57
Dedicated To The One I Love / Don't Be Ashamed	King 5098	2/57
The Feeling Is Real / Do The Cha Cha Cherry	King 5131	5/58
Double Or Nothing / Tell The Truth	King 5141	6/58
Don't Let It Be In Vain / The Slummer The Slum	King 5153	10/58
The Real Thing / Your Only Love	King 5162	1/59
Miracle Of Love / I Know It's Hard But It's Fair	King 5191	3/59
Wonder Where Your Love Has Gone / Tell Me You Care	King 5237	8/59
My Sugar Sugar / It Hurts Inside	King 5266	10/59
Don't Give No More Than You Can Take / I'm With You	King 5329	3/60
Why / Within My Heart	King 5357	6/60
Please, Please, Please / I Got To Know	HOTB 112	10/60
Dedicated To The One You Love / Miracle Of Love	King 5453	1/61
If You Don't Need Me / I'm Gonna Tell Them	HOTB 218	2/61
Not Going To Cry / Take Me With You Baby	HOTB 232	5/61
They Don't Know / Much In Need	HOTB 234	8/61
Goof Ball / Catch That Teardrop	HOTB 257	7/62
Much In Need / They Don't Know	Vee-Jay 412	1961
Help Me Somebody / Talk About My Woman	Vee-Jay 431	1962
Goof Ball / Catch That Teardrop	ABC 10348	1962
What's In The Heart / I Want It Like That	ABC 10368	9/62
I'm Standing In The Shadows / Doin' Everything	Todd 1086	1963
Baby Don't Do It / There's Somebody Over There	Todd 1088	10/63
Tears Of Joy / Dedicated To The One I Love	King 5756	1963

A SIDE/B SIDE	LABEL/CAT NO	DATE
I Need Your Lovin' Baby / Wonder Where Your Love Has Gone	King 5892	1964
Baby, Don't Do It / I Like It Like That	Smash 1936	9/64
Never Turn Your Back / Faith	Smash 1963	2/65

The Five Satins

One of the greatest rhythm and blues ballads of all time was a B side, and the Five Satins who recorded that B side, "In the Still of the Night," were actually only four Satins. But those Satins were undoubtedly one of the finest vocal groups of the '50s.

Fred Parris of 24 Sperry Street in New Haven, Connecticut, was expelled in 1953 from a vocal group known as the Canaries. The avid ball player (he once had a tryout with the Boston Braves) decided to form his own group and labeled them the Scarlets. The quintet of Hillhouse High School students included Sylvester Hopkins (first tenor), Nathaniel Mosely, Jr. (second tenor), Albert Denby (baritone), and William L. Powers (bass).

Since Fred wrote the songs the guys made him lead singer. They rehearsed under the influence of THE 5 ROYALES, THE CLOVERS, THE DOMINOES, and THE FIVE CROWNS. Fred was a particular fan of the Velvets and THE FOUR FRESHMEN.

As the group's leader, Parris was saddled with the responsibility of finding them a record label, but the 17-year-old had little idea how to go about it. He traveled to New York without so much as a tape in hopes of finding Red Robin Records (home of the Velvets), which was operated out of a record shop at 301 West 125th Street in Harlem. First he encountered Bob Shad, a record shop owner who also owned the Jax label (Bobby Hall and the Kings). Shad sent Fred down the block where he met Red Robin proprietor Bobby Robinson. When the Scarlets lead told Robinson of his group he got the same response elicited from Shad, which in effect was "go home and bring me a demo tape." When Fred did return with a tape of the self-penned "Dear One," Robinson still wasn't impressed, but his brother and partner Dan did like the group and convinced Robinson to record them.

In early spring of 1954 the Scarlets were given 15 minutes to cut "Dear One" and another ballad called "I've Lost." (This was done during the same session in which the Velvets spent over three hours

on what would become their last Red Robin single, "I Cried.")

"Dear One" had a classic rhythm and blues harmony sound. Fred's plaintive lead, shifting to falsetto riffing while the baritone and bass took over, helped make the record a New York hit in the spring of 1954. The flip, "I've Tried," was another solid ballad with more than a hint of the melody line from the 1948 Benny Goodman tune "Beyond the Sea."

The group got better with each release as December's "Love Doll" and the later "True Love" demonstrated. Even though "True Love" was almost a clone of "Dear One," the harmonies had a more confident sound.

Parris had his first hit as a writer with the B side, but not via the Scarlets. The rocker, "Cry Baby," was cut a year later by three moonlighting nurses from Bellevue Hospital called THE BONNIE SISTERS, reaching a healthy number 18 on the Pop charts.

The New Haven quintet was called by Uncle Sam in 1955 with the promise that they could stay together. Thus assured, the Scarlets foresaw a great time entertaining troops and officers. Instead, one member wound up in Alaska, one in Texas, another in Korea, and so on. After basic training in Texas the group returned to New York on leave and cut one farewell single for Red Robin called "Kiss Me." Fred was then stationed in Philadelphia and was able to return to New Haven for weekends. He formed a new group that included Lou Peebles (tenor), Ed Martin (baritone), Stanley Dortch (tenor), and Jim Freeman (bass). Fred wanted a new name since none of these new members had been in the Scarlets. He liked the idea of something soft and red like the Velvets and the Scarlets. The result: the Five Satins.

At around this time, New Haven teenager Marty Kugell, his partner Tom Zachariah, and their two-track tape recorder came together as a record label and asked the Satins to record for them. As Tom and Marty had no office, much less a studio, they hauled their precious two-track to a V.F.W. (Veterans of Foreign Wars) Post in New Haven on a hot summer day. The musicians never showed up (one rumor has it that their instruments fell off a truck), so they recorded the songs a cappella intending to add the music later. The songs were "All Mine" (written by Fred Parris) and "Rose Mary" (by Lou Peebles and Jim Freeman).

In an occurrence that could only happen in the imperfect world of 1950s rock and roll recording, the group left the hall door open in order to provide some ventilation, and toward the end of the beautiful ballad "All Mine" you can actually hear a truck rumbling—right on the finished record.

Music was later added to "Rose Mary" but not to "All Mine"; upon its release on Standard Records "All Mine" became the first rock and roll a cappella release. The sound was ahead of its time and few people ever heard it.

The group soon reorganized, with Peebles and Dortch out and Al Denby of the Scarlets in.

Fred came up with a rocker titled "The Jones Girl," but before the group could record again he was back at the army base in Philadelphia. One night he found himself on guard duty. At around 3 a.m., alone and pining for his sweetheart, Fred put down his rifle, picked up his pen, and wrote one of the greatest ballads of all time, "In the Still of the Night." After he returned to New Haven, he and the Satins went into the basement of St. Bernadette's church in East Haven on a December night in 1955 (this time the musicians showed up) and cut the two sides on Marty's trusty two-track. There were only four Satins on the date.

Standard put out "The Jones Girl" and its flip that spring, and when it started getting some New York reaction Herald Records prexy Al Silvers bought the masters and reissued them on his new Ember label. Meanwhile, Fred was in the studio on his last leave before being sent to Japan. At that time he recorded eight sides with the Satins including "Moonlight and I," "Sugar," "Oh Happy Day," and "Wonderful Girl."

By the summer, "Jones Girl" was getting some play but all of a sudden that B-side ballad with magical "sho doe" and "sho be doe" harmony started popping up on hundreds of radio stations. *Billboard*'s June 9th review of "The Jones Girl" called it an "enthusiastic vocal treatment of a bouncy rhythm opus with a strong solid beat." About "Still of the Night" they wrote, "The Satins chant with warm expressiveness on a smoothly paced ballad with dramatic lyrics."

On September 1, 1956, "In the Still of the Night" charted on *Billboard*'s R&B lists and one week later did the same on the Pop charts. The song has become such a symbol of the '50s that most listeners don't realize it never came close to being a number one record (except in New York and on various big-city charts); it only made it to number 24 Pop in the fall (#3 R&B). Still, its steady play on radio for over 35 years has made it a multi-million seller, though its author Fred Parris and the group were never honored with a gold record. It is usually among the top five songs on annual and holiday oldies shows and marathons.

While Fred was out guarding Japan, the label of "In the Still" was revised to read "(I'll Remember) In the Still of the Night" in order to differentiate it from Cole Porter's standard (now that the Satins' song was famous in its own right).

Two more beautiful ballads emerged on Ember: "Wonderful Girl" in late 1956 (with a bass player plucking on a cello since he showed up with the wrong instrument) and the Don Howard oldie "Oh Happy Day" in early 1957, but neither charted. Ember was running out of quality tracks to keep the Satins' name visible, so in May they added New Havenite Bill Baker on lead and sent him on tour with Freeman, Martin, newcomer Tommy Killebrew, and the Satins' pianist Jessie Murphy.

Meanwhile, to avoid boredom, Fred began singing with some army buddies in Japan when one guy brought in a copy of a record from the States. He started to teach everyone his version of it and chided Fred for singing a bass part that didn't blend with the record. The song was "In the Still of the Night," and Fred was having some fun singing the part the way he'd written it before it was recorded. When the guy found out who Fred was he never showed his face around the barracks again.

Back in the States, Bill Baker and company recorded Billy Dawn Smith's "To the Aisle." It took off in July 1957 and became another Five Satins standard, peaking at number 25 Pop (#5 R&B).

In 1958 Fred received his discharge, returned to New Haven, and formed yet another group with ex–Five Satins member Lou Peebles, ex-Scarlet Sylvester Hopkins, and former Starlarks (Ember) Richie Freeman and Wes Forbes. He called this group Fred Parris and the Scarlets and they recorded an excellent rhythm ballad titled "She's Gone" for Marty and Tom's Klik label (the label's small print read "Originally The Five Satins" directly below the name the Scarlets).

The Klik side didn't click, and since Marty didn't sell it to an active company there was no chance for promotion. Meanwhile, Bill Baker went on to sing with one of New Haven's best groups, THE CHESTNUTS ("Won't You Tell Me My Heart," Elgin, 1959).

Fred Parris and the Scarlets then became the Five Satins and moved to Ember for "A Night to Remember," a single that came and went with little play or support. Their next Ember release was "Shadows" (late 1959), a Parris-penned ballad and their strongest song since "She's Gone," but it only managed a number 87 Pop (#27 R&B). It also became their last R&B charter for 16 years as they began to lean more toward pop.

Ember then lent the Satins out to First Records for one single, the magnificent rhythm ballad "When Your Love Comes Along," with innovative "du wah wah" harmonies identical to those that showed up two years later in the Imaginations' "Hey You" (Musicmakers). Though this was a common practice in the '50s, try to imagine Sire Records lending Madonna out to a competing company today.

The Satins did three more Ember singles, the best being a splendid version of the number one 1944 Bing Crosby hit "I'll Be Seeing You," which reached number 79 on the Pop chart. The last Ember single ("Wishing Ring," 1961) wasn't really the Satins, as Fred and Lou were the only group members to show up for the session; three white musicians were drafted and taught the simplest of harmony parts. One of those musicians, the drummer Jerry Greenberg, later became president of Atlantic Records.

In 1960 the quintet joined Cub Records for "Your Memory," "A Beggar with a Dream," and "Can I Come Over Tonight" (THE VELOURS), but the label couldn't make them click. In 1961 Fred and company decided to keep making name changes until something stuck, so they became the Wildwoods ("When the Swallows Come Back to Capistrano," Caprice) and the New Yorkers, whose "Miss Fine" (Wall) reached number 69 Pop—not much recognition there for an act that's spent five years under another name, so they went back to the Five Satins for one side on United Artists ("On Lovers Island").

In 1962, the Five Satins signed with Bob Marcucci's Chancellor label for two singles, including a fine arrangement of "The Masquerade Is Over." The group then moved to the Warner Bros., Roulette, Lana, and Mama Sadie labels under their own name and to Checker and Green Sea as the Restless Hearts.

By 1971 the group was Fred, Wes, Richie, Jimmy Curtis of the Chestnuts (Elgin), and Corky Rogers of the Revalons (Pet). They recorded "Summer in New York" for RCA, and by 1972 were label shopping with two other sides, "Fate Has a Brother" and "He Ain't Heavy He's My Brother" (Hollies), produced by Five Satins fan Jay Warner.

In 1973 old New Haven mentor Marty Kugell hooked up with publisher Al Altman and the Satins to produce an ode to oldies that mentioned various groups and songs while slipping in a finale of "In the Still of the Night."

Two years later Kugell, Altman, and company were back at it for a soul LP on Buddah, and to counter radio aversion to anything older than their

disc jockey's morning donut, Fred renamed the group Black Satin. The 10-cut LP included a soulfully smooth version of "In the Still of the Night" and "Everybody Stand and Clap Your Hands" (#49), their first R&B chart single in 16 years.

With the oldies revival in full swing the Satins became a premier attraction, and following their November 22, 1969, rebirth in Richard Nader's Madison Square Garden Rock and Roll Revival show, they have been one of the most revered standard bearers of '50s music. They appeared in the movie *Let the Good Times Roll* doing a cappella renditions of "I'll Be Seeing You" and "In the Still."

In 1977 the group teamed with Southside Johnny and the Asbury Jukes for a solid cut on their *This Time It's for Real* LP, with "First Night." The group at that point was Fred, Richie, Jimmy, and Nate Marshall. Bill Baker formed Bill Baker and the Satins in around 1981 with three Hopkins brothers, Sylvester (former Scarlet and Satin), Carl, and Frank (formerly of the Chestnuts). In 1982 they cut another excellent version of "In the Still of the Night" b/w "Crying in the Chapel" on Clifton Records and continued to perform in the Connecticut area for years to come. In the mid-80s Baker's Satins included former members of the Modulations Harvey Potts, Jr., Anthony Hofler, and Octavio DeLeon. They recorded an LP in 1987 titled *I'll Be Seeing You*. No, it does not contain a version of "In the Still of the Night."

In 1982 Fred and company waxed another LP, this time as Fred Parris and the Satins on Electra, charting Pop for the first time in 21 years with a nostalgic look back on "Memories of Days Gone By," a medley that contained "Sixteen Candles," "Earth Angel," "A Thousand Miles Away," "Tears on My Pillow," "Since I Don't Have You," and guess which other song.

The group was still performing in the early '90s, and when Freddie held 60-second notes at the end of "I'll Be Seeing You," all was right with the world.

THE FIVE SATINS

A SIDE/B SIDE	LABEL/CAT NO	DATE
The Scarlets		
Dear One / I've Lost	RdRbn 128	5/54
Love Doll / Darling I'm Yours	RdRbn 133	2/55
True Love / Cry Baby	RdRbn 135	1955
Kiss Me / Indian Fever	RdRbn 138	9/55
The Five Satins		
All Mine / Rose Mary	Stndrd 100	2/56
In The Still Of The Night / The Jones Girl	Stndrd 200	3/56
In The Still Of The Night / The Jones Girl	Ember 1005	6/56

A SIDE/B SIDE	LABEL/CAT NO	DATE
Wonderful Girl / Weeping Willow	Ember 1008	1956
Oh Happy Day /		
Our Love Is Forever	Ember 1014	1957
To The Aisle / Wish I Had My Baby	Ember 1019	6/57
Our Anniversary / Pretty Baby	Ember 1025	9/57
A Million To One / Love		
With No Love In Return	Ember 1028	1957

Fred Parris and the Scarlets
She's Gone (With The Wind) /		
The Voice	Klik 7905	1958

The Five Satins
A Night To Remember /		
Senorita Lolita	Ember 1038	1958
Shadows / Toni My Love	Ember 1056	10/59
When Your Love Comes Along /		
Skippity Do	First 104	1959
I'll Be Seeing You /		
A Night Like This	Ember 1061	3/60
Your Memory / I Didn't Know	Cub 9071	6/60
Candlelight / The Time	Ember 1066	8/60
These Foolish Things /		
A Beggar With A Dream	Cub 9077	1960
Wishing Ring / Tell Me Dear	Ember 1070	1/61
Golden Earrings /		
Can I Come Over Tonight	Cub 9090	3/61

The New Yorkers
Miss Fine / Dream A Little Dream	Wall 547	4/61

The Wildwoods
When The Swallows Come Back		
To Capistrano / Heart Of Mine	Caprice 101	1961

The New Yorkers
Tears In My Eyes / A Little Bit	Wall 548	1961

The Five Satins
On Lovers' Island /		
Till The End	UA 368	1961
To The Aisle / Just To Be Near You	Msctn 1108	1961
The Masquerade Is Over /		
Raining In My Heart	Chnc 1110	1962
Downtown / Do You Remember	Chnc 1121	1962
All Mine / Rose Mary	TmsSq 4	1/63
Paradise On Earth /		
Monkey Business*	TmsSq 21	11/63
You Can Count On Me /		
Ain't Gonna Cry	Roul 4563	1964
Remember Me / Kangaroo	Wrnr 5367	6/63
Paradise On Earth /		
Monkey Business*	TmsSq 94	1964

Fred Parris and the Restless Hearts
Walk A Little Faster /		
No Use In Crying	Chkr 1108	4/65

The Five Satins
In The Still Of The Night /		
The Jones Girl	Lana 106	1965

Fred Parris and the Restless Hearts
A SIDE/B SIDE	LABEL/CAT NO	DATE
Bring It Home To Daddy /		
Land Of Broken Hearts	Atco 6439	9/66
Blushing Bride /		
Giving My Love To You	GrSea 106	1966
I'll Be Hanging On /		
I Can Really Satisfy	GrSea 107	1966
In The Still Of The Night '67 /		
Heck No (instrumental)	MamaS 1001	1967

The Five Satins
Summer In New York /		
Dark At The Top Of My Heart	RCA 74-0478	4/71
Very Precious Oldies /		
You Are Love	Kirsh 4251	12/73
Two Different Worlds /		
Love Is Such A Beautiful Thing	Kirsh 4252	5/74
The Voice / All Mine	NtTrn 901	1970
Wonder Why /		
No One Knows (a cappella)	TmMch 570	1970's
The Masquerade Is Over (a		
cappella) / Lonely Hearts	TmMch 571	1970's

Black Satin
Everybody Stand And Clap Your		
Hands / Hey There Pretty Lad	Buddah 477	1/75

The Five Satins
Everybody's Got A Home But Me /		
Heartache (Fred solo)	Sig 001	1990

* The Pharotones

The Five Sharps

The most widely sought rhythm and blues collectors' item of all time, "Stormy Weather," was recorded by a group that few people have heard of. Yet the Five Sharps were direct contributors to several successful vocal groups that followed.

Starting in 1952, a number of singers sang with the Jamaica, Queens, New York, group. Among them were Ronald Cussey (lead), Clarence Bassett (first tenor), Robert Ward (second tenor), Mickey Owens (bass), Johnny Jackson (baritone), and possibly Mickey Sorrence and Julius Brown, who also went under the name Julius McMichaels. James (Shep) Sheppard, later of THE HEARTBEATS, occasionally harmonized with the Sharps but did not record with them. Though one might expect their name to have come from music, the term "u sharp" was hip slang at the time, and since they thought they were sharp guys, they became the Five Sharps.

They were the first of the Jamaica High School groups to record (others were THE CLEFTONES, THE RIVILEERS, the Heartbeats, and the Harmonaires.) The group's main influences were THE MOONGLOWS, THE FIVE KEYS, and THE ORIOLES. They rehearsed songs like "Duck Butt Dottie" and a song Cussey and Bassett wrote called "Sleepy Cowboy."

Local shows at schools followed and the group eventually came in contact with Oscar Porter, a record producer who brought them to a Harlem recording facility to wax "Sleepy Cowboy" and the Arlen-Koehler standard "Stormy Weather." Porter arranged for the two sides to be issued on Jubilee; the group was thrilled to be on the label of their idols the Orioles.

In December 1952, "Stormy Weather" (Jubilee 5104) was issued and received some New York airplay from Hal Jackson and Dr. Jive. The consensus was that the record did not sell. Copies were few. Since the record company didn't give the singers any 78s, they each bought one. Robert Ward once stated that even friends and relatives didn't have any copies since "Nobody liked that record; nobody bought it." The recording itself was a slow blues version of the standard, with thunder, rain, and a soft piano intro leading to a melancholy performance by the Sharps. Hazy memories by group members are expected after the passage of many years, but the Sharps surpass most in this regard. Robert Ward, interviewed in 1974, stated that the group never made any personal appearances; in a 1972 interview with Clarence Bassett, he recalled that they performed in Washington, D.C., Philadelphia, and Richmond, Virginia. He also recollected the group performed at the Apollo with THE CADILLACS, the Five Keys, and Jimmy Reed, but the Cadillacs didn't first record until 1954.

After "Stormy Weather" disappeared as quickly as it arrived, the group split up and Clarence Bassett joined the service. Julius joined the legendary PARAGONS as lead and Sorrence died. The group kept harmonizing in the park and by 1958 Cussey, Bassett, and Jackson had formed the Videos (of "Trickle Trickle" fame—see THE HEARTBEATS). Ronald Cussey died soon after, and Clarence Bassett joined old friend James Sheppard in Shep and the Limelights from 1961 to 1970; at that point he joined THE FLAMINGOS and sang lead on a new recording of "At Night" (the Orioles) on the *Flamingos Today* LP.

Normally this is where the story of just another obscure vocal group would end, but the "Stormy Weather" single took on a life of its own, keeping the name the Five Sharps on thousands of lips and creating the greatest record hunt in recording history.

In 1961, nine years after the record's release, a collector named Bill Pensebini found a 78 of the now-obscure Five Sharps recording in Benny's Record Store on Fulton Street in Brooklyn. He brought it to Times Square Records dealer Irving "Slim" Rose, who had a radio show on WBNX where he played vocal group records of the '50s and early '60s. Slim agreed to play it, but the disc was destroyed before he had the chance. (Some say Slim sat on it, others that his pet raccoon broke it.) Feeling remorseful, he used his show to put out a call for anyone with a copy of "Stormy Weather" by the Five Sharps on Jubilee. If they had the record they could bring it in and get $25 credit. But no one brought it in.

In July 1962 Times Square Records' Top 150 list had the following notation: "For the first one who brings in 'Stormy Weather' by the Five Sharps (on Jubilee label—45 rpm) $150 cash! (on 78 rpm, $50 cash)." But collectors across the country and around the world had pooled their knowledge and concluded that no one had ever seen a 45 of that mysterious piece of plastic, even though Jubilee had issued 45s before and after that record number and were very consistent in the way they numbered their records.

Slim kept upping the ante till it reached $500, but still there were no finders. Magazine articles began to question whether a 78 ever existed and if so, why a hundred thousand worldwide record collectors couldn't find a single copy. They had checked everywhere—record stores, appliance stores, Salvation Army shops, toy stores, any place that ever sold a record in the entire country, but collectors were unable to locate even one.

Slim then turned to Jubilee owner Jerry Blaine in the hope of getting Blaine to license the "Stormy Weather" master so Rose could issue it on his own Times Square label. To his chagrin he was told that Jubilee 5104 was one of 80 masters destroyed by water damage due to a fire. Blaine and Rose then came up with an idea to rerecord the song in a similar slow '50s R&B style with a group they called the Five Sharps; thus in 1964 the public finally had a Five Sharps "Stormy Weather" to buy—and it was only a dollar. The trade was brisk until collectors realized it was not the original. To further confuse the issue Slim took a white group called the Intimates (possibly the same group that recorded as the second EXCELLENTS group on Blast), recorded "Stormy Weather" complete with opening and closing thunder and rain, and issued it in 1964 as Times Square number 35 by the Five Sharks.

Around this time, collector John Dunn wandered into the Pioneer Record Shop on Stone Avenue in Brooklyn and among a number of cracked 78s found a familiar blue and pink label staring up at him. Incredibly, he didn't take it thinking it was not of any great value. Several days later he returned, saw that the record was still there, and bought "Stormy Weather" for 50 cents. He took it to a recording studio and had a copy made on what is called a dub (a 10-inch metal disc with a coating that contains the record grooves), then locked away the original. When word spread, the calls and letters came flooding in. John's mail came in addressed to John "Stormy Weather" Dunn, and he became so protective of the recording he would only play half of the dub to people for fear someone might duplicate it.

In March 1972, nine years after he found "Stormy Weather," Dunn sold it and the dub for an undisclosed amount to *Bim Bam Boom* magazine, who issued it on their own Bim Bam Boom collectors label in 1973. In order to do so, a recording engineer had to spend over 50 hours removing almost 200 clicks from the cracked 78 while retaining the sound quality. After the transfer to tape, the record and dub were placed in a safety deposit box at the Chemical Bank of New York. Rather than satiating collectors' appetites, the finding of one copy and release of the Bim Bam Boom recording proved that a 78 existed and strengthened the resolve of collectors to find another copy.

During the '70s an East Coast radio station invited listeners to come in and help them clean out their obsolete record library of 78s. People were going home with handfuls of 78s and one such collector came upon the familiar record in his own stack. He had no idea of the record's value and filed it away in his collection. A few years later he moved to California and brought his old dusty 78s with him. One day in 1977 he brought them to Rowe's Rare Records in San Jose. The minute Gary Rowe saw what the lucky collector had he arranged an auction of the very-good-condition platter through *Record Exchanger* magazine. When word spread that the second copy of "Stormy Weather" to be found in 25 years was up for auction, the bids came in quicker than pigs at feeding time. The minimum bid was $1,000, and two Los Angeles coin dealers, Gary Wrubel and Dave Hall (who joined forces to avoid bidding against each other), bid the then unheard-of sum of $3,866. (The highest price ever paid for a record up to that point had been $800 for

the Hideaways' "Can't Help Loving That Girl of Mine" [Ronni, 1955].)

By 1980 one major price guide estimated that the value of a mint 78 copy would be over $5,000. No copies have appeared in the '80s or early '90s, but if one were found today, $10,000 would not be out of the ball park as an auction price. What about a 45? If one ever did surface, you'd have to hock your home!

As for the Five Sharps, the mystique of their rare record carried over to cult celebrity status among East Coast rhythm and blues music lovers, so the late '70s saw Bobby Ward, Tom Duckett (the piano player for that fateful session), Buzzy Brown, Robert Brown, and Pete LeMonier singing at oldies shows as the Five Sharps. One collector even started an oldies magazine that he named *Stormy Weather*.

On the basis of a single release issued 27 years before, on December 22, 1979, the Trax nightclub in New York City billed that night's show as "The a cappella event of all time: the Moonglows meet the Five Sharps in concert."

The Flamingos

Elegant vocals, musical pioneers, living legends, all terms used by legions of music lovers to describe the Flamingos. The simplest and most direct accolade would be that they were the best vocal group in history. Not the most successful, not having the most outstanding lead or deepest bass, but for breathtakingly beautiful harmonies enveloping and supporting a lead there were none better.

In 1950 cousins Jake and Zeke Carey moved to Chicago's Douglas community from their native Baltimore, where ORIOLES legend Sonny Til had been a childhood friend and neighbor. They joined the local black Jewish Church of God and Saints of Christ Congregation on 39th and State and met Paul Wilson and Johnny Carter (later cousins to the Careys through marriage).

The foursome began singing in the choir, eventually spilling out onto the streets near 35th and 36th and Lake Park, the same area where the Highway QCs and Sam Cooke sang. The group owes part of its uniqueness to their early singing of Jewish hymns. Minor key melodies were prevalent, giving the music a feeling of foreboding or sadness, perhaps contributing to the eerie quality of the group's later singing on ballads like "Whispering Stars."

One of the member's sisters was dating a guy named Earl Lewis (not the CHANNELS lead), who became the group's lead singer. Johnny and Zeke were tenors, Paul was baritone, and Jake was bass. The quintet called themselves the Swallows for about six months until they got wind of the King Records group out of Baltimore. Each member then submitted a new idea and Johnny came up with El Flamingos, which they changed to the Five Flamingos.

They moved from the streets to house parties and clubs after attending a picnic in the fall of 1952. Another picnicker, Fletcher Weatherspoon, Jr., heard them harmonizing and took the quintet to a friend who owned a club called Martin's Corner. The group entered the Thursday night talent contest and won, a minor achievement considering they were the only contestants. Still, the owner liked them enough to book them the following night. Fletcher started taking the group to house parties to entertain for experience and exposure (in other words, no money).

One night while the Flamingos were playing Martin's Corner a representative of the King Booking Agency caught their act and recommended them to his boss, Ralph Leon, who soon became their manager. Fletcher was on his way to heed Uncle Sam's call so there was little possibility of a conflict of management. But before he left he discovered 19-year-old Sollie McElroy of Gulfport, Mississippi, at a talent show held by the Willard Theatre. Fletcher brought him to the group at a party, and Sollie became the new lead. Earl was unceremoniously kicked out since he lacked the strict discipline or serious attitude of the others and often missed rehearsals. He went on to sing with the Five Echoes (Sabre, 1953).

By 1952 new manager Leon felt it was time to take his a cappella-trained music machine to a record company audition. He picked the most successful R&B label in Chicago at the time, United Records, but they weren't impressed with the technical perfection of the Five Flamingos, wanting a looser R&B group like all their others. The Five Flamingos (who ranged in age from 17, Paul, to 26, Jake) had strived to become qualitatively different (influenced by THE FIVE KEYS, ORIOLES, DOMINOES, CLOVERS, RAVENS, and FOUR FRESHMEN but intent on developing their own style) yet they had become too clean-sounding for United. While Leon was preparing his next move, *Billboard* noted in one of its columns that the Flamingos had signed with Savoy Records in 1952. This was not the same group, and curiously no recordings by an act named the Flamingos ever came out on Savoy.

In February 1953 Leon took the group to Art Sheridan's Chance label and they issued the ballad "If I Can't Have You" in the second week of March.

The label read "The Flamingos" even though they continued to perform as the Five Flamingos for almost two years. The quality of their vocals was immediately evident. Jake's bass notes were round and full, John's unique falsetto (which took to echo like a duck to water) was atmospheric and chilling, and Sollie's warm resonant lead was the perfect foreground for the Flamingos' background.

"If I" did well in Detroit, New York, Philadelphia, Columbus, and a number of other markets. The up-tempo flip, "Someday, Someway," was a good rocker but the group's true talent was obviously in ballads.

In July their second single came out, the Sammy Kaye hit (#2, 1947) "That's My Desire," which was done in a slow, controlled, yet sincere manner. It, too, did well regionally.

The third week of October ushered in the release of "Golden Teardrops," which many collectors call the most perfect-sounding single of all time. The Johnny Carter-penned balled opened with the most exquisite of intricate harmonies and soothed the listener with Sollie's passionate lead; Johnny and Jake roamed freely on top and bottom while Zeke and Paul tied it all together smoothly. In all, it was a breathtaking masterpiece that further spread their fame through the Midwest to the East, though it couldn't muster white radio interest in those days. (A reissue did go to number 108 on the Pop lists in the summer of 1961.) Unfortunately Art Sheridan felt that paying royalties was an acquired taste he'd never acquired, and the group had to live by their performances.

These were growing due to their new association with ABC (Associated Booking Company). They began doing shows with big jazz bands like the Lionel Hampton and Duke Ellington outfits at places like the Regal in Chicago on Christmas 1953 and the Apollo in New York on February 19, 1954.

The Flamingos were not satisfied with just being musically unique and a notch better vocally. They choreographed themselves into a visually exciting performing group that would later be emulated by such R&B artists as THE FOUR TOPS and THE TEMPTATIONS. They also learned early on that to last over the long haul they should polish their skills on instruments; the Flamingos thus became the first musically self-contained R&B vocal group. It's a good thing, too, because Art Sheridan's ability to run a record label was far below that necessary to promote the outstanding product he had (Chance also had THE MOONGLOWS and THE SPANIELS). The quality of Chance's releases coupled with their rarity due to Sheridan's inept marketing ability have made all vocal group releases on Chance expensive collectibles.

July 1954 brought the release of "Plan for Love," a straightforward blues number made uncommon by the Flamingos' pristine harmonies, but it's doubtful Sheridan sent out many copies. "Cross Over the Bridge" was next in March, but the former Patti Page hit (#2, 1954) had the same fate as "Plan for Love."

Their last Chance release came in November 1954. "Blues in a Letter" was an okay blues, but the flip, "Voit Voit (Jump Children)," was the group's best jump tune and one that deserved a better-than-dismal fate. Alan Freed liked it so much he included a Flamingos visual performance of it in his film *Go Johnny Go!* five years (1959) after the tune's original release.

One of the Flamingos' best Chance recordings, "September Song," was never issued on a single and wasn't out at all until a 1964 Constellation LP. So beautiful was their rendition that it's reported whenever Lionel Hampton would hear them perform it he'd break down in tears.

With Chance visibly failing, the group moved over to Chicago disc jockey Al Benson's Parrot label. Their first of three Parrot singles was a pop-ish sounding ballad called "Dream of a Lifetime" in January 1955.

The Flamingos tackled a variety of musical styles in their recordings and weren't afraid to venture outside the traditional R&B mold. From pop standards and blues to Latin they traveled, even testing country in their version of Eddie Arnold's "I Really Don't Want to Know." It had a flip that offered the debut of new lead singer Nate Nelson, formerly of a Chicago group known as the Velvetones (not the Aladdin group).

Sollie decided to leave; he often felt separate from the group since he was of a different religion and not part of their family. He did join a group with United called the Morroccos and went on to do several fine leads for them, especially on "Sad, Sad Hours" and "Over the Rainbow." In 1961 he joined the Chaunteurs, of which two members, Eugene Record and Robert Lester, later became part of THE CHI-LITES.

Nate Nelson did a duet with Johnny Carter on the Flamingos' last Parrot single, "Ko Ko Mo," which was an attempt to capitalize on what Al Benson felt would be a hit after he heard the Gene and Eunice version in California. The real prize was the "I'm Yours" B side, unquestionably their best Parrot

recording, but few heard it since "Ko Ko Mo" was the push side. The group was beginning to do better on the performing scene with tours of the U.S. and Canada arranged by agent Joe Glaser—including an appropriate stint in Las Vegas at the Flamingo Hotel.

During this period manager Ralph Leon was arranging a new deal with the Chess brothers' Checker label when he suddenly died. The group took over its own business activities at this time and closed the Checker deal. They began recording in Checker's funky office studios and then rerecorded sides like "When" in a real studio. Ironically, the studio sides lacked the warmth of the office tracks, and so their original takes were the ones released on the first few singles.

In the fourth week of April 1955, "When" was released to little response. "I Want to Love You" came in July and when it failed, its flip "Please Come Back Home," an even more potent ballad than "When," was released in September. Neither could break the national ice for the group.

Then in January 1956 Checker issued "I'll Be Home," supposedly written by disc jockey Fats Washington though New Orleans record distributor Stan Lewis got coauthor credit (Nate Nelson actually wrote all but the first line from his navy experiences). "I'll Be Home" was the record the Flamingos had been working for. The beautiful ballad, warmly led by Nelson, was a *Billboard* "Spotlight" pick in their January 14th issue. "The boys blend smoothly and sweetly on a pretty ballad with a relaxed romantic tempo and a stand out performance by the lead singer," wrote the reviewer. "This one should grab off plenty of attention from jocks, jukes and cross-counter buyers." It did become their first national R&B charter, reaching number five in March.

Phil Groia, in his book *They All Sang on the Corner*, states that during Nelson's navy days he would, when on leave in Newport News, Virginia, sit around, drink, and talk with an unknown vocal group who loved to sing Sonny Til and the Orioles songs. When Nate returned from overseas the local group had become THE FIVE KEYS.

Just before the release of "I'll Be Home," the Flamingos performed the song on a Tommy Small show which also included the nemesis of all R&B artists, Pat Boone. Several weeks after the show his pasteurized version came out and cancelled out the group's early crossover airplay, monopolizing the pop charts at number four. Decades later his version is virtually forgotten and rarely if ever played on oldies radio while the Flamingos' version is acknowledged as an R&B ballad standard.

"A Kiss from Your Lips" was their stunning ballad follow-up with haunting harmonies reminiscent of THE DIABLOS' "The Wind." *Billboard*'s May 12, 1956, reviewer didn't think much of the song, however, stating, "Though the material on both sides is below par for this fine group the renditions should carry them into the money. This one's a ballad with an especially tender voice handling the lead throughout." It reached number 12 R&B in June.

Two more love songs followed ("The Vow" and "Would I Be Crying") but mysteriously missed their mark. Still, Alan Freed made sure to include the Flamingos in his movie classic *Rock, Rock, Rock* in 1956 performing "Would I Be Crying." Freed, who loved the Flamingos, sensed their greatness and wanted them immortalized on celluloid even though they didn't have a hit at the time. (He also included "The Vow" in his 1959 film *Go Johnny Go!*) Others sensed their greatness as well. In 1956 Irving Feld was packaging the first integrated rock and roll show, which was akin to hiring the first African-American to play in the big leagues. They had to be the best of the time, justifying the continuation of integrated music into the future. The bill included Bill Haley and the Comets, THE PLATTERS, FRANKIE LYMON AND THE TEENAGERS, Clyde McPhatter, and artists of equal caliber. Oh yes, and the Flamingos.

After "Would I Be Crying" the group broke up due to Zeke and Johnny's draft commitment.

In 1957 they regrouped with Jake Carey, Nate Nelson, Paul Wilson, and former Five Echoes member (Sabre) Tommy Hunt. For the first time the group was a quartet. They signed with Decca Records, who then put a major promotion campaign together for their first 45, "The Ladder of Love," in July. Checker, however, still held a contract on Nate and effectively killed the chances of that single—and subsequent Decca releases—with legal entanglements; it was a truly unfortunate set of circumstances for the group and their pretty ballad. It's reported that around this time Nate moonlighted as lead on Steve Gibson and the Red Caps' ABC-Paramount single of "Silhouettes" (Rays).

In August 1958 Zeke Carey returned while Johnny Carter eventually went on to sing with THE DELLS. Zeke, knowing of George Goldner's interest in the Flamingos, mediated an arrangement between George and Chess Records thereby freeing up Nate and allowing the group to sign with End Records in late 1958. Though collectors and purists consider their best works to have been the Chance and Checker sides, the End recordings were some of their finest, most beautifully sung songs, the main difference stemming from the Flamingos' decision to change from recording originals to old standards in their full harmony style. This was Goldner's idea, according to Zeke Carey, who reports "George came up with the concept of an LP of standards for us. It was the only album we ever did that he picked every single song."

Their first End single, however, was a Paul Wilson-Isiah and Terry Johnson original (Terry was the group's guitarist and additional tenor) titled "Lovers Never Say Goodbye." One of the most beautiful of all doo wop love songs, "Lovers" reached number 25 R&B and became the Flamingos' first pop success, lifting their voices to number 52 in the spring of 1959.

"But Not for Me" was the next single, setting the stage for (as Zeke put it) the Flamingos' national anthem (and their favorite), "I Only (Shoo Bop Shoo Bop) Have Eyes for You." The 1934 Eddy Duchin recording (#4), written by Al Warren and Harry Dubin, was a spectacular ballad as done in the inimitable Flamingos style, awash in echoing harmonies, Nate's buttery delivery, and Terry Johnson's flowing falsetto. "Eyes" charted Pop on June 1st and R&B June 15th. By mid-summer it was a national hit, missing the Pop top 10 by one notch while flying to number three R&B. The record received international acclaim and even made the Australian charts at number 32. Those rehearsals in their rooms at the Hotel Cecil (118th Street and 7th Avenue) in Harlem had truly paid off. All this excitement caused Decca to continue releasing the 10 sides they'd recorded, coming out in May with "Kiss-A-Me" while Checker repackaged "Whispering Stars" b/w "Dream of a Lifetime" and put out an LP under the latter title's name.

In 1958 the Flamingos did a rare backup for Bo Diddley on an even rarer ballad performance for Bo titled "You Know I Love You," which was not released until 1990 when MCA put out a special Bo Diddley boxed set. It was the most subdued performance ever heard from Bo, and the Flamingos' prominent harmonies seem to have mellowed the rocker. Zeke maintains he was not on the Diddley backup though he did recall backing Gone artist Ral Donner with Jake on one long-since-forgotten single.

1959 to 1961 was the group's most prolific period chart- and album-wise. End put out four LPs in four years along with such outstanding singles as "Love Walked In" (#88 Pop, July 1959), "I Was Such a Fool" (#71 Pop, November 1959), "Mio Amore" (#74 Pop, #26 R&B, June 1960), "Your

Other Love" (#54 Pop, November, 1960), and "Time Was" (#45 Pop, June 1961).

By 1961 Tommy Hunt had left to pursue a solo career; he came up with a few minor hits for Sceptor including "Human" (#48, fall 1961).

In the spring of 1964 the Flamingos returned to Checker for a few sides. They recorded an incredible Latin-rhythmed version of Oscar Hammerstein's "Lover Come Back to Me" that would have established a whole new legion of Flamingos followers had radio given it a chance to be heard. (Proving the group's greatness no matter what some wacked-out A&R man handed them, the Flamingos recorded "Lover Come Back to Me" [Polydor, 1970] as a funk balled and still came out sounding good.)

In 1965 the veterans joined Phillips Records and released a funk/doo wop version of Bing Crosby's 1934 (number three) hit "Temptation."

In early 1966 they applied an "I Only Have Eyes for You" treatment to Hoagy Carmichael's song "The Nearness of You" and the effect was brilliant. It was the flip, however, that got the action: "The Boogaloo Party," a catchy dance tune sung mostly in unison, became their first R&B charter in six years (#22, #93 Pop). Trivia question: Out of all the fantastic Flamingos recordings ever made, which is the only single ever to make the British charts? Right! "The Boogaloo Party" (#26, and it took three and a half years to get there, charting in June of 1969).

By late 1966 Nate Nelson had left Atco, where he had recorded one excellent single with the Starglows (a Flamingos sound-alike) called "Let's Be Lovers." He shifted to Musicor Records as lead of the Platters, and one of his first singles was a beautiful remake of the song he'd sung years before with the Flamingos, "I'll Be Home."

The Flamingos' last charter was a 1970 ode to the black cavalry soldiers of the 1880s titled "Buffalo Soldier" (#86 Pop, #28 R&B). A few singles for Roulette, Worlds, Julmar, and their own Ronze label (including three LPs shifting between an old and new sound) and the Flamingos were finished with recording.

In the early '90s they were still performing with Zeke and Jake at the helm along with relative newcomers Archie Saterfield, Kenny Davis, and Ron Reace, and singing a wider variety of material than ever.

Though they've had only one national top 20 hit and only 11 national charters all told, the artists they've influenced (including THE TEMPTATIONS, Diana Ross and THE SUPREMES, THE JACKSON FIVE, THE SPINNERS, SMOKEY ROBINSON AND THE MIRACLES, HAROLD MELVIN AND THE BLUE NOTES, and GLADYS KNIGHT AND THE PIPS to name just a few) testify to their significance.

When Dick Clark wanted the best for his "Rock & Roll: The First Twenty-Five Years on TV," the Flamingos were there. When the 1988 Grammy Awards wanted the best of the '50s, the Flamingos were there. After almost 40 years it's good to know the best are still around.

THE FLAMINGOS

A SIDE/B SIDE	LABEL/CAT NO	DATE
Someday, Someway /		
If I Can't Have You	Chance 1133	3/53
That's My Desire /		
Hurry Home Baby	Chance 1140	7/53
Golden Teardrops / Carried Away	Chance 1145	10/53
Plan For Love / You Ain't Ready	Chance 1149	1/54
Cross Over The Bridge /		
Listen To My Plea	Chance 1154	3/54
Blues In a Letter / Jump Children	Chance 1162	11/54
Dream Of A Lifetime /		
On My Merry Way	Parrot 808	1/55
I Really Don't Want To Know /		
Get With It	Parrot 811	1955
I'm Yours / Ko Ko Mo	Parrot 812	1955
When / That's My Baby	Checker 815	4/55
Please Come Back Home /		
I Want To Love You	Checker 821	7/55
I'll Be Home / Need Your Love	Checker 830	1/56
A Kiss From Your Lips /		
Get With It	Checker 837	4/56
The Vow / Shilly Dilly	Checker 846	1956
Would I Be Crying /		
Just For A Kick	Checker 853	1956
The Ladder Of Love /		
Let's Make Up	Decca 30335	7/57
Helpless / My Faith In You	Decca 30454	10/57
Where Mary Go /		
The Rock And Roll March	Decca 30687	7/58
Lovers Never Say Goodbye /		
That Love Is You	End 1035	1958
But Not For Me /		
I Shed A Tear At Your Wedding	End 1040	1/59
Dream Of A Lifetime /		
Whispering Stars	Checker 915	1/59
Love Walked In / At The Prom	End 1044	1959
I Only Have Eyes For You /		
Goodnight Sweetheart	End 1046	4/59
Ever Since I Met Lucky /		
Kiss-A-Me	Decca 30880	5/59
I Only Have Eyes For You /		
At The Prom	End 1046	5/59
Yours / Love Walked In	End 1055	7/59
Jerri-Lee / Hey Now!	Decca 30948	8/59
I Was Such A Fool /		
Heavenly Angel	End 1062	11/59

A SIDE/B SIDE	LABEL/CAT NO	DATE
Mio Amore / You, Me And The Sea	End 1065	1/60
Nobody Loves Me Like You / You, Me And The Sea	End 1068	3/60
Besame Mucho / You, Me And The Sea	End 1070	1960
Mio Amore / At Night	End 1073	6/60
When I Fall In Love / Beside You	End 1079	1960
Your Other Love / Lovers Gotta Cry	End 1081	11/60
That's Why I Love You / Kokomo	End 1085	2/61
Time Was / Dream Girl	End 1092	6/61
My Memories Of You / I Want To Love You	End 1099	1961
It Must Be Love / I'm No Fool Anymore	End 1111	1961
For All We Know / Near You	End 1116	1962
Flame Of Love / I Know Better	End 1121	1962
True Love / Come On To My Party	End 1124	1962
Ol' Man River Part 1 / Ol' Man River Part 2	Roul 4524	1963
Lover Come Back To Me / Your Little Guy	Chkr 1084	6/64
Goodnight Sweetheart / Does It Really Matter	Chkr 1091	9/64
A Lovely Way To Spend An Evening / Walking My Baby Back Home	TmsSq 102	12/64
I Only Have Eyes For You / Love Walked In	End 1046	12/64
Temptation / Call Her On The Phone	Phlps 40308	7/65
The Boogaloo Party / Nearness Of You	Phlps 40347	1966
Brooklyn Boogaloo / Since My Baby Put Me Down	Phlps 40378	6/66
Itty Bitty Baby / She Shook My World	Phlps 40413	11/66
Koo Koo / It Keeps The Doctor Away	Phlps 40452	4/67
Do It, To It / Oh Mary Don't You Worry	Phlps 40496	10/67
Dealin' / Dealin' All The Way	Julmar 506	1969
Buffalo Soldier (short version) / Buffalo Soldier (long version)	Poly 14019	1/70
Lover Come Back To Me / Straighten It Up	Poly 14044	9/70
Welcome Home / Gotta Have All Your Lovin'	Ronze 111	1971
Think About Me / Think About Me	Worlds 103	1974
Buffalo Soldier Part 1 / Buffalo Soldier Part 2	Poly 14019	2/74
Heavy Hips / Someone To Watch Over Me	Ronze 115	1975
Love Keeps The Doctor Away / Love Keeps The Doctor Away	Ronze 116	1976
If I Could Love You / I Found A New Baby	Skylark 541	

The Fleetwoods

The Fleetwoods were one of the most underrated vocal groups in rock and roll history. Their soothing style was taken for granted and eclipsed by acts that created more pronounced emotional outbursts from their fans. But the Fleetwoods had such an identifiable mellow sound that even today they would sound distinctive (and a little out of place and time).

The trio started out as a duo of Barbara Ellis and Gretchen Christopher, both 18-year-old seniors in 1958 at Olympia High School in Olympia, Washington, about as far as you can get from the recording centers of New York and Hollywood. The high school cheerleaders were born nine days apart (Barbara on February 20, 1940, and Gretchen on February 29, 1940) and for a few days were actually in the same maternity ward together. The duo started singing in music class and began auditioning other girls to create a trio. When none fit the bill they remained a duo and called themselves the Saturns as kind of a sister group to a local rock act called the Blue Comets. It was through the Comets that they met trumpet player Gary Troxel. The girls discovered that Gary's singing style far outdistanced his trumpet playing, and he was added as the lead singer.

They called themselves, very imaginatively, "Two Girls and a Guy."

Meanwhile, Gretchen was doing a solo act at the Colony, a local club where Pat Suzuki was performing. Through the club owner, Gretchen met Bob Reisdorff, promoter for Suzuki's recordings on Liberty Records. He instructed her to make a tape of her group and bring it to him.

In the spring of 1958 the group did an a cappella tape of their new song "Come Softly," and Gretchen bused into Seattle to play it for Reisdorff.

He was immensely impressed and arranged for the recent high school grads to record for the Liberty-distributed Dolphin label of Seattle, which just happened to be owned by Reisdorff.

Feeling he had a hit in their first recording, Bob phoned Barbara to suggest the group come up with a catchier name. He then looked down at the phone and said, "Like Fleetwood," which was the Olympia area phone prefix. Henceforth, the Olympia trio sang as the Fleetwoods, and their first single, the cowritten song now called "Come Softly to Me," came out in January 1959.

The overnight success story never had a greater example than the Fleetwoods as "Come Softly" shot to number one in three weeks. It barely had enough time to be reviewed in *Billboard* on February 16th when their reviewer stated, "The kids have an interesting sound on this catchy folkish tune. It's of the ballad type and different enough to attract play and coin. There's already some West Coast action." What an understatement. It spent four weeks there, pushing "Venus," by teen idol Frankie Avalon, out of the top spot. The group performed on Dick Clark's April 11, 1959, Saturday night show in New York and were greeted and congratulated as they arrived by none other than the young man whose song they had just displaced from number one, Frankie himself.

By May 11th, when Dave "Baby" Cortez's "Happy Organ" replaced them at the chart pinnacle, the record was becoming a worldwide seller, reaching number six in England and number four in Australia. To top it off, the lily-white rhythm ballad even crossed to the R&B charts at number five.

The group had gone from beach parties and house parties to Dick Clark's and Ed Sullivan's TV shows, selling over a million copies of "Come Softly."

The next single out of 708 6th Avenue North in Seattle (Dolphin's headquarters, though now the label's name was changed to Dolton) was "Graduation's Here," which made it to number 39 in the spring. But their next release, the DeWayne Blackwell composition "Mr. Blue," became the typification of the Fleetwoods' "sad song" style and perched them once again atop the national charts, this time muscling Bobby Darin's six-weeks-at-number-one-hit "Mack the Knife" down to number two. "Mack" came back to retake the throne for another three weeks, but the Fleetwoods had proven their sales viability. Again the group crossed over to the R&B charts, this time rising to number three.

The Fleetwoods' sound was so appealing and in demand that disc jockeys started flipping "Mr. Blue"; the B side, "You Mean Everything to Me," reached number 84 in October 1959.

The composer of "Mr. Blue" had written the song for THE PLATTERS but hadn't known how to get it to them. He met a record promoter who knew Reisdorff and in a Washington hotel he was finally able to play the song live for the Fleetwoods.

Billboard picked up on the Fleetwoods by reviewing both of their new sides in the January 25th issue: "The trio has two hot sides to follow their big 'Mr. Blue.' The top tune, 'Magic Star,' penned by Bonnie Guitar, is presented along similar lines to

their current hit. Flip is an attractive reading of a gentle and plaintive ballad."

The B side, "Outside My Window," peaked on the Top 100 at number 28.

By the time Gary was drafted into the navy in September 1960 (the downfall of many great and near great vocal groups) the Washington wonders had scored another hit (#23) in "Runaround." The group then recorded only on Gary's occasional leaves but still scored with beautiful recordings of Thomas Wayne and the Delons' "Tragedy" (#10, 1961) and "(He's) The Great Imposter" (#30, 1961).

The group had done a substantial amount of recording during those first two years and had five LPs out through Gary's service time. The cover of one LP, *Deep in a Dream*, even has him pictured in uniform.

Though known for their pop recordings they recorded an album of personal favorites called *The Fleetwoods Sing the Best Goodies of the Oldies.* Seven of the 12 cuts were by R&B acts such as THE FIVE SATINS ("In the Still of the Night"), THE PENGUINS ("Earth Angel"), and THE HEARTBEATS ("A Thousand Miles Away").

Gary returned in 1962 and the group continued to create more of their trademark smooth ballads, such as "Lovers by Night, Strangers by Day" (#36, late fall 1962) and their last chart record, a remake of Jesse Belvin's 1956 classic "Goodnight My Love" (#32, summer of 1963).

By 1964 a combination of lesser material and the British beat monopoly on American radio had begun to force their 1964 through 1966 releases (all seven of them) into the 10-cent bins. Their contract with the Dolton label ran out in 1965 and was not picked up. Rather than pursue a new label the trio went their separate ways. They did a few oldies shows at the beginning of the '70s decade and in 1983 reunited for an LP that stayed true to their unique sound.

In 1990 Rhino Records issued a *Best of the Fleetwoods* LP that included two tracks from the reunion album and all the hits. Gary and Gretchen toured for a while with Cheryl Huggins as Barbara preferred to spend time with her family.

The trio went on to diverse lifestyles: Gary started working in a plywood mill in Anacortes, Washington, a small town near the Canadian border; Barbara became Barbara Ellis Pizzutello and went on to manage a mobile home park in Ontario, California. Gretchen became Gretchen Christopher Matzen, a part-time teacher of modern dance, an occasional solo act in Olympia, and a housewife.

THE FLEETWOODS

A SIDE/B SIDE	LABEL/CAT NO	DATE
Come Softly To Me /		
I Care So Much	Dolphin 1	1/59
Come Softly To Me /		
I Care So Much	Lbrty 55188	1959
Graduation's Here /		
Oh Lord Let It Be	Dolton 3	4/59
Mr. Blue / You Mean		
Everything To Me	Dolton 5	8/59
Outside My Window / Magic Star	Dolton 15	1/60
Runaround / Truly Do	Dolton 22	4/60
The Last One To Know /		
Dormilona	Dolton 27	9/60
Confidential / I Love You So	Dolton 30	11/60
Tragedy / Little Miss Sad One	Dolton 40	3/61
The Great Imposter /		
Poor Little Girl	Dolton 45	8/61
Billy Old Buddy / Trouble	Dolton 49	1961
Lovers By Night Strangers By		
Day / They Tell Me It's Summer	Dolton 62	9/62
You Should Have Been There /		
Sure Is Lonesome Downtown	Dolton 74	1963
Goodnight My Love /		
Jimmy Beware	Dolton 75	4/63
What'll I Do / Baby Bye-O	Dolton 86	1963
Ruby Red Baby Blue /		
Lonesome Town	Dolton 93	1964
Ska Light, Ska Bright /		
Ten Times Blue	Dolton 97	1964
Mr. Sandman / This Is My Prayer	Dolton 98	1964
Before And After /		
Lonely Is As Lonely Does	Dolton 302	1965
Come Softly To Me /		
I'm Not Jimmy	Dolton 307	1965
Just As I Need You / Rainbow	Dolton 310	1965
For Lovin' Me / This Is		
Where I See Her	Dolton 315	1966

The Four Aces

One of the '50s' most consistent chartmakers, the Four Aces had at least one top 20 record every year from 1951 to 1956 and remained Top 100 residents to the end of the decade. Half of the quartet came together in Newfoundland in 1946 when navy buddies Al Alberts and Dave Mahoney pacted to forge a vocal group upon their return to the States. With the help of Chester, Pennsylvania, music shop owner Marty Caruso, Al and Dave were soon teamed with Louis Silvestri and Rosario (Sod) Vaccaro.

They named themselves after Lou's local roller-skating club and began honing their harmonies and instrumental prowess. Al (lead and piano), Dave (tenor and sax), Sod (baritone and trumpet), and Louis (bass and drums) began playing for college kids at the Old Mill Inn in the late '40s.

Two Chester area songwriters named George Hoven and Chester Shull brought the Aces a song they'd written, confident it was a hit. Though George was a music shop owner specializing in polkas, the song "It's No Sin" was a ballad. The group agreed to try it for their audience; the response was so overwhelming that the Aces aimed to record it. Money was another matter, however, so the group continued performing till word reached the ears of two well-to-do collegians, Larry Pleet and Melvin Korn, who chipped in $500. Al and his fiancée Stella contributed their wedding money and the four gamblers headed off to Philadelphia's Reco-Art Studios to cut "It's No Sin," hooking up with pressing plant owner Dan Miller to produce copies on their own Victoria label.

The group had one ace in the hole: local disc jockey Jimmy Lynn of radio WVCH loved not only the song but songwriter Hoven's daughter Vera, and playing the record was one sure way into the family. "Sin" spread across the Pennsylvania countryside and by September 15, 1951, had popped onto the *Billboard* charts.

Although the song was ultimately covered by five other acts (Billy Williams Quartet [#28], Sammy Kaye [#25], the Four Knights [#14], Savannah Churchill [#5], and Eddie Howard [#1]), the Aces beat out four of them, doing it on a brand new label that had just issued its first record.

"It's No Sin" peaked at number four, attracting the attention of music executives as well as music lovers. Decca honcho Bob Brenner soon lured the group to the New York giant to record.

Their first Decca release, recorded on October 23, 1951, was the double-charting "Tell Me Why" (#2) b/w "A Garden in the Rain" (#14), putting the group solidly on the musical map.

The old Xavier Cugat hit "Perfidia (Tonight)" (#3, 1941) was next up the charts for the Aces in the spring of 1952 (#7), and the performing doors began swinging open from coast to coast. To assure the Old Mill performers were up to the task, Herb Kessler (manager of RCA's the Three Suns) was hand-picked by Decca to manage the act, and he quickly acquired the services of top Hollywood choreographer Jon Gregory to work with the boys. Herb figured if Jon could do it for Errol Flynn and Tyrone Power he could do it for the Four Aces.

The Aces totaled eight top-30-or-better singles in 1952, including "Should I" (#9) and a remake of

Larry Clinton's 1938 number one hit "Heart and Soul" (#11).

1953 was another hot year for the group that was fast becoming one of the most popular pop acts in the country: they scored nine more top 30 hits from "I'll Never Smile Again" (#21, originally #1 by Tommy Dorsey, 1940) and Sammy Kaye's 1946 number three hit "Laughing on the Outside" (#22) to "Stranger in Paradise" (#3).

In 1954 the group finally hit number one with a movie song also recorded by Frank Sinatra called "Three Coins in the Fountain." It went to number four for Old Blue Eyes, but the Aces' earlier release had enabled them to jump ahead and stay there, finishing at the top in the late spring of 1954. "Three Coins" became the first of seven Aces chart records in England, skyrocketing to number five in the summer. The group began performing on every TV show from Perry Como to Dick Clark.

1955 started with "Melody of Love" (#3) followed by their monumental smash (and theme song) "Love Is a Many-Splendored Thing" from the motion picture of the same name. The Sammy Fain–Paul Francis Webster tune was a perfect vehicle for the Aces, who took it to number one for six weeks in the fall (#2 U.K.).

The group toured England that year and found a whole new audience for their pop harmonies. They also played often in Canada and on various occasions at the Gattineau Club in Ottawa where they were visited by a young and aggressive songwriter trying to ply his wares. The songs were not in the Aces' style and they gently dismissed the young man. The writer was Paul Anka, who went on to greater success singing his own songs than he achieved giving them to others. In a twist typical of the music biz, Paul bought the Aces' publishing company years later; the Aces were now receiving their royalties from the guy whose songs they'd originally rejected.

In 1956 the group charted nine more times, but rock and roll was taking many of the top chart spots and the closest the foursome came to a real hit was "You Can't Run Away from It" (#20). The handwriting became a little clearer in 1957 with two mild charters, "Bahama Mama" (#53) and "You're Mine" (#76).

Trying to fit in, they recorded "Rock and Roll Rhapsody" (#66) and even wound up in Universal film's rock movie *The Big Beat* in 1958, but the kids weren't buying.

The group's July 30, 1958, recording session for "Hangin' Up a Horseshoe" and "Roses of Rio" was the last with Al Alberts, who decided to try a solo career. Unfortunately, the single's release passed with little fanfare.

Freddy Diodatti took Al's place. In late 1958 the Aces hit the charts with "The World Outside" from the 1942 film *Suicide Squadron*, but their version was beaten out by THE FOUR COINS (#21). The chief distinction of the Aces recording is that it became their first hit in Australia (#7) and did better in England for them (#18, 1959) than in the U.S.

By the '60s Dave and Sod were in private life, replaced by Joe Giglio and Tony Alessi. Lou left in 1976 and Jimmy Kapourellias (a.k.a. Jimmy Athens) took over.

The original members regrouped in the late '70s but ran into a legal roadblock from the existing Aces. The result was that the Alberts group would be called the Original Four Aces and the new group would perform as the Four Aces.

The originals stayed together longer as a reunited unit (1976 to 1987) than they did when they started (1948 to 1958) and in 1978 recorded one last LP for the faithful.

Al eventually went into TV hosting a children's variety show for WFIL and later WPIV in Philadelphia. David went into building and selling insurance. Sod became the tax collector and treasurer in Chester, Pennsylvania.

THE FOUR ACES

A SIDE/BE SIDE	LABEL CAT/NO	DATE
Garden In The Rain /		
Tell Me Why	Decca 27860	12/51
It's No Sin	Chester	1951
Perfidia / You Brought Me Love	Decca 27987	2/52
My Hero / Spring Is		
A Wonderful Thing	Decca 28073	1952
I Understand / I'm Yours	Decca 28162	1952
Should I / There's Only Tonight	Decca 28323	7/52
Heart and Soul /		
Just Squeeze Me	Decca 28390	10/52
I'll Never Smile Again /		
My Devotion	Decca 28391	10/52
Heaven Can Wait / Ti-Pi-Tin	Decca 28392	10/52
La Rosita / Take Me In Your Arms	Decca 28393	10/52
If You Take My Heart Away /		
You Fooled Me	Decca 28560	2/53
Honey In The Horn /		
Organ Grinder's Swing	Decca 28691	1953
Don't Forget Me / False Love	Decca 28744	1953
I've Been Waiting A Lifetime /		
Laughing On The Outside	Decca 28843	9/53
The Gang That Sang Heart Of My		
Heart / Stranger In Paradise	Decca 28927	1953
Amor / So Long	Decca 29036	3/54
Three Coins In The Fountain /		
Wedding Bells	Decca 29123	5/54

A SIDE/B SIDE	LABEL/CAT NO	DATE
Dream / It Shall Come To Pass	Decca 29217	7/54
It's A Woman's World / The Cuckoo Bird In The Pickle	Decca 29269	9/54
In Apple Blossom Time / Mister Sandman	Decca 29344	11/54
Melody Of Love / There Is A Tavern In The Town	Decca 29395	1/55
There Goes My Heart / You'll Always Be The One	Decca 29435	2/55
Heart / Slew Foot	Decca 29476	4/55
Love Is A Many Splendored Thing / Shine On Harvest Moon	Decca 29625	8/55
Of This I'm Sure / A Woman In Love	Decca 29725	10/55
The Xmas Song / Jingle Bells	Decca 29702	11/55
O Holy Night / Silent Night	Decca 29712	11/55
Charlie Was A Boxer / To Love Again	Decca 29889	4/56
Dreamer / I Only Know I Love You	Decca 29989	7/56
Friendly Persuasion / You Can't Run Away From It	Decca 30041	1956
Someone To Love / Written On The Mind	Decca 30123	11/56
Bahama Mama / You're Mine	Decca 30242	3/57
Yes Sir, That's My Baby / Three Sheets To The Mind	Decca 30348	6/57
Half Of My Heart / When My Sugar Walks Down The Street	Decca 30384	7/57
How Do You Say Goodbye / I Would Love You Still	Decca 30466	10/57
I Wish I May, I Wish I Might / Rock & Roll Rhapsody	Decca 30575	2/58
Saturday Swing Out / Take My Heart	Decca 30649	5/58
Hanging Up A Horseshoe / Roses Of Rio	Decca 30721	7/58
Heartache In Costume / Two Arms, Two Lips, One Heart	Decca 30659	7/58
How Can You Forget	Decca 30764	10/58
The Xmas Tree / Ol' Fatso	Decca 30775	11/58
Inn Of The Sixth Happiness / No Other Arms; No Other Lips	Decca 30822	1959
Paradise Island / Ciao, Ciao, Bambino	Decca 30874	4/59
Anyone Would Love You / The Five Pennies	Decca 30897	5/59
Waltzing Matilda / The Wonder Of It All	Decca 30989	10/59
Till Tomorrow / I Love Paris	Decca 31027	12/59
Poor Butterfly / You Are Music	Decca 31081	4/60
Beyond The Rule Horizon / Whatever Will Be, Will Be	Decca 25535	10/61

The Four Coins

They were a strong-voiced, tight-knit pop quartet, and three-fourths of them started out as band musicians, not singers. Coming from the small Pennsylvania town of Canonsburg (population about 10,000) the group included the Mahramas brothers, George and Michael, as well as George Mantalis and James Gregorakis.

The year 1952 saw George, George, and Jim playing in the orchestra of another son of Canonsburg, alto sax player Bobby Vinton (yes, *that* Bobby Vinton). Mahramas played trumpet, Mantalis played alto sax, and Gregorakis tenor sax. This professional music training was a key factor in the development of their later vocal style. During the Christmas season of that year the three plus Michael were doing some street-corner crooning just for fun when the realization hit them that singing could be their future.

The group began practicing at George Mahramas's house and calling themselves the Four Keys. The singing order was George Mahramas (lead), Mike (tenor), George Mantalis (tenor), and Jim (baritone). Though they worked to develop their own identity, style, and harmony, their influences were the likes of THE FOUR LADS and THE FOUR ACES.

The all-Greek quartet stayed a short while longer with Vinton and then struck out on their own. They took their sound to Pittsburgh for a year's worth of bookings—57 weeks at the Blue Ridge Inn for $250 a week.

By November 1953 they felt ready to record and went to George Heid's studio. Heid liked their vocalizing so much he issued their recording of "Hot Toddy" on his own local Carona label. In early 1954 he released another Keys single, "I'll Make the Best of It."

In the spring the group was performing at one of their numerous gigs, this time in Columbus, Ohio, when fate in the form of a honeymooning A&R exec came knocking. Danny Kessler of Columbia Records was enjoying his newly wedded bliss when he heard the group sing one night. Shifting from honeymooner to record exec with the speed of Clark Kent doffing his civvies, Danny committed the group to Columbia and became their manager (he was also the manager of Johnny Ray). It was Kessler who decided a name change was in order and came upon the Four Coins, culled from THE FOUR ACES' contemporaneous hit, "Three Coins in the Fountain."

The newly coined Coins released their debut disc in August 1954. "We'll Be Married (In the

Church in the Wood)" reached the *Billboard* charts on October 16th and topped out at number 30. Though not ultimately known as a typical mid-'50s white cover act, the Four Coins had their share of such releases. Their very next single was a cover of Charlie and Ray's "I Love You Madly," which escalated to number 28 nationally and set the group on the performance path. Other Coins covers didn't fare nearly as well: their versions of "Story Untold" (THE NUTMEGS, 1955) and "Cherry Lips" (THE ROBINS, 1956) didn't chart at all. This is probably why their label Epic (a Columbia subsidiary) fed them mostly original songs.

A film opportunity came in late 1955 with the release of "Memories of You," the title theme from *The Benny Goodman Story.* It had a big impact for the group, spending four months on the charts and peaking at number 22. A drought then set in for the group as they went through all of 1956 and the beginning of 1957 (six singles) without so much as a bottom-of-the-list title. Then in April they came out with a beautiful and powerfully sung ballad, "Shangri-La." In May it moved onto *Billboard's* chart, reaching number 11 and becoming their first (and only) million seller. Their follow-up, "My Sin," made it to number 28.

Either someone really liked their sound or they were brought in to balance out the collection of parent-threatening rockers, but whatever the reason the Four Coins managed to appear in the rock and roll movie *Jamboree,* which also starred Jerry Lee Lewis, LOUIS LYMON AND THE TEENCHORDS, Fats Domino, Buddy Knox, Jimmy Bowen, and Carl Perkins, among others. The group sang "A Broken Promise," which was their November 1957 single release preceding the film's December opening. The film, as it turned out, did better than the Coins' record, and that was their last rock and roll film. Still, they were quite busy going from TVers like "The Steve Allen Show," "The Ed Sullivan Show," and "Patti Page's Small Screen Showcase" to tours of the U.S., Europe, and Japan. They also managed to get on one Alan Freed show.

During the mid-to late '50s George and Mike's brother Jack proved to be an able tenor/baritone substitute when one of the members had to heed Uncle Sam's call.

The group placed two more singles on the charts in 1958, "Wendy Wendy" (#22) and "The World Outside" (#25), but white pop groups were facing a lot of new competition from rock and roll acts, rhythm and blues groups, and even white pop acts that were singing more of what the teens wanted to hear (like THE BELMONTS and THE ELEGANTS). The group did manage to rise to the occasion on "Angel of Love," reviewed February 23, 1959, by a *Billboard* observer who remarked, " 'Angel of Love' is a celestial type rock-a-ballad done in the group's familiar rockin' style. Strong vocal by the lead is nicely backed by the group." Where the reviewer got his definition of "rockin' style" is questionable, but there's no question that the record never picked up much play.

Jack became a regular in 1959 when Mike left to become an actor. His first single full-time was "Angel in the Rain" in September 1959.

Their last charter was "One Love, One Heart" (#87, 1958), and by 1960 they'd moved over to MGM with a new recording of Johnny Ace's hit (#17, 1955) "Pledging My Love." MGM decided if they couldn't reach the American teens they'd go after the Greek adults, issuing an LP aptly titled *Greek Songs by the Four Coins.*

A move to Jubilee in 1961 found them doing the outlandish "Gee Officer Krupkie" production number from *West Side Story.* Though the record never charted, the stage routine they created for it became a highlight of their performance for years to come.

Another mismatch was the placement of the Coins recording of the film theme *The War Lovers* with Vee-Jay Records in 1962. Vee-Jay was an established rock and roll and R&B-oriented label and rarely if ever dealt with film songs. To make matters worse, the tune was recorded too late to include in the film and only a distributor's resourceful decision to have the theme play after the movie ended (in some theaters) allowed the public to hear it at all.

Next, they recorded "Love Me with All Your Heart," only to be covered by the Ray Charles Singers. Ray's gang massacred the Coins with a national number three showing while the Coins couldn't even touch the Top 100.

After another Greek LP, this time for Roulette (1964), the Canonsburg quartet found themselves on Laurie Records (courtesy of manager Kessler, who'd now made six deals in seven years). One unlikely and unsuccessful remake of Ernie Maresca's hit "Shout Shout (Knock Yourself Out)" (#6, 1962), and the group was starting to show a kink in its armor.

The brothers George and Jack left to join brother Mike and formed a performing trio, the Original Three Coins, later known as the Brothers James. Newcomers Terry Richards (lead) and Ronnie Fiorento (tenor) from Cleveland took their places in the Coins.

In 1967 the group came full circle, signing with Epic's parent Columbia for one 45, "If You Love Me

(Really Love Me)." The group kept performing until 1970 when original members George Mantalis and Jim Gregorakis retired from singing (but remained active).

James went back to Canonsburg and at last count had four gas stations, two beer distributorships, three car washes, and seven laundries. Mike formed a new group and settled in Boca Raton, Florida. George Mantalis had a mobile phone company in West Palm Beach, Florida; George Mahramas became the maitre d' at Christopher's Restaurant in Pittsburgh; and his brother Jack became the manager of a Sternberger Paint Company store also in Pittsburgh.

The Four Fellows

A soft and soothing pop black group, the Four Fellows drew their style from a combination of jubilee spirituals and barbershop harmony.

The four Brooklynites became the Schemers in 1953 and included Jimmy Beckum (lead), Jim McGowan (first tenor), David Jones (second tenor), and Larry Banks (baritone/bass). McGowan, a worker in a metal factory, had sung in the Four Toppers (no recordings) with Harold Miller, later of THE RAYS ("Silhouettes," 1957). The Four Toppers developed out of a spiritual group, the Starlight Toppers, who had been influenced by such spiritual stars of the day as THE GOLDEN GATE QUARTET, the Dixiaires, THE MODERNAIRES, and THE PIED PIPERS. Jimmy Beckum had sung with a local teen gospel group, the Brooklyn Crusaders. (Most black spiritual music had been referred to as gospel music, while jubilee was a type of spiritual that usually stressed group singing rather than emphasizing a lead singer. Jubilee was also the name for secularized versions of black religious songs for concert audiences before it was termed race music.) Larry Banks, the group's driving force, had been influenced by the barbershop style since his father had sung with the Dunbar Barbershop Quartet.

The Schemers developed a MILLS BROTHERS style and, thanks to their manager Jimmy Johnson, began working clubs in 1954 such as Jamaica, Queens's Club Caribe.

Prior to a TV date on Ralph Cooper's "Spotlight on Harlem," Johnson told the group to come in with a better name. They returned as the Four Pals and he countered with the Four Fellows. By now, Beckum was missing rehearsals and was replaced by former Starlight Topper member Teddy Williams.

Their first recordings were done for Derby Records through A&R man "Ace" Adams; they did one unsuccessful single called "I Tried." Meanwhile, the group was regularly appearing on "Spotlight on Harlem," often alternating with THE CADILLACS. A new manager, Teddy "Cherokee" Conyers (sax man for Buddy Johnson's Band), had them record the Frank Loesser oldie "I Wish I Didn't Love You So" and took it to Coral Records exec Phil Rose. Rose was starting his own Glory label and the Four Fellows became the first act on it.

"I Wish I Didn't Love You" stiffed upon release in 1955 and the group was quickly paired with Betty McLaurin for "So Will I," another nonentity.

A breakthrough came when Phil Rose, after rejecting every song in their repertoire for a next single, hit upon a song called "Soldier Boy" that David Jones had written while serving in Korea. Phil moved McGowan into the lead and on July 2, 1955, "Soldier Boy" slipped onto *Billboard*'s national R&B charts, rising to number four while remaining visible for 15 weeks. The Four Fellows then performed in Alan Freed, Hal Jackson, and Dr. Jive's shows as well as on the black theatre circuit (including the Apollo theatre and the Brooklyn Paramount) with acts like THE MOONGLOWS, Etta James, THE NUTMEGS, Gene and Eunice, and Bo Diddley. More beautiful ballads were released in 1955 and 1956—"Angels Say," "In the Rain," "Darling You," and "Please Play My Song"—but the group never again came close to the success of "Soldier Boy." Their last single had them backing up Toni Banks on "You're Still in My Heart." Toni was originally Bessie White, who had sung with the group for a short while when they were Three Guys and a Doll prior to becoming the Four Fellows. Bessie later married Larry Banks onstage at the Royal Theatre in Baltimore.

In April 1956 Davey Jones left to join Hal Miller and the Rays. Jimmy Mobley of the Starlight Toppers took his place starting with the group's "Please Play My Song."

By the end of 1956 Larry and Jimmy had left, replaced by Gordon Payne and Alvin Scot (Payne had been with the Four Toppers).

The last lineup of McGowan, Williams, Payne, and Scott recorded an LP as backup vocalists for Josh White. They then broke up.

Payne moved to California where he died in 1974. Teddy Williams and Alvin Scott went to work for the New York Transit Authority and live in Brooklyn. Jimmy Beckum moved to North Carolina and Jimmy Mobley passed away in the '70s. Toni Banks recorded as Bessie Banks on Tiger. A song she recorded titled "Go Now," written by husband

Larry, became the tune that kicked the Moody Blues' career into gear in 1964. Jimmy McGowan was stabbed in a gang fight in 1951 and became permanently disabled, yet he graduated from Temple University with a B.A. in psychology (1978) and began a career in cytotechnology (the study of human cells for malignancies).

In 1979 the Four Fellows (Jimmy, Larry, Dave, and Teddy) reunited for an evening of song ranging from Fellows tunes to spirituals at a United in Group Harmony show in New Jersey.

In 1980 Ronnie I., founder of UGHA, issued a 1956 live performance of "Soldier Boy" on his own UGHA label, making it the first released record on the foursome in 23 years. The flip was a newly taped a cappella recording of THE CLOVERS' "Skylark."

THE FOUR FELLOWS

A SIDE/B SIDE	LABEL/CAT NO	DATE
I Tried / Bend Of The River	Derby 862	1954
I Wish I Didn't Love You So /		
I Know Love	Glory 231	1955
So Will I* / Grow Old		
Along With Me*	Glory 233	1955
Soldier Boy / Take Me Back, Baby	Glory 234	1955
Angels Say / In The Rain	Glory 236	1955
Just Come A LIttle Bit Closer* /		
A Love That's True*	Glory 237	1955
Fallen Angel / Hold 'Em Joe	Glory 238	1956
Petticoat Baby / I'm Past Sixteen	Glory 241	1956
Darling You / Please Don't		
Deprive Me Of Love	Glory 242	1956
Please Play My Song /		
Sit In My Window	Glory 244	1956
You Don't Know Me /		
You Sweet Girl	Glory 248	1956
Loving You, Darling /		
Give Me Back My Broken Heart	Glory 250	1956
You're Still In My Heart** /		
Johnny The Dreamer**	Glory 263	1957

* Bette McLaurin and the Four Fellows
** Toni Banks and the Four Fellows

The Four Freshmen

The Four Freshmen were the most innovative and emulated jazz vocal quartet ever to grace vinyl. Innovative because of their unique concept of singing "open" harmony, moving the third and fifth notes of a chord an octave higher or lower, or using ninths and elevenths while dropping root notes of a chord. Emulated because every type of artist heard something fresh and exciting in their sound—not only jazz groups, but acts as diverse as THE HARPTONES in the '50s, THE BEACH BOYS of the '60s, and THE MANHATTAN TRANSFER in the '70s heard a redefinition of harmony that stirred their own imaginations. That doesn't count THE HI-LOs, THE HILLTOPPERS, THE LETTERMEN, SPANKY AND OUR GANG, and THE MAMAS AND THE PAPAS.

The group started out as Hal's Harmonizers, with brothers Don and Ross Barbour, Hal Kratzsch, and Marvin Pruitt. All four members were students in 1947 at the Arthur Jordan Conservatory of Music, a division of Butler University in Indianapolis. Hal convinced his music theory classmates that forming a barbershop quartet would be a great source of income.

Hal, from Warsaw, Indiana, sang and played bass as well as trumpet and mellophone. Don and Ross were raised in Columbus, Indiana; Don sang second tenor and played guitar while his younger brother Ross sang baritone and played trumpet. The top voice was Marvin's. Decked out in Gay '90s apparel (armbands, exaggerated false moustaches, and waiters' aprons) the quartet began singing "Sweet Adeline" at fairs and conventions until they became bored with the confinement of barbershop chords. Not wanting to give up the income base they became a second group, the Toppers.

As fans of Stan Kenton they began using diminished and augmented chords, creating a jazz vocal style, and sang at local malt shops near the school. They graduated to the LVL Club where an audition with a ribald army classic, "They Stole My Wife While I Lay Sleeping," earned them a three-night-a-week job for the astounding sum of $5 a night each.

As their popularity grew so did the audiences and so did their first real problems: Marvin developed acute phobia of the masses—in other words, stage fright.

By the spring of 1948 Marvin and his nervous condition had resigned from both groups. The Toppers then dropped the Harmonizers and with Nancy Sue Carson, Ross's girlfriend (and future wife), pressed on. It became apparent that a fourth male voice was more appropriate for their sound, so Don and Ross contacted their cousin Bob Flanigan, who had sung with them as kids and lived 90 miles up the road from Columbus in Greencastle. Bob was in a high school quintet singing MODERNAIRES-styled songs. He also played trombone and had a reverence for jazz greats Charlie Parker and big-band trombonist Jack Teagarden. Bob's phrasing, pitch, and musical ear sold the group on him as their new lead.

With combined influences ranging from Stan Kenton and Woody Herman to Mel Torme's Meltones and the Pastels, the quartet developed a style of singing five-note chords with four voices; one voice would be shifting. None of the foursome were arrangers, so they worked out each song by ear, rehearsing in a parked car with the windows closed.

The group soon dropped out of school and drove to Chicago where they met agent Dick Shelton. The agent already had a group called the Cottontoppers, so he renamed the ex-first-year students the Freshmen Four. The guys reversed the words and debuted at the 113 Club in Fort Wayne, Indiana, on September 20, 1948. They nearly lost the job since the owner had never heard jazz chords, but his daughter had a crush on Hal and saved the day—actually the week.

While playing the Midwest lounge circuit they shifted their instrumentation, with Hal and Bob alternating bass playing and brass solos and Ross moving from piano to drums while Don remained on guitar.

Their big break came on March 21, 1950, while playing the Esquire Lounge in Dayton, Ohio. Stan Kenton, who had been told at his own show earlier that night about a quartet in town that sounded like his 43-piece ensemble, was sitting in the audience. He was sufficiently impressed to send the Freshmen to New York to make a demo which he would take to Capitol Records president Glen Wallichs.

The demo was produced by Kenton's former arranger, Pete Rugolo, and it contained "Laura," "Basin Street Blues," "Dry Bones," and two other songs. In May, Kenton sent a letter telling the group to come west, and when they arrived their mentor arranged to have them perform at Jerry Wald's Studio Club on Sunset Boulevard. The entertainment industry packed the club nightly to hear vocalizing as they'd never heard before; the one week job turned into eight weeks.

On October 13, 1950, the Freshmen recorded a rhythm and blues number called "Mr. B's Blues," which was released in November and became an instant collectors' item. Next, Steve Allen took the quartet to New York for his new TV show, but after one week of grumbling from New York's musicians union over the group's nonmembership status, he sent them back to Los Angeles where they landed their first and only motion picture appearance in *Rich, Young and Pretty* with Jane Powell and Vic Damone.

Their second single, a soft ballad called "Now You Know" (January 1951), also failed to grab radio's attention.

In their only session of 1951 the group recorded a Kenton-suggested "Tuxedo Junction," but the vocal work was so intricate they had to lay down the instrumental track first and then do their complex scat vocals separately, reportedly the first time this kind of multitracking had been done. The second song, "It's a Blue World," had been a Tony Martin 1940 hit (#2), and upon completing the recording the group knew the song epitomized their style.

Capitol didn't agree, canning the tape and dropping the Freshmen in December.

In May 1952 the group met up with Kenton in Chicago. Furious that Capitol gave up on his find, he demanded Capitol send demo copies of the songs to the group so they could promote it. That's just what they did, breaking the record of "Blue World" in Detroit at WJBK and then at every other Detroit station.

By the time Capitol re-signed the quartet and issued the single in July it had lost some momentum but still became their first national chart record reaching number 30 in late August.

In the spring of 1953 after several years on the road, Hal Kratzsch decided he'd had enough of touring and asked the group to replace him.

In May they came up with Ken Errair of Redford Township, Michigan, and his first session in July was their next chart single, "It Happened Once Before" (#29, September 1953). The year ended with the group winning the coveted *down beat* poll as Best Jazz Vocal Group of 1953.

In August 1954 the Freshmen issued their first LP, titled *Voices in Modern*. It gave birth to their next chart single, the beautiful "Mood Indigo," which reached number 24 on November 27, 1954.

In 1955 the group did a Jay Livingston-Ray Evans song called "How Can I Tell Her" for the film *Lucy Gallant* starring Charlton Heston and Jane Wyman. It came off so well they decided to try it as a single. The flip side, hastily chosen at the last minute, was Frank Sinatra's 1946 hit "Day by Day" (#5). They gave the ballad an up-tempo Latin feel and waited to see what happened. Following a June release, radio gave cursory response to the film song and flipped the 45 to "Day by Day," making it a number 42 chart single—their fourth. The next Freshmen release, a Guy Lombardo 1927 smash (#1), gave them their first and only back-to-back top 100 number, reaching number 69 in December 1955.

The February 1956 *Four Freshmen and Five Trombones* LP set a standard for modern jazz vocal groups; it reached number six nationally and resided on the charts for over eight months.

Ken Errair, who had only a year before married actress Jane Withers, begged off of the road and was replaced by Ken Albers of Pitman, New Jersey, a member of the Stuarts jazz vocal group.

With Ken firmly in place, the Freshmen decided to break ground with new audiences and became one of the first groups to play college auditoriums and field houses. Now pursuing a younger audience, they came up with the relevant "Graduation Day," their biggest chart hit at number 17 in the spring and summer of 1957. It might have been a top five hit had the song's publisher not given it to Canada's Rover Boys, who not only used it to get an ABC-Paramount record deal, but early on beat slow-moving Capitol to the marketplace with a version that finished at number 16.

In 1960 the group recorded the masterful "Their Hearts Were Full of Spring." It so enchanted a young Brian Wilson that he lifted the vocal arrangement note for note, first as "A Young Man Is Gone" (*Little Deuce Coupe* LP) and then under the original title for the *Live Beach Boys '69* LP. (Wilson even dropped by the Freshmen's office in Hollywood during the Beach Boys' formative years to secure copies of their vocal charts.) The Beach Boys ultimately found their niche playing Chuck Berry rhythms with Four Freshmen harmonies, but they did direct credit to the Freshmen.

In 1960 Don Barbour became the next to leave, replaced by Bill Comstock from Delaware, Ohio (also of the Stuarts). The group stayed with Capitol till 1965, then moved briefly to Decca and Liberty. In 1972 Bill Comstock left and in 1977 Ross Barbour followed. By 1982 Ken Albers had also retired from the group.

In 1986 they received a Grammy nomination for their 41st LP *Fresh* in the category of Best Jazz Vocal Performance Duo or Group.

Today, Bob Flanigan keeps the name and values of the Four Freshmen alive touring with three new and highly talented members, Autie Goodman, Mike Beisner, and Greg Stegeman. Hal Kratzsch went on to sing with THE SIGNATURES and died of cancer in November 1970. Don Barbour never finished the work he started on his solo LP for Capitol having died in a car accident on October 5, 1961. Capitol issued *The Solo Voice of Don Barbour* the following year. Ken Errair did one Capitol solo album in 1957 called *Solo Session* and then went into California real estate. He died in a small plane crash on June 14, 1968.

The Four Freshmen legacy is based not only on the music they created but also on their unswerving determination and courage in establishing a new sound that would make them a cornerstone of vocal group history.

THE FOUR FRESHMEN

A SIDE/B SIDE	LABEL/CAT NO	DATE
Mr. B's Blues / Then I'll Be Happy	Cap 1293	11/50
Now You Know / Pick Up Your Tears And Go Home	Cap 1377	4/51
It's A Blue World / Tuxedo Junction	Cap 2152	7/52
The Day Isn't Long Enough / Stormy Weather	Cap 2286	11/52
Poinciana / Baltimore Oriole	Cap 2398	4/53
Holiday / It Happened Once Before	Cap 2564	8/53
Seems Like Old Times / Crazy Bones	Cap 2745	2/54
I'll Be Seeing You / Please Remember	Cap 2832	6/54
We'll Be Together Again / My Heart Stood Still	Cap 2898	8/54
Mood Indigo / Love Turns Winter To Spring	Cap 2961	10/54
It Never Occurred To Me / Malaya	Cap 3070	3/55
Day By Day / How Can I Tell Her	Cap 3154	6/55
Charmaine / In This Whole Wide World	Cap 3292	11/55
Angel Eyes / Love Is Just Around The Corner	Cap 3359	2/56
Graduation Day / Lonely Night In Paris	Cap 3410	4/56
He Who Loves And Runs Away / You're So Far	Cap 3532	9/56
That's The Way I Feel / What's It Gonna Be	Cap 3652	2/57
Julie Is Her Name / Sometimes I'm Happy	Cap 3779	8/57
How Can I Begin To Tell / Granada	Cap 3832	11/57
Whistle Me Some Blues / Nights Are Longer	Cap 3930	3/58
Candy / Route 66	Cap 4341	2/60
Teach Me Tonight / Shangri-La	Cap 4749	6/62
I'm Gonna Go Fishing / Taps Miller	Cap 4824	9/62
Summertime / Baby Won't You Please Come Home	Cap 5007	6/63
Funny How Time Slips Away / Charade	Cap 5083	11/63
My Baby's Gone / Don't Make Me Sorry	Cap 5151	3/64
When I Stop Lovin' You / Nights Are Long	Cap 5401	4/65
Old Cape Cod / Men In Their Flying Machines	Cap 5471	8/65
Cry / Nowhere To Go	Cap 32070	12/66
Cherish, Windy / Come Fly With Me, Up Up and Away	Lbrty 56047	6/68
Blue World, Phoenix / My Special Angel	Lbrty 56099	4/69

The Four Lads

Probably the only group that ever made it by auditioning over a phone, the Four Lads were an early '50s pop harmony delight. They were originally choirboys at St. Michael's Cathedral Choir School in Toronto during the late '40s. The four included Bernie Toorish (lead), Jimmie Arnold (second tenor), Frank Busseri (baritone), and Connie Codarini (bass).

By day they attended school and by night their practices gave way to performances at local hotels. One such evening at the Toronto Hotel they did an imitation of the famed GOLDEN GATE QUARTET. Gates leader Orlando Wilson happened to be in the audience and was so impressed by the performance that he telephoned his manager Mike Stewart in New York right from the hotel. Holding the phone in the direction of the stage Stewart agreed with Wilson's assessment and agreed to sign the quartet sight unseen to a management contract.

The boys pooled their life savings for the New York trip and Stewart immediately put them into the fashionable Le Ruban Bleu nightclub for a tryout of two weeks. That tryout lasted 30 weeks and the Lads' reputation began to spread. Performances at the Paramount and on the Perry Como and Dave Garroway TV shows followed. During the Lads' appearance at Le Ruban Bleu, Columbia A&R guru Mitch Miller spotted them and brought them aboard.

They were originally signed to Columbia as a backup group and given the unique opportunity few acts ever get with a major label, that of choosing which of the roster's stars they'd like to sing backup for. In what can only be termed a fateful decision they passed over several name acts to back an unknown newcomer named Johnnie Ray.

In the fall of 1951 the group supported Ray's new two-sider "Cry" b/w "Little White Cloud that Cried." Even the most optimistic expectations didn't prepare the group or Ray for the incredible success, not just of "Cry" (number one for eleven weeks) but also "Little White Cloud" (number two for two weeks).

The Lads had three more hits with Ray "(Please Mr. Sun" [#6], "Here Am I Brokenhearted" [#8], and "What's the Use" [#13], all in 1952) before getting the opportunity to do it for themselves.

Their first single, "The Mockingbird," made it to number 23 in the summer of 1952 on Columbia's Okeh label. They moved up to the parent company starting with their next single, "Somebody Loves Me" (#22) from the musical *George White's Scandals of 1924*.

Five of their next 12 singles charted, including "Istanbul" (#10) and "Down by the Riverside" (#17), both in 1953. "Skokiaan," a South African song, became their first top 10 hit (#7) in the fall of 1954 followed by a charter behind Frankie Laine ("Rain Rain Rain," #21) at just about the same time. They also backed Columbia thrushes Jill Corey and Toni Arden.

The group continued on the national nightclub circuit but also did double duty wherever they were by officiating at early mass at a local church before going to bed (just like today's rockers and rappers).

Their biggest hit came in the fall of 1955 with "Moments to Remember" (#2), a pretty ballad done in their schmaltziest of styles. "No Not Much" had the same effect (#2) in early 1956. Though rock and roll was taking over, the group (much to its credit and talent) held their own into the late '50s, scoring another 16 pop charters including "Standing on the Corner (Watching All the Girls Go By)" (#3, spring of 1956).

With 28 chart singles between 1951 and 1959 the group was certainly a potent force in pop music of the period and their clean-cut harmonies attracted a large following.

By 1961 Connie was in the restaurant business. Lead singer Bernie Toorish left in the '70s to pursue the insurance business and Jimmy left in the '80s to teach voice in California. Baritone Frank continued on and in the early '90s was still performing to appreciative audiences, many of whom had fallen in love to the strains of Four Lads songs in the '50s.

THE FOUR LADS

A SIDE/B SIDE	LABEL/CAT NO	DATE
The Mockingbird	Okeh 6885	1952
Somebody Loves Me /		
Thanks To You	Col 39865	1952
Blackberry Boogie /		
The Girl On The Shore	Col 39902	1952
I Wonder, I Wonder, I Wonder /		
He Who Has Love	Col 39958	1953
Down By The Riverside /		
Take Me Back	Col 40005	1953
All I Desire / Lovers' Waltz	Col 40019	1953
I Love You / 900 Miles		
(From My Home)	Col 40042	1953
Anymore	Col 40081	1953
Istanbul (Not Constantinople) / I		
Should Have Told You Long Ago	Col 40082	1953

A SIDE/B SIDE	LABEL/CAT NO	DATE
YGotta Go To Fais Do Do /		
Harmony Brown	Col 40140	1953
Do You Know What Lips Are For /		
Cleo And Meo	Col 40177	1954
The Place Where I Worship		
(Is The Wide Open Space /		
Long John	Col 40204	1954
Oh, That'll Be Joyful /		
What Can I Lose (By Letting		
You Know I Love You)	Col 40220	1954
Gilly Gilly Ossenfeffer		
Katzenellem Bogem By The		
Sea / I Hear It Everywhere	Col 40236	1954
Skokiaan (South African Song) /		
Why Should I Love You?	Col 40306	1954
Two Ladies In De Shade Of De		
Banana Tree / Dance Calinda	Col 40402	1955
I've Been Thinking / Pledging My		
Love (Forever My Darling)	Col 40436	1955
Too Much! Baby, Baby! /		
The Average Giraffe	Col 40490	1955
I've Got Four Big Brothers (To		
Look After Me / Little Bit	Col 40532	1955
Moments To Remember /		
Dream On, My Love, Dream On	Col 40539	1955
Ain't It A Pity And A Shame /		
I Heard The Angels Singing	Col 40600	1955
No, Not Much! / I'll Never Know	Col 40629	1956
Herman And The Boys Sing:		
Standing On The Corner /		
My Little Angel	Col 40674	1956
The Bus Stop Song		
(A Paper Of Pins) /		
A House With Love In It	Col 40736	1956
The Stingiest Man In Town /		
Mary's Little Box Chile	Col 40788	1956
Who Needs You /		
It's So Easy To Forget	Col 40811	1957
Golly / I Just Don't Know	Col 40914	1957
The Eyes Of God /		
His Invisible Hand	Col 40974	1957
Put A Light In The Window / The		
Things We Did Last Summer	Col 41058	1957
There's Only One Of You /		
Blue Tattoo	Col 41136	1958
Enchanted Island / Guess		
What The Neighbors'll Say	Col 41194	1958
The Mocking Bird / Won'Cha		
(Give Me Somethin' In Return)	Col 41266	1958
The Girl On Page 44 / Sunday	Col 41310	1959
The Fountain Of Youth /		
Meet Me Tonight In Dreamland	Col 41365	1959
Together Wherever We Go /		
The Chosen Few	Col 41409	1959
Got A Locket In My Pocket /		
The Real Thing	Col 41443	1959
Happy Anniversary /		
Who Do You Think You Are?	Col 41497	1959

A SIDE/B SIDE	LABEL/CAT NO	DATE
You're Nobody Till Somebody		
Cares / Goona Goona	Col 41629	1960
Our Lady Of Fatima /		
The Sheik Of Chicago	Col 41682	1960
Two Other People /		
Our Lady of Fatima	Col 41733	1960

The Four Lovers

The Four Lovers were the forerunners of one of music's most famous groups but started out in a completely different musical direction.

Originally calling themselves the Variatones, they performed country and western numbers with some pop, rockabilly, and Italian love songs thrown in.

Joining together around 1955, the members were Francis Castelluccio a.k.a. Frankie Valli, Nick and Tommy DeVito, and Hank Majewski.

They did the New Jersey club circuit, places like the Broadway Lounge in Passaic, the Gondoleer in Orange, and the El Morocco in Newark.

One of their shows attracted an RCA representative who apparently liked the strange musical mix and Frankie's falsetto lead.

On April 12, 1956, the Variatones, now calling themselves the Four Lovers, recorded six sides for RCA. Nipper's execs decided to issue the first four sides in two singles to be released at the same time that April.

Billboard's reviewer on May 5th described "You're the Apple of My Eye" as "A catchy pop-styled rhythm & blues item with satiric overtones likely to get good play." The review of the flip, a Jesse Belvin-penned Cliques recording "The Girl of My Dreams," read, "This side is a ballad, nicely done, but without the impact of the flip." There was a writeup on the second single, "Honey Love," that read, "This was a big hit some months back in rhythm & blues as done by Clyde McPhatter and The Dominoes. The satiric style here may give it the edge to revive it for present day rock & rollers." A review of the flip, "Please Don't Leave Me," stated, "This one was a Fats Domino hit before that artist began to hit pop as well as the R&B charts. Again there's a satirical edge, but the side is potent rock and roll."

"Apple" (an Otis Blackwell song) got the most activity, reaching number 62 on *Billboard*'s national charts in May and June 1956 and earning them a shot on Ed Sullivan's Sunday night show. By August they were back in RCA's studios cutting four more sides, which became single number three, "Jambalaya" b/w "Be Lovey Dovey," followed by "Happy Am I" b/w "Never, Never" in December.

Neither single did well but an LP was issued anyway. Its contents ranged from harmony ballad versions of "For Sentimental Reasons" and "It's Too Soon to Know" to a wacky, fast-paced country version of "White Christmas."

Their last RCA single (January 1957) was the two leftover sides from their April 1956 session: "Shake A Hand" b/w "The Stranger."

In 1957 the Four Lovers had one single with Epic but it went the way of its RCA cousins.

In 1958, the Four Lovers became Frankie Valle and the Romans. Nick DeVito was replaced by arranger/singer Charlie Callelo for one single on Cindy, "Real (This Is Real)."

Frankie had a habit of changing his name and spelling almost as often as he had records out. Later in 1958 he went under the name Frankie Tyler for "I Go Ape" on Okeh. Before his Four Lovers days he recorded "My Mother's Eyes" as Frankie Valley on Carona in 1953 and "Forgive and Forget" as Frankie Valley and the Travelers on Mercury in 1954.

In 1959 Callelo was replaced by Royal Teens member Bob Gaudio. Hank also departed to join Chang Lee and the Zaniacs (not a joke) and Nick Massi came in. The group now consisted of Frankie Valle (22, lead), Bob Gaudio (17, tenor), Tommy DeVito (23, baritone), and Nick Massi (24, bass).

In the fall of 1959 the new foursome recorded a rhythm ballad single penned by Nick (Maciaci) Massi in an early '50s crooning group style called "Please Take a Chance" under the name Frankie Vally, though some pressings say the Four Lovers. Even though it received little airplay and practically no sales the group never gave up on developing their sound. Soon after, the New Jersey quartet would rename themselves after a local bowling alley called THE FOUR SEASONS.

THE FOUR LOVERS

A SIDE/B SIDE	LABEL/CAT NO	DATE
Frankie Valley		
My Mother's Eyes /		
The Laugh's On Me	Crna 1234	1953
Somebody Else Took Her Home /		
Forgive And Forget	Merc 70381	1954

A SIDE/B SIDE	LABEL/CAT NO	DATE
Frankie Vally and the Travelers		
It May Be Wrong /		
Please Take A Chance	Dca 9-30994	1955
The Four Lovers		
You're The Apple Of My Eye /		
The Girl of My Dreams	RCA 6518	4/56
Honey Love /		
Please Don't Leave Me	RCA 6519	4/56
Jambalaya / Be Lovey Dovey	RCA 6646	8/56
Happy Am I / Never Never	RCA 6768	12/56
The Stranger / Shake A Hand	RCA 6812	1/57
The Stranger / Night Train	RCA 6819	1957
My Life for Your Love / Pucker Up	Epic 9255	1957
Frankie Valle and the Romans		
Come Si Bella / Real	Cindy 3012	1959
Hal Miller and the Rays		
An Angel Cried /		
Hope, Faith and Dreams	Topic 6003	1960

The Four Preps

A pop-folk vocal group, the Four Preps probably could have sung anything from doo wop to white gospel if given songs in those styles. Formed in the mid-'50s at Hollywood High School in Los Angeles by Glen Larson (first tenor) and Bruce Belland (lead), the quartet was completed with the addition of Ed Cobb (bass) and Marvin Inabnett (second tenor). They practiced at a Hollywood church, sang songs by groups they admired like THE FOUR FRESHMEN, THE FOUR ACES, and THE FOUR LADS, and came up with a similar name in the Four Preps. They became proficient enough to begin playing the Los Angeles bar mitzvah and wedding circuit and by 1956 had worked up an act that included some vocal group parodies that would come in handy in later years.

On one Saturday night performance at a UCLA dance, the Preps had unknowingly been taped by their friend Howard Adelman. Not wanting a good thing to go to waste, Bruce and Glen ran the tape up and down Sunset Boulevard, where all the booking and management companies were. This led to their meeting with Les Paul and Mary Ford's manager Mel Shauer, who asked them to leave the tape.

In one of those Cinderella stories that can actually happen, the group was informed three days later that they had a record deal; they signed with Capitol only six days after friend Howard had taken the initiative to turn on his tape recorder.

Their single "Dreamy Eyes" landed on *Billboard*'s pop charts on December 22, 1956, reaching a respectable number 56. Several insignificant pop sides followed until their sixth single, a song Bruce started to write in junior high and didn't finish until their second recording session five years later (in about 15 minutes), when they were one song short for a four-song EP. The song was "26 Miles," which put the California coastal island of Santa Catalina in the national consciousness and became the Four Preps' biggest hit, reaching number two for three weeks. The follow-up by Bruce and Glen was a well-written "I was a jerk for letting you go" type of song with heavy piano chords and strong harmonies that made "Big Man" number three in the U.S. during the spring and summer of 1958 and number two in England.

The group next forayed into film songs reaching number 21 with "Lazy Summer Night" (from *Andy Hardy Comes Home*) and number 69 with "Cinderella" (from *Gidget*). Then they tried the cover route; *Billboard*'s January 12, 1959, reviewer stated about "She Was Five and He Was Ten": "Top side is a tune that was an almost hit a few years ago and should be a real hit with this fine reading." It wasn't, but three singles later they were back in the spotlight with a rewritten camp song called "Down By the Station" (#13, 1959).

In 1960, "Got a Girl" was a top 20 number (#24) that scored twice on the British charts (#28 in June and #47 in July; English hit lists often had a record enter, fall off and re-enter the Top 75).

Turning whimsical, the group created four minutes and 45 seconds of parody under the premise that if you could get rid of all the hit groups around there'd be "More Money for You and Me." With revised lyrics to songs like "Mr. Blue" (THE FLEETWOODS), "Smoke Gets in Your Eyes" (THE PLATTERS), "Alley Oop" (the Hollywood Argyles), and DION AND THE BELMONTS' "A Teenager in Love" ("each time I ask the stars without fail, why must I be a teenager in jail"), "More Money" lifted the group to number 17 and was surely heard by each of the seven groups they parodied. Even the Belmonts must have laughed at the Preps' notion that while Dion was on stage singing, the Belmonts were out in the parking lot stealing hubcaps off of cars. Apparently the British took hubcap theft more seriously as the record only made number 39 in the U.K.

The Preps tried the novelty route twice more. The first was "The Big Draft" featuring the Platters' "I'll Never Smile Again," THE MARCELS' "Heartaches," and another shot at Dion, this time with THE DEL-SATINS on "Runaround Sue," but it only made it to number 61.

The second was their last chart single, "The Letter to the Beatles," which reached number 85 on the charts before the Beatles' lawyers shot it down.

The quartet had nine more singles on Capitol between 1964 and 1966 when David Somerville (see THE DIAMONDS) joined, taking Ed Cobb's place. But by 1967 the group members had gone their separate ways in the entertainment business.

Bruce became a script writer ("McCloud" and "Mannix"), a TV producer for Ralph Edwards Productions, and eventually an executive at NBC-TV. Glen Larson also went into TV writing and producing and wrote the theme (with Somerville) for "The Fall Guy" in 1981. Ed went on to be a successful songwriter ("Every Little Bit Hurts," Brenda Holloway, #13, 1964, and "Tainted Love," Soft Cell, #8, 1982). While with the Preps he had moonlighted with arranger Lincoln Mayorga in a rock and roll band called the Piltdown Men (sometimes known as the Linc Eddy Combo) with a U.S. single on Capitol ("Brontasaurus Stomp," #75, 1960) and three chart singles in the U.K. on Capitol ("MacDonald's Cave," #14, 1960, "Piltdown Rides Again," #14, 1961, and "Goodnight Mrs. Flintstone," #18, 1961).

In the late '80s a TV producer suggested that Bruce, Ed, David Somerville, and Jim Pike (of THE LETTERMEN) re-form the Four Preps for the wrap party of a show Bruce had scripted called "Weekend Warriors." Dick Clark got involved after seeing them at the party, and the group has been touring ever since. 13 charters out of 38 singles along with four EPs and 12 LPs are only part of the Four Preps' story. As of 1992 there were still plenty of people who remembered and continued to enjoy the group's sound and satire.

THE FOUR PREPS

A SIDE/B SIDE	LABEL/CAT NO	DATE
Dreamy Eyes / Fools Will Be Fools	Cap F03576	1956
Moonstruck In Madrid /		
I Cried A Million Tears	Cap F03621	1957
Falling Star / Where Wuz You	Cap F03699	1957
Promise Me Baby /		
Again 'n' Again 'n' Again	Cap F03761	1957
Band Of Angels / How About That	Cap F03775	1957
26 Miles / It's You	Cap F03845	1957
Big Man / Stop Baby	Cap F03960	1958
Lazy Summer Night /		
Summertime Lies	Cap F04023	1958
Cinderella / Gidget	Cap F04078	1958
She Was Five And He Was Ten /		
Riddle Of Love	Cap F04126	1959
Big Surprise / Try My Arms	Cap F04218	1959

A SIDE/B SIDE	LABEL/CAT NO	DATE
I Ain't Never /		
Memories, Memories	Cap F04256	1959
Down By The Station /		
Listen Honey	Cap F04312	1959
Got A Girl /		
(Wait Till You) Hear It From Me	Cap F04362	1960
Sentimental Kid / Madelina	Cap F04400	1960
Kaw-Liga / The Sand And The Sea	Cap F04435	1960
I've A' Ready Started In / Balboa	Cap F04478	1960
Calcutta / Gone Are The Days	Cap F04508	1961
Grounded	Cap F05568	1961
More Money For You And Me (long		
version) / Swing Down Chariot	Cap F04599	1961
More Money For You And		
Me (edited version) /		
Swing Down Chariot	Cap F04641	1961
Once Around The Block /		
The Seine	Cap F04659	1961
The Big Draft / Sunny Cockroach	Cap F04716	1962
Alice / Goodnight Sweetheart	Cap F04792	1962
26 Miles / Big Man (reissue)	Cap X06030	1962
Charmaine / Hi Ho Anybody Home	Cap F04974	1963
Oh Where, Oh Where /		
Demons And Witches	Cap F05020	1963
I'm Falling In Love With A Girl /		
The Greatest Surfing Couple	Cap F05074	1963
Letter To The Beatles /		
College Cannonball	Cap F05143	1964
I've Known You All My Life /		
What Kind Of Bird Is That	Cap F05178	1964
Girl Without A Top / Two Wrongs		
Don't Make A Right	Cap F05236	1964
My Love, My Love /		
How To Succeed In Love	Cap F05274	1964
I'll Set My Love To Music /		
Everlasting	Cap F05351	1965
Our First American Dance /		
Now I'll Never Be The Same	Cap F05450	1965
Girl In The Shade Of A Striped		
Umbrella / Let's Call It A Day Girl	Cap F05687	1966
Something To Remember You By /		
Annie In Her Granny	Cap F05609	1966
Love Of The Common People /		
What I Don't Know Can't		
Hurt Me	Cap F05819	1966
Draftdodger Rag / Hitchhiker	Cap F05921	1966

Norman Fox and the Rob-Roys

Oone of the earliest interracial quintets, Norman Fox and the Rob-Roys were also one of the most underrated and overlooked groups ever to cut a 45.

With his distinctive lead voice, Norman Fox (16) of the Bronx hooked up with DeWitt Clinton High School friends Bob Trotman (16, first tenor), Andre Lilly (16, second tenor), Robert Thierer (17, baritone), and Marshall "Buzzy" Helfand (17, bass) in 1956 to form a dynamic vocal mix with their Jewish/black coalition. (Trotman and Lilly were originally members of the Harmonaires on Holiday.) They practiced in the school's bathroom, at Norman's house on Henry Hudson Parkway, and at Robert's Knolls Crescent address, sharpening their sound on songs like THE HEARTBEATS' "Rockin' and Rollin'" and their own "Tell Me Why."

Influenced by other groups like THE HARPTONES, THE EL DORADOS, THE CLEFTONES, THE TEENAGERS, and the Heartbeats, the Bronx quintet developed their own unique sound at the same time the racially mixed DEL-VIKINGS were getting it all together in Pittsburgh.

Early in 1957 Bob Trotman met Don Carter, New York agent for the Duke/Peacock organization, at Buddy's Record Shop on 167th Street in the Bronx, and told him of their group. After a live audition in that very same record store, the Bronx boys found themselves contracted to the Texas-based record label.

Originally called the Velvetones, they changed their name to the Rob-Roys (after the drink) and recorded their first single for Peacock's new Backbeat affiliate in April 1957 at Bell Sound Studios.

"Tell Me Why," written by bass Buzzy Helfand, became credited on all subsequent labels as Helford-Carter. (We all know who the freeloading Carter was, but how Helfand became Helford is a mystery. If it was a spelling mistake why wasn't it corrected on reprints over the years?) "Tell Me Why" was an exciting chime-harmony rocker that presented a perfect vehicle for Fox's powerful delivery, the group's tight harmonies, and Helfand's solid bass.

"Tell Me Why" came out in the summer of 1957. The single was well received by East Coast radio stations (particularly in New York and Philadelphia), but it was obvious that the gospel conglomerate had no idea of how to market rock and roll.

The Rob-Roys turned out to be Backbeat's first integrated group (Fox, Helfand, and Thierer were white, Lilly and Trotman black), but they performed at Harlem clubs to the surprise and delight of patrons lucky enough to see them. For the most part they played New York area record hops with deejays like Jocko while waiting for their next release, the Robert Thierer-Bob Trotman dance doo wop classic, "Dance Girl Dance."

In two singles Norman established himself as one of rock's most excitingly identifiable leads. Unfortunately, few people had the chance to concur thanks to Backbeat's inability or unwillingness to market another classic.

In late 1958 the group, weary of lost records, brought two Norman Fox originals to Capitol Records. They signed the group and issued "Pizza Pie" b/w "Dream Girl" in January 1959. Paul Schneller (another white Jewish bass) replaced Helfand on bass just before the Capitol sides were recorded.

On January 19th, *Billboard* reviewed "Pizza Pie," stating, "A rocker slightly dated in sound and approach, but the side is well made, the boys handle it nicely and the novelty interest is there. It ties the story of a lifetime in with a pizza pie. This could catch a spin." The minute the record came out, Don Robey of Backbeat showed up waving a still-valid contract with the Rob-Roys. Capitol chose to pull the single before it reached most radio stations.

In desperation, the group agreed to record five more Fox originals for Robey in order to be released from their deal, which they did, but by the time all was said and done Capitol still wouldn't reissue "Pizza Pie" and lost interest in the Rob-Roys. Ironically, Robey never issued the five sides he fought for and they remain in the MCA vaults.

In 1962 Fox and company did two sides, "Aggravation" and "Lonely Boy," for Bob Shad's Time label, but they were never issued.

The group broke up in 1963 but re-formed for a 1971 Hunter College "Oldies Revival" at the request of disc jockey legend Gus Gossert. All but Buzzy appeared that night.

In 1986 at the urging of Robert Thierer, a new Rob-Roys emerged with Norman back on lead along with veterans Stuart Morgan (first tenor) of an '80s touring DRIFTERS, Alex Augustine (second tenor) of the latterday CHARTS and ROOMMATES, and Leon McClain (bass) of the Quinns ("Hong Kong").

In the late '80s a couple of ardent collector/dealers happened upon two sides the group had cut for Capitol, "Lover Doll" and "That's Love," and one the Rob-Roys had done in 1974 ("Rainy Day Bells") and turned them into two singles on a bogus Backbeat label. A third Backbeat issue, "Do Re Mi" (somehow spirited from the Robey sides), came out in 1990 for the collectors' market.

Later, Robert Trotman became a motorman (since retired) for New York's E Train; Buzzy Helfand became the owner of a marina in Montauk, Long Island; Robert Thierer became a CPA; and Norman Fox gained success as a garment manufacturer when he and Robert weren't performing as the Rob-Roys. Not surprisingly, the group had greater popularity in the early '60s during the first oldies awareness period than when they were originally recording. "Tell Me Why" became a hit for THE BELMONTS in 1961 (#18).

In late 1991 the group recorded four songs a cappella for a Starlight Records CD. Three of the four were their own "Dream Girl," "Pizza Pie," and "Tell Me Why"; the fourth was the Heartbeats' "Your Way."

NORMAN FOX AND THE ROB ROYS

A SIDE/B SIDE	LABEL/CAT NO	DATE
Tell Me Why / Audrey	Backbeat 501	9/57
Dance Girl Dance / My Dearest One	Backbeat 508	5/58
Dream Girl / Pizza Pie	Cap 4128	1/59
Lover Doll / Little Star	Backbeat 499	1988
Rainy Day Bells / That's Love	Backbeat 500	1988
Do Re Mi / Lover Doll	Backbeat 501	1990

The Genies

The Genies originated in 1956 on the boardwalk at Long Beach, Long Island. The members were lead and first tenor Roy Hammond, second tenor Bill Gains, baritone Alexander "Buddy" Faison, and bass Fred Jones. The group actually started when Fred met Bill and Buddy and later discovered Roy singing on the Long Beach train. Fred called his friend Claude Johnson, who was from Brooklyn, to join the group on lead shortly after they formed. Claude was singing with an unnamed loose collection of Brooklynites that included Estelle Williams and Eugene Pitt (later lead of THE JIVE FIVE) but neither ever sang with the Genies, according to Claude. When Johnson joined the Long Beach bunch he named them the Genies though not for any particular reason except he felt that it sounded good.

The five 18- to 20-year-olds began rehearsing at Mrs. Henriata's Employment Agency after closing time. She'd give them the key and the Genies would wail through the night.

One evening in 1958 while they were singing on the boardwalk, a man came up and handed them his card. It was Bob Shad, president of Shad Records in New York, and the encounter led to an audition and a recording in June of the group's original song "Who's That Knockin'." It took Shad almost a year to put out "Who's That Knockin'," but on March 30, 1959, it proved worth the wait as the

R&B rocker hit *Billboard*'s charts. It became an East Coast favorite and a top five record in numerous cities, though it only made it to number 71 nationally.

Soon afterward, the Genies played a week at the Apollo Theatre with such groups as THE CHANNELS and THE CADILLACS. A few days into the engagement Bill Gains ran off to Canada with a girl and was never heard from again. The group had to move quickly to shift parts to cover Bill's second tenor spot for the remainder of the week. The Genies toured the East Coast and Canada while recording one single for Hollywood and three more for Morty Craft's Warwick label, the best one being the 1961 "Crazy Feeling." The group, however, had broken up by 1959.

Fred wound up in Brooklyn while Alexander remained in Long Beach driving a truck. Roy became Roy C and went on to solo R&B success in the soul era with "Shotgun Wedding" (#14 R&B, 1965). Claude met Roland Trone in a coffee shop in Long Beach in 1960 and the two began painting houses for a living. (Contrary to public opinion Roland never sang with the Genies.) While Claude and Roland were applying a coat of paint to an apartment building and singing their way through the work, a captivated tenant heard their vocalizing and put them in touch with agent Peter Paul who brought them to Big Top Records.

Their first single came out, but since the names Claude and Roland didn't have much magic, they became Don (Roland) and Juan (Claude) and hit the charts with Claude's song, "What's Your Name." It went to number seven nationally in the early spring of 1962 but subsequent singles went nowhere. In recent times Claude was still doing oldies clubs and shows with a new Juan (he decided his name should come first as he sings lead) in the person of Stanley Rogers, formerly of the '80s' version of THE PARAGONS.

THE GENIES

A SIDE/B SIDE	LABEL/CAT NO	DATE
Who's That Knockin' / The First Time	Shad 5002	1958
No More Knockin' / On The Edge Of Town	Hlywd 69-1	1959
There Goes That Train / Crazy Love	Warwick 573	1960
Just Like The Bluebird / Twistin' Pneumonia	Warwick 607	1960
Crazy Feeling / Little Young Girl	Warwick 643	1961

The Harptones

The Harptones, one of the most respected rhythm and blues groups of all time, never put one of their 29 singles on the national R&B lists. Yet many of their recordings are oldies standards today.

1953 was the year members of the Harps from downtown Manhattan joined up with members of THE SKYLARKS from uptown. The Harps consisted of Willie Winfield, his brothers Jimmy and Clyde, Bill "Dicey" Galloway, and Johnny Bronson. Willie, originally from Norfolk, Virginia, occasionally sang with his cousin Dickie Smith and his group THE FIVE KEYS before coming to New York but never recorded with them.

The Harps practiced under the Monroe Street underpass of the Manhattan Bridge (probably the largest echo chamber ever used) while the Skylarks—Bill Dempsey, Curtis Cherebin, Fred Taylor, Eugene "Sonny" Cooke, Raoul J. Cita, and the street singer remembered only as Skillum—hit their harmonies on 115th Street between 7th and 8th Avenues.

Early in 1953 Dicey Galloway went uptown to find a piano player who could work with the Harps and ran into the 115th Street Skylarks. In the midst of the Skylarks was Raoul Cita, a piano player, songwriter, arranger, baritone, and exactly the man the Harps needed. As time passed, a new Harps group emerged with Willie Winfield and Dicey Galloway of the original Harps and Curtis Cherebin, Bill Dempsey, and Raoul Cita of the Skylarks.

Soon after, Billy Brown replaced Cherebin, and Claudie "Nicky" Clark of the nearby FIVE CROWNS joined the group. The lineup now resembled the "Willie" club with Willie Winfield (24 and lead), Nicky Clark (20, second lead and first tenor), William "Bill" Dempsey (17 and second tenor), Bill "Dicey" Galloway (17 and baritone), Bill Brown (17 and bass), and Raoul Cita (25, tenor and baritone but usually piano player). Occasionally another Brown sang with the Harps—Johnny Brown—but his career direction became that of a comedian and he wound up as a cast member of the long-running '60s hit "Laugh-In."

The group's influences, especially Willie's, were the Five Keys, THE SWALLOWS, and THE LARKS, but what set them apart was the influence on Raoul of THE FOUR FRESHMEN. Their jazz harmony, tailored by Cita to fit the Harps' enormous talent, lifted them above most rhythm and blues groups and far above typical street-corner collaborations.

Their first paying performance was in New Jersey at the Piccadilly Club where the "huge" sum of $100 was garnered for two nights of singing. They branched out from there, working in Brooklyn, Manhattan, and New Jersey and even performing on the local New York TV show "Spotlight on Harlem." They also practiced extensively in Cita's 119th Street basement working on new Cita compositions like "My Memories of You."

Then in late 1953 came the big test. They felt ready for that equalizer of men and boys, the Apollo amateur night contest. The Skylarks had tried it in 1951 and had been booed off the stage. Willie remembered; he had been in the audience at the time. But this night would be different. The Harps sang a magical rendition of the Jo Stafford 1947 hit (#15) "Sunday Kind of Love" and were rousingly applauded.

If not for a twist of fate, many of the great Harptones recordings might have wound up on MGM. They met the label's representative at the show. They were to reconvene with him later in a hallway away from the Apollo crowd, but while singing in the hall they met Leo Rogers of Bruce Records. He took them to his partners, Morty Craft and Monte Bruce, who loved their sound. They knew that there was a group called the Harps recording on Savoy (Little David Baughn and the Harps), so Cita changed their name to the Harptones.

In December 1953 the song they had sung at the Apollo became their first single. From the eerie organ intro to the group's deep harmony to Willie's velvety vocalizing, "I Want a Sunday Kind of Love" was a classic. The record received large doses of airplay and was selling throughout the tri-state area when word reached the Harptones that a Baltimore group, Bobby Hall and the Kings, had covered "Sunday." Though the Kings' version did well in the Baltimore-Washington area, the Harptones' superior recording won out and sold as well as an R&B record could sell in 1954 without getting national attention. Even the flip ballad "I'll Never Tell" was getting airplay.

In January 1954 the first of the Cita-penned masterpieces came out. "My Memories of You" boasted five-part lyric harmony that was unique in R&B music of the time. The group had moved beyond doo wop into modern harmony, and Willie Winfield, the "Sultan of Smooth" (as Phil Groia called him), was fast becoming one of the most identifiable vocalists on the scene. "My Memories" became a solid seller in the group's East Coast realm though it was becoming noticeable that Bruce Records didn't have national clout.

"I Depended on You" was the next record and was led by Nicky Clark as Winfield missed the rehearsal that night. Only three musicians, Don Gardner (guitar), Jimmy Smith (organ), and Al Cass (sax), were on the session as Bruce tried to cut 10 sides one after the other to avoid a midnight January 1, 1954, musicians strike, and the other players had walked out.

The Harptones' fourth single, "Why Should I Love You," took them 22 takes while recording in Bruce's 1650 Broadway space. The 22 tries were not for the song itself but for the whistling intro and exit done over a modified boogie-woogie piano. By the time they got it done, THE FOUR LADS, whose offices were down the hall, had lifted it and put it on the B side of their "Skokiaan" hit. The pop up-tempo number had the Harptones' newly minted jazz-flavored harmonies. It gathered enough momentum to make the pop charts on September 18, 1954, reaching number 25. Though today it's one of the group's least remembered recordings it was their biggest national hit.

The Harptones did a number of backup sessions over the years. Their first was a loan by Bruce Records' Leo Rogers to friend Dave Miller and his Essex label so Dave could record Texas artist Bunny Paul on the Harptones' "I'll Never Tell." (Since Rogers owned the publishing rights he gained from the favor.) Essex issued it in August and the now sought-after collectors' item quickly vanished. Soon after, Dicey was drafted and replaced by Jimmy Beckum ("Laughing on the Outside," THE MAJORS, Derby).

In December, "Since I Fell for You" came out thanks to Buddy and Ella Johnson's suggestion to the Harptones after they met at the Apollo that the group try their song. Their unison-into-harmony intro, high-weaving vocals, and Willie's trademark pristine lead made for a memorable record—the standard version of the song—that Bruce was unable to take beyond the tri-state borders.

On January 14th the Harptones appeared at the historic Alan Freed Rock and Roll Ball at the St. Nicholas Arena in New York with an all-star lineup that included THE DRIFTERS, THE CLOVERS, Fats Domino, THE MOONGLOWS, and Joe Turner.

Their sixth and last Bruce release (March 1955) was the bluesiest of all Harptones singles, a remake of Ivory Joe Hunter's "I Almost Lost My Mind" with an exciting chime harmony intro.

By June the Harptones had signed with Hy Weiss's Old Town label and issued a song Cita had written almost two years earlier, the classic "Life Is But a Dream." With higher harmonies than previous Harptones sides and an almost angelic chorus of voices, the group's jazz leanings were becoming more predominant. The song has since become a street-corner classic and the solo singer's opening line "will you take part in" has become a measuring stick for group leads.

In September they played another historic gig (of their many one-nighters and package shows). The week-long Alan Freed Labor Day Rock and Roll Show at the Brooklyn Paramount featured the Moonglows, Chuck Berry, THE NUTMEGS, THE CARDINALS, and Tony Bennett, with Red Prysock and Sam "the Man" Taylor and their orchestras.

"(My Success) It All Depends On You" was the October 1954 Harptones issue. It lost momentum due to a Georgia Gibbs song with lyric similarities.

"What Is Your Decision," written by Ben Raleigh and Ben Weissman (the latter would go on to write 57 songs for Elvis Presley), became their only issue on Leo Rogers' Andrea label in April 1956. It was the most pop of their melodies, and *Billboard*'s April 21st reviewer commented, "The lads ask the big soulful question in slow emotional style. Winfield wails again and the group is with him all the way. This one should spin and spin."

By now the group consisted of Willie, Jimmy, Dempsey, and Bobby Spencer (THE CADILLACS, THE CHORDS, THE CRICKETS). "My Memories of You" was rerecorded by this version of the Harptones on the same session as "What Is Your Decision," and Rogers leased it to Tiptop Records for their September 1956 release.

Feeling their records weren't being promoted properly (and they weren't) the group moved over to George Goldner's complex in the summer of 1956. The first single for Rama was the minor classic "That's the Way It Goes." It was the group's favorite recording and was ahead of its time. Their tight harmony on the verses with part of the Raoul Cita chorus on the top (actually the Joytones and Lyrics were the chorus, in this case Joytones Lynn Middleton Daniels and Vickie Burgess) made this a jazz harmony jubilee. The ending had unison voices weaving upward until they broke into a full-blown harmony finale. The flip (actually the A side) "Three Wishes" was a superb pop-jazz ballad that had the smoothest of blends.

The Rama sides were the group's renaissance. "The Masquerade Is Over" followed in November 1956 and was a prime example of modern R&B jazz, with Cita's sax-led arrangement and peerless harmonies and lead.

In 1956 the Harptones appeared in the first rhythm and blues motion picture, *Rockin' the Blues*, along with THE WANDERERS, the Hurricanes, Linda Hopkins, the Miller Sisters, and disc jockey Hal Jackson.

They continued to tour and perform throughout the East with everyone from THE HEARTBEATS, THE FLAMINGOS, and THE SWALLOWS to Bo Diddley and Etta James, but they never got to the West Coast even though several of their records were getting play out there.

Watching their acrobatics in their cream-colored suits one wondered how they could sing at all. (Few people realize how innovative and talented the group was at dance routines, which they choreographed to Five Keys rockers like "Hucklebuck with Jimmy.")

At one point in 1956 Fred Taylor came in when Jimmy was ill, and Harriet "Toni" Williams Brown subbed for Dempsey while he helped his cancer-stricken father. Toni was the third member of the Joytones ("Gee What a Boy," Rama).

The Harptones' last Rama single, "The Shrine of St. Cecilia" (originally recorded by the Royals in 1952, Federal), had the most magnificent intro harmony of all their records. The full tenor harmonies descending like a cascading waterfall were truly memorable. It was also memorable as Bill Brown's last recording. He died soon after, and the group never could replace him.

The Harptones didn't issue another single until November 1957's "Cry Like I Cried." Released on Goldner's Gee label, the hard-to-sing ballad, a rhythm and blues grind number, had the group's first use of horns and a big-band intro.

In early 1959 the group returned to Morty Craft and his Warwick label. By now the lineup had changed to Willie, Dempsey, Toni, Curtis Cherebin (rejoined), and Milton Love (THE SOLITAIRES). Through all the labels and personnel changes Willie Winfield had always wanted to remain part of the group. Unlike many leads he never hungered to go solo.

In March 1959 Warwick released "Laughing on the Outside," the same song Jimmy Beckum had sung with the Majors back in 1953, but it saw little action. So too for "Love Me Completely" and their best Warwick single "No Greater Miracle" in May 1960.

One single in 1960 on Coed produced by Billy Dawn Smith (former lead of the Heralds) and one for Solitaires singer-turned-exec Buzzy Willis at MGM's Cub label ("Devil in Velvet") and the Harptones found themselves on Companion Records with two good sides ("The Last Dance" and "All in Your Mind") that *Billboard* noted in its February 13, 1961, issue: "The Harptones turn in a strong reading of something of an answer to 'Save the Last Dance for Me' on this pretty ballad. Side could easily take off. Flip is an answer to the current Maxine Brown ('All in My Mind') chart entry."

Their next single (the group's 22nd) took off—at least temporarily. "What Will I Tell My Heart" mustered enough across-the-country play and sales to reach number 96 on the pop charts in May 1961.

Their last new single with Willie came in 1964 on a song written by their lawyer's son, Ted Troob, titled "Sunset."

A year before, Bruce Records had issued a heretofore unreleased cut from 1953, called "Loving a Girl Like You." Why it was never released in the mid 50's is a mystery as it was a beautiful and competitive recording. In *They All Sang on the Corner*, Phil Groia wrote, " 'Loving a Girl Like You' was sung in the classic five-part Harptones harmony, the soft tenor lead, the smooth blend of second tenor and baritone, the high falsetto of the first tenor, the redoubtable bass and the mournfully heavy affirmation of the rhythm and blues piano chords."

In 1956 the Harptones backed Ruth McFadden (Old Town) on "Schoolboy," which was actually a female version of "Loving a Girl Like You."

In 1965 a group called the Soothers remade the Johnny Ray song "Little White Cloud that Cried" (Port). The Soothers were the Harptones without Willie—Bill Dempsey, Nicky Clark on lead, Fred, Curtis, Raoul, and Hank Jernigan. When you think about the group's heritage you realize that the last Harptones/Soothers single was cut by four members of the Skylarks and one of THE FIVE CROWNS.

In April 1970 the group with Willie, Dempsey, Jimmy, Curtis, Fred, and Raoul regrouped for the opening of the rock and roll revival at the Academy of Music and stayed together until 1972 when Willie and Raoul added Linda Champion and Lowe Murray (the Fitones, Angeltone) to form the current Harptones.

In November 1981 the group recorded an LP (Ambient Sound) which encompassed yesterday's feel with today's technology titled *Love Needs the Harptones*.

39 years later Willie, Raoul et al were still playing clubs in the East while disc jockeys across the country were still playing "Life Is But a Dream," "Memories of You," "Sunday Kind of Love," and other Harptones gems for the many thousands of faithful listeners.

The Harptones would undoubtedly be included on the top 10 vocal group list of anyone who remembers the '50s.

In 1971 Cita was asked, "How do you feel the Harptones compare to other groups?" He replied, "The only groups I feel are up there with us (musically) are the Flamingos, the Platters, and the Four Freshmen." Many would agree.

THE HARPTONES

A SIDE/B SIDE	LABEL/CAT NO	DATE
A Sunday Kind Of Love / I'll Never Tell	Bruce 101	12/53
My Memories Of You / It Was Just For Laughs	Bruce 102	1/54
I Depended On You / Mambo Boogie	Bruce 104	2/54
Why Should I Love You / Forever Mine	Bruce 109	7/54
I'll Never Tell* / Honey Lover*	Essex 364	8/54
Since I Fell For You / Oobidee-Oobidee-Do	Bruce 113	12/54
I Almost Lost My Mind / Oo Wee Baby	Bruce 126	3/55
Life Is But A Dream / You Know You're Doing Me Wrong	Prds 101	6/55
(My Success) It All Depends On You / I've Got A Notion	Prds 103	10/55
Schoolboy** / United We Stand**	OldTn 1030	1956
What Is Your Decision / Gimme Some	Andrea 100	4/56
Three Wishes / That's The Way It Goes	Rama 203	8/56
My Memories Of You / High Flying Baby	Tip Top 401	9/56
On Sunday Afternoon / The Masquerade Is Over	Rama 214	11/56
The Shrine Of Saint Cecilia / Oo Wee Baby	Rama 221	2/57
When Will I Know† / What Did She Do Wrong†	Gee 1029	1957
Cry Like I Cried / So Good, So Fine	Gee 1045	11/57
Laughing On The Outside / I Remember	Warwick 500	3/59
Love Me Completely / Hep Teenager	Warwick 512	1959
No Greater Miracle / What Kind Of Fool	Warwick 551	5/60
Rain Down Kisses / Answer Me, My Love	Coed 540	1960
Devil In Velvet / Your Love Is A Good Love	Cub 9097	1961
All In Your Mind / The Last Dance	Comp 102	2/61
What Will I Tell My Heart / Foolish Me	Comp 103	4/61
Sunday Kind Of Love / Mambo Boogie	Raven 8001	1962
Loving A Girl Like You / High Flying Baby	Bruce 123	1963

A SIDE/B SIDE	LABEL/CAT NO	DATE
Sunset / I Gotta Have Your Love	KT 201	1964
Until The Real Thing Comes		
Along / Not Harptones	RbnHd 131	1976
Loves Needs A Heart	AmbiS	1982

* with Bunny Paul
** with Ruth McFadden
† with Carol Blades

The Heartbeats

One of the premier harmony groups of the '50s, the Heartbeats' biggest hit would never have happened had it not been for the persistence of their fan club.

Originally calling themselves the Hearts, the group formed as a quartet from Jamaica, Queens, New York, in 1954. Albert Crump (lead), Vernon Seavers (baritone), and Wally Roker (bass) were students at Woodrow Wilson High School while Robby Tatum (tenor) attended Andrew Jackson. The foursome rehearsed in either Vernon's basement or Robby's house, practicing songs by THE ORIOLES, THE RAVENS, and THE HARPTONES. Other inspirations were THE CARDINALS, THE LARKS, the Four Buddies, THE FIVE KEYS, THE MOONGLOWS, and THE FLAMINGOS.

The group took singing very seriously and usually practiced after school up to five hours a night. When not rehearsing they were down in St. Alban's Park vocally battling it out against the likes of Jamaica neighborhood group members from THE CLEFTONES and THE RIVILEERS.

One such battle pitted members of the Hearts against a less-than-polished, unnamed group of singers with a marvelous lead singer named James Sheppard. When the harmonic highlights were finished for the evening, the Hearts had a new lead and Al shifted to first tenor.

In January 1955 a female group from Harlem started getting airplay on their soon-to-be hit "Lonely Nights." As the group was called the Hearts, the Queens quintet renamed itself the Heartbeats and soon performed their first show at Woodrow Wilson.

The Heartbeats had not only acquired a smooth-as-silk lead in James "Shep" Sheppard; he was also a talented composer of ballads. Songs like "Your Way" became part of their performing repertoire as they played Jamaica's Club Ruby and the Linden Manor in St. Alban's. They also performed at

Woodrow Wilson's graduation ceremonies, various weddings and basement parties, and got their first break when Wally met noted jazz musician Illinois Jacquet. Now calling themselves the Heartbeat Quintet, they rehearsed in Jacquet's basement. He introduced them to his brother Russell, who arranged their first recording of the James Sheppard ballad "Tormented" issued on Philadelphia's Network Records. The fledgling label provided little help and the record was hardly heard over Philadelphia's airwaves, let alone anywhere else. The group, once again calling themselves the Heartbeats, continued practicing and shortly came to the attention of Hull Records' William Miller, who lived across the street. He took the quintet to Bea Caslin, Hull's owner, and she signed them up, recognizing the group's unique, smooth, and extremely tight harmony.

In September 1955 the Heartbeats had their first Hull release, a beautiful James Sheppard ballad titled "Crazy for You," written while in his bathtub (where he wrote all his songs). Extensively played, it became a Northeast favorite and introduced the public to Shep's warmly identifiable lead, Wally's mellow bass, and the group's distinctive background chants.

The group's second ballad single "Darling How Long" surfaced in February 1956, and just a short time later, on March 3rd, *Billboard* reviewed it saying, " 'How long must I wait' is the theme of this wailing plaint. Group gives a good legitimate R&B feel, deep bass delivers some pleading spoken words."

Their spring release was one of the classic four-part harmony R&B ballads, the Shep gem "Your Way," with its heartfelt a cappella intro of "you always will remember, you never will forget," its harmony echoes, talking bridge, falsetto answers that made each vocalist's contribution important, and the ascending "her way" chime ending, all earning "Your Way" a street-corner legend status that few oldies have ever received. The song has become one of the ultimate tests of vocal group prowess.

Its flip, a slightly bluesy ballad titled "People Are Talking" gave disc jockeys a tough choice; many of them played both sides of the Shep-penned single.

The exposure of and response to the first two singles of this quintet, though not national hits, enabled them to perform at the Brooklyn Fox with Alan Freed.

To widen the group's scope, Bea Caslin hired famed choreographers Atkins and Coles to teach the boys some up-tempo steps for their next single "Oh Baby Don't" in the fall of 1956. They also tended to clothing: the group began performing the new single in their red corduroy jackets with blue velvet collars and black pants.

No one could have predicted that tradition-minded Heartbeats fan clubs would spring up all over the New York area after only two Hull releases. When "Oh Baby Don't" started getting airplay, fans began calling the stations' disc jockeys requesting (and in some cases demanding) they flip it to the other side, a Shep ballad entitled "A Thousand Miles Away." When deejays did flip the 45 to play the song about Shep's feelings for his girl who had moved to Texas, it began to sweep the nation. The group's innovative harmonies and Shep's soaring lead made "A Thousand Miles" a classic.

On November 17th it charted nationally R&B and on December 22nd it hit the Pop Top 100. It finished at number five R&B and number 53 Pop, setting the stage for tours and club dates from Boston to Los Angeles. They performed with all the stars of the day including the Flamingos, THE DELLS, the Five Keys, and THE VALENTINES, once doing a college stadium for 4,000 fans with B.B. King and Ray Charles. Bandleaders and musicians that backed them were just as legendary, including Dizzy Gillespie, Buddy Johnson, Sil Austin, Red Prysock, and Count Basie.

Tour-wise, all was not milk and honey for the Heartbeats. Not much of their work was financially rewarding. In *They All Sang on the Corner*, Phil Groia wrote, "In one experience their 1947 Olds blew up in the Cumberland Mountains while en route to a show in Fairmont, West Virginia. They sold the car for $15 for the bus fare to Fairmont believing that compensation from the show would facilitate the return trip. Arriving at the Hotel Magnolia they found the promoter had absconded with the preliminary receipts. The Heartbeats were driven back to New York by the El Dorados who were also on the bill."

The group's first national hit became their last release for Hull. When Shep went to Bea Caslin asking for the publishing rights to his songs he was turned down. This may have prompted the Hull owner to sell both the group and publishing to the Roulette conglomerate; the Heartbeats' next record, "I Won't Be the Fool Anymore" (which, like all their Hull and Rama sides, was recorded at Regent Sound Studios in New York City), came out on Rama in early 1957. In fact, once the preceding "A Thousand Miles Away" took off, it showed up on Rama for the extent of its run.

Their next effort was "Everybody's Somebody's Fool" in June 1957, and it was another exceptionally polished ballad, charting July 15th and reaching only number 78 with the usual extensive Eastern airplay. They moved internally to Gee in late 1957 and to Roulette in 1958 with their best effort being "After New Year's Eve" and a follow-up to their hit titled "500 Miles to Go."

"Down on My Knees" in 1958 was a blues-gospel single that deserved national status. With piano-bass chord runs reminiscent of JESTERS and PARAGONS records this outstandingly sung composition came during the group's fragmentation period.

The membership split into two camps, Shep and his oversized ego versus the Heartbeats, culminating in the latter leaving a Philadelphia gig and returning to New York when Shep incredibly fell asleep in the middle of singing the song "A Thousand Miles Away" and Albert adroitly picked up the lead. Shep awoke to finish the song at the uptown theatre but the embarrassment to the group was too great to be repaired. To fulfill commitments at places like the Apollo Theatre, the group would sing standards and then Shep would come out to sing only the group's hits.

Their last such appearance was at the Howard Theatre in 1959, though one more new Heartbeats single did surface in January (of 1959).

The group was offered guaranteed performance income for 35 weeks singing behind Rayna Shine, the former Steve Gibson's Red Caps thrush, but they turned it down. Robby Tatum went back to school and became a teacher; Albert Crump joined the psychology department of a New York college; Vernon Seavers became an electrical engineer; and Wally Roker went to California, working in the business end of the music business. Shep opened a restaurant in Jamaica and sang solo in clubs. Unlike most groups, the Heartbeats had the same five members throughout their history with no substitutions.

Almost as a tribute, the public gave "A Thousand Miles Away" another shorter chart run when Rama 216 was reissued in October 1960 and scratched the bottom of the *Billboard* Pop charts, (#96).

In 1960 Shep teamed with old friend Clarence Bassett (first tenor) and Clarence's friend Charles Baskerville (second tenor) to form Shep and the Limelites. Charles and Clarence had been with the Videos. Clarence had also been in THE FIVE SHARPS, who had met at the Jamaica Projects near New York Boulevard and 120th Avenue.

The Videos included Ron Woodhall (lead), Clarence (first tenor), Ronald Cussey (second tenor), Charles (second tenor), and Johnny Jackson (baritone). The quintet of 17-year-olds formed in 1957 and got their break singing THE ORIOLES' hit "At Night" at the Apollo's amateur night showcase, where they finished second. A patron that night, Sid Wick, liked the Videos and brought them to WWRL's "Jocko" Henderson who in turn arranged a record deal with Casino Records of Philadelphia. Their doo wop classic "Trickle Trickle" emerged from Casino in 1958 but before two more sides could be released Ronnie Woodhall and Ronald Cussey passed away, hastening the Videos' demise.

Shep and the Limelites went back to Hull, and Bea Caslin signed them, starting off with Shep's latest addition to his "A Thousand Miles Away" story, "Daddy's Home." "Daddy's" took the number two spot on *Billboard*'s charts (#4 R&B). 12 more Hull singles were released between 1961 and 1965, but only one other of Shep and the Limelites' ultra-smooth ballads charted: "Our Anniversary" went to number seven R&B in February 1962.

Once again Shep's ego and attitude intervened until even his friend Charles couldn't sing with him anymore; by 1966 the Limelites were no more.

Charles joined the Players and Clarence spent some time with the latter-day Flamingos.

On January 24, 1970, shortly after Shep and the Limelites had reunited and begun performing on the oldies revival circuit, James Sheppard was found shot to death and robbed in his car alongside the Long Island Expressway.

THE HEARTBEATS

A SIDE/B SIDE	LABEL/CAT NO	DATE
Tormented /		
After Everybody's Gone	Ntwrk 71200	1955
Crazy For You / Rockin' 'n' Rollin'		
'n' Rhythm 'n' Blues	Hull 711	9/55
Darling How Long /		
Hurry Home Baby	Hull 713	2/56
Your Way / People Are Talking	Hull 716	1956
A Thousand Miles Away /		
Oh Baby Don't	Hull 720	10/56
A Thousand Miles Away /		
Oh Baby Don't	Rama 216	11/56
I Won't Be The Fool Any More /		
Wedding Bells	Rama 222	1957
Everybody's Somebody's Fool /		
I Want To Know	Rama 231	6/57
When I Found You /		
Hands Off My Baby	Gee 1043	1957
After New Year's Eve /		
500 Miles To Go	Gee 1047	12/57

A SIDE/B SIDE	LABEL/CAT NO	DATE
Down On My Knees /		
I Found A Job	Roul 4054	1958
One Day Next Year /		
Sometimes I Wonder	Roul 4091	1958
One Million Years /		
Darling, I Want To Get Married	Guyden 2011	1/59
Crazy For You /		
Down On My Knees	Roul 4094	1959
Your Way / People Are Talking	Gee 1061	1960
Darling, How Long /		
Hurry Home, Baby	Gee 1062	1960

Shep and the Limelites

A SIDE/B SIDE	LABEL/CAT NO	DATE
To Young To Wed /		
Two Lovin' Hearts	Apt 25039	1960
I'm So Lonely /		
One Week From Today	Apt 25046	1961
Daddy's Home / This I Know	Hull 740	1961
Ready For Your Love /		
You'll Be Sorry	Hull 742	1961
Three Steps From The Altar /		
Oh, What A Feeling	Hull 747	1961
Our Anniversary /		
Who Told The Sandman	Hull 748	1962
What Did Daddy Do /		
Teach Me How To Twist	Hull 751	1962
Everything Is Going To Be Alright /		
Gee, Baby, What About You	Hull 753	1962
Remember Baby / The Monkey	Hull 756	1963
Stick By Me / It's All Over Now	Hull 757	1963
Steal Away / For You My Love	Hull 759	1963
Why, Why Won't You Believe Me /		
Easy To Remember	Hull 761	1963
I'm All Alone /		
Why Did You Fall For Me	Hull 767	1964
Party For Two / You Better Believe	Hull 770	1965
I'm A Hurting Inside /		
In Case I Forget	Hull 772	1965

The Highway QCs

Some have said the Highway QCs were like a farm team for lead singers going on to THE SOUL STIRRERS, but that would be an insufficient description of this fine gospel group.

Formed in 1945 by their manager Charles Copeland in Chicago, the membership included Spencer Taylor, Jr. (lead), Sam Cooke (first tenor and lead), Lee Richardson (second tenor), Creadell Copeland (baritone), and Charles Richardson (bass). They were all students at Q.C. High School and practiced singing at the Highway Baptist Church on 48th and Indiana in the church's basement, giving them the name the Highway QCs.

Practicing songs like "Amazing Grace" and "What a Friend," the group was heavily influenced by the Stirrers. The QCs did local church performances and eventually branched out to perform throughout the Midwest and South.

By 1950 young Sam Cooke had moved over to R. H. Harris's Soul Stirrers, where Harris continued his training. Johnnie Taylor, singer with the secular Five Echoes (Sabre) in 1953–54 joined the QCs as Sam's replacement. The QCs' smooth sweet style sounded in between THE SWAN SILVERTONES and the Soul Stirrers. In fact, many of their 1950s performances turned out to be with the latter group.

The QCs began the recording portion of their career in 1955 when they signed to Chicago's Vee-Jay label.

Their first single was "Somewhere to Lay My Head" with Johnnie Taylor on lead sounding very similar in style to Sam Cooke. "Somewhere" is probably the best example of Taylor's gospel side.

The group's next single, "He Lifted My Burdens" b/w "I Dream of Heaven," was a "Spotlight Pick" for spirituals in *Billboard* on June 30, 1956. The reviewer noted, "Chalk up two commercially potent sides for this top-notch crew. On top is a touchingly expressed song of gratitude to the Lord. Lead singer is tops on this as well as the flip, where the tempo is picked up to a surging climax."

Vee-Jay issued seven singles and a 1963 LP titled after their first and most successful 45. By 1964 they'd moved to Peacock Records in Texas.

In 1956 the Richardsons and Copeland left and were replaced by what has become known as the classic QCs group with Spencer Taylor, Jr. on lead, Ray Crume on tenor, James Davis on tenor and second lead, Chris Flowers on baritone, and James Walker on bass. Their most popular singles came during the Vee-Jay days, such as "Do You Love Him" (1961) and "Teach Me How to Pray" (1959).

In 1958 or 1959 Overton Vertis (O.V.) Wright, Jr. spent some time with the QCs before going off to Duke Records' Sunset Travelers and in 1964 to a solo secular career, first on Goldwax and then on Don Robey's Backbeat, where he hit with 12 R&B charters including "You're Gonna Make Me Cry" (#6, 1965) and "Eight Men, Four Women" (#4, 1967).

The QCs' first major live performance was at the Apollo Theatre in New York in 1960 with the Gospel Harmonettes, the Swannee Quintet, and the Harmonizing Four. Johnnie Taylor had left the QCs in 1956 to join the Soul Stirrers, again taking Cooke's place as Sam moved into the world of Pop music. Cooke, beginning in late 1957, ran up a string of 43 Pop chart records, becoming probably the most successful gospel pop solo artist ever. His hits included "You Send Me" (#1, 1957), "Chain Gang" (#2, 1960), "Wonderful World" (#12, 1960), "Twistin' the Night Away" (#9, 1962), and "Another Saturday Night" (#10, 1963).

Meanwhile, Taylor moved away from the religious sound in 1960, although not in the most ethical manner. In 1963 a Los Angeles artist named Little Johnny Taylor had an R&B hit with "Part-time Lover" (#1, Galaxy). Little Johnny's inefficient management failed to launch a tour for him but Johnnie stepped into Little Johnny's shoes, touring the South as Little Johnny Taylor and becoming established as a blues artist. This allowed him to sign with Stax Records in 1966. He then had a hit of his own on "Who's Makin' Love" (#1, 1968).

After one LP for Peacock (*Be at Rest*, 1966) the QCs, with Spencer Taylor on lead and Will Rogers (who joined in 1961) on second lead, did one LP for ABC Dunhill in 1973 and entered their most prolific recording era in 1976, signing with Savoy Records and doing seven LPs between 1976 and 1983.

Their most successful album was Savoy's *Stay with God* (1976), which sold over 50,000 copies, and the most memorable single of their Savoy releases was "Oh How Wonderful" (1976). Before any of this happened, however, Will Rogers left the QCs in 1963 for military service and then (you guessed it) tenure with the Soul Stirrers.

Between 1984 and 1990 the group recorded for the Talk of the Town, Messiah, Meltone, and Wajji labels and were still going strong some 46 years after their forming. In July 1991 they left the U.S. to perform at a festival in Italy.

In the early '90s the members were Spencer Taylor, Jr. (lead and manager), Stanley Richardson (lead and tenor, no relation to Lee or Charles Richardson), Joe L. Britt (tenor), Spencer B. Taylor III (and baritone Spencer, Jr.'s son), David Jackson (guitarist), and Steven Gardner (bass guitarist). Of the original members, Spencer Taylor, Jr. still sang with the group on occasion, Sam Cooke and Charlie Copeland passed away, Creadell Copeland and Lee Richardson retired in Chicago, and Charles Richardson died in the early '80s.

The Hilltoppers

The Hilltoppers were a pop vocal quartet that lit up the hit lists in the early '50s to the tune of 25 charters in five and a half years, but in early 1952 Jimmy Sacca (23, lead), Seymour Spiegelman

(21 and tenor), and Don McGuire (21 and bass) were just three students at Western Kentucky State College.

They sang barbershop harmony at the Goal Posts, the campus candy store and hangout. What turned the barbershop banter into serious singing was Jimmy's association with a piano player in the Ace Dinning band, Billy Vaughn. The college was located in Bowling Green where Ace's band played, and Jimmy would occasionally sit in. (Ace, by the way, was the brother of Lou, Ginger, and Jean, the Dinning Sisters of Chicago whose 1948 million seller "Buttons and Bows" helped keep girl groups visible in the late '40s.)

In the spring of 1952 Billy wrote a song he felt would be terrific for Jimmy's voice called "Trying" but wanted a group to sing it with him. Now the college barbershop boys had both a purpose and a fourth member since 30-year-old Vaughn turned out to be the baritone they were missing.

On a Saturday in April the campus cutups cut a session in Van Meter Auditorium on the school grounds. Vaughn then took the ballad to local disc jockey Bill Stamps at WLBJ (no, it was not owned by President Lyndon Baines Johnson), who programmed it and received enough phone call response to warrant sending it on to his old boss Randy Wood at Dot Records in Gallatin, Tennessee. Wood liked the group so much he shuffled off to Bowling Green to sign the boys. The no-name group was then christened the Hilltoppers, after the nickname of their school athletic team.

In May "Trying" came out and by August it was as if it hadn't. Wood had a meeting with the group to decide on a new single the same day the record broke in both Cleveland and Cincinnati. The success of "Trying" happened so quickly that the boys were called to perform on Ed Sullivan's show the same week and didn't know what to wear. They threw together a wardrobe of gray flannel pants, white buck shoes (the "in" thing in those days), and their college sweaters, with one borrowed for the newest man on campus, Billy Vaughn. When they arrived in New York one of the booking agents supplied them with beanies as an added touch. After they did Sullivan's show other variety hours started asking for them but demanded they wear their sweaters and beanies. A gimmick was born, and so was a hit as "Trying" charted on August 16th, reached number seven, and sold nearly a million copies (almost exclusively in the East as Dot had no distributors in the West).

Their second single "I Keep Telling Myself" b/w "Must I Cry Again" was a double-sided charter in

January 1953 with the top reaching number 26 and the flip rising to number 15.

Jimmy Sacca's strong, masculine, and expressive lead led the group's solid harmonies through "If I Were King" (#22, 1953). Then he and his vocal cords were drafted. Wood then sequestered the group in a studio until they'd recorded enough sides to carry them through a good part of Jimmy's stay with Uncle Sam. Though the group had no chance in the next year or two to record fresh material, and though some of their already-recorded songs may have sounded dated a year or two later, they had more hits and bigger charters during that period than they did when Jimmy returned to record anew.

Their first single when Jimmy was on his way to Okinawa was the Johnny Mercer-Gordon Jenkins-penned Rudy Vallee hit from 1934 (#12), "P.S. I Love You" (#4). Even the flip side scored ("I'd Rather Die Young," #8).

They had nine more successes, including "Love Walked In" (#8, 1953) from the Goldwyn Follies, "From the Vine Came the Grape" (#8, sung in English and Italian), THE MILLS BROTHERS' 1944 hit "Till Then" (#10, 1954), and THE INK SPOTS' 1939 smash "If I Didn't Care" (#17, 1954).

When Jimmy returned in March 1955 Uncle Sam drafted both Seymour and Don. They were replaced by Fred Waring group member Clive Dill and Bob Gaye of Four Jacks and a Jill.

Vaughn then became musical director of Dot but continued to record with the group. Eddie Crowe took Vaughn's spot on the road. Gaye soon left to be replaced by Karl Garvin, a former studio musician. Their first charter with the newly returned Jimmy was the title song from the Burt Lancaster film *The Kentuckian* (#20, 1955).

In late 1955 the Hilltoppers entered the cover sweepstakes, releasing THE PLATTERS' "Only You." Despite the fact that the Los Angeles pop R&B group charted on October 1, 1955, almost six weeks ahead of the western Kentucky wonders, the Hilltoppers managed to reach number eight on the Pop lists while the Platters made it to number five. In England, they had their first and biggest hit at number three. A tour of England was next through the spring and summer of 1956. While there the group heard a cover of the G-Clefs' current hit by a group on Dot called the Hilltoppers—quite a shock since our boys didn't record it. Apparently Randy Wood had formed a second Hilltoppers led by Chuck Schroder to do their own version of the song; it lost the chart race to the superior G-Clefs record 24 to 38.

The original Hilltoppers returned to knock out a calypso hit called "Marianne" (#3 in the spring of 1957).

Seymour and Don were then released from Uncle Sam's grasp and with Jimmy and newcomer Doug Cordoza (Seymour's brother-in-law) formed the newest Hilltoppers.

With music rapidly changing, the Hilltoppers found it harder to chart. Their last hit was "The Joker" (#22, 1957). They continued to tour until 1960 and then packed it in. Jimmy and Seymour went to work in Dot's distributing operation.

By 1965 Jimmy Sacca was back with another Hilltoppers and in 1967 cut two singles for 3 J Records.

In 1968 Karl Garvin came back along with Jack Gruebel and Chuck Ayre.

The group rang in the '70s by taking over the management of a food and beverage concession at the Holiday Inn on Okaloosa Island at Fort Walton, Florida. They then played there for most of the next two years.

Their last recordings were on MGM in 1973 and the group continued touring until they broke up in 1976. Don McGuire went into real estate in Lexington, Kentucky. Billy Vaughn stayed with Dot for many years as arranger/conductor for Pat Boone, Gale Storm, the Fontane Sisters, and many other artists. He had more instrumental hits as an orchestra leader (28 from 1954 to 1966) than he did with the Hilltoppers and more than any instrumentalist in the rock era. Jimmy Sacca became a booking agent in Jackson, Mississippi; Karl Garvin retired to Florida; and Eddie Crowe went to work for Lockport High School in Lockport, New York. Seymour Spiegelman died in 1987.

THE HILLTOPPERS

A SIDE/B SIDE	LABEL/CAT NO	DATE
Trying / You Made Up My Mind	Dot 15018	1952
Must I Cry Again /		
I Keep Telling Myself	Dot 15034	1952
If I Were King /		
I Can't Lie To Myself	Dot 15055	1953
P.S. I Love You /		
I'd Rather Die Young	Dot 15085	1953
To Be Alone / Love Walked In	Dot 15105	1953
From The Vine Came The Grape /		
Time Will Tell	Dot 15127	1954
Alone / You're All That I Need	Dot 15130	1954
Till Then / I Found Your Letter	Dot 15132	1954
Poor Butterfly /		
Wrapped Up In A Dream	Dot 15156	1954

A SIDE/B SIDE	LABEL/CAT NO	DATE
Alone With My Heart /		
Mansion On The Hill	Dot 15163	1954
Sweetheart (Will You Remember) /		
The Old Cabaret	Dot 15201	1954
At Sundown / Stormy Night	Dot 15218	1954
If I Didn't Care / Bettina	Dot 15220	1954
Time Waits For No One /		
You Try Somebody Else	Dot 15249	1954
D-A-R-L-I-N / Frivolette	Dot 15318	1955
The Door Is Still Open /		
Teardrops From Your Eyes	Dot 15351	1955
The Kentuckian Song /		
I Must Be Dreaming	Dot 15375	1955
Searching / All I Need Is You	Dot 15415	1955
Only You / Until The Real		
Thing Comes Along	Dot 15423	1955
My Treasure /		
The Last Word In Love	Dot 15437	1955
Do The Bop / When You're Alone	Dot 15451	1956
So Tired / Faded Rose	Dot 15459	1956
Eyes Of Fire, Lips Of Wine /		
I'm Walking Through Heaven	Dot 15468	1956
Ka-Ding-Dong / Into Each		
Life Some Rain Must Fall	Dot 15489	1956
No Regrets / Until You're Mine	Dot 15511	1956
Marianne / You're Wasting Your		
Time (Trying To Lose The Blues)	Dot 15537	1957
I'm Serious / I Love My Girl	Dot 15560	1957
A Fallen Star / Footsteps	Dot 15594	1957
Dedicated To You /		
My Cabin Of Dreams	Dot 15626	1957
The Joker (That's What They		
Call Me) / Chicken Chicken	Dot 15662	1957
Starry Eyes /		
You Sure Look Good To Me	Dot 15712	1958
Peggy's Sister /		
Signorina	Dot 15814	1958
Trying / You're Nobody Till		
Somebody Loves You	Dot 15857	1958
I'd Rather Die Young /		
Welcome To My Heart	Dot 15889	1959
Lots Of Luck / Lizzie Darlin'	Dot 15958	1959
Alone / The Prisoner's Song	Dot 16010	1959
P.S. I Love You / Trying	Dot 16022	1959
From The Vine Came The Grape /		
Love Walked In	Dot 16024	1959
Only You (And You Alone) /		
Till Then	Dot 16025	1959
Marianne / To Be Alone	Dot 16039	1959
P.S. I Love You / To Be Alone	Dot 16054	1960
Only You / No Longer Lonely	Dot 16556	1963
P.S. I Love You / Trying	Dot 112	1963
From The Vine Came The Grape /		
Love Walked In	Dot 113	1963
Only You / Till Then	Dot 114	1963
Marianne / To Be Alone	Dot 115	1963
All These Things /		
The World Outside	3J 1000	1967

A SIDE/B SIDE	LABEL/CAT NO	DATE
The Hurt / I've Been There Too	3J 1007	1967
Jamaica Fairwell / Sunshine and Love	MGM K14515	1973
Little Things You Do / Sunshine and Love	MGM K14603	1973
P.S. I Love You / Trying	ABC P 2694	1974
Only You / Till Then	ABC P 2715	1974

The Hi-Lo's

One of the most innovative jazz/pop vocal groups of all time, the pioneering Hi-Lo's influenced countless pop, R&B, and doo wop groups from the '50s right up to the present.

They formed in December 1953 when Gene Puerling of Milwaukee and friend Bob Strasen met Clark Burroughs and Bob Morse. The latter two were vocalists with the Encores, the vocal group for the Billy May Band. When Billy's band stopped traveling, the Hi-Lo's were born. Reportedly named because of their extreme vocal and physical ranges (Strasen and Morse were tall, Gene and Clark were short), the Hi-Lo's practiced at Clark and Gene's Los Angeles apartment, refining their revolutionary voicings. The group were themselves influenced by such artists as THE FOUR FRESHMEN, THE MODERNAIRES, and Mel Torme's Mel-Tones.

With Clark on lead, Bob and Bob on tenors, and Gene on bass, the Hi-Lo's fractured the traditional definition of vocal group structure with a tonal blend rarely equalled by any quartet.

In 1954 the group came in contact with orchestra leader Jerry Fielding, which initiated their recording career.

In the spring of 1954 their recording of "My Baby Just Cares for Me" (Trend) became their first and only chart single, reaching number 29, but pop singles for the emerging rock and roll generation were not what the Hi-Lo's were about. A *Billboard* review of "Too Young for the Blues" (Starlite) from March 10, 1956, summed it up: "The top swing vocal group has yet to find itself a piece of mass market material, but this attractive side will register with the faithful."

Their audience was a more sophisticated album-buying public that appreciated the intricacies and splendor of their harmonies and arrangements.

The group's first big performing gig was at Fack's in San Francisco in 1954, and from there it was on to the worldwide jazz club scene.

Their first LP, *Listen* (Starlite) in August of 1955, was a landmark of fresh musical interpretations that led to 26 more LPs over the next nine years for such companies as Columbia, Reprise, and Kapp.

During their formative stage, the group performed as backup to Italian actress/singer Anna Maria Albergetti. The Hi-Lo's were nobody's backup in years to come. As a matter of fact, their only other performing collaborations were on record—one on a single for Herb Jeffries on Trend and one for Dean Martin on Reprise.

In the mid-'50s the group's star rose when Judy Garland took them on tour and presented their new singing style to a wide audience.

In 1959 Don Shelton became their only replacement member as Bob Strasen left. Between 1962 and 1981 the quartet earned three Grammy nominations and performed in the Jack Lemmon film *Good Neighbor Sam*. They appeared on such TV shows as "The Andy Williams Show," "The Steve Allen Show," and put in an amazing 39 performances on Rosemary Clooney's TV show. In 1962 the group made their last appearance performing at the Tropicana Hotel in Las Vegas. When rock and roll eclipsed their traditional audience, the Hi-Lo's retired in 1963.

Gene went on to produce commercials in San Francisco and in 1967 left for Chicago to form THE SINGERS UNLIMITED with Don Shelton. Clark continued singing in studio sessions, and Bob Morse went into the antique business.

In 1977 the group was asked to perform at the Monterey Jazz Festival and reunited after 14 years. The Hi-Lo's fell back into their unique harmonies as if they were putting on a comfortable pair of shoes. This led to their first recording venture since 1964, the *Back Again* LP in 1978 for Pauso Records.

The Hollywood Flames

During their career, the Hollywood Flames recorded under no fewer than seven names for 19 different record companies. Through it all they remained solid and versatile; they were one of the West Coast's earliest rhythm and blues groups.

They were first called the Flames and consisted of Robert Byrd (lead, tenor, baritone, and bass),

David Ford (lead), Willie Ray Rockwell (second tenor), and a bit later, Curley Dinkins (baritone and bass). They formed at the Largo Theatre in Los Angeles at a talent show during 1949. Their first paying gig was at Johnny Otis's Barrelhouse Club, where THE ROBINS also came together around the same time. In January 1950 the group recorded its first single, the jump blues tune "Young Girl" with Bobby on lead.

They became the Hollywood Four Flames after the "Young Girls" release, doing three singles for Unique. One of those, "Tabarin," was issued on Fidelity as the Four Flames in late 1951. *Billboard* gave it this less-than-glowing response in a December review: "A new male quartet, specializing in the wobbly note bending style, gives out with a rather feeble ballad."

One single backing Patty Anne as Patty Anne and the Flames and one as the Four Flames for Specialty (tracks licensed from Unique) and the group was back as the Hollywood Four Flames on John Dolphin's Recorded in Hollywood label for three singles in 1952, the best of which was a nice cover of THE FIVE KEYS' "Glory of Love." They also did a solid rerecording of "Young Girl" for that label.

By now, Willie Ray Rockwell had left and joined THE LAMPLIGHTERS (Federal). His replacement was second tenor Clyde "Thin Man" Tillis, who added a bit of zaniness to the group as a dancer and comedian. Then over the next few years the scorecard became unintelligible: the group recorded for Spin (as the Jets in 1952), 7-11 (as the Flames in 1953), Aladdin (as the Jets and as Patty Anne and the Flames in 1954), and Lucky, Hollywood, and Money (as the Hollywood Four Flames in 1954 and 1955). The membership was even more muddled as Gaynel Hodge (THE PLATTERS), Leon Hughes, and Curtis Williams (the Flamingos, but not the Chicago hit group) sang at different times.

During the Aladdin, Lucky, Hollywood, Money, and Decca periods, the group was usually Dave Ford (first tenor), Gaynel Hodge (second tenor), Curtis Williams or Curley Dinkins (baritone), and Bobby Byrd (bass).

The group recorded some interesting rhythm and blues sides during this period, including "I'll Hide My Tears" (reportedly written by Murray Wilson, father of THE BEACH BOYS' Brian Wilson) and "Peggy" with Hodge on lead.

Curtis Williams, who was a member of the Flames before he joined THE PENGUINS, offered them "Earth Angel," but the Flames never got around to recording it.

The group always received local airplay on their releases and by 1955 were considered a successful act in the L.A. area though they didn't have a hit.

Groups in those days had loose membership; Bobby Byrd recorded under the name the Voices (Cash, 1955), singing lead and bass with only the help of Earl Nelson on tenor about the same time he was with the Flames.

In 1957 the group became yet another entity when they signed with Leon Rene's Class label. Leon's son Googie Rene (Leon's A&R director and producer) renamed Bobby Byrd "Bobby Day" and also renamed the Flames et al "The Satellites."

Their first single in the fall of 1957 was a Bobby Day-penned rocker called "Little Bitty Pretty One," which looked like a smash until Thurston Harris and the Sharps outclassed it, reaching number six Pop and number two R&B on Aladdin; the Satellites' single crashed and burned on takeoff. The group didn't have time to sulk. Their November release on Ebb Records as the Hollywood Flames (keep those scorecards handy) of the Bobby Byrd-penned "Buzz-Buzz-Buzz" entered *Billboard*'s Hot 100 on November 25, 1957, reaching number 11 Pop and number five R&B.

All this name shuffling was rarely the doing of the group. When they recorded for a new record company they had little knowledge of or control over the name that eventually showed up on the label. For example, in the fall of 1957 the group stopped by Dolphin's of Hollywood record store where Dick "Huggy Boy" Hugg, a well-known Los Angeles disc jockey, was broadcasting from the window. Dick asked if they had any new tunes, motivating Bobby to go home that night and knock out a 15-minute quickie called "Buzz-Buzz-Buzz." On October 21st the group recorded it for Dolphin with Earl Nelson singing lead and promptly forgot about it. At the time they were with Class Records as the Satellites. Earl and Bobby had day jobs at the Revell Toy factory and were working away when the radio in the shop blared out a familiar sound. It was "Buzz-Buzz-Buzz" by *the Hollywood Flames*, and a disc jockey gushed that it was the hottest record in Los Angeles. Dolphin had sold it to Lee Rupe (wife of Specialty Records' Art Rupe) for her new Ebb label, and the Flames were rising again. (The group at that time, besides Earl and Bobby, was Dave Ford, Curtis Williams, and Clyde Tillis.)

Obviously doing better as the Hollywood Flames than as the Satellites, the group decided to record several singles for Ebb, but they went nowhere.

By now, with a dual lack of identity, the group recorded on Ebb with Bobby Day and behind him (sometimes without credit) on Class. One such recording was his summer of 1958 hit "Rockin Robin" (#2 Pop, #1 R&B). The group on "Rockin Robin" was Day, Davis Ford, Earl Nelson, and Curtis Williams, who had left THE PENGUINS for a time. The MOONGLOWS/Moonlighters and VIBRATIONS/Marathons dual personalities had nothing on this bunch; they toured as Bobby Day and the Satellites, the Hollywood Flames, and Bob and Earl, all on one bill!

By late 1959 the Hollywood Flames consisted of Dave Ford, Curtis Williams, Donald Height, and Ray Brewster. The group did a few good sides for Atco, Chess, Coronet and Goldie, the best being a humorous take on Elizabeth Taylor called "Elizabeth," with Height on lead even though the label said Dave Ford and the Hollywood Flames.

When the 1960 Atco sides failed, the group went home to Los Angeles but Brewster stayed on and joined THE CADILLACS in New York. An early to mid-'60s photo of the Flames shows the members as Nelson, Ford, Brewster, and Eddie Williams (of the Aladdins on Aladdin).

The group's last recording lineup was in 1965 for Symbol and included Dave Ford, John Berry, George Home, and a forgotten bass. Having gone many years without a hit, the group finally split up in 1967.

Earl Nelson joined Bobby Relf and had hits as Bob and Earl (Earl and Bobby Day had been the original Bob and Earl) on "Harlem Shuffle" (#44, 1963) and later as Jackie Lee (Jackie was Earl's wife's name and Lee his own middle name) on "The Duck" (#14 Pop, #4 R&B, 1965). Earl was later living in Los Angeles, as was Curley Dinkins. Bobby Day performed at oldies shows up until his death in the early '90s. Willie Rockwell, Clyde Tillis, Curtis Williams, and Dave Ford also passed away.

THE HOLLYWOOD FLAMES

A SIDE/B SIDE	LABEL/CAT NO	DATE
The Flames		
Please Tell Me Now / Young Girl	Slctv 113	1/50
The Hollywood Four Flames		
Dividend Blues / W-I-N-E	Unique 003	1950
Tabarin / Cryin' For My Baby	Unique 009	
Please Say I'm Wrong / The Masquerade Is Over	Unique 015	1950
The Four Flames		
Tabarin / W-I-N-E	Fdlty 3001	12/51

A SIDE/B SIDE	LABEL/CAT NO	DATE
Patty Anne and the Flames		
The Bounce / The Bounce Part II	Fdlty 3002	12/51
The Four Flames		
The Wheel Of Fortune / Later	Spec 423	2/52
The Hollywood Four Flames		
I'll Always Be A Fool / She's Got Something	RIH 164	10/52
Young Girl / Baby Please	RIH 165	1952
Young Girl / Glory Of Love	RIH 165	1952
The Flames		
Strange Land Blues / Cryin' For My Baby	Spin 101	1952
The Jets		
Volcano / Comen Nasai	7-11 2102	3/53
The Flames		
Keep On Smiling / Baby Baby Baby	7-11 2106	1953
Together / Baby Pretty Baby	7-11 2107	9/53
Patty Anne and the Flames		
Sorrowful Heart / Beginning To Miss You	Aldn 3198	7/53
The Jets		
I'll Hide My Tears / Got A Little Shadow	Aldn 3247	6/54
The Hollywood Flames		
One Night With A Fool / Ride Helen Ride	Lucky 001	4/54
I Shall Return	Lucky 002	1954
Peggy / Ooh-La La	Lucky 006	7/54
Let's Talk It Over / I Know	Lucky 009	1954
Peggy / Ooh La La	Decca 29285	9/54
Let's Talk It Over / I Know	Decca 48331	12/54
Peggy / Ooh La La	Hlywd 104	1954
Fare Thee Well / Clickety Clack I'm Leaving	Money 202	1955
The Flames		
So Alone / Flame Combo	Aldn 3349	1957
Bobby Day and the Satellites		
Little Bitty Pretty One / When The Swallows Come Back To Capistrano	Class 211	10/57
Beep Beep Beep / Darling If I Had You	Class 215	1957
Sweet Little Thing / Honeysuckle Baby	Class 220	1958
The Tangiers		
Don't Try / Schooldays Will Be Over	Class 224	1958

A SIDE/B SIDE	LABEL/CAT NO	DATE
Bobby Day and the Satellites		
Saving My Love For You /		
Little Turtle Dove	Class 225	7/58
The Satellites		
Heavenly Angel /		
You Ain't Sayin' Nothin'	Class 234	1958
Bobby Day and the Satellites		
The Bluebird, Buzzard And Oriole /		
Alone Too Long	Class 241	1958
Say Yes / That's All I Want	Class 245	1958
Got A New Girl /		
Mr. & Mrs. Rock 'n' Roll	Class 252	1958
Ain't Gonna Cry No More /		
Love Is A One Time Affair	Class 255	1958
Three Young Rebs From Georgia /		
Unchained Melody	Class 257	1958
The Hollywood Flames		
Buzz Buzz Buzz / Crazy	Ebb 119	11/57
A Little Bird /		
Give Me Back My Heart	Ebb 131	1/58
Strollin' On The Beach /		
Frankenstein's Den	Ebb 144	3/58
A Star Fell / I'll Get By	Ebb 149	10/58
I'll Be Seeing You / Just For You	Ebb 153	11/58
There Is Something On		
Your Mind / So Good	Ebb 162	2/59
Now That You've Gone /		
Hawaiian Dream	Ebb 163	6/59
If I Thought You Needed Me /		
Everyday Every Way	Atco 6155	11/59
Ball And Chain / I Found A Ball	Atco 6164	5/60
Devil Or Angel /		
Do You Ever Think Of Me	Atco 6171	7/60
Money Honey / My Heart's On Fire	Atco 6180	10/60
Gee / Yes They Do	Chess 787	3/61
Believe In Me /		
I Can't Get A Hit Record	Crnt 7025	1962
Elizabeth / Believe In Me	Goldie 1101	1962
Letter To My Love /		
Drop Me A Line	Vee-Jay 515	1963
Annie Don't Love Me No More /		
Dance Senorita	Symbol 211	1965
I'm Coming Home /		
I'm Gonna Stand By You	Symbol 215	1966

The Impalas

The Impalas were a Brooklyn vocal group with the distinction of being one of the few white groups with a black lead singer. The distinction was blurred by the fact that Joe "Speedo" Frazier sounded as white as the rest of the group. Lenny Renda (second tenor), Richard Wagner (baritone),

and Tony Carlucci (first tenor) began practicing in the back room of a Canarsie candy store and on local street corners in the late 1950s; they were often heard by teenager Speedo. His offer to help their harmonies turned into a full-fledged front-running spot with the group. Their name idea was inspired by one of the teen's dad's new car, a Chevy Impala.

They issued a song called "First Date" on the small Hamilton label; it went unnoticed and they were back in the candy store in a flash.

One evening their street-corner singing attracted the attention of Artie Zwirn and Aristedes Giosasi (Gino of the act Gino and Gina, "Pretty Baby," #20, Mercury, 1958) who liked their sound and also had an original song titled "Sorry, I Ran All the Way Home."

In early 1959 an introduction to Alan Freed led to an MGM audition and a record deal with their Cub subsidiary. "Sorry" became their first single, charting at number two Pop. (Only Dave "Baby" Cortez's "Happy Organ" was in front of the up-tempo tune.) It managed to make it to England at number 28 by the summer.

In less than two months the Impalas had gone from Canarsie corners to big-time touring with THE SKYLINERS, Chuck Berry, and Frankie Avalon, playing Alan Freed concerts, the Brooklyn Fox, and the Ed Sullivan and Dick Clark TV shows.

With a million-seller under their belts the group issued "Oh What a Fool," another teen Top 40 pleaser penned by Zwirn and Giosasi. It started out swimmingly, but the record died at number 86 during the summer of 1959 (it possibly did too well on its own at first, prompting Cub to stop promoting).

Their last Cub single, "All Alone" (which was the first single to read Speedo and the Impalas), never had a chance although *Billboard*'s March 28, 1960, review called it "a tender ballad, with chick chorus lending a good touch to the arrangement," and gave it four stars.

In 1966 the group did a fine MAGNIFICENT MEN-styled recording for Dave Rick on Red Boy titled "I Can't See Me Without You."

By the '80s the membership included Speedo, Randy Silverman of VITO AND THE SALUTATIONS, Ricky Shaw, and John Monforte. Of the originals, Richard Wagner became a phone company lineman in New Mexico, Lenny Renda became a New York City cop, and Tony Carlucci dropped out of sight, but the Impalas can be heard almost any time you turn on oldies radio in America; "Sorry, I Ran All the Way Home" is a rock and roll standard.

THE IMPALAS

A SIDE/B SIDE	LABEL/CAT NO	DATE
First Date / I Was A Fool	Hmltn 5006	1958
Sorry I Ran All The Way Home /		
Fool, Fool, Fool	Cub 9022	1959
Oh What A Fool /		
Sandy Went Away	Cub 9033	1959
Peggy Darling / Bye Everybody	Cub 9053	1959
Speedo and the Impalas		
All Alone / When My Heart		
Does All The Talking	Cub 9066	1960
The Impalas		
I Can't See Me Without You /		
When You Dance	Red Boy 113	1966
My Hero / There Ain't		
Nothing Like A Dame	UGHA 17	1982

The Jacks

The Jacks started out as a spiritual group in Los Angeles under the guidance of former DIXIE HUMMINGBIRDS baritone Lloyd McCraw. Lloyd came to Los Angeles from Chicago in 1947. By 1954 he had joined up with Willie Davis (lead and first tenor), Ted Taylor (first tenor), Aaron Collins (second tenor), and Will "Dub" Jones (bass). Lloyd sang baritone and became the group's manager, bringing them to Modern Records' Culver City studios. When Modern's president Joe Bihari heard the group's potential and adaptability he conceived the idea of creating two groups out of one, giving the Jacks a new additional name. Henceforth they would do cover records of mostly up-tempo songs as THE CADETS; for the Jacks he envisioned using the writing talents of Aaron Collins and others to bring the group hit originals. This was not as far-fetched a plan as it seemed; there was a big difference between the sound of the Jacks with Davis singing lead and the tougher sound of the Cadets when the harmony followed Collins or Jones.

But this concept would have to wait for at least one record. Bihari and his sidekick arranger Maxwell Davis handed the Jacks a beautiful ballad titled "Why Don't You Write Me?" that was getting some attention on the Showtime label as recorded by the Feathers. The Feathers' original came out in the fourth week of April 1955 and the Jacks' copy came out one week later (on the Modern affiliate RPM). But the Jacks' version wasn't merely a copy; it was a vast improvement. Though the arrangements were similar, the Jacks' harmonies were

stronger and more appealing and Willie Davis sang it as if it had been written for him. The flip "Smack Dab in the Middle" was actually cut as the Cadets and wound up on their first LP. The Jacks' "Write Me" hit the R&B charts on August 6th, almost a year before the Cadets charted with "Stranded in the Jungle."

It took the record three months to build up enough national steam to make *Billboard*'s hit list (and when it did Joe Bihari immediately bumped the B side for another ballad, called "My Darling"). The Jacks jumped up to number three R&B by September and even managed to cross over to the Pop charts to reach number 82. Unfortunately, their first hit would be their last. "I'm Confessin'" followed in June while "Write Me" was still building momentum. Apparently RPM had little faith or little patience with records that took months to succeed and abandoned "I'm Confessin'" the minute "Write Me" hit the charts. If the group was flying high from their instant success, they were brought to earth rapidly; a fourth single didn't have either of their names on it. They backed vocalist Donna Hightower on two ill-fated sides, "Bob-O-Link" and "Since You," just as they had on their second single "Love Me Again."

Their next three releases were all original ballads, the best of which, "Why Did I Fall in Love," had a nice PLATTERS-PENGUINS feel. A *Billboard* review gave it an 81 rating. (Most *Billboard* reviews were rated between 80 [high] and 60 [low], and a rating above 80 was rare.) Their last single, in July 1956, was "Let's Make Up," a catchy mid-tempo rock and roll ditty that followed the path of every single since "Write Me"; the group was now officially relegated to full-time Cadets status.

In March 1957, eight months after their last release and 22 months after the release of their only hit, RPM put out the *Jumpin' with the Jacks* LP containing ten sides of which three ("You Belong to Me," "Do You Wanna Rock," and "Wiggie Waggie Woo") were released on singles by the Cadets! (At least they weren't cut by Milli Vanilli.)

Though their recordings were for the most part fine examples of original rhythm and blues ballads, it's ironic that their only hit came from what they weren't supposed to be doing as the Jacks— cover records.

THE JACKS

A SIDE/B SIDE	LABEL/CAT NO	DATE
Why Don't You Write Me /		
Smack Dab In The Middle	RPM 428	4/55

A SIDE/B SIDE	LABEL/CAT NO	DATE
Love Me Again* / Dog Gone It*	RPM 432	5/55
I'm Confessin'* /		
Since My Baby's Been Gone*	RPM 433	6/55
Why Don't You Write Me /		
My Darling	RPM 428	8/55
Bob-O-Link / Since You	RPM 439	8/55
This Empty Heart /		
My Clumsy Heart	RPM 444	11/55
So Wrong / How Soon	RPM 454	1/56
Why Did I Fall In Love /		
Sugar Baby	RPM 458	4/56
Let's Make Up / Dream		
A Little Longer	RPM 467	7/56

* with Donna Hightower

The Jaguars

From low-rider rock and roll to classical-meets-doo wop, the Jaguars, one of America's first interracial rock vocal groups, were a very versatile Los Angeles quartet.

The Freemont High School foursome included Herman "Sonny" Chaney, lead, of Dallas, Texas; Valerio "Val" Poliuto, tenor, from Detroit; Manuel "Manny" Chavez, baritone, of Los Angeles; and Charles Middleton, bass, of Lafayette, Louisiana. Freemont was a harmony haven for mid-'50s groups. Few schools in America have generated as many recorded groups; the Jaguars' schoolmates included Don Julian and the Meadowlarks (Dooto, probably the first integrated group), THE MEDALLIONS (Dootone), THE DREAMERS (Flip), THE FLAMES (later the Hollywood Flames, Ebb), and the Calvanes (Dootone).

The Jaguars first called themselves the Miracles. In 1955, big-band trumpeter turned would-be record exec Bob Ross formed Aardell Records at the office of his sheet music service. He signed up the Miracles and had them back his daughter Patti on a song written by his partner Buddy Ebsen (the actor on the "Davy Crockett" series and later star of TV's "Barnaby Jones"). "Rocket, Davey, Rocket" was then rerecorded by the group and issued as the flip side of the Manny Chavez-penned ballad "I Wanted You" issued in June 1955.

Prior to the record's release Ross and the group decided to change their name but were stumped for an idea. Then comedian Stan Freberg came in the office, heard of their dilemma, and after a bit of contemplation over a candy bar volunteered "the Jaguars" (no bird names for this group!)

"I Wanted You," a ballad too close in melody to the Richard Barrett and THE CHANTELS' 1959 "Summer's Love" classic not to have influenced that recording, took off in Los Angeles and the group appeared on the first West Coast R&B TV show, Hunter Hancock's "Rhythm and Bluesville Show." But Aardell's distribution was limited and the record became strictly a local item.

"You Don't Believe Me" was issued in November and earned a review in *Billboard* on January 21, 1956 that read, "The group tries hard here with slow paced rhythm and blues ballad material, but the overall effect is doubtful." The boys went back to the drawing board for a new song to record.

Val and Sonny found it in a Los Angeles nightclub, where they heard a female vocalist performing the 1936 Fred Astaire hit "The Way You Look Tonight" (#1) over rock and roll triplets at the piano. Val, a classically trained pianist who had once led an orchestra back in Detroit before he was 17, recognized the potential of the Jerome Kern-penned standard. He created a "Moonlight Sonata" (Beethoven) intro for the evergreen with a few classic harmony changes while turning it into a rock and roll ballad.

Released in mid-1956, the record got plenty of radio play and was their biggest seller. In October R-Dell (Ross had now revised the label's spelling, but unfortunately not its distribution) issued it again with more echo; it came out at least twice more (Baronett [1962] and Original Sound [1965]), each time with variable changes.

By 1957 the group had moved over to Ebb Records where they cut one single, "Hold Me Tight," and sang backup for Johnny Mathis's younger brother Ralph on a solid rocker called "Never Let You Go." When the single was issued later in 1958 it read "By Ralph Mathis and the Ambers," but the group never adopted that name.

In late 1959 the Jaguars moved to Art Laboe's Original Sound label and recorded "Thinking of You." They also became a temporary quintet: Manny missed the session but Tony Allen ("Nightowl," Specialty, 1955) and his fabulous falsetto along with Richard "Louie Louie" Berry on bass came in to beef up the harmony. Original Sound's distribution was better than R-Dell's, and "Thinking of You" was extensively played around the country. Consequently the group performed with acts like Chuck Berry, Little Richard, and Jackie Wilson in venues from Long Beach Municipal Auditorium to the Hollywood Bowl.

Through all this, the group had never experienced a personnel change, a near miracle given the constant-state-of-flux that surrounded many Los Angeles groups.

By 1961 the Jaguars had become the T-Birds on Chess—just as the Jaguars name was getting national recognition due to Art Laboe's inclusion of "The Way You Look Tonight" on his first *Oldies But Goodies* LP.

It stayed on the charts for 184 weeks while Top 40 radio disc jockeys started playing the Jaguars and others from the LP—the first of the '50s rockers to be exposed to the white masses via the oldies LP route.

From 1960 to 1966 Uncle Sam always had at least one Jaguar out of action; by 1966 the two black (Sonny and Charlie), one Chicano (Manny), and one Polish-Italian (Val) group decided to retire.

Val stayed in the business recording with the Nuggets (RCA) and playing piano on countless other records. In February 1962 when THE BEACH BOYS recorded a session that included "Surfin', Surfin' Safari" and "Little Surfin' Girl," the performers were actually Brian and Dennis Wilson and Val Poliuto. Val then became a solo performer. Charles Middleton went on to work on TV and film as a character actor, and Manny went to work for the *LA Times*. Sonny retired in the '80s after going blind, but it didn't stop him and the group from reuniting to perform in 1987.

THE JAGUARS

A SIDE/B SIDE	LABEL/CAT NO	DATE
Rock It, Davy, Rock It /		
The Big Bear	Ardl 0002	6/55
I Wanted You /		
Rock It, Davy, Rock It	Ardl 0003	6/55
Be My Sweetie /		
You Don't Believe Me	Ardl 0006	11/55
The Way You Look Tonight /		
Moonlight And You	RDell 11	1956
The Way You Look Tonight /		
Baby Baby Baby	RDell 11	10/56
The City Zoo /		
I Love You, Baby	RDell 16	2/57
Hold Me Tight / Piccadilly	Ebb 129	1/58
Thinking Of You /		
Look Into My Eyes	OrigS 06	9/59
Girl Of My Dreams /		
Don't Go Home	RDell 117	7/60
The T-Birds		
Come On, Dance With Me /		
Green Stamps	Chess 1778	1/61
The Jaguars		
It Finally Happened /		
Fine Fine Fine	Rndvs 159	1961

A SIDE/B SIDE	LABEL/CAT NO	DATE
Thinking Of You /		
Look Into My Eyes	OrigS 20	1962
The Way You Look Tonight /		
Baby Baby Baby Baby	OrigS 59	1965

The Jesters

The Jesters exemplified the New York City vocal group sound of the mid-'50s. Their strong and vibrant street harmonies were an influence on groups for years to come, primarily early '60s white aggregations like THE EXCELLENTS and THE IMAGINATIONS.

The Jesters were students at Cooper Junior High School in Harlem on 120th Street and started practicing under a nearby elevated railway station in 1956. The members were Leonard "Lenny" McKay (lead), James "Jimmy" Smith (second tenor), Leo Vincent (baritone), and Noel Grant (bass). Meanwhile, 17-year-old Adam Jackson was attending Samuel Gompers High School in the Bronx and was singing in a quintet called the Continentals. Adam managed a TV performance later that year with the Continentals singing THE FLAMINGOS' "I'll Be Home," and he knew then and there that he wanted to be a performer.

In early 1957 Adam joined up with the Jesters, who had been named by Noel after his favorite movie, Danny Kaye's *The Court Jester*. The group's singing style was a reflection of the influence groups like the Flamingos had on them. Adam soon became the co-lead and main songwriter. The group performed at the Apollo amateur night contest. After winning first prize three times, they were spotted and signed by Winley Records owner Paul Winley. Prior to the Apollo appearance, they had auditioned for and been turned down by Columbia.

The Jesters' first single was "So Strange," a slow, bluesy doo wop arrangement that became a New York favorite and charted on a variety of East Coast disc jockey lists. On July 15th, it built up enough steam to jump onto the national Pop chart for a single week at number 100. Its flip side, "Love No One But You," was an equally arresting recording, a rhythm ballad with an a cappella "bong" harmony intro that showcased the incredibly round, full, and smooth blend of which the Jesters were capable. "Love No One But You," with Lenny McKay on lead and Adam on falsetto, saw as much (if not more) action in the tri-state area as "So Strange" did.

Their next 45 came in October with the release of the classic rhythm ballad "Please Let Me Love You." Once again Lenny took the tenor lead and Adam the falsetto on what is often considered the epitome of mid-'50s New York doo wop. Jesters records were of such high quality that none of the flips sounded like typical B sides. The flip of "Please" was no exception. "I'm Falling in Love" was an exciting Latin-rhythm rocker that earned its own following.

By that time, the Jesters had begun touring the chitlin circuit. They returned to the Apollo as professionals in shows alongside label mates THE PARAGONS as well as Ben E. King, Ruth Brown, Jimmy Jones, THE OLYMPICS, and Dante and the Evergreens.

Their third single was a solid remake of the CHANTELS ballad "The Plea" with Adam on solo lead, and it too stirred national interest—enough to reach number 74 Pop in March 1958. Its flip "Oh Baby" was a rousing jump side that showed no matter how hot the tempo, the Jesters' harmonies could still dominate the track.

The arranger for all those recordings was former Pearls and VALENTINES vocalist David Cortez Clowney. He became more known to the public some 14 months after "The Plea" under the name Dave "Baby" Cortez with the instrumental hit "Happy Organ" (#1, 1959).

In June 1958 the original Jesters had their fourth and final single, another two-sided classic, "Now That You're Gone" and the rockin' "I Laughed," patterned after THE SPANIELS' "Everyone's Laughing."

By the summer of 1958 McKay and Grant had left and Vincent had been drafted. To replace them, Adam Jackson and Jimmy Smith brought in baritone Melvin Lewis (the Climbers on J&S) along with his brother Donald on bass. In the meantime, Paul Winley noticed his release schedule of label issues seemed to always have a Paragons single followed by a Jesters single. This, along with the increasing popularity of "battle of the groups" shows and street-corner sing-offs, gave him the idea for the classic *The Paragons Meet the Jesters* LP with its vocal duels and a cover depicting members of a hotshot street gang. Issued around 1959, it was one of the first rock and roll compilation LPs and sold very well on the East Coast.

By May 1960 the new Jesters quartet had its first single, a revision of THE DIABLOS' classic "The Wind." Though not as magical as the Diablos ver-

sion and lacking the fifth harmony part that was such an integral part of the earlier Jesters sound, "The Wind" was still excellently done and well-received in their tri-state stronghold, even reaching number 110 on Billboard's June 20, 1960, national chart.

Their last two singles, though good, were not of the caliber of their earlier 45s and never charted. The group did some backup work for other Winley artists, namely Charlie White of THE CLOVERS ("Nobody's Fault But Mine," 1958) and Ann Fleming, Winley's wife ("Jive Time Baby," 1960). During the early '60s they also backed Ben E. King onstage at the Apollo.

The group, much to its credit, never really broke up, working occasional gigs through the '60s, '70s, and '80s and often performing in a routine based on their LP with the Paragons.

In 1974 they again became a quintet when Adam's brother Ronald (former lead of the Youngtones, Xtra, 1957) joined up.

In 1991 the group was still around, with Adam Jackson on lead, Ronald Jackson on tenor, Melvin Lewis on baritone, Donald Lewis on bass, and Marshall Cherry on second tenor. Marshall was a hairstylist when the group found him to replace Jimmy Smith. When not harmonizing, Ronald Jackson was a metal spinner, Melvin a manager of a photo company, Donald the manager of a D'Agostino's market, Marshall a New York high school custodian, and Adam an inspector for the New York City Environmental Department. The whereabouts of Lenny McKay, Leo Vincent, and Noel Grant are not known.

For three decade the Jesters' recordings have been played whenever a disc jockey wanted to demonstrate the New York sound.

THE JESTERS

A SIDE/B SIDE	LABEL/CAT NO	DATE
So Strange / Love No One But You	Winley 218	5/57
Please Let Me Love You / I'm Falling In Love	Winley 221	10/57
The Plea / Oh Baby	Winley 225	1/58
I Laughed / Now That You're Gone	Cycln 5011	6/58
The Wind / Sally Green	Winley 242	5/60
That's How It Goes / Tutti Frutti	Winley 248	1960
Uncle Henry's Basement / Come Let Me Show You How	Winley 252	1961

▲ MAURICE WILLIAMS AND THE GLADIOLAS　　▼ FOUR FRESHMAN　▲ THE CHORDETTES

▼ THE MOONGLOWS ▲ THE JAGUARS ▲ THE FIVE KEYS ▼ THE CHANTELS

The Jive Bombers

The Jive Bombers were a distinctive blues-jazz quartet formed in 1952. The lead was Clarence Palmer, whose performing experience went back to the '30s when he was a member of the Palmer Brothers (Dick, Ernest, and Clarence) of Pawtucket, Rhode Island. They were a self-contained trio that joined the vocal group set when they performed at Connie's Inn in Harlem. Acts like THE PIED PIPERS, THE MERRY MACS, and THE MODERN-AIRES were often part of the audience enjoying their original vocal blend. They became one of the first harmony trios to sing with big bands, including those of Count Basie and Cab Calloway, recording as the Cabaliers on Okeh when they were with Cab.

By 1949 Dick and Ernest retired but Clarence couldn't kick the performing bug. He formed a group with members of Sonny Austin's Jive Bombers. In 1949 they recorded two singles for Coral, "125th Street New York" and "Brown Boy," issued in January and May, respectively, as Al Sears and the Sparrows.

In 1952 they became Clarence Palmer and the Jive Bombers, but their first three singles on Lou Parker's Citation Records of Detroit went nowhere. The group went through some changes, eventually winding up as Clarence Palmer, Earl Johnson, Al and William "Pee Wee" Tinney by 1956. The Tinney Brothers had been a successful tap dance duo and brought an added dimension to the group's mellow vocal style.

Clarence himself sang in a Louis Armstrong style, and the group developed almost as a stylistic tie between THE MILLS BROTHERS and the OLYMPICS.

Manager Cliff Martinez introduced the group to Herman Lubinsky of Savoy Records and the Bombers were in the studio on November 30, 1956, recording. By December they had their first Savoy single, the Lil Armstrong-penned "Bad Boy" (which in 1936 was originally called "Brown Gal").

On February 2, 1957, "Bad Boy" charted Pop, and the unusual stuttering sound of Clarence on the laid-back jazz-blues ballad proved a winner for listeners, reaching number 36 Pop and number seven R&B.

Clarence (who was 39 by the time "Bad Boy" hit) and company were the toasts of the town and their performance card was full, highlighted by an Easter week headlining at the Loew's State Theatre in New York City for Jocko's Rock and Roll Show.

More strong singles (like "Cherry," also done by THE DIAMONDS in 1953 and later by THE RIVINGTONS in 1963) featured Clarence sounding like a muted trumpet but could not follow up "Bad Boy."

The ballad "Is This the End" and the group's pleasantly jazzy interpretation of "Stardust" in 1959 missed their deserved marks.

Still, due to "Bad Boy's" success, the polished performers stayed on the club scene through the late '60s before calling it a career.

THE JIVE BOMBERS

A SIDE/B SIDE	LABEL/CAT NO	DATE
It's Spring Again /		
Pork Chop Boogie	Cit 1160	1/52
Brown Boy / Pee Wee's Boogie	Cit 1161	1/52
Saturday Night Fish Boy	Cit 1162	1/52
Bad Boy / When Your Hair		
Has Turned To Silver	Savoy 1508	12/56
If I Had A Talking Picture /		
The Blues Don't Mean A Thing	Savoy 1513	1957
Cherry / You Took My Love	Savoy 1515	1957
Is This The End /		
Just Around The Corner	Savoy 1535	1958
Stardust / You Give		
Your Love To Me	Savoy 1560	1959
Anytime / Days Of		
Wine And Roses	Mdl Tn 020	1963

The Jordanaires

As Elvis was the king of rock and roll, the Jordanaires were the kings of background vocals. As their name implies, they started as a gospel group in their hometown of Springfield, Missouri. They also sang barbershop songs when they formed in 1948.

The members were Gordon Stokes (first tenor), Neal Matthews (second tenor), Hoyt Hawkins (baritone), and Hugh Jarrett (bass).

They moved to Nashville in the early '50s and started applying the influences they had grown up with (THE GOLDEN GATE QUARTET, the Dinning Sisters, and THE AMES BROTHERS) in order to get work. Not long after reaching Music City they were hired as regulars at the Grand Old Opry. They also recorded some spirituals for Decca including "Just a Closer Walk with Thee" with Red Foley.

By 1953 they were appearing on "Eddy Arnold Time," the first syndicated TV series that used Nashville music people, even though the show was done in Chicago.

In 1954 the group was appearing with Arnold at the Cotton Carnival in Memphis when a young, outlandishly dressed (pink shirt, white shoes, and black pants) fan came backstage and told the quartet, "If I ever get to cut a record, I want to use you guys singing background with me."

The Jordanaires thought little of the flattery until two years later when that same youngster signed with RCA and remembered his promise. It was Elvis, who had enjoyed the Jordanaires' music on both Arnold's show and at the Grand Old Opry, particularly appreciating their gospel material, which was Elvis's first love. Another of Elvis's loves was the sound of rhythm and blues groups, and singing with the Jordanaires afforded him the opportunity to stretch out with his R&B side. The quartet supported him with some great doo wop background on songs like "I Was the One" (the B side of "Heartbreak Hotel") in 1956.

Also in 1956 the group put out "Sugaree," a record that went Top 10 Country on Capitol. But they withdrew as featured artists, partly because of a Capitol exec's opinion that they'd be better off staying behind the scenes doing backup work.

It's ironic that the single greatest boost given to the income and legitimacy of backup groups was by a single artist, Elvis. After he and the Jordanaires had hits like "Too Much," "All Shook Up," "I Got Stung," "A Fool Such As I," "It's Now or Never," "Are You Lonesome Tonight," and "Indescribably Blue" (with the Imperials Quartet), every act wanted a studio backup group. In fact, the Jordanaires did so many Elvis sessions, he might technically have been considered their lead singer.

The quartet became active to the point of doing four sessions a day, five days a week for artists ranging from Patsy Cline, Hank Snow, Marty Robbins, and Jim Reeves to Connie Francis, Steve Lawrence, and Julie Andrews. Just a few of the hundreds of hits they've sung on include Ricky Nelson's "Poor Little Fool" and Jimmy Dean's "Big Bad John." In some cases—Johnny Horton and Rick Nelson, for example—they sang on all of an artist's hits.

In 1958 Ray Walker replaced Hugh Jarrett, and then the group remained intact into the '90s. Though no one knows precisely how many songs the Jordanaires have recorded, simple arithmetic shows if they did one song a session (and they probably did more) the total would equal 1,000 songs a year over 50 weeks. Add 35 years of recording and you have the astounding total of 35,000 recordings, surely one of the most, if not *the* most prolific of all recording acts.

The quartet sang on all the soundtracks for Elvis's 28 movies and toured with him on the rare occasions he went out. Even on TV the group was never more than a few feet out of camera range, and that's the way Elvis liked it; he always felt more comfortable on TV when the Jordanaires were singing with or near him.

In 1970 Elvis looked toward Las Vegas, but the group's lucrative Nashville lifestyle of commercials and background work (and their home lives and families) were too much to give up and they parted company.

The group continued into the '90s with everyone from Jerry Lee Lewis to the Judds, and whether the session required gospel, country, pop, or rock and roll, after almost 40 years the Jordanaires remained the behind-the-scenes vocal kings.

The Kodaks

An early male R&B group with a female lead, the Kodaks' chief asset was the uncanny similarity of Pearl McKinnon's voice to that of FRANKIE LYMON.

Pearl's first group got together in Newark, New Jersey, at Robert Trent Junior High and consisted of 15-year-old Pearl, Marian Patrick, and Jean Miller. The boys, who grew up in the Baxter Terrace housing project, included Marian's brother James (lead, tenor, and brother of Charles Patrick of THE MONOTONES), William Franklin (second tenor), Larry Davis (baritone), and William Miller (bass). The guys met Pearl in 1957 and felt she would be the unique twist that would differentiate them from the volume of vocal acts singing throughout Newark. The group's influences included THE HARPTONES, THE SPANIELS, THE HEARTBEATS, and Frankie Lymon's Teenagers. Whether conscious or not, Pearl's amazing ability to sound like Frankie made the group a popular quintet around the Baxter Terrace recreation hall where they rehearsed. They called themselves the Supremes (over four years before the Detroit superstars) and when they felt confident enough headed for Harlem to audition for Fury label owner Bobby Robinson.

Since Bobby had reportedly missed out on signing Frankie Lymon because he had been late for an appointment with Richard Barrett (who had then taken Lymon downtown to George Goldner's Gee label), he made up for it by grabbing the Supremes and recording "Teenager's Dream," a ballad Pearl and he collaborated on. At this time the group decided to change their name to the Kodaks after the camera company.

Both "Teenager's Dream" and its flip, the rollicking "Little Boy and Girl," were immediate New York airplay favorites, and the group's smooth yet enthusiastic harmonies gave both the songs and Pearl's lead an aura of quality not found in many of the Lymon-like groups.

The group's second single, "Oh Gee Oh Gosh," written by Pearl when she was 12, became their best-known effort; it did well in the Northeast and reached number eight R&B on their hometown chart in June 1958. They performed a number of times at the Apollo, did the chitlin circuit from Philadelphia's Uptown Theatre to the Howard in Washington, and appeared on Dick Clark's "American Bandstand." Around this time Franklin and Davis left to join the Sonics ("This Broken Heart," Harvard, 1959). They were replaced by Harold "Curly" Jenkins and Richard Dixon.

The group had two more Fury singles, neither of which reached the level of the previous efforts, and within a year the Kodaks had disbanded. Pearl married and stopped performing; James Patrick joined his brother in the Monotones. Miller, along with his wife Jean, Harold Jenkins, and Renaldo Gamble (the Schoolboys, Okeh), formed a new Kodaks and recorded one single for Zell Sanders' J&S label in 1960 and two for Sol Winkler's Wink label, the best side being "Love Wouldn't Mean a Thing."

In 1960 Pearl, along with Carl Williams (first tenor), James Straite (second tenor), Luther Morton (baritone), and Aaron Broadnick (bass), became Pearl and the Deltars and did another version of "Teenager's Dream" for Robinson's Fury label.

In the mid-'70s Pearl joined Second Verse (IX Chains label), but in one of the great ironies of rock lore wound up singing lead with Frankie Lymon's old group the Teenagers after his death.

THE KODAKS

A SIDE/B SIDE	LABEL/CAT NO	DATE
Teenager's Dream /		
Little Boy And Girl	Fury 1007	1957
Oh Gee Oh Gosh /		
Make Believe World	Fury 1015	1957
My Baby And Me / Kingless Castle	Fury 1019	1958
Guardian Angel /		
Run Around Baby	Fury 1020	1958
Don't Want No Teasing /		
Look Up To The Sky	J&S 1683	1960
Twista Twistin' / Let's Rock	Wink 1004	1961

A SIDE/B SIDE	LABEL/CAT NO	DATE
Mister Magoo / Love		
Wouldn't Mean A Thing	Wink 1006	1961
Pearl and the Deltars		
Teenager's Dream /		
Dance, Dance, Dance	Fury 1048	1961

The Kool Gents

Though some groups were named by disc jockeys after themselves (THE MOONGLOWS by Alan "Moondog" Freed and THE MAGNIFICENTS by "The Magnificent" Montague), the Kool Gents named *themselves* after a local disc jockey and in the process gave birth to one of pop's best solo vocalists.

Cicero Blake (lead), James Harper (first tenor and baritone), Howard McClain (second tenor), Teddy Long (second tenor), and John Carter (bass) started singing together at Marshall High School in Chicago during 1951. The fledgling quintet first called themselves the Golden Tones. By 1953, Harper, McClain, and Blake were out and Delecta "Dee" Clark (lead), John McCall (first tenor), and Doug Brown (second tenor) were in. Dee, born in Blytheville, Arkansas, came to Chicago with his family at the age of three and at age 13 was a member of the Hambone Kids, performers of "Hambone" with the Red Saunders Orchestra on Okeh Records.

The Golden Tones were inspired by a combination of rhythm and blues and gospel acts, among them THE CLOVERS, THE FIVE ROYALES, and THE HIGHWAY QCs.

In 1955 Clark and company went to see local disc jockey Herb "Kool Gent" Kent at WGS hoping he would manage them. He was too busy to handle the new group but didn't mind their request to use his nickname, so the Golden Tones became the Kool Gents. He also introduced them to Cal Carter (Vee-Jay Records A&R director), who eventually signed them after they returned to audition with original songs.

They issued "This Is the Night," in late 1955, a fine rhythm and blues record that showcased Dee's tenor. The 45 only reached the public in the Chicago area. The same went for their 1956 ballad "I Just Can't Help Myself," though *Billboard*'s June 23rd reviewer liked the flip, "Do You Do," describing it as a "catchy item. Kool Gents vocal is backed by smart rhythm work." "This Is the Night" was tersely dispatched by the reviewer as a "bluesy ballad, adequately done."

Next, the Kool Gents became the Delegates on Vee-Jay's whim and recorded "The Convention," a novelty record built around an election year campaign. Another single, "Mother's Son," did little and a change was on the horizon.

Dee then asked Carter if he could become a solo act and Vee-Jay obliged, issuing singles on their Falcon and Abner affiliates in 1957 and 1958. The group was understandably upset when they heard that Vee-Jay had supported their lead singer's defection, so to placate them Carter arranged for the Kool Gents/Delegates to become the new EL DORADOS, convincing them there was more money to be made by becoming a group that had already had a hit than there was as a leaderless quartet of Kool Gents. Since the original El Dorados had separated, the Kool Gents could back the group's original lead and all would be well. As it turned out, they didn't earn much money as the new El Dorados and lasted only a year or two.

John Carter formed a new Kool Gents that hung on till 1965 but never recorded. Dee Clark hit the pop charts (as he always professed to be a pop singer more than an R&B stylist) in 1958 with "Nobody But You" (#21), "Just Keep It Up" (#18, 1959), and "Hey Little Girl" (#20, 1959), all on Abner. Transferred to the parent Vee-Jay label by 1960 he hit the big time with a 1961 classic "Raindrops" (#2) featuring his trademark soaring falsetto. Dee went on to record for seven more labels through 1975 including Constellation, Columbia, Wand, Liberty, United Artists, Rocky, and Chelsea, where he hit #16 in late 1975 in England on Kenny Nolan's "Ride a Wild Horse." On December 7, 1990, Dee died of a heart attack in Atlanta at the age of 52.

The Lamplighters

A notoriously self-destructive group of talents, the Lamplighters also served as the starting point of the '60s act THE RIVINGTONS.

Formed in 1952 in Southeast Los Angeles at Jordan High School, the members were Leon Hughes, Matthew Nelson, and Willie Ray Rockwell. They began singing at talent shows, and on one such evening were performing at Johnny Otis's Barrell House at Wilmington Avenue and 106th Street in Watts when they lost the $25 prize to a solo vocalist from Indianapolis, Indiana, named Thurston Harris. Thurston, who had sung with the gospel groups the Canaan Crusaders and the Indiana Wonders, claimed to have been the lead of THE FIVE ROYALES (he wasn't), and sang their song "Help Me Somebody" to win the prize.

The three vocalists convinced Thurston to join them. The new brash, ragged, and rough quartet started playing gigs, one of which was at the Club Alimony on 101st Street and Main. Between shows they went into the men's room, where they met Mellomoods (1949, not the Red Robin group) former vocalist Al Frazier. Al, who had somewhat more experience, gave them some tips on unison hand claps and facing the audience. Before he knew it he was the fifth member of the no-named group and wound up doing a second show with them. (Al had previously sung with another group who hadn't been able to decide on a name and had come up with the Emanons, which is "no name" spelled backwards.) The new quintet soon met Ralph Bass of Federal Records, but they lost Leon Hughes before they could record. Bass then signed them and issued their first single "Part Of Me," a bluesy ballad that stirred little attention.

Up to the time of that release they still had no name and never got a chance to choose one; Bass and/or Johnny Otis came up with the Lamplighters, and that's what appeared on the label. Their second disc, "Bee Bop Wino" (with Rockwell on lead) turned out to be their best-received single, especially in San Francisco.

From the beginning the group was its own worst enemy; wine and women distracted all but Frazier from a serious approach to their music. Harris wound up having fights onstage with patrons, Nelson was jailed by his wife for nonsupport, and Rockwell's drinking ended in tragedy when he crashed into a telephone pole and killed himself. But the same outrageous behavior made for some wild performances: Nelson was prone to removing his shoes and socks and playing piano with his toes; the group would jump into the audience on instrumental breaks and dance with any good-looking woman in sight; and their onstage gymnastics (back flips and all) were something to behold.

In late 1954 the Lamplighters toured the South with Joe Liggins and his band. Eddie Jones and Harold Lewis stepped in for Willie Rockwell and Matthew Nelson but by the time they reached Griffin, Georgia, Thurston Harris decided to go home after being paid less than what he thought he was worth. The group was left stranded. Finally back in Los Angeles, Al Frazier had just about given up on groups when Rockwell called him over to his house to sing with two newcomers, Carl White and Sonny Harris (no relation to Thurston, but he did sing with the Feathers on "Why Don't You Write Me," Showtime, 1955). Rockwell lasted for one rehearsal, and soon Matthew Nelson was back. The group went through the Federal Records new-name routine again: when the new foursome's single "Kissing Bug" was issued in March 1955 their name was now the Tenderfoots.

Four unremarkable issues later (the best being "Cindy," their last 45) the group decided to drive to Cincinnati to pick up some overdue royalties from Federal's home base, and since they were within driving distance of Indianapolis they dropped in on Thurston. The timing couldn't have been better: he was itching to get back on the road. The group wound up driving back to Los Angeles with Thurston back on board.

Since Thurston was back they decided to record again as the Lamplighters and did three singles in late 1955 and early 1956 for Federal. During this time the group's high point was a San Francisco performance with SONNY TIL AND THE ORIOLES and a few shows with a young, then unknown comedian named Flip Wilson.

It wasn't long before Thurston became too difficult to work with and the group replaced him with Turner "Rocky" Wilson III.

The Lamplighters soon became the Sharps, with members Carl White (who had sung all the leads when the group was the Tenderfoots), Sonny Harris, Al Frazier, and Rocky Wilson.

Thurston Harris was living in the early '90s in Pomona, sometimes performing with Big Jay McNeely and Johnny Otis's band. Matthew Nelson died. The Sharps became relatively active backup singers and even helped give Thurston a hit (without credit) on the smash "Little Bitty Pretty One." Had they taken their music more seriously, they might have had a success long before that 1957 hit.

THE LAMPLIGHTERS

A SIDE/B SIDE	LABEL/CAT NO	DATE
Turn Me Loose / Part Of Me	Fed 12149	9/53
Be-Bop Wino / Give Me	Fed 12152	11/53
Sad Life* / Move Me Baby*	Fed 12156	12/53
Smootchie / I Can't Stand It	Fed 12166	2/54
I Used To Cry Mercy, Mercy /		
Tell Me You Care	Fed 12176	4/54
Salty Dog / Ride, Jockey, Ride	Fed 12182	5/54
Five Minutes Longer / You Hear	Fed 12192	8/54

A SIDE/B SIDE	LABEL/CAT NO	DATE
Yum Yum / Goody Good Things	Fed 12197	10/54
I Wanna Know / Believe In Me	Fed 12206	1954
Love, Rock And Thrill / Roll On	Fed 12212	3/54
The Tenderfoots		
Kissing Bug / Watussi Wussi Wo	Fed 12214	3/55
My Confession /		
Save Me Some Kisses	Fed 12219	4/55
Those Golden Bells /		
I'm Yours Anyhow	Fed 12225	6/55
Cindy / Sugar Ways	Fed 12228	7/55
The Lamplighters		
Don't Make It So Good /		
Hug A Little, Kiss A Little	Fed 12242	11/55
Bo Peep / You Were Sent		
Down From Heaven	Fed 12255	2/56
It Ain't Right /		
Everything's All Right	Fed 12261	1956

* Jimmy Witherspoon and the Lamplighters

The Larks

Ask any R&B vocal group fan his opinion of the best groups of the '50s and he'll probably include the Larks on a list of top 10. Yet the original Larks lasted only two years, releasing 11 highly collectible 45s.

The Larks' roots go way back to the late '30s in the form of a well-schooled gospel group known as the Selah Jubilee Singers of Durham, North Carolina. The membership included Thurmon Ruth, Allen Bunn, Junius Parker, Jimmy Gorham, and Melvin Coldten. The group recorded for Decca from 1939 through 1944 with their most well-remembered recording being "I Want Jesus to Walk Around."

In the mid-'40s the group met Eugene Mumford of the gospel group the Four Internes and, recognizing his splendid tenor as unique, attempted to bring him onboard. But before they could, Gene was charged with the attempted rape of a white woman and sent to work for two years in 1947 as a member of a North Carolina chain gang. It was hard to forget Gene's pristine vocals and harder still because Thurmon Ruth would drive past the highway Gene was working on each day on his way to radio station WPT, where the Selahs had a 15-minute show each weekday.

In the late '40s, Allen (baritone) and Thurmon (lead) left the Selahs and returned home to Wilson, North Carolina, and formed the Jubilators, with

Raymond "Pee Wee" Barnes (tenor), Hadie Rowe, Jr. (tenor), and David McNeil (bass).

In June 1949 Gene Mumford was released with a full pardon from North Carolina's governor; it had taken two years for the state to substantiate his alibi by a drugstore owner. He quickly joined the Jubilators, and the quintet (Rowe, Jr. was eliminated by the draft) began to create their incomparable sound.

Ruth, the group's organizer, had been influenced by THE DEEP RIVER BOYS and THE FOUR VAGABONDS and was planning a move into the secular world for the Jubilators when he and the group drove to New York in the fall of 1950. For a start, however, they began recording gospel tunes, which led them to a variety of opportunities. On one occasion the group, hoping to earn some quick advances, recorded four times for four labels—in the same day. In order to do it they sang as the Jubilators on Regal, the Selah Singers for Jubilee, the Four Barons for Savoy, and the Southern Harmonaires for Apollo. They were finally caught at Apollo Records when an agent told owner Bess Bermen that the same guys had recorded there earlier (at Mastertone Studios) under another name.

By December 1950 Apollo had turned the gospel Jubilators into the Five Larks, a name the group chose in keeping with THE ORIOLES/RAVENS bird group trend.

Their first single, in January 1951, was the jump tune "Coffee, Cigarettes and Tears" accompanied by a pop ballad, the Percy Faith-Carl Sigman-penned "My Heart Cries for You."

Their second single initiated the group's rise as legendary balladeers. "Hopefully Yours," written by Mumford, was well-received on East Coast radio and sold enough to reach number 10 on a New York chart. The flip side was a bluesy ballad titled "When I Leave These Prison Walls," written by Mumford while incarcerated.

Their doorway to immortality was opened by the next release. "My Reverie," the Larry Clinton (#1, 1938) pop ballad, took on a whole new inspirational rhythm and blues tone in the hands of the Larks. Mumford's lead was mesmerizing and the five-part vocal harmony blend was exquisite. A vocal orchestra, the Larks needed only a piano for accompaniment; McNeil's incredibly round and full bass notes improved on any standup bass that Apollo might have chosen to use. The Larks' "My Reverie" ranks with THE FLAMINGOS' "Golden Teardrops" as the most beautifully performed rhythm and blues ballad ever. Collectors have thought so for decades, and one even turned to crime over it.

Slim Rose, proprietor of New York's Time Square Records, obtained an excruciatingly rare orange plastic copy of the disc in the early '60s and played it on his radio show, then promptly placed it on his rare record wall with the words "Not For Sale" printed on the sleeve. This was the only time in the famous oldie emporium's history that a record was not purchasable. Two weeks later Slim announced on the air that the store had been broken into. To his and his audience's astonishment, only one record had been stolen out of all the thousands of rarities: the Larks' "My Reverie."

Back in 1951, however, the single could be had for less than a dollar; there were plenty of copies since it was the Larks' biggest New York seller and sold fairly well up and down the East Coast at rhythm and blues record stores.

A change of pace brought the group their first national R&B charter. The blues shuffle "Eyesight to the Blind," with Allen Bunn on lead, reached number five on *Billboard*'s July 28th Best Seller list.

The group performed on a surprising number of TV shows for a 1951 black act but they were so superior to most other performers it must have been hard to ignore them, especially when they had a chart record. They appeared on Perry Como's "Chesterfield Superclub Show," "The Ted Steele Show," "Spotlight on Harlem," "The Zeke Manners Show," and "Arthur Godfrey's Talent Scouts," where they wiped out the competition singing Patti Page's "Tennessee Waltz" with Gene on lead.

The "Little Sidecar" single, their fifth, was a bouncy blues tune that also reached number 10 on the country's rhythm and blues charts on October 6th.

By the time it reached the national hit list, Apollo had released a tune brought to the group by bandleader Lucky Millinder called "I Don't Believe in Tomorrow." Probably the last thing songwriter Ben Weisman expected was an R&B group recording one of his songs, but the Larks made "Tomorrow" their own as Allen and Gene traded leads. Had "Little Sidecar" not still been gathering sales momentum in the summer and fall, "Tomorrow" might have made some chart noise of its own.

The Larks continued to have solid singles on Apollo like "My Lost Love," "Darlin'," "In My Lonely Room," and "I Live True to You."

Unfortunately, they couldn't earn enough to continue as performers and the Larks went their separate ways in late 1952. Gene went back to religious music with the granddaddy of gospel greats, THE GOLDEN GATE QUARTET, but soon hungered to sing in the secular style. In early 1954 a new Larks was formed which was actually half Golden Gaters (Gene Mumford and Orville Brooks) and half the King Odom Four (Isaiah Bing and David Bowers).

The sides they recorded (six singles for Apollo's new Lloyds affiliate) sounded nothing like Larks records or even like rhythm and blues; the group's new direction was straight pop and generated little if any activity.

The second Larks disbanded by the end of 1955 and Gene Mumford joined the Serenadors on Whiz (Old Town). He finally hit the big time when he replaced Jackie Wilson in THE DOMINOES and went on to have two major hits with "Stardust" (#12 Pop, 1957) and "Deep Purple" (#20 Pop, 1957). He then went out as a solo on several labels, was reported to be singing with THE INK SPOTS in the early '70s, and since passed away. David McNeil went on to sing with the Dominoes in 1952 on some of their early and best records (including a bass lead on "Pedal Pushin' Papa"). Raymond Barnes became a guitar player, mostly working with bands in the South; Thurmon Ruth went back to gospel; and the late Allen Bunn formed and sang with the Wheels ("My Heart's Desire," 1956) and took the stage name Tarheel Slim (Fury) while singing with Little Ann as the Lovers (Lamp).

The Larks influenced groups from THE HARPTONES to THE MOONGLOWS (especially McNeil's bass singing, which replaced the standup bass sound that anchored countless doo wop records of the '50s and '60s), and their legacy has survived and flourished because their fans keep passing the sound on to others.

Eddie Gries and Donn Fileti of Relic Records issued two LP's of Larks Apollo and Lloyds sides in the late '80s from master tapes that were miraculously found in excellent condition in the closet of a Chicago dress factory.

THE LARKS

A SIDE/B SIDE	LABEL/CAT NO	DATE
Coffee, Cigarettes And Tears /		
My Heart Cries For You	Apollo 1177	1/51
Hopefully Yours / When I Leave		
These Prison Walls	Apollo 1180	4/51
My Reverie / Let's Say A Prayer	Apollo 1184	5/51
Eyesight To The Blind / I Ain't		
Fattenin' Frogs For Snakes	Apollo 427	6/51
Hey Little Girl / Little Side Care	Apollo 429	6/51
I Don't Believe In Tomorrow /		
Ooh . . . It Feels So Good	Apollo 430	7/51
My Lost Love /		
How Long Must I Wait For You	Apollo 435	12/51

A SIDE/B SIDE	LABEL/CAT NO	DATE
Darlin' / Lucy Brown	Apollo 437	1/52
Shadrack / Honey In The Rock	Apollo 1189	1/52
Stolen Love / In My Lonely Room	Apollo 1190	2/52
Hold Me / I Live True To You	Apollo 1194	7/52
Margie / Rockin' In The Rocket	Lloyds 108	3/54
If It's A Crime / Tippin' In	Lloyds 110	5/54
When You're Near /		
Who Walks In When I Walk Out	Lloyds 111	6/54
No Other Girl / The World Is		
Waiting For The Sunrise	Lloyds 112	7/54
Os-Ca-Lu-Ski-O / Forget It	Lloyds 114	10/54
Johnny Darlin' /		
You're Gonna Lose Your Gal	Lloyds 115	1954
Honey From The Bee /		
No Mama No	Apollo 475	1955

Little Anthony and the Imperials

A superb vocal group, Little Anthony and the Imperials were also one of the few '50s acts to survive and prosper during the ever-changing '60s. Anthony Gourdine was born and brought up in the Fort Green Projects in the Greenpoint section of Brooklyn and determined early on to make singing a way of life. With a dad who played alto sax professionally and a gospel-singing mom, the youngster (born Jan. 8, 1940) was well-schooled in music. He admired artists from Ella Fitzgerald and Nat King Cole to George Shearing and his favorite singing group, THE FLAMINGOS. Anthony started out singing legit pop songs on the "Startime Studio Shows" but by his mid-teens wanted to be doing what other teens in Boys High School were doing: singing with a group. (Both THE VELOURS and the Fitones would soon come from Boys High.)

Anthony put together a quartet with William (Doc) Dockerty (tenor), William Delk (baritone), and William Bracy in 1954. Gourdine knew Delk from the choir of the Church of the Open Doors.

Practices included an obligatory version of "Gloria" (THE CADILLACS) at places like the Red Hook Projects and would occasionally include neighborhood friends chiming in. One of them was Tommy Davis, who turned out to be a better ballplayer than a singer, ultimately playing for the Dodgers.

Anthony's group performed at local shows that offered $5 prizes to the winners and on one such show ran up against a young Harlem group named

FRANKIE LYMON AND THE TEENAGERS. At that point Anthony's quartet was called the DuPonts, having seen a sign for DuPont textiles.

Doc Dockerty's dad knew a writer/producer named Paul Winley (who had written for THE CLOVERS and Joe Turner and was the brother of the Clovers' Hal Winley). After hearing the DuPonts he committed to record them for his own Winley label—which didn't even exist until after he recorded the group. He put out their first single "You" in August 1955. The Anthony-led rhythm ballad had a distinct Frankie Lymon sound and was backed with "Must Be Falling in Love," a Teenagers-styled rocker. The session at New York's Regent Studios included a who's who of the day's top musicians, including Dave "Baby" Cortez on piano, Mickey "Guitar" Baker, and Sam "The Man" Taylor on sax.

Promotion by the fledgling label was insufficient and the DuPonts' first single never got a shot. Once again Doc's dad took things in hand and introduced the boys to songwriter Otis Blackwell, who brought them to Alan Freed's manager Jack Hook. Jack signed them to Royal Roost Records in February 1957 and by March "Prove It Tonight," a pop/R&B rocker, hit the streets and stayed there. Hook then arranged for the DuPonts to do Alan Freed's Easter Show at the New York Paramount, and the group became the opening act for THE CLEFTONES, Ruth Brown, THE PLATTERS, Frankie Lymon and the Teenagers, Buddy Knox, Jimmy Bowen, and THE CADILLACS.

Three days into the show Anthony came down with laryngitis, so the group covered his parts. When the Paramount shows ended so did the DuPonts. They did re-form in 1958 without Anthony for one single on Roulette called "Screamin' Ball at Dracula Hall."

During 1957 Anthony connected with a neighborhood foursome looking for a lead singer. The new quintet became the Chesters. The lineup consisted of Anthony (lead), Tracy Lord (tenor), Ernest Wright, Jr. (second tenor), Clarence Collins (baritone), and Glouster "Nate" Rogers (bass). They went nowhere fast until one day the five jumped on their bikes and took the lengthy ride to Jamaica, Queens, searching out some female friends. On the outing they also met a member of THE CELLOS who sent them to Charles Merenstein at the Apollo label. Merenstein was captivated by the group, especially Anthony's tenor, and had them practice a ballad of Gourdine's called "The Fires Burn No More." When it came time to record, Keith Williams replaced Clarence, whose father made him resign in order to spend more time on schoolwork.

In February 1958 "Fires" came out blazing, helped in part by heavy Alan Freed play, but Apollo couldn't stoke the flames and it died.

The group then went to see Richard Barrett, an A&R man for End Records who had been too busy to do anything with them when they had come to him earlier in the year. Hearing "Fires Burn No More" must have helped open up his schedule; he arranged for the group to record two of Ernest's songs, "Two People in the World" and "Cha-Cha Henry."

By now Clarence had come back to the Chesters and Williams had left to eventually join the gospel group THE HIGHWAY QCs. Originally Ernest Wright had been singing the Chesters' lead, but George Goldner, Ends owner, shifted Anthony into the featured position. Not satisfied with the two songs they'd recorded as A sides, Goldner agreed to listen to a Sylvester Bradford-Al Lewis composition right in the middle of the session. The song was "Tears on My Pillow," and though the Chesters were negative, George loved the tune. Coaxing a high-voiced vocal out of Anthony, the End prexy knew he had a hit.

"Tears" was issued in July 1958 under the name the Imperials; End promo man Lou Galley had renamed them just before the record was released. The song hit the airwaves like a rocket and spread across the country. Anthony was sitting on a Brooklyn park bench one evening and heard Alan Freed coming over the radio. Alan often gave credit to the lead singers on vocal group records he played. That night he announced, "And here's a new record that's making a lot of noise, 'Little Anthony and the Imperials' and 'Tears on My Pillow.'" That bit of creativity had Goldner rushing to redo the label so it read just that, and Little Anthony was born.

So was a national hit, as "Tears" charted on August 11th and rose to number four Pop by October 4th and number two R&B. The flip, "Two Kinds of People," made it one of the most popular double-sided ballad singles in vocal group history. "Tears" was number four in New York and the 13th most popular single in the Big Apple during 1958 according to a WINS year-end survey.

Others tried to capitalize on the Imperials' good fortune. Savoy Records acquired the earlier Winley masters and rushed out "You" with the label reading Little Anthony Gourdine and the DuPonts.

In the fall of 1958 a young songwriter named Neil Sedaka, who was on the charts at that time with Connie Francis's "Stupid Cupid," brought a new song of his to Goldner. "The Diary" was perfect for the Imperials and the group recorded it. Goldner had to leave town but left instructions with Richard Barrett to issue the record as the next single. Instead, Barrett issued another song titled "So Much," which just happened to be written by someone named, ahem, Richard Barrett. When Sedaka found out he was doubly annoyed: he hadn't really liked the Imperials' recording of "The Diary" and now it wasn't even coming out, so he took his version to RCA, recorded it himself, and saw it reach number 14 and launch his incredible recording career. Meanwhile, "So Much," a pretty ballad in its own right, didn't chart until two weeks after Sedaka's single and only reached number 87 Pop and number 24 R&B. When Goldner returned he was furious (not furious enough to fire Barrett, however) and tried to salvage the situation by issuing "The Diary," but it was too late. The group's version was excellent, and had they had a shot they would have given Sedaka a run for his money.

Three more singles passed relatively unnoticed ("Wishful Thinking," #79, "A Prayer and a Jukebox," #81, and a gospel rocker in THE ISLEY BROTHERS' "Shout" mode titled "I'm All Right"). Then came a November 1959 release that to this day Anthony still refers to as "stupid"—the group's recording of the novelty "Shimmy, Shimmy, Ko-Ko Bop." It took off on December 7th, giving the group their second hit (#24 Pop, #14 R&B). "Shimmy" was the last record Alan Freed played when he resigned on the air in 1960 after being made the scapegoat for record label payola practices.

On March 14, 1960, *Billboard* picked both sides of their new single as contenders, commenting, "Little Anthony and crew come through with two strong sides. 'Bayou' is a spiritual type rocker that is sold with verve. 'My Empty Room' is a warmly delivered rock-a-ballad, based on a Tchaikovsky theme." "My Empty Room" won the battle but the prize was only a number 86; it became their last End charter.

Several 45s followed, including a captivating reading of *Billboard* "Spotlight" winner "Please Say You Want Me." Their 13th End issue was a harmony classic practiced by every doo wop group for years to come and usually done a cappella, the start-and-stop sizzler "Traveling Stranger."

By the end of 1961, disappointed over failing singles and pressured to go solo, Anthony left the Imperials and did two less-than-magical singles for Roulette. Richard Barrett moved over to Carlton Records in 1961, taking along THE CHANTELS and the Imperials minus Anthony. Tracy Lord and Nate Rogers left prior to Carlton and Barrett replaced them with Sammy Strain (THE CHIPS on Josie, the

Fantastics on RCA) and new lead George Kerr (the Serenadors on Chock Full of Hits).

The Imperials' "Faithfully Yours" was a quality ballad that went nowhere as did two releases on Newtime and one on Capitol through 1963. They also backed Pookie Hudson (THE SPANIELS) on "I Know I Know" (without credit) for Lloyd Price's Double L label. Still, the group worked consistently and expanded its music to include modern harmony, some of which must have been generated by the ground-breaking LP they did with Anthony for End (*Shades of the Forties*) in which they sang all old '40s standards.

In 1963 Anthony reunited with the Imperials, now older, wiser, and possessing better stage presence. Anthony and the Imperials then honed their skills on countless Catskill mountain jobs while their manager, Ernie Martinelli, brought them ace songwriter and former THREE CHUCKLES member Teddy Randazzo. Teddy loved Anthony's sound and had a song just perfect for him called "I'm on the Outside (Looking In)."

The group's members were now Anthony (lead), Sammy Strain (first tenor), Ernie Wright (second tenor), and Clarence Collins (baritone/bass), so they ended up with two Boys High alumni (Anthony and Clarence) and two Alexander Hamilton grads (Sam and Ernie).

Though not really sure about "I'm on the Outside," the group rehearsed it for a Murray the K show at the New York Paramount. Murray was a fan of the group, and even though the Imperials didn't have a record out, he wanted them on. He promoted the appearance as the return of Little Anthony and the Imperials. While they practiced "I'm on the Outside" backstage, encouragement from JAY AND THE AMERICANS that the song was a hit gave them the confidence to cut it. Recorded for DCP Records (Don Costa Productions, where Randazzo was A&R Director), the song was not only their first chart record in four years, it became so when almost everything else on pop radio was British. "I'm on the Outside" (a Weinstein-Randazzo song) charted on August 22, 1964, and reached number 15, their biggest record since "Tears on My Pillow."

Their next single traveled all the way from Rome to reach them. Randazzo wrote "Goin' Out of My Head" there after a breakup with his wife. The Randazzo-Weinstein classic rose to number six Pop on December 26th and number 22 R&B in a week when four of the top 10 singles were by American groups ("Come See about Me," THE SUPREMES, #2; Imperials #6; "Dance, Dance, Dance," THE BEACH BOYS, #8; "The Jerk," THE LARKS, #9).

Anthony's favorite recording was their next single, "Hurt So Bad," a Randazzo-Weinstein-Harchman song that reached number 10 Pop (#3 R&B). The Imperials were on top of the musical world at a critical juncture in pop music evolution. Few of the '50s groups had so successfully re-emerged in a new musical environment, but here was Anthony and company alongside the Mo-towners, the British rockers, and the emerging American bands. They might have stayed there were it not for some badly timed political fallout.

The group ran into problems with Don Costa, who was having his own problems with distributor United Artists. "Take Me Back" (#16, 1965) and "I Miss You So" (#34, 1965) were the last relatively successful recordings for the Imperials, and they flew pretty much on their quality and the group's reputation as promotion began to disappear. "Hurt" was their last DCP charter (#51) and it wasn't until March 14, 1966, that UA recorded them again.

Now on UA's Veep label in place of the now defunct DCP, the group debuted with a Broadway styled rock-a-ballad called "Better Use Your Head." With Randazzo at the helm again, "Better" reached only number 54 Pop and strangely became their first and only chart single in England (#42). The group began to expand their performance base from Las Vegas to the Copacabana and from TV's Dick Clark to Ed Sullivan. But they went through 11 more Veep releases with nothing landing higher than "It's Not the Same" (#92) in 1966 (the first song to list the group as Anthony and the Imperials).

Meanwhile Veep reissued all six of their DCP singles in September 1966 along with a rerecorded version of "Tears on My Pillow" by Anthony and company.

In 1969 the group moved up to the parent company, United Artists, became Little Anthony and the Imperials again, and went back to their roots, recording solid singles of "Out of Sight, Out of Mind" (#52 Pop, #38 R&B, originally by THE FIVE KEYS) and "Ten Commandments of Love" (#82 Pop, originally by THE MOONGLOWS) before moving back to originals.

Though hits eluded them, an ever-growing legion of fans bought hundreds of thousands of their LPs, making them one of the mid-'60s' best at tightrope walking between teens and the adult fans.

Kenny Seymour took Ernest's spot for their Janus releases in the early '70s, and by 1974 the group shifted to Avco with Bobby Wade in for Seymour.

In 1972 the group hooked up with writer/producer Thom Bell and even did some demos for him. One of them was "Break Up to Make Up," but the song wound up with THE STYLISTICS rather than the Imperials.

After four Avco sides the group decided they had come as far as they could and amicably parted ways. Their last chart single was "Hold On (Just a Little Bit Longer)" (#106 Pop, #79 R&B), but the group couldn't.

17 years later, there was still a performing Imperials and a performing Little Anthony who would often tell his audience that despite public opinion his first name was not "Little." The two entities would often find themselves working down the road from each other (as in Las Vegas) and Anthony would occasionally hit some harmony with them. Those Imperials included Bobby Wade and Harold Jenkins (formerly of THE KODAKS) who replaced Sammy Strain in the early '70s. Clarence was with the group until around 1988, Sammy Strain went on to great success as a member of THE O'JAYS, and Ernest joined one of the Platters' groups.

Statistics like 17 Pop and 12 R&B charters don't begin to tell the story with a group like Anthony and the Imperials. Their sound made them a cut above, and as for their "little" lead singer (who's actually five-foot-ten inches), he sounds even better today than he did then.

LITTLE ANTHONY AND THE IMPERIALS

A SIDE/B SIDE	LABEL/ CAT NO	DATE
The Duponts		
You / Must Be Falling In Love	Winley 212	1956
Prove It Tonight / Somebody	RylRst 627	1957
The Chesters		
The Fires Burn No More /		
Lift Up Your Head	Apollo 521	1958
Little Anthony and		
the Imperials		
Tears On My Pillow /		
Two People In The World	End 1027	7/58
So Much / Oh Yeah	End 1036	11/58
The Diary / Cha Cha Henry	End 1038	1/59
Wishful Thinking /		
When You Wish Upon A Star	End 1039	2/59
A Prayer And A Juke Box /		
River Path	End 1047	5/59
So Near And Yet So Far /		
I'm Alright	End 1053	1959
Shimmy Shimmy Ko-Ko-Bob /		
I'm Still In Love With You	End 1060	11/59
My Empty Room /		
Bayou, Bayou, Baby	End 1067	3/60
I'm Taking A Vacation From Love /		
Only Sympathy	End 1074	1960

A SIDE/B SIDE	LABEL/CAT NO	DATE
Limbo Part 1 / Limbo Part 2	End 1080	1960
Formula Of Love / Dream	End 1083	1960
Please Day You Want Me /		
So Near Yet So Far	End 1086	2/61
Traveling Stranger / Say Yeah	End 1091	1961
A Lovely Way To Spend		
An Evening / Dream	End 1104	1961
Faithfully Yours / Vut Vut	Carlton 566	12/61
A Short Prayer /		
Where Will You Be	Nwtm 503	1962
The Letter / Go And		
Get Your Heart Broken	Nwtm 505	1962
I'm On The Outside / Please Go	DCP 1104	1964
Goin' Out Of My Head /		
Make It Easy On Yourself	DCP 1119	1964
Hurt So Bad / Reputation	DCP 1126	1965
Take Me Back / Our Song	DCP 1136	6/65
I Miss You So / Get Out Of My Life	DCP 1149	1965
Hurt / Never Again	DCP 1154	1965
Better Use Your Head /		
The Wonder Of It All	Veep 1228	1966
You Better Take It Easy Baby /		
Gonna Fix You Good	Veep 1233	8/66
Tears On My Pillow /		
Who's Sorry Now	Veep 1239	9/66
I'm On The Outside Looking In /		
Please Go	Veep 1240	9/66
Goin' Out Of My Head /		
Make It Easy On Yourself	Veep 1241	9/66
Hurt So Bad / Reputation	Veep 1242	9/66
Our Song / Take Me Back	Veep 1243	9/66
Get Out Of My Life / I Miss You So	Veep 1244	9/66
Hurt / Never Again	Veep 1245	9/66
It's Not The Same / Down On Love	Veep 1248	10/66
Don't Tie Me Down /		
Where There's A Will There's		
A Way To Forget You	Veep 1255	1/67
Hold On To Someone /		
Lost In Love	Veep 1262	4/67
You Only Live Twice /		
My Love Is A Rainbow	Veep 1269	1967
Beautiful People /		
If I Remember To Forget	Veep 1275	11/67
I'm Hypnotized / Hungry Heart	Veep 1278	11/67
What Greater Love /		
In The Back Of My Heart	Veep 1283	4/68
Yesterday Has Gone /		
My Love Is A Rainbow	Veep 1285	5/68
The Gentle Rain /		
The Flesh Failures	Veep 1293	1968
Goodbye Goodtimes / Anthem	Veep 1303	1969
Out Of Sight, Out Of Mind /		
Summer's Comin' In	UA 50552	6/69
The Ten Commandments Of		
Love / Let The Sunshine In	UA 50598	9/69
Don't Get Close /		
It'll Never Be The Same Again	UA 50625	1970
World Of Darkness / The Change	UA 50677	1970

A SIDE/B SIDE	LABEL/CAT NO	DATE
If I Love You / Help Me Find A Way	UA 50720	10/70
Father, Father /		
Each One, Teach One	Janus 160	5/71
Universe / Madeline	Janus 166	6/71
Love Story / There's An Island	Janus 178	1972

Frankie Lymon and the Teenagers

Frankie Lymon and the Teenagers were true trendsetters in the early days of rock and roll. They were the yardstick by which hundreds of kiddie vocal groups gauged their capabilities in order to bring themselves to the public's attention. Groups like the Students (Checker), THE CHANTERS (Deluxe), RONNIE AND THE HI-LITES (Joy), Nicky and the Nobles (Gone), THE KODAKS (Fury), THE DESIRES (Hull), Tiny Tim and the Hits (Roulette), and even Frankie's brother's group LOUIS LYMON AND THE TEEN CHORDS, are just some of the many who tried for the brass ring in the footsteps of Frankie and company. Some of those fans that made it big include Diana Ross, Millie Jackson, Ronnie Spector, and Tim Hauser (THE MANHATTAN TRANSFER).

Their story began in the Washington Heights section of New York City in 1954 as Jimmy Merchant (second tenor) and Sherman Garnes (bass), both ninth graders at Edward W. Stitt Junior High School, formed a group called the Earth Angels (named after THE PENGUINS' hit). That group was short-lived, but the two black teens were not discouraged and they were soon talking with two neighborhood Puerto Ricans, Herman Santiago (first tenor) and Joe Negroni (baritone), whom Sherman had met.

A fateful meeting on 164th Street (where Sherman lived) led to the foursome calling themselves the Coupe De Villes. Across the street lived a family with four brothers, Howie, Timmy, Louis, and Frankie Lymon, all of whom would sing with groups in the future.

The four Coupe De Villes became the Premiers and alternated their practices between Joe's hallway on 153rd Street, Sherman's on 165th and Edgecombe Avenue, and Jimmy's on 156th, depending on how long they lasted without being chased away by complaining neighbors. Their practices led to performances at neighborhood talent shows, and one was scheduled for the school auditorium. The

Premiers decided to get in some extra practice after a dress rehearsal and entered one of the classrooms. A young teen who was also scheduled to perform with his brother's mambo band came in and asked to sing a few songs with the group. It was Herman's neighbor from across 164th Street, 12-year-old Frankie Lymon. They sang "Why Don't You Write Me" (THE JACKS), "Painted Pictures" (THE SPANIELS), and "Lily Maebelle" (THE VALENTINES), and had such a good time they agreed to do it again, but no one formally asked young Frankie to join.

After the talent show (where Frankie played bongos and his brother Howie played congas with their Latin group), Frankie just started hanging out with the older guys and became first tenor to Herman Santiago's lead.

Frankie came from a gospel background. His father Howard sang with the Harlemaires and Frankie, Louie, and Howie sang with the Harlemaires Juniors. This seemed to have little impact on his early occupation as a 10-year-old hustler of prostitutes in Harlem. His father was a truck driver and mother a domestic, and it wasn't easy to feed a family of seven. Frankie also worked in a grocery on his corner as a delivery boy, so pimping was not necessarily his preferred source of income.

By 1955 the quintet was calling themselves the Ermines when they weren't lapsing back to the Premiers. On one fateful evening the hallway kids (as they were designated by neighbors) were practicing in Sherman's hall when they were confronted by a man named Robert, who often stopped and listened to them before entering his apartment. According to author Phil Groia, he said, "My old lady [her name was Delores] sends me letters in the form of poems. Being that you're always singing the same old songs, why don't you get some original material of your own? I'm giving you some of these poems; see what you can do with them." The Premiers/Ermines sorted through them and started working on one in particular called "Why Do Birds Sing So Gay." Frankie worked on a melody line and the others formulated a harmony while tenor Jimmy Merchant came up with a vocal bass intro. It started out as a ballad but soon evolved into an uptempo rocker.

Many evenings later they were rehearsing their repertoire at Stitt's Night Community Center when in walked the revered Valentines, who also practiced there. Lead singer Richard Barrett had heard there was a hot neighborhood group doing his song and was very impressed by the Premiers' interpretation.

Barrett's version of his meeting with the group is slightly different: he claims they camped under his 161st Street window and sang until he came down and agreed to hear them audition at Stitt's the following Monday.

There are also three versions of how they went from Barrett to George Goldner's Gee Records. The Barrett version states that on the day of the audition for Goldner, Herman Santiago caught a cold and the only one who knew the words was Frankie. Barrett knew Goldner was preoccupied with recording a new group called the Millionaires, so he threatened that he would not rehearse the group if George didn't sign his new find, the Premiers. Supposedly, the Gee exec agreed and let the Premiers record two songs during the Millionaires' dinner break. (The Millionaires were actually Ben E. King and several of THE FIVE CROWNS, who later went on to become THE DRIFTERS.)

Another version is attributed to Hy Weiss, a legendary figure of the golden days of rock and owner of the Old Town label. He claimed that Barrett brought the Premiers to him, but Hy had too many acts so he recommended the group go see his friend George Goldner.

The final (and most probable) version was that Barrett took the group to Goldner, auditioned right after THE CLEFTONES had done so, and were told they had a deal. Herman sang lead on "Why Do Birds Sing So Gay," "That's What You're Doin' to Me" (THE DOMINOES), and one of his originals, "I Want You to Be My Girl." He also sang a duet with Frankie. Then Lymon sang a song he'd done with brother Howie's group. Goldner then suggested Frankie sing "Why Do Birds," changed the title to "Why Do Fools Fall in Love," moved Herman to first tenor, and told the teens they had a deal.

In the spring of 1955 the Premiers began recording at Bell Sound Studios with Gee musical director and sax man Jimmy Wright. He decided they needed a more imaginative name, so he suggested they become the Teenagers.

By the fall of 1955 all but Frankie were attending George Washington High School and their record had still not come out. They went downtown to find Goldner busy with other projects. By Christmas their school friends doubted they had ever recorded at all.

Then in January 1956 Jimmy Merchant strolled through the school corridor when he heard a girl singing a very familiar refrain. He asked where she heard that and she replied, "On the radio last night."

The record had been released on January 10, 1956, and the floodgates had opened. "Why Do Fools Fall in Love" sold a hundred thousand copies in three weeks. *Billboard* wrote, "Here's a hot new disc, which has already sparked a couple of covers in the pop market. The appealing ditty has a frantic arrangement, a solid beat and a sock lead vocal by 13-year-old Frankie Lymon. Jockeys and jukes should hand it plenty of spins and it could easily break Pop."

The covers *Billboard* referred to were tough competition—Gale Storm (#9), Gloria Mann (#59), and THE DIAMONDS (#12). But the Teenagers' single was destined for greatness and beat out all comers; it rose to number six (#1 R&B).

The original first pressing read "The Teenagers featuring Frankie Lymon," with Frankie's name printed at twice the size of his vocal mates. The song credit listed "Lymon-Santiago-Goldner," but George took care of that quickly: the second pressing read only "Lymon-Goldner."

In February 1956 the Teenagers played their first paying gig at the State Theatre in Hartford, Connecticut, alongside the Valentines, Bo Diddley, THE BONNIE SISTERS, THE HARPTONES, THE TURBANS, Fats Domino, and their idols, THE CADILLACS. In fact it was Earl Wade of that group who took them aside between shows to give them a few pointers on dance steps and instructed them to seek out Cholly Atkins, who had taught the Caddies their dance routines.

Within months the record and group were international hits: "Fools" reached number one in England, the first R&B/rock and roll record by an American vocal group to do so. Not bad for three 16-year-olds (Jimmy, Joe, and Sherman), one 15-year-old (Herman), and one 13-year-old (Frankie).

In April their second 45, "I Want You to Be My Girl," hit the airwaves. Once again the first printing read "The Teenagers featuring Frankie Lymon," but the second was changed to read "Frankie Lymon and the Teenagers." Herman Santiago wrote "Girl"; given the typical practices of the day, it's not surprising that the writer's credit was given to Goldner-Barrett. "I Want You to Be My Girl" skyrocketed like its predecessor, reaching number 13 (#3 R&B).

Their first big tour started on a dubious note: the Teenagers and co-billed acts THE FLAMINGOS, THE PLATTERS, THE CLOVERS, THE FLAIRS, and Carl Perkins all stood around the Hotel Theresa in New York ready to hit the road except for one small detail. Frankie Lymon was nowhere to be found. Sherman Garnes then marched the group up to the High School of Music and Art to recruit their friend Jimmy Castor (of the Juniors, Wing), who had a style similar to Frankie's. Jimmy left school that same day and the tour got underway. Frankie

showed up later on with little in the way of explanation.

A similar incident happened on another tour when Richard Barrett stepped in as lead in Detroit.

On a Canadian tour the group was approached backstage by a youngster who had a song he wanted them to record. They weren't interested since it appears they didn't record songs Goldner couldn't put his name on. The kid left a copy anyway and then went next door to see the Platters, and heard a similar response. Shortly after, the song and the kid became national hits. If the Teenagers had gone ahead and recorded "Diana," Paul Anka might never have become a hit artist. (On March 25, 1958, Frankie and an unknown vocal group recorded "Diana," but it was never issued on a single.)

In the summer of 1956 Gee cajoled the group into doing Jimmy Castor and the Juniors' "I Promise to Remember." It reached only number 56 (#10 R&B) and its solid rocker flip "Who Can Explain" made R&B number seven.

The "ABCs of Love" was another strong jump tune that Frankie and the group put over solidly, and it reached number eight R&B but only number 77 Pop. The flip side "Share" showcased the Teenagers' polished harmonies and Sherman's bass. (Almost 30 years later the U.G.H.A. organization did a massive East Coast vote-in for the 500 most popular oldies among devotees of group harmony, and "Share" was voted number one.)

The group appeared in Alan Freed's classic teen film *Rock, Rock, Rock*, which was filmed in the Bronx at the Bedford Park Studios and the nearby botanical gardens. They sang "I'm Not a Juvenile Delinquent" (written by Bobby Spencer of the Cadillacs and the Valentines, though the label credit read "Goldner") and "Baby Baby," which became their next single.

The British loved "Delinquent." It reached number 12 in Britain in early 1957 (and the flip "Baby Baby" reached number four), but U.S. kids nixed the cutesy rocker and it failed to chart.

The group also did a British tour in 1956 that included a performance at the world-famous London Palladium and a command performance in the Queen's chambers for Princess Margaret. The outstanding ballad "Out in the Cold Again" became their last R&B chart record, reaching number 10.

While still on the six-week European tour, Goldner started tampering with the chemistry that made the quintet so successful. Frankie began recording solo; the results were languid and desperately in need of the Teenagers' enthusiastic backing. Though the label of the 1957 single

"Goody Goody" read "Frankie Lymon and the Teenagers," the Harlem teens were nowhere to be found on the released recording. It reportedly had the pasteurized harmony of the Ray Charles Singers accompanying Frankie. It reached number 20 Pop and number 24 in England but never made the R&B chart.

The quintet continued to tour through mid-1957 and Gee then moved Frankie to Roulette Records for a series of lackluster singles like "So Goes My Love," "Little Girl," "Footsteps," and Elvis's "Jailhouse Rock."

In 1960 Frankie charted for four weeks with a remake of Thurston Harris's "Little Bitty Pretty One" (#58).

Meanwhile, the Teenagers were mismatched with Bill Lobrano, a white-sounding cross between Frankie Avalon and an imitation Elvis, for two singles, "Flip Flop" (which it did) and "Mama Wanna Rock" (which didn't wanna rock). In 1960 they recorded a credible cover of THE SHIRELLES' "Tonight's the Night" with Kenny Bobo, formerly of the Juniors, on lead and a second single (both for End), "A Little Wiser Now" with Johnny Houston upfront sounding like Jackie Wilson leading the Flamingos. The Teenagers certainly had diversity, but it didn't help them sell records.

The Teenagers and Frankie reunited in 1965 for a brief period but no recordings resulted. The four Teenagers performed one last time in 1973 with Pearl McKinnon of the Kodaks on lead (whose vocal likeness to Frankie was startling). Sherman Garnes passed on after a heart attack in 1977, and Joe Negroni died of a cerebral hemorrhage in 1978.

In 1981, the 25th anniversary of their first hit, the Teenagers were re-formed at the suggestion of Herbie Cox and Charlie James (the Cleftones), Ronnie Italiano (U.G.H.A. founder), and Joel Warshaw. The members were Jimmy Merchant, Herman Santiago, Eric Ward (of the soul group Second Verse), and Pearl McKinnon. The group, managed by Warshaw and helped by Ronnie I., began performing to overwhelming adulation.

By 1983 Ward had been replaced by Derek Ventura, and in 1984 Phil Garrito took over for Derek. Roz Morehead replaced Pearl, and Marilyn Byers moved into Roz's lead spot.

In the early '80s they opened for Manhattan Transfer, thanks to Tim Hauser, who tracked them down and arranged the gig.

The group did a PBS documentary as a tribute to their music and to Frankie, who died of a drug overdose in his grandmother's apartment at the age of 26. The show was aired on August 14, 1983.

In 1983 Pearl McKinnon discovered that Frankie was buried in an unmarked grave at St. Raymond's Cemetery in the Bronx.

In September 1985, thanks to Ronnie Italiano, a benefit was held to raise money and a headstone was bought. It now sits in the window of Ronnie's Clifton Music at 1135 Main Avenue in Clifton, New Jersey, while three so-called widows of Lymon's, Emira Eagle, Zola Taylor (formerly of the Platters), and Elizabeth Waters, fight over Frankie's half a million dollars in royalties.

FRANKIE LYMON AND THE TEENAGERS

A SIDE/B SIDE	LABEL/CAT NO	DATE
Why Do Fools Fall In Love /		
Please Be Mine	Gee 1002	1/56
I Want You To Be My Girl /		
I'm Not A Know It All	Gee 1012	4/56
I Promise To Remember /		
Who Can Explain	Gee 1018	6/56
The ABC's Of Love / Share	Gee 1022	9/56
I'm Not A Juvenile Delinquent /		
Baby, Baby	Gee 1026	11/56
Paper Castles / Teenage Love	Gee 1032	1957
Love Is A Clown /		
Am I Fooling Myself Again	Gee 1035	1957
Out In The Cold Again /		
Miracle In The Rain	Gee 1036	6/57
Goody Goody /		
Creation Of Love	Gee 1039	7/57
The Teenagers		
Flip-Flop / Everything To Me	Gee 1046	1957
My Broken Heart /		
Mama Wanna Rock	Roul 4086	1958
Tonight's The Night / Crying	End 1071	1960
A Little Wiser Now /		
Can You Tell Me	End 1076	1960
Joey and the Teenagers		
What's On Your Mind / The Draw	Col 42054	6/61

Louis Lymon and the Teenchords

Louis Lymon, brother of legendary Teenagers lead FRANKIE LYMON, was 12 years old when he and some neighborhood friends took a cue from the big guys and started singing in 1956. The members of the Harlem quintet included Louis (lead), Rossilio

Rocca (19, second tenor), Lyndon Harold (15, baritone), and David Little (17, bass).

They came up with the name the Teenchords in keeping with Louis's famous brother's group.

One day in the fall of 1956 the four were hanging out at the back of the Apollo Theatre where Frankie was performing. In need of a first tenor, the Teenchords were about to audition 15-year-old Ralph Vaughan when Charles Sampson of the Velvets (Red Robin) passed by. Charles told his friend Ralph that his manager Bobby Robinson of Red Robin Records was looking for talent and asked if that was his group. Wanting to record, the Teenchords told Sampson that Ralph was their first tenor, and all involved went around the corner to Robinson's record shop on 125th Street near 8th Avenue to audition. Singing "Who Can Explain," a Teenagers recording, the Teenchords appealed to Robinson, and he liked Louis's vocal similarity to his brother. Soon he was rehearsing them on a song he wrote expressly for the Teenchords called "I'm So Happy," which captured the high-energy exuberance of the group. Louis wrote a lyric about a girl in his building, Lydia Perez, which Robinson finished as the B side. In November 1956 he launched his new Fury label with the Teenchords' "I'm So Happy" b/w "Lydia." Radio response was immediate, and an ad for Fury in the trade papers stated that over 40,000 singles were sold in the New York, Philadelphia, and Boston areas in the first 10 days. "I'm So Happy" later became a New York doo wop street-corner classic that was sung as a warmup by hundreds of groups. The song also became Phil Spector's first New York doo wop production (see THE DUCANES).

On Friday January 3, 1957, Louis Lymon and the Teenchords performed on the Apollo stage with THE CHANNELS, Jerry Butler and THE IMPRESSIONS, THE HEARTBEATS, Jesse Belvin, Clarence "Frogman" Henry, Micky and Sylvia, all emceed by WOV's Jocko Henderson. Because they were naturally energetic performers who actively wooed the tough Apollo audiences, they wound up playing the historic venue many times over the next year and a half. They also did shows with WLIB's Hal Jackson, WWRL's Dr. Jive, and others.

In February 1957 their second single, "Honey, Honey," received a strong response on East Coast radio but did not do as well as their first.

Their last single for Fury was "I'm Not Too Young to Fall in Love" recorded on July 22nd and issued soon after.

In July they performed at Alan Freed's Summer Festival at the New York Paramount along with

Frankie Lymon and the Teenagers, THE DUBS, the Everly Brothers, Chuck Berry, Screamin' Jay Hawkins, and Jodie Sands. They were billed above the Everly Brothers but below Jodie Sands. Their stage outfits were black pants with red sweaters (imprinted with the word "Teenchords") along with white shirts, black bow ties, and white bucks.

During the summer, David and underaged Lyndon were caught sitting in a stolen car and David was hauled in. The group quickly enlisted Jimmy Merchant to sing bass for a four-week tour of Jamaica in the West Indies, and when they returned, according to a trade paper announcement of September 14, 1957, George Goldner had signed Louis et al to End Records. But Louis never actually signed; his mother refused to let him do anything if David was associated with the group. David was then eliminated from the lineup, but Lymon's mother never got around to signing for Louis (though she did let him record).

The first single on End, "Your Last Chance" b/w "Too Young," had actually been recorded earlier by Robinson, indicating that he and Goldner must have struck a deal.

The group's high point was a performance in the Warner Bros. rock and roll film *Jamboree* with Jerry Lee Lewis, THE FOUR COINS, Fats Domino, Connie Francis, Frankie Avalon, Slim Whitman, Charlie Gracie, and more disc jockeys in the film than recording artists (18), including Dick Clark, Joe Smith (WVDA-Boston, later a honcho at Warner Bros. Records), Barry Kaye (WJNS-Pittsburgh), Jocko Henderson (WOV-New York), Robin Seymour (WKMK-Detroit), and Dick Whittinghill (KMPC-Hollywood). The group sang "Your Last Chance."

In November 1957 the Teenchords did an answer record to the Teenagers' "Why Do Fools Fall in Love" called "I Found Out Why," but it wasn't a real contender. Another song that *was* a contender came out in 1958. The Les Cooper-penned "Dance Girl" was the original version of this song, not released until after THE CHARTS' classic recording. In less than two years the group broke up.

In 1961 Louis recorded with the Townsmen ("I Can't Go," P.J. Records). In 1962 he appeared at the Apollo singing duets with Frankie, but the collaboration lasted only one day; he and his brother never got along due to the older Lymon's adult attitude in a young teen body.

In 1971 Louis formed a new Teenchords for *Rock* magazine's "Collectors' Show" with Ralph Ramos (first tenor), Louis Vasquez (second tenor), Velmont Miller (baritone), and Frank San Pietro (lead). Louis sang baritone and occasional lead.

In 1973 the re-formed Teenagers did a show in Philadelphia with Louis singing lead on "I'm So Happy," but it never developed into a regular thing as Pearl McKinnon took over Frankie's old spot.

Over the years, Louis worked as a typist, a mail clerk, and a messenger and in the early '80s was a waiter.

He re-formed the Teenchords in 1983 and in 1984 recorded a sparkling a cappella treatment of the Teenagers' "I Want You to Be My Girl" for Starlight Records.

In 1985 they did an a cappella 45 of their original "Dance Girl." The members then were Louis (lead), John O'Keefe (first tenor), Mike Nicoletti (second tenor), Thomas Camuti (baritone), and Andre Garnes (bass and brother of Teenagers bass Sherman Garnes).

Louis later left to co-author a book (unpublished as of 1991), and Beverly Warren took over lead.

LEWIS LYMON AND THE TEENCHORDS

A SIDE/B SIDE	LABEL/CAT NO	DATE
Lydia / I'm So Happy	Fury 1000	11/56
Honey, Honey / Please Tell The Angels	Fury 1003	2/57
I'm Not Too Young To Fall In Love / Falling In Love	Fury 1006	8/57
Too Young / Your Last Chance	End 1003	9/57
I Found Out Why / Tell Me Love	End 1007	11/57
Dance Girl / Them There Eyes	Juanita 101	1958
I Found Out Why / Too Young	End 1113	1962
I Want You To Be My Girl* / Please Tell The Angels*	Strlt 21	1984
Dance Girl* / Honey Honey*	Strlt 25	1985

* A cappella

The Magnificents

The Magnificents had the unfortunate experience of having their talent tinkered with to the point of destruction. But that was later. In 1953 the denizens of the predominantly white Hyde Park High School in Chicago were beginning to hear a new sound echoing through its hallways and bathrooms. That sound was rhythm and blues and it was being put into practice by four black youths, Johnny Keyes (lead), Thurman "Ray" Ramsey (tenor), Fred Rakeshaw (tenor), and Willie Myles (bass).

They called themselves the Tams (long before the ABC group of the early '60s) and sang songs by

their favorites, THE HARPTONES, THE MOONGLOWS, THE PENGUINS, and THE EL DORADOS. They graduated from the bathroom to talent and variety shows, and at one such event WAAF disc jockey Nathaniel Montague, a.k.a. the Magnificent Montague, heard them and became their manager. He then changed their name to the Magnificents after himself (no egotist he) and took them to Vee-Jay Records with a song called "Up on the Mountain."

Unlike many disc jockeys of the '50s who listed themselves on record labels as collaborators with the actual writers, Montague actually had a hand in the writing of "Up on the Mountain." It started out as a street practice piece known as "Newborn Square." Vee-Jay A&R man extraordinaire, Cal Carter, edited the over seven-minute song and the group recorded it in the spring of 1956.

By June it was rocking Chicago radio and was spreading through the country. From its "num de numbi do" bass intro to Keyes's lead, "Up on the Mountain" was a unique R&B jump tune that captivated listeners. It was one of the most bass-dominated singles of all times and had an infectious rhythm. *Billboard*'s June 25th issue had it as the week's "Best Buy," adding, "Quietly this record has been moving up in various territories and now is a chart threat. It has been on the Cincinnati territorial chart and is now reported a very good seller in New York, New England, Philadelphia, Chicago, St. Louis, Durham and Pittsburgh." The same week it was number seven in Cincinnati, number eight was "In the Still of the Night" by THE FIVE SATINS, and number six was "A Kiss from Your Lips" by THE FLAMINGOS. On July 14th it reached number nine on the national Jukebox Chart and number 14 R&B Best Seller.

Then the tinkering began. Montague, not satisfied with his hit combination, replaced Ramsey with Sam Cooke's brother L. C. Cooke and added a fifth member, a female, Barbara Arrington. Their next single "Caddy Bo" sounded nothing like "Up on the Mountain" or even the Magnificents, and it flopped. (Barbara's lightweight lead was out of place with the high-powered harmony of the original four.) Their third single should have been their second since "Off the Mountain" was a continuation of "Up on the Mountain" with Keyes back on lead. But Myles's bass was relegated to the back of the mix and the magic was gone.

Disgusted with Montague's meddling, the group left the disc jockey and Vee-Jay. Keyes and Rakeshaw formed a new Magnificents with Reggie Gordon (tenor) and Rufus Hunter (bass) but they never recorded, doing only performances. Gordon joined

THE RAYS and Hunter the Cameos when the group became stagnant. Keyes and Rakeshaw then joined Thurston Harris as backups and sang on his "I'm Out to Getcha" (1958, Aladdin). Meanwhile, Vee-Jay released one more Magnificents single to capitalize on the group's name but "Don't Leave Me," though a good rocker, sounded more like the Prodigals (Abner) than the Magnificents.

In 1960 Vee-Jay reissued "Up on the Mountain" with a flip by another unknown Magnificents that sounded like the original group. The song "Let's Do the Cha-Cha" is probably the only vocal group record about a particular dance that is not actually in that dance's style; "Let's Do the Cha-Cha" was done to a street R&B beat with terrific vocal work from the group, whoever they were.

In 1962 another mystery Magnificents surfaced on Checker with "Do You Mind" but it too was someone other than the "Mountain" men.

Ray Ramsey formed the Emeralds in 1965 with Clarence Jasper and James Pleasants. When Richard Dixon (the Dukays) joined they became another of the many Magnificents but they never recorded. Johnny Keyes continued in the business singing on a variety of recording sessions. In 1959 he paired up with Reggie Gordon as the Shell Brothers (End) for one single titled "Shoom a Dom Dom." From 1968 until 1970 he became Isaac Hayes's road manager and in 1970 had a million seller (#13 Pop) as writer of "Too Weak to Fight" for Clarence Carter on Atlantic.

Arthur Lee Maye and the Crowns

The only vocal group that ever spawned a successful major league baseball player, the Crowns were also a skilled rhythm and blues quintet with one of the finest tenor leads on the West Coast in the 1950s.

Formed in the fall of 1951 at Jefferson High School in Los Angeles, the Debonairs (as they originally called themselves) included Arthur Lee Maye (lead), Johnny Morris (first tenor), Joe Moore (tenor), Richard Berry (tenor and baritone), and Johnny Coleman (bass).

The 16-year-olds rehearsed mostly in Lee's home at 1641 East Vernon or at Richard Berry's place on 22nd and Naomi, a mere stone's throw

from where they attended high school. Although West Coast vocal groups did not have the same street-corner image as East Coast groups, the Crowns had their share of nights under the streetlights in East Los Angeles.

The group's early influence included THE CLOVERS, THE DRIFTERS, THE DOMINOES, and THE FLAMINGOS. They practiced such hits of the day as "Fool, Fool, Fool" (the Clovers) and "The Bells" (the Dominoes) while Lee began writing original songs like "Set My Heart Free."

Arthur Lee (who preferred to be called Lee) spent the summer of 1954 playing baseball in Boise in Idaho's Pioneer League, batting a mighty .319 with nine homeruns in his first try at professional baseball.

Later in 1954 Richard Berry, who had recorded with the Hollywood Blue Jays in 1953, brought the Debonairs to the Bihari brothers, owners of Crown, Modern, and RPM Records. After their audition, Jules Bihari renamed them and Saul Bihari signed them to Modern in mid-November on the strength of a beautifully done a cappella rendition of Berry's song "Truly."

Their first single soon followed with the Lee Maye composition "Set My Heart Free," recorded at Modern's Studios on Washington Boulevard. For this session Randolph Jones (a part-timer from THE PENGUINS) sang bass. It was typical of the Los Angeles vocal group scene in the 1950s that members of other acts or friends would unofficially drop in on a session or cover for a missing member. At one time or another second tenor John Favors, first tenor Charles Colbert, bass Charles Holm, and even Lee's brother, first tenor Eugene Maye, sang with the group. The latter two were mostly on the later Dig sides.

The Crowns' first performances took place at the Lincoln Theatre on Central Avenue and the El Monte Legion Stadium appearing with the Johnny Otis Band. In 1955 the group shifted over to RPM for three fine singles released in February, June, and October, respectively, but none of these lit up the charts (though Crowns records were getting Los Angeles airplay). Lee spent the summer in more cities as a ball player than his group did as performers. He finished the season at Yakima in the Northwest League hitting .320, while the Crowns finished 1955 right back where they started, in East Los Angeles.

The group met Specialty Records owner Art Rupe and moved from Modern's factory-style digs in Culver City to Specialty's Hollywood address on Sunset Boulevard. They recorded four sides in

February 1956, with "Gloria" (no relation to the CADILLACS classic) emerging as the single. An appealing rhythm ballad akin to various CHANNELS records ("The Girl Next Door" in particular), the Crowns' fifth single was their most popular record to date, although primarily a West Coast affair.

Lee was again off to the minors where he hit a terrific .330 with 24 homeruns and 99 R.B.I.'s for Evansville, but it still didn't earn him a ticket to the big leagues. After Lee returned home in the fall of 1956, he and the Crowns hooked up with Johnny Otis (if you had a singing group in Los Angeles in the '50s, sooner or later you ran into the multi-talented Otis) and recorded for his Dig label.

Their first Dig single "This Is the Night for Love" was a New York-New Jersey styled doo wop ballad replete with a soaring falsetto and ultra-smooth harmonies, making this one of the Crowns' best and Lee's favorite. Their next Dig release was "A Fool's Prayer," another ably done single.

As spring 1957 rolled around Lee was back in the minors but having an off-season, hitting only .264 at Jacksonville. A couple of the group's sides ("Cause You're Mine Alone" and "Hey Pretty Girl") wound up on Flip Records where for several years Richard Berry had been recording and writing for such groups as THE DREAMERS and the Pharoahs when not bringing his versatile tenor-to-baritone talents to Crowns sessions.

In 1958 Milwaukee Braves minor-leaguer Maye hit .318 at Louisville in the American Association, but the chances of him cracking the Braves' outfield of Aaron, Bruten, and Covington was as likely as expecting Aaron to retire one homerun short of Babe Ruth's record. Still, Lee felt confident he would make it.

The group, meanwhile, had little excuse to come together since they were seeing less and less of their driving-force lead singer. That year Otis convinced Lee to make an album with Jessie Belvin, Richard Berry, Mel Williams, and Otis himself under the group name the Jayos. That LP, *Great Hits of the Fifties*, went unreleased though it contained some very credible cuts including "Earth Angel," "Sincerely," and "Only You."

By 1959 Lee Maye was hitting .339 with 17 homeruns and Milwaukee could no longer ignore him. Singing would have to wait. Lee joined the club and responded by hitting an even .300 in 51 games.

By the summer of 1960 Lee was a full-fledged Brave and triumphantly arrived in Los Angeles to play the Dodgers. While in town he hooked up with the Crowns to record four sides for Cash Records.

The first single was a doo wop ballad several years out of date. "Will You Be Mine" sported the name Lee Maye on the label, ignoring the Crowns, and was intended to take advantage of Lee's newfound fame on the diamond. The B side, "Money Honey," was a reworking of a tune they had recorded for Dig in 1956. The record saw little action and was followed soon after by "All I Want Is Someone to Love," a ballad that had "pop hit" written all over it. The label must have blundered through their promotional efforts to lose this one, but that's what they did.

Lee went back to hitting baseballs and the Crowns went back to hitting the streets. In 1961 Imperial Records issued "Will You Be Mine" but it stiffed. In 1964, Lee appeared on "Truth or Consequences," stumping the panel with the question "Who's the only major league ball player whose second career is that of a hit singer?" (At the time Lee had out his biggest solo record, "Have Love Will Travel.")

Lee continued in baseball for 12 years, leaving the Braves in 1965 and playing for Houston, Cleveland, Washington, and the Chicago White Sox before heading home to Los Angeles with a lifetime .274 batting average. He continued to record as a solo soul artist through the '60s and in 1986 recorded a doo wop ballad titled "Moonlight" backed by the Dream-Airs (actually Kendall Floyd of a latter-day COASTERS and two members of the Calvanes) on the Antrell label.

Some 30 years after their last recording together the Crowns appeared at The Hop in Lakewood, California, in April 1990 and were shocked to find how many people remembered not only the group but songs like "Truly," "Love Me Always," and "All I Want Is Someone to Love."

Today Charles Colbert owns a cleaning store, Johnny Coleman works at a Los Angeles Veterans Hospital, Joe Moore passed away in the early '80s, and Johnny Morris has not been heard from for many years. Richard Berry and Arthur Lee Maye continue to make music in the Los Angeles area, occasionally performing on the same bill in local clubs. As Lee says about appearing before an enthusiastic audience, "It just reminds me of those good old doo wop days."

ARTHUR LEE MAYE AND THE CROWNS

A SIDE/B SIDE	LABEL/CAT NO	DATE
Set My Heart Free /		
I Wanna Love	Modern 944	11/54
Truly / Oochie Pachie	Modern 424	2/55

A SIDE/B SIDE	LABEL/CAT NO	DATE
Love Me Always /		
Loop De Loop De Loop	RPM 429	6/55
Please Don't Leave Me /		
Do The Bop	RPM 438	10/55
Gloria / Oh-Rooba-Lee	Spec 573	1956
This Is The Night For Love /		
Honey Honey	Dig 124	1956
A Fool's Prayer /		
Whispering Wind	Dig 133	1957
Cause You're Mine Alone /		
Her Pretty Girl	Flip 330	1958
Honey Honey /		
Will You Be Mine	Cash 1063	1960
Pounding / All I Want Is		
Someone To Love	Cash 1065	1960
Will You Be Mine /		
Honey Honey	Imprl 5790	1961
Earth Angel /		
Honey Love	Dig 146	1970
Gee / Only You	Dig 146	1970
Sh-Boom /		
Sincerely	Dig 149	1970

The McGuire Sisters

Any group that can perform for five presidents and a queen has got to be both nonpartisan and very good. And the McGuire Sisters were very good indeed.

The family trio from Middletown, Ohio, began singing together in 1935 when Phyllis was four, Dorothy was five, and Christine was six. Their early training came at the First Church of God in Miamisburg, Ohio, where their mother, an ordained minister, was the pastor. Throughout their high school years, the girls sang together at Sunday school picnics, church socials, weddings, and even funerals.

They found out at an early age that they had an uncanny ability to harmonize. Renowned musician Jerry Herman called it instant harmony, as Phyllis could start singing in any key while Dot and Chris would immediately pick up the appropriate part and chime in. Their voices blended so uniformly that even their own mother couldn't tell them apart over a telephone.

As they were forbidden by their parents to listen to secular songs, they had to sneak a listen to their favorites like the Dinning Sisters and THE ANDREWS SISTERS over the radio.

They graduated from hymns to pop songs in 1949 and in 1950 toured military bases and veterans hospitals around the country for the U.S.O. What thoroughly convinced them to make pop a career was an incident in 1950 when they were broadcasting hymns in their own three-part harmony style from the First Church of God on West 3rd Street. An agent and bandleader Karl Taylor and his wife Inez were driving in their car when they heard the girls' performance. They turned the car around and headed straight for the church. During the service Karl waited in the back and when the girls came out (all dressed alike) he told them they were wonderful, gave them his card, and said if they'd like to sing pop music to call him. In a month the girls were singing with Taylor's band at the Van Cleef Hotel in Dayton, Ohio.

They went on to appear at supper clubs and on local TV. From there they did eight weeks on Kate Smith's radio show in 1952 and by December 1st were the winners on "Arthur Godfrey's Talent Scouts" having auditioned with "Mona Lisa" and "Pretty-Eyed Baby." Invited to appear on his morning show for a week, they replaced THE CHORDETTES and remained for six years.

Before 1952 was over they were signed to Coral Records and had their first single release, "One, Two, Three, Four."

Their fifth single became their first chart record as "Pine Tree, Pine Over Me" with Johnny Desmond and Eileen Barton reached number 26 in April 1954. Their follow-up, "Goodnight Sweetheart, Goodnight," became their first top 10 hit (#7) in the summer of 1954 and first by the group alone. "Muskrat Ramble" made number 10 next by the fall of 1954 and the whirlwind touring life began from New York's Waldorf Astoria to Las Vegas's top casinos.

Their lucky 11th single was a cover of THE MOONGLOWS' classic "Sincerely," and the group rode the Harvey Fuqua-penned ballad to number one in January 1955 where it resided for an incredible 10 weeks. Even the flip side, "No More," reached number 17 indicating a developing case of McGuire mania among the general public. "Sincerely" went to number 14 in the U.K., and in a rare case of an American record's B side also charting, "No More" reached number 20.

With Phyllis consistently on lead the group continued its hot hit pace with songs like "Something's Gotta Give" (#5, 1955), "He" (#10, 1955), "Sugar Time" (#1, 1957, #14 U.K., 1958), "May You Always" (#11, 1958), and "Just for Old Time's Sake" (#20, 1961).

The group was so popular that as commercial representatives for Coca-Cola they received the highest fee in advertising history up to that time.

The trio's last chart record was "Just Because" in 1961 (#99), and in mid-1963 they moved to Reprise for six singles and then to ABC for two more, with their last in September 1966 appropriately titled "Via Con Dios."

In 1968 they performed for what they thought would be the last time on "The Ed Sullivan Show," broadcast from Ceasar's Palace in Las Vegas.

An excellent entertainer and skilled comedian, Phyllis went solo and performed with everyone from Johnny Carson to Sammy Davis, Jr. She also appeared in the film *Come Blow Your Horn* with Frank Sinatra.

In 1985 the sisters made a comeback and the fans were still enthusiastic. Their first appearance was at Harrah's in Reno, Nevada. In 1989 they performed at the inauguration of President George Bush and they continued to do the Las Vegas/Reno circuit into the 1990s. They did a sparkling performance on Jerry Lewis's Labor Day Telethon in 1991.

In recognition of their popularity, MCA Records reissued their greatest hits album on CD. In the early '90s they were in the process of recording their first LP in over 20 years with their original producer, Bob Thiele.

When not entertaining Phyllis lives in Las Vegas and gives endless hours of time to humanitarian causes. Christine lives in Scottsdale, Arizona, and has business interests in movie theatres, pubs, and diet centers. Dorothy also lives in Scottsdale with her husband of 30 years, Lowell Williamson, and the two are extensively involved in community affairs and philanthropic work.

THE McGUIRE SISTERS

A SIDE/B SIDE	LABEL/CAT NO	DATE
One Two Three Four / Picking Sweethearts	Coral 60917	12/52
Tootle-Loo-Siana / Miss You	Coral 60969	12/52
You Never Know Till Monday / Are You Looking For A Sweetheart	Coral 61073	3/53
Hey Mr. Cotton Picker / Tell Us Where The Good Times Are	Coral 61002	5/53
Pine Tree Pine Over Me / Cling to Me	Coral 61126	2/54
Goodnight Sweetheart Goodnight / Heavenly Feeling	Coral 61187	8/54
Uno Due Tre / Lonesome Polecat	Coral 61239	9/54
Muskrat Ramble / Not As A Stranger	Coral 61258	10/54

A SIDE/B SIDE	LABEL/CAT NO	DATE
Muskrat Ramble / Lonesome Polecat	Coral 61278	10/54
Christmas Alphabet / Give Me Your Heart For Christmas	Coral 61303	11/54
Sincerely / No More	Coral 61323	12/54
Melody Of Love / Open Up Your Heart	Coral 61334	12/54
Hearts Of Stone / Naughty Lady Of Shady Lane	Coral 61335	12/54
It May Sound Silly / Doesn't Anybody Love Me	Coral 61369	2/55
Something's Gotta Give / Rhythm And Blues	Coral 61423	5/55
Kiss Me And Kill Me With Love / If It's A Dream	Coral 61454	7/55
Heart / Young And Foolish	Coral 61455	7/55
Sweet Song Of India / Give Me Love	Coral 61494	9/55
He / If You Believe	Coral 61501	10/55
Littlest Angel / I'd Like To Trim A Tree With You	Coral 61531	12/55
Baby Be Good To Me / My Baby's Got Such Loving Ways	Coral 61532	1/56
Missing / Tell Me Now	Coral 61587	3/56
Picnic / Delilah Jones	Coral 61627	4/56
Weary Blues / In The Alps	Coral 61670	7/56
Everyday Of My Life / Endless	Coral 61703	9/56
Goodnight My Love Pleasant Dreams / Mommy	Coral 61748	12/56
Kid Stuff / Without Him	Coral 61771	2/57
Blue Skies / He's Got Time	Coral 61798	3/57
Drowning In Memories / Please Don't Do That To Me	Coral 61815	4/57
Rock Bottom / Beginning To Miss You	Coral 61842	5/57
Around The World / Interlude	Coral 61856	7/57
Kiss Them For Me / Forgive Me	Coral 61888	9/57
Santa Claus Is Coming To Town / Honorable Congratulations	Coral 61911	11/57
Sugartime / Banana Split	Coral 61924	12/57
Since You Went Away To School / Ding Dong	Coral 61991	5/58
Volare / Do You Love Me Like You Kiss Me	Coral 62021	6/58
Sweetie Pie / I'll Think Of You	Coral 62047	10/58
May You Always / Achoo-Cha-Cha	Coral 62059	11/58
Summer Dreams / Peace	Coral 62106	4/59
Red River Valley / Compromise	Coral 62135	8/59
Some Of These Days / Have A Nice Weekend	Coral 62155	11/59
Livin' Dangerously / Lovers' Lullaby	Coral 62162	1/60
The Unforgiven / I Give Thanks	Coral 62196	4/60
The Last Dance / Nine O'Clock	Coral 62216	6/60
To Be Loved / I Don't Know Why	Coral 62235	11/60
Just For Old Time's Sake / Really Neat	Coral 62249	1/61
Tears On My Pillow / Space Ship	Coral 62276	6/61

A SIDE/B SIDE	LABEL/CAT NO	DATE
Just Because / I Do I Do I Do	Coral 62288	9/61
Time / I Can Dream Can't I	Coral 62296	11/61
Sugartime . . . / More Hearts Are Broken That Way	Coral 62305	2/62
I Really Don't Want To Know / Mama's Gone Goodbye	Coral 62333	9/62
Cordially Invited / Summertime	Rprs 20197	6/63
Now And Forever / Never	Rprs 0256	2/64
I Don't Want To Walk Without You / That's Life	Rprs 0310	10/64
Dear Heart / Candy Heart	Rprs 0330	12/64
I'll Walk Alone / Ticket To Anywhere	Rprs 0338	1/65
Somebody Else Is Taking My Place / Run To My Arms	Rprs 0354	3/65
Truer Than You Were / Grazia	ABC 10776	2/66
My Happiness / Via Con Dios	ABC 10826	9/66

The Medallions

The Medallions' image was far larger than their actual success thanks to the extensive play of their West Coast hits "The Letter" and "Buick '59" years after they were first released.

The original Medallions formed in Los Angeles during 1954 as the result of a fortuitous walk taken by Vernon Green. He was strolling down an East Los Angeles street singing out loud when a passerby said he sounded pretty good and muttered something to the effect of "why don't you get a group together." Normally that kind of advice was merely flattering, but since the man was Dootsie Williams, owner of Dootone Records, it was also an instant contact for young Vernon. He wasted no time in getting to Will Rogers Park in Watts and putting together a quartet of Andrew Blue (tenor), Randolph Bryant (baritone), and Ira Foley (bass). They became the Medallions because of Vernon's penchant for jewelry around his neck.

Vernon began writing and within a month the group was recording for Dootone.

Their first single was "The Letter," a ballad in the style of THE DIABLOS' "The Wind." It had more talking than singing and was immortalized by Vernon's lines "let me whisper sweet words of pismatality" (don't look it up—Vernon invented the word "pismatality," but oldies listeners didn't know it for years to come).

"The Letter" and its flip "Buick '59" received extensive airplay in Los Angeles and started a

Medallions trend: the group went on to create a series of car-oriented songs like "Coupe De Ville Baby" in January 1955 (with a follow-up to "The Letter" on the flip, "The Telegram").

By now Willy Graham had replaced Andrew Blue. In 1955 Donald Woods joined to make it a quintet. Then, with Randolph on lead, "Edna" b/w "Speedin'" (another automobile rocker) was issued ("Edna" had already been recorded before Woods' arrival).

By the time "Edna" hit the airwaves the Medallions were no more; Woods and the others had left Vernon to form the Vel-aires (Flip). Undaunted, Green grabbed tenors Kenneth Williams and Frank Marshall, formed the Cameos, and quickly issued "Only for You" on Dootone the same month as "Edna" was released (June 1955).

Dootsie then paired Vernon with THE DOOTONES, made them the new Medallions, and sent them on a Canadian tour. Their promo photo was actually a Dootones photo with a cutout of Vernon's head glued to the lower lefthand corner.

In the fall of 1955, the Medallions backed Johnny Morrisette on a 45 called "My Pretty Baby," but this Medallions now consisted of Vernon and brother Jimmy (tenor), Charles Gardner (tenor, of the Dootones), Albert Johnson (tenor), and Otis Scott (bass).

Two more singles with Morrisette ("Dear Darling," "I Want a Love," the latter with Otis singing lead) and the group became Vernon Green and the Medallions, doing three singles for Dootsie's new Dooto label. According to Vernon, those members were Vernon, Jimmy, Charles, and Jimmy Evans, but Don Julian has claimed it's his group, the Meadowlarks. (Imagine who'd claim to be on the records if they were hits.) Not making much money (and not making any recorded successes since "The Letter"), Vernon jumped to Art Rupe's Specialty Records in 1957 and formed the Phantoms. Their masquerade gimmick of wearing hoods was a bit transparent: Vernon was the only known lead singer at the time who walked with a cane (he had polio as a child in Denver, Colorado).

Later in 1957 Vernon drifted back to Dooto with yet another Medallions, this time made up of Billy Foster (tenor), Jimmy Green (tenor), and Joe Williams (bass).

In February 1959 the Medallions finally came out with a car song, "Volvo '59," that was relevant to its year and model. ("Buick '59" hadn't been. There never was a Buick 1959 model, and the only explanation for Vernon's singing about having a 1959 car in 1954 can be that he hoped the record would still be popular in 1959). The "Volvo" song was conjured up at the request of a Los Angeles area disc jockey whose brother owned a Volvo dealership. The flip "Magic Mountain" was their best effort on a ballad and got some play back East.

Even without a modest chart record the Medallions toured from Los Angeles to Washington, D.C. with shows in Illinois, Arizona, and Texas. They appeared on Dick Clark's "American Bandstand" doing "The Letter," but where most groups try to break their current release, the Medallions were doing it years later when it was an oldie.

In 1962 Vernon and Jimmy, along with Gardner, Johnson, and Scott, recorded for Pan World, and in 1964 Jerome Evans, Ed Carter, Jimmy, and Vernon did the group's next Medallions single for Minit.

Vernon had a car accident in the mid-'60s and shunned singing for nine years, returning to (where else?) Dootsie Williams in 1973 with Evans, Maxine Green (Vernon's sister-in-law), and Doris Green (both altos) for "Can You Talk" on Dooto.

In 1989 Vernon performed at the first show established by Los Angeles's Doo Wop Society and demonstrated that his ability was intact. He still had his pismatality.

THE MEDALLIONS

A SIDE/B SIDE	LABEL/CAT NO	DATE
Buick 59 / The Letter	Dootone 347	11/54
The Telegram /		
Coupe De Ville Baby	Dootone 357	1/55
Speedin' / Edna	Dootone 364	6/55
Johnny Twovoice and the Medallions		
My Pretty Baby /		
I'll Never Love Again	Dootone 373	10/55
The Medallions		
Dear Darling / Don't Shoot Baby	Dootone 379	11/55
I Want A Love / Dance And Swing	Dootone 393	4/56
Vernon Green and the Medallions		
Pushbutton Automobile /		
Shedding Tears For You	Dooto 400	8/56
Did You Have Fun / My Mary Lou	Dooto 407	11/56
For Better Or For Worse /		
I Wonder, Wonder, Wonder	Dooto 419	6/57
The Medallions		
Lover's Prayer / Unseen	Dooto 425	1957
Magic Mountain / 59 Volvo	Dooto 446	2/59
Behind The Door / Rocket Ship	Dooto 454	1959
Deep, So Deep /		
Shimmy Shimmy Shake	PnWld 10000	1962

A SIDE/B SIDE	LABEL/CAT NO	DATE
Look At Me / Am I Ever Gonna		
See My Baby Again	Minit 30234	1962
Can You Talk /		
You Don't Know	Dooto 479	1973

The Meditation Singers

The Meditation Singers were one of the best of all-female gospel quartets and the first to sing gospel in major nightclubs. Despite claims that the Clara Ward Singers were first, the Meditation Singers backed former member Della Reese at the Flamingo Hotel in Las Vegas several weeks before the Ward Singers came to town in 1962.

The Meditations were formed in April 1950 at the New Liberty Missionary Baptist Church in Detroit by Pastor E. Alan Rundless II and pianist Emory Radford.

Originally known as the Moments of Meditation after Pastor Rundless's weekly radio broadcast, the foursome were picked from the church's larger choir and included Ernestine Rundless (lead soprano), Dellareese Early (lead, first soprano), Marie Waters (alto), and DeLillian Mitchell (tenor). Della was attending Wayne State University at the time and had been singing at the church since she was six. At the time of forming, the group's ages ranged from 16 to 35. They practiced songs like "Get Away Jordan" and "By and By" and were influenced by the Clara Ward Singers.

Their popularity grew statewide through performances and radio broadcasts and in 1952 they won the Golden Cup Jubilee, competing against many of the nation's top gospel acts, the Ward Singers among them.

By then, Della had left for a solo career. Having performed on the road since she was 13 with gospel legend Mahalia Jackson (for about five years), Della was ready for the challenge of the secular world. She was replaced by Laura Lee Newton, and Carrie Williams was added as a fifth voice.

The incomparable Reverend James Cleveland joined to arrange and write for the group.

Now known as the Meditation Singers, they played across the country from the Apollo Theatre in New York to Las Vegas and then on to Paris where they were the only gospel act at the International

Jazz Festival, playing with Ella Fitzgerald, Lionel Hampton, and Horace Silver.

The group recorded for Hob and Specialty Records during the late '50s and early '60s with some of their best works being "I'm Only One River to Cross" and "He's Done Something for Me."

Their performances attracted the likes of Sammy Davis, Jr., Tony Bennett, Brook Benton, and Elvis Presley (who, while they were in Las Vegas, came by every morning after finishing his own show).

The group continued to spread its musical magic right into the '90s with the most recent group consisting of original members Ernestine Rundless, Marie Waters, and Laura Lee Newton along with relative newcomers Donna Hammonds and Valerie Rogers.

Laura Lee Newton (sometimes known as Laura Lee Rundless) became soul singer Laura Lee in 1967, achieving her biggest success with "Woman's Love Rights" (#36 Pop, #11 R&B, Chess). She also had a number three R&B hit in 1972 ("Rip Off") that also reached number 68 Pop (Hot Wax). Laura turned in 15 R&B chart records between 1967 and 1976.

Della Reese went on to fame with such hits as "Don't You Know" (#2 Pop, #1 R&B, RCA 1959) and "Not One Minute More" (#16 Pop, #13 R&B, RCA 1960). She became a well-known actress and had her own TV series, "Della," in 1970. From 1976 to 1978 she played Della Rogers on the TV series "Chico and the Man."

Both have returned to and supported the Meditation Singers over the years.

The Mello-Kings

One of the blackest-sounding white groups of the '50s, the Mello-Kings are most affectionately known for a two-million-plus-selling single that never made the top 40. That seemingly contradictory set of circumstances came about through the efforts of five teenagers from Washington High School in Mt. Vernon, New York in 1956.

The boys were brought together as a result of tryouts for a school production of *South Pacific*. The arranger, Dick "King" Levister, liked their harmonies and decided to help them form a group. The quintet included Jerry Scholl (15, lead), Robert Scholl (18, first tenor and Jerry's brother), Eddie Quinn (16, second tenor), Neil Arena (16, baritone), and Larry Esposito (16, bass). Between the

influences of LITTLE ANTHONY and the Duponts and FRANKIE LYMON AND THE TEENAGERS and the musical direction of their young black manager Dick Levister, it's not surprising that the group started to sound like the Teenagers. In order to create a style of their own they shifted brother Bob Scholl into the lead spot.

Originally calling themselves the Mellotones, the Mt. Vernon boys became active on the amateur talent show rounds and met a songwriter at one such showcase who made them an offer they couldn't refuse. He'd arrange an audition with a record company if they'd sing his song at the audition. They agreed and in July 1957 found themselves standing in the offices of Herald Records at 1697 Broadway in New York City singing for president Al Silver. He liked the group and signed them on the spot, but unlike in the movies, Silver hated the mystery writer's song and that composer was never heard from again. Herald staff writer Billy Myles then played the Mellotones several songs, only one of which they cared for titled "Tonite, Tonite." The group rehearsed it, recorded it, and saw it issued, all within a month from the time the teens had walked in Herald's door.

On August 19, 1957, it charted Pop but everyone (including this writer) thought it was by a black group. As it started to sell and gain airplay, the Mellotones' "Tonite, Tonite" ran into trouble of an unexpected kind in the form of Gee Records president George Goldner, who told Al Silver he'd run his company better if he looked at the charts occasionally. Sure enough, rising on the Pop chart was a group called the Mello-Tones singing "Rosie Lee" on Goldner's Gee Records (which eventually reached number 24). With one thousand "Tonite, Tonite" 45s already on the street, Silver immediately issued a new single with the group's quickly chosen new name, the Mello-Kings (after Dick Levister's middle name). Airplay intensified, the record sold well in the New York, Boston, Washington, and Philadelphia areas (it was number one in Philly), but somehow the charts reflected only a number 77 peak while it hung around the Top 100 for 10 weeks. Still, "Tonite, Tonite" became a solid Pop/R&B harmony classic and consistently sold for years, tallying well over two-and-a-half million sales and invariably winding up in the top 10 oldies surveys year after year.

When Art Laboe put out the first *Oldies but Goodies* LP in 1959, "Tonite, Tonite" was featured with established classics like "In the Still of the Night" and "Earth Angel."

In January 1961, when the first wave of oldies nostalgia took hold, "Tonite, Tonite" mustered enough airplay and sales in a reissue to chart nationally at number 95. Ironically, the Gee Records Mello-Tones only had one more release and were never heard from again while the *Herald* Mello-Tones earned legendary status with a record that couldn't make the top 60.

Their next single, "Sassafras," written by Bob Crewe and Frank Slay and released in September 1957, was an up-tempo Everly-Brothers-meets-the-CLEFTONES rocker that went nowhere. (The group felt they should have stayed in the ballad vein with songs like the flip "Chapel on the Hill" done in a style similar to the FIVE SATINS' "To the Aisle.") Still, the group played a myriad of one-nighters, and each release garnered them a shot on Dick Clark's "American Bandstand." They toured doing numerous live radio shows and for a while practically lived on buses, where Jerry, who was short, would sleep in the luggage rack. On one occasion the same rack was slept in by another short dynamo, Paul Anka.

Many of the group's performances were at black venues, but they always went over well. Besides the Regal and Howard Theatres on the chitlin circuit, they played the Apollo five times.

Levister, who had a great musical influence on the group, must have also had some influence on their stage wardrobe. Few other white groups would dare appear in black shirts and trousers with white shoes, ties, and jackets. Their jackets carried a diamond-shaped emblem with an "M" on it.

Each of their subsequent 45s were solid singles that failed to match the success of "Tonite." "Baby Tell Me Why, Why, Why" was a vocal doo wop delight and demonstrated how much better the group was than its material and arrangements. Their harmony in the subsequent HEARTBEATS-styled ballad "Valerie" and "Our Love Is Beautiful" put them on a par with the best R&B groups of the era, and marked them as forerunners of white groups like THE PASSIONS and THE MYSTICS.

After "Valerie," Neil and Larry left to be replaced by Louis Janacone and Tony Pinto.

The reviews in response to the group were always good but Herald couldn't compete in the promo game by the late '50s. Soon after the 1959 release of "Chip, Chip," Bobby was drafted, ending all hopes of moving to a powerhouse label.

Their last single, "Love at First Sight," was released in 1961 though actually recorded in 1957, so even their surplus had been exhausted.

The group survived through personnel changes and continued to perform in the New York area into the '90s with Jerry Scholl on lead.

Eddie Quinn went into hotel management in Las Vegas, Larry Esposito into construction, and Neil Arena became an insurance agent. Sadly, Bob Scholl, who had the sound to be a star, died in a boating accident in 1975.

THE MELLO-KINGS

A SIDE/B SIDE	LABEL/CAT NO	DATE
The Mellotones		
Tonite, Tonite / Do Baby Do	Herald 502	7/57
The Mello-Kings		
Tonite, Tonite / Do Baby Do	Herald 502	7/57
Chapel On The Hill / Sassafras	Herald 507	9/57
Baby Tell Me Why, Why, Why /		
The Only Girl	Herald 511	1/58
Valerie / She's Real Cool	Herald 518	4/58
Chip, Chip / Running To You	Herald 536	2/59
Our Love Is Beautiful /		
Dear Mr. Jock	Herald 548	1960
Kid Stuff / I Promise	Herald 554	1960
Penny / Till There Were None	Herald 561	1961
Love At First Sight / She's Real Cool	Herald 567	1961

The Mello-Moods

Over four years before FRANKIE LYMON AND THE TEENAGERS brought teen groups to prominence, the Mello-Moods formed and became the first of the true teen groups. The quintet was so young that they were all still attending Resurrection Grammar School on West 151st Street in Manhattan when the 13- and 14-year-olds began practicing at Macombs Dam Park across the bridge in the Bronx, right behind Yankee Stadium. The eighth graders included Ray "Buddy" Wooten (lead), Bobby Williams (second lead, tenor, and piano), Bobby Baylor (second tenor and baritone), Monteith "Monte" Owens (tenor and guitar), and Jimmy Bethea (bass).

The group's main influence was SONNY TIL AND THE ORIOLES, so it was no surprise that they included songs like "I Miss You So," "So Much," and "It's Too Soon to Know" in their rehearsals. The teen quintet started singing in early 1951 (or late 1950 depending on the information source) and soon heard that a local record store owner, Bobby Robinson, was starting a record company. Buddy's mother knew Robinson and arranged an audition, which led to a session and their being named the Robins after Bobby's new Robin label.

By December 1951 the group had become the Mello-Moods and their single "Where Are You" was receiving a significant amount of radio response, enough so that the fledgling label and group found themselves debuting on *Billboard*'s national R&B charts on February 23, 1952, reaching number seven. The soft ballad, with Buddy's mellow tenor lead, became the first teen group national R&B charter, but unlike later teen groups' singles it offered nary a hint of the group's age thanks to their mature sound. Since there was not yet a marketable teen audience, the kids were singing mature love lyrics convincingly to older audiences, though it's doubtful Buddy knew what he was singing.

Jimmy Keyes, a friend of the group (later with THE CHORDS on Cat), became their manager and wangled some appearances at the Apollo Theatre as well as clubs usually reserved for adults. They also did an early "Spotlight on Harlem" TV show.

The group next issued "I Couldn't Sleep a Wink Last Night," another ballad (as were all their A side recordings) that received some airplay but didn't chart. New manager Joel Turnero, writer of the single's B side, took the group down to the Prestige Records office at 446 West 50th Street where they put together "I'm Lost," probably their best vocal effort. When "I'm Lost" and its follow-up "Call on Me" both failed to chart in 1952, the youngsters began drifting toward other goals.

Baylor, Williams, and Owens became the nucleus of the legendary SOLITAIRES, and the Mello-Moods disappeared into history.

THE MELLO-MOODS

A SIDE/B SIDE	LABEL/CAT NO	DATE
How Could You / Where Are You	RdRbn 105	12/51
I Couldn't Sleep A Wink Last Night / And You Just Can't Go Through Life Alone	RdRbn 104	1952
I'm Lost / When I Woke Up This Morning	Prestige 856	1953
Call On Me / I Tried, Tried And Tried	Prestige 799	1953

The Mellows

One of the first female-led male R&B groups (THE CAPRIS with Renee Hinton recorded a few months earlier), the Mellows were also one of the best. Johnny "Tiny" Wilson (first tenor), Harold Johnson (second tenor), and Norman "Polecat" Brown (bass) were three teens from the Morrisania section of the Bronx attending Morris High School (the same institution that yielded THE CHORDS [Cat], the Twilighters [MGM], NORMAN FOX AND THE ROB ROYS [Backbeat], and THE LIMELIGHTERS [Josie]).

One evening in 1954 the three were harmonizing in a hallway outside a party. 17-year-old Lillian Leach came out to hear them sing and found herself harmonizing with them. Harold, who had sung on Joe Davis's Jay Dee label with Dean Barlow and THE CRICKETS, commented on how mellow they sounded with the addition of Lillian, and a group was born. Wanting to call themselves the Mello-Tones, they shortened it to the Mellows when they learned the name was already used. Lillian, whose favorites included Big Maybelle, THE SOUL STIRRERS, Jeri Southern, and Ella Fitzgerald, had a smooth-as-glass voice that even male-group devotees enjoyed when the first oldies revival hit in 1960. None of the members who were now practicing with Lillian four or five times a week knew that they were one of the first to try this vocal combination.

Harold took the group to several companies for auditions before going back to his old Jay Dee Records base at 441 West 49th Street. Joe Davis liked the group and issued their first single, a Johnson-penned ballad called "How Sentimental Can I Be?" If Doris Day or Patti Page had recorded it the song would have been a smash, but a young black group with an almost-pop single that its small label was unable to promote was doomed to failure. The radio play in New York fathered only one performance for the group, at the club Baby Grand at 125th Street in Harlem.

Their second single was the Harold-penned ballad "Smoke from Your Cigarette," again with Lillian's pristine vocal leading an elegant yet unobtrusive harmony. This time New York took notice; even Jay Dee's ineptness couldn't keep "Smoke" from becoming a regional hit.

Alan Freed gave the record a lot of play and even posed for a now-legendary photo with the group in which he held a 78 of the waxing. Surprisingly, the Mellows never appeared on any of Freed's shows or even at the Apollo, though they did have a moment of glory on April 2nd performing at a 1955 rock and roll festival at St. Nicholas Arena with THE CADILLACS, Varetta Dillard, Red Prysock, Otis Blackwell, and the Joe Morris Combo.

The Mellows' third single was their weakest and was received accordingly, but their fourth single, a solid doo wop rhythm ballad called "Yesterday's Memories" that was issued in August, was overlooked unjustly.

Norman Brown left the group at this time and was replaced by Gary Morrison. Arthur Crier of THE CHIMES (Royal Roost) also joined, making the Mellows a quintet.

In late 1955 the group left Davis and signed with David Levitt's 43 Harrison Avenue, Brooklyn, label, named Celeste. Levitt had even less market clout than Jay Dee, and two excellent 45s, "My Darling" and "I'm Yours," disappeared into collectors' paradise.

Next was "Moon of Silver" a rhythm ballad produced by Otis Pollard for Ron Zinsser's Candlelight label that featured a more mature-sounding Lillian. It ended the group's recording career; the Mellows lead left for marriage and motherhood in the spring of 1957. Harold and Arthur went on to form the Halos, who had a national hit in the summer of 1961 with "Nag" (7 Arts), but they made their real money as a vocal group behind a variety of soloists like Gene Pitney ("Every Breath I Take," #42, 1961) and Curtis Lee ("Pretty Little Angel Eyes," #7, 1961). Arthur later joined Motown as a producer/writer working with THE FOUR TOPS, THE TEMPTATIONS, and THE SPINNERS. Gary Morrison became a jazz vocalist.

The first wave of '60s nostalgia brought such interest in the Mellows' Jay Dee sides that their reissues outsold the originals.

In 1984 Lillian, Arthur, Gary, and Eugene Tompkins (the Limelighters, Josie) re-formed the Mellows and earned such a strong response to their sophisticated R&B sound that the group began working more in the '80s (at places like Radio City Music Hall and the Beacon Theatre in New York) than they did in the '50s.

By 1987 Gary Morrison had died and was replaced by former Limelighters lead Sammy Fain. In the '90s the group was still entertaining listeners with their Mellows sound.

THE MELLOWS

A SIDE/B SIDE	LABEL/CAT NO	DATE
How Sentimental Can I Be /		
Nothing To Do	Jay-Dee 793	1954
Smoke From Your Cigarette /		
Pretty Baby, What's Your Name	Jay-Dee 797	1955
I Still Care /		
I Was A Fool To Let You Go	Jay-Dee 801	1955
Yesterday's Memories /		
Loveable Lily	Jay-Dee 807	1955
Lucky Guy / My Darling	Clst 3002	1956
I'm Yours / Sweet Lorraine	Clst 3004	1956
You've Gone /		
Moon Of Silver	Cndlt 1011	1956

Harold Melvin and the Blue Notes

One of the many groups who started on the street corners of Philadelphia in the 1950s, Harold Melvin and the Blue Notes were also one of the few to continue beyond their doo wop infancy. Starting out as the Blue Notes in 1955, they recorded their first song, "If You Love Me," for the New York-based Josie Records. Known for the soaring falsetto lead of John Atkins, early Blue Notes releases like "O Holy Night," and "My Hero," carried on the tradition of what was known in the '50s and '60s as the Philadelphia Sound (long before the Gamble and Huff days of the '70s gave it new meaning), established by such acts as THE CASTELLS, THE CAPRIS, and the Universals. The trademark of that sound was high tenor harmonies and lead vocals.

Besides lead singer John Atkins, the group consisted of Bernard Wilson, Lawrence Brown, and Harold Melvin. Although Harold was the group's founder it was a little misleading to feature his name (as happened when they joined Philadelphia International Records), since he never actually sang lead.

They recorded only eight singles between 1956 and 1971, but two of those records, "My Hero" on Val-ue and "Get Out" on Landa, hit the national R&B charts and kept them working one nighters. Finally they caught a break and signed with the William Morris Agency, reportedly due to enthusiastic lobbying on their behalf by one Martha Reeves (of MARTHA AND THE VANDELLAS). They were then transformed from a rhythm and blues group to a lounge act playing Las Vegas and Reno night clubs.

In 1970, a 20-year-old drummer named Teddy Pendergrass joined the group and soon replaced John Atkins on lead vocal. A fifth member, Lloyd Parks, was added and by 1972 they had become Harold Melvin and the Blue Notes. That same year the group signed with Gamble and Huff's Philadelphia International Records (their sixth label in 16 years) and started issuing a string of hits including "If You Don't Know Me By Now," "The Love I Lost," "Wake Up Everybody," and "Hope That We Can Be Together Soon," all number one R&B records. After 10 hit records in a row, Pendergrass left to pursue a solo career in 1976. New member David Ebo took over lead vocals at that time and brought the group another 10 chart records; the last was "I Really Love You" in 1984. However, none of their releases after the 1977 recording of "Reaching for the World" (#74 Pop, #6 R&B) could dent the top 10 charts. But between 1956 and 1984 the group had an enviable 23 chart singles out of 29 releases.

HAROLD MELVIN AND THE BLUE NOTES

A SIDE/B SIDE	LABEL/CAT NO	DATE
The Blue Notes		
If You Love Me / There's		
Something In Your Eyes, Eloise	Josie 800	7/56
The Retribution Blues /		
Wagon Wheels	Josie 823	1957
The Letter / She Is Mine	LstNt 104	1960
My Hero / A Good Woman	Value 213	9/60
O Holy Night / Winter Wonderland	Value 215	1960
If You Love Me / There's		
Something In Your Eyes, Eloise	Port 70021	1961
You May Not Love Me / Get Out	Landa 703	1962
My Hero / A Good Woman	Red Top 135	3/63
Go Away / What Can A Man Do	Arctic 135	1967
Never Gonna Leave You /		
Hot Chills, Cold Thrills and Fever	Dash 5005	1972
Harold Melvin and		
the Blue Notes		
I Miss You Part 1 /		
I Miss You Part 2	Phila 3516	3/72
Let Me Into Your World /		
If You Don't Know Me By Now	Phila 3520	9/72
Ebony Woman /		
Yesterday I Had The Blues	Phila 3525	2/73
The Love I Lost Part 1 /		
The Love I Lost Part 2	Phila 3533	8/73
I'm Weak For You /		
Satisfaction Guaranteed	Phila 3543	2/74
Let It Be You /		
Where Are All My Friends	Phila 3552	10/74
Bad Luck Part 1 / Bad Luck Part 2	Phila 3562	2/75
Be For Real / Hope That		
We Can Be Together Soon	Phila 3569	5/75
Wake Up Everybody Part 1 /		
Wake Up Everybody Part 2	Phila 3579	10/75
You Know How To Make Me Feel		
So Good / Tell The World How		
I Feel About Cha Baby	Phila 3588	2/76
Reaching For The World /		
Stay Together	ABC 12240	12/76

The Monotones

If, as many believe, having a hit record has as much to do with luck and timing as it does with talent, then the Monotones owe their place in history to a kid playing ball outside their rehearsal room.

Their story started in 1955 at the Baxter Terrace housing projects where they lived in Newark, New Jersey. From the beginning the group was a little different. Unlike most groups who originated a name, they took theirs from a local group that was breaking up. And unlike the usual rhythm and blues quartets and quintets covering the street corners and school halls they were a sextet with two basses. And most unusual of all, though they were influenced by THE HEARTBEATS, THE FLAMINGOS, THE SPANIELS, THE MOONGLOWS, and THE CADILLACS, they sang only for fun and had no aspirations to record.

The six friends and neighbors began singing as part of the New Hope Baptist Choir along with other choir members Dionne and Dee Dee Warwick, Judy Clay, Cissy Houston, Leroy Hutson (later of THE IMPRESSIONS), and several of THE SWEET INSPIRATIONS. Cissy was the choir director and Dionne and Dee Dee were cousins of Jim and Charles Patrick of the Monotones.

The group's unique lineup included Charles Patrick (17, lead), Warren Davis (16, first tenor), George Malone (15, second tenor), Warren Ryanes (18, baritone), Frank Smith (17, bass), and John Ryanes (15, Warren's brother and second bass). Jim Patrick, Charles's brother, also subbed on a regular basis. The group practiced at the Baxter Terrace Recreation Hall singing four-part harmony with Frank and John both bassing away.

The Monotones' determination to perform anywhere and everywhere brought them to local hops and dances and in 1956 to New York City's "Ted Mack's Amateur Hour," where they sang THE CADILLACS' "Zoom" and won the show. They got another shot the following week but lost. Content with their performing role, the group took little notice of brother James joining another Newark group called THE KODAKS (from Charles Evan Hughes High School) in 1957, until James's new group negotiated a recording deal with Bobby Robinson's Fury label and started playing places like the Apollo Theatre. This propelled Charles to write some originals for the group.

There are two schools of thought as to how he came to write their classic. One is that he was in a music store looking at the sheet music to a FOUR LADS song, the Al Stillman composition "Book of Love," when the store radio played an old Pepsodent toothpaste commercial that said "You'll *wonder* where the yellow went . . .," and he went home and collaborated on the "Book of Love" with Davis and Malone, using only the word "wonder" from the commercial. The other more practical explanation is that his brother told him of a song 15-year-old

Kodaks lead Pearl McKinnon had written titled "Book of Love." Liking the title (much the same way Georgia Dobbins of THE MARVELETTES liked the title brought to her called "Please Mr. Postman" four years later), Charles wrote his version with some help from his brother.

Either way, they cut a demo of "Book of Love" along with a beautiful Patrick-penned ballad "You Never Loved Me" in the summer of 1957.

They ran their demo to a number of companies including Robinson's Fury. Atlantic Records wanted "Book of Love" for THE BOBBETTES but the group was now determined to record it themselves. Brother James helped Charles and company by taking them to Bea Caslon's Hull Records, home of their heroes, the Heartbeats. She loved the whole package and told them they would be recording in September (1957). The group went into rehearsals, and according to doo wop folklore, they were practicing their now legendary intro, "Oh I wonder wonder ohm ba doo doo who," when a baseball came crashing through the window (though another report is that a mike fell on the floor, and still a third that something slammed against an outside wall). When the boys played their rehearsal tape back, there it was: "Oh I wonder wonder ohm ba doo doo who—BOOM!" It fit, they liked it, and it was used in the form of a solitary bass drum during their session at Bell Sound Studios.

Three months later "Book of Love" was issued on Hull's subsidiary Mascot. By January it was too big for cash-poor Hull/Mascot so they licensed it to Chess Records, who issued it on their affiliate Argo Records.

All of a sudden the Monotones were touring with the gods, Frankie Lymon and Bobby Darin. They still thought they were on Mascot till the record was well on its way up the charts. On March 24, 1958, "Book" climbed onto *Billboard*'s Top 100 and did the same to the R&B lists on April 7th. By late spring it was number five Pop and number three R&B, spending 18 weeks competing with the other 99 of the nation's best. "Book" even read number five in Australia. Their reading of "Book's" flip "You Never Loved Me" showed them to be a solid ballad harmony group as well as a rocking sextet. It should have been saved as a second or third A side, for as they returned to the studio on June 1, 1958 they had no idea that their first hit would be their last.

The Monotones now felt they had found a niche and began writing more rock novelties like their second single "Tom Foolery," but its constant rhythm stops and weak hook made it a poor dance record and a poorer radio record.

On July 15, 1958, their third session yielded two monster tracks, "The Legend of Sleepy Hollow" and "Soft Shadows." "Legend" was a raucous recap of Washington Irving's story about Ichabod Crane and his encounter with the headless horseman. Starting with high-speed horse clip-clops, a potent vocal, and a sax solo right out of a cavalry charge, "Sleepy Hollow" had hit written all over it. The flip was an exquisite ballad and, like "Legend," was another group-written affair.

Though recorded in July 1958, "Legend" wasn't issued until December since Hull was wrapped up in its leased hit "Little Star" (see THE ELEGANTS) through the summer and fall of 1958. Then Argo seriously dropped the ball on "Legend": promotion was nonexistent.

In October 1958 the group found out that for one release they were the Terrace Tones when another of their July 15th novelty history numbers, "The Ride of Paul Revere," rode out of Apt Records courtesy of Hull's usual licensing deals, but it took the road to nowhere. As there was an actual group called the Terrace Tones that included Robert Johnson and Andrew Cheatham, both writers of "Paul Revere" with three other Toners, it's possible some or all of both groups were on this recording.

On June 4, 1959, four new sides were recorded, with yet another novelty, "Tell It to the Judge," coming and going quickly in its June release. The flip was "Fools Will Be Fools," a "Why Do Fools Fall in Love"-styled rocker written by the boys. Another song from that session that posed the intriguing question "What Would You Do If There Wasn't Any Rock and Roll?" was inexplicably never issued until a 1980s Monotones anthology LP (Murray Hill) hit the streets. Perhaps Hull thought it had been too long since the March 1958 charting of DANNY AND THE JUNIORS' "Rock and Roll Is Here to Stay" for "What Would You Do" to have impact, or maybe they figured the song was a melodic clone of "McNamara's Band."

In 1960 the boys had their first true Hull single with the issue of a two-year-old answer record, "Reading the Book of Love." Monotones records were now becoming more sporadic; their last single was from a January 27, 1960, session and wasn't released till June 1961. But this time they outdid themselves, coming up with an answer record to an answer record called "Daddy's Home, But Mama's Gone" (answering Shep and the Limelites' "Daddy's Home" answer to "A Thousand Miles Away").

Their last session was on February 14, 1962. They recorded two titles, "Book of Dance" and "Toast to Lovers," that weren't released until a Hull compilation LP in late 1962.

They disbanded that year but re-formed for oldies shows in the '70s and '80s. Both Ryanes brothers died, but in 1992 there were still Charles and James Patrick, Warren Davis, Frank Smith, and George Malone to answer the favorite question of 1958, "Who Wrote the Book of Love?"

THE MONOTONES

A SIDE/B SIDE	LABEL/CAT NO	DATE
Book Of Love /		
You Never Loved Me	Mascot M-124	12/57
Book Of Love /		
You Never Loved Me	Argo 5290	2/58
Tom Foolery / Zombie	Argo 5301	6/58
The Terrace Tones		
Ride Of Paul Revere /		
Words Of Wisdom	Apt 15037	10/58
The Monotones		
Legend Of Sleepy Hollow /		
Soft Shadows	Apt 5321	12/58
Fools Will Be Fools /		
Tell It To The Judge	Apt 5339	6/59
Reading The Book Of Love /		
Dream	Hull 735	2/60
Daddy's Home But Mama's Gone /		
Tattletale	Hull 743	6/61

The Moonglows

One of the most innovative vocal groups, the Moonglows perfected a blend that practically defines blow harmony.

It was around 1950 when Harvey Fuqua (nephew of INK SPOTS great Charlie Fuqua) and Bobby Lester began singing for fun in their hometown of Louisville, Kentucky.

By 1952, Harvey and Danny Coggins (lead), both just out of the service, found themselves in Cleveland harmonizing with Prentiss Barnes. The trio was jazz-oriented originally and called themselves the Crazy Sounds. They soon brought in Bobby Lester from Louisville and Alexander "Pete" Graves of Cleveland; Coggins dropped out.

The lineup in late 1952 was Bobby Lester (22, lead), Pete Graves (17, tenor), Harvey Fuqua (22, baritone), and Prentiss Barnes (31, bass), who was the brother of SPANIELS lead "Pookie" Hudson.

Influenced by groups like THE RAVENS and ORIOLES, the new quartet started to develop that deep warm sound they would later be famous for, and Harvey began writing songs with Bobby working

out the vocal leads. The group would then go into clubs and ask if they could perform. Some said no but the ones that said yes gave them a chance to perform the rhythm and blues hits of the day like "Crying in the Chapel" (Orioles) and "I Woke Up This Morning" (B. B. King).

It was at one such club, the Chesterfield Lounge in Cleveland, where they were heard by Al "Fats" Thomas. He was so knocked out that he called his friend, a local disc jockey at WJW, and had him listen to the group over the phone while they were performing. The disc jockey was none other than Alan Freed, and he liked what he heard enough to bring the group right into WJW to record what would become their first single, the Fuqua-Lester composition "I Just Can't Tell No Lie," on Freed's own instantly created Champagne label. He also changed their name to reflect his own on-air "Moondog" persona by renaming them the Moonglows. The label read "Al Lance" as writer, which was Freed's pen name.

Released in late 1952 the blues ballad gave the world the first taste of Bobby Lester's incredibly smooth and soulful lead and a rough introduction to Moonglows harmonies of the future.

The record did well within the range of Freed's voice and sold almost 10,000 copies, but he mysteriously never followed up with another.

Contrary to popular opinion, according to Fuqua, Freed did not take the group to Chance Records. When the Moonglows saw nothing happening after their first release (except for the stage shows they were doing for Freed), they went to Chicago on their own to Chess Records (Phil Chess had been in the WJW office, probably promoting Chess product, when the Moonglows first recorded). They never got to see Chess, but since the Chance label was only a few blocks away (1151 East 47th Street to Chess's 950 East 49th Street), the group walked over to Chance and sang three new Fuqua compositions, "Hey Santa Claus," "Baby Please," and "I Was Wrong" for Ewart Abner, general manager of the label. He and owner Art Sheridan liked every song and signed them. They cut the blues ballad "Baby Please" (which was Harvey's favorite of the Chance sides) and a harmony-filled jumper, "Whistle My Love" as the group's first single, issued the fourth week of October 1953. It sold well in the Chicago and Cleveland areas. The Alan Freed connection was obviously still active since both sides of their first and subsequent Chance originals had the writer credits Fuqua-Freed. ("I Was Wrong" actually read Freed-Fuqua. It was just the way things were done in those days, and a resigned Harvey has stated, "Alan would sit there and throw a word in every now and then so, ya know, we'd give him credit for that, sometimes all the credit.")

For Christmas, Chance issued two Moonglows originals, the rockin' "Hey Santa Claus" and another soulful blues ballad, "Just a Lonely Christmas." They are R&B Christmas standards today.

In February 1954 their third Chance release was the only nonoriginal, a cover of the January 1954 Doris Day-sung, Fain-Webster song "Secret Love," done in a beautiful Moonglows setting. Though B-side rockers were mandatory, "Real Gone Mama" was a first-class jazz-tinged jump side.

Their biggest Chance single was their next 45, "I Was Wrong" in June 1954, a rhythm ballad with a bluesy melody, a great bass part, and a jumpin' bridge that was another solid example of the Moonglows carving their own vocal niche.

The group's last Chance side "219 Train" was during Chance's decline and so the song received no promotion, relegating a good R&B record to instant extinction.

The Moonglows left Chance after those five classics for the standard reason: no royalties and no royalty statements.

In the fall of 1954 the quartet signed with Chess for records and the Shaw agency for bookings, and two years of struggling started to pay off.

"Sincerely," another Fuqua-penned ballad (that naturally read Fuqua-Freed) was issued in November 1954 and in March 1955 made the national Jukebox top 20. It reached number one R&B in early 1955 and stayed there two weeks. Had they not been covered by THE MCGUIRE SISTERS (#1 Pop) they no doubt would have had a bigger hit, though some maintain the McGuire's access to white radio gave the song its status as a standard. (Harvey acknowledges that the bridge on "Sincerely" is almost exactly the bridge of THE DOMINOES' 1952 rocker "That's What You're Doin' to Me," so whether they knew it or not, the McGuire girls covered two R&B groups in one song.)

The same month that Chess released "Sincerely," they issued a Lester-Fuqua duet, "Shoo Doo Be Doo," as Bobby Lester and the Moonlighters. Feeling they had an up-tempo hit but not wanting to wait for "Sincerely" to die down and not wishing to distract from the ballad image they were projecting, Chess's sister label Checker became home to the Moonlighters.

Though not charting nationally, "Shoo Doo Be Doo" received extensive airplay and sales in pockets of the country, and booking agents looking to hire the group found out that to get them, they had to take the Moonglows too (I wonder why).

The Moonlighters' schizophrenia lasted for one more single in 1954. "Hug and a Kiss" failed and they went back to being full-time Moonglows.

Ever since signing with Shaw, the group had been doing tours with THE CLOVERS, THE CHARMS, Joe Turner, Bill Doggett, and the Paul Williams Orchestra. On one Alan Freed show, Harvey mentioned that the Moonglows backed up Jesse Belvin.

While the Moonglows were appearing at the New Orleans Municipal Auditorium in February 1955, LaVern Baker was making an appeal to her representative Charles Diggs (Democrat-Michigan) which could have had an effect on the Moonglows and many of the day's black artists. She asked him to study the possibility of authoring a bill in Congress that would revise the 1909 copyright act, which did not prohibit the duplicating of arrangements on records, such as Georgia Gibbs' identical cover of LaVern's "Tweedle Dee." Needless to say, LaVern got nowhere.

In February 1955, a simple "doe doe doe" bass intro led listeners into "Most of All," one of the most beautiful of all Moonglows masterpieces. With Bobby's soaring lead and the group doo wopping through the bridge, "Most of All" and its four-part harmony "ooh wah" ending reached number five R&B but mysteriously failed to chart Pop. (It's possible that the existence of Don Cornell's pasteurized and maudlin version [#14 Pop] kept the white jocks from the Moonglows original.) On April 18th the Moonglows spent a week in Alan Freed's "Rock & Roll Easter Jubilee" at the Paramount in Brooklyn along with THE PENGUINS, LaVern Baker, and THE THREE CHUCKLES, among others. Though the Moonglows, when queried, had stated that Alan always paid them what he could, that show seemed to tell a different tale. The gross was reportedly $107,000, of which Freed received $50,000; the total paid to all the talent was $11,000.

In June 1955 "Foolish Me," with its ascending and descending slur harmonies and Bobby's potent lead, came out but couldn't chart.

On September 10th *Billboard* reviewed the Moonglows' "Starlite" and "In Love," writing, "The boys come through with showmanly vocal performances on two fine songs. 'Starlite' is a dreamy ballad with a poignant warbling stint by the group's lead singer. 'In Love' is a delightful rhythm ballad, highlighted by a fascinating phrasing gimmick on the title. The platter has a bright future." Wishful thinking for the reviewer and countless music lovers. "Starlite" stiffed. Apparently Chess was in a "don't spend a dime on promotion" period.

If "Starlite's" failure was a sin, the loss of its follow-up, the fluid bluesy rhythm ballad "In My

Diary," was pure sacrilege. The last Moonglows single of 1955, its beauty was heard only in scattered spots throughout the country. The record sold more as a collector's favorite in the '60s and '70s than it did upon release.

The ultra-commercial "We Go Together" in March 1956 was next and by the summer it was number nine R&B.

Their next became their only two-sided charter. "When I'm with You," with its chime harmony, sent kids swooning to the tune of number 15 R&B. Written by Fuqua and Dallas (Bobby Lester's real name), it is acknowledged by Harvey as being one of his favorite Chess sides.

The "See-Saw" flip had unfamiliar credits (Davis-Sutton and Pratt); Freed's name was no longer showing up on Moonglows sides. Pratt, by the way, was Harry Pratt, a.k.a Harvey Fuqua. "See-Saw" outdistanced "When I'm with You" and by the fall of 1956 had reached number six R&B. "See-Saw" was the Glows' first record with a jazz group backing in the form of James Moody's rhythm section.

Harvey admits with a chuckle that he kept writing up-tempo B sides in hopes he'd get a chance to sing lead; he readily acknowledged no one could touch Bobby on a ballad.

In 1956 the group had its first appearance in a film when Alan Freed brought them to the sound-stage of the teen classic *Rock Rock Rock*, along with THE FLAMINGOS, Chuck Berry, and Tuesday Weld in her screen debut (with Connie Francis singing for her). The two songs the Moonglows sang in the film were the Ben and Al Weisman ballad "Over and Over Again" and "I Knew from the Start," which became their next two-sider in 1956 (but not until a fast version of "Over and Over Again" was recorded and released around the same time with the same record number.)

Their last single of 1956, "Don't Say Goodbye," cast the Moonglows as one of the first R&B groups to use strings.

The summer of 1957 saw Harvey on a rare ballad lead for the Percy Mayfield-penned "Please Send Me Someone to Love." Harvey's solid interpretation brought the song to number five R&B and number 73 Pop despite a subdued performance by the Moonglows. Bobby Lester's last lead was on "The Beating of My Heart," which he and Harvey wrote. Any records issued after "Beating" with Bobby on lead had been recorded earlier.

By 1958 Bobby's voice was conspicuous in its absence, a problem magnified by the lack of quality material except for one gem supposedly written by a mysterious M. Paul titled "Ten Commandments of Love." The group was now called Harvey and the Moonglows, and their harmony intro and Harvey's listing of the commandments of love made the record a favorite love song of 1958 and an all-time classic. It ultimately charted number 22 Pop and number nine R&B. M. Paul turned out to be the nine-year-old son of one of the Chess brothers, but before you consider him a protégé, note that when the legal smoke cleared, it turned out that Fuqua had actually written the song.

"I'll Never Stop Wanting You," recorded in 1956, was issued in January 1959. *Billboard*'s January 19th issue reported, "This one starts with some pleasant vocal harmonies, followed by a devoted lead performance [Lester] in a slow rock tempo. The cat really put his heart in this. Watch it!" Without Bobby Lester, the Moonglows lacked vibrancy and a sense of purpose, and Fuqua knew it.

During one period, Harvey and the guys were performing at the Howard Theatre in Washington when a 14-year-old kid came up to Harvey before the show and asked if he would listen to the teen's group. Harvey was mainly interested in eating at the moment so he told Prentiss Barnes to talk to the kid. When Fuqua returned, Prentiss had brought the youngster into the dressing room. Harvey was now cornered so he asked, "Where's your group?" "Outside," the teen replied. Harvey went to the Howard Theatre alleyway where the Marquees, to quote Harvey, "sang me in the gutter—with our own songs!" The kid, by the way, was one of two lead singers. His name was Marvin Gaye. The Marquees (who recorded one great rocker in 1957, "Hey Little Schoolgirl" b/w "Wyatt Earp" for Okeh) were fresh and exciting. So Harvey finished up the week with the Moonglows, but instead of going to Baltimore to continue the tour he folded the group and took the Marquees with him to Chicago. The members besides Gaye (baritone) were Reese Palmer (first tenor), James Nolan (first tenor), and Chester Simmons (first tenor/baritone).

In Chicago, Mr. Harvey (as Marvin used to call him) added Chuck Barksdale of THE DELLS to the group on bass and proceeded to cut the next "Moonglows" single, the ballad "12 Months of the Year," with Marvin doing a bland talking intro. Despite Harvey's enthusiasm, Barksdale's bass, and a budding Marvin Gaye, the new Moonglows couldn't shine the old Moonglows' shoes.

While in Chess's studios doing their own sides, the group put background vocals on Chuck Berry's "Almost Grown" and "Back in the U.S.A."

The next single with Marvin on lead ("Mama Loocie") was their worst.

In 1960 the new Moonglows dispersed and Harvey and Marvin went off to Detroit. While there Harvey married the sister of the young songwriter who had cowritten a late Moonglows trifle called "Soda Pop." Her name was Gwen and his name was Berry, as in Gordy.

In 1961 Harvey set up his own Tri-Phi label signing groups like the Five Quails and THE SPINNERS, whom Harvey trained as a cross between the Moonglows (blow harmony and all) and a soulful HI-LOs-type group.

Meanwhile Chess issued its last Moonglows single, a 1956 recording and one of the group's most beautiful ballads, "Blue Velvet."

Harvey molded the Spinners so well that their recording of "That's What Girls Are Made For" (with Marvin Gaye playing drums) sounded like Harvey was on lead even though it was Bobby Smith. Harvey sang on all the Five Quails and Spinners records on Tri-Phi.

In 1964 Pete Graves formed another Moonglows including Doc Green (THE FIVE CROWNS, Rainbow), George Thorpe, and Bearle Easton (both from the Velvets, Red Robin). They tried to recreate the old group's sound on five singles for Lana (from the Chess days), one single for Times Square, and one for Crimson.

In 1970 Bobby Lester, who was now managing a Louisville nightclub, returned to perform with a local group called the Aristocrats. Within a year he turned the quintet into a new Moonglows with Albert Workman, Bobby's cousin Gary Rodgers, Robert Ford, and Billy McPhatter (son of the late DRIFTERS lead Clyde McPhatter). They performed at the Academy of Music in 1971 but after the show the backups wanted to go home to Louisville while Bobby wanted to continue on. He contacted Fuqua and they went about the task of restructuring the group.

In 1972, three-fourths of the original Moonglows group (Fuqua, Lester, and Graves), along with Chuck Lewis and Doc Williams, recorded an LP for Philadelphia deejay George Woods' Big P label. The album was then bought by RCA. The LP was called *Return of the Moonglows* and had remakes of "When I'm with You," "Most of All," "I Was Wrong," "Ten Commandments of Love," and "Sincerely '72," which started like the original and then got funky after one verse. The latter song reached number 43 on the R&B chart in the summer of 1972 and became the Moonglows' last chart record.

Fuqua couldn't tour due to his Motown commitments, but the other four did until the oldies boom slowed down in the mid-'70s.

In 1978 Bobby, his cousin Archie Bailey, Rodgers, and Ford once again revived the Moonglows' name.

A performance in Boston in January 1979 was taped and issued as the relic LP, Bobby Lester and the Moonglows' *One More Time*, featuring many of the old favorites. These Moonglows stayed together until Bobby's sad demise in October 1980 of cancer. The group was to appear at Madison Square Garden on November 14th, so to keep the tradition alive, Billy McPhatter rejoined the group and performed for the five-thousand-plus fans who had come to hear the Moonglows, a group that hadn't had a pop hit in 22 years.

In 1983 Fuqua was invited to appear at the Grammy Awards and brought the remainder of his RCA version of the group. It was this same foursome that appeared at Radio City Music Hall in April 1986.

Billy McPhatter's group of Moonglows, with Robert Lee Davis, Gary Rodgers, Peter Lawford, and Bruce Martin carried the tradition into the late '80s. Entering the '90s the newest member was none other than Bobby Lester's son.

Today, Prentiss Barnes is retired and living in Macomb, Mississippi. Alexander Graves is also retired. Harvey Fuqua is anything *but* retired. After selling his Tri-Phi operation to his brother-in-law Berry Gordy, Jr., he became the head of Motown's Artist Development Department. He discovered Tammi Terrell, wrote and produced numerous hits including "What Does It Take" for Junior Walker (an original Tri-Phi artist), and produced "Someday We'll Be Together" for THE SUPREMES.

Today he is still writing and works closely with Smokey Robinson. His song "Sincerely" was nominated for a 1990 Grammy for Best Female Vocal Performance by a Country Group known as the Forrester Sisters (who had a top 10 country hit with it). And as recently as 1991 the Moonglows original was used in the box office smash *Good Fellas*. The Moonglows are simply an American vocal legend, and deservedly so.

THE MOONGLOWS

A SIDE/B SIDE	LABEL/CAT NO	DATE
I Just Can't Tell No Lie /		
I've Been Your Dog	Chmp 7500	1952
Whistle My Love /		
Baby Please	Chance 1147	10/53

A SIDE/B SIDE	LABEL/CAT NO	DATE
Just A Lonely Christmas /		
Hey Santa Claus	Chance 1150	12/53
Secret Love / Real Gone Mama	Chance 1152	2/54
I Was Wrong /		
Ooh Rocking Daddy	Chance 1156	6/54
219 Train / My Gal	Chance 1161	1954
Sincerely / Tempting	Chess 1581	11/54
So All Alone* /		
Shoo Doo-Be Doo*	Checker 806	11/54
Hug And A Kiss* / New Gal*	Checker 813	12/54
Most Of All / She's Gone	Chess 1589	2/55
Foolish Me / Slow Down	Chess 1598	6/55
Starlite / In Love	Chess 1605	9/55
In My Diary / Lover, Love Me	Chess 1611	11/55
We Go Together /		
Chickie Um Bah	Chess 1619	3/56
See Saw / When I'm With You	Chess 1629	7/56
Over And Over Again		
(fast version) /		
I Knew From The Start	Chess 1646	1956
Over And Over Again		
(slow version) /		
I Knew From The Start	Chess 1646	1956
Don't Say Goodbye / I'm Afraid		
The Masquerade Is Over	Chess 1651	1956
Please Send Me Someone		
To Love / Mr. Engineer	Chess 1661	5/57
Confess It To Your Heart /		
The Beating Of My Heart	Chess 1669	1957
Too Late / Here I Am	Chess 1681	1957
Soda Pop /		
In The Middle Of The Night	Chess 1689	3/58
This Love / Sweeter Than Words	Chess 1701	1958
Ten Commandments Of Love** /		
Mean Old Blues**	Chess 1705	8/58
I Want Somebody /		
Ga Ga Goo Goo	Chess 1713	1959
I'll Never Stop Wanting You /		
Love Is A River	Chess 1717	1/59
Twelve Months Of The Year /		
Don't Be Afraid	Chess 1725	1959
Unemployment** /		
Mama Loocie**	Chess 1738	1959
Beatnik / Junior	Chess 1770	1960
Blue Velvet† / Penny Arcade†	Chess 1811	1961
Secret Love / Real Gone Mama	Vee-Jay 423	1962
Sincerely / Time After Time	Lana 130	1964
Most Of All /		
What A Difference A Day Makes	Lana 131	1964
See Saw / Love Is A River	Lana 133	1964
We Go Together /		
Shoo Doo Be Doo	Lana 134	1964
Ten Commandments Of Love /		
Half A Heart	Lana 135	1964
Baby, Please / I've Got The Right	TmsSq 30	1964
Gee / My Imagination	Crmsn 1003	1965
Sincerely '72 / You've Chosen Me	Big P 101	1971
Sincerely '72 / I Was Wrong	RCA 74-0759	6/72

A SIDE/B SIDE	LABEL/CAT NO	DATE
When I'm With You /		
You've Chosen Me	RCA 74-0839	10/72

* Bobby Lester and the Moonlighters
** Harvey and the Moonglows
† Bobby Lester and the Moonglows

The Mystics

There have been many groups who have passed on the opportunity to record a song, only to watch it become a hit for someone else. But rarely has an act been given a song that they *wanted* and then had it taken away and recorded by another artist.

Such is the saga of the Mystics, but fortunately their story had a happy ending.

The Bensonhurst section of Brooklyn, New York, was home to a number of would-be vocalists. A particular group of 10 or more would hang out at Kelly's pool room on 86th Street and Bay 19th Street and sing in the nearby park on Bay Parkway and Cropsey Avenue. The teens were Tony Armato (first tenor), Vinnie Acierno (baritone), Albie Galione (second tenor), Nicki Lombardi, John Pungi, Joe Strobel (lead), Allie Contrera (bass), Bob Ferrante (first tenor), Albie Cracolici (baritone), Phil Cracolici (lead), and George Galfo (second tenor). By now you may have surmised the groups from this neighborhood were Italian.

In 1957 Contrera, Ferrante, Albie Cracolici, Tony Armato, and Joe Strobel formed the Overons. They won a local talent contest but soon splintered apart. In 1958 Ferrante (22, first tenor), Cracolici (22, baritone), and Contrera (18, bass) joined with Albie's brother Phil (21, lead) and George Galfo (18, second tenor) as a revised Overons. A good many of the other guys went on to become THE PASSIONS.

After auditioning live for several labels and being turned down, the group made a demo at Broadway Studios but never even got a chance to take it for auditions. Manager Jim Gribble (THE CLASSICS) heard the tapes and brought the group to Laurie Records in the spring of 1959. They changed their name by picking it out of several thrown in a hat and became the Mystics.

As the group had no original material, Laurie's brass, Gene and Bob Schwartz, contacted song pros Doc Pomus and Mort Shuman to create some Mystics magic. They outdid themselves and two weeks later showed up with a song that everyone felt was a homerun. The group was excited, the writers were excited, and the Schwartzes were ecstatic, but concerned. A song like that should go to a name act, they thought. So it was that DION AND THE BELMONTS (also on Laurie) wound up with "A Teenager in Love."

To calm and placate their disappointed quintet, Laurie asked the dynamic writing duo to make lightning strike twice, and that's just what they did. "Little Star" had been a big hit by THE ELEGANTS not long before, and the Schwartz brothers felt a song in that style would work perfectly for the Mystics' soft harmonies, so that was the task given to Pomus and Shuman. The very next day Doc and Mort brought in "Hushabye." The Mystics' recording was released in April and charted Pop on May 25th, one week after the Belmonts' "Teenager" peaked at number five. The Mystics did pretty well with their nursery rhyme rock-a-ballad, going to number 20.

Sticking with a celestial style, the Brooklyn boys' August release was another nice rock-a-ballad, "Don't Take the Stars," but it barely scratched the Top 100 (#98) before it was gone.

The February 15, 1960, issue of *Billboard* reviewed their third single: "The Mystics can click again with either of these potent bids. 'I Began' is a pretty rock-a-ballad that is warmly warbled by the group over a soft arrangement. 'All Through the Night' is the old tune done with a rock-a-ballad approach and this too, has the sound." They also had the added backup voice of another Jim Gribble client named Paul Simon (yes, *that* Paul Simon). "All Through the Night" became an East Coast favorite but never dented the national Top 100, though it tried, reaching number 107.

Staying in the "stars" and "night" bags, the boys did an excellent "Hushabye"-styled rhythm ballad called "Blue Star" that was overlooked by radio. Another disappointment was the Mystics' rockingest side of all, "Goodbye Mr. Blues." All the elements were there—a hit melody and hook, solid vocals, and wailing sax.

Their last single, a nice ballad reworking of THE HARPTONES' "Sunday Kind of Love," came and went, and by mid-1961 the group's six-record career was all but over.

In the 1980s the group finally got their first compilation LP with their six previous singles and never-before released versions of "Over the Rainbow" and "Again."

In 1982 the corporation of Cracolici, Cracolici, Contrera, Ferrante, and John Tarangelo (in for George Galfo) released an LP on Ambient Sound

that featured an '80s version of "Hushabye" titled "Hushabye My Darling," along with some oldies remakes.

Today four of the five Mystics are engineers living in the New York area while George Galfo is living in Florida.

THE MYSTICS

A SIDE/B SIDE	LABEL/CAT NO	DATE
Hushabye / Adam And Eve	Laurie 3028	4/59
Don't Take The Stars / So Tenderly	Laurie 3038	8/59
All Through The Night / To Think Again Of You	Laurie 3047	2/60
Blue Star / White Cliffs Of Dover	Laurie 3058	4/60
Goodbye Mister Blues / Star-Crossed Lovers	Laurie 3086	3/61
Sunday Kind Of Love / Darling I Know Now	Laurie 3104	1961

Nino and the Ebb Tides

One of the first purveyors of rock nostalgia, Nino and the Ebb Tides started as the Ebbtides from the Bronx, New York, in 1956. Schoolmates Antonio "Nino" Aiello (lead) and Vinnie Drago (bass) drafted Tony Delesio (baritone) and a guy remembered only as Rudy. They met talent scout Murray Jacobs, who cut two sides with them in 1957: "Franny Franny" b/w "Darling I Love Only You," both written by Nino and Vinnie.

By the fall of 1957 the quartet (now Nino and the Ebb Tides) found themselves on Bill Miller's West 44th Street Acme label, and "Franny Franny" was getting some solid rotation from New York jocks like Alan Fredericks and Alan Freed. Their next single, "Puppy Love," saw a 50 percent change in the group as Rudy and Tony D. were replaced by Ralph Bracco (tenor) and Tony Imbimbo (baritone), formerly of Tony and the Imperials (not Little Anthony's group).

That wasn't the only change, as Murray Jacobs decided to set up his own Recorte record label in March 1958. Nino got a chance to sample the new Recorte setup as he sang backup vocals for the Rockin Chairs' spring 1958 regional classic, "A Kiss Is a Kiss."

"Puppy Love," unlike frantic "Franny," was a nice ballad on Recorte that surfaced in October

1958 and saw a lot of local activity, but nothing more (though you could certainly sell a lot of records in the New York area of the late '50s with its population of over five million).

The Tides' next single became their rarest ("The Meaning of Christmas"), quickly passing into history. The group was still rough-edged and learning its craft when they did two more singles for Recorte ("I'm Confessin'" and "Don't Look Around") as well as a backup job on the Rockin' Chairs' third release, "Memories of Love" b/w "Girl of Mine."

By 1960 Tony DiBari was at tenor for Ralph Bracco, and the group moved to the Marco label for one ill-fated (but better sounding) ballad called "Someday."

Their next stop was Larry Uttal's Madison label, whose claim to fame was the Tassels' charter "To a Soldier Boy" (#55, 1959) and the Al Browne and the Tunetoppers hit "The Madison" (#23, 1960).

The Ebb Tides' first Madison single was a song called "Those Oldies But Goodies Remind Me of You" that was starting to get action on the West Coast. The Ebb Tides revised it slightly by adding quick harmony references to such past hits as "Deserie" (THE CHARTS) and "That's My Desire" (THE CHANNELS) and singing the title lines of oldies like "Glory of Love" (THE FIVE KEYS), "Silhouettes" (THE RAYS), and "Over the Mountain" (Johnnie and Joe) behind Nino's talking bridge. They recorded on a Friday and the record was out that Monday (today it takes that long for some musicians to program their drum machines!). "Those Oldies" was reviewed by *Cashbox* on May 13, 1961, 12 days after the LITTLE CAESAR AND THE ROMANS version hit the *Billboard* charts.

Nino's group outdistanced Caesar's in *Cashbox*'s Top 100 but *Billboard* gave a slice of pie to Caesar at number nine (#28 R&B) with Nino and company nowhere to be found. New York was evenly split, giving both versions heavy airplay.

The battle for nostalgia bragging rights continued through both groups' next releases. The Romans tried for another brass ring with "Memories of Those Oldies But Goodies," which never got off the ground. The Ebb Tides' summer release was a revision of the Tex Beneke, Marion Hutton, and MODERNAIRES (with Glenn Miller) masterpiece of merriment, "Juke Box Saturday Night" (#7, 1942). It *did* get off the ground, complete with imitations of THE MONOTONES' "Book of Love" and THE SILHOUETTES' "Get a Job" replacing the '40s versions of classics by THE INK SPOTS and Harry James. On September 4, 1961, "Juke Box" charted on *Billboard*'s Top 100, reaching number 57 and becoming another East Coast hit.

It's likely that the references to earlier songs in these recordings helped to fuel the first wave of rock nostalgia that soon cropped up on Top 40 radio and on oldies compilations by Original Sound, Roulette, and many other labels in the early '60s.

It's unusual for a group to leave a label after their biggest success, but Nino and the boys had no choice since Madison was going out of business. Toward the end of 1961 they fell in with Mr. Peacock Records, cutting one of their best singles, "Happy Guy." By this time their sound was polished, and the Belmonts/DEL-SATINS-styled rocker seemed like a winner until Mr. Peacock laid an egg in support of its single. At around this time, Bronx songwriter Ernie Maresca wrote a rocker that the guys heard and passed on. Ernie took it next to Dion, who recorded it with the Del-Satins and made it a number two record in the nation. The Ebb Tides must still be smarting over the loss of "The Wanderer."

A few more singles on various labels and the group members were back to their separate lifestyles by 1965. Unlike many groups, even when they were on the charts the Ebb Tides kept working at their regular jobs and never became full-time performers.

They regrouped in 1971 for the start of that decade's rock revival and disbanded soon after, returning to their professions: Vinnie at a TV and radio sales company, Tony Imbimbo as a New York City policeman, Tony D. for American Express, and Nino as a record distributor.

In the '80s the group would occasionally get together to give fans of the '50s and '60s a taste of those oldies but goodies.

NINO AND THE EBB TIDES

A SIDE/B SIDE	LABEL/CAT NO	DATE
The Ebb-Tides		
Franny, Franny /		
Darling I'll Love You Only	Acme 720	11/57
Nino and the Ebb Tides		
Puppy Love / You Make Me		
Wanna Rock And Roll	Recorte 405	10/58
The Meaning Of Christmas /		
Two People Shadows The Snow	Recorte 408	12/58
I'm Confessin' / Tell The World I Do	Recorte 409	1959
Don't Look Around / I Love Girls	Recorte 413	7/59
Those Oldies But Goodies /		
Don't Run Away	Madison 162	5/61
Juke Box Saturday Night /		
I'll Fall In Love	Madison 166	1961
Little Miss Blue / Someday	Marco 105	1961
Happy Guy / Wished I Was Home	MPcok 102	1961
Lovin' Time /		
Stamps, Baby Stamps	MPcok 117	1962

A SIDE/B SIDE	LABEL/CAT NO	DATE
Nursery Rhymes / Tonight	MrPk 123	1963
Automatic Reaction /		
Linda Lou Garrett	Mala 480	1964

The Nutmegs

One of the finest of the '50s R&B groups, the Nutmegs unwittingly became the founders of the a cappella craze that swept the East Coast between 1963 and 1966. The street-singing troubadours formed into a quintet from a loose collection of singers in the 1953 New Haven, Connecticut, home of THE FIVE SATINS (Ember), the Scarlets (Red Robin), THE CHESTNUTS (Davis), and the Four Haven Knights (Atlas).

All would soon record, but for now the individuals were getting their feet (and vocal chords) wet in the stockmarket of sound, where their fortunes as a vital part of a quartet or quintet rose or fell with the sweetness and resonance of their tone.

Leroy Griffin, James "Sonny" Griffin (Leroy's brother), Dieder Cobb, and a second Leroy Griffin (now that's a first) who became Leroy Gomez, all sang together with Walter Singleterry, Bill Emery, and Gomez's brother Tommy moving in and out. When Griffin, Griffin, Cobb, and Gomez sauntered down to the corners of Webster and Dixon Streets to ask Jimmy "Co Co" Tyson if he'd join their tentative foursome, Tyson agreed, leaving behind his quintet of Ruby Whittaker (lead), Eddie Martin (first tenor), Lyman Hopkins (second tenor), and Reuben White (bass). All but Martin eventually went on to form the Chestnuts.

A few more changes and a group called the Lyres was formed, which included Bill Emery (lead), Walter Singleterry (first tenor), Sonny Griffin (second tenor), Jimmy Tyson (baritone), and Leroy Griffin (bass). The Gomez brothers went on to form the Four Haven Knights.

A promoter named Charlie Johnson met the group and recorded two of Leroy's songs, "Ship of Love" and "Playboy," for his miniscule J&G label after the local Klik label (where the record was recorded) passed on the group. J&C issued "Ship of Love" in 1953 and it promptly sank out of sight; Johnson had no funds for marketing the record.

By 1954 the group revised its singing order with Leroy on lead, Sonny as first tenor, Jimmy second tenor, Bill baritone, and added Leroy McNeil on bass. This new lineup was extraordinary: they practiced endlessly, their hunger for success often transcending their need to leave their Eureka Spa hangout for dinners. Leroy's young nephew Harry James used to sit and listen endlessly, little knowing what part he would play in carrying on the group's tradition many years later.

In late 1954 the quintet went to New York and met RCA-Groove artists THE DU DROPPERS, who introduced them to Herald Records exec Al Silver. The group had just recorded four sides ("Story Untold," an updated version of "Ship of Love," "Whispering Sorrows," and "Betty Lou," the first three of which would become singles). Silver opted for a name change, since he didn't think the Lyres sounded right. When no one could come up with a name, somebody asked where they were from; since Connecticut was known as the Nutmeg State, the quintet used that for the name.

In March 1955 they issued "Story Untold" on Herald, a beautiful harmony ballad that Leroy's emotion-packed lead helped to leap onto the R&B charts. By July it was number two in the nation. THE CREWCUTS covered "Story" (#16), effectively eliminating the 'Megs' Pop market chances.

In August "Ship of Love" was released and reached number 13 R&B and number five in New York by October. The group then ran into a problem when they were accused of doing an obscene dance at the Apollo Theatre. When Alan Freed got wind of it he pulled the Nutmegs release off the air. McNeil and Emery went to New York and apologized to Freed explaining they were only doing "The Hunch," a dance that centered around pulling your arms in and out at your sides. Freed apparently forgave them as they appeared at his next Brooklyn Paramount show and then spent 90 days touring with THE MOONGLOWS, THE HARPTONES, Chuck Berry, THE SPANIELS, and others on one of Freed's road shows.

The compelling ballad "Whispering Sorrows" was next with another exciting Leroy Griffin lead, but Herald pushed the flip "Betty Lou" and got no response. Bill Emery then left, replaced by Sonny Washburn, formerly of the Five Dukes ("Cross Your Fingers," Atlas, 1955).

The Nutmegs' fourth single, entitled "Key to the Kingdom," was reviewed in the June 16, 1956, *Billboard* as "a ballad in the refined, celestial groove, garnished with a few ecstatic sighs." December's "Comin' Home" was a good rocker, but the group had lost its momentum. "My Story," their next to last Herald single, was just not of the calibre of their earlier sides.

By now Sonny Griffin had departed, replaced by Eddie Martin.

A single as the Rajahs on Connecticut's Klik label (1958) bore the same poor results, and so did one on Morty Craft's Tel Records in 1960.

Leroy Griffin's nephew Harold James joined the group in 1962, yielding a membership of Uncle Leroy, Sonny Washburn, Leroy McNeil, and Jimmy Tyson. This aggregation returned to Herald for one more single, "Rip Van Winkle," before a phenomenon occurred. Times Square Records started issuing 45s of the Nutmegs made from mid-'50s vocal demos that had no music accompaniment (see The "Acappella" Era), calling these singles a cappella records. The Nutmegs soon became the foremost exponents of a new subculture that held their quality cuts as the standard of the new craze. Six singles were issued in 1963 and 1964, and they sold heavily among collectors and group enthusiasts. "Let Me Tell You" reached number five on Times Square's January 1963 Top 150 Survey; "The Way Love Should Be" made number three in July 1963; "Why Must We Go to School" hit number four in December 1963; "Down in Mexico" jumped to number five in January 1964; and "You're Crying" reached number four in December 1964. Other surveys up and down the coast registered similar successes and prompted Lana Records to have the group overdub vocals on preexisting tracks and vocals of "Story Untold" and "Ship of Love" in 1964 for two singles. Sadly, the heart of the Nutmegs was cut out in the mid-'60s when Leroy Griffin died in a factory accident. Harold James, who had painstakingly worked to duplicate his uncle's sound, took over the lead.

In 1972 the Nutmegs did a superlative a cappella LP with versions of all their hit material and a terrific rendition of "Over the Rainbow" in a Moonglows style. Billy Vera, noted musician and singer ("At This Moment," #1, 1986), whose band used to back many oldies acts, has said the Nutmegs were the finest a cappella group he'd ever seen. Many would agree.

THE NUTMEGS

A SIDE/B SIDE	LABEL/CAT NO	DATE
Story Untold /		
Make Me Lose My Mind	Herald 452	3/55
Ship Of Love / Rock Me	Herald 459	8/55
Whispering Sorrows /		
Betty Lou	Herald 466	12/55
Key To The Kingdom /		
Gift O' Gabbin' Woman	Herald 475	6/56
Comin' Home / A Love So True	Herald 492	12/56

The Rajahs

Shifting Sands / I Fell In Love	Klik 7805	1/58

A SIDE/B SIDE	LABEL/CAT NO	DATE
The Nutmegs		
Story Untold /		
Make Me Lose My Mind	Herald 452	1/59
My Sweet Dream /		
My Story	Herald 538	3/59
A Dream Of Love /		
Someone Somewhere	Tel 1014	1960
Rip Van Winkle /		
Crazy 'Bout You	Herald 574	1962
Let Me Tell You / Hello	TmsSq 6	1963
The Way Love Should Be /		
Wide Hoop Skirts	TmsSq 14	1963
Down To Earth /		
Coo Coo Cuddle Coo	TmsSq 19	1963
Why Must We Go		
To School / Ink Dries Quicker		
Than Tears	TmsSq 22	1963
Down In Mexico /		
My Sweet Dreams	TmsSq 27	1964
You're Crying / Wa-Do-Wa	TmsSq 103	1964
Beautiful Dreamer /		
Story Untold	Lana 128	1964
Ship Of Love / Ting A Ling	Lana 129	1964
Story Untold / Tell Me	BbyGr 800	1972
The Rajahs		
Roseann / You're Crying	Klik 1019	1973
The Nutmegs		
Over The Rainbow /		
In The Still Of The Night	Pyramid 162	1970's

The Olympics

The Olympics were an R&B, dance, and novelty group often considered a COASTERS clone. They formed in Compton, California, during 1956 at Centennial High School and originally called themselves the Challengers.

The pecking order was Walter Ward (lead), Eddie Lewis (tenor and cousin of Walter), Charles Fizer (baritone), and Walter Hammond (baritone). Since Ward was also a baritone the group had three, but they usually sang a shrill unison, so few got to hear their deeper side, and the group never even had a ballad A side 45 out of their 34 career singles.

Their first record was on the small Melatone label ("I Can Tell," 1958) and became instantly extinct.

They soon met writer/artist Jesse Belvin, who took an interest in the quartet now called the Olympics and introduced them to talent agent John

Criner and his wife, blues singer Effie Smith. Within three months they had inked a record deal with Si Aronson's Demon Records of Hollywood. Demon issued "Western Movies," a parody of TV westerns that the Coasters took to the next step in a 1959 mimicry called "Along Came Jones." "Western Movies" became an international hit, reaching number eight Pop and number seven R&B while shooting to number 12 in Britain.

The group then had its first important national appearance on Dick Clark's "American Bandstand." Though an obvious R&B group, their novelty approach transcended ethnic boundaries and they eventually wound up with more Pop charters (14) than R&B (5).

Their second Demon disc, "Dance with the Teacher," reached number 71 Pop. By then Fizer had left, replaced by bass Melvin King; by 1959, however, Fizer had returned to replace Hammond.

The group had one clinker titled "Chicken" on Demon before moving over to Richard Vaughn's Los Angeles-based Arvee Records and charting with "Hully Gully" (#72 Pop, February 1960). The Arvee period (1960 to 1965) was the group's golden age in terms of their finest recorded material. They turned out singles like "Big Boy Pete" (#50 Pop, #10 R&B, 1960), "Shimmy Like Kate" (#42 Pop, #45 U.K., 1960) and their best record, "Dance By the Light of the Moon" (#47 Pop). Their follow-up "Little Pedro" only reached number 76 but Arvee kept trying, issuing six more singles including a remake of Ray Charles's "What'd I Say."

Their last Arvee single was a remake of their own song, "Big Boy Pete '65."

In August of that year Charles Fizer was killed during the Watts riots in Los Angeles and was replaced by Julius McMichael (Mack Starr), former lead of THE PARAGONS from Brooklyn, New York (Winley).

The group continued on with a variety of labels. In 1966, King dropped out and was replaced by Kenny Sinclair of THE SIX TEENS in 1970. They kept on cutting energetic dance songs like "The Bounce" (#40 Pop, #22 R&B), "Bounce Again," "The Duck," and "Baby Do the Philly Dog," their last charter (#63 Pop, #20 R&B, 1966).

In March 1965 they released a solid rocker on Loma called "Good Lovin'." It never charted, but Felix Cavaliere heard it on his car radio over WWRL in New York and a little over a year later the song was number one by his Young Rascals.

The Olympics never had hits (except for "Western Movies") like the other novelty honchos, but they recorded from 1958 to 1973, giving them 15 years as contenders.

THE OLYMPICS

A SIDE/B SIDE	LABEL/CAT NO	DATE
Walter Ward and the Challengers		
I Can Tell / The Mambo Beat	Mlatn 1002	1958
The Olympics		
Western Movies / Well	Demon 1508	1958
Dance With The Teacher / Everybody Needs Love	Demon 1512	1958
Chicken / Your Love	Demon 1514	1959
Private Eye / Hully Gully	Arvee 562	1959
Big Boy Pete / The Slop	Arvee 595	1960
Shimmy Like Kate / Workin' Hard	Arvee 5006	1960
Dance By The Light Of The Moon / Dodge City	Arvee 5020	1960
Little Pedro / Bull Fight	Arvee 5023	1961
Dooley / Stay Where You Are	Arvee 5031	1961
The Stoap / Mash Them Taters	Arvee 5044	1969
Everybody Likes To Cha Cha Cha / Twist	Arvee 5051	1962
Baby, It's Hot / The Scotch	Arvee 5056	1962
What'd I Say Part 1 / What'd I Say Part 2	Arvee 5073	1964
The Boogler Part 1 / The Boogler Part 2	DDsc 104	1964
Return Of Big Boy Pete / Return Of The Watusi	DDsc 105	1964
Big Boy Pete '65 / Stay Where You Are	DDsc 6501	1965
I'm Comin' Home / Rainin' In My Heart	Loma 2010	1/65
Good Lovin' / Olympic Shuffle	Loma 2013	3/65
Baby I'm Yours / No More Will I Cry	Loma 2017	7/65
We Go Together / Secret Agents	Mrwd 5504	1966
Mine Exclusively / Secret Agents	Mrwd 5513	3/66
Western Movies / Baby Do The Philly Dog	Mrwd 5523	1966
The Duck / The Bounce	Mrwd 5525	1966
The Same Old Thing / I'll Do A Little Bit More	Mrwd 5529	1966
Big Boy Pete / Hully Gully	Mrwd 5523	1967
Good Things / Lookin' For Love	Pkwy 6003	1967
The Cartoon Song / Things That Made Me Laugh	Jubi 5674	1969
Please Please Please / Girl, You're My Kind Of People	Wrnr 7369	5/70
The Apartment / Worm In Your Wheat Germ	MGM 14505	2/73

The Paragons

Brother group to the legendary JESTERS, the Paragons were an equally fine tenor-led quintet. The members, mostly students at Jefferson High School in the Bedford-Stuyvesant section of Brooklyn, were Julius McMichael (tenor lead), Ben Frazier (second lead and tenor), Donald Travis (second tenor), Rickey Jackson (baritone), and Al Brown (bass). The group of 17- to 22-year-olds wrote much of their material soon after they formed in 1956.

By 1957 they had met Paul Winley, owner of Winley Records, who already had the Jesters and was trying to get THE DUBS, who were controlled by Hiram Johnson. When Winley failed to get permission to sign the Dubs, he signed the Jesters-styled Paragons and had them record the McMichael-Winley ballad "Florence." It became a radio favorite and a classic New York doo wop oldie, ultimately selling a few hundred thousand.

True to the Winley tradition, the flip was an excellent jump tune, titled "Hey Little Schoolgirl." One of the features of Paragons and Jesters up sides was the groups' penchant for singing "bop bow du bop bop oo oop" and other assorted phrases right through the instrumental sections, keeping the record's high energy at a peak. This was demonstrated on "Schoolgirl."

"Let's Start All Over Again," from the summer of 1957, had the same exciting style of "Florence" and has also become a cherished doo wop classic.

Later that year a solid rhythm ballad called "Two Hearts Are Better Than One" was issued and followed by the New York mini-classic, "Twilight."

By now the group was performing in a variety of venues from Philadelphia's White Horse Roller-skating Rink to New York's Apollo Theatre, often with their labelmates the Jesters. Their best and hardest-to-find Winley single was their fifth release, the brilliant ballad "So You Will Know." Its simple two-note piano repetition set the tone for a made-for-radio melody superbly sung by the Paragons with Bill Witt ("Mexico," THE ROCKETONES, Melba) singing lead. Why it failed can be attributed to the age-old story of a label that couldn't promote it beyond their own limited borders.

Still, the Paragons were immortalized when Winley issued its *Paragons meet the Jesters* LP, the most successful "battle of the groups" and doo wop compilation of all time, selling hundreds of thousands over the years.

In 1959 the group backed solo act Tommy Collins on "Doll Baby," an ordinary mid-tempo jump tune in comparison to their earlier efforts.

By 1960 the group had experienced major changes. Julius left, replaced by the deep tenored Alan Moore, and the group began cutting standards for Andy Leonetti's Musicraft label.

They released "Blue Velvet," which canvassed pop radio in many major cities and charted at

number 103. "If" did better, peaking at number 82. Cole Porter's "Begin the Beguine" and the Sammy Cahn-Julie Styne standard "Time After Time" followed. Both were competent versions but neither got out of the New York area.

In 1961 Winley issued one more Paragons single (reading Mack Starr and the Paragons) on "Just a Memory," which was all that was left of their great releases. Mack Starr was the new *nom de plume* of Julius McMichael.

By 1964 the group consisted of Alan Moore (lead), Ernest Burnside (first tenor), Glen Mosley (second tenor), and Joseph Pitts (baritone). That group lasted into the '70s when Bill Witt showed up again. By the mid-'80s their tradition was being continued by Ray Neal (lead) of the Exploits (Fargo), John Epps (tenor lead) of THE CHIPS ("Rubber Biscuit," Josie), Robert Honey (second tenor, "Doom Lang," the black Tokens, Gary), and Teddy Olds (baritone of the same Tokens).

They recorded the first new single under the Paragons' name in 21 years when Starlight Records issued "Florence" b/w "Blue Velvet" to the collectors' market.

Julius McMichael went off to California and joined THE OLYMPICS in the late '60s. He was killed in a motorcycle accident in the early '80s.

Entering the '90s you can still find the current Paragons group battling it out with Adam Jackson and the Jesters at oldies shows in the New York area, and at least during those magic moments it's still 1957.

THE PARAGONS

A SIDE/B SIDE	LABEL/CAT NO	DATE
Florence / Hey Little Schoolgirl	Winley 215	1957
Let's Start All Over Again / Stick With Me Baby	Winley 220	7/57
Two Hearts Are Better Than One / Give Me Love	Winley 223	1957
Twilight / The Vows Of Love	Winley 227	1958
So You Will Know / Don't Cry Baby	Winley 228	1958
Doll Baby* / Darling I Love You*	Winley 236	1959
So You Will Know / Doll Baby	Winley 240	1960
Blue Velvet / Wedding Bells	Mscrft 1102	1960
Just A Memory / Kneel And Pray	Winley 250	1961
If / Hey Baby	Tap 500	1961
Begin The Beguine / In The Midst Of The Night	Tap 503	1961
Time After Time / Baby Take My Hand	MsClf 3001	1963
So You Will Know / Don't Cry Baby	TmsSq 9	1963
Blue Velvet / Florence	Strlt 23	1984

* Tommy Collins and the Paragons

The Pastels

One of only a few American vocal groups to form outside of the continental United States (the Pharoahs in West Germany and the Lucky Charms in Hawaii were some others), the Pastels came together in the most unlikely of places, Narsarssuak, Greenland.

In the summer of 1955 (Dee Irwin stated, "You could tell it was summer because you could see the ground through the snow") four air force members, Airman Second Class J. B. (James) Willingham of New York City (20), Richard Travis of St. Paul, Minnesota (19), Private First Class Tony Thomas of Cleveland, Ohio (19), and Private First Class Gerald Craig of Buffalo, New York (19), began singing just for fun (and to avoid boredom) on the Narsarssuak base. Sgt. DiFosco (Dee) Irwin, recently stationed at Semiutak, Greenland (with 40 men, two dogs, and a cat), was transferred to the main base in July and began singing and playing piano at the service club when the four airmen approached him to form a quintet they had named the Rocketeers. With little else to do, the quintet polished up their sound on songs like "The Nearness of You" and "Stormy Weather."

The singing order was Dee on lead (originally called "Fat Daddy" when he was singing solo), Richard Travis first tenor, Tony Thomas second tenor, J. B. Willingham on baritone, and Gerald Craig on bass. J. B., by the way, had a sister Joan who spent some time as a member of the all-girl group the Hearts (Baton) and who sang that unforgettable bridge solo "You great big lump of sugar" in "Lonely Nights," and a brother Gus, who served time with THE CADILLACS (Josie).

The Rocketeers pared down to a quartet when Craig dropped out. The backup vocalists were all transferred to Andrews Air Force Base (in Washington, D.C.) late in 1955 and their lead, Sgt. Ervin, was sent to the same base about three months later, allowing the quartet to resume its singing. They played service clubs and USOs in the Washington area for the next several months.

Dee's unique sound and vocal delivery gave what might have been considered a competent vocal group an identifiability that often raises groups to star status. (It helped to have influences like THE RAVENS, Chuck Willis, Ivory Joe Hunter, and Amos Milburn.)

The Rocketeers won the local competition of "The Tops in Blue" at Andrews and went on to the final round in the summer of 1956 at Mitchell Air

Force Base on Long Island, New York. They performed "The Nearness of You" but were beaten by a Pittsburgh air force group calling themselves THE DEL-VIKINGS. (Six months later a song written by Sgt. Clarence Quick and recorded by the Del-Vikings would go on to be a top five hit record titled "Come Go with Me.")

After the competition, the Rocketeers decided to travel to Manhattan and bang on some record company doors. It didn't take much banging. They entered 1619 Broadway and walked into the offices of Hull Records. (They picked the 1619 building because J. B.'s sister's label, Baton, was in that building, but they never made it that far.) Bea Caslon, owner of Hull, heard the quartet sing a newly-penned song by Dee and J. B. titled "Been So Long" and signed them on the spot. Since Bea didn't like the name the Rocketeers (and there was a Rocketeers on Herald starting in 1953), the group began scrambling for ideas right in her office. As Dee recollects, "The members were brainstorming, we looked around the room, we said well gee, Jimmy's dark, Dee's light, Tony's light, oh my goodness, pastel colors—The Pastels." Dee and J. B. both acknowledge that they had never heard of the Chicago group the Pastels (United Records, 1955) until this writer mentioned it to them in 1991.

By October 1956 the Pastels were in the studio recording "Been So Long" with Bea producing and old pro Teacho Wilshire arranging. The record wasn't released until a year later on Mascot, a Hull affiliate. The mystically beautiful "Been So Long" started to break out just as Washington, D.C., record store owner "Waxie Maxie" Silverman (a reported one-time silent partner in Atlantic Records) brought the Mascot masters to the attention of the Chess brothers of Chicago, who owned Argo Records. They licensed the recording from Bea Caslon and distributed "Been So Long" nationally on Argo in January 1958.

By now, all but Dee had been discharged from the air force, and the Pastels lead emerged from the service in February 1958. Less than a month later the magical melody of "Been So Long" was on radios across the nation reaching number four R&B by April and number 24 Pop by May. Amazingly, the group had been together over two years before recording "Been So Long" and had never recorded so much as a home tape of anything before their first record's success.

While Dee was still at Andrews he and the group did their first major performance at Washington's renowned Howard Theatre and soon after played the Apollo with Sam Cooke.

In the coming months they performed with the likes of Little Richard, Frankie Lymon, THE FLAMINGOS, THE SPANIELS, THE PLATTERS, and the Cadillacs on shows like Alan Freed's and Dick Clark's TV shows.

Of course touring had its bizarre side. One time an Alan Freed show took them to Louisiana. After a performance with Larry Williams of "Bony Maronie" fame, the group was sitting around the club when a man waving a gun approached Larry and threatened his life for alleged advances toward the gunslinger's wife. Dee came up behind him, pushing the gun arm toward the ceiling as the Pastels pounced on the pickled patron and threw him out. Then there was the time in Baton Rouge, Louisiana, when the group performed uninterrupted with the Lee Allen Band ("Walkin' with Mr. Lee," #54, February 1958) for 25 minutes on a dance floor singing songs ike "That's My Desire" (CHANNELS) and "Gee" (CROWS) while the entire crowd surrounding them participated in a brawl. The safest place, according to J. B., was right where they were.

Their next single was "You Don't Love Me Anymore," a bluesy ballad that listed the group as the writers (like the "Been So Long" label) even though Dee and J. B. were the actual creators. Released in the spring of 1958 on Argo (all of the Pastels' singles were recorded for Hull/Mascot but licensed to Argo) it received very little airplay. In September, "So Far Away" (Dee's personal favorite), an attempt to recapture the "Been So Long" sound, failed and by 1959 the Pastels decided that with little performance work, no competent management, and no label, they would go home.

Richard Travis returned to St. Paul and went to work for the post office. Tony Thomas returned to Cleveland and has not been heard from since. J. B. stayed in New York along with Dee and the two continued to write and sing. Dee backed up Chubby Checker on an early Parkway release and in June and July 1963 had a hit as a solo act (#38 Pop) on "Swinging on a Star" (the 1944 number one Bing Crosby hit that included the Williams Brothers with seven-year-old Andy Williams in support) under the name Big Dee Irwin. Dee also had support on his record by Little Eva along with the Cookies ("Don't Say Nothin' Bad," #7, 1963).

Dee had two other singles for Dimension backed by the Cookies that should have been hits, the tongue-in-cheek "Happy Being Fat" (1963) and his first post-Pastels effort, the name-dropping (from James Brown to the Isley Brothers) "Everybody's Got a Dance But Me."

In November Dee and J. B. sang back-up on the co-penned Wilson Pickett charter (#95 Pop), "I'm Down to My Last Heartbreak."

When J. B. finally left the business he became a member of the New York Transit Authority and is now living in New Jersey and has retired. Dee went on to a diversified series of careers from air traffic controller, executive at the Los Angeles Musicians Union, to writer for such acts as Ray Charles and the DELLS. He also recorded for Liberty and 20th Century (as Jason Grant in 1966 with the Harry Simeone Chorale backing) and had an R&B chart record as late as August 1976 ("Face to Face," #89) on Wes Farrell's Roxbury Records.

Today Dee is a music publisher in Hollywood and still writes an occasional song.

The Pastels, a fine quartet, had a short life span like many of the '50s' best groups. And if it hadn't been for the U.S. Air Force, we would have been deprived of one of the classic ballads of the '50s.

THE PASTELS

A SIDE/B SIDE	LABEL/CAT NO	DATE
Been So Long /		
My One And Only Dream	Mascot 123	11/57
Been So Long /		
My One And Only Dream	Argo 5287	1/58
You Don't Love Me Anymore / Let's		
Go To The Rock And Roll Ball	Argo 5297	7/58
So Far Away / Don't Knock	Argo 5314	9/58
Oh Me, Oh My / Human	Owl 332	1970's

The Penguins

The Penguins created America's favorite oldie, "Earth Angel" (though some would argue it was "In the Still of the Night" by THE FIVE SATINS), which was actually an unfinished, garage-made, one-track demo recording. In fact, the worldwide hit has the first five seconds of the intro clipped off and starts abruptly (though no one noticed).

If that had been their biggest disappointment, the Penguins might have gone on to superstardom like fellow Angelenos THE PLATTERS. But the Penguins wound up involved in almost as many lawsuits as they had Dootone releases, and only the enormity of their single hit kept them visible outside of the record-collecting community.

Fremont High Schooler Cleveland "Cleve" Duncan was doing a local talent show at the California Club on Santa Barbara Avenue (one of several he'd entered) in Los Angeles in late 1953. He was approached by aspiring songwriter Curtis Williams (bass) of Jefferson High School who liked his distinctive and mellow tenor lead and asked him if he'd like to form a group. Curtis had previously been in an historic though unrecorded embryonic group called the Flamingos in 1951 (not Chicago's famed quintet). The Flamingos were Richard Berry (who founded the Flairs), Cornelius Gunter (who cofounded the Flairs, the Hollywood Blue Jays, and sang with ARTHUR LEE MAYE AND THE CROWNS), Gaynel Hodge (later of THE HOLLYWOOD FLAMES), and brother Alex Hodge who was a founding member of the Platters. Curtis brought baritone Bruce Tate of Jefferson, Cleve drafted tenor Dexter Tisby of Fremont, and another quartet was born.

While pondering a name that the teens thought would be cool, they noticed Dexter's pack of Kool cigarettes with Willie the Penguin on the front. The very cool Penguins now had their identity.

Curtis Williams had also brought a song to the group called "Earth Angel." The history of this song is clouded by conflicting opinion, although over the years a consensus has been reached that its roots can be traced, at least in part, to the pen of Los Angeles R&B writer Jesse Belvin. Curtis either wrote or cowrote with Gaynel Hodge a revised "Earth Angel" which included the line "a vision of your loveliness" from a Patti Page song, "I Went to Your Wedding" (#1, summer 1952). Cleve Duncan's recollection was that by the time it reached him the melody sounded like Jesse and Marvin's "Dream Girl" (Jesse Belvin and Marvin Phillips, Specialty, 1953) and he didn't like it so he rewrote the melody; as far as he knew, only Curtis wrote the lyrics. But Cleve couldn't know the origin of the song prior to his involvement, so the mystery continued.

The Penguins practiced "Earth Angel" along with an uncontested Curtis Williams song called "Hey Señorita" (originally known as "Ese Chiquita"). Through Cleve's uncle Ted Brinson, mailman and former bass player for the Jimmie Lunceford Band, they met local Dootone label owner Dootsie Williams (no relation to Curtis).

Dootsie took them into Ted Brinson's backyard garage at 2190 West 30th Street and recorded them backing blues artist Willie Headon on "Ain't No News Today." He then signed them when he heard "Hey Señorita" (rhythm tunes were the rage) and recorded it on Brinson's Ampex one-track machine along with a demo of "Earth Angel." It had to be redone seven or eight times because the recording acoustics were so crude. Every time Brinson's

neighbor's dog barked at passing cars his voice leaked onto the tape. Brinson would then turn on the tape, leap up, grab his bass, and with Curtis Williams on piano, Preston Epps on bongos (supposedly), and a long-since-forgotten drummer, begin recording.

Dootsie Williams then decided to take the demo disc to John Dolphin at Dolphin's of Hollywood All Night Record Shop for an opinion. Dolphin would broadcast a rhythm and blues radio show right from his store window. Sitting in at the time was white KGFJ disc jockey Dick "Huggy Boy" Hugg. Dootsie barely had time to tell Dolphin it was a demo before he handed it directly to Hugg and told him to play both sides over the air. Then Dootsie took his demo and went home. The next morning Huggy Boy called Williams to tell him that people were calling up and going crazy over the ballad. Dootsie sprang into action and pressed as many 78s and 45s as he could, but was still convinced "Hey Señorita" was the A side. When it came out in October of 1954 the record label read Dootone 348-A, and that's the side that got initial airplay. But Williams soon found that you can't hold back a tidal wave, and when jocks started flipping the "Señorita" for the "Angel," orders came in faster than Dootsie could keep up with them. He knew there were two kinds of records on the market, those that had to be promoted and the rare natural hit that everyone wanted. He now knew he and the Penguins had the latter.

On December 18th it charted R&B nationally and on Christmas Day crossed over to pop. Even when the pop establishment jumped on the bandwagon in the form of THE CREW-CUTS' (Mercury) cover, they couldn't slow "Earth Angel" down (though the white version went to number three). The Penguins reached number eight Pop Best Seller in early 1955, becoming the first West Coast R&B group to dent the previously off-limits Pop top 10. "Earth Angel" also reached number one R&B for three weeks, finally being eased out by Johnny Ace's "Pledging My Love."

On December 31, 1954, the literally overnight sensations found themselves on the other side of the country for a New Year's Eve show at the Howard Theatre in Washington with THE 5 ROYALES.

By mid-January problems were already looming for the new stars. When the group reportedly couldn't get any advances from Dootone they acquired lawyer/arranger/songwriter Buck Ram (now there's a combination) to manage them. Ram had originally been an arranger for Duke Ellington and Count Basie, among others, and fronted his own combo on Savoy Records in 1944. Various industry trades wrote in January 1955 that Dootone denied reports the Penguins were moving to a major label and cited a three-year contract with the group backing them up.

At the same time Dootone released another Penguins ballad penned by Curtis called "Love Will Make Your Mind Go Wild," but "Love" was nowhere as strong as "Earth Angel" and never even charted.

On February 21st the group was back in Los Angeles playing the Savoy Ballroom with label-mates THE MEDALLIONS and the Meadowlarks. The show was called "The Ookey Ook Dance Party," named after the Penguins' current flip side. The group was using it for a stage dance similar to a penguin walk.

They were across the country again on April 8th in Alan Freed's Rock & Roll Easter Show at the Brooklyn Paramount with THE MOONGLOWS, LaVern Baker, and THE THREE CHUCKLES, along with Red Prysock's Orchestra. The next day the Penguins, directed by Ram, signed with Mercury Records. But Ram was a sly businessman: it so happened he was using his power as representative of the Penguins to get a deal with Mercury for another of his L.A. groups, a yet unknown quintet (despite nine single releases on Federal) called the Platters. It was one of those "if you want this, you have to take that" deals, and Mercury took both.

Meanwhile the Penguins' "Earth Angel" had sold about two million copies (over the next 30 years it would go on to sell as many as 10 million, and as recently as 1983 was reportedly still selling a thousand singles a week around the world).

Mercury's confidence was bolstered by a court decision that Dootone's contract was invalid since three of the four Penguins had been minors at the time they signed to Dootsie's label. Before the last session for Dootone in early 1955 Bruce Tate accidentally hit a pedestrian with his car and was so shook up by the experience he dropped out of the group. He was replaced by Randolph Jones (baritone).

In April 1955, two Penguin ballad singles were released: Mercury's "Be Mine or Be a Fool" and Dootone's "Kiss a Fool Goodbye." Neither received much response. "Be Mine" was a particularly fine record and how Mercury lost it is a mystery.

Curtis Williams put another nail in the Penguins coffin in April when he sued Dootone for $100,000, claiming damages to his career because he signed a record contract when he was a minor. If he hadn't signed with Dootone he probably

would not have had a career at all, but the suit was most likely instigated by Ram.

Two weeks later (May 13, 1955) Dootone sued Mercury for inducing the Penguins to break their contract and for taking the publishing rights for its copyright and giving it to its own publishing affiliate, Peer International. That same week Jesse Belvin and supposed cowriter Johnny Green sued Curtis Williams over "Earth Angel," and the court ordered Dootone to put all related writer/publisher monies in trust until the situation was dealt with. The upshot was that Dootone won the publishing rights, Mercury kept the Penguins, and depending on what label copy you read, several people were credited as the writer. In 1961 Art Laboe's historic first *Oldies but Goodies* LP listed the writers as "Williams-Hodge-Belvin." A mid-'80s collectibles album, the WCBS-FM 101 *For Lovers Only* oldies LP, has the writer as (are you ready?) Dootsie Williams.

Nothing that followed for the Penguins seemed to work. Good recordings like "Devil that I See," "A Christmas Prayer" and "My Troubles Are Not at an End" failed to generate activity, probably because Ram was now concentrating heavily on his new hit act, the Platters, who were busily singing Ram-penned songs like "Only You."

The group even tried re-cutting "Earth Angel" with strings but all it did was serve to sell more of the Dootone original. (That August 1956 issue on Mercury became a collectible.) In August 1956 Dootone released one of the first R&B vocal group compilation LPs, *Best Vocal Groups of Rhythm and Blues*, featuring cuts by the Penguins, the Meadowlarks, the Medallions, and THE DOOTONES.

Mercury then tried a release on its Wing affiliate in early spring 1956. BILLBOARD's May 12th issue gave "Dealer of Dreams" good marks: "A moving reading by the boys on a serenely paced ballad with imaginative lyrics, excellent job by the lead singer." It was moving, all right, but not up the charts.

In early 1957 the Penguins moved over to Atlantic for one single, "Pledge of Love," which reached number 15 R&B and then disappeared quickly. The group returned to Los Angeles broke and disheartened. Cleve needed a throat operation for tonsillitis, Curtis had fled California to avoid being jailed for nonsupport and wound up singing with the Hollywood Flames (his is the first voice on Thurston Harris's "Little Bitty Pretty One" that the Flames backed without credit). Teddy Harper joined the group, and when they re-formed (Cleve Duncan, Dexter Tisby, Randy Jones, and Teddy

Harper), the Penguins went to the only contact they had, Dootsie Williams, hoping that since they were older and wiser they'd cut a better deal. It didn't matter; three less-than-stirring singles and the *Cool Cool Penguins LP* drew little attention.

In late 1959 "Earth Angel" was issued again by Dootone and amassed enough play and sales to reach number 101 on the Pop 100 in early 1960. In 1959 Cleve tried one record on Dootone with a Dexter-and-two-girls backup under the name Cleve and the Radiants (Gladys and Vesta White), but "To Keep Our Love," a good ballad, didn't move.

In 1963 a soon-to-be controversial character named Frank Zappa from Lancaster, California, talked them into cutting his song "Memories of El Monte" (actually cowritten with Ray Collins, later of Zappa's the Mothers of Invention). The record received strong radio play and good sales in a variety of markets but failed to chart nationally. Zappa reportedly used the royalties he earned to bail his girlfriend out of jail; she had allegedly made a sex tape with him and had been caught by the San Bernardino Vice Squad.

After one more Penguins single in 1966 on Original Sound, "Heavenly Angel," their recording days were through. Tisby, Jones, and Harper went off to be Cornelius Gunter's COASTERS.

In 1969 Cleve, who now owned the Penguins name, added Walter Saulsbury and Glenn Madison (formerly of the Delcos, Ebony, 1962).

In 1984 Ace Records did a live LP titled *Big Jay McNeely Meets the Penguins*, and Cleve's trio did seven sides with a "Memories of El Monte"/"Earth Angel" medley and highlighted by a rendition of "Ookey Ook."

Dexter Tisby eventually moved to Hawaii. Curtis Williams and Bruce Tate passed away. Dootsie Williams, ever the entrepreneur, made a fortune selling Redd Foxx party albums.

Cleve Duncan still has that fine distinctive sound some 37 years after he first sang "Earth Angel."

THE PENGUINS

A SIDE/B SIDE	LABEL/CAT NO	DATE
No There Ain't No News Today / When I Am Gone	Dootone 345	8/54
Earth Angel / Hey Senorita	Dootone 348	10/54
Love Will Make Your Mind Go Wild / Ookey Ook	Dootone 353	1/55
Kiss A Fool Goodbye / Baby Let's Make Some Love	Dootone 362	4/55
Be Mine Or Be A Fool / Don't Do It	Merc 70610	4/55

A SIDE/B SIDE	LABEL/CAT NO	DATE
It Only Happens With You / Walkin' Down Broadway	Merc 70654	7/55
Devil That I See / Promises Promises Promises	Merc 70703	9/55
A Christmas Prayer / Jingle Jingle	Merc 70762	12/55
My Troubles Are Not At An End / She's Gone, Gone	Merc 70799	1/56
Dealer Of Dreams / Peace Of Mind	Wing 90076	5/56
Earth Angel / Ice	Merc 70943	8/56
Will You Be Mine / Cool Baby Cool	Merc 71033	1/57
Pledge Of Love / I Knew I'd Fall In Love	Atln 1132	3/57
That's How Much I Need You / Be My Loving Baby	Dooto 428	12/57
Let Me Make Up Your Mind / Sweet Love	Dooto 432	1/58
Do Not Pretend / If You're Mine	Dooto 435	3/58

Cleve and the Radiants

To Keep Our Love / My Heart	Dooto 451	8/59

The Penguins

Believe Me / Pony Rock	SnSt 001	1962
Memories Of El Monte / Be Mine	OrigS 27	1963
Heavenly Angel / Big Bobo's Party Train	OrigS 54	1965

The Platters

The most successful vocal group of the '50s, the Platters helped immeasurably in putting black groups on the pop map. Their biggest assets were Tony Williams's sweet tenor and their pop radio acceptability, fostered by some early hits from the pen of manager Buck Ram.

Buck had a long career as an arranger for big bands like Duke Ellington, Tommy Dorsey, Cab Calloway, Glenn Miller, and Count Basie after earning a law degree at the University of Illinois and studying music at Southwestern University.

He turned to management in the early '50s in Los Angeles, building a roster of local talent like THE PENGUINS, the Flairs, THE COLTS, Young Jessie, and Linda Hayes.

Meanwhile, a quartet was formed in Los Angeles by Cornel Gunter along with Joe Jefferson and Alex and Gaynel Hodge. Tony Williams met them at the Club Alabama in Watts and soon became their lead singer.

Tony, who was originally from Elizabeth, New Jersey, was working in a car wash when he was brought to Ram in 1953 by his recording artist sister, Linda Hayes (actually Bertha Williams), who in February 1953 hit with an answer record to Willy Mabone's "I Don't Know" titled "Yes I Know (What You're Putting Down)" (#2 R&B, R-I-H Records).

Ram thought Tony's warm, rich tenor was terrific but knew he couldn't sell a black solo tenor in those times, so he asked Williams if he'd be interested in joining a group. Since Tony already had one called the Platters, an audition was arranged. Though they sounded amateurish, Ram began working with them and with a few key changes made the pieces fall into place. After a few practices Gaynel Hodge and Joe Jefferson left and in came Herb Reed of Kansas City, Missouri, from the famous gospel group the Wings Over Jordan. Also hired was David Lynch of St. Louis, Missouri, who was working as a cab driver when he joined.

The Platters were now Tony on lead, David tenor, Alex baritone, and Herb bass. Ram arranged a record deal with Federal Records and cut several sides that included the Ram-penned ballad "Only You." Syd Nathan, president of Federal, thought it was so bad he swore he wouldn't issue it, so the Platters' first single became the gospel-ballad turned rocker "Give Thanks," which went nowhere. But it did show the potential of 25-year-old Tony Williams.

Their second single was the solid rhythm and blues ballad "I'll Cry When You're Gone." Five more Federal releases boosted their local stature and a few sold around 20,000 copies on the West Coast. Though the group would wind up with a pop harmony style, their early Federal 45s were R&B and gospel oriented. To soften the group's sound, Ram added Zola Taylor from one of his other acts, Shirley Gunter and the Queens (Shirley was Cornel's sister). She recorded on the last few sides the Platters did for Federal, including a 1955 backup for Linda Hayes on "Please Have Mercy." Alex then left and Paul Robi of New Orleans took over the baritone position.

Ram kept the group working and polishing its sound, so much so that another Los Angeles group, the Penguins, seeing how much money a group like the Platters was making without a hit, decided to sign with Ram.

The first thing he did with the "Earth Angel" group was move them to the Chicago major label Mercury, but in order for the Windy City label to have them, they had to accept Buck's now famous two-for-one deal. "If you want the Penguins you have to take the Platters," he said, and Mercury reluctantly agreed, privately celebrating over their acquisition of the proven hit Penguins while tolerating their purchase of the no-hit Platters.

The first session for Mercury's Platters included a rerecording of "Only You." Mercury's A&R man, Bob Shad, was ready to drop the song from the session until Buck volunteered to play piano for the musician who had to leave early. It was the only session Buck ever played on, but he was determined to get it recorded and knew the song could be a hit.

On July 3, 1955, "Only You" hit the charts and was soon at number one R&B (for an amazing seven weeks) and number five Pop. It stayed on the charts for 30 weeks and was the first rock and roll record to beat out a white cover in the race for the top 10 (THE HILLTOPPERS reached number eight).

Buck's beautiful ballad and his persistence convinced Mercury to continue promoting the black group as if they were a pop white act, and to keep the momentum going Ram told Shad of a terrific new song he had that was even better than "Only You." When pressed to name it he quickly replied "The Great Pretender." Now all he had to do was write it, and that's what he did.

"The Great Pretender" was issued in November 1955 and became their second number one R&B single and first number one Pop hit (the first R&B ballad to reach the top Pop spot). The song also began a streak of 11 two-sided hits (its flip "I'm Just a Dancing Partner" reached number 87 Pop) making the Platters the number one American vocal group in that category. "Great Pretender" launched their career as American ambassadors of music when it reached number five in England (with "Only You" on its flip side) and spread around the world. Meanwhile, Federal's Syd Nathan choked on his own words in order to make a quick dollar and put out his badly recorded version of "Only You." (*Billboard*'s January 7, 1956, issue noted that Federal hoped to cash in by reissuing "Tell the World" newly backed by "I Need You All the Time," two previous A-side singles.)

Ballad hits like "The Magic Touch" (#4 Pop and R&B, 1956), "My Prayer" (#1 Pop and R&B, and #4 U.K., 1956), "You'll Never, Never Know" (#11 Pop, #9 R&B, and #23 U.K., 1956), and "I'm Sorry" (#23 Pop, #15 R&B, and #18 U.K., 1957) established the Platters in a way few black groups had ever been perceived by the general public, save for THE INK SPOTS and MILLS BROTHERS.

The Platters became the first rock and roll group to ever have a top 10 LP, and worldwide tours became the order of the day.

In 1958 they debuted "Twilight Time" on Dick Clark's "American Bandstand" Saturday night TV show. A film of the Platters performing the song was used for promotion on TV shows. If you've seen it, you were looking at what may have been the first precursor of music videos.

A super seller, "Twilight Time" was number one Pop and R&B in the spring of 1958, number three in the U.K., and number one in Australia.

In October 1958 Mercury issued the legendary ballad "Smoke Gets in Your Eyes" (originally by Paul Whiteman in 1933–34, #1, Victor), recorded in Paris, France, while the group was on tour. It reached number one Pop on June 19, 1959, for three weeks (Lloyd Price's "Stagger Lee" finally displaced it) and number one R&B, while it became their only number one record in Britain and also hit the top spot in Australia.

The group delivered excellent records like "Enchanted" (#12 Pop, #9 R&B) and "Remember When" (#41 Pop) in 1959.

The Platters weren't immune to the perils of their business and touring lifestyle. They (the four male members) were arrested in Cincinnati, Ohio, in August for an encounter with four 19-year-old women, three of whom were white. By December they had been acquitted, but not before shocked and outraged disc jockeys (a proven pristine lot themselves) had removed the Platters' current single "Where" from many play lists, causing it to die at number 44.

On March 28, 1960, "Harbor Lights," the Francis Langford 1937 hit (#6), became the Platters' last top 10 charter (#8 Pop, #15 R&B, #11 U.K.) and "Sleepy Lagoon" their last flip side charter (#65).

After 20 Mercury singles the label changed the credit to read "The Platters Featuring Tony Williams." It appeared on the 1953 (#2) Frank Chacksfield hit "Ebb Tide," but the warm reading only reached number 56.

More great standards followed: "Red Sails in the Sunset" (#36, 1960), "To Each His Own" (#21, 1960), and "If I Didn't Care" (#30, 1961).

By early 1961 Tony Williams had decided to record on his own and signed with Reprise Records. *Billboard*'s July 10th review noted the change on their new single "I'll Never Smile Again," saying, "The group, with its new lead, Sonny Turner, wrap up the tender oldie in a smooth, expressive vocal treatment. An effective side."

Mercury continued issuing Williams-led Platters singles with "It's Magic" (#91) the last charter in early 1962. Then Mercury refused to release any

product with a lead other than Williams. Buck "I'll sue 'em" Ram did exactly that, and 1961 ended in legal turmoil.

By 1962 Paul Robi and Zola Taylor left and were replaced by Nate Nelson (THE FLAMINGOS) and Sandra Dawn, respectively.

The group always worked but it took four years to put them back on the charts while Mercury continued to issue old sides from the can right up to 1964, the last being "Little Things Mean a Lot."

In April 1966 "I Love You a Thousand Times" was issued by Musicor and reached number 31 Pop (#6 R&B), their biggest hit since 1961's "I'll Never Smile Again" (#25). They issued several more platters on Musicor, the most successful being "With This Ring" (#14 Pop, #12 R&B).

In the early '70s there were at least four related Platters groups and who-knows-how-many "pretender" acts. One had original bass Herb Reed with Nate Nelson, Liz Davis, Ron Austin, and Duke Daniels. Another billed as the Original Platters had Paul Robi, David Lynch, and Zola Taylor. Tony Williams formed his own Platters and as of 1989 they consisted of he and his wife Helen, Bobby Rivers, Ted E. Fame, and Ricky Williams.

Buck Ram had no intention of being left out and formed the Buck Ram Platters with Monroe Powell, Ella Woods, Chico LaMar, Craig Alexander (a cousin of Zola Taylor), and Gene Williams. Last but not least, Sonny Turner formed his own group now billed as Sonny Turner, formerly of the Platters and Sounds Unlimited.

David Lynch died in 1981 and Paul Robi passed on in 1989, both of cancer. In 1990 the Platters were inducted into the Rock and Roll Hall of Fame. The group not only helped break the musical color barrier, they set a standard of quality that groups would try to reach in coming decades. By the time their recording days were done they'd amassed 16 gold singles and three million-selling LPs. They performed in cities and countries that most Americans never dreamed had even heard a Platters disc, taking American music to appreciative audiences all over the world.

THE PLATTERS

A SIDE/B SIDE	LABEL/CAT NO	DATE
Give Thanks / Hey Now	Fed 12153	11/53
I'll Cry When You're Gone /		
I Need You All The Time	Fed 12164	1/54
Roses Of Picardy /		
Beer Barrel Polka	Fed 12181	5/54
Tell The World / Love All Night	Fed 12188	1954

A SIDE/B SIDE	LABEL/CAT NO	DATE
Shake It Up Mambo /		
Voo-Vee-Ah-Bee	Fed 12198	10/54
Take Me Back, Take Me Back /		
Maggie Doesn't Work		
Here Anymore	Fed 12204	12/54
Please Have Mercy* /		
Oochi Pachie*	King 4773	2/55
Only You / Bark, Battle And Ball	Merc 70633	11/55
The Great Pretender /		
I'm Just A Dancing Partner	Merc 70753	11/55
Only You / You Made Me Cry	Fed 12244	12/55
Tell The World /		
I Need You All The Time	Fed 12250	12/55
The Magic Touch / Winner Take All	Merc 70819	2/56
My Prayer / Heaven On Earth	Merc 70893	6/56
You'll Never Never Know /		
It Isn't Right	Merc 70948	8/56
Give Thanks /		
I Need You All The Time	Fed 12271	1956
One In A Million /		
On My Word Of Honor	Merc 71011	11/56
I'm Sorry / He's Mine	Merc 71032	1/57
My Dream / I Wanna	Merc 71093	4/57
Only Because /		
The Mystery Of You	Merc 71184	8/57
Helpless / Indiff'rent	Merc 71246	12/57
Twilight Time / Out Of My Mind	Merc 71289	4/58
You're Making A Mistake /		
My Old Flame	Merc 71320	6/58
Twilight Time / For The First Time	Merc 30075	1958
I Wish / It's Raining Outside	Merc 71535	9/58
Smoke Gets In Your Eyes /		
No Matter What You Are	Merc 71383	10/58
Enchanted /		
The Sound And The Fury	Merc 71427	2/59
Remember When /		
Love Of A Lifetime	Merc 71426	5/59
Wish It Were Me / Where	Merc 71502	9/59
What Does It Matter / My Secret	Merc 71538	11/59
Harbor Lights / Sleepy Lagoon	Merc 71563	1/60
Ebb Tide / Apple Blossom Home	Merc 71624	5/60
Red Sails In The Sunset /		
Sad River	Merc 71656	8/60
To Each His Own / Down The		
River Of Golden Dreams	Merc 71697	10/60
If I Didn't Care / True Lover	Merc 71749	1/61
Trees / Immortal Love	Merc 71791	3/61
I'll Never Smile Again /		
You Don't Say	Merc 71847	7/61
Song For The Lonely /		
You'll Never Know	Merc 71904	11/61
It's Magic / Reaching For A Star	Merc 71921	1/62
More Than You Know /		
Every Little Movement	Merc 71986	1962
Memories / Heartbreak	Merc 72060	11/62
I'll See You In My Dreams /		
Once In A While	Merc 72107	1963

A SIDE/B SIDE	LABEL/CAT NO	DATE
Here Comes Heaven Again /		
Strangers	Merc 72129	6/63
Viva Ju Juy /		
Cuando Calienta El Sol	Merc 72194	1963
Java Jive / Row That Boat Ashore	Merc 72242	2/64
Sincerely / P.S. I Love You	Merc 72305	6/64
Love Me Tender /		
Little Things Mean A Lot	Merc 72359	1964
Won't You Be My Friend /		
Run While It's Dark	Entree 107	1965
I Love You 1000 Times /		
Don't Hear, Speak, See No Evil	Mscr 1166	4/66
Devri / Alone In The Night	Mscr 1195	8/66
I'll Be Home / The Magic Touch	Mscr 1121	11/66
With This Ring / If I Had A Love	Mscr 1229	2/67
Washed Ashore / What Name		
Shall I Give You My Love	Mscr 1251	6/67
Sweet, Sweet Lovin' / Sonata	Mscr 1275	10/67
Love Must Go On /		
How Beautiful Our Love Is	Mscr 1288	1968
So Many Tears /		
Think Before You Walk Away	Mscr 1302	1968
Hard To Get A Thing Called Love /		
Why	Mscr 1322	7/68
Fear Of Loving You / Sonata	Mscr 1341	1968
Be My Love / Sweet, Sweet Lovin'	Mscr 1443	6/71

* Linda Hayes and the Platters

The Playmates

A music and comedy trio in the style of THE FOUR PREPS, the Playmates were college students at the University of Connecticut in the early '50s when their act came together. Coming from Waterbury, Connecticut, members Donny Conn, Chic Hetti, and Morey Carr initially did straight comedy and toured around Canada in 1952 as the Nitwits. Over the next four years they developed into a musical group and renamed themselves the Playmates. They signed with Roulette Records in 1957 as the label's first vocal group. Their early spring single "Pretty Woman" was only Roulette's third single issued.

Both "Woman" and its follow-up failed, but their third single reached number 19 on the Best Seller lists. It was a dreamy, Paul Anka-styled ballad, a cover of the Twintones (Johnny and James Cunningham) recording "Jo-Ann."

"Don't Go Home," with its folksy, childlike melody, reached number 22 on the D.J. charts and number 36 on the Top 100, while establishing the group.

The novelty side of their talents surfaced on "Beep Beep," the classic turtle and hare story switched to a Cadillac and a Nash Rambler. By December 8th the tale of two autos was their biggest hit at number four.

In the summer of 1959 the group struck again with a pop pleaser that asked the teenage male question, "What Is Love?" The answer, "five feet of heaven in a pony tail," touched on both sex and fashion in 1959 America. "What Is Love?" reached number 15. It was a year until their next chart ride, a touching counterpoint to the PONI-TAILS' "Born Too Late" called "Wait for Me" (#37), in which a young girl implored Johnny to wait for her to grow up so he could love her.

Their next single was a Paul Vance-Lee Pockriss-penned number that told of "Little Miss Stuckup" (#70), who's too snobbish to give her male schoolmate a turn though he's positive she'll belong to him before long. Their last charter was the tongue-in-cheek novelty number "Keep Your Hands in Your Pockets" (#88, 1962).

In 1963 the group signed to ABC and in 1964 to Colpix, but their novelty style and innocent teen-love approach was derailed by the British invasion.

Though not a powerhouse act, they were tuned to what teens were thinking. That gave them 10 chart singles in five years (1958–62), the last five innocent years in America.

THE PLAYMATES

A SIDE/B SIDE	LABEL/CAT NO	DATE
Pretty Woman / Barefoot Girl	Roul 4003	1957
Darling It's Wonderful / Island Girl	Roul 4022	1957
Jo-Ann / You Can't Stop		
Me From Dreaming	Roul 4037	1958
Let's Be Lovers /		
Give Me Another Chance	Roul 4056	1958
Don't Go Home /		
Can't Get It Through Your Head	Roul 4072	1958
While The Record Goes Around /		
The Day I Died	Roul 4100	1958
Your Love / Beep Beep	Roul 4115	1958
Star Love / The Thing-A-Ma-Jig	Roul 4136	1959
What Is Love / I Am	Roul 4160	1959
First Love / A Ciu-E	Roul 4200	1959
On The Beach /		
Song Everybody's Singing	Roul 4211	1959
Second Chance /		
These Things I Offer You	Roul 4227	1960
Our Wedding Day /		
Parade Of Pretty Girls	Roul 4252	1960
Eyes Of An Angel / Wait For Me	Roul 4276	1960
Real Life / Little Miss Stuck-Up	Roul 4322	1961

A SIDE/B SIDE	LABEL/CAT NO	DATE
Tell Me What She Said /		
Cowboys Never Cry	Roul 4370	1961
One Little Kiss / Wimoweh	Roul 4393	1961
Bachelor Flat / A Rose And A Star	Roul 4417	1962
The Cop On The Beat / Keep		
Your Hands In Your Pockets	Roul 4432	1962
Petticoats Fly /		
What A Funny Way To Show It	Roul 4464	1963
Just A Little Bit / My Name Is Alice	ABC 10422	1963
But Not Through Tears /		
She Never Looked Better	ABC 10468	1963
I'll Never Get Over You /		
I Cross My Fingers	ABC 10492	1963
Guy Behind The Wheel /		
Only Guy Left On The Corner	ABC 10522	1964
Piece Of The Sky /		
Fiddler On The Roof	Colpix 760	1964
One By One The Roses Died /		
Spanish Perfume	Colpix 769	1965
Ballad Of Stanley The Lifeguard /		
Should I Ask Someone Else		
To Tell Her	Colpix 245	1965

The Poni-Tails

The wispy innocence of the Poni-Tails' harmony has been heard on oldies radio for over 30 years, thanks largely to one timely hit.

The threesome of Toni Cistone on lead, LaVerne Novak on the top, and Karen Topinka on the bottom were students at Brush High School in Lyndhurst, Ohio, near Cleveland, when they started harmonizing in 1956. They performed at school functions and benefits, and it was at one such show that they were spotted by an attorney, John Jewitt, who gave them an introduction to music publisher Tom Illius. Tom liked the soft style of the trio and their original song "Que La Bozena." He took them to the local Point label, who issued their first single "Your Wild Heart" b/w "Que La Bozena" in January 1957. Unfortunately, even innocent white girls were subject to being covered: "Your Wild Heart" became a hit for Mercury artist Joy Lane (#20) while the version by the Poni-Tails (named for the hairstyle they wore at the time) became an instant collectible.

With Illius managing the group, they had one more single on the Marc label, "Can I Be Sure" in 1958.

Karen's father put his foot down and it landed on her career with the Poni-Tails. Tony and LaVerne held auditions for a replacement and came up with former Regina High student Patti McCabe.

Now they had the first names of two-thirds of THE ANDREWS SISTERS (Patti and LaVerne), a nice sound, and no record deal.

Illius fixed that by getting ABC Records' Don Costa interested in the group. ABC released "It's Just My Luck to Be 15" by the end of 1957 and it disappeared quickly.

With a similar theme, the Fred Tobias/Charles Strouse composition "Born Too Late" made the Poni-Tails a part of rock and roll history. It reached number seven on *Billboard*'s Top 100 and number five in England. The group might still be anonymous, however, if ABC had had its way. They were promoting the flip, "Come on Joey, Dance with Me." When several Cleveland disc jockeys pushed "Born Too Late" instead, the record took off.

The three gals were the model of what parents of the '50s called "the safe look," and their appearances on shows like Dick Clark's "American Bandstand" further fostered that image.

Their next single, "Seven Minutes to Heaven," reached only number 87 in December 1958, and they had their last charter, "I'll Be Seeing You," in late fall of 1959.

Still, ABC wanted to renew the girls' contract for another five years in 1960, but the Poni-Tails unanimously agreed to call it a career and settle into family life.

Their last 45 was "Who, When and Why" in 1960.

The girls turned in their ponytails for husbands. In 1991 LaVerne (Novak) Glivic was working for a real estate agent in Menor, Ohio, and had five grandchildren. Toni (Cistone) Costabile was working at a high school in Shaker Heights, Ohio. Patti (McCabe) Barnes died in January 1989 of cancer. Tom Illius went on to become a top executive with the William Morris Agency in Los Angeles.

The Prisonaires

One of the most unusual of vocal group stories, this one is made all the more poignant by the extremes of sadness and momentary success that permeated the group members' lives.

The Prisonaires were formed at the Tennessee State Penitentiary in 1940 by Ed Thurman. They were encouraged by Warden James E. Edwards.

By 1943, when Johnny Bragg was incarcerated, the quintet consisted of Bragg on lead, John Drue as first tenor, Ed Thurman as second tenor, William Stewart singing baritone and playing guitar, and Marcell Sanders rounding out the quintet on bass. Bragg, who was blind until age seven, was reportedly jailed at the age of 11 for rape and given 99 years, which meant no hope of parole. For a black man in 1940s Tennessee, rape could have meant anything from a casual relationship with a white girl to an actual rape, but whatever the circumstances the sentence was stiff. Most of the other Prisonaires (who were all black) were serving 99-year sentences for crimes ranging from a 14-year-old committing armed robbery to a member killing someone who killed his dog.

The talented quintet was influenced by a cross-section of performers from Louis Jordan and Muddy Waters to THE INK SPOTS and Perry Como. Their repertoire included blues, hillbilly, spiritual, and pop songs. Warden Edwards arranged for the group to perform at various civic functions (under armed guard, of course) as part of the state's rehabilitation program, and then he contacted Jim Bullett and Red Wortham, talent scouts for Sam Phillips and his soon-to-be-legendary Sun Records of Memphis.

During the long hours of incarceration with little to do, Bragg would sing in his cell and write songs incessantly, often putting a bucket over his head so he wouldn't bother other prisoners. One song was entitled "Just Walkin' in the Rain," which he collaborated on with inmate Robert Riley. Warden Edwards and Governor Frank Clement agreed to let the group record for Sun and authorized the trip on June 1, 1953. 10 years after Bragg had taken up residence in the Nashville penitentiary, the Prisonaires were driven to Memphis and recorded for Sun at their 706 Union Avenue address.

"Just Walkin' in the Rain," with only a soft and simple guitar accompaniment, was issued by July, and WSOK Nashville was the first station to start the musical landslide. The record took off, selling over a quarter of a million copies, nowhere near what it might have sold had Columbia artist Johnny Ray not covered it, selling over two million copies himself. Despite that, the Prisonaires became unique celebrities and performed at schools, radio stations, other prisons, on TV shows (in suits and ties), and other functions. In less than a year they left the prison grounds 75 times to perform, driving in a car purchased for their use by the Deputy Warden. Legend has it that their armed guard contingent was reduced to one since the inmates never tried any kind of escape. On one occasion they had more trouble getting back in than getting out. After a particular performance, the audience was so enthusiastic they tried to get the boys away from their guard; the group and its "security" became separated so the guys just returned to the prison.

For their second single, Sam Phillips brought the recording equipment right to the prison and on August 3, 1953, recorded "My God Is Real" and "Softly and Tenderly."

"My God Is Real," a departure from their first gospel-tinged single, sold well but not close to the figures of "Walkin'."

A third single, "I Know" b/w "A Prisoner's Prayer," was cut at Sun's studios in Memphis, and a young unknown singer dropped by to hear them only to be chased out of the studio by Phillips. He came back at their lunch break to chat since "Just Walkin' in the Rain" was one of his favorite songs. The singer was a newcomer named Elvis Presley. He visited the group in prison and asked Bragg if there was anything he could do for him. Bragg, whose pride overruled his needs, said he was fine, but Elvis made sure to have the group appear on a show with him.

After the third single, several members of the group were paroled, so Bragg formed a new Prisonaires renamed the Sunbeams that included Hal Hebb (brother of Bobby Hebb, "Sunny," #2 Pop, #3 R&B, 1966), Al Brooks, Willy Wilson, and Henry "Dishrag" Jones.

Meanwhile, in July 1954, Sun issued the last Prisonaires single "There Is Love In You," which *Billboard* described as a "pretty ballad sung skillfully, sparked by a baritone lead. This is one of the group's best to date."

In 1955 the Sunbeams became the Marigolds and recorded in Nashville for Excello Records.

The Excello-released "Rollin' Stone" became a number eight R&B hit while the group was still based in the Tennessee penitentiary.

Three more singles failed to chart and by 1956 Bragg was released, ending the Prisonaires/Marigolds story.

In the '70s Charly Records of England put together a superb collection of the Prisonaires' Sun recordings. Its 16 tracks included a great, previously unreleased version of Louis Jordan's "That Chick's Too Young to Fry" (and they were not talking about Colonel Sanders) and most of their Sun singles.

Bragg recorded a few R&B singles for Decca in 1959–60 and then was unjustly reincarcerated for parole violations when he was arrested for being in the back seat of a car with a white girl, who happened to be his wife. He spent six and a half years in prison on that charge. While in, he started a third Prisonaires, an integrated group that Bragg felt deserved to record. The members other than Bragg were Sullivan Hayes, Jimmy Doyle, Clarence McHeel, and Acie Horton. In 1967 Bragg was again free and recorded two singles for ElBe-Jay. In the '70s, Johnny Bragg was working at a cemetery. The Prisonaires were never again to record, but at least they were free.

THE PRISONAIRES

A SIDE/B SIDE	LABEL/CAT NO	DATE
Baby Please /		
Just Walkin' In The Rain	Sun 186	7/53
My God Is Real /		
Softly And Tenderly	Sun 189	9/53
I Know /		
A Prisoner's Prayer	Sun 191	11/53
There Is Love In You /		
What Do You Do Next	Sun 207	7/54
The Marigolds		
Rollin' Stone /		
Why Don't You	Exelo 2057	1955
Two Strangers /		
Love You, Love You, Love You	Exelo 2061	1955
Johnny Bragg and the Marigolds		
Foolish Me /		
Beyond The Clouds	Exelo 2078	1956
Juke Box Rock 'n' Roll /		
It's You Darling, It's You	Exelo 2091	1956

The Quin-Tones

Across between THE BOBBETTES and THE CHANTELS, the Quin-Tones created one of rock's most enduring "drags" (rock-a-ballads), "Down the Aisle of Love." The York, Pennsylvania, quintet consisted of lead Roberta Haymon, Carolyn "Cissy" Holmes, Jeannie Crist, Phyllis Carr, and Kenny Sexton, although photos of the group show six people, with the second male being piano player/arranger Ronnie Scott.

The 16- and 17-year-olds were all students at William Penn Senior High School when they started to develop their angelic-sounding style. Originally calling themselves the Quinteros, the group played the usual round of teen dances in their formation year of 1957. They came in contact with a Harrisburg disc jockey, Paul Landersman of WHGB, who promoted dances. When he saw them perform he was sufficiently impressed to become their manager. He made the boast that if they stayed with him, they'd be on "American Bandstand" within a year.

In February 1958 the group, now called the Quin-Tones, recorded several sides at Philadelphia's Reco-Art Studios. Landersman arranged for their first single, "Ding Dong," to be issued on Chess Records, but the song was a dead issue by the spring.

Their next session contained "Down the Aisle of Love," a song that the group had written performing on the road. Landersman thought it was so terrific that he arranged a new release deal with Irv Nathan and Marvin "Red Top" Schwartz's Red Top label of Philadelphia.

Opening with an organ interpretation of "Here Comes the Bride," the classic beat ballad took off on radio. It was soon licensed to the larger Hunt label since Red Top couldn't keep up with the demand. "Down the Aisle," complete with wedding vows, charted Pop on August 18, 1958, and reached number 18 only 10 months after the Quin-Tones met their manager.

Not surprising for the times, the group never received any royalties even though the record reportedly sold close to a million copies.

On August 28, 1958, the high point of the Quin-Tones' performing career came with an appearance alongside the Chantels as well as THE SPANIELS, THE COASTERS, and THE OLYMPICS at New York's Apollo Theatre.

"There'll Be No Sorrow," another group-penned ballad, failed, and so did their remake of Edna McGriff's 1952 single (#4 R&B) "Heavenly Father."

With the long pervasive (but shortsighted) record industry attitude that you're only as good as your last hit, the Quin-Tones found themselves with no one to record them.

In 1960 Roberta married and the group disbanded. The guys, Kenny and Ronnie, joined the service, with Ron then moving to Arkansas and Kenny to San Diego.

In 1986, the group reunited and began performing again, with Roberta, Carolyn, Jeannie, and Phyllis's brother Vince and Rob Webb. Today, Carolyn Holmes is a receptionist, Phyllis Carr is a case worker for the Department of Public Welfare, Jeannie Crist is active in the church, and Roberta Haymon works in a Harrisburg, Pennsylvania, hospital.

THE QUIN-TONES

A SIDE/B SIDE	LABEL/CAT NO	DATE
Ding Dong / I Try So Hard	Chess 1685	1958
Down The Aisle Of Love / Please Dear	Hunt 321	1958
There'll Be No Sorrow / What Am I To Do	Hunt 322	9/58
Down The Aisle Of Love / Please Dear	Red Top 108	6/58
Oh, Heavenly Father / I Watch The Stars	Red Top 116	1959

The Rainbows

An R&B teen group that gave the world more than its share of solo stars, the Rainbows were a quartet, quintet, sextet, and sometimes even more.

Formed during the early '50s in Washington, D.C., a hotbed of rhythm and blues activity going on at the time, the original members of the group were John Berry (lead and second tenor), Henry "Shorty" Womble (first tenor), Ronald "Poosie" Miles (lead and first tenor), James "Sally" Nolan (baritone), and Frank "Jake" Hardy (bass). The Rainbows' early influences included THE MIDNIGHTERS, THE TURBANS, and THE CADILLACS. Henry and Frank had sung with the Serenaders, who had recorded demos in 1952 that were issued on Roadhouse Records in 1974. They also became the Five Vultures on Roadhouse, who released "Soldier in Korea" as a single in 1953.

In 1954 the group went to New York to audition for Bobby Robinson's Red Robin label, but he felt they were too ragged and inexperienced. With egos deflated they returned to Washington to polish their sound and went back to New York a year later. This time Robinson signed them.

Their first single, the rousing "Mary Lee," came out in June 1955. The title came from one of the member's girlfriends Marion Lee, who was reportedly the only girl allowed at rehearsals. Popular in the Baltimore, Washington, New York, and Philadelphia areas, "Mary Lee" was licensed to Pilgrim Records of Boston, which finally had it reviewed in the March 10, 1956, issue of *Billboard*: "There is a trace of West Indian and also of gospel flavor in this effectively rendered rhythm and blues chant. Good disc that could take off if it gets circulated enough." It apparently wasn't circulated enough to make the national charts.

Soon after, Henry went off to school and Berry's friends Don Covay and Chester Simmons joined. Billy Stewart and Marvin Gaye also sang with the group in 1956, although it's not certain they sang on any of the group's recordings. The then sextet was Berry, Miles, Covay, Simmons, Stewart, and Gaye.

The group's manager, Jay Perry, apparently made a deal directly with Pilgrim after "Mary Lee," so the group recorded "Shirley" in New York for a June 1956 release. "Shirley" was a lot like "Mary Lee" but much improved, and is the best remembered of their three singles. After the short life of "Shirley" they did "Minnie," another rocker for Rama. The ballad B side "They Say" is considered their best-sung group effort.

By early 1957, the Rainbows were not making money and split up. Nolan (of "Mary Lee") and Simmons (of "Shirley") joined with Gaye and Reese Palmer to form the Marquees. They were discovered by Bo Diddley and brought to Okeh Records for one great 1957 rocker, "Hey Little Schoolgirl," that never saw extensive radio exposure.

The Marquees then met Harvey Fuqua and became the new MOONGLOWS.

Miles formed a new Rainbows in 1961 consisting of Joe Walls (tenor), Duval Potter (tenor), Layton McDonald (baritone), Victor English (bass), and Miles on lead. They recorded "I Know" with Potter on lead for the Dave label and "It Wouldn't Be Right" with Miles leading, both in 1963.

By 1965 Donald Watts had replaced Walter McDonald. Chester Simmons became a talent coordinator for a Charlotte, North Carolina, recording studio, Reflection Sound, and then joined Reese's '70s group Choice of Color. Henry Womble went to work with the Department of Human Resources along with John Berry. James Nolan went to live in Louisville, Kentucky, and Frank Hardy became a truck driver. Billy Stewart (who was influenced by THE HEARTBEATS' lead James Sheppard) went on to be one of the finest soul talents of the '60s, signing with Chess and turning out doo wop soul like "I Do Love You" (#26 Pop, #6 R&B, 1965), "Sittin' in the Park" (#24 Pop, #4 R&B, 1965), and "Summertime" (#10 Pop, #7 R&B, 1966). He died in a car crash on January 17, 1970. Don "Pretty Boy" Covay, who recorded solo under that name in mid-1956 for Atlantic while still with the Rainbows, went on to become a premier writer/singer. He wrote "Letter Full of Tears" for Gladys Knight and the Pips, "Pony Time" for Chubby Checker, and "Chain of Fools" for Aretha Franklin, and many others. The Little Richard-influenced Covay had several hits of his own including "Mercy" (#35, 1964), "Seesaw" (#44 Pop, #5 R&B, 1965), and "I Was Checkin' Out, She Was Checkin' In" (#6 R&B). Marvin Gaye left the Moonglows with Harvey Fuqua to start an illustrious career as one of soul music's greats with 62 R&B charters between 1962 and 1985. Among them were "Pride and Joy" (#10 Pop, #2 R&B, 1963), "How Sweet It Is" (#6 Pop, #4 R&B, 1965), "Ain't That Peculiar" (#8 Pop, #1 R&B, 1965), "I Heard It Through the Grapevine" (#1 Pop and R&B, 1968), "What's Goin' On" (#2 Pop, #1 R&B, 1971), and "Sexual Healing" (#3 Pop, #1 R&B, 1982).

The Rays

The Rays were probably the music business's most fortunate beneficiaries of the effects of a subliminal message.

The group formed after the breakup of another R&B group from the mid-1950s, THE FOUR FELLOWS ("Soldier Boy," #4 R&B, 1955). Second tenor Davey Jones left that group in late 1955 and joined up with metal worker and lead singer Hal Miller, formerly of the Four Toppers (a forerunner of the Four Fellows), first tenor Walter Ford, and baritone Harry James to form a group named the Rays by their vocal arranger, Jimmy Duggan.

The Brooklyn, New York-based quartet immediately fell in with writers-producers Bob Crewe and Frank Slay, and recorded and released a single for Chess in January 1956 called "Tippity Top," a big-band styled pop-jazz rocker.

Most accounts of the group being discovered by Slay and Crewe have them auditioning in mid- to late 1957 at Philadelphia's Cameo Records, where Slay had an office as an employee of Cameo but also had his own XYZ record label with Crewe (the term "conflict of interest" hadn't yet come into vogue). When the group was passed on by Cameo and left the building, the story goes, Slay ran outside asking if they'd like to record for his XYZ label and they said yes. He was supposedly so excited because he and Crewe had written a great song called "Silhouettes" that he felt the group was perfect for. The problem with this version of the story is that if the Rays met Slay and subsequently Crewe in mid- to late 1957, how does one explain the fact that Slay and Crewe wrote both sides of the group's first single almost two years earlier on Chess Records? (And if Slay was so excited about the Rays recording "Silhouettes," why did he and Crewe not issue it right away? They saved it for the Rays' second single on XYZ, the first being "My Steady Girl"—unless the record numbers were out of order.)

In 1957 Chess issued a second Rays single, "Second Fiddle," and reissued it on Argo the same year. After XYZ issued "Silhouettes," Crewe ran a copy to Philadelphia's most successful disc jockey, Hy Lit of WFIL, who took the record home with a bunch of others to listen to. He put it on top of the stack on his turntable and fell asleep as they played. "Silhouettes," the last record, played over and over until he awoke and shut off the machine. The subliminal effect had already registered. The next day, with the melody running through his head though he didn't know why, he chose to play it on his show. The switchboard lit up and the record took off. Ironically, Cameo got involved anyway and picked up distribution on the hot-selling single. It eventually reached number three on both the Pop and R&B charts. If THE DIAMONDS hadn't covered it (#10 Pop), it might have been the biggest record of the year.

Cameo issued two more Rays records and XYZ issued three more: another Slay/Crewe composition called "Mediterranean Moon" barely charted (#95 Pop) in January 1960; it was followed by "Magic Moon (Clair de Lune)" (#49, 1961).

Crewe recorded the group on his Topix and Perri labels in 1961 and 1962, respectively, but the public passed on their post-"Magic" works. The group worked on into the '80s with varying personnel, though Hal remained as lead.

THE RAYS

A SIDE/B SIDE	LABEL/CAT NO	DATE
Tippity Top / Moo-Goo-Gai-Pan	Chess 1613	1955
How Long Must I Wait / Second Fiddle	Chess 1678	1957
Second Fiddle / How Long Must I Wait	Argo 1074	1957
My Steady Girl / Nobody Loves You Like I Do	XYZ 100	1957
Silhouettes / Daddy Cool	XYZ 102	1957
Silhouettes / Daddy Cool	Cameo 117	1957
Crazy Girl / Dressin' Up	Cameo 127	1958
Triangle / Rendezvous	Cameo 128	1958
Rags To Riches / The Man Above	Cameo 133	1958
Souvenirs Of Summertime / Elevator Operator	XYZ 2001	1958
Why Do You Look The Other Way / Zimba Lulu	XYZ 600	1959
It's A Cryin' Shame / Mediterranean Moon	XYZ 605	1959
Magic Moon / Louis Hoo Hoo	XYZ 607	1960
Silver Starlight / Old Devil Moon	XYZ 608	1960

A SIDE/B SIDE	LABEL/CAT NO	DATE
Hal Miller and the Rays		
An Angel Cried / Hope, Faith, And Dreams	Topix 6003	1961
Are You Happy Now / Bright Brown Eyes	Perri 1004	1962

The Rivieras

An excellent harmony group that made its short-lived contribution to music via standards, the Rivieras were a late-'50s pop R&B quartet with a sound that fit somewhere between THE SPANIELS and THE PLATTERS.

Homer Dunn (lead), Andy Jones, Ronald Cook, and Charles Allen joined forces in 1957 to take a serious stab at stardom. Dunn had sung with a recording group before named the Bob-O-Links (Okeh, 1953).

One evening they were performing at a closed party in their home base of Englewood, New Jersey. The foursome were seen by the manager of THE AVONS (Hull), who thought they had a Broadway style and recommended the unnamed group call themselves the Four Arts. They worked clubs and dances for almost two years under that name until they met talent scout Warren Lanier, who took the group on for management and changed their name to the El Rivieras.

But the El Rivieras themselves made the contact leading to their recording career. Actually it was Andy Jones who, needing extra money, went out to shovel snow from in front of some houses one winter day in early 1958. One property owner was nice enough to offer him a hot cup of coffee, and while Andy stood in the hallway drinking, he began singing to himself. Commenting on his voice, the homeowner asked if Andy was a professional. After listening to the young man's El Rivieras story he introduced himself. He was William Fix, manager of THE AMES BROTHERS.

Sometime later, Fix invited the whole group over to audition and, liking their warm pop-flavored R&B style, took them to New York's George Paxton, publisher and owner of Coed Records. They sang the oldie "Count Every Star" and Paxton signed them to a three-year contract. "Count" was their first single, issued in June.

On August 25, 1958, it reached number 73 on *Billboard*'s Top 100. Their performance calendar suddenly and predictably filled up, including shows from the Top Club in Boston to the Regal Theatre in Chicago.

Continuing to sing standards, they next cut the Glenn Miller-Mitchell Parish hit (#3, 1939) "Moonlight Serenade." *Billboard*'s January 24th, 1959 reviewer liked both sides, first calling "Neither Rain Nor Shine" "a pretty rock-a-ballad, stylishly rendered. Flip is a ballad-with-a-beat sing of the Glenn Miller theme that also provides excellent listening. Either can make it for pop and R&B loot."

On February 9th "Moonlight" stepped out front and became their biggest record, reaching number 47 and hanging around for 11 weeks.

Five more solid singles followed, but only "Since I Made You Cry" (#93, 1960) charted, leaving such stalwart performances as "Moonlight Cocktails," "Our Love," and "Easy To Remember" to go unnoticed.

By 1961 Coed was going under; the Rivieras, lacking enough survivability to surface anywhere else, disappeared into rock's pages of history.

THE RIVIERAS

A SIDE/B SIDE	LABEL/CAT NO	DATE
Count Every Star /		
True Love Is Hard To Find	Coed 503	1958
Moonlight Serenade /		
Neither Rain Nor Snow	Coed 508	1958
Our Love / True Love		
Is Hard To Find	Coed 513	1959
Our Love / Midnight Flyer	Coed 513	1959
11th Hour Melody /		
Since I Made You Cry	Coed 522	1959
Moonlight Cocktails /		
Blessing Of Love	Coed 529	1960
Great Big Eyes / My Friend	Coed 538	1960
Easy To Remember /		
Stay In My Heart	Coed 542	1960

The Robins

One of the earliest of West Coast R&B groups, the Robins were the forerunners (and roots) of THE COASTERS. They formed in 1947 in San Francisco and featured smooth harmony often contrasted with a bass lead.

The original trio was Ty Terrell (tenor), Billy and Roy Richards (bass and baritone). They moved to Los Angeles in 1949 under the name the A Sharp Trio and began playing at Johnny Otis's Barrelhouse Club. He helped them develop by adding bass Bobby Nunn to their lineup.

Otis first called them the Four Bluebirds. By the time they first recorded for the Aladdin label in 1949 they had changed their name to the Robins.

Their first single, "Don't Like the Way You're Doin'," was reviewed by *Billboard* in September with the comment, "The Robins aren't the Ravens though they give it a try." By the end of the year they were on Savoy and clicking with "If It's So, Baby" (#10 R&B). That recording made them one of the first West Coast R&B acts to make the top ten.

In April 1950 *Billboard* said of their new single, "There Ain't No Use Beggin'," "Ballad with catchy figure is handled in Ink Spots style." Though the Robins were strongly influenced by the Ravens, they at one point influenced their idols, if only instrumentally, as the Robins used vibes on a couple of sides and soon after so did the Ravens.

In 1951 they moved to Recorded In Hollywood and moonlighted on RPM as the Nic Nacs. Also in 1951, during a short stint with Modern Records, they recorded "That's What the Good Book Says," the first recorded Leiber and Stoller song.

In December 1951 one of their older Aladdin sides, "Round About Midnight" surfaced on its Score subsidiary.

In 1953 they moved again, this time to RCA, and their style became a more polished R&B sound though they still laid into those blues tales of trouble like "Ten Days in Jail" and "Empty Bottles."

In 1954 they recorded for their ninth label in six years, the newly formed Spark Records owned by songwriters Jerry Leiber and Mike Stoller. By now the Robins were a sextet with additional members Carl Gardner and Grady Chapman.

Their first single on that label was a bass-led talk/singing story of prison life. Leiber and Stoller felt that Nunn's base wasn't threatening enough to handle their hardcore song so they substituted Richard Berry (later of "Louis Louis" fame).

A June 1956 review in *Billboard* commented about "Riot in Cellblock Number Nine," "A new group, a new label, a song with a bright set of lyrics and a good performance by the Robins make this a strong new release." Though not a national hit it sold over 90,000 copies, mostly in Los Angeles. Berry then went over to Modern Records for his own rewritten version called "The Big Break"; then Bobby Nunn copied Berry's narrative nuances for the Robins' follow-up, "Framed." The classic tongue-in-cheek R&B number was the tablesetter for all "legalese" tunes to follow, like Herb and

Lou's "The Trial" and "Here Comes the Judge" (the Magistrates).

In August 1955 the Robins issued "Smokey Joe's Cafe," their last and most notorious record on Spark.

Around this same time Leiber and Stoller sold Spark to Atlantic's Atco label; "Smokey Joe" wound up on this label, and Atco's added clout brought the record to number 79 Pop and number 10 R&B at the end of 1955.

The Robins' consensus, however, was to pass on joining the new East Coast label (Leiber and Stoller were moving to New York). Leonard, Chapman, the Richards brothers, and new member H. B. Barnum (THE DOOTONES) moved to the Whippet label owned by Los Angeles TV personality Gene Norman. Gardner and Nunn, meanwhile, joined with Billy Guy and Leon Hughes to work with Leiber and Stoller as the Coasters.

The Robins became more of a pop group, doing seven singles from 1956 through 1958 for Whippet, the most successful being "Out of the Picture." They recorded through 1961 for the Knight, Arvee, and Gone labels without any success and finally disbanded. Grady Chapman, who chose to stay with the Robins in 1957 rather than join the Coasters, wound up singing lead for a Coasters group in the 1980s.

THE ROBINS

A SIDE/B SIDE	LABEL/CAT NO	DATE
Don't Like The Way You're Doing /		
Come Back Baby	Aldn 3031	9/49
If I Didn't Love You So /		
If It's So Baby	Savoy 726	12/49
I'm Not Falling In Love With You	Regent 1016	1950
Turkey Hop Part I /		
Turkey Hop Part II	Savoy 732	1950
Our Romance Is Gone /		
There Ain't No Use Beggin'	Savoy 738	1950
I'm Living O.K. /		
There's Rain In My Eyes	Savoy 752	1950
I'm Through /		
You're Fine But Not My Mind	Savoy 762	1950
Race Of Man / Bayou Baby Blues	RIH 112	1951
A Falling Star /		
When Gabriel Blows His Horn	RIH 121	1951
School Girl Blues /		
Early Morning Blues	RIH 150	1951
Round About Midnight /		
You Sure Look Good To Me	Score 4010	12/51
A Food Such As I /		
My Heart's The Biggest Fool	RCA 47-5175	2/53
All Night Baby / Oh Why	RCA 47-5271	4/53

A SIDE/B SIDE	LABEL/CAT NO	DATE
Let's Go To The Dance /		
How Would You Know	RCA 47-5434	8/53
My Baby Done Told Me / I'll Do It	RCA 47-5486	10/53
Ten Days In Jail / Empty Bottles	RCA 47-5489	10/53
Don't Stop Now /		
Get It Off Your Mind	RCA 47-5564	12/53
I Made A Vow /		
Double Crossin' Baby	Crown 106	2/54
Riot In Cell Block #9 / Wrap It Up	Spark 103	6/54
Framed / Loop De Loop Mambo	Spark 107	10/54
If Teardrops Were Kisses /		
Whadaya Want	Spark 110	2/55
One Kiss / I Love Paris	Spark 113	1955
I Must Be Dreamin' /		
The Hatchet Man	Spark 116	6/55
Smokey Joe's Cafe /		
Cherry Lips	Spark 122	8/55
Smokey Joe's Cafe /		
Just Like A Fool	Atco 6059	10/55
Out Of The Picture / Cherry Lips	Whpt 200	3/56
Hurt Me / Merry-Go-Rock	Whpt 201	6/56
Since I First Met You /		
That Old Black Magic	Whpt 203	1956
A Fool In Love / All Of A		
Sudden My Heart Sings	Whpt 206	1957
Every Night / Where's The Fire	Whpt 208	1957
In My Dreams /		
Keep Your Mind On Me	Whpt 211	1957
Snowball / You Wanted Fun	Whpt 212	1958
A Quarter To Twelve /		
Pretty Little Doll	Knight 2001	1958
Little Bird Told Me /		
It's Never Too Late	Knight 2008	1958
Just Like That /		
Whole Lot of Imagination	Arvee 5001	1960
Live Wire Suzie / Oh No	Arvee 5013	12/60
Baby Love / We Loved	Gone 5101	1961

The Rocketones

Many groups have been considered one-hit wonders. The Rocketones were one-*record* wonders. That record, "Mexico," became an East Coast legend among doo wop lovers.

Starting at Junior High School 178 in Brooklyn, Allen Days (first tenor), Ronald Johnson (second tenor), Harold Chapman (baritone), and Arthur Blackman (bass) originally called themselves the Avalons.

In 1955 Bill Witt, another Brooklyn teen, came aboard as lead singer, and the group commandeered the corners of Saratoga Avenue and Dean Street for their rehearsals. This same neighborhood gave birth to other recording groups like THE SHELLS (Johnson), THE VELOURS (Onyx), the Tokens (the black group on Gary), the Continentals (Rama), and the Fantastics (RCA).

In 1956, armed with several Bill Witt-written songs, they trudged to Manhattan and visited several labels, finally soliciting some interest from Morty Craft's Melba records. Bill wrote "Mexico" as a change of pace from all the love songs of the time. The flip, "Dee I," was written for his girlfriend Delores and titled after her nickname.

The record took six months to come out, and when it did the group barely recognized it. First of all, Craft had changed their name to the Rocketones; the first the Avalons learned of it was when they saw the record label. Second, the intro was a fully orchestrated bull fight theme; it came to an abrupt stop and was followed by Arthur Blackman's "bo bo bo bo" bass and two minutes and 45 seconds of street-corner rock and roll. New York radio (especially Jocko and Dr. Jive) played it heavily and it sold well in the tri-state area. Immersed in other projects, Craft never issued another Rocketones single.

By 1958 Allen Days had been drafted; Ron Johnson had followed by 1959. Bill took the opportunity to join THE PARAGONS, replacing Julius McMichaels (who had gone west to join THE OLYMPICS). The Rocketones' brief career was over.

Bill sang lead on the Paragons' classic "So You Will Know" and then moved to Herald with the Townsmen in 1963 ("Is It All Over").

In the mid-'70s Bill went back to the Paragons to perform on the revival circuit, and he was lead singer of the group as recently as 1991.

The Sensations

The Sensations were a quartet out of Philadelphia that originally called themselves the Cavaliers. Formed in 1954, they were one of the first of the rock and roll era groups with an all-male background and a female lead. That lead, Yvonne Mills, had a sweet-but-strong tone quality that made her immediately identifiable. The foursome had only been together a short time when she, tenor Tommy Wicks, bass Alphonso Howell, and one other long-since-forgotten member signed with Atco Records in 1955. Considering the group's sound something of a sensation, Atco execs renamed the group just that.

The old Gene Austin 1925 number one standard "Yes Sir, That's My Baby," done in a style similar to that of THE CLOVERS' 1950 Rainbow release, was their first single, released in November 1955. It charted number 15 R&B on February 18, 1956. The group picked up some worthwhile bookings from the exposure of "Yes Sir," including a November 17, 1955 show at Town Hall in Philadelphia with Ray Charles.

Billboard reviewed the follow-up, "Ain't She Sweet" on April 14, 1956, saying: "Yvonne Mills handles the evergreen in a tasteful jazz style that was so appealing in the last effort by the group. Many will like listening to this effort in both Pop and R&B markets." Of the flip, "Please Mr. Disc Jockey," the reviewer wrote, "Tailormade bittersweet ballad about love messages delivered by platter spinners. It's also sung sweetly, the backing tasteful and appropriate. This too could move." It charted number 13 R&B in May and remained a staple of oldies radio stations for decades.

Their next four singles made little noise. The group then disbanded as Yvonne became Mrs. Yvonne Baker and started raising a family.

In 1961 Alphonso, feeling that vocal groups were once again in demand, convinced Yvonne to re-form the Sensations. Tenor Richard Curtain (the Hideaways, MGM) and baritone Sam Armstrong were added, and the group convinced local Philadelphia disc jockey Kae Williams (who had managed THE SILHOUETTES of "Get a Job" fame) to handle them. He arranged a record deal with Chess's Argo affiliate, and by the summer of 1961 the jazz-tinged rock and roll recording of Teresa Brewer's 1950 number one hit "Music, Music, Music," complete with walking bass and rockin' sax solo, had reached number 54 (#12 R&B). It was The Sensations' first R&B charter in five years and their first Pop hit ever.

In the winter of 1961 a Yvonne Baker-penned fast and bouncy slice of fun came out titled "Let Me In." Once again radio loved Yvonne as she pleaded to be let in the party where all the fun was. The catchy "wee-oop-oop-we-ou" harmony helped to make "Let Me In" their biggest hit, rising to number four (#2 R&B) in early 1962.

As happens so often after finally having major success, the group couldn't seem to *buy* a hit to sustain their chart momentum. A slow jazzy version of "That's My Desire" (THE CHANNELS, 1957, Gone) made it to number 69 in 1962, and there were two additional Argo releases along with several on Kae Williams's own Junior label. But nothing could bring the group back.

THE SENSATIONS

A SIDE/B SIDE	LABEL/CAT NO	DATE
Sympathy /		
Yes Sir, That's My Baby	Atco 6056	11/55
Ain't He Sweet* /		
Please Mr. Disc Jockey*	Atco 6067	3/56
Cry Baby Cry /		
My Heart Cries For You	Atco 6075	7/56
Little Wallflower* / Such A Love*	Atco 6083	11/56
My Debut To Love* /		
You Made Me Love You*	Atco 6090	4/57
Romance In The Dark* /		
Kiddy Car Love*	Atco 6115	1958
Music, Music, Music /		
A Part Of Me	Argo 5391	7/61
Let Me In / Oh Yes, I'll Be True	Argo 5405	11/61
That's My Desire** / Eyes**	Argo 5412	3/62
Party Across The Hall** /		
No Changes**	Argo 5420	8/62
You Made A Fool Out Of Me /		
That's What You've Gotta Do	Junior 986	1962
We Were Meant To Be /		
It's Good Enough	Junior 1002	1962
That's What You've Gotta Do /		
You Made A Fool Out Of Me	Junior 1005	1/63
Baby	Junior 1006	1963
When My Lover Comes Home** /		
Father Dear**	Argo 5446	1963
We Were Meant To Be /		
It's Good Enough For Me	Junior 1021	1964
You Made A Fool Out Of Me /		
That's What You've Gotta Do	Tollie 9009	1964

* Yvonne Mills and the Sensations
**Yvonne Baker and the Sensations

The Shells

In one of the more unusual success stories, the Shells owe their one-hit status to a pair of New York record collectors. The group formed in Brooklyn, New York, in the mid-'50s and consisted of Nathaniel Bouknight (lead), Bobby Nurse (first tenor), Randy Alston (second tenor), Gus Geter (baritone), and Danny Small (bass).

The Shells barely managed to attract attention at Hiram Johnson's Johnson Records. Not really excited by the group, Johnson gave them 20 minutes to record at the end of a session by THE DUBS, and with some coaching from that group, the Shells recorded "Baby Oh Baby" and "What Do You See in an Angel's Eyes."

"Baby Oh Baby" was issued by Johnson in August 1957 and managed some New York area play before dying out.

After one more single for Johnson ("Don't Say Goodbye"), Shells lead singer "Little Nat," as Bouknight was called, left. Nat came back in 1958 for a few sides with End Records, the best being the doo wop single called "Sippin' Soda." Roy Jones then took over the Shells' lead, and they did the Roulette one-shot "She Wasn't Meant for Me," which stiffed.

In late 1959 record collectors and high school students Donn Fileti and Wayne Stierle ventured beyond the usual hunt for records. They went hunting for out-of-print master recordings of vocal groups that stores like Slim Rose's Times Square Records considered hard to get and would pay to get copies of. The best way to get quantities of such recordings was to find the record label owners (usually small label proprietors) and convince them to press up a few hundred to a few thousand copies so Donn and Wayne could act as middlemen between the record label and the store.

One of their favorite doo wops was the little-known 1957 single "Baby Oh Baby," so in the beginning of 1960 the duo sought out Johnson Records, now run by Jim McCarthy. He was more than happy to press copies of the Shells' single for them. They sold it to Slim, who put it on Alan Frederick's "Night Train" show, of which the Times Square store was a sponsor. Soon New York's heavyweight disc jockeys like Bruce Morrow were playing it, and Alan Freed, who was now on the West Coast, began airing it when it took off.

On December 19, 1960, it charted on *Billboard*'s Top 100 and started climbing. The semi-retired Shells had to re-form quickly to get themselves ready. "Baby Oh Baby" reached number 21 in the nation.

Their follow-up single, "Explain It to Me," went nowhere, and two subsequent 45s fared no better.

Nat left after a spat about being featured on the label, and the group, with record-collector-turned-producer Stierle at the helm, recorded THE CRESTS' "Sweetest One." It received some pop AM radio attention while its flip, "Baby Walk on In," received some R&B play.

A few more singles went by unnoticed. Stierle talked the group into doing an a cappella LP in 1966 that included a number of their previous sides.

THE SHELLS

A SIDE/B SIDE	LABEL/CAT NO	DATE
Baby Oh Baby / Angel's Eyes	Johnson 104	8/57
Pleading No More /		
Don't Say Goodbye	Jnita 106	1958

A SIDE/B SIDE	LABEL/CAT NO	DATE
Pleading No More /		
Don't Say Goodbye	Johnson 106	1958
Sippin' Soda / Pretty Little Girl	End 1022	1958
Shooma Dom Dom /		
Whispering Wings	End 1050	1959
She Wasn't Meant For Me /		
The Thief	Roul 4156	1959
Baby Oh Baby /		
What In An Angel's Eyes	Johnson 104	11/60
Explain It To Me /		
An Island Unknown	Johnson 107	1961
Better Forget Him / Can't Take It	Johnson 109	4/61
O-Mi Yum-Mi Yum-Mi /		
In The Dim Light Of The Dark	Johnson 110	1961
Sweetest One / Baby, Walk On In	Johnson 112	9/61
Sippin' Soda / Pretty Little Girl	Gone 5103	1961
Deep In My Heart / Happy Holiday	Johnson 119	10/62
A Toast To Your Birthday /		
The Drive	Johnson 120	1963
On My Honor / My Royal Love	Johnson 127	1963
Our Wedding Day /		
Deep In My Heart	Josie 912	8/63

The Signatures

The Signatures were a very appealing jazz vocal group that, unlike most such ensembles, was instrumentally self-contained. They met at the Servicemen's Center in Seattle, Washington, in 1954 and originally included Cathi Hayes (lead), Ruth Alcivar (alto), Lee Humes (tenor), Jerry Hayes (baritone, Cathi's older brother), and Bob Alcivar (bass, later to be Ruth's husband).

The teenagers (they were all between 16 and 18) picked the name because they felt it sounded musical and classy. Their influences were THE HI-LOS, the Mel-Tones, THE FOUR FRESHMEN, and the Pastels of Stan Kenton's band. The group's practices were initially at Bob's home in Montlake Terrace in Seattle, where they rehearsed standards and originals that he arranged.

When local jazz disc jockey and promoter Norm Bobrow began organizing a big-band show for colleges, he opened the door for the group's career by having them front the band. Bob introduced the Signatures to a variety of jazz greats, including Stan Kenton, who in turn advised them to be self-contained.

The group soon became instrumentally proficient, with Cathi on vibes, Ruth on drums, Bob on piano, Les on bass, and Jerry playing guitar.

After a year on the jazz club circuit, Cathi and Jerry Hayes left and were replaced by Bunny Phillips (lead) and Hal Kratzsch (bass, mellophone, trumpet, and former member of the Four Freshmen).

In 1956 the group played a date at Jazz City in Hollywood on Hollywood Boulevard and met Four Freshmen manager Sid Garris, who introduced them to record exec Gene Norman. The Signatures had their first recording session in Los Angeles on the July 4th weekend of 1956 for Whippet Records. The session, held at Gene Norman's studio in the basement of the Pantages Theatre, was a baptism of fire: the air conditioning broke down, leaving the girls to steam (literally) over the boys' ability to work stripped to the waist. But the group did cut a hot album, and it turned out to be the only one in which they played their instruments.

By August, *The Signatures, Their Voices and Instruments* LP was on the market, selling several thousand copies, and they began playing jazz clubs in New York as arranged by new manager Sid Garris. Their first single, the easygoing ballad "Julie Is Her Name," was also released in August.

Their appearances at the Left Bank Club attracted Count Basie, who became a fan. On one occasion he brought down Roulette Records head Morris Levy to sign the group, but the quintet felt a loyalty to Stan Kenton, who was touting the new Warner Bros. label. In late 1958 the Signatures signed with the Bugs Bunny company; they recorded the LP *The Signatures Sign In* in November with George Avakian producing. Their only regret in singing with Warner's was knowing they would not get to record with Roulette artist Basie.

The January 1959 LP release signalled the start of their coast-to-coast jazz club circuit tours, through Chicago, Reno, Tahoe, Las Vegas, and New York. In the Big Apple they played the Village Vanguard, alternating shows with Dizzy Gillespie and Anita O'Day.

A group reorganization took place in January 1959 with Dottie Dunn taking over lead for Bunny and Don Purdy replacing Lee Humes. The first LP of this aggregation sold over 50,000 units, a good start for a jazz album.

They issued the Warner Bros. single "Playboy" b/w "Ain't We Got Fun" in July 1959 and began work on a new LP. It was to be a tribute album to Duke Ellington and Billy Strayhorn. Eight sides were cut and the first four were sent to Los Angeles from New York. Somehow those recordings were lost in transit, leaving only four sides for a never-to-be-finished LP.

In the fall of that year the Signatures recorded another LP for Warner Bros. titled *The Signatures—Prepare to Flip*. (Jazz LPs were cut much more quickly and less expensively than pop releases, and as long as there was public demand jazz groups cut rather frequently.)

The group went to the Playboy Jazz Festival in Chicago and were voted number one vocal group by the Jazz Critics Poll in *Down Beat*. Their last Warner Bros. single was "Please Don't Play the Cha-Cha," released in January 1960. Although 45s were never the Signatures' forte (the group sounded better in large doses—shows and LPs), one song they recorded that should have been a single was "This Can't Be Love" (Benny Goodman, #2, 1939). It had more harmonic variety than you'll hear on most LPs. Bob's superlative arrangement showed off the full range of the group's abilities, from chime harmony to jazz phrasing and beyond. Among the early pioneers in jazz to open up and spread out their harmony, the Signatures were a sophisticated, innovative quintet.

The group continued to tour (even hitting some harmony using a dry swimming pool as a makeshift stage with fellow vocalists the Four Freshmen after a gig in Hanover, Pennsylvania) until the early '60s when rock and roll convinced them to hang it up.

Bunny Phillips went to live in Ojai, California. Dottie Dunn continued to sing and live in Detroit. Lee Humes kept playing bass but also worked in real estate in Hawaii. Jerry Hayes became an art critic in Los Angeles, and Cathi Hayes recorded a jazz solo album and worked with the Johnny Hamlin Trio. Hal Kratzsch died in the mid-'60s. Bob and Ruth Alcivar live in Los Angeles where he became a film composer and occasionally sat in with various jazz groups. In the late '60s Bob was highly successful as an arranger for pop groups like THE ASSOCIATION and THE FIFTH DIMENSION, and you'll hear plenty of Signatures-style harmony in their arrangements thanks to Bob. Jazz's answer to Karen Carpenter, drummer Ruth Alcivar has returned to her arts and paints.

THE SIGNATURES

A SIDE/B SIDE	LABEL/CAT NO	DATE
Julie Is Her Name / Someone In Love	Whpt W210	8/56
Playboy / Ain't We Got Fun	Wrnr WB5089	7/59
Please Don't Play The Cha Cha / Cling To Me	Wrnr WB5055	1/60

The Silhouettes

One of the most memorable of all rock and roll hits, "Get a Job" was recorded by a gospel group. That's what the Silhouettes were even though they were forced to sing secular songs to earn a living.

In 1955 Philadelphia, Bill Horton of Hickory, North Carolina, and local vocalists Raymond Edwards, Earl Beal, and a guy whom history only remembers as Shorty joined together to become a gospel group called the Gospel Tornadoes. While the better gospel acts of the '30s and '40s still singing in the '50s were eking out a living, new groups of the '50s that didn't have the calling, even though they had the desire, found a need to earn a living. One of the better ways to make a living was by singing secular music.

So it was that on Sunday the Gospel Tornadoes sang in church and on Monday (and so on) the "Thunderbirds" sang in nightclubs.

By 1956, the Gospel Tornadoes had a new fourth member: Shorty left; James Jenkins entered; Jenkins was then replaced by former TURBANS roadie Richard Lewis. The lineup then read Bill Horton (lead), Richard Lewis (tenor), Earl Beal (baritone), and Raymond Edwards (bass). It was the influence of Lewis that headed the group towards rhythm and blues and rock and roll. The group's own influences on the secular side were other converted gospel singers THE DOMINOES and THE DRIFTERS.

The Thunderbirds worked up a few songs including one Lewis wrote while stationed in the army in West Germany that would become the most famous song written by a soldier since Fred Parris penned "In the Still of the Night." The group searched all over Philadelphia and New York for a deal but no one was interested. Even Cameo/Parkway—the home of Philadelphia groups—turned them down, and co-owner Bernie Lowe described the Lewis-penned rocker "Get a Job" as "nothing." The group tried the disc jockey/manager direction, but Hy Lit was too busy working with LEE ANDREWS AND THE HEARTS.

In 1957 a break finally came: the technician of the Uptown Theatre (Philadelphia's equivalent to New York's Apollo) saw the group perform in a small club and arranged a date for them at the Uptown. The show's emcee was Kae Williams, a local disc jockey (WDAS) and the owner of Junior Records, who liked their style and signed them. Renaming them after THE RAYS' hit single "Silhouettes," Kae got them into Robinson Recording Labs in Radio WIP, located in the same building as Gimbel's Department Store. There they recorded the pretty pop blues ballad "I Am Lonely" and the raucous song "Get a Job."

"I'm So Lonely" was issued in late 1957 on Junior and due to Kae's radio play became a Philadelphia hit. Other jocks started flipping it and "Get a Job" began blaring out of radios all over. When it sold 9,000 copies in a few days, Al Silvers' Ember Records of New York picked up the distribution and Dick Clark played it on his show. The very next day Silver walked in to find orders for 300,000 records on his desk and knew a phenomenon had been triggered. The song, with its "Sha na na na" syllables, was everywhere, and in three weeks "Get a Job" had sold one million copies. It charted both Pop and R&B on January 30, 1958, and hit number one on both charts by February. The record became such a '50s standard that a '70s group gained fame parodying '50s rock records under the name SHA NA NA.

As big as the record was it might have been even bigger had it not been covered by a group that had already made its millions, THE MILLS BROTHERS. Their version, as homogenized as it was, reached number 21 nationally.

The greatest acknowledgment of a hit in the '50s was the issuing of answer records by other acts. It wasn't long before record players were spinning discs like "I Found a Job" by THE HEARTBEATS (Roulette), "I Got Fired" by the Mistakes (Lofi), "I Lost My Job" by the Supreme Four (Sara), and "Got a Job" by a young group with their first record, THE MIRACLES (End).

The Silhouettes followed up with "Heading for the Poor House," a toned-down rocker by comparison. It never clicked but the Silhouettes were too busy on the tour circuit to notice. 1958 saw them performing with Jackie Wilson, Paul Anka, Clyde McPhatter, THE MONOTONES, Sam Cooke, and many others. They also appeared on the Patti Page and Dick Clark TV shows.

In a reversal of the usual course of events, Kae Williams refused to issue a track the group had recorded while on the road. They had heard Jerry Butler and THE IMPRESSIONS' "For Your Precious Love" when it first came out and had cut it. But because of Kae's friendship with Abner Records exec Ewart Abner, he decided not to release the cover version.

In the summer they issued "Bing Bong," which had been written in the car between New York and Philadelphia while they had been searching for a record deal in 1957. The chime-harmony rocker

went nowhere except in Philly, where jocks like Jerry Blavit have made it a Philadelphia area standard for more than 30 years.

For their fourth single they released the ballad "I Sold My Heart to the Junkman" on Junior (the Ember distribution deal was apparently over). Ace Records then picked it up, but it soon slid into limbo. Three years later THE BLUEBELLES would build a career on an up-tempo version of it.

A few more singles surfaced, but by the 1962 release of "Rent Man," Horton and Edwards had departed to find another way to pay the rent, and John Wilson and Cornelius Brown had taken their places. The group eventually separated from Kae Williams. They did a few more singles and a concept LP for Goodway Records, *The Original and New Silhouettes—'58/'68, Get a Job*, that had oldie recordings by the original Silhouettes and new releases by the latest foursome.

In 1964 members Horton, Joe Moody, Robert Byrd, and George Willis sang "Like to See You in the Mood" on Lawn as Bill Horton (misspelled on the label as Harton) and the Dawns, but the record went nowhere.

The Silhouettes went their separate ways in 1968, but the original four re-formed in 1980 for "The Royal New York Doo Wop Show" in October. They have been known to perform on occasion ever since.

THE SILHOUETTES

A SIDE/B SIDE	LABEL/CAT NO	DATE
Get A Job / I Am Lonely	Junior 391	12/57
Get A Job / I Am Lonely	Ember 1029	12/57
Headin' For The Poorhouse / Miss Think	Ember 1032	1958
Bing Bong / Voodoo Eyes	Ember 1037	8/58
I Sold My Heart To The Junkman / What Would You Do	Junior 396	1958
I Sold My Heart To The Junkman / What Would You Do	Ace 552	1958
Evelyn / Never Will Part	Junior 400	1959
Evelyn / Never Will Part	Ace 563	1959
Never / Bull Frog	20th 240	1959
Rent Man / Your Love	Junior 993	1962
Wish I Could Be There / Move On Over	Grand 142	1962
The Push / Which Way Did She Go	Imprl 5899	1962
Climb Every Mountain / We Belong Together	Jamie 1333	1967
Not Me Baby / Gaucho Serenade	Goodway 101	1968

The Six Teens

An interesting vocal combination, the Six Teens were rock and roll's first male/female sextet, dominated on most of their singles by the three female harmonizers.

Formed in 1955 as the Sweet Teens, the Los Angeles Catholic school contingent was the brainchild of 17-year-old Ed Wells. He wanted at least one girl to round out the three males' sound since he liked the smoothness that Zola Taylor gave another Los Angeles group, THE PLATTERS. What Ed got were *three* females when Beverly Pecot joined and Louise Williams auditioned along with her 12-year-old sister Trudy. The members finally included Trudy and Louise Williams, Beverly Pecot, Ed Wells, Darryl Lewis, and Kenneth Sinclair.

At the time, the nation's radios were playing FRANKIE LYMON AND THE TEENAGERS' "Why Do Fools Fall in Love." The group shifted leads from Ed to Trudy, and they started singing Teenagers tunes.

Also interested in the Lymon sound was Flip Records owner Max Freitag, who discovered the Sweet Teens and recorded "Don't Worry About a Thing" in late 1955. When it went unnoticed on its early 1956 release, Max made a name change to the Six Teens and in early spring issued an Ed Wells song called "A Casual Look" (that the Students borrowed from for their 1958 classic "I'm So Young"). The top side of the Six Teens' single was really "Teenage Promise," but disc jockeys decided to do what the label name said and flipped the record.

Billboard's April 21, 1956, issue made both sides a "Spotlight Pick," saying, "The new mixed vocal group has come through here with a strong coupling. 'Promise' is keyed right to the current rock & roll groove. It has a winning, lilting melody and an appealing relaxed beat. On the flip there's an equally strong bit that has beautiful harmony and a saleable teenage love theme. With exposure these can be big." Reviewed that same issue were the Wheels' "My Heart's Desire," the Cliques' (actually Jesse Belvin) "Girl in My Dreams," the Solitaires' "The Honeymoon," the Harptones' "What Is Your Decision," and the Jacks' "Why Did I Fall in Love." The Week's "Best Buys" were Frankie Lymon and the Teenagers' "I Want You to Be My Girl" and the Drifters' "Ruby Baby."

By June 9th, with Trudy and Ed trading leads à la Shirley and Lee, "A Casual Look" charted nationally R&B and went Pop on July 14th. Though its initial response was in L.A., it broke big in the East out of Pittsburgh, New York, Baltimore, and Philadelphia. By late summer it was number seven R&B and number 25 Pop and the Six Teens (ages 12 to 17) found themselves performing with THE COASTERS, Shirley and Lee, Etta James, Jesse Belvin, and Richard Berry. They only played on weekends in the Los Angeles area since they were all still in school and wards of the court.

When summer came they made the blunder of their career. Instead of touring east where the popularity had been, the went west to Hawaii. True, the song "Send Me Flowers," their second single out of Flip's 618 South Ridgeley Drive address, had hit number one there, but you couldn't build a career playing Hawaii (unless you were Don Ho).

"Arrow of Love" was issued in early 1957. It was an up-tempo tune (which read "The Six Teens featuring Trudy Williams") that finally reached number 80 Pop after building up steam for four months. After "Arrow" Louise and Beverly sang with Richard Owens (later of the Jayhawks and THE VIBRATIONS) and two girls from THE DREAMERS (also on flip and later to become THE BLOSSOMS) for a Flip single written by Wells titled "Beware of Love." They were billed as the Ivy Leaguers featuring Richard Owens.

Summer 1957's "My Surprise" (recorded in 1956) read "The Six Teens featuring 14-year-old Trudy Williams." That was its chief distinction.

The group's last recordings were in the late '50s. Their 1959 single "Why Do I Go to School" went nowhere. A similar fate befell their last two singles in 1960. Still, the group performed off and on till the late '60s when Ed moved to New York. Beverly became a school teacher in Los Angeles, Darryl moved to Sacramento and Kenneth planted himself in Southern California. Louise entered a convent to become a nun but changed her mind, married, and moved to the Midwest. Trudy married and had a child. Ed Wells, who wrote all the group's songs (unusual for the time), became a San Francisco accountant.

The Skyliners

If you were to put together the harmonies of the best '50s R&B groups and mix them with THE FOUR FRESHMEN and THE HI-LOS, the result would be the Skyliners, an unbelievably perfect blend of voices emanating from five white Pittsburgh teenagers.

The group was formed of members from three different local groups, the Crescents, the Montereys, and the El Rios. In 1958, the Crescents attended St. George's Catholic School in the Allentown area of Pittsburgh's South Hills. Former vocalist (the Marquees, studio singers) Joe Rock, now a promo man, heard the group and took note of the promising 13-year-old Wally Lester on tenor (although the group as a whole wasn't completely together). Sometime later, Rock attended a local record hop hosted by Al "Nickles" Noble of KTV's "Jukebox." He saw an a cappella group called the Montereys and flipped over the 14-year-old bass singer, promptly drafting him for the Crescents. The kid's name was Jimmy Beaumont, and as good as he was on bass, when he sang in tenor voice he floored everyone; he immediately became the Crescents' new lead singer.

Around this time, the Crescents heard about a young South Hills High School guitarist. Jackie Taylor's Hank Ballard guitar style was warmly received, and he too joined the group.

After doing a demo tape of a few originals along with "Sympathy" (THE CADILLACS) and "Please Don't Tease" (THE SPANIELS), Rock sent the tape to ABC-Paramount. The company eventually offered them a contract. In the interim they auditioned for Atlantic's Jerry Wexler, Jerry Leiber, and Mike Stoller, who also wanted the teenage group; Leiber and Stoller even volunteered to write for them. But somehow both deals were blown.

At Rock's request, a promotion man from Specialty Records came to Pittsburgh to hear the group, but half of the demoralized Crescents decided to go joy riding rather than meet with him. The three who showed up were Jimmy, Wally, and Jackie. Jimmy was so upset about the missed opportunity he sought out another local quartet that included Janet Vogel (top tenor), Joe VerScharen (baritone), and Richie Atkins (bass), and asked the three if they'd like to join the Crescents. Janet and Joe jumped at the offer and Richie declined. The group had everything but a bass until Jimmy realized their rockin' guitar player Jackie had a voice that could cover a range from bass to falsetto.

In mid-1958 the Crescents were now Jimmy Beaumont (17, lead), Janet Vogel (16, top tenor), Wally Lester (16, tenor), Joe VerScharen (17, baritone), and Jackie Taylor (17, bass).

Joe Rock, while sitting in his car between stoplights, wrote a lyric titled "Since I Don't Have You" about the girl who had just left him. Jimmy wrote the music the next night. Someone brought in a tape recorder and a rough a cappella demo was done.

Janet, thinking the tape had been turned off, kept riffing at the end, weaving up to an incredible high C finale.

It was this tape that Rock sent to 13 established labels, including Chess, ABC, Imperial, and RCA. All 13 came back with rejection notes. One said the song was negative and should have been "Since I Have You." Another wrote, "A song with 13 'yous' at the end will never sell!" Undaunted, the group thumbed through the phone book and came up with Calico Records, which was owned by Lou Caposi and Bill Lawrence and had Lenny Martin as A&R head and arranger. The Crescents, who were influenced by the Cadillacs, the Spaniels, THE EL DORADOS, the Four Freshmen, and the Hi-Los, practiced their hearts out and on November 3, 1958 jumped into a member's 1952 Dodge, sped off, and promptly became involved in a head-on collision. Miraculously, no one was hurt and they arrived in time to audition. After singing "Since I Don't Have You" and "One Night, One Night," Martin said, "Hold it, no need to go any further. That's my group."

"Since I Don't Have You" was recorded on December 3, 1958, at Capitol Studios in New York. 18 musicians were used, an awesome number for a teen vocal group at that time and the first time a full orchestra had been used with a rock group. When the test pressing came back there was no group name on the label, which prompted Rock and the Crescents to think about a new permanent moniker. They came up with the title of an old Charlie Barnett 1945 hit (#19), "Skyliner."

"Since I Don't Have You" was released the day after Christmas 1958. The record was soon number one in Pittsburgh, and Dick Clark invited the Skyliners to appear on his February 13th "American Bandstand" show (after their performance he announced the song was an old standard—a tribute to the songwriting of Rock and Beaumont). Within three days of the Dick Clark performance "Since" had charted on *Billboard*'s Top 100 and had sold 100,000 records. Beaumont and company's debut single did better R&B (#3) than Pop (#12), and the group began to perform on the chitlin circuit, including the Apollo on eight occasions. In the early days stunned silence usually greeted them until they began singing and converting black audiences to instant fans. The Skyliners became the first white group ever to top the R&B charts ("Since" went to number one in Cashbox).

"This I Swear," another dreamy Beaumont-Rock love ballad, was issued in May from Calico's 1409 Fifth Avenue Pittsburgh offices. (Appearing at the New York recording session was a young writer/artist/producer and member of the Teddy Bears named Phil Spector; he later cited "Since I Don't Have You" as an influence on his production style in the '60s.) Like "Since I Don't Have You," "This I Swear" did better on the black charts (#20 R&B to #26 Pop).

Though all the originals issued on Calico read "Skyliners," Rock and Beaumont actually wrote the songs, occasionally with VerSharon.

"It Happened Today" was their third 45. It reached only number 59 Pop in the fall, but oldies radio played it for the next 30 years as if it had been a top 10 hit. Another goodie was the flip ballad "Lonely Way," which reached number one in Hawaii and was one of their most requested performance songs. As recorded by THE ZIRCONS in 1963, "Lonely Way" helped to start the '60s a cappella craze in America. It became a favorite tune of THE MANHATTAN TRANSFER (as the Skyliners were one of their favorite groups).

The January 18, 1960, issue of *Billboard* cited both sides of the follow-up single ("How Much" and "Lorraine from Spain") as "Spotlight" Winners of the Week, commenting, "The group has two fine outings. 'How Much' is a nicely chanted rock-a-ballad. 'Lorraine' is a Latin-ish rocker. Their deliveries on both are smooth and winning and either side can take off." "How Much" had been written by Rock and Beaumont between shows (five a day) at the Regal Theatre in Chicago. They played the test pressing for Alan Freed, who loved it. The record broke quicker than their previous releases but never charted nationally.

In the spring of 1960 the Skyliners released an up-beat version of the Arthur Johnson-Johnny Burke standard "Pennies from Heaven," putting the group back in the spotlight at number 24 on the pop chart. Following their next single, "Believe Me," the group moved over to Colpix Records, the home of yet another great Pittsburgh quintet, THE MARCELS.

The Skyliners' first single on Colpix, "The Door Is Still Open," failed to chart. The follow-up, "Close Your Eyes," only reached number 105.

VerScharen got tired of living out of a suitcase and left shortly after getting married. The group signed to Cameo for the single "Three Coins in the Fountain" and then moved on to Viscount Records for "Comes Love," their best ballad since the early Calico days, masterfully arranged by Jim Drake and sung to perfection by the group. It managed to chart nationally at number 128 on February 16, 1963.

Meanwhile, Jimmy Beaumont left briefly to record a few solo sides for Colpix and its affiliate May, without success.

In June 1963 Jimmy and the group recorded a beautiful version of THE HARPTONES "Since I Fell for You" on Atco that was overlooked. The group then disbanded.

In 1965 Jackie Taylor formed a new Skyliners on Jubilee, issuing a blue-eyed soul ballad called "The Loser," produced by Mike Lewis (of THE CONCORDS) and Stu Wiener. It reached number 34 R&B and number 72 Pop in the summer of 1965.

After two more ballad singles failed to hit, nothing more was heard from the Skyliners until 1970, when Beaumont, Janet Vogel Rapp (now married), Lester, and VerScharen re-formed for Richard Nader's Madison Square Garden oldies revival and kept on playing the oldies circuit. The foursome then recorded a Buddah LP in 1970 called *The Skyliners Featuring Jimmy Beaumont "Once Upon a Time,"* but no single was issued.

A 1975 single, "Where Have They Gone," looked promising, but its fate was summed up in a note from Joe Rock to this writer: "Here's a copy of the record Capitol is losing for us." The record stopped dead at number 100 on March 22nd, becoming their last chart single.

In 1978, Jimmy, Janet, and two newcomers, Bobby Sholes and Jimmie Ross, did an LP for Tortoise International of Southfield, Michigan. As recently as the early '90s, Beaumont, Sholes, Rick Morris, and Donna Groom were playing the oldies circuit and keeping the Skyliners' name alive (oldies radio continued to spin "Since I Don't Have You" and "This I Swear" as if they were new records).

Jackie Taylor became a captain in the army in Vietnam and then went into computers. Wally Lester became a VP for the Clairol Corporation and Joe VerScharen delved into real estate and insurance. Joe Rock continued to manage the Skyliners with Jimmy Beaumont sounding as good as ever. Janet Vogel, wife, mother, and soprano supreme, died on February 21, 1980, at the age of 37.

THE SKYLINERS

A SIDE/B SIDE	LABEL/CAT NO	DATE
Since I Don't Have You / One Night, One Night	Calico 103,4	1/59
This I Swear / Tomorrow	Calico 106	5/59
It Happened Today / Lonely Way	Calico 109	10/59
How Much / Lorraine From Spain	Calico 114	1/60

A SIDE/B SIDE	LABEL/CAT NO	DATE
Pennies From Heaven /		
I'll Be Seeing You	Calico 117	5/60
Believe Me / Happy Time	Calico 120	1960
The Door's Still Open /		
I'll Close My Eyes	Colpix 188	2/61
Close Your Eyes /		
Our Love Will Last	Colpix 613	9/61
Three Coins In The Fountain /		
Everyone But You	Cameo 215	1962
Comes Love / Tell Me	Visct 104	1962
Since I Fell For You / I'd Die	Atco 6270	1963
The Loser / Everything Is Fine	Jubi 5506	1965
Get Yourself A Baby /		
Who Do You Love	Jubi 5512	1965
I Run To You / Don't Hurt Me Baby	Jubi 5520	1966
Where Have They Gone? /		
I Could Have Loved You So Well	Cap 3979	1975
The Day The Clown Cried /		
The Day The Clown Cried	Drive 6250	1976
Oh How Happy /		
We've Got Love On Our Side	Tort 11343	1978
Another Lonely New Year's Eve /		
You're My Christmas Present	ClsArt 123	12/90

The Solitaires

No matter which of their several singers sang lead, the Solitaires' solid New York-styled harmony made them immediately identifiable.

In the early '50s, a variety of vocalists would congregate on 142nd Street between Lenox and 7th Avenues in Harlem, form quartets and quintets, and pursue ritual battles of the groups. One such aggregation consisted of Eddie Jones, Nick Anderson, Winston "Buzzy" Willis, Rudy Morgan, and Pat Gaston, who called themselves the Solitaires. After some shuffling, a lineup emerged that included Herman Dunham (lead), Bobby "Schubie" Williams (first tenor), Bobby Baylor (second tenor), Monte Owens (tenor and guitar), Buzzy Willis (baritone), and Pat Gaston (bass).

Dunham (real name Herman Curtis) had sung lead for the Vocaleers on Red Robin. Baylor, Owens, and Williams had all been members of THE MELLO-MOODS on Red Robin. Gaston had performed with the Four Bells on Gem. Willis had been hanging out and singing with THE CROWS, though he never recorded with them.

Willis, who served as the spokesman for the group, worked as a record librarian for Hal Jackson's WLIB radio show out of the Hotel Teresa. He told Hal of the Solitaires, and Jackson arranged an audition for them with Old Town Records' Hy Weiss at a theatre on 125th Street and Lexington Avenue. Weiss's practice was to review the latest talents at midnight after the theatre closed.

Weiss liked the group's strong vocals (which had to carry them since they weren't a dance act like so many of the other up-and-comers) and signed them up. He arranged recording sessions similar to a Hollywood cattle call; he would have five or six groups standing by for sessions that started in the early evening and often ran till daylight. Each group would sing two to four songs. The perk was a curious arrangement in which the act with the most recent hit record had the opportunity to record first and then go home. The Solitaires' 15- and 16-year-old members wrote much of their recorded material, which helped them develop a distinctive style of harmony and separate them from many of the other street-corner groups.

In February 1954 the Solitaires issued the fragile ballad "Wonder Why," the first record on the Old Town label. They then performed on Old Town's second release as backup to Ursula Reed on "You're Laughing 'Cause I'm Crying."

In July 1954 Old Town issued a Latin-rhythmed version of "South of the Border" with Baylor on lead, showcasing the Solitaires' versatility. The ballad flip "Please Remember My Heart," had Herman Dunham pleading as hard as possible short of breaking into tears. Their last 1954 single was the rock-a-ballad "Chances I've Taken," another group-penned effort.

In January 1955 their haunting version of the Bing Crosby 1933 hit (#5) "I Don't Stand a Ghost of Chance" held its few listeners spellbound. Unfortunately, it disappeared like its previous sister singles.

Still, the group was getting airplay and building a fantastically loyal following among R&B group lovers who showed up to see them wherever they played. On February 5, 1955, for example, they performed to an overflow audience at the Second Annual Festival of Negro Music, broadcast live from the Savoy Ballroom in New York City.

By mid-1955 Herman was in the air force and Milton Love (THE CONCORDS) had taken his spot, beginning with the harmony duet (with Bobby Baylor) "The Wedding." Milton's fragile falsetto lead gave the group a slightly altered sound on ballads. The record did well in the East and charted locally for the group.

In early 1956 the Solitaires masqueraded (through no control of their own) as the Supremes behind Ruth McFadden's superior single "Darling Listen to the Words of This Song." The real Supremes were a black male group on Old Town who recorded a minor key rhythm ballad masterpiece entitled "Tonight" later that summer.

Milton and Bobby duetted again in March 1956 on "The Honeymoon," a sequel to "The Wedding." Another local success, "The Honeymoon" was the best of the new crop of Solitaires issues.

When the group performed "The Wedding" and "The Honeymoon" live, Milton wore a mop over his head to play the female role.

In January 1957 the group came as close as they ever would to a hit, with the group-penned rocker "Walkin' Along." The record slowly built momentum but couldn't sustain national play and ultimately became another Solitaires single relegated to the shelves of hardcore collectors, though it picked up some notoriety almost two years later when THE DIAMONDS took their version to number 29. By now, Herman had returned from the military, but Milton Love continued doing most leads. Gaston also went into the air force around this time and was replaced by Fred Barksdale (THE CRICKETS).

In February 1959 the group was scheduled to perform at Ted Steel's show at the Paramount in New York with Buddy Holly, the Big Bopper, and Frankie Avalon. Holly and the Bopper never made it—their plane went down on February 3rd.

The changing of the guard had become more regular by 1958, but Milton Love remained a constant. Wally Roker of THE HEARTBEATS sat in for Barksdale on bass for a while. Bobby Williams left in mid-1956, and Herman Dunham left after 1958's "No More Sorrows." Willis and Baylor went into the army in 1960, and Cecil Holmes and Reggie Barnes (both from the Fi-Tones, Atlas) took their places.

After "Lonesome Lover" in 1961 Milton Love also joined Uncle Sam's singing soldiers, and the group became somewhat inactive. The best of the Solitaires' remaining sides with Old Town from 1959 through 1963 was the quality ballad "Embraceable You." The members at that time were Love, Baylor, Willis, Owens, and Barksdale. By the time Milton returned from army duty in 1963 the membership was Love, Baylor, Barksdale, and a girl named Cathy Miller, who was soon replaced by a returning Herman Dunham.

Buzzy Willis became a record producer and later a record executive with RCA and vice president of R&B operations for Polydor. At RCA he supervised LPs by THE MAIN INGREDIENT and the Friends of Distinction. In the '80s, Buzzy became the Minority Marketing Consultant to the Department of Defense and by the '90s, was the manager of Kool and the Gang.

In 1963 the group once again had a different name, backing Ray Brewster as the Cadillacs ("Fool," Artic). The Solitaires even toured for a while as both the Cadillacs and THE DRIFTERS, with Bobby Baylor doing his best Clyde McPhatter impression. Their last single as the Solitaires was "Fool that I Am" for MGM in 1964.

In the same year they became the Chances for their last single with Love on lead and Baylor, Barksdale, Barnes, Roland Martinez, and Cecil Holmes singing backup. Buzzy Willis helped the group get on Roulette for one ill-fated single, "Through a Long and Sleepless Night."

By 1965 the Solitaires were only a memory. Cecil Holmes worked as an executive at several record companies, including Buddah. Fred Barksdale and Monty Owens went to work for the Post Office. Bobby Baylor became a transit conductor in the New York City subway system. Herman Dunham joined a band as an organist. Reggie Barnes played drums on numerous record sessions, including Jimmy Caster's hit "Hey Leroy." Pat Gaston became the Commissioner of the Department of Corrections in New York City. Milton Love became a medical technician.

In the early '70s Baylor, Barksdale, and Love performed again as the Solitaires; in January 1973 Buzzy Willis joined them onstage at New York's Academy of Music for an enthusiastically received show.

As recently as September 1990 the Solitaires, with Milton on lead and Barksdale on bass, were performing in the New York/New Jersey area.

THE SOLITAIRES

A SIDE/B SIDE	LABEL/CAT NO	DATE
Wonder Why / Blue Valentine	OldTn 1000	2/54
Please Remember My Heart /		
South Of The Border	OldTn 1006/7	7/54
Chances I've Taken / Lonely	OldTn 1008	11/54
I Don't Stand A Ghost Of		
A Chance / Girl Of Mine	OldTn 1010	1/55
What Did She Say / My Dear	OldTn 1012	7/55
The Wedding / Don't Fall In Love	OldTn 1014	9/55
Magic Rose / Later For You Baby	OldTn 1015	12/55
The Honeymoon /		
Fine Little Girl	OldTn 1019	3/56
You've Sinned /		
You're Back With Me	OldTn 1026	8/56
You've Sinned / The Angels Sang	OldTn 1026	8/56

A SIDE/B SIDE	LABEL/CAT NO	DATE
Give Me One More Chance /		
Nothing Like A Little Love	OldTn 1032	11/56
Walking Along /		
Please Kiss This Letter	OldTn 1034	1/57
I Really Love You So /		
Thrill Of Love	OldTn 1044	11/57
Walkin' And Talkin' /		
No More Sorrows	OldTn 1049	1958
Big Mary's House /		
Please Remember My Heart	OldTn 1059	1959
Embraceable You /		
Round Goes My Heart	OldTn 1066	1959
Helpless /		
Light A Candle In The Chapel	OldTn 1071	1959
Lonesome Lover / Pretty Thing	OldTn 1096	1961
Money Babe / The Time Is Here	OldTn 1139	3/63
Ray Brewster and the Cadillacs		
Fool / The Right Kind Of Lovin'	Arctic 101	1963
The Solitaires		
Fool That I Am /		
Fair Weather Lover	MGM 13221	1964
The Chances		
Through A Long And Sleepless		
Night / What Would You Say	Roul 4549	1964

The Spaniels

It was the R&B and rock and roll sound of the Spaniels that brought about the formation of one of R&B's legendary labels, Vee-Jay Records.

Gary, Indiana, natives Ernest Warren (first tenor), Opal Courtney, Jr. (baritone), Willie Jackson (second tenor), and Gerald Gregory (bass) met and started singing in Roosevelt High School. The unnamed quartet had heard schoolmate James "Pookie" Hudson sing, and they convinced him to sing with them for the school talent show. They debuted as Pookie Hudson and the Hudsonaires for the Christmastime 1952 show and fared so well they decided to continue as a quintet.

The 11th-graders began rehearsing and performing Pookie-penned songs like "Baby It's You" at local churches and talent show performances, with Pookie's smooth and smoky lead marvelling the masses. The group was looking for a new name when Gregory's wife heard them singing and told them they sounded like a "bunch of dogs." Not wanting to join the bird group club they went for the name the Spaniels.

In the spring of 1954 the group visited a local record shop owned by James Bracken and Vivian Carter Bracken of WWCA. The group's singing convinced the Brackens to start their own label named after the couple's first-name initials (V. J.). The Brackens moved their operation to Chicago and on May 5, 1953, the Spaniels recorded "Baby It's You" and "Bounce." The 45, issued as Vee-Jay 101 in July 1953, had a bouncy ballad piano, bass, and melody line that surfaced in numerous later recordings (THE CAPRIS' "Oh My Darling" [1954] and THE JESTERS' "So Strange" [1957]). "Baby It's You" started getting enough radio response and sales in the Chicago area to interest the larger Chance label. (In later years, Vee-Jay would own and distribute all of Chance's recordings.) On September 5th "Baby" hit number 10 on the national R&B Best Seller and Jukebox charts.

The follow-up, "The Bells Ring Out" was a mellow bluesy ballad with lots of vocal harmony but it received only some local play.

The Spaniels were the first of the successful Midwestern R&B groups. They were also one of the first (if not the first) R&B groups to perform with the lead singer on one mike and the group on another and they initiated a trend toward using tapdance routines in live shows. In terms of original material, Pookie's songs did not come about through the traditional formula. Normally the group would just walk down a street and harmonize till something came together.

In March 1954 Vee-Jay released "Goodnight, Sweetheart, Goodnight," about which *Billboard*'s reviewer wrote, "Almost pop-like piece of material. The imitation of the sounds of a sax by the bass singer gives this side a gimmick which helps greatly. Strong wax." (In a 1970s interview with Alan Lee and Donna Hennings, Pookie Hudson stated that Gregory was not attempting to imitate a sax but rather trying to keep the guys on pitch.) The success of "Goodnight" prompted THE MCGUIRE SISTERS (#7) to cover it for the white market, stealing a lot of the Spaniels' thunder. But their version still managed to peak at number five R&B in the summer of 1954. It became one of the most requested records on oldies radio.

Pookie and company's next single, "Let's Make Up," earned more for writer Hudson as someone else's B side than it did as his A side. That's because the voice of Walter Schumann had it on the flip of the hit "The Ballad of Davy Crockett" (#14, 1955).

On June 11, 1954, the Spaniels made the first of numerous appearances at the Apollo in New York, along with Joe Turner and Arnett Cobb's Orchestra. In August they toured with the second annual "Biggest R&B Show" through the Midwest with THE DRIFTERS, the Counts, Erskine Hawkins, Roy Hamilton, and King Pleasure, winding up on September 12th at the Brooklyn Paramount.

Their mid-tempo "Do Wah" single of May 1955 failed, but the follow-up "You Painted Pictures" reached #13 R&B in October and kept the Spaniels working.

Opal Courtney, Jr. was then drafted and replaced by Vee-Jay A&R man Cal Carter for a few months until James "Dimples" Cochran took over. Shortly thereafter, Ernest Warren was drafted and the group continued recording as a quartet. Two subsequent singles, "False Love" and "Dear Heart," drifted off into obscurity.

With records not selling, Pookie and Willie left. The roster now read Carl Rainge (lead), Gerald Gregory (bass), James Cochran (baritone), and Don Porter (second tenor). This contingent lasted for only one single in 1956 ("Since I Fell for You") until Pookie rejoined and began creating some of the group's most outstanding sides: "Peace of Mind," "Everyone's Laughing" (which became their one and only Pop charter at number 69, July 1957), the solid rhythm number "Tina," and an exciting fast version of the standard "Stormy Weather." The story goes that in 1958 Pookie Hudson was performing with the group at the Casbah Club in Washington, D.C., at a time when a gospel act, the Nightingales, were also there. The 'Gales had a song called "The Twist" that they offered to the Spaniels since they couldn't record secular songs and still keep their gospel following. The Spaniels passed on it, and HANK BALLARD put it out shortly thereafter. When Chubby Checker had his hit version of it, the Spaniels must have kicked themselves for letting it get away. It's unclear how the Nightingales came upon the song, though they probably had heard Hank and the Midnighters performing it before it was released since Hank is the acknowledged author of the song and the Nightingales never publicly claimed to have created it.

By 1960 the Spaniels were Hudson, Ernest Warren (who was back again), Gerald Gregory, Bill Carey, and Andy McGruder (former lead of the Five Blue Notes on Sabre). They recorded the group's last Vee-Jay single, "I Know," in 1960, and it reached number 23 R&B that summer.

By 1961 McGruder and Gregory had left. Road manager Ricky Burden took over on bass for "For Sentimental Reasons" (Neptune). Pookie did a few solo sides for Jamie and in 1962 cut "I Know, I

Know" backed by THE IMPERIALS minus Little Anthony for Lloyd Price's Double-L label. In the late '60s Pookie formed his own North American Records and issued "Fairytales" (with the Imperials backing again). It was picked up by Nat McCalla's Calla Records (distributed by Roulette), becoming Pookie's last chart single (#45 R&B) in the fall of 1970.

Two more North American singles were issued in the early '70s with a new Spaniels lineup of Hudson, Charles Douglas (first tenor), Alvin Wheeler (second tenor), Alvin Lloyd (baritone), and the group's former guitarist Pete Simmons (bass). Douglas was replaced by Andrew Lawyer (the Truetones), and the group recorded a remake of "Goodnight, Sweetheart, Goodnight" for Buddah.

Their last release was for Henry Farag's Canterbury label of Gary, Indiana, in 1974 when Hudson, Rainge, Cochran, and Porter recorded a contemporary version of "Peace of Mind" and two B sides, "She Sang to Me" and an a cappella arrangement of "Danny Boy."

Pookie and the Spaniels remained active and were one of the more in-demand acts on the oldies circuit. Though they never had a pop hit, oldies radio made them popular far beyond the R&B audience. Their recordings remain excellent examples of fine R&B and rock and roll, and Pookie's sound remains unique.

THE SPANIELS

A SIDE/B SIDE	LABEL/CAT NO	DATE
Baby, It's You / Bounce	Vee-Jay 101	7/53
Baby, It's You / Bounce	Chance 1141	1953
The Bells Ring Out / House Cleaning	Vee-Jay 103	10/53
Goodnight, Sweetheart, Goodnight / You Don't Move Me	Vee-Jay 107	3/54
Let's Make Up / Play It Cool	Vee-Jay 116	10/54
Do-Wah / Don'cha Go	Vee-Jay 131	5/55
You Painted Pictures / Hey Sister Lizzie	Vee-Jay 154	9/55
Painted Picture / Hey Sister Lizzie	Vee-Jay 154	10/55
False Love / Do You Really	Vee-Jay 178	1956
Dear Heart / Why Won't You Dance	Vee-Jay 189	1956
Since I Fell For You / Baby Come Along With Me	Vee-Jay 202	7/56
You Gave Me Peace Of Mind / Please Don't Tease	Vee-Jay 229	12/56
I.O.U. / Everyone's Laughing	Vee-Jay 246	1957
You're Gonna Cry / I Need Your Kisses	Vee-Jay 257	1957
I Lost You / Crazee Babee	Vee-Jay 264	1958
Tina / Great Googley Moo	Vee-Jay 278	4/58

A SIDE/B SIDE	LABEL/CAT NO	DATE
Stormy Weather /		
Here Is Why I Love You	Vee-Jay 290	8/58
Baby It's You / Heart And Soul	Vee-Jay 301	12/58
Trees / I Like It Like That	Vee-Jay 310	1959
100 Years From Today /		
These Three Words	Vee-Jay 328	9/59
People Will Say We're In Love /		
The Bells Ring Out	Vee-Jay 342	1959
I Know / Bus Fare Home	Vee-Jay 350	1960
For Sentimental Reasons* /		
Meek Man*	Neptune 124	7/61
John Brown* /		
Turn Out The Lights*	Parkway 839	4/62
Maybe / Goodnight Sweetheart	Buddah 153	1969
Fairy Tales / Jealous Heart	NoAmr 001	1970
Fairy Tales / Jealous Heart	Calla 172	1970
Stand In Line / Lonely Man	NoAmr 002	1970
Money Blues /		
Come Back To These Arms	NoAmr 3114	1970
This Is A Lovely Way To Spend		
An Evening / Red Sails In		
The Sunset	LstNt 307	1970
Little Joe / The Posse	Owl 328	1970
Peace Of Mind / She Sang To Me /		
Danny Boy	Cant 101	9/74

* Pookie Hudson and the Spaniels

The Spiders

Avery successful mid-'50s R&B group, the Spiders of New Orleans nevertheless had a short-lived career. They were without a doubt the most well-known and popular of the Crescent City's vocal groups (including the Barons, Fat Man Matthews and the Four Kittens, the Kidds a.k.a. the Pelicans, the Dukes, and the Bees).

The Spiders started out as the gospel group the Zion Harmonizers in 1947. The members were Leonard "Chick" Carbo (lead and baritone), Joe Maxon (first tenor), Matthew West (baritone), and Oliver Howard (bass). Hayward "Chuck" Carbo (Chick's brother) joined on lead soon after and by 1950 the group had become the Delta Southernaires, with a home base of the historic Second Baptist Church. Some say the group was discovered by a Mrs. Phyllis Boone, who worked at J&M Recording Studios and who offered them an audition after hearing Leonard Carbo playing piano. Other people claim the group was discovered by someone from Imperial Records while they were performing at the local Pelican Club. In either case it is known that the group almost got its name by the conventional method of placing names in a hat. After three rounds of doing that, they were still unable to agree on a name until Chuck's wife, who was standing in the garage with them, saw a big spider on the wall and said, "Stop arguing, there's a name for you." On that they agreed.

When the group originally auditioned in 1953 they believed they were going to record as a gospel group. But the powers that be at Imperial wanted a rhythm and blues group and sent them home to write songs in an R&B style. They came back with "I Didn't Want to Do It" and "You're the One," which became their first single in December 1953.

The Spiders' smooth style gained them immediate attention and both sides of their first single charted and went R&B top 10 ("I Didn't Want to Do It," #3, February 20, 1954, and "You're the One," #8, April 17, 1954).

For a time they kept their secular identity a secret from the gospel community so they could continue as the Delta Southernaires and still sing in church. But a New Orleans disc jockey on WWEZ let the cat out of the bag and the Delta group was banned from singing at the Second Baptist Church. But they never stopped singing gospel on their own. They met Ray Charles in 1955 at a show in Evansville, Indiana, and discovered mutual enthusiasm for religious music; they sang throughout the night (after their regular show) with Ray singing tenor and baritone harmony and some leads.

Imperial continued to issue Spiders singles. In the summer of 1954 their third 45, "I'm Slippin' In," reached number six on *Billboard*'s R&B chart. Two singles later "Twenty-One" made the national Jukebox top 10 (#9) in early 1955.

They performed all over the country, from New York's Apollo to the West Coast. Dissension and jealousy set in during 1954 when Imperial owner Lew Chudd asked New Orleans A&R exec Dave Bartholomew to bring Chuck Carbo to Los Angeles so he could meet him. The group felt left out, prompting Chudd (who probably planned it all along) to suggest Chuck go solo.

In late 1955 the Spiders had one more R&B top 10, the rocker "Witchcraft" (#5 DJ and #7 Best Seller).

Four more singles were issued through early 1957, including a good rhythm version of the Kresa-Loveday standard "That's My Desire" (which reads "The Spiders with Chuck Carbo" on the label) but the hits stopped coming and the group soon broke up.

Chuck recorded two singles for Imperial ("Poor Boy" and "I Miss You") and then moved over to Rex and Ace through the early '60s. Chick soloed on Atlantic, Vee-Jay, and Instant between 1956 and 1962 with an equal lack of record activity. Chuck eventually became a dump truck driver.

THE SPIDERS

A SIDE/B SIDE	LABEL/CAT NO	DATE
I Didn't Want To Do It /		
You're The One	Imprl 5265	12/53
I'll Stop Crying /		
Tears Began To Flow	Imprl 5280	4/54
I'm Slippin' In / I'm Searchin'	Imprl 5291	1954
The Real Thing /		
Mmm Mmm Baby	Imprl 5305	9/54
She Keeps Me Wondering / 21	Imprl 5318	11/54
That's Enough /		
Lost And Bewildered	Imprl 5331	1955
Sukey Sukey Sukey /		
Am I The One	Imprl 5344	3/55
Bells In My Heart / For A Thrill	Imprl 5354	7/55
Witchcraft / Is It True	Imprl 5366	10/55
Don't Pity Me / How Can I Feel	Imprl 5376	1/56
A-1 In My Heart / Dear Mary	Imprl 5393	6/56
Goodbye /		
That's The Way To Win My Heart	Imprl 5405	9/56
Honey Bee / That's My Desire	Imprl 5423	1/57
Tennessee Slim /		
You're The One	Imprl 5714	10/60
Witchcraft /		
True, You Don't Love Me	Imprl 5739	1961

The Staple Singers

The most successful gospel group ever to cross into rhythm and blues and pop, the Staples were a family affair. Roebuck "Pop" Staples started singing and playing guitar on a plantation in his hometown of Winona, Mississippi, during the late '20s. Pop fine-tuned his guitar style by learning the licks of the likes of Barbecue Bob and Big Bill Broonzy, and he sang with the Golden Trumpets of Mississippi.

By the 1940s he and his wife Oceola had moved to Chicago; Pop started working in the Armour meat factory. During the '40s he set up a gospel group made up of his children Pervis, Cleotha, and Mavis, the youngest, singing bass. They started performing at churches and, thanks to a tight sound that only a family of voices could produce, began to earn acclaim throughout black communities as a rousing folk gospel group.

In 1952 or early 1953, the Staple Singers gathered around a small microphone and two-track recorder to tape "These Are They" and "Faith and Grace," which Pop pressed up on his own Royal label. These 78s were sold at their programs right from the stage. About 500 were pressed and were the informal start of a more than 30-year recording career. The label read "The Staples Singers" as they first called themselves.

In September 1953 they signed with Chicago's United label. They issued one unheralded 78 out of nine sides recorded, so it was mainly through performances that the group continued to build its following until they recorded again in September 1956. This time it was for Vee-Jay. With Mavis singing lead the Staples recorded "Uncloudy Day," which became an immediate gospel classic and introduced the world to Mavis's deep contralto. Influenced by Dorothy Love Coates of the Gospel Harmonettes, Mavis began a long string of high-powered vocals through the Vee-Jay days on songs such as "Don't Drive Me Away" and "Pray On."

By the early '60s Pop's third daughter Yvonne had joined to make the group a quintet. The Staples had left Vee-Jay behind and along with it some of their strict gospel styling; they signed to Riverside Records and started playing white establishment folk-gospel at folk festivals. They became the first black act to record Bob Dylan tunes (Dylan was often quoted as saying Mavis Staples was his favorite soul vocalist). When Riverside went under, the quintet signed to Epic and charted Pop on June 3, 1967, with "Why" (#95) more than three years before they eventually charted R&B.

Their next Pop charter was in September with a cover of Buffalo Springfield's "For What It's Worth." Though they were mixing gospel with mainstream R&B music they continued to choose material that would convey their social and moral point of view. The result was that they were now performing with established rock acts. This did not sit well with hardcore churchgoers who felt a gospel group couldn't sing anything but gospel and still have its road to heaven assured. In the late '60s they performed their hearts out at a gospel appearance and received only polite applause from an unforgiving audience.

In 1968 they made the full transition to secular music (with a message) by signing with Memphis-based Stax Records. Their first R&B chart hit was "Heavy Makes You Happy (Sha Na Boom Boom)" which reached number six R&B and number 27 Pop, paving the way for such hits as "Respect Yourself" (#12 Pop, #2 R&B, 1971), "I'll Take You

There" (#1 Pop and R&B, 1972), "This World" (#38 Pop, #6 R&B, 1972), "If You're Ready (Come Go with Me)" (#9 Pop, #1 R&B, 1973). The group had successfully combined Memphis-style soul shufflers with "message" lyrics.

They toured in 1971 with the Bee Gees, and Pervis then left for the service. The group performed internationally from Europe to Iran, and while in Ghana their performance was filmed and used in the motion picture *Soul to Soul* with Santana and Wilson Pickett.

In January 1973 the family was featured in the film *Wattstax* with Richard Pryor and Isaac Hayes.

With all its success, Stax still managed (or mismanaged) to fold by the mid-'70s, and the Staple Singers signed with Curtis Mayfield's Curtom label in time to strike gold with "Let's Do It Again" (#1 Pop and R&B, 1975) keeping the group a hit international item.

Despite their crossover celebrity status, the quartet retained their gospel loyalties, though the gospel community rarely saw it that way.

By 1976 they were the Staples, signing to Warner Bros. and reaching number 11 R&B with "Love Me Love Me." In the '80s Mavis's magnificent leads were weaving through rock tracks on Private I Records as produced by Gary Goetzman and "Cowboy" Mike Piccirillo. Records like the Talking Heads' "Slippery People" (#109 Pop, #22 R&B, 1984) and the Goetzman-Piccirillo-penned funk tune "Nobody Can Make It on Their Own" (#89 R&B, 1985, the Staples' last chart record) were exciting efforts, merging different styles of music. The best of their '80s cuts, however, was the former Pacific, Gas & Electric single (#49 R&B, 1970) "Are You Ready" (#39, R&B, 1985). In all, the Staples were one of the luckier gospel acts to cross into R&B and Pop to the extent they did, although luck had nothing to do with their enormous talent.

The Sultans

Nebraska is known for wheat, cows, and 74,000 farms, but it is not known for singing groups. Still, one group managed to emerge from the city of Omaha and even spawned the solo career of a talented '60s hitmaker.

In 1946, 11-year-old Kellom public school student Eugene McDaniels decided to form his own gospel group, calling it the Echoes of Joy. Having trained in a church choir, young Gene felt qualified

to form such an entity and set about schooling two of his classmates on the fine points of singing. By the time the group was in Omaha Technical High School it was called the Five Echoes and consisted of Gene and Willie Barnes (lead vocalists), James Farmer (baritone), Rosenwald Alexander (tenor), and Jimmy Mims (bass). Wesley Devereaux (son of Omaha blues great Wynonie Harris) and Richard Beasley soon joined in place of Alexander and Mims.

The group practiced whenever possible at Gene's house at 30th and Franklyn and on the schoolgrounds at 33rd and Cummings. Gene's diverse musical tastes ran the gamut, from the SWAN SILVERTONES and Sam Cooke's SOUL STIRRERS to THE HI-LO'S and THE FOUR FRESHMEN. This made for some interesting group harmony.

By 1953 the five Echoes had attracted the attention of Paul Allen, a local record shop owner and uncle of James Farmer. Allen owned a club named the Showcase, which provided the five Echoes with a place to present their talents.

It was around this time that Gene and company changed their name to the Sultans. The group also gradually changed its musical direction from gospel to R&B. At one of their performances, they met saxophone player Preston Love, a friend of Duke Records A&R man Johnny Otis; by January 1954 they were driving the 894 miles from Omaha to Don Robey's Houston-based Duke label.

Their first recordings were overseen by Otis. They included "Good Thing Baby," a mid-tempo blues tune written by Otis's wife, and "How Deep Is the Ocean," the 1932 Rudy Vallee hit written by Irving Berlin. (The former was led by Wesley while the latter's lead was Willie.) The release came out in June but received little attention.

The group then left for a road tour as part of Johnny Otis's show. Over the coming months they picked up a road manager in the person of Ohio newspaperman Welton Barnett.

Also yielded by the January recording session was a second single, "I Cried My Heart Out," with a B-side jump tune that was Eugene McDaniels' first recorded lead. By mid-summer 1954 the group had recorded four more sides, this time in the basement of an Omaha drummer named Walter Harrold. The emerging pattern was that Wesley would lead on the jump tunes like their third single "Boppin' with the Mambo" and Willie would front the ballads like the blues B side "What Makes Me Feel This Way." Neither side clicked, however. A year after their first recording the group was struggling through Columbus, Ohio, when they ran into

Wesley's dad, Wynonie Harris. He brought the quintet to New York to meet Henry Glover, A&R man for King Records of Cincinnati.

In the '50s, when you weren't doing too well and felt you could do better by recording for another company, little complications such as recording contracts were dealt with by changing your group's name. So it was that in January of 1955 the Sultans on Duke became the Admirals on King.

Their first King single was the Wes Devereaux-led up-tempo tune "Oh Yes," with exuberant harmonies and an enjoyable sax solo. The flip side, with a lead by Willie, was a melodic pop-blues ballad called "Left with a Broken Heart." Their second King release was a cover of the FIVE KEYS ballad "Close Your Eyes," this time with Devereaux singing lead. The flip side, an up-tempo pop song formerly recorded by Don Cherry ("Give Me Your Love"), was led by McDaniels and gave indication of his solo potential. The Admirals' "Close Your Eyes" never competed with the Five Keys version, and it became their last featured release. Soon after, they backed white artist Kathy Ryan on "It's a Sad, Sad Feeling" and did four backup sides for Robert "Bubber" Johnson while still in New York.

By April 1955 the Admirals/Sultans were back in Omaha doing clubs and hanging out. Gene McDaniels remembers Sam Cooke coming through town and singing with the group on occasion but the Sultans didn't record again until more than two years later. Back in Houston in June 1957 the once-again Sultans cut their last two sides for Duke, "If I Could Tell" with Willie up front and "My Love Is So High" written and led by Eugene. But the group separated soon after, precipitated by Jimmy Farmer joining the armed forces. Wesley and Willie formed a short-lived singing duo into 1958 until Roy Hamilton's manager Bill Cook spotted Willie and added him to the Hamilton tour. Willie wound up in New York cutting a few recordings for the United Artists label as Billy Barnes. Meanwhile T. J. Pruitt and his Pinewood, Mississippi, singers came through Omaha, met Eugene, and asked him to join the act as a lead and first tenor.

They toured west and reached San Francisco, where Eugene (now Gene) began singing with jazz musicians. After working his way down to Los Angeles's Jazz Cellar near Hollywood Boulevard, he met Les McCann. During an audition for McCann he was asked what key and tempo on the song "Never Be Another You" and replied, "Your key, your tempo." Gene, now about 20, sang with Les's combo until discovered by talent scout Don Reardon. At one point Gene worked in the mail room of

Liberty Records until he convinced A&R Director Snuff Garrett he knew more about singing and songs than mail. He recorded for Liberty in 1959 and by May 1961 had the number three record in the United States with "A Hundred Pounds of Clay." He went on to have eight more chart records between 1961 and 1963 including "Tower of Strength" (#5, 1961) and "Chip Chip" (#10, 1962), all produced by Snuff Garrett.

In 1962 he appeared in the motion picture *It's Trad, Dad* and in 1974 wrote the number one jazz-influenced hit for Roberta Flack (another Les McCann discovery), "Feel Like Makin' Love."

On October 7, 1989, the Sultans/Admirals came together in the form of Willie Barnes, Wesley Devereaux, Gary Lewis (also a member of THE CADILLACS), and Lou Courtney to perform at Ronnie I's Collectors Group Concert Volume 3. Singing as if they were still in 1955, the quartet got an ovation from a large audience of appreciative record collectors. The group was amazed that so many people were aware of their sometimes obscure recordings. Today those recordings are prized among collectors.

Entering the '90s Willie Barnes was managing acts, singing, and driving a cab in New York. Devereaux was living in Omaha and occasionally performing as a singer and guitarist. Beasley was also living in Omaha. Farmer died around 1975. Gene McDaniels was living in Philadelphia, writing, producing, and working on the next "Feel Like Makin' Love" while no doubt taking an occasional fond look over his shoulder at his early days as a member of the Sultans/Admirals.

The Swallows

A favorite among collectors of early rhythm and blues recordings, the Swallows were a Baltimore, Maryland, sextet that formed in 1946. Originally calling themselves the Oakaleers, the original members were all 13 years old and included Lawrence Coxson (lead), Earl Hurley (first and second tenor), Herman "Junior" Denby (second tenor and baritone), Frederick Johnson (baritone), Irving Turner (tenor and baritone), and Norris "Bunky" Mack (bass).

The Oakaleers were heavily influenced by the Vibranaires, another Baltimore singing group whose lead singer Sonny Til lived just across the street from tenor Earl Hurley. This was all before the Vibranaires had recorded and changed their name to THE ORIOLES.

By the late '40s, Coxson had gone, Eddie Rich had become the lead, and the group had become known around town as the Swallows. Though most fans assume they became a bird group as a tribute to the Orioles, the name was actually recommended by Fred Johnson's mother, who loved the song "When the Swallows Come Back to Capistrano."

The group attracted the attention of record store owner Ike Goldstick and his associate Bill Levinson after they played some local shows and appeared at an Alan Freed show in Cleveland.

In 1951 the Swallows were signed to King Records of Cincinnati through Goldstick and Levinson (now managing the young group). Before their first session in May 1951, Turner left and the quintet recorded "Dearest," a soft rhythm and blues ballad that garnered appreciable airplay and sales in the Baltimore, Washington, New York, and Philadelphia area, but it turned out that the flip would be their most successful single.

In June 1951 the B side "Will You Be Mine" was reviewed by *Billboard*: "A first rate new group debuts most promisingly with a glowing performance. This disking could set this group up for big things." It reached number nine R&B in August 1951.

"Since You've Been Away" and "Eternally," were next as the best of their early sides.

By their fifth single, "Beside You" (#8 R&B Jukebox, #10 Best Seller, August 1952), Junior Denby was singing lead. The best of the Denby-led sides was a pleasing version of the Warren-Dubin standard "I Only Have Eyes for You" in May 1952.

After 11 singles with King and some personnel changes the group recorded one single for After Hours titled "My Baby." The membership now included Hurley (lead), Eddie Rich, Dee Ernie Bailey, Money Johnson, Irving Turner, and Al France.

In 1956 France and Turner were gone; Bobby Hendricks and Buddy Crawford replaced them, but this contingent never recorded any released product. Later that year Bailey and Hendricks joined the Flyers (Atco), and the Swallows, already in disarray, disbanded.

In 1957 Rich sang with the Honey Boys but they didn't last out the year. One night at a Baltimore club a makeshift group was put together to cover for one of the acts that didn't show, and the group included Rich and Calvin Kollette (lead of the Honey Boys), Buddy Bailey of the local group the Capitols, and former Swallows Earl Hurley and Money Johnson. They liked the way they sounded

and decided to give it a shot as the new Swallows, returning to the King organization's Federal label in 1958. It led to the release of four singles that year, the best being the last release "Who Knows, Do You." Its flip, a cover of Bobby Hendricks's "Itchy Twitchy Feeling," garnered crossover appeal and managed to make the national Top 100 on September 22, 1958 (#100). It was not only their sole Pop chart record, it was simply their *last* record. The group soon disbanded.

In 1988 Eddie Rich and several other members rerecorded "Since You've Been Away" for Val Shively's Starborn label, and the group began appearing on the collectors' series circuit in the New York and Baltimore-Washington area.

THE SWALLOWS

A SIDE/B SIDE	LABEL/CAT NO	DATE
Dearest / Will You Be Mine	King 4458	6/51
Since You've Been Away / Wishing For You	King 4466	8/51
Eternally / It Ain't The Heat	King 4051	12/51
Tell Me Why / Roll Roll Pretty Baby	King 4515	12/51
Beside You / You Left Me	King 4525	4/52
I Only Have Eyes For You / You Walked In	King 4533	5/52
Where Do I Go From Here / Please Baby Please	King 4579	11/52
Our Love Is Dying / Laugh	King 4612	11/52
Nobody's Lovin' Me / Bicycle Tillie	King 4632	5/53
Trust Me / Pleading Blues	King 4656	9/53
I'll Be Waiting / It Feels So Good	King 4676	11/53
My Baby / Good Time Girls	AftrH 104	1954
Oh Lonesome Me / Angel Baby	Fed 12319	1958
We Want To Rock / Rock-A-Bye Baby Rock	Fed 12328	1958
Beside You / Laughing Boy	Fed 12329	1958
Itchy Twitchy Feeling / Who Knows, Do You	Fed 12333	1958
Have Mercy Baby / Since You've Been Away	Strbd 8607	1988

The Teddy Bears

Many ideas for hit songs have come from unusual places or circumstances. Jerry Lee Lewis's "Whole Lot of Shakin' Going On," for example, was inspired by a drunken binge in a rowboat, while Chuck Berry's "Ida Red" was changed to "Maybellene" when he remembered a childhood nursery rhyme in which Maybellene was a cow. But none have as macabre an origin as the Teddy Bears' hit "To Know Him Is to Love Him," a title that came from the headstone on a grave in the Beth David cemetery at Elmont, Long Island.

The group was formed at Fairfax High School in Los Angeles in early 1958 by 17-year-old Phil Spector (born the day after Christmas 1940). The quartet included lead singer Annette Kleinbard, Marshall Leib (tenor), Harvey Goldstein (bass), and Spector (tenor). The group practiced songs Spector had written in the garage of his girlfriend, Donna Kass. After the group had sufficiently rehearsed, each member chipped in $10 to record for two hours at Gold Star Studios. It seemed that if Annette (Donna's close friend) and Harvey hadn't kicked in their share, they probably would have been left off that first Spector four-part harmony demo "Don't You Worry My Little Pet" since he was prepared to do it with Marshall and overdub their harmonies.

One of Spector's songs was conceived when his mother took him to the gravesite of his father, Ben. The legend on the grave marker read "To Know Him Was to Love Him."

Teenaged Phil, his mother, and sister moved to Los Angeles, where he played guitar, wrote songs, and put together his first, short-lived group, the Sleep Walkers.

Soon after the Teddy Bears formed, the foursome recorded "Don't You Worry" on May 20, 1958. Phil then got an introduction to Lew Bedell and his cousin Herb Newman (owners of Era Records) from a friend Donnie Kartoon, who lived on the same street as Bedell. (Era Records' claim to fame at that point was Googie Grant's 1956 number one hit "The Wayward Wind.") Bedell and Newman liked the demo and cut a deal to lease the master, a ploy used in lieu of a recording contract that included hauling all four minors and their parents into court for approval under Hollywood's "Jackie Coogan" law pertaining to working minors.

The group went into the studio to cut another Spector side, "Wonderful, Lovable You," but when it didn't come off in the allotted two hours Phil switched to the tombstone song. With an extra half hour graciously granted by Gold Star owner Stan Ross, Phil cut "To Know Him Is to Love Him" in two takes, with Annette singing her innocent and pleading lead for the trio. It was a trio because Harvey was doing Army Reserve duty at Ford Ord, but his contribution to the group had come prior to the session when he named them after Elvis Presley's number one hit of the previous year, "(Let Me Be Your) Teddy Bear."

On August 1st the single was issued on Dore (an Era subsidiary), and "Don't You Worry" went nowhere.

Marshall and Harvey went on to Los Angeles City College, Annette went into her senior year at Fairfax High, and Phil began business school with designs on being a court reporter. Then in September the flip side "To Know Him Is to Love Him" broke out of Fargo, North Dakota, and Minneapolis, Minnesota, and on September 22nd debuted at number 88 on *Billboard*'s Top 100. The single took off after its initial play on "American Bandstand," and the group headed to Philadelphia to perform on Dick Clark's show as part of a promo tour during Thanksgiving. (They were still only a trio: Harvey was apparently passed over since he hadn't performed on the now flipped B side hit.)

By December 1st "To Know Him" was at number one and stayed there three weeks, selling about one and a half million copies. It hit number 10 R&B and number two in England. Phil's sister Shirley became the group's manager, though Marshall and Annette had great misgivings over her involvement, which caused ever-widening friction.

Having made the mistake of not signing the group to a contract but only licensing masters, Dore lost the Teddy Bears after a disagreement over the quality of Spector's next song, "Oh Why," which they refused to issue. With "To Know Him" at number three in *Billboard*, the group signed with Imperial Records.

The Teddy Bears had that rare opportunity to sign with a new label while they were hot; Imperial allowed them to record an LP, unheard-of for a one-record group.

Their first Imperial single was "Oh Why." Bedell and Newman were proven right in not wanting to issue it when the ballad reached only number 91 in March 1951 while its flip, "I Don't Need You Anymore," spent one week at number 98 in February. The LP was rushed into production, but with nothing magical like their first single to recommend it, it failed. Two more Imperial singles, "You Said Goodbye" and "Don't Go Away," along with the finally finished "Wonderful, Lovable You" that Dore had in the can, were all released in 1959. They stirred no interest, hastening the Bears' disintegration as a one-shot group.

In September 1959 Annette was severely injured when her MG convertible rolled down a hillside off of Hollywood's Mulholland Drive. It's reported that Phil never visited her during her recuperation, and this too probably hastened the group's separation.

Harvey went on to be an accountant. Marshall toured with the Hollywood Argyles, produced acts like Timi Yuro, and became a film music supervisor in the '70s, working on such projects as *Ode to Billy Joe* and *Take This Job and Shove It*. Annette Kleinbard became Annette Bard, who in turn became Carol Connors, a top-notch songwriter who cowrote the Billy Preston and Syreeta hit "With You I'm Born Again" (#4, 1979) and the theme from *Rocky* (with Bill Conti), "Gonna Fly Now" (#1, 1977), as well as the theme for *Mr. Mom*.

Phil, of course, went on to legendary status as a producer for acts like THE RONETTES, THE CRYSTALS, and the Righteous Brothers, and is the subject of a number of books.

THE TEDDY BEARS

A SIDE/B SIDE	LABEL/CAT NO	DATE
To Know Him Is To Love Him /		
Don't You Worry My Little Pet	Dore 503	7/58
Oh Why /		
I Don't Need You Anymore	Imprl 5562	12/58
You Said Goodbye /		
If You Only Knew	Imprl 5581	3/59
Till You'll Be Mine /		
Wonderful Loveable You	Dore 520	4/59
Don't Go Away /		
Seven Lonely Days	Imprl 5594	1959

The Three Chuckles

A vocal/instrumental act that also started as a comedy group, the Three Chuckles were formed in 1949. Tommy Romano and Tommy Gilberto were both residents of the Red Hook section of Brooklyn, New York, when they met playing sandlot baseball. Romano had left Brooklyn Special Trades School and Gilberto was employed by his father in the tombstone business when they decided to form a group with accordionist Phil Benti. Gilberto sang lead and played bass and Romano sang the middle and played guitar. To avoid the "Tommy" confusion Gilberto changed his name to Russ. The threesome met booking agent Charlie Bush who told them they first needed a name; when a mother and son arrived to audition for Bush and the child was noticed eating a Chuckles bar, the group had its name.

The Three Chuckles toured from 1950 to 1952, polishing their craft in every kind of venue from clubs to bowling alley lounges. They would travel to their destinations in a 1936 Oldsmobile, which once broke down right in New York's Holland Tunnel, forcing them to leave the car and walk out, instruments in hand.

While showcasing in the South, Phil decided a more stable life was in order and decided to quit. Russ and Tom checked with the New York musicians union and came up with 15-year-old Teddy Randazzo of 115th Street in Manhattan, who had just joined the union that month. Russ was 27 and Tom 24 when they reorganized the Three Chuckles in 1953. The group's influences, according to Teddy, were THE FOUR ACES, Tony Bennett, and Johnny Ray, while some of their early songs included "Stardust," "You Belong to Me," and "How High the Moon."

Their first show with Teddy was at the Crystal Lake Lounge in Newburgh, New York. Still leaning heavily on comedy, they tipped TV newcomer Soupy Sales (whose show they performed on) to their gag of throwing shaving cream pies. At one show on the Jersey Shore the group was approached by an aspiring songwriter, Cirino Colacrais, who gave them a song written on a napkin titled "Runaround." They took it with little enthusiasm and forgot about it until they played a bowling alley lounge in Detroit in the summer of 1953. There they were "discovered" by Ray Gayhan, a promotion manager who arranged a record deal with his local Great Lakes label and their new subsidiary, Boulevard Records. The two songs they cut were "At Last You Understand" and "Runaround." While recording, the engineer, hearing Teddy prompting Russ on the melody, suggested Teddy sing the lead as his voice was more suited to the ballad. Teddy then became the full-time lead—at least on records. "Runaround" took off, breaking out of Boulevard's Detroit home base. It was bought by RCA's X-division along with their management and recording contract for over $50,000, a huge sum in those days.

On November 13, 1954, "Runaround" charted nationally and reached number 20, opening the door to bigger and more lucrative appearances from New York to Las Vegas. They performed on the TV shows of Ernie Kovacs, Perry Como, and Steve Allen, and reportedly sold over a million copies of "Runaround."

They built a solid relationship with disc jockey Alan Freed. When Alan began casting for his 1955 movie *Rock, Rock, Rock*, the Three Chuckles were chosen to perform and Teddy was given the male lead opposite Tuesday Weld.

Several singles followed but none with the impact of "Runaround." In 1955 they were given the song "Ivory Tower" but passed it over for a tune called "Times Two, I Love You," which reached number 67 in November. "Ivory Tower" became a hit for THE CHARMS (#11 Pop) in early 1956.

The Three Chuckles spent a few minutes on camera in the 1958 film *The Girl Can't Help It* starring Mamie Van Doren and then returned from Hollywood to record an LP of mostly standards for RCA Records. The LP reportedly sold a few hundred thousand copies. By 1956 the Three Chuckles had moved to RCA's Vik affiliate and charted once more with the 1939 number one Benny Goodman hit "And the Angels Sing" (#70). Three singles later Randazzo opted for a solo career; Russ and Tommy replaced him with Jackie Farrell but the trio never released another single.

By the early '70s Tommy Romano was performing with Karen Gayle as A Chuckle and a Chicklet. Russ passed away and Teddy Randazzo had a short-lived solo career with his biggest record being "The Way of a Clown" (#44, 1960, ABC Paramount). Randazzo, however, went on to great fame as a songwriter, penning hits for LITTLE ANTHONY AND THE IMPERIALS ("Goin' Out of My Head," #6, 1964, and "Hurt So Bad," #10, 1965, both on DCP).

THE THREE CHUCKLES

A SIDE/B SIDE	LABEL/CAT NO	DATE
Runaround /		
At Last You Understand	Blvd 100	1953
Runaround /		
At Last You Understand	X 0066	9/54
Foolishly /		
If You Should Love Again	X 0095	1/55
So Long /		
You Should Have Told Me	X 0134	4/55
Blue Lover / Realize	X 0150	6/55
Still Thinking Of You /		
Times Two, I Love You	X 0162	8/55
The Funny Little Things We		
Used To Do / Anyway	X 0186	12/55
Tell Me / And The Angels Sing	X 0194	2/56
Anyway / The Funny Little		
Things We Used To Do	Vik 0186	1956
Tell Me / And The Angels Sing	Vik 0194	1956
Gypsy In My Soul /		
We're Still Holding Hands	Vik 0216	6/56
Midnight Till Dawn /		
Fall Out Of Love	Vik 0232	9/56
We're Gonna Rock Tonight /		
Won't You Give Me A Chance	Vik 0244	11/56

The Tune Weavers

The Tune Weavers earned a place in rock and roll history with their classic ballad "Happy, Happy Birthday Baby," but the group itself was really a pop-jazz outfit.

Margo Sylvia and her brother Gilbert Lopez performed around Boston as a duet in the mid-'50s. They were eventually joined by Margo's husband John Sylvia and her cousin Charlotte Davis doing a repertoire of R&B songs and jazz vocalese.

They went by the name the Tone Weavers until one night a waiter at a club was told by his boss to introduce the act. He was so nervous about standing up in front of a crowd that he introduced them as the Tune Weavers, and they decided to keep it. They performed songs by THE FOUR FRESHMEN and the Jackie Gleason Orchestra, two of their influences.

In late 1956 the foursome, Margo (20, lead), Charlotte (20, obbligato), Gil (22, tenor), and John (21, bass) came to the attention of former bandleader Frank Paul, whose brother-in-law had raved about the group. Frank, who had his own small record label, Casa Grande (named after his old band), finally agreed to hear them and went to his brother-in-law's home where they were set to audition. After they played some tapes and sang some a cappella tunes, Margo and company sang a song she wrote at the age of 16 called "Happy, Happy Birthday Baby." Frank came to life and said "That's the one we're going to record."

On March 7, 1957, the Tune Weavers recorded "Happy" and the standard "Old Man River" as eight-months-pregnant Margo crooned her way through the songs. The record came out soon afterward, but Frank Paul's promotion was minor league in comparison to what was necessary and the birthday song went nowhere. Then in July a Philadelphia disc jockey played the record and suddenly the phones were ringing off the hook. Checker Records (distributed by Chess) picked up the distribution rights from Casa Grande and by September 16th "Happy, Happy Birthday Baby" was chart bound, eventually reaching number five Pop and number four on the R&B chart while selling over two million copies.

Their first big performance was at one of Alan Freed's rock and roll shows at the Brooklyn Paramount with Paul Anka, Little Richard, THE DIAMONDS, Della Reese, and the blonde bombshell Joann Campbell. The group maintained a one-record touring career with artists like the Everly

Brothers, Buddy Holly and the Crickets, Johnny Mathis, Tony Bennett, THE AMES BROTHERS, THE SPANIELS, LaVern Baker, THE CLEFTONES, Jerry Lee Lewis, THE DEL-VIKINGS, Ricky Nelson, THE CHANTELS, and many more. Several quality recordings followed on both Checker and Casa Grande (including "I Remember Dear" and "My Congratulations Baby") but the group never charted again.

In 1958 Charlotte left and was replaced by William Morris, Jr.

The group broke up in 1962 but re-formed for some '70s oldies shows. In 1988 Margo recorded under the Tune Weavers name singing all the harmony parts on two singles for Bruce Patch's Classic Artist Records. One was a remake of "Happy, Happy Birthday Baby" done as a Christmas song titled "Merry, Merry Christmas Baby."

Today Margo lives in San Francisco and occasionally performs. Her ex-husband John has been a therapist at Boston State College. Charlotte became a housewife and Gil the manager of an electrical plant. Margo's son Mark Sylvia has his foot firmly planted in the music business as a record producer working with Howard Huntsberry and Klymaxx.

THE TUNE WEAVERS

A SIDE/B SIDE	LABEL/CAT NO	DATE
Happy, Happy Birthday Baby / Ol' Man River	CasaG 4037	1957
I Remember Dear / Pamela Jean	CasaG 4038	1957
Happy, Happy Birthday Baby / Ol' Man River	Checker 872	1957
Happy, Happy Birthday Baby / Yo Yo Walk	Checker 872	1957
Ol' Man River / Tough Enough	Checker 880	1957
I'm Cold / There Stands My Love	CasaG 4040	1958
Little Boy / Look Down That Lonesome Road	CasaG 101	1958
My Congratulations Baby / This Can't Be Love	CasaG 3038	1960
Your Skies Of Blue / Congratulations On Your Wedding . . .	Chkr 1007	1/62
Margo Sylvia and the Tune Weavers		
Come Back To Me / I've Tried	ClsArt 104	1988
Merry, Merry Christmas Baby / What Are You Doing New Year's	ClsArt 107	1988
Merry, Merry Christmas Baby / What Are You Doing New Year's / You're My Christmas Present (Skyliners)	ClsArt 116	1989

The Turbans

A top-quality R&B harmony group out of Philadelphia, the Turbans turned a mambo rhythm into a rock and roll standard.

In 1955 the members were Al Banks (lead), Matthew Platt (tenor), Charlie Williams (baritone), and Andrew "Chet" Jones (bass). They were discovered by manager Herman Gillespie, who took them to Al Silver at Herald Records in New York to audition. Al Banks's soaring falsetto impressed Silvers (and it probably influenced such singers as Russell Tompkins, Jr. of THE STYLISTICS and THE DELFONICS, two later Philadelphia star groups).

Herman wanted to give them a name similar to another Philadelphia group, Steve Gibson and the Red Caps. Charlie didn't agree and said, "I'd rather wear a turban than a cap." You know the rest.

They recorded a Chet Jones song, "When You Dance," which had one of the slickest mambo rhythms of the year and featured a searing, ear-catching sax instrumental along with the group's solid harmonies and Al's stratospheric falsetto. It was issued in August 1955 and took a long, slow climb before finally reaching number 33 Pop and number three R&B.

On December 23rd the Turbans tore the house down at Doctor Jive's Brooklyn Paramount Christmas Show. That show also featured Ruth Brown, THE FIVE KEYS, Bo Diddley, and Willis Jackson and his orchestra.

The group followed up with an interesting rhythm tune with nice melody changes and their now trademark rhythm change in the sax solo. "Sister Sookey" did well in the East and South but never made the national Top 100.

Their third single, "I'm Nobody's," was a strong ballad and showed the Turbans to be more than an up-tempo quartet. *Billboard*'s May 26th reviewer wrote, "The crooning, screaming tenor lead makes this side stand out sharply. The guy is a great performer and his chanting with a solid backup makes this a strong contender." Sadly it did not sell enough (and was not promoted enough) to chart nationally.

The same fate befell their next three Herald Singles, the last of which was the classic Turbans ballad "Congratulations." Despite limited activity in 1958, it went on to become an East Coast doo wop standard today.

The group moved on to Red Top, Roulette, and eventually Philadelphia's Parkway Records in 1961 with a modified version of "When You Dance" (added strings and less Latin rhythm), which was a mere shell of its 1955 predecessor except for the group's great harmony and Al's still stimulating lead. Its flip, "Golden Rings," was a solid ballad that deserved more attention than it got.

The group finished its career on Imperial Records. One of Art Laboe's *Oldies But Goodies* LPs (Volume II, spring of 1960) contained "When You Dance" and helped further ensure its place as a rock and roll classic.

In the late '60s the Turbans finally got an LP when Relic Records' Eddie Gries, Donn Fileti, and Little Walter issued *The Turbans' Greatest Hits*, which included all six A and B sides from their Herald days.

Al Banks went on to sing with Charlie Thomas's DRIFTERS after the Turbans broke up, but as late as the mid-'80s a Turbans group was performing on the oldies scene.

THE TURBANS

A SIDE/B SIDE	LABEL/CAT NO	DATE
When You Dance /		
Let Me Show You	Herald 458	8/55
Sister Sookey /		
I'll Always Watch Over You	Herald 469	2/56
I'm Nobody's . . . / B-I-N-G-O	Herald 478	5/56
It Was A Nite Like This /		
All Of My Love	Herald 486	8/56
Valley Of Love / Bye And Bye	Herald 495	1/57
Congratulations / The Wadda-Do	Herald 510	12/57
I Promise You Love / Curfew Time	RedTop 115	1959
Diamonds And Pearls / Bad Man	Roul 4281	1960
I'm Not Your Fool Anymore /		
Three Friends	Roul 4326	1961
When You Dance / Golden Rings	Prkwy 820	3/61
Six Questions /		
The Lament Of Silver Gulch	Imprl 5807	12/61
Clicky Clicky Clack /		
This Is My Story	Imprl 5828	3/62
I Wonder / The Damage Is Done	Imprl 5847	6/62

The Valentines

Agroup that never had a national chart record yet is widely known among lovers of '50s rhythm and blues, the Valentines created some fondly remembered 45s while serving as a launching pad for a few important careers.

The group began in 1952 across from the Polo Grounds (at the Colonial Projects on 8th Avenue) in New York City, home of the National League pennant winners, the New York Giants.

The original members Raymond "Pop" Briggs (tenor), Carl Hogan (second tenor), Mickey Francis (first tenor and lead), and Ronnie Bright (bass) would practice on the playground on 128th Street and Amsterdam Avenue in Harlem and on a number of street corners from 130th to 161st Street in the Sugarhill section of town (also known as Washington Heights). Though none had any musical training (though Carl's grandfather Broadus Hogan wrote the gospel classic "Amen"), they managed an enthusiastic street blend.

The quartet originally called themselves the Dreamers and began performing at house parties. At one of these, according to one source, they met a young writer/singer up from his hometown of Philadelphia named Richard Barrett who sang with a Philly street group called the Angels (no recordings). Phil Groia, in *They All Sang on the Corner*, states the group actually met Barrett in a Riverside Drive park while he was serenading park lovers with his ukulele. Whatever the meeting place, he made his way into the group because they wanted his song "Summer Love," and Richard's lead vocals came with the song. (The distinctive tone of that voice gave the Valentines a colorful recorded sound that would still be appreciated years later.) With Barrett aboard, the Dreamers opted for a new name and came up with the Valentines, courtesy of Mickey's fondness for the song "My Funny Valentine."

Their friend Raoul Cita of THE HARPTONES brought them to Monte Bruce of Bruce Records where they did a "Summer Love" demo, and though the tape was played on local radio, Bruce never issued it or recorded the group again.

In 1954 the group turned professional the day they made their first dollar, which was all each member received for performing at Bowman's on 155th Street and St. Nicholas Avenue. (Considering that only two of the 12 people there applauded, they were lucky to be paid at all.) Influenced both musically and in showmanship by THE CADILLACS, THE SOLITAIRES, and THE FLAMINGOS, the Valentines did a variety of "battle of the groups" shows: there was the night they took on the Harptones at the Englewood Jewish Center, and another time they fought for bragging rights against the Cadillacs and the Opals at the Rockland Palace. Then there was the date at an Apollo Theater amateur night contest when they lost out to a belly dancer with a snake. Even their rendition of THE DRIFTERS' "Money Honey" couldn't sway the audience from the snake charmer.

Donald Razor (the Velvets, Red Robin) came in to replace Hogan. The group went to see Hy Weiss, who ran Old Town Records out of the cloak room of the Triboro Theatre on 125th Street and 3rd Avenue in Harlem. Weiss signed the Valentines and issued "Summer Love," along with the beautiful Barrett-penned love song "Tonight Kathleen," in December 1954, but Old Town had no distribution and the record went unnoticed.

Eddie Edgehill was in at second tenor when the group moved to George Goldner's Rama label and issued the chime harmonied "Lily Maebelle" in September 1955. Some say the street tune was written by Barrett and Briggs about Raymond's sister Lil, though others remember it as a long-standing neighborhood tune that Donald Razor came up with. Either way it became an East Coast favorite, allowing the hoofing Valentines to work Alan Freed shows at the Academy of Music and Brooklyn Paramount along with stints at the Apollo (minus the snake dancing competition), Howard, and Royal Theatres, and dates with disc jockeys Hal Jackson and Jocko.

A beautiful and haunting holiday ballad was next with the November release of "Christmas Prayer." Appearing on stage in white jackets with red valentines on the pockets, red shirts, black shoes, and pink bowties, the debonair dancers were a top performance attraction though their in-person harmonies were not always sharp.

In April 1956 the group blanketed the East Coast with "Woo Woo Train," (an Alan Freed favorite). The group would open its shows coming on-stage in a chugging conga line to its driving beat.

David Clowney (the Pearls, Onyx) replaced Raymond Briggs in 1956. Carl Hogan, who had been singing with the Miracles (the original group on Fury a year before Smokey Robinson's group recorded), rejoined for a last session which produced the Hogan-Barrett ballad "Don't Say Goodbye."

In between, the Valentines sang with the Wrens on their Rama rarity "C'est la Vie" and did a radio promotional song for Boston disc jockey Joe Smith, who later went on to become head of Warner Bros. Records.

The group broke up in 1958 after one more Apollo appearance out of frustration brought on by a lack of hits. David Clowney became Dave "Baby" Cortez, arranger for many groups like THE PARAGONS and THE JESTERS and performer of his own instrumental monster hit ("Happy Organ," #1, 1959). Carl Hogan then became a writer, often cowriting with Barrett on sides like "So Much" (the Imperials), "What's My Chances" (Alvin Robinson), and "Be Sure My Love" (THE DUBS). Bass

Ronnie Bright joined the Cadillacs and in 1963 had a hit (#16) with Johnny Cymbal as the immortal "Mr. Bass Man." He then joined THE DEEP RIVER BOYS and later Carl Gardner's COASTERS. Richard Barrett became the legendary A&R Director for Goldner's End and Gone labels and recorded acts like LITTLE ANTHONY AND THE IMPERIALS, THE CHANTELS, and later the Three Degrees.

THE VALENTINES

A SIDE/B SIDE	LABEL/CAT NO	DATE
Summer Love / Tonight Kathleen	OldTn 1009	12/54
Lilly Maebelle / Falling For You	Rama 171	9/55
Christmas Prayer / K-I-S-S Me	Rama 186	11/55
I Love You Darling / Hand Me Down Love	Rama 181	12/55
The Woo Woo Train / Why	Rama 196	4/56
Twenty Minutes / I'll Never Let You Go	Rama 201	6/56
Nature's Creation / My Story Of Love	Rama 208	9/56
Don't Say Goodnight / I Cried Oh, Oh	Rama 228	4/57

The Velours

One of the most polished of the '50s street-corner groups, the Velours built an 11-record career that began in Brooklyn's Bedford-Stuyvesant section during early 1956.

The members, all around 19 years old, were Jerome "Romeo" Ramos (lead), John Cheetom (first tenor), Donald Heywood (second tenor), Kenneth Walker (baritone), and Marvin Holland (bass). Their influences ranged from THE RAVENS to the Harmonizing Four.

During the late spring the group met Jerry Winston, a former employee of Malverne Record Distributors who had been dabbling in mambo and cha-cha records with his Mardi Gras label out of 5544 Avenue D in Brooklyn. With the acquisition of the exceptional Velours, Winston launched his new Onyx label in June 1956 with their original rhythm ballad "My Love Come Back." The best of all Velours records, that first effort became a regionally popular single, spreading up and down the East Coast and becoming a New York City favorite.

Their second single, the ballad "Romeo," received some local airplay but disappeared quickly, making it the rarest of Velours vinyl offerings.

By the spring of 1957 Holland had left, as had Walker. They were replaced by Charles Moffitt (bass) and John Pearson (baritone). The Velours then issued their third ballad and biggest single, "Can I Come Over Tonight." It established a strong sales and airplay pattern, particularly in the East, and by July 8th had charted in *Billboard* at number 83. Though kids weren't buying Velours records in droves, the radio play they received kept them working the theatre circuit from the Apollo and the Brooklyn Paramount to the Howard Theatre in Washington and the Royal in Baltimore. Unlike most of the favorite son groups of Brooklyn, the Velours got work beyond the tri-state area due to their extensive airplay; they also performed in the West, the Carolinas, and even Mexico.

"This Could Be the Night" followed in the fall of 1957. A strong ballad with another gem of a Jerome Ramos lead, it couldn't hit its mark. Their next single, "Remember," was the group's first up-tempo A side. Like "Come Over Tonight" it peaked at number 83 Pop (March 1958).

The group that started Onyx also closed it down when the label folded in February. The distribution of "Remember" was picked up by MGM, who transferred the side to its Orbit satellite.

For their next releases the group added another tenor, Troy Keyes, and transferred to MGM's Cub label. After "I'll Never Smile Again" in 1958 (with Keyes on lead doing an INK SPOTS-styled vocal), Troy left and Keith Williams (tenor) joined. Keyes went on to join the High Keys (Atco, 1963) and later charted as a solo artist with "Love Explosion" (#92 Pop, #43 R&B, ABC 1968). The group did one more Cub single, a nice though lusterless version of THE CLOVERS' "Blue Velvet" in 1959.

One single on the small Studio label ("I Promise") and the group found itself with the distinction of being on three George Goldner labels in a row with three different singles (and little else to show for it). The best of the three was a remake of "Can I Come Over Tonight."

By 1961 Moffitt, Williams, and Pearson had abandoned ship, with the latter becoming road manager for THE FLAMINGOS. The three tenors, Ramos, Cheetom, and Heyward, added a fourth tenor, Richard Pitts (the Newtones, Baton), and cut one last Velours single titled "Don't Pity Me."

The group then decided to take their chances as part of the soul explosion in England. In May 1968 they released "Baby Make Your Own Sweet Music" as the Fantastics on MGM. Three singles on Deram made no great waves, but their first release for Bell ("Something Old, Something New") in early 1971 was a U.K. chart winner at number nine and got some exposure in the U.S. Their new soul sound

was a far cry from their sweet R&B style of the Onyx days.

In the mid-'70s Cheetom began working in a European version of THE PLATTERS; Heywood kept the group going, while Ramos returned to the United States.

In March 1984 the Velours (with Ramos and Moffitt) performed at a U.G.H.A. show in New Jersey and did justice to the songs that had become doo wop classics. The group performed on occasion, but in the late '80s Moffitt died, the victim of a senseless attack.

THE VELOURS

A SIDE/B SIDE	LABEL/CAT NO	DATE
My Love Come Back / Honey Drop	Onyx 501	6/56
Romeo / What You Do To Me	Onyx 508	2/57
Can I Come Over Tonight / Where There's A Will	Onyx 512	5/57
This Could Be The Night / Hands Across The Table	Onyx 515	10/57
Remember / Can I Walk You Home	Onyx 520	2/58
Remember / Can I Walk You Home	Orbit 9001	3/58
Crazy Love / I'll Never Smile Again	Cub 9014	8/58
Blue Velvet / Tired Of Your Rock and Rollin'	Cub 9029	8/58
I Promise / Little Sweetheart	Studio 9902	1959
Can I Come Over Tonight / Where There's A Will	Gone 5092	1960
Sweet Sixteen / Daddy Warbucks	Goldisc 3012	1960
Lover Come Back / The Lonely One	End 1090	4/61
Don't Pity Me / I'm Gonna Change	MGM 13780	7/67

The Fantastics

Baby Make Your Own Sweet Music / Who Could Be Loving You	MGM 1434	5/68
Face To Face With Heartache / This Must Be My Rainy Day	Deram 264	6/69
Waiting Round For The Heartaches / Ask The Lonely	Deram 283	1/70
For The Old Times' Sake / Exodus Main Theme	Deram 334	1/71
Something Old, Something New / High And Dry	Bell 1141	3/71
Something Wonderful / Man Made World	Bell 1162	6/71
(Love Me) Love The Life I Lead	Bell 45157	1971
The Best Of Strangers Now	Bell 45279	1971
Baby Make Your Own Sweet Music / Who Could Be Loving You	Poly 2027004	8/71

The Wanderers

A pop-jazz group, the Wanderers were probably too pop for the rock and roll era and too jazzy for success as rhythm and blues artists. Alfonso Brown (lead), Frank Joyner (second tenor), Robert Yarborough (baritone), and Shephard Grant (bass) started out as the Barons on 116th Street and Lenox Avenue in New York's Harlem, circa 1952. For a short while they were the Larks (not the Apollo group) and changed to the Singing Wanderers after appearing at an Apollo amateur night show and winning. Their early style was based on a MILLS BROTHERS sound.

By 1953 Alfonso Brown was not taking rehearsals seriously, so Joyner asked returning Korean vet Ray Pollard to take over the lead spot. (Pollard and Joyner had both attended Cooper Junior High School.) With Pollard's powerful bass-to-tenor flexibility the group sounded better than ever and by mid- to late 1954 found themselves on Savoy Records for the single "We Could Find Happiness."

In the fall of 1954 the Singing Wanderers joined Decca for two totally opposite-sounding singles, the novelty number "Say Hey Willie Mays" and the strong ballad "The Wrong Party Again."

Lee Majid, Savoy's A&R director, found their sound to his liking and took on the managerial reins, booking them with such luminaries as Eartha Kitt, Ethel Merman, and Martha Raye. Even without a hit they appeared numerous times on Ed Sullivan's TV show. Though their sound was more polished than that of the average black group of the era, they were not spared the trials and tribulations of the touring life. On one trip the quintet found itself snowbound in Kansas. When they finally made it to a small nearby town, the hotels were filled up with other trapped travelers, forcing them to hole up in the one available place of lodging in the burg, the town jail.

In late 1957 the group, now called the Wanderers, signed to Onyx Records for one superb pop outing called "Thinking of You." It received good response in the New York area and established Pollard's powerful pipes as among the elite of the mid-'50s group leads.

MGM acquired Onyx records. Since they also owned Orbit and Cub, "A Teenage Quarrel" followed on those two labels. The group usually proved to be superior to the ballads they issued in 1958 and 1959, though the Stallman-Jacobson song "Only When You're Lonely" and the jazz influenced "I'm Waiting in Green Pastures" were exceptions.

By 1961 someone finally got the idea to pair the power of the Wanderers with some powerful past hits, a combination that yielded the group's biggest success, "For Your Love." It was reviewed on March 27, 1961, by *Billboard*, with the reviewer observing, "Ed Townsend's 1957 hit rock-a-ballad is wrapped in emotion-packed vocal by lead singer and group. Good side."

On May 15, 1961, it charted nationally at number 93 but attained greater acceptance in the New York area. Their follow-up was the rhythm and blues, doo wop-oriented "I'll Never Smile Again."

Their best single was a rhythm ballad issued in late summer of 1961 called "Somebody Else's Sweetheart," credited to someone named David Bacharach. That writing entity was understandably unknown; it was their first recorded song, partially explaining the dash left out between the two names Hal David and Burt Bacharach.

The Wanderers' last and highest chart record was "There Is No Greater Love" (#88 Pop) in the summer of 1962. As the single took off it was transferred to the parent company MGM, and the group's reward for MGM's inept promotion was to be dropped.

The Wanderers continued to perform until 1970, when bass Shep Grant died. Pollard continued singing and landed a role in the Broadway play "Purlie" in 1971. In 1972 he joined the Joe Cuba Sextet.

During the '80s Ray sang with an INK SPOTS group, but on November 24, 1989, he jumped in his time machine and turned the clock back to the '50s, re-forming the Wanderers with Robert Yarborough for a 13th anniversary United in Group Harmony show in North Bergen, New Jersey.

THE WANDERERS

A SIDE/B SIDE	LABEL/CAT NO	DATE
The Singing Wanderers		
We Could Find Happiness /		
Hey Mae Ethel	Savoy 1109	1953
Say Hey, Willie Mays /		
Don't Drop It	Decca 29230	1954
The Wrong Party Again /		
Three Roses	Decca 29298	1954
The Wanderers		
Thinking Of You /		
Great Jumpin' Catfish	Onyx 518	1957
A Teenage Quarrel /		
My Shining Hour	Orbit 9003	1958

A SIDE/B SIDE	LABEL/CAT NO	DATE
A Teenage Quarrel / My Shining Hour	Cub 9003	1958
Two Hearts On A Window Pane / Collecting Hearts	Cub 9019	1958
Please / Shadrach, Meshach And Abednego	Cub 9023	1958
I'm Not Ashamed / Only When You're Lonely	Cub 9035	1959
I Walked Through A Forest / I'm Waiting In Green Pastures	Cub 9054	1959
I Need You More / I Could Make You Mine	Cub 9075	1960
For Your Love / Sally Goodheart	Cub 9089	1961
I'll Never Smile Again / A Little Too Long	Cub 9094	1961
She Wears My Ring / Somebody Else's Sweetheart	Cub 9099	1961
There Is No Greater Love / As Time Goes By	Cub 9109	1962
There Is No Greater Love / As Time Goes By	MGM 13082	1962

Billy Ward and His Dominoes

A group's career longevity is often based on its ability to find and hold onto that one great vocal interpreter. The Dominoes' career was blessed with three of the greatest leads ever, Clyde McPhatter, Jackie Wilson, and Eugene Mumford. Along the way, the Dominoes became one of the most influential R&B groups of the early '50s.

Founder Billy Ward was born in Los Angeles, the son of a preacher and a choir-singing mother. He began composing classical and gospel works when the family took up residence in Philadelphia and at age 14 composed "Dejection," a serious piece that won a citywide competition and was performed by a symphony orchestra conducted by Walter Damrosch. After leaving the army, where he was the Director of the Coast Artillery Choir, he ventured to New York, went to the Juilliard School of Music, and became a vocal coach and arranger. A suggestion from songwriter Rose Marks that he start a singing group led to the formation of a short-lived unit whose commitment turned out to be questionable. Ward realized that the best way to ensure a stable and motivated group was to assemble the best of his pupils. So it was that in 1950 the

Ques were born, consisting of Clyde Ward (lead), Charlie White (tenor), Joe Lamont (baritone), Bill Brown (bass), and Billy Ward accompanying on piano. Clyde Ward was actually Clyde McPhatter, posing as Billy's brother.

Before he joined the Ques, later called the Dominoes, Clyde had won the Apollo's amateur night contest as a solo artist. He got a chance to win again as he and the heavily rehearsed Dominoes played Amateur Night in mid-1950 as a gospel quartet, winning in a walk. This led to an October appearance on Arthur Godfrey's "Talent Scouts," where they won singing Billy Ward's unique arrangement of "Goodnight Irene."

By the end of 1950 all this attention resulted in their signing with Syd Nathan's King Records.

In December 1950 they inaugurated King's new Federal label with "Do Something for Me," an instant R&B smash (#6 Best Seller, #8 Jukebox). What set the Dominoes apart was their blend of gospel and blues, and this was apparent from their first release. In February 1951 they tried a ballad, the beautiful Frances Langford 1937 standard "Harbor Lights," and though it was an impressive recording highlighted by Clyde's brilliant tenor lead, "Harbor Lights" was not a big seller.

The group returned to its up-tempo roots later in 1951 with a record that practically defined R&B in the '50s, "Sixty Minute Man." It had a raunchy lyric about a guy named Dan who boasts of his prowess with the ladies ("I rock 'em, roll 'em all night long," the bass proudly stated). Though McPhatter was to become a legendary lead singer and was featured on most of the Dominoes' singles, bass Bill Brown stole the show as the lead on this landmark release.

On May 26, 1951, "Sixty" entered the R&B charts and spent three and a half months at number one, stayed for 30 weeks on the hit list, and sold over a million copies. It's probably the first R&B vocal group record to cross over as a pop hit, reaching number 17.

The follow-up, "I Am with You," was a bluesy McPhatter-led ballad that went to number eight R&B in November 1951. At about the same time they issued a single as their second try with Little Esther (Phillips) titled "Heart to Heart."

The group's next single was an exciting rocker that reached number seven R&B but whose greatest distinction would not be realized until three years later when the Harvey Fuqua composition "Sincerely" became a big hit for THE MOONGLOWS. The midsection of "Sincerely" was note-for-note and almost word-for-word from the middle of "That's What You're Doing to Me."

Even though the Dominoes were hot in 1951, Charlie White left to join THE CLOVERS and Bill Brown just left. His replacement was David McNeil of THE LARKS and White's tenor substitute was James Van Loan, brother of THE RAVENS' Joe Van Loan.

In April 1952 the Dominoes conquered the charts again with a blues rocker ("Have Mercy Baby") that gave them their second number one R&B blast in eight tries, spending seven weeks at number one Best Seller and 10 weeks on top of the Jukebox charts. The public couldn't get enough of them; their June 14, 1952, schedule—an afternoon gig at the Washington Auditorium followed by an evening performance at the Coliseum Arena in New Orleans—typified their glorious in-demand days.

In October, Federal, feeling the power of its act, released "No Room" and "Yours Forever" in the same week and they promptly killed each other off. The label returned to sanity with the November issuance of "I'd Be Satisfied" (#8). "The Bells," released Christmas week 1952, was the Dominoes' strangest record. Complete with an uncontrollably crying Clyde and dirge-like doo wops, this musical funeral march grabbed the public to the tune of a number three hit. The flip was no slouch either, taking a ride to number four on its own merit. With an intro and harmonies straight out of "Sixty Minute Man," "Pedal Pushin' Papa" kept Ward and his Dominoes right up there with the Clovers in popularity. They played everywhere and with everyone, even headlining shows around the country with boxer-turned-singer Sugar Ray Robinson.

Their next single, "These Foolish Things," was a beautiful rendition of the Billie Holiday and Teddy Wilson Orchestra's 1936 number five hit. Clyde and company coincidentally took their version to the same level (R&B), but the song also had the distinction of being Clyde's last Dominoes 45. After a show in Providence, Rhode Island, McPhatter decided to quit. He was earning little of what the group (Billy Ward, that is) was taking in and wanted a new start. Soon after, Ward held an afternoon audition at the Fox Theater in Detroit. A young, brash Golden Gloves boxing champ showed up and stated that he was a better singer than McPhatter, belting out a soulful rocker to prove his point. So impressive was this outstanding vocalist that Ward hired him on the spot. Not only could he sing in Clyde's league, he sounded an awful lot like Clyde.

So it was that 19-year-old Jackie "Sonny" Wilson took over the Dominoes' reins. Wilson had been discovered in 1951 at a talent show by the best talent finder in Los Angeles, Johnny Otis. Clyde stayed with the Dominoes for a few weeks to break Jackie in, but the two never recorded or performed together.

In May, McPhatter signed with Atlantic and formed THE DRIFTERS.

In June, Dominoes bass David McNeil joined the armed forces. The second week of July signaled the Dominoes' first release with Wilson. "You Can't Keep a Good Man Down" charted in September moving to number eight; a month later Clyde and his Drifters released their first single, "Money Honey," on Atlantic.

In November, Federal issued the Dominoes' biggest Jackie Wilson-led single, "Rags to Riches" (#2). (That same week Federal's owner King Records released the Checkers' "White Cliffs of Dover" with two ex-Dominoes, Charlie White and Bill Brown, and Little David Baughan, a McPhatter sound-alike.) "Rags" was an exquisite remake of Tony Bennett's number one hit from earlier in 1953, with an emotion-packed, high-voltage performance by Jackie. The Dominoes' ballad on King was their last chart single for a while. So varied was the group's capability that King decided to issue the group's 45s for both the R&B and pop markets separately; over the next two years Dominoes records alternated between Federal and King.

In November 1953 Jackie Wilson collapsed onstage in Charlotte, North Carolina, and was rushed to a hospital in Detroit for surgery. It would sadly not be his last onstage disaster.

On the following Thanksgiving the Dominoes were to perform at the Music Festival in Quincy, Illinois, with Sugar Ray at eight and 10 o'clock shows. When they showed up at 10:30 the promoter withheld payment, causing Ward to pull a gun on Robinson. Though no one was hurt, it was obvious that the strain of touring and mistrust of booking agents and record companies was taking its toll.

Dominoes records kept coming from both labels at regular intervals. By the beginning of 1954 the lineup of the Dominoes (who had been billed since 1952 as Billy Ward and His Dominoes though Billy hardly ever sang lead) had been completely made over from the McPhatter days. Jackie Wilson was on lead, James Van Loan was on second tenor, Milton Merle was the baritone, with Cliff Givens on bass and, of course, Billy Ward on piano.

More great recordings came in 1954, but ballads like "Tenderly," "Three Coins in a Fountain," and "Little Things Mean a Lot," despite hypnotic renditions by Wilson and the group, could not gain a foothold on the charts. Still, their popularity was such that by summer, Ward, Wilson, and company had signed a two-year deal with the Sahara Hotel in

Las Vegas for the astronomical sum of $5,000 a week. Ward was also doing pretty well writing many of the group's B sides and even a few of the hits ("Sixty Minute Man" with collaborator Rose Marks). This didn't stop him from announcing how unhappy he was with King; with a year still to go on his contract, he started shopping for a new company in June 1954.

That month King released the Checkers' "Over the Rainbow," which more than likely was the inspiration for Jackie Wilson and the Dominoes' own magnificent version in 1955. In August 1954 the Dominoes signed with Jubilee, releasing the flop "Gimme Gimme Gimme" in the second week of October (the same week "Earth Angel" by THE PENGUINS and "Ubangi Stomp" by Earl Bostic came out).

In January 1955 they jumped to Decca. By now the sound was a little more pop, with a religious theme in their first release "St. Theresa of the Roses." It became the group's first pop hit, scoring a number 13 on the Disc Jockey charts and number 20 on the Best Seller lists, hanging in for almost four months. Five more Decca singles yielded no follow-up, though the group did a few excellent sides such as "I Don't Stand a Ghost of a Chance," "September Song," and "Will You Remember," the latter featuring a guitar intro that later showed up as the intro on THE FLAMINGOS' "Lovers Never Say Goodbye" (they were label mates of the Dominoes on Decca in 1957).

Meanwhile, Federal kept issuing R&B sides. About "How Long, How Long Blues," *Billboard*'s May 19, 1956, reviewer stated, "Ward pours much heart into this wailing blues job. There's a distinct Eckstine touch to the vocalizing and the Dominoes are in there pitching too. Fans will like."

In late 1957 Wilson opted for a solo career, signing with Brunswick Records. This necessitated a search for another lead, a quest that ended with the discovery of Eugene Mumford, former lead of the Larks (Apollo) and the Serenaders (Whiz) who had just moved to the West Coast. When the Dominoes joined Liberty Records in 1957, Eugene was singing open-voiced power leads, a far cry from his fragile falsetto sound on such Larks classics as "My Reverie."

The first single was "Star Dust," a 1931 Isham Jones number one standard written by Hoagy Carmichael and Mitchell Parish. The Dominoes' version was an early example of a "power ballad"; the strings swelled in full orchestra support of the Dominoes' warm harmonies and Gene's strong vocal culminating in an exhilarating falsetto on the song's final notes.

The cut also had a unique intro in which the group sang an entire verse with only a tambourine and strings as accompaniment. "Star Dust" became the biggest hit of the group's seven-year career going to number 12 Pop (Disc Jockey), number 13 Top 100, and number five R&B. In August they hit the charts again with a DeRose-Parish classic, the number one 1939 Larry Clinton smash, "Deep Purple," which reached Pop top 20. In April 1958 Billy Ward's wonders tried the standard formula again with a Tommy Dorsey 1938 number one hit, "Music, Maestro Please," in an up-tempo vein. To their shock the B side, an out-of-character cover of Jan and Arnie's "Jennie Lee" (#8) hit the Pop charts on June 2nd and went to number 55. It became their last chart single. King/Federal continued issuing Dominoes sides both unreleased and re-released cuts into 1965.

By 1960 the group members were Monroe Powell (lead and first tenor), Robbie Robinson (second tenor), Milton Merle (baritone), and Cliff Givens (bass), with Ward still at the helm. Mumford had been induced by Liberty to go solo at around the same time the group left the label to sign with ABC and later Ro Zan.

By 1984 all three legendary leads had died. McPhatter had gone on to tremendous success as lead of the Drifters and as a solo artist. He died on June 13, 1972. Wilson collapsed on stage during his performance on September 25, 1975 at the Latin Casino in Cherry Hill, New Jersey, and died after a long coma on January 21, 1984. His tremendous solo successes, including 54 chart singles such as "Lonely Teardrops," "Night," and "Baby Workout," added to the legacy he started as a member of the Dominoes. He earned every bit of the title "Mr. Excitement."

Mumford went from Liberty to Columbia and then worked with several INK SPOTS groups and the Jubilee Four. He died in 1978.

BILLY WARD AND HIS DOMINOES

A SIDE/B SIDE	LABEL/CAT NO	DATE
Do Something For Me /		
Chicken Blues	Fed 12001	12/50
Harbor Lights / No Says My Heart	Fed 12010	2/51
Other Lips, Other Arms* /		
The Deacon Moves In	Fed 12016	1951
Sixty Minute Man /		
I Can't Escape From You	Fed 12022	4/51
Heart To Heart* /		
Lookin' For A Man	Fed 12036	1951
I Am With You /		
Weeping Willow Blues	Fed 12039	10/51

A SIDE/ B SIDE	LABEL/CAT NO	DATE
That's What You're Doing To Me / When The Swallows Come Back To Capistrano	Fed 12059	2/52
Have Mercy Baby / Deep Sea Blues	Fed 12068	4/52
That's What You're Doing To Me / Love, Love, Love	Fed 12072	5/52
I'd Be Satisfied / No Room	Fed 12105	1952
Yours Forever / I'm Lonely	Fed 12106	10/52
The Bells / Pedal Pushin' Papa	Fed 12114	12/52
These Foolish Things Remind Me Of You / Don't Leave Me This Way	Fed 12129	4/53
You Can't Keep A Good Man Down / Where Now Little Heart	Fed 12139	1/54
Rags To Riches / Don't Thank Me	King 1280	1953
Christmas In Heaven / Ringing In A Brand New Year	King 1281	1953
Until The Real Thing Comes Along / My Baby's 3-D	Fed 12162	1/54
The Outskirts Of Town / Tootsie Roll	Fed 12178	1954
A Little Lie / Tenderly	King 1342	1954
One Moment With You / Handwriting On The Wall	Fed 12184	5/54
Three Coins In The Fountain / Lonesome Road	King 1364	6/54
Little Things Mean A Lot / I Really Don't Want To Know	King 1368	1954
Above Jacob's Ladder / Little Black Train	Fed 12193	8/54
Gimme Gimme Gimme / Come To Me Baby	Jubi 5163	10/54
Can't Do Sixty No More / If I Never Get To Heaven	Fed 12209	2/55
Love Me Now Or Let Me Go / Cave Man	Fed 12218	4/55
Learnin' The Blues / May I Never Love Again	King 1492	7/55
Sweethearts On Parade / Take Me Back To Heaven	Jubi 5213	8/55
Over The Rainbow / Give Me You	King 1502	9/55
Bobby Sox Baby / How Long, How Long Blues	Fed 12263	5/56
St. Theresa Of The Roses / Home Is Where You Hang Your Heart	Decca 29933	6/56
Will You Remember / Come On, Snake, Let's Crawl	Decca 30043	10/56
Evermore / Half A Love	Decca 30149	12/56
Till Kingdom Come / Rock Plymouth Rock	Decca 30199	3/57
Star Dust / Lucinda	Lbrty 55071	5/57
St. Louis Blues / One Moment With You	Fed 12301	7/57
To Each His Own / I Don't Stand A Ghost Of A Chance With You	Decca 30420	8/57
Deep Purple / Do It Again	Lbrty 55099	1957
Have Mercy Baby / Love Love Love	Fed 12308	9/57

A SIDE/B SIDE	LABEL/CAT NO	DATE
My Proudest Possession / Someone Greater Than I	Lbrty 55111	1957
September Song / When The Saints Go Marching In	Decca 30514	12/57
Solitude / Sweeter As The Years Go By	Lbrty 55126	4/58
Jennie Lee / Music, Maestro Please	Lbrty 55136	4/58
Please Don't Say No / Behave Hula Girl	Lbrty 55181	1959
The World Is Waiting For The Sunrise / You're Mine	ABC 10128	1960
The Gypsy You	ABC 10156	1960
Have Mercy Baby / Sixty Minute Man	King 5322	1/60
Lay It On The Line / That's How You Know When You're Growing Old	King 5463	2/61
Man In The Stained Glass Window / My Fair Weather Friend	RZan 10001	1961
I'm Walking Behind You / This Love Of Mine	King 6002	1965
What Are You Doing New Year's Eve / O Holy Night	King 6016	1965

* with Little Esther (Phillips)

Maurice Williams and the Gladiolas

A spontaneous-sounding rhythm and blues group, the Gladiolas boasted the writing and singing talents of Maurice Williams. The group started out in Barr Street High School in Lancaster, South Carolina, during 1955. It was there that Maurice and Earl Gainey began singing in the Junior Harmonizers gospel group. They soon formed a secular quintet with Maurice on lead, Earl on tenor, William Massey also on tenor, Willie Jones on baritone, and Norman Wade on bass. They called themselves the Royal Charms, combining the names of two vocal favorites, THE 5 ROYALES and THE CHARMS.

Winning a local talent show enabled them to get a job singing the R&B hits of the day on a WLCM Saturday morning radio show in Lancaster. Thanks to the show, which they did for about a year, and club gigs, they earned a statewide reputation. Maurice contacted Excello Records owner Ernie Young in Nashville, who was glad to arrange an audition. All they had to do was get to Nashville, some 511 miles away. The enterprising group began a neighborhood fundraiser among businessmen, friends, and relatives and came up with about $40—enough to make the trip in Willie's old Chrysler. Ernie Young signed them on the basis of two of Maurice's songs, "Sweetheart Please Don't Go" (for an A side) and "Little Darlin'" (for the B side). Ernie had one prerequisite for working with them, and that was that they change the name from the Royal Charms to the Gladiolas.

Maurice was into West Indian and Latin rhythms and combined them with American rhythm and blues on "Little Darlin'" (and what would become their second single, "Run Run Little Joe"). Most disc jockeys preferred "Little Darlin'" to the "Sweetheart" A side, and before long, Mercury Records copycats THE DIAMONDS had covered it in an exaggerated though effective version. Though Maurice and company eventually reached number 41 (#11 R&B), their version was obscured by the Diamonds' better produced and slicker recording, which reached number two Pop.

Excello issued three more Gladiolas goodies but none received any notable attention. The best of the three was "Shoop Shoop." The last two Gladiolas singles had Bob Robertson as an additional tenor.

Upon their exit from Excello they were informed that Ernie owned their name and they could only use it for performing, not recordings. This handicap was overcome on the group's next road trip while they were waiting for their car to be repaired in a small West Virginia town. Their manager Harry Gains was thumbing through a newspaper when he saw an ad for a new foreign car called the Zodiac.

They recorded as Maurice Williams and the Zodiacs on the small South Carolina Cole label in 1959 with Henry Gaston replacing Earl Gainey. "Golly Gee" came and went as did "Lover Where Are You" and "College Girl" for Selwyn, another equally obscure record label. Massey then joined the air force and Wade decided enough was enough, precipitating the Zodiacs' demise.

Maurice wouldn't give up; soon a new and improved Zodiacs was assembled with Henry Gaston (tenor), Wiley Bennett (tenor), and Charles Thomas (baritone). They recorded two singles for Soma in 1960, a novelty takeoff on "Little Darlin'" called "Another Little Darlin'" and "Anything," but neither was noticed.

By mid-1960 Maurice and company hooked up with two would-be Columbia, South Carolina, record producers, Phil Gernhard and Johnny Mc-

Cullough. They recorded a few of Maurice's songs in what used to be an old TV studio, and after half of the city's companies had passed on them Maurice brought the recordings to New York's Al Silvers, head of Herald Records. A one-minute-and-37-second selection got the most attention from Silvers, but he found two of the song's features requiring changes. First, the line that went "Let's have another smoke" had to go since 1960 American radio wouldn't play it. Second, the song was recorded so badly it barely made the volume needle move on a tape machine. After numerous attempts at bringing it up to Silver's standards the single was finally released in August.

One side, "Do You Believe," began getting play in the South. But "Believe" was not the A side Silver was pushing. The top side, "Stay," finally broke out of Detroit and on October 3rd climbed onto *Billboard*'s Hot 100. On November 21st "Stay" (the shortest single in rock history) made number one (#3 R&B), starting the group on a whirlwind of performances with acts like Chuck Berry, THE DRIFTERS, and James Brown. Maurice kept penning rhythmic numbers, but follow-up singles like "I Remember" (#86, 1961) and "Come Along" (a "Stay" sound-alike, #83, 1961, despite this strong review in the March 13 issue of *Billboard*: "Maurice Williams sings this righteous tale about a guy pleading for his girl's companionship with fervor, aided by a vocal group with style. Strong wax here.") couldn't sustain the staying power of "Stay," and three more singles in 1961 didn't chart at all.

Atlantic, Scepter, and Sphere Sound were all whistle stops for the Zodiacs from 1963 to 1965. Marshall Seahorn, a mainstay of New Orleans music, recorded the catchy Williams tune "May I" and leased it to Vee-Jay just as they were going out of business. He then issued it on his own Deesu label. Though the record never charted on any national listing, the R.I.A.A. saw fit to certify "May I" a million seller. Two years later Bill Deal and the Rhondels recorded Maurice's "May I" (Heritage) and it reached number 39 on the Hot 100. The group stayed with Seahorn's Deesu for 1967 and 1968, and on a few occasions Marshall arranged for THE PIPS (Gladys Knight's group) to back Maurice, as on the "May I" flip "This Feeling" and the 1969 release "My Baby's Gone" b/w "Return" (Sea-Horn).

By now John Mobley was alternating tenor with Wiley Bennett.

By then "beach music" was becoming a part of mid-south coast music history and Zodiacs recordings were in the thick of it.

In 1985 Maurice and company were inducted into the Beach Music Hall of Fame. "Stay" became a standard and was covered by acts like THE FOUR SEASONS, Jackson Browne, and the Hollies. Williams's "Little Darlin'" is also a rock standard and was covered by Elvis Presley for his *Moody Blue* LP.

Willingness to change with the times kept the group going throughout its career. And the hit song "Stay" has kept Maurice Williams's music in the public ear, thanks to its inclusion in the 1987 hit film *Dirty Dancing*.

MAURICE WILLIAMS AND THE GLADIOLAS

A SIDE/B SIDE	LABEL/CAT NO	DATE
The Gladiolas		
Little Darlin' /		
Sweetheart Please Don't Go	Exelo 2101	1/57
Run Run Little Joe /		
Comin' Home To You	Exelo 2110	1957
Hey! Little Girl /		
I Wanta Know	Exelo 2120	1957
Shoop Shoop /		
Say You'll Be Mine	Exelo 2136	1958
Maurice Williams		
and the Zodiacs		
Golly Gee / "T" Town	Cole 100	1959
Lover (Where Are You) She's Mine	Cole 101	1959
College Girl / Say Yeah	Selwyn 5121	1959
Another LIttle Darlin' / Lita	Soma 1410	1960
Little Sally Walker /		
Anything	Soma 1418	1960
Stay / Do You Believe	Herald 552	8/60
Always / I Remember	Herald 556	1960
Come Along / Do I	Herald 559	3/61
Some Day / Come And Get It	Herald 563	1961
High Blood Pressure /		
Please	Herald 565	1961
Here I Stand* / It's All Right*	Herald 572	1961
Loneliness / Funny	Atln 2199	1963
Nobody Knows / I Know	Scptr 12113	1965
So Fine / The Winds	Sphr 707	1965
May I / Lollipop	Vee-Jay 678	
Being Without You* /		
Baby Baby*	Deesu 302	1967
May I / This Feeling	Deesu 304	1967
Surely / Don't Ever Leave Me	Deesu 309	1968
How To Pick A Winner /		
Don't Be Half Safe	Deesu 311	1968
Stay / Dance, Dance, Dance	Deesu 318	1968
My Baby's Gone / Return	SeHrn 503	1969
I'd Rather Have A Memory		
Than A Dream / Try	SeHrn 440,1	1969
The Four Corners /		
My Reason For Livin'	Veep 1294	1969

* Maurice Williams only

The Willows

A pioneering R&B doo wop group from Harlem, the Willows were idols and inspirations to many from the neighborhood who followed, like THE HARPTONES, THE FIVE CROWNS (later THE DRIFTERS), THE BOP CHORDS, THE CHARTS, the Keynotes, the Ladders, and the Laddins.

Though the streets of Harlem would soon be teeming with groups, in 1950 only a comparative few were cluttering the halls and street corners near 115th Street and Lenox Avenue.

Originally called the Dovers, the members of the Willows were Richie Davis, Ralph and Joe Martin (who were twin brothers), John Thomas "Scooter" Steele, and Bobby Robinson. Bobby opened a record store on 125th Street where he later established the legendary Whirlin' Disc, Red Robin, and Fury labels.

In 1952 a young would-be boxer from the neighborhood, Tony Middleton, was invited to the home of Mrs. Clarisse Martin on 115th Street to practice with her son Joe and the other Dovers. Mrs. Martin's philosophy was simple: if they're singin', they can't be swingin' in street gangs. The lineup now read Middleton (lead), Richie Davis (first tenor), Ralph Martin (second tenor), Joe Martin (baritone), and John Steele (bass). Another neighbor, Doc Green, also sang with them before moving on to the Five Crowns.

The group itself idolized the sounds of THE ORIOLES, THE DOMINOES, the Checkers, THE SWALLOWS, and Clyde McPhatter's original Drifters. They practiced day in and day out singing at hospital dances, Chelsea Vocational High School, and church benefits. (They occasionally rehearsed with a female group called the Delltones, who had among its members Gloria Lynne, who would go on to acclaim as a top jazz vocalist.) The group's taste for vocal battles was legendary, and they would often walk as far as the Sugarhill section and back again to sing against the likes of THE MELLO-MOODS and the Velvets.

In 1953 the Dovers met Pete and Goldie Doraine, who became their managers. They changed their name to the Five Willows and issued their first single, led by Richie Davis on Pete Doraine's own Pee Dee label. "Love Bells" was a typical rhythm and blues ballad with lots of harmony and a smokey blues sax solo.

Three singles followed on the Allen label, and on all of these Doraine was partnered with Victor Allen.

The first single on Allen, "My Dear Dearest Darling" (a collectors' favorite among early rhythm and blues ballads), with Middleton singing the lead part, credits the group and someone named Wright as the writers but doesn't include Middleton's name. Fred Taylor of the Skylarks has always maintained he wrote the song. Its performance at the Apollo amateur night contest in 1951 by the Skylarks lends credence to his claim. *Billboard* wasn't impressed no matter who wrote the song, noting in a June 1953 review that the record was "Kind of weird and somewhat hypnotic." "My Dear Dearest Darling" took a quick ride to oblivion, as did the follow-up record "Dolores."

"The White Cliffs of Dover" was their last release on the Allen label. Middleton walked the group to Al Silver's Herald label for two singles in 1954, the best being "Look Me in the Eyes," though it was becoming obvious that ballads were not the group's forte.

In 1955 Middleton met mogul-to-be Morty Craft and was signed to Morty's new Melba label, recording a rocker titled "Church Bells Are Ringing," which was written by Middleton and practiced as a ballad.

Billboard's February 25, 1956, reviewer stated, "Happy jump ballad is chanted with force and a joyful beat by the group. Gimmick sounds help for a side that could move up if it's handed sufficient exposure. Has pop potential too." By March 17th it was cited as a "Best Buy" in *Billboard*, with the comment, "After a fast start in several Eastern cities this item has begun to sweep out across the country with almost unqualified success. Figuring now on the New York territorial charts, it is also a strong seller in Boston, Los Angeles, Baltimore, Philadelphia, Cleveland, St. Louis and other important cities."

The record was a natural, indicating that the Willows (they dropped the "Five" in case they wound up performing with fewer members) had polished their craft thanks to Morty's production and help with their vocals. From Middleton's powerful lead to the talk-singing bass bridge, "Church Bells May Ring" (as it was now titled) was a doo wop delight. Ironically, that famous bass line was sung by Richard Simon, a neighborhood friend who was drafted just for the one song (since Scooter had missed the session) and was never a permanent member of the group. The chimes used on the recording were played by the as-yet-unknown lead singer of another Melba group called THE TOKENS (forerunners of the "Lion Sleeps Tonight" group) whose name was Neil Sedaka.

By May, "Church Bells Are Ringing," now retitled "Church Bells May Ring," had reached number 11 R&B Best Seller, number 14 Disc Jockey, and number 62 Pop, spending 11 weeks on the Pop charts and reportedly selling a million copies. It might have done better were it not for one of the "vulture" groups (as they were known in the R&B marketplace). THE DIAMONDS covered "Church Bells" and took it up to number 14 on the Pop charts. THE CADETS and Sunny Gale also had versions but they did not fare well enough to chart.

The group's career went downhill from "Church Bells." "Do You Love Me" and "Little Darlin'," another solid rocker on Melba, failed to sustain interest beyond New York.

There were additional recordings in 1957 and 1958 for Club, El Dorado, Gone, and Warwick (two LP cuts, a rerecording of "My Dear Dearest Darling" and "You"), but by then Middleton had left to go solo. Richie Davis went into the army in 1958. Scooter was let go by the group after the Melba sides. The Warwick Records group then included the Martin brothers, Freddie Donovan, and Dotty Martin (Joe's wife) on lead. Donovan joined THE SOLITAIRES for a short while but returned to singing with the Willows soon after.

In 1964, with Richie on lead, they signed to Heidi Records for two singles and then surfaced in the '70s and '80s with Middleton for the oldies revival shows. Meanwhile, Tony had been earning a living recording demos with the likes of Dionne Warwick and did a demo for a song called "Big Hunk of Love" that Elvis learned the words and music from for his own version.

THE WILLOWS

A SIDE/B SIDE	LABEL/CAT NO	DATE
The Five Willows		
Love Bells / Please Baby	PeeDee 290	1953
My Dear Dearest Darling /		
Rock Little Francis	Allen 1000	6/53
Dolores / All Night Long	Allen 1002	1953
The White Cliffs Of Dover /		
With These Hands	Allen 1003	1953
Baby Come A Little Closer / Lay		
Your Head On My Shoulder	Herald 433	8/54
Look Me In The Eyes /		
So Help Me	Herald 442	11/54
The Willows		
Church Bells Are Ringing /		
Baby Tell Me	Melba 102	2/56
Church Bells May Ring /		
Baby Tell Me	Melba 102	3/56

A SIDE/B SIDE	LABEL/CAT NO	DATE
Do You Love Me /		
My Angel	Melba 106	1956
Little Darlin' /		
My Angel	Melba 115	1957
This Is The End / Don't Pull,		
Don't Push, Don't Shove	Club 1014	1956

A SIDE/B SIDE	LABEL/CAT NO	DATE
Tony Middleton		
and the Willows		
The First Taste Of Love /		
Only My Heart	Eld 508	1957
Let's Fall In Love /		
Say Yeah	Gone 5015	1958

THE 1960s

LITTLE ANTHONY AND THE IMPERIALS

THE MAMAS AND THE PAPAS

ON AND THE BELMONTS

THE BELMONTS

hile the '50s saw the birth of rock and roll and the development of rhythm and blues, the '60s kept the momentum going at a rapid pace.

As in the '50s, there were three developmental phases of almost equal length. The period 1960 to 1963 saw veteran black vocal groups reach their greatest level of pop success. Some of them were the Drifters, Anthony and the Imperials, the Dells, Hank Ballard and the Midnighters, the Vibrations (who were the Jayhawks in the '50s), the Olympics, the Sensations, the Cleftones, the Shells, the Coasters, the Flamingos, and the Platters. In the '50s they were considered mostly R&B acts, but by the early '60s they were creating pop records, thanks to some musical sweetening. Those that were staying closer to their rhythm and blues roots were furthering the development of the early sounds of soul. Among these acts were the Impressions, the Isley Brothers, Gladys Knight and the Pips, the Marcels, Maurice Williams and the Zodiacs, the Falcons, and the Fiestas.

At the same time, new black vocal groups emerged in the '60s that combined doo wop and R&B with gospel and soul to create the smoother, more widely accessible style called pop R&B. Acts like the Manhattans, the Chi-Lites, the Jive 5, Ruby and the Romantics, the O'Jays, and later in the decade the Delfonics, the Drewvels, and the Fifth Dimension made pop R&B a viable music style of its own.

The second period, the mid-'60s, saw the development of distinctive regional sounds. Where the New York and Los Angeles vocal group sounds led the way in the '50s, the '60s belonged to Chicago (the Impressions, the Chi-Lites, and the Dells); Philadelphia (the Tymes, the

Delfonics, and Harold Melvin and the Blue Notes); and of course, the Motown sound of Detroit, which dominated the rest of the decade due to the overwhelming success of pop, R&B, and soul acts like the Temptations, the Supremes, the Miracles, the Marvelettes, Martha and the Vandellas, the Contours, and the Velvelettes.

The '60s also yielded one of pop music's most enjoyable trends, the "girl group" phenomenon. Starting in the '50s as a trickle represented by the Hearts, the Blossoms, the Joytones, the Clickettes, the Deltairs, the Quintones, the Chantels, and the Bobbettes, it became a flood of groups in the '60s, including the Shirelles, the Chiffons, the Shangri-Las, the Crystals, the Ronettes, the Angels, Reparata and the Delrons, the Exciters, the Cookies, the Supremes, the Marvelettes, and Patti LaBelle and the Blue Belles.

The Phil Spector era was also ushered in during the early and middle '60s, bringing us his "wall of sound" and overdubbed harmonies by predominantly female groups like the Ronettes and the Crystals. Spector's production techniques changed recording forever and made groups sound larger-than-life.

The last period of the decade (1967 to 1969) ushered in the progressive era. It was a time of musical expansion in American song and of lyrics that reflected social and moral concerns. Vocal groups like the Temptations and the Fifth Dimension on the soul side and the Mamas and the Papas on the pop/rock side contributed to the intense musical activity.

White groups flourished in four main arenas: pop, doo wop, rock, and folk. Pop groups, despite a weakening of the influence they had on early '50s radio prior to rock and roll, still made strong contributions in the '60s, led by acts like the Lettermen, Jay and the Americans, the Fleetwoods, the Dimensions, the Duprees, the Four Seasons, the Mamas and the Papas, and Spanky and Our Gang.

Doo wop groups were usually teens who were continuing the emulation of early R&B groups that acts like Dion and the Belmonts and Danny and the Juniors were imitating in the late '50s. The large doo wop community included the Earls, the Capris, the Del-Satins, the Passions, the Regents, Randy and the Rainbows, Vito and the Salutations, the Dovells, Nick Addio and the Plazas, and the Tokens, who were actually the first folk rock group.

Rock vocal groups developed quickly into vocal bands when the British invasion of 1964 hit. There were the Brooklyn Bridge, the Association, Crosby, Stills and Nash, and the Beach Boys, who almost single-handedly created the West Coast "surf" sound of the early '60s. The doo wop groups were hurt more than the pop and vocal bands in that they were invariably of draft age and couldn't stay together long enough to succeed before the Viet Nam buildup started. Of course, the British band penchant for ignoring harmony didn't help doo wop prosper in those changing times.

From 1962 through approximately 1966, an East Coast phenomenon occurred in which harmony lovers were brought in contact with hundreds of acappella vocal groups and their recordings created just for that audience. What would later be called oldies radio started playing these often unknown artists, and without any promotion, thousands upon thousands of records were sold and many groups became local celebrities.

Folk music thrived in the '60s. As the antiwar and civil rights movements gathered steam, groups like Peter, Paul and Mary helped provide a folk music soundtrack. Other folksmiths of this era were the Mitchell Trio, the Kingston Trio, the Highwaymen, and the Limelighters.

In all, it was a decade that came and went like the month of March in reverse: in like a lamb and out like a lion. ∎

The Accents

Before they turned to doo wop, the Accents began their brief career as a pop group sounding somewhat like THE LETTERMEN and THE FOUR COINS.

The members were Shelly Weiss (first tenor), Ian Kaye (baritone), Allan Senzan (second tenor), and Mike Lasman (lead). They met on the boardwalk of Brighton Beach in Brooklyn, New York, and were students at Erasmus and Lincoln high schools when they formed the group in 1960. Lasman had previously recorded as the lead singer of Mike and the Utopians on the Ceejay label. Weiss had recorded for JDS Records in early 1960 as a member of Bobby Roy and the Chord-a-roys, who also backed Barry Mann on various demos that reportedly included "Who Put the Bomp (In the Bomp Bomp Bomp)." The four boardwalk vocalists originally called themselves the Dreamers and practiced regularly on the corner of Church and Flatbush Avenues. They met Jerry Halperin, owner of Halperin Music on Flatbush Avenue in Brooklyn, who liked their intricate pop harmonies and became their manager. Henceforth the group practiced right in his record store.

Their polished pop sound soon earned them a deal with Guaranteed Records of New York, a subsidiary of Carlton Records. The first release was the old standard "Canadian Sunset," but the bland production and lack of promotion doomed it almost from inception.

Dropped after only one release, the group changed its name to the Accents and its style to doo wop, putting together a reworking of the old ballad "Rags to Riches." They also began practicing an old Jewish ballad entitled "Where Can I Go," complete with middle section sung in Hebrew, and it was this song that they performed in an audition for Sultan Records. The audition was a success, and "Rags to Riches" b/w "Where Can I Go" became their first single release as the Accents. "Rags" became a Brooklyn favorite among doo wop enthusiasts but never charted. It did, however, give them enough exposure to land them a spot in an Allan Freed Show at the Ambassador Hotel in the Catskill Mountains.

Between local gigs Kaye and Senzan sang backup with the Del Satins on Dion's hit "Ruby Baby" in late 1962. Weiss began singing with JAY AND THE AMERICANS and became the group's road manager for a period in 1965.

The group's last effort was disappointing: they were forced to back up the inept vocal of Scott English on a tune called "High on a Hill." The Accents broke up soon after.

Today, Weiss is a writer for *Cashbox* magazine in Los Angeles. Ian Kaye is a teacher in Brooklyn, Alan Senzen is a plumber on Long Island, and Lasman is nowhere to be found, although rumor has it he resides somewhere in South America.

The Ad Libs

The doo wop group the Ad Libs distinguished themselves in two ways. First, they were one of the few '60s groups with a female lead and male backups, and second, their sound prefigured the jazz-styled doo wop of several later groups like THE MANHATTAN TRANSFER. The Ad Libs' birth can be credited to John (J. T.) Taylor, a saxophone player who worked with various big bands as far back as the 1930s. By the early 1960s, J. T. (already in his early 50s) had mothballed his saxophone for a teaching career. Then he came across a street-corner quintet in Hudson County, New Jersey. They called themselves the Creators and consisted of Hugh Harris (lead), James Wright, John Alan, Danny Austin, and Chris Coles. By mid-1963 the Creators had already released their first record on the small local TK Records label without any chart results. A single on Phillips ("I'll Stay Home") later that year had the same fate.

By 1964, the Creators had re-formed in Newark, New Jersey, with Harris and Austin teaming up with Norman Donegan and Dave Watt. They added Mary Ann Thomas (who had been part of another short-lived New Jersey group) and renamed themselves the Ad Libs. J. T.'s jazz and big-band flavored songwriting blended with the group's natural harmonic sound and a modified boogie-woogie rhythm to create "The Boy from New York City."

Demo tape in hand, Taylor confidently approached Red Bird Record chiefs Jerry Leiber and Mike Stoller. The Ad Libs were signed to their affiliate, Blue Cat Records. "The Boy from New York City" was released in December 1964 and by March 1965 had reached number eight on the pop charts (#6 R&B). Their follow-up of May 1965 barely made number 100 Pop. The next single was an ode to street-corner life written by John Linde and Pete Antell entitled "On the Corner" (originally recorded by the Expressions on Parkway in 1964), but the single saw little activity, and after one more unsuccessful release the group was dropped by Blue Cat.

Three labels (AGP, Karen, and Interphone) and three singles later, the group, still determined, signed with Share Records of New York and recorded the 1964 GLADYS KNIGHT AND THE PIPS ballad "Giving Up." It went to number 34 on the R&B charts, outdistancing the Pips' original (#38).

"Giving Up" was the group's last chart record. The Ad Libs made various member changes over the next 20 years and managed a few more releases, but none with the success of "Boy from New York City." In 1984 John Taylor set up his own label, Passion Records, to record the Ad Libs, and in the fall of 1988 he came up with the Johnny-Boy label for the group's next single "I Stayed Home (New Years Eve)" (a remake of their Creators single "I'll Stay Home"). In 1989, they released another seasonal 45 on Johnny-Boy entitled "Santa's on His Way."

THE AD LIBS

A SIDE/B SIDE	LABEL/CAT NO	DATE
The Boy From New York City / Kicked Around	Bl Ct 102	1964
He Ain't No Angel / Ask Anybody	Bl Ct 114	1965
On The Corner / Oo-Wee Oh Me Oh My	Bl Ct 119	1965
Johnny My Boy / I'm Just A Down Home Girl	Bl Ct 123	1965
Human / New York In The Dark	A.G.P. 100	1966
Every Boy And Girl / Thinking Of Me	Karen 1527	1966
Don't Ever Leave Me / You're In Love	Phlps 40461	1967
Giving Up / Appreciation	Share 104	1969
The Boy From New York City / Nothing Worse Than Being Alone	Share 106	1969
Love Me / Know Well About You	Cap 2944	1970
Spring And Summer	Passion 1	1984
Santa's On His Way	Johnnie Boy	1989

Alive and Kicking

Alive and Kicking was a Brooklyn group formed in 1968. They played the New York club circuit, gaining recognition for their emphasis on vocal harmony. The membership included Sandy Todar, Peppie Cordova, Bruce Sudano, Woody Wilson, Vito Albano, and John Parisio.

Their big break followed a strange succession of contacts linking them to hit recording artist Tommy James. It seems that Sandy Todar's brother's wife

(who ultimately became the group's manager) knew the wife of Tommy James. Tommy got the word to go see the group, and go he did. He began writing songs for them, one of which was called "Tighter, Tighter." James also played them a composition he wrote entitled "Crystal Blue Persuasion" but wisely kept it for himself; it went to number two in the summer of 1969.

Signed with Roulette Records (James's label) in 1970, Alive and Kicking's first release was "Tighter, Tighter." By June it was all over the national airwaves and by early summer had broken the top 10, peaking at number seven. This mercurial beginning presaged the group's end: their next release, "Just Let It Come," peaked at number 69, and their last single, "Good Old Lovin' Back Home," failed to chart. They broke up later that year. The group was partially reformed in 1976 with Cordova, Wilson, and Albano joined by newcomers Richie Incorvaia and Steve Spagis.

Bruce Sudano went on to form the group BROOKLYN DREAMS in 1976 and married superstar Donna Summer.

As of this writing, the most recent incarnation of Alive and Kicking is living up to its name, playing clubs in the New York area. The group has not recorded since 1970.

The Angels

The early and mid-'60s can be described as the golden age of female vocal groups. But for every name act like THE SHIRELLES, THE RONETTES, THE CRYSTALS, THE SUPREMES, and THE CHANTELS, there were many more like the Deltairs, THE HEARTS, THE QUINTONES, the Clickettes, the Secrets, the Carousels, and the Cotillions that went nearly nowhere. One of the latter type germinated the seed for a true '60s success story.

A group called the Starlets from Orange, New Jersey, recorded the old standard "P.S. I Love You" in a pleasing enough version on the obscure Astro label; predictably the single went nowhere. Shortly thereafter, two of the members, Barbara and Phyllis "Jiggs" Allbut, joined Linda Jansen and went to New York to do vocal session work.

By the summer of 1961 the girls had raised enough money to record a demo of the song "Till," originally a top 30 hit for Roger Williams some five years earlier. They took the demo to Caprice Records and, just like in the movies, were signed up. To choose a name, they each placed a piece of paper in a hat and drew out the name Blue Angels, later eliminating the "Blue" portion. Barbara left Juilliard School of Music and Phyllis abandoned college. Soon their first release, "Till," enhanced with a scintillating string arrangement by Hutch Davie, took off like a rocket and hit the national charts in October 1961, peaking at number 14.

Their second release, "Cry Baby Cry," also hit the charts, but only got as high as number 38. Linda left the Angels and Peggy Santiglia replaced her as lead singer. Peggy was already a seasoned professional, having appeared in the play *Do Re Mi* on Broadway, but even her expertise couldn't stop the group's slide; inferior material for the next three singles kept them off the charts for almost a year and left them in the spring of 1963 with no record label. Then two major events took place: they were signed to Mercury Records and almost simultaneously came up with a song written by Jerry Goldstein, Rich Gottehrer, and Bobby Feldman. The writers were aware of the group, since they had written the B side of the Angels' last Caprice single "I'd Be Good for You." They convinced Mercury to let them produce the group on a contagiously singable little ditty they'd written, and by late summer of 1963 "My Boyfriend's Back" was a number one record in America on Mercury's Smash label affiliate. It even went to number two on the R&B charts.

Their next single, "I Adore Him," went to number 25, and the B side, "Thank You and Good Night," became the sign-off theme on Murray the K's WINS radio show for months thereafter.

The Angels' success enabled them to tour the country and Europe through 1964, performing with acts like Gerry and the Pacemakers. More versatile than their hits led people to believe, the group did numerous recording sessions backing up artists ranging from Jackie Wilson to Sal Mineo, and were the vocal group that helped Lou Christie make "Lightnin' Strikes" a number one record in early 1966. Their angelic harmonies were so high that on one recording ("A Moment Ago," the B side of "Till") you could play the 45 at 33 rpm speed and swear you were hearing an R&B male group. Performing backup sessions and commercials kept them busy from the summer of 1964 (when their last smash release failed to chart) until they signed with RCA in 1967. Six singles and two years later the group broke up, when RCA efforts (or lack of same) resulted in no further chart activity.

The early '70s nostalgia movement brought the Angels back together for rock and roll revival shows, and in 1974 they even cut another single, this time on Polydor, entitled "Papa's Side of the Bed." They are reportedly still doing occasional oldies shows on the East Coast.

THE ANGELS

A SIDE/B SIDE	LABEL/CAT NO	DATE
Till / A Moment Ago	Caprice 107	1961
Cry Baby Cry /		
That's All I Ask Of You	Caprice 112	1962
Everybody Loves A Lover /		
Blow Joe	Caprice 116	1962
I'd Be Good For You /		
You Should Have Told Me	Caprice 118	1962
Irresistible / Cotton Fields	Ascot 2139	1963
My Boyfriend's Back / Now	Smash 1834	6/63
Thank You And Goodnight /		
I Adore Him	Smash 1854	9/63
Wow Wow Wee /		
Snowflakes And Teardrops	Smash 1870	12/63
Java / Little Beatle Boy	Smash 1885	4/64
Dream Boy / Jamaica Joe	Smash 1915	7/64
What To Do /		
I Had A Dream I Lost You	RCA 47-9129	2/67
Go Out and Play / You'll Never		
Get To Heaven	RCA 47-9246	6/67
With Love / You're The Cause Of It	RCA 47-9404	12/67
If I Didn't Love You / The Model	RCA 47-9541	5/68
But For Love / The Boy With		
The Green Eyes	RCA 47-9612	8/68
Merry-Go-Round / So Nice	RCA 47-9681	11/68
Papa's Side Of The Bed /		
You're All I Need To Get By	Polydor 14222	1974

The Arbors

Although the late '60s were considered the psychedelic era, musical tastes were still diverse enough to allow groups with a mellower sound, like THE VOGUES and THE LETTERMEN, to cut through the fuzz-tone guitars and Farfisa organ sounds and have an impact on the charts. Such was the case with two pairs of brothers who met at the University of Michigan. Edward and Fred Farren began rehearsing with Thomas and Scott Herrick on pop standards in early 1966. They named themselves after their home town of Ann Arbor, Michigan, and built a local following, leading to a record deal with Columbia's Date Records affiliate. Their first single, "A Symphony for Susan," went to number 51 on the national charts in the fall of 1966. With a sound reminiscent of THE FOUR COINS and THE FOUR ACES they recorded standards like "When I Fall in Love" and "My Foolish Heart," but only charted once more in the next two years with the syrupy ballad "Graduation Day" (#59, June 1967).

The quartet then made a radical departure for an MOR group. After five singles and two LPs they started recording songs by contemporary "hip" artists. Their own brand of MOR and psychedelia merged with the Box Tops' year-and-half-old "The Letter" brought them their biggest chart single in February 1969. Their LP *The Letter* contained a mixed bag of songs and approaches: a Beatles "Eleanor Rigby" sound applied to Dylan's "Like a Rolling Stone"; a Harpers Bizarre touch added to Blood, Sweat and Tears' "I Can't Quit Her." Even THE MOONGLOWS' R&B and doo wop classic "Most of All" succumbed to the Arbors metamorphosis: they made it sound like the Lettermen meeting THE MAMAS AND THE PAPAS. They tackled the Doors' "Touch Me" and the Leaves' "Hey Joe," while their "I Can't Quit Her" became their fourth and last chart record in the spring of 1969.

With the onset of the '70s the group moved to Chicago and carved a very lucrative career doing commercials. All told, they batted a very respectable .500, with four of their eight singles charting. They were able to bow out voluntarily, with the satisfaction of knowing they created one of the more innovative pop vocal sounds of the late '60s.

THE ARBORS

A SIDE/B SIDE	LABEL/CAT NO	DATE
A Symphony For Susan /		
Love Is The Light	Date 1529	1966
Just Let It Happen / Dreamer Girl	Date 1546	1967
Graduation Day /		
Win The Whole Wide World	Date 1561	1967
With You Girl /		
Love For All Seasons	Date 1570	1967
Valley Of The Dolls /		
You Are The Music	Date 1581	1967
The Letter / Most Of All	Date 1638	1969
I Can't Quit Her /		
Lovin' Tonight (Maybe Tonight)	Date 1645	1969
Touch Me / Motet Overture	Date 1651	1969

The Archies

The brainchild of music publisher/producer Don Kirshner, the Archies were formed to capitalize on the success of TV's cartoon show of the same name. The New York quartet was made up entirely of professional studio singers and was probably the first vocal group put together to record and not tour. They opened the floodgates for other groups based on TV shows (e.g., the Globetrotters, the Partridge Family, the Brady Bunch, and the Monkees).

The Archies' vocalists included, at various times, Ellie Greenwich and Jeff Barry (Jeff was also the Archies' producer), Tony Wine (cowriter of Tony Orlando's hit "Candida"), Andy Kim (hit artist on "Baby I Love You," #9, 1969), Ray Stevens (artist on "Everything Is Beautiful," #1, 1970), Bobby Bloom (second tenor of THE IMAGINATIONS), and Tony Passalaqua (lead singer of the Fascinators on Capitol). The lead, however, was always Ron Dante, who simultaneously sang lead for the Cufflinx in 1969–70 ("Tracy," #9 in 1969 on Decca) and was formerly the lead of the Detergents in 1964–65 ("Leader of the Laundromat," #19, Roulette).

Their first release, "Bang-Shang-A-Lang," went to number 22 on the national charts in September 1968. Their third single, "Sugar Sugar," became an international number one hit in the summer of 1969, selling over six million records.

The Archies lasted from 1968 through 1972, yielding six chart hits out of 11 releases. Ellie and Jeff (also one of the great writing teams of the '60s; see THE RONETTES) soon separated; Ellie stayed in New York, doing commercials and creating the Off-Broadway play *Leader of the Pack* in 1987, while Jeff moved to Los Angeles and wrote music mostly for television (*The Jeffersons* theme). Tony Wine married record producer Chips Moman and moved to Nashville. Andy Kim moved to Los Angeles, issuing a string of solo hits on Steed and Capitol from 1968 through 1974, including the number one "Rock Me Gently." Bobby Bloom had a top 10 solo hit in the fall of 1970 (produced by Jeff Barry) entitled "Montego Bay." He died of accidental causes in 1974. Tony Passalaqua continued to sing on and off, and as recently as 1989, appeared at a U.G.H.A. Concert in Clifton, New Jersey, performing Fascinators oldies with a sound-alike backup group.

Ron Dante went on to record several releases for Bell and RCA Records: he did stints as lead of Ronnie and the Dirt Riders ("Yellow Van" on RCA in 1976), Pearly Gate ("Daisy" on Decca in 1970), and Dante's Inferno ("Ain't Miss Behavin'" on Infinity in 1979). In 1972 he hooked up with a then unknown singer and musical conductor for Bette Midler named Barry Manilow. Ron and Barry, along with Melissa Manchester and Valerie Simpson (of Ashford and Simpson), were called in to sing on a commercial for a New York jingle firm. After that session Ron and Barry teamed up and began a string of tremendously successful co-productions for Manilow into the early '80s, with Dante singing backup on most of Barry's records. Barry returned the favor in 1975 when they coproduced a new version of Ron's 1969 hit "Sugar Sugar."

Though the Archies' records are often put down as mindless bubblegum music, there is no questioning the quality of the recordings and the success of the sound. The fact that the Archies never had faces (except for cartoon characters) may have worked against them, but the vocal expertise of the group certainly didn't.

THE ARCHIES

A SIDE/B SIDE	LABEL/CAT NO	DATE
Bang-Shang-A-Lang / Truck Driver	Clndr 1006	1968
Feeling So Good / Love Light	Clndr 1007	1968
Sugar Sugar / Melody Hill	Clndr 1008	1969
Jingle Jangle / Justine	Kirsh 5002	1969
Who's Your Baby / Senorita Rita	Kirsh 5003	1970
Sunshine / Over and Over	Kirsh 1009	1970
Together We Are Two / Everything's Alright	Kirsh 5009	1971
This Is Love / Throw A Little Love My Way	Kirsh 5011	1971
Maybe I'm Wrong / Summer Prayer For Peace	Kirsh 5014	1971
Love Is Living In You / Hold On To Lovin'	Kirsh 5018	1971
Stangers In The Morning / Plum Crazy	Kirsh 5021	1972

The Association

Although many bands of the late '60s and early '70s emphasized instruments over harmony vocals, the Association came across more as a vocal group than a band, even though they were both.

The group was formed by Terry Kirkman with three members of his original band the Men. Russ Giguere, Ted Bluechel, Jr., Brian Cole, and Terry were joined by Gary Alexander and Jim Yester in 1964 and performed for the first time together at a club called the Icehouse in Pasadena, California. They soon signed with a local label, Davon Records. Not yet skilled as writers (group members, particularly Kirkman, would later write most of their recordings), they first released a Bob Dylan composition entitled "One Too Many Mornings." The release of their May 1966 recording "Along Comes Mary" set the table for a feast of subsequent hits. "Mary" went top 10 and wound up on the larger Valiant label when Davon couldn't handle the huge response. A unique-sounding record for its time, the soft vocals balanced against a hard-edged track made the Association almost instant successes. But if "Mary" was a home run, their next single was a grand slam. Emphasizing even greater use of intricate harmonies, the Association's "Cherish" became a standard almost as quickly as it became number one in the summer of 1966.

Their next two singles missed the mark ("Pandora's Golden Heebie Jeebies," #35, and "No Fair at All," #51), but the group's unmistakable harmonies (even though their label was touting them as a band) made them a vocal group on a par with their contemporaries THE MAMAS AND THE PAPAS.

By 1967, Warner Brothers had absorbed Valiant Records and the group found itself climbing the chart to number one with "Windy" and to number two with the Addrissi brothers' "Never My Love."

The group spent most of its rehearsal time polishing the intricate harmonies that they felt set their sound apart. The culmination of those efforts is generally regarded by fans to be the recording "Everything that Touches You" (#10, 1968).

Because the group was adept at recreating its recorded sound on stage, bookings over the long term were assured. Even after the string of chart records ended in 1969 with "Goodbye Columbus" (#80) the group continued to perform into the 1970s. The group signed with Mumms Records in 1973 and RCA in 1975, but various personnel changes led the group in a hard-rock direction. Kirkman, however, was determined to get back to the original sound and in 1981 reformed the Association minus Brian Cole, who died in 1972. Early in 1981 they had their first charter in eight years on Elektra with "Dreamer."

15 million record sales, 24 singles, and nine LPs later, their place as one of the best vocal groups of the '60s is assured.

THE ASSOCIATION

A SIDE/B SIDE	LABEL/CAT NO	DATE
Forty Times / One Too Many Mornings	Valiant 730	1966
Along Comes Mary / Your Own Love	Valiant 741	1966
Cherish / Don't Blame The Rain	Valiant 747	1966
Pandora's Golden Heebie Jeebies / Standing Still	Valiant 755	1966
No Fair At All / Looking Glass	Valiant 758	1966

A SIDE/B SIDE	LABEL/CAT NO	DATE
Windy / Sometime	Wrnr 7041	1967
Never My Love /		
Requiem For The Masses	Wrnr 7074	1967
Everything That Touches You /		
We Love Us	Wrnr 7163	1968
Time For Living / Birthday Morning	Wrnr 7195	1968
Six Man Band / Like Always	Wrnr 7229	1968
Goodbye Columbus /		
The Time It Is Today	Wrnr 7267	1969
Under Branches / Here In Here	Wrnr 7277	1969
Yes, I Will / Am Up For Europe	Wrnr 7305	1970
Are You Ready / Duduquet Blues	Wrnr 7349	1970
Just About The Same /		
Look At Me, Look At You	Wrnr 7372	1970
Along The Way	Wrnr 7429	1970
P.F. Sloan / Traveler's Guide	Wrnr 7471	1971
Bring Yourself Home /		
It's Gotta Be Real	Wrnr 7515	1971
That's Racin' / Makes Me Cry	Wrnr 7524	1971
Come The Fall /		
Kicking The Gong Along	Col 45654	1972
Names, Tags, Numbers and		
Labels / Rainbow's Bent	Mums 6061	1973
Dreamer	Elektra 47094	1973

The Beach Boys

An American musical institution, the Beach Boys parlayed a repertoire of songs about surfing, cars, and girls into the basis for one of the country's longest-lasting success stories.

The group formed in Hawthorne, California, in 1961 and included brothers Brian, Dennis, and Carl Wilson, their cousin Mike Love, and friend Al Jardine. Mike Love sang most of the leads while Brian led on many ballads. Dennis and Al also led on various songs.

The group started out as Kenny and the Cadets, Carl and the Passions, and finally the Pendletones (named after an "in" shirtmaker at that time). Brian, who was a fan of George Gershwin, Stephen Foster, and THE FOUR FRESHMEN, began teaching the others intricate Freshmen-styled harmonies. Murray Wilson, father of the three brothers and a sometime songwriter, took the boys to his publisher Hite Morgan who in turn took the group to Keen Recording Studios. Dennis, as the only member of the group who surfed, thought the sport would be a good subject for a song and suggested it to Brian. Brian then wrote "Surfin'" and with Mike wrote "Surfin' Safari," the songs they made into demos on a fall day in 1961.

Murray then took the demos to Herb Newman, who owned Candix and Era Records. On December 8th Newman signed the group, and Era's promo man Russ Regan (later president of 20th Century Fox Records) suggested they change their name to the Beach Boys. (The group wanted the name the Pendletones and Candix wanted the Surfers; Regan pointed out there already was a group called the Surfers.) In December 1961 "Surfin'" by the Beach Boys was issued on X Records (Morgan's Label) as a promo issue and on Candix.

On February 17, 1962, "Surfin'" hit the national pop charts and reached number 75. (On December 31st the group had performed at its first important show under the Beach Boys name at the Long Beach Municipal Stadium in a memorial concert for Richie Valens, where they earned $300.)

In February 1962 Jardine left to study dentistry. On February 8th, Brian, Dennis, and Val Poliuto of THE JAGUARS recorded six songs for Hite Morgan's Deck Records. The songs were "Surfin'," "Surfin' Safari," "Karate," "Little Surfin' Girl," "Luau," and "Judy." In May the Candix label folded and Murray Wilson, now acting as the group's manager, started taking their demos around. Several labels, including Liberty, Dot, and Decca, passed on the group, but Capitol's Nick Venet liked the demo of "Surfin' Safari" and signed the boys in June. A master of "Surfin' Safari" was quickly recorded (actually the February 8th demo, with several Beach Boys overdubbing harmony parts) with new member David Marks, who'd replaced Jardine. On August 11, 1962, the song reached number 14 while the flip, a hotrod racing song called "409," charted at number 76. The boys were cashing in on two American fads, and the formula of double-sided hits rolled on from there.

In early 1963 Jardine returned after apparently concluding that the safety of dentistry didn't have the same allure as celebrity status with a rock and roll group. Marks, his earlier replacement, departed.

The February release of "Surfin' U.S.A." marked the beginning of the unique harmonies the group came to be known for. Brian was producing a new style of rock and roll with Chuck Berry rhythms and Four Freshmen harmony. "Surfin' U.S.A.," which read "Wilson-Love" as writers on the label's first pressing, was so close to Chuck's "Sweet Little Sixteen" that all it took was the threat of a lawsuit to have later pressings list Chuck Berry as sole writer. *Billboard*'s March 9, 1963, review stated, "The boys scored with their last 'Surfin' side and this one will go right up after it. The side has strong beat and can be expected to blast off in Los Angeles."

By May 25th the powerpacked single was number three in the U.S.A.; it went on to reach number 32 in England and number nine in Australia. The flip, another hotrod song called "Shut Down," reached number 23.

The next surfing/drag-racing two-sider was the group's first ballad, "Surfer Girl" (#7 Pop, #18 R&B, #8 Australia), along with "Little Deuce Coupe" (#15 Pop).

Wilson and company were hitting the top of the music world; when their *Surfin' U.S.A.* LP hit number two, the number one record in the country was Jan & Dean's "Surf City," written by their friend Brian Wilson. The group's popularity was such that two nearly simultaneous LPs produced by Brian hit the top 10: the surf-themed *Surfer Girl* (#7) and the car-titled *Little Deuce Coupe* (#4).

"Be True to Your School," a rocking paean to school loyalty, with the Honeys cheerleading alongside the boys' contagious harmony, reached number six on December 21, 1963 (#27 R&B), while its flip, the ballad "In My Room," rose to number 23.

"Fun, Fun, Fun," one of their brightest rockers, with Love on lead and a Chuck Berry-style guitar intro, reached number five on March 21, 1964, and number six in Australia.

Their first number one came next as "I Get Around," again with Mike on lead, hit the top spot most appropriately on July 4, 1964 (#7 U.K.), pushing Peter and Gordon's "A World Without Love" from the pinnacle.

The exemplification of the Beach Boys' rich, full, harmony was on the flip, "Don't Worry, Baby" (#24), which Mick Jagger of the Rolling Stones called one of the greatest singles ever.

More great rock and roll followed in 1964 with "When I Grow Up" (#9 U.S., #44 and #27 on two U.K. chartings, #20 Australia) and "Dance, Dance, Dance" with Brian on lead (#8 U.S., #24 U.K., #36 Australia). On December 23rd, while on a plane trip from Los Angeles to Houston, Brian suffered a nervous breakdown brought on by an overwhelming schedule of writing, producing, recording, and touring. To help his recovery he stopped touring with the band, and guitarist/singer Glen Campbell joined to perform on the road.

With original material in short supply, 1965 ushered in a remake of an oldie, the Bobby Freeman hit "Do You Wanna Dance" (#5, 1958) with Dennis leading the way; it danced up to number 12. By April Bruce Johnston (the Ripchords, "Hey Little Cobra," #4, 1963) had replaced Glen Campbell.

"Help Me Rhonda" entered the scene in the spring of 1965 and became their second number

one, pushing the Beatles' "Ticket to Ride" out of first place.

Despite a hearing loss in his right ear, Brian continued to write and produce commercial vocal harmony hits. One of them, "California Girls," had the most readily identifiable keyboard intro of any '60s hit, and with Love on lead it reached number three on August 28, 1965. The spontaneous-sounding party recording of the Regents' "Barbara Ann" soared to number two nationally, with Dean Torrence of Jan and Dean guesting on lead.

Meanwhile, a 1927 folk song with Jardine on lead, "Sloop John B.," sailed to number three on May 7, 1966.

It was followed by the bouncy Brian Wilson and Tony Asher-penned slice of life, "Wouldn't It Be Nice" (#8 U.S., #2 Australia). The flip side, "God Only Knows," earned a distinction beyond its number 39 chart position when Paul McCartney called it the greatest love song ever written. It reached number two in England, where "Wouldn't It Be Nice" was totally ignored.

All the hits up to this time were simply appetizers to the main course, a song Brian and Mike wrote and that Brian spent six months working on. The song, recorded in 17 different sessions in four Los Angeles studios (Western, Gold Star, RCA, and Columbia) and costing the then unheard-of sum of over $16,000 to produce, was titled "Good Vibrations." Influenced by Phil Spector (Brian had already recorded THE CRYSTALS' "There's No Other" with the Beach Boys and would later record other Crystals and RONETTES songs), Brian built a heavily overdubbed and echoed rock symphony that appealed to the public, complexities and all. It reached number one on December 10, 1966. In the U.K. it reached number one and in Australia number two.

The group then toured the U.K. and was promptly voted the world's best group in the annual NME poll, displacing the Beatles.

It was no easy task following "Good Vibrations," and it took 10 months for Capitol to issue the next Beach Boys single. The British didn't wait as long, issuing an LP cut, the Beach Boys' version of the Crystals' "Then He Kissed Me" retitled "Then I Kissed Her." It went to number four and number 28 in Australia.

"Heroes and Villains," a complex but less commercial composition, finally reached the American airwaves, climbing to number 12 (#8 U.K., #11 Australia).

The group returned to straight-ahead rock and roll with recordings like "Wild Honey" (#31 U.S., #29 U.K., #10 Australia, 1967), "Darlin'" (#19

U.S., #11 U.K., 1967), "Do It Again" (#20 U.S., #1 U.K., #1 Australia, 1968), and "I Can Hear Music" (#24 U.S., #10 U.K., #30 Australia.)

In the summer the last record they recorded for Capitol, "Break Away," reached number 63; the Beach Boys then signed with Warner Bros./Reprise, reestablishing its Brother label (which "Heroes and Villains" first appeared on) and by March 7, 1970, were back on the charts with "Add Some Music to Your Day" (#64).

The group's image suffered in the late '60s in performance; they were perceived more as an oldies group in the midst of the progressive rock movement. They rectified the situation in 1970 when they appeared at the Big Sur Festival in North California, making fans of the new hip rock crowd. They solidified that status in February 1971, playing Carnegie Hall in New York to overwhelming positive response and splitting the bill in April at the Fillmore East with the Grateful Dead.

The Beach Boys were starting to look different in 1972. Dennis was sidelined after a mishap with a windowpane that put his right hand out of action. Bruce Johnston left for a solo career. The two were replaced by Rick Fataar and Blondie Chaplin of the South African group Flame.

Meanwhile, their Warner Bros. records were proving not to be of the caliber of the Capitol sides. As if to prove the point, a reissue by Capitol of "Surfin' U.S.A." in the summer of 1974 reached number 36, higher than any of the six singles Warner Bros. had issued to date. The Warner Bros. material was getting more creative input from the group and less from Brian. Brian's return to producing a full LP's worth of music (*15 Big Ones*, titled after their 15th anniversary) brought the group back to the top five for the first time in 10 years. His simple formula? Back to Chuck Berry for "Rock and Roll Music" (#5 U.S., #36 U.K., #30 Australia) in the summer of 1976. The LP contained mostly oldies like "In the Still of the Night" and "A Casual Look" but it hit number eight in the nation so it was obvious what the public wanted from the Beach Boys.

By then Dennis was back and Fataar and Chaplin were out.

That year, through the Beach Boys' relationship with longtime fan and Chicago producer James William Guercio, the group sang backup for Chicago's hit "Wishing You Were Here" (#11, 1974).

In 1977 the Beach Boys signed with Guercio's Caribou label and by 1979 charted with a disco-flavored remake of "Here Comes the Night" (#44) originally on their 1968 *Wild Honey* LP.

Johnston rejoined the group in 1979. On July 4, 1980, the Beach Boys played a free concert in Washington, D.C., before half a million people, which became an annual event through the '80s.

In 1981 the "Stars on 45" craze prompted Capitol to edit a bunch of the group's early hits into "The Beach Boys Medley" that reached number 12 (#47 U.K., #2 Australia). This in turn encouraged Caribou to issue the old DEL-VIKINGS hit "Come Go with Me" (#18, 1981—the dark ages of doo wop).

In December 1983, Dennis Wilson drowned while swimming alongside his boat at Marina Del Ray Harbor in Los Angeles, an ironic twist of fate for the only actual surfing Beach Boy.

In 1985 the group got its act back together for the best original since the early days. With Mike Love on lead and Brian's falsetto sounding strong, "Getcha Back" and its harmony intro right out of THE MYSTICS' "Hushabye," reached number 26. The energy remained high with "Rock 'n' Roll to the Rescue" (#68, 1986) and a remake of THE MAMAS AND THE PAPAS' "California Dreamin'" (#57, 1986).

The Beach Boys enjoyed a number of recording collaborations. In 1984 they did a 45 with THE FOUR SEASONS on "East Meets West" (FBI). In 1987 they teamed with Little Richard on "Happy Endings" (Critique) and in 1988 with the Everly Brothers on another recording of "Don't Worry Baby" (Mercury). The weirdest pairing was their 1987 hit with the Fat Boys, "Wipe Out" (#12, Tin Pan Apple).

The Beach Boys came full circle in 1988 with "Kokomo," the Jamaica-rhythmed number one hit from the film *Cocktail*, with Mike on lead.

An amazing barometer of their appeal is the fact that between 1962 and 1981 they were only off the charts for two years, 1972 and 1977. They started a new streak in 1985 and charted at least once each year through 1989.

THE BEACH BOYS

A SIDE/B SIDE	LABEL/CAT NO	DATE
Surfin' / Luau	X 301	1961
Surfin' / Luau	Candix 301	1961
Surfin' Safari / 409	Cap 4777	1962
Ten Little Indians / Country Fair	Cap 4880	1962
Surfin' U.S.A. / Shut Down	Cap 4932	1963
Surfer Girl / Little Deuce Coupe	Cap 5009	1963
Be True To Your School / In My Room	Cap 5069	1963
Little Saint Nick / The Lord's Prayer	Cap 5096	1963
Spirit Of America / Boogie Woodie	Cap Promo	1963

A SIDE/B SIDE	LABEL/CAT NO	DATE
Fun, Fun, Fun /		
Why Do Fools Fall In Love?	Cap 5118	1964
I Get Around / Don't Worry, Baby	Cap 5174	1964
When I Grow Up /		
She Knows Me Too Well	Cap 5245	1964
Dance, Dance, Dance /		
The Warmth Of The Sun	Cap 5306	1964
The Man With All The Toys /		
Blue Christmas	Cap 5312	1964
Do You Wanna Dance? /		
Please Let Me Wonder	Cap 5372	1965
Help Me, Rhonda / Kiss Me, Baby	Cap 5395	1965
California Girls / Let Him Run Wild	Cap 5464	1965
Be True To Your School /		
In My Room	Cap 6059	1965
Ten Little Indians /		
She Knows Me Too Well	Cap 6060	1965
Salt Lake City /		
Amusement Parks U.S.A.	Cap 2936/37	1965
There's No Other /		
The Little Girl I Once Knew	Cap 5540	1965
Barbara Ann / Girl, Don't Tell Me	Cap 5561	1965
Sloop John B. /		
You're So Good To Me	Cap 5602	1966
Wouldn't It Be Nice /		
God Only Knows	Cap 5706	1966
Help Me, Rhonda /		
Do You Wanna Dance?	Cap 6061	1966
Surfin' U.S.A. / Shut Down	Cap 6094	1966
Surfin' Safari / 409	Cap 6095	1966
Good Vibrations /		
Let's Go Away For Awhile	Cap 6676	1966
Help Me, Rhonda /		
Do You Wanna Dance?	Cap 6081	1967
Heroes And Villains /		
You're Welcome	Brthr 1001	1967
Dance, Dance, Dance /		
The Warmth Of The Sun	Cap 6105	1967
Fun, Fun, Fun /		
Why Do Fools Fall In Love	Cap 6106	1967
Surfer Girl / Little Deuce Coupe	Cap 6107	1967
Wild Honey / Wind Chimes	Cap 2028	1967
Darlin' / Here Today	Cap 2068	1967
Friends / Little Bird	Cap 2160	1968
Do It Again / Wake The World	Cap 2239	1968
Bluebirds Over The Mountain /		
Never Learn Not To Love	Cap 2360	1968
I Can Hear Music /		
All I Want To Do	Cap 2432	1969
Break Away / Celebrate		
The News	Cap 2530	1969
Good Vibrations / Barbara Ann	Cap 6132	1969
Cotton Fields /		
The Nearest Faraway Place	Cap 2765	1970
Add Some Music To Your Day /		
Susie Cincinnati	Rprs 0894	1970
Slip On Through /		
This Whole World	Rprs 0929	1970

A SIDE/B SIDE	LABEL/CAT NO	DATE
Tears On The Morning /		
It's About Time	Rprs 0957	1970
Cool, Cool Water / Forever	Rprs 0998	1971
Wouldn't It Be Nice /		
(B side by Merry Clayton)	Ode 66016	1971
Long Promised Road / Deirdre	Rprs 1015	1971
Long Promised Road / 'Till I Die	Rprs 1047	1971
Surf's Up /		
Don't Go Near The Water	Rprs 1058	1971
You Need A Mess Of Help To		
Stand Alone / Cuddle Up	Rprs 1091	1972
Marcella / Hold On, Dear Brother	Rprs 1101	1972
Sail, On Sailor / Only With You	Rprs 1138	1973
Sail On, Sailor / The Trader	Rprs 557	1973
California Saga / Funky Pretty	Rprs 1156	1973
Sloop John B. /		
Wouldn't It Be Nice	Rprs 0101	1973
God Only Knows / Caroline, No	Rprs 0102	1973
Good Vibrations /		
Heroes And Villains	Rprs 0103	1973
Darlin' / Wild Honey	Rprs 0104	1973
Friends / Be Here In The Morning	Rprs 0105	1973
Do It Again / Cotton Fields	Rprs 0106	1973
I Can Hear Music /		
Bluebirds Over The Mountain	Rprs 0107	1973
I Can Hear Music /		
Let The Wind Blow	Rprs 1310	1974
Child Of Winter / Susie Cincinnati	Rprs 1321	1974
Surfin' U.S.A. /		
The Warmth Of The Sun	Cap 3924	1974
When I Grow Up (To Be A Man) /		
She Knows Me Too Well	Cap 6204	1974
Little Honda / Wendy	Cap 6205	1974
Barbara Ann / Little Honda	Cap 6259	1974
Little Honda / Hawaii	Cap 4093	1975
Barbara Ann / Little Honda	Cap 4110	1975
Sail On, Sailor / Only With You	Rprs 1325	1975
Wouldn't Be Nice / Caroline, No	Cap 1336	1975
Rock And Roll Music / TM Song	Cap 1354	1976
It's O.K. / Had To Phone Ya	Cap 1368	1976
Susie Cincinnati /		
Everyone's In Love With You	Cap 1375	1976
Graduation Day /		
Be True To Your School	Cap 4334	1976
Rock And Roll Music / It's O.K.	Rprs 0118	1977
Honkin' Down The Highway /		
Solar System	Rprs 1389	1977
Peggy Sue / Hey, Little Tomboy	Rprs 1394	1978
Mt. Vernon and Fairway	Rprs 2118	1978
Here Comes The Night /		
Baby Blue	CrbuZS89026	1979
Good Timin' / Love Surrounds Me	CrbuZS99029	1979
Lady Lynda / Full Sail	CrbuZS99030	1979
It's A Beautiful Day /		
Sumahama	CrbuZS99031	1979
Goin' On / Endless Harmony	CrbuZS99032	1980
Livin' With A Heartache /		
Santa Ana Winds	Crbu 9033	1980

A SIDE/B SIDE	LABEL/CAT NO	DATE
School Day (Ring! Ring! Goes The Bell) / School Day (Ring! Ring! Goes The Bell)	Crbu 9034	1981
Come Go With Me / Don't Go Near The Water	Crbu2Z502633	1981
Beach Boy Medley / God Only Knows	Cap 5030	1981
Getcha Back / Male Ego	Crbu2Z404913	1985
It's Gettin' Late / It's O.K.	Crbu 05433	1985
She Believes In Love / It's Just A Matter Of Time	Crbu 05624	1985
Rock And Roll To The Rescue / Good Vibrations	Cap 5595	1986
California Dreamin' / Lady Liberty	Cap 5630	1986
Happy Endings / California Girls	Crtq 799392	1987
Kokomo / (B-side by Little Richard: Tutti Frutti)	Elek 769385	1988

The Blue Jays

Rarely (if ever) has an R&B group been discovered by a rockabilly vocalist wanting to record them on his country and western label. Such was the fate of the Blue Jays, a group formed in Venice, California, in 1958.

Former Venice High School student and track star Leon Peels spent a lot of his spare time playing basketball at the Oakwood Playground. That's where he met Alex Manigo, Van Earl Richardson, and Len Davidson. In between basket stuffing the four had some fun imitating THE PLATTERS and other favorite groups.

22-year-old Peels and his community center friends practiced on and off for almost three years. Peels loved the tenor sound of Jackie Wilson and tried to utilize certain aspects of his style—like his high-note riffing—in his own vocal work. The group began singing originals after Leon and Alex wrote a song entitled "Lover's Island," which was reminiscent of the Sheppards' 1958 "Island of Love."

Soon after, the Blue Jays showed up at a talent contest at the Fox Venice Theater and were spotted by veteran A&R man and Specialty Records producer Bumps Blackwell. He told the guys their harmonies weren't tight enough to record but to call him when they had it together. That day never came because the group met country and western singer Werly Fairburn a short time later. Werly was a seasoned performer and recording artist who counted among his friends and associates the king himself—Elvis Presley. Alex Manigo actually met

Fairburn first and brought him to the old playground to hear the group sing. Werly owned a small rockabilly record company called Milestone but he'd gotten the bug to do black groups after his third release, the Paradons' recording of "Diamonds and Pearls," became a hit (#18, 1960). Fairburn liked the park performers, raw as they were, and offered to do a record with them. The quartet realized they'd better come up with a name fast and by that same evening had christened themselves the Blue Jays.

By mid-summer 1961 the Jays had recorded "Lover's Island" at Master Recorders on Fairfax Avenue in Los Angeles with Leon on lead.

In the 1950s and early '60s, records could be and often were recorded on one day and pressed and released on the next. "Lover's Island" was one of those discs, especially when a company had access to local disc jockeys like Hunter Hancock as Milestone did. By August 14th, the Blue Jays were on the charts and hovering at number 31. The resulting notoriety brought the group a local performance with Chubby Checker and Bobby Rydell at the Hollywood Bowl. But the Jays' management was practically nonexistent and Leon, who had been a cook at the Goody Goody Drive-in before the hit, was still working there during and after the charting. No one capitalized on the record's exposure and consequently the group had no television, no tours, no clubs, and no further hits.

They tried to recapture the magic of "Lover's Island" with such similar compositions as "Tears Are Falling" and "Venus My Love," but to no avail. After five singles in 1961 and 1962, the group went back to their wives and jobs.

On April 22, 1989, members of the Blue Jays appeared together for the first time in decades at the Hop in Lakewood, California for the Doo Wop Society show. On June 17, 1989, Leon appeared at the Ronnie I Collectors Concert Volume II in New Jersey with Vito and two of his Salutations (Eddie Pardocci and Shelly Buchansky) ably acting as his Blue Jays.

In December 1989 their first record in 27 years, "Once Upon a Love," was released on Classic Artists Records. A nostalgia-filled ballad, it transported those with a memory back to the much simpler days of "Lover's Island."

THE BLUE JAYS

A SIDE/B SIDE	LABEL/CAT NO	DATE
Lover's Island / You're Gonna Cry	Mlstn 2008	1961
Tears Are Falling / Tree Tall Len	Mlstn 2009	1961
Let's Make Love / Rock Rock Rock	Mlstn 2010	1961

A SIDE/B SIDE	LABEL/CAT NO	DATE
The Right To Love / Rock Rock Rock	Mlstn 2012	1962
Tall Len / Venus, My Love	Mlstn 2014	1962
Once Upon A Love / Alice From Above	ClsArt 111	1989

The Brooklyn Bridge

Rarely has the lead singer of one successful group dropped out of sight only to surface as the lead singer of another successful act. Yet that's exactly how the Brooklyn Bridge came to be. Johnny Maestro was the lead singer of the popular late '50s group THE CRESTS. He left to pursue a solo career in 1961 and vanished from the public eye for more than six years. In 1968 he reemerged as the lead of a revamped quartet of DEL-SATINS with Les Cauchi (first tenor), Mike Gregorio (second tenor), and Fred Ferrara (baritone).

The group entered a talent contest at a Farmingdale, Long Island, nightclub known as the Cloud Nine and were pitted against a jazzy band called the Rhythm Method led by Tom Sullivan and featuring his wife, Carolyn Woods, on vocals and keyboards. In one of the more spontaneous mergers in rock history, the two groups met after the show and joined forces the next day. Now 11 members strong, they hadn't been long in search of a name when a friend quipped that Johnny's entourage had about as good a shot at success with a group that size as they would have selling the Brooklyn Bridge.

The newly named group's "shot" came in April 1968 when they were the opening act for the Rascals at the Westbury Music Fair. Soon after, they began appearing at Cheetah, New York's hottest discotheque, where the patrons were delighted by the combination of a pop vocal group fronting a contemporary jazz ensemble. In short order the Brooklyn Bridge was signed to Buddah Records, and their first release came in the fall of 1968 under the unlikely title of "The Little Red Boat by the River."

The "Boat" promptly sank and Wes Farrell was brought in to produce the group. He feverishly set about looking for stronger material. What he came up with was a Jimmy Webb masterpiece buried in a FIFTH DIMENSION LP. "The Worst that Could Happen" hit the pop charts in December 1968 and didn't stop until it propelled the Bridge to number three in the nation.

With the advent of the big horn groups in the late '60s, Farrell could easily have been tempted to imitate them by mixing down the harmonies and pulling up the brass, thus losing the essence of the song. Yet he had the taste to let the song rest on his talented vocal section, and his mixes magnified this aspect of the group. Interestingly, the Brooklyn Bridge reached the charts several months before the two most successful horn groups of the late '60s, Blood, Sweat and Tears (March 1969) and Chicago (August 1969). When the record reached a million sales, a gold record was cemented into the sidewalk in front of Cheetah.

Their next single, "Blessed Is the Rain," was on the charts in March of 1969 before "Worst that Could Happen" had a chance to fall off. Maestro was masterful and the group's intricate harmonies showed through even with the horns more in evidence than on "Worst." But the song might have been too elegant for the pop charts; "Blessed" peaked at number 45 while disc jockeys started flipping the record over to play "Welcome Me Love," a song with a more commercially viable hook and an equally strong Farrell production. The B side charted for a longer period than "Blessed," but it only made it up to number 48.

Meanwhile Johnny Maestro had evolved from a respected vocalist with the Crests to one of pop music's premier white leads, rivaling Jay Black of JAY AND THE AMERICANS and Jimmy Beaumont of THE SKYLINERS. Maestro, however, had an R&B grittiness that lent his sound an extra dimension.

"Your Husband—My Wife" was another brilliant Farrell production, written by Tony Wine and Irwin Levine of "Candida" fame. (The song had to do with two people trying to reckon with their consciences in the throes of an affair they can't untangle, while knowing they can't be together forever.) Equal in quality to its predecessors, "Your Husband" was lost in the myriad of successful songs that were on the market (such as "In the Year 2525" and "Spinning Wheel") and only went to number 46. The Bridge's next single, "You'll Never Walk Alone" from Rodgers and Hammerstein's *Carousel*, was a lead singer's showcase, tailor-made for Johnny's vocal gymnastics. The backup singers' open-voiced "Ah" harmonies helped Maestro build to a crescendo; the sustained sound of a Farfisa organ accompanied his clear falsetto on the words "You'll never walk alone." Artistically, "Walk Alone" was Wes Farrell's crowning achievement with the Bridge. Commercially, the record stalled on the charts at number 51.

Their early 1970 release was "Free as the Wind," a bouncy, poor man's version of "Up, Up and Away" that became the first of the group's last five singles to miss the charts entirely. Still, the group's popularity enabled them to appear in the movie version of the musical *Hair* (1970) and begin work on a new LP with producer Stan Vincent at the helm. Vincent changed the group's direction by having them record such rock-oriented songs as Neil Young's "Down by the River," the Moody Blues' "Nights in White Satin," and Buffalo Springfield's "For What It's Worth." These recordings were more in tune with the time than the Bridge's preceding few singles, but covering other acts' relatively recent successes wasn't working in 1970. "Down by the River" only reached number 91 in July, and a 180-degree shift in direction with PETER, PAUL AND MARY's 1969 hit "Day Is Done" (#21) yielded the group's last chart record at number 98 in October.

Whether it was due to lack of promotion, changing times, or a changing creative direction, Johnny and the Bridge's last three singles (including a version of "Nights in White Satin" two years before the Moody Blues single charted) went nowhere.

Ten years passed before the group recorded again for the small collector-oriented label Harvey Records. The 1981 album was a rerecording of all of Johnny Maestro's hits with the Crests and Brooklyn Bridge using original members of both groups. A two-record set, the new recording also featured a medley of Dion songs ("Ruby Baby," "Runaround Sue," and "The Wanderer") as well as a dynamic rendition of Little Anthony's "Goin' Out of My Head," all backed by the Del-Satins/Brooklyn Bridge vocalists. Since Dion's backup group on those 1961 to 1963 hits was the Del-Satins, the album offered evidence of the group's consistently high quality over the years.

On June 20, 1987, Maestro and the Bridge performed at Radio City Music Hall along with Dion to honor his return to New York for the first time in 15 years. The concert, which also included Fred Parris and THE FIVE SATINS, had the Bridge/Del-Satins backing both Dion and Johnny Maestro along with one of the original BELMONTS, Carlo Mastrangelo.

In December 1988 the Bridge surfaced on record again with a beautiful Christmas original "Christmas Is" backed with a typically brilliant Maestro reading of the holiday standard "Oh Holy Night."

More than 20 years after they first appeared the Brooklyn Bridge were still in demand for live performances and remained one of the most popular of the golden '60s groups.

THE BROOKLYN BRIDGE

A SIDE/B SIDE	LABEL/CAT NO	DATE
Little Red Boat By The River / From My Window	Buddah 60	1968
Worst That Could Happen / Your Kite, My Kite	Buddah 75	1968
Blessed Is The Rain / Welcome Me Love	Buddah 95	1969
Your Husband—My Wife / Upside Down	Buddah 126	1969
You'll Never Walk Alone / Minstral Sunday	Buddah 139	1969
Free As The Wind / He's Not A Happy Man	Buddah 162	1970
Down By The River / Look Again	Buddah 179	1970
Day Is Done / Opposites	Buddah 193	1970
Nights In White Satin / Cynthia	Buddah 199	1970
Wednesday In Your Garden	Buddah 230	1971
Yours Until Tomorrow / Man In A Band	Buddah 236	1971
Bruno's Place / Man In A Band	Buddah 293	1972
Christmas Is / O Holy Night	Bklyn Brdg	1980

Billy Butler and the Chanters

The idea for the Chanters first came up in the home of one of the IMPRESSIONS. In 1956, Jerry Butler (original lead) and Curtis Mayfield (later lead) of the Impressions would rehearse in Jerry's house in Chicago. An avid fan and listener was Jerry's 11-year-old brother Billy, who decided this was also the life for him. When he reached Wells High School, Billy joined a group of schoolmates and began taking singing seriously. The members of the group were Billy on lead, Errol Bates on first tenor, John Jordan on second tenor, Jesse Tillman on baritone, and Alton Howell on bass.

They called themselves Billy Butler and the Four Enchanters. In 1963 the quintet put a few songs together and hit Chicago's version of Music Row looking for a record deal, but found no takers. Encouraged by brother Jerry, Billy and company kept working at it with new material and when the elder Butler returned from a series of performances he was sufficiently impressed with their strong harmony sound to have Curtis Mayfield listen to them. He in turn introduced them to Okeh (a Columbia subsidiary) A&R director Carl Davis.

The end result of subsequent demo sessions was a record deal, with the Billy Butler-penned "Found True Love" emerging as the group's first single in

September 1963. Despite a prominence of horns, the vocal group's sound on "Found" was much in evidence (more so than on later recordings) in those early days of Chicago soul. Its heavy sales in the Chicago and Midwest belied the fact that it was not doing well anywhere else and it only peaked at number 134 on November 2nd.

Disappointed with the overall results, Alton and John left the group soon after and the Chicago kids became Billy Butler and the Enchanters for their next release. "Gotta Get Away" (a Curtis Mayfield song), released in April 1964, made it to number 101 on *Billboard*'s Bubbling Under, but by now the group had become aware of Garnet Mimms and the Enchanters on the strength of their hit, "Cry Baby" (#4 Pop, #1 R&B, October 12, 1963).

Once again, Billy's group underwent a name change, its third in three releases. They became Billy Butler and the Chanters for "Can't Live Without Her," their third Bubbling Under record with a peak of number 130 in September 1964.

They finally broke the mold when "I Can't Wait No Longer" (another Mayfield song) reached the R&B charts on June 12, 1965, rising to number six with a number 60 position on the Pop charts.

Unlike writers in most acts, Billy did not always hold back his best songs for his own group. His tunes were turned into chart hits by artists like Gene Chandler ("Bless Our Love," #39 R&B, October 1964) and Otis Leavill ("Let Her Love Me," #31 R&B, February 1965).

In September 1965 the trio hit the Bubbling Under chart for the last time with "(I've Got a Feelin') You're Gonna Be Sorry" at number 103.

Billy and the Chanters broke up after an incident in which Errol Bates missed a show, opting to get married instead. Billy continued on as a solo for Okeh on one more record, "Right Track," which turned out to be his biggest individual success, hitting number 24 R&B in late summer of 1966.

Three years after Billy's solo charter he formed a new group that included Errol Bates (obviously forgiven), Larry Wade, and Phyllis Knox, and renamed them Infinity. They signed with brother Jerry's new Fountain Records, landing "Get on the Case" on the R&B charts (#41) in November 1969. Their last and best effort, "Hung on You," found itself on Pride Records of Hollywood in the spring of 1973. The STYLISTICS-styled ballad reached number 48, but with no significant success by 1974, Infinity (actually half of the Chanters) broke up.

Still, Billy Butler and the four Enchanters/Chanters made some fine soul harmony records at soul's infancy in the early '60s.

The Camelots

The Camelots were a good four-part harmony, rhythm and blues group from the Coney Island section of Brooklyn, New York. The Lincoln High School teens were David Nicholas (lead and first tenor), Milton (Bright) Pratt (lead, second tenor, and baritone), Joe Mercede (first tenor), Elijah Summers (baritone), and Julius Williams (bass, the Tremaines, Old Town, 1958).

They began harmonizing at a local YMCA in the late '50s and by 1962 had attracted the attention of producers/managers Bill and Steve Jerome, who arranged a deal with the local Aanko label.

The group, whose heroes included THE HEARTBEATS and THE MIRACLES, had no name when they traveled to New York City for their first recording session. That changed when they stepped out of the subway station onto 42nd Street and saw a billboard right in their path advertising the new hit musical *Camelot*.

Their first single (1963) was a reworking of the Heartbeats' "Your Way" that received a degree of airplay in the New York area but was treated more like an instant oldie.

Their next Aanko 45, "Sunday Kind of Love" (THE HARPTONES), was also solid but got less exposure than "Your Way."

The group hit with "Pocahontas" on Ember in 1984, telling the story of the Indian maiden in a doo wop/R&B setting and taking it to several cities' charts. The Camelots then played the Apollo with THE TEMPTATIONS and the Contours. Curiously, "Pocahontas" became their only single for Ember, though that same year they did record an excellent neo-gospel-flavored a cappella rocker called "Don't Leave Me Baby" for Cameo.

In 1964 the group recorded an original a cappella ballad, "Dance Girl," for the Times Square label, and when Relic Records bought out Times, "Dance Girl" and "Chain of Broken Hearts" were issued as singles. Both were popular with oldies and a cappella lovers in the tri-state area.

By the mid-'60s the group had separated, put out of business by the British invasion.

In February 1981 a re-formed Camelots emerged, with Milton Pratt (lead and second tenor), Michael Regan (lead, first, and second tenor), Joe Pitts (lead, second tenor, and baritone), Ernest Burnside (lead and first tenor), and Julius Williams (lead and bass). As with the original group, all were from Coney Island in the Mermaid and Neptune Avenue areas. All had sung with local groups; Joe and Ernest had sung with THE PARAGONS on Musictone (Milton and Julius were from the original Camelots). They hooked up with Clifton Records' Ronnie Italiano and began performing with acts like THE JIVE FIVE, THE CHANNELS, THE FIVE SATINS, the Paragons, and THE JESTERS on oldies shows in the tri-state area. In 1981 they recorded their only single, an EP of new versions of "Pocahontas" and "Don't Leave Me Baby" along with two previously unissued 1963 tracks, "Music to My Ears" and "Daddy's Going Away."

The group had such enthusiasm for their music that on a 1982 trip to New Jersey for a recording session their practicing made them miss their stop and they wound up in Philadelphia. Another time they were so into rehearsing that they became late for their radio appearance on a Don K. Reed show; while rushing through traffic they could hear Reed over the radio asking, "Where are the Camelots?"

By October 1984 the group had dissolved. Milton and Joe both died, Ernest went to work for the New York City school system, Julius settled in Brooklyn, and Mike became a City inspector also residing in Brooklyn.

The Carnations

One of only two vocal groups that are known to have been discovered in a men's room (the other being THE FIESTAS), the Carnations are all the more intriguing in that they had quite a bit of public exposure before they were finally noticed harmonizing in the lavatory.

The group formed in 1954 in the Yellow Mill River ghetto of Bridgeport, Connecticut. The members were Matthew Morales and Carl Hatton (both leads), Harvey Arrington, Alan Mason, and Arthur Blackwell. They called themselves the Startones and went to Watersville Junior High School, starting out as a quintet of 13-year-olds.

Their first record was "Betty" b/w "No Time for Tears" on a long-since-forgotten local label. By 1957, three members, Carl, Arthur, and Harvey, were in the service, but after a two-year hitch only Carl and Harvey came out. The group reformed with Arthur's younger brother Tommy taking his place and by 1959 they had added Edward Kennedy (no, the Massachusetts Senator was not moonlighting) to replace Alan Mason, who had hooked up with a different group during the Carnations' service time.

Now called the Teardrops, the group parlayed its local hop experience into tours performing with such notables as Robert & Johnny, THE CHANNELS,

and Bo Diddley. When Diddley (actually Ellas Bates, as he was known in his hometown of McComb, Mississippi) went to Chicago to record in early 1959 he took the group with him and they sang backup on the songs "I'm Sorry" and "Crackin' Up." The former was Bo's fifth R&B chart record and his first in over three years ("Pretty Thing," #4, 1956). An uncharacteristic ballad for Bo, it was cowritten with Harvey Fuqua of THE MOONGLOWS and contained prominent harmony by the group (though the only name on the label was Bo Diddley's); it peaked at number 17. Bo's "Crackin' Up" did even better, going to number 14 R&B and becoming the first Diddley tune to hit the Top 100, climbing to number 62 in August. The mid-tempo cha-cha also made the quintet's presence evident although it too carried only Bo's name.

At the turn of the decade, the Teardrops found themselves in New York appearing in the Apollo's amateur night contest where they reportedly won it an impressive six weeks in a row. Yet the group remained invisible; not one record company approached them to record. Taking the bull by the horns, Carl and company went door to door (or rather office building to office building) looking for a recording contract. The closest they got was some interest from George Goldner's Gone label to sign co-lead Matthew Morales. After a particularly frustrating day of record company rhetoric, the five disgruntled youths decided to stop searching the building at 1650 Broadway and just relieve their tensions by hitting some harmony in the building's men's room. Also present was Beltone Records A&R director Joe René. Apparently liking what he heard, René asked them back to his office. The group sang several songs including an original titled "Long Tall Girl"; the Beltone brass signed them up for a one-year deal. The group had accomplished more in a bathroom than they had on stage at the Apollo.

Beltone asked the boys to change their name, however, so the Teardrops became the Carnations. "Long Tall Girl" was recorded on March 2, 1961 and released in October, along with the B side ballad "Is There Such a World," for Beltone's Lescay subsidiary (named after Beltone founder Les Cahan).

"Long Tall Girl" was a simple, hooky, rock and roll jump tune that merited chart attention. Replete with solid wall-to-wall harmony and an enthusiastic lead by Carl Hatton, "Long Tall Girl" should have sold more than the estimated 75,000 records claimed by Beltone.

Still the group squeezed some more performance work out of their new release and reveled in their all-too-brief local hero status in Bridgeport. In the fall of 1961 they cut two more sides for Lescay, "Arlene" and "Crying Shame," but neither was ever released.

Beltone never picked up the group's option and they disbanded when Tommy Blackwell (the booming bass on the intro of "Girl" and the youngest member) followed in his brother Arthur's footsteps and joined the service. Tommy later joined another Bridgeport group, the Friegos, in the mid-'60s. "Long Tall Girl" went on to outlive its group, developing a cult following after repeated radio play from the late New York disc jockey Gus Gossert around 1972, more than 11 years after its release. Since then it's been a staple of doo wop radio shows (often acting as a show opener) from Boston to Baltimore and has been reissued several times.

The Carolons

The Carolons were a Brooklyn vocal group formed in a time of musical change. With the initial goal of keeping the vocal harmony sound of the '50s on the airwaves in new recordings of the '60s, Jay Wax got together with Artie Indursky and a guy named Ray in the summer of 1963.

The Tilden High School grads started singing some old favorites like "My Juanita" (THE CRESTS), "In the Still of the Night" (THE FIVE SATINS), "The Wind" (THE DIABLOS), and "Seven Wonders of the World" (the Key Tones). By November, Gary Banks had joined, and on the 10th they began their first rehearsal in earnest, adding such doo wop standards as "Life Is But a Dream" to their repertoire. Over the next few months the quartet's rehearsal spot became an informal gathering place; various friends added their blend to the group, including Stu Nadel and Stephanie Deustch and a guy everyone remembered only as Sinclair.

By their December 8th rehearsal, the as-yet-unnamed quintet included Jay, Gary, Stu, and newcomer Ruben Crespo (with his dynamite vibrato lead) along with another Tildenite, Joe Cooper. Songs like THE TYMES' "So Much in Love" and THE DANLEERS' "One Summer Night" now entered the repertoire, and for the first time, the group began singing a street-corner favorite, "Let It Please Be You" (THE DESIRES, 1957). They practiced in a variety of places, but one of their favorites was "The Pit," an infamous Brooklyn Pool Hall on Empire Boulevard and Utica Avenue, strategically placed between Mario's Pizza and the local White Castle.

The highlight of the group's gatherings were the nights at Sid Gordon's Bowling Alley on King's Highway and Utica Avenue. Gordon's was named after the great one-time New York Giants third baseman, who actually managed the alley for some time. It had a unique oval-shaped hallway with stone walls on two opposite sides, floor-to-ceiling glass by the entrances and a stone floor. The echo was fantastic, and on Friday nights a variety of groups would sing against the walls while listeners stood in the middle surrounded by vocalists and song. No one stood on ceremony then, and known acts who had chart records sang next to acts that didn't even have recording deals. On any given Friday, the likes of THE IMPALAS (Cub Records), VITO AND THE SALUTATIONS (Herald Records), THE TOKENS (RCA Records), and THE JESTERS (Winley Records), would be singing alongside the Carolons, who finally got their name when Jay came up with it while trying to fall asleep. He didn't hear about Lonnie and the Carollons (from 1959) until many years later.

On December 29, 1963, the group recorded what was only remembered as a radio rehearsal tape of "Let It Please Be You." It was sent off to local radio station WFUV in the Bronx at Fordham University, since the station had a signal that reached three states and was playing vocal group recordings. By the middle of January things started happening fast. The group scheduled a real studio session to record two songs a cappella on Saturday, February 1st, and they planned their last rehearsal for Wednesday night, January 29th. The trouble was that by the 29th, Gary and Stu had quit the group, so Joe Cooper suggested Paul Rothenberg join; Stephanie Deutsch was redrafted. The group rehearsed several songs that night, including "Tell Him" (THE EXCITERS) and "If You Want To" (the Carousels) with Stephanie as lead, but the group decided the recordings would be "Let It Please Be You" with Ruben on lead, coupled with a five-part harmony tune called "Let's Make Love Tonight," originally recorded by the Tymes. When Thursday rolled around the Carolons found out their December demo tape was going to be played on WFUV's "Time Capsule" show that night. Nerves became frayed as they settled around a radio and the first 50 minutes of the one-hour show came and went without the strains of "Let It Please Be You." Suddenly the announcer stated, "We've got a new group for you tonight with a terrific unreleased demo, so let's listen to the Carolons and 'Let It Please Be You.'" Half the song was gone before the screams stopped, and although it wasn't stardom, the group's spirits were at fever pitch. By Saturday morning, however, fever had turned to panic; Stephanie had decided to drop out two hours before the session. The "quartet" now scrambled to replace her, and with an hour to spare, Paul came up with Nat Schliefer, former bass of Bobby and the Consoles ("My Jelly Bean"). (Bobby later went on to become Robert John of "The Lion Sleeps Tonight" fame.) When Nat couldn't learn his parts quickly enough, the other singers shifted around during note pauses on "Let It Please Be You" to take up the slack. At any given time during the song you would hear Jay or Nat on bass or Joe and Nat on baritone. The intended lineup was Reuben (lead), Paul (first tenor), Joe (second tenor), Jay (baritone), and Nat (bass).

When the smoke cleared, the Carolons had recorded two songs in one hour at Richcraft Studios on 63rd Street, and had time left over to do an a cappella version of the Drifters hit "Please Stay" with only 10 minutes of rehearsal time.

Fresh from their first collision with recording, the group nominated Jay to get a record deal. Since the only record label he had the nerve to go to was the Times-Square Label and record store in the subway of the Avenue of the Americas station in New York City (where each Saturday he'd go to buy records), Jay tucked his acetates under his arm on Saturday, February 15th, confidently strolled into the busy shop looking for the proprietor, Slim. There was a record player on the counter and Jay, trying to get Slim's attention, yelled out, "Slim, my group just cut a great demo; got a minute?" Slim didn't seem to hear or didn't have a minute, but a big stocky guy standing next to him said, "I've got a label; I'd like to hear what you've got." Jay was nervous; his group's recording was about to get its first "professional" listen. But as the strains of "Let It Please Be You" and its last falsetto note faded from Slim's stereo, Billy Shibilsky, owner of Mellomood Records, announced that he liked it. Billy's label was in the forefront of the new East Coast a cappella craze, having released records by THE DEL STARS and THE ZIRCONS (who at the time had one of the biggest a cappella recordings on the East Coast, entitled "Lonely Way"). Jay figured that the Carolons would be recording his next a cappella release. Shibilsky, however, had expansion plans, having recently bought and reissued a 1959 master with music by THE FIVE DISCS entitled "Roses." Now he wanted the Carolons recording to be his first new release with band backing, and that suited Jay just fine. The quintet quickly put together a backup band of Tilden alumni, including music prodigy Lenny Hirsch, and on February 29th went back to Richcraft Studios. They re-recorded the two songs, this time with guitar, bass, drums, and sax accom-

paniment, and signed a recording contract with Mellomood on March 6th.

On March 31st, five nervous teenagers played their first gig at the Hillcrest Center in Jamaica, Queens, along with Vito and the Salutations, the Percells ("What Are Boys Made Of," ABC Records, 1963), and local favorite Joanne Engel ("Mirror, Mirror on the Wall," Sabrina, 1963). The Carolons sang both songs along with "Babalu's Wedding Day" (THE ETERNALS, 1958); the audience response was tremendous.

The record was released April 8, 1964, and by April 9th the A side, "Let It Please Be You," was on the "Time Capsule" show being heard all over New York, New Jersey, and Connecticut. The record then began to receive regular airplay on WNJR's Danny Styles "Kit Cat Club" show. By April 18th it was on Townhall distributor's "New Records to Watch" list. The problem was that the record listed was "Let's Make Love Tonight," the B side.

Meanwhile, "Let It Please Be You" built radio momentum, reaching number 36 on Danny Styles's Top 100 in July and climbing to number six in *Blues Train* magazine, right below "Under the Boardwalk" by THE DRIFTERS and above "Alone" by THE FOUR SEASONS.

But it was all local activity, and the record wasn't moving beyond the five boroughs and parts of New Jersey. By mid-July the group decided to try something in a more contemporary Four Seasons style, rehearsing a song Jay wrote titled "I'm Through with You." The Carolons would diligently gather in Jay's apartment and practice the song on an old Ampex two-track while Paul pounded out a rhythm on a twin-blade fan in the sweltering summer heat. By the end of July the group was becoming less active; the Mellomood Records operation was grinding to a halt, and the group members had to start thinking of jobs and careers.

"Let It Please Be You" continued to get play, having remained on the "Kit Cat Club" radio survey from July to November 1964. But the fun and dreams were over. It was almost as if the group had attempted to prove they could get a record out and then having done so, went their separate ways.

Joe Cooper stayed in music, working as a keyboard player in a Latin band and eventually becoming a music monitor for the American Society of Composers, Authors, and Publishers (ASCAP). Paul got married and became a glazier. He kept on singing, joining a group called the Triboros and performing in August 1990 on the Don K. Reed "Doo Wop Shop" show. Nat disappeared many years ago; Ruben moved to Chico, California, and became an insurance salesman. Jay became a music publisher and author and moved to Los Angeles. Ironically, the Carolons' last-rehearsed and only original song, "I'm Through with You," was recorded by the Tokens on RCA Records in 1988, some 24 years later, on both an LP and single. For some, the dreams are never over.

The Cascades

The Cascades were a quintet from San Diego, California, who formed in the late '50s. Their roster included John Gummoe (lead), Eddie Snyder, Dave Stevens, Dave Zabo, and Dave Wilson.

In 1962, after several years of developing their sound and musicianship (each was an instrumentalist as well as a singer), they played a local night spot called the Peppermint Stick. With Gummoe on guitar, Stevens on bass, Snyder on piano, Zabo on drums, and Wilson playing sax, the group was spotted by a representative of Valiant Records (distributed by Warner Bros.). Toward the fall of 1962 the five San Diego lads (ranging in age from teens to early 20s) were brought into Los Angeles's Gold Star Studios around the same time Phil Spector was starting to record some of his Crystals releases.

Their late-1962 release of "There's a Reason" failed, but the holiday season "Rhythm of the Rain," a soft pop harmony effort featuring a celesta, charted on January 12, 1963, rising to number three by March 9th on *Billboard*'s Pop charts. What really surprised record watchers was the success of the white-sounding single on the black charts as it rose to number seven at about the same time. Meanwhile, Cascades fever caught on in England where "Rain" reached number five and hung onto the British Isles charts for four months. Its biggest numbers were posted "down under," where it was number two on Australia's Best Sellers chart.

The group was now being booked by the prestigious William Morris Agency and managed by industry vet Andy Dimartino, Jr.

During a national tour they reached number 91 with "Shy Girl," and lifted to number 60 with the haunting flip-side FOUR PREPS-styled rhythm recording of "Last Leaf" (probably their best vocal effort).

"My First Day Alone," released in the late spring of 1963, made no noise at all and suddenly the Cascades, former toasts of the town, were moving to RCA. Their second of four soft-sounding singles made a slight three-week dent on the charts, losing steam at number 86 ("For Your Sweet

Love"), and the group became label vagabonds by mid-1964, moving through Charter, Liberty, Arwin, Smash, Probe, UNI, London, and Can Base until 1972. Playing as a band helped them persevere without a hit, although only Dave Wilson was still a member by the late '60s. The highlight of their later releases was Smash Records' "Flying on the Ground," with a youthful Neil Young on guitar.

Their last charter was "Maybe the Rain Will Fall" on UNI in the summer of 1969 (#61).

A mellow-sounding early '50s white vocal blend with an early '60s rhythm section enabled the Cascades to produce 20 singles in their quest for stardom.

The Cashmeres

The Cashmeres were a gospel group in rock and roll clothing. The members were neighbors all living on or near St. John's Place in Brooklyn, New York in 1959. Jean Reeves, Arnita Arnold, William Jordan, and Bobby Bowers made up the mixed gender quartet, practicing their combination of street-corner harmony and church gospel anywhere they could.

Word spread of the foursome until a young bartender at Queenie's Bar in the Flatbush section of Brooklyn got wind of them. The barkeep, Windsor King, had been a first tenor with the '40s gospel group the Royal Sons of Winston-Salem, North Carolina, who had come to New York in 1948 and become THE 5 ROYALES R&B group in the '50s. King had also sung with a family group called the Cozy Tones in 1956 consisting of brother Ralph, sisters Eloise and Katheryn, and Mitchell McPhee. They recorded for Melba and Willow while King continuously wrote songs, including "Tears of Happiness" recorded by THE CHARMS in 1958.

He went to see the group as a potential outlet for his songs, and by the time the evening was over he emerged as both their writer and their new lead singer. With their smoother sound, they agreed on the name the Cashmeres.

Since bartending kept him from some rehearsals, King recorded a demo at Broadway Studios. The song was titled "Satisfied," and it was overheard by Lake Records' owners Alan Lorber and Ernest Kelley. When they heard he had a group that wasn't yet ready to record, the Lake execs told King to see them when his group was ready. Buoyed by the interest, King rehearsed the group so much that the police were often called by neighbors to quiet them down.

King felt comfortable with the Cashmeres because they had gospel roots; he was writing gospel tunes with a contemporary backbeat. When the Isley Brothers' "Shout" charted in September 1959, King felt he was headed in the right direction.

Returning to Lake Records, the group put out its first release, "Everything's Gonna Be All Right," a call-and-response rocker with no hook and an endless verse. This pale "Shout" imitation never got off the ground, so Lake went to "Satisfied," the song they originally liked in the studio. The only problem was that "Satisfied" was four minutes and 19 seconds long—too long—so Lorber and Kelley cut it in half and titled the halves "Satisfied Part I" and "Satisfied Part II."

Though no more polished than the first single, "Satisfied" had more energy, a hook, and great gospel rock harmony dominated by the girls. Airplay was instantaneous, and the East Coast of 1960 was jumping to "Satisfied," so much so that Lake had to pick up additional distribution from the Amy-Mala-Bell organization. And so much that an unlikely cover by Debbie Reynolds soon surfaced on Dot. The Cashmeres' recording reached #64 Pop in December.

Hal Jackson, Dr. Jive, and Jocko all had the group performing in their rock and roll shows. Lake Records' Kelley and Lorber, knowing the limitations of their label, took the Cashmeres to Laurie Records to get even greater exposure. Three releases later all were thoroughly disappointed.

In 1961 the group found itself on Josie with another shouter titled "Lifeline," reportedly King's least favorite Cashmeres cut. Apparently disc jockeys agreed with him. When Bobby Bowers was diagnosed with a brain tumor in 1963 it seemed to be the straw that broke the Cashmeres back, and they disbanded. Bowers eventually recovered and became manager of a New York nightclub. He had songs recorded over the years by such artists as THE FLAMINGOS, THE FIVE KEYS, Joey Dee, and J.J. Jackson (of the Cordials), who coproduced Johnny Maestro's "Try Me" (Parkway 987) with Windsor King.

In 1964 King hooked up with a group called the Sharpettes for a last try ("How Do I Stand Today," Aldo) before settling into the moving business with his brother John, Jr. (Johnson's Practical Movers of New York) while attempting to write the next "Satisfied."

THE CASHMERES

A SIDE/B SIDE	LABEL/CAT NO	DATE
Everything's Gonna Be All Right /		
Four Lonely Nights	Lake 703	1960
Satisfied Part 1 / Satisfied Part 2	Lake 705	1960
A Very Special Birthday /		
I Believe In St. Nick	Laurie 3078	12/60
I Gotta Go / Singing Waters	Laurie 3088	4/61
Baby Come On Home /		
Poppa Said	Laurie 3105	10/61
Life-Line / Where Have You Been	Josie 894	1961

The Castells

The Castells (no relation to the Philadelphia CASTELLES) were a white pop trio formed in Santa Rosa, California, during the late fall of 1958. The threesome members were Chuck Girard, Tom Hicks, and Joe Kelly.

In early 1959 Bob Ussery joined and the group played the usual local gigs until they met mentor and disc jockey Dan Dillon, who whisked a demo of theirs to Era Records' Herb Newman in Los Angeles.

Their first single for this HILLTOPPERS/CREWCUTS-styled quartet was "Romeo," which prompted *Billboard*'s reviewer of January 30, 1961, to comment, "Pleasant teen appeal ditty is wrapped up in melodic vocal by lead singer and group." Local airplay lifted the cut only to number 101 on *Billboard*'s Bubbling Under in February 1961, so the Castells tried again with "Sacred" in April, a beautiful full-harmonied tune with Chuck Girard's soft-as-butter lead vocal and a sticks-on-bamboo rhythm right out of Ernie Kovacs's Nairobi Trio. The cha-cha rhythmed pop pleaser shot to number 20 nationally by the summer of 1961. A hit is no guarantee of the next single's success, however, and the Castells' next 45, "Make Believe Wedding," reached only number 98; it had a nice semi-ballad arrangement and satisfying vocals, but the song was weak. The group did not write and were dependent on the label for material. After one more failure, "Vision of You," they came upon a dreamy Steve Howard rhythm ballad right out of the 1955 FOUR COINS-FOUR LADS bag called "So This Is Love."

It charted on April 14, 1962, finishing one notch shy (#21) of "Sacred" on the national hit list.

Their last charter was a remake of the Frank Sinatra number one hit from 1946, "Oh What It Seemed to Be," which floated to number 91 in August and sank soon after. Their next single, "Echoes in the Night," had a chime intro and a musical feel that was possibly borrowed three months later for THE EMOTIONS' hit "Echo." The Castells' B side was a castanets-filled, Spanish-guitar-laden, up-tempo 45 called "Only One," which was arranged by Jack Nitzsche about the same time he became Phil Spector's arranger for "Zippity-Doo-Dah." This new Castells direction didn't impress radio, so in June 1963 Era retreated, reissuing their first single's B side "Little Sad Eyes." A reviewer in *Billboard* wrote, "The smooth-sounding group with the harmony touch has another neat ballad effort here. It's a tender side and it gets a meaningful performance. Watch it!" The Castells did but it went nowhere.

By early 1964 the quartet was on Warner Bros. Records with an exciting Brian Wilson arranged, written, and produced single titled "I Do." Its melody was note-for-note the same as THE BEACH BOYS' 1962 "County Fair," but with a "Spectorized" production, Brian created something like a male RONETTES record out of "I Do." With the cut playing in both the East and West, Warner Bros. must have truly dropped the ball to let this one get away.

When their solid rendering of THE DUBS' 1957 classic "Could This Be Magic" failed in 1964 to get label support the Castells were doomed to travel the desert of record deals, coming upon the occasional oases of Decca, Laurie, and United Artists but with no further success.

An excellent pop group, their legacy to most listeners is "Sacred."

Cathy Jean and the Roommates

Thanks to the sizeable hit "Please Love Me Forever," the teen world of 1961 perceived Cathy Jean and the Roommates as a collection of friends singing their way to stardom. The truth was that the Roommates and Cathy Jean recorded "Please" without ever meeting each other.

The Roommates were from Kew Gardens, Queens, and were formed by 15-year-old Steve Susskind and Bob Minsky of Russell Sage Junior High School. Bob originally sang with a local quartet called the Sparklers, but in 1959 he and Steve became a duo called the Roommates (they were in the same homeroom at Sage). Later that year they competed at Forest Hills High School and took second place, losing to a duo that was already considered professional. That act, Tom and Jerry,

had scored a hit in 1957 titled "Hey Little School-girl" (#49). Years later they would be known as Simon and Garfunkel.

The Roommates duo decided to become a group. Several short-termers came and went until the 1960 lineup included Steve Susskind (lead), Jack Carlson (first tenor and falsetto), Felix Alvarez (second tenor), and Bob Minsky (bass).

The group practiced after school and began writing original songs. Unlike most groups who wrote, however, the Roommates were honest enough to admit their own songs were not very competitive, so they went through the group's 45s to find workable material and came up with songs like "One Summer Night" (THE DANLEERS) and "Glory of Love" (THE FIVE KEYS). The group was heard on several occasions singing in the lobby of the Forest Hills apartment building where Jody Malis lived. Jody was the record librarian at WMGM radio, which had one of the nation's first top 40 formats. Jody and her husband Gene had a similar idea about resurrecting standards for '60s teens and signed the Roommates to a management deal.

The Roommates' first single was not a pop standard but a country hit from the '50s by Muriel Deason a.k.a. Kitty Wells titled "Making Believe." Complete with harmonica, "Making Believe" got some airplay but soon disappeared from the scene.

The Roommates, whose smooth harmonies put their sound somewhere between THE HILLTOPPERS and THE PASSIONS, soon found themselves in an unexpected situation. On May 3, 1960, Jody and Gene Malis recorded another new act for their recently established Valmor label. The act, 14-year-old Cathy Jean, recorded the Malone/Blanchard ballad "Please Love Me Forever," but something was missing so Jody brought the Roommates in and they reluctantly overdubbed harmony parts. Since Cathy Jean had left the studio by the time the Roommates recorded, the singers never met her. Following in the footsteps of the West Coast's Kathy Young and the Innocents, Jody felt that if she had a hit she would have two acts instead of one, so she was sure to credit both on the label.

The group hated the song and their work on it. Yet it won Murray the K's "Boss Record of the Week" honor on WINS in New York City in the late winter of 1960. On February 27th its momentum carried it onto the *Billboard* Hot 100 and by April it was at number 12, reaching number two in New York.

"Please" was followed in March by the Roommates' own recording of one of their '50s favorites, "Glory of Love." While "Please" was still in the Top 20, "Glory of Love" charted and rose to number 49.

The Roommates were off and running on the tour circuit with Ral Donner, Tony Orlando, Cathy Jean, and B. Bumble and the Stingers.

The Roommates became regulars at Palisades Park (once jumping off the stage and into the pool while fully dressed), playing lip-synced shows for disc jockeys Cousin Bruce Morrow, Hal Jackson, and Dick Clark.

Their next single, "Band of Gold," made it into the top 20 in New York but failed to chart nationally for a technical reason. A microphone pop caused by Steve's voice on the word "prove" resulted in a skip on all the deejay pressings (New York stations received acetate dubs that didn't skip). A rushed second pressing failed to correct the problem and by a third pressing the momentum was lost. Its fall follow-up, a solid rendition of the 1950 Gordon Jenkins number three hit "My Foolish Heart," also failed to chart.

The group also backed Cathy on "Make Me Smile Again," her fall release, but they were given no label credit.

Valmor closed in late 1962 but Malis retained faith in the quartet and moved them over to Cameo Records for the single "Sunday Kind of Love" (THE HARPTONES). Added vocalist George Rodriguez made them a quintet. The song won Murray's "Boss Record of the Week" contest in the fall of 1962 but did little else.

By 1963 the Roommates were on Philips for two strong revised oldies, "Gee" (THE CROWS, #14, 1953) and "The Nearness of You" (#5, Glenn Miller, 1940), but their chart days were over.

Their last single (on the Canadian American Records label, where Gene Malis was now the general manager, Jody Malis was the A&R director, and Steve Susskind was the national promotion manager) was "My Heart" (1964), a song similar to the Volumes' second single (1962) "Come Back into My Heart," but the Roommates did rockin' good justice to it.

By the end of 1965 the Roommates had called it quits and, unlike many who reunited for the late '60s and early '70s oldies revivals, never re-formed. Cathy Jean went on to form her own Roommates and continued performing in the New York area into the '90s.

CATHY JEAN AND THE ROOMMATES

A SIDE/B SIDE	LABEL/CAT NO	DATE
The Roommates		
Making Believe /		
I Want A Little Girl	Promo 2211	1960

A SIDE/B SIDE	LABEL/CAT NO	DATE
Please Love Me Forever* /		
Canadian Sunset*	Valmor 007	11/60
Glory Of Love /		
Never Knew	Valmor 008	3/61
Make Me Smile Again** /		
Sugar Cake	Valmor 009	5/61
Band Of Gold /		
O Baby Love	Valmor 10	6/61
My Foolish Heart /		
My Kisses For Your Thoughts	Valmor 13	9/61
Please Tell Me* / Sugar Cake*	Valmor 16	1962
Sunday Kind Of Love / A Lonely		
Way To Spend An Evening	Cameo 233	11/62
Answer Me, My Love / Gee	Phlps 40105	6/63
The Nearness Of You /		
Please Don't Cheat On Me	Phlps 40153	1963
My Heart / Just For Tonight	Can Am 166	1964

* Cathy Jean and the Roommates
** with Cathy Jean

The Chaperones

A polished pop doo wop group, the Chaperones were from the ELEGANTS school of vocalizing. They were formed from two separate Long Island aggregations who were attending a Sunday afternoon battle of the groups at the Lindenhurst Ballroom in 1958.

The lead singer of the Fabulous Exquisites, Tony Amato, got into a conversation with another group that needed a lead singer. The new lineup was Tony (lead, from Deer Park, New York), Roy Marchesano (first tenor, Farmingdale, New York), Tommy Ronka (second tenor, Farmingdale), Nick Salvato (baritone from Bethpage), and Dave Kelly (bass).

Originally called the Sharptones and then the Fairlanes, they finally settled on the Chaperones because of its relevance to the proms and dances that were so popular at the time. The quintet practiced a combination of doo wop and barbershop harmony, and since Tony's favorites at the time were the Elegants, the Chaperones' sound reflected that style. Their starry-eyed idol worship carried over into their first demo, a song that the group wrote called "Cruise to the Moon."

When they finished the recording in May 1959 (Nick Salvato was 20 at the time; the others were between 16 and 18), Nick played it for C.W. Post College classmate Steve Blaine, son of Josie Records head Jerry Blaine. He signed the group, but the record was not an immediate release, so when Tommy Ronka's friend Lee Adrian needed some backup for his recording, the group pitched in and cut "Barbara, Let's Go Steady" at Brooklyn's dungeon-like Richcraft Studios (2314 63rd Street).

To the surprise of the Chaperones, "Barbara" came out on Richcraft Records soon after. It credited only Lee Adrian, but technically it was the Chaperones' first release since "Cruise" didn't hit the airwaves until the summer of 1960. When it did, airplay was substantial, especially in the East, but the chime harmony intro and exit ballad didn't match its airplay in sales. And a bit of confusion was added to the early pressings as the group's name was misspelled Cahperones on the label.

Still, the group got a taste of performing when they became the kings of supermarket openings on Long Island. They also did the theme park circuit with Murray the K's shows at Frontierland in Patchogue and Freedomland in the Bronx; Bruce Morrow extravaganzas that co-billed THE EARLS, VITO AND THE SALUTATIONS, and THE FIVE DISCS; and several Palisades Park appearances that included a July 3, 1960, date with THE FIVE SATINS and Jimmy Jones. (One of these shows had them backing Paul Anka.)

By the time "Cruise" was released, Rich Messina of Bethpage was on bass replacing Dave Kelly.

Their next single, "Shining Star," was a cross between "Little Star" and "Hushabye" (THE MYSTICS) and although it was a nice, pop up-tempo opus, radio did not take it to heart.

Their next release was another uncredited affair backing vocalist Lou Jordan on "Paradise for Two" in 1961, also on Josie.

Their last Josie 45 was a remake of "Blueberry Sweet" (the Chandeliers, 1958) in 1961 with a flip titled (still touting stars-and-skies) "Man from the Moon."

The group then wrote "Memories," but when their career with Josie seemed to be at an end the song wound up recorded by THE BOB KNIGHT FOUR. The Chaperones went their separate ways soon after but did eventually reunite, and by the mid-'80s consisted of Tony and Nick along with Kim Chlandra (first tenor) and Danny Sasatori (second tenor).

In 1985 this group recorded a slow-to-rockin' version of THE ROB ROYS' "Pizza Pie" for Tabor Records. It was the group's last release.

Today, Nick is a plant engineer, Roy is an electrician, Richie is a teacher on Long Island, and Tommy is performing in Las Vegas. Lead singer Tony Amato died in the late '80s.

His legacy, "Cruise to the Moon," turned out to have a greater afterlife, becoming the theme song for New York radio personality Jocko Henderson.

The Chiffons

Throughout rock and roll history, vocal groups (especially the non-writing variety) have spent entire careers in search of hit-bound melodies and captivating lyrics. In a reverse of that equation, the Chiffons garnered their greatest success because a hit song was in search of a group.

In 1960 the Chiffons formed at James Monroe High School in the Bronx. The lead singer was 14-year-old Judy Craig, and she sang along with Patricia Bennett and Barbara Lee, both 13. They met writer/manager/entrepreneur hopeful Ronnie Mack at the after-school center. Up to that time Mack's claim to fame was a 1959 local Philadelphia hit by Little Jimmy (Rivers) and the Tops (V-Tone Records) entitled "Puppy Love." Though partial to his own songs, Mack got wind of a new Luther Dixon–Shirley Owens composition in the summer of 1960. Shirley was the leader of THE SHIRELLES, so it was logical that they would be the ones to record "Tonight's the Night." Mack decided that one way to get publicity would be to have a cover record by an unknown group fight it out with the version by a more established act.

The girls chose the name the Chiffons out of a hat. Mack then signed the trio to Big Deal Records, a Chatsworth, California, label. They recorded "Tonight's the Night," and both versions hit the charts on September 12th. The Shirelles, having a stronger lead vocalist and fuller harmonies (not to mention greater label promotion), climbed to number 39 while the Chiffons' first release managed only a number 76 ranking. For some reason no further releases emanated from Big Deal.

In the fall of 1962 Ronnie Mack, ever hustling his songs, dropped his wares at the doorstep of a new production team in New York City. The company was called Bright Tunes and the producers were Phil and Mitch Margo, Jay Siegel, and Hank Medress a.k.a. THE TOKENS. They liked one song he had called "He's So Fine" and asked if he had a group to sing it. Fearing a negative response would end their interest he said he had a terrific group. The Bright Tunes crew said, "Great. Bring them in tomorrow." Scrambling back to the Bronx, Ronnie knew he had no such group, but he also knew the Chiffons had heard and even sung the song around the school. To bolster the harmonies he brought in one new girl, Sylvia Peterson, who had sung with Little Jimmie and the Tops.

Several months passed until the quartet was called in to record the single. Finally, in December 1962, it was released on Laurie Records (via the

Tokens' production agreement). From that point on the intro line of "doo lang doo lang doo lang" became the newest nonsensical addition to rock and roll vernacular. By March 30th "He's So Fine" was the number one record in America on both the Pop and R&B charts and reached number 16 in England, making the Tokens the first vocal group to produce a number one record for another group. The one downbeat footnote to the Chiffons' success was that their manager/writer, Ronnie Mack, was dying of Hodgkins disease and would be gone before 1963 was over.

The next single, "Lucky Me," was as big a flop as "He's So Fine" was a hit. But not wanting to waste any momentum, the Tokens immediately produced a third single, the sparkling "One Fine Day." "One Fine Day" proved to have the same simple appeal as "He's So Fine," and the Carole King-Gerry Goffin composition rocketed up the charts to number five Pop in June and to number six R&B. By July it was also on the British Best Seller list peaking at number 29.

The Tokens decided to create a multiple personality for the group, so at the same time "One Fine Day" was being released, they recorded the Chiffons on Laurie's Rust subsidiary as the Four Pennies.

"My Block" was their first single as the Pennies, and it reached the charts only three weeks after "One Fine Day." It was a cha-cha rhythmed, castanet-spiced slice of life à la THE CRYSTALS' "Uptown," incorporating DRIFTERS-styled kettle drums into a sound reminiscent of Phil Spector's productions. Unfortunately it only went to number 67 Pop. But 1963 remained the year of the Chiffons; they charted top 40 in September with their third Laurie single in four tries, the catchy "A Love So Fine." Meanwhile, back as the Four Pennies, their September release of "When the Boy's Happy" reached number 95 Pop in November.

The group was greatly in demand and, having honed their craft into an excellent blend of four-part harmony, had been playing everything from TV's "American Bandstand," "Hullabaloo," and "Shindig" to Murray the K's Brooklyn Fox live show, and had been singing commercials for the likes of Great Shakes drinks.

In the fall of 1963 the Chiffons released "I Have a Boyfriend," considered by some to be their best recording. Written by Jeff Barry, Ellie Greenwich, and the Tokens, the rhythm ballad was a RONETTES-styled mix of early '60s rhythm and blues and doo wop. It charted in November, reached #36 on *Billboard*'s Best Seller list, and was gone 10 weeks later.

Several strong Chiffons recordings followed ("Tonight I Met an Angel," "Sailor Boy" [#81, 1964], and the Goffin-King song "What Am I Gonna Do with You," 1964) but the charts now seemed to belong more to the British than to the Bronx. Still, a good song is a good song, and in the spring of 1966 the Chiffons struck again with "Sweet Talkin' Guy," a top 10 record in June.

The Tokens pulled the group from Laurie in 1968 for one single on their own B.T. Puppy label called "My Secret Love," which remained a secret to the public since radio never gave it a shot.

By 1970 the girls were on Buddah singing the old TYMES hit "So Much in Love," while George Harrison was (unconsciously) plagiarizing Ronnie Mack's "He's So Fine" while writing his first solo hit "My Sweet Lord." In an act of sarcastic retribution Laurie Records and producer Bill Frenz recorded the Chiffons in 1975 singing—you guessed it— "My Sweet Lord," and released the single that same year.

Another Chiffons twist of fate occurred in March 1972, six years after their last chart record. It seems someone in Britain felt the old "Sweet Talkin' Guy" deserved another shot at the top 10 (in keeping with a common *modus operandi* in England) and so London Records issued the original recording on the U.K. label Statesides. To everyone's surprise the record went skyrocketing to number four in the U.K. when the Chiffons were working small clubs and didn't even have a U.S. record deal.

In 1976, Laurie issued the last Chiffons single, "Dream, Dream, Dream" with "Oh My Lover" (the "He So Fine" B side) on the flip. By the 1970s Judy Craig (Mann) had left the act. Pat Bennett married and Barbara Lee did the same. The Chiffons continued to perform locally into the '80s, perhaps hoping the girl group sound of the '60s might reemerge in the '90s.

THE CHIFFONS

A SIDE/B SIDE	LABEL/CAT NO	DATE
Tonight's The Night / Do You Know	BgDl 6003	1960
Never Never / No More Tomorrows	Wildcat 601	1962
After Last Night / Doctor Of Hearts	Rprs 20103	1962
He's So Fine / Oh My Lover	Laurie 3152	12/62
Lucky Me / Why Am I So Shy	Laurie 3166	1963
One Fine Day / Why Am I So Shy	Laurie 3179	1963
My Block* / Dry Your Eyes*	Rust 5071	5/63
A Love So Fine / Only My Friend	Laurie 3195	1963
When The Boy's Happy* / Rockaday Part 1*	Rust 5070	9/63
I Have A Boyfriend / I'm Gonna Dry My Eyes	Laurie 3212	1963

A SIDE/B SIDE	LABEL/CAT NO	DATE
Tonight I Met Angel / Easy To Love	Laurie 3224	1963
Sailor Boy /		
When Summer's Through	Laurie 3262	1964
What Am I Gonna Do With You /		
Strange Strange Feelin'	Laurie 3275	1964
Nobody Knows What's Goin' On /		
The Real Thing	Laurie 3301	1965
Nobody Knows What's Goin' On /		
Did You Ever Go Steady	Laurie 3301	1965
The Heavenly Place /		
Tonight I'm Gonna Dream	Laurie 3318	1965
Sweet Talkin' Guy /		
Did You Ever Go Steady	Laurie 3340	1966
Out Of This World / Just A Boy	Laurie 3350	1966
Stop, Look And Listen / March	Laurie 3357	1966
My Boyfriend's Back /		
I Got Plenty O'Nuttin'	Laurie 3364	1966
Keep The Boy Happy /		
If I Knew Then	Laurie 3377	1967
Just For Tonight / Teach Me Now	Laurie 3423	1967
Up On The Bridge / March	Laurie 3460	1968
Love Me Like You're Gonna Lose		
Me / Three Dips Of Ice Cream	Laurie 3497	1969
Secret Love /		
Strange, Strange Feeling	BTP 558	1969
So Much In Love /		
Strange, Strange Feeling	Buddah 171	1970
My Sweet Lord / Main Nerve	Laurie 3630	1975
Dream, Dream, Dream /		
Oh My Lover	Laurie 3648	1976

* The Four Pennies

The Chi-Lites

The Chi-Lites were one of the most popular of the Chicago soul quintets on the scene in the late '60s and early '70s.

Formed in 1960, the group included Marshall Thompson (baritone), Creadel Jones (bass), Robert "Squirrel" Lester (tenor), Clarence Johnson (tenor), and Eugene Record (lead). Thompson and Jones were originally in an unrecorded group called the Desideros, and Chi-Lites founder Marshall Thompson was a drummer playing the Regal Theatre behind such notables as THE FLAMINGOS and THE DELLS. Lester, Johnson, and Record were with a group called the Chantours before joining up with Thompson and Jones.

They originally called themselves the Hi-Lites in 1963 and had an undistinguished single for Mercury called "Pots and Pans." Due to an earlier group with the Hi-Lites name, they added a C for Chicago and became Marshall and the Chi-Lites in 1964.

In 1965 they signed with Blue Rock Records for three less-than-competitive singles, but in 1967 they joined MCA's Dakar label and turned out a strong Gerald Sims-produced rock-a-ballad, "Baby It's Time," which gave them some local exposure. With Eugene Record (who was originally a cab driver) writing and singing lead, the group moved to MCA's Revue label with the ballad "Love Is Gone," and by 1969 they had worked their way up to Brunswick Records.

Their first single there was "Give It Away," a cross between an IMPRESSIONS and a FIVE STAIRSTEPS sound, charting February 8, 1969, R&B at number 10 (#88 Pop). Carl Davis and Eugene Record were now producing the group.

Their second single established the close-harmony ballad style as their forte; "Let Me Be the Man My Daddy Was" reached number 15 R&B in the summer of 1969.

Their breakthrough record was the TEMPTATIONS-styled "Give More Power to the People" (#26 Pop, #4 R&B, #32 U.K., their first of 10 U.K. charters) in 1971.

By later that year they were back to their trademark ballad style with back-to-back major hits, the talk-singing "Have You Seen Her" (#3 Pop, #1 R&B, #3 U.K., written by artist Barbara Acklin and Record, her husband) and the harmony-filled harmonica-led "Oh Girl" (#1 Pop, #1 R&B, #14 U.K., 1972).

When "Oh Girl" hit number one Pop on May 27, 1972, the top five were owned by black artists: Sammy Davis, Jr. ("Candy Man," #5), Al Green ("Look What You Done for Me," #4), Roberta Flack ("The First Time Ever I Saw Your Face," #3), and THE STAPLE SINGERS ("I'll Take You There," #2).

The group went on to have other top 20 R&B hits like "Stoned Out of My Mind" (#30 Pop, #2 R&B, 1973), "Homely Girl" (#54 Pop, #3 R&B, #5 U.K.), and "Toby" (#78 Pop, #7 R&B), but they never again crossed into the Pop top 20.

In 1973 Jones left and was replaced successively by Stan Anderson, Willy Kensey, and Doc Roberson in 1975. In November 1975 the group charted with an exciting Temptations-styled soul rocker, "Don't Burn No Bridges," with label-mate Jackie Wilson singing lead (#91 R&B). November was also the month Record decided to go solo, but his only chart release was 1977's "Laying Beside You" (#24 R&B, Warner Bros.).

David Scott and Danny Johnson, both tenors, were then added to the group, and Vandy Hampton replaced Johnson in 1977.

▲ THE FOUR SEASONS

▼ THE BROOKLYN BRIDGE ▲ THE ORLONS

▼ PETER, PAUL AND MARY   ▼ THE LETTERMEN   ▲ THE HIGHWAYMEN

In 1976 the Chi-Lites moved to Chicago's Mercury label with "Happy Being Lonely" (#30 R&B) as their biggest record.

In late 1980 original members Thompson, Lester, Jones, and Record re-formed and recorded for Eugene's own Chi-Sound label as well as for 20th Century, but it wasn't until they joined Joe Isgro's Hot Larc label that they reached the top 10 for the first time in nine years with "Bottoms Up" (#7 R&B). In 1983 Creadel Jones retired and the group continued on as a trio.

In 1984 they had their last chart single, "Gimme Whatcha Got" (#41 R&B), for another Isgro company, Private I Records distributed by Epic. By the late '80s the group had once again disbanded after chalking up 41 soul charters from 1969 to 1984.

The Chimes

"**F**rom pool room to pop hits" accurately encapsulates the Chimes' career. A Brooklyn street-corner group formed in 1957, they originally called themselves the Capris until they found out that friends of theirs from Rockaway Beach in Long Island were already using the name. (That group turned out to be the "There's a Moon Out Tonight" Capris). So Lenny Cocco and company renamed themselves the Chimes. They didn't hear of the Chimes on Specialty Records of Los Angeles ("Zindy Lou," 1955) until well after they recorded, and probably never heard at all of the Chimes on Reserve ("Nervous Heart," 1957) and Flair ("Love Me, Love Me," 1954).

The original Brooklyn quintet consisted of Cocco (lead), Pat DePrisco (first tenor), Richard Mercardo (second tenor), Joe Croce (baritone), and Pat McGuire (bass). Lenny was into standards at an early age since his father was a professional accordion player. He thought Tommy Dorsey's 1937 number one hit "Once in a While" would work well in a vocal quintet arrangement, so the group began practicing it at a local pool hall that had a piano.

In 1960 the five Italian lads recorded a demo of "Once in a While," attracting the interest of the studio's engineer. While the Chimes were still in the studio the engineer called a friend at Tag Records and within an hour Andy Leonetti was there listening to the quintet's first recording.

By the fall of 1960 "Once in a While" was hitting *Billboard*'s national charts. It finished one spot shy of the top 10, spent 18 weeks on the charts, and sold over a million copies. Though they had a white doo wop sound by today's standards, in 1960 the Chimes were thought by many to be a black group. Their first major bookings were thus in black theatres (the Howard in Washington, the Regal in Chicago, and the Apollo in New York).

Their second single was "I'm in the Mood for Love," another standard (Little Jack Little, #1 in 1935). Performed in a similar style to "Once," it charted on March 27th and rose to number 38 nationally. By spring, the group was on its third standard in three tries, the 1934 Eddy Duchin number one smash "Let's Fall in Love," but apparently radio and the public weren't buying it (possibly due to a deviation in vocal arrangement from the first two releases—"Let's" had the group up front with the lead).

The Chimes tried a Cocco original ("Paradise") in 1962, and when it failed they moved over to Metro Records for one 1963 release, "Whose Heart Are You Breakin'." The group was now a quartet; bass Pat McGuire had died in a car accident.

In November, Laurie Records picked up the Metro sides and released them with no success.

In 1964, the Chimes wound up on a label in transition: Vee-Jay Records. The '50s R&B vocal group powerhouse was now putting out top-selling British and American rock and roll in the form of the Beatles ("Do You Want to Know a Secret," #2) and THE FOUR SEASONS ("Candy Girl," #3). With this kind of competition, the label was distracted enough to virtually ignore the Chimes' summer of 1964 release, "Two Times Two." By 1965 the Chimes had separated only to come together again in 1970 for the rock and roll revival shows.

By 1973 they had split again, lacking any real recording opportunities. In the early '80s Lenny took another stab at it, but the guys were not up for the rigors of performance, so Cocco formed a new Chimes consisting of Rocky Marsicano (first tenor), Joe Locicero (second tenor), Joe Ficarotto (baritone), and Joe Amato (bass and keyboards).

In 1986, the group went contemporary with "New York City Lady" on Freedom (their own label). An LP of all the old Chimes '60s singles came out in the late '80s. The group still performs all over the East Coast as Lenny Cocco and the Chimes.

The Classics

Though the Classics were active in the '60s, their style was reminiscent of the groups of the late '40s and early '50s. This was especially true of lead singer Emil Stucchio's crooning leads.

Apart from Emil, the group consisted of first tenor Tony Victor, second tenor John Gambale, and bass Jamie Troy. They came from Garfield Place in Brooklyn and were all between 14 and 16 years of age when they formed as the Perennials in 1958. While they were playing the club Illusion on New Utrecht Avenue, the show's host, comedian Sam Sardi, tried in vain to introduce the group but couldn't pronounce "Perennials." He called the group onstage and asked whether they could come up with a simpler moniker. When they couldn't, he introduced them as "the Classics." The group continued playing teen hops, developing a style of white doo wop similar to a group they would later hear of from Jersey City, THE DUPREES.

In late spring 1959, baritone Louis Rotundo of THE PASSIONS (who were neighborhood friends of the Classics) recommended the group see their manager Jim Gribble. Unbeknownst to the Passions, they were only five months away from "Just to Be with You," their only national chart record. The Classics took Louis's advice and went to audition with several other groups at Gribble's office. They didn't realize at the time that Roger Sherman, owner of the Manhattan-based Dart Records (640 Tenth Avenue) was sponsoring the audition in search of a new act. They were immediately signed and went about writing a song in a novelty vein under Sherman's direction.

The group came up with an idea from a movie classic—"Cinderella"—that they interpreted in teenage street-corner terms. The song ended up a fun-filled rock doo wopper in the style of early EARLS (the idea seems to have paved the way for THE DEVOTIONS' 1961 recording of "Rip Van Winkle"). "Cinderella" was cut in late summer of 1959 at Bell Sound Studios in New York City. The band on "Cinderella" was reportedly the Virtues of "Guitar Boogie Shuffle" fame (#5, May 1959). The record started out strong but never charted nationally, with sources claiming it sold over 50,000 copies in the tri-state area as well as in Philadelphia.

Late in 1959 the group cut two more Dart sides: "Angel Angela," a badly mixed, less-than-competitive ballad, and a B side that droned along under the title "Eenie, Meenie, Meinie and Mo." It was not released until Dart was about out of business more than a year later. Their third Dart session was "Life Is But a Dream" b/w "That's the Way It Goes"—both HARPTONES songs. Soon after they were issued on Dart in 1961, the masters were sold to Mercury Records, then somehow the "Life" side also wound up on the Streamline label. This gave the Classics the same recording released on three different labels in the same year. Although it was a

good up-tempo record, the Earls version on the small independent Rome Records blew it away on the East Coast.

Mercury then "lent" the Classics to its affiliate, Promo Records, to back up rhythm and blues vocalist Herb Lance for a similarly styled rendition of THE MARCELS' recent hit "Blue Moon."

Over a year passed before the Classics got another opportunity with a label. Andy Leonetti (manager of THE CHIMES and THE PARAGONS) set up his own Musicnote label, and asked the Classics to record for him. Larry Lucie, an arranger with heavy R&B tendencies, was directed to give a pop rhythm and blues treatment to the old standard "Till Then" for the group; this transformed them from a '60s doo wop act into a '50s-styled quartet of crooners.

The song was recorded on January 25, 1963. On June 22nd the record, replete with walking vocal bass and Emil's best-ever lead, hit the pop charts 19 years after the MILLS BROTHERS version had reached number eight. The Classics recording went to number 20. Their next single, in late 1963, was the standard "P.S. I Love You." Lacking the same magic and radio support, it failed to chart nationally.

Several more releases for Stork, Josie, and Piccollo between 1965 and 1967 had the same results, and the group drifted apart.

In 1971, Emil, Jamie, former Passions baritone Lou Rotundo, and tenor Steve Misciagno formed a new Classics renamed the Profits, recording a midtempo version of THE DIABLOS' "The Wind" for Sire Records. By the summer of 1972 the group was down to a trio of Emil, Lou, and Kenny Gill but was again called the Classics. A decade later the trio was still doing occasional shows with Albie Galione (another former Passion) taking Kenny Gill's place.

Later Tony Victor took a seat on the New York Stock Exchange, Jamie Troy went into the scrap iron business, John Gambale became a commercial artist, and Emil Stuccio became a policeman for the New York City Transit Authority.

The Classics last recording came from the miniscule Bed-Stuy label in 1972 when they did two standards, "Again" and "The Way You Look Tonight."

The Classics' up sides were early examples of white novelty rock while their ballad style served as a bridge between acts like THE FOUR ACES of the '50s and the Duprees of the '60s.

THE CLASSICS

A SIDE/B SIDE	LABEL/CAT NO	DATE
So In Love / Cinderella	Dart 1015	1960

A SIDE/B SIDE	LABEL/CAT NO	DATE
Angel Angela /		
Eenie, Meenie, Meinie and Mo	Dart 1032	1961
Life Is But A Dream /		
That's The Way It Goes	Dart 1038	1961
Life Is But A Dream Sweetheart /		
That's The Way It Goes	Merc 1038	5/61
Life's But A Dream /		
Nuttin' In The Noggin	Strm 1028	1963
Blue Moon* / Little Lost Boys*	Promo 1010	2/61
Till Then / Eenie, Meenie, Meinie		
and Mo	MscNt 1116	1963
P.S. I Love You /		
Wrap Your Troubles In Dreams	MscNt 118	1963
You'll Never Know /		
Dancing With You	Stork STL2A	1965
Over The Weekend /		
Dancing With You Josie	Josie 939	1965
I Apologize / Love For Today	Pclo 500	1967
Wind / Vagabond	Sire 353	1971
Again / The Way You Look Tonight	BdSty 222	1972

* Herb Lance and the Classics

The Concords

Many street-corner groups had successful records even though those acts were not what you would consider professional-sounding. On the other hand, a few groups that never had a significant hit were actually top-sounding pros. One of the latter was the Concords, a solid quintet formed in 1959 in the Brighton Beach area of Brooklyn, New York.

The original fivesome included Mike Lewis (lead and tenor), Dickie Goldman (lead and tenor), Charles "Chippy" Presti (second tenor), Murray Moshe (baritone), and Steve Seider (bass). The teens were students at Lincoln High School, the same educational institution that gave birth to THE TOKENS at about the same time. In fact it was the Tokens' tenor Hank Medress who taught Mike Lewis how to harmonize (they had sung together for a time in Darrell and the Oxfords before they recorded "Picture in My Wallet" on Roulette). Mike was inspired to form the Con-Cords (as they originally called themselves), because it meant "with chords" in Spanish and was in keeping with their emphasis on harmony. They changed the name to Concords when everyone seemed to mispronounce it.

The Concords were influenced by THE FLAMINGOS, THE CADILLACS, and DION AND THE BELMONTS, among others, and practiced songs like "Teenager in Love," "Little Star," and "Sincerely" in Chippy's basement and on every street corner in Brighton Beach.

Through a series of introductions they met Roy and Julie Rifkind, who landed an RCA singles deal for them on a frantic MARCELS-styled reworking of the standard "Again" with Mike Lewis on lead. The record was widely played in New York but didn't receive even the slightest attention elsewhere.

The Concords then met songwriter Stu Wiener, who arranged for them to record for his father's small Gramercy label. The late 1961 single "Cross My Heart" and the early 1962 45 "My Dreams" had no chance in the competitive marketplace. Dickie Goldman then left.

The group recorded one of its best singles as a quartet, "Away," for Rust in the spring of 1962, again with Lewis on lead.

Mike Lasman, formerly of Mike and the Utopians (CeeJay), came aboard as lead during late 1962, and the group signed with Herald Records.

"Marlene," their first Herald single, was a stylistic forerunner of THE FOUR SEASONS' alter ego "The Wonder Who" and became their most successful single, hitting the top five in such markets as Pittsburgh and Detroit.

While the record was number two in the latter city the Concords did a show there with a new group called THE SUPREMES. On one occasion, their lead Diana Ross commented to Mike Lewis, "I hope our record gets as big as yours."

By 1963 the group had splintered. Lewis then formed the Planets but by early 1964 decided to reform the Concords with Seider, Teddy Graybill (formerly of the Stardrifts [Goldisc] and the Planets), Sal Tepedino (the Travelers [Decca] and the Planets), and Bobby Ganz.

On March 13th the new Concords with Teddy on lead recorded a polished up-tempo doo wop rocker called "Should I Cry," issued by Epic Records in June.

By 1965 Mike Lewis and his partner Stu Wiener had hit the charts by producing Roddie Joy on "Come Back Baby" (Redbird, #86 Pop).

It was more than two years before the Concords did their next and last single, a remake of THE QUINTONES' 1958 number 18 hit "Down the Aisle of Love."

In 1991 the Concords' first and only LP was issued, a collection of all their A and B side singles (Crystal Ball Records).

In recent years the Concords were scattered across the country in diverse lifestyles, Dickie Goldman as a lawyer in Woodstock, New York; Murray Moshe in the garment business and living in Florida; Charles Presti as a beautician in Hollywood; Steve Seider in the appliance business in Phoenix, Arizona; and Mike Lewis writing and producing while living in California's San Fernando Valley and recently returning to performing as part of a duo called Mike and Renate.

THE CONCORDS

A SIDE/B SIDE	LABEL/CAT NO	DATE
Again / The Boy Most Likely	RCA 47-7911	6/61
Cross My Heart /		
Our Last Goodbye	Grmcy 304	1961
My Dreams / Scarlet Ribbons	Grmcy 305	1962
Away / One Step From Heaven	Rust 5048	1962
Marlene /		
Our Love Wasn't Meant To Be	Herald 576	1962
Should I Cry /		
It's Our Wedding Day	Epic 9697	1964
Cold And Frosty Mornings /		
Don't Go Now	Herald 578	7/70
Down The Aisle Of Love /		
I Feel A Love Comin' On	Boom 60021	10/66

The Corsairs

Another fine North Carolina rhythm and blues group (see THE LARKS, THE 5 ROYALES, and THE CASANOVAS) the Corsairs were three brothers and a cousin. Hailing from La Grange, Jay Uzzell (lead), Moses Uzzell, James Uzzell, and George Wooten originally called themselves the Gleems during their high school days as members of the glee club.

After the usual run of talent shows and local performances the quartet felt the limitations of a small town; they decided that since their objective was to record, they'd be better off moving to New York City. They wound up across the Hudson River in nearby Newark, New Jersey. Playing clubs at night while running to the city during the day to interest a label in their sound, Jay and company knocked on every door that had a record company name on it in early 1961.

During one performance the Gleems were spotted by producer Abner Spector who had his own small label, Tuff Records. By August, the group was renamed the Corsairs by Abner. Two songs, "Time Waits" and "It Won't Be a Sin," both written by James with friend Lona Stevens, became their first record, released that same month.

First out on Tuff (distributed by Mercury) and then Smash (also distributed by Mercury) "Time Waits" was a rock-a-cha-cha effort loosely borrow-

ing its melody from Jodie Sands' 1957 (#15) hit "With All My Heart" and its feel from the group's DRIFTERS influence. When it received little attention, Abner took the group back in the studio on a composition of his own called "Smokey Places." The group was perfectly suited to sing this story of two lovers having to meet secretly to share their stolen moments. From its bass-led intro of "I believe, tang-tang-be-do-do" right through the continuous "dull thud" African rhythm sounding like Ernie Kovacs's Nairobi Trio, the record was chock full of hooks (not to mention Jay "Bird" Uzzell's terrific lead, soaring to unexpected falsettos).

"Smokey Places" became so hot that Chess Records not only picked up Abner's record for distribution, they picked up his label, sharing logos on the same recording (an unusual arrangement in the growing record business).

The October 1961 release was fated to chart on Christmas Day, soaring all the way to number 12 Pop and number 10 R&B.

Their next single, "I'll Take You Home," didn't have the magic of "Smokey Places" but did reach number 68 nationally and number 26 R&B that spring. The follow-up, "Dancing Shadows," was an attempt to recapture "Smokey Places," but not a successful one. Abner Spector tried various exotic musical sounds to revive the Corsairs, including mandolins on "Dancing Shadows" and vibraphones on its pretty ballad B side, "While." But after "Stormy," originally written by Spector for the Prophets on Atco in 1956, the group was nearing the end of its recording career.

In 1965 Landy McNeil joined, leading the group on a last shot with "On the Spanish Side," an engrossing combination of "Smokey Places" and Ben E. King's "Spanish Harlem." Times had changed, and Latin-styled rhythms would not predominate again until Tony Orlando and DAWN's Drifters-influenced "Candida" hit in 1970.

THE CORSAIRS

A SIDE/B SIDE	LABEL/CAT NO	DATE
Time Waits / It Won't Be A Sin	Tuff 1715	8/61
Time Waits / It Won't Be A Sin	Smash 1715	8/61
Smokey Places / Thinkin'	Tuff 1808	10/61
I'll Take You Home /		
Sittin' On Your Doorstep	Tuff 1818	3/62
Dancing Shadows / While	Tuff 1830	7/62
At The Stroke Of Midnight /		
Listen To My Little Heart	Tuff 1840	10/62
Stormy /		
It's Almost Sunday Morning	Tuff 1847	2/63

A SIDE/B SIDE	LABEL/CAT NO	DATE
Save A Little Monkey /		
Save A Little Money	Tuff 375	1964
Landy McNeil and the Corsairs		
On The Spanish Side /		
The Change In You	Tuff 402	1965

The Cowsills

Proponents of the late '60s "good time" sound in rock and roll, the Cowsills were the quintessential American family group, consisting of five brothers, a sister, and their mother. To round it out, dad managed the Newport, Rhode Island, septet. Bob (17), Bill (19), Barry (13), Paul (15), John (11), Susan (7), and mama Barbara began their odyssey into entertainment doing local shows and landing a one-shot record deal with recording artist Johnny Nash's Joda label. Their only single with Joda, "All I Really Want to Be Is Me," never got off the ground, but performance-wise they were becoming regulars on the New York City club circuit.

The Cowsills, who had probably the widest age gap between members (little Susan was 7 in 1967 and mom was 38) since Pop Staples and his Staple singing daughters, were spotted by MGM Records, who soon had them in the studio recording their first of eight LPs.

Artie Cornfeld was producing and writing with songwriter Steve Duboff when they hit upon the ideal vehicle for the septet. "The Rain, the Park and Other Things" was recorded that summer and ascended to number two on the *Billboard* Pop charts the week of December 2nd. Only the Monkees' "Daydream Believer" kept it from the top chart position.

Their lively and youthful harmonies along with their fresh-scrubbed good looks set them up as immediate teen idol material, and their top 20 second single "We Can Fly" kept the image alive and thriving in early 1968. ("We Can Fly" was similar to THE 5TH DIMENSION's "Up, Up And Away" from the summer of 1967.) Bright, energetic arrangements on their first two LPs by such industry pros as Jimmy Wisner, Herb Bernstein, and Charlie (FOUR SEASONS) Calello, coupled with surprisingly tight, high, up-front harmony, gave the Cowsills an upbeat identity. Add that to a collection of teen-dream contemporary songs and you had a niche carved out that one reviewer called "psychedelic pop."

"In Need of a Friend" (March 1968) paid homage to the sound of THE MAMAS AND THE PAPAS, but the Cowsills' writing and production effort ran out of steam at number 54, prompting MGM to look for an outside producer. They came up with boy wonder Wes Farrell, who had just turned a band from Greenwich Village into a top 10 success for MGM with "Come on Down to My Boat" (#6, July 1967). Farrell put songwriter Tony Romeo on the case and he came up with a delightful piece of hook-laden pop titled "Indian Lake." The Farrell-produced "trip to the country" was an instant radio favorite in the summer of 1968, reaching *Billboard*'s number 10 position. From teen magazines and milk commercials to Las Vegas and their very own TV special on NBC, the Cowsills had in less than a year become a phenomenon.

With the group's Bill and Bob back at the production helm in early 1969, the Cowsills recorded the title song from the nationally acclaimed Broadway musical *Hair*. The song, alternately stirring, driving, and bouncy, was perfectly suited for the Rhode Island family. *Hair* locked onto the charts on March 15th and reached number two the week of May 19th. Ironically, the record keeping them out of the number one spot was another song from *Hair*, "Aquarius/Let the Sun Shine In" by the 5th Dimension.

There was talk of a TV series based on their lives, but the group nixed it when TV honchos wanted to use an established star to play Barbara.

By mid-1969 the group's recordings were becoming less and less commercial as indicated by their titles: "The Prophecy of Daniel and John the Divine," "Six Six Six" (#75), and "Silver Threads and Golden Needles" (#74).

In 1970 that TV show was made, with Shirley Jones (as mom) and David Cassidy leading the Partridge Family through three years of pop hits and high ratings.

In 1970 the Cowsills became tired of touring, and with no chart singles to carry their clean-cut image into the emerging antihero '70s, the act disbanded.

Barbara died in 1985 while working on the night shift at a nursing home in Rhode Island. By the late '80s, Susan was living in Burbank, California, doing backup singing for Dwight Twilley and Tom Petty. Bob was also living in California, married with five kids and performing in local clubs. John was performing with Jan & Dean. Paul, married with two children, was Helen Reddy's roadie and then entered the construction business. Bill was living in Canada and performing. Barry was in

Monterey, California, with his wife and two children. The Cowsills finally felt it was time to regroup when a deejay at WZLX-FM in Boston did an interview with Bob in 1989. They had turned down numerous offers to reform as an oldies act in the '70s and '80s but on July 3, 1990, the Cowsills played their first concert together in 20 years at a club called Zanzibar in Boston. The group consisted of original members Bob, Paul, John, Sue, and bass player Cecil Duke. The night was enhanced by the presence of fans like the Beach Boys and Paula Abdul. Buoyed by the experience, the group began work on original material for a comeback LP.

The Crystals

One of the most popular of the '60s girl groups, the Crystals were the first act producer Phil Spector gave full attention to while establishing his Philles label.

The group was not your typical collection of friends singing together in the neighborhood; they were mostly from different sections of Brooklyn. The eventual quintet was the creation of Benny Wells, a former big-band musician and by 1960 a manager. Benny rehearsed his acts in the music room of P.S. 73 on MacDougal Street.

Deciding in the fall of 1960 to form a female passel, Benny recruited his niece, 17-year-old Barbara Alston from Lexington Avenue in the Bedford-Stuyvesant section of Brooklyn. Kate Henry, who worked at P.S. 73, brought in her 15-year-old daughter Delores (Dee Dee) Kennibrew, who lived on Bergen Street in the Crown Heights section and went to Wingate High School. Barbara Alston recommended 17-year-old Mary Thomas of Sumner Avenue in Williamsburg and 17-year-old Merna Girard of Kingston Avenue, thus making the group a foursome.

Since Benny Wells didn't write, he acquired material from various songwriters such as Skank Avenue's Leroy Bates. When the bevy of Brooklynites wasn't rehearsing at P.S. 73 they'd go to Leroy's sister-in-law's house (where Leroy was living with his wife and newborn child), where there was a piano. His sister-in-law was 17-year-old Pat Wright of Bushwick High School; she then became the fifth member. They became the Crystals when they named themselves after Leroy's baby daughter, "Crystal" Bates.

Leroy wrote a song titled "There's No Other" which Barbara sang lead on. At this time the usual group order was Barbara or Pat on lead, Dee Dee on soprano, Merna on second tenor, and Mary on contralto.

Early in 1961 Benny Wells brought the five singers to the Celebrity Club in Freeport, Long Island, to get the feel of a stage and live performing, but that was the group's only public showcase until after their first record. During their manager's continuing quest for hit material he met Hill and Range songwriters Bill Giant and Bernie Baum, who arranged for the girls to rehearse at the publishing company's office in midtown Manhattan.

It was on a March evening in 1961 while rehearsing "There's No Other" that the group met Phil Spector. "There's No Other" was originally done up-tempo, but Spector slowed it down, creating an entirely different feel.

The group continued to rehearse until late June and were finally called in to Mira Sound on West 47th Street in New York City to record on the night of their high school graduation prom. Barbara, Mary, and Merna showed up at the studio after 10 P.M., still in the prom dresses they wore at Central Commercial High School, to lay down "There's No Other" and "Oh Yeah, Maybe Baby." The session was unusually smooth. Dee Dee states, "We did all the tracks and vocals in three hours. Our first session turned out to be my favorite and 'There's No Other' my favorite Crystals song as it had more of an R&B feel than anything we did after that." The scheduled September release had "Oh Yeah" as the A side.

When the single came out, *Billboard* described the Crystals as "a wild sounding new girl vocal group with much of the excitement of the Shirelles. On top, they tie into a swingin' rocker with great backing. Flip is a strong rock-a-ballad reading with an equal chance. Watch both."

The first in a series of surprising events in the Crystals' career happened when the record came out not on Liberty as they expected (since Spector was seemingly involved with that label) or even on Big Top (which was affiliated with Hill and Range, for which Spector was expected to do some productions). It came out on Philles, a label started by *Phil* Spector and *Lester* Sill. By the time it reached radio, "There's No Other," with its solo intro by Barbara and Chantels-styled delicate harmony, was the popularly elected A side. Barbara's beautiful lead on this catchy throwback to the late '50s' "Maybe" days entered *Billboard*'s Pop listings on November 20th and peaked at number 20 in January 1962, also hitting number five R&B. Their first major live performance was at a place none of them had ever even seen a show at—the Apollo Theatre.

Though influenced by THE BOBBETTES, THE CHANTELS, and THE SHIRELLES, the Crystals sound was being shaped by Spector to redefine the girl group style. The first real hint of that came with their second single, the Barry Mann/Cynthia Weil-penned "Uptown." The Flamenco-styled pastiche of plucked violin strings dueling with acoustic guitars and castanets was a colorful setting for a jewel of a melody. The lyric, about a girl whose battle-weary man finds strength and pride when he comes "uptown" to her arms, was ahead of its time in its raw realism and interpreted with vulnerability and passion by Barbara, backed by the Crystals. There were six of them on this date; 16-year-old Dolores (Lala) Brooks had been brought in to replace the pregnant Mèrna Girard, who had just enough muscle control to last through the "Uptown" session before departing.

"Uptown" jumped onto the charts in the same month of its release (March) in 1962, stopping inexplicably at number 13 Pop (#18 R&B). Despite six voices, the harmonies were not particularly prevalent; Spector had apparently chosen to let the instruments overshadow the voices on a brilliant recording that stopped just short of becoming too busy.

If "Uptown" was lyrically ahead of its time, their next single, "He Hit Me (and It Felt Like a Kiss)" has not yet seen its time. The song, written by Carole King and Gerry Goffin, was based on a story their babysitter told them about being beaten by her boyfriend. (The babysitter, by the way, was Eva Boyd, who by August of the same year would have the number one record in the U.S., "The Locomotion," under the name Little Eva and written and produced by her employers Goffin and King.)

The production of "He Hit Me" was another notch closer to Spector's eventual "wall of sound" approach, with a stark intro building to a bolero-like finale in the quintet's strongest harmony effort to date. *Billboard*'s July review said, "Much thought went into the lyrics on these two unique sides by the vocal group. The first is a serious ballad with a telling message, while the second sets a mood much like 'Uptown,' the group's most recent hit. It notes the pain and complexity of life. Either or both could be winners."

The B side they were referring to was "No One Ever Tells You," another haunting Goffin/King (and Spector) slice of life, though not of "He Hit Me" caliber. Despite its good reviews and instant airplay the Crystals hated it, and so did Spector's

partner, Lester Sill, feeling it was a depressing, negatively influenced song. The public at large never got a chance to decide; the self-professed watchers of the nation's morals started bombarding radio stations with complaints over the alleged sadistic implications of the lyrics.

Philles immediately pulled the record, and today it's a lucky collector who has one of the few deejay copies released.

The Crystals' next career surprise was the recording of "He's a Rebel," a song previously turned down for the Shirelles by Scepter Records' head Florence Greenberg as being too adventurous. Dee Dee states, "From 'Uptown' on, he [Spector] would bring in the tracks, not finished, but enough for you to put your part down so we did everything in segments, so I could not tell you how or what he kept of ours."

What Spector apparently kept on that killer Gene Pitney song was Darlene Love and THE BLOSSOMS' vocals.

"He's a Rebel" came out as Philles 106 in August 1962 immediately after "He Hit Me," and to the surprise of some, the label listed the Crystals. The record, featuring Darlene Love's gutsy lead, Al Delory's tinkling double-time piano, and a host of hooks, took off to number one the week of November 3, 1962. (Coincidentally, the number two record that week was sung by Gene Pitney himself ["Only Love Can Break a Heart"].) "Rebel" also went to number two R&B in the fall of 1962 and to number 19 at the same time in England. The song became the national anthem for teen girls who secretly longed for good-hearted bad guys. The Crystals, meanwhile, had their biggest hit but weren't sure that any of their harmony work was actually on the record (they could tell the lead was not Barbara or Lala).

After "Rebel" Mary left to get married, and the group remained a quartet.

By now the Crystals had been doing extensive touring and Lala was singing lead on almost everything. "She went over very well and was a much stronger singer," Dee Dee claims.

That summer, the Crystals recorded the original version of the Mann/Weil/Leiber/Stoller song "On Broadway" that later became a hit for THE DRIFTERS (#9, April 1963) with Spector playing guitar on the track. The Crystals' version was relegated to their first LP, *He's a Rebel*, in March 1963.

The odd circumstances surrounding the production of "Rebel" were repeated for the Crystals' next single, "He's Sure the Boy I Love," another successful spoken-intro Mann/Weil tune (#11 Pop,

1963, #18 R&B). Darlene Love and the Blossoms were the actual performers on the cut.

Spector was now doing most of his recording at Gold Star Studios on Santa Monica Boulevard in Los Angeles, although he did return to New York to do the Crystals in January 1963 at Mira Sound for five minutes and 45 seconds of "The Screw, Part I," an obnoxious, unreleased single of which only a few copies were made. The record was apparently designed to aggravate his partners. With a monotonous male talking chorus and a boring mid-tempo dance rhythm, it (and its even worse half-speed B side "The Screw, Part II") must have had its effect since Spector was soon partnerless.

In March 1963 the Crystals' producer seemed to have finally discovered Lala Brooks and flew her to Los Angeles to do lead vocals over Darlene Love's original track on the Jeff Barry/Ellie Greenwich/Phil Spector song, "Da Doo Ron Ron." As Dee Dee describes the production, "We did vocals on rough tracks for that and 'He's Sure the Boy I Love,' but I don't know how many voices were there by the time Phil finished."

Released in April under the Crystals' name, it was basically Lala and the Blossoms. The nonsense title didn't stop the driving beat and leave-it-to-the-imagination lyrics from going all the way to number three on the charts by the week of June 8th. Only Leslie Gore's "It's My Party" and one-shot Kyu Sakamoto's "Sukiyaki" had more chart power. It reached number five R&B while spending four months on the British charts, also peaking at number five. The Crystals name was more successful than ever, but the group was frustrated by their producer's game of label-credit roulette.

Their seventh single, however, was a full Crystals affair, and the Jeff/Ellie/Phil concoction "Then He Kissed Me" entered the *Billboard* Hot 100 on August 17th. The recording was an astounding balance of powerful girl-group rock and roll in symphonic overdrive. The production officially established the "wall of sound," using more echo than any previous Spector effort, and probably more than any previous non-Spector effort. Horns and strings were painted across a brilliant canvas of teen rock sound, with galloping castanets, maracas, and bass drums that sounded like kettle drums. Only the power of Lala's voice survived the symphonic onslaught.

By September 14th it was number six Pop and number eight R&B at a time when seven of the top 10 records were by British groups. It became their biggest international hit, reaching number two in England and number one in Australia. The group performed from Japan to Germany with the likes of Johnny Mathis, Jackie Wilson, THE FLAMINGOS, the Drifters, James Brown, and THE CADILLACS.

In the fall of 1963 a compilation of Philles' best, including the Crystals cuts "Then He Kissed Me," "Da Doo Ron Ron," and "Oh Yeah, Maybe Baby," hit the streets.

At the same time Philles was planning its now-legendary Christmas compilation. Lala provided lead vocals for three Crystals tracks on the Christmas LP: "Santa Claus Is Coming to Town," "Rudolph the Red-Nosed Reindeer," and "Parade of the Wooden Soldiers," each with a spirited Crystals (and Spector) trademark sound carrying the evergreens into the realm of '60s teen relevance.

January 1964 opened with the girls' release of yet another Barry/Greenwich/Spector heart tugger, "Little Boy." *Billboard's* reviewer predicted, "The big, rolling, almost overwhelming sound backs the girls again on this powerful side arranged by Jack Nitzsche. Side builds to a wild frenzy. It's chart destined!" Well not quite. The record had two striking weaknesses. First, it was "over-produced." Everything crashed together and obscured the lyric, the melody, and the group. Unfortunately, a fine arrangement and song were lost. Second, Philles was now preoccupied with its newest talents, THE RONETTES. In short, "Little Boy" saw little play and died at number 92 in February.

By now, Pat had left to marry and was replaced by Frances Collins, who had first appeared on the Crystals' February 1964 British tour. When "Little Boy" failed, Philles made an effort to capitalize on the girls' English trip by immediately releasing "I Wonder." This rousing rocker, with its pop-sounding string section riding over a volcanic rhythm track, was musically somewhere between "He's Sure the Boy I Love" and "Then He Kissed Me." The Crystals never sounded better, and Hal Blaine dropped in every drum riff he'd invented for the Ronettes' "Be My Baby." Strangely, Philles never released it in America, and it topped out at only number 36 in the U.K.

Their last Spector record came as a result of another Jeff Barry and Ellie Greenwich song (as "I Wonder" had been) titled "All Grown Up," which the group had recorded a year before. Written in a similar vein to Chuck Berry's "Almost Grown," it was not like anything the Crystals had previously recorded. Had it not been for the fact that Barry and Greenwich wanted to release it on a track they cut with THE EXCITERS, Philles #122 might never have come out at all. As it is, it belly-flopped at number 98 on August 1, 1964.

In 1965 the Crystals signed with United Artists Records and released two singles, the better of the two being "My Place," a cross between "Uptown," "Downtown" (Pet Clark), and "On Broadway," with a soul feel and no traces of a wall of sound. The Paul Tannen-produced and Charlie Calello-arranged 45 quickly dropped out of sight. Soon thereafter Barbara married; the Crystals split up around 1967.

Dee Dee also got married, but around 1971 she reformed the group with Lala, Barbara, and Mary for a Richard Nader rock and roll revival show. From 1971 to 1973, Barbara, Mary, and Dee Dee toured and performed until motherhood and husbands once again took over. Barbara left after a 1973 U.K. tour but Dee Dee carried on the Crystals' tradition and kept on performing with two new Crystals, Darlene Davis (since 1978) and Marilyn Byers (since 1989). Marilyn was the former lead of THE TEENAGERS, replacing Frankie Lymon's soundalike Pearl McKinnon. In 1986, Lala (on lead), Dee Dee, Darlene, and Gretchen Gale-Prendatt recorded a 10-song LP in Nashville for Jango Records titled *The Crystals: He's a Rebel*, featuring many of the Philles 45s. In 1974 "Da Doo Ron Ron" was reissued in England 11 years after it went top five; this time it reached number 15.

Nowadays, Lala lives in Vienna, Austria, with her jazz musician husband (her high school sweetheart). Barbara is married in Brooklyn with four kids. Mary is also still in Brooklyn. Pat married a serviceman and reportedly lives out west. Dee Dee, when she's not touring, lives in Atlanta.

THE CRYSTALS

A SIDE/B SIDE	LABEL/CAT NO	DATE
There's No Other /		
Oh Yeah, Maybe Baby	Philles 100	10/61
Uptown / What A Nice Way		
To Turn Seventeen	Philles 102	3/62
He Hit Me / No One Ever Tells You	Philles 105	7/62
He's A Rebel / I Love You Eddie	Philles 106	8/62
He's A Sure The Boy I Love /		
Walkin' Along	Philles 109	12/62
The Screw Part 1 /		
The Screw Part 2 (not released)	Philles 111	1/63
Da Doo Ron Ron / Git It	Philles 112	4/63
Then He Kissed Me /		
Brother Julius	Philles 115	7/63
Little Boy / Harry and Milt	Philles 119	1/64
All Grown Up / Irving	Philles 122	7/64
My Place / You Can't		
Tie A Good Girl Down	UA 927	9/65
I Got A Man / Are You Trying		
To Get Rid Of Me Baby	UA 994	2/66

The Delfonics

If you were to ask fans of 1970s rhythm and blues who their favorite group was, you can be sure a large number would say Michael Jackson and THE JACKSONS. If you asked Michael Jackson who his favorite group is, he'd say the Delfonics. At least that's what he said back in the late '60s, and he wasn't alone.

One of the most popular of the newly emerging slick soul groups, the Delfonics started out as the Orphonics of Overbrook High School in Philadelphia during 1964. The original group was a quartet consisting of William Hart (17, lead and tenor), Wilbert Hart (William's brother, 15, lead and baritone), Richard Daniels (second tenor), and Ricky Johnson (bass).

By 1965 Daniels had answered the draft board's call and Johnson the call to become a minister. The Orphonics then added Herbert Randal (Randy Cain III) as a second tenor and began rehearsing in the Harts' basement at 5442 Media Street in Philadelphia. The teenagers were heavily influenced by LITTLE ANTHONY AND THE IMPERIALS as well as FRANKIE LYMON AND THE TEENAGERS and practiced songs like "Tears on My Pillow" and "Goin' Out of My Head."

They began their performing career doing college homecomings and local high school talent shows.

In 1966 the trio came to the attention of manager Stan Watson, who brought the group to Cameo Records and also introduced them to young writer/ arranger Thom Bell. At this time Watson convinced the group to change their name since there already was an Orphonics; they came up with the Delfonics.

In 1967 they released a Thom Bell-William Hart ballad called "You've Been Untrue," which saw some regional activity. They also recorded a celesta- and kettle drum-filled power ballad, "He Don't Really Love You," in August of 1966.

Their first single for the Philly Groove label was a song by Bell and Hart, "La-La-Means I Love You," that came from Hart listening to his young son. The smooth ballad with the stratospheric falsetto lead charted on February 10, 1968, eventually reaching number four Pop (#2 R&B). Their first performance was in front of the home folks at the Uptown Theatre along with THE INTRUDERS, the Soul Survivors, and Billy Stewart.

While appearing in Chicago in 1968 the Delfonics let a new untested group appear on their show who had just had a single out called "Big

Boy"/"You've Changed" on the Steeltown label of Gary, Indiana. It was the first release for a family of boys calling themselves the Jackson 5, and their 10-year-old lead singer was so enamored of the Delfonics (it's reported he ran out to bring tea and honey for the group) that he told everyone they were his favorite group.

Before they could issue their second Philly Groove single a chart record came out from a most unexpected place. The Moon Shot "He Don't Really Love You" 45 that they had recorded two years earlier was released and went to number 92 Pop (#33 R&B) in the spring, just as their Philly Groove "I'm Sorry" reached number 42 Pop (#15 R&B). Later on in 1968 the group played in Las Vegas and had the opportunity to sing backup for Sammy Davis, Jr. on stage.

With each release Thom Bell built bigger and more colorful orchestrations around the songs he and William were writing. Staccato strings and foreboding bassoons introduced "Ready or Not Here I Come" and continued through the song to maintain a dramatic feeling. "Ready" reached number 35 Pop (#14 R&B) in late 1968 and early 1969.

"You Got Yours and I'll Get Mine" opened with an orchestral flourish, lifting the Delfonics to another hit (#40 Pop, #6 R&B) and their seventh straight chart smash.

Their eighth became an all-time classic. The first two notes on an echoed French horn conjured up images of the Vikings readying for a battle. Then the celesta and piano intro led to the most melodic of all Delfonics singles, "Didn't I Blow Your Mind." "Didn't I" charted on January 17, 1970, reaching number 10 Pop (#3 R&B) and crossing the ocean a year later to become the Delfonics' first U.K. hit at number 22. This precipitated the reissue of "La La" in England and a chart ranking of number 19 by the summer of 1971. The group continued having American hits through 1970 ("Trying to Make a Fool of Me," #40 Pop, #8 R&B) and 1971 ("Over and Over," #52 Pop, #9 R&B).

Around this time, the group started touring Europe with THE FOUR TOPS and in 1971 won a Grammy as best R&B group of the year.

In 1973 former Jarmels member Major Harris joined when Randy became ill and stayed on until 1974 when he went solo and had a 1975 hit, "Love Won't Let Me Wait" (#5 Pop, #1 R&B).

Harris was with the group through their last chart record ("Lying to Myself," #60 R&B, summer 1974) and was replaced by John Johnson. Major eventually returned to the group and in the early '90s the quartet of William, Wilbert, Randy, and Major were still touring and planning a new record with Thom Bell. That would be a long-overdue return for a group with a smooth soul sound that placed 20 singles on the charts between 1968 and 1974.

The Del-Satins

The Del-Satins were one of the finest white male doo wop groups of all time. Though not as well known as THE EARLS, JAY AND THE AMERICANS, or THE FOUR SEASONS, in their own style (which was rhythm and blues and rock and roll) they were every bit as good. Unfortunately, they received no credit on any of their 13 hit records, although they did have the chance to make a few excellent singles under their own name.

Formed in 1958 in the Yorkville section of Manhattan, the quintet consisted of Stan Ziska (lead), Leslie Cauchi (first tenor), Bobby Fiela (second tenor), Fred Ferrara (baritone), and his brother Tom Ferrara (bass). Les attended Power Memorial while Fred and Tom went to Machine and Metals Trade School. Influenced by R&B groups like THE HEARTBEATS, THE DUBS, and THE FLAMINGOS, the Del-Satins, aged 15 to 17, would practice on Tom and Fred's stoop on 69th Street when they weren't searching for a good overpass or bathroom to provide that perfect echo.

Early on they were called the Jokers, not as a singing group but rather as a basketball team playing in a house league for the Lenox Hill Neighborhood House. They decided on the name Del-Satins by putting together two of their favorite groups, THE DELLS and THE FIVE SATINS. They then made their own first break by participating in a talent show at the Empire Hotel on New York's West Side. The first prize, which they won, was a record deal with George Goldner's End Records, and so it was that the Del-Satins' first single, "I'll Pray for You," was released in 1961. The record received good local response, especially from WADO disc jockey Alan Fredericks, leading to some shows for Fredericks at the Levittown Arena.

Around this time Jim Gribble, manager for other New York-area harmony groups like THE PASSIONS, took on the Del-Satins. He brought the quintet to Bob and Gene Schwartz at Laurie Records when he heard Dion was looking for a new backup group. (Dion's most recent three releases had been sugar-coated pop platters with female and mixed choruses that were losing more ground on the charts with each record. "Lonely Teenager" [#12, 1960], "Havin' Fun" [#40, 1961], and "Kissin' Game" [#82, 1961] were all done without THE BELMONTS, who Dion figured weren't rock and roll enough for his new vision; but neither were the resulting efforts.) On the spot, the Del-Satins started rehearsing a new Dion song that began with a talk/sing intro followed by the group singing a "hey hey, woo oh oh," background. Little by little, "Runaround Sue" was brought to life.

On October 23, 1961, the Del-Satins, who'd recorded only one other record to date, saw their first number one hit. (In England it rose to number 11 and in Australia to number four. It was even a hit in France and made number two in South Africa and number one in Israel.) "Sue" made it to the top spot in only five weeks, staying there for two weeks while denying the high-water mark to THE DOVELLS' "Bristol Stomp."

The rhythm and blues community also liked the Dion and Del-Satins combination; "Runaround Sue" reached number four on the R&B charts. But even though the record owed a great deal to the driving harmonies of the Del-Satins (especially that now-famous unison-to-harmony "ah" in the bridge), Dion got all the credit.

Since the group was not actually signed to Laurie, Jim Gribble made a deal with the tiny Winn label for a Del-Satins single titled "Counting Teardrops." It sounded like a cross between THE CRESTS' "Step by Step" and Dion's "Runaround Sue" ("Counting Teardrops" even went so far as to mention "Runaround Sue" in the lyric).

Their next single with Dion was a two-sided classic. The teen rebel national anthem, "The Wanderer" worked its way up to number two after three months on the charts, and only "The Duke of Earl" kept Dion and the Del-Satins from the very top. ("The Wanderer" also traveled to Europe, going to number 10 in the U.K. and number one in Australia.) Written by one Italian (Ernie Maresca) and sung by a bunch of others, it's not surprising that the rhythm was that of an old Italian dance called the Tarantella.

"Lovers Who Wander" was another instant winner, establishing Dion as the king of the scat-singing rock and rollers. The Del-Satins' harmony and unison singing was so powerful and such an integral part of the Dion songs that the lead and background worked together as a group no matter what the label said. "Lovers Who Wander" hit the *Billboard* charts on April 21, 1962, and reached a peak of number three. R&B-wise it went to number 16. The "I Was Born to Cry" flip side, with Dion's

pleading lead, the Del-Satins' intense harmony, and a snarling saxophone, had a new sound that combined doo wop and blues.

After three singles (and five chart sides) with Dion, the Schwartz's were finally with them and they released a Stan Vincent rocker called "Teardrops Follow Me." This Del-Satins doo wopper jumped on East Coast radio and coincidentally found itself pitted against their new release with Dion, "Little Diane," on Murray the K's nightly new-release contest. "Diane" won that night, but "Teardrops" went top 10 in several Eastern cities and gave the group a following under its own name. They began doing a lot of performances for Murray the K and for Alan Freed's TV dance shows. Les Cauchi remembers: "We were driving up to Hartford, Connecticut, to do a TV show and were running late. We all crammed into my Chevy Nova and realized we didn't have time to get there, dress, and make up. So we literally cut my back seat to get to the shaving gear in the trunk and at 65 miles an hour on the Merritt Parkway shaved and changed in the car. The minute we got to Hartford we ran from the car and jumped in front of the cameras with a minute to spare."

"Little Diane" returned the group to the formula they had developed on "The Wanderer," that is, a double harmony where part of the group would sing a sustained "ooh" while the rest did some driving stop-and-go sound that gave the record "wall-to-wall" vocals. Besides being an outstanding song and having a great lead by Dion, this record is immortalized as having the first kazoo-led instrumental section in rock history. "Diane" made it to number eight nationally on August 18th and the group just kept on working. "One time we were picked up in a limo by promo man Pete Bennett for a trip to perform at a school in Easton, Pennsylvania," Les recalls. "We stopped to pick up a young girl trio on the way who turned out to be the Ronettes, but nobody knew them yet [it was 1962]. Over 3,000 people showed up, about 80 percent girls, and when the Ronettes went on they were just about ignored. We did our best and came off well, but then on came Fabian and the sound of all those girls was the loudest sound I ever heard."

Their second Laurie release, "Does My Love Stand a Chance," came out in the fall of 1962 and never got off the ground. But their next single with Dion, "Love Came to Me," became the group's fifth top 10 entry, reaching number 10 on December 22nd.

By the end of 1962 the Del-Satins were backing Dion in his move to Columbia and wondering when their own opportunity would come again. Their first

Columbia shot was a 1956 DRIFTERS song, "Ruby Baby." Dion's patented blues-rock style led the way while the Satins' tough yet smooth harmony solidified the groove that took the song to number two Pop and number five R&B (not to mention number four in Australia).

Laurie, meanwhile, decided to use the good Dion/Del-Satins tracks it had in the can to compete with Columbia. Thus in the early spring of 1963 Laurie's "Sandy" and Columbia's "This Little Girl" raced to a dead heat at number 21, giving two chart songs to a group that no one knew about.

Around this time, a series of introductions (one being an encounter on the street with Heartbeats bass Wally Roker) led the group to a meeting with Phil Spector. The group auditioned for Phil at his New York apartment, singing several songs a cappella, including "Teardrops Follow Me." Spector wanted to sign them and take them in a FOUR SEASONS direction, but the group decided against it.

Soon after, Dion cowrote and produced a single for them on Columbia. That song, "Feeling No Pain," came on like a musical gang war. If West Side Story had been done with '60s rock and roll, this song would have been the Jets' war theme. Jerry Blavit, the Philadelphia emperor of rock and roll radio, used "Feeling No Pain" as his sign-off song for over 20 years, but back in 1963 it was lost among the glut of lesser recordings. Even so, it was one of the most awesome and powerful white doo wop recordings ever made.

The Del-Satins became a regular on Clay Cole's weekly TV show and came up with two more hits with Dion in the last half of 1963, the Dion-penned "Donna the Prima Donna" (written about his sister) and a classic R&B remake of the Drifters' 1957 hit "Drip Drop."

In 1964 their new manager Jay Fontana took the group to Mala Records after Dion curtailed his own recordings. Following one up-tempo harmony effort ("Two Broken Hearts"), the Del-Satins signed with B.T. Puppy Records by auditioning a cappella for THE TOKENS (who owned B.T.) The best of their three singles was another Drifters tune, "Sweets for My Sweet." Soon after, Stan left (and changed his name from Ziska to Sommers), eventually emerging as lead singer of THE MAGNIFICENT MEN. Carl Parker of Detroit sang lead for a while but never recorded on a Del-Satins single.

In 1966 the group did some backup work for Len Barry, and then Les Cauchi and Tommy Ferrara joined Uncle Sam in Vietnam. Mike Gregorio took Les's place and, together with Richard Green, Johnny Maestro, and original member Fred Ferrera, continued to play gigs while Tommy was slugging it out in the Iron Triangle and Les was in the middle of the Tet offensive at Da Nang.

The Del-Satins cut two sides for Diamond Records and recorded "Ebb Tide" and "Goin' Out of My Head" with Johnny Maestro on lead in 1967 (Harvey Records LP).

When Les returned in 1968 he and the Del-Satins formed the BROOKLYN BRIDGE.

In the '90s Les and Fred were in their fourth decade with the Brooklyn Bridge. Tommy Ferrera became a member of THE CAPRIS ("There's a Moon Out Tonight"). Stan (Sommers) Ziska joined Charlie Aiello, a musical computer whiz, and the two worked together from 1970 on. Bobby Fiela freelanced as a singer. Richard Green passed away in the early '70s.

In 1991 the original group re-formed for a few shows. While each member continued with his own vocal career, the foursome (produced by Johnny Maestro) created an LP and the first Del-Satins recording in more than 24 years.

Though Dion and the Belmonts became a household name as a *mellow* pop vocal group, Dion turned to the Del-Satins when he wanted to sound tough. Even without Dion, the Del-Satins proved to be the truest exponent of power doo wop.

THE DEL-SATINS

A SIDE/B SIDE	LABEL/CAT NO	DATE
I'll Pray For You /		
I Remember The Night	End 1096	1961
Counting Tear Drops / Remember	Win 102	1961
Runaround Sue* / Runaway Girl*	Laurie 3110	1961
The Wanderer* / The Majestic*	Laurie 3115	1961
Lovers Who Wander* /		
(I Was) Born To Cry*	Laurie 3123	1962
Teardrops Follow Me / Best		
Wishes, Good Luck, Good-Bye	Laurie 3132	6/62
Little Diane* / Lost For Sure*	Laurie 3134	1962
Love Came To Me* / Little Girl*	Laurie 3145	1962
Ballad Of A Dee-Jay /		
Does My Love Stand A Chance	Laurie 3149	10/62
Sandy* / Faith*	Laurie 3153	1963
Come Go With Me* /		
King Without A Queen*	Laurie 3171	1963
Ruby Baby* / He'll Only Hurt You*	Col 4-42662	1962
Lonely World* / Tag Along*	Laurie 3187	1963
This Little Girl* /		
Loneliest Man In The World*	Col 4-42776	1963
Little Girl* / Shout*	Laurie 3240	1963
Feelin' No Pain / Who Cares	Col 42802	5/63
Donna The Prima Donna* /		
You're Mine*	Col 4-42852	1963
Drip Drop* /		
No One's Waiting For Me*	Col 4-42917	1963
Two Broken Hearts / Believe In Me	Mala 475	1964

A SIDE/B SIDE	LABEL/CAT NO	DATE
Hang Around /		
My Candy Apple Vette	B.T. Puppy 506	1965
Sweets For My Sweet /		
A Girl Named Arlene	B.T. Puppy 509	1965
Relief / The Throwaway Song	B.T. Puppy 514	1965
A Little Rain Must Fall /		
Love, Hate, Revenge	Diamond 216	1/67
A Girl Named Arlene /		
I'll Do My Crying Tomorrow	B.T. Puppy 563	1969

* with Dion

The Demensions

The most beautiful recording coming out of transistor, home, and car radios in the summer of 1960 was "Over the Rainbow" by the dynamic new vocal group the Demensions. The ultra-talented quartet started at Christopher Columbus High School in the Bronx as members of the Melody Singers, the school's premier choral group. Lenny Del Giudice (Lenny Dell) and Howard Margolin decided to form a group in the beginning of 1960. They felt the aggregation would be more unique if a female voice were added so they sought out Melody Singers soprano Marisa Martelli. The last member added was another choral member, Charlie Peterson. As the group wanted a name that suggested the depth of their talent, Howie came up with the Demensions, but to be unique he spelled it with an e.

They started practicing songs like "In the Still of the Night" (THE FIVE SATINS), and "Over the Rainbow." Though they strived for a sound of their own, their sophisticated harmonies and structure showed the influence of THE SKYLINERS and THE PLATTERS. Often rehearsing at Howie or Lenny's house in the Pelham Parkway-Laconia Avenue sections of the Bronx, the new quartet began getting some help from Lou Dell, a professional trumpet player and father of Lenny. Lou helped to rehearse the group, and when he felt they were ready he brought word of them to his friend Irv Spice, owner of Mohawk Records (distributed by Laurie).

They auditioned right in Lenny's house for Irv, singing "Over the Rainbow," and the mesmerized Spice set a date to record in April at Dick Charles Studios.

One week before the session Charlie Peterson decided to drop out to more seriously pursue his education. A desperate Lenny asked his parents what to do and they calmly responded, "Call Uncle Phil." Uncle Phil Del Giudice was an accomplished first tenor who had sung opera and classics for many years. Lenny at first thought his parents were crazy. After all, Uncle Phil was twice his age (though he looked very young). Besides, he wouldn't want to sing rock and roll! He finally called, and to his shock his uncle was flattered and eager to join. Thus the recording Demensions became Lenny (17, lead and second tenor), Marisa (18, soprano), Howie (18, baritone/bass), and Uncle Phil Del Giudice (34, first tenor).

In May 1960 the unique block-harmony, off-the-melody version of Judy Garland's 1939 number five hit "Over the Rainbow" came out and immediately started getting airplay in the East. By July 4, 1960, the Demensions had become the first act in 21 years to hit the national charts with it (although over 60 different single versions of the song had been released between 1939 and 1960, the most recent being the one by LITTLE ANTHONY AND THE IMPERIALS in 1959). By summer's closing the subtle yet powerful Demensions harmonies had driven the evergreen to number 16, spending 15 weeks in the rarefied air of success.

Their first dividend from the "Rainbow" chart run was a performance on Dick Clark's "American Bandstand" during the summer. They went on to perform throughout the East Coast alongside Bobby Rydell, Frankie Avalon, THE ELEGANTS, DION AND THE BELMONTS, and Tony Orlando.

In October Mohawk issued their second single, a bright up-tempo harmony-filled 45 of "Zing Went the Strings of My Heart," with Lenny, Marisa, and Howie trading leads. On the flip side was another refurbished oldie ballad, "Don't Take Your Love from Me," which further showcased the group's voices (especially Phil's) but was generally a bad choice of material for the teen set.

Their third single was an even worse choice of material: Mohawk tried to put the group's stirring Italian reading of "Ave Maria" on American holiday season radio.

In March 1961 Mohawk released the fourth single from the Demensions, an "Over the Rainbow"/Seymour Barab arrangement titled "Teresa." *Billboard*'s March 20th reviewer noted, "The boys have another good chance to climb chartward with this listenable ballad over a combo that has both a beat and unusual harmonies." When it didn't click, Mohawk made the unusual move of selling the group's contract to Coral Records. On June 9, 1961, the Demensions began recording their first session of three songs with producer/arranger Henry Jerome.

Coral envisioned a return to standards, so the first single was a shuffling, "Rainbow"-styled ballad version of the Doris Day 1949 (#2) hit "Again" with Irving Berlin's "Count Your Blessings Instead of Sheep" on the flip. "Again" the harmonies were impeccable and the off-the-melody arrangement unique to the Demensions' style, but Coral couldn't sell it to the kids.

The same held true for their November 1961 release of the Rudy Vallee 1931 number 15 (and 1943 #1) hit "As Time Goes By" and the July 1962 single of Frank Sinatra's 1954 number two hit "Young at Heart."

Coral might have done better promoting the flip, a rock harmony effort that revitalized the Hank Williams country hit "Your Cheatin' Heart" and gave the first indication after seven singles that the Demensions could do something other than a ballad.

In January 1963 Henry Jerome finally came up with a standard that could mix the old and new workably. With a "shoo do and shooby do" background right out of the Five Satins' "In the Still of the Night," a brilliant Lenny Dell lead, Marisa's dominating soprano riding the top, and the best overall harmonies since THE SKYLINERS, "My Foolish Heart" filled East Coast radios and managed to muster enough action to finally chart on March 2nd, reaching number 95.

Two more excellent outings followed in May, a remake of Joe Harnell's 1963 hit (#14) "Fly Me to the Moon," complete with "ra ta tas" from the Elegants "Little Star" (which they in turn borrowed from the Heartbeats' "A Thousand Miles Away"), and a rockin' version of the Mack Gordon/Harry Warren-scribed Sinatra song (#2, 1943) "You'll Never Know."

From this point through 1965 the group recorded mostly originals like "A Little White Gardenia" and their last single, "Ting Aling Ting Toy (China Girl)." Conspicuous was the absence of Marisa's top notes; she had left the group to get married toward the end of 1963.

The threesome of Lenny Dell, Phil Del Giudice, and Howie Margolin continued performing mostly at hotels and resorts throughout New York state and in the Catskill Mountains.

By 1965 teen hearts were being captured by the British rather than by standard love songs, so the group disbanded.

During the '80s a friend of Lenny's, Johnny Faster, convinced him to reform the group. With Phil, Johnny, and Cathy O'Brien the group commenced a series of appearances that included a live in-studio performance on Don K. Reed's CBS-FM radio show. Cathy left soon after and dashed any hopes of a comeback. Around 1990 Faster, who had

been a motivating force in group reunions, died in a car accident.

In the early '90s Phil Del Giudice was retired from City service and living in Dix Hills, New York. Howie Margolin was living in Florida and Marisa Martelli was on City Island in the Bronx. Lenny, based in Commack, Long Island, was performing as a solo artist in the New York area.

THE DEMENSIONS

A SIDE/B SIDE	LABEL/CAT NO	DATE
Over The Rainbow / Nursery Rhyme Rock	Mohawk 116	5/60
Zing Went The Strings Of My Heart / Don't Take Your Love From Me	Mohawk 120	10/60
Ave Maria / God's Christmas	Mohawk 121	12/60
A Tear Fell / Theresa	Mohawk 123	3/61
Again / Count Your Blessings	Coral 62277	7/61
As Time Goes By / Seven Days A Week	Coral 62293	11/61
Young At Heart / Your Cheatin' Heart	Coral 62323	7/62
My Foolish Heart / Just One More Chance	Coral 62344	1/63
Fly Me To The Moon / You'll Never Know	Coral 62359	5/63
Just A Shoulder To Cry On / Don't Worry About Bobby	Coral 62382	1963
A Little White Gardenia / Don't Cry Pretty Baby	Coral 62392	1/64
My Old Girl Friend / This Time Next Year	Coral 62432	1964
Once A Day / Ting Aling Ting Toy (China Girl)	Coral 62444	1965

The Devotions

In the early '60s, record companies put out oldies LPs containing hits from recent years. The Devotions were the only act to have a failed single get on one such compilation and *then* become a hit because of it.

Starting out as a sextet in 1960, the Astoria, Queens, half-dozen were pared down to a fivesome with the loss of Billy Crache and Ray Herrera and the gain of Ray Sanchez on bass. The other members were Ray's brother Andy, Bob Hovorka, and Joe and Frank Pardo.

For a time the group (whose name must have reflected their devotion to rehearsals) was practicing seven days a week, even though three were working and two were still in high school. Sometime between this starting point and their first recording Bob Weisbrod replaced Andy Sanchez. Almost a half a year of practicing passed before they met record promoter Joe Petralia, who lived down the street from Joe and Frank. He introduced them to Bernie Zimming, owner of the Delta Recording Company. The Devotions auditioned with a few well-chosen vocal group classics such as "Life Is But a Dream" and "Sunday Kind of Love" (both by THE HARPTONES), and "Ten Commandments of Love" (THE MOONGLOWS).

Zimming liked the group but felt a reworking of an old standard from the '30s or '40s would be a more likely choice for a hit single. (Records like THE MARCELS' radical arrangement of "Blue Moon" were topping the charts at this time.) The group came back to him with a nice but far-from-unique interpretation of the Nat King Cole 1946 number one record "For Sentimental Reasons." Zimming began to lose interest; he knew he wanted something gimmicky that would sell to teens but he didn't seem to know how to convey it to the Devotions.

In a last-ditch effort, Ray Sanchez wrote a novelty song in keeping with the kind that were popular at the time (e.g., "Mr. Custer" by Larry Verne and "Stranded in the Jungle" by THE CADETS). What emerged was "Rip Van Winkle," the story of an old man who slept for 20 years. It sounded like a cross between "Babalu's Wedding Day" and an old Ajax Cleanser commercial. Zimming liked it so much he whisked them into the studio to record the rock and roll fable along with "For Sentimental Reasons" as the B side. Reflecting the indecision of the newly formed record company, "Sentimental" became the A side sometime between the recording and the release. Fate, in the form of THE CLEFTONES' recent mid-tempo version of "Sentimental," relegated the Devotions' A side once again to the flip side, and "Rip" was ready to hit the streets.

The group, with no concept of what it took to expose a record, would give out copies on the street and leave signs in record stores that they would be giving away autographed copies on a future date.

Despite these efforts, "Rip" became an immediate obscurity until late in 1962 when Slim Rose started playing it on his oldies show. It reached number one on the Time Square Records Top 100 sales list in September 1962 and stayed on that chart for eight months. This activity enabled the Devotions to appear on Slim's rock and roll show in September 1962 at Palisades Park (New Jersey), one of the first oldies shows and years ahead of Richard Nader's late '60s successes.

The quintet performed their two sides alongside acts like THE SHELLS ("Baby Oh Baby"), the Summits (Slim's own group doing "Go Back Where You Came From"), and the Interiors ("Darling Little Angel").

Late in 1962, Roulette bought the Delta masters and gave them a half-hearted release. By 1963, the group called it quits having played few dates and earned little money though retaining fond memories.

In 1964 the folks at Roulette were compiling an "oldies but goodies" LP collection titled *Golden Goodies*. Why an obvious flop like "Rip" was included among all those top 20 hits is still not known, but when the LP reached a particular disc jockey in Pittsburgh, he started playing the Devotions cut and the request line lit up.

Word got back to Roulette, and within a week of release "Rip Van Winkle" had sold 15,000 copies in Pittsburgh. A rush call from the record company found two members of the quintet in the armed forces overseas, so a new Devotions was formed featuring new lead Louis DeCarlo, Larry Frank, and originals Bob Hovorka and the Pardo boys.

On February 8, 1964, the four-year-old record hit *Billboard*'s Top 100 charts reaching number 36 in March. Though Roulette brought the boys in to record again, neither "Sunday Kind of Love" (recorded at the original group's session) or "Snow White" received any attention from radio.

The fact that the label had accidently tripped over the "Rip Van Winkle" hit was still no guarantee of their long-term interest in the Devotions, and realizing this, the group once again disbanded.

The group re-formed in the '70s with Andy Sanchez on lead, and ironically the Devotions performed more in that decade than when they had their one and only hit.

Dion and the Belmonts

Without question one of the best of the late '50s early '60s vocal groups, the Belmonts were actually two aggregations. First known as Dion and the Belmonts, the four Italian lads were the darlings of pop doo wop sound in the late '50s. When Dion left for a solo career they became strictly the Belmonts and continued to crank out great sounding, harmony-dominated rockers and ballads. The members were Dion DiMucci (lead), Carlo

Mastrangelo (bass), Fred Milano (second tenor), and Angelo D'Aleo (first tenor).

The Belmonts (naming themselves after Belmont Avenue in the Bronx, where they honed their early harmonies) originated as a trio. Although Dion knew them in and out of Roosevelt High School, he did not record with them at first even though the foursome often hit some harmony in the vicinity of Cratona Avenue and 187th Street. Given that tough neighborhood it is not surprising that their first groups were not singing groups at all, but street gangs, Dion with the Fordham Daggers and Freddie and Carlo with the Imperial Hoods.

Dion's first opportunity to record came with Mohawk Records in 1957 on a song titled "The Chosen Few" (Mohawk 105), with vocal accompaniment by a group he never met known only as the Timberlanes. Around the same time the Belmonts also got an opportunity to record, coincidentally, for Mohawk; their single of "Teenage Clementine" (Mohawk 106) was released to the same minimal response as Dion's first effort.

The group then joined forces and recorded their first single as Dion and the Belmonts in late 1957, entitled "We Went Away" (Mohawk 107). Undaunted by the record's failure (and buoyed by their newfound status as neighborhood celebrities), the group continued to practice at any time or place including the platforms of the southbound Sixth Avenue D train. With so many diverse influences (Dion loved country music, Carlo was a jazz aficionado, Freddie a doo wop diehard, and Angelo an operatic stylist) it's amazing that the group could create such a tight, original pop sound.

By the spring of 1958 they had signed with the newly formed Laurie Records as their first act and wasted no time in climbing the charts to number 22 with their debut single "I Wonder Why." They followed with seven more chart records out of only seven releases including the top five hit "A Teenager in Love." Except for their first Laurie Record, all the group's single releases were ballad standards from the 1930s ("No One Knows" and "Where or When" by the Hal Kemp orchestra from 1937, "In the Still of the Night" by Tommy Dorsey from 1937) and the 1940s ("When You Wish Upon a Star" by the Glenn Miller Orchestra in 1940).

Their unique harmony gave many people the impression they were a black group, so it wasn't surprising that agents in places like the traditionally black venue, the Howard Theater in Washington, D.C., booked them for performances. In 1958, they were the first white group ever to work the famed Apollo Theater in Harlem. Between 1958 and 1960, the group did many one-nighters and tours around the country, and became an obscure footnote in history when they went out on the road through the Northwest in January 1959, riding in a dilapidated bus with the Big Bopper, Ritchie Valens, and Buddy Holly. Known as the "Winter Dance Party" the continual bus breakdowns and freezing cold made it anything but a party. On a fateful day in February when Buddy Holly could take no more, he asked Dion to fly with him to the next show rather than rumble on in the bus. Had Dion said yes, four legends would have died in that plane crash rather than three.

By 1960, the role of rock and roll balladeers suited the Belmonts just fine, but Dion preferred to "rock out" more, so after "In the Still of the Night" went to number 38 in August 1960, he decided to begin a solo career (see THE DEL-SATINS). The Belmonts regrouped with Carlo taking over lead and did one more record for Laurie in 1961, a reworking of the 1958 Robert and Johnny ballad "We Belong Together." Although it failed to chart, the up-tempo B side, "Such a Long Way," laid the groundwork for their '60s-style up-beat doo wop rockers. Having learned how to hit the charts with reworked oldies, the Belmonts tried out their formula on an up-tempo song with the NORMAN FOX AND THE ROB ROYS rocker "Tell Me Why," which immediately joined the top 20 of the national charts as the first release on their new label Sabrina (later renamed Sabina).

The formula proved to be a good one; five of their next six singles charted, with the lone non-charter a ballad ("I Confess," Sabina 503).

After recording "Come on Little Angel" in 1962, Carlo decided on a solo career, and with Laurie records looking for a replacement for Dion (who left the same year to sign with Columbia) the reunion (with Laurie) seemed to be of mutual benefit. Laurie even used Carlo's first name only on the label to keep the Dion mystique alive. He recorded four singles backed by another Bronx group, the Tremonts. The highlight of these releases was the pulsating up-tempo harmony gem "Baby Doll," which, like the others, saw little exposure.

Carlo's place in the Belmonts was taken by Frank Lyndon for the remaining six singles on Sabina. Their last chart record for that label was "Ann Marie," which got some airplay in the East but only managed to reach number 86 in April 1963. Four singles and a year later, the group moved on to United Artist Records and recorded four mediocre singles between 1964 and 1966, all destined for obscurity.

Then, in late 1966 Dion and Carlo reteamed with Freddie and Angelo for the first Dion and the Belmonts recording in six years. The result was the

Together Again LP on ABC Records with two excellent singles, "Moving Man" (cowritten by the future head of Arista Records Publishing Company, Billy Meschel) and the scat, jazz-blues doo wop "My Girl, the Month of May." With little understanding of what to do with a revitalized group of street crooners, ABC soon let a potentially classic LP go down the drain. Dion went solo again, back to Laurie, and up the charts with his comeback hit "Abraham, Martin and John." The Belmonts (with Frank Lyndon again replacing Carlo) moved on to Dot Records in 1968 for an LP entitled *Summer Love* with the singles "Reminiscences" and "Have You Heard/Worst That Could Happen," a medley of the Duprees and Brooklyn Bridge signature songs. Uninspired production by Gerry Granahan doomed the recordings to an obvious fate. Carlo continued with Laurie as lead singer of a group known only as "Endless Pulse" through 1968 and 1969, recording three spirited but behind-the-times singles.

In 1972, the magic returned for the Belmonts as Bobby Feldman (a knowledgeable doo wopper and coproducer with Jerry Goldstein and Rich Gottehrer of many hits like "My Boyfriend's Back" by THE ANGELS) produced a glorious LP entitled *Cigars, A Cappella, Candy*. More than 16 years before THE NYLONS gave national recognition to a cappella doo wop via their "Na Na Hey Hey Kiss Him Goodbye" hit, the Belmonts had created the consummate professional a cappella record (which coincidentally contained a version of "Na Na Hey Hey" along with instrument-less versions of their original recordings "Where or When," "That's My Desire," and "We Belong Together"). Coming right in the midst of the oldies revival the record was well-received though not a national trend-setter.

The revival also brought the Belmonts and Dion back together in a performance at Madison Square Garden on the night of June 2, 1972. The Garden was packed with adoring fans as the group performed together unrehearsed for the first time since the days of the Winter Dance Party. Although Angelo, Carlo, and Freddie were all there with Dion, pictures of that evening show a fourth Belmont, Frank Lyndon, at the harmony mike. The evening was preserved on record by Dion's manager, Zack Glickman, and released by Warner Brothers as the *Dion and the Belmonts Live at Madison Square Garden—1972 Reunion* album. The seven minute, 42 second version of "Runaround Sue" by the then quintet was alone worth the price of the LP. The reunion was only momentary, and Dion and the Belmonts once again separated. As in the past, all roads seemed to lead to Laurie Records: the Bel-

monts cut one single for the label entitled "A Brand New Song," released in 1975.

By the mid-'70s Warren Gradus had replaced Frank Lyndon for the two singles and LP on Strawberry Records (1976). The group continued to perform on the East Coast and in 1981 again joined up with producer Bobby Feldman for a rousing ode entitled "Let's Put the Fun Back in Rock 'n' Roll." This time, however, the magic harmonies and Freddie Cannon's lead singing led to the first chart record for the Belmonts in over 18 years. Cannon himself (hit artist on "Palisades Park" and "Tallahassee Lassie") hadn't had a chart record since "The Dedication Song" in 1966, and the pairing of these two energetic entities proved visionary. It also proved the Belmonts still maintained a vocal sound that had a ready audience.

DION AND THE BELMONTS

A SIDE/B SIDE	LABEL/CAT NO	DATE
The Belmonts		
Teenage Clementine / Santa Margarita	Mohawk 106	1957
We Went Away* / Tag Along*	Mohawk 107	1957
I Wonder Why */ Teen Angel*	Laurie 3013	1958
No One Knows* / I Can't Go On*	Laurie 3015	1958
Don't Pity Me* / Just You*	Laurie 3021	1958
A Teenager In Love* / I've Cried Before*	Laurie 3027	1959
Every Little Thing I Do* / A Lover's Prayer*	Laurie 3035	1959
Where Or When* / That's My Desire*	Laurie 3044	1959
Wonderful Girl* / When You Wish Upon A Star*	Laurie 3052	1960
In The Still Of The Night* / A Funny Feeling*	Laurie 3059	1960
We Belong Together / Such A Long Way	Laurie 3080	1961
Smoke From Your Cigarette / Tell Me Why	Srprs 1000	1961
Smoke From Your Cigarette / Tell Me Why	Sabina 500	1961
Don't Get Around Much Anymore / Searching For A New Love	Sabina 501	1961
I Need Someone / That American Dance	Sabina 502	1961
I Confess / Hombre	Sabina 503	1962
Diddle-Dee-Dum / Farewell	Sabina 507	1962
Ann-Marie / Ac-Cent-Tchu-Ate-The Positive	Sabina 509	1963
Let's Call It A Day / More Important Things To Do	Sabina 517	1964
Why / C'Mon Everybody	Sabina 519	1964
Summertime / Nothing In Return	Sabina 522	1964

A SIDE/B SIDE	LABEL/CAT NO	DATE
You're Like A Mystery / Come Go With Me	Sabina 526	1965
I Don't Know Why, I Just Do / Wintertime	UA 809	1964
Then I Walked Away / Today My Love Has Gone Away	UA 904	1965
I Got A Feeling / To Be With You	UA 966	1965
Come With Me / You're Like A Mystery	UA 50007	1966
My Girl The Month Of May* / Berimbau*	ABC 10868	1966
Movin' Man* / For Bobbie*	ABC 10896	1967
Reminiscences / She Only Wants To Do Her Own Thing	Dot 17173	1968
Answer Me My Love / Have You Heard / Worst That Could Happen	Dot 17257	1969
A Brand New Song / Story Teller	Laurie 3631	1975
Cheek To Cheek / The Voyager	Straw 106	1976
I'll Never Fall In Love Again / Voyager	Straw107	1977
Let's Put The Fun Back In Rock 'n' Roll / Your Mama Ain't Always Right	MiaSd 1002	1981

* Dion and the Belmonts

The Dixie Cups

The Dixie Cups were a short-lived though successful trio from New Orleans. In the space of 11 months they had five national chart records and in the span of two-and-a-half years they had come and gone. Such was the fate of sisters Barbara Ann and Rosa Lee Hawkins and their cousin Joan Marie Johnson.

They began singing together in their public school days and tagged themselves the Meltones. When they reached their mid-teens a local performance caught the eye of hit-artist-turned-manager and New Orleans native Joe Jones ("You Talk Too Much," #3, 1960), who took the group under his wing. Jones, who at one time in the '50s had been the valet for B.B. King, took the trio to Jerry Leiber and Mike Stoller, who in 1964 were starting their own new label with industry vet George Goldner (Leiber and Stoller had run Spark Records in the 1950s).

By 1964, Barbara (21) and Rosa (18) were enrolled at Southern University in New Orleans and Joan (19) was going to Booker T. Washington High School in the Crescent City, but the lure of recording was too great to ignore when the chance to sign with Red Bird came. The strength of Red Bird was

its philosophy that the song is everything; its two biggest contributors were not Leiber and Stoller as you might expect, but the writing and producing silent partners Jeff Barry and Ellie Greenwich.

Jeff, Ellie, and Phil Spector had written a song recorded by THE RONETTES in 1964, but Spector had refused to release it. Not wanting what they felt was a hit song to go to waste, they agreed to give "Chapel of Love" to the light-voiced, innocent-sounding Dixie Cups.

The Cups recording was two minutes and 51 seconds of pure teen pop pleasure with an ever-so-simple and catchy hook. "Chapel" took off like a rocket after its April 1964 release, charting on May 2nd and reaching number one on June 6th while pushing the Beatles' "Love Me Do" out of first place. It stayed at the top for three weeks and went to number one R&B. "Chapel" fever caught on internationally as the Dixies found themselves peaking at number 22 in England and number 21 in Australia that summer.

Their next single, "People Say," jumped out in June and was also bounding up the charts by July 18th. "People Say" had all the hook elements of "Chapel," with a Cookies-styled vocal sound that was the group's best harmony recording. It went to number 12 on both the Pop and R&B charts before the summer ended. An LP titled *Chapel of Love* soon hit the market, and among its 11 cuts were two more Jeff-Ellie-Phil songs that had been languishing in the can at Philles: "All Grown Up," released in July 1964 as THE CRYSTALS' last single for Philles, and "Girls Can Tell," also by the Crystals and unreleased until 1976 when it was issued in England on a Phil Spector International (Polydor) LP titled *Phil Spector's Wall of Sound Volume V, Rare Masters*.

Their next two releases ("You Should Have Seen the Way He Looked at Me," #39, and "Little Belle," #51) were lesser recordings whose success was probably hampered slightly by the tremendous success of their new label mates, THE SHANGRI-LAS.

The Dixie Cups temporarily salvaged their hit reputation with the unlikely New Orleans-styled Mardi Gras chant "Iko Iko" in March 1965. With just a bass and rhythm accompaniment, the Dixie Cups and their Creole concoction attained number 20 Pop and R&B and number 23 in the U.K. during the spring.

Red Bird's philosophy seemed to be, "If it doesn't go Top 100, drop the group," so when their sixth single ("Gee the Moon Is Shining Bright") became the only one to miss the 100 mark (it peaked at number 102 on *Billboard*'s Bubbling

Under) in July, the Dixie Cups found themselves homeless.

Joe Jones and company quickly rebounded onto ABC Records for four single releases, but the magic of the songs wasn't up to those of the Red Bird writing academy, and by Christmas of 1966 the Dixie Cups were resigned to record industry retirement.

The Dovells

An excellent white vocal group, the Dovells made their mark as the kings of early '60s dance records. They started out in 1959 as the Brooktones, named after their educational institution, Overbrook High School in Philadelphia.

The group may have started out as a singing group, but the fact that each member adopted a different name made it seem as if they were going for a theatrical career. The members were Len Borisoff (Len Barry) on lead, Jerry Gross (Jerry Summers) on lead and first tenor, Mike Freda (Mike Dennis) on second tenor, Arnie Silver (Arnie Satin) on baritone, and Jim Mealey (Danny Brooks) on bass, with part-timer Mark Gordesky (Mark Stevens) on tenor. The Brooktones (all 17 years of age except for 18-year-old Len) rehearsed at their houses and occasionally at John Madara's record shop on 60th and Market. (Madara was cowriter of "At the Hop" for Danny and the Juniors.) All the members were into rhythm and blues, numbering among their favorites Jackie Wilson and FRANKIE LYMON AND THE TEENAGERS. The group even recorded several Teenagers songs, including "Why Do Fools Fall in Love" and "I Want You to Be My Girl."

By the summer of 1960 Jerry and Mike had left to form a new group called the Gems with Mark Stevens and Alan Horowitz. While the Gems were negotiating to sign with Bob Marcucci's Chancellor Records (the home of teen idols Fabian and Frankie Avalon), the Brooktones had added William Shunkwiler and Jerry Sirlin and through an attorney arranged a live audition for the quintet with Cameo/Parkway execs Bernie Lowe, Kal Mann, and A&R head Dave Appell. They were signed in late 1960 and began recording two of Lenny's songs at Reco Art (now Sigma Sound) on 12th Street.

When they ran into harmony problems, Jerry recalls, "Len called me and asked me to come back and help out. I told him we could use Mike too who was a great singer, and so we came back and replaced Shunkwiler and Sirlin."

The Dovells' first single, "No, No, No," written by Len Barry (though the label read "Len Borisoff"), was released in March and was described in *Billboard* as "a rocker, with drums, chimes and other instruments contributing a busy quality."

In late spring the quintet returned to the studio (this time Cameo's studios at 1405 Locust) to record their new A side, the 1957 Teenagers ballad "Out in the Cold Again." While the session was proceeding, Parkway promotion man Billy Harper excitedly entered the studio babbling on about a hot new dance kids were doing called "the Stomp" at the Goodwill Fire Hall in Bristol, just outside of Philadelphia. Jerry remembers, "Billy put on the Students record of 'Everyday of the Week,' and you'll notice the guitar riff at the beginning sounds familiar, and that's what they were dancing to. Kal and Dave went hey, we should write a song called 'The Bristol Stomp,' and they did it overnight (and practically over 'Everyday of the Week'). We came in the next day and they said, 'Let's record this,' so we did." "Out in the Cold" became the B side.

"Bristol Stomp" spent the better part of the summer of 1961 doing nothing, and then it broke out of the Midwest. On September 11th it gained enough momentum to go national and by October 23rd was the number two seller in America, right behind Dion and THE DEL-SATINS' "Runaround Sue." It also reached number seven on the R&B chart.

Parkway had found the Dovells' niche, and they kept filling it following "Bristol." "Do the New Continental," with the same kind of dance orientation, made *Billboard*'s Pop chart on January 27, 1962, and reached number 37. In fact, their next three singles were all dance titles that all charted, including "Bristol Twistin' Annie" (which they did in a mere 29 takes), number 27, "Hully Gully Baby," number 25, and "The Jitterbug," number 82, all in 1962, giving them five different charters to five different dances in a little over a year.

Sounding to many like a black group, the Dovells performed more at black shows and theatres than in white venues. Their first large-scale performance, upon the release of "Bristol Stomp," was at the Fox Theatre in Detroit with Ray Charles, Timi Yuro, Gloria Lynne, and Fabian.

While taking a break behind the theatre the Dovells encountered three young girls singing on a fire escape. In a gesture of encouragement Jerry said to the lead, "Keep pluggin', man, you girls are gonna make it; you're good." A little over a year later "the girls" had their first of 45 chart singles as THE SUPREMES ("Your Heart Belongs to Me," #95).

The career pace became so fast and furious that on one trip between Washington's Howard Theatre and the Apollo Theatre in New York City the group was brought into Philadelphia by Parkway and cut a whole album in two days. Even when they got some time off it was short-lived. Toward the end of 1965, the group was vacationing in Florida when they were called back to perform in the film *Don't Knock the Twist* with Dion, Chubby Checker, and THE MARCELS.

During 1962, while the Dovells were immortalizing on record every dance Dave Appell and Kal Mann could think of, they were also touring the country by bus with black bands and artists like James Brown. Since they were the only white group on some of these shows they must have appeared to be civil rights activists, especially while touring through the South. On one occasion near Atlanta the bus was fired upon.

After the below-standard "Save Me Baby" in January 1963, the Dovells came back with a powerful tune in Phil Upchurch's performance "break" song, "You Can't Sit Down." By June 15th it had hit number three Pop and finished at number 10 on the R&B chart. Their next single, "Betty in Bermudas," was another goodie in the "You Can't Sit Down" vein, and the Kal Mann/Dave Appell-penned song (the writers of many Dovells recordings) was a perfect summer rocker. Unfortunately, by the time it built up enough steam to chart, summer was already over, and it only managed a climb to number 50.

In the fall, "Stop Monkeyin' Aroun'" became the group's last chart single, reaching number 94. Around this time, they heard a tape of an English group's record leased to Swan Records. The Dovells and Parkway thought the song was a natural for them and immediately recorded it, but procrastination on Parkway's part cost them a hit. The Swan release came out in January 1964 and went to number one. The group was the Beatles and the song was "She Loves You." The Dovells' version was never released and to this day is sitting in a vault somewhere.

Earlier group differences exploded at a Christmas show performance in Las Vegas. According to Jerry, a dispute arose over whether or not to tailor their talents to the Vegas crowd. Most of the group wanted to, and they threatened to quit after the show. Len, the dissenting voice, saw that he was outnumbered and quit instead. The group, now a trio, returned to Philly and recorded three Parkway singles in 1964, including the BEACH BOYS-styled "Be My Girl," the LETTERMEN-influenced "Happy Birthday Just the Same," and the up-tempo, harmony-filled FOUR SEASONS-styled "What in the World's Come Over You."

Their best record since "You Can't Sit Down," "What in the World" was a blending of pop, rock, and folk with Jerry's outstanding (though brief) lead. Unfortunately it came out of too few radios and, like its predecessors, never charted.

During their tenure at Parkway they recorded as an uncredited vocal group behind Chubby Checker on his hit "Let's Twist Again" and performed as backups to Fabian, Chubby Checker, and with Jackie Wilson at the Brooklyn Fox.

The group moved to Swan in 1965 for one record ("Happy") that included backup vocals by 23-year-old Danny Hutton, later to become a member of THREE DOG NIGHT.

Meanwhile, Len Barry signed with Decca as a solo act and placed six singles on the Pop charts between 1965 and 1966, including a bit of bubblegum titled "One, Two, Three" (#2, November 20, 1965).

In the spring of 1968, while driving home on the New Jersey Turnpike from a show, Jerry came up with an idea for a song based on a segment of TV's "Laugh-In" show known as "Here Comes the Judge." He and Mike finished the song in the car, recorded it the following night with a female lead named Jean Hillery, and went to New York the very next day to place it. Not having slept in 48 hours, Jerry and Mike walked dazed into MGM's suite and made a beeline for A&R director Lenny Sheer's office. Interrupting a meeting, they announced, "We have a hit record," to which Sheer responded, "Great! But who the hell are you?" After a quick exchange of amenities Sheer asked the guys to wait outside. A few minutes later he emerged to inform them that they did indeed have a hit, and he signed them on the spot. The act was to be called the Magistrates. It was a Thursday, a mere 48 hours after the concept was born on the Turnpike. The following Saturday the Dovells were driving to New York across the George Washington Bridge and listening to WABC when "Here Comes the Judge" came blaring out of the radio, putting them into such a frenzy that they nearly drove off the bridge.

For the summer of 1968 the Dovells toured with Jean, and when she came out they'd become the Magistrates. "The Judge" became an East Coast smash and made it up the *Billboard* scale to number 54 Pop. Around this time, Mike Dennis left and Mark Stevens became a regular. No further Magistrates releases followed, however, and the group went back to being full-time Dovells.

By 1972 Mark (who had been in and out on various occasions) and Arnie Satin recorded a duo LP for Lion Records (an MGM subsidiary) titled *Silver-Stevens Dusty Roads*.

In 1974 the Dovells went out (record wise) the way they came in, with a rockin' dance record. It was "Dancin' in the Street," from the MARTHA AND THE VANDELLAS hit of 1964. The Event release was picking up national action (number 105) when European parent company Polydor stepped in and fired Event's promo people, leaving the group with a record the deejays couldn't play because the record honchos weren't supplying 45s to the stores.

The group continued to perform until a gig at Hershey's Lodge in Hershey, Pennsylvania, when Arnie gave his two-weeks' notice. Mark and Jerry continued the group without skipping a beat, having band members filling in on vocals and developing a Dean Martin/Jerry Lewis-styled stage act to go with their million-selling hits. The approach enabled them to work 16 weeks a year in Las Vegas.

In 1991 Len rejoined Jerry and Mark for an LP, recording many of their original hits. Arnie became general manager of a Lincoln/Mercury dealership in Atlantic City. Mike began doing landscaping in Jacksonville, Florida. Jim died in the mid-'70s. Len was bartending in Philadelphia. Jerry was producing corporate events when not performing with Mark.

THE DOVELLS

A SIDE/B SIDE	LABEL/CAT NO	DATE
No No No / Letters Of Love	Prkwy 819	3/61
Bristol Stomp /		
Out In The Cold Again	Prkwy 827	6/61
Bristol Stomp / Letters Of Love	Prkwy 827	9/61
Do The New Continental /		
Mope-Itty Mope Stomp	Prkwy 833	1/62
Bristol Twistin' Annie / The Actor	Prkwy 838	4/62
Hully Gully Baby /		
Your Last Chance	Prkwy 845	7/62
The Jitterbug /		
Kissin' In The Kitchen	Prkwy 855	10/62
Save Me, Baby / You Can't		
Run Away From Yourself	Prkwy 861	1/63
You Can't Sit Down /		
Stompin' Everywhere	Prkwy 867	3/63
Betty In Bermudas /		
Dance The Froog	Prkwy 882	7/63
Stop Monkeyin' Aroun' / No No No	Prkwy 889	10/63
Be My Girl /		
Dragster On The Prowl	Prkwy 901	1/64
Happy Birthday Just The Same /		
One Potato-Two Potato-Three		
Potato-Four	Prkwy 911	3/64
What In The World's Come Over		
You / Watusi With Lucy	Prkwy 925	7/64
Happy / Alright	Swan 4231	1965
Our Winter Love / Blue	Jamie 1369	1965

A SIDE/B SIDE	LABEL/CAT NO	DATE
There's A Girl /		
Love Is Everywhere	MGM 13628	11/66
The Magistrates		
Here Come The Judge / Girl	MGM 13946	5/68
The Dovells		
Roll Over Beethoven /		
Something About You Boy	Event 3310	3/70
Sometimes / Far Away	Verve 10701	12/72
Mary's Magic Show /		
Don't Vote For Luke McAbe	MGM 14568	6/73
Dancing In The Streets /		
Back On The Road Again	Event 216	1974

The Dreamers

The Dreamers had two short careers marked by one of the most outrageous reworkings any standard ballad has ever undergone. The original group included Frank Cammarata (lead and tenor), Bob Malara (tenor), Luke "Babe" Berardis (tenor and baritone), John "Buddy" Trancynger (baritone and bass), and Dominic Canzano (baritone and bass).

They formed in 1958 at a family wedding (all but John were cousins) and the encouraging response to their singing was all they needed to make a serious go of it. The group, aged 16 ("Babe") to 22 (Bob) years old and all from Yonkers and White Plains in New York, won a local talent show that qualified them for the "Ted Mack Amateur Hour" in 1959. The Dreamers sang a combination of CHANNELS and BELMONTS versions of "That's My Desire" but lost out to a female tap-dancing drummer. All was not lost, however. George Goldner of End Records was sitting in the audience, and he signed the group to his newest label, Goldisc.

In the fall of 1960 they recorded "Teenage Vows of Love." It became a New York area hit and received some excellent radio and sales response throughout the East and Midwest. When the creative rewards started seeming greater than the financial ones, the group signed to the Cousins label. By now Luke and Dom had been replaced by Frank Nicholas (the Meridians) and Frank DiGilio, and their harmony was at its strongest.

In early 1962 Cousins released the Dreamers' off-the-wall mutation of Tony Bennett's 1951 "Because of You" number one hit. If Bennett had been dead he would have turned in his grave, but teens loved it—that is, those who got a chance to hear it. The arrangement was actually very creative, the harmonies were excellent, and the track moved at an exciting pace, with Cammarata's lead sparkling throughout. But Cousin's distributor (Colpix) dropped the ball when they transferred the single to their May affiliate, and one of rock's most enjoyable revisions of a standard was lost.

The group performed mostly at promotional shows and at local army bases and the West Point Military Academy, often appearing with THE BOBBETTES ("Mr. Lee," Atlantic) in Detroit, Chicago, and the obligatory Palisades Park, New Jersey.

In 1963 the group broke up when recording opportunities became scarce. 20 years later Frank Cammarata, Jr., the son of the Dreamers' lead singer, was working as a producer for Don K. Reed's WCBS-FM oldies show. When it was revealed that Frank's dad was the singer, Reed invited the group to sing on his show. All they had to do was regroup after 20 years. Three of them did: Frank, Sr., John Trancynger, and Frank Nicholas were joined by Tony Federico and Bruce Goldie (the Meridians), and the practice grind started again. The Dreamers performed on Reed's show and the phone response was so strong that the group decided to record their first LP, *Yesterday Once More*, which they put out on their own Dream Records of Yonkers. The 12-song LP was one of the vocal group highlights of 1987, and it included remakes of their own "Teenage Vows of Love" and "Because of You" along with strong versions of "This I Swear" (THE SKYLINERS), "Little Darlin'" (THE GLADIOLAS), and their first single in 25 years, "Tonight" (the Velvets) b/w "Been So Long" (THE PASTELS).

Bruce Goldie moved to Florida (now singing with THE FIVE BOROUGHS) and Dario Bianchini came aboard, later replaced by Sam Casarella.

By 1989 they had disbanded for good. In recent years Dom Canzano was going under the name Dom Cannon as a Philadelphia disc jockey. Luke was in computer sales, John was serving as a Yonkers fireman, and Frank Cammarata was retired as a Yonkers firefighter. Tony Federico became a New York architect, Frank Nicholas was working as an iron worker, and Frank DiGilio was in the air conditioning business. Bob Malara died in a boat accident in the late '70s.

The Dreamlovers

An excellent street-corner group, the Dreamlovers were the unsung heroes of the 1960s Philadelphia sound. They came together as a group at Northeast High School, having been street-corner friends since 1956. Originally calling themselves the Romancers, the members included William Johnson (lead), Tommy Ricks (first and second tenor), Cleveland Hammock, Jr. (second tenor), Clifton Dunn (baritone), and his brother James Ray Dunn (bass). The group was just beginning to get its sound together when a senseless turn of events left William Johnson dead, shot several times outside a party by some hothead. This was the price William paid for talking to the guy's girl.

Morris Gardner took Johnson's place and the group moved on to defining its style based on admiration for acts like THE FLAMINGOS, THE MOONGLOWS, and THE FIVE KEYS. They renamed themselves after a single vocalist's current hit—Bobby Darin's "Dream Lover" in mid-1959.

By 1960 they had come to the attention of Philadelphia upholstery shop owner and record label entrepreneur Venton Len "Buddy" Caldwell, who signed them to his Len label and released their bongo-led, up-tempo 45 of "For the First Time." Buddy moved the group to his V-Tone label for their next release, a harmony-filled rocker "Annabelle Lee," with Donald Hogan on lead. Don joined the group just in time to duet on the first single. "Annabelle" didn't sell but their name started getting around Philadelphia.

Cameo/Parkway Records heard a tape the quintet sent them and called them in to record. The group was not aware that they wouldn't be recording as the Dreamlovers but rather as a backup to some new kid with a name that sounded like Fats Domino. They recorded a Hank Ballard song, got paid for backup work, and didn't think much about it until the summer of 1960 when that record, "The Twist" sung by Chubby Checker, became the hottest single in America, going to number one on September 19th.

Even though their harmonies were prominent, the group received no credit on the record. But that success did give them plenty of backup work with Cameo/Parkway, including most of Chubby's hits ("Pony Time," "Let's Twist Again," and more) and Dee Dee Sharp's recordings.

With no chance to record under their own name at Parkway they turned their attention toward a new label named Heritage started by Murray Wecht and Jerry Ross.

In the meantime V-Tone released their third single, "May I Kiss the Bride," a DRIFTERS-influenced, up-tempo, string-laden affair with close doo wop harmonies. In addition to that, by the time the Dreamlovers' first single on Heritage surfaced, the group had sung on seven Chubby Checker charters anonymously.

On July 31, 1961, "When We Get Married" (written by Don Hogan) hit the *Billboard* lists and shot up to the top 10.

The next, "Welcome Home," failed. But the flip, "Let Them Love (And Be Loved)," was a well-crafted production sung in the "When We Get Married" mold, and it managed to bubble under at number 102.

In March 1962 the Dreamlovers jumped on the up-tempo bandwagon with a recording of the Collegians' 1956 rocker, "Zoom, Zoom, Zoom." *Billboard*'s reviewer enthusiastically proclaimed, "Here's a bright rocker done in close to the Marcels' style over pounding percussion backing. Early reports already show action and the side could easily step out. Bears watching." Unfortunately, "Zoom" didn't bear watching; it flopped.

They moved the group over to the better established New York indy End Records for a super-smooth ballad called "If I Should Lose You," with ultra-warm harmonies accompanying Don's lead. It scored a Pop number 62.

By now, Chubby Checker had 15 chart records (including "The Fly," "Slow Twistin'," and "Let's Twist Again"), most of which were backed by the Dreamlovers as before and all conspicuously missing a group credit.

Strangely, "If I Should Lose You" was their only End release. Their next single was on the small Casino label, which was picked up by Swan in 1963.

The group moved to the majors in 1963 (and Morris Gardner left about this time) starting with Columbia, Warner Bros., and Mercury, but only their 1965 Walker Brothers-styled rhythm ballad "You Gave Me Somebody to Love" made enough noise to reach even a low chart rung (#121).

In 1964, after they'd rung up backing successes on some 20-odd Cameo/Parkway hits, they finally got to do one single for that organization called "Oh Baby Mine."

In 1973 they changed their name for a one-shot as a Brothers Guiding Light (Mercury) and then disbanded only to regroup in 1980.

They remained together afterwards and played Philly area clubs and oldies shows from time to time with the same five guys—James, Clifton, Tommy, Cleveland, and Don, who was still writing songs.

THE DREAMLOVERS

A SIDE/B SIDE	LABEL/CAT NO	DATE
For The First Time /		
Take It From A Fool	Len 1006	1960

A SIDE/B SIDE	LABEL/CAT NO	DATE
Home Is Where The Heart Is /		
Annabelle Lee	V-Tone 211	1960
Time / May I Kiss The Bride	V-Tone 229	1961
When We Get Married /		
Just Because	Heritage 102	7/61
Welcome Home / Let Them Love	Heritage 104	1961
Zoom Zoom Zoom /		
While We Were Dancing	Heritage 107	3/62
If I Should Lose You / I Miss You	End 1114	5/62
Together / Amazons And Coyotees	Swan 4167	1963
Sad Sad Boy /		
If I Were A Magician	Col 42698	2/63
Black Bottom / Sad Sad Boy	Col 42752	3/63
Pretty Little Girl /		
I'm Through With You	Col 42842	8/63
Together / Amazons And Coyotees	Casino 1308	1964
Oh Baby Mine / These Will Be		
The Good Old Days	Cameo 326	1964
You Gave Me Somebody To Love /		
Doin' Things Together With You	Wrnr 5619	3/65
The Bad Times Make The Good		
Times / Bless Your Soul	Merc 72595	10/66
Calling Jo-Ann / You Gave		
Me Somebody To Love	Merc 72630	11/66

The Ducanes

If you asked anyone in America under 40 who the Ducanes were, odds are you'd get blank stares. Yet the quintet of teenagers were notable if only for the fact that they were the next rung up the ladder to superstardom for America's greatest record producer.

The Ducanes were five friends who loved basketball, spending countless hours practicing near their homes at Bergenfield Memorial Field. In between games the guys would harmonize on some of the better (though often obscure) doo wops of the day such as "I Laughed" by THE JESTERS, "Zoom" by the Collegians, and "When I Fall in Love" by THE FLAMINGOS (who were their favorite group). The only actual hit they sang at the time was their first practiced song, "Diamonds and Pearls" by THE PARADONS.

The Bergenfield, New Jersey, quintet consisted of leader Eddie Brian (baritone) and Rick Scrofan (second tenor), both from Bergen Catholic High School, along with Louis Biscardi (lead), Jeff Breny (first tenor), and Dennis Buckley (bass), all from Bergenfield High School.

In 1961 the group won a talent contest at Northern Valley High and met a publisher from Hill and

Range Music who suggested they come by and audition. Taking his advice, the Ducanes (who named themselves without knowing what a Ducane was except that it sounded hep) went up to Hill and Range's office on Broadway in New York City with their lone original composition "On My Vision Screen." The song went over like a lead balloon, but given another chance the group fell back on the comfortable oldie "Zoom, Zoom, Zoom." Unbeknownst to the Bergenfield bunch, standing outside the door was a young record producer who was in New York looking for material. He came in, sat at the piano, and proceeded to work on a slower version of "Zoom" with the Ducanes. The 20-year-old producer—whose name was Phil Spector—rebuilt "Zoom" until it became "Yes, I Love You." Next, as if it came from their collective fantasies, Spector asked if they'd like to record the song.

Soon after, Phil signed the boys to one of the first independent production contracts. Back then artists were signed directly to record labels, not producers, but Spector had his own formula. The Los Angeles-bred boy genius was just starting to get recognition as a unique talent, producing hits such as "To Know Him Is to Love Him" in 1958 (as a member of the Fairfax High singing trio THE TEDDY BEARS) and the Ray Peterson 1960 top 10 scoring "Corrina, Corrina." Still, Phil had never produced a doo wop group, and the Ducanes had never heard of him before their chance encounter. Eddie and the group spent the next few months commuting by bus into Hill and Range's offices to rehearse "Yes I Love You" and a ballad Spector had written entitled "Little Did I Know."

One day in June, the Ducanes decided to warm up at their rehearsal with a 1957 rocker originally by LOUIS LYMON AND THE TEENCHORDS. They had gotten no further than six bars into the song (including the now famous "tra-la-la-la-la-la-la" intro) when Phil barged through the door and asked, "What is that song you're singing?" The guys told him it was called "I'm So Happy." They cut the song with Phil one week later at Bell Sound Studios. Eddie Brian recalls, "The group idolized Spector because he was so hep. He was a great producer, on top of the whole sound. A few weeks earlier he asked us to listen to a tape he had made. It was 'Pretty Little Angel Eyes' [by Curtis Lee, which later went to number seven nationally], and we knew half way through the tape it would be a monster hit. There and then the group became Phil Spector fans."

The sound of "I'm So Happy" was pure pandemonium. Louis Biscardi sang the lead entirely in falsetto. The record's pace was frantic. Hand claps, piano glisses, and uninhibited sax solos abounded, and the guitar of Jimi Hendrix (*that* Jimi Hendrix) filled all the spaces. The group sang its way through two minutes and 36 seconds of the best rock doo wop 1961 had heard, and to top it all off, Spector brought in Duane Eddy's 300-plus-pound "shouter" to let out two wailing "yeeaas" in the instrumental section that were guaranteed to send any teen's parents heading for the safety of a padded cell.

Even in 1961 Spector had little patience with B sides, and "Little Did I Know" was done in only two takes, cracked notes and all, along with "Yes I Love You" (which remains unreleased to this day).

Spector must have enjoyed the Ducanes experience and liked the music since he recorded other doo wop oldies in 1961 including "When You Dance," "Dear One," "Honey Love," and "A Kiss from Your Lips," all by Billy Storm and the Valiants on Atlantic. Even his later classics by THE RONETTES, THE CRYSTALS, and the Righteous Brothers were heavily laced with harmonic oohs and ahs, a touch that almost certainly came from his days of doo wopping with the Ducanes.

In a contrast of worlds, while Phil was making his arrangements to license the recordings to George Goldner's Goldisc label and was recording his first cuts with the Crystals, the Ducanes were performing at their senior prom. As a matter of fact, Eddie Brian's date that evening was friend Linda Scott (Linda Joy Sampson), who a month before had scored a top three national hit with "I've Told Every Little Star." She sang "He's Gone" (THE CHANTELS) and "Please Say You Want Me" (the Schoolboys) backed by the Ducanes in an impromptu performance that was the highlight of the prom.

In short order "I'm So Happy" was on the airwaves in many parts of the country. All three of New York's top stations went on it (WABC, WMCA, and WINS) although Murray the K (WINS) originally went on the flip "Little Did I Know." By July 17th "Happy" was on *Billboard*'s national Bubbling Under listings. It spent three weeks on the charts and peaked at number 109.

The East Coast airplay gave the Ducanes an opportunity to perform with THE EARLS, THE CAPRIS, Chubby Checker, THE JIVE FIVE, and THE DREAMLOVERS. On one such show emceed by Murray the K and Clay Cole at the Teaneck, New Jersey, Armory, the quintet performed with Dion, Bobby Lewis, and THE CLEFTONES.

After a few months of popularity the boys wanted to get back in the studio. Spector was now splitting his time between his own secret projects (like the Crystals for his yet-undisclosed Philles label) and working in A&R for Liberty Records. Liberty gave Phil an appalling country song for the group entitled "Tennessee," that elicited their best barnyard imitations. Trouble was, the head of Liberty walked into the studio just when this irreverent response was being bestowed upon his planned future hit. The group was unceremoniously tossed from the studio, and even Spector couldn't help them (although it's questionable whether he really had any further interest in the group since he was preparing to jump Liberty and put all his time into Philles).

The Ducanes had no idea what to do next, so they did nothing. As a result of that inaction the group of 16-year-olds never recorded again. But it turned out they were right about "Tennessee." It was later recorded twice (by the Todds and Jan and Dean) and it flopped both times.

In 1991 Louis Biscardi was living in Las Vegas and had reportedly been a studio musician. Rich Scrofan was in construction and Jeff Breny was with United Parcel Service in Tenafly, New Jersey. Dennis Buckley was an executive with Metropolitan Life Insurance in Westbury. Eddie Brian sang with the Connotations and the Autumns on Bab Records in the mid-'80s and was still performing as of 1991.

Back in 1961 Phil Spector had two more hits, "I Love How You Love Me" by THE PARIS SISTERS and, more importantly to Phil, a top 20 hit with the first Philles release "There's No Other (Like My Baby)" by the Crystals. His star was just beginning to rise, while the Ducanes had only memories—but *what* memories.

The Duprees

If Glenn Miller and his Orchestra were backing acts like THE HILLTOPPERS or THE FOUR PREPS in the early '60s on song standards, the results probably would have sounded like the Duprees. This teen quintet from Jersey City, New Jersey, made every ballad sound like an old standard.

In 1956, 16-year-old Tommy Bialoglow and 13-year-old Joey Canzano formed a group with three black teens that evolved into the Utopians with Joey (lead), Tom (tenor), Jackie Smith (tenor), and Brian Moran (bass). By 1959 Joey and Tom had formed the Parisiennes with three members of another vocal group, Joe Santollo (16, tenor), John Salvato (19, tenor), and Mike Arnone (16, baritone). Canzano

was soon going by the name of Joey Vann, and the Parisiennes were becoming proficient at performing standard ballads.

The group recorded a demo tape that included "My Own True Love" and "As Time Goes By," and in 1962 it was sent to Coed Records. Coed's owners, Marvin Cane and George Paxton, liked their harmonies and signed the group. Coed had turned out hits with THE CRESTS and THE RIVIERAS in the late '50s, and their success with groups was well-known. Cane and Paxton weren't interested in changing this group's musical direction, but they did want the boys to change their name. Trying to keep a French sound, they named themselves after an old black singer named Dupree.

Their first single was "You Belong to Me," a warm-sounding version of the Jo Stafford hit from 1952. With its Glenn Miller-styled orchestration it soon breached the Pop charts, hitting number seven the week of September 22nd.

One of Joey Canzano's finest performances was on their second single, "My Own True Love" (Tara's theme from *Gone with the Wind*) in which his voice rivaled that of Jimmy Beaumont of THE SKYLINERS. "True Love" made it to number 13 in the holiday season of 1962.

The Duprees generated mediocre chart action until Coed had them record another 1952 gem, the Jonie James number one hit "Why Don't You Believe Me." It reached number 37, prompting them to dip in to Jonie James's repertoire yet again. They reworked her 1953 number four hit "Have You Heard." It got them back on track at number 18 around Christmastime 1963 and was their last top 20 single. The group became a quartet following Tommy's departure in November.

By mid-1965 the Duprees had moved to Columbia Records and totally changed their style thanks to an Artie Ripp-produced tune titled "Around the Corner." Sounding now like JAY AND THE AMERICANS, the Duprees rode "Around the Corner" (a cross between THE DRIFTERS' "On Broadway" and the Americans' "Come a Little Bit Closer") to number 91 in the summer of 1965.

The group also sounded different because Joey Vann had left before they signed to Columbia and had been replaced by Mike Kelly. (Joey, meanwhile, recorded one solo single called "My Love, My Love," which ironically was Coed's last release before closing down in 1965.) The group recorded four more singles for Columbia through the spring of 1967 but none charted. The best of these were two Jay and the Americans-styled songs, the uptempo "She Waits for Him" and an interesting ballad of "The Exodus Song."

In 1968 they signed with Heritage for four singles that placed them somewhere between their old and new sound.

By 1970 music had changed so much they thought a new name might give them a fresh start and a chance to change musical directions. Deciding to drop their French name and emphasize their national origin, they renamed themselves the Italian Asphalt and Pavement Company. Their single "Check Yourself" got enough sporadic East Coast play to reach number 97 Pop before disappearing.

In 1980 Joey Vann returned to the music world as lead of a new vocal band, Vintage, recording a Duprees medley titled "Joey Vann Medley" under his own name on Chubby Records in the summer of 1982.

Joe Santollo died in 1981 of a heart attack at the age of 38. Joey Vann and his gifted voice were stilled on February 28, 1984, at the age of 41.

As of 1989 the Duprees were still performing in the New York, New Jersey, and Connecticut area.

THE DUPREES

A SIDE/B SIDE	LABEL/CAT NO	DATE
You Belong To Me /		
Take Me As I Am	Coed 569	7/62
My Own True Love / Ginny	Coed 571	9/62
I'd Rather Be Here In Your Arms /		
I Wish I Could Believe You	Coed 574	12/62
Gone With The Wind /		
Let's Make Love Again	Coed 576	2/63
Take Me As I Am /		
I Gotta Tell Her Now	Coed 580	1963
Why Don't You Believe Me /		
The Things I Love	Coed 584	1963
Why Don't You Believe Me /		
My Dearest One	Coed 584	1963
Have You Heard / Love Eyes	Coed 585	1963
It's No Sin /		
The Sand And The Sea	Coed 587	1963
Where Are You /		
Please Let Her Know	Coed 591	1964
So Many Have Told Me /		
Unbelievable	Coed 593	1964
It Isn't Fair / So Little Time	Coed 595	1964
I'm Yours / Wishing Ring	Coed 596	1965
Around The Corner /		
They Said It Couldn't Be Done	Col 43336	6/65
She Waits For Him / Norma Jean	Col 43464	11/65
The Exodus Song / Let Them Talk	Col 43577	3/66
It's Not Time Now /		
Didn't Want To Have To Do It	Col 43802	9/66
I Understand / Be My Love	Col 44078	4/67
My Special Angel / Ring Of Love	Hrtg 804	8/68
Goodnight My Love / Ring Of Love	Hrtg 805	8/68
My Love, My Love /		
The Sky's The Limit	Hrtg 808	10/68

A SIDE/B SIDE	LABEL/CAT NO	DATE
Two Different Worlds / Hope	Hrtg 811	12/68
Have You Heard / Have You Heard	Hrtg 826	3/69
Check Yourself	Colo 110	4/70
Delicious / The Sky's The Limit	RCA 10407	1975
Have You Heard /		
Around The Corner	Shwbt 100	1983
The Christmas Song /		
It's Christmas Once Again	1stCh FCA	1989

The Earls

A truly innovative vocal group, the Earls interpreted rhythm and blues ballads in their own white rock and roll style, much the same way the Beatles interpreted Chuck Berry. The Earls of the Bronx, New York, were formed thanks to a young Philadelphian named Larry Figueiredo. In the mid-'50s Larry attended high school in South Philadelphia with such household names as Ernest Evans, Danny Rapp, and Frankie Avaloni. Not impressed? Ernest became Chubby Checker, Danny was the lead of Danny and the Juniors, and Mr. Avaloni changed his last name to Avalon.

Larry's first group was the Coronas, named after the cigar, but they were strictly for fun and for learning. When Larry finished high school his family moved to the Bronx and in 1957 he started singing with a few guys he met at the Tecumsa Social Club. They called themselves the High Hatters, complete with canes and hats for dramatic effect. Though influenced early on by Philadelphia neighbors THE TURBANS and the Treniers, Larry led the High Hatters (Bob Del Din on first tenor, Eddie Harder on second tenor, Larry Palumbo on baritone, and John Wray on bass) in a style that was his own interpretation of street vocalizing.

Many Earls fans have for years been under the impression that Larry Palumbo died during a parachute jump in the army (which he joined in 1959). But in 1977 Larry Figueiredo stated that Larry died of a blood clot that developed due to jumping. He died in 1960 after a two-month-long coma.

The remaining High Hatters went on singing from corner to corner. It was at a subway station entrance in the fall of 1959 that would-be producer Johnny Powers first heard the High Hatters. He brought them into A-1 Studios on their own money. The group's backup "band" consisted of Powers' partner in their miniscule Rome label, Trade Martin, who played drums, bass, piano, and guitar. The session cost under a hundred dollars and produced four sides, "Looking for My Baby," "Cross My Heart," "It's You," and "Life Is But a Dream."

It was time for a new name so Larry opened a dictionary to the letter E and found Earl.

The newly christened Earls had to wait more than a year for their first release. Rome Records had no distribution until it hooked up with Bill Buchanan's (he of Buchanan and Goodman's Flying Saucer Records) Trio-Dex operation in 1961.

The first 45 was "Life Is But a Dream" (THE HARPTONES, 1955) done with a raucous swirl of harmonies and rhythms backing up Larry's exuberant lead. The Earls unknowingly became the forerunners of white doo wop groups who took standards done by rhythm and blues balladeers and brought them to the attention of a new generation. Acts like THE CONCORDS doing "Again" (the Universals), THE ACCENTS on "Rags to Riches" (Jackie Wilson and THE DOMINOES), and the Magnificent Four covering "The Closer You Are" (THE CHANNELS) all followed the Earls in 1961.

An immediate airplay favorite, "Life Is But a Dream" became a top 10 hit in New York, although it only reached number 107 on *Billboard*'s Bubbling Under chart in June. This led to a week with Murray the K at the Brooklyn Fox and an appearance on Dick Clark's "American Bandstand."

Their second single was another rockin' cover, this time of an unknown recording by Tony Marra and the Du-Wells on the Du Well label titled "Looking for My Baby" (1960), done in a mere 22 takes. The stuttering bass intro and Larry's vocal made this rocker a teen pleaser. Unfortunately, Rome was not able to do the marketing job and "Looking" looked in vain for sales.

In between their second and third Rome releases, Trio-Dex borrowed the Earls for backup work on "Jimmy Love" by Cathy Carroll and "Teenage Tears" by James MacArthur (later to do a better job on TV's "Hawaii Five-O" than he did as a singer).

In 1962 producer Stan Vincent, who had heard "Looking," joined forces with the quintet and started reworking a song that had already been reworked numerous times called "Remember When." Vincent did some work on it until it became "Remember Then" and took the Earls' recording to every major label. Everyone passed. Next, he tried the indy labels and Hy Weiss, honcho of Old Town Records. Weiss saw "Remember Then" for what it was, a hit record, and released it to a spectacular radio reception. From its catchy "Re-mem-mem, re-mem-ma-member" bass part to Larry's driving lead, the song proved to be a high-energy doo wop winner. It climbed to number 24 on the charts by early 1963.

Their second Old Town 45 rang in the new year and was surveyed as a "Spotlight Pick" in *Billboard* on February 23rd. The reviewer commented, "The Earls just coming off their hit 'Remember Then' should do it again with this zingy little rocker that shows off some bright harmony and stylish vocalizing. Sock teen wax." The zingy little rocker "Never," penned by Larry and Bobby along with Stan Vincent, made it to the top five in New York and top 50 in one national trade, though it only "bubbled under" at number 119 in *Billboard*'s March issues.

The spring 1963 "Eyes," written by Vic Thomas and Stan Vincent, was another top-notch recording. It became their last chart single (#123 in July) even though it was being played from Massachusetts to Alabama. The group did seven more singles for Old Town through 1965, the best being a stunning vocal rendition of the Jane Froman (#11, 1953) and Frankie Laine (#2, 1953) ballad standard "I Believe." Figueiredo wrote the stirring lyrical intro and bridge that helped make this demonstration record—flaws and all—an East Coast classic. (The Earls had not expected the demo to be released as a finished master.) The song continued to be an emotional high point of the group's live performances for almost 30 years.

The record "Kissin'," released just before "I Believe," had Larry featured on the label for the first time. Hy Weiss wanted him to step out front, and though Figueiredo was reluctant, Weiss and his super salesmanship convinced him to take a chance when he said, "I'm gonna call you Larry Chance." He went on to release a Larry Chance single ("Let Them Talk") on his Barry affiliate in 1964.

The group continued to perform while making changes and adapting. Wray and Del Din left, replaced by Bob Moricco and Ronnie Calabrese (Ronnie was the group's original drummer). The Earls also became self-contained by playing their own instruments, which helped them stay active while other singers-only units were dispersing. Meanwhile Stan Vincent liked the Earls' sound so much he formed two other groups (the Crowns and the Barons) and recorded his Earls-like originals with them. The Barons did "Remember Rita" on Epic in 1964 and the Crowns (who really sounded like Larry and company) did "Possibility" on Old Town, also in 1964. Larry repeatedly stated he had not recorded with either.

In 1967 the Earls surfaced on Mr. G Records (an Audio Fidelity affiliate) with "If I Could Do It Over Again." When the public didn't get much of a chance to hear it on radio, the group moved over to ABC for one release called "It's Been a Long Time Coming." The recording became a royal affair when two guest artists, Clarence Collins and Kenny Seymour of THE IMPERIALS, joined the Earls on vocals.

The quickly changing music scene of the late '60s forced the group to reassess its recording plans. When they emerged in 1973 they were a nine-piece band called Smokestack. One single on Daisy convinced the group to return to their roots and by 1975 they had redone "Sunday Kind of Love" for the small Harvey label, owned by Harvey Mandel.

In 1976 three previously unreleased Rome records and a new 10-inch dance single, "Get Up and Dance the Continental" (Woodbury), were issued. An album on Woodbury (really Hy Weiss in disguise) surfaced in 1977 with additional cuts added to an LP called *Remember Me Baby* that had first come out in 1965 on Old Town.

Their best single since the Old Town days hit the airwaves in 1977, a very effective remake of the Velvets' 1961 hit "Tonight."

By 1983 the Earls were Larry, Ronny Calabrese, Colon Rello (first tenor), Bobby Tribuzio (tenor), and Butch Barbella (baritone). They recorded the LP *Larry Chance and the Earls—Today* in 1983, redoing a number of their '60s songs. Among the new oldies was a take-off of "In the Still of the Night." The writer credit went to Geraldo Santana Banana, a fictional radio station manager who regularly appeared on WNBC in New York. Geraldo was none other than Larry Chance, diversifying his career.

THE EARLS

A SIDE/B SIDE	LABEL/CAT NO	DATE
Life Is But A Dream / It's You	Rome 101	4 /61
Life Is But A Dream / Without You	Rome 101	5/61
Looking For My Baby / Cross My Heart	Rome 102	9/61
My Heart's Desire / Sunday Kind Of Love	Rome 5117	1962
My Heart's Desire / I'll Never Cry	Rome 5117	3/62
Remember Then / Let's Waddle	OldTn 1130	11/62
Never / I Keep Tellin' You	OldTn 1133	1/63
Eyes / Look My Way	OldTn 1141	5/63
Kissin' / Cry Cry Cry	OldTn 1145	1963
I Believe / Don't Forget	OldTn 1149	1963
Oh What A Time / Ask Anybody	OldTn 1169	1964
Remember Me Baby / Amor	OldTn 1182	1965
If I Could Do It Over Again / Papa	Mr. G 801	1967

A SIDE/B SIDE	LABEL/CAT NO	DATE
It's Been A Long Time Coming / My Lonely Room	ABC 11109	1968
Wall Between Us / Take A Look (Smokestack)	Daisy 1010	1973
Wall Between Us / Take A Look (Smokestack)	Dakar 4503	1973
Sunday Kind Of Love / Teenager's Dream	Harvey 100	1975
Goin' Uptown / Mrs. Women	Columbia 10225	1976
Get Up And Dance The Continental / Love Epidemic	Woodbury 1000	1976
Stormy Weather	Rome 111	5/76
Little Boy and Girl / Lost Love	Rome 112	6/76
All Through Our Teens / Whoever You Are	Rome 114	6/76
Tonight / Meditation	Woodbury 101	1977
Daddy's Home / If I Could Do It Once Again	Bo-P-C 100	1978

The Echoes

A pop trio that made the most of listening to their teachers, the Echoes were a Brooklyn group hunting for a hit in 1960.

Meanwhile, miles away, Long Island High School assistant principal Val Lageux and music teacher Sam Guilino were analyzing current pop music trends and concluding that what the teen world needed was a misspelled love song titled "Baby Blue." They just happened to have such a song, complete with "B-b-a-b-y B-b-l-u-e" as the opening line.

The duo of educators gave their new creation to one Johnny Powers of a local group called the Jokers, but he gave the song a failing grade and opted instead for his own "Do-Re-Mi Rock," which the Jokers recorded for Harvard Records. Johnny then passed "Baby Blue" to Brooklyn friend Tommy Duffy of the Laurels. The members of the trio included Duffy on lead, with Harry Doyle and Tommy Morrissey. His group sound was just right for the song, so the Laurels made an a cappella demo of it and took it to Jack Gold of Paris Records. Not wanting to spend the money for a complete rerecording, Jack sped up the tape and added some instrumentation, particularly a "Hush-a-Bye" (THE MYSTICS) styled guitar intro.

Meanwhile the group renamed themselves the Echoes. Jack Gold then set up his own SRG Label (named after Steven Richard Gold, his son), and early response encouraged him to move the record to a more established indy, Seg-Way Records.

In February 1961 Seg-Way issued "Baby Blue," and on March 6th two school teachers and three Brooklyn teens found themselves in *Billboard*'s Top 100. By the spring the Echoes had the number 12 record in the country.

Their second release was tailor-made for Murray the K airplay. The opening lines were sung in "Mia Suri" talk, a language Murray invented for kids so they could talk to each other without parents knowing what they were saying. The title was "Sad Eyes (Don't You Cry)." It was another New York hit but only reached number 88 nationally.

The Echoes' last Seg-Way single was a FLEETWOODS-styled rhythm ballad called "Gee Oh Gee." When it couldn't pass the competition tests the group moved to Smash Records for three unnoticed 45s between 1962 and 1963.

During the '70s Tom and Harry formed a group called Red Hook and Tommy Duffy continued on, leading a new Echoes through their paces.

There is no truth to the rumor that teachers Guilino and Lageux went on to teach Madonna how to sing.

THE ECHOES

A SIDE/B SIDE	LABEL/CAT NO	DATE
Baby Blue / Boomerang	SRG 101	1/61
Baby Blue / Boomerang	Seg-Way 103	2/61
Sad Eyes / It's Rainin'	Seg-Way 106	6/61
Gee Oh Gee / Angel Of My Heart	Seg-Way 1002	1961
Bluebirds Over The Mountain / A Chicken Ain't Nothin But A Bird	Smash 1766	7/62
A Million Miles From Nowhere / Keep An Eye On Her	Smash 1807	6/63
Annabelle Lee / If Love Is	Smash 1850	11/63

The Emotions

The Emotions were a white doo wop group from Brooklyn who got their start at a party in late 1959. That's when they met songwriter Henry Boye ("Call Off the Wedding," Sunny Gale, 1954) who encouraged them to practice.

The quintet consisted of members Joe Favale (lead), Tony Maltese (first tenor), Larry Cusimano (second tenor), Joe Nigro (baritone), and Dom Collura (bass). Henry Boye decided to get more involved and started writing songs with Joe. Through a friend of Henry's at Beechwood Music Publishing, a real estate mogul was convinced to put up the money to start a record company with the boys

as their first act. The label became PIO after the gentleman's initials, and the group named themselves the Runarounds.

They rehearsed at a beauty parlor on Nostrand Avenue until they had their new songs, "Nearest Thing to Heaven" and "Lover's Lane," ready to record. In August 1961 the record came out and died. Later that year they changed their name to the Emotions since they felt they sang with a lot of feeling. They cut a few new songs in 1962 and played them for every label they could find until Kapp Records, known mostly for pop instrumentalist Roger Williams (originally Louis Wertz of Omaha, Nebraska) signed them.

In September 1962 they released "Echo," their chime harmony ode to car crashes similar in theme to Mark Dinning's "Teen Angel" (1959) and Ray Peterson's "Tell Laura I Love Her" (1960). It immediately hit airwaves across the nation. New York's Murray the K made it a co-pick hit of the week (with THE FOUR SEASONS' "Big Girls Don't Cry") when the Emotions, their friends, and their relatives "stuffed the ballot box" by flooding the station with phone calls.

It rose to number 76 in December of that year, but Kapp was unfamiliar with promoting that kind of record and lost it after it had sold over 250,000 copies in New York. Kapp then signed Ruby and the Romantics, and when Ruby's "Our Day Will Come" charted on February 9, 1963, the Emotions' new single, "A Million Reasons," was ignored.

The Italian quintet went through one change when Tony Maltese left to get married and was replaced by Sal Covais (the Hytones on Fonsca, 1961).

The Emotions signed for a one-shot with Gene and Bob Schwartz's Laurie Records, creating a light rocker in a CRESTS/MYSTICS/PASSIONS style called "Starlit Night." When that failed they moved again, this time to 20th Century Fox to redo THE NUTMEGS' classic "Story Untold" (#2 R&B, 1955) in an up-tempo Four Seasons style. The record became popular in New York during the summer of 1963 but created little interest elsewhere. After a few more singles for 20th, Karate, and Calla with minimal radio response, the group decided to call it quits in 1970.

As sometimes happens when fans turn into patrons, the year 1981 rolled around and Marty Pekar, a former Brooklyn kid who used to stand at a certain beauty shop and marvel at the harmonies of a group called the Runarounds, became president of the rock and roll label Ambient Sound, distributed by the giant Columbia Records. What was different about Marty's label was the fact that he wanted to sign only '50s and '60s acts recording mostly new songs (a practice picked up and continued in the '80s and '90s on the West Coast by Bruce Patch and Classic Artists Records).

Marty contacted Joe Favale, who was now working for Blue Cross. Joe and Tony jumped at the chance but the others weren't interested, so a new group was formed with some of Joe's coworkers who used to sing in the men's room at Blue Cross. For what might have been legal reasons the group could not use the name the Emotions, so they craftily came up with an alternative . . . the Blue Emotions.

In 1982, Joe, Tony, Joe Cavanna, Eddy Balen, and John Van Soest recorded their first and only LP titled *Doo-Wop All Night Long*.

THE EMOTIONS

A SIDE/B SIDE	LABEL/CAT NO	DATE
The Nearest Thing To Heaven /		
Lover's Lane	PIO 107	8/61
Echo / Come Dance Baby	Kapp 490	9/62
Love / A Million Reasons	Kapp 513	1/63
Starlit Night / Fool's Paradise	Laurie 3167	3/63
A Story Untold /		
One Life, One Love, One You	20th 430	1963
Little Miss Blue / Rainbow	20th 452	1963
Boomerang / I Love You Madly	20th 478	1964
Heartstrings / Everytime	20th 623	1964
Hey Baby / I Wonder	Karate 506	1964
Baby I Need Your Loving /		
She's My Baby	Calla 122	1965
Are You Real /		
You're A Better Man Than I	Johnson 746	1970
Color My World /		
You're A Better Man Than I	SPrk 1000	1970
Sincerely / Sincerely	Ambient Sound	1982

The Escorts

They were an early '60s white vocal group that produced a doctor, lawyer, a famous producer, and a nearly famous female rock singer.

Originally called the Legends, a trio of Richards from Brooklyn's Poly Prep High School—Richard Berg (tenor), Richard Rosenberg (baritone), and Richard Perry (bass)—joined together in 1961. They each played instruments and worked the local bar mitzvah circuit. A schoolmate liked their sound and arranged to get them an audition with Decca Records, where his dad was an executive. Thinking they needed more vocal muscle, the

Legends brought in Rodney Garrison, who worked in Perry's dad's musical instrument business, as lead singer. In Perry's basement they practiced songs by such influences as THE HEARTBEATS and VITO AND THE SALUTATIONS. It was a Salutations song, a doo wop ballad called "Gloria," that they picked for their Decca audition. To spice it up they did an up-tempo interpretation with a rambling bass intro à la THE MARCELS' "Blue Moon." The formula worked, and Decca signed them to their Coral affiliate. By now, they had become the Escorts, though Richard Perry said it was decided on at an uninspired moment. They always wanted to change it but never did. For a flip, they recorded a song suggested by a record collecting friend, "Seven Wonders of the World" (the Keytones, Old town, 1957). Both songs were recorded at Decca's West 57th Street studios on January 2, 1962.

"Gloria" came out soon after and was well-represented on radio but didn't sell at the time, though it did well years later as an oldie.

Their second 45, "Gaudeamus," was another Marcels-styled up-tempo reworking, this time of the traditional graduation march. It's probably the only rock and roll record sung in Latin, which didn't help its sales.

The Escorts' first big gig was at Trudy Heller's on 6th Avenue and 9th Street in New York City in July 1962. They also performed at the Lollipop Lounge on Coney Island Avenue in Brooklyn. It was there that Perry met a vivacious would-be vocalist named Goldie Zelkowitz. Since female-fronted male groups were popular at the time (CATHY JEAN AND THE ROOMMATES, Cathy Young and the Innocents, for example), Goldie moved into the Escorts and Rodney Garrison moved out. With their new lead the group released two topical sides in the fall of 1962, "Somewhere" from the current Broadway hit *West Side Story* and "Submarine Race Watching," WINS deejay Murray the K's favorite pastime for his listeners, which was a thing you did as an excuse to do some "making out" with your girlfriend. "Somewhere" reached number one in Detroit, and the group did a Thanksgiving show with Chuck Jackson and THE FOUR SEASONS in the Motor City. Other than in Detroit, the activity of "Somewhere" was minimal.

By the fall the boys were off to college and Coral issued their fourth single, another song from *West Side Story*, "One Hand, One Heart." The labels now read "The Escorts Featuring 'Goldie.'" When "One Hand" won Murray the K's "Record of the Week" honors, Murray contacted Goldie about having the group do his Easter show. Since the boys were at school she rejected the offer. When the boys found out, a dispute arose that had Goldie going her own way. The group then replaced Goldie with singer/writer Bobby Lance, and he sang lead on their last two Coral issues.

Goldie, meanwhile, formed the all-girl group Goldie and the Gingerbreads (Atco, 1965) for two unsuccessful singles. She went on to put together the rock band Ten Wheel Drive ("Morning Much Better," #74, Polydor, 1970) and became well-known in the recording community as one of rock's first female record producers (in 1980 she recorded Ronnie Spector for her own Polish label) and as a rock vocalist under the name of Genya Ravan.

The Escorts ended it in 1963 to pursue their educations. Richard Rosenberg became a doctor (on Long Island). Richard Berg became an attorney (in Westchester). Richard Perry went into record production and over 20-plus years produced hits for such superstars as Barbra Streisand, Carly Simon, the Pointer Sisters, Ringo Starr, and countless more. In 1989 he returned to his roots to produce an LP titled *Rock, Rhythm and Blues* with current stars recording hit oldies. Some of the highlights of that LP were THE MANHATTAN TRANSFER's "I Wanna Be Your Girl" (THE TEENAGERS), Rick James's "This Magic Moment"/"Dance with Me" medley (THE DRIFTERS), and Michael McDonald's "For Your Precious Love" (THE IMPRESSIONS). As for Rodney Garrison, the original lead, it's only known that he became a laborer.

THE ESCORTS

A SIDE/B SIDE	LABEL/CAT NO	DATE
Gloria / Seven Wonders Of The World	Coral 62302	1962
Gaudeamus / As I Love You	Coral 62317	1962
Submarine Race Watching / Somewhere	Coral 62336	1962
One Hand, One Heart / I Can't Be Free	Coral 62349	1962
Back Home Again / Something Has Changed Him	Coral 62372	1963
My Heart Cries For You / Give Me Tomorrow	Coral 62385	1963

The Essex

The Essex started out as a duo entertaining their fellow marines in Okinawa in 1961. Rodney Taylor (19) from Gary, Indiana, and Walter Vickers (19) from New Brunswick, New Jersey, decided to make the duo a quartet when they were shipped stateside to Camp Lejune in North Carolina. They added Billie Hill (19) from Princeton, New Jersey, and Rudolph Johnson (19) from New York City and were practicing rhythm and blues tunes with a touch of jazz when they met 20-year-old Anita Humes, also a marine who was singing at the base's non-commissioned officers (NCO) club. Anita, a native of Harrisburg, Pennsylvania, had a crystal-clear voice that the boys felt really complemented their sound, so they convinced her to join.

Performing both on and off the base for experience, the quintet finally made a demonstration tape of some ballads and sent it to Roulette Records in New York. Roulette replied that they were interested enough to set up a live audition and would like to hear more up-tempo originals from the group. Walter then asked a fellow marine who professed to be a songwriter if he would come up with something. That marine, one William Linton from the post's communications department, began creating a song with a cowriter named Larry Huff. The song they composed was probably the only song in rock history to be written to the rhythm of a teletype machine, which was what Linton spent his time working on each day.

When in 1963 the entire group was finally able to go on leave together, they went to New York to audition at Roulette. As it happened, they did not perform Linton and Huff's song. Roulette liked the girl/guy combination and put them in the studio with Henry Glover and George Goldner to see what they could come up with. The Essex agreed to put the "teletype song" on the flip side of a Rudolph Johnson original titled "Are You Going My Way?" They had to edit and splice Linton and Huff's recording in order to make it long enough for its eventual two-minute-and-eight-second use.

The single came out in May 1963, but the disc jockeys' consensus was to play the flip, "Easier Said than Done." On June 8th that same flip charted and by July 6th it was number one in the nation.

Performances became a problem because the group always needed special permission for a leave to appear anywhere, and when they did go out it was usually in uniform. One show in Connecticut during 1964 had the Essex and Linda Scott on the bill. When Anita came down with a sore throat Linda subbed for her on the Essex songs.

Roulette followed the hit with "A Walking Miracle," and it went to number 12 in the late summer of 1963. Despite these two hits the first Essex LP only rose to number 119. Their third single reached number 56 in the winter of late 1963 ("She's Got

Everything") and their next Roulette single, "Curfew Lover," didn't chart at all. One more issue in 1966 on Bang and the group faded into history.

THE ESSEX

A SIDE/B SIDE	LABEL/CAT NO	DATE
Easier Said Than Done / Are You Going My Way	Roul 4494	5/63
A Walking Miracle / What I Don't Know Won't Hurt Me	Roul 4515	8/63
She's Got Everything / Out Of Sight, Out Of Mind	Roul 4530	10/63
Curfew Lover* / What Did I Do*	Roul 4542	1964
The Eagle / Moonlight, Music And You	Bang 537	1966
Are You Going My Way* / Everybody's Got You*	Roul 4750	1967

* Anita Humes and the Essex

The Excellents

The Excellents *were*. Excellent, that is. But it didn't keep their career going when their label pulled a fast one and left them in the cold.

The Bronx, New York, group started out as the Premiers in 1960 and evolved into the Excellents, practicing at the Bronx Park Community Center in Pelham Bay Park. One of the few white sextets, the members were John Kuse (17, lead), Denis Kestenbaum (14, falsetto), George Kuse (15, first tenor and John's brother), Phil Sanchez (17, second tenor), Joel Feldman (15, baritone), and Chuck Epstein (15, bass).

All were students at Christopher Columbus High School except for Chuck, who attended Dewitt Clinton. So many people commented on their excellent sound that they decided to bestow the compliment on themselves via their name.

The Bronx was an active place for vocal groups in the early '60s, and new acts like the Excellents were greatly encouraged by more established groups like THE BELMONTS, THE DEMENSIONS, NINO AND THE EBB TIDES, and THE REGENTS, whose lead singer Guy Villari at one time worked at Western Union with John Kuse. Though not directly influenced by any one group the boys did like THE CHANNELS, THE CLEFTONES, THE JESTERS, and THE PARAGONS as well as the sound of their white group neighbors.

In late 1960 John began approaching numerous record companies in New York City with a demo tape. He finally received some interest from Sinclair Records' Vinny Catalano, who liked their vocal blend and their rockin' version of the Al Jolson 1926 number one standard, "When the Red, Red Robin Comes Bob, Bob Bobbin' Along."

Their first session, in January 1961, included an up-tempo a cappella version of "Sunday Kind of Love" (THE HARPTONES) and an original, "Helene (Your Wish Came True)," but neither was released at that time. "Helene" was unusual in that it began a cappella and the band entered halfway through, as if they showed up late. Actually the band had rhythm trouble and so parts of their track were removed.

During the summer "Red Red Robin" and the Jesters' 1957 classic "Love No One But You" were cut and issued on Mermaid Records. Some local airplay resulted and the group went back to record two more sides, the Cleftones' "You, Baby You" and a Catalano original "Coney Island Baby," that was inspired by Lili Loftus, a hostess at Astro Land in Coney Island.

The Excellents did a breakneck-speed interpretation of "You" with prominent harmonies. Released in 1961 on Catalano's own Blast label, the rocker went nowhere. In April 1962 it was released again, and *Billboard*'s May 26th reviewer described it as "an old style rocker, complete with bomp bomp and high voice gimmicks in the background all set to a good swinging rhythm. Side is said to be getting action already in certain markets." For "Coney Island Baby" the reviewer waxed enthusiastically, "This is not the old barbershop standard, but a new dramatic vehicle for a belting shouting lead. Side also employs the familiar high and low gimmick sounds. Watch this one."

Released at the same time as TICO AND THE TRIUMPHS' "Express Train," THE BOB KNIGHT FOUR's "Memories," and THE ORLONS' "Wah-Watusi," "You, Baby You" started to get airplay attention but soon died off. Instead, New York disc jockeys began playing "Coney Island Baby" in conjunction with bathing suit contests at the famous amusement park.

Then in the fall of 1962 "Coney Island Baby" started getting unpromoted national airplay. The love song gathered momentum and on November 24th hit *Billboard*'s Hot 100, rising to number 51 nationally. The group was flying high, doing shows with disc jockey Bruce Morrow and at Palisades Amusement Park in New Jersey. Their first big gig was at Palisades with VITO AND THE SALUTATIONS, THE DEL-SATINS, Clay Cole, and Freddie Cannon (whose current hit was coincidentally titled "Palisades Park" [#3, 1962]).

During the record's peak, the Excellents were supposed to go to Philadelphia to appear on Dick Clark's "American Bandstand." They were expected to take care of their own financial arrangements, which would have been fine except that they *had* no finances. When they complained, they were quietly but quickly replaced by a bogus Excellents, who also recorded the last single to come out under their name in early 1963, "I Hear a Rhapsody" (Blast).

Needless to say, this put a damper on their spirits and career.

In March 1964 that half a cappella, half accompanied recording of "Helene" came out on Bobby Records under the name the Excellons. Two of the members (Joe and Chuck) had requested the Excellents name not be used since they were pursuing new recordings. Those new recordings never came, however, and although the group was still performing in the '90s they never released another Excellents record.

The most recent group was a quintet of John, Denis, Phil, Jerry Pilgrim (formerly of B.Q.E. on Starlight), and Les Levine (also of B.Q.E.). John spent some time in the '80s as lead of both the Excellents and Grand Central Echo.

Today, when not harmonizing, John is a supervisor at an investment banking firm, George is a foreman at the Department of Water Supply, Phil is a city engineer, Joel is a doctor of psychology, Chuck is a lighting consultant, and Denis is a manager in the city housing projects.

THE EXCELLENTS

A SIDE/B SIDE	LABEL/CAT NO	DATE
Red Red Robin /		
Love No One But You	Mermaid 106	1961
Coney Island Baby / You Baby You	Blast 205	4/62
The Excellons		
Helene / Sunday Kind Of Love	Bobby 601	3/64

The Exciters

The first of the vocally aggressive girl groups, the Exciters led the way for acts like THE RONETTES and THE SHANGRI-LAS. Though the trio of girls (Brenda Reid on lead, Lillian Walker, and Carol Johnson) sang with male bassman Herb Rooney, his vocal contributions were not as audible as the basses in other groups, serving more to solidify the blend. When Herb met them in the early '60s, the original group was a quartet of 17-year-olds, including Sylvia Wilbur, who were high school classmates in Queens, New York, calling themselves the Masterettes ("Follow the Leader," Lesage, 1961). Coincidentally, Herb was singing with a "brother" group called the Masters ("Lovely Way to Spend an Evening," Bingo, 1960) who did local shows with the Masterettes. (Herb had started his singing career with the Beltones on Hull Records with the New York doo wop classic, "I Talk to My Echo," in 1957.) He found the Masterettes' harmonies to be solid and felt that Brenda's powerhouse pipes made the group an exciting find.

The girls soon came to the attention of producers Jerry Leiber and Mike Stoller (THE COASTERS, THE ROBINS), who were so excited they renamed the quartet the Exciters. To round out the sound they added Herb Rooney (who was there to help out with arrangements) on bass. It went back to being a quartet when Sylvia Wilbur decided to leave.

The group signed with United Artists Records in the fall of 1962 and by December 1st had entered the *Billboard* charts with "Tell Him," eventually reaching number four Pop on January 26, 1963, and number five R&B.

Brenda's no-nonsense tough-girl vocal, the group's vocal blend, and a surefire Bert Berns composition made "Tell Him" a whole new direction in girl-group rock and roll. It also charted R&B (#5) and was number five in Australia though only #46 in the United Kingdom.

Their follow-up was even stronger. "He's Got the Power," an Ellie Greenwich song written with Tony Powers before she began working with Jeff Barry, was a driving teen rocker that opened with "Yeah, yeah, yeah" two years before the Beatles made those words their international trademark. It rose only to number 57 in the spring of 1963 but did a lot better in Australia (#15). Ellie Greenwich once stated in effect that Brenda had one of the best female voices she'd ever heard.

"Get Him," their third single, had a dynamite lyric and driving melody that were set in an overly sweet arrangement, thereby nullifying Brenda's pleading lead and relegating the Exciters to number 76 during the summer.

Their fourth U.A. single was an overlooked gem written by Greenwich and Barry (#78)—overlooked, that is, until Paul Jones of the British rockers Manfred Mann heard it, cut it, and took "Do Wah Diddy Diddy" to number one internationally in the fall of 1964, a mere eight months after the Exciters first charted with it.

When the group's next U.A. 45, the up-tempo "Havin' My Fun," failed to chart, the exciters moved over to Roulette for a remake of the FRANKIE LYMON AND THE TEENAGERS hit, "I Want You to Be My Boy." It spent one week at number 98.

Meanwhile the Exciters were performing on tours with artists like Wilson Pickett and as an opening act for the Beatles.

In early 1966 the group charted once more with a remake of the Jarmels' hit (#12, 1961) "A Little Bit of Soul" (#58).

Herb and Brenda were married in the late '60s. By the early '70s Lillian and Carol left and were replaced by Skip McPhee and Ronnie Pace. The group toured the U.S., the U.K., and Europe over the years and during the '80s shrank to a duo of Brenda and Herb ("Tonight I'm Gonna Make You a Star," #70 R&B, H&L Records, 1978).

By the mid-'80s Herb was separated from Brenda and owned a cosmetics company on Long Island. Brenda kept the Exciters going with her children on backup vocals and instruments. One son, Mark, became a famous producer for acts like Lisa Lisa, Eric B, and Rakim, going under the name of L.A. Reid.

THE EXCITERS

A SIDE/B SIDE	LABEL/CAT NO	DATE
Crying My Heart Out / I'm Searching*	Lesage 714	1961
Follow The Leader / Never, Never**	Lesage 711	1961
Tell Him / Hard Way To Go	UA 544	10/62
He's Got The Power / Drama Of Love	UA 572	2/63
Get Him / It's So Exciting	UA 604	5/63
Do Wah Diddy Diddy / If Love Came Your Way	UA 662	11/63
We Were Lovers (When The Party Begins) / Having My Fun	UA 721	1964
I Want You To Be My Boy / Tonight, Tonight	Roul R4591	12/64
Are You Satisfied / Just Not Ready	Roul R4594	1965
My Father / Run Mascara	Roul R4614	1965
There They Go / I Knew You Would	Roul R4632	1965
A Little Bit Of Soap / I'm Gonna Get Him Someday	Bang B515	1966
You Better Come Home / Weddings Make Me Cry	Bang B518	1966
Number One / You Know It Ain't Right	Shout 205	10/66
Soul Motion / You Know It Ain't Right	Shout 214	5/67
If You Want My Love / Take One Step	RCA 47-9633	9/68

A SIDE/B SIDE	LABEL/CAT NO	DATE
Blowing Up My Mind / You Don't Know What You're Missing	RCA 47-9723	1/69
Learning How To Fly / Life, Love And Peace	Today 1002	1971
You Don't Know What You're Missing	Today	1972
Alone Again (Naturally)	Fargo 1400	1972
Reaching For The Best	20th 1005	1975

* The Masters
**The Masterettes

The Fiestas

The Fiestas were important as one of the early soul groups to grow out of '50s rhythm and blues and doo wop.

Formed in Newark, New Jersey, in 1958 the quartet consisted of Tommy Bullock (lead), Eddie Morris (first tenor), Sam Ingalls (baritone), and Preston Lane (bass). An early influence on the group was THE COASTERS.

Legend has it that in 1959 the Fiestas (who apparently chose that name because they liked to have a good time) were rehearsing in a restroom at the Triboro Theatre on 125th Street in New York City. This happened to be next door to the offices of Hy and Sam Weiss of Old Town Records (which, in its early days, was a converted cloakroom). Hy heard them through the wall, went in, and signed them up to his label. Hy loves to recount how their first session cost him only $40, yet became a major hit. That hit was "So Fine," written by Jesse Belvin and recorded four years earlier by the Sheiks on Federal. (The Old Town release credited manager Jim Gribble as the writer, and a 1974 recording listed Johnny Otis.)

Sung from beginning to end without the traditional up-front lead, the soul rocker was an instant smash, making it to number 11 Pop and number three R&B. "So Fine" became one of Old Town's biggest records, but not strictly on its own merit. The doo wop flip, "Last Night I Dreamed," got the initial airplay and was selling well when jocks started flipping the 45 to see what else the Fiestas could do. The catchy pre-soul era single delighted radio and its listeners and piggybacked on the sales base of "Last Night."

Their follow-up, "Our Anniversary," was a ballad in the mid-'50s R&B vein. It couldn't match the chart performance of "So Fine." Nor could its "So Fine"-styled flip, "I'm Your Slave."

The Fiestas continued with a variety of soul-style singles ("Anna"), gospel/soul sounds ("Try It One More Time"), Sam Cooke-type "Chain Gang" songs ("The Railroad Song"), "So Fine" similes ("Fine as Wine"), and doo wop soul ("You Could Be My Girlfriend"), but to no avail. Their only other popular piece was the ISLEY BROTHERS/OLYMPICS-styled soul rocker "Broken Heart" (#81 Pop, #18 R&B, fall 1962). "Broken Heart" was a perfect example of the Fiestas' great ability to go from a soul-sounding section of a song to a strong full blow-harmony doo wop sound in the same record.

The Fiestas had 15 singles for Old Town (1959 to 1965), but never released an LP until the British company Ace Records issued an Old Town package in 1986 titled *The Oh So Fine Fiestas*. By that time Randy Stewart was part of the lineup. Randy was also the manager of Old Town girl group the Gypsies (later the Flirtations, Deram, 1969).

Tommy Bullock left the group after the Old Town days and became half of Tommy and Cleve (Cleveland Horne, later of the Fantastic Four on Rick Tick). Bullock later rejoined the relatively inactive Fiestas for a slower soul revision of "So Fine" on Vigor in 1974. Their last single was "Tina (The Disco Queen)," written by Mack Rice of the Falcons, another early soul group and issued by Chimneyville in 1977.

The number of '60s soul acts influenced by the Fiestas in general and by "So Fine" in particular is anybody's guess. But it's safe to say these early innovators left an everlasting impression on many.

THE FIESTAS

A SIDE/B SIDE	LABEL/CAT NO	DATE
Last Night I Dreamed / So Fine	OldTn 1062	3/59
Our Anniversary / I'm Your Slave	OldTn 1069	1959
Good News / That Was Me	OldTn 1074	1959
Dollar Bill / It Don't Make Sense	OldTn 1080	1960
You Could Be My Girl Friend / So Nice	OldTn 1090	1960
Mr. Dillon, Mr. Dillon / Look At That Girl	OldTn 1104	1961
She's Mine / The Hobo's Prayer	OldTn 1111	1961
Broken Heart / The Railroad Song	OldTn 1122	1962
I Feel Good All Over / Look At That Girl	OldTn 1127	1962
The Gypsy Said / Mama Put The Law Down	OldTn 1134	2/63
The Party's Over / Try It One More Time	OldTn 1140	1963
Foolish Dreamer / Rock-A-Bye Baby	OldTn 1148	1963
All That's Good / Rock-A-Bye Baby	OldTn 1166	1964
Anna / Think Smart	OldTn 1178	1965

A SIDE/B SIDE	LABEL/CAT NO	DATE
Ain't She Sweet / I Gotta Have Your Lovin'	OldTn 1189	1965
So Fine / Darling You've Changed	Vigor 712	1974
Tina (The Disco Queen) / I'm No Better Than You	Chim 10216	1977

The 5th Dimension

Whether you believe an artist launches a songwriter's career or vice versa, it's undeniable that the talented 5th Dimension had a creative formula that benefitted writers, the public, and themselves.

The group formed because of a beauty contest winner and a photographer. Lamonte McLemore was a photographer and his subject was Miss Bronze America of 1963, Marilyn McCoo. They decided to merge their gospel singing interests and form a group with fellow Los Angeles residents Harry Elston and Floyd Butler. The foursome hooked up with Ray Charles for a six-month tour but Elston and Butler left to form a separate group, the Friends of Distinction (RCA). Lamonte went back to picture-taking and Marilyn became an executive trainee at a department store.

In to the picture came Lamonte's cousin Billy Davis, Jr. from St. Louis (formerly of the Emeralds on Bobbin, 1959–60), and the seeds of a new group were planted. Lamonte and Billy brought in Ron Townson, Marilyn, and a teacher from Grant Elementary School in Hollywood named Florence LaRue. Lamonte knew Florence because she was Miss Bronze America 1962 and was the one who crowned her successor Marilyn McCoo the day Lamonte was photographing them.

The group now called themselves the Versatiles and met with producer Johnny Rivers at his Soul City label. Johnny liked the group but not what he felt was a passé name, so Ron and his wife, Babette, came up with the 5th Dimension.

The first single, in November 1966, was by Willie Hutch, and the song was "I'll Be Loving You Forever." The producers must have been Motown fans, because the song sounded like a FOUR TOPS record along the lines of "Reach Out." When that single failed, their second record was done in a black MAMAS AND PAPAS direction using a forgotten John Phillips cut called "Go Where You Wanna Go" from a Mamas and Papas LP.

Bypassing the R&B charts, "Go" went straight up the Pop listings on January 14, 1967, stopping at number 16.

Their third single, the P. F. Sloan/Steve Barri song "Another Day, Another Heartache," was back in the black Mamas and Papas groove but by now you could hear their harmonies developing into the more familiar 5th Dimension sound of later hits. "Another Day" made it to number 45 Pop, and by May the group began working on its first LP. Fate stepped in when Rivers decided to stop production to participate in the San Remo Song Festival, and young session pianist Jimmy Webb took the weekend off to attend a fair. It was there that he saw a hot-air balloon taking off, inspiring him to write "Up-Up and Away." When the group heard it their reaction was so enthusiastic that Webb wound up with that and four more songs on the LP.

"Up" was immediately cut and released, logging on to *Billboard*'s Top 100 on June 3rd and rising to number seven by July 8th. The free-and-easy big band, jazz, pop flavor of the song lifted it to standard status and made it their first million seller. It went on to win five Grammys in 1968, for Best Song of the Year, Record of the Year, Best Contemporary Group of the Year, Best Contemporary Single, and Best Performance By a Group of Two to Six.

The 5th Dimension continued to issue intricately arranged singles. Among them were "Paper Cup" (#34), and "Carpet Man" (#29), both by Jimmy Webb. They were particularly successful in 1968 with "Stoned Soul Picnic" (#3, Pop, #2 R&B) and "Sweet Blindness" (#13 Pop, #45 R&B) by New York writer Laura Nyro.

Another twist of fate provided the 5th Dimension with their biggest hit of all time. During a booking at New York's Americana Hotel in 1968 Billy lost his wallet while shopping. It turned out to have been left in a taxi, and the finder cheerfully returned it to him. Billy was grateful and invited the gentleman and his wife to a 5th Dimension performance at the hotel. The honest man turned out to be one of the producers of a hit Broadway play titled *Hair*. He reciprocated by inviting the whole group to see his play, where they heard the incredible opening number "Aquarius" and immediately resolved to record it. When producer Bones Howe heard it he felt it was only half a song and needed additional material, possibly a gospel-styled ending. Bones then traveled to New York to see the play for himself and hit upon the needed ending. It was the final section of "The Flesh Failures" ("Let the Sunshine In"), and though the group had doubts

about the coupling, Bones and former SIGNATURES vocalist (Warner Bros.) and jazz arranger extraordinaire Bob Alcivar connected the two halves, thus creating one of the most exciting records of the late '60s, "Aquarius/Let the Sunshine In."

"Aquarius" took off for its meteoric rise to number one on March 8, 1969. It spent six weeks there, selling over two million copies in less than a month. "Aquarius" also went to number 11 in the U.K. and became a worldwide best seller.

The Neil Sedaka-penned follow-up, "Working on a Groovy Thing," went to number 20, followed by the Laura Nyro winner "Wedding Bell Blues" (#1) in the fall of 1969. Wedding bells were on everyone's mind: Marilyn married Billy and manager Marc Gordon married Florence.

In 1970, the group moved over to New York City's Bell Records, which signaled a softer easy-listening style for the quintet. They alternated between Webb and Nyro songs for charters "Puppet Man" (Webb, #24) and "Save the Country" (Nyro, #27) until they hit it big again on January 2, 1971, with the ballad "One Less Bell to Answer," a Bacharach/David song (#2).

The group continued to record quality sides for Bell, including 1971's "Never My Love" (THE ASSOCIATION) which hit number 12 Pop (#45 R&B) and "(Last Night) I Didn't Get to Sleep At All" (#8 Pop, #28 R&B) in 1972.

In November of that year the 5th Dimension performed at the White House for President Nixon.

In the fall of 1975 Marilyn and Billy went out as a duet, and both they and the 5th (now with Marjorie Barnes and Danny Beard as replacements) signed with ABC Records.

The group's last Pop chart record was "Love Hangover" for ABC (#80) in the spring of 1976. Meanwhile, Marilyn and Billy hit gold with "You Don't Have to Be a Star" (#1 Pop and R&B) and went on through 1977 with four charters, the last being "Look What You've Done to My Heart" (#51) and "Shine on Silver Moon" (#86, 1978).

The 5th Dimension moved over to Motown in 1978 for a few unsuccessful LPs and singles. In June 1977 Marilyn and Billy co-hosted a six-week CBS TV variety show, which led to Marilyn having a successful run as host of 1980's "Solid Gold."

The 5th Dimension continued to be a popular performance attraction through the '80s, when Michael Bell replaced Ron Townson.

Their vocal flexibility made them an ideal producer's group and a great vehicle for sophisticated songs that otherwise might never have reached the masses.

THE 5TH DIMENSION

A SIDE/B SIDE	LABEL/CAT NO	DATE
I'll Be Loving You Forever /		
Train Keep On Movin'	SI Cty 752	11/66
Go Where You Wanna Go /		
Too Poor To Die	SI Cty 753	12/66
Another Day, Another Heartache /		
Rose Crans Blvd.	SI Cty 755	3/67
Up, Up And Away /		
Which Way To Nowhere	SI Cty 756	5/67
Paper Cup / Poor Side Of Town	SI Cty 760	9/67
Carpet Man / The Magic Garden	SI Cty 762	1/68
Stoned Soul Picnic /		
The Sailboat Song	SI Cty 766	4/68
Sweet Blindness / Bobbie's Blues	SI Cty 768	9/68
California Soul /		
It'll Never Be The Same Again	SI Cty 770	11/68
Aquarius-Let The Sunshine In /		
Don'tcha Hear Me Callin' To Ya	SI Cty 772	2/69
Workin' On A Groovy Thing /		
Broken Wing Bird	SI Cty 776	6/69
Wedding Bell Blues / Lovin' Stew	SI Cty 779	9/69
Blowing Away / Skinny Man	SI Cty 780	12/69
The Declaration / A Change		
Is Gonna Come / People Gotta		
Be Free	Bell 860	1/70
The Girls' Song /		
It'll Never Be The Same Again	SI Cty 781	3/70
Puppet Man / A Love Like Ours	Bell 880	3/70
Save The Country / Dimension 5	Bell 895	5/70
On The Beach / This Is Your Life	Bell 913	7/70
One Less Bell To Answer /		
Feelin' Alright	Bell 940	9/70
Loves Lines, Angels And Rhymes /		
The Singer	Bell 965	1/71
Light Sings / Viva	Bell 999	5/71
Never My Love / A Love Like Ours	Bell 134	8/71
Together Let's Find Love /		
I Just Wanna Be Your Friend	Bell 170	12/71
I Didn't Get To Sleep At All /		
The River Witch	Bell 195	3/72
If I Could Reach You / Tomorrow		
Belongs To The Children	Bell 261	8/72
Living Together, Growing		
Together / What Do I		
Need To Be Me	Bell 310	12/72
Everything's Been Changed /		
There Never Was A Day	Bell 338	3/73
Ashes To Ashes / The Singer	Bell 380	7/73
Flashback / Diggin' For A Livin'	Bell 425	11/73
Harlem / My Song	Bell 612	11/74
No Love In The Room / I Don't		
Know How To Look For Love	Arista 0101	1/75
Lean On Me Always /		
Magic In My Life	ABC 12136	1975
Speaking With My Heart /		
Walk Your Feet In The Sunshine	ABC 12168	1/76
Love Hangover /		
Will You Be There	ABC 12181	3/76

The Five Stairsteps

A smooth pop/R&B group, the Five Stairsteps were the forerunners of such family acts as THE SYLVERS and THE JACKSON FIVE. The Burke family vocalists included Clarence, Jr. (16, lead), Alohe (17, contralto), James (15, first tenor), Kenneth (13, second tenor), and Dennis (14, baritone). All attended Harlan High School in Chicago but were singing together before that. They had been encouraged and tutored by their police officer dad, Clarence Burke, Sr., while their mom, Betty Burke, had coached them on their harmonies.

They were named during a rehearsal after their mother noticed that when they sat on a couch in order of size they looked like stairsteps.

In 1966 the group entered a talent show at the renowned Regal Theatre and won. Proud Papa Burke was boasting of his group's prowess to old associate Fred Cash in a food store when he discovered Fred was a member of THE IMPRESSIONS. Cash agreed to set up an audition with Impressions producer/lead singer Curtis Mayfield and the result was that Curtis took them to his newly formed Windy C label distributed by Philadelphia's Cameo Records. Curtis began producing for the act, and in the spring of 1966 they had their first single and hit, "You Waited Too Long" (#94 Pop, #16 R&B). "You Waited" initiated a string of ballad charters throughout 1966 and 1967. Six of their seven Windy C releases made both the R&B and Pop hits list, the biggest being "World of Fantasy" (#49 Pop, #12 R&B) in the summer of 1966.

In 1967 Mayfield established a relationship with Buddah Records of New York and brought them the Five Stairsteps, who now included the youngest member of any group on record. Michael Jackson started his career as an elder statesman compared to two-year-old Cubbie Burke, who first appeared on the December 1967 "Something's Missing" (#88 Pop, #17 R&B).

At the other end of the age scale, Papa Burke began playing bass for the group.

In 1970, Stan Vincent took over production and created their biggest hit, the rhythm ballad "O-o-h Child" (#8 Pop, #14 R&B).

Often billing themselves as "America's First Family of Soul," the Five Stairsteps began to diversify into rock and pop, reducing public interest and creating disputes among the members.

Their last hit was "From Us to You" in 1976 for George Harrison's Dark Horse label (#102 Pop, #10 R&B). They disbanded soon after.

The four boys, with Clarence on lead (minus Cubbie and Alohe), formed the Invisible Man's Band in 1980 and came up with one hit ("All Night Thing," #45 Pop, #9 R&B, Mango) and two also-rans, "Really Wanna See You" (#79 R&B, Boardwalk, 1982) and "Sunday Afternoon" (#77 R&B, Move'n, N.G., 1983).

Kenneth "Keni" Burke went out on a solo career around the same time, with his biggest single being "Rising to the Top" (#63, RCA, 1982).

The closeness that made the family work as a group in early years disappeared as each member developed in a different musical direction. But they were quite a success while it lasted, posting 17 R&B and 12 Pop charters out of their 24 Stairsteps releases.

The Four-Evers

One of the finest of the '60s white doo wop groups, the Four-Evers' distinctive harmony sound was originally fashioned in a FOUR SEASONS mold by Seasons producer/writer Bob Gaudio.

The Brooklyn quartet included Joe Di Benedetto (lead), John Cipriani (first tenor), Steve Tudanger (second tenor), and Nick Zagami (baritone). John and Steve (of Boody Junior High School) were originally in the Vocal Lords on Abel and later the Taurus label with a local charter, "At 17," in 1960.

At the same time, Joe and Nick (who attended Lafayette High School) were part of a group called the Palladiums that featured Jimmy Gallagher on lead. When Jimmy left to form THE PASSIONS, John and Steve of the Vocal Lords joined up with Joe and Nick to form the Four-Evers in 1961. The Bensonhurst boys first rehearsed at Saint Finbar's Church on 19th Avenue and Bath Avenue on songs like "I'll Be Seeing You" and "You Belong to Me." It was the latter, done with an up-tempo Mexican flavor, that earned the four 15-year-olds their first single on the Columbia label in January 1962. The record had top 20 written all over it, but "You" still went nowhere.

In fewer than eight months a ballad version of the song by THE DUPREES (summer of 1962) went to number seven nationally. "You Belong to Me" and the Four-Evers' subsequent recordings were arranged by songwriter/manager Al Kasha (he later went on to win an Academy Award for cowriting with Joel Hirschhorn the number one Maureen McGovern hit "The Morning After" from *The Poseidon Adventure*). The group had auditioned for Al

in his office in Columbia Records back in 1961, and the song they had performed was their up-tempo version of "You Belong to Me." When Al decided to introduce the quartet to Bob Crewe and Bob Gaudio, a perfect match was made between their high harmonies, Joe's commercial tenor, and Gaudio and Crewe's writing and producing skills. It led to a record deal with Mercury subsidiary Smash Records.

In September 1963 they released an original written by the group in a Latin groove titled "It's Love," with a flip that was a remake of the 1929 Rudy Vallee number nine hit "Lover Come Back to Me." When radio missed its opportunity to immortalize a hot new group, it was back to the studio in early 1964 with a new Bob Gaudio composition, "Please Be Mine." This one put the Brooklynites on the map, going top 10 in New York. It spread across the country and hit the *Billboard* national charts on May 30th, but only made it to number 75. Soon after its release "Please Be Mine" was retitled "Be My Girl."

The group began performing throughout the U.S. and Canada and did vocal backup for Leslie Gore, Bobby Rydell, Diane Renee, and Terry Stafford at different times.

Their last Smash single was the up-tempo rocker "Say I Love You (Doo Bee Dum)," which received airplay in the East but went no further.

The Four-Evers did some backup vocals on record for acts like Eddie Rambeau ("Come on Come Closer") and Vinnie Monte ("What's the Matter with Marilyn") in which Frankie Valli sang in the background with them.

Singles with Constellation, Red Bird, and Columbia yielded no hits for the Four-Evers, and they disbanded in 1968.

Soon after, Joe and Steve formed a studio group called Playhouse with Marietta Martinez and Judy Moroulis and began working with writer/producer Jeff Barry. As a backup group they had more success (though less visibility) than the Four-Evers, becoming THE ARCHIES behind Ron Dante on "Jingle Jangle" (#10, 1969), backing Andy Kim on "Baby I Love You" (#9, 1969), and supporting Robin McNamara on "Lay a Little Lovin' on Me" (#11, 1970). They recorded two singles as Playhouse, "Just We Two" and "You Don't Know It" on Barry's Steed label, but the group decided to pack it in by 1970.

Joe became a member of the Joe Casey Orchestra in New York. John went to work for the Board of Education. Nick went into the computer business. Steve began writing commercial jingles.

THE FOUR-EVERS

A SIDE/B SIDE	LABEL/CAT NO	DATE
You Belong To Me / Such		
A Good Night For Dreaming	Col 42303	1/62
It's Love / Lover Come Back To Me	Smash 1853	9/63
Please Be Mine /		
If I Were A Magician	Smash 1887	2/64
Be My Girl / If I Were A Magician	Smash 1887	3/64
(Doo Bee Dum) Say I Love You! /		
Everlasting	Smash 1921	7/64
Out Of The Crowd / Stormy	Const 151	1965
You Never Had It So Good /		
What A Scene	RdBrd 078	1966
A Lovely Way To Say Goodnight /		
The Girl I Wanna Bring Home	Col 43886	12/66

The Four Seasons

Powered by Bob Gaudio's ability to write and produce hit songs and Frankie Valli's distinctive falsetto, the Four Seasons were one of the most popular and successful vocal groups of all time.

The group formed from members of three other acts in 1959. Frankie Valli and Tommy DeVito were with THE FOUR LOVERS. Nick Massi was a member of the Hollywood Playboys and was later a replacement for Hank Majewski in the Four Lovers. Bob Gaudio was with the Royal Teens ("Short Shorts," #3, 1958). Bob left the Royal Teens because of a desire to write more, but Frankie convinced him he could do that for the Four Lovers and still be a regular member of the group.

Frankie, born Francis Castelluccio in 1937, was originally encouraged by Texas Jean Valley, a country singer who heard him perform "White Christmas" at a school play; consequently Francis Castelluccio adopted the name Frankie Valley. He was busy doing demos when publisher Paul Kapp discovered him and arranged a record deal for the 16-year-old on Mercury's Corona affiliate ("My Mother's Eyes").

In 1954 Frankie and an unknown studio group recorded "Forgive and Forget" as Frankie Vally and the Travelers on Mercury. Neither was a success and Frankie went on to join the Variety Trio, which became the Variatones and, in 1956, the Four Lovers. Tommy DeVito and Nick Massi were part of that group.

Bob Gaudio met Frankie briefly in 1958 when both were performing with their respective groups (Frankie with the Romans promoting "Come Si Bella" and Bob with the Royal Teens while they were promoting "Big Name Button" on the Buddy Deane TV show in Baltimore), but had no idea they'd soon become lifetime partners.

Gaudio was born in the Bronx. He and his family moved to Bergenfield, New Jersey, when he was 14, and there he hooked up with Billy Crandell, Tom Austin, and Billy Dalton to form the Royal Teens. The manager of the Three Friends saw them at a church basement dance and got them the audition that led to their hit "Short Shorts." Bob left the Royal Teens after they recorded the ballad "Believe Me" (Capitol, 1959) and began writing songs while working in a printing factory. His friend Joe Pesci (later an actor and a star of 1990's *GoodFellas*) brought him to a friend's house thinking they'd work well together. Pesci's friend was Frankie Valli.

Another key player in the Seasons' success met Frankie on the road. He was Bob Crewe, the writer of Frankie's 1958 Okeh recording "I Go Ape," and he was working as a recording artist at the time.

From 1957 to 1962 Frankie did backup vocals for various acts, most notably on Danny and the Juniors' "Rock and Roll Is Here to Stay" (1957).

As the decade turned, the group auditioned for a job in the lounge of a Union, New Jersey, bowling alley known as the Four Seasons. They didn't get the job but they did get the name.

They began recording some of Bob Gaudio's compositions as demos. While shopping them around for a record deal they ran into Bob Crewe as he was leaving Larry Uttal's office at Madison Records in New York. Crewe asked to hear their cuts after Uttal. The Madison Records man expressed interest but didn't make the Seasons an offer. Crewe did, signing them to a three-year artist agreement.

Bob Crewe was working on numerous productions and used the Four Seasons on a variety of backup sessions, including "Cry Myself to Sleep" by Matthew Reid (Topix) and "Cupid's Poison Dart" by Scott Oberle (Atco).

Gaudio and Valli had by now shaken hands on what would become a famous show of faith. They agreed on an even split of all their earnings from writing, producing, and performing. They never signed a piece of paper but maintained the agreement from then on.

Bob Crewe came up with a deal for the Seasons with George Goldner's Gone records, and in January 1962 the Four Seasons' first single, "Bermuda," was released in a cover battle with a version by Linda Scott. The flip side was "Spanish Lace," which Gaudio had recorded in 1961 for Topix under the name Turner DiSentri. No one got to hear it; the A side "Bermuda" never left the gate.

The group's unique harmonies were rooted in a FOUR FRESHMEN style with modern rhythms.

In 1962 Gaudio wrote a song called "Jackie," named after Jacqueline Kennedy. It was written in about 15 minutes, and only after group pressure did Crewe relent and tag it on the fourth cut of their four-song session. At the last minute the name was changed from Jackie to "Sherry." Recognizing the recording's potential, Crewe took the Seasons cuts to a record convention and arranged a deal with indy label Vee-Jay Records.

"Sherry" was released in the summer and moved slowly until the group performed on Dick Clark's "American Bandstand." The power of that show was demonstrated by the fact that the day after the Four Seasons' appearance, "Sherry" sold almost 200,000 records. By September 15th it had pushed Tommy Roe's "Sheila" out of first place on the Billboard Top 100 chart. "Sherry" sat firmly in the number one spot for five weeks until it was finally dislodged by Bobby "Boris" Pickett's hit "Monster Mash." In the meantime it hit number one on the R&B chart and number eight in the U.K.

Frankie's three-and-a-half octave range, the group's tight harmonies, and the success of "Sherry" made the Four Seasons household names on an international level.

The title of the group's next single came from an old John Payne western that Crewe was watching. When Payne walloped a girl and asked "What do you think of that?," she dusted herself off and said, "Big girls don't cry." The resulting Crewe-Gaudio composition charted on October 20th and hit number one on November 17th, only four weeks after "Sherry" dropped out of first. "Big Girls" bumped THE CRYSTALS and their "He's a Rebel" out of first place and spent five weeks atop the charts. R&B-wise it went to number one for three weeks. It reached number 13, in England and number one in Australia, and number four in Israel.

By January 1963 the Gaudio-Crewe writing machine had turned out another monster, "Walk Like a Man," and it marked the first of several hits arranged by former Four Lovers member Charlie Callelo. Like its predecessors, it reached number one (#3 R&B, #12 U.K.).

The group issued its last R&B charter in summer 1963, a mid-tempo, Latin-flavored arrangement (another Callelo classic) of Larry Santos' "Candy Girl" (#3 Pop, #13 R&B). Its flip, a "Sherry"-styled tune called "Marlena," reached number 36.

The quartet was touring England when they heard a song on BBC radio that was by a band that had no U.S. record deal. The song was called "Please, Please Me," and the Seasons considered covering it until Bob Gaudio came up with "Walk Like a Man." Frankie suggested to Randy Wood at Vee-Jay that he check out this new group, which resulted in the label acquiring some of the first masters to be released in the United States by the Beatles.

At this point Vee-Jay began releasing some quality oldies that the Seasons had recorded for them. Actually they had no choice, since the group, feeling they were being short-changed on royalties, signed with Mercury's Philips affiliate. While the Seasons' hit-making days had only numbered 14 months, Vee-Jay already issued a Golden Hits of The 4 Seasons LP in October 1963 (it reached number 15).

Reverting to the "Sherry" formula, Bob Gaudio and Sandy Linzer, with Callelo arranging and Crewe producing, created the masterpiece "Dawn," and "The 4 Seasons Featuring the Sound of Frankie Valli" (as the label now read) carried it to impressive heights. On February 22nd it was at number three, right behind the Beatles' "I Wanna Hold Your Hand" at number one and "She Loves You" at number two. (Ironically, after three weeks, the number four song was "Please, Please Me" by the Beatles . . . on Vee-Jay.) "Dawn," with its driving melody and rhythm, exciting vocals, and stirring lyric, became another million seller.

The Seasons' eight singles had shown they were one of the few American acts able to weather the British invasion.

In January Vee-Jay dug into the vaults for those Four Seasons oldies, starting off with the 1960 MAURICE WILLIAMS AND THE ZODIACS hit, "Stay." The Seasons' version fit Frankie's falsetto to a T and went to number 16.

Meanwhile, the follow-up to "Dawn" on Philips was another Gaudio and Crewe rocker, "Ronnie," and it rode up the charts like most of the others, this time to number six in the spring. Vee-Jay tried to stay neck and neck, releasing "Alone" (Sheppard Sisters, #18, 1957), which made it to number 28.

The inspiration for their next hit came from an incident that took place in 1964 when Gaudio was driving to a New York recording studio. Stopped for a long light off one of the Westside Highway exits, his car was approached by a small young girl with a dirty face and tattered clothes. Like many other street people of New York, she cleaned car windows to make some tips, and she was cleaning Bob's when the light changed. Panic gripped him as he rifled through his pockets to find nothing smaller than a 10-dollar bill. He handed it to her, and though she said not a word, her eyes lit up. That image haunted Gaudio for days until he sat down to write "Rag Doll."

From the four-part harmony intro to the drum beat right out of THE RONETTES' "Be My Baby," "Rag Doll" was classic rock and roll. On July 18, 1964 it bypassed THE BEACH BOYS' "I Get Around" to reach first place for two weeks. It was their fourth number one in less than two years and their seventh top 10 hit. "Rag Doll" brought them back to the international spotlight as well, reaching number two in England and Australia.

"Save It for Me" was another top 10 hit for the group, charting the same day Vee-Jay launched another of its canned cuts (August 29, 1964), the old MOONGLOWS classic, "Sincerely," which managed to make it only to number 75.

The group continued on through 1964 and 1965 with a string of terrific rock and roll records like "Big Man in Town" (#20), "Bye Bye Baby" (#12), and "Let's Hang On" (#3 Pop, #4 U.K.).

Vee-Jay repackaged some cuts into a "battle of the groups" two-record set titled *The Beatles Versus the Four Seasons*, but the album reached only number 142. Later it became a valuable collector's item.

Meanwhile, Vee-Jay finally ran out of Four Seasons sides after issuing five more after "Sincerely." Of particular note were versions of "Tonight Tonight" (THE MELLO-KINGS) and "Since I Don't Have You" (THE SKYLINERS), as well as Vee-Jay's last Four Seasons charter, "Little Boy" (#60).

In May 1965 Nick Massi, who did all the vocal arrangements for the group, departed and was temporarily replaced by Charlie Callelo until Joe Long came aboard.

Toward the end of 1965 "The Wonder Who" surfaced with "Don't Think Twice, It's All Right" from an LP of Bob Dylan songs in exaggerated novelty form (a cold had forced Frankie to exaggerate his already famous falsetto). Of course, nobody "wondered who" for long, when "Don't Think Twice" went to number 12. Philips, apparently, didn't want to issue the oddly appealing single under the Four Seasons name while "Let's Hang On" was so hot and "Working My Way Back to You" was ready for follow-up, so the group invented the Wonder Who.

This was around the time Frankie began his solo career on Smash, a Phillips affiliate. His first single was the Gaudio-Crewe song "The Sun Ain't Gonna Shine Anymore" (one of Gaudio's personal favorites), which was a hit several months later by

the Walker Brothers (#13, 1966). Frankie's first solo hit was the rhythm ballad "Can't Take My Eyes Off of You" (#2, 1967).

Frankie and the Seasons continued turning out hits through 1967, including "Opus 17" (#13), "I've Got You Under My Skin" (#9 and Gaudio's other personal favorite), "Tell It to the Rain" (#10), "Beggin'" (#16), and "C'mon Marianne" (#9), along with near hits "Watch the Flowers Grow" (#30) and THE SHIRELLES' "Will You Love Me Tomorrow" (#24).

In early 1969 Gaudio made a deal for his own label with Columbia (Gazette Records) and started recording acts like Lock, Stock and Barrel. This maneuver was a prelude to taking the Seasons in a "social relevance" direction that AM radio wouldn't accept from the favorite purveyors of pop rock. The eclectic *Genuine Imitation Life Gazette* LP, coproduced by Jake Holms and Bob Gaudio, failed in comparison to their hit albums (this one charted at number 85).

By the fall of 1969 Crewe had started his own label and taken the Seasons with him for one chart single, "And That Reminds Me" (#45).

Numerous changes took place in the '70s starting with Tommy DeVito's departure. Bill Deloach, Clay Jordon, Paul Wilson, and Demitri Callas all came and went.

In early 1972 Gaudio stopped performing to spend more time writing and producing. Around this time the group signed with Motown affiliate Mowest, but a couple of potential charters managed to slip away.

In 1974 the Seasons escaped Motown. Frankie's faith in one recording he did there convinced him to buy the track and license it to Larry Uttal's Private Stock Records. The song was "My Eyes Adored You," and it became Frankie's first solo number one record. Valli followed it with "Swearin' to God" (#6).

Renewed success gave Frankie and Bob the initiative to create a new Four Seasons. Don Ciccone (the Critters), John Pavia (the Classaires), Gerry Polci, and Lee Shapiro joined forces, with Frankie and Polci now sharing leads. Gaudio was writing, producing, and singing background.

They hooked up with Mike Curb at Warner Bros. Records and recorded "Who Loves You" with a driving disco beat, Frankie's lowest notes ever, and a hot instrumental and harmony tradeoff. The Bob Gaudio/Judy Parker song rose to number three (#6 U.K.) but was only a prelude to their biggest record since "Big Girls Don't Cry." On December 27, 1975, "December 1963 (Oh What a Night)" hit the charts and didn't stop selling for 27 weeks, longer than any Four Seasons single in history. It knocked THE MIRACLES' "Love Machine" out of first place on March 13, 1976, and held on for three weeks, rising also to number one in the U.K. (#4 Australia). The cut was the first Seasons 45 to feature three different leads—Frankie, Don, and Gerry. Warner Bros. chose to issue only one more U.S. single, the double-time, western-styled rocker "Silver Star." With its tempo changes, *Star Wars* orchestrations, rock opera harmonies, spaghetti western guitar lines, and shades-of-Procol-Harum organ riffs, "Silver Star" was a Seasons symphony and, as it turned out, their chart swan song. The Gaudio-Parker masterpiece sadly stalled at number 38. (In Britain it went to number three.) Nothing ever reached as high again in the U.S., and it took a recording of "Silver Star's" magnitude to usher Frankie out of the lead for the first time ever.

In the summer of 1977 "Down the Hall" (from the new *Helicon* LP) was issued. Another step in the transition from a pop vocal group to a rock vocal band, "Down the Hall" was a Gaudio-Parker collage of beautiful harmonies and melodies that Warner Bros. lost at number 65 (#34 U.K.). The label didn't even try for another single, though they had some magnificent music like "Helicon," "Rhapsody," and "New York Street Song (No Easy Way)," which opens with 16 bars of flawless a cappella harmony and then becomes a high-powered rocker.

It took the Seasons three more years—until 1980—to get their last charter, "Spend the Night in Love" (#91), out of Warner Bros.

In September 1977 Frankie announced he was leaving the group and then scored another solo hit with the title song from *Grease* (#1) in 1978, but failing hearing caused by otosclerosis forced him to have several operations. His hearing was eventually restored.

In 1981 the group reunited for a tour, added former Sugarloaf lead Jerry Corbetta, and recorded their first live LP.

In 1984 Frankie and Bob formed F.B.I. Records and put out a single with THE BEACH BOYS titled "East Meets West." in 1985 their *Street Fighting* LP for Curb/MCA gave birth to a contemporary version of THE MONOTONES' "Book of Love."

In the summer of 1988 the group was still touring successfully, and in the spring of 1991 they began work on another Bob Gaudio-produced album. The Four Seasons sold 85 million records and had 46 chart hits, yet in 1991 they and their sound were very much alive, and poised to hit the charts at any time.

THE FOUR SEASONS

A SIDE/B SIDE	LABEL/CAT NO	DATE
Spanish Lace / Bermuda	Gone 5122	1/62
Sherry / I've Cried Before	Vee-Jay 456	7/62
Big Girls Don't Cry / Connie-O	Vee-Jay 465	10/62
Santa Claus Is Coming To Town / Christmas Tears	Vee-Jay 478	12/62
Walk Like A Man / Lucky Lady Bug	Vee-Jay 485	1/63
Ain't That A Shame / Soon	Vee-Jay 512	4/63
Candy Girl / Marlena	Vee-Jay 539	6/63
New Mexican Rose / That's The Only Way	Vee-Jay 562	9/63
Peanuts / Stay	Vee-Jay 576	11/63
Dawn / No Surfing Today	Phlps 40166	1/64
Stay / Goodnight My Love	Vee-Jay 582	1/64
Ronnie / Born To Wander	Phlps 40185	3/64
Alone / Long Lonely Nights	Vee-Jay 597	5/64
Rag Doll / Silence Is Golden	Phlps 40211	6/64
Save It For Me / Funny Face	Phlps 40225	1964
Sincerely / One Song	Vee-Jay 608	8/64
Happy Birthday Baby / Apple Of My Eye	Vee-Jay 618	9/64
Big Man In Town / Little Angel	Phlps 40238	10/64
I Saw Mommy Kissing Santa Claus / Christmas Tears	Vee-Jay 626	12/64
Never On Sunday / Connie-O	Vee-Jay 639	4/65
Bye Bye Baby / Searchin' Wind	Phlps 40260	12/65
Toy Soldier / Betrayed	Phlps 40278	3/65
Since I Don't Have You / Tonight Tonight	Vee-Jay 664	1965
Girl Come Running / Cry Myself To Sleep	Phlps 40305	1965
Let's Hang On / On Broadway Tonight	Phlps 40317	9/65
Little Boy In Grown Up Clothes / Silver Wings	Vee-Jay 713	11/65
Working My Way Back To You / Too Many Memories	Phlps 40350	1/66
Stay / My Mother's Eyes	Vee-Jay 719	1966
Opus 17 / Beggar's Parade	Phlps 40370	4/66
I've Got You Under My Skin / Huggin' My Pillow	Phlps 40393	8/66
Tell It To The Rain / Show Girl	Phlps 40412	11/66
Beggin' / Dody	Phlps 40433	2/67
C'mon Marianne / Let's Ride Again	Phlps 40460	1967
Watch The Flowers Grow / Raven	Phlps 40490	10/67
Will You Still Love Me Tomorrow / Around And Around	Phlps 40523	1968
Saturday Father / Goodbye Girl	Phlps 40542	6/68
Electric Stories / Pity	Phlps 40577	11/68
Idaho / Something's On Her Mind	Phlps 40597	1969
And That Reminds Me / The Singles Game	Crewe 333	1969
Patch Of Blue / She Gives Me Light	Phlps 40662	1970
Lay Me Down / Heartaches And Raindrops	Phlps 40688	9/71
Where Are My Dreams / Any Day Now-Oh Happy Day	Phlps 40694	11/71

A SIDE/B SIDE	LABEL/CAT NO	DATE
Walk On, Don't Look Back /		
Sun Country	Mowest 5026	1972
How Come / Life And Breath	Motown 1255	5/73
Hickory / Charisma	Motown 1288	1974
Who Loves You / Who Loves You	Wrnr 8122	1975
December 1963 / Slip Away	Wrnr 8168	12/76
Silver Star / Mystic Mr. Sam	Wrnr 8203	1976
We Can Work It Out /		
Harmony (British)	Wrnr 16845	1976
Rhapsody / Helicon (British)	Wrnr 16932	1977
Down The Hall /		
I Believe You	Wrnr 8407	1977
Spend The Night In Love /		
Slip Away	Wrnr 49597	1980
Heaven Must Have Sent You /		
Silver Star	Wrnr 49685	1981
Book Of Love / Book Of Love	MCA/Curb	1985
Streetfighter /		
Deep Inside Your Love	MCA 52618	1986

**The Four Seasons and
the Beach Boys**

East Meets West / Rhapsody	FBI 7701	1984

The Four Tops

One of the premier soul groups of all time, the Four Tops were a mainstay of the Motown sound. Levi Stubbs, Abdul "Duke" Fakir, Renaldo "Obie" Benson, and Lawrence Payton were boyhood friends in Detroit who gave it a go at a friend's birthday party in 1954 and found they were pretty good at it. They started practicing the next day and called themselves the Four Aims. Starting with school parties and church socials they worked their way onto the small club circuit and with the help of a talent agency began performing as a backup group for Billy Eckstine, Brook Benton, and Della Reese, among others.

By 1956 they became the Four Tops, thus avoiding confusion with THE AMES BROTHERS, and signed for one single with Chicago's Chess Records. They were then signed by John Hammond to Columbia (in 1960), but only lasted long enough to cut one less-than-exciting single called "Ain't That Love."

By 1962 Levi and company were working in Las Vegas with Billy Eckstine when the Tops recorded a version of "Pennies from Heaven" for the jazz-based Riverside label. Still, they were unable to find a radio audience until they met up with Berry Gordy, Jr. and his hot Motown label.

Working first in a jazz vein, the group was used mainly to back up THE SUPREMES until Berry and company could find the right song and musical direction for them. Their first hit turned out to be the Supremes' "When the Lovelight Starts Shining Through His Eyes" (#23).

In 1964 Motown songwriting stars Holland, Dozier, and Holland came up with a song for the Tops called "Baby I Need Your Lovin'." Its charting in August went to number 11 Pop and R&B.

In early 1965 the Tops issued "Ask the Lonely," one of their finest recordings. Though not one of their biggest hits (#24 Pop, #9 R&B), the gospel-tinged inspirational rhythm ballad piqued the ears of listeners and set the Tops up for their first monster hit. In the spring of 1965, "I Can't Help Myself" spent two weeks at number one Pop (#1 R&B, #23 U.K.). The contagious, pounding rhythm of the song most buyers called "Sugar Pie Honey Bunch" helped establish the Tops as mid-'60s favorites in the music world. In a throwback to music business style of the '50s, fast-moving Motown recorded their follow-up, "The Same Old Song," on a Thursday and had it on radio by Saturday and in the stores on Monday. It reached number five Pop and number two R&B.

Soul hits like "Something About You" (#18 Pop, #9 R&B), "Shake Me, Wake Me" (#18 Pop, #5 R&B), and "Loving You Is Sweeter than Ever" (#45 Pop, #12 R&B) made the Tops familiar faces across the country. They also were popular in England, and when they went there in 1965, that part of their tour was handled by Beatles manager Brian Epstein.

In the late summer of 1966 their most outstanding single was issued. With a Middle Eastern sound grafted on to an American soul beat, "Reach Out" made it to number one on both the Pop and R&B charts, edging THE ASSOCIATION's "Cherish" out of first place on October 15th. It also made number one in the U.K., becoming the fourth of 29 chart appearances there (by 25 different singles), making them second only to THE BEACH BOYS in the number of British hits by an American vocal group.

While Motown had the Supremes doing light, breezy material and THE TEMPTATIONS recording mostly easygoing pop-soul, Berry Gordy reserved the rockers for the Tops. "Reach Out" was followed by a series of similarly driving recordings like "Standing in the Shadows (of Love)" (#6 Pop, #2 R&B), "Bernadette" (#4 Pop, #3 R&B), and "Seven Rooms of Gloom" (#14 Pop, #10 R&B).

In 1967 the group diversified their sound and cut an uncharacteristic live LP that contained standard songs like "Climb Every Mountain" and "If I Had a Hammer." This was followed by an LP called *The Four Tops on Broadway* that offered several covers of show tunes.

By the end of 1967 Holland, Dozier, and Holland had left Motown to form their own label and the Tops were turning to other sources for songs. Focusing on covers of other artists' songs, the group hit with the Left Banke's 1966 number five hit "Walk Away Renee" in 1968 (#14 Pop, #15 R&B) and Bobby Darin's 1966 winner (#8), "If I Was a Carpenter" (#20 Pop, #17 R&B) also in 1968.

In 1970 the historic pairing of the Four Tops and the Supremes in an LP titled *The Magnificent Seven* yielded a soul version of Phil Spector's Ike and Tina Turner classic, "River Deep, Mountain High" (#14 Pop, #7 R&B).

In 1972 Motown moved to Los Angeles, and the Tops, after 30 Pop hits and 28 R&B winners with Gordy's company, moved over to Dunhill. They did this largely because of the writing talents of Dennis Lambert and Brian Potter, who in the late fall of 1972 had had a hit with the Tops on their song "Keeper of the Castle" (#10 Pop, #7 R&B). Lambert and Potter's "Ain't No Woman (Like the One I Got)" kept their star rising in 1973 (#4 Pop, #2 R&B) while "Are You Man Enough" (from the film *Shaft in Africa*) finished at number 15 Pop and number two R&B.

In 1976 they moved over to Dunhill's parent label ABC for a few good sides, most notably "Seven Lonely Nights" (#71 Pop, #13 R&B) and "Catfish" (#71 Pop, #7 R&B).

In 1981 they moved again, this time to Casablanca, and their release "When She Was My Girl" was their first R&B number one hit since "Reach Out" (also going to number 11 Pop).

In 1983 the Tops performed on Motown's 25th Anniversary TV spectacular and soon after resigned with Gordy's company while touring internationally with the Temptations.

Their last Motown R&B charter was "Sexy Ways" (#21). In September 1988 they signed with Arista Records, and the single "Indestructible" became their 45th Pop hit (#35).

In 1986 Levi became the voice of Audrey II, the man-eating plant in the film version of *Little Shop of Horrors*.

In 1991, more than 35 years after they started, the same four vocalists were still recording and performing. Unlike other acts who had their biggest successes in the '60s, whenever a new Four Tops record came out it was treated like the release of a hot new group.

THE FOUR TOPS

A SIDE/B SIDE	LABEL/CAT NO	DATE
Could It Be You / Kiss Me Baby	Chess 1623	1956
Ain't That Love / Lonely Summer	Col 41755	7/60
Pennies From Heaven / Where You Are	Rvrsd 4534	1962
Baby I Need Your Loving / Call On Me	Mtwn 1062	7/64
Without The One You Love / Love Has Gone	Mtwn 1069	1964
Ask The Lonely / Where Did You Go	Mtwn 1073	1965
I Can't Help Myself / Sad Souvenirs	Mtwn 1076	1965
It's The Same Old Song / Your Love Is Amazing	Mtwn 1081	1965
Something About You / Darling, I Hum Our Song	Mtwn 1084	1965
Shake Me, Wake Me / Just As Long As You Need Me	Mtwn 1090	1966
Loving You Is Sweeter Than Ever / I Like Everything About You	Mtwn 1096	1966
Reach Out (I'll Be There) / Until You Love Someone	Mtwn 1098	1966
Standing In The Shadows / Since You've Been Gone	Mtwn 1102	1966
Bernadette / I Got A Feeling	Mtwn 1104	1967
Seven Rooms Of Gloom / I'll Turn To Stone	Mtwn 1110	1967
You Keep Running Away / If You Don't Want My Love	Mtwn 1113	9/67
Walk Away Renee / Your Love Is Wonderful	Mtwn 1119	1968
If I Were A Carpenter / Wonderful Baby	Mtwn 1124	1968
Yesterday's Dreams / For Once In My Life	Mtwn 1127	1968
I'm In A Different World / Remember When	Mtwn 1132	1968
What Is A Man / Don't Bring Back Memories	Mtwn 1147	1969
Don't Let Him Take Your Love From Me / The Key	Mtwn 1159	1969
Love / It's All In The Game	Mtwn 1164	1970
Still Water (Love) / Still Water (Peace)	Mtwn 1170	1970
Just Seven Numbers / I Wish I Were Your Mirror	Mtwn 1175	1970
In These Changing Times / Right Before My Eyes	Mtwn 1185	1971
MacArthur Park Part 1 / MacArthur Park Part 2	Mtwn 1189	1971
A Simple Game / L. A.	Mtwn 1196	1972
Happy / I Can't Quit Your Love	Mtwn 1198	1972
Nature Planned It / I'll Never Change	Mtwn 1210	1972
Keeper Of The Castle / Jubilee With Soul	Dnhl 4330	1972
Guardian De Tu Castillo / Jubilee With Soul	Dnhl 4334	1973

A SIDE/B SIDE	LABEL/CAT NO	DATE
Ain't No Woman /		
The Good Lord Knows	Dnhl 4339	1973
Are You Man Enough /		
Peace Of Mind	Dnhl 4354	1973
Sweet Understanding Love /		
Main Street People	Dnhl 4366	1973
I Just Can't Get You Out Of My		
Mind / Am I My Brother's Keeper	Dnhl 4377	1973
One Chain Don't Make No Prison /		
Turn On The Light Of Your Love	Dnhl 4386	1974
Midnight Flower / All My Love	Dnhl 15005	1974
Seven Lonely Nights	ABC 12096	1975
We All Gotta Stick Together /		
Drive Me Out Of My Mind	ABC 12123	1975
I'm Glad You Walked Into My Life /		
Mama You're All Right With Me	ABC 12155	1976
Catfish	ABC 12214	1976
Catfish / Look At My Baby	ABC 12223	9/76
Feel Free	ABC 12236	1/77
The Show Must Go On	ABC 12315	11/77
H.E.L.P.	ABC 12427	11/78
When She Was My Girl	Casa 2338	8/81
Let Me Set You Free	Casa 2344	12/81
Tonight I'm Gonna Love You All Over	Casa 2345	2/82
Sad Hearts	Casa	8/82
I Believe In You And Me	Casa 2353	12/82
I Just Can't Walk Away	Mtwn 1706	10/83
Sexy Ways	Mtwn 1790	6/85
Indestructible	Arista 9706	1988

The Happenings

With a pop style that seemed to fall somewhere between THE FOUR SEASONS and THE TOKENS, the Happenings gave new life to old standards.

The group formed in 1961 in Patterson, New Jersey, and called themselves the Four Graduates. Bob Miranda (lead), Tom Giuliano (first tenor), Ralph DiVito (baritone), and Dave Libert (bass) began singing together in the army at Fort Dix, New Jersey. Developing a versatility that enabled them to sing barbershop as well as jazz and doo wop, they became proficient enough to work in local clubs and begin doing background work on recording sessions. In late 1962 they met Bob Crewe, who had just produced the huge hit "Sherry" for the Four Seasons. He used the Four Grads on a variety of sessions, including some by the Seasons.

They signed with Rust (distributed by Laurie) in 1963 and, produced by Lor Crane, cut a rhythm version of THE INK SPOTS' 1944 ballad hit (#16) "A Lovely Way to Spend an Evening." At Rust the Tokens met the quartet and were impressed with their sound, especially the stylistic possibilities they heard in the group's recording of "Lovely Way." (The Tokens were fond of reworking oldies in a new tempo.) The group was producing THE CHIFFONS (as the Four Pennies) and RANDY AND THE RAINBOWS for Rust in 1963 but kept the Four Grads on mental "hold."

In the early summer of 1964 the Tokens formed B.T. Puppy Records. A little over a year later, after recording such obscurities as the Cinnamons, the Three Pennies, and the English Muffins, the Tokens signed the Four Graduates.

At that time Miranda and company opted for a name change to the Happenings.

When their first single, "Girls on the Go," came and went, the Tokens (Jay Siegel, Phil and Mitch Margo, and Hank Medress), decided to pull a familiar oldie out of the hat. They took an MOR ballad from 1959, the Tempos' number 23 hit "See You in September," gave it a stylish vocal intro, some rhythm, a neat Herb Bernstein arrangement, and off it went. "See You," a song tailor-made for Bob Miranda's tenor lead, was the first single that showcased a distinct Happenings vocal style. By August 27th it was number three in the nation.

Next up was another rearranged recent oldie, the Goffin/King-penned Steve Lawrence number one smash from 1962, "Go Away Little Girl," which the Happenings took to number 12.

Shifting from a successful formula, the Happenings recorded an original for their third single. When "Goodnight My Love" failed, the Tokens made sure the next one wouldn't. They went to the Gershwin songbook and came up with a masterful arrangement of "I Got Rhythm" in a "See You" mode. On May 27, 1967, "Rhythm" rose to number three, right behind Aretha Franklin's "Respect" and the Rascals' "Groovin'."

Their next reclamation project went further back. The double-time arrangement of Al Jolson's theme song "My Mammy" (1928), a hit as far back as 1921 for the Peerless Quartet, propelled the group to another hit. With its a cappella barbershop harmony intro, "Mammy" climbed to number 13.

By now, Ralph DiVito had departed and been replaced by Bernie Laporte. The group was touring all over the nation and doing TV with Clay Cole, Johnny Carson, and "Where the Action Is." They traveled to the San Remo Song Festival, where the Italian teens went wild when the Happenings broke into "See You in September" in Italian. The group was at the crest of its career.

Six subsequent B.T. singles had mediocre activity, and the group, trying for a new lease on life, switched to Jubilee for a summer of '69 medley from *Hair*, "Where Do I Go"/"Be In." It brought them back on the charts for the first time in a year, but at number 66 became their last charting song.

In 1970, after their fifth Jubilee single, the group was ready for a change. They recorded "Sweet September" as the Honor Society, but it didn't work.

In 1972 they did two singles for Big Tree and then switched to Musicor as Sun Dog.

Bob and company had one more single on Midland International in 1977, "That's Why I Love You." 15 years later the group was still keeping evergreens alive via performances in the tri-state area.

THE HAPPENINGS

A SIDE/B SIDE	LABEL/CAT NO	DATE
The Four Graduates		
A Lovely Way To Spend An Evening / Picture Of An Angel	Rust 5062	1963
Candy Queen / A Boy In Love	Rust 5084	1964
The Happenings		
Girls On The Go / Go-Go	BTP 517	2/66
See You In September / He Thinks He's A Hero	BTP 520	6/66
Go Away Little Girl / Tea Time	BTP 522	9/66
Goodnight My Love / Lillies By Monet	BTP 523	11/66
I Got Rhythm / You're In A Bad Way	BTP 527	3/67
My Mammy / I Believe In Nothing	BTP 530	6/67
Why Do Fools Fall In Love / When The Summer Is Through	BTP 532	9/67
Have Yourself A Merry Little Christmas / Have Yourself A Merry Little Christmas	BTP 181	12/67
Music Music Music / When I Lock My Door	BTP 538	1/68
Randy / The Love Song Of Mommy And Dad	BTP 540	4/68
Sealed With A Kiss / Anyway	BTP 542	5/68
Breaking Up Is Hard To Do / Anyway	BTP 543	6/68
Girl On A Swing / When I Lock My Door	BTP 544	8/68
Crazy Rhythm / The Love Song Of Mommy And Dad	BTP 545	9/68
That's All I Want From You / He Thinks He's A Hero	BTP 549	11/68
Where Do I Go / Be-In / Hare Krishna	RCA 7002	1969
Where Do I Go / Be-In / Hare Krishna / New Day Comin'	Jubi 5666	6/69

A SIDE/B SIDE	LABEL/CAT NO	DATE
El Paso County Jail / Won't Anybody Listen	Jubi 5677	9/69
Answer Me, My Love / I Need A Woman	Jubi 5686	1969
Tomorrow Today Will Be Yesterday / Chain Of Hands	Jubi 5698	1970
Crazy Hands / Chain Of Hands	Jubi 5702	1970
Sweet September / Condition Red	Jubi 5703	1970
Lullaby In The Rain / I Wish You Could Know Me	Jubi 5712	1971
Make Your Own Kind Of Music	Jubi 5721	1971
Workin' My Way Back To You / Strawberry Morning	BigTr 146	9/72
Me Without You / God Bless Joanna	BigTr 153	1972
We're Almost Home*	Mscr 1482	1973

Bob Miranda and the Happenings		
That's Why I Love You / Beyond The Hurt	Md Int 10897	1977

* as Sun Dog

The Highwaymen

Johnny Cash, Waylon Jennings, Kris Kristofferson, and Willie Nelson are not the Highwaymen of this story, and if it hadn't been for some quick thinking on Waylon's part, one of the most popular of the early '60s folk groups would have made sure that Cash and company never used that name again.

The original folk-singing Highwaymen included Dave Fisher (lead), Bob Burnett (tenor), Steve Trott (tenor/baritone), Chan Daniels (baritone), and Steve Butts (baritone/bass). Fisher had originally sung with the Academics ("Darla My Darling," Ancho, 1957), a doo wop group from Connecticut.

In 1958 the folkies got together at Wesleyan University in Middletown, Connecticut, and performed a skit at their fraternity E. Q. V. (*Esse Quam Videre*, or for the layman, "To be, rather than to seem"). They originally called themselves the Clansmen but the negative connotation of that name became apparent. They renamed themselves after Alfred Noyes' poem *The Highwaymen* since they were looking for something that reflected their repertoire of songs from around the world.

The quintet of 18-year-olds practiced and performed through their freshman, sophomore, and junior years for a collection of preoccupied pool players in their frat house basement.

Influenced by the Weavers and the Kingston Trio, the five honor students decided at the end of one semester to go into New York City and find a few summer bookings. What they found instead was manager extraordinaire Ken Greengrass, who knew that quality folk groups were a hot commodity. He took them to RCA studios, cut a demo, and made a deal with Don Costa at United Artists Records.

Their first single was the 19th-century folk tune "Michael (Row the Boat Ashore)." By September 4, 1961 the Highwaymen had pushed Joe Dowell's "Wooden Heart" out of the number one spot in the nation. "Michael" also spread around the world, reaching number one in England and number two in Australia.

Even though they were offered tours (including a world tour with comedian Mort Sahl), the group was steadfastly against leaving school. They performed only on the weekends, mostly at colleges.

Their first big performance was at East Carolina College in Greenville, North Carolina, during the fall of 1961.

The late fall of 1961 produced a two-sided charter, "Cotton Fields" (#13) b/w "Gypsy Rover" (#42).

"I'm on My Way" (#90, 1962) and a unique recording called "The Bird Man," with a narration by Burt Lancaster as the bird man of Alcatraz (#64, 1962), were their third and fourth singles and last two chart records, though they followed them with excellent adaptations of "I Know Where I'm Goin'," "I Never Will Marry," "All My Trials," and "Universal Soldier."

Their last single was "Michael '65," but by 1963 the group had decided to focus on their higher education.

Steve Trott had already gone on to Harvard Law School and had been replaced in 1961 by Gil Robbins, formerly of the Cumberland Three. Bob Burnett went on to Harvard Law, Chan Daniels went to Harvard Business School, and Steve Butts entered Columbia, while Dave Fisher stayed in the music business. Daniels became an executive at Capitol Records after securing his degree from Harvard. He died on August 2, 1975, from complications caused by pneumonia.

In 1991 Bob Burnett was a bank vice president in Barrington, Rhode Island; Steve Butts, a Ph.D. in Chinese Politics, was Director of Planning at Grinnel College in Iowa; Dave Fisher was a songwriter, arranger, record producer, and TV composer for Glen Larson Productions in Los Angeles; Gil Robbins became a successful Broadway actor

(his son Tim also became an actor); Steve Trott became the Associate Attorney General of the United States and was an active Federal Judge of the U.S. Court of Appeals for the 9th Circuit.

But that wasn't the end. In 1989 Dave Fisher attended a concert in Houston by some new so-called Highwaymen, the aforementioned outlaws Messrs. Cash, Jennings, Kristofferson, and Nelson. Seeing all the ancillary merchandise labeled "The Highwaymen," Fisher notified the honorable Steve S. Trott and the other original Highwaymen and a lawsuit was filed. Jennings's novel solution (prior to trial) was for the original group to appear as an opening act for the new Highwaymen, and the latter would then be granted a nonexclusive, nontransferable right to use the name in perpetuity. The originals would also have the right to use the name.

The irony is that if the case had gone to court and then to appeal it would have been heard in the U.S. Court of Appeals for the 9th Circuit. And we know who was sitting on that prestigious seat.

In 1990 the two-group concert at Universal Amphitheater in Los Angeles went off without a hitch. Even the District Court Judge who was scheduled to hear the case, Robert M. Takasugi, attended.

THE HIGHWAYMEN

A SIDE/B SIDE	LABEL/CAT NO	DATE
Michael (Row The Boat Ashore) / Santiano	UA 258	1961
Cotton Fields / Gypsy Rover	UA 370	1961
I'm On My Way / Whiskey In The Jar	UA 439	1962
Cindy Oh Cindy / The Bird Man	UA 475	1962
I Know Where I'm Going / Well, Well, Well	UA 540	1962
All My Trials / Midnight Train	UA 568	1963
I Never Will Marry / Pretoria	UA 602	1963
Nellie / Sweet Mama Tree Top Tall	UA 752	1964
Michael '65 / Puttin' On The Style	UA 801	1965

The Imaginations

One of the finer of the lesser-known '60s groups, the Imaginations also served as the starting point for one member's short-lived stardom.

Formed in Bellmore, Long Island, at a luncheonette near Mepham High School, the group included Frank Mancuso (lead) of Mepham High along with Wantagh High Schoolers Bobby Bloom (first tenor), Phil Agtuca (second tenor), Pete Agtuca (baritone), and Richard LeCausi (bass). The members, aged 15 to 17 in 1961, practiced songs by THE PARAGONS, THE JESTERS, THE DUBS, the Blue Notes, THE DEL-VIKINGS, and THE DRIFTERS. As their harmony became tighter, the group began working on originals.

A casual conversation between Frank and his record collecting friend Tony Sarafino, who was working at Sam Goody's record store in Valley Stream, Long Island, led to the boys auditioning in a basement for Tony and Sam Meltzer, partners in a new production company. Tony and Sam recognized the boys were special and decided to spend their own money to prove it.

On March 9, 1961, the group trekked to New York City to record at Music Makers Studio's 6 West 57th Street address. They cut "Hey You," "Never Let You Go," "The Search Is Over," and "Goodnight Baby," all originals. The last of these, with its two minutes and 14 seconds of the most free-form doo wop since DION AND THE BELMONTS' "I Wonder Why," hit the airwaves in April. (The instrumentation included King Curtis on sax and Mickey Baker on guitar.) "Goodnight Baby" scored up and down the East Coast, particularly in Philadelphia, Washington, Baltimore, and New York, where it went to number 19 on WABC's "Swingin' Sound" Survey of May 25, 1961.

The group became regulars on the WMGM-sponsored Saturday shows at Palisades Park, New Jersey, and on Murray the K's shows with the Belmonts, THE HARPTONES, THE CLEFTONES, Adam Wade, LITTLE ANTHONY, and Chuck Jackson.

On May 23rd, the group was back in the studio to sing backup for young Darlene Day, who was doing her best to sound like Kathy Young of the Innocents ("A Thousand Stars," #3, 1960). With some time left to kill, Tony Sarafino decided the Selections' song "Guardian Angel" would be great for the Imaginations, so they worked it up and recorded it. They also cut "Hey You," a definitive doo wop recording.

"Hey You" cracked WABC's top 20 and was starting to spread across the country when "Guardian Angel" also began getting airplay. Music Makers licensed the single to Duel Records for greater distribution, but they ran into cash-flow problems and the record's chances died. Nonetheless, "Hey You" sold over 30,000 records and enabled the Queens quartet to perform on Clay Cole's TV show alongside Dion, Chubby Checker, and Baby Washington in 1962.

"Hey You" became a New York favorite and almost a year later reached number 12 on Times Square's top 150 survey of the most popular vocal group records. An interesting first was established on the "Hey You"/"Guardian Angel" label when the group members' names and parts they sang were listed under the title and Imaginations name. Only Al Catabiani's Avenue D Records, formed in 1980, has continued the practice of crediting the vocalists in such a manner.

Music Makers closed down and the group found themselves in limbo, especially when Frank decided to join the air force. The Imaginations then added Bobby Caupin and renamed themselves the Ebonaires for two sides ("Chapel Bells" b/w "My Little Girl"), but the tracks were never placed with a label and Bobby soon left.

Bobby Bloom then assumed leadership of the group and with his R&B-sounding tenor took the Imaginations/Ebonaires in that direction with an exciting original titled "Wait a Little Longer Son." Issued on the Ballad label in December 1962 it hit all the cities that had supported other Imaginations singles and was a WABC pick hit. Reaction was strong enough for Laurie Records to arrange national distribution, but they were slow to promote it and another potential hit single failed to reach the buyers.

In January 1963 the group separated but reformed under the guidance of Pete Antell and John Linde, two local record producers. Now consisting of Bobby, Phil, and Richie, along with new first tenor John Governale and baritone Pete Lanzetta, the group renamed themselves the Expressions to go along with their blacker sound. At Cameo/Parkway Studios in Philadelphia they recorded two sides written by Antell and Linde titled "On the Corner" and "To Cry." (At about the same time, Richie sang bass for the Antell/Linde-produced ABC group the Percells, who had the charter "What Are Boys Made Of" [#53, March 1963]. Richie also sang an exuberant bass part under the three girls' high harmonies on their last single, "The Greatest." Meanwhile, the Expressions backed Tommy Boyce on a 1963 recording for RCA titled "Don't Be Afraid.")

"On the Corner," an ode to street-corner singing, came and went, and the Expressions/Imaginations went into retirement.

Bobby Bloom kept at it, however, and in September 1970 he cracked the pop charts as a solo artist with "Montego Bay," cowritten with Jeff Barry. By November 28th it was number eight nationally and number three in England. Bobby reached the lower end of the pop charts three more times before taking his own life on February 28, 1974.

Frank was later reported to be playing in a band in Florida. Pete Agtuca became involved in a Honda motorcycle dealership on Long Island. Richie LeCausi became an operations manager for the Genovese drug chain and was living on Long Island.

Those wondering if a little-known group can leave any kind of long-term legacy need only note a recording of "Hey You" released on Crystal Ball Records in 1990 by a West German group called the Microgrooves.

THE IMAGINATIONS

A SIDE/B SIDE	LABEL/CAT NO	DATE
Goodnight Baby /		
The Search Is Over	MsMkr 103	4/61
Will* / I Love You So*	MsMkr 106	8/61
Hey You / Guardian Angel	MsMkr 108	9/61
Hey You / Guardian Angel	Duel 507	9/61
Wait A Little Longer Son /		
Mama's Little Boy	Ballad 500	12/62
On The Corner** / To Cry**	Parkway 892	12/63

* Darlene Day and the Imaginations

** as the Expressions

The Impressions

Two schools of soul were started in the late '50s by THE FALCONS, who promulgated a ragged-edged shouting style, and the Impressions, who gave birth to soul's intense-yet-soft side. The Impressions were actually made up of members of two groups: Arthur and Richard Brooks (tenors) and Sam Gooden (baritone) of the Roosters, and Jerry Butler (baritone) and Curtis Mayfield (tenor) of the Northern Jubilee Gospel Singers.

The three Roosters splintered from their original quintet when they moved to Chicago from Chattanooga, Tennessee, in 1957. The Jubilees' Jerry and Curtis were Chicago residents who were traveling the gospel circuit and performing in the Traveling Souls Spiritualist Church, of which Mayfield's grandmother was a pastor. To help out with the family finances, both boys sang with secular groups on the side, Jerry with the Quails and Curtis as part of the Alphatones.

When the Roosters came on the scene, Jerry convinced Curtis to join, and soon they had both a sound and a manager named Eddie Thomas.

During 1957 Thomas came up with an unusual gig for the teenagers: a downtown fashion show. Performing their usual set of rhythm and blues doo wop songs, the group also did an original with music by the Brooks brothers and lyrics by Butler titled "For Your Precious Love." It caught the attention of one Mrs. Vi Muzinski, who arranged an audition with Calvin Carter of Vee-Jay Records. A more elaborate version of the Vee-Jay encounter was described by Curtis Mayfield in an interview. It seems the group was standing knee-deep in snow at the door of Chess Records, but the secretary, seeing them through the window, refused to let them in. Rather than freeze, they went across the street to Vee-Jay Records, entered, and were greeted by a great dane that held them at bay until Carter came down. They auditioned with "For Your Precious Love" right in the hallway and wound up recording for the label a few days later. (It was Carter who changed the name of the Roosters to the Impressions.)

Whichever version is correct, "For Your Precious Love" was released on Vee-Jay in May 1958. It was an unusual all-verse ballad that never repeated the title, had no hook, and had a quiet gospel tone. With Butler's baritone lead, it is, arguably, the first recognizable soul-styled ballad. There were immediate complications: before many copies of the Impressions' single could be pressed on Vee-Jay, Ewart Abner, the label's general manager, arranged for "Precious Love" to wind up on a Vee-Jay distributed label called Falcon, which some say Ewart owned a piece of. To further complicate matters, Falcon then had to change its name or face an infringement suit, so it became Abner Records, with the exact same logo and artwork (a picture, not surprisingly, of a falcon). The song was now on three labels, each of which read "Jerry Butler and the Impressions" since Vee-Jay recognized his distinctive style and wanted him out front.

By July 28th "For Your Precious Love" was at number 11 Pop and number three R&B. Its flip side, the more traditional doo wop rocker "Sweet Was the Wine," became a street-corner vocal group favorite over the years.

In September, their second single, "Come Back My Love," with a similarity to "Precious Love," came out and went to #28 R&B but never crossed into Pop.

By the fall of 1958, Jerry Butler decided to go solo. Three remaining Ewart Abner singles under the name the Impressions went nowhere, including "At the County Fair," the first recording with a Curtis Mayfield lead.

When Butler's solo career finally managed to take off, it was due in part to his writing and duetting collaboration with Curtis on "He Will Break Your Heart" (Butler's fifth solo single and his first on Vee-Jay).

Meanwhile, Fred Cash of Chattanooga, a Rooster before that group moved north, took Jerry's place in the Impressions. When Vee-Jay left them out in the cold, re-signing only Butler, their manager arranged for the recording of two short-lived singles, "Shorty's Got to Go" on Bandera and "Don't Leave Me" on Swirl, both in 1958. Curtis, now clearly the lead voice and writer, took the quintet to New York and established a record deal with ABC Paramount in 1960.

Their first ABC single established them as distinct from other vocal groups, thanks to Curtis's unique, fragile-sounding falsetto. "Gypsy Woman" reached number 20 Pop while rising to number two R&B. A few more singles were issued, but none with the impact of "Gypsy," so in February 1963 Curtis, Sam, and Fred opted to return to Chicago while the Brooks brothers chose to stay in New York. The Impressions were now a trio, and their first 45 release under that configuration was "Sad, Sad Girl and Boy" (#84).

Mayfield began to write in a more spiritual and black-awareness vein, and September's "It's All Right" catapulted the group into the high reaches of stardom (#4 Pop, #1 R&B). Gospel-styled recordings like "Keep on Pushin'" (#10 Pop, 1964), "Amen" (#7 Pop, #17 R&B), "People Get Ready" (#14 Pop, #3 R&B), and "Meeting Over Yonder" (#48 Pop, #12 R&B) followed in 1965.

Mayfield was wearing numerous professional hats. He wrote for other artists (Jan Bradley, "Mama Didn't Lie," #14 Pop, #8 R&B, 1963) and became Okeh Record's head producer, working with and writing for Major Lance ("Monkey Time" with the Impressions backing, #8 Pop, #2 R&B, 1963) and Gene Chandler ("Rainbow," #47 Pop, #11 R&B, 1963), among others. He continued to pen love songs for the Impressions while singing lead on "Woman's Got Soul" (#29 Pop, #9 R&B, 1965) and "I'm So Proud" (#14 Pop and R&B, 1964), and in 1966 he started his own short-lived Windy C label (seven singles) that recorded THE FIVE STAIRSTEPS.

In 1967 Curtis addressed black political issues in his Impressions recording of "We're a Winner," which was banned on radio in many parts of the U.S. It still made number one R&B and number 14 Pop. (Mayfield had another shorter-lived label called Mayfield Records, the chief success of which was the Fascinations' "Girls Are Out to Get You" [#92 Pop, #13 R&B, 1967].) "We're a Winner" was the Impressions' last ABC single. Their contract expired and they signed with the new Curtom label that was distributed by Buddah and just happened to be owned by Curtis Mayfield. ABC issued a few more canned sides and the trio then went on a streak of 19 R&B charters for Curtom from 1968 to 1976, 12 of which crossed over to Pop. They included "Fool for You" (#22 Pop, #3 R&B, 1968), "This Is My Country" (#25 Pop, #8 R&B, 1969), "Choice of Colors" (#21 Pop, #1 R&B, 1969), and "Check Out Your Mind" (#28 Pop, #3 R&B, 1970).

In the summer of 1970, Mayfield left the group to go solo but continued writing and producing for them. Leroy Hutson of the Mayfield Singers (on Mayfield) took the lead, but the group's popularity declined without Mayfield's familiar sound, much as it did in the early days after Jerry Butler left.

In 1973 Leroy Hutson opted for a solo career. The group then became a quartet with the addition of Ralph Johnson and Reggie Torian. The Impressions hit it big again with the Ed Townsend-produced "Finally Got Myself Together" (#17 Pop, #1 R&B) in the spring of 1974. Follow-up records like "Sooner or Later" (#68 Pop, #3 R&B) and "Same Thing It Took" (#75 Pop, #3 R&B) kept them in the public's consciousness.

The group recorded the soundtrack for the film *Three the Hard Way* in 1973 and in 1976 moved over to Atlantic's Cotillion affiliate.

Johnson left at that time to form the group Mystique, and Nate Evans took his place. Coming full circle, the quartet charted in 1981 with a remake of "For Your Precious Love" (#58, Chi-Sound), and by the late '80s was recording for MCA with its most recent charter being "Can't Wait 'Till Tomorrow" (#91 R&B, 1987).

In 1983 Jerry and Curtis joined with the original Impressions for a reunion tour.

Curtis Mayfield had a very successful solo career from 1970 through 1985, charting R&B 29 times and crossing Pop 11 of those times with songs like "(Don't Worry) If There's a Hell Below We're All Going to Follow" (#29 Pop, #3 R&B, 1970), "Freddy's Dead" (#4 Pop, #2 R&B), and "Superfly" (#8 Pop, #5 R&B), both from the 1972 film *Superfly*.

Butler became an international star with an incredible 54 black charters after his Impressions days and 37 Hot 100 residents, including "Moon River" (#11 Pop, #14 R&B, 1962), "Make It Easy on Yourself" (#20 Pop, #18 R&B, 1962), "Let It Be Me" with Betty Everett (#5 Pop, 1964), "Hey Western Union Man" (#16 Pop, #1 R&B, 1968), and "Only the Strong Survive" (#4 Pop, #1 R&B, 1969).

Combine Mayfield's and Butler's hits with the Impressions' 50 R&B chart songs and 37 Pop sides and you have three entities rooted in one group that had a total of 133 R&B chart singles and 85 on the Pop list. Add that to their position as one of the early proponents of soul and you've got an impressive set of accomplishments.

THE IMPRESSIONS

A SIDE/B SIDE	LABEL/CAT NO	DATE
Jerry Butler and the Impressions		
For Your Precious Love / Sweet Was The Wine	Vee-Jay 280	5/58
For Your Precious Love / Sweet Was The Wine	Falcon 1013	5/58
For Your Precious Love / Sweet Was The Wine	Abner 1013	5/58
Come Back My Love / Love Me	Abner 1017	9/58
The Gift Of Love / At The County Fair	Abner 1023	1958
The Impressions		
Don't Leave Me / I Need Your Love	Swirl 107	1958
Listen For Me / Shorty's Got To Go	Band 2504	1958
Senorita I Love You / Say That You Love Me	Abner 1025	1959
Say That You Love Me / A New Love	Abner 1034	1959
Gypsy Woman / As You Love Me	ABC 10241	11/61
Can't You See / Grow Closer Together	ABC 10289	2/62
Little Young Lover / Never Let Me Go	ABC 10328	7/62
You've Come Home / Minstrel and Queen	ABC 10357	1962
I'm The One Who Loves You / I Need Your Love	ABC 10386	2/63
Sad, Sad Girl & Boy	ABC 10431	5/63
It's All Right / You'll Want Me Back	ABC 10487	10/63
Talking About My Baby / Never Too Much Love	ABC 10511	1/64
I'm So Proud / I Made A Mistake	ABC 10544	4/64
Keep On Pushing / I Love You	ABC 10554	5/64
You Must Believe Me / See The Real Me	ABC 10581	9/64
Amen / Long Long Winter	ABC 10602	1/65
People Get Ready / I've Been Trying	ABC 10622	2/65
Woman's Got Soul / Get Up and Move	ABC 10647	4/65
Meeting Over Yonder / I've Found That I've Lost	ABC 10670	6/65
I Need You / Never Could Be You	ABC 10710	9/65

A SIDE/B SIDE	LABEL/CAT NO	DATE
Just One Kiss From You / Twilight Time	ABC 10725	10/65
You've Been Cheating / Man Oh Man	ABC 10750	12/65
Since I Lost The One I Love / Falling In Love With You	ABC 10761	2/66
Too Slow / No One Else	ABC 10789	4/66
Can't Satisfy / This Must End	ABC 10831	8/66
You Always Hurt Me / Little Girl	ABC 10900	2/67
You've Got Me Runnin' / It's Hard To Believe	ABC 10932	5/67
I Can't Stay Away From You / You Ought To Be In Heaven	ABC 10964	8/67
We're A Winner / It's All Over	ABC 11022	12/67
We're Rolling On Parts 1 & 2	ABC 11071	4/68
I Loved And Lost / Up Up and Away	ABC 11103	7/68
Fool For You / I'm Loving Nothing	Curtom 1932	8/68
Don't Cry My Love / Sometimes I Wonder	ABC 11135	11/68
This Is My Country / My Woman's Love	Curtom 1934	11/68
My Deceiving Heart / You Want Somebody Else	Curtom 1937	2/69
Just Before Sunrise / East Of Java	ABC 11188	1969
Seven Years / The Girl I Find	Curtom 1940	4/69
Choice Of Colors / Mighty Mighty Spade and Whitney	Curtom 1943	6/69
Say You Love Me / You'll Always Be Mine	Curtom 1946	10/69
Amen / Wherever She Leadeth Me	Curtom 1948	12/69
Check Out Your Mind / Can't You See	Curtom 1951	4/70
Baby Turn On To Me / Soulful Love	Curtom 1954	8/70
Ain't Got Time / I'm So Proud	Curtom 1957	1/71
Love Me / Do You Wanna Win	Curtom 1959	7/71
Inner City Blues / We Must Be In Love	Curtom 1964	10/71
This Love's For Real / Our Love Goes On And On	Curtom 1070	3/72
I Need To Belong To Someone / Love Me	Curtom 1973	6/72
Times Have Changed / Preacher Man	Curtom 1982	2/73
Thin Line / I'm Loving You	Curtom 1985	4/73
If It's In You To Do Wrong / Times Have Changed	Curtom 1994	1974
Finally Got Myself Together / I'll Always Be Here	Curtom 1997	1974
Something's Mighty Wrong / Three The Hard Way	Curtom 2003	1974
Sooner Or Later / Miracle Woman	Curtom 0103	1975
Same Thing It Took / I'm So Glad	Curtom 0106	1975
First Impressions / Loving Power	Curtom 0110	1975
I Wish I'd Stayed In Bed / Sunshine	Curtom 0116	1975
This Time / I'm A Fool For Love	Cot 44210	1976
Silent Night / I Saw Mommy Kissing Santa Claus	Cot 44211	1976

The Intruders

The quintessential Philadelphia soul group, the Intruders were the original foundation for the Gamble and Huff musical empire.

Merging in 1960, Philadelphia's Sam "Little Sonny" Brown (lead), Phil Terry, Eugene "Bird" Daughtry, and Robert "Big Sonny" Edwards recorded a single for the small Gowen label. Little Sonny's distinctive, straining tenor was evident even on this cut, the Latin-rhythmed "I'm Sold on You." With its doo wop flip side "Come Home Soon," the record quickly disappeared among the competition.

In 1964 the group met Leon Huff and by 1965 they had a regional success with "Gonna Be Strong" on Excel.

During 1966 Huff partnered with Kenny Gamble, set up the Gamble label, and signed the Intruders as their first act. Gamble and Huff then began writing for the quartet, yielding a soul-styled ballad called "United" that charted at number 78 on *Billboard*'s Pop charts (#14 R&B). The group had continued success with "Together" (#48 Pop, #9 R&B, 1967) and "Baby I'm Lonely" (#70 Pop, #28 R&B, 1967).

Gamble and Huff seemed to have a habit of borrowing instrumental intros from Motown. "Baby I'm Lonely" had an opening similar to that of THE FOUR TOPS' "Ask the Lonely." The Intruders' third Gamble single, "Check Yourself," was right in the mode of THE TEMPTATIONS' "Get Ready."

The group became more original with their first single of 1968, the clever Gamble-and-Huff-penned rhythm ballad "Cowboys to Girls." With Little Sonny's distinctive wailing and a smart Bobby Martin arrangement (the previous arrangements were by the king of Upper Black Eddy, P. Joe Renzetti), the Intruders went to number six Pop and number one R&B during the spring.

"(Love Is Like a) Baseball Game," a mix of America's two favorite pastimes, followed soon after and rose to number 26 on the pop chart and number four R&B.

Other worthy singles followed, including the harmony-filled "Slow Drag" (#54 Pop, #12 R&B, 1968), "Me Tarzan, You Jane" (#41 R&B, 1969), "Lollipop" (#101 Pop, #22 R&B, 1969), "When We Get Married" (#45 Pop, #8 R&B, 1973) and that perennial Mother's Day favorite, "I'll Always Love My Mama, Part I" (#36 Pop, #6 R&B, and their first U.K. charter at #32, 1973).

Their biggest overseas single was "(Win, Place or Show) She's a Winner," which was number 12

R&B in the U.S. during 1972 and number 14 in Britain two years later.

In 1972 the group moved to Gamble and Huff's Philadelphia International label with no successes and in 1974 shifted to their TSOP label, where "A Nice Girl Like You" reached number 21 R&B.

They earned their last chart single in the spring of 1975 with "Rainy Days and Mondays" (#81 R&B).

Though never a superstar act, their consistent chart appearances made them a mainstay of soul and disco in the late '60s and early '70s.

The Isley Brothers

Coming from a gospel background, the Isley Brothers successfully entertained several generations of R&B and rock and roll lovers.

The Isley family was from Cincinnati, Ohio, and the original group was a quartet consisting of four Isley sons of Kelly and Sallye Isley. They were Ronald (b. 5/21/41, lead), O'Kelly (b. 12/25/37), Rudolph (b. 4/1/39), and youngest brother Vernon.

In 1944, three-year-old Ronald won a $25 war bond for singing in a spiritual contest at the Union Baptist Church, and by the time he was seven he was singing on stage at the Regal Theatre alongside Dinah Washington and others. With their mother accompanying them, the Isleys toured churches throughout Kentucky and Ohio, but activities ground to a halt in the 1950s when young Vernon was killed in a traffic accident. A year later their parents convinced them to regroup, and the trio set about crafting a balance of gospel, rhythm and blues, and doo wop into an energetic style.

In 1957 they left for New York with bus fare and $20 out of the family fund. A woman on the bus liked their harmonizing and recommended they see an agent in New York that she knew. The introduction allowed the teens to work and earn money for food and lodging.

Through their local shows they met Bill (Bass) Gordon, former lead singer of the Colonials (Gee, 1956) and owner of Teenage Records. He recorded the group and issued their first single, the doo wop, tenor-led ballad "The Angels Cried."

A year later they crossed paths with George Goldner and recorded the Ron Isley-penned JESTERS/"So Strange" styled ballad "Don't Be Jealous."

Three more Goldner singles (two on Gone and one on Mark-X) went nowhere. The group was then spotted by Howard Bloom of RCA at the Howard

Theatre in Washington, D.C., and in the spring of 1959 they signed with that label.

On July 29th the trio made the historic recording of "Shout, Parts I and II," the song that epitomized the merging of gospel and rock and roll. With a high-energy rhythm, gospel shouts, insistent tambourines, Professor Herman Stephens (their hometown church organist) on the keys, and the Isleys' now-famous "hey-ey-ey-ey" call-and-response section, "Shout" charted Pop on September 21, 1959, and reached number 47. It never made it to the R&B chart, but in years to come it sold over a million copies as a standard rock and roll oldie and became one of oldies radio's most popular plays.

In 1962 it charted again (#94), but their other RCA releases didn't fare as well even though they included such gospel rockers as "Respectable," which the Outsiders (another Ohio group, this one from Cleveland) took to number 15 in 1966, and the rousing "Tell Me Who."

They moved to Atlantic Records in 1961 and were produced by Leiber and Stoller, but they couldn't come up with a commercial package for the group's gospel power. Four singles failed. In 1962 the brothers switched over to Wand (a division of Florence Greenberg's Scepter operation) and hit with a Bert Berns song and production called "Twist and Shout" (#17 Pop, #2 R&B, #42 U.K.). The Beatles made it a number two hit in 1964.

In 1964 the group set up their own T-Neck label named after the New Jersey city where they and their family now lived. They issued only one single at the time, "Testify, Parts I and II," a recording that featured a 22-year-old touring band member named Jimi Hendrix on guitar.

By 1966 the Isleys had signed with Motown's Tamla affiliate and recorded some of their best material, including the Holland, Dozier, and Holland song "This Old Heart of Mine" (#12 Pop, #6 R&B, #47 U.K.).

In 1968 the group toured England and "This Old Heart" was reissued for a chart climb to number three. The group wasn't on Tamla anymore, so they resurrected T-Neck, arranged distribution through Neil Bogart's Buddah label, and in 1969 hit with "It's Your Thing," which turned out to be their biggest record ever (#2 Pop, #1 R&B, #30 U.K.). Their *It's Your Thing* LP eventually sold over two million copies.

Meanwhile, in the U.K., Tamla releases that did little in the U.S. began to hit the upper reaches of the charts. "I Guess I'll Always Love You" hit number 11 in early 1969 and "Behind a Painted Smile" went to number five in the spring of 1969—just two of the eventual charters the Isleys would accumulate in Britain.

By the fall of 1969 the family trio had been joined by brothers Marvin (bass), Ernie (guitar and drums), and cousin Chris Jasper (keyboards).

The group began producing other acts for T-Neck like Dave "Baby" Cortez (of THE VALENTINES, Rama) and Judy White.

They also began covering rock and folk-rock material, adding their own gospel flavor to songs like Stephen Stills's "Love the One You're With" (#18 Pop, #3 R&B, 1971) and Bob Dylan's "Lay, Lady, Lay" (#71 Pop, #29 R&B, 1971), while doing a whole LP of covers (*Giving It Back*) that included James Taylor's "Fire and Rain."

In 1973, T-Neck moved from Buddah to Columbia and the initial release, "That Lady," became one of their biggest hits (#6 Pop, #2 R&B).

From 1974 to 1984 the group scored 27 times on the R&B chart and 12 times on the Pop list with songs like Seals and Crofts' "Summer Breeze" (#60 Pop, #10 R&B, 1974), "Fight the Power" (#4 Pop, #1 R&B, 1975), "The Pride" (#63 Pop, #1 R&B, 1977), "Take Me to the Next Place" (#1 R&B, 1978), "I Want to Be with You" (#1 R&B, 1979), and "Don't Say Goodnight" (#39 Pop, #1 R&B, 1980).

In 1984 the younger brothers, Ernie and Marvin, along with cousin Chris, formed the Isley, Jasper, Isley group and hit number 51 in late 1985 with the gospel-influenced "Caravan of Love." The House Martins in England did an a cappella version in 1986 and reached number one there.

The split of the family into two groups may have taken the wind out of the original trio's sales for a while but in late 1985 they mothballed T-Neck, signed with Warner Bros., and reached number 12 R&B with "Colder Are My Nights."

On March 31, 1986, O'Kelly died of a heart attack at age 48, and little Isley Brother action happened after that.

A previous cut, "Smooth Sailing Tonight," became their last top five R&B single (#3) in the spring of 1986, and in 1990 Ron Isley and Rod Stewart teamed up for a strong remake of "This Old Heart of Mine" (#10 Pop).

THE ISLEY BROTHERS

A SIDE/B SIDE	LABEL/CAT NO	DATE
The Cow Jumped Over The Moon / The Angels Cried	Teen 1004	1/57
Don't Be Jealous / This Is The End	Cindy 3009	6/58

A SIDE/B SIDE	LABEL/CAT NO	DATE
I Wanna Know / Everybody's Gonna Rock And Roll	Gone 5022	1958
My Love / The Drag	Gone 5048	1958
Turn To Me / I'm Gonna Knock At Your Door	RCA 47-7537	5/59
The Drag / Rockin' MacDonald	Mark-X 8000	12/59
Shout Part 1 / Shout Part 2	RCA 47-7588	8/59
Respectable / Without A Song	RCA 47-7657	12/59
How Deep Is The Ocean / He's Got The Whole World In His Hands	RCA 47-7718	3/60
Open Up Your Heart / Gypsy Love Song	RCA 47-7746	6/60
Tell Me Who / Say You Love Me Too	RCA 47-7787	9/69
Jeepers Creepers / Teach Me How To Shimmy	Atln 2092	2/61
Your Old Lady / Write To Me	Atln 2100	4/61
A Fool For You / Just One More Time	Atln 2122	10/61
Fight Now / The Snake	Wand 118	1962
Twist And Shout / Spanish Twist	Wand 124	1962
Twistin' With Linda / You Better Come Home	Wand 127	1962
Nobody But Me / I'm Laughing To Keep From Crying	Wand 131	1/63
Hold On Baby / I Say Love	Wand 137	1963
Tango / She's Gone	UA 605	1963
Surf And Shout / Whatcha Gonna Do	UA 638	1963
Please Please Please / You'll Never Leave Him	UA 659	1963
Who's That Lady / My Little Girl	UA 714	1964
The Last Girl / Looking For Love	Atln 2263	10/64
Testify Part 1 / Testify Part 2	T-Neck 501	1964
Wild As A Tiger / Simon Says	Atln 2277	2/65
Move Over And Let Me Dance / Have You Ever Been Disappointed	Atln 2303	9/65
This Old Heart Of Mine / There's No Love Left	Tamla 54128	1/66
Take Some Time Out For Love / Who Could Ever Doubt My Love	Tamla 54133	5/66
I Guess I'll Always Love You / I Hear A Symphony	Tamla 54135	6/66
Love Is A Wonderful Thing / Open Up Her Eyes	Veep 1230	1966
Got To Have You Back / Just Ain't Enough Love	Tamla 54146	4/67
That's The Way Love Is / One Too Many Heartaches	Tamla 54154	6/67
Take Me In Your Arms / Why When Love Is Gone	Tamla 54164	3/68
All Because I Love You / Behind A Painted Smile	Tamla 54175	10/68
Just Ain't Enough Love / Take Some Time Out For Love	Tamla 54182	4/69
It's Your Thing / Don't Give It Away	T-Nk 901	2/69

A SIDE/B SIDE	LABEL/CAT NO	DATE
I Turned You On / I Know Who You Been Socking It To	T-Nk 902	5/69
Black Berries Part 1 / Black Berries Part 2	T-Nk 906	8/69
Was It Good To You / I Got To Get Myself Together	T-Nk 908	9/69
Give The Women What They Want / Bless Your Heart	T-Nk 912	11/69
Keep On Doin' / Same Me	T-Nk 914	1/70
If He Can, You Can / Holdin' On	T-NK 919	4/70
Girls Will Be Girls, Boys Will Be Boys / Get Down Off Of The Train	T-Nk 921	7/70
Warpath / I Got To Find Me One	T-Nk 929	3/71
Love The One You're With / He's Got Your Love	T-Nk 930	5/71
Spill The Wine / Take Inventory	T-Nk 932	9/71
Lay Lady Lay / Vacuum Cleaner	T-Nk 933	11/71
Lay-Away / Feel Like The World	T-Nk 934	2/72
Pop That Thang / I Got To Find Me One	T-Nk 935	6/72
Work To Do / Beautiful	T-Nk 936	9/72
It's Too Late	T-Nk 937	4/73
That Lady Part 1 / That Lady Part 2	T-Nk 2251	6/73
The Highways Of My Life / What It Comes Down To	T-Nk 2252	11/73
Summer Breeze Part 1 / Summer Breeze Part 2	T-Nk 2253	2/74
Live It Up Part 1 / Live It Up Part 2	T-Nk 2254	7/74
Midnight Sky Part 1 / Midnight Sky Part 2	T-Nk 2255	10/74
Fight The Power Part 1 / Fight The Power Part 2	T-Nk 2256	5/75
For The Love Of You / You Walk Your Way	T-Nk 2259	10/75
Who Loves You Better Part 1 / Who Loves You Better Part 2	T-Nk 2260	4/76
Harvest For The World	T-Nk 2261	8/76

Jay and the Americans

One of the most popular groups of the '60s, Jay and the Americans brought a distinctive sound and clean-cut image to the music scene.

Lead singer John Traynor was originally a member of THE MYSTICS of "Hushabye" fame but left to form his own group in 1959. He and Howard Kirshenbaum, Kenny Rosenberg, and Sandy Yaguda christened themselves the Harbor Lights. The Brooklyn quartet recorded two singles, one for

Mala Records and one for Jaro Records in 1960, neither receiving notable exposure.

In 1962, they met producer/writers Jerry Leiber and Mike Stoller via an audition, resulting in a United Artists recording contract. Leiber and Stoller built on the group's natural doo wop ability; they broadened its appeal by emphasizing John's lead and the pop flavor of the sound. United Artists came up with a new name for the group: Binky Jones and the Americans. A compromise changed it to Jay and the Americans, using John's nickname.

Their first recordings were in October of 1961, and from those sessions emerged the *West Side Story* single "Tonight." It failed to chart nationally, though it did receive considerable New York airplay. Their second single, "She Cried," was one of the eeriest, most haunting 45s released during the '60s, and it headed straight up the charts to number five in the spring and early summer of 1962. The next single, "This Is It," failed to chart. Jay decided to leave and by 1963 had begun a solo career on Coral Records. His first release, "How Sweet It Is," was a sugary, punchless Bobby Rydell/Frankie Avalon-style shuffle that nearly initiated his retirement. His last single came three years later on ABC-Paramount Records. "The Merry Go Round Is Slowing You Down" was a better recording then "How Sweet It Is," but suffered the same chartless fate.

The Americans, meanwhile were without a lead singer. Guitarist Marty Sanders, the group's backup vocalist since the "She Cried" session, brought in his friend to audition. The friend, David Blatt, was currently lead singer for the Empires, an all-Jewish vocal group from Tilden High School in Brooklyn who had just released a single on Epic entitled "(A) Time and a Place." David won the spot. The remaining Empires (Gary Kessler, Phil Horowitz, Richie Kaufman, and Eddie Robbins) were upset over his departure from their group and renamed themselves the Squires, recording a single for Congress Records in 1964 entitled "Joyce." In between, they worked as stage hands for the long-running Broadway smash *Hello Dolly.*

Leiber and Stoller were reluctant to change the group's name to David and the Americans, so David Blatt became Jay Black. Other names changed as well: Kenny Rosenberg became Kenny Vance; Howard Kirshenbaum (a mortician when he wasn't singing) became Howie Kane. With a new lead and three new names, the group resumed its career. Unfortunately the next two singles, "Tomorrow" and "Strangers Tomorrow," failed to make the top 100.

Even "Tomorrows'" B side, "Yes," with its Latin feel and simple though catchy hook, deserved to see some chart activity. The group didn't realize it at the time, but "Yes" was the first of several future connections they would have to THE DRIFTERS. While Leiber and Stoller had been working with the Americans they simultaneously had a chart record with "When My Little Girl Is Smiling," a song with an almost identical feel to "Yes" as recorded by the Drifters.

Jay Black's soaring vibrato and powerful mid-range were just waiting for the right song. It came through an unusual set of circumstances. Early in 1963, the Drifters (produced since 1959 by Leiber and Stoller) were recording a song titled "Only in America," written by the producers with the legendary team of Barry Mann and Cynthia Weil. It looked like a sure smash until Atlantic Records decided not to release it. The original Drifters vocals were wiped from the track and replaced by Jay and the Americans. The unreleased (and eventually erased) Drifters version of "Only in America" surfaced on a compilation album packaged in Europe in the 1970s, and is a much sought after collector's item. Jay and the Americans' version was released in July 1963, and it became their first chart hit with Jay Black as lead, reaching number 25 by late summer.

One year and two singles later they hit with their biggest record, "Come a Little Bit Closer" (#3). This resulted in the group's participation in the Beatles' first American tour in 1964, along with the Righteous Brothers.

"Let's Lock the Door" (#11) and "Think of the Good Times" (#57), two Wes Farrell-penned compositions, kept them on the charts into the summer of 1965. At that time they began the second phase of their career with their recording of David Whitfield's 1954 opera-styled hit, "Cara, Mia"; it soared up the charts to number four. Starting with this song, the group found extended chart life covering successful oldies. Their next release was another operatic gem, "Some Enchanted Evening" from the musical *South Pacific.* It reached number 13 and was followed by Neil Diamond's first songwriting success "Sunday and Me" (#18).

The 10 singles released between 1966 and 1968 produced only one top 30 record, a powerful remake of Roy Orbison's classic "Crying" (#25). They had gone back to originals during this period, but in what had become the psychedelic era the public wasn't buying Jay and the Americans without a familiar song. They dipped back into the oldies bag, reworking the eight-year-old hit by the

Drifters, "This Magic Moment," which became their biggest hit since "Cara, Mia" and even outdistanced the original (number six to the Drifters' number 16).

From 1968 thru 1971, they charted with three more remakes, including THE TURBANS' "When You Dance" (#70), the Mystics' "Hushabye" (#62) (original lead Jay Traynor must have gotten a kick out of that), and THE RONETTES' "Walking in the Rain" (#19). Ironically, their last chart record was an original song, "Capture the Moment" (#57), in the spring of 1970, and their last single was another Drifters classic, "There Goes My Baby."

In the early '70s the oldies revival gave the group new performance opportunities; Jay Black stayed on as lead into the 1980s while other members dropped out. Two band members at the time, Walter Becker and Donald Fagen, went on to form the hit rock group Steely Dan. Kenny Vance began working with record producer Joel Dorn (Roberta Flack) and recorded one of the last doo wop classics in 1975, "Looking for an Echo." His backup group included Eddie Brigati of the Rascals, David Brigati of the Hi-Five, Pete Anders of the Trade Winds, and most of the Americans minus Jay.

More than any group of the '60s, Jay and the Americans paid tribute to the '50s vocal sound, filling their repertoire with songs by THE HARPTONES, THE PASSIONS, THE CLEFTONES, THE PLATTERS, THE SKYLINERS, and THE IMPRESSIONS. They also drew from such '60s groups as THE ANGELS, THE TYMES, THE MAMAS AND THE PAPAS, and of course the Drifters. Whether by circumstance or design, Jay and the Americans were one of the few successful groups to spend their entire career with one record label: all of their 32 singles and numerous LPs (18 of which were top 100) were with United Artists.

JAY AND THE AMERICANS

A SIDE/B SIDE	LABEL/CAT NO	DATE
The Harbor Lights		
Angel Of Love / Tick-a Tick-a-Tock	Mala 422	1960
What Would I Do Without You /		
Is That Too Much To Ask	Jaro 77020	1960
Jay and the Americans		
Tonight / The Other Girls	UA 353	1961
She Cried / Dawning	UA 415	1962
This Is It / It's My Turn To Cry	UA 479	1962
Tomorrow / Yes	UA 504	1962
Strangers Tomorrow /		
What's The Use	UA 566	1962
Only In America /		
My Claire De Lune	UA 626	1963

A SIDE/B SIDE	LABEL/CAT NO	DATE
Baby, This Is Rock and Roll	UA 629	1963
Come Dance With Me /		
Look In My Eyes Maria	UA 669	1963
Friday / To Wait For Love	UA 693	1964
Come A Little Bit Closer /		
Goodbye Boys Goodbye	UA 759	1964
Let's Lock The Door /		
I'll Remember You	UA 805	1964
Think Of The Good Times /		
If You Were Mine, Girl	UA 845	1965
Cara Mia / When It's All Over	UA 881	1965
Some Enchanted Evening / Girl	UA 919	1965
Sunday And Me /		
Through This Doorway	UA 948	1965
Why Can't You Bring Me Home /		
Baby Stop Your Cryin'	UA 992	1966
Crying / I Don't Need A Friend	UA 50016	1966
Living Above Your Head /		
Look At Me, What Do You See	UA 50046	1966
Baby Come Home /		
Stop The Clock	UA 50086	1966
The Reason For Living /		
Raining In My Sunshine	UA 50094	1966
Nature Boy / You Ain't		
As Hip As All That Baby	UA 50139	1967
Yellow Forest /		
Got Hung Up Along The Way	UA 50196	1967
French Provincial /		
Shanghai Noodle Factory	UA 50222	1967
No Other Love /		
No, I Don't Know Her	UA 50282	1968
Gemini / You Ain't		
Gonna Wake Up Crying	UA 50448	1968
Since I Don't Have You /		
This Magic Moment	UA 50475	1968
No, I Don't Know Her /		
When You Dance	UA 50510	1969
Gypsy Woman / Hushabye	UA 50535	1969
Learnin' How To Fly /		
For The Love Of A Lady	UA 50567	1969
For The Love Of A Lady /		
Walkin' In The Rain	UA 50605	1969
Do You Ever Think Of Me /		
Capture The Moment	UA 50654	1970
Do You Love Me / Tricia	UA 50683	1970
There Goes My Baby /		
Solitary Man	UA 50858	1971

The Jive Five

The street corners of Brooklyn, New York have probably seen more vocal groups come and go than any other locale. From black groups like THE PARAGONS, THE ROCKETONES, THE IMPERIALS, THE

VELOURS, THE DANLEERS, THE SHELLS, the Fantastics, and THE CHIPS, to white quartets and quintets like THE TOKENS, THE PASSIONS, THE MYSTICS, THE CLASSICS, THE FOUR-EVERS, THE QUOTATIONS, and VITO AND THE SALUTATIONS, many an act pursued street singing as a way of life.

That way of life led Eugene Pitt through four groups starting in 1954, from the Top Notes on the Cooper Projects streets of Frost and Jackson to the Zip-Tones and the Akrons of Bedford and Jefferson Avenues. Pitt sang backup baritone in the days when the Akrons' backup included two guys named Murphy—the father and uncle of comedian Eddie Murphy.

Though he sang with a variety of groups, Gene never really had to leave the house. His four brothers and nine sisters made up two gospel aggregations that were drilled constantly by their dad.

Borough-wide battles of the groups brought Gene in contact with four vocalists looking for a fifth, so he, Estelle Williams, Fred Jones, Claude Johnson, and Haskell Cleveland began a quintet. Some claim that they named themselves THE GENIES and that Gene Pitt sang with them on their 1958 chart record "Who's That Knockin'." In fact, Fred Jones moved to Long Beach, formed a quartet, and asked Claude Johnson to join him. That group became the Genies. Both Johnson and Pitt claim that he (Pitt) never recorded or even sang with that Long Island quintet. But that's as far as facts go when you get down to who named the Genies and when. Johnson states that the Brooklyn bunch was unnamed and that he named the Long Island group the Genies after joining. Others state the Pitt's Brooklyn party called themselves the Genies because of Gene and long before the Long Island doo woppers were together.

With the unnamed Brooklyn Genies (now there's a compromise) depleted, Pitt formed still another group around 1959 with Jerome Hanna (first tenor), Thurmon "Billy" Prophet (second tenor), Richard Harris (baritone), and Norman Johnson (bass) at the night center of P.S. 54.

(Estelle Williams and Haskell Cleveland went on to form Jeannie and Her Boyfriends [Warwick] for a rockin' 1959 answer to "Who's That Knockin'" titled "It's Me Knockin'.")

Pitt's new group had two priorities—singing and attracting girls. Emphasizing the latter, they began running into the same group of girls almost daily until one of them in exasperation said something to the effect of "There they are, following us again. Those guys are jive—five jive guys." With a little imaginative revision, the group became the Jive Five.

Gene (whose main vocal group influence was THE SPANIELS) was working in a Nostrand Avenue supermarket when a patron, Mrs. Oscar Waltzer, told him about her songwriter/arranger husband. That introduction led to Waltzer bringing the five to Joe René at Beltone Records, owned by Les Cahan.

The Jive Five auditioned live, singing several songs that elicited bored looks. Finally René asked if they had any songs they really liked, so the group sang a Gene Pitt original titled "My True Story." Cahan enthusiastically announced that he thought it was a hit. The song was recorded in December 1960 but wasn't released until the spring of 1961.

By July 3rd "My True Story" was on the national charts and by September 11th it had reached number three Pop and number one R&B. With harmonies reminiscent of the mid-'50s, the Jive Five seemed almost like a standard bearer of a past era. The group hit the chitlin circuit, and by the time they surfaced from a myriad of Howard, Regal, and Apollo Theatre dates to drive to their next recording session, they found halfway there that they were missing something—namely, a song to record. While the group fought the traffic, Gene fought the clock and wrote "Never Never" in the car. A ballad with more prevalent harmonies than "My True Story," it charted in November 1961 but only reached number 74.

Their third single, "Hully Gully Calling Time," was reviewed by *Billboard* on March 3, 1962, as an "attractive hunk of teen wax with the lead selling the hully gully effort solidly over listenable support by the group." Heavily played in the New York area, it never went national.

In the late summer of 1962 the five returned to their ballad style with a song by Bobby Feldman, Jerry Goldstein, and Rich Gottehrer. But there were some personnel changes before they hit the studio: Jerome Hanna died and was replaced by Andre Coles, Casey Spencer came on for Billy Prophet, and Beatrice Best subbed for Richard Harris.

That song, "What Time Is It," was an immediate East Coast smash and the best of all Jive Five recordings, but it failed to do better than number 67 nationally. (It was also the first record on which the label read "The Jive Five with Eugene Pitt.") Their next 45, "These Golden Rings," managed a number 27 on the R&B chart in late 1962.

By now only Gene and a returning Billy Prophet were left. They teamed with three CADILLACS (J. R. Bailey, Bobby Phillips, and Buddy Brooks) to record another strong ballad called "Rain."

It was issued in March 1963 but flopped. The group continued to work constantly, however, doing one-nighters and Dick Clark tours with the likes of Chubby Checker, THE SHIRELLES, Paul Anka, Tom Jones, and Linda Scott.

Shuttling to the local Sketch label, Gene brought back the team of Harris, Best, and Spencer as the new Jive Five, even though there were only four. A cover of the Love Notes' 1957 ballad "United" elicited a purchase of the master by United Artists. One of their finer cuts, it garnered only New York airplay. But its UA follow-up, recorded on February 15, 1965, and issued in the summer, gave new life to the Jive Five (or "Jive Four" if you want to be as precise as one club owner was—but that's a later story). "I'm a Happy Man" became their biggest hit since "My True Story" (#36 Pop, #26 R&B).

Five more singles were released in 1965–66 but UA couldn't get the required response, so in 1967 the group moved on to Musicor for their last chart record as the Jive Five, "Sugar (Don't Take Away My Candy)" (#119 Pop, #34 R&B) in 1968.

As for the previously mentioned club owner, he refused to pay the group for a performance because they were called the Jive Five but were only four singers. Gene Pitt then decided to alter the name without losing the group's recognition and re-spelled it the Jyve Fyve.

Recordings with Decca, Avco, and Brut failed to create a stir, but the group kept on performing through the '70s and '80s. During the early '70s the Jive Five included Gene, Casey Spencer, Richard Fisher, and Webster Harris of the Persians (Richard's brother). Johnny Watson also sang with them in 1971. In 1974 Gene and Casey did backup vocals on Gloria Gaynor's "Never Can Say Goodbye" hit and LP.

At one point in 1975 they changed their name to Ebony, Ivory and Jade (Columbia) and made a startling transition from '60s doo wop to contemporary disco in the song "Sampson." The Tony Bongiovi-produced single, with its doo wop disco arrangement, Gene's strong-as-ever lead, and hair-raising background vocals, made this new Jive Five sound a radio favorite, but it reached only number 92 R&B in September.

By 1979 the Jive Five quartet was Eugene (lead), Casey (first tenor), Richard Harris (second tenor), and Beatrice Best (baritone and bass).

In 1982 they became a quintet again with Herbert and Frank Pitt (Gene's brothers) replacing Casey and Richard and with the addition of Charles Mitchell. In 1982 Ambient Sound (Columbia) released two Jive Five singles and an LP, *Here We Are*. Part of this output was a sequel to the 21-year-old "My True Story" titled "Never, Never Lie" and a

cut called "Don't Believe Him Donna" with additional vocals by Arlene Smith and THE CHANTELS.

Another LP in the "new sound, old style" genre on Ambient Sound in 1984 closed out the group's recorded product, but into the '90s the Jive Five remained one of the most polished and enjoyable acts to see live. For example, on October 20, 1990, they tore up the audience of the "Royal New York Doo-Wopp (East Coast spelling) Show" at Radio City Music Hall, which featured THE FLAMINGOS, THE CHIFFONS, and the first-ever all-lead singing girls supergroup consisting of Arlene Smith (the Chantels), Lillian Leach (THE MELLOWS), Baby Washington (THE HEARTS), and Pearl McKinnon (THE KODAKS).

THE JIVE FIVE

A SIDE/B SIDE	LABEL/CAT NO	DATE
My True Story /		
When I Was Single	Bltn 1006	5/61
Never, Never /		
People From Another World	Bltn 1014	10/61
Hully Gully Callin' Time /		
No Not Again	Bltn 2019	3/62
What Time Is It /		
Beggin' You Please	Bltn 2024	8/62
These Golden Rings /		
Do You Hear Wedding Bells	Bltn 2029	11/62
Lily Marlene / Johnny Never Knew	Bltn 2030	1963
Rain / She's My Girl	Bltn 2034	3/63
United / Prove Every		
Word You Say	Sketch 219	1964
United / Prove Every		
Word You Say	UA 807	1964
I'm A Happy Man / Kiss, Kiss, Kiss	UA 853	1965
A Bench In The Park /		
Please, Baby, Please	UA 936	1965
Goin' Wild / Main Street	UA 50004	1966
In My Neighborhood /		
Then Came Heartbreak	UA 50033	1966
Ha Ha / You're A Puzzle	UA 50069	1966
You / You Promised		
Me Great Things	UA 50107	1966
Crying Like A Baby /		
You'll Fall In Love	Mscr 1250	1967
No More Tears / You'll Fall In Love	Mscr 1270	1967
Sugar / Blues In The Ghetto	Mscr 1305	1968
You Showed Me The Light Of		
Love / If You Let Me Make		
Love To	Decca 32671	1970
I Want You To Be My Baby /		
If I Had A Chance To Love You	Decca 32736	1970
Come Down In Time / Love Is Pain	Avco 4568	1971
Follow The Land /		
Let The Feeling Belong	Avco 4589	1972
Follow The Land / Lay, Lady, Lay	Avco 4589	1972
All I Ever Do /		
Super Woman Part 2	Brut 814	1974

A SIDE/B SIDE	LABEL/CAT NO	DATE
Magic Maker Music Maker / Oh Baby	AmbiS 2742	1982
Don't Believe Him Donna	AmbiS 3053	1982
Hurry Back / You Know What I Would Do	Bltn 3001	1990

The Bob Knight Four

Against a backdrop of Brooklyn street gangs like Pigtown, the Chaplins, and the Canarsie Boys; drag racing on Ralph Avenue, Kings Highway, and Cross Bay Boulevard; fashions like black leather jackets, garrison belts, black chinos, and D.A. hairstyles; and hangouts like clubrooms, record hops, White Castle drive-ins, and Nathan's Hot Dog stand in Coney Island, thousands of vocal groups were spawned.

One of Brooklyn's best was the Bob Knight Four, a group that formed in 1956 as the Bobby Dells (named after a race horse). As fans of THE MOONGLOWS, THE FLAMINGOS, and THE RAVENS, they practiced songs like "A Simple Prayer" (The Ravens) and "Crazy for You" (THE HEARTBEATS) on Pitkin Avenue near the Kinema Movie Theatre or John's Ice Cream Parlor on Cleveland Street. The quintet's members were Bob Bovino (lead), Paul Ferrigno (first tenor), Charlie Licarta (second tenor), Ralph Garone (baritone), and John Ropers (bass).

In 1960 the group met Julie and Roy Rifkind of Dome Records and cut one side called "Hymn of Love" which was never released. Charlie then joined the service and the group decided on a name change. Since Bob wanted to perform under the name Bob Knight they became the Bob Knight Four. They appeared at local hops like St. Fortunato's (with the Heartbeats and THE CADILLACS) and the 111th Street Hall's "Friday Night Battle of the Groups" with such acts as THE FIVE DISCS, THE CAPRIS, and the Fascinators. Through contacts they met Laurel Records owner Tony Seppe. He put their voices on a track for the song "Good Goodbye," which became an East Coast favorite, becoming a regular sign-off song for many disc jockey's shows.

In 1961 the group backed Madison artist Eddie Delmar on a rock and roll record called "Love Bells" but received no label credit. The same held true for three other Delmar sides, "Blanche" (Josie), "Garden in the Rain," and "My Heart Belongs to You" (Vegas Records). Their next single, "For Sale," was a group-written ballad that received some split airplay with its flip side "You Gotta Know." Meanwhile Seppe got some additional mileage out of "Good Goodbye" when he pulled Bob's lead off of the track and put on female artist Sandy Lynn backed by the Bob Knight Three on what became "So, So Long" (Taurus Records).

In 1962 the group moved over to Josie Records, recording with full orchestra on "Memories." The doo wop tune "Two Friends" followed on Josie's parent label Jubilee but, like its predecessors, was unable to match the success of their first single.

Their last 45 was "Tomorrow We'll Be Married" in 1964, produced and accompanied by THE TOKENS (with THE ANGELS providing hand claps).

By now, Bovino had left and been replaced by Frank Iovino, and Charlie Licarta had returned and replaced Paul Ferrigno.

During 1964 the group disbanded but re-formed for the WCBS Revival Show in New York's Central Park on July 14, 1973, with Bovino, Ferrigno, Garone, and Ropers still singing solidly.

In recent years Frank Iovino was a Deputy Sheriff in Broward County, Florida, and singing with THE FIVE BOROUGHS (Classic Artists Records). Paul Ferrigno owned a carpet and tile business in New York, Charles Licarta was a New York police officer, John Ropers was a sculptor, and Ralph Garone was an executive at R. H. Donnelly Publishing Company before his death. Bob (Knight) Bovino was in car repair.

In the '90s, the group (with Bob, Paul, John, and Ralph's brother Michael) was still performing in the New York area.

THE BOB KNIGHT FOUR

A SIDE/B SIDE	LABEL/CAT NO	DATE
Good Goodbye / How Must I Be	Laurel 1020	1961
For Sale / You Gotta Know	Laurel 1023	1961
So So Long / You Tease Me	Taur A-100	1961
I'm Selling My Heart / The Lazy Piano	Taurus 356	1962
Memories / Somewhere	Josie 899	1962
Two Friends / Crazy Love	Jubi 5451	1963
Tomorrow We'll Be Married / Willingly	Goal 4	1964

Gladys Knight and the Pips

One of the earliest and finest of the family-based rhythm and blues groups, Gladys Knight and the Pips originally formed at an impromptu 10th birthday party of Gladys's brother

Merald in 1952. The bunch included two sisters, a brother, and two cousins. The members, all from Atlanta, Georgia, were sisters Gladys and Brenda Knight, brother Merald ("Bubba") Knight, and cousins Eleanor and William Guest.

Gladys, only eight at the time, was already an experienced performer, having begun singing with the Mount Mariah Baptist Church choir at the age of four and having toured the church circuit with the Morris Brown Choir by five. She ran off with the $2,000 top prize by singing "Too Young" (Nat King Cole) at the ripe old age of seven on "The Ted Mack Amateur Hour," and she subsequently did a number of other TV shows.

Another cousin (James "Pip" Woods) lent the quintet his nickname and the group was off and running. Gladys's soulful, church-trained alto lead, accompanied by the Pips' warm harmony, helped the Atlanta teens crack the tour circuit without a record, and by 1957 they'd been on the road with Sam Cooke, B.B. King, and Jackie Wilson. Wilson (godfather of singer Jody Watley) arranged an introduction to his label, Brunswick Records, and the group ended up releasing one single for them "Whistle My Love," in early 1958.

By 1959 Eleanor and Brenda left to get married and the Pips drew on their reservoir of cousins to fill out the quintet, enlisting Edward Patten (22) and Langston George.

A local Atlanta club owner named Clifford Hunter (who had booked the group at his Builders Club) started his own label with a friend, Tommy Brown (Griffin Brothers), called it Huntom, and recorded the group on the 1952 Johnny Otis-penned "Every Beat of My Heart" (the Royals). It was released in early 1961.

The song took off in Atlanta so quickly that Hunter didn't have time to sign the group. Huntom then sold the rights to Vee-Jay Records. In the meantime an Atlanta disc jockey named James Patrick sent a copy to his friend Bobby Robinson at Fury Records in New York.

In an instant the group was in New York re-recording the song at Beltone Studios for Fury. They copied the Huntom Vee-Jay version, though that original was more soulful and had more pervasive harmonies than the new recording, a sultry, pseudo-supper-club interpretation. Both versions sounded like they were sung by a mature woman rather than a 16-year-old girl.

The Vee-Jay and Fury 45s raced up the charts, first hitting Pop (May 15, 1961) and then R&B (May 29, 1961) on both labels at the same time. By July 10th the group found itself in the unusual position of having the same song on two different labels and two different recordings on the charts—Vee-Jay's at number six Pop and number one R&B and Fury's at number 45 Pop and number 15 R&B. Adding to the public's confusion was the fact that Vee-Jay's label listed the group as the Pips while the Fury single named them Gladys Knight and the Pips.

When their second Fury single failed to chart (Jessie Belvin's "Guess Who"), Bobby Robinson came up with their best Fury release, the Don Covay classic "A Letter Full of Tears" (#19 Pop, #3 R&B).

Despite their initial success, Gladys and company did only one more single for Fury ("Operator") which reached number 97 Pop in early 1962. "Letter Full of Tears," however, prompted Robinson to issue a Gladys Knight and the Pips LP in 1962, a great tribute in the early '60s to an R&B group with only two hits. When Langston George left the group they became the quartet that would remain in place, with the same foursome, into the '90s.

Gladys soon married and had a child, and the Pips went on to record two singles without her magical lead. In 1964 Gladys returned and the foursome signed with Larry Maxwell's Maxx label. In April 1964 they issued one of the group's more memorable records, the majestic "Giving Up." The dramatic, beautifully sung Van McCoy-penned ballad reached number 38 Pop. Bobby Robinson then issued an answer record to "Letter Full of Tears" from the can on his Enjoy label, but "What Shall I Do" never charted. Three more Maxx singles surfaced through 1965 with only "Lovers Always Forgive" (#89 Pop) receiving any interest. Soon after, Maxx went under.

The group itself never lacked work and in 1966 were hired as special guests on a Motown package tour. That's where they caught Berry Gordy's attention.

By the summer of 1966 they were on Gordy's subsidiary Soul label issuing the single "Just Walk in My Shoes." Their second release on Soul, "Take Me in Your Arms and Love Me," only rose to number 95 Pop, but it became the first of their 21 British charters, reaching number 13 in the summer of 1967.

The group's first major American chart single was their third soul release, "Everybody Needs Love" (#39 Pop, #3 R&B), in 1967.

Perhaps more famous was "I Heard It Through the Grapevine," the original hit version that came out a year before Marvin Gaye went to number one with it. The Pips made it their second number one R&B hit and took it to number two Pop on December 16th (the Monkees' "Daydream Believer" was number one), selling over one million copies. Soul follow-ups included "The End of the Road" (#15 Pop, #5 R&B, 1968), "I Wish It Would Rain" (#41 Pop, #15 R&B, 1968, issued only a half a year after THE TEMPTATIONS' hit version), the great Leon Ware/Pam Sawyer/Clay McMurray-penned "If I Were Your Woman" (#9 Pop, #1 R&B, 1970), and the Jimmy Wetherly country song "Neither One of Us (Wants to Be the First to Say Goodbye)" (#2 Pop, #1 R&B, 1973).

Despite their successes, the group had a complaint that was common among Motown acts like MARTHA AND THE VANDELLAS and THE MARVELETTES: they felt neglected while other acts were catered to and given priority. So Gladys and the Pips moved to Buddah Records when their Motown contract ran out at the end of 1972. Due to the brilliant maneuvering of Sidney Seidenberg (Gladys and the Pips' accountant turned manager) and his able sidekick Floyd Lieberman, Gladys and company were brought to Buddah with a (then) incredible multi-million-dollar contract.

The group then issued a new string of winners, starting out with a formula that succeeded for them at Motown. They took a Jim Wetherly country tune, sang it soulfully, and then reaped the chart rewards on tunes like "Where Peaceful Waters Flow" (#28 Pop, #6 R&B, 1973) and the million seller "Midnight Train to Georgia" (#1 Pop and R&B, 1973). The latter was originally titled "Midnight Plane to Houston" before Atlanta producer Sonny Limbo changed it and recorded it with Cissy Houston (mother of Whitney Houston).

Their next single was "I've Got to Use My Imagination," produced by the dynamic musical talent Tony Camillo. It sold a million plus while reaching number four Pop and number one R&B in 1974.

In March 1974 the group earned two Grammy awards, one for "Neither One of Us" (Best Pop Vocal Performance by a Group) and the other for "Midnight Train to Georgia" (Best R&B Vocal Performance by a Group).

More hit songs followed, like "Best Thing that Ever Happened" (#3 Pop, #1 R&B, 1974), the Camillo-penned "I Feel a Song (In My Heart)" (#21 Pop, #1 R&B, 1975) and "The Way We Were"/"Try to Remember" medley (#11 Pop, #6 R&B, 1975).

Also in 1974 they did the soundtrack LP for the film *Claudine*, which went gold, and by 1975 had their own four-week summer replacement variety TV show on NBC. Gladys then branched out to acting by starring in the film *Pipe Dreams* in 1976, while she and the group sang the songs featured in the film on a soundtrack LP that reached number 47.

In 1977 complex legal maneuvers began between Motown, Buddah, Gladys Knight and the Pips, and Columbia Records, where the family foursome was attempting to move. The result was that Gladys was not able to record with the Pips.

Instead, the group recorded two LPs (with no chart singles) for Casablanca and Gladys did one solo album for Buddah. In 1980 they reunited on Columbia and hit with "Landlord" (#46 Pop, #3 R&B), but through 1986 only "Save the Overtime (For Me)" (#66 Pop, #1 R&B) and its accompanying gold LP did well for them.

In 1986 the group switched to MCA and came up with their biggest record since the 12-year-old "The Way We Were" medley with "Love Overboard" (#13 Pop, #1 R&B) showing they'd lost none of their class, polish, or hitmaking ability.

After 58 R&B charters and 41 trips up the Pop Top 100 ladder, Gladys Knight and the Pips, one of soul's worthiest successes, continued to turn out quality music in performance and on record.

GLADYS KNIGHT AND THE PIPS

A SIDE/B SIDE	LABEL/CAT NO	DATE
Ching Chong* / Whistle My Love*	Brns 55048	2/58
Every Beat Of My Heart* /		
Room In Your Heart*	Huntom 2510	1961
Every Beat Of My Heart* /		
Room In Your Heart*	Vee-Jay 386	4/61
Every Beat Of My Heart /		
Room In Your Heart	Fury 1050	4/61
Guess Who /		
Stop Running Around	Fury 1052	1961
Letter Full Of Tears /		
You Broke Your Promise	Fury 1054	11/61
Operator / I'll Trust In You	Fury 1064	1962
Darling* / Linda*	Fury 1067	1962
Happiness* /		
I Had A Dream Last Night*	Ever 5025	1963
Queen Of Tears /		
A Love Like Mine	Vee-Jay 545	1963
Giving Up / Maybe Maybe Baby	Maxx 326	4/64
What Shall I Do / Love Call	Enjoy 2012	1964
Lovers Always Forgive /		
Another Love	Maxx 329	7/64
Either Way I Lose /		
Go Away, Stay Away	Maxx 331	1964
Who Knows /		
Stop And Get A Hold Of Myself	Maxx 334	2/65
If I Should Ever Fall In Love /		
Tell Her You're Mine	Maxx 335	1965
Just Walk In My Shoes /		
Stepping Closer To Your Heart	Soul 35023	7/66
Take Me In Your Arms And Love		
Me / Do You Love Me Just		
A Little Honey	Soul 35033	3/67

A SIDE/B SIDE	LABEL/CAT NO	DATE
Everybody Needs Love /		
Stepping Closer To Your Heart	Soul 35034	6/67
I Heard It Through The		
Grapevine / It's Time To Go Now	Soul 35039	9/67
The End Of Our Road / Don't Let		
Her Take Your Love From Me	Soul 35042	1/68
It Should Have Been Me /		
You Don't Love Me No More	Soul 35045	5/68
I Wish It Would Rain / It's Summer	Soul 35047	8/68
Just A Closer Walk With Thee /		
His Eye Is On The Sparrow	Motown 1128	9/68
Didn't You Know / Keep An Eye	Soul 35057	2/69
The Nitty Gritty /		
I Got Myself A Good Man	Soul 35063	5/69
Cloud Nine / Friendship Train	Soul 35068	10/69
You Need Love Like I Do /		
You're My Everything	Soul 35071	2/70
If I Were Your Woman /		
The Tracks Of My Tears	Soul 35078	10/70
I Don't Want To Do Wrong /		
Is There A Place	Soul 35083	5/71
Make Me The Woman That		
You Go Home To / It's All		
Over But The Shoutin'	Soul 35091	11/71
Help Me Make It Through The		
Night / If You Gonna Leave	Soul 35094	3/72
Neither One Of Us /		
Can't Give It Up No More	Soul 35098	12/72
Daddy Could Swear, I Declare /		
For Once In My Life	Soul 31505	4/73
Where Peaceful Waters Flow /		
Perfect Love	Buddah 363	5/73
All I Need Is Time / The Only		
Time You Love Me Is When		
You're Losing Me	Soul 35107	7/73
Midnight Train To Georgia /		
Midnight Train To Georgia		
(instrumental)	Buddah 383	8/73
Midnight Train To Georgia /		
Window Raising Granny	Buddah 383	8/73
I've Got To Use My Imagination /		
I Can See Clearly Now	Buddah 393	11/73
Best Thing That Ever Happened /		
Once In A Lifetime Thing	Buddah 403	2/74
On And On / The Makings Of You	Buddah 423	5/74
Between Her Goodbye And		
My Hello / This Child Needs		
Its Father	Soul 35111	5/74
I Feel A Song /		
Don't Burn Down The Bridge	Buddah 433	9/74
Silent Night /		
Do You Hear What I Hear	Buddah	12/74
Love Finds Its Own Way /		
Better You Go Your Way	Buddah 453	1/75
The Way We Were / Try To		
Remember / The Need To Be	Buddah 463	4/75
Street Brothers /		
Money	Buddah 487	8/75

A SIDE/B SIDE	LABEL/CAT NO	DATE
Part Time Love /		
Where Do I Put His Memory	Buddah 513	10/75
Make Yours A Happy Home	Buddah 523	1976
So Sad The Song /		
So Sad The Song	Buddah 544	8/76
Baby Don't Change Your Mind	Buddah 569	1977
Sorry Doesn't Always		
Make It Right	Buddah 584	1977
The One And Only	Buddah 592	1978
It's A Better Than Good Time	Buddah 598	1978
I'm Coming Home Again	Buddah 601	1978
Am I Too Late	Col 10922	1979
Landlord	Col 11239	1980
Taste Of Bitter Love	Col 11330	1980
Bourgie Bourgie	Col 11375	1980
Forever Yesterday		
(For The Children)	Col 02113	1981
It That'll Make You Happy	Col 02143	1981
I Will Fight	Col 02549	1981
A Friend Of Mine	Col 02706	1982
Save The Overtime (For Me)	Col 0361	1983
You're Number One (In My Book)	Col 04033	1983
Hero	Col 04219	1983
When You're Far Away	Col 04369	1984
My Time	Col 04761	1985
Keep Givin' Me Love	Col 04873	1985
Till I See You Again	Col 05679	1985
Send It To Me	MCA 53002	1986
Love Overboard	MCA 53210	1987
Lovin' On Next To Nothin'	MCA 53211	1988
It's Gonna Take All Our Love	MCA 53351	1988

* The Pips

Patti LaBelle and the Blue Belles

The Blue Belles were one of the most dynamic female vocal groups of the '60s, yet they might never have had a career if it hadn't been for another group's recording.

In the fall of 1961, Patricia Holt and Cindy Birdsong (late of a group called the Ordettes) joined with Sarah Dash and Nona Hendryx (formerly of the Del Capris) to create the Blue Belles in Philadelphia.

Around the same time another female quartet, THE STARLETS from Chicago, were on tour thanks to the success of their single "Better Tell Him No." The Starlets stopped in Philadelphia for some one-nighters, and before you could say "Better Tell Him No," they were convinced to go in the studio by a used car salesman and came out with a recording of "I Sold My Heart to the Junkman." The recording was an infectious up-tempo version of THE BASIN STREET BOYS' 1946 rendition.

Whether the Blue Belles heard the recording before its release is subject to conjecture, but suffice it to say that when Newtown Records released the Starlets' recording in late 1961/early 1962 the name on the label was "The Blue-Belles." (For a time in 1962 the group was known as Patti Bell & the Blue Bells, according to an ad in a May issue of *Billboard* magazine.) By June, the record was number 15 (Pop) and number 13 R&B, giving the Philadelphia females their first hit without stepping foot in the studio. Their actual initial recordings didn't fare nearly as well even though they tried to keep the same feel and tempo as "Junkman." But their second "real" release, a ballad simply titled "Go On," gave a taste of things to come, and their harmonies on the old Cowboys song "Cool Water" indicated that they could sing better given better material. Their third single of 1963 met those qualifications as Patti Holt (now Patti LaBelle) soared through the melody of "Down the Aisle" accompanied by the Blue Belles' angelic-sounding higher-than-high warblings. It went to number 37 pop and number 14 R&B, setting the stage for the quartet to record every big ballad they could find, and the biggest were the old standards. Their January 1964 release was the brilliant Rodgers and Hammerstein classic "You'll Never Walk Alone," which went to number 34 on both the Pop and R&B charts. What "Down the Aisle" did to establish the group, "You'll Never Walk Alone" did to establish Patti as one of the most powerful and distinctive lead vocalists ever.

Patti began incorporating her high-note finale into new recordings such as the memorable 1855 Irish classic "Danny Boy," which peaked at #74 on both the pop and R&B charts. The B side was the evergreen "I Believe." "Danny Boy" turned out to be their last of three singles for the Philadelphia-based Parkway Records since the English invasion took its toll of small indie labels. By mid-1965, the Belles had made it to New York and signed with the major label Atlantic Records. It was then they found out they were not the first Blue Belles group, and not even the first on Atlantic. Another female aggregation had used that name to record their one and only single "The Story of a Fool" some 12 years earlier.

Not fazed in the least, the group began the task of cutting the first of 12 singles that they would do for Atlantic. "All or Nothing," cut October 7, 1965, charted nationally on December 4th, but only made it to number 68. Relying more on a contemporary soul feel and less on their gospel roots, the Burt Burns production took the edge off the girls' sound and added punchy horns to a Pam Sawyer-Laurie Burton composition that should have fared better. Hoping for better luck they went back to standards with the *Wizard of Oz* classic, "Over the Rainbow." The rendition was emotionally charged, becoming one of Patti's favorite songs, so much so that she recorded it for a single release more than 15 years later on Philly International Records. The flip side of "Rainbow" was the original version of Tony Wine's and Carol Bayer's (later Carol Bayer Sager Bacharach) "Groovy Kind of Love," which was released weeks ahead of the Mindbenders recording.

With all this going for them neither side charted and the Mindbenders surged on to the airwaves with a number two money maker. The Blue Belles went back to recording standards ("Ebbtide," "Unchained Melody"), soul, and offbeat versions of contemporary hits such as Lou Johnson's "Always Something There to Remind Me."

Cindy Birdsong got an opportunity to become a member of THE SUPREMES by replacing disgruntled backup vocalist Florence Ballard. Patti, Nona, and Sarah continued as a trio but never again had a chart record as the Blue Belles despite six more quality releases on Atlantic.

In 1970, British TV producer Vickie Wickham ran into the girls, and remembering their stints on her "Ready, Steady, Go" English show agreed to manage the group. The first change under the Wickham regime was the name. Gone were the Blue Belles and in was the name LaBelle. Next came a new record label, Warner Brothers, and tours with white rockers like the Who instead of the usual soul circuit survivors. The sound became funkier (à la Sly Stone) and their trademark harmony reserved more for B sides like "Shades of Difference."

Late in 1971, the trio, ever mindful of its roots, teamed up in Philadelphia with Bronx-born white soul singer/songwriter Laura Nyro and in one week cut a 10-track LP at Sigma Sound Studios entitled *"Gonna Take a Miracle,"* Laura Nyro and LaBelle. The LP included cuts ranging from a mostly a cappella version of the SHIRELLES' "I Met Him on a Sunday" and various Motown tunes ("You've Really Got a Hold on Me," "Jimmy Mack," and "Nowhere to Run") to doo wop standards like the DIABLOS' "The Wind" and a haunting rendition of THE CHARTS' "Deserie." Despite all the changes, the two LPs, the three Warner Brothers singles, and the two RCA releases garnered little public interest.

As the glitter era of rock's early '70s took hold, LaBelle jumped on the bandwagon with all six feet and began appearing in their now famous silvery space suits and luminescent makeup.

In 1974, New Orleans producer Alan Toussaint took over the production reigns of LaBelle. His creole creativity culminated in a collection of exciting songs that formed their first Epic LP *Night Birds*. The album's crowning touch was the Kenny Noland and Bob Crewe-penned ode to creole ladies of the night, "Lady Marmalade," which the trio debuted at New York's Metropolitan Opera House (the first time a black vocal group had ever appeared at the historic venue). By December 1974, "Lady Marmalade" was riding up the Pop and R&B charts, reaching number one in 1975 and number 17 in England. It became the group's first and last million seller, and for many Americans its lyrics ("voulez-vous coucher avec moi ce soir?") became the only French they ever learned. Their follow-up "What Can I Do for You," riding largely on the heels of "Marmalade," went to number 48 Pop and number eight R&B, in the spring of 1975. Three of their next four singles charted R&B, but none with anything resembling the excitement generated by "Lady Marmalade." Musical differences between Patti and Nona began to pull the trio apart.

By 1977, their last single, aptly titled "Isn't It a Shame," came out unnoticed and the group separated. Sarah moved on to Kirshner Records for two low-chart releases in 1979, "Sinner Man" and "(Come and Take This) Candy from Your Baby." Nona became a rock and roller, playing with New York bands Propaganda and Material. In 1983, she signed to RCA and ran a streak of five chart singles though none went above number 22 (her first release was "Keep It Confidential"). Her biggest hit was for EMI America in the spring of 1987 with "Why Should I Cry."

Patti continued on Epic garnering the most solo success with eight chart singles between 1977 and 1980, though none went above number 26 ("I Don't Go Shopping"). Her solo career took off when she signed with Philadelphia International Records, and she copped top R&B charts honors with "If Only You Knew." A succession of duets ("Love Has Finally Come at Last" with Bobby Womack and "On My Own" with Michael McDonald) and songs from movies ("New Attitude" and "Stir It Up" from *Beverly Hills Cop*, "Something Special" from *Outrageous Fortune*, and "Just the Facts" from *Dragnet*) kept her in the spotlight ever since.

As for the Blue Belles/LaBelle entity, any act that stuck it out for 16 years with no member additions and only one defection deserves recognition.

PATTI LaBELLE AND THE BLUE BELLES

A SIDE/B SIDE	LABEL/CAT NO	DATE
The Blue Belles		
I Sold My Heart To The Junkman / Itty Bitty Twist	Nwtwn 5000	1962
Pitter Patter / I Found A New Love	Nwtwn 5006	1962
Go On / I Found A New Love	Nwtwn 5006	1962
Go On / Tear After Tear	Nwtwn 5007	1962
Cool Water / When Johnny Comes Marching Home	Nwtwn 5009	1963
Decatur Street / Academy Award	Nwtwn 5019	1963
Patti LaBelle and the Blue Belles		
Down The Aisle / C'est La Vie	King 5777	1963
Down The Aisle / C'est La Vie	Nwtwn 5777	1963
You'll Never Walk Alone / Where Are You	Nctwn 5020	1963
You'll Never Walk Alone / Decatur Street	Nctwn5020	1963
You'll Never Walk Alone / Decatur Street	Parkway 896	1963
One Phone Call / You Will Find My Eyes No More	Parkway 913	1964
I Believe / Danny Boy	Parkway 935	1964
All Or Nothing / You Forgot How To Love	Atln 2311	1965
Over The Rainbow / Groovy Kind Of Love	Atln 2318	1965
Ebbtide / Patti's Prayer	Atln 2333	1966
Family Man / I'm Still Waiting	Atln 2347	1966
Take Me For A Little While / I Don't Want To Go On	Atln 2373	1966
Tender Words / Always Something There To Remind Me	Atln 2390	1967
Unchained Melody / Dreamer	Atln 2408	1967
Oh My Love / I Need Your Love	Atln 2446	1967
Wonderful / He's My Man	Atln 2548	1968
He's Gone / Dance To The Rhythm Of Love	Atln 2610	1969
Pride's No Match For Love / Loving Rules	Atln 2629	1969
Suffer / Trustin' In You	Atln 2712	1970
LaBelle		
Morning Much Better / Shades Of Difference	Wrnr 7512	1971
If I Can't Have You / Moon Shadow	Wrnr 7579	1972
Ain't I Sad It's All Over	Wrnr 7624	1972
Going On A Holiday / Open Up Your Heart	RCA 0956	1973
Mr. Music Man / Sunshine	RCA 0157	1974
Lady Marmalade / Space Children	Epic 50048	1974
Night Bird / What Can I Do For You	Epic 50097	1975
Messin' My Mind / Take The Night Off	Epic 50140	1975
Far As We Felt Like Goin' / Slow Burn	Epic 50168	1975
Get You Somebody New	Epic 50262	1976
Isn't It A Shame / Gypsy Moths	Epic 50315	1977

▼ REPARATA AND THE DELRONS   ▲ THE DOVELLS   ▼ THE CAROLONS

MELLOMOOD
RECORD CO., N.Y.C.

GS-1003-B
Keel Music
(BMI)

A BILLY SNELL
RELEASE
Time: 2:12

LET IT PLEASE BE YOU
(White-Whitier-Smith-Hirston-Powell)
CAROLONS
G-BT-NG

Howie   Phil   Larry

Marise

▲ THE TOKENS   ▲ THE DEMENSIONS   ▼ THE BEACH BOYS

THE BEACH BOYS

The Lettermen

The Lettermen sound went up against the rock era and provided some calm in the frantic '60s.

Original members Tony Butala, Mike Barnett, and Talmadge Russell came together in 1958. Tony had been a child performer with the Mitchell Boys Choir, which performed in such films as Bing Crosby's *White Christmas* and Doris Day's *On Moonlight Bay* in the early '50s. He was also the singing voice for actor Tommy Rettig in the "Lassie" TV series.

In 1954, while attending Hollywood Performing School (where some of his schoolmates were Jill St. John and Brenda Lee), Tony formed a pop quartet called the Fourmost with Jimmy Blaine, Art Westgate, and lead singer Concetta Ingolia. They stayed together for about three years and recorded the single "Give Me the Simple Life" for P.I.V. Records. The group was down to a male trio when Concetta opted for acting, but she would have something to do with the Lettermen later on when she became known as actress/singer Connie Stevens.

In 1958 Tony met Mike Barnett at a party and was asked to join a group that Mike was in called the Lettermen. By the first rehearsal the others had dropped out, so Tony brought in his friend Talmadge Russell and a trio took shape. The group lasted about four weeks, until Barnett and Russell opted for nonmusic careers. Tony scrambled to form a new Lettermen with friends Gary Clark, who was dating the vivacious Connie, and Jerry Paul.

In the spring of 1958 the group decided to try recording, but by the time they entered Gold Star Studios in Los Angeles Jerry had been replaced by ex-Fourmost member Jimmy Blaine. Needing to earn a living while waiting for the Lettermen to be discovered, Tony and Gary joined Bill Norvis and the Upstarts to perform in Las Vegas. Gary soon left the Upstarts and in walked Jim Pike for an audition, promptly winning the spot.

With Tony and Jim in place, only one piece of the puzzle remained. Connie provided it. Now starring in TV's "Hawaiian Eye" as Cricket Blake, she was signed as a singer to Warner Bros. Records in 1959 and was paired with producer Carl Engemann. She began dating his brother Bob and after hearing him sing contacted Tony.

The Lettermen began practicing in Tony's garage on North Hatteras in North Hollywood, drawing on the influence of THE FOUR FRESHMEN for their delicate three-part harmony and practicing songs like "Love Is a Many-Splendored Thing."

The group had its first recording opportunity with Warner Bros. in 1959, but their two singles ("The Magic Sound" and "Their Hearts Were Full of Spring") failed to excite radio and the singers were dropped. (Before that occurred the enthusiastic trio sang backup on Mel Blanc's "Blymie, Blymie, Blymie.")

In 1961 Tony heard that the new A&R man at Capitol was looking for talent, so he went up there to find it was an old friend, Nick Venet. Nick loved the group but told Tony that Capitol already had too many vocal groups. Soon after, Nick called to say that if they could put the group together in an hour they should meet him at Capitol Studios. It seems THE FOUR PREPS were busy disputing which song to record and weren't using the studio time they had booked. Venet smuggled in the Lettermen on the Preps' studio time and they recorded "Glory of Love," "When," "That's My Desire," and "The Way You Look Tonight."

The 1947 Sammy Kaye number two hit "That's My Desire" was issued first. It had a Jimmy Haskell arrangement that put the group somewhere between DION AND THE BELMONTS and THE FOUR SEASONS, giving the group a sound that was close to doo wop. On its release, disc jockeys started flipping the 45 to the Jerome Kern/Dorothy Fields-penned Evergreen, "The Way You Look Tonight."

It charted and reached number 13 on the *Billboard* Top 100 by fall 1961. It became the only British charter of their 59 career releases, reaching number 36 in November 1961.

The soft harmonies employed on "Tonight" became a Lettermen trademark, copied by many '60s and '70s groups like THE VOGUES and the Sandpipers.

Their version of the 1952 number 20 Doris Day hit "When I Fall in Love" became their biggest single, reaching number seven on January 27, 1962. It established a niche for the Lettermen that didn't rely on trends. Their third single, "Come Back Silly Girl," was noted by a *Billboard* reviewer with the comment, "A persuasive piece of material and a winning reading of the moody ballad by the Lettermen make this a potent discing. Good wax for teen and young adult set." In the week of February 17th the song charted eventually reaching number 17.

The trio followed up with a variety of standard ballads like "Where or When" and "I Only Have Eyes for You," and by the end of 1967 they had recorded 23 LPs. The medley "Going Out of My Head"/"Can't Take My Eyes Off You" (#7, February 10, 1968) became their second biggest hit, and by then they were performing all over the world.

In late 1967 Bob Engemann retired from the group and was replaced by Jim Pike's brother Gary. The group continued recording LPs and putting out singles like Paul Anka's "Put Your Head on My Shoulder" and LITTLE ANTHONY AND THE IMPERIALS' "Hurt So Bad." Between 1962 and 1970 they earned the dubious distinction of amassing more records that hit the *Billboard* Bubbling Under chart without crashing the Top 100 (11) than any other American vocal group. The first was "Turn Around, Look at Me" (#105, 1962) and the last was "Hey Girl" (#104, 1970).

By 1969 Jim, who had developed voice problems, had been replaced by Doug Curran and later by Jim's other brother Donnie.

In 1981 Donovan Scott Tea and Mark Preston replaced the Pike brothers and in 1988 Bobby Poynton came aboard for Mark, bringing the group to its most recent lineup.

Tony and company continued to maintain a grueling worldwide performance pace more than 30 years after the idea of a pop trio popped into his head. With 20 chart singles and 55 LPs, the most recent being from 1990, the Lettermen retained a strong following.

THE LETTERMEN

A SIDE/B SIDE	LABEL/CAT NO	DATE
The Way You Look Tonight / That's My Desire	Cap 4586	1961
When I Fall In Love / Smile	Cap 4658	1961
Son Of Old Rivers / Dutchman's Gold	Cap 4760	1962
Come Back Silly Girl / A Song For Young Love	Cap 4699	1962
How Is Julie? / Turn Around Look At Me	Cap 4746	1962
Silly Boy (She Doesn't Love You) / I Told The Stars	Cap 4810	1962
A Tree In The Meadow / Again	Cap 4851	1962
Heartache, Oh Heartache / No Other Love	Cap 4914	1963
Allentown Jail / Two Brothers	Cap 4976	1963
Where Or When / Be My Girl	Cap 5091	1963
Seventh Dawn Theme / Put Away Your Teardrops	Cap 5218	1964
You Don't Know Just How Lucky You Are / When Summer Ends	Cap 5273	1964
It's Over / Girl With The Little Tin Heart	Cap 5370	1965
Theme From *A Summer Place* / Sealed With A Kiss	Cap 5437	1965
Secretly / The Things We Did Last Summer	Cap 5499	1965
Sweet September / I Believe	Cap 5544	1966

A SIDE/B SIDE	LABEL/CAT NO	DATE
You'll Be Needin' Me / Run To My Lovin' Arms	Cap 5583	1966
I Only Have Eyes For You / Love Letters	Cap 5649	1966
Chanson D'Amour / She Don't Want Me Now	Cap 5749	1966
Our Winter Love / Warm	Cap 5813	1967
Volare / Mr. Sun	Cap 5913	1967
Somewhere My Love / Theme From *A Summer Place*	Cap 6916	1967
Goin' Out Of My Head—Can't Take My Eyes Off You / Believe	Cap 2054	1967
Sherry Don't Go / Never My Love	Cap 2132	1968
All The Grey Haired Men / Anyone Who Had A Heart	Cap 2196	1968
Holly / No Other Love	Cap 2203	1968
Love Is Blue—Greensleeves / Where Were You When The Lights Went Out	Cap 2218	1968
Sally Le Roy / Playing The Piano	Cap 2254	1968
Put Your Head On My Shoulder / Mary's Rainbow	Cap 2324	1968
I Have Dreamed / The Pendulum Swings Both Ways	Cap 2414	1969
Blue On Blue / Sittin' Pretty	Cap 2476	1969
Hurt So Bad / Catch The Wind	Cap 2482	1969
Shangri-La / When Summer Ends	Cap 2643	1969
Traces-Memories / For Once In A Lifetime	Cap 2697	1969
Hang On Sloopy / For Love	Cap 2774	1970
She Cried / For Love	Cap 2820	1970
Hey Girl / Worlds	Cap 2938	1970
Morning Girl / Here, There And Everywhere	Cap 3006	1971
Everything Is Good About You / It's Over	Cap 3020	1971
The Greatest Discovery / Since You've Been Gone	Cap 3097	1971
Feelings / Love Is A Hurtin' Thing	Cap 3098	1971
Love / Maybe Tomorrow	Cap 3192	1971
Oh My Love / An Old-Fashioned Love Song	Cap 3285	1971
Spin Away / Maybe We Should	Cap 3449	1972
Sandman / Love Song	Cap 3512	1973
MacArthur Park / Summer Song	Cap 3619	1973
Goodbye / The You Part Of Me	Cap 3810	1974
Touch Me—*The Way We Were* / Isn't It A Shame	Cap 3912	1974
Eastward / To Love And Be Loved—*Some Came Running*	Cap 4005	1975
You Are My Sunshine Girl / Make A Time For Lovin'	Cap 4096	1975
Love Me Like A Stranger / If You Feel The Way I Do	Cap 4161	1976
The Way You Look Tonight (Disco) / Storms Of Troubled Times	Cap 4226	1976
What I Did For Love / I'll Be Back	Cap 0101	1977
World Fantasy / Just Say I Love You	Cap 20566	1979

A SIDE/B SIDE	LABEL/CAT NO	DATE
In The Morning I'm Coming Home / Midnight Blue	Cap	1980
It Feels Like Christmas / I Believe	A78501	1985
Proud Lady Of America / The Star-Spangled Banner	A078601	1986
One More Summer Night / Theme From *A Summer Place*	A078701	1987
All I Ask Of You (from *Phantom Of The Opera*) / Why I Love Her	A078801	1988

Little Caesar and the Romans

Around the time the term "oldies but goodies" was coined, Little Caesar and the Romans turned the phrase into a hit record.

Little Caesar was actually David "Caesar" Johnson of Chicago. He cut his musical teeth on gospel music and later did doo wop street-corner duty with some high school friends. When he joined the air force the young Windy City resident formed a gospel act called the Northern Crusaders, and upon his discharge he created a secular group in San Diego named the Ivory Tones after member Ivory Wemberly. David headed for Los Angeles and joined up with Johnny Simmons (first tenor), Early Harris (second tenor), Leroy Sanders (bass), and someone named Curtis (second tenor) to form the Cubans in 1955 (though none of the members were Cuban).

They signed with Charlie Reynolds' Watts-based record label/record store, Flash Records.

The Cubans' only single out of Flash's 623 East Vernon Avenue address was an enjoyable ballad called "Tell Me," with Early on lead, backed by a blues-styled jump tune similar to THE PARAGONS' later "Stick with Me Baby" titled "You've Been Gone So Long," featuring David. Except for some local play it went unnoticed.

In 1959 the Cubans disbanded (they would not have been too popular under that name anyway during Castro's Cuban revolution), and David hooked up with Lummtone Records, owned by Lummie Fowler.

He formed the Upfronts (a name Lummie came up with), who included Harris and Sanders of the Cubans, Bobby Relf of the Laurels (lead and second tenor), and a mystery man remembered only as Theotis (first tenor). It's interesting to note that neither group had a baritone, instead carrying two second tenors.

Their first 45, "It Took Time," got a good L.A. response, but their second, "Too Late to Turn Around," did nothing.

When not singing or recording David and company would hang around and drink with the likes of Johnny "Guitar" Watson and Jesse Belvin. When they ran out of wine money, Jesse would go to the piano like it was an instant teller machine, knock out a song in 15 or 20 minutes and drive off to Hollywood where he'd unload his rights for a quick 50 to 100 dollars.

One evening in 1961 at Lummie's house David met songwriter Paul Politti, who played him his composition "Those Oldies But Goodies (Remind Me of You)." When David agreed to record it, the 17-year-old writer went to Art Laboe at Original Sound Records, who had started his own series of "oldies but goodies" LPs in 1959. Laboe passed on the song. Politti then sold the idea to Del Fi's Bob Keene, so David had to secure a release for his Upfronts from Lummie. When he did, a new act was formed with Johnson, Early Harris, Leroy Sanders, former Cuban Johnny Simmons, and David's first baritone, Carl Burnett. A new Upfronts was formed by Lummie Fowler that included a young bass singer from the area named Barry White.

Now dubbed Little Caesar and the Romans by Paul Politti, David and company (complete with togas, which the group despised) recorded and released the ode to oldies in the spring of 1961. By July 3rd it was number nine in the nation, heavily outscoring NINO AND THE EBB TIDES' East Coast version.

The Romans began touring the country with artists like Etta James, THE VIBRATIONS, and the amazing Jackie Wilson. They appeared on Dick Clark's "American Bandstand," togas and all. On one show in Philadelphia the group lost their togas to overexuberant fans and finished the show in their shorts.

Their follow-up 45, a takeoff on THE OLYMPICS' "Hully Gully Baby" titled "Hully Gully Again," made it to number 54 in August. Their third single on Del Fi was their most nostalgic, combining the most memorable phrases from a whole host of oldies including "A Thousand Miles Away," "In the Still of the Night," "Oh What a Night," "Earth Angel," and the only slow version of "Stranded in the Jungle" ever recorded.

The record only "bubbled under" at number 101 in September 1961. Del Fi was losing interest in the group.

The Romans recorded an LP that included their fourth single, a nice reworking of the MOONGLOWS classic, "Ten Commandments of Love," along with versions of THE COASTERS' "Searchin'," THE COLTS' "Adorable," and THE ELEGANTS' "Little Star."

The group broke up in 1962 and Caesar became a solo act in the '60s and '70s. In 1977 a new Romans backed Caesar for "Disco Hully Gully" on Essar.

In the late '70s, the Romans became a supporting act for Marvin Gaye and in 1978 took on a young female member who sang with the group for six months until she was signed to a solo contract by Warner Bros. The girl was Rickie Lee Jones, and by the spring of 1979 her hit "Chuck E's in Love" was number four nationally.

Today, Caesar's group is still going strong, with new Romans Larry Tate, Laurie Ratcliff, and Nathaniel Johnson. Leroy Sanders went on to sing with one of the touring DRIFTERS groups, John Simmons began pursuing an acting career, and Carl Burnett settled in Los Angeles.

In the summer of 1991 a new LP came out titled *There's No Doubt about It, It's David Johnson* (Trom Records), with the energized singer doing contemporary rhythm and blues.

LITTLE CAESAR AND THE ROMANS

A SIDE/B SIDE	LABEL/CAT NO	DATE
The Cubans		
Tell Me /		
You've Been Gone So Long	Flash 133	1959
The Upfronts		
It Took Time /		
Benny Lou And The Lion	Lumtn 103	1960
Too Late To Turn Around /		
Married Jive	Lumtn 104	1960
Little Caesar and the Romans		
Those Oldies But Goodies /		
She Don't Wanna Dance	Del Fi 4158	3/61
Hully Gully Again /		
Frankie And Johnny	Del Fi 4164	7/61
Memories Of Those Oldies		
But Goodies / Fever	Del Fi 4166	8/61
Ten Commandments Of Love /		
C C Rider	Del Fi 4170	10/61
Baby Let's Wait / Black Lantern	GJM 9000	1960s

The Magnificent Men

During the '60s, three acts exemplified the term "blue-eyed soul": the Righteous Brothers, the Walker Brothers, and the Magnificent Men. But only the latter got so close to R&B roots that they were able to perform on the chitlin circuit and receive standing ovations.

Very few white artists have achieved a degree of popularity with black audiences comparable to that attained by this seven-member vocal band from York and Harrisburg, Pennsylvania. The Mag Men (as they were often called) merged the rhythm section of a doo wop group called the Endells ("Vicky," Heigh Ho, 1963), with the vocalists (Dave Bupp and Buddy King) from a band called the Del-Chords ("Everybody's Gotta Lose Someday," Impala, 1964). Their common ground was the soulful sounds of groups coming out of Chicago and Detroit like THE IMPRESSIONS and THE TEMPTATIONS.

The Endells and the Del-Chords began to cross paths in 1964 while performing in the Harrisburg area. Bupp and King had great respect for the tight sound of the Endells (created by Bob Angelucci, Jim Seville, Tom Hoover, Terry Crousare, and Tom Pane), and they started to play clandestine gigs with the instrumentalists. With Tom Pane added to the vocals, the group called themselves the Magnificent Seven and began playing at the Raven on Harrisburg's East Shore. They became the house group by mid-1965, toured New York state, and eventually reached the famed Peppermint Lounge, where they met manager Ron Gittman.

Since there were several Magnificent Seven groups around the New York area, they opted for a name change after walking along 42nd Street and noticing a theatre marquee advertising the film *Those Magnificent Men in Their Flying Machines*.

Gittman then arranged an audition with Capitol Records after label reps had heard a demo of the group singing an original called "Peace of Mind" and the Arlen/Koehler standard "Stormy Weather." Intent on confirming that the sound on the demo really emanated from seven white kids, Capitol stopped the group after they played only about 10 bars and signed them.

"Peace of Mind" was released at the end of 1965 and received most of its favorable radio response on R&B stations.

When the Mag Men arrived to play at Philadelphia's rhythm and blues venue the Uptown Theatre, they were told "You're not playing here" by the theatre manager, who remained insistent until he was informed that they were indeed the group listed on the marquee.

Their second single was the high-powered, soulful rhythm ballad "Maybe, Maybe Baby," which sold well in the Northeast and helped bring the group face to face with the toughest, most critical audience in America at New York's Apollo Theatre. Their performance was so exciting that

James Brown jumped onstage and did 45 minutes of his own music with the group.

Their terrific version of "Stormy Weather" followed but somehow failed, and their fourth single, "I Could Be So Happy," only managed to reach number 93 in July 1967.

They became the only white group ever to tour with the Motortown Revue, which led to "The Sweet Soul Medley," a tribute to several of their favorite black groups mixed into Arthur Conley's "Sweet Soul Music." The record died at number 90. (Reverse racism may have affected sales. Some black disc jockeys jumped on their records and then dropped them after learning that the act was white. One Los Angeles disc jockey went so far as to break it into pieces and send it back to Capitol.)

The best of their remaining four singles were a bluesy version of Jimmy Webb's "By the Time I Get to Phoenix" and the powerful original "I Found What I Wanted in You."

In 1969 the group moved to Mercury with Ted Cooper producing "Holly Go Softly." It failed along with their last single, a version of Bob Dylan's "Lay, Lady, Lay." While trying to find its niche in a changing rock marketplace, the group met an act on tour that told them the four Magnificent Men LPs had inspired and influenced their music. The group was the Chicago Transit Authority, later known simply as Chicago.

Soon after, Dave Bupp decided they had missed their opportunity and he left. Stan Sommers of THE DEL-SATINS came in and the group continued, now limiting themselves to performing.

By 1974 they had disbanded. In the mid-'80s, Dave, Buddy, Bob, and Tom did a few reunion concerts in York, Pennsylvania, while Dave worked as a disc jockey at WOYK spinning rhythm and blues discs of the '50s and '60s.

In 1987 the Magnificent Men hired a new backup behind Bupp and King with Dusty Rhoades, Kent Craley, Jim Inners, Larry Green, and Bobby Seiberling, and issued a single ("I Wanna Know") on Major League Records, the label of longtime manager and friend Ron Gittman.

In the '90s, the Magnificent Men were still performing their blue-eyed soul.

THE MAGNIFICENT MEN

A SIDE/B SIDE	LABEL/CAT NO	DATE
Peace Of Mind / All Your Lovin's Gone To My Head	Cap 5608	1966
Maybe Maybe Baby / I've Got News	Cap 5732	1967

A SIDE/B SIDE	LABEL/CAT NO	DATE
Stormy Weather / Much Much More Of Your Love	Cap 5812	1967
I Could Be So Happy / You Changed My Life	Cap 5905	1967
Sweet Soul Medley Part 1 / Sweet Soul Medley Part 2	Cap 5976	1967
Forever Together / Babe, I'm Crazy 'Bout You	Cap 2062	1967
By The Time I Get To Phoenix / Tired Of Pushing	Cap 2134	1967
I Found What I Wanted In You / Almost Persuaded	Cap 2202	1968
Save The Country / So Much Love Waiting	Cap 2319	1968
Holly, Go Softly, Open Up And Get Richer	Merc 72988	1970
Lay Lady Lay / What Ever It Takes	Merc 72988	1970
I Wanna Know / There's Something On Your Mind	MjrLg 4411	1987

The Majors

Though they were short-lived, one-time winners, there was no mistaking the sound of the Majors. The ear-piercing falsetto of Rick Cordo and the warm harmonies of the group were easy to identify in a sea of similar-sounding singers.

They first called themselves the Premiers and hung around Harlan Street in Philadelphia in 1959. Robert Morris, Gene Glass, Frank Troutt, Rick Cordo, and Ron Gathers made up the original quintet, with Idella Morris soon replacing her brother Robert.

A meeting with would-be producer Buddy Caldwell led to their first session recording the originals "I'll Whisper in Your Ear" and "Lundee Dundee" in 1960. They entered the studio as the Premiers but came out as the Versatiles. The record, a treasured doo wop collectors' item today, was issued on Rocal Records and was quickly followed by a trip back to Harlan Street for the group.

Two years later they met Philadelphia producer Jerry Ragovoy (producer of THE CASTELLES). He was looking for a sound, and the newly christened Majors had it. Ragovoy had heard "Lundee Dundee" and knew the group couldn't write the hit he wanted, so he searched until he came up with "A Wonderful Dream." The song transformed the Majors from a rhythm and blues group to a pop, FOUR SEASONS-like ensemble.

Imperial Records signed the act and "A Wonderful Dream" rose to number 22 Pop and number 23

R&B. An LP came out, followed by their next single at the end of 1962, a bouncy tune in the "Wonderful Dream" mold called "A Little Bit Now." The single peaked at number 63.

"She's a Troublemaker" reached number 83 in late 1962. Three of their remaining five Imperial sides breached the Bubbling Under list ("Anything You Can Do," #117, February 1963, "Your Life Begins at Sweet Sixteen," #125, September 1963, and "I'll Be There," #113, February 1964), but Imperial gave up after those seven singles.

Ragovoy used the Majors' hit to launch his producing career. He worked with acts like Freddie Scott, Bobby Freeman, Irma Thomas, and Garnett Mimms while writing for Janis Joplin.

In 1966 the Majors got one more chance. This time it was with producer Pete De Angelos, who placed them on ABC-Paramount for "Love Is the Answer." The song wasn't the answer, and the group disbanded.

In the early '90s, three of the five (Cordo, Idella, and her husband, Gene Glass) were still performing as the Majors, occasionally joined by Gathers or Troutt.

THE MAJORS

A SIDE/B SIDE	LABEL/CAT NO	DATE
Lundee Dundee** /		
I'll Whisper In Your Ear**	Rocal 1002	1960
A Wonderful Dream /		
Time Will Tell	Imprl 5855	1962
She's A Troublemaker /		
A Little Bit Now	Imprl 5879	1962
Anything You Can Do /		
What In The World	Imprl 5914	1963
Tra La La /		
What Have You Been Doin'	Imprl 5936	1963
Get Up Now / One Happy Ending	Imprl 5968	1963
Your Life Begins /		
Which Way Did She Go	Imprl 5991	1963
Ooh Wee Baby / I'll Be There	Imprl 66009	1963
Love Is The Answer / Just Dance*	ABC P 107777	1966

* as the Performers
** as the Versatiles

The Mamas and the Papas

The title of the Mamas and the Papas' first LP—*If You Can Believe Your Eyes and Ears*—was appropriate. Looking at them, you might not believe that this combination of two mustachioed folkies, a would-be model, and a hefty jazz enthusiast could change the sound of vocal harmony in the '60s.

The group evolved from four previous groups started in the early '60s. Denny Doherty was a member of a group in New York known as the Halifax Three that included Zal Yanovsky (later to become a member of the Lovin' Spoonful). John Phillips, active on the Greenwich Village scene, was in a folk group known as the Journeymen, one of whose members was Scott McKenzie (famous for the 1967 John Phillips-penned ode to flower power, "San Francisco (Be Sure to Wear Flowers in Your Hair)." Michelle Gilliam of Long Beach, California, came to New York in 1962 to be a model, but that career was cut short when she met Phillips and joined the Journeymen.

In 1963, Doherty and Yanovsky got together with Jim Hendricks and his wife, Cass Elliot, to become Cass Elliot and the Big Three. After an uneventful release the group added John Sebastian and renamed themselves the Mugwumps. In 1964, they recorded an eponymous LP and released a single, "I'll Remember Tonight," that went nowhere. With no imminent release plan for the LP, the key figures of the Mugwumps split in four separate directions. Doherty became a member of the Journeymen with John Phillips and Michelle Gilliam (by now Michelle Gilliam Phillips, John's wife). Yanovsky and Sebastian founded the Lovin' Spoonful, and Cass Elliot joined a short-lived jazz act. Jim Hendricks joined a new group called the Lamp of Childhood.

By 1965 the Journeymen had decided their fortunes would be better served elsewhere and migrated to the Virgin Islands. Cass Elliot did a stint in the islands at the same time (as a waitress, not a singer) and in 1965 relocated to Los Angeles. The Journeymen headed west soon after, and Cass ended up as the fourth and final member.

By the end of 1965 they were called the Mamas and the Papas. After doing some Los Angeles background singing (including recordings with Barry McGuire of "Eve of Destruction" fame) they signed with Dunhill Records. John Phillips emerged as the group leader and songwriter, coming up with a string of chart records beginning in January 1966. The first one, "California Dreamin'," went to number four and became a pop standard in the midst of what was rapidly becoming the psychedelic era. "Monday, Monday" followed and went to number one, firmly establishing the group as the hippest of contemporary harmonizers.

The Mamas and the Papas' success lasted for only a short time, but in that period (from January 1966 to January 1969) all 13 of their single releases charted, including two B sides, "Look Through My Window" (#24) and "Dancing in the Street" (#73). They also had a hit backing up Cass Elliot on "Dream a Little Dream of Me" in 1968 (#12). Their first six singles all became top five hits. Along with "California Dreamin'" and "Monday, Monday," they had "I Saw Her Again" (#5), "Words of Love" (#5), "Dedicated to the One I Love" (#2), and "Creeque Alley" (#5).

There was gold in them thar hills, and in mid-1967, ex-Mugwump Jim Hendricks recorded a Mamas and the Papas sound-a-like with his group Lamp of Childhood entitled "Two O'Clock Morning." The song lacked the magic of John Phillips' compositions. Warner Bros., meanwhile, finally released the Mugwumps' LP (three years after its recording) to capitalize on Cass's and Denny's success.

In late 1968 John Phillips's inability to keep writing great songs seemed to signal the beginning of the group's demise. Their last single, "Do You Wanna Dance," was a reworking of the Bobby Freeman 1958 hit, and it peaked at number 76. Cass continued to record for Dunhill after the group split up and had several minor charters including "It's Getting Better" (#30) and "Make Your Own Kind of Music" (#36) in 1969. In late 1971, the group reunited to record the *People Like Us* LP, which included a February 1972 release called "Step Out." Although the album lacked the magic of their earlier efforts, the "Step Out" B side, "Shooting Star," had a vibrancy and persistence that, given a chance, might have reestablished the group. By 1972, the group had again disbanded, with Denny recording solo for Columbia and John going into seclusion. Cass recorded for Dunhill and (from 1972 on) for RCA until her death in 1974. Her last single was "Listen to the World" in 1973. Michelle had the most growth through the '70s, building an acting career in films like *Dillinger* and *Brewster McCloud*. Her 1977 solo LP for A&M contained a rock doo wopper entitled "Victim of Romance" that was in a Phil Spector–Bob B. Soxx and the Blue Jeans mode.

When the '80s rolled around, John again reformed the group, this time replacing Michelle with his daughter, actress McKenzie Phillips, and replacing Cass with Spanky McFarlane, the personable lead singer of SPANKY AND OUR GANG. Doherty came all the way from his home in Nova Scotia to rejoin, and the foursome started performing around the country. By 1987 Doherty had been replaced by original Journeymen member Scott McKenzie.

Though the Mamas and the Papas didn't record after 1972's *People Like Us*, their contrapuntal har-

monies, unique arrangements, and singable songs helped make them a significant part of rock and roll history in general and vocal group history in particular.

THE MAMAS AND THE PAPAS

A SIDE/B SIDE	LABEL/CAT NO	DATE
The Mugwumps		
I'll Remember Tonight /		
I Don't Wanna Know	Wrnr 5471	1964
Jug Band Music /		
Bald-Headed Woman	Sidewalk 900	1966
Searchin' / Here It Is Another Day	Wrnr 7018	1967
Season Of The Witch / My Gal	Sidewalk 909	1967
The Mamas and the Papas		
California Dreamin' /		
Somebody Groovy	Dnhl 4020	1966
Monday Monday / Got A Feelin'	Dnhl 4026	1966
I Saw Her Again / Even If I Could	Dnhl 4031	1966
Look Through Any Window /		
Once Was A Time I Thought	Dnhl 4050	1966
Words Of Love /		
Dancing In The Street	Dnhl 4057	1966
Dedicated To The One I Love /		
Free Advice	Dnhl 4077	1967
Creeque Alley /		
Did You Ever Want To Cry	Dnhl 4083	1967
Twelve Thirty (Young Girls Are		
Coming To The Canyons) /		
Straight Shooter	Dnhl 4099	1967
Glad To Be Unhappy / Hey Girl	Dnhl 4107	1967
Dancing Bear / John's Music Box	Dnhl 4133	1967
Safe In My Garden / Too Late	Dnhl 4125	1968
Dream A Little Dream Of Me* /		
Midnight Voyage	Dnhl 4145	1968
For The Love Of Ivy	Dnhl 4150	1968
Do You Wanna Dance / My Girl	Dnhl 4171	1968
Step Out / Shooting Star	Dnhl 4301	1972

* Mama Cass

The Manhattans

One of the most enduring of the soul doo wop groups of the '60s, the Manhattans stayed at it for almost 30 years. Their story goes back to 1961, when a 19-year-old Macon, Georgia, GI named Edward "Sonny" Bivins (tenor) came to the New York area (after an air force stint in West Germany) with his friend Richard Taylor. They formed the Dulcets, an R&B group whose only recording, "Pork Chops," became a legendary item among R&B record collectors. Meanwhile, Jersey City, New Jersey, residents Kenny Kelly (18, second tenor), and Winfred "Blue" Lovett (18, bass) were singing with rival vocal groups. When the Dulcets dispersed in 1961, Bivins and Taylor met up with Kelly and Lovett. One trip into New York provided an encounter with George "Smitty" Smith (lead), and the Manhattans were born.

They chose the name because they liked its classy sound and spent so much time singing on 116th Street in Harlem.

In 1963 they came to the attention of Danny Robinson's Enjoy label and recorded "Come on Back" as Ronnie and the Manhattans.

In 1964 they performed at the Apollo's amateur night contest, finishing third. Newark's Carnival Records owner Joe Evans heard the youngsters and signed them. Bivins and Lovett wrote most of the group's songs, though not always in collaboration. The Manhattans' first single on Carnival, "For the Very First Time," did as little as their second 1964 release, "There Goes a Fool," an up-tempo, transitional soul/doo wop number. But "I Want to Be" (written by Blue) rode its New Orleans soul sound to number 12 on the R&B chart and crossed over to number 68 Pop in early 1965.

Their Marvin Gaye-styled follow-up, "Searchin' for My Baby," went to number 20 R&B and number 135 Pop, but it was the flip side that established the group's "soul balladeers" reputation. "I'm the One Love Forgot," penned by Bivins, became a huge record in New York and Philadelphia.

Their next four singles all charted R&B ("Follow Your Heart," #20, "Baby I Need You," #22, "Can I," #23, and "I Betcha," #23), taking the group to the end of 1966. Their string of six charters ended with the holiday ballad "Alone on New Year's Eve" followed by the harmony-filled failure, "Our Love Will Never Die."

The group bounced back with their most beautiful ballad to date, the George Smith/Joe Evans-penned classic "When We're Made as One." Though it only made number 31 R&B (and number 128 Pop) the group liked it so much they recorded it again 18 years later on their *Too Hot to Stop It* LP in an a cappella arrangement.

After two more releases, the quintet moved over to the King Family's Deluxe label. Seven of their 11 Deluxe singles charted R&B between 1970 and 1973, with the highlights being "One Life to Live" (#3, 1972) and "From Atlanta to Goodbye" (#48).

In 1970 the Manhattans appeared on a show at North Carolina's Kittrell College with the New Imperials (not Little Anthony's group), who included student Gerald Alston. The Manhattans were so impressed with Gerald that they asked him to join their group, but he graciously declined. However,

fate refused to let young Gerald's decision stand. Smitty became ill that year and died. Alston joined the group in 1971.

When Deluxe went out of business the group signed to Columbia. "There's No Me Without You" was released in April 1973 and outdistanced all their previous singles, going to number 43 Pop and tying "One Life to Live" at number three R&B. The record became their first million seller.

Through 1974 and 1975 they continued to chart R&B but after 10 years of recording still hadn't seriously crossed over to the Pop charts (their highest reading was 1974's "Don't Take Your Love" at #37). That changed in the spring of 1976 with the release of the ballad "Kiss and Say Goodbye."

Reaching number one on both the R&B and Pop charts, "Kiss" also crossed national boundaries to score in England (#4) and Australia (#5). "Kiss" became the second single in history to be certified RIAA platinum under the new two million sales standard ("Disco Lady" by Johnny Taylor was the first).

In 1977 the group was selected to perform at the President's Inaugural Ball at the White House. During that year baritone Taylor left to become a Muslim and the group decided to continue on as a quartet.

In 1980 the group performed at a concert broadcast live from Citicorp Plaza on WABC Radio, the first live broadcast at the station since the Beatles. By then "Shining Star" had become the Manhattans' third million-plus seller (#5 Pop, #4 R&B).

While the Manhattans improved their pop appeal, the group never lost its solid rhythm and blues base. In fact, every one of their Pop singles also charted R&B.

The same four men were still performing in 1991 after more than 18 years with Columbia, and they were still bent on improving their record beyond 24 Pop single charters and 41 R&B chart successes.

The Marcels

One of the best vocal groups of all time, the Marcels produced more good recordings in their tragically short career than many groups did in their long careers.

Their tale starts in 1959 Pittsburgh, Pennsylvania, where baritone Richard F. Knauss of a local unnamed ensemble conceived the idea of putting together a Pittsburgh supergroup when he heard bass Fred Johnson sing. They added second tenor

Gene J. Bricker from a third group and soon found their first tenor, Ron "Bingo" Mundy. The toughest part was finding an exciting lead, but when they heard Cornelius Harp they knew they had something special.

They practiced on Woodstrun Avenue on Pittsburgh's north side while attending Oliver Allegheny High School. Sometime during their formation Dick Knauss auditioned for another group, the Dynamics ("Don't Leave Me," Dynamic, 1959), but wound up telling their manager Jules Kruspir about an even more exciting quintet he was working with. Jules went to hear the mixed fivesome (Knauss and Bricker were white; Harp, Johnson, and Mundy black) at Johnson's house and liked what he heard. At this time the group decided to call themselves the Marcels after a popular hairstyle of the day that Cornelius wore.

The Marcels practiced songs by many of the '50s' best R&B acts, including such influences as THE HARPTONES, THE SPANIELS, THE CADILLACS, LITTLE ANTHONY AND THE IMPERIALS, and THE DELVIKINGS. Several of these numbers wound up on a demo tape that Jules sent to Colpix Records, a division of Columbia Pictures. They had no original songs, so the purpose of the tape was strictly to showcase their singing ability. Little did they know that the vocal arrangements on the Cadillacs' "Zoom" from that 1960 tape would help give them immortality.

Stu Phillips, A&R director for Colpix, liked the demo enough to bring the group to New York. Though he was under orders to concentrate solely on another Colpix act, he liked the Marcels so much he snuck them into the studio after the other artist's session. They began recording several oldies at RCA Studios on February 15, 1961. Stu asked them to do "Heart and Soul" but no one knew the song, so they opted for an evergreen called "Blue Moon" that had been a 1935 number one hit for alto sax man Glen Gray. Apparently the bass intro arrangement from the demo tape of "Zoom" was still buzzing around in Phillips's head since he had Johnson apply the now-famous intro note-for-note to the Rogers and Hart standard. That intro went something like "Bomp baba bomp, ba bomp ba bomp bomp, baba bomp baba bomp, da dang da dang dang, da ding a dong ding." Sound familiar?

The recording was done in two takes, which was lucky for the Marcels since they only had eight minutes left in the studio. An overzealous promo man for Colpix heard the Marcels master and played it for WINS disc jockey Murray the K. The soon-to-be "fifth Beatle" was so knocked out by it he reportedly played "Blue Moon" 26 times during his four-hour show. (He never did that with a Beatles song. Perhaps they should have named him the sixth Marcel.) Reaction was so terrific that Colpix rush-released the single in February. *Billboard*'s February 20th reviewer wrote, "Here's a wild and woolly old time rock & roll treatment of the well-known standard. There's a great deal happening on this arrangement and the side figures to have a strong chance."

Even the label wasn't prepared for what happened next. In four weeks it was number one on both the Pop and R&B charts, having pushed no less than Elvis Presley out of the top spot. It took Del Shannon's historic "Runaway" to displace the Marcels on April 24th. "Blue Moon" didn't stop there. It reached number one in England, number four in Australia, number seven in Holland, number seven in Sweden, number six in French Belgium, number five in Denmark, number two in New Zealand, and went top 10 in such locales as Israel, Norway, Spain, South Africa, and France.

Not only had half the world gotten a healthy dose of American doo wop, but America itself had a rekindling of interest in a bass vocal tradition that had been slowly disappearing from U.S. recordings since the mid-'50s.

On March 16th, a month and a day after their first session, the Marcels recorded six more gems that included "Over the Rainbow," "Two People in the World," "Sweet Was the Wine," and "Teeter Totter Love." On April 11th they recorded five more sides, coming up with their well-timed second single, the Porgy and Bess classic, "Summertime."

Its 'ba-oo' bass intro, Cornelius's velvety baritone lead, and a solid wall of Marcels vocals made this the best group version of the Gershwin classic ever recorded, but it only reached number 78 Pop and number 46 in the U.K.

During that summer the Marcels appeared in a rock and roll movie for Columbia titled *Twist Around the Clock* with Dion and Chubby Checker. In the film they sang "Blue Moon" and a number called "Merry Twistmas."

In July the LP *Blue Moon* was issued containing all the sides from the March 16th session, their hit and its flip, a strong version of THE CHANTELS' "Goodbye to Love," and some doo wop and R&B standards cut at the first session including "Peace of Mind" (the Spaniels), "I'll Be Forever Loving You" (THE EL DORADOS), "Most of All" (THE MOONGLOWS), and "Sunday Kind of Love" (the Harptones). In all, the LP was a strong showcase for the Marcels' vocal talents.

Unfortunately, the 18 recordings made at those three sessions were the sum total of the original group's output. Some mysterious goings on between Jules Kruspir and Richard Knauss caused the latter to leave with Gene Bricker in August. They were replaced by Alan Johnson (baritone, Fred's brother) and Walt Maddox (second tenor).

The now all-black quintet's first session, on September 1, 1961, yielded their fourth single, a remake of the 1931 Guy Lombardo number 12 hit "Heartaches." By November 27th it ranked seventh in the nation on the Pop chart (#19 R&B).

1962 opened with their self-parody, "My Melancholy Baby." Although a *Billboard* reviewer enthused, "The great standard is wrapped up in their amusing bomb de bomp styled delivery and a rockin' beat. Watch it," "Melancholy Baby" only reached number 58 Pop in March 1962, becoming their last Top 100 chart 45.

By the end of 1961 Mundy had left and their February 1962 release, "Twistin' Fever," had stalled at number 103. Colpix continued to issue older secondary sides through 1963, of which "That Old Black Magic" and "One Last Kiss" were strong cuts.

Cornelius Harp, the heart of the Marcels, left at the end of 1962. The group then left Colpix, picking up a few singles between Kyra and 888, two Pittsburgh labels, in 1964. Then Alan Johnson dropped out, leaving acting leader Fred Johnson to add William Herndon and Richard Harris (formerly of THE ALTAIRS).

The quartet now included Walt Maddox (lead), Richard Harris (baritone), William Herndon (first tenor), and Fred Johnson (bass).

The Marcels recorded again in 1973, but without Harp's strong lead they turned in a mediocre traditional ballad performance of "In the Still of the Night" (Queen Bee).

In 1975 the Marcels shined once again with their formula sound on "Lucky Old Sun," with Harp back on lead and Johnson on bass, but the Pittsburgh-based St. Clair label had no marketing capability and the record faded into collectors' dreamland.

That same year Val Shively issued three great sides for the collectors' market from the group's first LP. But by now the Marcels were working the oldies circuit even though they were capable of a contemporary R&B hit in the SPINNERS or O'JAYS mode.

On January 14, 1973, the original members held a reunion at an oldies club called the Villa Madrid in Pittsburgh. Ron Mundy and Dick Knauss continued singing there in a group called the Memories. Ironically, the hit Marcels lasted only a few years while the Maddox, Harris, Herndon, and Fred Johnson grouping lasted on and off for over two decades.

In the early '90s Cornelius Harp was living in Pittsburgh. Ron Mundy worked for Pittsburgh's Port Authority as a bus driver. Dick Knauss was a school janitor. Gene Bricker died in the '80s. Walt Maddox continued to perform in nightclubs, doing a musical tribute to Nat King Cole. Alan Johnson was working for the University of Pittsburgh. Fred Johnson continued leading modern-day Marcels through their bomp baba bomps.

THE MARCELS

A SIDE/B SIDE	LABEL/CAT NO	DATE
Blue Moon / Goodbye To Love	Colpix 186	2/61
Summertime / Teeter Totter Love	Colpix 196	6/61
You Are My Sunshine / Find Another Fool	Colpix 606	9/61
Heartaches / My Love For You	Colpix 612	10/61
Don't Cry For Me This Christmas / Merry Twist-Mas	Colpix 617	11/61
My Melancholy Baby / Really Need Your Love	Colpix 624	1/62
Twistin' Fever / Footprints In The Sand	Colpix 629	2/62
Flowerpot / Hold On	Colpix 640	5/62
Friendly Loans / Loved Her The Whole Week Through	Colpix 651	8/62
All Right, Okay, You Win / Lollipop Baby	Colpix 665	11/62
That Old Black Magic / Don't Turn Your Back On Me	Colpix 683	3/63
Give Me Back Your Love / I Wanna Be The Leader	Colpix 687	5/63
One Last Kiss / Teeter Totter Love	Colpix 694	7/63
Comes Love / Your Red Wagon (You Can Push It, Or Pull It)	Kyra 888	1964
How Deep Is The Ocean / Lonely Boy	Kyra 101	1964
In The Still Of The Night / High On A Hill	QnBee 47001	1973
Lucky Old Sun* / (You Gave Me) Peace Of Mind*	StClr 13711	1975
That Lucky Old Sun* / (You Gave Me) Peace Of Mind*	Rocky 13711	1975
A Fallen Tear / I'll Be Forever Loving You	Monogram 112	1975
Sweet Was The Wine / Over The Rainbow	Monogram 113	1975
Two People In The World / Most Of All	Monogram 115	1975

Walt Maddox and the Marcels

A Letter Full Of Tears / How Do You Speak To An Angel	SprM 203073	1982
Blue Moon / Clap Your Hands (When I Clap My Hands)	SprM 304027	1983

* as the Fabulous Marcels

Martha and the Vandellas

One of the most aggressive-sounding girl groups, Martha and the Vandellas were originally formed because the brother of 19-year-old Martha Reeves would not let her sing with his group. Martha's early background in music came from her father's Methodist church, where she was schooled in the sounds of THE SOUL STIRRERS, THE FIVE BLIND BOYS, and Clara Ward, among others. At Northeastern High School she was vocally trained by the same man who later taught Mary Wilson and Florence Ballard of THE SUPREMES (Abraham Silver). She then began doing solo work in clubs as Martha LaVelle.

In 1960 Martha, Gloria Williams, Rosalind Ashford, and Annette Sterling, having been friends from high school, formed the Del-Phis. In 1961 the group did one 45 for Checkmate Records (a division of Chess) called "I'll Let You Know" and then Martha went to Motown Records to audition. Instead she was offered a secretarial job in the A&R Department and she took it, hoping it would lead to an opportunity. As assistant to producer Mickey Stevenson, one of Martha's jobs was to book studio time for upcoming recording sessions. On one occasion when Mary Wells couldn't make a session, Martha brought in the Del-Phis and they recorded "There He Is at My Door." Since the group was technically still signed to Chess, Motown named them the Vels and issued the 45 on their Melody affiliate. Gloria sang lead at the time. When the Melody release went nowhere she quit the group, leaving them a trio with Martha as lead.

Their real break came in July 1962 when the group backed new Tamla artist Marvin Gaye on his fourth single, "Stubborn Kind of Fellow." When it took off, the trio knew they'd finally get their chance. Martha came up with a new name, a combination of Van Dyke Street (where her grandmother lived) and the name of one of her favorite singers, Della Reese.

They released the single "I'll Have to Let Him Go" in September 1962, but it received little attention. The beginning of their collaboration with songwriters Holland, Dozier, and Holland led in February 1963 to their second single, the rhythmic "Come and Get These Memories." It charted on April 27th, eventually reaching number 29 (#6 R&B). With the 1963 hit "Heat Wave," the girls established their forceful formula: power vocals

with a tinge of gospel laid over the emerging Motown trademark bass and drums. It burned its way up the *Billboard* Hot 100 and reached number four (#1 R&B). More hot rockers followed, including "Quicksand" (#8) and "Live Wire" (#42).

Toward the end of 1963, Annette left to marry and was replaced by Betty Kelley.

Martha and the Vandellas were easily the most popular in-person act in the Motown stable, and they rocked audiences at such shows as the Labor Day week performance at the Brooklyn Fox with Murray the K and the Supremes, Marvin Gaye, and THE SHANGRI-LAS.

In the summer of 1964 Martha and company had their biggest hit with "Dancing in the Street," which reached number two on October 17, right behind Manfred Mann's "Do Wah Diddy Diddy." In February 1965 "Nowhere to Run" was issued just as the group took off for England as part of Motown's first European package tour alongside THE TEMPTATIONS, the Supremes, Marvin Gaye, THE MIRACLES, and Stevie Wonder. "Nowhere" rose to number eight Pop and number five R&B.

In 1966 Lois Reeves, Martha's sister and formerly with the Orlons, replaced Kelly. The group then continued to soar with hits like "My Baby Loves Me" (#22 Pop, #3 R&B) and "I'm Ready for Love" (#9 Pop, #2 R&B).

1967 opened with the smash "Jimmy Mack" (#10 Pop, #1 R&B). Another change occurred when Sandra Tilley replaced Rosalind Ashford that year.

In the fall of 1967 Gordy labels began reading "Martha Reeves and the Vandellas" with the release of "Honey Chile," their last top 10 R&B hit (#5 R&B, #11 Pop). On September 15th the group appeared on the debut episode of NBC-TV's "Soul" with Lou Rawls and Redd Foxx.

The group had three more chart singles in 1968 and two in 1969, but it was becoming increasingly clear that Berry Gordy's energies were primarily directed toward the Supremes.

Martha suffered a breakdown in the spring of 1969 but fought her way back by 1971. Upon returning to Detroit from an overseas tour she learned that Motown had moved to Los Angeles but no one had the courtesy to inform her.

On July 15, 1972, "Tear It Down" became the group's last charter, reaching number 37 R&B and number 103 Pop. It was also the group's last single. On December 31, 1972, Martha and the Vandellas performed a farewell concert at Cobo Hall in Detroit. The group broke up in early 1973 and Martha went out as a solo. In 1974 Martha had her biggest solo success, "Power of Love" (#76 Pop, #27 R&B) on MCA, produced by the legendary Richard Perry.

In 1978 the group reunited for a benefit for actor Will Geer in Santa Cruz, California.

Martha later settled in Detroit and often toured with "The Legendary Ladies of Rock and Roll," including THE CRYSTALS and Ronnie Spector, among others.

The Marvelettes

Despite 21 R&B chart hits, 23 Pop hits, and Motown's first number one single, the Marvelettes, much to their consternation, were never the darlings of Motown that they aspired to be.

The girls started out as a quintet in rural Inkster, Michigan.

The original 1961 lineup included leads Gladys Horton and Georgia Dobbins with Georgeanna Tillman, Juanita Cowart, and Katherine Anderson.

The five 17-year-olds attended Inkster High and entered the school's talent show, where the first three prizes were auditions at Detroit's Motown Records. The girls called themselves the Marvels and finished fourth in the contest (though in a 1980 interview Gladys Horton stated they came in first), but their teacher, Mrs. Sharpley, convinced the principal to let them go to the audition.

The group's early influences were THE SHIRELLES and THE CHANTELS, so it was no surprise when they auditioned with "I Met Him on a Sunday" and "He's Gone."

Berry Gordy and Smokey Robinson were impressed but sent them home to come up with an original hit song. Since none of the Marvels had ever written, Georgia asked William Garrett, a songwriting friend, if he had anything in the hopper. He showed them a blues tune titled "Please Mr. Postman." Georgia rewrote the entire song overnight, keeping only the title. She then gave it to Gladys to learn and dropped out of the group to take care of her ailing mother. The Marvels then added second lead Wanda Young, a graduate of Inkster, and were soon knocking on Motown's door again.

Gordy rechristened them the Marvelettes and issued "Please Mr. Postman" in the summer of 1961 on Tamla, around four months after the first single by Motown's other girl group, THE SUPREMES.

On September 4th the Inkster girls hit the *Billboard* charts and one week later jumped on the R&B listings. Their recording then took the longest ride to number one of any single in chart history

up to that time. For 14 weeks "Postman" kept trying to deliver the goods until December 11th, when it pushed "Big Bad John" and Jimmy Dean from the top spot. The background of "Please Mr. Postman" was notably similar in feel to the Primettes' 1960 obscurity "Tears of Sorrow" (Lupine). The connection was most likely the producers Holland and Bateman, since they knew of the Primettes and their record before that group became known as the Supremes.

An immediate rivalry arose between the Supremes and the country girls from Inkster. It was ironic that the girls being groomed for stardom with songs written for them by Motown's top writers had two releases and two failures, while the novices from the sticks not only recorded a hit but were also the writers.

On January 20, 1962, *Billboard* reviewed their follow-up: "The 'Postman' girls pound out the wild rocker, 'Twistin' Postman,' tied in with their current hit, but with a more heavily accented blues beat." It ultimately reached number 34 Pop and number 13 R&B. Meanwhile, the group was becoming popular on tour, but underlying tensions and internal competition were taking their toll.

Billboard's April 21 issue again took note of a Marvelettes song: "The gals have another potential hit that follows in the footsteps of their 'Postman' hit. This is done in a similar rockin' tempo, with a good gospel piano in the backing. Watch it!" "Playboy" was the record in question, but there was no question about its hit potential; it reached number seven Pop and number three R&B on June 23rd. The Supremes were still three weeks away from their first Pop charter ("Your Heart Belongs to Me," #95).

"Beechwood 4-5789" became the most famous phone number in the country in the summer of 1962 (#17 Pop, #7 R&B). Then "Strange I Know" reached number 49 Pop (#10 R&B) in early 1963, but the rest of the year was a chart disappointment, with "Locking Up My Heart" doing the best at number 44 Pop (#25 R&B).

By 1965 the group was back in the limelight with records like "Too Many Fish in the Sea" (#25 Pop, #15 R&B), "I'll Keep Holding On" (#34 Pop, #11 R&B), and "Don't Mess with Bill" (#7 Pop, #3 R&B), written by Smokey Robinson and led by Wanda (who did most of the later leads).

The group made a major mistake by passing on a song brought to them in 1964 by Holland, Dozier, and Holland. The writers then took "Baby Love" to the Supremes, giving those singers their second number one hit in a row.

In 1965 Juanita left the group reportedly following a nervous breakdown. When Georgeanna fell ill soon after and had to leave the roadwork behind, the group continued as a trio.

In 1967 the Marvelettes hit with three in a row, "The Hunter Gets Captured by the Game" (#13 Pop, #2 R&B), "When You're Young and in Love" (#23 Pop, #9 R&B, #13 U.K., their only British charter), and "My Baby Must Be a Magician" (#17 Pop, #8 R&B).

Gladys then left the group after giving birth to her first son, and Anne Bogan came on board.

Their last chart record came in late 1968 with "Destination: Anywhere" (#63 Pop, #28 R&B).

In 1969 Wanda decided to stay in Detroit when Motown moved to Los Angeles. That was the end of the group, but four more singles were issued through 1971, the last being "A Breathtaking Guy."

Georgeanna married Billy Gordon of the Contours and died in 1980 of sickle cell anemia. Wanda married Bobby Rogers of THE MIRACLES, Katherine wedded Joe Schaffner, road manager for THE TEMPTATIONS, and Gladys settled in Los Angeles.

THE MARVELETTES

A SIDE/B SIDE	LABEL/CAT NO	DATE
Please Mr. Postman / So Long Baby	Tamla 54046	7/61
Twistin' Postman / I Want A Guy	Tamla 54054	1/62
Playboy / All The Love I've Got	Tamla 54060	1962
Beechwood 4-5789 / Someday Someway	Tamla 54065	8/62
Strange I Know / Too Strong To Be A Strung Along	Tamla 54072	11/62
Locking Up My Heart / Forever	Tamla 54077	3/63
My Daddy Knows Best / Tie A String Around Your Finger	Tamla 54082	7/63
As Long As I Know He's Mine / Little Girl Blue	Tamla 54088	10/63
He's A Good Guy / Goddess Of Love	Tamla 54091	2/64
You're My Remedy / A Little Bit Of Sympathy, A Little Bit Of Love	Tamla 54097	6/64
Too Many Fish In The Sea / A Need For Love	Tamla 54105	11/64
I'll Keep Holding On / No Time For Love	Tamla 54116	5/65
Danger Heartbreak Dead Ahead / Your Cheating Ways	Tamla 54120	8/65
Don't Mess With Bill / Anything You Wanna Do	Tamla 54126	12/65
You're The One / Paper Boy	Tamla 54131	4/66
The Hunter Get Captured By The Game / I Think I Can Change You	Tamla 54143	12/66

A SIDE/B SIDE	LABEL/CAT NO	DATE
When You're Young And In Love / The Day You Take One You Have To Take The Other	Tamla 54150	4/67
My Baby Must Be A Magician / I Need Someone	Tamla 54158	12/67
Here I Am Baby / Keep Off, No Trespassing	Tamla 54166	5/68
Destination: Anywhere / What's Easy For Two Is Hard For One	Tamla 54171	10/68
I'm Gonna Hold On As Long As Can / Don't Make Hurting Me A Habit	Tamla 54177	1968
That's How Heartaches Are Made / Rainy Morning	Tamla 54186	1969
Marionette / After All	Tamla 54198	1970
A Breathtaking Guy / You're The One For Me Baby	Tamla 54213	1971

The Mighty Clouds of Joy

The Mighty Clouds of Joy were one of the best of the modern young gospel groups and one of only a handful who successfully crossed over to soul and pop.

Though the members were from different parts of the U.S., they all met at Jefferson High School in Los Angeles in 1960. Joe Ligon of Troy, Alabama, was the lead; Johnny Martin from Los Angeles was the tenor; Richard Wallace from rural Georgia was on baritone; and Elmo Franklin from Louisiana performed on bass. Other early members included David Walker, Ermont Franklin, and Jimmy Jones.

Joe Ligon was heavily influenced by sensational Nightingales lead Julius Cheeks (as was the great '60s soul singer Wilson Pickett). With high harmonies abounding, the group sounded much like THE IMPRESSIONS. The Clouds started out doing small gospel concerts and came to the attention of Houston-based Peacock Records, where they did their first of 11 albums through the decade.

From the outset the group wanted to be different from the typical gospel act in both image and sound. They wore green suits, yellow ties, and red shoes at their appearances, and when gospel began to wane on black radio in the '70s, their musical versatility allowed them to sign with the more pop-oriented ABC Records. They were reportedly the first black gospel act to have a drummer as part of their regular group.

Their fourth ABC LP (*It's Time*, 1974) yielded the ground-breaking single "Time" (produced by Philadelphia's Gamble and Huff), which reached number 32 R&B and number 102 on *Billboard*'s Bubbling Under chart in late 1974.

Another single, "Mighty Cloud of Joy," went to number 47 R&B. Despite the group's increased popularity, the religious message in their music allowed them to maintain a strong gospel following.

Their biggest single success came in February 1976 with the release of "(Ride the) Mighty High," which charted on February 14th and reached number 69 Pop (#22 R&B).

By 1978 they received a Grammy nomination for the ABC LP *God Is Not Dead* and a Grammy for the *Live and Direct* LP.

When ABC went under, they moved to Epic and won a 1979 Grammy for the LP *Changing Times* produced by former JACKSON 5 producer Frank Wilson.

In 1980 it was another label (Word) and another Grammy nominated LP (*Cloudburst*), produced by Earth, Wind & Fire's Al McKay.

Former gospel Keynotes member Paul Beasley joined the Clouds and was later replaced by Michael Cook.

After a tour of Japan in 1987, Johnny Martin died and was replaced first by Dwight Gordon and then by Michael McGowan.

In an age when acts would normally release an LP once every 18 months, the Clouds had three records out in 1982. They were *Request Line*, a compilation of their earlier ABC recordings; *Miracle Man*, which received two Grammy nominations; and *Mighty Clouds Above*, recorded live at the Montreux Jazz Festival in Switzerland.

Over the years they regularly crossed the lines between gospel and R&B, opening for acts as diverse as the Rolling Stones, Earth, Wind & Fire, Andrea Crouch, and the Reverend James Cleveland.

Entering the '90s, the Clouds were still going strong. They were performing more than 200 concerts a year around the world and had a catalog of 27 albums. The Mighty Clouds were one group that had no trouble spreading their message.

The Miracles

The group most responsible for establishing the Motown sound, the Miracles featured the singer Smokey Robinson, who would go on to become one of America's premier songwriters.

William "Smokey" Robinson founded the Miracles in 1954, while the quintet was attending Morgan High School in Detroit. They included Warren "Pete" Moore (bass), Ronnie White (baritone), Bobby Rogers (tenor), and his brother Emerson Rogers (tenor).

Smokey Robinson was initially influenced by another great Detroit group, Nolan Strong and THE DIABLOS. In 1955 Robinson and the Matadors (as the Miracles originally called themselves) did an a cappella demo of the Diablos' "Adios, My Desert Love" that revealed a distinctive though rough Robinson falsetto already taking shape. That demo managed to wind up on a rare late 1960s LP titled *Roadhouse Presents the Great Unreleased Group Sounds* that included cuts by the Parakeets, the Fascinators, and "Smokey and Group" (billed that way to avoid legal complications).

In 1956 Emerson joined the army, so the group drafted someone they knew the service couldn't touch, Emerson's sister Claudette Rogers.

The Matadors played local shows and in 1957 auditioned for Jackie Wilson's manager, who turned them down because he felt they sounded too much like THE PLATTERS. A young writer (who was also a Ford assembly line worker) was also there and liked the Matadors. His name was Berry Gordy, Jr., and by early 1958 he and Jackie Wilson's cousin Tyrone Carlo had written an answer song to the SILHOUETTES hit "Get a Job" called "Got a Job." By now the group had renamed themselves the Miracles, no doubt hoping for one.

Berry helped get "Got a Job" recorded on George Goldner's End Records in March 1958. The Silhouettes spoof sold some records and led to another End release, the rocking, Latin-rhythmed "Money" (not the Barrett Strong song), decorated with Robinson's easily identifiable lead. With no "Money" action, Berry produced a side cowritten with Smokey titled "Bad Girl" and licensed it to Chess in 1959. He then issued it locally on his own experimental Motown label. When the smooth ballad reached number 93 nationally, Robinson convinced Gordy to start his own record label. On 800 borrowed dollars in 1960, Gordy formed the Tamla label and signed the Miracles, whose bombing first single "Way Over There" made the company look like a bad investment.

Things turned around dramatically for the fledgling group and label when the Robinson song "Shop Around" was released in October 1960 and charted on the Pop and R&B lists on December 12th. A commercial dance tune with clever lyrics, "Shop Around" went to number two Pop on February 20, 1961 (#1 R&B). *Billboard* reviewed both sides of the Miracles' follow-up, "Ain't It Baby" b/w "The Only One I Love," citing them as "two strong ones from the Miracles, who could follow 'Shop Around' with the lively rock & roll first side. The second is a strong rock-a-ballad that's tenderly sung by the lead singer. Sock dual-sider." "Ain't It Baby" reached number 15 R&B and number 49 Pop. The group, the first act signed to Tamla, also became the act that established its chart base. Smokey Robinson, in recognition of his work with both the Miracles and other Motown acts, was made a Tamla vice president by the end of 1961.

In 1962 the Miracles came out with two in a row of their best, the soulful, mid-tempo "What's So Good about Good-bye" (#35 Pop, #16 R&B) and the swirling, cha-cha flavored "I'll Try Something New" (#39 Pop, #11 R&B).

In November 1962 the Miracles carved their permanent niche with the release of "You Really Got a Hold on Me," a slow grind that tore up radio and the charts (#8 Pop, #1 R&B). "Mickey's Monkey" followed in the summer and became their third top 10 Pop hit (#8 Pop, #3 R&B).

By the beginning of 1964 Claudette, who had married Smokey in 1963, had retired from the group.

The British invasion had little affect on the Motown explosion, and the Miracles kept up the activity with singles like the classic ballad "Ooo Baby Baby" (#16 Pop, #4 R&B, 1965), "The Tracks of My Tears" (#16 Pop, #2 R&B, 1965), and their first U.K. charter, the dance hit "Going to A Go-Go" (#11 Pop, #2 R&B, #44 U.K., 1966). Robinson also found time to pen hits for other Motown acts like Mary Wells ("My Guy," #1) and THE TEMPTATIONS ("The Way You Do the Things You Do," #11). 1966 ended with their last hit as the Miracles, "I'm the One You Need" (#17 Pop, #4 R&B, #45 U.K.), because in 1967 they became Smokey Robinson and the Miracles.

Their first public release under the new name was "The Love I Saw in You Was Just a Mirage" (#20 Pop, #10 R&B) (a special pressing of "I Care About Detroit" was issued on a limited basis just prior to "Mirage").

In July 1967 Tamla released the Smokey-penned "More Love" (#23 Pop, #5 R&B), which Kim Carnes later took to number 10 Pop in 1980. The single after "More Love" was one of their biggest, "I Second that Emotion" (#4 Pop, #1 R&B, #27 U.K.).

More strong sides followed, including "If You Can Want" (#11 Pop, #3 R&B, #50 U.K.), "Yester Love" (#31 Pop, #9 R&B), and a solid version of Dion's single "Abraham, Martin and John" (#37 Pop, #16 R&B).

Their next big hit broke not in Detroit or even the U.S., but in England. In 1967 the Miracles had cut a song titled "Tears of a Clown." Three years later, British Motown exec John Marshall needed a follow-up to "The Tracks of My Tears" and heard "Clown" off the 1967 *Make It Happen* LP. Issued in September 1970 it sold an incredible 900,000 copies and reached number one on the British charts. In December Motown released it in the states, and by December 12th it was the Miracles' biggest hit ever (#1 Pop and R&B), selling over one million singles.

On July 16, 1972, at the end of a six-month U.S. tour, Robinson made his last appearance as a Miracle in Washington, D.C.

The Miracles' final single with Smokey was "I Can't Stand to See You Cry" (#45 Pop, #21 R&B) and after 42 Pop chart singles, Smokey began his solo career.

Billy Griffin of Baltimore took Robinson's place, and the Miracles issued seven more Tamla singles that included "Do It Baby" (#13 Pop, #4 R&B), and "Don'tcha Love It" (#78 Pop, #4 R&B).

In late 1975 the group had its longest running chart hit when "Love Machine" (#1 Pop, #5 R&B, #3 U.K.) stayed active for 28 weeks.

In 1977 the group left Motown for Columbia and added Billy's brother Don. The Miracles became a quintet for the first time in 14 years.

Their last chart single was "Mean Machine" in 1978 (#55 R&B).

On May 16, 1983, they reunited with Smokey Robinson for Motown's 25th anniversary TV special. Robinson continued recording and from 1973 to 1989 had 24 Pop and 38 R&B chart 45s, including "Baby That's Backatcha" (#26 Pop, #1 R&B, 1975), "Cruisin'" (#4 Pop and R&B, 1979), "Bein' with You" (#2 Pop, #1 R&B, 1981), and "Just to See You" (#8 Pop, #2 R&B, 1987).

In January 1987 Smokey Robinson (conspicuously without the Miracles) was inducted into the Rock and Roll Hall of Fame.

THE MIRACLES

A SIDE/B SIDE	LABEL/CAT NO	DATE
Got A Job /		
My Mama Done Told Me	End 1016	1958
I Cry / Money	End 1029,84	1958
Bad Girl / I Love You Baby	Chess 1734	1959
Bad Girl / I Love You Baby	Motown G1/G2	9/59
All I Want / I Need A Change	Chess 1768	3/60

A SIDE/B SIDE	LABEL/CAT NO	DATE
The Feeling Is So Fine /		
You Can Depend On Me	Tamla 54082	7/60
Way Over There / Depend On Me	Tamla 54082	7/60
Shop Around / Who's Lovin' You	Tamla 54034	10/60
Ain't It Baby / The Only One I Love	Tamla 54036	3/61
Broken Hearted /		
Mighty Good Lovin'	Tamla 54044	7/61
I Can't Believe / Everybody's		
Gotta Pay Some Dues	Tamla 54048	10/61
What's So Good About Good-		
Bye / I've Been Good To You	Tamla 54053	12/61
I'll Try Something New /		
You Never Miss A Good Thing	Tamla 54049	4/62
Way Over There /		
If Your Mother Only Knew	Tamla 54069	8/62
You've Really Got A Hold On Me /		
Happy Landing	Tamla 54073	11/62
A Love She Can Count On /		
I Can Take A Hint	Tamla 54078	3/63
Mickey's Monkey /		
Whatever Makes You Happy	Tamla 54083	7/63
I Gotta Dance To Keep From		
Crying / Such Is Love,		
Such Is Life	Tamla 54089	11/63
The Christmas Song /		
Christmas Everyday	Tamla Ex-009	11/63
(You Can't Let The Boy		
Overpower) The Man In You /		
Heartbreak	Tamla 54092	2/64
I Like It Like That /		
You're So Fine And Sweet	Tamla 54098	6/64
That's What Love Is Made Of /		
Would I Love You	Tamla 54102	9/64
Come On Do The Jerk /		
Baby Don't You Go	Tamla 54109	11/64
Ooo Baby Baby / All That's Good	Tamla 54113	3/65
The Tracks Of My Tears /		
A Fork In The Road	Tamla 54118	6/65
My Girl Has Gone /		
Since You Won My Heart	Tamla 54123	9/65
Going To A Go-Go /		
Choosy Beggar	Tamla 54127	12/65
Whole Lot Of Shakin' In My Heart		
(Since I Met You) /		
Oh Be My Love	Tamla 54134	5/66
(Come Round Here) I'm The One		
You Need / Save Me	Tamla 54140	10/66

Smokey Robinson and the Miracles

A SIDE/B SIDE	LABEL/CAT NO	DATE
The Love I Saw In You Was Just		
A Mirage / Come Spy With Me	Tamla 54145	1/67
More Love / Swept For You Baby	Tamla 54152	5/67
I Second That Emotion /		
You Must Be Love	Tamla 54159	10/67
If You Can Want / When The		
Words From Your Heart Get		
Caught Up In Your Throat	Tamla 54162	2/68
Yester Love / Much Better Off	Tamla 54167	5/68

A SIDE/B SIDE	LABEL/CAT NO	DATE
Special Occasion / Give Her Up	Tamla 54172	8/68
Baby, Baby Don't Cry /		
Your Mother's Only Daughter	Tamla 54178	12/68
Here I Go Again / Doggone Right	Tamla 54183	5/69
Abraham, Martin And John /		
Much Better Off	Tamla 54184	6/69
Point It Out / Darling Dear	Tamla 54189	11/69
Who's Gonna Take The Blame /		
I Gotta Thing For You	Tamla 54194	5/70
The Tears Of A Clown / The Love I		
Saw In You Was Just A Mirage	Tamla 54199	9/70
I Don't Blame You At All / That Girl	Tamla 54205	3/71
Crazy About The La La La /		
Oh Baby Baby I Love You	Tamla 54206	6/71
Satisfaction / Flower Girl	Tamla 54211	11/71
We've Come Too Far To End It		
Now / When Sundown Comes	Tamla 54220	5/72
I Can't Stand To See You Cry /		
With Your Love Came	Tamla 54225	11/72

The Miracles

A SIDE/B SIDE	LABEL/CAT NO	DATE
Don't Let It End ('Till You Let It		
Begin) / Wigs And Lashes	Tamla 54237	7/73
Give Me Just Another Day /		
I Wanna Be With You	Tamla 54240	11/73
Do It Baby / I Wanna Be With You	Tamla 54248	6/74
Don'tcha Love It / Up Again	Tamla 54256	11/74
Gemini / You Are Love	Tamla 54259	4/75
Love Machine (Part 1) /		
Love Machine (Part 2)	Tamla 54262	10/75
Night Life / Smog	Tamla 54268	5/76
Women (Make The World Go		
Round) / Spy For Brotherhood	Col 10515	1977
Mean Machine / The Magic Of		
Your Eyes (Laura's Eyes)	Col 10706	1978
Embraceable You / After All*	Tamla 54022*	1982

* Unauthorized Issue

The O'Jays

An R&B/doo wop group of the first magnitude, the O'Jays persevered for 14 years before they had a number one R&B record.

The O'Jays started singing together at McKinley H.S. in Canton, Ohio, during the semester of 1958. The quintet consisted of Eddie Levert on lead along with William Powell, Walter Williams, Bob Massey, and Bill Isles.

The 16-year-olds first took the name the Triumphs and by their own admission began performing at YMCA shows and hops just to hear the girls scream. Levert and Williams had previously been in a more sedate vocal combination, the gospel group the Levert Brothers.

A local songwriter named Andriotto gave the group some songs that included "The Story of My Heart," "(Do the) Wiggle" (cowritten with Gene Redd of the Fi-Tones), "Lonely Rain," and "That's the Way I Feel," and before long the Canton quintet was off to New York to audition for Decca. The label passed on them. Their next stop was King Records, where prexy Syd Nathan signed them and renamed them the Mascots in 1959. When no releases were immediately forthcoming, the group hooked up with Cleveland disc jockey Eddie O'Jay who in turn put them together with Detroit producer Don Davis (later to produce hits with THE DRAMATICS on Stax/Volt). O'Jay then rechristened the Mascots the O'Jays for good luck.

The result of Davis's session was "Miracles," issued on the tiny Daco label in 1960 and then leased to New York's Apollo Records.

By the fall of 1960 (almost a year later), King had issued the Mascots' "The Story of My Heart" to little response. They released "Lonely Rain" in January 1961, and though the song was an outstanding, harmony-filled rocker, King lost it in their flood of new releases.

O'Jay then sent the group to Little Star Records in Los Angeles, which was owned by arranger and former member of THE DOOTONES (Dootone) H. B. Barnum. H. B. fine-tuned the quintet's harmonies and did four singles with them, including 1963's "Love Is Wonderful" in which they backed up Jimmy Norman. He then made a deal for them with Imperial Records, and in the summer of 1963 the O'Jays' self-penned rhythm ballad "Lonely Drifter" became their first chart single. Reminiscent of both "This Magic Moment" and "Dance with Me," "Drifter" suggested a DRIFTERS influence. It reached only number 93 Pop but was the start of a career in which the O'Jays would place 27 singles on the Pop lists and 47 on the R&B charts.

The group continued with some excellent sides for Imperial through 1966 including "The Storm Is Over" (a "Lonely Drifter" sequel and a beautiful ballad) and "Oh How You Hurt Me," but their best-received singles were "Lipstick Traces" (#48 Pop, #28 R&B, 1965) and "Stand in for Love" (#95 Pop, #12 R&B). (The flip of "Stand in" was another Drifters-styled tune written by then-newcomer Randy Newman.) In the summer of 1960 Isles left to be a full-time songwriter and the group stayed a quartet while returning to Cleveland.

For many acts the Apollo Theatre played an important role in their success as performers, but for the O'Jays it also had a profound effect on their record label status. On one occasion a deejay named Rocky Gee heard them and suggested they do some new demos with a producer named Richard King. The subsequent demos earned the O'Jays a record deal with Larry Utall's Bell Records. George Kerr (formerly lead of the Serenaders, Chock-Full-Of-Hits) became their producer.

The first Bell single, "I'll Be Sweeter Tomorrow," went to number eight R&B and number 66 Pop. But the honeymoon with Bell ended after the O'Jays proved unable to find a hit formula in their next four singles. They played the Apollo again (September 1969), and some good advice, this time from their bill-mates THE INTRUDERS, led them to two hot young producers/label owners named Kenny Gamble and Leon Huff. The first O'Jays/Gamble/Huff collaboration was "One Night Affair" in the summer of 1969. Released on the Chess-distributed Neptune affiliate, it reached number five R&B and number 68 Pop. But even though the O'Jays placed four of their six Neptune releases on the charts over the next year and a quarter, Neptune went under when Chess owner Leonard Chess died, and the O'Jays once again returned to Cleveland.

Meanwhile Gamble and Huff had regrouped and set up the Philadelphia International label, and that's where the O'Jays moved in 1972 despite offers from Motown and Invictus. Their first 45 was a departure from the group's previous love-song style. "Back Stabbers" had a socially conscious lyric, but the chugging beat, Levert's rugged vocal, the minor-key harmony, and Thom Bell's arrangement made the record a monster hit that reached number one R&B, number three Pop, and number 11 U.K. a mere 14 years after the resolute Canton kids had begun their career.

A series of smashes followed that included "Love Train" (#1 Pop and R&B, #9 U.K.), "Put Your Hands Together" (#10 Pop, #2 R&B, their second million seller), "For the Love of Money" (#9 Pop, #3 R&B), "Give the People What They Want" (#45 Pop, #1 R&B), and "I Love Music" (#5 Pop, #1 R&B, #13 U.K.). Between "I Love Music" and their next number one, "Livin' for the Weekend" (#20 Pop, #1 R&B, Spring 1976), the O'Jays lost the services of William Powell, who was stricken with cancer and left the group in early 1976 (he died on May 26, 1977). His place was taken by the only replacement the O'Jays ever had, Sammy Strain, formerly of LITTLE ANTHONY AND THE IMPERIALS.

In 1978 the group had its fifth and last million seller, "Use Ta Be My Girl" (#4 Pop, #1 R&B), and they performed at Hollywood's Greek Theatre for their 20th anniversary celebration. The trio remained with the Gamble and Huff organization through the next decade and as recently as 1987 had a number one R&B hit with "Lovin' You." Their last Top 100 single was "Girl, Don't Let It Get You Down" in 1980.

The Orlons

Fun-filled dance tunes were the Orlons' specialty, making them one of the most popular groups ever to come out of Philadelphia. The group was originally called Audrey and the Teenetts in the early '50s, and it included Audrey, Jean, and Shirley Brickley along with Rosetta Hightower and Marlena Davis. When Mama Brickley refused to let the youngest, Audrey, sing with the others in one of Philadelphia's small clubs, she and sister Jean quit the group.

Shirley, Rosetta, and Marlena continued singing at Overbrook High School and were heard by student Stephen Caldwell, who sang with a local unrecorded group called the Romeos. Stephen brought his baritone lead to the girls' attention and soon turned the unnamed trio into a quartet. The girls subsequently followed in the footsteps of their Overbrook rivals the Cashmeres (who later became the famous DOVELLS) by calling themselves the Orlons.

They practiced at Shirley's house on songs like "Mama Said" (THE SHIRELLES) and "Stormy Weather" (THE SPANIELS). They were also influenced by acts like THE CHANTELS, Ray Charles, and THE MOONGLOWS.

In the fall of 1961, thanks to an introduction made on their behalf by Len Barry of the Dovells, the Orlons auditioned for Kal Mann of Cameo Records and were signed almost immediately. A&R director Dave Appell started writing songs for the group and decided to feature Rosetta (alto), with Shirley (alto), Marlena (soprano), and Stephen (baritone) supporting her.

Their first single was "I'll Be True," which *Billboard* described as a "sincere piping by the young-sounding femme lead on a wistful rock-a-ballad about a gal's message to her GI sweetheart. Wax has a chance." It elicited little interest; ditto their early 1962 follow-up "Happy Birthday 21."

In early 1962 the Orlons had their first hit. But no one knew it; they were backing up Dee Dee Sharp, another Cameo artist, on the dance tune "Mashed Potato Time" (#2 Pop, #1 R&B).

In the spring, buoyed by their dance hit with Dee Dee, the Orlons moved in their own dance direction with "The Wah Watusi." On May 26th *Billboard* cited it as "a solid item for teen buyers. The group sells the rhythmic swinger with enthusiasm and drive, while the combo provides effective backing. Watch it!" In July it danced to number two, with only Bobby Vinton's "Roses Are Red" above it.

The group had two top 10 records at the same time when Dee Dee Sharp's second hit "Gravy (For My Mashed Potatoes)" went to number nine with the Orlons again backing her (again without credit).

They followed up with the Mann/Appell-penned "Don't Hang Up," which climbed the charts in the fall and winter of 1962 to number four Pop, number three R&B, and number 39 U.K.

Their first major performance was at New York's Apollo Theatre with THE CRYSTALS, Bobb B. Soxx and the Blue Jeans, Chuck Jackson (who the Orlons backed onstage), Tommy Hunt (of THE FLAMINGOS), and Gene Chandler.

The quartet kept up their chart barrage into 1963 with "South Street" (#3 Pop, #4 R&B), "Not Me" (#12 Pop, #8 R&B), and "Crossfire" (#19 Pop, #25 R&B).

By 1964 their style was being swept aside by the British invasion, and three of their four releases that year only rose to the 60s on the Pop listings ("Shimmy Shimmy," #66, "Rules of Love," #66, and "Knock Knock," #64). They recorded for Cameo through 1965 but couldn't break back into the charts.

In 1966 they moved to Calla and in 1967 to ABC, but the story was the same. Still, with nine chart records and three top five hits, the group was able to work right into the '70s until Rosetta decided to move to England. Shirley died that same year.

By the early '90s Marlena had become Marlena Davis Easley, word processing expert and executive secretary. Stephen, whose growling baritone/bass added an interesting color and dimension to the tight harmony of the girls, had worked for Philadelphia's Board of Education for 20 years.

THE ORLONS

A SIDE/B SIDE	LABEL/CAT NO	DATE
I'll Be True / Heart Darling Angel	Cameo 198	1961
Happy Birthday Twenty-One / Please Let It Be Me	Cameo 211	1962
The Wah-Watusi / Holiday Hill	Cameo 218	1962
Don't Hang Up / The Conservative	Cameo 231	1962
South Street / Them Terrible Boots	Cameo 243	1963
Not Me / My Best Friend	Cameo 257	1963
Crossfire! / It's No Big Thing	Cameo 273	1963

A SIDE/B SIDE	LABEL/CAT NO	DATE
Bon-Doo-Wah /		
Don't Throw Your Love Away	Cameo 287	1963
Shimmy Shimmy / Everything Nice	Cameo 295	1964
Rules Of Love / Heartbreak Hotel	Cameo 319	1964
Goin' Places / Knock Knock	Cameo 332	1964
I Ain't Coming Back / Envy	Cameo 346	1964
I Ain't Coming Back /		
Come On Down Baby Baby	Cameo 352	1965
I Can't Take It /		
Don't You Want My Lovin'	Cameo 372	1965
Envy / No Love But Your Love	Cameo 384	1965
Spinnin' Top /		
Anyone Who Had A Heart	Calla 113	1966
Everything /		
Keep Your Hands Off My Baby	ABC 10894	1967
Kissin' Time / Once Upon A Time	ABC 10948	1967

The Paris Sisters

The Paris Sisters were a soft-voiced sister trio who formed in the early '50s due to the aspirations of their opera-singing mother. She had quit her career at San Francisco's Milano Opera Company to raise the three as singers, training them around the family piano. When the earlier-vintage trio THE ANDREWS SISTERS came to San Francisco to perform, Mom had the girls, Sherrell, Albeth, and Priscilla, all dressed alike and sitting down in front, mouthing the words to Andrew Sisters songs for the full three weeks of their engagement.

The Andrews Sisters couldn't help but notice and finally put the girls onstage to perform. The three pre-teens then proceeded to knock out the audience with their version of the Sister's "Rum and Coca-Cola" (#1, 1945).

An MCA agent saw them and in no time had the toddlers out on the road playing USO shows and fairs along the California coast.

Soon after, the trio found themselves on the slave shift as a lounge act in Las Vegas, working from midnight to seven A.M. at the ages of 9 (Priscilla), 10 (Albeth), and 15 (Sherrell). Wigs, padded bras and hips, lots of makeup, and false eyelashes hid their youth, and their dad was reportedly able to revise their birth certificates since he was employed at the hospital where they were born. The girls sang with Frank Sinatra at the Dunes and were summoned to the Frontier by a young Elvis Presley, who wanted to meet them.

By 1959 the group had met Jess Rand (later to be manager of THE LETTERMEN). Rand brought them

to Imperial Records, where they issued the two singles "Old Enough to Cry" and "My Original Love." Both went unnoticed. Lester Sill of Sill/ Hazelwood Productions then saw the act and acquired their contract from Rand in 1961. Sill's claim to fame at the time was a young writer named Phil Spector, whom he brought from New York to Los Angeles just to produce the girls.

The Paris Sisters had always sung three-part harmony and rarely featured anyone up front, but Spector saw a similarity between Priscilla's breathy voice and that of Annette Kleinbard (now Carol Connors) of THE TEDDY BEARS, Spector's former group. He envisioned a new Teddy Bears style.

He had the group come to New York and stay in his apartment while he moved across the street to the Plaza Hotel. In typical Spector fashion he reportedly woke the girls in the wee hours and took them through Central Park in a horsedrawn carriage to rehearse songs.

Back in Los Angeles they recorded "Be My Boy," a song he co-wrote (Spector/Sands) which was Ray Peterson's B side to "Corinna, Corinna" (#9, 1960) under the title "Be My Girl." It had just fallen off the charts around the time the girls were recording it (February-March 1961).

When Sill shopped around with negative results (Capitol and Liberty, among others, passed), he issued it on his own newly formed Gregmark label. By April 24th it had charted, reaching number 56 on the *Billboard* Top 100.

Sill then went to New York in search of a followup and found it at Don Kirshner's Aldon Music. Artie Ripp, a professional manager at Aldon before his Kama Sutra Productions days, sat at the piano and sang a Barry Mann/Larry Kolber ballad titled "I Love How You Love Me" for Sill and Spector.

It became the Sisters' second Gregmark single and a precursor to Spector's yet-to-develop "wall of sound." The song was appropriately titled; 15-year-old Priscilla was pregnant at the time of recording and eventually married her studio engineer boyfriend.

"I Love How You Love Me," with Priscilla whisping her way through the lead and the girls' hypnotic harmony weaving though the swirling strings, rose to number five on October 30th. Spector's first girl-group success encouraged him to pursue productions with other female aggregations like THE CRYSTALS.

The Goffin/King-penned single "He Knows I Love Him Too Much" prompted a January 1962 *Billboard* reviewer to write: "A slow, dreamy rock-a-ballad is sold with feeling and heart by the lead canary, with fluid backing by strings and an effective offbeat ork arrangement. A strong side." It eventually rose to number 34. Meanwhile the group recorded a Spector-produced LP of similar sides that mysteriously disappeared (it was reported to have been accidentally discarded by Sill's assistant along with a group of unneeded dubs). Without an LP to follow the hits, the girls were effectively sent back to square one. They did one backup session for Gary Crosby yielding "That's All Right Baby" (Gregmark, 1962), and then due to disagreements over royalties due them, soon found themselves label-less.

They appeared in a British rock and roll movie produced by Richard Lester (who later did the Beatles' films) titled *Ring-A-Ding Rhythm* and performed on the U.S. rock circuit with DION AND THE BELMONTS and THE MARVELETTES, among others. They also toured Southeast Asia on several occasions.

In 1964 Nick Venet produced the girls on a strong pseudo-Spector rock-a-ballad version of Bobby Darin's "Dream Lover" for MGM, but the record lost its momentum and peaked at number 91 in June.

An LP and five singles in 1966 and 1967 failed, and by the early '70s the Paris Sisters had decided to go separate musical ways.

Sherrell formed a band called Sherrell Paris and the New People that toured until the late '70s. Sherrell then married for the second time and became an executive assistant on Bob Barker's TV show, "The Price Is Right."

Albeth went into independent TV production with her husband, and Priscilla moved to Paris, France. She began conducting motivational seminars in French and English for salespeople in the hotel business. Over the years she recorded several solo LPs, including a tribute to Billie Holiday titled *Priscilla Loves Billie.*

THE PARIS SISTERS

A SIDE/B SIDE	LABEL/CAT NO	DATE
Old Enough To Cry / Tell Me More	Imprl 5465	1959
My Original Love / Someday	Imprl 5487	1959
Be My Boy / I'll Be Crying Tomorrow	Gregmark 2	1961
I Love How You Love Me / All Through The Night	Gregmark 6	1961
He Knows I Love Him Too Much / A Lonely Girl's Prayer	Gregmark 10	1962
That's All Right, Baby* / Who	Gregmark 11	1962
Let Me Be The One / What Am I To Do?	Gregmark 12	1962
Yes, I Love You / Once Upon A While Ago	Gregmark 13	1962
Dream Lover / Lonely Girl	MGM 13236	1964
Sincerely / Too Good To Be True	Rprs 0440	1966
You / I'm Me	Rprs 0472	1966
My Good Friend / It's My Party	Rprs 0511	1966
Some Of Your Lovin' / Long After Tonight Is All Over	Rprs 548	1966

* with Gary Crosby

The Passions

One of the best of Brooklyn's white doo wop groups, the Passions helped to further the careers of two top writer/artists.

The group members were among those vocalists whose harmony haven was the alley of the Loew's Oriental Theatre in the Bensonhurst section of Brooklyn. The nearby Kelly's pool room served as an occasional rehearsal hall. When five of the bunch formed the Overons (who later became THE MYSTICS), the remaining members became the Sinceres. They included Tony Armato, Albie Galione, Vinny Acierno, Nicky Lombardi, and John Pangi.

The quintet recorded a few demos in 1958, at which time Tony, Albie, and Vinny began looking for replacements who were more career-minded. Another group in Bensonhurst had what they needed; when the three Sinceres heard Run-arounds lead singer Jimmy Gallagher, they knew he was the one for them. (Jimmy's previous group, the Palladiums, included Joe Di Benedetto, who later formed THE FOUR-EVERS.)

The Sinceres weren't sure how to approach Jimmy, so they followed him home one night and knocked on his door. After convincing his mother that they only wanted to sing with her son, not mug him, the foursome went to a nearby park and ended up harmonizing for hours. They were now a quartet, with Jimmy on lead, Tony on first tenor, Albie on second tenor, and Vinny on baritone.

In 1959, while the Mystics were recording "Hushabye" at their first session, their friend Tony Armato was there cheering them on and promoting his own group to their manager, Jim Gribble.

Gribble soon signed the Sinceres and renamed them the Passions. He gave them a demo by a duo of studio singers who called themselves the Cousins. The song was "Just to Be with You" written by Marv Kalfin. The Cousins were Paul Simon and Carole King.

Released in August 1959 on Sol Winkler's Audicon label, the Passions' impeccable harmonies and Gallagher's impassioned lead put "Just to Be with You" on radios across America. It was a top 20 hit in many eastern cities and it charted nationally, rising to number 69.

The follow-up out of Audicon's 1674 Broadway digs was twice as good. Both sides—the harmony-filled "I Only Want You" and the beautiful Billy Dawn Smith ballad "This Is My Love"—vied for radio play and sales throughout the states. A reviewer in the January 11, 1960, issue of *Billboard* commented, "The group could score again via either of these rock-a-ballads. On both, the lead comes through with fine readings, and he gets good group assists. Both remind of their previous hit, 'Just to Be with You.'" "I Only Want You" eventually took the lead, but the split play killed any hopes of one single becoming a national hit. "I Only Want You" stopped at number 113 in March 1960.

"This Is My Love" later became a doo wop classic and part of the repertoire of countless harmony groups. (The song is often called "Sweeter Than," from its opening line.)

The group attracted a great deal of attention from these singles and toured with some of the industry's top talent, including Chubby Checker, DION AND THE BELMONTS, THE SKYLINERS, THE ISLEY BROTHERS, and of course their Kelly's pool room pals the Mystics. They also appeared on Dick Clark's TVer, Alan Freed's "Big Beat" TV show, and Clay Cole's show while performing at the Brooklyn Fox with Alan Freed.

For their third release the Passions showed their mettle by tackling "Gloria," a street-corner classic that few white groups had been able to pull off as well as the original by THE CADILLACS. The Passions did an excellent version that became the yardstick by which other white groups measured their ability to handle the song.

By the time the group recorded "Gloria" Vinny had left and been replaced by Gallagher's friend Lou Rotondo. Also in 1960 Lou Rotondo and Albie Galione, along with Albie Contrera of the Mystics, sang behind Clay Cole on "Here, There, Everywhere" (Roulette), a single that became popular in the New York area.

Audicon Records lost the group's next release, the harmony rocker "Made for Lovers." The group recorded a few more sides for Audicon which were leased to Jubilee and Octavia.

By 1962, Gallagher had joined the navy and Gribble had died. The group signed with producer Teddy Vann, ABC Records, and drafted Joey O'Neal for the lead. Before Joey could sing, however, Jimmy returned on leave and joined with the Passions to record "The Bully" (ABC, 1963) and an up-tempo version of THE CRESTS' "Sixteen Candles" (Diamond, 1963). When both went out unpromoted, Gallagher returned to the navy. Graham Lee True (the Hitones, Fonsca) took over the lead, but they only recorded unreleased demos. The group broke up in 1963.

In 1970 Tony, Albie, and Lou sang with Emil Stuccio as THE CLASSICS (Emil was the Classics' original lead) on "Again" b/w "The Way You Look Tonight" for Bedstuy Records. Then Emil, Albie, and Lou became the Profits' on Sire for an interesting revision of THE DIABLOS' "The Wind."

Jimmy Gallagher eventually moved to Florida and became part of the Miami doo wop scene of the '80s, recording a remake of "Made for Lovers" as lead singer of Reunion. In the '80s Tony joined the Mystics while Albie and Lou stayed with Emil as the Classics.

THE PASSIONS

A SIDE/B SIDE	LABEL/CAT NO	DATE
Just To Be With You / Oh Melancholy Me	Audicon 102	1959
I Only Want You / This Is My Love	Audicon 105	1960
Gloria / Jungle Drums	Audicon 106	1960
Beautiful Dreamer / One Look Is All It Took	Audicon 108	1960
You Don't Love Me Anymore / Made For Lovers	Audicon 112	1961
Lonely Road	Jubi 5406	1961
I Gotta Know / Aphrodite	Octva 8005	1962
Sixteen Candles / The Third Floor	Diamond 146	1963
The Bully / The Empty Seat	ABC 10436	1963

Peter, Paul and Mary

In 1961 fate brought a folk singer, a comedian, and a Broadway actress (for one week) together to create contemporary folk music for the masses.

New York-born Peter Yarrow (23), with his guitar and a psychology degree from Cornell, met Baltimore, Maryland, standup comic Noel Paul Stookey (24) in New York City's creative melting pot of Greenwich Village. Peter was the veteran, having already played the Newport Folk Festival in 1960. Noel introduced Peter to actress/singer Mary Travers (24), who lived in New York (her parents were both Greenwich Village writers) though she was born in Louisville, Kentucky. Mary had just ended a starring one-week run in the Broadway revue *The Next President*. She had been singing with a Village group called the Song Swappers that had recorded four LPs with folk legend Pete Seeger when she was only 14.

They spent the next seven months rehearsing 18 songs, usually in Mary's three-flight walkup. They drew the attention of Milt Okun and folk impresario Albert Grossman (who became their manager), and soon they were debuting their three-part harmony brand of social-protest folk music at the Bitter End café.

They agreed to become Peter, Paul and Mary since it sounded catchier than Peter, Noel and Mary (and already had a familiar ring from a folk song lyric that went, "I saw Peter, Paul and Moses playing ring-around-the-roses"). The group's name and music came to the attention of Warner Bros. Records and in early 1962 they recorded the single "Lemon Tree." The simplicity of their sound caught on and "Lemon Tree" charted on May 5, 1962, reaching number 35.

With the release of "If I Had a Hammer" in August 1962, Peter, Paul and Mary found themselves in the forefront of a protest movement that, for them, would address everything from world hunger and homelessness to civil rights, apartheid, and war.

By October 13, 1962, "If I Had a Hammer" had reached number 10 in the nation and was spreading to the shores of Australia (#10) and beyond.

Their first LP proved they could bring folk music and a substantive message to a large audience. It made the top 10, staying there for an incredible 10 months. It took over three years for it to finally fall out of the Top 100. "If I Had a Hammer" became an anthem for the civil rights movement and the three-some became its musical ambassadors.

A song that evolved from a poem Lenny Lipton left in Yarrow's typewriter at Cornell in 1959 became one of the group's biggest hits. "Puff the Magic Dragon" reached number two nationally on May 11, 1963. It also made number 11 in Australia and surprisingly reached number 10 on the U.S. R&B charts while becoming the national camp song anthem.

Their next single was the powerful "Blowin' in the Wind." It's ironic that the ultimate song of right and wrong should be clouded in its own controversy. To this day there is still speculation about whether Bob Dylan wrote the song or whether it was penned by a Milburn, New Jersey, high school student named Lorre Wyatt, who reportedly sold the song to

Dylan for a thousand dollars under the condition that Wyatt deny any involvement in the composition. Regardless of its authorship, its message was clear and universally accepted in the context of Peter, Paul and Mary's harmony version. "Blowin'" was another number two hit Stateside, and became their first hit in England (#13).

In 1963, in keeping with the viewpoints expressed in their songs, the trio marched with Dr. Martin Luther King in Selma, Alabama, and Washington, D.C., for civil rights.

Their music continued to reach a growing number of fans, keeping Peter, Paul and Mary messages a part of America's daily life. They issued such recordings as "Don't Think Twice, It's All Right" (#9, 1963), "Tell It on the Mountain" (#13 U.S. and U.K., #2 Australia, 1964), "The Times They Are A-Changin'" (#44 U.K., 1964), "For Lovin' Me" (#30 U.S., 1965, #18 Australia), and "The Cruel War" (#52, 1966).

Their influence was not only felt in the realm of social causes. Songwriters' careers (including those of Gordon Lightfoot and John Denver) were often launched by having their compositions recorded by the new folk hitmakers.

In 1967 the trio did an admirable job of parodying THE MAMAS AND THE PAPAS and Donovan, among others, in the hit "I Dig Rock and Roll Music" (#9 U.S., and #8 Australia).

In 1969 the group charted with the beautiful "Day Is Done" and had their last Top 100 hit with their only number one song, John Denver's "Leaving on a Jet Plane" (#2 U.K.). That year Yarrow co-organized a peace march on Washington where the trio sang before over half a million people.

By 1970 the group, in need of outlets for their individual expression and a break from the more than 200 performances they were doing a year, disbanded.

Mary recorded five solo LPs; produced, wrote, and starred in a BBC-TV series; and did concerts and lectures across the nation. Paul (who preferred to be known as Noel Stookey when not associated with Peter, Paul and Mary) formed a Christian music group called the Body Works Band. Peter remained the most visible, staying politically active while cowriting and producing Mary Mac-Gregor's "Torn Between Two Lovers" (#1, 1977). He also earned an Emmy for his three animated TV specials based on "Puff the Magic Dragon."

In 1978, Peter asked Paul and Mary to join him at an anti-nuclear concert at the Hollywood Bowl in Los Angeles. Though they hadn't sung together in over six years they "got back on the horse" as if they'd never been off and renewed their performance schedule as a trio with a modified (for them) average of 60 shows a year. In 1985, they did a single, Yarrow's "Light One Candle," in support of Soviet Jews trying to emigrate from the U.S.S.R.

In 1986 they returned to the LP side with a collection called *No Easy Walk to Freedom*, for Gold Castle Records, focusing attention on the anti-apartheid cause. That same year they appeared on PBS-TV in a special concert to mark their 25th anniversary.

In 1990, they recorded the *Flowers and Stones* LP, including songs by Tom Paxton, Bob Dylan, and Pete Seeger.

Though the trio garnered eight gold and five platinum LPs, along with 19 chart hits (all 10 of the group's LPs were artfully remixed for CD by Peter and remained brisk sellers), numbers fail to tell the whole story of Peter, Paul and Mary.

Though they attained legendary status as performers and recording artists, their motives reached beyond the desire for wealth, as indicated by the time and energy they devoted to nonprofit activities and benefits. They were more than just entertainers. With two guitars, three voices, and a lot of integrity, they became one of the most respected groups in the history of pop vocal music.

The Quotations

Most late '50s and early '60s American vocal groups formed in schools, parks, friends' houses, night centers, or street corners. The additional few that got together in the unusual surroundings of a pool room all seemed to come from Brooklyn, New York, and included THE MYSTICS, THE PASSIONS, and the Quotations.

In the Quotations' case, they started out at Barney's Pool Room on Kings Highway and East 14th Street. The members included Larry Kaye (Kassman) on lead, Richie Schwartz as first tenor, Lou Arno on second tenor, and Harvey Hershkowitz as baritone. The Madison High School quartet discovered their mutual interest in late 1958, and they practiced in local haunts, from Sid Gordon's Kings Highway Bowling Alley to the boardwalk of Brighton Beach. Larry was 16 at the time, Lou and Harvey were 15, and Richard was 14. They got their name from the song "Quotations of Love."

Their break came when they met Helen Miller, a songwriter associated with MGM Records. She agreed to manage them and found that their ener-

getic doo wop style was easily adaptable to standards. Since THE MARCELS had successfully revived "Blue Moon" around that time, Helen chose the Johnny Burke/Jimmy Van Heusen classic "Imagination" as the group's first single, which she had them do in a wildly up-tempo style with a stuttering intro. Released on MGM's Verve affiliate in November 1961, "Imagination" saturated East Coast radio and on January 27, 1962 registered on the *Billboard* Bubbling Under chart at number 105. The flip, "Ala-Men-Sy," was a nursery-rhyme-styled rocker that deserved an A side of its own and became a wasted track on the back of "Imagination."

The group's early 1962 follow-up, "This Love of Mine," was a good doo wop rocker in an "Imagination" arrangement that went unnoticed by Verve and consequently the public. The same fate awaited a remake of the Tempos' "See You in September."

The group then moved to Kapp Records in 1963 for the rock-a-ballad "Is It True What They Say about Barbara," whose chief distinction is that its cowriter, Charles Koppelman, later became co-chairman of SBK-EMI Music Publishing, one of the world's major publishing conglomerates. The activity of "Barbara" was certainly no help to Koppelman's or the Quotations' careers, and the group's name was not even on the record since they were backing up former Chord-A-Roys lead Mike Regal. Except for a single recorded in 1962 ("In the Night") released in 1964 on Admiral, the group's recording career was kaput. For a while the Quotations performed locally and in the South, but by 1963 the fun was over.

Harvey became art director for *Teen World* magazine and Lou went on to run a patio furniture company. Both settled in Freehold, New Jersey. Richard became a paint company vice president and Larry went on to run a delivery organization.

THE QUOTATIONS

A SIDE/B SIDE	LABEL/CAT NO	DATE
Imagination / Ala-Men-Sy	Verve 10245	1961
We'll Reach Heaven Together / This Love Of Mine	Verve 10252	1962
See You In September / Summertime Goodbye	Verve 10261	1962
Is It True What They Say About Barbara* / Too Young	Kapp	1963
In The Night / Oh No I Still Love Her	Admiral	1964
Night / Why You Do Me Like You Do	Dwnst 1003	1974

* Mike Regal and
   the Quotations

Randy and the Rainbows

One of the last pop doo wop groups to hit the top 10 before the Beatles barnstormed American radio (actually Dion and THE DEL-SATINS were the last, reaching number six with "Drip Drop" on December 28, 1963), Randy and the Rainbows were a Maspeth, Queens, quintet with hopes of lasting success that were dashed by the death of a president and a foreign "invasion."

In 1959, 12-year-olds Dominick Safuto, his brother Frank, cousin Eddie Scalla, and Rosalie Calindo on lead formed the Dialtones. They managed one obscure single, "Till I Heard It from You," for George Goldner's Goldisc label in 1960. The highlight of that session might have been the period the Dialtones spent sitting in the studio waiting room with idols LITTLE ANTHONY AND THE IMPERIALS awaiting their turn to record.

In 1961 Goldisc tried again, releasing the Dialtones single for another shot at the charts. It didn't work.

Dom (lead) then joined up with friend Mike Zero (baritone) to form a new group with Mike's brother Sal (second tenor) and Ken Arcipowski (bass) as the Encores.

When the Grover Cleveland High School quartet decided to fill out their sound as a quintet, Dom convinced his brother and ex-Dialtone member Frank (first tenor) to join, and they renamed themselves Junior and the Counts.

The Counts started playing church festivities, sweet sixteens, and the like until they came to the attention of Fran Carrarie, who became their manager and introduced them to songwriter Neil Levenson. Neil brought them to Bright Tunes Productions, which was really the creative base of singing-group-turned-producers THE TOKENS.

The Tokens produced the group on two songs written by Levinson titled "Denise" and "Come Back," but before they could issue them on Rust subsidiary Laurie Records, a more commercially acceptable group name had to be chosen. The Schwartz brothers, owners of Laurie, renamed them Randy and the Rainbows.

Dom became Randy and "Denise" became a monster hit. By August 24th it was number 10 nationally. With its gust-of-wind styled "oohs" on the intro, a FOUR SEASONS type of arrangement, and Randy's attractive lead, "Denise" crossed over to the R&B chart on September 14th and peaked at number 18. It reached as high as number two on New York's local radio charts.

A cross-country tour grew out of "Denise's" success, and the five 16-year-olds were living in fantasyland performing alongside Dionne Warwick, THE CHIFFONS, Timi Yuro, Darlene Love, and the Four Seasons. They also did Murray the K's Brooklyn Fox Labor Day show for 10 days and were in awe of the talent around them, including Ben E. King, THE RONETTES, THE MIRACLES, THE DOVELLS, the Chiffons, THE TYMES, Little Stevie Wonder, THE ANGELS (whose "My Boyfriend's Back" beat them out of the top spot in New York), THE SHIRELLES, Jan and Dean, Gene Pitney, and for one day only (as the poster said), THE BEACH BOYS.

The Rainbows' next release, "Why Do Kids Grow Up," was a similarly infectious doo wop rocker that was released in the fall of 1963. It stopped, along with the country's heartbeat, when one week later President John F. Kennedy was assassinated. The record was affected (as were countless others); due to lack of interest during the country's turmoil, it barely charted nationally (#97, December 14, 1963).

From there on Rust singles like "Dry Your Eyes," "Little Star" (the ELEGANTS song), and "Joy Ride" had little support and not much of a chance when the British invasion hit America.

The group continued to perform, but mostly on New York area one-nighters. They appeared on Jerry Blavat's Philadelphia TV show as well as on Clay Cole's New York TVer.

Three releases on Mike and a return to the Tokens and their B.T. Puppy label in 1966 for "I'll Be Seeing You" brought them little more than sporadic airplay.

After the B.T. Puppy sides, Sal and Kenny left, leaving Dom, Frank, Mike, and sometimes Vinnie Corella as the nucleus.

To find a record deal in the '70s the group had to change its identity, so while they played oldies shows as Randy and the Rainbows they also recorded as Triangle for two singles on Paramount in 1970–71. In 1977 they produced their own self-financed single, "Mr. Minstrel Man," as Madison Street and wound up on Millenium Records. The commercial results were not encouraging.

Also in 1977 Crystal Ball Records issued an a cappella single of Randy and the Rainbows doing DION AND THE BELMONTS' "I Wonder Why." Although the record was musically pleasing, the recording quality indicated that it was a demo record or a practice tape not intended for release. It even ended abruptly, without the traditional fadeout.

At one point they performed as a progressive rock band, hiring four musicians and calling themselves Them and Us.

In 1978 the New York new wave group Blondie, featuring Deborah Harry, had their first British chart success with "Denis," a remake of the Rainbow's "Denise." Later that year Debbie Harry showed up in a silver limo at New York's Mudd Club where Randy and the group were playing and asked for their autographs.

In 1982 Randy and the Rainbows were contacted to do what they did best, sing doo wop, so Dom, Frank, Mike, and Vinnie Corella recorded an LP for Marty Pekar's Ambient Sound Records (Columbia) titled *C'mon Let's Go*. The LP included a reworking of "Till I Heard It from You" from 22 years before, "Debbie" (a "Denise" and "Sherry"-styled rocker), and "Try the Impossible" (LEE ANDREWS AND THE HEARTS).

In 1984 they did another Ambient Sound LP titled *Remember* and later a Crystal Ball LP titled *Joy Ride*.

In the spring of 1990 the group split and became two Randy and the Rainbows contingents, one with Dom (Randy) and Frank and the other with Vinnie.

RANDY AND THE RAINBOWS

A SIDE/B SIDE	LABEL/CAT NO	DATE
The Dialtones		
Till I Heard It From You / Johnny	Goldisc 3005	1960
Randy and the Rainbows		
Denise / Come Back	Rust 5059	1963
Why Do Kids Grow Up? /		
She's My Angel	Rust 5073	1963
Happy Teenager / Dry Your Eyes	Rust 5080	1964
Little Star / Sharin'	Rust 5091	1964
Joyride / Little Hot Rod Susie	Rust 5101	1964
I'll Forget Her Tomorrow /		
Lovely Lies	Mike 4001	1966
Quarter To Three / He's A Fugitive	Mike 4004	1966
Bonnie's Part Of Town /		
Can It Be?	Mike 4008	1966
I'll Be Seeing You /		
Oh, To Get Away	BTP 535	1967
Triangle		
Jacqueline / Your Love		
Comes Shinin' Through	Prmnt 0055	1970
Judge And Jury /		
Midnight Magic Man	Prmnt 0123	1971
Madison Street		
Mr. Minstrel Man / King Of Love	Mill 605	1977
Simple Love Song /		
We're Falling In Love	Mill 621	1978

A SIDE/B SIDE	LABEL/CAT NO	DATE
Randy and the Rainbows		
Angel Face / I Wonder Why	CrysB 106	1978

The Regents

Another talented Italian doo wop group from the Bronx, the Regents started in 1958 under the name the Montereys. Guy Villari (lead), Sal Cuomo (first tenor), Ernie Maresca (baritone), and Chuck Fassert (second tenor) fashioned their sound at Sloopy Sam's candy store on Prospect Avenue with songs written by Maresca. They signed with Danny Kessler and Murray Sporn of the New York-based Seville label and recorded two sides, "Story of Love" and "I Ask You," which were promptly shelved. Soon after, Ernie left the group to concentrate on writing and Donnie Jacobucci came aboard.

The group continued to record demos at New York's Regent Sound Studios. To change their luck they renamed themselves the Regents.

Their next one-hour session used only 50 minutes for a ballad Guy had written. With 10 minutes left the group ran down a song, written by Chuck's brother Fred Fassert, that up until that time had been relegated to the status of a warmup tune. The song was "Barbara-Ann." A friend named Ronnie Lapinsky sat in on the session and sax player Tony Gravagna may have also sung on it. After using that 10 minutes to full advantage, the group set out to place the recording.

50 labels later they'd been turned down by every conceivable New York-area company. Before 1958 was over, it was over for the Regents.

By early 1961 Donnie Jacobucci's younger brother Eddie had joined a group known as the Consorts. Looking for songs to demo he found his brother's old dub of "Barbara-Ann," so he and the Consorts cut their own version. Consorts member Sal Donnarumma took it to a local record-shop-turned label, Cousins Records on Fordham Road. Lou Cicchetti, the owner, liked the demo, which resulted in songwriter Fred Fassert bringing in his copy of the Regents' recording. Since that version was more polished and almost ready to release, Cicchetti agreed to issue the Regents record with the addition of some bass overdubbing. The only remaining problem was that there was no B side and no group.

The Regents were quickly reunited, minus Guy who was down with pneumonia and Ronnie who was off with his own quartet, the Tremonts. Donnie's brother Eddie joined temporarily, and "I'm So Lonely" was cut as the flip side.

In March 1961 "Barbara-Ann" was issued on Cousins. The record was an immediate radio favorite and became number one in New York in short order, bringing '60s "stuttering" into musical vogue. Cousins had to lease it to the larger Roulette/Gee complex to keep up with the orders. By May 15th it was on the *Billboard* Top 100 and it reached number 13 Pop and number seven R&B. It also received extensive play overseas and even took the top spot in the Philippines. "Barbara-Ann" was translated into French and German for successful versions under the titles "Maryleen" by Martin Circus (Roulette) and "Barbara-Ann" by Die Tories (Decca).

An LP was rushed so quickly that one of the cuts listed, "Over the Rainbow," was not recorded in time to make the disc. Though the LP lists "Cuomo, Fassert, Gravagna, Villari, and (D.) Jacobucci as the Regents, at different sessions Ronnie Lapinsky (the Tremonts), Al Reno (the Selections), Bob Falcone (the Camerons), and Donny Dee all participated.

The group did the usual run of teen shows from Palisades Park to Dick Clark. Their second single, "Runaround," got off to a great start but leveled off at number 28 nationally, number nine in New York, and number 30 R&B. Its flip side, "Laura, My Darling," was the quintessential pop doo wop ballad of 1961 along with THE IMAGINATIONS' "Hey You" (Musicmakers).

Their single of the Sal Cuomo-penned "Liar" was a step down from previous efforts, not charting on *Billboard*'s Top 100 at all.

When their follow-up "Oh Baby" received no radio response, the group separated but reemerged in 1964 as the Runarounds, named after their second release.

This contingent contained Villari and Fassert of the Regents along with Lapinsky and Sal Corrente. Their single, the Ernie Maresca-Pete Baron song "Unbelievable" (in an EARLS style), saw lots of New York airplay but limited sales on Nat Cole's K.C. label.

Ditto for the FOUR SEASONS-styled "Carrie" (Felsted).

The group appeared regularly on WMCA hops, and in exchange their records were played like hits. This activity translated into releases on Capitol and MGM, but none with the magic of "Barbara-Ann."

Once again they separated, regrouping in 1970 with Warren Gradus for one ill-conceived release as Cardboard Zeppelin on Laurie ("Ten Story Building").

Later Corrente became lead of the Dials (Phillips) and then teamed with Lapinsky in the Johnny Law Four (Providence).

In 1973 Villari, Falcone, and Lapinsky reformed as the Regents, working regularly in the tri-state area for years to come.

THE REGENTS

A SIDE/B SIDE	LABEL/CAT NO	DATE
Barbara-Ann / I'm So Lonely	Csns 1002	3/61
Barbara-Ann / I'm So Lonely	Gee 1065	4/61
Runaround / Laura My Darling	Gee 1071	7/61
Don't Be A Fool / Liar	Gee 1073	11/61
Oh Baby / Lonesome Boy	Gee 1075	1962
The Runarounds		
Unbelievable / Hooray For Love	KC 116	2/63
Are You Looking For A Sweetheart / Let Them Talk	Tarheel 065	5/63
Carrie / Send Her Back	Flstd 8704	1964
You're A Drag / Perfect Women	Cap 5644	1966
You Lied / My Little Girl	MGM 13763	6/67

Reparata and the Delrons

St. Brendan's High School in Brooklyn could not exactly be called a mecca for vocal groups, but it did produce one of note, the memorably named Reparata and the Delrons. Fashioned in 1962, the original quartet included Mary Aiese on lead along with Regina Gallagher, Anne Fitzgerald, and Nanette Licari.

Two years later the Delrons (as they christened themselves) sported a whole new look, with only Mary remaining from the originals, now singing with Sheila Reillie, Kathy Romeo, and Carol Drobnicki. In 1964 there were not many places a Catholic school quartet could sing with the blessings of parents and teachers, except for dances. It was at one of them that record producers Bill and Steve Jerome got wind of this interesting teen tetrad. Almost before you could say "Catholic schoolgirls," the Delrons had demos in hand and were in the office of Laurie Records. Resident songwriting guru Ernie Maresca provided the trio (Kathy was dropped from the group) with the song "Your Big Mistake," a CRYSTALS-CHIFFONS-styled shuffle with a RONETTES-like intro. On its July release it sank like a stone.

The Jeromes wasted no time in taking the trio to World Artists Records, whose claim to fame was the British duo Chad and Jeremy ("A Summer Song," #7, 1964). When the recording session ended a half hour early, another Ernie Maresca tune, "Whenever a Teenager Cries," was thrown in and hastily cut. The last minute throw-in became the first single on World Artists. The Delrons then became Reparata and the Delrons thanks to Mary Aiese's appropriation of the name of her elementary school choir leader, Sister Mary Reparata.

"Teenager" entered the *Billboard* Pop charts on January 9, 1965, topping out at number 60. The trio then began a grueling pace of one-nighters on Dick Clark's "Caravan of Stars."

Their next tour for Clark (which included LITTLE ANTHONY AND THE IMPERIALS, among others) was to start as soon as the first one ended, but when it came time for the girls to leave from the Park Sheraton Hotel, only Reparata showed up. Apparently, the pressure had panicked Carol and Sheila, and Reparata ended up doing the tour as a solo.

World Artists then released another group single, "Tommy," followed by two Reparata solos, "The Boy I Love" and "He's the Greatest." Each failed to inspire buyers, so the Jeromes packed up and moved over to RCA in 1965. RCA wanted a group sound, however, and began a search that eventually turned up ex-original Delron Nanette Licari. Their first RCA release, "I Can Tell," reportedly included Lesley Gore to round out the trio. Soon after, Mary and Nanette found a third regular member, singer/pianist Lorraine Mazzola, at the neighborhood glee club.

They recorded five singles for Nipper's label between late 1965 and the summer of 1967, but none made a mark. Their last RCA single, the Lou Stallman and Lang Martine oft-recorded powerhouse ballad "I Can Hear the Rain," was Reparata's best vocal performance and included background assistance from an as-yet-unknown Melba Moore. "Rain" deserved a chart run but it was not to be, and the group moved on to Larry Utall's Mala Records in 1967.

"I Believe," done in a style similar to that of THE EARLS' 1963 release, received indifference from broadcasters. Their next Mala single, in January 1968, had Lorraine debut as a lead on "Captain of Your Ship," which stopped dead at number 127 on

the *Billboard* Bubbling Under list in February yet became a hit in England at number 13.

The popularity of "Captain" forced the girls out of their Brooklyn college classrooms and onto a plane for a British tour, highlighted by a hotel reception hosted by none other than two of the Liverpool mop tops, John Lennon and Ringo Starr of the Beatles.

Once again, the pressures were building up for the Delrons, and Lorraine left the group in mid-tour for some R&R. After she rejoined the girls in the States, Nanette departed. She returned in time for a remake of the Ronettes' "Walkin' in the Rain" in late 1969 which was then eclipsed by JAY AND THE AMERICANS' hit version (#19) at the same time. This time it was Mary's turn to leave. She eventually married, had several kids, and in 1972 started a teaching career while occasionally recording.

In 1970 Lorraine became the new Reparata, working with another Brooklyn girl named Cookie Sirico. They did one LP of girl-group oldies for Avco-Embassy titled *Rock and Roll Revolution* and then broke up in the summer of 1973. By 1974, Lorraine resurfaced as part of the trio known as LADY FLASH, Barry Manilow's backup vocal group.

Of the original Delrons, Carol is reported to have joined a California band and Sheila by all accounts became a Catholic school teacher. Nanette became a cashier in a department store in Brooklyn, and Cookie was working as a secretary in a brokerage stock cage. Mary occasionally performed with a re-formed Reparata and the Delrons.

REPARATA AND THE DELRONS

A SIDE/B SIDE	LABEL/CAT NO	DATE
Your Big Mistake / Leave Us Alone	Laurie 3252	1964
Whenever A Teenager Cries / He's My Guy	WldArt 1036	1964
Tommy / Mama Don't Allow	WldArt 1051	3/65
The Boy I Love / I Found My Place	WldArt 1062	1965
I Can Tell / Take A Look Around You	RCA 47-8721	11/65
Loneliest Girl In Town / I'm Nobody's Baby Now	RCA 47-8820	4/66
He Don't Want You / Mama's Little Girl	RCA 47-8921	8/66
Boys And Girls / The Kind Of Trouble That I Love	RCA 47-9123	2/67
I Can Hear The Rain / Always Waitin'	RCA 47-9185	4/67
I Believe / It's Waiting There For You	Mala 573	9/67
Captain Of Your Ship / Toom Toom	Mala 589	1968
Saturday Night Didn't Happen / Panic	Mala 12000	1968
Weather Forecast / You Can't Change A Young Boy's Mind	Mala 12016	1968

A SIDE/B SIDE	LABEL/CAT NO	DATE
Heaven Only Knows / Summer Laughter	Mala 12026	1968
That's What Sends Men To The Bowery / I've Got An Awful Lot Of Losing You To Do	Kapp 989	1969
We're Gonna Hold The Night / San Juan	Kapp 2010	6/69
Walking In The Rain / I've Got An Awful Lot Of Losing You To Do	Kapp 2050	1969

Ricky and the Hallmarks

Despite their street-gang background, the Hallmarks were a talented vocal group. They evolved in 1961 from a neighborhood gang that "hung out" at a candy store called D.J.'s on 43rd Street and Greenpoint Avenue in Long Island City, Queens. The members were Rick Lisi (15, lead), Dennis McMahon (16, first tenor, and replacement for Beverly Warren, 14, in 1962), Tom "Bix" Boyle (17, second tenor), and Jack Scandura (17, baritone/bass). An earlier form included Tommy Oliveri (17) and a guy known only as Tony (17, bass).

Though Jack and Dennis were from a rival gang on Skillman Avenue, singing groups had a kind of diplomatic immunity under gangland's code of ethics and could cross "turf" boundaries without being hassled. Some of the "gang groups" that enjoyed this immunity were THE DELROYS (Apollo), the Symbols (Kape), the Selections (Mona-Lee), THE DEVOTIONS (Roulette), and the Newports (Guyden), plus groups that never recorded, like the Pharoahs, the Chiefs, and the Dedications.

All the members had either been kicked out of or quit their respective schools (though Jack and two others eventually finished their educations). That gave the Hallmarks (named after the greeting card section at the candy store) plenty of spare time to practice at Greenpoint Avenue Park or under the Flushing Avenue El on Queens Boulevard.

The group patterned itself after THE SKYLINERS and initially sang mostly Skyliners tunes. When Jack Scandura and Dennis McMahon joined with their CHANNELS, HEARTBEATS, and MOONGLOWS influences, the repertoire broadened.

They recorded four songs at Variety Studios, and Ricky started shopping for a label on New York City's Record Row. In the Brill Building (1619 Broadway), he met Wemar Music Publishing's Stu Weiner and Johnny Brandon, who introduced the act to producer/artist Mike Lewis (lead of THE CONCORDS on "Again," RCA, 1961). They recorded a Mike Lewis rocker, "Wherever You Are," that featured Rick's tough-sounding lead, the group's full harmonies, and a persistent sax. It was recorded at Stea-Phillips Studios in Manhattan in November 1962 with Stu Phillips (of Colpix Records) as engineer. "Joanie Don't You Cry" was the flip side, adapted from the spiritual "Oh Mary Don't You Weep," and that side was mistakenly the one that became Murray the K's "Pick of the Week" in early 1963. Unfortunately, the career path went downhill from there. Had the label pushed "Wherever," Ricky and the Hallmarks could have made substantial chart noise.

Performance opportunities were limited. As the group was underage, they could only work local high school dances. (But they did manage to bluff their way into the Sea Hunt nightclub in the Bronx.)

Jack and Rick are reported to have returned the favor for Lewis by singing backup with the Concords on "Cold and Frosty Morning" while that group was on Herald in 1963. They (Jack and Rick) also sang with Mike Lewis and a girl remembered only as Laura on a Rick original ("Send Him to Me") for Roulette under the name the Uniques in 1963.

When the Hallmarks single failed, the group splintered in March 1963. Rick did a solo on Roulette produced by Lewis and titled "The River," and he continued to write. He had a national chart breaker in March 1985 with the Roddie Joy single "Come Back Baby" on Redbird (#86). Ricky moved to Los Angeles circa 1969. Dennis, Jack, and Bix formed a group called the Blend-Aires in 1963. Beverly Warren recorded solo for United Artists and B.T. Puppy and joined a later formation of the Blend-Aires in the late '70s. Tommy Oliveri sang with the 1963 Blend-Aires before settling into antique car restoration.

The Rivingtons

An R&B group with a long history and a short period of success, the Rivingtons were an outgrowth of a Los Angeles group known as THE LAMPLIGHTERS (Federal) in 1953.

It was as the Sharps (Combo) in 1956 that Al Frazier, Carl White, John "Sonny" Harris, and Turner "Rocky" Wilson, Jr. became the group that would emerge as the '60s Rivingtons.

One of the quartet's first recordings was as a backup group for a 15-year-old singer whose session was financed by his father. The song, "I Confess," was written by the young singer, named Paul Anka, and it wound up on L.A.'s RPM label. That year the group did its first single as the Sharps for Tag Records on "Six Months, Three Weeks" in 1956, which later wound up on Chess Records in 1958.

The journeymen harmonizers had releases on Jamie, Lamp, Vik (purchased from Jamie), and Aladdin, all in 1957. All were strong R&B records for the time, but their one successful record that year was one that didn't have their name on it. Thurston Harris, an old friend from their Lamplighter days, was signed to Aladdin in 1957 and had them back him on "Little Bitty Pretty One." Now a rock and roll classic, it went to number six Pop and number two R&B.

The group also recorded a superb blues ballad on Combo with non-member Joe Green subbing on lead for Carl White (a common practice of the L.A. "clique" groups of the '50s) titled "All My Love."

It was music publisher Lester Sill who named the group the Sharps, and through Sill the group began doing backup vocals (again unidentified) for instrumentalist Duane Eddy on such hits as "Rebel Rouser."

By January 1961 the Sharps had renamed themselves the Crenshaws (most likely after the Los Angeles street) and had recorded one single for Warner Bros., a reworking of the Billy Butterfield 1945 number 15 hit "Moonlight in Vermont."

Their real break came when producers Jack Levy and Adam Ross renamed the quartet the Rivingtons after Rivington Street on New York's Lower East Side. Signed to Liberty Records, the group first released "Papa-Oom-Mow-Mow," a nonsense rock and roll record that went top 10 in a variety of East Coast cities and registered number 48 Pop in late 1962. The song also became a popular European dance tune and helped start the "bird" dance craze. It was covered as "Je Suis Contaminé" (EMI) in 1984 by Jerry Smash et les Snappeuses, a three-girl, one-guy French vocal group.

The Rivingtons followed with more dance tunes like "Kickapoo Joy Juice" and "Mama-Oom-Mow-Mow," but only their 1963 release "The Bird's the Word" made any noise, reaching number 52 Pop and finally giving them an R&B charter at number 27.

In October 1963 the group went back to its roots for a stirring harmony-filled ballad single called "Cherry," which saw more action in France than in America.

Al Frazier became the group's manager in 1965 and Darryl White took his vocal spot.

The Rivingtons spent the '60s cutting credible dance sides for a slew of companies like Columbia, RCA, Vee-Jay, and Reprise and in 1973 even recut a new version of "Papa," but they never charted again.

The lineup in the late '70s consisted of Carl White, Madero White (Carl's brother), Rocky Wilson, Jr., and Sonny Harris. Since then, Carl White passed away. Al Frazier occasionally performed with the Rivingtons and was last heard to be writing a book on the Los Angeles rhythm and blues scene.

THE RIVINGTONS

A SIDE/B SIDE	LABEL/CAT NO	DATE
The Sharps		
Love Me My Darling /		
Heaven Only Knows	Mikes 101	1954
Six Months, Three Weeks /		
Cha Cho Hop	Tag 2200	1956
Come On / Sweet Sweetheart	Jamie 1040	1/57
Sweet Sweetheart / Come On	Vik 0264	2/57
Our Love Is Here To Stay /		
Lock My Heart	Lamp 2007	6/57
What Will I Gain / Shugglin'	Aldn 4301	10/57
6 Months, 3 Weeks, 2 Days,		
2 Hours / Cha-Cho Hop	Chess 1690	2/58
All My Love /		
Look What You've Done To Me	Combo 146	1958
All My Love /		
Look What You've Done To Me	Dot 15806	8/58
Look At Me! /		
Have Love, Will Travel	Jamie 1108	1958
Here's A Heart / Gig-A-Lene	Jamie 1114	1958
The Rivingtons		
Papa-Oom-Mow-Mow /		
Deep Water	Lbrty 55427	3/62
My Reward / Kickapoo Joy Juice	Lbrty 55513	1962
Mama-Oom-Mow-Mow / Waiting	Lbrty 55528	12/62
The Bird's The Word /		
I'm Losing My Grip	Lbrty 55553	1963
The Shaky Bird Part 1 /		
The Shaky Bird Part 2	Lbrty 55585	1963
Cherry / Little Sally Walker	Lbrty 55610	10/63
Wee Jee Walk / Fairy Tales	Lbrty 55671	1964
I Tried / One Monkey	Rprs 0293	7/64
All That Glitters /		
You Move Me Baby	AREA 100	8/64
You Move Me Baby /		
All That Glitters	Vee-Jay 634	1964

A SIDE/B SIDE	LABEL/CAT NO	DATE
I Love You Always / Years Of Tears	Vee-Jay 649	12/64
The Willy / Just Got To Be More	Vee-Jay 677	5/65
Tend To Business /		
A Rose Growing In The Ruins	Col 43581	4/66
Yadi-Yadi-Yum-Dum /		
Yadi-Yadi Revisited	Col 43772	8/66
You're Gonna Pay /		
I Don't Want A New Baby	Quan 1379	1967
Pop Your Corn Part 1 /		
Pop Your Corn Part 2	RCA 74-0301	11/69
Papa-Oom-Mow-Mow /		
I Don't Want A New Baby	Wand 11253	1973

Rochell and the Candles

Rochell and the Candles were a typical one-hit wonder with an atypical image. The group was formed in 1958 in Los Angeles by Rochell Henderson (lead and tenor) along with Johnny Wyatt (lead and first tenor), Melvin Sasso (tenor), and T. C. Henderson (no relation) (bass). Both Hendersons were from Louisiana, and Rochell had sung with the Chosen Gospel Singers, who included Lou Rawls. Sasso was an L.A. lifer and Wyatt was from Texas. Wanting a name that conjured images of light, fire, and excitement, Rochell picked the Candles. The foursome played clubs until they had enough original material to record and then went to the backyard studio of Ted Brinson in Watts (the same place THE PENGUINS cut "Earth Angel" many years earlier), recording four songs.

One of the hottest rhythm and blues disc jockeys in Los Angeles at the time was Hunter Hancock of KGFJ, who had started his own Swingin label in 1959.

In 1960 the Candles brought their best cut, the ballad "Once Upon a Time" (written by Swingin artist Jimmy Johnson), to Hancock, who tested it out on his show by playing their acetate. When the studio phones rang off the hook the Candles became the newest members of the Swingin family. "Once Upon a Time" left the gate in October and slowly gathered national momentum until five months later (February 6, 1961) it slipped onto Billboard's Hot 100, reaching number 26.

The feminine tenor lead was beautifully done and dominated the group's harmonies. But the record was not in keeping with the group's image: on the disc, not only was Rochell not the lead, "Rochell" wasn't even a girl. That heavenly falsetto was none other than Johnny Wyatt. Though the label of this and subsequent singles did read "Rochell and the Candles featuring Johnny Wyatt," disc jockeys rarely mentioned Johnny, let alone that the lead wasn't Rochell or even a female.

Still, the group got plenty of work out of their hit, performing with acts like Hank Ballard, James Brown, and Brook Benton.

Their second single, "So Far Away," another ballad, didn't have the ingredients that made "Once" a hit, and except for Los Angeles and surrounding areas it didn't really get much play.

Their third Swingin single was recorded in Downey, California, using HANK BALLARD'S MID-NIGHTERS as backup musicians. "Beg of My Heart" was a bluesier number than the previous two but it went nowhere. The group found itself in mid-1962 recording for the Los Angeles-based Challenge label, whose claim to fame had been the instrumentals of the Champs, such as "Tequila."

It was the Champs (with Glen Campbell on guitar) who backed the Candles on their June release, "Each Night," which Billboard reviewed on July 28th saying, "Rochell and the Candles bow on this label with their first disc in quite a while. It's a strong ballad sung in the lads' warming style over an ear-catching background."

When "Every Night" and their pre-funk era funky recording of "Let's Run Away and Get Married" crashed on takeoff, it was pretty much over for Rochell and company.

Two older cuts released on Bingo, "Are You the Future" and "The Girl Is All Right," along with Swingin's last shot from the can, an odd arrangement of THE OLYMPICS' "Big Boy Pete" in 1964, and the Candles were snuffed out.

Johnny Wyatt recorded three singles for Josie in 1966 with a group called Johnny and the Expressions, the best of which was a terrific soul ballad, "Now that You're Mine."

A few more unsuccessful solo singles for Mustang affiliate Bronco and Johnny's recording days were over. He died in 1983.

Rochell and the remaining Candles have not been able to light the fire since then.

ROCHELL AND THE CANDLES

A SIDE/B SIDE	LABEL/CAT NO	DATE
Once Upon A Time /		
When My Baby Is Gone	Swingin 623	10/60
So Far Away / Hey, Pretty Baby	Swingin 634	4/61
Beg Of My Heart /		
Squat With Me Baby	Swingin 640	11/61
Each Night / Turn Her Down	Ching 9158	6/62

A SIDE/B SIDE	LABEL/CAT NO	DATE
Annie's Not An Orphan Anymore /		
Let's Run Away And Get Married	Chlng 9191	1963
Big Boy Pete / A Long Time Ago	Swingin 652	9/64
You Are The Future /		
The Girl Is Alright	Bingo	1964

The Ronettes

No girl group set male hearts pounding in quite the way the Ronettes did. Most female aggregations, from THE BONNIE SISTERS, THE ANDREWS SISTERS, and THE CHANTELS to THE ANGELS, THE CHIFFONS, and THE SHIRELLES presented the picture of innocence. Not so for the group that many consider the first bad girls of rock and roll.

Veronica (Ronnie) Bennett, her sister Estelle, and their cousin Nedra Talley grew up in New York City's Washington Heights listening to rock and pop, especially fancying FRANKIE LYMON AND THE TEENAGERS, LITTLE ANTHONY AND THE IMPERIALS (Ronnie), and Rosemary Clooney (Nedra).

On those occasions, starting in 1959, when the young girls weren't being little ladies, their grandmother would sequester the trio in a room for an indefinite period and encourage the threesome to harmonize. They became surprisingly proficient on songs like "Red Red Robin" and "Goodnight Sweetheart."

The girls, aged 13 to 16, called themselves the Darling Sisters and took their act—with Grandma's encouragement—to the Apollo Theatre amateur night contest. When they won, Grandma packed them off for singing lessons. Phillip Halikus heard the look-alike vocalists, saw their potential, and became their manager. He started out by arranging appearances at hops and charity shows.

On a fateful night in 1961 the girls, dressed in tight skirts and with their hair piled high, stood on line at Joey Dee's Peppermint Lounge on New York's 45th Street. The manager mistook them for a singing trio that hadn't arrived, and the three were whisked inside. They were ushered onstage, where they took advantage of the moment and belted out a stimulating version of Ray Charles's "What'd I Say," even using the choreography they had been working on. The girls took the club by storm and were signed to appear regularly for the sum of $10 a night.

The Darling Sisters were also booked to perform at the Miami Peppermint Lounge. They were spotted there by New York disc jockey Murray Kaufman, who converted the trio into Murray the K's dancing girls for his touring company and his Brooklyn Fox shows. They also did duty with Clay Cole's "Twist-A-Rama" tour, and when those tough-looking young girls started wiggling and singing onstage, pandemonium broke loose even before they had a record.

Meanwhile, Phillip Halikus set up their first recordings through Stu Phillips at Colpix Records (though in a mid-'70s interview Nedra stated her mother's contact arranged it). Colpix renamed the girls Ronnie and the Relatives and issued their first single in the summer of 1961, an up-tempo piece titled "I Want a Boy."

Their next single, "I'm on the Wagon," listed the girls as the Ronettes. Around this time they recorded an LP's worth of material for Colpix/May, but it went unreleased until their glory days.

In early 1963 they did a good Exciters-styled teen rocker called "Good Girls," arranged by Bert Keyes, which showed continued recording maturity and a developing sound.

In between their other activities, the girls found themselves backing artists like Bobby Rydell, Del Shannon, and Joey Dee on record.

At this juncture two conflicting stories emerge. One has it that Estelle, while dialing a phone number for confirmation of a recording session, dialed the *wrong* number and wound up talking to Phil Spector. One thing led to another and he supposedly asked the group to do a demo for him. After hearing them, he went immediately to thoughts of producing a finished Ronettes record. The other, less romantic version is that *16* magazine staffer Georgia Winters introduced Spector to the girls when he was in New York talent hunting. Whichever is true, Spector was taken with Ronnie's hard-but-sweet sound and saw the "bad girls" in bouffants as an act he could finally build an image around. Up to that time girl groups rarely had an identity or even their pictures on the sleeves of their 45s. That certainly changed with the Ronettes.

Their first single on Spector and Lester Sill's new Philles label in July 1963 was a classic, the Ellie Greenwich/Jeff Barry/Phil Spector-penned collage of castanets, maracas, strings, and Hal Blaine drumwork titled "Be My Baby." Ronnie's distinctive, seductive vocal delivery, along with her now-legendary "woh-oh-oh-oh," drove teen boys wild while Spector's production drove the single to chart success. The July review in *Billboard* stated, "This is the best record the Ronettes ever made, and more than that, it's one of the strongest records of the week. It was made by Phil Spector, and he has transformed the gals into a sock singing group who handle this dramatic piece of material with flair. Backing has a stunning, rolling rock sound that's bound to make the disc score with the kids."

Brian Wilson of THE BEACH BOYS went further. He called it "the most perfect pop record of all time."

By October 12, 1963, it was at number two, denied the top spot by Jimmy Gilmore's "Sugar Shack." "Be My Baby" became an international hit, reaching number four in England.

In November, earth-shaking hand claps, thousand-pound drums, and Leon Russell's insistent piano playing introduced the most powerful wall-of-sound record yet, "Baby I Love You." If "Be My Baby" was a musical storm, "Baby I Love You" was a symphonic hurricane. The Ronettes held their own in a sea of orchestration, but not without some support: Spector added the backing voices of Darlene Love and THE BLOSSOMS, Ronnie herself, and Cher, overdubbing them until he had 20 to 25 voices balancing out the dense instrumental tracks. "Baby I Love You" charted on December 21, 1963, but only reached number 24, though the British took it to number 11.

In November the group joined Dick Clark's Caravan of Stars and then returned to New York to participate in one of the most memorable Christmas LPs ever made, Spector's *A Christmas Gift for You.* Of the 12 seasonal songs, they recorded "Sleigh Ride," "I Saw Mommy Kissing Santa Claus," and "Frosty the Snowman," all in true "Be My Baby"/ "Baby I Love You" style. The LP's climb to greatness was halted by the death of President Kennedy.

On the wings of two solid U.K. hits, the group flew to Britain in February 1964 and toured with the Rolling Stones. While there, they also met the newest sensations, the Beatles. They were the first girl group to produce anything resembling hysteria among audiences; the headlines in the British press read, "Girls scream at Stones, boys at Ronettes."

That same month they released their third wall of sounder, "The Best Part of Breaking Up." It reached number 39 in the U.S. and number 43 in England before Spector returned to high-powered orchestral teen rock with "Do I Love You," a Vinnie Poncia/Pete Androli/Spector masterwork that had one of the most power-driven intros ever recorded. Despite its U.S. peak of number 34 and a British high of number 35, "Do I Love You" became known as one of their best recordings.

When the Ronettes returned to the U.S., the Beatles were right behind them. Murray the K, who prided himself on being the self-proclaimed fifth Beatle, met them because of the Ronettes. Murray called the girls and asked to meet the mop-tops, so

the Ronettes brought the starstruck disk jockey along with them to the group's hotel. Also during 1964, Spector apparently test-marketed Ronnie as a solo act, issuing two singles under the name Veronica on his Phil Spector label. The first was a remake of the Students' ballad classic "I'm So Young," and the second was a Barry/Greenwich/ Spector composition, "Why Don't They Let Us Fall in Love," each backed by the Ronettes and each pulled from the marketplace almost immediately after its release.

In November 1964 the group released "Walking in the Rain," their most dramatic ballad. The Mann/Weil/Spector-penned record (done in one vocal take by Ronnie) reached number 23 and won a Grammy for Best Sound Effects—the only Grammy Spector ever received.

Working on the road held the same perils for the Ronettes as it did for others, even though they always traveled with a family member. On one jaunt they were playing Wildwood, New Jersey, for two weeks and the show owners demanded they stay on for a third. When threats of holding them against their will surfaced, the Ronettes' five-foot-tall aunt stepped in and called the troops—the girls' seven burly uncles—to come and take the trio home.

Their next two singles, "Born to Be Together" (#52) and "Is This What I Get for Loving You" (#25) were worthy of greater response then they got back in 1965. Meanwhile, the girls did some backup work on other Spector projects including the Righteous Brothers' classic ballad, "You've Lost that Loving Feeling." Their LP *Presenting the Fabulous Ronettes Featuring Veronica* reached only number 96 though cut for cut it was the best Philles album.

Spector's practice was to put an instrumental B side on Ronettes singles (as he'd done with earlier Philles acts) to keep the disc jockeys from flipping the record and taking attention away from his "push" side. Titles like "Bee Bee and Su Su" (the names of Ronnie's and Nedra's moms) and "Chubby Danny D." (the name of some long-since-forgotten promo man) graced those early B sides. But from the single "Is This What I Get" forward, an actual Ronettes recording was paired with the A side. In this case it was "Oh I Love You," which was the last side Spector produced with the Ronettes before he married Ronnie in 1966.

Prior to that, the Ronettes (minus Ronnie, who stayed behind with Phil), with another cousin named Elaine, toured the U.S. with the Beatles.

In September 1966 Jeff Barry was given the reins for the Ronettes' only non-Spector produced single on Philles (and their last Philles 45), "I Can

Hear Music" (#100). The song was later covered by the Beach Boys.

By the end of 1966 the Ronettes had disbanded. Nedra married WINS program director Scott Ross and Estelle married producer/songwriter Teddy Vann. Ronnie, forced into retirement by Spector, managed to emerge with an occasional single like "You Came, You Saw, You Conquered," a Toni Wine/Irwine Levine composition. It was released on Spector/A&M in 1969 with the backing of studio singers under the name "the Ronettes featuring the voice of Veronica" and produced by Phil.

In 1971, again under Spector's direction, Ronnie recorded "Try Some, Buy Some" for the Beatles' Apple label. It became her last chart record, with a peak of number 77 in the spring of 1971.

In 1973, her marriage with Phil almost at an end, Ronnie returned to performing and appeared as Ronnie and the Ronettes at Richard Nader's "Rock and Roll Revival" show at New York's Madison Square Garden with a new female trio that included Denise Edwards and Chip Fields.

In the fall, Stan Vincent produced two singles on the new Ronettes for Buddah; "I Wish I Never Saw the Sunshine" was a rerecording of a song the original Ronettes recorded for Spector in 1965 (and Ronnie's favorite). Spector didn't release it until his 1976 *Rare Masters II* LP came out in the U.K.

There were two Ronettes recordings of special note that were not issued as singles by Spector. One was the legendary rock-a-ballad "Paradise," penned by Harry Nilsson and Spector. Finally issued on the *Rare Masters* LP, the recording was in such demand it was openly bootlegged in 1979 on a bogus Philles label. The other masterpiece was the driving, exciting, wall-of-sound winner, "I Wonder," from the girls' *Fabulous Ronettes* LP.

In 1976 Ronnie sang backup for Bruce Springsteen at his New York Palladium performance. (Bruce acknowledged her and the Ronettes as an influence on his music.) This led to E Street Band member Miami Steve Van Zant producing and arranging a 1977 single with Ronnie Spector and the E Street Band titled *Say Goodbye to Hollywood*. The Billy Joel-penned powerhouse (Joel was also heavily influenced by Ronnie and company) rocked with Ronnie's most inspired vocals since the early Spector days. It never charted.

In 1978 Ronnie tried again with an Australian song called "It's a Heartache," produced by Kyle Lehning and Steve Popovich. The record was beaten to the charts by Bonnie Tyler's version (#3).

In 1980 rock and roll mover and shaker Genya Ravan (real name Goldie Zelkowitz; see THE ESCORTS) produced Ronnie on a fuzz-toned wall-of-

sound rocker called "Darlin'" for her own Polish label. (Ronnie also did the Polish LP *Siren*.) In 1986 she reemerged in the song "Take Me Home Tonight" with Eddie Money, which put her back in the spotlight at number four.

In 1987 Columbia issued a new Ronnie Spector LP with the song "Dangerous" backed up by THE BANGLES.

Through the '80s Ronnie performed as one of the legendary ladies of rock and roll. She got her due on December 11, 1990, when CBS-TV aired a special titled "Grammy Legends" that included a segment with Ronnie singing "Say Goodbye to Hollywood."

While the Ronettes were unique musically, they were also the first really seductive girl group. Others before them seemed to be singing to their friends about the boys they desired ("Maybe," the Chantels; "I Met Him on a Sunday," the Shirelles; "He's So Fine," the Chiffons). The Ronettes, on the other hand, sang directly to the boys ("Be My Baby," "Baby I Love You"). Performer-to-audience relations have never been the same since.

THE RONETTES

A SIDE/B SIDE	LABEL/CAT NO	DATE
Ronnie and the Relatives		
I Want A Boy / Sweet Sixteen	Colpix 601	1961
The Ronettes		
My Guiding Angel / I'm Gonna Quit While I'm Ahead	May 111	1961
I'm On The Wagon / I'm Gonna Quit While I'm Ahead	Colpix 646	1962
Silhouettes / You Bet I Would	May 114	1962
Good Girls / Memory	May 138	1963
Be My Baby / Tedessco And Pitman	Philles 116	7/63
Baby I Love You / Miss Joan And Mr. Sam	Philles 118	11/63
Breakin' Up / Big Red	Philles 120	2/64
Do I Love You / Bee Bee And Su Su	Philles 121	6/64
Do I Love You / (The Best Part Of) Breaking Up	Spec 377	1964
I'm So Young / Larry L.	PSpec 1	1964
Why Don't They Let Us Fall In Love / Chubby Danny Dee	PSpec 2	1964
Walking In The Rain / How Does It Feel	Philles 123	10/64
Born To Be Together / Blues For Baby	Philles 126	1/65
Is This What I Get For Loving You / Oh I Love You	Philles 128	4/65
I Can Hear Music / When I Saw You	Philles 133	9/66
I Can Hear Music / How Does It Feel	PSpec 2010014	1966

A SIDE/B SIDE	LABEL/CAT NO	DATE
You Came You Saw You Conquered / Oh I Love You	A&M 1040	3/69
Ronnie Spector and the Ronettes		
Lover Lover / Go Out And Get It	Buddah 384	1973
The Ronettes		
I Wish I Never Saw The Sunshine / I Wonder What He's Doing	Buddah 408	1974
(I'm A) Woman In Love / When I Saw You	PSpec 2010009	1975
Paradise / When I Saw You	W-Spec 0409	1976
Girls Can Tell / Be My Baby*	Philles 116	1979
Keep On Dancing / Baby, I Love You*	Philles 118	1979
A Woman In Love / Do I Love You?*	Philles 121	1979
Paradise / Walking In The Rain*	Philles 123	1979

* Bootleg

Ronnie and the Hi-Lites

An overlooked group of the early '60s, Ronnie and the Hi-Lites had a short career but a lot of talent. That talent was developed in the late 1950s in Jersey City, New Jersey, where Sonny Caldwell (18, first tenor), John Witney (17, second tenor), Stanley Brown (17, baritone), and Kenny Overby (17, bass) started out as the Cascades.

The teenagers made their singing headquarters at Public School 14. John saw a young vocalist named Ronnie Goodson in a school play and knew that he'd make a great "kiddie" lead. 12-year-old Ronnie joined up and the group began practicing FRANKIE LYMON AND THE TEENAGERS songs in John's basement. Ronnie, whose style came from his soloing at the Salem Baptist Church, led the group members through their first talent contest (which they won) singing LITTLE ANTHONY and Frankie Lymon songs at P.S. 14.

The Cascades then came to the attention of arranger Hal Weiss and his songwriting spouse Marian. The group auditioned with the Starlites' "Valerie," and Mrs. Weiss was so impressed by Ronnie's charisma and professional sound that she began to write a song for him. She renamed them Ronnie and the Hi-Lites and spent months crafting just the right vehicle for Ronnie's lead.

The song that finally emerged was "I Wish that We Were Married," a ballad that invited an emotion-laden treatment. And that's exactly what Ronnie brought to their recording of the song.

In 1961 Atlantic and ABC Records both passed on the Hi-Lites' cut, but Eddie Joy of Joy Records liked it and issued the single in the early winter of 1962. On March 10th, a *Billboard* reviewer commented: "The 14-year-old lad sings with feeling and heart on moving rock-a-ballad with teen-appeal lyrics about young couples who are too young to wed."

"I Wish" broke out of Philadelphia and Trenton with an extra boost from the group's appearance on "American Bandstand." On March 31st it charted and rose to number 16 nationally. Selling over half a million copies, the song put 14-year-old Ronnie and company on the map, paving the way for performances alongside THE CRYSTALS and THE SPANIELS at such venues as the Apollo and Palisades Park. But their rise to the big time lasted only a short time. The follow-up single "Be Kind" received good airplay but died at number 120 in July. Then a single on Raven failed, and a doo wop ballad called "A Slow Dance" fizzled out at number 116 in August 1963, even though it went top 10 in several eastern cities. "A Slow Dance" was the first release on Hal and Marian Weiss's own Win label, based at 27 Stegman Place in Jersey City.

By now Bill Scruggs had replaced Stan Brown. Scruggs himself was soon replaced by Richmond Charles.

Two 1963 releases, "The Fact of the Matter" and "High School Romance," were unsuccessful. Still, the group kept working, and they appeared opposite Stevie Wonder, Major Lance, and Ronnie's girlfriend Eva Boyd, better known as Little Eva ("The Locomotion").

When the group graduated from high school, some joined the service and others went to work. Ronnie did one solo single, "You Keep Me Guessin'," for the Uptite label (Hal Weiss had become ill and Marian had shut down Win to take care of him).

Ronnie had been ill on and off for years and had undergone several operations for a recurring benign tumor. But he kept working, giving his all in every performance. On one night he couldn't continue, and rather than deny the audience a full show he asked Mrs. Weiss, who was a singer and knew all his songs, to fill in on lead with the Hi-Lites.

Sonny Caldwell became a computer programmer in California. Kenny Overby also ended up out West. John Witney became a diesel mechanic in Harrisburg, Pennsylvania. Richmond Charles became a phone company representative and Bill Scruggs a Secaucus, New Jersey, security guard.

Ronnie Goodson died in his sleep at the age of 33 on November 4, 1980.

RONNIE AND THE HI-LITES

A SIDE/B SIDE	LABEL/CAT NO	DATE
I Wish That We Were Married /		
Twistin' And Kissin'	Joy 260	2/62
Send My Love / Be Kind	Joy 265	6/62
Valerie / The Fact Of The Matter	Raven 8000	1962
A Slow Dance /		
What The Next Day May Bring	Win 250	7/63
The Fact Of The Matter /		
You Keep Me Guessin'	Win 251	9/63
High School Romance /		
Uptown-Downtown	Win 252	11/63
Too Young / High School Romance	ABC 10685	1965

The Royalettes

The Royalettes were a pop R&B quartet from Baltimore, Maryland, that came together at Edmondson High School. The members were Sheila Ross on lead, her sister Anita Ross, cousin Ronnie Brown, and friend Terry Flippen.

The four girls practiced the hits of the day and emulated the sounds of THE CHANTELS and THE SHIRELLES in particular.

In 1962 they came to the attention of the decision makers at Bob Marcucci's Chancellor Records in Philadelphia and recorded two singles. "No Big Thing," released in late 1962, had an up-tempo soul sound in an ORLONS, Shirley Matthews and the Big Town Girls style. Its flip, "Yesterday's Lovers," had a surprising pop group sound not unlike the Sheppard Sisters. When it went nowhere Chancellor issued "Blue Summer" in early 1963 with the same results.

In 1964 the girls won a talent contest on Buddy Deane's TV show in Baltimore and were noticed by local promo man Harold Berkman. He brought the group to producer/writer Teddy Randazzo (formerly of THE THREE CHUCKLES), who started creating material for them that was similar in sophistication to the songs Burt Bacharach and Hal David were writing and producing for Dionne Warwick in the early and middle '60s. He also sprinkled some appropriate sounding oldies between the new songs that they rehearsed at the office Teddy shared with producer/arranger Don Costa on 54th Street above Bell Sound. Harold Berkman then took the group to MGM and struck a deal. The result was a late 1964

remake of the Chantels' "He's Gone" that came and went. So did their second try, titled "Poor Boy."

In June 1965 the original ballad "It's Gonna Take a Miracle" was issued, charting on July 17th and rising to number 41 nationally.

The girls, who were between 17 and 21 when they met Randazzo, got their first taste of big-time touring when they played the Royal Theatre in Baltimore with THE SUPREMES, HANK BALLARD AND THE MIDNIGHTERS, THE COASTERS, MARTHA AND THE VANDELLAS, Marvin Gaye, and Wilson Pickett.

Their fall follow-up, "I Want to Meet Him," made it to number 72 nationally, but five subsequent singles for MGM did little.

They moved to Roulette in 1967 for the single "River of Tears," but by the early '70s they were off the scene. The members went to marriage and families while Sheila reportedly became a Playboy bunny.

Ruby and the Romantics

Ruby and the Romantics epitomized the pop black sound of the early '60s. The quintet started out as an all-male quartet in Akron, Ohio, in 1961 and included Ed Roberts (first tenor), George Lee (second tenor), Ronald Mosley (baritone), and Leroy Fann (bass).

The group called themselves the Supremes (obviously not having heard of the male groups of the same name on Kitten and Old Town in 1956).

Meanwhile, Akronite Ruby Nash, her sister, and two female friends had their own group playing talent shows.

The Supremes went off to New York looking for recording success but came back empty-handed. Fann then ran into the smooth-sounding 22-year-old Ruby, and knowing how groups like THE MIRACLES and THE PLATTERS had enjoyed success with a female member, asked her to join.

Thanks to music arranger Leroy Kirkland, the group was given an audition at Kapp Records in front of A&R director Alan Stanton. Stanton agreed to sign them and picked Ruby to sing lead with the proviso that they change their name pronto. (It's possible Stanton had heard of a young female quartet out of Detroit named THE SUPREMES who already had four singles released.) Stanton didn't wait for them to come up with a new name; within a few days he had christened them Ruby and the Romantics.

The Romantics' first single was a sophisticated Mort Garson/Bob Hilliard-penned tune called "Our Day Will Come." The writers were so reluctant to give it to this new group that they made Stanton promise that if the Romantics record failed he'd issue it with another Kapp artist, Jack Jones. They needn't have bothered. Ruby (who'd never been in a recording studio before) and company did two versions of the song, one on a bossa nova rhythm (which was a hot fad at the time) and the other in a strong mid-tempo arrangement. The bossa nova version won out and on February 9, 1963, it charted on the *Billboard* Hot 100. Six weeks later it was the number one record in the country. It also made number one R&B and was an international success at number 11 in Australia and number 38 in England. Jack Jones would have to look elsewhere for a hit.

It was prime time for vocal groups. Five of the top seven singles were by quartets or quintets, including THE CHIFFONS, THE FOUR SEASONS, THE CASCADES, and THE ORLONS.

"Moonlight and Music," penned by Leroy Fann and the flip side of "Our Day," was one of the most beautiful and haunting songs the group would ever record. With Ruby's top-note harmony floating over the male voices, "Moonlight" was unique and should have been an A side single.

More silky-smooth harmonies filled the grooves of "My Summer Love," which reached number 16 in the summer of 1963.

The follow-up "Hey There Lonely Boy" was a velvety rhythm ballad that helped establish the cleaner brand of pop that would later be known as MOR (middle of the road). "Hey There" made it to number 27 on *Billboard*'s national charts.

Despite excellent recordings and songs the group was losing ground on the charts with each release. "Young Wings Can Fly," a beautiful Hilliard/Garson rhythm ballad released in October 1963, reached only number 47. "Our Everlasting Love" reached number 64 in the spring of 1964.

Trying to put the group back on track, Kapp tried a slightly different approach with a mid-tempo pop R&B side titled "Baby Come Home," but the slide continued and the cut peaked at number 75.

The cozy, satiny "When You're Young and in Love" followed (#48), and a slightly tougher rhythm ballad, "Does He Really Care for Me," ended their chart career, earning only a number 87 ranking in February 1965.

One of the group's best performances, Larry Weiss's "Your Baby Doesn't Love You Anymore," didn't even make the charts.

By 1967 the group had signed on with ABC Records for two singles, the better one a reworking of the Platters' "Twilight Time." By this time the entire male contingent had been replaced by Vincent McLeod, Ronald Jackson, Robert Lewis, and Richard Pryor (not the comedian).

In 1968 the group was not only a trio, it was an *all-girl* trio with Ruby, Cheryl Thomas, and Denise Lewis.

Their last single was the striking Geld/Udell-penned rhythm ballad "Hurting Each Other."

The recordings of Ruby and the Romantics are today considered prime examples of early '60s black pop. Their songs became hits in later years in versions by other performers. THE MARVELETTES made "Young and in Love" a number 23 Pop and number nine R&B hit in 1967. "Hey There Lonely Boy" became "Hey There Lonely Girl" for Eddie Holman, reaching number two Pop and number four R&B in 1969. The Carpenters made "Hurting Each Other" number two nationally in 1972. Frankie Valli rode "Our Day Will Come" to number 11 Pop in 1975.

Ruby and the Romantics finally called it a career in 1971 and Ruby retired to raise a family. In the early '90s she was living in Akron and working for AT&T. Ed Roberts was residing in New York and working in a bank. George Lee was driving a truck. Leroy Fann died in 1973.

RUBY AND THE ROMANTICS

A SIDE/B SIDE	LABEL/CAT NO	DATE
Our Day Will Come / Moonlight And Music	Kapp 501	1/63
My Summer Love / Sweet Love And Sweet Forgiveness	Kapp 525	4/63
Hey There Lonely Boy / Not A Moment Too Soon	Kapp 544	8/63
Young Wings Can Fly / Day Dreaming	Kapp 557	10/63
Our Everlasting Love / Much Better Off Than I've Ever Been	Kapp 578	1964
Baby Come Home / Everyday's A Holiday	Kapp 601	1964
When You're Young And In Love / I Cry Alone	Kapp 615	1964
Does He Really Care For Me / Nevertheless	Kapp 646	1965
Your Baby Doesn't Love You Anymore / We'll Meet Again	Kapp 665	1965

A SIDE/B SIDE	LABEL/CAT NO	DATE
Imagination / Nobody But My Baby	Kapp 702	1965
Remember Me / We Can Make It	Kapp 759	1966
Hey There Lonely Boy / Think	Kapp 773	9/66
I Know / We'll Love Again	Kapp 639	7/67
Twilight Time / Una Bella Brazilian Melody	ABC 10911	1967
More Than Yesterday Less Than Tomorrow / On A Clear Day You Can See Forever	ABC 11065	1968
Hurting Each Other / Baby I Could Be So Good At Lovin' You	A&M 1042	1969

The Safaris

A soft pop group from Los Angeles, the Safaris trekked through four names and three labels before reaching their one-hit status.

The original group was formed in 1959 and called themselves the Mystics. When the East Coast MYSTICS hit that spring, Sandy Weisman, Marv Rosenberg, and Richard Clasky became the Enchanters. Marv was a student at Fairfax High School and Richard was from Hamilton High. They met at a party and launched the Enchanters as a vehicle for their mutual interest in songwriting.

After one single on Orbit Records ("Touch of Love") that sounded like an early Kathy Young and the Innocents, the trio added Fairfax High student Sheldon Briar and became the Dories on Dore. Their solo single, "I Love Him So," stood still. Sandy, the Dories' female lead, decided marriage was more fun than singing, so the boys replaced her with San Fernando Valley vocalist Jim Stephens, who had graduated Van Nuys High School. Jim's innocent-sounding lead fit right into the group's quiet style of vocalizing.

In late 1959 the Dories met a trumpet player who was starting his own label with a friend, at which point the Dories became the Angels. The label was Tawny Records and the friend was soon-to-be-legendary producer Lou Adler. The trumpet player was named Herb Alpert.

While all were looking for material for the Angels to record, Marv was lying on his girlfriend's bed suffering an anxiety attack brought on by her ultimatum of "me or your music." Lying alone in the room, listening to the loud ticking of her clock and water dripping in the bathroom, he began to formulate the song "Image of a Girl."

Herb Alpert didn't like the song and opted instead for "A Lover's Poem (To Her)," which was recorded with Darlene Love and THE BLOSSOMS backing the Angels, with Alpert on trumpet. The record never left the gate, but Adler and Alpert salvaged the instrumental track and in 1959 had the Untouchables record "Poor Boy Needs a Preacher" over it (Madison Records).

The Angels managed to do a variety of San Bernardino record hops and came to the attention of Eldo Records.

In April 1960 "Image of a Girl," with its clock intro sound (made by hitting two ends of a wooden block), was released by the newly christened Safaris and on June 6th charted on *Billboard*'s Hot 100. When it reached number six on August 1st, the California quartet became an "overnight" sensation. In Australia, "Image" made it to number 26, and in Japan, to number one. The group performed mostly in California and played with THE DRIFTERS, THE TURBANS, THE MEDALLIONS, THE OLYMPICS, THE PENGUINS, and THE PLATTERS, and appeared on Dick Clark's "American Bandstand" when it was done in California.

Even with a big hit the Safaris found themselves playing schlock shows like the one at the notorious El Monte Legion Stadium, where fights were a constant and many of the teens carried razor blades. Sheldon was so terrified he bought a gun.

"The Girl with the Story in Her Eyes" was their second Safaris single, and it managed to reach number 85 before falling off the charts. When their manager tried to send the group out on a three-week promo tour with no pay, all but Jim returned to college, while he and three friends did the tour and recorded the last single as the Safaris, the FIVE SATINS classic "In the Still of the Night."

Jim moved on to a folk group. Later in 1961 Briar, Rosenberg, and Clasky joined with Lee Forrester for one single as the Suddens on Sudden ("China Love") and one on Valiant in 1963 called "That's Where the Difference Lies."

In 1989, 29 years after "Image," the Safaris (with Jimmy Stephens on lead) issued an "Image" sound-alike with different lyrics titled "My Image of a Girl (Is You)."

Today Richard Clasky has a market research company in Vancouver, Canada; Sheldon Briar is a criminal attorney; Marv Goldberg has a Ph.D. in Psychology and works at a hospital insurance company; and Jim Stephens is sales manager for a bottled water company.

Marv found out that nostalgia always has a value. A month after "Image of a Girl" became a hit, his girlfriend called and said she and her mom were moving. Would he like to buy the bed he wrote that song on?

THE SAFARIS

A SIDE/B SIDE	LABEL/CAT NO	DATE
The Enchanters		
Touch Of Love / Cafe Bohemian	Orbit 532	1959
The Dories		
I Love Him So / Tragedy Of Love	Dore 528	1959
The Angels		
A Lover's Poem (To Her) /		
A Lover's Poem (To Him)	Tawny 101	1959
The Safaris		
Image Of A Girl /		
Four Steps To Love	Eldo 101	4/60
The Girl With The Story In		
Her Eyes / Summer Nights	Eldo 105	8/60
In the Still Of The Night / Shadows	Eldo 110	1/61
The Suddens		
China Love / Childish Ways	Sudden 103	1961
That's Where The Difference Lies /		
Funny Thing Happened	Valiant 6033	1963
The Safaris		
My Image Of A Girl Is You /		
C'mon Everybody	DeeJay 203	1989

The Shangri-Las

The queens of teen melodrama, the Shangri-Las were the most broadly appealing of all '60s girl groups. What they sang had a lot to do with it (dating, dealing with parental conflicts, and so forth). Their "hip" look combined with a measure of innocence also helped convince the kids of the sincerity of the Shangri-Las' message.

The group of four were sisters Mary (lead) and Liz (Betty) Weiss, and identical twins Marge and Mary Ann Ganser. All were 15 and 16 when they started singing at Andrew Jackson High School in the Cambria Heights section of Queens, New York, around 1963. Influenced by LITTLE ANTHONY AND THE IMPERIALS and THE FOUR SEASONS, they began playing school shows, talent shows, and teen hops. The girls came to the attention of Artie Ripp (formerly of the Four Temptations, ABC, 1958), who arranged the group's first record deals with Smash, where they cut the live sounding Tony Michaels-penned single "Simon Says," and with Spokane for "Wishing Well." (It's also rumored that they recorded two singles as the Bon Bons in late 1963 or early 1964 for Coral Records, produced by Henry Jerome.)

"Wishing Well" (another Michaels song) gave a taste of the future with its talking intro over a cappella harmony. The body of the song had chime harmonies and call-and-response recitations of 12 wishes similar to what Harvey and THE MOONGLOWS did in "Ten Commandments of Love."

Meanwhile, an as-yet-unproven self-professed songwriter named George Morton bluffed his way into a meeting with Brill Building professional Jeff Barry through Jeff's wife Ellie Greenwich, whom Morton knew from Long Island. Without even a song, he presented himself to Barry, who in turn challenged him to bring in a hit. George then put together a few musicians and went to see the Shangri-Las, whom he also knew from some of their local Queens appearances. He convinced them he could produce a hit.

Morton now had all his pieces in place and smugly drove to the demo session. He claims that the only thing he forgot to do was write a song, so he pulled to the side of the road and created "Remember (Walking in the Sand)."

The demo done (with a young Billy Joel on piano), Morton rushed to Greenwich and Barry's office. Stunned that this upstart actually had a strong record, they called in Jerry Leiber and Mike Stoller from their offices next door, where they ran Red Bird Records with George Goldner.

"Remember" was released on July 20, 1964. With its seagull sound effects, the Shangri-Las' chilling harmonies, and Mary's nostalgic tale of lost love, "Remember" shot up the charts to reach number five on September 26th. It also reached the British charts by the fall, rising to number 14.

To keep the momentum going, Barry and Greenwich worked with Morton to write and produce the next tapestry of torment, "Leader of the Pack."

With this song, the Shangri-Las initiated their practice of killing off more people on records than youth gangs did on L.A. streets. What emerged from the recording sessions was a modified Phil Spector record. Mary's tortured vocal lead and the girls' spine-tingling harmonies worked in concert with screeching tires, car crashes, and the eventual demise of one biker. (Engineer Joe Veneri had even brought his motorcycle into the studio's echo chamber and recorded as he revved his engine.) With its memorable talk intro ("Is she really going out with him? . . ."), "Leader of the Pack" quickly became just that, reaching number one on November 28th. It skyrocketed to number one in Australia and number 11 in England, where it recharted in 1972 (#3) and 1976 (#7). It became the only American vocal group record ever to hit the upper reaches of the British charts three times.

The record spawned a parody called "The Leader of the Laundromat" by the Detergents (a pre-ARCHIES Ron Dante group) that hit number 19 in early 1965.

Though the nation was caught up in the British invasion, the week of November 28, 1964, belonged to American vocal groups. The top three records were "Leader of the Pack" (the Shangri-Las), "Baby Love" (THE SUPREMES), and "Come a Little Bit Closer" (JAY AND THE AMERICANS).

Following their chart-topper, the group became a fixture on the Murray the K tours, even performing with the Beatles.

The Shangri-Las lightened up on their third Red Bird release; "Give Him a Great Big Kiss" had a pasteurized soul sound, and it reached number 18.

The group appeared on TV's "Hullabaloo," "Shindig," and "Hollywood a Go Go," and on shows hosted by Steve Allen, Soupy Sales, Bruce Morrow, Clay Cole, and the guru of the groove tube, Dick Clark.

When Morton, Barry, and Greenwich needed a break to write another teen soap opera, Red Bird issued the '50s CHANTELS classic "Maybe," done up in perfect '60s style by Mary and company, but it only reached number 91.

In December 1964 the girls came back with a tough teen tale called "Out in the Streets." The mini-epic rose no higher than number 53.

By now, most public performances were being done as a trio with Mary and the Ganser girls, since Betty was on and off.

The body count rose on their next outing, which had Mary pleading with her folks to let her marry Jimmy or else they'd run away. "Give Us Your Blessings" was another (Barry/Greenwich-penned) tune produced by "Shadow" Morton, a name George Goldner stuck him with when he couldn't find the elusive producer.

Shadow penned "I Can Never Go Home Anymore," released in the fall of 1965. The talk-singing, tear-jerking, mini-opera must have ripped a million hearts apart when Mary screamed "Mama"; "Go Home" shot to number six in the nation, but not before Shadow had "Mom" die of loneliness at the loss of her runaway-though-repentant daughter.

"Long Live Our Love" lived long enough to reach number 33, and then the group re-cut the ballad "She Cried" (Jay and the Americans, #5, 1962) retitled "He Cried" (#65).

"Past, Present and Future" (#59, summer of 1966) was the Shangri-Las' last Red Bird single. Fans would have been better served if deejays had flipped the record to the Nilsson-penned B side "Paradise." The group's most exciting ballad,

"Paradise" was a record of epic proportions and a crowning achievement for Shadow Morton, though few heard it.

In spite of its success, Red Bird was going under, so Shadow and the Shangri-Las moved to Mercury for two ill-fated singles, the better of which was "Sweet Soft Sounds of Summer" (#123, January 1967) with its touch of psychedelia.

Morton and cowriter/producer Tony Michaels (from the early Shangri-Las singles) did another record for Mercury in a Shangri-Las style with a mysterious group only known as the Nu Luvs ("So Soft, So Warm"), which was issued before the two Shangri-Las releases. Perhaps the Nu Luvs were really the Shangri-Las.

By 1968, the Shangri-Las were no more. Betty married artist/writer Jeremy Storch and later became Mrs. Betty Weiss Nelson. Marge became Mrs. Marge Ganser Droste, and her sister Mary Ann died in 1971. Mary Weiss became an interior decorator and was running a furniture store in the mid-'80s as Mrs. Mary Weiss Stoker.

In 1989, the three surviving Shangri-Las performed for the first time in over 20 years for Cousin Brucie at his first Palisades Amusement Park Reunion on June 3rd at the Meadowlands Arena in East Rutherford, New Jersey. The show featured Little Anthony, Leslie Gore, Freddy Cannon, THE CHIMES, the Tokens (the East Coast version), and Bobby Rydell. The closing act, dressed in black leather, was the Shangri-Las. They performed several songs, left the stage, then returned on motorcycles and tore the house down with "Leader of the Pack." And that's what they always will be.

THE SHANGRI-LAS

A SIDE/B SIDE	LABEL/CAT NO	DATE
The Shangra-Las		
Simon Says / Simon Speaks	Smash 1866	12/63
The Shangri-Las		
Wishing Well /		
Hate To Say I Told You So	Spkn 4006	1964
Remember / It's Easier To Cry	RdBrd 008	7/64
Leader Of The Pack /		
What Is Love	RdBrd 014	10/64
Give Him A Great Big Kiss /		
Twist And Shout	RdBrd 018	12/64
Maybe / Shout	RdBrd 019	12/64
The Boy / Out In The Streets	RdBrd 025	2/65
Heaven Only Knows /		
Give Us Your Blessings	RdBrd 030	5/65
Right Now And Not Later /		
The Train From Kansas City	RdBrd 036	8/65
I Can Never Go Home Anymore /		
Sophisticated Boom Boom	RdBrd 043	10/65

A SIDE/B SIDE	LABEL/CAT NO	DATE
I Can Never Go Home Anymore /		
Bull Dog	RdBrd 043	10/65
Long Live Our Love /		
Sophisticated Boom Boom	RdBrd 048	1/66
He Cried / Dressed In Black	RdBrd 053	1966
Past, Present And Future /		
Paradise	RdBrd 068	1966
Past, Present And Future /		
Love You More Than Yesterday	RdBrd 068	1966
Sweet Soft Sounds Of Summer /		
I'll Never Learn	Merc 72645	11/66
Take The Time /		
Footsteps On The Roof	Merc 72670	3/67

The Bon-Bons
(possibly the Shangri-Las)

Everybody Wants My Boyfriend /		
Each Time	Coral 62435	1964
What's Wrong With Rings /		
Come On Baby	Coral 62402	1964

The Shirelles

The Shirelles were the most popular of the early '60s girl groups and were the mold from which many of the decade's female aggregations were cast. The quartet of 16- and 17-year-olds were all friends from Passaic High School in Passaic, New Jersey, and began singing together in 1957. The girls were fans of THE FLAMINGOS, THE CHANTELS, and LITTLE ANTHONY AND THE IMPERIALS as well as THE BOBBETTES, and received a large part of their musical education by listening to New York's premier R&B station at the time, WWRL.

They originally called themselves the Poquellos (meaning birds).

The members were Shirley Owens, Addie "Micki" Harris, Beverly Lee, and Doris Coley. Their harmonizing in the school gym resulted in a teacher suggesting they direct their energy to the school talent show. The quartet then set about creating an original song for the show and wrote a story of young love (which typically lasted only a week) called "I Met Him on a Sunday." The girls sang the infectious hand clapper a cappella in the show and were an immediate sensation. Their friend Mary Jane Greenberg wanted to introduce the girls to her mother Florence Greenberg, who owned the tiny company Tiara Records, but the girls weren't interested and actually turned her down. After repeated requests by Mary Jane, the Poquellos (who were singing just for fun) finally auditioned in Florence's living room with "I Met Him on a Sunday." On February 7, 1958, they found themselves in a recording studio doing "Sunday" and "I Want You to Be My Boyfriend." Florence then decided she wanted them to have a more commercial name, so the group came up with the Shirelles, a frilly version of Shirleys.

The single—flat notes and all—came out in March and created sufficient activity for Decca to buy the masters. On April 21st, "Sunday" reached the *Billboard* charts, rising to number 49. The orchestral direction credit on the label went to "Stan Green"—actually Stanley Greenberg, Florence's son.

The gals began performing on the chitlin circuit, but their moms demanded the teens be accompanied by chaperones. Two of the tour's older performers, Etta James and Ruth Brown, became the designated den mothers (probably not what the mothers had in mind, but the ladies did steer the girls away from any pitfalls).

Decca issued two more singles from an April 22, 1958, session. "My Love Is a Charm," a "Lonely Nights"-styled doo wop ballad (with musical direction by Bud Johnson), and "I Got the Message" both failed to chart.

After Decca dropped the Shirelles, Greenberg started up Scepter Records in the spring of 1959 and brought in producer/writer Luther Dixon to work with the girls. Luther was best known for his cowritten hit "Sixteen Candles" (THE CRESTS).

The Shirelles' first Scepter single was a remake of THE 5 ROYALES' 1957 45 "Dedicated to the One I Love," which reached number 83 in July.

Two lightweight singles followed and went nowhere. The group then came out with a Shirley/Luther-penned composition, "Tonight's the Night," that charted on September 12th and reached number 39 Pop and number 14 R&B. (The flip "The Dance Is Over" was the issued A side, and nothing happened until disc jockeys started to flip over "Tonight's the Night.")

In late summer of 1960, two Brooklyn writers named Carole King and Gerry Goffin (the label later read Carol King and Jerry Goffin) brought Dixon a song titled "Tomorrow." The girls didn't like it, feeling it was too white, and they had to be pressured to record it by Dixon. By the time it was released, in the fall of 1960, it had become "Will You Love Me Tomorrow," an up-tempo pop song with an exciting string arrangement and lyrics that were ahead of their time in subject matter. (The lyric is actually "Will you *still* love me tomorrow.")

On November 21, 1960, "Tomorrow" (with Carole King playing drums) charted Pop and in two months reached the hallowed number one spot, the first record by a black all-female group to hit the top. It also reached number four in England and number six in Australia. Its flip, the Wes Farrell/Luther Dixon-penned "Boys" later became a favorite of the Beatles and wound up on their first LP. (The Beatles went on record to say the Shirelles were their favorite American group.)

The girls followed up with a reissue of "Dedicated," and it climbed the Hot 100 so fast that "Tomorrow" was still at number three when "Dedicated" entered the top 10.

The group's tours and performances paired them with all the hitmakers of the day from Dion, Chubby Checker, Ray Charles, Neil Sedaka, and THE COASTERS to Fats Domino, THE DRIFTERS, and Bo Diddley. They did the Dick Clark Caravan of Stars with Dick right on the bus sitting near the cooler of sodas he brought for everyone.

Shirley's distinctively innocent sound was now fully developed and the girls' harmonies were polished and smoothly commercial. As a result, the Shirelles charted Pop more times in their career than they did R&B (26 to 20).

"Mama Said" scored in the spring of 1961 (#4 Pop, #2 R&B). (In their entire career, the group turned in four number two R&B singles and two number three's but never hit number one on the R&B chart.) The Shirelles were doing so well that Decca tried to grab some of the pie by reissuing "I Met Him on a Sunday" in early 1961, but they found out the record only had one life.

Their next release, the Goffin/King-penned "What a Sweet Thing that Was," found unexpected competition from its B side, "A Thing of the Past," and the split play killed the hit ("Past" reached number 41 and "Sweet Thing" hit number 54.)

The group did one of Alan Freed's infrequent West Coast tours and on June 25, 1961, played the Hollywood Bowl in an outdoor extravaganza with Jerry Lee Lewis, Brenda Lee, and Bobby Vee.

In early 1962 three new writers, Hal David, Burt Bacharach, and Barney Williams gave Dixon a hypnotic rock-a-ballad called "I'll Cherish You," which developed into "Baby It's You." It charted at number eight Pop and number three R&B. (The Beatles recorded "Baby It's You" on their debut LP issued two years later.) Despite the group's enormous popularity, TVers like "The Ed Sullivan Show" were off limits to four black girls in 1962 (it would be several years before THE SUPREMES would break that barrier). Still, teen fare was open to them and the group did numerous Dick Clark shows.

In early 1962 Luther Dixon and Florence Greenberg hammered out a quick country-styled tune. It was added to the girls' session at the last minute and was put down in a few takes. The tune was "Soldier Boy," and it became their second number one record.

By now every publisher and writer in town was trying to get a song recorded by the act. Florence passed on two songs they could have had. One was called "The Shoop Shoop Song" (a number six hit for Betty Everett in 1964), and song publisher Aaron Schroeder brought them "He's a Rebel" written by Gene Pitney, which THE CRYSTALS took to number one in 1962.

The Shirelles continued to appear on the charts in 1962 with Luther Dixon productions like "Welcome Home Baby" (#22 Pop, #20 R&B), "Stop the Music" (#36 Pop), and "Everybody Loves a Lover" (#19 Pop, #15 R&B, formerly #6 by Doris Day in 1958), but in 1963 Dixon left to work at Capitol and Florence's favorite, Stan Green, began producing the group. He managed a strong entry, the Helen Miller/Howard Greenfield song "Foolish Little Girl" (#4 Pop, #9 R&B, #38 U.K.), but subsequent releases contained weaker songs. Still, the group remained in demand, recording several songs for the film comedy spectacular *It's a Mad, Mad, Mad, Mad World* and completing their first tour of England with Little Richard and Duane Eddy.

Somehow Shirley found time to become Shirley Owens-Alston, and Doris became Doris Coley Kenner. A relative newcomer helped out by subbing at performances for the newlyweds. At the same time, she was building her own career at Scepter as Dionne Warwick.

In 1983 Dionne had the Shirelles sing backup for her on "Will You *Still* Love Me Tomorrow" (Arista LP).

Sceptor continued to issue Shirelles sides through 1968, but after "Foolish Little Girl" the closest they came to the top 20 out of 23 singles was "Don't Say Goodnight and Mean Goodbye" (#26) in the summer of 1963. One song that had a good shot was "Sha La La" (early 1964), which charted and started to build momentum when Manfred Mann covered it at the beginning of the British invasion and disc jockeys opted to play the foreign version.

Their last chart single was "Last Minute Miracle" (#99 Pop, #41 R&B, August 1967), but there wasn't any. The group was already signed to Mercury's Blue Rock affiliate, recording soul funk like "Don't Mess with Cupid."

In 1968 Doris left the group and they carried on as a trio. In 1969 the girls had three singles as Shirley and the Shirelles for Bell and on November

29th appeared on Richard Nader's first "Rock & Roll Revival" concert at the Felt Forum in New York with THE PENGUINS, Chuck Berry, Bill Haley and the Comets, THE FIVE SATINS, SHEP AND THE LIME-LITES, THE SPANIELS, THE MELLO-KINGS, and Gary U.S. Bonds.

The rock revival had officially begun, and although the Shirelles were still making contemporary records, their eight- or nine-year-old hits made them a part of the nostalgia craze.

In 1970 the group signed to United Artists and came up with a medley of "There Goes My Baby"/"Be My Baby." In the fall of 1971 they signed with their last label, RCA, for four singles and continued touring.

In 1975 Shirley went solo, in a way. She teamed with producer and former Shirelles manager Randy Irwin for a unique concept LP titled *Shirley Alston with a Little Help from Her Friends* (Prodigal Records). The friends were famous doo wop groups who backed Shirley while she sang lead on their biggest hits, e.g., "I Only Have Eyes for You" with the Flamingos, "Where or When" with THE BELMONTS, "Save the Last Dance for Me" alongside the Drifters, and "In the Still of the Night" with the Five Satins. In the meantime Doris returned, and the group continued performing until June 10, 1982, when Mickey Harris died of a heart attack while performing with the group on stage in Atlanta.

Entering the '90s there were at least three different Shirelles groups, each with one original member.

THE SHIRELLES

A SIDE/B SIDE	LABEL/CAT NO	DATE
I Met Him On A Sunday / I Want You To Be My Boyfriend	Tiara 6112	3/58
I Met Him On A Sunday / I Want You To Be My Boyfriend	Decca 30588	3/58
My Love Is A Charm / Slop Time	Decca 30669	6/58
I Got The Message / Stop Me	Decca 30761	1958
Dedicated To The One I Love / Look Here Baby	Scptr 1203	6/59
A Teardrop And A Lollipop / Doin' The Ronde	Scptr 1205	1959
Please Be My Boyfriend / I Saw A Tear	Scptr 1207	1960
Tonight's The Night / The Dance Is Over	Scptr 1208	8/60
Tomorrow / Boys	Scptr 1211	11/60
Will You Love Me Tomorrow / Boys	Scptr 1211	11/60
Dedicated To The One I Love / Look Here Baby	Scptr 1203	1/61
Mama Said / Blue Holiday	Scptr 1217	3/61

A SIDE/B SIDE	LABEL/CAT NO	DATE
A Thing Of The Past / What A Sweet Thing That Was	Scptr 1220	6/61
Big John / Twenty-One	Scptr 1223	9/61
Baby It's You / The Things I Want To Hear	Scptr 1227	11/61
Soldier Boy / Love Is A Swingin' Thing	Scptr 1228	3/62
Welcome Home Baby / Mama, Here Comes The Bride	Scptr 1234	6/62
Stop The Music / It's Love That Really Counts	Scptr 1237	8/62
Everybody Loves A Lover / I Don't Think So	Scptr 1243	11/62
Foolish Little Girl / Not For All The Money In The World	Scptr 1248	3/63
Don't Say Goodnight And Mean Goodbye / I Didn't Mean To Hurt You	Scptr 1296	1/65
What Does A Girl Do / Don't Let It Happen To Us	Scptr 1259	8/63
It's A Mad, Mad, Mad, Mad World / 31 Flavors	Scptr 1260	8/63
Tonight You're Gonna Fall In Love With Me	Scptr 1264	12/63
20th Century Rock 'N' Roll Sha-La-La / His Lips Get In The Way	Scptr 1267	3/64
Thank You Baby / Doomsday	Scptr 1278	7/64
Maybe Tonight / Lost Love	Scptr 1284	9/64
Are You Still My Baby / I Saw A Tear	Scptr 1292	12/64
Shhh, I'm Watching The Movies / Shhh, I'm Watching The Movies	Scptr 1255	5/63
March / Everybody's Goin' Mad	Scptr 12101	5/65
My Heart Belongs To You / Love That Man	Scptr 12114	8/65
Soldier Boy / My Soldier Boy Is Coming Home	Scptr 12123	11/65
I Met Him On A Sunday '66 / Love That Man	Scptr 12132	3/66
Que Sera Sera / Till My Baby Comes Home	Scptr 12150	6/66
Look Away / Shades Of Blue	Scptr 12162	8/66
After Midnight / Shades Of Blue	Scptr 12162	8/66
When The Boys Talk About The Girls / Shades Of Blue	Scptr 12162	9/66
Teasin' Me / Look Away	Scptr 12178	11/66
Don't Go Home / Nobody Baby After You	Scptr 12185	1/67
Too Much Of A Good Thing / Bright Shiny Colors	Scptr 12192	5/67
Last Minute Miracle / No Doubt About It	Scptr 12198	6/67
Wild And Sweet / Wait Till I Give The Signal	Scptr 12209	1/68
Hippie Walk Part 1 / Hippie Walk Part 2	Scptr 12217	3/68
Don't Mess With Cupid / Sweet Sweet Lovin'	Bl Rk 4051	6/68

A SIDE/B SIDE	LABEL/CAT NO	DATE
Call Me / There's A Storm		
Going On In My Heart	Bl Rk 4066	10/68
A Most Unusual Boy* / Look What		
You've Done To My Heart*	Bell 760	1969
Playthings* / Looking Glass*	Bell 787	1969
Go Away And Find Yourself* /		
Never Give Up*	Bell 815	1969
There Goes My Baby / Be My		
Baby / Strange, I Still Love You	UA 50648	3/70
Lost / It's Gonna Take A Miracle	UA 50693	1970
Dedicated To The One I Love	UA 50740	12/70
Strange, I Still Love You /		
No Sugar Tonight	RCA 48-1019	10/71
Brother, Brother /		
Sunday Dreaming	RCA 48-1032	6/72
Let's Give Each Other Love /		
Deep In The Night	RCA 74-0902	1/73
Touch The Wind /		
Do What You've A Mind To	APBO 0192	11/73

* Shirley and the Shirelles

Spanky and Our Gang

A counterpoint to late '60s psychedelic music, Spanky and Our Gang's folk/pop/rock sound was a reinforcement of what THE MAMAS AND THE PAPAS had started earlier. Lead singer Elaine McFarlane of Peoria, Illinois, was a member of an electric jug band, the New Wine Singers, in the early '60s, along with Malcolm Hale of Butte, Montana. Elaine had met Mamas and Papas member Cass Elliott around that time and the two seem to have had much in common musically.

Vacationing in Florida, Elaine met Kenny Hodges of Jacksonville (vocalist and guitarist), Eustace Britchforth a.k.a. Lefty Baker of Roanoke, Virginia (vocalist, guitarist), and Pontiac, Michigan's Nigel Pickering (vocalist and bass player). The foursome began playing clubs like the Mother Blues.

Chicago's Mercury Records got wind of the unusual group that was now calling themselves Spanky and Our Gang (from the famous Little Rascals of the '30s and '40s) and signed them to record. John Seiter, a vocalist-drummer from St. Louis, Missouri, then joined along with "Spanky" McFarlane's guitar-playing vocalist friend Malcolm Hale.

The group was looking for material to record when songwriter Terry Cashman brought in a tune

he and Gene Pistilli had written called "Sunday Will Never Be the Same," a sound tailor-made for the powerful Spanky and her harmony five.

The record climbed *Billboard's* Hot 100 in the spring of 1967 reaching number nine, and the whole country seemed to be singing the Jimmy Wisner-arranged "Sunday."

Spanky's sextet adopted the image of their namesakes, dressing in clothes of the '20s, '30s, and '40s.

Their next single, "Making Every Minute Count," was in keeping with the sunny, good-time feeling of their music and made a respectable showing at number 31. It was more of the same when their harmony-filled George Fischoff/Tony Powers-penned "Lazy Day" rose to number 14 in the fall of 1967. Their "safe" look and sound offered a contrast to the day's psychedelic bands and earned them popularity.

Spanky and company's first LP included the first three singles and an arrangement of "Leavin' on a (Jet Plane)," two years before the Peter, Paul and Mary number one version came out.

By January 1968 "Sunday Morning" had charted and reached number 30, followed by the group's concession to the soft side of psychedelic music, "Like to Get to Know You," with its enchanting harmonies and Spanky's vibrant lead alternating between soft and loud dynamics, culminating in an instrumental blur.

Their second LP was produced by Stu Scharf and Bob Dorough and ranged in content from Leonard Cohen's "Suzanne" to Hoagy Carmichael and Mitchell Parrish's "Stardust." Their light, frivolous period ended with the mid-1968 protest song, "Give a Damn." The powerful performance only reached number 43, held back by the numerous stations that banned it.

During 1968 Malcolm died and the group remained a quintet. The wind was out of the group's sails (and out of their record sales) by late 1968 with the best of their last few singles being "Yesterday's Rain" (#94).

Their last chart record was "And She's Mine" (#97, 1969), followed by Mercury's last single on the group, "Everybody's Talking."

The group separated in 1970 but Spanky and Nigel re-formed the Gang in 1975 with Bill Plummer, Marc McClure, and Jim Moon. Old fan Eddie Wenrich put together a deal with Epic Records that culminated in a terrific country-styled comeback LP featuring "I Won't Brand You" and Gene Clark's "L.A. Freeway."

By 1980 the group had dissolved again. For some reason they weren't thought of as part of the

'60s nostalgia revival and never really worked that circuit. One group that did was the Mamas and Papas, and standing in the place of Mama Cass in 1982 was none other than Spanky McFarlane.

SPANKY AND OUR GANG

A SIDE/B SIDE	LABEL/CAT NO	DATE
Sealed With A Kiss /		
And Your Bird Can Sing	Merc 72598	1967
Sunday Will Never Be The Same /		
Distance	Merc 72679	1967
Making Every Minute Count /		
If You Could Only Be Me	Merc 72714	1967
Lazy Day / Byrd Avenue		
(It Ain't Necessarily)	Merc 72732	1967
Sunday Morning /		
Echoes (Everybody's Talkin')	Merc 72765	1967
Like To Get To Know You /		
Three Ways From Tomorrow	Merc 72795	1968
Give A Damn /		
Swinging Gate	Merc 72831	1968
Yesterday's Rain /		
Without Rhyme Or Reason	Merc 72871	1968
Anything You Choose /		
Mecca Flats Blues	Merc 72890	1969
And She's Mine /		
Leopard Skin Phones	Merc 72926	1969
Everybody's Talkin'	Merc 72982	1969
I Won't Brand You	Epic 50170	1975
L.A. Freeway	Epic 50206	1975

The Sparrows Quartette

The Sparrows Quartette had a "retro" concept. While music was changing rapidly and pressing forward in the early '60s, the Sparrows were trying to go backwards. Their object was to recapture the sound of early '50s rhythm and blues groups such as THE ORIOLES, THE CROWS, and THE RAVENS. Adding to their unusual challenge was the fact that the boys were all white Catholics and Jews.

The concept was the brainchild of R&B record collector Dominick (Dom) D'Elia, a 19-year-old from Jackson Heights, Queens, who spent his spare time in the subway arcade of 42nd Street in Manhattan collecting 45 rpm vinyl at Times Square Records in 1961. Also congregating at TSR were fellow collectors Sam Wood, 18, and James Brady, 19. When the threesome decided to sing some of the obscure songs they were collecting, like "Is It a Dream" by THE VOCALEERS (Red Robin), "My Plea

for Love" by the Starlings (Josie), and "Miss You" by THE CROWS (Rama), it became obvious this was not going to be the next JAY AND THE AMERICANS.

When Dom's brother Billy, 11, joined up, the lineup that practiced in the back room at Times Square Records included Dom (lead), Billy (tenor), James (baritone), and Sam (bass). Another hardcore collector, Bob Freedman (formerly of the Squires on Gee), joined the group as lead tenor. Though there were usually five members, they persisted in calling themselves the Sparrows Quartette (named after the Sparrows on Jay Dee).

When not at Times, the singing collectors practiced at a park on Broadway in Jackson Heights and recorded their first tape at Dom's house in 1962. Dom then hooked up with drummer Spence Wooten and a few other musicians and recorded the group in Spence's basement, issuing their first single, "Merry Christmas Baby," on his own Broadcast label in 1963.

In 1965, Sal Mondrone replaced Brady. In that same year Dom formed the Jet Records label and put out the first of three Sparrows Quartette singles, "Deep in My Heart," which was also the group's first a cappella release. Sal sang lead on the Jet sides while Dom was the predominant lead on the Broadcast sides.

The group disbanded in 1969 and then reformed in 1971 and recorded their first Jet LP, titled *Sparrows Quartette Rehearsal Session*. Released in 1974, it featured some old-sounding covers of "Most of All" and "Just a Lonely Christmas" (both by THE MOONGLOWS) and "Close Your Eyes" (THE FIVE KEYS).

The group's trademark baritone/bass lead applied to extremely slow ballads made for many unusual records. Their recordings were so slow that you could play an LP at 45 rpm and it sounded like a normal tenor group doing a slow ballad.

Their first single in eight years was "I Love You So Much I Could Die," followed in 1974 by "We Sing for Fun." Both were a cappella. That year the group moonlighted on the Blue Sky label as Mel Dark and the Giants doing "Darling," another super slow ballad.

In 1975 they released the LPs *Rehearsal Session, Volume II* and *Volume III* and cut their last Jet single, "The Christmas Song."

In 1974 Freedman moved to Chicago and the group disbanded, having fulfilled their musical objectives.

In 1976 the Sharks Quintette was formed with Dom and Billy of the Sparrows, Dino DeAngelo (Dino and the Heartspinners), Buzzy Garland (the Five Sharks), and John Monforte (the Gold Bugs,

Coral). They recorded three singles in the Sparrows Quartette mold for Broadcast: "For Sentimental Reasons," "I'll Be Home," and "The Glory of Love."

In 1983 Sal, Dom, Billy, and Bob (who was in New York for a short time) reunited for the last time to sing at a UGHA (United in Group Harmony) show in Clifton, New Jersey.

Sal became a New York City bus driver, Sam an insurance salesman in Queens, and Dom an employee of the Transit Authority.

A number of vocal groups starting in the '80s, like the Blue Stars (Arcade) and the Blend-Aires (Story Untold), were influenced by the Sparrows Quartette. In their small way they helped to keep diversity in group singing.

THE SPARROWS QUARTETTE

A SIDE/B SIDE	LABEL/CAT NO	DATE
Merry Christmas Baby	Broadcast	1963
Deep In My Heart / Love My Baby	Jet 3000	1965
I Love You So Much I Could Die / Please Come Back To Me	Dltn 3001	1973
We Sing For Fun / The Christmas Song	Jet 3021	1974
Darling*	Blue Sky 108	1974
The Christmas Song / He Is My Friend	Jet 3020	1975

* as Mel Dark and the Giants

The Spinners

The Spinners, an excellent harmony quintet, were out of Detroit and formed in the late '50s. The members, all from Ferndale High School, were Bobbie Smith (tenor), George Dixon (tenor), Billy Henderson (tenor), Henry Fambrough (baritone), and Pervis Jackson (bass). They originally called themselves the Domingoes and were discovered by legendary writer/producer Harvey Fuqua, the second lead of THE MOONGLOWS.

Harvey took the youngsters and molded them into his concept of a soulful HI-LO'S-styled group in 1961. He then eased them into the marketplace by singing lead himself on his own Tri-Phi label with a song he and his wife Gwen Gordy (Berry Gordy's sister) wrote, titled "That's What Girls Are Made For." A Moonglows-styled ballad with mandolin accompaniment (rare for an R&B record), it rose to number five R&B and number 27 Pop by mid-summer of 1961.

In the fall they followed with the soulful "Love (I'm So Glad) I Found You."

In November 1961 it charted on *Billboard*'s Top 100 at number 91 with Harvey again on lead. Bobby Smith then took over the featured spot on four more Tri-Phi 45s between 1961 and 1962, each a superb example of soul doo wop.

George Dixon became the first to leave, and Edgar Edwards replaced him.

Fuqua soon linked his operation in with that of brother-in-law Berry Gordy and brought the Spinners along, but the group didn't record for Motown until 1964, when Harvey produced the rhythm ballad "How Can I." They followed up with "I'll Always Love You" (#35 Pop, #8 R&B), produced and written by Ivory Joe Hunter and Mickey Stevenson. "Truly Yours" followed in 1966 and reached number 16 R&B and number 111 Pop. In 1967 Edwards left and G. C. Cameron took over lead vocals.

In 1969 the group was moved to Motown's V.I.P. label with Johnny Bristol producing, and their initial single there was a tribute to the Moonglows with Smith doing his best Bobby Lester impression on "In My Diary."

Two singles later Stevie Wonder took over production and brought the group back to the charts with "It's a Shame" (#14 Pop, #4 R&B, #20 U.K.), their biggest record to date. But since they had been relegated to V.I.P. and weren't getting the top star treatment, the group was motivated to look elsewhere. Still, their next Wonder-produced 45, "We'll Have It Made," charted in early 1971 (#89 Pop, #20 R&B).

By now the group was known in England as the Motown Spinners to avoid confusion with a longtime Liverpool folk group also known as the Spinners.

Avco Embassy and Stax, among others, were interested in the quintet, but longtime friend Aretha Franklin encouraged them to sign with Atlantic, the label she recorded for.

G. C. Cameron decided to stay with Motown as a solo act, and Phillipe Wynne took over the lead chores.

Thom Bell, producer of THE DELFONICS and THE STYLISTICS, began producing the group and turning out a string of commercial hits: "I'll Be Around" (#3 Pop, #1 R&B, 1972, issued as the B side of their first Atlantic single "How Could I Let You Get Away" but preferred by deejays), "Could It Be I'm Falling in Love" (#4 Pop, #1 R&B, #11 U.K., 1972), "One of a Kind (Love Affair)" (#11 Pop, #1 R&B, 1973), "Ghetto Child" (#29 Pop, #4 R&B, #7 U.K., 1973), "Mighty Love, Part I" (#20 Pop, #1 R&B, 1974), and "I'm Comin' Home" (#18 Pop, #3 R&B, 1974).

By now their records were being issued in England under the name the Detroit Spinners.

In 1974 the group was the opening act for Dionne Warwick on a summer tour. Bell suggested they duet with her, and the result was "Then Came You," their only Pop number one record.

More hits followed, like "Love Don't Love Nobody" (#15 Pop, #4 R&B, 1974) and "They Just Can't Stop It (The Games People Play)" (#5 Pop, #1 R&B, 1975), as well as the catchy dance tune, "Rubberband Man" (#2 Pop, #1 R&B, #16 U.K., 1976).

In 1977 Phillipe Wynne decided to pursue a solo career, and John Edwards was chosen to help perpetuate the Spinners tradition.

In 1979 Michael Zager (formerly with Genya Ravan in Ten Wheel Drive, Polydor) took over production for the group and came up with an unusual formula for a medley and a hit. He strung together a past hit, "Working My Way Back to You" (THE FOUR SEASONS) with an original song titled "Forgive Me Girl." The combination worked; "Working" hit number six R&B and number two Pop and became their biggest hit in England at number one in early 1980. It also became their seventh and last million-selling single.

The group continued to turn out quality chart singles and LPs though the mid-'80s with their last hit being "Right or Wrong" (#104 Pop, #22 R&B) in 1984.

Four months after it charted (July 14, 1984), former lead Phillipe Wynne died.

In May 1988 the Spinners joined numerous Atlantic acts for that label's 40th anniversary show at Madison Square Garden in New York.

There's little doubt that the Spinners will be hitting the charts in their fourth decade and adding to their 38 R&B and 29 Pop chart hits in the '90s.

THE SPINNERS

A SIDE/B SIDE	LABEL/CAT NO	DATE
That's What Girls Are Made For /		
Heebie Jeebies	Tri 1001	1961
Love / Sudbuster	Tri 1004	1961
What Did She Use /		
Itching For My Baby, But I Don't		
Know Where To Scratch	Tri 1007	1/62
She Loves Me So /		
Whistling About You	Tri 1010	1962
I've Been Hurt /		
I Got Your Water Boiling Baby	Tri 1013	1962
She Don't Love Me* /		
Too Young, Too Much, Too Soon*	Tri 1018	1962
Sweet Thing / How Can I	Mtwn 1067	1964

A SIDE/B SIDE	LABEL/CAT NO	DATE
I'll Always Love You /		
Tomorrow May Never Come	Mtwn 1078	1965
Truly Yours / Where Is That Girl	Mtwn 1093	1966
For All We Know /		
I Cross My Heart	Mtwn 1109	1967
Bad Bad Weather / I Just Can't		
Help But Feel The Pain	Mtwn 1136	1968
At Sundown / In My Diary	V.I.P. 25050	1969
At Sundown /		
Message From A Black Man	V.I.P. 25054	1970
It's A Shame / Together We Can		
Make Such Sweet Music	V.I.P. 25057	1970
We'll Have It Made /		
My Whole World Ended	V.I.P. 25060	1960
I'll Be Around /		
How Could I Let You Get Away	Atln 2904	7/72
Could It Be I'm Falling In Love /		
Just You And Me Baby	Atln 2927	12/72
One Of A Kind / Don't Let		
The Green Grass Fool You	Atln 2962	4/73
Together We Can Make		
Such Sweet Music /		
Bad, Bad Weather	Mtwn 1235	3/73
Ghetto Child / We Belong Together	Atln 2973	7/73
Mighty Love Part 1 /		
Mighty Love Part 2	Atln 3006	12/73
I'm Coming Home /		
He'll Never Love You Like I Do	Atln 3027	4/74
Then Came You** /		
Just As Long As We Have Love**	Atln 3029	6/74
Then Came You** /		
Just As Long As We Have Love**	Atln 3202	7/74
Love Don't Love Nobody Part 1 /		
Love Don't Love Nobody Part 2	Atln 3206	8/74
Living A Little, Laughing A Little /		
Smile, We Have Each Other	Atln 3252	2/75
Sadie / Lazy Susan	Atln 3268	4/75
They Just Can't Stop It /		
I Don't Want To Lose You	Atln 3284	7/75
Love Or Leave /		
You Made A Promise To Me	Atln 3309	12/75
Wake Up Susan /		
If You Can't Be In Love	Atln 3341	6/76
The Rubberband Man /		
Now That We're Together	Atln 3355	8/76
You're Throwing A Good Love		
Away / You're All I Need	Atln 3382	2/77
Me and My Music /		
I'm Riding Your Shadow	Atln 3400	5/77
Heaven On Earth /		
I'm Tired Of Giving	Atln 3425	8/77
Easy Come, Easy Go /		
One Step Away	Atln 3462	1/78
If You Wanna Do /		
Once In A Life Proposal	Atln 3493	6/78
Are You Ready For Love /		
Once You Fall In Love	Atln 3546	2/79
I Love The Music	Atln 3590	1979
Body Language / With My Eyes	Atln 3619	9/79
Working My Way Back / Disco Ride	Atln 3637	11/79

A SIDE/B SIDE	LABEL/CAT NO	DATE
Medley: Cupid / Pipedream / I've Loved You For A Long Time	Atln 3664	5/80
Now That You're Mine / Love Trippin'	Atln 3757	8/80
I Just Want To Fall In Love / Heavy On The Sunshine	Atln 3765	10/80
Medley: Yesterday Once More / Nothing Remains / Be My Love	Atln 3798	1/81
Working My Way Back To You / Cupid (medley)	Atln 13220	3/81
Long Live Soul Music / Give Your Lady What She Wants	Atln 3814	4/81
The Winter Of Our Love / The Deacon	Atln 3827	6/81
You Go Your Way / Got To Be Love	Atln 3865	9/81
Love Connection / Love Is Such A Crazy Feeling	Atln 3882	11/81
Never Thought I'd Fall In Love / Send A Little Love	Atln 4007	1/82
Funny How Time Slips Away / I'm Calling You Now	Atln 89922	11/82
Magic Is In The Moonlight / So Far Away	Atln 89962	9/82
I'm Coming Home / He'll Never Love You Like I Do	Atln 13171·	12/82
City Full Of Memories / No Other Love	Atln 89862	3/83
Our Time For Love / All Your Love	Atln 89648	6/84
Right On Wrong / Lover Is In Season	Atln 89689	3/84
Love Don't Love Nobody Part 1 / Part 2	Atln 84982	9/85
Put Us Together Again / Show Me Your Magic	Atln 99604	9/85
She Does / The Witness	Atln 99580	11/85

* The Spinners and Bobby Smith
** Dionne Warwick and the Spinners

The Starlets

In baseball terms you could say the Starlets batted .500. They had one hit under their own name and one hit under someone else's. The latter helped launch the career of one of rock's best girl groups, PATTI LABELLE AND THE BLUE BELLES.

Chicago resident Jane Hall joined forces with Maxine Edwards (both girls worked in a pecan processing plant), Mickey McKinney, and Jeanette Miles in early 1961. Hall rehearsed the quartet and took them to Bernice Williams, a local songwriter who had been writing for Gene Chandler's Dukays (Vee-Jay). (One of the Dukays, Earl Edwards, was Maxine's brother.) Williams felt the group needed beefing up and added Liz Walker (sometimes

known as Dynetta Boone). Bernice wrote a song called "Better Tell Him No," and with Maxine on lead the quintet of teens (the girls were all 18 and 19 years old) recorded it for the local Pam label (owned by Bill Sheppard and Carl Davis) on Chicago's South Side.

On April 24, 1961, the girls were startled to see that their little record had entered *Billboard*'s Pop charts and was steadily rising, finally peaking at number 38. It lasted two weeks on the R&B list, reaching number 24.

The group began touring with the likes of Jackie Wilson, THE SPINNERS, GLADYS KNIGHT AND THE PIPS, and Mary Wells.

In August Pam issued their second single "My Last Cry" but it went nowhere.

The following April the group pulled into Philadelphia for an appearance. A fast-talking car salesman named Harold Robinson convinced the Starlets to come to his studio and cut a couple of sides for him. His studio was right on the car lot, and the smooth talker used local producer Phil Terry (later of THE INTRUDERS) to record the oldie "I Sold My Heart to the Junkman" in an exciting up-tempo version with Maxine on lead. Since the group wasn't doing much with Pam they figured they had nothing to lose. Several weeks later "Junkman" was all over the radio, but the label read "The Blue-Belles." It soared to number 15 in 1962 and to number 13 R&B. The girls then sued Harold Robinson, and so did Phil Terry. According to one article, Robinson claimed he used the Blue-Belles in the background, wiping off the Starlets' vocals, though it did come out that Maxine was the lead voice. Terry disagreed, stating that all the voices were the Starlets. Apparently the girls won out, and each received about $5,000.

Carl Davis moved to Okeh Records in the A&R department and did one more single with the girls that read Dynetta and the Starlets ("You Belong to Me") and had Liz Walker on lead. Released in the summer of 1962 it quickly disappeared. The group was dropped soon after, but seemingly as punishment for the "Junkman" situation, they were told they couldn't record anywhere else as a group. The bluff worked and the girls broke up.

The Supremes

The most successful female group of all time, the legendary Supremes started out as a quartet known as the Primettes. In 1959, two 15-year-olds, Florence Ballard of Northwestern High School and

Mary Wilson of Northeastern High School, met at a talent show. Mary sang Frankie Lymon songs like "I'm Not a Juvenile Delinquent" while Flo belted out "Ave Maria." Local manager Milton Jenkins, who had a doo wop group called the Primes (see THE TEMPTATIONS), wanted a sister group to accompany the Primes for stage performances, and he asked Flo to put together such an act. She remembered Mary. The two of them then brought in 16-year-old Betty Travis while Primes member Paul Williams recommended a 15-year-old from Detroit's Brewster Housing project, Diane Ross of Cass Technical High School. Jenkins christened them the Primettes after Diane was given permission by her parents to join, and the quartet started doing club dates.

Travis was yanked from the Primettes by her parents, who wanted her to pay more attention to her studies. Then Barbara Martin joined, only to exit shortly after—along with Florence—under the same parental conditions. Mary and Diane worked as a duo until Florence and Barbara improved their grades and rejoined.

The group's influences ranged from THE MCGUIRE SISTERS to FRANKIE LYMON AND THE TEEN-AGERS, and unlike most black groups of the day, they were not largely influenced by gospel music.

Florence, Mary, and Diane could all sing lead; Florence's voice was considered the best and most powerful.

In 1960 they met Diane's neighbor William "Smokey" Robinson and auditioned for him in the basement of the home of his girlfriend Claudette Rogers (later his wife and an original member of THE MIRACLES) in hopes of getting to Motown's Berry Gordy, Jr. That audition turned into a dead end for the group, but they managed to try out for Gordy later on, singing THE DRIFTERS' "There Goes My Baby." He told them to return when they finished high school.

Undaunted, the foursome began camping out in Motown's Grand Boulevard office reception room, but no one took any special notice. They continued doing local talent shows and were spotted by Richard Morris, who brought them to Lupine owner/producer Bob West. Bob recorded two sides on the Primettes, "Pretty Baby" with Mary on lead and "Tears of Sorrow" featuring Diane. Released in 1960, the Lupine single went nowhere, and soon the girls were hanging around Motown again, doing occasional hand claps on Marvin Gaye's early sides and singing some backups for blues artist Mabel John.

In January 1961 Gordy finally signed the quartet but required they change their name. The girl who formed the group, Florence, was also the one to name it the Supremes, which Mary and Diane initially disliked, but Gordy approved. By now, Diane had upscaled herself to Diana, which was what her birth certificate incorrectly read.

Their first single, issued on Tamla in April 1961, was the undistinguished "I Want a Guy," and the second was an R&B dance tune called "Buttered Popcorn" with Florence on lead. Both releases failed.

Their next three sides barely touched the bottom of the Hot 100. In fact, by the middle of 1962 the Supremes were doing so badly Diana took a job in the cafeteria of Hudson's Department Store in Detroit and later in the year Barbara left to get married, leaving the group a trio.

In the fall of 1963 came the best of their early releases, "When the Lovelight Starts Shining," (#23) but by the spring of 1964 the "no-hit Supremes," as they were called by their hit-making stablemates, had seen eight of their Tamla/Motown singles come and go without a single one making it to the top 20.

It took a Marvelettes reject to jumpstart the Supremes' career. Holland, Dozier, and Holland brought their new song "Where Did Our Love Go" to the Supremes after Gladys Horton, the Marvelettes lead, rejected it with the comment that she "wouldn't sing that junk." Gladys told Diana she passed on it, which may explain why the Supremes didn't even like the recording when it was finished on April 8, 1964.

Nonetheless, by August "Where Did Our Love Go" was at number one Pop and R&B, number three in the U.K., and number 19 in Australia. In a matter of weeks the group went from no billing on a Dick Clark Caravan of Stars show (which included THE SHIRELLES and Gene Pitney) to top billing.

Diana was now doing all the lead vocals, which did not always sit well with Florence.

More Holland/Dozier/Holland magic followed. "Baby Love," issued in September 1964, also went to number one Pop, R&B, and in the U.K. and to number 38 in Australia. With "Baby Love," the Supremes became the first all-girl group to reach number one in England.

"Come See about Me," released in October, also reached number one, and the Supremes became the first American group to have three number ones from the same LP.

With "Stop! In the Name of Love," the Supremes became the first group to have four number ones in a row on the *Billboard* Hot 100. The song also rose to number two R&B and number seven in England, where the girls spent the "Stop" chart run thrilling the British fans on the historic Motown Revue tour through Europe. The group developed their now-familiar hand motions (resembling a traffic cop stopping oncoming cars) for "Stop! In the Name of Love" in the men's room of a London TV studio with the help of Berry Gordy and the Temptations' Paul Williams and Melvin Franklin prior to a live appearance.

On June 12, 1965, "Back in My Arms Again" became the girls' fifth million-selling single, their fifth number one, and the fifth mega-hit in a row from the pens of Holland, Dozier, and Holland.

The Supremes were not only competing head-on with the British invasion, they were accomplishing the greater feat of gaining superstar status in the realm of the pop establishment. The groundswell picked up strength when they appeared as head-liners at New York's famed Copacabana nightclub on July 29, 1965.

That same month, "Nothing But Heartaches" was issued and broke the string of number ones, reaching only number 11 Pop (#6 R&B). But it was a short-lived decline; "I Hear a Symphony" reached number one on November 20th.

"My World Is Empty Without You" (#5) and "Love Is Like an Itching in My Heart" (#9) kept the hot Supremes in the top 10 in early 1966. Then they returned to number one with "You Can't Hurry Love" (#1 Pop, #3 U.K., September 10, 1966).

A new string of number ones started. The hard-edged side of the Supremes surfaced with one of their best records, "You Keep Me Hangin' On" (#1 Pop, #8 U.K., November 19, 1966), followed by "Love Is Here and Now You're Gone" (#1 Pop, #17 U.K., March 11, 1967) and "The Happening" (#1 Pop, #6 U.K., May 13, 1967).

"The Happening" was the last of 10 chart toppers produced and written by Holland/Dozier/Holland for the trio. They left Motown to form their own labels, called Hot Wax and Invictus.

By that time the friction between Ballard and Ross had taken its toll on Florence and she missed two shows in New Orleans and Montreal. During July, part way through their performance stay at the Flamingo Hotel in Las Vegas, Florence was fired by Gordy and replaced by Cindy Birdsong of the Blue-Belles.

With Ballard gone, Gordy took the opportunity to rename the trio Diana Ross and the Supremes. Though Diana was gaining stature on her way to a solo career, the new lineup was not nearly as popular saleswise as the old. Over the next two years Motown issued 12 singles and only one, the powerful message song "Love Child," hit number one (November 30, 1968).

Their first two singles as the new trio, "Reflections" (#2) and "In and Out of Love" (#9), were carryovers from the H/D/H days.

The group did several good remakes with the Temptations, including "I'm Gonna Make You Love Me" (#2, originally by Madeline Bell), "I'll Try Something New" (#25, the Miracles), and "The Weight" (#46, the Band).

Their final record together provided for a series of lasts. "Someday We'll Be Together," issued in October 1969, became the last of the group's 12 number one records (#13 U.K.), on December 27, 1969, which also made it the last number one of the turbulent '60s. It was the trio's last single together, and they performed it in the last of 20 appearances on Ed Sullivan's show. Additionally, it was the last song they sang together when they appeared at the Frontier Hotel in Las Vegas on January 14, 1970. Then, on stage, Diana dramatically introduced her replacement, Jean Terrell (the sister of boxer Ernie Terrell), and an era was over.

The song that pulled together all these elements was not, as many believe, written to be Diana's swan song as a Supreme. It was written and recorded in 1960 by Johnny Bristol, Jackie Beavers, and Harvey Fuqua. Johnny and Jackie sang it and Harvey produced it on his Tri Phi label, which was bought out by Gordy with Bristol coming over as a writer.

In the late '60s Bristol dug out a tape copy and showed it to Gordy, who immediately recognized its possibilities for the Supremes. Ironically, it was not the Supremes who sang it on the hit record. If the label had been accurate it would have read "Diana Ross and the Waters." Julia and Maxine Waters, two pro backup vocalists, recorded it with the added depth of Johnny Bristol's male tones.

To keep pace with their singles popularity over the years, Motown recorded the Supremes on a series of concept LPs. Some of the many were *A Bit of Liverpool* (featuring recordings of British bands' songs); *The Supremes Sing Country, Western and Pop*; *We Remember Sam Cooke*; *The Supremes at The Copa*; *The Supremes A-Go-Go*; *The Supremes Sing Disney*; *The Supremes Sing Motown*; and *The Supremes Sing Rodgers and Hart*.

On March 7, 1970, the Jean Terrell-led Supremes hit the *Billboard* charts with "Up the Ladder to the Roof" (#10) and proved the name still had power even without Diana Ross. In fact, their *Right On* LP with Terrell did better (#25) than the double live farewell LP with Ross (#46).

Their third single as the new Supremes, the Frank Wilson-produced "Stoned Love," was a million seller in 1970, and the number seven Pop hit became the eighth number one R&B charter under the Supremes' name.

The group did two LPs with the Four Tops in the early '70s and hit with a remake of the Ike and Tina Turner 1966 single "River Deep, Mountain High" (#14 Pop, #7 R&B, #11 U.K.).

In June 1972 Cindy Birdsong left for home and family and was replaced by Lynda Lawrence.

A succession of replacements for Lawrence included Sherrie Payne (Freda's sister), Cindy again, and Susaye Greene.

In December 1976 Mary Wilson, who'd been there from the beginning, left and was replaced by Karen Jackson.

Their last Pop chart single was "You're My Driving Wheel" (#85, 1976), and the group soon disbanded.

Florence Ballard, after leaving the group in 1967, did two singles for ABC and then spent several years fighting Motown in a lawsuit over her dismissal. She lost the suit and spent some time on welfare while trying to support her three children. On February 21, 1976, an overweight and despondent Florence Ballard died of a heart attack at the Mount Carmel Mercy Hospital in Detroit at the age of 32.

In complete contrast, the driving, aggressive Diana Ross realized her every dream and then some as a superstar performer and actress of the '70s and '80s. Her 41 Hot 100 hits included "Ain't No Mountain High Enough" (#1, 1970), Michael Masser's "Touch Me in the Morning" (#1, 1973), "Do You Know Where You're Going To" (theme from the film *Mahogany*, which she starred in), "Love Hangover" (#1, 1976), "Upside Down" (#1, 1980), "It's My Turn" (#9, 1980), "Endless Love" (#1, 1981), and Frankie Lymon's "Why Do Fools Fall in Love" (#7, 1981). Her movie career included roles in *Lady Sings the Blues* and *The Wiz.*

Mary Wilson later went on to form her own group called Mary Wilson and the Supremes, with Karen Jackson and Karen Ragland. She lost her right to use the name sometime after.

In May 1983, she, Diana, and Cindy reunited for Motown's 25th Anniversary TV show.

In 1984 Mary wrote her story, titled *Dream Girl: My Life as a Supreme.*

In 1988 the group was inducted into the Rock and Roll Hall of Fame.

The number one female group scored 18 Hot 100 hits as the Supremes, nine as Diana Ross and the Supremes, three as Diana Ross and the Supremes and Temptations, 12 as the Supremes (after Diana), and two as the Supremes and the Four Tops (also after Diana). Obviously, the whole was always greater than its parts to their fans, and the group sounded as top-notch at the end as they did when the hits started.

THE SUPREMES

A SIDE/B SIDE	LABEL/CAT NO	DATE
The Primettes		
Tears Of Sorrow /		
Pretty Baby	Lupine 120	1960
The Supremes		
I Want A Guy /		
Never Again	Tamla 54038	4/61
Buttered Popcorn /		
Who's Loving You	Tamla 54045	7/61
Your Heart Belongs To Me /		
(He's) Seventeen	Mtwn 1027	5/62
Let Me Go The Right Way /		
Time Changes Things	Mtwn 1034	11/62
My Heart Can't Take It No More /		
You Bring Back Memories	Mtwn 1040	3/63
A Breathtaking, First Sight, Soul Shaking, One Night Love Making, Next Day Heart Breaking Guy /		
(The Man With The) Rock And Roll Banjo Band	Mtwn 1044	6/63
A Breath Taking Guy /		
(The Man With The) Rock And Roll Banjo Band	Mtwn 1044	6/63
When The Lovelight Starts Shining Through His Eyes / Standing At The Crossroads Of Love	Mtwn 1051	11/63
Run, Run, Run /		
I'm Giving You Your Freedom	Mtwn 1054	2/64
Where Did Our Love Go /		
He Means The World To Me	Mtwn 1060	6/64
Baby Love / Ask Any Girl	Mtwn 1066	9/64
Come See About Me /		
Always In My Heart	Mtwn 1068	10/64
Stop! In The Name Of Love /		
I'm In Love Again	Mtwn 1074	2/65
Back In My Arms Again /		
Whisper You Love Me Baby	Mtwn 1075	4/65
Nothing But Heartaches /		
He Holds His Own	Mtwn 1080	7/65
I Hear A Symphony /		
Who Could Ever Doubt My Love	Mtwn 1083	10/65
Children's Christmas Song /		
Twinkle Twinkle Little Me	Mtwn 1085	12/65
My World Is Empty Without You /		
Everything Is Good About You	Mtwn 1089	12/65
Mother You, Smother You /		
Mother You, Smother You	Mtwn 294M05	1966
Love Is Like An Itching In My Heart / He's All I Got	Mtwn 1094	4/66
You Can't Hurry Love /		
Put Yourself In My Place	Mtwn 1097	7/66

A SIDE/B SIDE	LABEL/CAT NO	DATE
You Keep Me Hangin' On /		
Remove This Doubt	Mtwn 1101	10/67
Love Is Here And Now		
You're Gone / There's No		
Stopping Us Now	Mtwn 1103	1/67
The Happening /		
All I Know About You	Mtwn 1107	3/67

Diana Ross and the Supremes

Reflections /		
Going For The Third Time	Mtwn 1111	7/67
In And Out Of Love /		
I Guess I'll Always Love You	Mtwn 1116	10/67
Forever Came Today /		
Time Changes Things	Mtwn 1122	3/68
Some Things You Never		
Get Used To / You've Been		
So Wonderful To Me	Mtwn 1126	5/68
Love Child / Will This Be The Day	Mtwn 1135	9/68
I'm Gonna Make You Love Me* /		
A Place In The Sun*	Mtwn 1137	11/68
I'm Livin' In Shame / I'm So Glad		
I Got Somebody Like You Around	Mtwn 1139	1/69
I'll Try Something New* / The Way		
You Do The Things You Do*	Mtwn 1142	2/69
The Composer /		
The Beginning Of The End	Mtwn 1146	3/69
No Matter What Sign You Are /		
The Young Folks	Mtwn 1148	5/69
Stubborn Kind Of Fellow* /		
Try It Baby*	Mtwn 1150	8/69
The Weight* / For Better Or Worse	Mtwn 1153	9/69
Someday We'll Be Together /		
He's My Sunny Boy	Mtwn 1156	10/69

The Supremes

Up The Ladder To The Roof /		
Bill, When Are You Coming Back	Mtwn 1162	2/70
Everybody's Got The Right To		
Love / But I Love You More	Mtwn 1167	7/70
Stoned Love / Shine On Me	Mtwn 1172	10/70
River Deep, Mountain High** /		
Together We Can Make		
Such Sweet Music**	Mtwn 1173	11/70
Nathan Jones /		
Happy Is A Bumpy Road	Mtwn 1182	4/71
You Gotta Have Love In Your		
Heart** / I'm Glad About It	Mtwn 1181	5/71
Touch / It's So Hard For		
Me To Say Good-Bye	Mtwn 1190	9/71
Floy Joy / This Is The Story	Mtwn 1195	12/71
Automatically Sunshine /		
Precious Little Things	Mtwn 1200	4/72
Your Wonderful, Sweet Sweet		
Love / The Wisdom Of Time	Mtwn 1206	7/72
I Guess I'll Miss The Man /		
Over And Over	Mtwn 1213	10/72
Bad Weather / Oh Be My Love	Mtwn 1223	5/73
He's My Man /		
Give Out, But Don't Give Up	Mtwn 1358	7/75

A SIDE/B SIDE	LABEL/CAT NO	DATE
Where Do I Go From Here /		
Give Out But Don't Give Up	Mtwn 1374	10/75
I'm Gonna Let My Heart Do The		
Walking / Early Morning Love	Mtwn 1391	5/76
You're My Driving Wheel /		
You're What's Missing In My Life	Mtwn 1407	10/76
Let Yourself Go /		
You Are The Heart Of Me	Mtwn 1415	2/77
Medley Of Hits /		
Where Did We Go Wrong	Mtwn 1488	6/80

* with the Temptations
** with the Four Tops

The Sweet Inspirations

The Sweet Inspirations took up where THE JOR-DANAIRES left off as backup singers for Elvis Presley, but that was by no means their only accomplishment. They grew out of what would become an all-star team's worth of celebrity singers that began as the Drinkard Sisters. The Drinkards were a gospel group spawned by the chorus of the New Hope Baptist Church in Newark, New Jersey. It included Marie Dionne Warwick, sister Dede Warwick, Emily "Cissy" Houston (their aunt), Judy Guions (later Judy Clay), and her sister Sylvia Guions (also called Sylvia Shemwell).

The group sang gospel music in the '50s and recorded for RCA. The Warwick sisters (who were influenced by gospel-great professor Alex Bradford) and Aunt Cissy also sang as the Gospelaires along with friend Doris Troy ("Just One Look," #10, 1963). By the early '60s the Gospelaires were moonlighting to earn some money by doing recording sessions. Soon, Cissy teamed with Sylvia, Estelle Brown, and Myrna Smith to specialize in backups for Atlantic while Dionne and Dede worked more for Scepter (where Dionne established herself as a major star).

Jerry Wexler of Atlantic used the girls' expertise to enhance the recordings of everyone from Aretha Franklin to Wilson Pickett, and he fondly named them the Sweet Inspirations. No less than Aretha herself once called them the finest vocal group in the country.

They continued to back such artists as Dusty Springfield, Don Covay, Neil Diamond, and Solomon Burke until 1967, when Wexler decided to put them out front with Cissy doing lead. The first chart single for the four girls was "Why Am I Treated So Bad," which charted Pop on June 3, 1967, and R&B on June 17th, eventually reaching number 57 and number 36, respectively.

Their biggest hit came in the spring of 1968 when the Sweet Inspirations reached number five R&B and number 18 Pop with "Sweet Inspiration."

In 1968 Elvis began his comeback and the Sweet Inspirations were picked to tour with him. They even sang with the King in his Las Vegas shows. They also appeared on their own in settings as varied as New York's Apollo and a party in Portugal for Bolivian millionaire Antenor Patino.

Although they created some quality recordings like "Walk in My Shoes" and "Unchained Melody" (#73 Pop, #41 R&B, 1968), the Inspirations never attained chart success under their own power. They did sing behind others on such major hits as Aretha Franklin's "Chain of Fools" (#2, 1967) and "Storybook Children" (#54 Pop, #20 R&B, 1967) for ex-Drinkards member Judy Clay with Billy Vera.

In 1970, Cissy (mother of renowned vocalist Whitney Houston) toured with Darlene Love and Dede Warwick behind Dionne and then went solo, charting R&B five times between 1970 and 1978, with her biggest record reaching number 31 R&B and number 92 Pop ("Be My Baby," Janus, 1971). Myrna, Estelle, and Sylvia continued on as backup vocalists through the '70s.

The Tams

Out of the ghettos of Atlanta rose the Tams, and their perseverance should serve as a model for all vocal groups. Formed while in high school in the late '40s, the group included five friends, Joe and Charlie Pope, Floyd Ashton, Bob Smith, and Horace Key. Their level of poverty was so great that they couldn't even afford the kind of matching outfits that were required of vocal ensembles at the time. They began performing in local clubs, with their only concession to dress conformity being a set of inexpensive multicolored hats known as Tam-o-Shanters. Thus the inspiration for their name.

The group perfected their harmony and kept working local gigs, since that seemed to be the only way out of the treadmill of ghetto life. They performed for over a decade before their first record opportunity.

That came in 1960, yielding one single for Philadelphia's Swan Records titled "Sorry." The record passed unnoticed, and it was two more years before they walked into Atlanta's Lowery Music. Bill

Lowery liked the act and Joe South, a Lowery employee, became their producer.

By the fall of 1962 the Tams' first single, "Untie Me," came out on Harry Finfer's Arlen label (Harry later wound up a partner in the Delite label, home of Kool and the Gang), and by October 20, 1962, it had charted both R&B and Pop, leveling off at number 12 and number 60, respectively.

The Tams finally had a chance to make some money and began the Southern tour circuit while Arlen issued three more singles that brought them back to earth. Lowery and South didn't give up on the boys, however, and in late 1963 a deal was struck for them with ABC-Paramount. At that time Floyd left, opening a slot for the group's only replacement, Albert Cottle, Jr.

The first of an eventual 19 ABC singles, "What Kind of Fool" reached number nine on February 22, 1964 (Billboard had no R&B chart in 1964, but "Fool" would undoubtedly have done well had there been one). "You Lied to Your Daddy" followed (#70), and by the summer they'd registered their second biggest and their catchiest charter, "Hey Girl, Don't Bother Me" (#41).

All told, the quintet had seven chart records, their last being "Be Young, Be Foolish, Be Happy" (#26, 1968, and #32 in the U.K. in 1970).

The unexpected reissue of "Hey Girl" in England seven years after it had been a hit in the U.S. gave the Tams a number one hit there in the summer of 1971 and another market in which to earn a living.

In 1973 the group left ABC for Lowery's own MGM South, doing a remake of the Hollywood Argyles' "Alley Oop."

In the early '90s they were still performing in the South and doing occasional local label releases.

The Temptations

One of the most enduring and popular of all vocal groups, the Temptations were the end result of the merging of two groups in 1960. Edward James Kendricks and Paul Williams formed a high school group in Birmingham, Alabama, called the Cavaliers with Cal Osborne and Wiley Waller. After graduating school they moved to Cleveland and met manager Milton Jenkins, who felt the group would do better based out of Detroit. Eddie, Paul, and Cal did so and then changed their name to the Primes.

▲ MARTHA AND THE VANDELLAS   ▼ THE MIRACLES ▲ GLADYS KNIGHT AND THE PIPS   ▼ THE TEMPTATIONS

▲ THE SHIRELLES ▶ THE SUPREMES

Meanwhile, Otis Miles of Texarkana, Texas, moved to Detroit in 1950 and in 1959 formed the street-corner group the Elegants with Elbridge Bryant, Melvin Franklin (whose real name was David English), his cousin Richard Street, and Albert Harrell, all friends from Northwestern High School. At some point they must have gotten wind of the white ELEGANTS and became the Questions and then the Distants.

In 1960 they recorded "Always" for the small Northern label, with Richard singing lead.

The Primes met the Distants at a house party thrown by Janette Poole, a friend of the Distants. Street and Harrell soon departed, and the two groups merged into one consisting of Otis Miles (who was now calling himself Otis Williams, despite the fact that there was a known group named Otis Williams and His CHARMS on King), Melvin Franklin, Eddie Kendricks, Paul Williams, and Elbridge "Al" Bryant.

Jenkins arranged some local club work and shortly thereafter the group became the Elgins. It was at one of those club dates that Berry Gordy, Jr. spotted the group and signed them to his Motown subsidiary, Miracle Records. While standing on the porch of Motown's Hitsville office, Otis Williams and label employee Billy Mitchell came up with the Elgins' new name, the Temptations.

In July 1961 the up-tempo, gospel-influenced single "Oh Mother of Mine" was issued with little fanfare and to less response. At the time, the group's influences ranged from HANK BALLARD AND THE MIDNIGHTERS, THE CADILLACS, and FRANKIE LYMON AND THE TEENAGERS to Jerry Butler and THE IMPRESSIONS. (Their second single "Your Wonderful Love," sounded a lot like the Impressions' "For Your Precious Love.")

In April 1962 the Temps were moved to Gordy's new namesake label and issued a contagious rocker that had a "walking" vocal bass, a frantic gospel falsetto, and ascending harmonies. "Isn't She Pretty" was unique, all right, but the flip got most of the attention: the shuffle ballad "Dream Come True" reached number 22 R&B.

After five singles with only one marginal chart number, Al Bryant decided to leave in early 1963, and his place was taken by another vocalist from Berry's Miracle label, David Ruffin (Voice Masters, Anna).

In January 1964 the Temps, with Kendricks's delicate falsetto lead, came out with a Smokey Robinson-produced pleaser "The Way You Do the Things You Do." (Previous sides were, for the most part, produced by Gordy.)

On February 29th "Things You Do" charted Pop and R&B. The catchy melody and clever comparison-style lyrics made the Temps new radio favorites with a number 11 chart ranking for their lucky seventh single.

Around the time "The Way" was debuting on the charts, the group backed soul soloist Liz Lands on a gospel flavored ballad "Keep Me."

In August, the Temps and the Motown horn section had a field day with "Girl (Why You Wanna Make Me Blue)." More driving than most Smokey Robinson-produced records, "Girl" reached number 26 in the fall of 1964. In September the Temps played the Brooklyn Fox with Murray the K's "Rock and Roll Super Show," featuring THE RONETTES, the Searchers, Marvin Gaye, THE SUPREMES, and MARTHA AND THE VANDELLAS.

In December the Temptations became a household name with the soul rock-a-ballad "My Girl," again produced by Smokey Robinson. Containing the most famous three-part chime harmony in soul history, "My Girl" shot to number one Pop and to number 43 U.K. (the first of their 20 U.K. charters). It was also the lead debut for David Ruffin; with two lead singers, the Temptations had a one-two punch of rough and raw with Ruffin and sweet and smooth with Kendricks.

Smokey continued to crank out great sides with the quintet like "Since I Lost My Baby" (#17 Pop, #4 R&B, 1965) and "Get Ready" (#29 Pop, #1 R&B, 1966 and #10 U.K., 1969). He then turned the production over to Norman Whitfield and Brian Holland, who gave the group a harder edge with "Ain't Too Proud to Beg" (#13 Pop, #1 R&B, 1966), "Beauty Is Only Skin Deep" (#3 Pop, #1 R&B, #18 U.K., 1966), "I'm Lovin' You" (#8 Pop, #1 R&B, 1966), "All I Need" (#8 Pop, #2 R&B, 1967), "You're My Everything" (#6 Pop, #3 R&B, #26 U.K., 1967), "It's You that I Need" (#14 Pop, #3 R&B, 1967), and a change of pace, the beautiful ballad "I Wish It Would Rain" (#4 Pop, #1 R&B, #45 U.K., 1968).

In mid-1968 Ruffin left to record solo on Motown, and Dennis Edwards took over.

In late 1968 Norman Whitfield decided to cross into the relatively uncharted waters of psychedelic music for a black group by producing "Cloud Nine" on the Temps, and it rose to number six Pop and number two R&B, winning a Grammy for Best Group R&B Performance (Motown's first Grammy).

Next, the group teamed up with the Supremes to do the LP *Diana Ross and the Supremes Join the Temptations*, and the successful combo went to number two and included a number two hit single,

"I'm Gonna Make You Love Me" and a revised version of the Miracles hit "I'll Try Something New" (#25 Pop, #8 R&B).

Whitfield (who had been with Motown's Popcorn and the Mohawks in 1960) began to create psychedelic and socially conscious songs and productions with the Temptations that included "Run Away Child, Running Wild" (#6 Pop, #1 R&B), "Don't Let the Joneses Get You Down" (#20 Pop, #2 R&B), and "Ball of Confusion" (#3 Pop, #2 R&B, #7 U.K.), but they also slipped in a great soul rocker of denied love with each member singing lead, called "I Can't Get Next to You" (#1 Pop and R&B, #13 U.K.).

In 1970 they broadened their appeal by doing the LP *On Broadway with the Temptations and the Supremes* (#38) featuring show tunes.

In the spring of 1971 the group briefly returned to its roots with the classic "Just My Imagination" (#1 Pop and R&B, #8 U.K.). It became Kendricks's swan-song lead since he left soon after for a solo career on Motown. Paul Williams left at the same time due to ill health.

Now both original Primes were gone from the Temptations. Damon Harris (the Vandals, T-Neck) and Richard Street (the Distants and later the Monitors on Miracle) took their places, and around this time Ricky Owens of THE VIBRATIONS sang with them for a short while.

In September 1972 Gordy issued the gospel soul masterpiece "Papa Was a Rollin' Stone," which had been released unsuccessfully four months earlier by another Motown act called Undisputed Truth. Edited down from an 11-minute LP cut "Papa" reached number one Pop on December 2nd and hit number one R&B and number 14 in England. The flip side, which was the recording's instrumental section, marked a first when it won a Grammy as Best Instrumental.

More monster hits followed with "Masterpiece" (#7 Pop, #1 R&B, 1973), "Let Your Hair Down" (#27 Pop, #1 R&B, 1973), "Happy People" (#40 Pop, #1 R&B, 1974), and "Shakey Ground" (#26 Pop, #1 R&B, 1975).

In 1975 Glenn Leonard (the Unifics, Kapp) took Damon Harris's place.

Temptations records in 1976 and 1977 did not do as well as previous releases, and the group decided in 1978 to sign with Atlantic. Then Edwards left for a solo career and Louis Price took his place. The Atlantic releases did nothing to reestablish the group, and in 1980 the lineup included a returned Dennis Edwards, Otis Williams, Melvin Franklin, Richard Street, and Glenn Leonard.

Berry Gordy convinced them to reenter the Motown fold, but they went two years without a top 10 record until they hooked up with Melvin's nephew, James Johnson, better known as Rick James. He wrote, produced, and sang lead for "Standing on the Top, Part I," with a revised Temps octet that had Eddie Kendricks, David Ruffin, Dennis Edwards, Richard Street, Otis Williams, Melvin Franklin, and Glenn Leonard. "Standing" reached number six R&B, their first top 10 in six years.

In 1983 the group performed on the Motown 25th Anniversary TV special trading medleys with THE FOUR TOPS. They were so well received, the two veteran acts decided to do an international tour together.

The group continued through the '80s, chalking up "Treat Her Like a Lady" (#48 Pop, #2 R&B, 1984), "Lady Soul" (#47 Pop, #4 R&B, 1986), and "Look What You Started" (#8 R&B, 1987).

The 1991 Temptations included Ali-Ollie Woodson, Damon Harris, Richard Street, Ron Tyson, and Louis Price. Otis and Melvin, the last two originals, retired from the group in 1986. The Temptations' amazing legacy includes 76 R&B chart singles and 52 Pop counterparts. An incredible 41 of those R&B charters were in the top 10 over a period of 25 years (1962 to 1987).

THE TEMPTATIONS

A SIDE/B SIDE	LABEL/CAT NO	DATE
Oh, Mother Of Mine / Romance Without Finance	Mrcl M5	7/61
Check Yourself / Your Wonderful Love	Mrcl M12	11/61
Dream Come True / Isn't She Pretty	Gordy 7001	4/62
Paradise / Slow Down Heart	Gordy 7010	1/63
I What A Love I Can See / The Further You Look The Less You See	Gordy 7015	3/63
May I Have This Dance / Farewell My Love	Gordy 7020	7/63
The Way You Do The Things You Do / Just Let Me Know	Gordy 7028	1/64
Keep Me* / Midnight Johnny	Gordy 7030	2/64
The Girl's Alright With Me / I'll Be In Trouble	Gordy 7032	4/64
Girl (Why You Wanna Make Me Blue) / Baby, Baby, I Need You	Gordy 7035	8/64
My Girl / (Talking 'Bout) Nobody But My Baby	Gordy 7038	12/64
It's Growing / What Love Has Joined Together	Gordy 7040	3/65
Since I Lost My Baby / You've Got To Earn It	Gordy 7043	6/65

A SIDE/B SIDE	LABEL/CAT NO	DATE
My Baby / Don't Look Back	Gordy 7047	10/65
Get Ready / Fading Away	Gordy 7049	2/66
Ain't Too Proud To Beg /		
You'll Lose A Precious Love	Gordy 7054	5/66
Beauty Is Only Skin Deep /		
You're Not An Ordinary Girl	Gordy 7055	8/66
(I Know) I'm Losing You /		
I Couldn't Cry If I Wanted To	Gordy 7057	11/66
All I Need / Sorry Is A Sorry Word	Gordy 7061	4/67
You're My Everything /		
I've Been Good To You	Gordy 7063	6/67
(Loneliness Made Me Realize)		
It's You That I Need /		
Don't Send Me Away	Gordy 7065	9/67
I Wish It Would Rain /		
I Truly, Truly Believe	Gordy 7068	12/67
I Could Never Love Another		
(After Loving You) / Gonna Give		
Her All The Love I've Got	Gordy 7072	4/68
Please Return Your Love To Me /		
How Can I Forget	Gordy 7074	7/68
Cloud Nine / Why Did She		
Have To Leave Me (Why Did		
She Have To Go)	Gordy 7081	10/68
I'm Gonna Make You Love Me** /		
A Place In The Sun	Mtwn 137	11/68
Rudolf, The Red Nosed Reindeer /		
Silent Night	Gordy 7082	12/68
Run Away Child, Running Wild /		
I Need Your Lovin'	Gordy 7084	1/69
I'll Try Something New** / The		
Way You Do The Things You Do	Mtwn 1142	2/69
Don't Let The Joneses Get You		
Down / Since I've Lost You	Gordy 7086	5/69
I Can't Get Next To You / Running		
Away (Ain't Gonna Help You)	Gordy 7093	7/69
Stubborn Kind Of Fellow** /		
Try It Baby	Mtwn 1150	8/69
The Weight** /		
For Better Or Worse	Mtwn 1153	9/69
Psychedelic Shack /		
That's The Way Love Is	Gordy 7096	12/69
Ball Of Confusion (That's What		
The World Is Today) / It's Summer	Gordy 7099	5/70
Ungena Za Ulimwengu (Unite The		
World) / Hum Along And Dance	Gordy 7102	9/70
Just My Imagination (Running		
Away With Me) / You Make		
Your Own Heaven And Hell		
Right Here On Earth	Gordy 7105	1/71
It's Summer /		
I'm The Exception To The Rule	Gordy 7109	7/71
Superstar (Remember How		
You Got Where You Are) /		
Gonna Keep On Tryin'		
Till I Win Your Love	Gordy 7111	10/71
Take A Look Around /		
Smooth Sailing (From Now On)	Gordy 7115	2/72
Mother Nature / Funky Music		
Sho Nuff Turns Me On	Gordy 7119	6/72

A SIDE/B SIDE	LABEL/CAT NO	DATE
Papa Was A Rollin' Stone /		
Papa Was A Rollin' Stone		
(instrumental)	Gordy 7121	9/72
Masterpiece /		
Masterpiece (instrumental)	Gordy 7126	2/73
Plastic Man / Hurry Tomorrow	Gordy 7129	6/73
Hey Girl (I Like Your Style) / Ma	Gordy 7131	8/73
Let Your Hair Down /		
Ain't No Justice	Gordy 7133	12/73
Heavenly / Zoom	Gordy 7135	2/74
You've Got My Soul On Fire /		
I Need You	Gordy 7136	5/74
Happy People /		
Happy People (instrumental)	Gordy 7138	12/74
Shakey Ground	Gordy 7142	1975
Glasshouse / The Prophet	Gordy 7144	7/75
Keep Holding On / What You		
Need Most (I Do Best Of All)	Gordy 7146	1/76
Up The Creek (Without A Paddle) /		
Darling, Stand By Me		
(Song For My Woman)	Gordy 7150	5/76
Who Are You / Let Me Count		
The Ways (I Love You)	Gordy 7152	10/76
In A Lifetime /		
I Could Never Stop Loving You	Atln 3436	1977
Let's Live In Peace /		
Think For Yourself	Atln 3461	1978
Ever Ready Love /		
Touch Me Again	Atln 3538	1978
I Just Don't Know How To Let		
You Go / Mystic Woman	Atln 3567	1979
Power / Power (instrumental)	Gordy 7183	4/80
Struck By Lightning Twice /		
I'm Coming Home	Gordy 7188	7/80
Take Me Away / There's More		
Where That Came From	Gordy 1501	11/80
Aiming At Your Heart /		
The Life Of A Cowboy	Gordy 7208	8/81
Oh, What A Night /		
Isn't The Night Fantastic	Gordy 7213	10/81
Standing On The Top (Part 1) /		
Standing On The Top (Part 2)	Gordy 1616GF	4/82
More On The Inside /		
Money's Hard To Get	Gordy 1631GF	7/82
Silent Night /		
Everything For Christmas	Gordy 1654GF	12/82
Love On My Mind Tonight / Bring		
Your Body (Exercise Chant)	Gordy 1666GF	3/83
Surface Thrills / Made In America	Gordy 1683GF	5/83
Miss Busy Body (Get Your Body		
Busy) / Miss Busy Body (Get		
Your Body Busy) (Part 2)		
(instrumental)	Gordy 1707GF	10/83
Silent Night (6:03) /		
Everything For Christmas	Gordy 1713GF	12/83
Sail Away /		
Isn't The Night Fantastic	Gordy 1720GF	2/84
Treat Her Like A Lady /		
Isn't The Night Fantastic	Gordy 1765GF	10/84

A SIDE/B SIDE	LABEL/CAT NO	DATE
My Love Is True (Truly For You) /		
Set Your Love Right	Gordy 1781GF	2/85
How Can You Say That It's Over /		
I'll Keep My Light In My Window	Gordy 1789GF	5/85
Do You Really Love Your Baby /		
I'll Keep My Light In My Window	Gordy 1818GF	10/85
Touch / Set You Right	Gordy 1834GF	2/86
A Fine Mess / Wishful Thinking	Mtwn 1837MF	3/86
Lady Soul / Put Us Together Again	Gordy 1856GF	6/86
To Be Continued . . . /		
You're The One	Gordy 1871GF	11/86

* with Liz Lands
**with the Supremes

Tico and the Triumphs

No, Tico and the Triumphs were not a Latin band from the Los Angeles barrio but a white Jewish vocal group from Queens, New York, whose eventual leader went on to become one of the biggest names in rock music.

14-year-old Mickey Borack attended Parsons Junior High School and began singing for fun with schoolmates Marty Cooper and Gail Lynn. When the junior high prom at Forest Hills Jewish Center rolled around in June 1961 the three teens were put to the test by well-meaning friends. Marty and company performed Linda Scott's "I've Told Every Little Star" while Jerry Landis, the night's real entertainment, looked on. Liking the group, Jerry suggested they all meet at summer's end to work together. In the meantime, the trio practiced on street corners around 71st Street and Kissena Boulevard in Flushing, Queens.

By September the group (minus Lynn and plus Jamaica High friend Howie Beck) joined Jerry at his home in Flushing to work on a song he'd written titled "Motorcycle." Jerry (who had also recorded under the names Paul Kane, True Taylor, and Harrison Gregory) had an association with Larry Uttal's Madison Records and produced the single with himself on lead.

Feeling that car group names were in and liking the Tico record label name, he christened the group Tico and the Triumphs.

"Motorcycle," with its Harley-Davidson growling intro, was a teen pleaser extolling the virtues of cruising around town on a red chopper. The record started getting a lot of airplay in the New York, New Jersey, and Connecticut area, racing to number one in Baltimore and, of all places, Puerto Rico. "Motorcycle" gained enough steam to reach just above the bottom of the *Billboard* Hot 100 chart on January 6, 1962, anchoring at number 99. The recording was a nightly winner on Murray the K's WINS new releases contest but lost out on the weekly sweepstakes to Bobby "Boris" Pickett and the Crypt Kickers' "Monster Mash."

Their next release was "Express Train," with Jerry again writing, producing, and singing lead. Though not a national charter, "Express" was an even tighter harmony and musical production than "Motorcycle."

The group's airplay enabled them to appear with THE DREAMLOVERS and THE DRIFTERS in Camden, New Jersey, for a 1961 Christmas show and in Detroit with Del Shannon, Gene Pitney, and Ann-Margret. They must have sensed an irony in appearing on a Rhode Island TV show when they found themselves performing on the same bill with Linda Scott, the girl whose song started their career.

In September 1962 they released "Cry Little Boy Cry," a "Runaround Sue"-styled rocker with Marty singing lead. This time it won Murray the K's weekly contest but little else. Then Amy Records issued a novelty rocker by Jerry Landis titled "The Lone Teen Ranger." The Triumphs were prominent on the record but received no credit.

Their last Amy release, "Cards of Love," came out in early 1963 under the name "Tico."

Jerry then signed a solo deal with Canadian-American Records and the Triumphs backed him on "I Wish I Weren't in Love," a song originally written to be the B side of "Motorcycle."

During 1964 Tico and the Triumphs broke up and Jerry Landis went back to work with his old partner. Before finding the Triumphs Jerry had been half of the duo that charted pop in 1957 (#49) with "Hey Schoolgirl" as Tom and Jerry. Marty Cooper went on to become a psychologist and Mickey Borack became Mickey's Men to record a disco single for Buddah in 1979 called "Garbageman." In later years Mickey was the host of a doo wop radio show at WNYG on Long Island.

Jerry Landis, meanwhile, went back to his real name and within two years of Tico and the Triumphs' demise began a streak of 18 charters with "Sounds of Silence" (#1, 1965) as the Simon half of Simon and Garfunkel. Among their biggest hits were "Mrs. Robinson" (#1, 1968) and "Bridge over Troubled Water" (#1, 1970). In 1972 Paul Simon went solo and recorded another 18 chart hits that included "Kodachrome" (#2, 1973), "Love Me

Like a Rock" (with the Dixie Hummingbirds, #2, 1973), and "Fifty Ways to Leave Your Lover" (#1, 1975).

TICO AND THE TRIUMPHS

A SIDE/B SIDE	LABEL/CAT NO	DATE
Motorcycle / I Don't Believe Them	Madison 169	10/61
Motorcycle / I Don't Believe Them	Amy 835	1962
Wild Flower / Express Train	Amy 845	4/62
Cry, Little Boy Cry /		
Get Up And Do The Wobble	Amy 860	9/62
The Lone Teen Ranger / Lisa	Amy 875	1962
Cards Of Love / Noise	Amy 876	1/63
I'm Lonely /		
I Wish I Weren't In Love	Can Am	1963

The Tokens

Recording artists, performers, producers, songwriters, jingle writers, record executives, and trendsetters, the Tokens wore more hats successfully than any other group. Yet their greatest talent was as a superior vocal ensemble.

There is often confusion about their origin since the hit group was preceded by another Tokens unit.

In 1956, Lincoln High School (Brooklyn) students Henry "Hank" Medress and FOUR-FRESHMEN-inspired Neil Sedaka formed the Linc-Tones with Eddie Rabkin and Cynthia Zoliton. With Neil on lead and armed with two Sedaka and Howie Greenfield songs, "While I Dream" and "I Love My Baby," the group earned themselves a single on Morty Craft's Melba label. Before the release, they chose the name the Tokens, not from the famous subway coin, but from the phrase "token of affection." When "While I Dream" failed, Rabkin went off to college. Sedaka went out on his own, and Medress formed a new foursome called Darrell and the Oxfords with schoolmates Jay Siegel, Warren Schwartz, and Fred Kalkstein in 1958.

A single on Roulette, the rhythm ballad "Picture in My Wallet," showed off Jay's incredible tenor lead and instantly identifiable sound. "Picture" was a New York hit but went unnoticed elsewhere. After one more disappointing single, "Your Mother Said No" in 1959, the Oxfords were left with Jay and Hank.

On December 7, 1959, the hit Tokens story began. Hank and neighbors Phil and Mitch Margo all cut school that day to sing together. The first song they practiced was DION AND THE BELMONTS' "A Teenager in Love." The Margos and Hank began writing and came up with "Please Write" in the beginning of 1960, along with a song originally called "It's Imagination." By the summer, Hank had brought Jay in and the nameless foursome began to develop as a cross between the Weavers and Dion and the Belmonts. The lineup that summer was Jay (20, lead), Mitchell (13, first tenor), Hank (21, second tenor), and Phillip (18, bass).

Jay was influenced by the Weavers and brought their Carnegie Hall LP to one of the early practices. The Margos, in the meantime, looked to Ray Charles, THE SKYLINERS, and the Belmonts for inspiration. One of the Weavers' tunes, "Wimoweh," was actually an early Zulu chant called "Mbube," which means "lion." Its repeated haunting refrain came across in English as "wimoweh." In the '50s Miriam Makeba recorded a rendition in its original Zulu language. The Weavers recorded their hit version (#14) in 1952.

The group's career suddenly kicked into high gear when Hank met a Mrs. Gottesfield on the subway and told her of the quartet. She arranged for her son to bankroll a session, and they recorded four songs in three hours at Allegro Studios in the fall of 1960. The songs were "Please Write," "I'll Always Love You," "Wimoweh," and "It's Imagination," which was rewritten into "Tonight I Fell in Love."

The group produced the session themselves (gaining hands-on experience that would serve them well in the future). Hank, wanting everything to go perfectly, stood between Phil and Mitch with his hands on their necks and squeezed when he wanted the younger brothers to start and stop. When the tapes were completed, Mrs. Gottesfield took them to Morty Craft, who picked up the masters, and in late January "Tonight I Fell in Love" (Warwick) was issued. But before that, Craft asked what name should be put on the label. Hank, remembering his old group, suggested the Tokens, and since nobody disagreed, that's what it became. When the record started getting airplay, Jay was a buyer in a department store, Phil was an order clerk on Wall Street working for a stock firm, and Mitch was still in Lincoln High.

On February 13th *Billboard* reviewed the recording: "The lads turn in a snappy performance here on a bright rocker that is loaded with gimmicks, and it could easily happen. Watch it." By March 6th it was indeed happening, climbing *Billboard*'s Hot 100 and ascending to number 15. The sparse production (it only had drums, bass, piano, and three strings) didn't stop the record from selling over 700,000 copies.

The Tokens did two Dick Clark shows and a bunch of local hops while acquiring Seymour Barish as manager. He immediately called Hugo and Luigi, producers for RCA. Since there was a dispute over Warwick royalties, Barish felt he could break the contract. Upon hearing the news, a visibly irked Craft asked the Tokens, "What can RCA do for you that I can't?" "Pay us," was the reply.

The Tokens' ultra-tight and distinctive harmony was evident in their rocker "When I Go to Sleep at Night," the first single written by Margo and Medress for RCA. The doo wop flip "Dry Your Eyes," with a "Little Darlin'" intro, was also hot, but the record failed to generate any action. In August 1961 an up-tempo version of THE MOON-GLOWS' "Sincerely," done in a "Tonight I Fell in Love" style, was issued, but it reached only number 120 nationally.

With two misses in a row, the Tokens switched direction and performed "Wimoweh" live in Hugo and Luigi's office. The producers thought it could be a hit but felt it needed an English lyric, so they arranged for a translation. The song turned out to be about a lion hunt, so they wrote "The Lion Sleeps Tonight" around it. The group loved the record but had little faith that the song would be a hit. They were already concentrating more on becoming a production team when the record charted on November 13, 1961. Five weeks later it was at number one. The tune became their first and only R&B chart single (#7); it reached number one in most foreign countries and was number two in Australia and number eleven in Britain. The whole world was now aware of Jay's trademark falsetto (he was nicknamed "superthroat") and the Tokens' unusual harmony blend.

"The Lion Sleeps Tonight" sold over three and a half million records at the time (close to six million to date) and became immortalized as the 218th biggest hit of the rock era in *Billboard*'s top 1000 records. In retrospect the group can be seen as being among the founders of folk-rock years before it had a name. Not bad for four Jewish kids from Brooklyn who had also just made their first major appearance before 14,000 screaming fans at the University of Detroit.

In January 1962 "B'wa Nina" was issued, described by a *Billboard* reviewer as "a smart follow-up to the Tokens' recent smash 'The Lion Sleeps Tonight.' The material again has a touch of the veldt about it and employs the same high yodeling technique." "B'wa Nina" reached only number 55 Pop,

but the group had a fairly successful LP in *The Lion Sleeps Tonight*, filled with folk songs done in that now-famous Tokens style.

The group wasted no time in capitalizing on their talent. *Billboard*'s February 10th issue noted, "Tokens members ink pact as A&R team for Capitol." The group was now thoroughly immersed in producing and was one of the first independent teams (and certainly the youngest) to ink a deal for exclusive production with a major label. The article said the deal called for 12 singles a year, a hefty load for young shoulders who were still trying to follow up their big hit. In those early days they produced under their company name Bright Tune Productions, so people were not aware of their efforts. One example was their DRIFTERS-styled shuffle version of "Dry Your Eyes" by the Revlons for Capitol in 1962.

Meanwhile, RCA issued some excellent Tokens tunes like the Afro rock-a-ballad "I'll Do My Cryin' Tomorrow," "Tonight I Met an Angel," and the bossa nova-based "A Bird Flies Out of Sight" (a doo wop predecessor to the Beatles' "Fool on the Hill"). None of them charted.

In late 1962 the Tokens brought their 12th record to Capitol under their commitment deal, but the label turned it down. The group then shopped it, finally finding interest from Doug Morris at Laurie Records after nine other labels had passed. (Maybe that's how Morris became President of Atlantic Records.)

The record was "He's So Fine" by THE CHIFFONS, and its tenure at number one made the Tokens the first full vocal group to produce a number one record for another vocal group.

The Brooklyn boys finally had an opportunity to issue their first original composition, "Please Write." They recorded it for Laurie in 1963 after their RCA deal expired, but it only went as high as number 108 (October 12, 1962).

Later that year they put on record executive hats and formed their own B.T. Puppy label. They took the initials from their production company *B*right *T*unes and combined it with a modestly sized RCA dog to come up with their B.T. Puppy logo.

Their first Tokens single for B.T. was "Swing," which only charted nationally at number 105 (May 1964).

The group continued to produce hits for the Chiffons, and in the summer of that year they issued the Gerry Goffin/Carole King-penned "He's in Town" (#43), Jay's favorite Tokens recording.

The Tokens were even more productive behind the scenes, doing backup vocals for everyone from

Del Shannon, Mac Davis, Connie Francis, and Melissa Manchester to the Blues Project and even Bob Dylan on his *Highway 61 Revisited* LP. Their biggest uncredited backup record was Keith's 1966 hit "98.6" (#7).

In 1964 the group performed at New York's Paramount Theatre with the Beatles. They occasionally backed up others performing on the same bill, once working behind DANNY AND THE JUNIORS. They often crossed paths with other acts. On record they were paired with the Americans (without Jay) as the Rockaways for "Don't Cry" (Red Bird, 1964).

Part of the group's versatility came from their instrumental ability. Phil played drums, piano, and guitar; Mitch played 11 instruments, including drums, piano and guitar; Jay was a guitarist; Hank played bass and piano.

To expand their creative output the Tokens started the B.T. Puppy affiliate, Swing Records, and issued two teen rockers, "Remember Last Summer" as the Four Winds and the BEACH BOYS-styled "On the Go" as the Buddies, but there was no hiding the Tokens' distinctive style.

After "He's in Town" the group came back with the Goffin/King gem, "You're My Girl." By the mid-'60s the Tokens' voices were all over the airwaves but not usually on hit records.

They became the first successful vocal group production team to enter the commercial field, writing, producing, and singing spots like "Pan Am makes the going great," "Ban won't wear off," and "Hair so new" (for Clairol).

In the summer of 1966 the group produced B.T. Puppy's first top 10 hit, "See You in September" by THE HAPPENINGS (#3), and followed it with "I Got Rhythm" (#3) in 1967.

In early 1967 the Tokens teamed with the pop/jazz-styled Kirby Stone Four as the U.S. Double Quartet, releasing "Life Is Groovy" to a chart ranking of number 110 during January.

Since it was becoming more difficult to receive payment from their Jubilee distributor, the Tokens jumped their own label during 1967 and moved over to Warner Bros. Records for another up-tempo revision of an old hit ballad—this time "Portrait of My Love" (#36). Their *Portrait* LP contained a rocking version of "The Lion Sleeps Tonight" called "Wimoweh, Five and a Half Years Later," complete with a Motown-styled horn section right out of Stevie Wonder's "Uptight."

The medley "Go Away Little Girl"/"Young Girl" was their last Warner Bros. charter (#118, 1969).

In 1969 they issued a version of the Schoolboys' "Please Say You Want Me" on B.T. Puppy, but psychedelically charged AM radio wasn't paying attention.

In late 1969 they signed to Buddah for adaptations of the Beach Boys' "Don't Worry Baby" (#95) and Judy Collins's "Both Sides Now" (written by Joni Mitchell). Their recording of the Clairol commercial "She Lets Her Hair Down" reached number 61 and led to a harmony-filled LP that included a new recording of "The Lion Sleeps Tonight."

In 1973 the group transformed into a Crosby, Stills and Nash-styled contemporary rock group called Cross Country and did an LP they produced with Dave Appell for Atlantic. They also took the funky Wilson Pickett song "Midnight Hour" and slowed it down to a harmony-filled rhythm ballad that reached number 30.

Tokens recordings ended by the early '70s, when the group concentrated on producing hits with Tony Orlando and DAWN. But by the mid-'70s, after the mega-smash "Tie a Yellow Ribbon," Hank wanted to pursue his own production interests.

On October 3, 1981, the Four Tokens reunited for one show at Radio City Music Hall, appearing on an all-star bill with such contemporaries as THE ELEGANTS, THE CLEFTONES, THE FIVE KEYS, THE CHANNELS, and the Students, but it would be their last reunion.

Phil and Mitch moved to Los Angeles and in 1983 formed a new Tokens with Norm Bergen and Dennis Marcellino (with Mitch having mastered those high tenor leads). Jay went on to manage his own Mayfair Recording Studios and form an East Coast Tokens along with Billy Reid and Richie Grasso.

In 1988 both Tokens aggregations issued albums. Jay's group issued a memory-filled LP highlighted by an a cappella arrangement of "Morse Code of Love" along with strong versions of "Don't Worry Baby," "He's in Town," and a reggae version of the Gladiolas'/Diamonds' "Little Darlin'" issued as a single in 1986. Mitch and Phil's Tokens created a concept LP featuring several medleys of memorable doo wop tunes done with '80s rhythms. The LP was picked up by Rick Blieweiss's RBI Records of New York, and the "Re Doo Wop" single with a flip of a 24-year-old Carolons song titled "I'm Thru with You" started getting national airplay and became the most performed jukebox record during its release. As it was gaining momentum RBI ran into financial problems and sold the masters to, ironically, RCA. The Tokens had returned home after 25 years.

Hank went on to produce Tony Orlando and Dawn with Dave Appell and also produced a number three hit in 1972 on Robert John doing "The Lion Sleeps Tonight." Robert used to be Bobby Pedrick, lead of the Brooklyn group Bobby and the Consoles ("My Jellybean," Diamond, 1963). Hank joined the Entertainment Company (which became SBK) as a producer working with Buster Poindexter and Dan Hill. He later worked out of their Toronto office.

In 1989, Jay, Dion, Johnny Maestro (THE CRESTS), Ronnie Bright (THE VALENTINES and THE COASTERS), Ellie Greenwich (the Raindrops), and Carole King recorded "When the Radio's On" for Paul Shaffer's LP and debuted it on the David Letterman show at the end of July. Phil worked his way into management and handled TV star Robert Guillaume for seven years. He later wrote and produced for TV when not out with Mitch and company performing as the Tokens. Mitch continued to write and produce while keeping up his full-time involvement with the Tokens.

Apart from their role as door openers for other artists and producers, the Tokens were one of the great vocal groups of the '60s (and '70s).

THE TOKENS

A SIDE/B SIDE	LABEL/CAT NO	DATE
Tonight I Fell In Love /		
I'll Always Love You	Warwick 615	1/61
Dry Your Eyes /		
When I Go To Sleep At Night	RCA 47-7896	5/61
Sincerely /		
When Summer Is Through	RCA 47-7925	8/61
The Lion Sleeps Tonight / Tina	RCA 47-7954	10/61
B'wa Nina / Weeping River	RCA 47-7991	1/62
The Riddle / The Boat	RCA 47-8018	3/62
La Bomba / A Token Of Love	RCA 47-8052	6/62
I'll Do My Crying Tomorrow /		
Dream Angel Goodnight	RCA 47-8089	9/62
Wishing / A Bird Flies Out Of Sight	RCA 47-8114	11/62
Tonight I Met An Angel /		
Hindi Lullabye	RCA 47-8148	2/63
A-B-C 1-2-3 / Hear The Bells	RCA 47-8210	6/63
Please Write / I'll Always Love You	Laurie 3180	1963
Swing / A Girl Named Arlene	BTP 500	1963
Let's Go To The Drag Strip /		
Two Cars	RCA 47-8309	1/64
He's In Town / Oh Kathy	BTP 502	6/64
He's In Town / Oh Kathy	BTP 502	1964
You're My Girl / Havin' Fun	BTP 504	1964
Mr. Cupid / Nobody But You	BTP 505	1964
Sylvie Sleepin' /		
A Message To The World	BTP 507	1965
Only My Friend / Cattle Call	BTP 512	1965
The Bells Of St. Mary's /		
Just One Smile	BTP 513	1965

A SIDE/B SIDE	LABEL/CAT NO	DATE
The Three Bells /		
A Message To The World	BTP 516	1965
I Hear Trumpets Blow / Don't		
Cry, Sing With The Music	BTP 518	2/66
Breezy / Greatest		
Moments In A Girl's Life	BTP 519	5/66
Life Is Groovy* / Split*	BTP 524	12/66
Eulogy / Green Plant	BTP 525	1967
Portrait Of My Love /		
She Comes And Goes	Wrnr 5900	3/67
How Nice / It's A Happening World	Wrnr 7056	6/67
Bye, Bye, Bye / Ain't That Peculiar	Wrnr 7099	11/67
Till / Poor Man	Wrnr 7169	1/68
Mister Snail /		
Needles Of Evergreen	Wrnr 7183	3/68
Animal / Bathroom Wall	Wrnr 7202	5/68
Grandfather /		
The Banana Boat Song	Wrnr 7233	9/68
Walking Along* /		
The Happy Wanderer* /		
When I Lock My Door*	BTP 547	1968
Some People Sleep / The World		
Is Full Of Wonderful Things	Wrnr 7255	12/68
Go Away Little Girl / Young Girl /		
I Want To Make Love To You	Wrnr 7280	4/69
I Could Be / End Of The World	Wrnr 7323	1969
Do Re Me* /		
When I Lock My Door*	BTP 551	1969
Please Say You Want Me /		
Get A Job	BTP 552	1969
She Let's Her Hair Down /		
Oh To Get Away	Buddah 151	1969
Don't Worry Baby /		
Some People Sleep	Buddah 159	1970
Both Sides Now / I Could See Me	Buddah 174	1970
Groovin' To The Sunshine-Sesame		
Street / Listen To The Words	Buddah 187	1970
You And Me /		
I Like To Throw My Head Back	Bell 45190	1970
Little Darlin'** / Don't Worry Baby**	Downtown	1986
Re Do Wop Medley† /		
I'm Thru With You†	RBI 7002	1988
Re Do Wop Medley† /		
I'm Thru With You†	RCA 8749-7-R	1988

* The United States Double Quartet
  (The Tokens and the Kirby Stone Four)
** Jay's Tokens
† Mitch's Tokens

The Tymes

A pop-sounding R&B group, the Tymes were excellent rhythm balladeers from Philadelphia. Norman Burnett met George Hilliard at a Willow Grove, Pennsylvania, summer camp in

1955. When they returned home they met neighbors Albert Berry III and Donald Banks and formed the Latineers. Banks went to Benjamin Franklin High School while the others attended Northeast High School. In 1961 Norman met George Williams while working in the Einstein Medical Center. Now the quintet consisted of George (lead), Albert (first tenor), George Hilliard (second tenor), Norman (baritone), and Donald (bass).

The group rehearsed at Albert's house five nights a week in his basement. (It turned out that two of THE DREAMLOVERS were his next-door neighbors, though they never helped the act's career.) One of the group's biggest influences was Johnny Mathis, which helps explain the pop sound of the quintet.

In 1963 the Latineers were contestants in the Tip Top (bread) Talent Hunt and impressed judge Leroy Lovett enough to have him send them to A&R director of Cameo/Parkway Records, Billy Jackson. Williams had an unfinished song he called "The Stroll" that Jackson and fellow producer Roy Straigis revised, calling it "So Much in Love." The group then became the Tymes.

Because is was springtime and any record released would be for the summer, Jackson added the sounds of birds and waves lapping on the shore to go with the record's hypnotic finger snaps. In no time "So Much in Love" was on the *Billboard* Hot 100 (June 1st) and the R&B chart (June 29th). On August 3rd it pushed Jan and Dean's "Surf City" out of the number one spot (#4 R&B, #21 U.K.).

Their first major billing was at Philadelphia's State Theatre with Lloyd Price, the Dreamlovers, and Big Dee Irwin (of THE PASTELS).

In July they played the famed Apollo in New York alongside RUBY AND THE ROMANTICS, Brook Benton, and Moms Mabley and got a good lesson in stage preparedness. As the opening act, they came on to the huge stage to find only one mike off to the side. Not realizing it was the lead mike, they all gathered around it and started to sing. When the group mike came rising up out of the floor on the other side of the stage they had to scurry over in embarrassment.

Their next single was a remake of Johnny Mathis's "Wonderful! Wonderful!," with George doing his best Mathis mimic. The record took off, stopping at number seven Pop and number 23 R&B in a week (September 18, 1963) in which eight of the top 10 records were by vocal groups (the Jaynetts, THE RONETTES, THE VANDELLAS, THE ANGELS, THE CRYSTALS, the Tymes, THE MIRACLES, and the Enchanters). Only Bobby Vinton ("Blue Velvet,"

#1) and Trini Lopez ("If I Had a Hammer," #10) breached the vocal group dominance.

"Somewhere" was their next single, and its "So Much in Love" styling took the classical melody to number 19 Pop and R&B. The group was a natural for the day's popular packaged tours, and they criss-crossed the country with Dick Clark's "Caravan." On one show the group sang backup for Barbara Lewis ("Hello Stranger").

A remake of THE PLATTERS' "To Each His Own" was their next 45, but it only reached number 78 Pop in March 1964. "The Magic of Our Summer Love," in a Ruby and the Romantics style, did even worse (#99) in the summer of 1964 even though it was a very worthwhile record.

On one of their Apollo stops Norman met a young lead singer from a Detroit group whom he began dating and would see as they criss-crossed the country during their tour. He even asked her to marry him, but young Diana Ross was determined to make a career of it and wasn't ready to settle down.

Seeing Parkway's promo support eroding, the group started up their own Winchester label with ex-Parkway songwriters John Madara and Dave White ("At the Hop," DANNY AND THE JUNIORS) and Leon Huff (later of the Gamble-Huff conglomerate). (The Tymes also did backup for Johnny Maestro's Cameo single "I'll Be True" in 1963 and Joey Heatherton's "Live and Learn" recording in 1966.)

Their single of "These Foolish Things" failed to draw significant radio interest, so Billy Jackson took them to MGM and then Columbia. A rhythm version of Barbra Streisand's "People" got them back in the public eye in 1968, charting at number 39 Pop, number 33 R&B, and number 16 in the U.K. It also marked the group's emergence as a bona fide soul group. When their next three singles failed the group found themselves label-less but still able to work the soul circuit.

In the early '70s Hilliard left, replaced by Charles Nixon. In 1973 believer Billy Jackson spent his own money to record a few sides with the group and took them to RCA. The resulting 1974 single, "You Little Trustmaker" became their biggest hit (#12 Pop, #20 R&B, #18 U.K.) since "Wonderful! Wonderful!"

The follow-up, a John and Johanna Hall song called "Ms. Grace," placed poorly in the States (#91 Pop, #75 R&B) yet became a number one record in the U.K. in early 1975.

At the beginning of 1976 the Tymes had their last RCA charter, "It's Cool" (#68 Pop, #3 R&B), but continued to tour right into the '90s.

In the '70s Nixon and Berry left, replaced by two female vocalists, Melanie Moore and Terri Gonzalez.

In 1990 the act consisted of returning Al Berry, Norman Burnett, Donald Banks, and Dave James. George Williams left in the '70s and worked as a greeter and singer in a nightclub in London.

The group, always close friends, even formed a company together, Burnett's Painting of Palmyra, New Jersey, for the times when they were not performing.

You can bet that whenever one of their records came over Philadelphia radio (which was pretty often) they would put down their paintbrushes and take a break.

THE TYMES

A SIDE/B SIDE	LABEL/CAT NO	DATE
So Much In Love /		
Roscoe James McClain	Prkwy 871	5/63
Wonderful! Wonderful! /		
Come With Me To The Sea	Prkwy 884	7/63
Somewhere / View		
From My Window	Prkwy 891	11/63
To Each His Own /		
Wonderland Of Love	Prkwy 908	1/64
The Magic Of Our Summer Love /		
With All My Heart	Prkwy 919	2/64
Here She Comes / Alibu	Prkwy 924	9/64
Pretend / Street Talk	MGM 13536	5/66
A Touch Of Baby /		
What Would I Do	MGM 13631	11/66
These Foolish Things /		
This Time It's Love	Win 1002	1967
People / For Love Of Ivy	Col 44630	8/68
God Bless The Chile /		
The Love That You're		
Looking For	Col 44799	3/69
Find My Way /		
If You Love Me Baby	Col 44917	6/69
Love Child /		
Most Beautiful Married Lady	Col 45078	1/70
She's Gone /		
Someone To Watch Over Me	Col 45336	3/71
You Little Trustmaker /		
The North Hills	RCA 10022	7/74
Ms. Grace /		
The Crutch	RCA 10128	10/74
Interloop / Someway		
Somehow I'm Keepin' You	RCA 10244	3/75
If I Can't Make You Smile /		
God's Gonna Punish You	RCA 10422	9/75
Good Morning Dear Lord /		
It's Cool	RCA 10561	1/76
Goin' Through The Motions /		
Only Your Love	RCA 10713	5/76

The Vibrations

The Vibrations, a rhythm and blues harmony group whose career spanned the '60s and early '70s, had their biggest chart success in the '50s when they recorded for only two years as the Jayhawks.

Formed in 1955, the Los Angeles Jefferson High juveniles included Jimmy Johnson (lead), Carl Fisher (tenor), Dave Govan (baritone), and Carver Bunkum (bass).

In late 1955 they encountered Flash Records store owner Charlie Reynolds, who liked their ballad "Counting My Teardrops." Released on Charlie's Flash Records in January 1956, "Counting" failed on the large scale but received enough Los Angeles attention to warrant another shot.

In the late spring of 1956 the most successful record ever issued from Reynolds's 623 East Vernon Avenue address came out under the name the Jayhawks. The novelty rocker, "Stranded in the Jungle," written by Johnson and Smith, was an instant hit. Flash's tiny operation could barely keep up with the demand until Modern Records' Cadets jumped on the bandwagon with a more polished, better-recorded version and bypassed the Jayhawks, reaching number 15 Pop and number four R&B. The Jayhawks' version peaked at number 18 Pop and number nine R&B. (On the single, "Stranded" was listed as the B side, with the crude harmony ballad "My Only Darling" expected to take the radio play.)

The Jayhawks hit proved to be a one-shot. The follow-up, "Love Train," derailed early, and the group then found itself on Aladdin for the songs "Johnny's House Party" and "Everyone Should Know," neither of which received much airplay.

The Jayhawks had had it by the summer of 1957, and by 1960 Carver had left. The group then beefed up its sound and smoothed out its harmonies with the addition of tenor Ricky Owens (THE SIX TEENS, Flip) and bass Don Bradley.

That same year a much-improved harmony group calling themselves the Vibrations surfaced on the tiny Bet label with a haunting version of the Brown/DeSilva/Henderson minor-key ballad "So Blue." Checker Records picked up the master and rode it on to *Billboard*'s Bubbling Under chart at number 110 in June. A few more singles came and went until the Vibrations hit the charts with "The Watusi" (#25 Pop, #13 R&B) in the spring of 1961. Meanwhile, Arvee Records' ace A&R man H. B. Barnum had a timing problem: his hot act

THE OLYMPICS were away on the East Coast and he needed a new single immediately. He convinced the Vibrations to do a little moonlighting, and an Olympics-styled novelty titled "Peanut Butter" was cut by the Vibes as the Marathons. No one expected "Peanut Butter" to stick to radio as it did, and soon the Vibrations found themselves with two hits, two names, and two labels. For a while they were entering the stage to perform in sweaters with a big V, doing their set as the Vibrations, then exiting and returning with sweaters monogrammed with a big M to sing "Peanut Butter" and other songs. At one point "Watusi" was number 25 Pop while "Peanut Butter" was number 20. The problems arose when Checker filed a lawsuit against H. B. Barnum's Arvee Records. The resolution saw Checker winding up with the Marathons single and Arvee keeping the name for use with another unknown group to complete a Marathons LP.

By 1964 the Vibrations were progressing from a dance group with hits like "My Girl Sloopy" (#26 Pop) on Atlantic to a more ballad-oriented sophisticated soul sound on Okeh. In the fall of 1965 they hit with their trademark single, the Erroll Garner and Johnny Burke song "Misty," with Carl Fisher singing lead. "Misty" reached number 63 Pop and number 26 R&B by Christmas. In 1968 their final charter was a rhythm and blues rocker called "Love in Them There Hills" (#93 Pop, #38 R&B).

They signed to Neptune Records in 1969 and issued a number of strong sides, such as "Expressway to Your Heart" (the Soul Survivors) and "Smoke Signals." In 1971 they sang backup in one of history's odder pairings, supporting Ersel Hickey on "Look What They've Done to the Garden" (Black Pearl).

The Vibrations' last recordings were for North Bay Records in the 1970s.

THE VIBRATIONS

A SIDE/B SIDE	LABEL/CAT NO	DATE
The Jayhawks		
Counting My Teardrops /		
The Devil's Cousin	Flash 105	1956
My Only Darling /		
Stranded In The Jungle	Flash 109	1956
Love Train / Don't Mind Dyin'	Flash 111	8/56
Johnny's House Party Part 1 /		
Johnny's House Party Part 2	Aldn 3379	4/57
The Creature /		
Everyone Should Know	Aldn 3393	7/57
The Vibrations		
So Blue /		
Love Me Like You Should	Bet 001	1960

A SIDE/B SIDE	LABEL/CAT NO	DATE
So Blue /		
Love Me Like You Should	Chkr 954	1960
Feel So Bad / Cave Man	Chkr 961	1960
Doing The Slop /		
So Little Time	Chkr 967	1960
The Watusi / Wallflower	Chkr 969	1961
Continental / The Junkaroo	Chkr 974	3/61
The Marathons		
Peanut Butter / Talkin' Trash	Arvee 5027	3/61
Peanut Butter /		
Down In New Orleans	Chess 1790	4/61
The Vibrations		
Stranded In The Jungle /		
Don't Say Goodbye	Chkr 982	6/61
Stop Right Now /		
All My Love Belongs To You	Chkr 987	7/61
Let's Pony Again / What Made		
You Change Your Mind	Chkr 990	9/61
Over The Rainbow / Oh Cindy	Chkr 1002	1961
Anytime / The New Hully Gully	Chkr 1011	1962
Hamburgers On A Bun /		
If He Don't	Chkr 1022	1962
Since I Fell For You /		
May The Best Man Win	Chkr 1038	2/63
Between Hello And Goodbye /		
Lonesome Little Lonely Girl	Atln 2204	9/63
Dancing Danny / Dancing Danny	Chkr 1061	11/63
My Girl Sloopy / Daddy Woo-Woo	Atln 2221	9/63
Sloop Dance / Watusi Time	Okeh 7205	10/64
Hello Happiness /		
Keep On Keeping You	Okeh 7212	12/64
End Up Crying /		
Ain't Love That Way	Okeh 7220	4/65
If I Only Knew / Talkin 'Bout Love	Okeh 7228	8/65
Misty / Finding Out The Hard Way	Okeh 7230	9/65
Gina / The Story Of A Starry Night	Okeh 7238	1/66
Canadian Sunset /		
The Story Of A Starry Night	Okeh 7241	2/66
Gonna Get Along Without You		
Now / Forgive And Forget	Okeh 7249	5/66
And I Love her / Soul A Go-Go	Okeh 7257	8/66
Pick Me / You Better Beware	Okeh 7276	2/67
Together / Come To Yourself	Okeh 7297	10/67
Love In Them There Hills /		
Remember The Rain	Okeh 7311	3/68
Cause You're Mine /		
I Took An Overdose	Epic 10418	11/68
Expressway To Your Heart /		
Who's Gonna Help Me Now	Nptn 19	11/69
Smoke Signals /		
Who's Gonna Help Me Now	Nptn 21	1/70
Right On, Brother, Right On /		
Surprise Party For You Baby	Nptn 28	5/70
Wind Up Toy /		
Ain't No Greens In Harlem	Mndla 2511	1972
Make It Last / Shake It Up	Chess 2151	1974
Sneakin'	North Bay 307	1970s

Vito and the Salutations

The Salutations were originally a group from the Brownsville and Canarsie sections of Brooklyn who became known for reviving standards in a most unorthodox way.

Sometime in 1961, Bob De Pallo, Barry Solomon, and a long-since-forgotten third harmonizer were heard singing in a New York subway station (the Big Apple's stations are known for their natural echo—and not much else). The lady who listened was one Linda Scott, who recommended the singers to producer Dave Rick. Dave was holding auditions in three days and invited them down, putting Bob and Barry in the position of having to quickly put together a real group. Bob's younger brother played him a demo by neighborhood 14-year-old Vito Balsamo, and De Pallo tracked the teen to P.S. 230 to offer him the lead singing spot. Vito agreed and brought along baritone Bobby Mitchell. The group rehearsed with one day left and instantly became Vito and the Salutations after the line in disc jockey "Jocko" Henderson's nightly opening patter, "Greeting and salutations, ooh-pooh-pa-doo."

On the day of the audition, they were the last of 20 acts to perform for Dave Rick, but they caught his ear with a version of THE CRESTS' "My Juanita."

In December 1961 the group went into ODO Studios and recorded several songs. One of them came from a last-minute suggestion by Big Top Records exec David Mook, who heard the group warming up with the CADILLACS classic "Gloria" and recommended they cut it.

It became their first single in February 1962 and was a big New York favorite even though THE PASSIONS had cut a ballad version of it only a year before. The label issuing "Gloria," Rayna Records, had no real distribution or marketing capability beyond New York and the boys soon became disenchanted with them.

Group members De Pallo, Solomon, and Mitchell departed. Vito then built a new and improved Salutations with Randy Silverman (lead and first tenor), Shelly Buchansky (first and second tenor), Lenny Citrin (baritone), and Frankie Fox (bass).

The Salutations could usually be found harmonizing in the bathroom of their school, Jefferson High. At the time they were heavily influenced by the black groups of the mid- and late '50s like THE HEARTBEATS, the Cadillacs, THE FLAMINGOS, and THE MOONGLOWS, so it's no surprise that songs by

these groups (such as "Gloria") would become a staple of their repertoire.

Dave Rick took them to another tiny label, Kram, for a single on the Heartbeats gem "Your Way." Kram had even less power than Rayna and "Your Way" became an instant collectible.

In 1963 Rick took the boys to Al Silver's Herald Records, a label with proven power among indies. The group then decided to rearrange the oldies they were doing in a more attention-getting manner.

The standard "Unchained Melody" received a Salutations triple-time treatment with exaggerated bass and falsetto parts that could have been forerunners of THE 4 SEASONS' pseudonymous group the Wonder Who ("Don't Think Twice," Philips, 1965). In the summer, "Unchained Melody" hit the airwaves and went top 10 in many cities. The rapid-fire bass solo in the bridge and a modulation were just two of the record's many vocal gimmicks, and on October 26, 1963, "Unchained" charted nationally, rising to number 66.

A similarly styled original called "Extraordinary Girl" followed in early 1964 and airplay was instantaneous. Unfortunately, Herald was on the verge of folding and could not promote it.

The next stop was Wells Records, where the quintet tried unsuccessfully to ride along with the British invasion with "Liverpool Bound" and then followed with a wild reworking of Harry Belafonte's "Banana Boat (Day-O)," both arranged by Norm Bergen (who later arranged many of the DAWN hits).

Thanks mainly to "Unchained Melody," the group worked steadily in nightclubs and did a few Murray the K shows and Clay Cole and Dick Clark TVers. They performed with Marvin Gaye, Dionne Warwick, JAY AND THE AMERICANS, THE TOKENS, and THE RONETTES. A 1962 appearance at Harlem's Roosevelt Theatre had them backed by a young blind guitarist named Jose Feliciano.

Releases on Regina ("Get a Job," THE SILHOUETTES), Apt ("High Noon," a radical reworking of the western movie title song), and Red Boy ("So Wonderful," a blues ballad) did little and brought them up to their last single on Rust, a hilarious harmony-filled version of "Hello Dolly" that would have had Louis Armstrong gasping for breath to keep up.

The group disbanded around 1965. Randy joined the Attitudes for one single on Times Square, an a cappella version of "That Old Black Magic" in which he sang lead. Vito joined the Kelloggs, who sang on a morning TV show in Philadelphia and had a 1969 single on Laurie called "Snap, Crackle and Pop."

In 1971 the Salutations re-formed for a show at Hunter College during the oldies revival. By 1980, due to legal haggles over ownership of the name, Vito sang under the name Vito Balsamo and His New Group while Dave Rick's group of Salutations included Eddie "Vito" Pardocchi (formerly lead of THE FIVE DISCS), Frankie "Gee" Graziano (first tenor), Shelly Buchansky (second tenor), and Jimmy Spinelli (THE IMPALAS, baritone).

In 1973 Fred Kaplan at Kape Records issued Vito and the Salutations' first LP, a greatest hits package of 14 songs that included four old a cappella sides.

In 1980 the Pardocchi Salutations did a new LP, *From Doo-Wop to Disco* (Lifestream), and in the late '80s Madison Records issued a 14-side LP entitled *Extraordinary Group*, including their best original cuts from the '60s.

An innovative, exaggerated style gave them a trademark sound, and even though they had no major hits, that trademark was more than most groups came away with after years of recording.

VITO AND THE SALUTATIONS

A SIDE/B SIDE	LABEL/CAT NO	DATE
Gloria / Let's Untwist The Twist	Rayna 5009	1962
Your Way / Hey-Hey-Hey	Kram 1202	1962
Unchained Melody /		
Hey Hey Baby	Herald 583	1963
Eenie Meenie / Extraordinary Girl	Herald 586	1964
Can I Depend On You /		
Liverpool Bound	Wells 1008	1964
Day-O / Don't Count On Me	Wells 1010	1964
Get A Job / Girls I Know	Regina 1320	1964
High Noon / Walkin'	Apt 25079	1965
Bring Back Yesterday /		
I Want You To Be My Baby	Boom 60020	1966
So Wonderful / I'd Best Be Going	Red Boy 1001	1966
Hello, Dolly /		
Can I Depend On You	Rust 5106	1966
I'd Best Be Going / So Wonderful	Sandbag 103	1968

The Vogues

Originally known as the Val-Aires, this quartet from Turtle Creek, Pennsylvania, turned out some tasty early '60s pop rock and some late sixties M.O.R. Bill Burkette (lead), Charles "Chuck" Blasko (tenor), Hugh Geyer (tenor), and Don Miller (baritone) were the four friends who became the Val-Aires in the late '50s.

One record on Coral, "Laurie, My Love," and they were transformed into the Vogues.

In 1965 (when all were 22) they recorded a Petula Clark song titled "You're the One" on Blue Star Records. When its activity spread, Co and Ce Records of Pittsburgh (Herb Cohen and Nick Cenci) picked up the master and pushed it to number four in the nation. It was the Vogues' first chart record.

The group followed it with an English unison-styled rocker "Five O'Clock World" (#4), and soon the Pennsylvania pop rockers were a hot commodity on the rock and roll stock exchange.

The Barry Mann/Cynthia Weil-penned "Magic Town" followed, charting in February 1966 to number 21. Next to chart was "The Land of Milk and Honey" (#29), an up-tempo rocker that fell somewhere between Gary Lewis and the Playboys and the Outsiders. Its flip, "True Lovers," was a mid-tempo story of ill-fated love that deserved an A side of its own.

Their fifth single, the 1952 Johnnie Ray number six hit "Please Mr. Sun" (#48), was another strong harmony effort with a terrific flip, a Critters-styled cut called "Don't Blame the Rain."

Three more Co and Ce singles were issued but by 1967 interest in the group sound was waning. Their last Co and Ce release, "Brighter Days," was licensed to MGM but failed. The group then moved over to Reprise Records (distributed by Warner Bros.).

The Reprise single "Turn Around, Look at Me" (#7), originally a charter in 1961 for Glen Campbell, signalled a change to an M.O.R. LETTERMEN-styled direction.

The Bobby Helms 1957 number seven hit "My Special Angel" followed and reached number seven for the Vogues on October 12, 1968.

The group continued to chart through 1969 with remakes like "Till" (THE ANGELS, #14, 1962), which reached number 27, and "Earth Angel" (THE PENGUINS, #8, 1955) at number 42.

A Dick Glasser-produced, fully orchestrated single of Leonard Cohen's "Hey, That's No Way to Say Goodbye" might have been a hit had it not been on the flip side of the Vogues' best Reprise A side of "Over the Rainbow," a stunning single that was overlooked by radio programmers preoccupied with Blood, Sweat and Tears, Steppenwolf, and Led Zeppelin.

The group's last Reprise single was THE SKY-LINERS' 1959 hit (#12) "Since I Don't Have You." They continued to perform through the '70s as a self-contained vocal/instrumental band.

The Volumes

The Volumes came from Detroit, Michigan, in 1960 with tight harmonies and a strong desire to succeed. Motown was not yet a factor in Detroit, though Barrett Strong had their first big hit ("Money," #23 Pop, #2 R&B) in early 1960 on the Tamla and Anna Labels. The quintet's members were Eddie Union (lead), Elijah "Teenie" Davis (first tenor), Larry Wright (second tenor), Joe Truvillion (baritone), and Ernest Newson (bass).

All but Wright attended the same high school. The teens practiced and performed a cappella for months until they met Henry Reed, who helped book them with bands in Detroit and across the border in Canada. The group came up with their music-related moniker when at a rehearsal the guys asked Joe to turn down the volume on the overly loud radio playing in the room.

While performing in Toronto, Canada, they were spotted by Chex Records owner Willie Ewing. He signed them and sent them into a garage studio in Detroit with his A&R man, Richard "Popcorn" Wylie. Fate stepped in when they found out from Wylie that the song they wanted to record, "Answer Me," had already been recorded by the Distants (some of whom would later join members of the Primes to become THE TEMPTATIONS). The reason Wylie knew this was because he had produced the record. By default, their B side, "I Love You," then became their A side. A new, quickly composed tune called "Dreams" became the flip.

12 takes later the Volumes, with Popcorn playing rhythm on a suitcase, had a record. From Newson's solo opening bass notes, the group's doo wop soul harmonies, and the catchy rhythm guitar, to Eddie's buttery smooth lead, "I Love You" was a contagious piece of music.

After climbing to number one in Detroit, it charted nationally on April 28, 1962, and rose to number 22 in *Billboard*.

Soon after, the Volumes played New York's Apollo Theatre and then hit the chitlin circuit through Baltimore and Washington.

During the summer they recorded in a real studio with a real drum setup played by Lamont Dozier, and by July "Come Back into My Heart," another mix of catchy rhythms and great harmonies, had started receiving solid airplay, but it only reached number 118 by August.

The group them moved to Jubilee, Old Town, and American Arts for some undistinguished efforts. Eddie left in 1965, and his lead spot was taken over by Larry.

In 1966 they signed to Impact Records with Gerald Mathis on lead. They moved to Inferno Records in 1967 for three singles with Jimmy Burger on lead. But all the changes in the world couldn't help them dent the charts. The group continued working until the mid-'70s and then disbanded.

THE VOLUMES

A SIDE/B SIDE	LABEL/CAT NO	DATE
I Love You / Dreams	Chex 1002	4/62
Come Back Into My Heart / The Bell	Chex 1005	7/62
Teenage Paradise / Sandra	Jubi 5446	1963
Oh My Mother-In-Law / Our Song	Jubi 5454	1963
Why / Monkey Hop	Old Town 1154	1963
I Can't Live Without You / Gotta Give Her Love	AmArts 6	1964
I Just Can't Help Myself / One Way Lover	AmArts 18	1965
The Trouble I've Seen / That Same Old Feeling	Impact 1017	1966
You Got It Baby / A Way To Love You	Inf 2001	1967
My Road Is The Right Road / My Kind Of Girl	Inf 2004	1967
Ain't That Lovin' You / I Love You Baby	Inf 5001	4/68

THE 1970s

THE VILLAGE PEOPLE

THE POINTER SISTERS

THE EMOTIONS

T he 1970s ushered in the electronic age, and vocal harmony began to be deemphasized on recordings. The only areas that managed to sustain significant vocal group activity were soul music and the phenomenon called the oldies revival, which manifested a renewed interest in '50s and '60s music as performed by the original acts. Groups like the Cadillacs, the Drifters, the Five Satins, Danny and the Juniors, the Skyliners, the Flamingos, the Moonglows, Hank Ballard and the Midnighters, the Belmonts, the Crystals, the Jive Five, and Sonny Til and the Orioles found themselves working and even recording again, some for the first time in many years. This national wave of nostalgia started in 1969 with Richard Nader's first rock and roll revival show.

The soul sound was well-represented by new acts like Bloodstone, Chairmen of the Board, the Dramatics, LaBelle, the Hues Corporation, and Creative Source. Soul's softer side attracted new groups such as Blue Magic, the Main Ingredient, and the Stylistics.

Female groups were prevalent, especially in the soul and disco arenas (which took hold in the middle to late '70s), and they included the Emotions, Shalamar, High Inergy, First Choice, Honey Cone, and Sister Sledge.

Disco attracted a cross section of vocal acts, among them Tavares and the Sylvers; but white vocal groups were conspicuously absent from the disco scene unless they were put-ons like the Village People.

Successful '60s vocal groups that carried over into the '70s were predominantly soul and rhythm and blues acts like the Chi-Lites, Patti La Belle and the Blue Belles, Gladys Knight and the Pips, the Delfonics, the Isley Brothers, the Spinners, Harold Melvin and the Bluenotes, and gospel greats the Dixie Hummingbirds.

'60s pop groups that stayed active in the '70s included the Beach Boys, the Four Seasons, Crosby, Stills and Nash, the Association, the Lettermen, and Three Dog Night. New pop acts, though fewer than in the '60s, still brought some good music to their audiences via Tony Orlando and Dawn, Hamilton, Joe Frank and Reynolds, and the Starland Vocal Band.

A number of acts succeeded in the '70s by carving their own musical niche, such as the jazz/ doo wop Manhattan Transfer and the soul-rocking Lady Flash.

The Motown sound, though not what it was in the '60s, still had a strong presence in the '70s led by the Supremes, the Four Tops, the Temptations, High Inergy, and Gladys Knight and the Pips. Another soul stronghold emerged in the decade in the form of the Soul Train and subsequent Solar (Sound of Los Angeles Records) labels featuring Shalamar and the Whispers.

In the early and mid-'70s the '50s seemed far enough in the past for nostalgia specialists to pop up, like Sha Na Na and Flash Cadillac and the Continental Kids.

TV-established vocal groups were often successful even though they were usually visual concepts based around studio singers, like the Partridge Family, the Archies, and the Globetrotters.

Acappella vocal groups that died off during the '60s British invasion received renewed inter-est from a newly established group of oldies radio stations, particularly in the Northeast. The United in Group Harmony Association in New Jersey, established by Ronnie Italiano, served as a magnet for many new and re-formed vocal groups. With clubs in the Northeast and the South offering acappella nights and oldies shows that were well attended, more and more veteran groups found it worthwhile to return to the performing scene. There were also new groups like the Persuasions, the Ribitones, the Blue Stars, the Ecstasies, Joel and the Connotations, Fourteen Karat Soul, Street Corner Symphony, and Stormy Weather, singing '50s and '60s hits as well as originals in the acappella mode. Older groups who were not of the national hit calibre and couldn't regularly work the established oldies circuit (as the Four Seasons and the Association did), found a very substantial and well-supported underground of fans and clubs. When Ronnie Italiano began holding concerts at Schuetzen Park in North Bergen, New Jersey, in the late '70s, all sorts of groups came out of the woodwork to perform, including the Jesters, the Paragons, the Solitaires, the Sparrows Quartette, the Diablos, and the Excellents.

Record labels catering to this audience sprang up, such as Clifton, Pyramid, Arcade, Story Untold, Crystal Ball, Owl, Monogram, and U.G.H.A. They issued not only new recordings but reissues of long out-of-print records that fans and collectors gobbled up. Still, it was all a far cry from the days of vocal group supremacy in previous decades. Vocal groups were fewer in number on the charts, though they were still active and visible on the performing and recording scene. ◼

The Autumns

The Autumns were a late-'70s group with members from a number of '60s vocal aggregations. Formed in Bergen County, New Jersey, in the summer of 1978, the Autumns included Joel Katz on lead (later of the Wizards on Grecco, 1981, and Twilight on Jade, 1986), Dickie Harmon on tenor (the Connotations on Technichord, Windsong on Clifton, and the recent Del-Vikings on BVM), Eddie Brian on tenor (THE DUCANES on Goldisc, the Connotations), and Jackie Davis on bass (the Connotations).

The group practiced at Eddie's house in Bergenfield and Joel's place in Saddlebrook and on a summer night in 1979 recorded an Eddie Brian song titled "A 1950s Love Song."

Sounding somewhat like a PENGUINS recording (especially Joel's smooth yet powerful lead), "Love Song" came out on the small New Jersey-based J&M label in April 1979. A local radio favorite, had it been on a larger label it might have attained the status of other doo wop era nostalgia songs.

In the early '80s, Eddie Brian, fed up with the myriad of amateurs who were butchering old vocal group standards, brought together the Autumns and another New Jersey group called the Infernos to record a concept LP *The 1980 Doo-Wop Album*, with new, original songs. It took several years to complete, and at one time or another eight different vocalists, including three different basses (Chuck Hereford, Jackie Davis, and Dennis Rotunda) participated.

Upon its 1985 release the LP became a popular item among New York and New Jersey vocal group enthusiasts, but the Autumns themselves, never really a performing act, soon disappeared from the recording scene.

Bloodstone

A quintet formed in Kansas City, Missouri, Bloodstone became one of the few a cappella groups to turn to soul funk to achieve success, but they had to leave America to do it.

The group originally formed in high school in 1962 and called themselves the Sinceres. The five-member act consisted of Charles McCormick, Charles Love, Roger Durham, Willis Draffen, Jr., and Henry Williams. They performed a cappella for years until they felt the group was strong enough

and then moved lock, stock, and vocal cords to Las Vegas to perform as a nightclub act for over a year. By 1971 they had moved on to Los Angeles, learned to play various instruments, and renamed the group "Bloodstone," feeling the name the Sinceres didn't accurately reflect their newfound harder edge. (Most of their recordings continued to maintain a high vocal harmony presence, however.)

In 1972, on the advice of their management company, Bloodstone moved to England and began a long association with producer Mike Vernon. In early 1973 they signed with London Records and by the summer their first single, "Natural High," was at number four on the R&B charts, number 10 on the pop charts, and number 40 on the British charts. They followed "Natural High" with a series of rhythm and blues hits that included "Never Let You Go" (#7 R&B) and "Outside Woman" (#2 R&B).

In 1975, they appeared in and wrote the music for a motion picture titled *Train Ride to Hollywood*. From 1973 to 1984 the group scored 13 chart records with original songs. Their LPs usually contained reminders of their past like "Yakety-Yak," "So Fine," and "Sh-boom."

BLOODSTONE

A SIDE/B SIDE	LABEL/CAT NO	DATE
Natural High	Lndn 1046	4/73
Never Let You Go	Lndn 1051	9/73
Outside Woman	Lndn 1052	2/74
That's Not How It Goes	Lndn 1055	7/74
My Little Lady	Lndn 1061	2 /75
Give Me Your Heart	Lndn 1062	10/75
Do You Wanna Do A Thing	Lndn 1064	4/76
Just Like In The Movies	Lndn 1067	7/76
We Go A Long Way Back	T-Nk 02825	4/82
Go On And Cry	T-Nk 03049	8/82
My Love Grows Stronger (Part 1)	T-Nk 03394	12/82
Instant Love	T-Nk 04465	5/84
Bloodstone's Party	T-Nk 04592	9/84

Blue Magic

A mellow '70s soul group, Blue Magic found its niche in the circus-related titles of their biggest recordings. The group members were from the Philadelphia area and included Ted Mills (lead tenor), Keith Beaton (first tenor), Vernon Sawyer (second tenor), Wendell Sawyer (baritone), and Richard Pratt (bass). Ted attended Overbrook High

School (home of THE DOVELLS) and lived in North Philly while the rest were from Germantown and went to Ben Franklin High School. Though they knew each other from school the group did not form until the members were all out of school and working. They were aged 21 (Richard) to 24 (Ted).

Ted started with a group called the Topics while the other four had their own group called Shades of Love. In 1973 producers Al Rubens, Steve Bernstein, and Bruce Gable were working with Delfonics member Randy Cane. He brought Ted in to do some writing and the producers took note of his vocal potential. The Shades of Love soon came in to audition, and although all concerned felt they were good, they lacked a solid lead singer. That is, until Al Rubens got the idea to put Ted with the group.

They started rehearsing in earnest. The group's influences included THE STYLISTICS and THE DELFONICS, and their early practice songs were by those groups along with THE BLUE NOTES and THE O'JAYS.

Rubens wanted to use the word "magic" in the group's name, but "black magic" seemed too obvious. Looking for something hip or cool like ice they came up with Blue Magic. Rubens, Bernstein, and Gable, known as W.M.O.T. Productions (We Men Of Talent), had the group begin rehearsals at their apartment on Henry Avenue. Bringing in the best writing, producing, and arranging talent in Philadelphia, including Bobby Eli, Norman Harris, Allan Felder, Vinnie Barrett, and Vince Montana (all of whom worked with or as part of Gamble and Huff's MFSB group), the Philadelphia five were soon ready for a record deal arranged by Rubens and company with Atco Records.

They began recording in Sigma Sound Studios and by March 31st had their first R&B chart single, "Spell," which eventually reached number 30. Two singles later "Stop to Start" went to number 14 R&B and later peaked on the Pop charts at number 74.

They played their first gig at Philly's Uptown Theatre and rapidly developed into a tight performing act.

Their hitmaking status was established with the ballad "Sideshow," which reached number eight Pop and number one R&B. It was followed by the equally intriguing "Three Ring Circus," written by Eli and Barrett (#36 Pop, #5 R&B).

The group did one single with songstress Marge Joseph in early 1975 ("What's Come over Me") but it didn't score. They went in a disco direction à la THE SPINNERS on "Love Has Found Its Way to Me," reaching only number 45. During the summer Blue Magic backed up the Rolling Stones on their *It's Only Rock and Roll* LP.

It was back to ballads (as their fans preferred) when they reached number 15 R&B with the Eli/Barrett song "Grateful" in the spring of 1976. The group continued to record and in late 1976 moved over to the WMOT label for one charter, "Summer Snow" (#40 R&B).

After stints at Capitol and Mirage they concentrated on touring the U.S., Europe, and Japan. By 1978 Michael Buchanan and Walter Smith had replaced the Sawyers.

In 1989 they signed with Def Jam Records (Columbia) and had a May release, "Romeo and Juliet," followed by "It's Like Magic" in July.

In 1991 Blue Magic continued to demonstrate the vocal quality that had kept them active for two decades.

BLUE MAGIC

A SIDE/B SIDE	LABEL/CAT NO	DATE
Spell	Atco 6910	1973
Look Me Up	Atco 6938	1973
Stop To Start /		
Where Have You Been	Atco 6949	1973
Sideshow	Atco 6961	1974
Three Ring Circus	Atco 7004	1974
Love Has Found Its Way To Me	Atco 7014	1975
Chasing Rainbows	Atco 7031	1975
Grateful	Atco 7046	1976
Freak-N-Stein	Atco 7052	1976
Teach Me	Atco 7061	1976
Summer Snow	WMOT 4003	1976
Land Of Make Believe	Cap 4977	1981
Seems I Haven't Seen Her	Cap 5024	1981
One Two Three /		
Can I Say I Love You	Lbrty 56146	
Romeo And Juliet	DfJm 3868566	5/89
It's Like Magic	Col 68900	7/89

The Blue Stars

The Blue Stars managed to change from doo wop to rhythm and blues to jazz during their varied career.

They formed in 1974 and featured Louis De Carlo (lead and first tenor), Tony Millone (lead and second tenor), Jack Scandura (lead and second tenor), Bobby Thomas (lead and baritone), and Ken Mewes (lead and bass).

The members were from various parts of Queens and New York and several had sung with prior recording groups. Jack (from Sunnyside) had been with RICKY AND THE HALLMARKS ("Amy," 1962). Louis (from Astoria) had sung lead on "Snow White" with THE DEVOTIONS (Roulette, 1964) and had been with Mr. Bassman and the Symbols ("Rip Van Winkle," Graphic Arts, 1963). Bobby Thomas had sung with Jordan and the Fascinations ("If You Love Me," Josie, 1962) and the Boulevards ("Chop Chop Hole in the Wall," Everest, 1959). Tony (from Manhattan) had sung with Jack in a band called the Fulton Fish Market prior to forming the Blue Stars.

The group started as an a cappella quintet, tracing their roots back to favorite groups like THE HEARTBEATS and THE CLEFTONES. Tony left soon after they formed. His place was taken by Larry Galvin, who had sung with the Velvet Five ("Shop Around," Nostalgia, 1971).

During that year the group recorded three singles for Arcade Records of Jackson Heights, Queens. Each had them accompanied by instruments, although their harmonies were strong and prominent. The first was a version of "My Love Will Never Die" (THE CHANNELS), done very true to the original. Next came a reworking of "I Only Have Eyes for You" (THE FLAMINGOS). The last was an elegant interpretation of "Your Way" (the Heartbeats) along with a reading of the Cleftones' "Can't We Be Sweethearts."

Soon after, the Blue Stars went into hibernation, with three-fifths of the group surfacing as the Blendairs in 1976 with a more vintage R&B-oriented sound. Johnny "Ace" Acuino (lead and first tenor), a former blues bass player for John Lee Hooker and Elvin Bishop, wanted to start a rhythm and blues doo wop group and found willing accomplices in the three Blue Stars, Jack (first tenor), Larry (second tenor), and Ken (bass). When Eddie Conway (Astoria) came aboard, the group began rehearsals at John's house in Sunnyside.

By 1976 Sam Wood (bass of THE SPARROWS QUARTETTE) had replaced Ken Mewes. Between Ace and Wood the Blendairs were now a decidedly early '50s-styled rhythm and blues group in the mold of THE SOLITAIRES. The Blendairs were set to record for Roy Adams's Arcade label when Ace received an offer to work with Elvin Bishop again. The group then had to overdub one part to retain the quintet sound on the single "Sweet Sue" (THE CROWS) b/w "Call on Me" (THE MELLO-MOODS). (The former was led by Jack, the latter by Larry.) Though the label had Manny Giz listed along with the other four (Arcade credited each singer under the Blendairs name), Manny, now of the Del Monicos on Clifton, only sang on one unreleased side called "Tell Me You're Mine."

When Eddie was required to move to Houston for business, the group sat out 1977. In 1978 Jack, Sam, and Larry decided their next musical challenge should be to lean more towards doo wop with modern jazz harmony, but before the group could coalesce, Larry moonlighted on an imaginative rendition of THE BOP CHORDS' "When I Woke Up This Morning" with the group Oasis (Joe Del Pizzo, Dennis Cahill, Charley Ferrari, and Al Vieco) for Arcade. Al was then convinced to join the revamped Blendairs and soon thereafter Beverly Warren, Jack's old friend from the early Ricky and the Hallmark days, also joined. She had since recorded with Vince Vance and the Valiants in the '70s ("Bomb Iran").

With Beverly's addition the direction changed to an R&B doo wop style. The group recorded "He's Gone" on Story Untold Records (1978) followed by singles on "Gee Whiz" (Carla Thomas) and, in March 1979, "Don't Leave Me."

They performed on Don K. Reed's "Doo Wop Shop" radio show that same month.

Sam then decided to retire and by 1980 the Blendairs were no more. However, in keeping with the Jack Scandura seesaw, 1983 ushered in a revamped Blue Stars that included Jack (lead), Anthony Millone (first tenor), Bix Boyle (second tenor), Bobby Thomas (baritone), and Jay Ortsman (bass).

By the time the revolving-door Blue Stars won Rookie Group of the Year at U.G.H.A. in 1986, the quintet consisted of Jack, Larry Galvin, Anthony, Rick Wakeman, and Don Raphael. Finally getting into jazz-based, four-part chords on songs like "Please Mr. Sun" and "Goodnight My Love," they also recorded jazz-styled tunes for Clifton such as "Route 66" (unreleased).

In 1987 they became U.G.H.A.'s Veteran Group Award winner.

The group found a performing niche backing many top oldies leads such as Vernon Green (THE MEDALLIONS), Jimmy Gallagher (THE PASSIONS), Lee Maye (THE CROWNS), Tony Passalacqua (the Fascinators), and LITTLE CAESAR (the Romans) at U.G.H.A. shows.

In 1989 they were co-winners of U.G.H.A.'s Veteran Group of the Year Award with REUNION, and in 1991 they released the *Blue Velvet A Cappella* LP on Clifton in an R&B style.

Though they separated in 1990, there was always the possibility that the Stars/Blendairs might resurface.

As of 1991 Louis De Carlo was in Tampa, Florida, employed in construction. Anthony Millone was in New York City and retired. Bobby Thomas was in Ronkonkoma, New York, in the catering business. Ken Mewes was living in Connecticut and working in computer sales. Rick Wakeman was with New York's Department of Sanitation. Sam Woods was residing in Woodside, Queens, and working in insurance while singing with the Companions. Beverly Warren was last singing with THE TEEN CHORDS. Al Vieco was in Freeport, Long Island, doing clubs. Jay Ortsman was living in Nesconset, Long Island, and singing with East River Drive. Bix Boyle was residing in Arizona. Larry Galvin was living in Woodside and singing with the Companions. Jack Scandura was living in Lynbrook, Long Island, and was a member of THE FIVE DISCS of "I Remember" fame.

Brooklyn Dreams

Brooklyn Dreams was a disco soul-rock group whose roots were in Brooklyn, New York, though they formed 3,000 miles away in Los Angeles. The trio joined forces in the mid-'70s though all three knew each other from back East when Joe "Bean" Esposito and Ed Hokenson went to Erasmus Hall High School and Bruce Sudano went to a nearby Catholic high school. Bruce originally sang with ALIVE AND KICKIN' in 1970 ("Tighter and Tighter," #7, Roulette) while Joe and Ed sang with a few local unrecorded groups.

The threesome called themselves the Movements, Little Mike and the Mysteries, and Alfalfa before coming up with Brooklyn Dreams, the result of a brainstorming session in which one person suggested Brooklyn Queens Expressway and another said something about dreams.

They began practicing songs in Bruce's Laurel Canyon Boulevard apartment, applying their Marvin Gaye and TEMPTATIONS influence to original songs like "Music, Harmony and Rhythm" and "Sad Eyes" that would eventually wind up on their first LP. They did some demos, came in contact with manager Susan Munao, and by 1977 were signed to Millenium Records through exec Jimmy Ienner, who heard their demo and felt the group was right for the burgeoning disco market.

Brooklyn Dreams recorded their first LP at Iam Studios in Newport Beach during May 1978. Their first chart single was "Sad Eyes" in November (#63). Through Bruce's association with Donna Summer the group toured with the disco queen throughout the world, from Europe to Japan.

The Dreams' best single, "Music, Harmony and Rhythm," charted in March 1978 and made it to number 57.

In January 1979 the group recorded with Donna Summer and issued "Heaven Knows," their biggest record (#4) and a million seller. Their last chart single came soon after with the release of "Make It Last" (#69, March 1979).

The trio continued to record and perform but after four LPs they decided to disband in 1983. As Joe said, "The fire and excitement seemed to be gone." In 1991 Joe was writing and doing commercial jingles while looking for a new record deal. Bruce (who married Donna Summer) and Ed were producing and writing for artists on Bruce's Purple Heart label.

Chairmen of the Board

By the 1970s many vocal groups were stocked with veterans of old ensembles as new combinations seemed to be required to meet the demands of a changing music scene.

Such was the case with Chairmen of the Board, formed by General Norman Johnson in Detroit in 1969. Johnson was a member of the Showmen of "It Will Stand" fame (1961) while still in high school in Norfolk, Virginia. Another former Showman, Danny Woods, became a Board member along with ex-LEE ANDREWS AND THE HEARTS vocalist Eddie Curtis and Harrison Kennedy, ex of the Stone Soul Children.

They signed with Invictus Records, owned by former Motown writers Holland, Dozier, and Holland, and their first record, "Give Me Just a Little More Time," started off the new decade by going all the way to number eight R&B and number three on the Pop chart. The group went on to have 11 more R&B chart records between 1970 and 1974, including "Pay to the Piper" (#4 R&B) and the group's namesake title "Chairmen of the Board" (#10 R&B).

All of their 17 single releases were on Invictus Records, but when the hits stopped happening the group disbanded. Johnson developed into a top-notch songwriter, having hits with Clarence Carter ("Patches") and the HONEY CONE ("Want Ads"), among others.

CHAIRMEN OF THE BOARD

A SIDE/B SIDE	LABEL/CAT NO	DATE
Give Me Just A Little More Time /		
Since The Days Of Pigtails	Invcts 9074	1969
Danglin' On A String /		
I'll Come Crawling	Invcts 9078	1970
Everything's Tuesday / Patches	Invcts 9079	1970
Pay To The Piper / Bless You	Invcts 9081	1970
Chairman Of The Board / When		
Will She Tell Me She Needs Me	Invcts 9086	1971
Hanging On To A Memory /		
Tricked and Trapped	Invcts 9089	1971
Try My Love On For Size /		
Working On A Building Of Love	Invcts 9099	1971
Men Are Getting Scarce /		
Bravo, Hooray	Invcts 9103	1971
Bittersweet, Elmo James	Invcts 9105	1972
Everybody's Got To Sing /		
Working On A Building Of Love	Invcts 9122	1972
Let Me Down Easy /		
I Can't Find Myself	Invcts 9126	1972
Finders Keepers /		
Finders Keepers	Invcts 1251	3/73
Life and Death /		
Live With Me, Love With Me	Invcts 1263	2/74
Everybody Party All Night /		
Morning Glory	Invcts 1268	4/74
Let's Have Some Fun /		
Love At First Sight	Invcts 1271	8/74
Skin I'm In / Love At First Sight	Invcts 1276	3/75
Someone Just Like You /		
You've Got Extra Added Powder	Invcts 1278	5/76

Crosby, Stills and Nash

Known as the first so-called supergroup (because all three members came from successful acts), Crosby, Stills and Nash might never have come together if two of their three members hadn't become disenchanted with their previous groups, coincidentally, for the same reason. In 1964, David Crosby was a member of the Byrds, one of the first folk-rock groups. When Crosby wrote a song in 1967 called "Triad" that the Byrds did not feel enthusiastic about and didn't want to record, he left. Graham Nash, a member of the Hollies, decided to move on when his group refused to record Nash's "Marrakesh Express." In 1968 both joined forces with former Buffalo Springfield member Stephen Stills to develop what became an immediately recognizable three-part harmony vocal style. Though all three were guitarists (Stills was the "hot" lead player), the concentration on tight vocals gave them a fresh, country-rock sound that seemed all the more original as the psychedelic era began to wind down in the early '70s. Ironically, "Marrakesh Express" became CSN's first release and first hit in July 1969 (#28).

Neil Young (also of the now-defunct Buffalo Springfield) joined the group soon after. Neil had been a member of a doo wop group known as Danny and the Memories (Valiant Records, 1964) whose recording of the standard "Can't Help Loving That Girl of Mine" gave little indication of his future direction (though it had a solid group harmony sound).

Practically unrehearsed as a performing unit, CSN appeared at the legendary Woodstock festival in August 1969.

Their next five singles all did well, including "Suite: Judy Blue Eyes" (#21), written by Stephen Stills for Judy Collins; "Woodstock" (#11), written by Joni Mitchell; "Teach Your Children" (#16) and "Our House" (#30), both written by Nash; and Neil Young's tribute to those killed at Kent State University, "Ohio" (#14). "Our House" was the last chart single before their first breakup in late 1970.

Largely due to the new exposure medium of FM radio (playing mostly LP cuts in the late '60s and early '70s), the group enjoyed tremendous album success without the usual necessary top 10 record. They didn't score one until they regrouped in 1977, with "Just a Song Before I Go."

They continually regrouped and worked in various configurations through the '70s and '80s, sometimes recording as duos (Crosby and Nash LPs in the early '70s, Stills and Young's *Long May You Run* LP in 1976, and so on). In 1982, the trio saw their *Daylight* LP yield their second top 10 hit, "Wasted on the Way" (#9).

CROSBY, STILLS AND NASH

A SIDE/B SIDE	LABEL/CAT NO	DATE
Marrakesh Express /		
Helplessly Hoping	Atln 2652	1969
Suite: Judy Blue Eyes /		
Long Time Gone	Atln 2676	1969
Woodstock / Helpless	Atln 2723	1970
Teach Your Children / Carry On	Atln 2735	1970
Ohio / Find The Cost Of Freedom	Atln 2740	1970
Our House / Deja Vu	Atln 2760	1970
Just A Song Before I Go /		
Dark Star	Atln 3401	1977
Fair Game / Anything At All	Atln 3432	1977

A SIDE/B SIDE	LABEL/CAT NO	DATE
I Give You Give Blind / Carried Away	Atln 3453	1978
Carry On	Atln 3784	1980
Wasted On The Way	Atln 4058	1982
Southern Cross	Atln 89969	1982
Too Much Love To Hide	Atln 89888	1983
War Games	Atln 89812	1983

Dawn

In May 1970 record producer and TOKENS member Hank Medress and his partner Dave Appell (former A&R executive at Cameo/Parkway Records) produced a recording of a song written by Toni Wine and Irwin Levine. Medress and Appell brought the DRIFTERS-styled recording to Bell Records president Larry Uttal, who loved the song but not the singer. Hank then hoped that his friend Tony Orlando (actually Michael Anthony Orlando Cassivitis, son of a Greek furrier), who had sung demos for Goffin and King songs that ended up being recorded by the Drifters ("When My Little Girl Is Smiling" and "Some Kind of Wonderful"), would help him out and put his voice on the recording. Tony, however, was now working as a music publisher for April-Blackwood, the publishing arm of Columbia Records, and was not about to jeopardize his job just to cut a vocal, even though singing was his first love. In the early '60s Tony had recorded for his current company's affiliate, Epic, garnering hits with "Half Way to Paradise" (#39, 1961) and "Bless You" (#15, 1961), but when the hits had stopped coming, Tony had joined the working class.

Tony finally agreed to spend an hour in the studio, with Ellie Greenwich (the Raindrops, Jubilee), Toni Wine, Jay Siegel (lead of the Tokens), and Robin Grean doing backup vocals. With Hank producing and Phil Margo (also of the Tokens) on drums, it was almost a Tokens affair.

By July, Tony had totally forgotten the session. But then he saw the record bulleting up the charts in *Billboard*. He didn't recognize the group name Dawn, but he did think there was something familiar about the song title "Candida."

When he finally heard the record he almost fell on the floor.

For a short time, Dawn's record had some competition from a Bill and Steve Jerome-produced version on Musicor by the Corporation, a Drifters-styled group. They had obviously heard Toni Wine's original piano/voice demo of the song, a slower version than Dawn's. The Corporation's disc faltered as the Bell release took off in July.

By October 3rd it was number three in the nation (#9 U.K., and #13 in Australia) and Hank was back on Tony's doorstep with a new Irwin Levine and Larry Brown song called "Knock Three Times." Still, no one knew who Dawn was (they were named by Bell Records promotion VP Steve Wax after his daughter Dawn) let alone who was singing lead. Tony, fearing for his job, wanted to remain anonymous since he found it hard to explain why he was recording for a competing label. He changed his mind when Hank offered him a royalty. Beyond that, he thought the song was terrible and would never get off the ground, thus ending his crisis of conscience.

In the fall it was back to the studio with Jay, Toni Wine, and Robin doing "Knock Three Times." At least this time Tony knew who the group was (at the "Candida" session, Tony had left the studio before the background vocals were put on). On January 23, 1971, the song knocked George Harrison's "My Sweet Lord" out of the number one spot and stayed there for three weeks, selling over six million records. It also went to number one in England and number four in Australia. Tony had to face the enviable but embarrassing fact that he'd just had two million sellers back to back.

Though there was no group, Bell Records wanted to expose somebody, so Dawn's performing debut was arranged for a Christmas show at Carnegie Hall. The Dawn that appeared turned out to be Tony along with Norm Bergen (the arranger for many of Dawn's hits and now a member of the Tokens), Mitchell Brown, Ronnie Amodea, and Lois Griffiths.

Tony finally told his Columbia boss Clive Davis. Waiting to be lambasted, he was told that as long as he wasn't going on the road it was okay to moonlight, but he'd better put some April-Blackwood's songs on the forthcoming Dawn LP. With the job pressure off, Tony started enjoying the LP recording. He then quit his job in preparation for a European tour. The only problem was there was no Dawn to tour with. Thanks to producer Tony Camillo (GLADYS KNIGHT AND THE PIPS), Orlando met Telma Hopkins and her cousin Joyce Vincent. The two had done studio work for Motown, backing THE FOUR TOPS on "Reach Out" and "Bernadette." The girls only went with the understanding that after the European tour Tony would be on his own again, but the trio hit it off and upon returning to America decided to stay together and record.

Sides recorded before the girls joined continued to hit: "I Play and Sing" (#25, spring of 1971) and "Summer Sand" (#33, summer of 1971). Another Pocketful of Tunes single (Wes Farrell's company and publisher of all the hits to date), "What Are You Doing Sunday" (now credited as "Dawn Featuring Tony Orlando," #39, fall of 1971), was a clever teen top 40 tune which peaked in the U.K. at number three. The group's singles and LPs usually read "Produced by the Tokens and Dave Appell" or "Produced by Hank Medress, Dave Appell, and the Tokens."

Telma and Joyce finally recorded as Dawn on the sixth single, a medley of "Runaway" (Del Shannon)/ "Happy Together" (the Turtles) done in alternatingly slow and fast sections. It only peaked at number 79 in early 1972. Their next two releases, "Via Con Dios" (#95) and "You're a Lady" (#70), did little to bolster the trio's career.

The group was on the verge of separating when Hank Medress arrived in the nick of time with the song "Tie a Yellow Ribbon Round the Ole Oak Tree." Tony hated it and tried to give it to Bobby Vinton, who wouldn't touch it either. Needless to say, Tony and company finally acquiesced, and the result was their second number one hit and the top record of 1973. Internationally, it gave them their fourth hit in Britain (#1) and another number one in Australia and New Zealand.

The new series of Dawn 45s in 1973 brought a new "ragtime" sound to top 40 with "Say Has Anybody Seen My Sweet Gypsy Rose" (#3), "Who's in the Strawberry Patch with Sally" (#27), and "Steppin' Out (Gonna Boogie Tonight)" (#7), all written by Irwin Levine and Larry Brown. Speaking of Levine and Brown, their future was assured when a tape containing the last tune they owed in their writing commitment to Pocketful of Tunes couldn't be found; company president Wes Farrell (or one of his executives) had somehow lost it and couldn't prove the song ever fell under their songwriting agreement. The song? "Tie a Yellow Ribbon," of course.

At the height of Tony and Dawn's popularity, CBS gave them a summer replacement TV variety show in 1974 that ran until December 1976.

By the end of 1974, "Look in My Eyes Pretty Woman" was on its way up the charts to reach an eventual number 11 spot. The group then moved to Elektra Records where they felt they could create more R&B-influenced records. They did just that, and their version of the Jerry Butler 1960 hit "He Don't Love You (Like I Love You)" (originally titled "He Will Break Your Heart") became their third

number one hit on May 3rd. By early 1975 Bell Records became Arista Records and they issued one LP and one single, both titled "Skybird" (#49). Four more Elektra singles were released and charted, the best being "Morning Beautiful" (#14) and "You're All I Need (To Get By)" (#34).

The pressures of success combined with personal tragedies in Tony's life (the death of his sister to cerebral palsy and the suicide of friend Freddie Prinze) overcame the singer, and while on stage in Cohasset, Massachusetts, on July 27, 1977, he broke down and announced that he was retiring. He went through months of rest and rehabilitation while Joyce (now married) left the entertainment business and Telma became an actress doing the TV sitcoms "Bosom Buddies" from 1980 through 1984 followed by "Gimme a Break" from 1984 through 1987.

In July 1988 Tony and Dawn did a reunion tour that found their sound and their friendship as strong as ever. Though not taken very seriously by listeners who put down top 40 and bubblegum acts, Tony Orlando and Dawn were nonetheless thoroughly professional singers who combined to make an excellent vocal group.

Not one of the singles in their seven-year recording career failed to make the national pop charts. Few acts can make that claim.

DAWN

A SIDE/B SIDE	LABEL/CAT NO	DATE
Candida / Look At	Bell 903	1970
Knock Three Times / Home	Bell 938	1970
I Play And Sing / Get Out From Where We Are	Bell 970	1971
Summer Sand / Sweet Soft Sounds Of Love	Bell 45107	1971

Dawn Featuring Tony Orlando

A SIDE/B SIDE	LABEL/CAT NO	DATE
What Are You Doing Sunday / Sweet Soft Sounds Of Love	Bell 45141	1971
Runaway-Happy Together (medley) / Don't Act Like A Baby	Bell 45175	1972
Vaya Con Dios / I Can't Believe How Much I Love You	Bell 45225	1972
You're A Lady / In The Park	Bell 45285	1972
Tie A Yellow Ribbon Round The Old Oak Tree / I Can't Believe How Much I Love You	Bell 45318	1973
Say, Has Anybody Seen My Sweet Gypsy Rose / The Spark Of Love Is Kindlin'	Bell 45374	1973

Tony Orlando and Dawn

A SIDE/B SIDE	LABEL/CAT NO	DATE
Who's In The Strawberry Patch With Sally / Ukulele Man	Bell 454524	1973

A SIDE/B SIDE	LABEL/CAT NO	DATE
It Only Hurts When I Try To Smile / Sweet Summer Days Of My Life	Bell 45450	1974
Steppin' Out (Gonna Boogie Tonight) / She Can't Hold A Candle To You	Bell 45601	1974
Look In My Eyes Pretty Woman / My Love Has No Pride	Bell 45620	1974
He Don't Love You Like I Love You / Pick It Up	Elek 45240	1975
Mornin' Beautiful / Dance Rosie Dance	Elek 45260	1975
You're All I Need To Get By / I Know You Like A Book	Elek 45275	1975
Skybird / That's The Way A Wallflower Feels	Arista 0156	1975
Cupid / You're Growin' On Me	Elek 45302	1976
Sing / Sweet On Candy	Elek 45387	1977

The Dramatics

A solid soul vocal group, the Dramatics started out as the Dynamics. The Detroit teenagers were all from Pershing High School except for lead singer Ron Banks, 13, who was attending Cleveland Junior High when they formed in 1964. The group was originally a sextet that included Banks, Larry Reed (16, second tenor), Elbert Wilkins (17, first and second tenor), Larry "Squirrel" Demps (15, baritone), Robert "Duke" Ellington (the nephew of Duke Ellington, baritone), and Rob Davis (17, bass).

The group began practicing on Pershing's tennis courts doing songs by THE MIRACLES, THE IMPRESSIONS, THE TEMPTATIONS, and the Contours. Ron himself was influenced by artists ranging from Sammy Davis, Jr. and Nancy Wilson to the Temptations and Curtis Mayfield. Before long, Ellington dropped out of the group.

The Dramatics began playing talent shows. They played a cabaret called Mr. Kelly's and met the niece of Ed Wingate, who owned Wingate Records. Wingate auditioned the group on a Sunday and signed them the next day. When little happened at Wingate after a spring of 1965 recording session, the group moved on to Sport Records and by 1967 had their first modest charter, "All Because of You" (#43, R&B).

They renamed themselves the Dramatics in a time-honored tradition: each member threw a name in a hat and Larry Demps's choice was pulled out. Their first major performance was at the B.I.M.A.

auditorium in the fall of 1965 appearing with LITTLE ANTHONY AND THE IMPERIALS.

In 1969 the revised lineup included Banks, Wilkins, Demps, William Howard (20), and Willie Ford, Jr. (20). They signed with the Stax/Volt label that year, and though they would become almost exclusively balladeers, their first single (October 1969) was an up-tempo Temptations-styled soul screamer called "Your Love Was Strange." When it failed, it took the Dramatics almost two years to get another chance, but they made the most of it with the release of "Whatcha See Is Whatcha Get," another Temps-styled rhythm number that had the right radio ingredients. By July 3, 1971, it charted, reaching number three R&B and number nine Pop. Two singles later they had their biggest record ever, the beautifully soulful ballad "In the Rain" (#5 Pop, #1 R&B, 1972). In 1973, L. J. Reynolds and Lenny Mayes replaced Howard and Wilkins.

The group continued to chart for Volt (four of their last five singles) with only their last single, "I Made Myself Lonely," missing the lists. They also recorded, uncredited, on a variety of Mavis Staples and Johnny Taylor singles ("Jody's Got Your Girl" and "Gone," 1971). After a short run at Cadet Records they moved to ABC and hit with "Me and Mrs. Jones" (#47 Pop, #4 R&B) in the spring of 1973. They also did a unique LP with THE DELLS, and from it came "Love Is Missing in Our Lives" (#46 R&B, 1975). Their biggest ABC single was "Be My Girl" (#53 Pop, #3 R&B) toward the end of 1976. Though their recording of Hall and Oates' "Do What You Wanna Do" was one of their finest and Ron Banks's favorite, it only reached number 56 R&B in the fall of 1978.

The group continued recording for MCA, Capitol, and Fantasy through the '80s with their last charter being "One Love Ago" (#61 R&B, Fantasy) in 1986. L. J. Reynolds went solo in 1981 but later rejoined the group. In 1991 the lineup consisted of Banks, Reynolds, Lenny Mays, and Willie Ford.

The Emotions

One of the most successful female groups of the '70s, the Emotions were originally a gospel group made up of three sisters, Sheila, Wanda, and Jeanette Hutchinson. The Chicago siblings were performing at the respective ages of three, four, and five under the guidance of their father, Joe, Sr.

Originally called the Heavenly Sunbeams, the trio later became the Hutchinson Sunbeams and hosted a radio show of spiritual music in the '60s (later to evolve into a Sunday TV show) while in their early teens. Joe, Sr. taught his daughters how to sing, harmonize, and read music, and their repertoire ran the gamut of gospel, blues, folk music, and secular songs.

In 1958 the trio made their first TV appearance on the Jerry Van Dyke show. They performed in "The Passion Play" in Chicago for two years and shared a stage with gospel great Mahalia Jackson on numerous occasions. At one point in the mid-'60s, while attending Parker High School, the act was called Three Ribbons and a Beau (Joe, Sr. was the Beau, a guitarist/vocalist).

As the Sunbeams' talent and experience grew over the years, they had the opportunity to record for One-der-ful, Twin Stax, and Vee-Jay.

It's reported that in 1968, while the oldest in the trio was only 18, the group won a talent contest at the Regal Theatre in Chicago. The first prize was a contract with Stax Records of Memphis for a single recording, but once Stax heard the girls they were given an LP deal instead. Other reports differ, however, saying that while the group was on tour they met the Staple Singers, who helped them acquire a contract with Stax/Volt.

The Parker High School grads now became the Emotions to convey a more soulful image (listeners would tell their dad how emotional they felt when they heard the girls).

Their first Volt release, "So I Can Love You," hit the R&B charts on May 3, 1969, and the Pop charts on May 24th, going all the way to number three R&B and number 39 Pop. With Isaac Hayes and David Porter of Stax producing and often writing for the sisters, the Emotions became an important act in the Stax stable of stars.

During 1970 the trio became a foursome with the addition of Teresa Davis. Between 1969 and 1974, the Emotions registered 13 R&B charters out of 17 releases, all with that identifiable soul-gospel feel the group had become so well-known for. Their biggest recordings of that period were "Show Me How" (#52 Pop, #13 R&B, 1971) and "My Honey and Me" (#113 Pop, #18 R&B, 1972). In 1973 the Emotions appeared in the film *Wattstax*.

In 1974 Stax went under, so the girls began to write songs, added brother Joe, Jr. on guitar, and spent a year woodshedding. During the early '70s the group toured with such stars as Stevie Wonder, B. B. King, Sly and the Family Stone, and THE JACKSON 5, among others.

The former drummer of the Jazz Interpreters asked about their availability to record in November 1975. The drummer was Maurice White, later of Earth, Wind and Fire. He brought the Emotions to Columbia, produced their first LP, *Flowers*, in February 1976, and took the girls on tour with his group and Ramsey Lewis.

The first single was a two-sided R&B hit, "Flowers" (#87 Pop, #16 R&B) b/w "I Don't Wanna Lose Your Love" (#51 Pop, #13 R&B), and the LP went gold. Their next LP, recorded in March 1977 and titled *Rejoice*, contained what would become the mother of all hits for the Emotions, "Best of My Love." Charting on May 29, 1977, it reached number one on both the Hot 100 and R&B charts by August 20th. It also hit number four in England in the fall of 1977. The group began a college tour that year with younger sister Pamela replacing Jeanette, who opted to stay home with her family. "Best of My Love" won a Grammy that year. The girls then turned in two more R&B top 10s, "Don't Ask My Neighbors" (#44 Pop, #7 R&B) and "Smile" (#102 Pop, #6 R&B) in late 1977 and early 1978.

In the spring of 1979 Maurice, who had started his own Arc label (distributed by Columbia) produced the energetic "Boogie Wonderland," combining Earth, Wind and Fire with the Emotions for their second biggest hit (#6 Pop, #2 R&B).

The girls stopped recording as a unit in the mid-'80s but continued to perform together. They appeared together in the play "Wicked Ways" in 1991 while working on a pop spiritual LP.

THE EMOTIONS

A SIDE/B SIDE	LABEL/CAT NO	DATE
So I Can Love You /		
Got To Be The Man	Volt 4010	1969
The Best Part Of A Love Affair /		
I Like It	Volt 4021	1969
Stealing Love /		
When Tomorrow Comes	Volt 4031	1969
Heart Association /		
The Touch Of Your Lips	Volt 4045	1970
Black Christmas / Black Christmas	Volt 4053	1970
You Make Me Want To Love You /		
What You See Is What You Get	Volt 4054	2/71
If You Think It /		
Love Ain't Easy One Sided	Volt 4062	1971
Show Me How / Boss Love Maker	Volt 4066	9/71
My Honey And Me / Blind Alley	Volt 4077	1972
I Never Could Be Happy /		
I've Fallen In Love	Volt 4083	1972
From Toys To Boys /		
I Call This Loving You	Volt 4088	11/72

A SIDE/B SIDE	LABEL/CAT NO	DATE
Runnin' Back /		
I Wanna Come Back	Volt 4095	7/73
Peace Be Still / Runnin' Back	Volt 4100	10/73
What Do The Lonely Do At		
Christmas / What Do The		
Lonely Do At Christmas	Volt 4104	12/73
Put A Little Love Away /		
I Call This Loving You	Volt 4106	2/74
Baby I'm Through /		
I Wanna Come Back	Volt 4110	8/74
Anyway You Look At It / There Are		
More Questions Than Answers	Volt 4113	12/74
Flowers / I Don't Wanna		
Lose Your Love	Col 10347	9/76
Best Of My Love / A Feeling Is	Col 10544	5/77
Don't Ask My Neighbors /		
Love's What's Happenin'	Col 10622	9/77
Smile / Changes	Col 10791	7/78
Whole Lot Of Shakin' /		
Time Is Passing By	Col 10828	9/78
Walking The Line /		
Ain't No Doubt About It	Col 10874	12/78
Boogie Wonderland*	Col 10956	1979
What's The Name Of Your Love? /		
Laid Back	Col 11134	10/79
Where Is Your Love? / Laid Back	Col 11205	2/80
Turn That Out /		
When You Gonna Wake Up	Col 02239	7/81
Now That I Know /		
Here You Come Again	Col 02535	9/81
You're The One	Rd Lbl 001	1984
You're The Best	Rd Lbl 002	1984
Are You Through With My Heart	Rd Lbl 003	1984

* Earth, Wind and Fire with the Emotions

Flash Cadillac

There was a nostalgia craze in the '70s, as maturing baby boomers yearned for the good old '50s and '60s epitomized by the music of those eras. One of the better-known groups catering to the demand was Flash Cadillac and the Continental Kids, who played and sang new songs in the style of the previous decades. They even took on '50s-style names. In 1970 "Flash" Samuel McFadden (lead and guitar), "Angelo" Chris Moe (lead and drums), "Spike" Lin Phillips (vocals and guitar), "Wally" Jeff Stuart (vocals and drums), "Butch" Warren Knight (vocals and bass), and "Spider" Dwight Bement (sax) formed on the campus of the University of Colorado in Boulder.

They began playing fraternity parties and then branched out to local clubs. Buoyed by their warm reception, the 18-to-30-year-olds packed up and drove to Los Angeles, where they lined up an appearance at the legendary Troubador. As the jobs piled up, they began opening for a variety of rock acts and in 1972 came to the attention of Epic Records. They issued an LP in 1973 and then appeared in the prom scene of the George Lucas film *American Graffiti*. A follow-up LP, *There's No Face Like Chrome*, included the single "Dancin' (On a Saturday Night)" (#93) in the spring of 1974.

By 1975 the Kids had signed to Larry Uttal's Private Stock Records, recording *The Sons of the Beaches* LP produced by veteran Toxey French. The key single was "Good Times, Rock & Roll," and the BEACH BOYS-styled group took it to number 41 in the spring of 1975. Their best and biggest single came toward the end of summer 1976 with the HAPPENINGS-styled Joe Renzetti/Dave Chackler-produced doo wop tune "Did You Boogie (With Your Baby)," that was interspersed with raps by Wolfman Jack. The 45 made it to number 29 but the group couldn't keep the momentum going on record and wound up on the club scene through the late '70s and the '80s.

Fourteen Karat Soul

Once called "the best teenaged singing group in America" by a *Village Voice* columnist, Fourteen Karat Soul was the brainchild of Glen "Glenny T" Wright, a 16-year-old from Essex County Vocational and Technical High School in Bloomfield, New Jersey.

On a fateful November day in 1975 Glenny T attended a registration for a talent show at East Orange High to enroll his band. While there, a vocal group with eight members came on stage to audition, singing "Me and Mrs. Jones" (Billy Paul, 1972) a cappella. Enthralled by this new experience, Glen ran home and announced his intention to form a singing group. The original members came from three different schools but each was in the Mount Olive Baptist Church Young Adult Choir in East Orange. Besides Glen there was Russell Fox II (13, baritone, from William S. Heart Middle School), Brian Simpson (13, first tenor natural), David Thurmond (16, first tenor falsetto), and Reginald "Briz" Brisbon (16, bass) (the latter three were of East Orange High School).

Briz was found at the school playground and he auditioned singing "The Sun," a song by THE PERSUASIONS. When he sailed through the song in baritone, Glenny told him they were really looking for a bass. Briz finished off the ballad by dropping to a lower register, and Glenny T's smile told Briz he'd made the group.

They began rehearsing at Glen's Chestnut Street home in East Orange, practicing songs from the '70s' "Me and Mrs. Jones" to the '50s' "Why Do Fools Fall in Love."

Their name came from a brainstorming session with David and his girlfriend, Denise Washington (later actress Miesha McCay). He thought of "Fourteen Karat Gold" and she adapted "Gold" to "Soul."

Their humble debut was a performance at the dedication for the East Orange Public Library on March 14, 1976. After that they played local gigs and practiced what could best be described as sounds of the '50s and '60s turned into '70s soul music.

In November 1977 they played a United in Group Harmony Association (U.G.H.A.) show for the newly formed oldies organization at Schuetzen Park in North Bergen, New Jersey. Former Persuasions producer Stan Krause saw them and immediately recognized the above-average talent. Stan brought in producer Skip Jackson to record FKS, and rather than going in an obvious a cappella oldies direction, he recorded the group in a disco mode on the song "Doo-Wop Disco." (Skip also recorded their version of "The Sun" for the doo wop diehards in early 1979.) Due to their contemporary harmony sound with '50s roots, the quintet found themselves performing with a wide cross section of acts. On the oldies side there were THE CADILLACS, THE HARPTONES, THE FLAMINGOS, THE SPANIELS, THE MOONGLOWS, and THE CHARTS. The unexpected side included soul rockers B. T. Express and Brass Construction, soul acts BLUE MAGIC and Al Green, and rockers Southside Johnny and the Asbury Jukes as well as Bruce Springsteen's E Street Band.

Confidence was building when Glenny T got word that Ray Charles would be appearing at Newark's Symphony Hall. Glenny managed to reach Ray by phone hoping for an opening spot on his bill, but the forthright R&B legend passed, saying he'd never heard of the group. Glen replied that their record was currently being played on WNJR. On June 2, 1979, FKS opened for Ray Charles. Apparently he had turned on his radio and liked what he heard.

Playwrights Bob Telson and Lee Breuer saw the quintet perform almost a year later at that same Symphony Hall (March 9, 1980), which led to Fourteen Karat Soul appearing in a doo wop operetta produced by Joseph Papp called *Sister Suzie Cinema*. When the show moved out of the Public Theater in New York the group went with it to travel on the road to San Francisco, Los Angeles, and European stopovers in France, Switzerland, Holland, and Belgium.

By 1982 they had also toured the U.K. and had an LP out on Catamount titled *Lovers' Fantasy*. As an inspiration to others, their album was encased in glass for display at the East Orange Public Library. They also appeared three times on NBC's "Saturday Night Live," on "Sesame Street," sang backup for Robert Plant on stage, and did a U.K./European tour with Whitney Houston, and all without a hit record.

In 1983 the soulful foursome met Stray Cats lead Brian Setzer in London. He was so intrigued by the group's sound that they were brought in to do the harmony on the Stray Cats' EMI recording "I Won't Stand in Your Way," which charted on October 29th and went to number 35, unfortunately without any credit to FKS. The performance was done with such perfection that the B side of the single was the A side's vocal tracks without instruments. The record marked the beginning of a five-month tour (October 1983 to February 1984) for the group with the Cats.

During April 1986 Fourteen K performed at a music industry party in London and met a gentleman who was interested in bringing them to Japan. It took a year, but the group finally got to perform at several Tokyo clubs in 1987. They went on to record three albums released only in Japan.

Fourteen Karat Soul had only a few member changes in its career. In 1991 the group included Glenny T, Russell, and David, along with Tony-Zeke Holding (replacing Simpson in 1986 at first tenor) and Mykle Alexander (on bass, replacing Brisbon in 1984). Mykle was a former member of the a cappella group Charm, which is often credited with having backed Billy Joel on his 1984 hit "The Longest Time." It has since come to light that Mykle was the only Charm on Joel's record.

Though they didn't have a hit, Fourteen Karat Soul was one of the premier soul vocal groups of the '70s and '80s.

FOURTEEN KARAT SOUL

A SIDE/B SIDE	LABEL/CAT NO	DATE
Doo Wop Disco / Doo Wop Disco (instrumental)	Catamount	1979

A SIDE/B SIDE	LABEL/CAT NO	DATE
Boogie Woogie Bugle Boy / The Sun	Catamount	1979
Please Say You Want Me / The Trouble With Love	Catamount	1979
This Boy / Ain't Too Proud To Beg	Discafrique	1987
The Girl In White / This Boy	Pony Canyon	1988
Stand By Me	Pony Canyon	1989
Get Back In Love / I Want You To Stay	Pony Canyon	1990

Hamilton, Joe Frank and Reynolds

Hamilton, Joe Frank and Reynolds were a pop-rock trio whose career was launched from an Alka-Seltzer commercial. The threesome, Dan Hamilton, Joe Frank Carollo, and Tommy Reynolds, were all accomplished musicians who recorded in a studio band called the T-Bones. Hamilton of Wenatchee, Washington, moved to Los Angeles and by the age of 15 was regularly playing guitar on recording sessions for Jerry Lee Lewis, Johnny Rivers, and others. While working on the TV show "Shindig" he put the T-Bones together with Carollo of Leland, Mississippi, and Reynolds of New York City.

In 1965 Alka-Seltzer had an immensely popular television campaign with an instrumental melody that caught the attention of record producer Joe Saraceno. He recorded it with the T-Bones and in December 1965 "No Matter What Shape Your Stomach's In" hit the *Billboard* charts and kept bubbling up until the Alka-Seltzer song had dissolved all challengers on the Hot 100 except THE BEACH BOYS' "Barbara Ann" and Petula Clark's "My Love." A few months later the T-Bones went on from indigestion to digestion when they charted with "Sippin' 'N Chippin'" (#62) from the Nabisco Sip 'N Chip commercial.

After years of studio work and anonymity as the T-Bones (how do you tour doing antacid commercials?), Hamilton, Joe Frank and Reynolds formed Hamilton, Joe Frank and Reynolds.

In 1971 they hooked up with Dunhill Records and hit it big with "Don't Pull Your Love," which climbed to number four on July 17th right behind James Taylor's "You've Got a Friend" (#3), the Raiders' "Indian Reservation" (#2), and Carole King's "It's Too Late" (#1).

By the end of 1971 it seemed as if their vocal group career was over; their only other Dunhill charters were "Annabella" (#46) and "Daisy Mae" (#41).

In 1972 Reynolds, convinced it was over, became a Texas minister and Alan Dennison of Marion, Ohio, replaced him.

By 1975 the determined trio signed with *Playboy* magazine's record company, Playboy Records, and in the summer of 1975 took a Dan and Ann (his wife) Hamilton song, "Fallin' in Love," to number one on August 23rd for one week (#33 U.K.). To do it they had to displace the hot Bee Gees "Jive Talkin'" from the top spot, and a week later they were evicted by K.C. and the Sunshine Band with "Get Down Tonight." "Winners and Losers" (#21) followed, and in 1976 they charted again with "Everyday Without You" (#62).

During this time (more than a year after "Fallin' in Love" was issued) they were still going by the name Hamilton, Joe Frank and Reynolds. It wasn't until the summer of 1976 and the release of "Light Up the World with Sunshine" that they charted under the name Hamilton, Joe Frank and Dennison, reaching number 67.

After one more single, "Don't Fight the Hands (That Need You)" (#72), the group drifted back into studio background obscurity.

High Inergy

At the height of their six-year career, the High Inergy members were touted as the Miss American Teenagers of Soul. The exceptionally pretty foursome were schoolmates Vernessa Mitchell (lead), her sister Barbara, Michelle Martin, and Linda Howard. They all attended Blair High School in Pasadena, California.

Upon graduation the teen queens entered a federally funded bicentennial performing arts program in 1976.

Spotted by Gwen Gordy, sister of Motown legend Berry Gordy, the group was given the royal packaging treatment, from what to wear to how to dance.

In the summer of 1977 their first single, the suggestive "You Can't Turn Me Off (In the Middle of Turning Me On)" was on the national airwaves, charting on September 3rd and reaching number two R&B and number 12 Pop in the fall. The danceable hit spent six months on the charts, but its rapid rise created an unattainable goal for their follow-ups.

In 1978, after the group's LP *Steppin' Out*, Vernessa left and the girls continued as a trio.

"Love Is All You Need," released in January 1978, reached number 20 R&B and only number 89 Pop while "We Are the Future" did even worse (#77 R&B). Apparently, the public preferred their seductive side to their love or message records.

Six of their next 17 singles hit the lower reaches of the R&B charts, meaning either the songs were off or Motown's promotion wasn't doing the job, because the girls' vocal work was outstanding. Some of their best tracks were "Shoulda Gone Dancin'" (#50, 1979), "First Impressions" (#50, 1982), and their last single, a remake of THE SUPREMES' "Back in My Arms Again" in 1983.

The group appeared on Motown's 25th Anniversary show in 1983, and after eight LPs and 20 singles they called it a recording career. Barbara then joined Capitol Records that same year, but no successful recordings were forthcoming.

HIGH INERGY

A SIDE/B SIDE	LABEL/CAT NO	DATE
You Can't Turn Me Off (In The Middle Of Turning Me On) / Save It For A Rainy Day	Gordy 7155	9/77
You Can't Turn Me Off (In The Middle Of Turning Me On) / Let Me Get Close To You	Gordy 7715	9/77
Love Is All You Need / Some Kinda Majik	Gordy 7157	2/78
We Are The Future / High School	Gordy 7160	6/78
Lovin' Fever / Beware	Gordy 7161	8/78
Shoulda Gone Dancin' / Peaceland	Gordy 7166	3/79
Skate To The Rhythm / Midnight Music Man	Gordy 7174	9/79
Come And Get It / Midnight Music Man	Gordy 7172	10/79
I Love Makin' Love (To The Music) / Somebody, Somewhere	Gordy 7178	1/80
Make Me Yours / I Love Makin' Love (To The Music)	Gordy 7187	8/80
Hold On	Grdy G8996M1	8/80
Hold On To My Love / If I Love You Tonight	Gordy 7192	10/80
I Just Wanna Dance With You / Take My Life	Gordy 7201	4/81
Goin' Through The Motions / I Just Can't Help Myself	Gordy 7207	8/81
Don't Park Your Loving / Now That There's You	Gordy 7211	9/81
First Impressions / Could This Be Love	Grdy 1613GF	4/82

A SIDE/B SIDE	LABEL/CAT NO	DATE
Wrong Man, Right Touch / Beware	Grdy 1632GF	7/82
Journey To Love / Could This Be Love	Grdy 1641GF	9/82
So Right / Don't Let Up On The Groove	Grdy 1656GF	1/83
He's A Pretender / Don't Let Up On The Groove	Grdy 1662GF	1/83
Blame It On Love / Even Tho'	Tamla 1684TF	6/83
Back In My Arms Again / So Right	Grdy 1688GF	7/83

The Honey Cone

What do Hale and the Hushabyes, Ike and Tina Turner's Ikettes, and the Girlfriends have in common? Each group had a member who later became a part of the hitmaking soul trio Honey Cone. Honey Cone was the first of the '70s sassy sisters whose show-of-independence song lyrics (ironically, mostly written by men) paved the way for more assertion of female rights in music of the '70s and '80s.

The three girls were Edna Wright (sister of Darlene Love; see THE BLOSSOMS), Shellie Clark, and Carolyn Willis.

By the time they came together in 1969 to do background vocals on an Andy Williams TV special, each girl had apprenticed for five to nine years with different groups and done a lot of professional studio singing.

Edna, from L.A., started in 1960 with a gospel group called COGIC, standing for Church of God in Christ, and in 1964 recorded as the lead of Hale and the Hushabyes ("Yes Sir, That's My Baby," Apogee). That gig had been an honor considering that the other singers on the date had been Sonny, Cher, Brian Wilson, Jackie De Shannon, and Darlene Love. Edna later went on to sing backup for the Righteous Brothers, Johnny Rivers, and Ray Charles's Raelettes.

Shellie, from Brooklyn, New York, won a scholarship to the University of Southern California in Los Angeles and wound up singing background for Dusty Springfield, Little Richard, and as an Ikette.

Carolyn was in the Girlfriends on Colpix in 1963 doing two David Gates-penned records, "My One and Only Jimmy Boy" (#49 Pop, 1963) and "Baby Don't Cry." She also did some singing with Phil Spector's Bob B. Soxx and the Blue Jeans and as backup for O. C. Smith and Lou Rawls.

▲ THE MANHATTAN TRANSFER

▼ THE OSMONDS

▼ CROSBY, STILLS AND NASH

▲ LADY FLASH

▲ SISTER SLEDGE

▼ THE PERSUASIONS

While the three were lighting up the boob tube behind Burt Bacharach on the Williams show that fateful night, songwriter/producer Eddie Holland of Holland, Dozier, and Holland was watching and was impressed by the girls. The three superwriters who had created lyrics, melody, and momentum for the voices of the three SUPREMES and THE FOUR TOPS decided to leave Motown and start their own labels called Invictus and Hot Wax Records.

The first acts they signed were three females (the Honey Cone) and four males (CHAIRMEN OF THE BOARD), in keeping with what they were accustomed to. Eddie named the girls after a favorite childhood ice cream. They put out their first single in 1969, a tell-him-where-it's-at slice of life called "While You're Out Looking for Sugar (Somebody's Gonna Take Your Honey)," with Edna on lead. It showed up on the charts June 28th, reaching number 62 Pop and number 26 R&B.

Most of the group's early hits were produced and written by General Johnson and Greg Perry of Chairmen of the Board, since lawsuits with Holland, Dozier, and Holland's previous monarchs dragged on for some time and inhibited their production activities.

In late 1969 the girls reached *Billboard*'s R&B top 10 with "Girls, It Ain't Easy" (#8 R&B, #68 Pop), but they didn't click with a hit until 1971 when they became the fourth act to try the Johnson-Perry tune "Want Ads." Johnson and Perry tried it first on Sherrie Payne (Freda's sister) and Glass House, an Invictus group, and then on Freda herself, but it didn't work right until Honey Cone cut it.

On June 12, 1971, "Want Ads" was number one Pop and R&B across America. The group that some were calling a pop-gospel Supremes were using their flashy guitar-dominated soul to send a message to the woman who no longer wanted to sit home and cry while her man was out cheating or playing cards. She was going to take out a want ad for a new guy.

A few more slickly produced singles ventured forth like "Stick-Up" (#11 Pop, #1 R&B, 1971), "One Monkey Don't Stop No Show" (#15 Pop, #5 R&B), "The Day I Found Myself" (#23 Pop, #8 R&B, 1972), and "Sittin' on a Time Bomb (Waitin' for the Hurt to Come)" (#96 Pop, #33 R&B, 1972).

The girls' last chart single, "Innocent Till Proven Guilty" (#101 Pop, #37 R&B, 1972) proved the formula wasn't as effective as before, and the group disbanded by 1973 to return to the more secure and lucrative world of background singing.

THE HONEY CONE

A SIDE/B SIDE	LABEL/CAT NO	DATE
While You're Out Looking For Sugar / The Feeling's Gone	HtWx 6901	1969
Girls It Ain't Easy / The Feeling's Gone	HtWx 6903	1969
Take Me With You / When Will It End	HtWx 7001	1970
When Will It End / Take Me With You	HtWx 7005	1970
Want Ads / We Belong Together	HtWx 7011	1970
Stick-Up / V.I.P.	HtWx 7106	1971
One Monkey Don't Stop No Show Part 1 / One Monkey Don't Stop No Show Part 2	HtWx 7110	1971
The Day I Found Myself / When Will It End	HtWx 7113	1972
Sittin' On A Time Bomb / It's Better To Have Loved And Lost	HtWx 7205	1972
Innocent Till Proven Guilty	HtWx 7208	1972
O-o-o Baby, Baby / Ace In The Hole	HtWx 7212	1972
The Truth Will Come Out / Somebody Is Always Messing Up A Good Thing	HtWx 9255	1976

The Hues Corporation

A soul pop trio from Los Angeles, the Hues Corporation's members were all from different parts of the country. Hubert Ann Kelly was from Fairchild, Alabama; Bernard "St. Clair" Lee Calhoun Henderson (no kidding) came from San Francisco; and Karl Russell hailed from Columbus, Ohio.

They came together in Los Angeles in 1969 and became a lounge act. Flint, Michigan's Fleming Williams soon took Karl's place and the group hooked up with producer Wally Holmes, who wanted to call them the Children of Howard Hues. When that wouldn't fly legally Wally adjusted it to the Hues Corporation. They performed locally and in 1970 were signed to Liberty Records for one awful single titled "Good Footin'."

They moved their act to Las Vegas's Circus Circus casino and were then picked up by RCA in 1973 based on several of Wally's productions. Their LP *Freedom for the Stallion* yielded a single of the same name, which cracked the Hot 100 (#63) in the summer. Curiously, the group was totally overlooked by black radio and the black charts. Tommy Brown was now in, replacing Fleming on lead, and the group got a new life when RCA executive David Kershenbaum saw them perform at a Los Angeles club. Audience reaction to one of their songs, "Rock the Boat," convinced him to put it out as their next single. "Rock the Boat" promptly sank upon its release to the public, but then a strange underground movement—later classified as the disco craze—took hold of the record and generated the sale of 50,000 copies from play in dance clubs in the New York area alone. When radio picked it up this time, people came to buy it in droves and by July 6, 1974, "Rock the Boat" had sailed to number one on the Hot 100 and number two R&B, forcing Gordon Lightfoot's "Sundown" into a rapid chart sunset.

"Rock the Boat" reached number six in England and number 18 in Australia, selling over two million copies worldwide. "Rockin' Soul" followed, finishing at a very respectable number 18.

Tommy then decided on a solo career, which didn't pan out for him or the Hues Corporation. Their next single, "Love Corporation," only reached number 62, but tours of Europe, the U.S., Australia, and South America kept them working and earning.

The group appeared in the film *Blacula* just before Holmes took them to Warner Bros. for their last charter, "I Caught Your Act" (#92 Pop, #61 R&B, spring of 1977).

The hits soon stopped and the group went back to the club circuit hoping to find another "Rock the Boat," but they never did.

The Jackson 5

The Jackson 5 were one of the most successful pop/soul groups of the '70s. The famous family started out as a trio of Jermaine, Sigmund "Jackie," and Toriano "Tito," the sons of Joe and Katherine Jackson of Gary, Indiana. Papa Joe had been a guitar player with THE FALCONS and encouraged the formation of his singing offspring in 1963. By 1964 younger brothers Marlon and Michael Joe were singing with the group and appeared at their first nightclub performance that year when Michael was only five.

The story goes that they were paid only $8 for the whole night's work, but money thrown onto the stage added up to over a hundred dollars. A neighborhood woman gave them the name the Jackson 5

and it stuck. After winning a local talent show at Roosevelt High School while performing THE TEMPTATIONS' "My Girl," daddy Joe decided to play the bigger cities and brought them to New York City, where they won the Apollo Theatre's amateur night contest.

In 1968 they were seen by Ben Brown and signed to his Gary, Indiana-based Steel-Town label, and Gordon Keith produced their first single, called "Big Boy." It garnered regional airplay extending to Chicago, and the group was soon working at clubs and theatres like the Regal opening for such hit acts as Jerry Butler, THE MIRACLES, THE DELFONICS, and the Temptations.

Though the belief persists that Diana Ross discovered the group in Gary, it was actually GLADYS KNIGHT of the Pips and Bobby Taylor of the Vancouvers who told Motown mentor Berry Gordy, Jr. of the sibling prodigies after performing with them during the summer of 1968.

In 1969 Gordy finally did see the Jackson 5 perform in Gary at a benefit concert. He signed them to the label and the family moved to Los Angeles to be "professionalized" by Motown's star-grooming staff. Some of the members lived with Berry Gordy for a period of time and Michael stayed at Diana Ross's home.

Meanwhile, former school teacher and piano player Freddie Perren was working with collaborators Fonce Mizell and Deke Richards on a new song called "I Wanna Be Free" and felt it was the right tune for Gladys Knight and the Pips. They played the song for Gordy who liked the melody but suggested they rewrite it for his new act the Jackson 5. They did and it was released in October 1969 under the new title "I Want You Back."

On October 18th the quintet played their first live performance as a Motown act with THE SUPREMES at the Hollywood Palace, and 11-year-old Michael and company tore the house down. So did "I Want You Back," which became their first number one record on January 31, 1970, also reaching number one R&B and number two in England.

Their follow-up, "ABC," took the same trip up the charts, reaching number one Pop and R&B on April 25th, number eight in the U.K., and number nine in Australia. It dethroned the Beatles' "Let It Be" when it took over the top spot.

Their third single by Perren, Mizell, and Richards, "The Love You Save," had writing and production credits that read "The Corporation" rather than the three writers' actual names. Gordy may have been gun shy about crediting writers since his ace team of Holland, Dozier, and Holland had left him (an unfortunate reaction since writers' futures depend on their current and past credits). "The Love You Save" also shot to number one, this time on June 27th, once again displacing the Beatles ("The Long and Winding Road") from the top position. In the U.K. it reached number seven.

Their fourth single was the ballad "I'll Be There," a reversal of direction after three high-energy soul rockers. It rose to the top of both the Pop and R&B charts and to number four in the U.K. It not only was Motown's largest-selling single to date (over four million), but when it hit number one on October 17, 1970, the Jackson 5 became the first and only act of any kind to have their first four single releases reach the top. In less than a year they'd sold over 14 million records.

Their fifth Motown single, "Mama's Pearl," came as close as you can get without making it five number ones in a row but was kept out of the top by THE OSMONDS' "One Bad Apple," a recording that cloned the style of the Jackson 5's "I Want You Back."

The Jackson 5 also charted number two R&B, giving them five records in a row, finishing exactly the same on both charts.

Follow-ups were "Never Can Say Goodbye" (#2 Pop, #1 R&B, #33 U.K., 1971), "Maybe Tomorrow" (#20 Pop, #3 R&B, 1971), "Sugardaddy" (#10 Pop, #3 R&B, 1972), and a remake of the Thurston Harris and the Sharps' 1957 hit (#6 Pop, #2 R&B) "Little Bitty Pretty One" (#13 Pop, #8 R&B, 1972).

In September 1971 a Jackson 5 animated TV series first aired on ABC-TV, and by November Michael's first solo disc, "Got to Be There," was out, eventually reaching number four Pop and R&B.

Steel-Town Records issued some old Jackson 5 tracks. Among them was an up-tempo "We Don't Have to Be Over 21," with 10-year-old Michael's undisciplined but intriguing lead, and a single titled "Let Me Carry Your Schoolbooks," with the group going by the name of the Ripples and Waves Plus Michael.

In the fall of 1972 Jermaine had his first taste of solo success, scoring with "That's How Love Goes" (#46 Pop, #23 R&B). Several months later he released a remake of Shep and the Limelites' 1961 number two hit "Daddy's Home" (#9 Pop, #3 R&B) in doo wop style.

More Jackson 5 hits followed: "Lookin' Through the Windows" (#16 Pop, #5 R&B, #9 U.K., 1972), "Get It Together" (#28 Pop, #2 R&B, 1973), "Dancing Machine" (#2 Pop, #1 R&B,

1974), and "I Am Love" (#15 Pop, #5 R&B, 1975).

In 1974 they backed Stevie Wonder on his mega-hit "You Haven't Done Nothin' " (#1 Pop and R&B).

By 1976 the group was craving more artistic control, so they signed with Epic. Jermaine, who married Gordy's daughter Hazel, stayed with Motown and continued his solo career. Brother Randy took Jermaine's place and sisters Rebbie and La Toya also joined for a time. They struck gold with some funk and roll entitled "Enjoy Yourself" (#6 Pop, #2 R&B). It was their first million seller since "Dancing Machine" two years earlier.

The Jacksons (as they were now called, because Motown owned the Jackson 5 name) starred in a four-week variety show on CBS television in 1976. More Epic hits followed afterward for the family with "Shake Your Body" leading the pack (#7 Pop, #3 R&B).

By the early '80s several of the Jacksons were involved in solo careers but the group kept on churning out chart hits: "State of Shock" (#3 Pop, #4 R&B, 1984), with Michael and Mick Jagger featured; "Torture" (#17 Pop, #12 R&B, 1984), with Michael and Jermaine trading leads; and the group's last chart single, "Time Out for the Burglar" (#88 R&B) from the film *Burglar*.

In 1983 Michael and Jermaine (the latter now signed to Arista Records) got together with their brothers to perform on Motown's 25th anniversary television show.

All six Jackson brothers toured in the celebrated 1984 "Victory" concert series of 40 shows grossing over $5.5 million. Sister Janet, who spent only a brief time with the group in 1973, signed to A&M and racked up five number one R&B hits including "Nasty," "Control," and "The Pleasure Principle" between 1986 and 1987. Jermaine had 21 charters through 1987, including "Let's Get Serious" (#9 Pop, #1 R&B, 1980) and "Dynamite" (#15 Pop, #8 R&B, 1984). La Toya signed with Polydor, Larc, and Private I during the '80s with her biggest records being "Betcha Gonna Need My Lovin' " (#23 R&B, 1983) and "Heart Don't Lie" (#56 Pop, #29 R&B, 1984). She also made a hit with the exposure she got from a layout in *Playboy* magazine in the late '80s. Marlon charted on Capitol with "Don't Go" (#2 R&B, 1987) and Rebbie with "Centipede" (#24 Pop, #4 R&B, 1984) on Columbia, produced and written by Michael.

As for Michael, he became the top star of the '70s and '80s, registering as many chart hits solo (31) as he did with the Jackson 5/Jacksons. He had 11 number one Pop smashes including "Ben"

(1972), "Don't Stop Till You Get Enough" (1979), "Rock with You" (1979), "Billie Jean" (1983), "Beat It" (1983), "Say Say Say" (1983), "I Just Can't Stop Lovin' You" (1987), "Bad" (1987), "The Way You Make Me Feel" (1987), "Man in the Mirror" (1988), and "Dirty Diana" (1988). His 1982 LP *Thriller* sold over 40 million copies and won 11 Grammy Awards. The biggest winner in the Jackson family sweepstakes, Michael made a deal worth $1 billion in a multimedia contract with Sony software in early 1991.

THE JACKSON 5

A SIDE/B SIDE	LABEL/CAT NO	DATE
Big Boy / You've Changed	Stltn 681	1968
I Want You Back /		
Who's Lovin' You	Mtwn 1157	10/69
ABC / The Young Folks	Mtwn 1163	2/70
The Love You Save /		
I Found That Girl	Mtwn 1166	5/70
I'll Be There / One More Chance	Mtwn 1171	8/70
Santa Claus Is Coming To Town /		
Christmas Won't Be The		
Same This Year	Mtwn 1174	11/70
Mama's Pearl / Darling Dear	Mtwn 1177	1/71
Never Can Say Goodbye /		
She's Good	Mtwn 1179	3/71
Maybe Tomorrow /		
I Will Find A Way	Mtwn 1186	6/71
We Don't Have To Be Over 21 (To		
Fall In Love) / Jam Session	Stltn 682	1971
You Don't Have To Be Over 21		
(To Fall In Love) / Some Girls		
Want Me For Their Lover	Dynamo 146	1971
Let Me Carry Your Schoolbooks /		
I Never Had A Girl	Stltn 688	1971
Sugar Daddy / I'm So Happy	Mtwn 1194	11/71
Little Bitty Pretty One /		
If I Have To Move A Mountain	Mtwn 1199	4/72
Lookin' Through The Windows /		
Love Song	Mtwn 1205	6/72
The Corner Of The Sky To Know	Mtwn 1214	10/72
You Made Me What I Am /		
Hallelujah	Mtwn 1224	2/73
Get It Together / Touch	Mtwn 1277	8/73
Dancing Machine / It's Too		
Late To Change The Time	Mtwn 1286	2/74
Whatever You Got, I Want /		
I Can't Quit Your Love	Mtwn 1308	10/74
I Am Love / I Am Love Part 2	Mtwn 1310	12/74
Forever Came Today /		
All I Do Is Think Of You	Mtwn 1356	6/75

The Jacksons

Enjoy Yourself / Style Of Life	Epic 850289	9/76
Show You The Way To Go /		
Show You The Way To Go	Epic 850350	3/77

A SIDE/B SIDE	LABEL/CAT NO	DATE
Goin' Places /		
Do What You Wanna	Epic 850454	9/77
Find Me A Girl /		
Different Kind Of Lady	Epic 850496	1/78
Blame It On The Boogie /		
Do What You Wanna	Epic 850595	8/78
Shake Your Body (Down To The		
Ground) / That's What You Get	Epic 850656	12/78
Bless His Soul /		
Lovely One	Epic 950938	9/80
Things I Do For You /		
Heartbreak Hotel	Epic 1950959	11/80
Can You Feel It /		
Wondering Who	Epic 01032	1981
Walk Right Now / Your Ways	Epic 1902132	5/81
Things I Do For You /		
Working Day and Night	Epic 1902720	2/82
Your Ways / State Of Shock	Epic 3404503	6/84
Body / Body	Epic 3404673	10/84
State Of Shock /		
Torture	Epic 1505536	7/85
Torture / Torture	Epic 3404575	8/87
Nothin' (That Compares 2 U) /		
Alright With Me	Epic 3468688	4/89
When I Look At You /		
2300 Jackson Street	Epic 3469022	7/89

Lady Flash

Lady Flash was a trio of professional singers originally formed as the backup vocalists for then newcomer Barry Manilow. The original group consisted of Lorraine (Reparata) Mazzola, Debra Byrd, and Ramona Brooks. The three girls were from diverse backgrounds when fate in the form of Manilow brought them together.

Reparata was from Brooklyn, New York, learning piano at St. Agnes Seminary for Girls. While at Brooklyn College she sang with the baroque Brooklyn College Chorus by day and pop vocal groups at night. Her teen group, REPARATA AND THE DELRONS, had a big British hit with "Captain of Your Ship" (#13, March 1968), and when they toured the U.K. Reparata stayed on to work as a background singer for a year. After returning to the U.S., she pursued a career in television and became a producer of Pat Collins's news program (CBS) and later "A.M. New York."

The daughter of a Harlem Globetrotter and a fashion model, Cleveland, Ohio's Debra Byrd formed and directed a 50-member choir called the Community Voices of Faith while in high school. A scholarship to Kent State University immersed her in music theory and led to her becoming musical director of the Black Theatre Workshop (Karamu Theatre). She then joined the Jean Austin Singers, a gospel group, and later the Interpreters, who recorded for Columbia. Ramona Brooks came from Akron, Ohio, and had Broadway aspirations. She played the club circuit as a strong solo vocalist until New York beckoned.

In September 1974, 28-year-old Barry Manilow was at a career crossroads. He had several unsuccessful singles and an LP on Bell Records and he was about to have the first single from his new album released. Barry had been Bette Midler's musical arranger and had toured briefly with the Harlettes (Bette's backup singers). Now he was determined to put his own money into a short tour to break his new single. He wanted a backup act that would enhance his identity, one that, in Reparata's words, ". . . could look tough in contrast to Barry's clean, lily-white boyish image. Girls that look like they could eat nails!" Barry called Reparata, who he remembered had auditioned at one time for the Harlettes; though she hadn't been picked he had always liked her sound. He also liked the idea of having Reparata and the Delrons back him, and Reparata jumped at the chance; singing was her first passion—so much so that she was ready to quit her TV producing job for only a four-week tour that would culminate at Carnegie Hall.

The Delrons were not as enthused, however. Not wanting to leave home, Nanette (who was working as a cashier in a department store on Utica Avenue at the time) and Cookie (working as a secretary in a brokerage stock cage) declined.

With Reparata on hold, Barry decided to hold auditions at a rehearsal studio in New York. Debra, who by now had made it from Kent State to New York (and who turned down a part in *The Wiz* for *Raisin*, only to be subsequently denied both parts) read of Barry's cattle call in *Back Stage*. Arriving late, she was assigned number 165; she figured that she had little chance since one of the 164 girls ahead of her must have been chosen. Halfway through her rendition of "Walk on By" she was stopped . . . and hired.

Ramona also saw the *Back Stage* ad, and her beautiful and full-voiced sound made her the other one chosen out of the 164—before Debra even arrived.

Barry started rehearsals in the living room of his 27th Street apartment. He even supervised the girls' costume shopping trip down the block for their now-famous long black skirts and black glitter lurex tops. Aside from Barry's originals, the girls rehearsed a few past hits like "Nowhere to Run" and "Heat Wave" (MARTHA AND THE VANDELLAS). Prepped and ready, Barry and the Flashy Ladies (that's what they had decided on for their name) set out for Philadelphia and the Bijou Theatre to promote Barry and his new single, "Mandy."

While sitting in the balcony of the Bijou watching the opening act, Reparata nearly went into shock. The act on stage was a little-known comedian named Andy Kaufman. Reparata remembered how a year before, a manager had brought Kaufman to her for an audition on "A.M. New York." She liked his Elvis imitation but was told that to get him she had to take the manager's other client as well, Zippy the Chimp. The deal fell through, but now here Kaufman was, performing for Reparata without even knowing it. He went on to become the lovable Latka on the popular TV series "Taxi."

When it was Barry and the ladies' turn, they spared no energy to put across a dynamic show, and it was well-received. Their Boston stop was another matter, however. Booked at a jazz club, the girls decided if there were more people on stage than in the audience they'd call off the second show. Barry and the girls bowled them over at their next stops of Nashville and Memphis, and by the time they returned to New York "Mandy" was on the move.

By January 1975 Ramona had left the scene for a solo career (one LP for Manhattan Records in 1978), and her replacement was multi-talented Monica Burruss. Born to show business parents who were gospel singers. Monica went to the High School of Music and Art and later sang backup for artists such as Melanie, Joan Baez, and Edgar Winter.

The girls' first LP work was a makeover job of Barry's first LP, and now that Barry was a hit ("Mandy" went to number one on January 18, 1975), remixing and adding Flashy Ladies vocals made sense. A lot of sense, as it turned out: the first single with the girls ("Could It Be Magic") went to number six on September 20, 1975. They went on to have nine hit singles with Barry, including two number ones ("I Write the Songs" and "Looks Like We Made It") and three more top 10s ("Trying to Get the Feeling," "Weekend in New England," and "Can't Smile Without You") between 1975 and 1978, and recorded seven LPs with Barry.

A performance at the Troubador at the beginning of Barry and the Flashy Ladies' tenure together had a tremendous impact on their careers. After a week at the Troub, Barry and the Oreos (that's what he fondly called his one white and two black backups) refused to sign an option letter for Doug Weston's club, so Weston refused to pay them. Almost broke, the group's only recourse was to work their way across the country from college to college. Barry built such a following from this maneuver that most of his future records began breaking in colleges, where he was becoming the Sinatra of the '70s.

Unlike most backup groups that recorded behind many acts in their careers, Flashy Ladies only recorded behind Barry and on one rare occasion in 1978 behind Greek superstar Demis Roussos for his *Mercury* LP.

In the spring of 1976 Flashy Ladies, with Barry's help, made a record deal with Polydor and created a multi-styled LP titled *Beauties in the Night*. Polydor execs didn't like the group's name, however, and changed it to Lady Flash. The LP was full of goodies, from the disco/R&B rocker "The Thunderbolt" and the gospel/rock "Right Now If You Believe" to the folk/rock sound of "Arms of Mary" and the jazz/blues "Jumpin' at the Woodstock." The LP's centerpiece was "Street Singin'," sounding like THE POINTER SISTERS doing power doo wop. Lady Flash laid into a tribute to "Street Singin'" with kudos to THE CLEFTONES, THE SHANGRI LAS, and THE RIVINGTONS, and it reached number 27 Pop in late summer of 1976. Unfortunately, the next single, a revival of "Dancin' in the Street," danced into a ditch and stayed there. Before anyone could regroup, it was back on the road with Barry.

One show at the Troubador in Los Angeles found the girls singing behind Martha Reeves, who spontaneously came on stage to sing her hit with the girls. Another stage backup they did was for Jose Feliciano in 1977.

In late 1977 Monica decided to move on, and Muffy Hendricks took her place for the group's first European tour with Barry.

By 1978, the members of Lady Flash, squeezed by the lack of recording opportunities coupled with Barry's desire to tour less, had gone in separate directions. Monica went back to New York and became the first female vocalist winner of "Star Search." Debra, also back in New York, married an editor at the Daily News and continued to do backup vocals on record for everyone from the Eurythmics to Bob Dylan.

Reparata settled in Los Angeles, went into acting, appeared in the 1989 movie *Dark Before Dawn*, and coauthored the best-selling book *Mafia Kingpin*.

Had Lady Flash continued, they might well have been one of the top female groups of the '70s.

The Main Ingredient

The Main Ingredient was a soul group formed in Harlem during the mid-'60s. Their membership included Donald McPherson of Indianapolis, Indiana, on lead; Enrique Antonio "Tony" Sylvester of Colon, Panama; and Luther Simmons, Jr. and Cuba Gooding, both of New York City. The foursome, all in their early 20s, joined forces as the Poets and had one single on Redbird Records in December 1965, a rhythm ballad called "Merry Christmas Baby," that had hints of an IMPRESSIONS influence that would later blossom fully with Cuba on lead. Gooding had left before that recording to finish his education in college.

In 1967 Buzzy Willis of THE SOLITAIRES, then A&R director of rhythm and blues for RCA, signed the trio. Now called the Insiders, they did one harmony effort that didn't click ("I'm Better Off Without You") and decided another name change might bring them better luck. After reading the writing on a Coke bottle they became the Main Ingredient.

In the spring of 1970, their fourth single as the Main Ingredient, "You've Been My Inspiration," climbed to number 64 Pop and number 25 R&B. Their next single was an August 1970 rerecording of their Insiders cut "I'm Better Off Without You."

Their first R&B top 10 hit came from the March 1971 release of "Spinning Around" (#7 R&B, #52 Pop). Before they could chart again Donald McPherson died of leukemia on July 4, 1971, five days short of his 30th birthday. Cuba came back to take over the lead and the group did an LP, *Black Seeds*, as a eulogy and a tribute to Donald.

They scored a career-maker hit in the summer of 1972 when "Everybody Plays the Fool" went to number three Pop, and number two R&B. It peaked on October 14th, with only Bill Withers' "Use Me" and Michael Jackson's "Ben" ranked higher. All of their next 10 releases charted, including the soft soul hits "Just Don't Want to Be Lonely" (#8 R&B, 1974), "Happiness Is Just Around the Bend" (#35 Pop, #7 R&B, 1974), and "Rolling down a Mountainside" (#92 Pop, #7 R&B, 1975).

With the disco era approaching, Tony went into production with Bert DeCouteaux and they produced Ben E. King's "Supernatural Thing" (#5 Pop, #1 R&B, Atlantic, 1975) and SISTER SLEDGE'S "Love, Don't You Go Through No Changes on Me" (#92 Pop, #31 R&B, Atlantic, 1974).

The group broke up in 1977 and Cuba barely charted as a solo act on "Mind Pleaser" (#98 R&B) in 1978 (Motown). In 1980 they reunited on RCA and had one charter, "Think Positive" (#69 R&B) in a very distinctive Impressions vein with another charter six years later on Zakia ("Do Me Right," #69 R&B).

Still sounding good in the '90s, they signed with Polygram and issued the single "I Just Wanna Love You." By then Simmons had retired, so Cuba and Tony added Jerome Jackson to the trio. The Main Ingredient tallied 17 R&B chart records in their 25 singles career, and the potential was there to add to that total at any given time.

THE MAIN INGREDIENT

A SIDE/B SIDE	LABEL/CAT NO	DATE
The Poets		
Merry Christmas Baby	Red Bird	1965
The Insiders		
I'm Better Off Without You /		
I'm Just A Man	RCA 9225	1967
The Main Ingredient		
I Was Born To Lose You /		
Psychedelic Ride	RCA 47-9748	5/69
Brotherly Love / Get Back	RCA 74-0252	9/69
The Girl I Left Behind /		
Can't Stand Your Love	RCA 74-0313	1/70
You've Been My Inspiration /		
Life Won't Be The Same	RCA 74-0340	4/70
I'm Better Off Without You /		
Need Her Love	RCA 74-0382	8/70
I'm So Proud / Brotherly Love	RCA 74-0401	10/70
Magic Shoes / Spinning Around	RCA 74-0456	3/71
Black Seeds Keep on Growing /		
Baby Change Your Mind	RCA 74-0517	7/71
I'm Leaving This Time /		
Another Day Has Come	RCA 74-0603	11/71
Everybody Plays The Fool /		
Who Can I Turn To	RCA 74-0731	5/72
You've Got To Take It /		
Traveling	RCA 74-0856	11/72
I'm Better Off Without You /		
You Can Call Me Rover	RCA 74-0939	3/73
Girl Blue / Movin' On	RCA 0046	7/73
Just Don't Want To Be Lonely /		
Goodbye My Love	RCA 0205	12/73
Happiness Is Just Around The		
Bend / Why Can't We All Unite	RCA 0305	5/74
California My Way /		
Looks Like Rain	RCA 10095	9/74
Rolling Down A Mountainside /		
Family Man	RCA 10224	2/75
The Good Old Days /		
I Want To Make You Glad	RCA 10334	6/75

A SIDE/B SIDE	LABEL/CAT NO	DATE
Shame On The World		
(short version) / Shame		
On The World (long version)	RCA 10431	10/75
Shame On The World / Lillian	RCA 10431	11/75
Instant Love /		
Let Me Prove My Love To You	RCA 10606	2/76
Think Positive	RCA 12060	7/80

The Manhattan Transfer

A vocal group that proved the '40s, '50s, and '60s weren't absent from the music of the '80s, Manhattan Transfer was a very successful act in that decade. Deriving their name from a novel about 1920s New York, the original group formed in New York City in 1969 and included Erin Dickens, Pat Rosalia, Gene Pistilli (later with Cashman, Pistilli, and West on Capitol Records in 1971), and Tim Hauser. Hauser sang with a Brooklyn doo wop group in 1959 called THE CRITERIONS, who recorded the obscure releases "Don't Say Goodbye" and "I Remain Truly Yours" on Cecilia Records. Ironically, the lead singer of the Criterions, one Tommy West, became the West of Cashman, Pistilli, and—some 12 years later. The Transfer's earlier releases could best be described as a cross between "let's not take ourselves too seriously" and folk doo wop with a touch of country. Recordings like "Chicken Bone Bone," "Java Jive," and "Rosianna" didn't have much commerciality, but the group still managed to get a Capitol Records recording contract.

By 1972, Hauser's then current occupation as a cab driver had led to a fateful meeting with Janis Siegel through an introduction by a passenger in Hauser's cab. At the time Siegel was singing with the group Laurel Canyon and had been in the Young Generation on Red Bird Records in 1965. Hauser's cab proved to be a mecca for talent; that's where he also met singer Laurel Masse. He filled out the foursome with an acquaintance of Masse's, Alan Paul, who was then appearing in the original cast of *Grease*.

With a common taste for four-part harmony that was uncharacteristic for a group in the early and mid-'70s, they landed a recording contract with Atlantic Records. Their second single, a gospel/

pop recording titled "Operator" (1975), showed Atlantic's faith was well placed. It went up to number 22 on the pop charts and garnered the group the opportunity to star in their own TV summer replacement series (it ran for three weeks.)

While American chart hits were hard to come by for the group after "Operator," their December 1976 recording of "Chanson D'Amour" (the Art and Dottie Todd hit from 1959) became a number one record in France and England by April 1977. In 1979, Laurel Masse left for a solo career and Cheryl Bentyne, formerly of the New Deal Rhythm Band (1975) took her place.

Changing vocal direction with almost every LP through the '70s and '80s, the group's most successful chart single was a jazz-flavored doo wop remake of THE AD LIBS' 1965 hit "The Boy from New York City," reaching number seven in the summer of 1981.

The group's flexibility and growing expertise enabled them to perform music from the '30s to the '80s, touching on bebop, fusion jazz, doo wop, Latin melodies, pop/rock, and so on. Although never considered a superstar act, their accomplishments (such as having each of their six studio LPs between 1980 and 1989 contain at least one Grammy-winning performance, and being the first group to win Grammys in the same year in both the jazz and pop categories) won them a loyal worldwide following. Due to their varied style, Manhattan Transfer's recordings placed on the pop, R&B, and jazz charts and registered 10 chart singles in England.

Through 1989, the group recorded 12 LPs and nine singles (two R&B charters and seven pop charters) and won 10 Grammys.

THE MANHATTAN TRANSFER

A SIDE/B SIDE	LABEL/CAT NO	DATE
Care For Me / Rosianna	Cap 2968	1970
Winterlude / Maybe Mexico	Cap 3036	1970
Chicken Bone Bone / Java Jive	Cap 3108	1971
Clap Your Hands / Sweet Talking Guy	Atln 3277	1975
Operator / Tuxedo Junction	Atln 3292	1975
Helpless / My Cat Fell In The Well	Atln 3349	1976
Chanson D'Amour / Poinciana	Atln 3374	1976
Don't Let Go	(UK)	1977
Where Did Our Love Go / Single Girl	Atln 3472	1978
Walk In Love	(UK)	1978
On A Little Street In Singapore	(UK)	1978
Where Did Our Love Go / Je Voulais The Dire	(UK)	1978

A SIDE/B SIDE	LABEL/CAT NO	DATE
It's Not The Spotlight / Farm Brothers	Atln 3491	1978
Birdland / The Shaker Song	Atln 3636	1979
Nothing You Can Do About It / Wacky Dust	Atln 3756	1979
Twilight Zone / Twilight Zone / Body and Soul	Atln 3649	1980
Trickle Trickle / Foreign Affair	Atln 3772	1980
Boy From New York City / Confirmation	Atln 3816	1981
Smile Again / Until I Met You	Atln 3855	1981
Spies In The Night / Kafka	Atln 3877	1981
Route 66 / On The Boulevard	Atln 4034	1982
Spice Of Life / The Night		
The Monk Returned To Heaven	Atln 7-89786	1983
American Pop* / Why Not*	Atln 7-89720	1983
Baby Come Back To Me / That's The Way It Goes	Atln 89594	1984
Mystery / Goodbye Love	Atln 89695	1984

* with Frankie Valli

Memory

Through the decades, pop vocal groups have come together in a variety of ways. From the typical "we all met in high school" like THE FLEETWOODS, THE MAGNIFICENTS, or THE MARVELETTES, to the not-so-typical "we met in a men's room" like members of the original DRIFTERS, to the outrageous "we met in prison" like THE PRISONAIRES or THE ESCORTS, the stories of how these groups formed have always been of interest to music enthusiasts.

The distinction of Memory is that they are the only group (in memory) that was formed in the board room of an insurance company.

In the fall of 1976, six computer data processors working for the New York Life Insurance Company in Lebanon, New Jersey, met in the board room after hours to cultivate their vocal group aspirations. The multiracial, multiethnic, unisex group consisted of Jaime de Jesus (lead), Lesley Uhl (falsetto), Bobby "Bobby Hep" Hepburn (first tenor), Otis "Big O" Harper (second tenor), Herb "Iceman" Olson (baritone), and Lou "Big Lou" Benito (bass). The 30-something sextet decided on the name Memory because computers have it, and the name reflected the content of their material. They did oldies, particularly songs by the Drifters ("Under the Boardwalk") and Shep and the Limelites ("Daddy's Home"), though their main influences were the a cappella experts THE PERSUASIONS and THE MANHATTAN TRANSFER.

They first performed at the insurance company's Christmas party in 1976 and then began the New Jersey club circuit in 1978. They also did a performance and interview hour on Don K. Reed's "Doo-Wop Shop" radio show in September 1981.

In February 1981 the group recorded for Avenue D Records in New York, thanks to Bobby Hep's moonlighting as a disc jockey in the Easton area of Pennsylvania.

Their single "Street Corner Serenade" came out in March 1981. Around this time they picked up a new baritone, Greg Restivo, at a wedding while practicing in the men's room at the Commodore Inn in New Jersey.

On June 1st of 1981 their second and last single, "Under the Boardwalk" (the Drifters) b/w "Daddy's Home" (the Limelites), was issued. Both singles were a cappella and were well received by the doo wop community.

Memory continued to perform through the tri-state area until 1987 when conflicting work schedules put a halt to rehearsals.

In 1991 only Bob, Jaime, and Herb were still with New York Life. Lou was with Off-Track Betting, Greg was with a cable TV company, Otis was working for a storage company, and Lesley was a housewife, though all were still involved in the computer data processing field for their respective companies. The data processing doo woppers certainly added their own unique wrinkle to the chronicle of vocal group origins.

The Moments

The Moments formed in Hackensack, New Jersey, but may have been having thoughts of Philadelphia, where Thom Bell and THE DELFONICS were creating great soft-soul recordings like "La-La-Means I Love You" in 1968. That was the same year Mark Greene (lead), John Morgan, and Richie Horsely were signed to Stang Records as the Moments and began production with Sylvia Robinson, co-owner with her husband, Joe Robinson, of the All Platinum group of companies and its Stang subsidiary. Sylvia was also the female half of the legendary "Love Is Strange" duo, Mickey and Sylvia (#11 Pop, #1 R&B, 1957).

The group's first single, a delicate soul ballad titled "Not on the Outside," gave notice that the Moments were serious contenders for chart spots.

On November 30, 1968, "Outside" was inside the R&B hit circle, finishing at number 13 and crossing over to Pop number 57. By the time they charted with "Sunday" in April 1969 (written by Sylvia), two thirds of the lineup had changed. William Brown (of the Broadways, Lenny Welch's group) was on lead replacing Greene, and Al Goodman (the Corvettes) was in for Horsely. Unlike groups like the Magnificents (who had personnel changes after their first hit and disappeared due to a lack of identity), the new Moments sounded just like the old (if you can call a two-record group old) and scored the same R&B chart ranking (#13).

"I Do," a rhythm ballad with lots of falsetto wailing, was their third charter and first R&B top 10 tune, and it featured the addition of Sylvia's brother-in-law Johnny Moore in place of John Morgan.

Probably their most memorable work was the Sylvia/Bert Keyes-penned ultra-slow "Love on a Two-Way Street" (1970). It hit number one R&B for five weeks and reached number three Pop by May 30, 1970, with only Ray Stevens's "Everything Is Beautiful" and the Guess Who's "American Woman" at higher positions.

At the height of their success and with their first million seller under their belts, Moore was replaced by Harry Ray, and when Brown developed a sore throat Ray became the group's third lead singer in two and a half years.

Next, the New Jersey trio reached number seven R&B and number 44 Pop with their reading of THE INK SPOTS' 1939 hit "If I Didn't Care." Brown and Ray alternated leads over the next few years, turning in some stylish performances, most notably "All I Have" (#56 Pop, #9 R&B, 1970), "Sexy Mama" (#17 Pop, #3 R&B, 1971), "Sho Nuff Boogie" (#80 Pop, #45 R&B, with Sylvia on lead in 1974), and "Look at Me" (#39 Pop, #1 R&B, #42 U.K., their second U.K. charter), and the Bruce Roberts/Carole Sager song "I Don't Wanna Go" (#18 R&B). Their biggest U.K. issue, "Girls" (with the Whatnauts instrumental group), made number three in Britain while only going to number 25 R&B in the U.S.

After a legal battle with Stang that lasted over two years, the group re-formed as Ray, Goodman and Brown, signed with Polydor, and came out singing soft soul for the '80s in the form of "Special Lady" (#5 Pop, #1 R&B) in late 1979.

By the time R, G & B's third Polydor charter, a remake of the PLATTERS and Ink Spots standard "My Prayer," had fallen off the charts (#47 Pop, #31 R&B), Stang (now Sugarhill) had issued their last Moments chart single, "Baby Let's Rap Now (Part I)" (#39 R&B).

Ray, Goodman and Brown continued to delight their audiences in concert but "My Prayer" was their last Hot 100 chart song. "Happy Anniversary" was their best after that (#16 R&B) and the mid-'80s found them on Panoramic and then EMI, where they went to number eight R&B with "Take It to the Limit."

Carrying a résumé of 28 R&B and 11 Pop charters as the Moments, along with nine R&B and three Pop charters as Ray, Goodman and Brown, this dual-named trio left a noticeable mark on contemporary soul music.

The Osmonds

One of the most talented families ever, the Osmonds were eight brothers and a sister. The first four boys became the original group in 1959, with Alan (10, baritone), Wayne (8, bass), Merrill (6, tenor), and Jay (4, lead).

They were originally called the Osmond Brothers Boy Quartet.

A very close-knit family, much of their life was centered around music and education. Their dad began teaching them to sing in the car to help pass the time while traveling. They practiced church hymns and barbershop songs in their home on North Washington Street in Ogden, Utah. Some of those first songs included "Side by Side" and "The Old Oaken Bucket." They began performing at local events, and the uniqueness of the family quartet led to a part in the 1962 Disney special "Disney after Dark." Andy Williams's father saw the Utah youngsters and convinced his son to audition them.

The group, now known as the Osmond Brothers, guested on Andy's show, and mail response was so overwhelming that Williams made them regulars. They became his backup group, even in live performances, creating the widest age gap (21 years) between lead singer and group in show business.

In 1963 the brothers recorded their first LP, *Songs We Sang on the Andy Williams Show*. The first big live performance for the Elvis Presley-influenced vocalists was at the Tropicana Hotel in Las Vegas, opening for Nancy Sinatra.

In 1963 a fifth Osmond, six-year-old Donny, joined the group. In that same year the group appeared in a TV show about Eddie Foy and his famous vaudeville family. Jimmy Osmond joined the troupe on stage in 1966 when he was only three, and sister Olive Marie (the eighth of nine Osmond kids and named after their mom) debuted at six (1965), although she didn't become a regular part of the act until 1973.

When their contract with Williams's show ended in 1967 they joined "The Jerry Lewis Show" as regulars. Alan joined the army soon after, bringing the group down to a quartet of Merrill, Wayne, Jay, and Donny.

TV opened more doors than records ever could; the Osmonds became worldwide household names.

In April 1969 they toured Japan and were received enthusiastically. During that tour little Jimmy broke his arm in a revolving door but went on to perform with a microphone in his left hand and cast and sling on his right. Jimmy recorded a song for the Japanese market in Japanese, which became the first Osmond family gold hit.

The Osmonds were all accomplished musicians (Jay on drums; Alan, Wayne, and Merrill on guitars; and Donny on keyboards), and their sound evolved from barbershop harmony to rock and roll. In 1970 they recorded "One Bad Apple" in Muscle Shoals, Alabama, and were signed by Mike Curb to MGM. By January 2, 1971, "Apple" had charted. The JACKSON 5-styled bubblegum dance tune shot to number one on February 13th, and even reached number six R&B. Wearing trademark white jumpsuits, the Osmond Brothers now became international rock and roll stars, appearing as a quintet and then a sextet when Jimmy was aboard.

They studied karate with Chuck Norris, incorporating their black belt status into dance routines. In one show Alan connected with Jay's nose. He spent the next three months performing with a bandage wrapped around his broken proboscis, and karate rock was eventually phased out.

Meanwhile other hits like "Yo-Yo" (#3, 1971) and "Down by the Lazy River" (#4 U.S., 1972, #40 U.K., the first of 10 British charters) kept the famous family on a whirlwind of shows and tours.

In 1975 they went on their first world tour, which included a command performance for the Queen of England. Their popularity in the U.K. was such that no hotel would have them because of the security risk posed by the thousands of teens who were chasing after them, so the group had to stay at a country estate.

In 1972 the group backed Steve Lawrence and Eydie Gorme on "We Can Make It Together" (#68, MGM). Marie joined the act, and they became strictly the Osmonds.

In 1973 four different entities from the same family had chart hits: Jimmy ("Tweedle Dee," #59), Donny ("The Twelfth of Never," #8), Marie ("Paper Roses," #5), and the Osmonds ("Let Me In," #36 Pop, #2 U.K.), all on MGM.

All told, those four had nine chart singles in 1973. Donny had already laid claim to teen idol status in 1971 with his number one hit of the former Steve Lawrence smash, "Go Away Little Girl," and with "Puppy Love" (#3) and "Hey Girl" (#9).

In 1974 the group broke through in England with "Love Me for a Reason" (#1 U.K., #10 U.S.). Their sixth charter in Britain included the number two hit "Crazy Horses" (#14 U.S., 1972).

Donny and Marie paired up for mid-'70s duets, taking the old Dale and Grace hit "I'm Leaving It Up to You" to number four in 1974. They went on to have their own TV variety hour, "The Donny and Marie Show."

In the early '80s Alan, Jay, Wayne, and Merrill turned to country music (as did Marie), while Donny emerged with the rock hit "Soldier of Love" (#2, Capitol) in 1989.

In 1985 the group and family came together for a two-hour TV special celebrating their 25 years in show business. That same year Jay retired from the group and became a corporate executive with Morris Travel in Salt Lake City, leaving the Osmond Brothers as a trio.

By 1991, Alan and Merrill each owned companies that produced live events, pageants, and corporate shows. Wayne was working with a film and television production company, and Jimmy was in television and movie production with the Ventura Entertainment Group. The group performed together in a 1991 summer reunion concert with Andy Williams at the Stadium of Fire in Provo, Utah.

The brothers went on to raise their own families, ultimately resembling a small battalion of Osmonds. Alan's sons, christened the Osmond Boys, recorded for Mike Curb and his Curb Records. The Boys offered the promise of continuing entertainment from the long line of Osmonds.

The Persuasions

The kings of '70s a cappella recording, the Persuasions are often credited as influences of FOURTEEN KARAT SOUL, the FORCE M.D.'S, and many other '70s and '80s groups.

The five members all had previous singing experience with doo wop groups, and their influences ranged from gospel music to groups like THE TEMPTATIONS and Fantastic Four of the 1960s, THE FLAMINGOS and THE DELLS of the '50s, and THE MILLS BROTHERS of the '40s.

The quintet was from the Bedford-Stuyvesant section of Brooklyn, New York. They got together in 1966 after discovering their common interest in harmony singing. The team was led with a hard-edged, gospel vocal style by Jerry Lawson (the Five Bs). The other members were bass Jimmy Hayes (also of the Five Bs), first tenor Jay Otis Washington ("Darling Little Angel," the Interiors on Worthy, 1961), second tenor Joe Russell, and baritone Herb "Tubo" Rhoad (both on "Sunny Side of the Street," the Parisians on Pova, 1962).

The first song they practiced was THE FIVE SATINS' "In the Still of the Night." The group finally settled on a name Jimmy came up with and the Persuasions were born. They practiced in the traditional "rehearsal halls" of their forefathers, that is, subways, parks (like Fort Greene Park), and street corners (such as Lafayette Avenue and Fulton Street).

The Persuasions met Catamount Records owner Stan Krause, who recorded the group on a number of sides but didn't issue anything until a single of "Stardust" was shipped in 1970. Meanwhile, back in 1967, Krause had introduced them to doo wop group fan David Dashev, who became their manager. The Persuasions, 19 to 23 years of age when they started, recorded a live Jersey City performance for Dashev who took it to Frank Zappa's Straight Records. The *A Cappella* LP was issued in 1968 and a following began to develop.

When Warner Bros. Records bought Straight Records they offered to record the Persuasions with instrumental backing but the a cappella specialists declined, so Warner's Reprise affiliate recorded them on one a cappella single, "Without a Song" (THE RAVENS, THE ISLEY BROTHERS) in 1971. That same year David Dashev took the group to Capitol, and for two years they turned out fine 45s that included a hard gospel-styled version of the Beatles' "Let It Be," a reproduction of the Flamingos' "Buffalo Soldier," and THE MOONGLOWS' "Ten Commandments of Love."

Also during 1972 a single of Kenny Vance's "Looking for an Echo" was issued by "The Four Persuasions."

In 1973 the group backed a Blue Sky vocalist named Donna on "In the Still of the Night" (the Five Satins), marking the beginning of a long history of backup work for the Persuasions behind such artists as Don McLean, Stevie Wonder, and Phoebe Snow.

In 1973 they cut an LP for MCA called *We Still Ain't Got No Band*, and that title remained their theme over the years.

In 1974 Washington left and was replaced by Willie Daniels. The group signed with A&M and began recording music produced by another doo wop lover, Jeff Barry.

Their first A&M single, the laid-back, soul-blues rhythm ballad "I Really Got It Bad for You," brought the Persuasions a new audience when it entered the R&B chart on July 6, 1974, and reached number 56, spending 11 weeks on the listing. Their best A&M effort was the solid Tony Camillo-produced, Evie Sands/Richard Germanero-penned single "One Thing on My Mind," which managed a number 84 chart spot in the summer of 1975.

In 1977 Washington returned and replaced Daniels, and the group continued its backup recording work.

They signed with Elektra in 1977 and issued a vibrant version of THE RIVINGTONS' "Papa-Oom-Mow-Mow" without any hint of instrumentation.

In 1979 they toured with Joni Mitchell and recorded on her *Shadows and Light* live LP doing THE TEENAGERS' "Why Do Fools Fall in Love."

They continued as performers and recording artists into the '90s and were still highly revered after more than 25 years of bringing a cappella to a wider audience.

In 1990 they performed on Spike Lee's nationally syndicated TV special "Do It A Cappella" with such contemporary a cappella acts as True Image, Take 6, and ROCKAPELLA. The show yielded an Elektra CD that had the Persuasions singing "Up on the Roof" and "Looking for an Echo."

THE PERSUASIONS

A SIDE/B SIDE	LABEL/CAT NO	DATE
Stardust / I Could		
Never Love Another	Cata 1957	1970
Without A Song /		
Since I Fell For You	Rprs 0977	1971
It's You That I Need /		
Let It Be	Cap 3162	1971
Tempts Jam /		
Don't Know Why I Love You	Cap 3242	1971
Buffalo Soldier /		
People Get Ready	Cap 3317	1972
The Ten Commandments		
Of Love / Good Times	Cap 3425	1972
Three Angels Looking For Love	Cap 3492	1972

A SIDE/B SIDE	LABEL/CAT NO	DATE
(Looking For An) Echo /		
I Won't Be The (Fool No More)	Pay-4 100	1972
In The Still Of The Night* /		
For Your Love*	Blue Sky 103	1973
We're All Goin' Home /		
I Really Got It Bad For You	A&M 1531	1974
With This Ring /		
Somewhere To Lay My Head	A&M 1631	1974
I Just Want To Sing With My		
Friends / Somewhere To		
Lay My Head	A&M 1658	1975
Darlin' / One Thing On My Mind	A&M 1698	1975
Papa-Oom-Mow-Mow /		
Papa-Oom-Mow-Mow	Elek 45396	1977

* Donna and the Persuasions

The Pointer Sisters

Given that the Pointer Sisters, Ruth, Anita, Bonnie, and June, were raised strictly on gospel music and couldn't go to the movies or wear makeup, they were successful with remarkably diverse styles of music, dress, and performance.

They started as members of their parents' choir at the Church of God in Oakland, California. They also sang in the Northern California State Youth Choir. When their parents (Elton and Sarah) were out, the foursome would secretly swing into some secular songs.

In 1969, 18-year-old Bonnie and 15-year-old June began performing in nearby San Francisco, calling themselves Pointers, a Pair. They were soon joined by Anita (21), who gave up her job as a legal secretary to make them a trio. By the dawn of the new decade the group had come to the attention of producer Dave Rubinson, who was fascinated by their ability to sing pop, R&B, country, and jazz. He used the girls on a wide variety of recording sessions backing such artists as Chicago, Grace Slick, Boz Scaggs, Dave Mason, Esther Phillips, Dr. Hook, the Tubes, and Elvin Bishop, often touring with them as well.

It was at a performance in L.A.'s Whiskey A Go Go backing Elvin Bishop that the group was spotted by Atlantic Records' Jerry Wexler and signed to the company.

"Don't Try to Take the Fifth," produced by Wardell Quezergue, was released in 1971 but failed to sell heavily. Not wanting to be compared with that other big trio (THE SUPREMES) the Pointers asked older sister Ruth (a keypunch operator) to join.

Using their vast repertoire and a penchant for outlandish costumes of the '40s, including print dresses, feather boas, and platform shoes, the Pointers began to be compared to THE ANDREWS SISTERS (you can't win!). One more single for Atlantic failed, and Rubinson took the group to Blue Thumb Records.

A Lee Dorsey R&B song (#46, 1970), "Yes We Can Can," reached number 11 Pop and number 12 R&B and gave the sisters their first gold record. Their next release was the Willie Dixon Chicago blues standard "Wang Dang Doodle," which made number 61 Pop and number 24 R&B.

The group was a delight to see and hear. Their close harmony, fast scat singing, precocious manner, and colorfully nostalgic wardrobe made them initially popular with the gay scene and then rock audiences. Extensive TV bookings followed.

In September 1974 they became the first pop act ever to perform at the San Francisco Opera House and recorded a double live LP there.

The Pointers also became accomplished songwriters. In late 1974 Blue Thumb issued a country song written by Bonnie and Anita called "Fairytale," which made number 13 Pop and number 37 Country. The group then became the first black female act ever to appear on the stage at the Grand Old Opry in Nashville. "Fairytale" also won a Grammy as 1974's Best Country Vocal Performance by a Duo or Group. In the same year PBS did a documentary on the group.

"How Long (Betcha' Got a Chick on the Side)" brought them back to the R&B side, going to number one in the summer of 1975 (#20 Pop). In 1976 the group appeared in the film *Car Wash*.

A few more singles charted between 1975 and 1977 ("Going Down Slowly" [#61 Pop, #16 R&B], "You Gotta Believe" [#103 Pop, #14 R&B], and Sam Cooke's 1962 hit "Havin' a Party" [#62 R&B]), but the group became preoccupied with June's nervous breakdown and a lawsuit against ABC/Blue Thumb for past-due royalties.

In February 1977 the Pointers performed on Dick Clark's 25th anniversary show.

Bonnie went solo with Motown in 1978, charting on "Free Me from My Freedom" (#58 Pop, #10 R&B) and the Elgins' number nine R&B hit of 1966, "Heaven Must Have Sent You" (#11 Pop, #52 R&B).

Meanwhile June, Anita, and Ruth signed with long-time fan Richard Perry and his new Planet label in late 1978.

The first chart song on that label was Bruce Springsteen's "Fire." The hot single hit on January 20, 1979, and reached number two Pop and number 14 R&B (#34 U.K.)

A variety of hits followed, including "He's So Shy" (#3 Pop, #10 R&B, 1980), "Slow Hand" (#2 Pop, #7 R&B, #10 U.K., 1981), "Automatic" (#5 Pop, #2 R&B, #2 U.K., 1984), "Jump (For My Love)" (#3 Pop, #3 R&B, #6 U.K., 1984), "Neutron Dance" (from the film *Beverly Hills Cop*, #6 Pop, #13 R&B), and their greatest single of all, "I'm So Excited" which charted first in 1982 (#30 Pop, #46 R&B) and later with a remix (#9 Pop, #11 U.K., 1984).

In 1985 the sisters, now on RCA after Planet's closing, reached number 11 Pop, number six R&B, and number 17 U.K. with "Dare Me," their last big hit. They also took part in the recording of U.S.A. for Africa's "We Are the World" that same year. Their final Pop chart song was "Be There" (#42) from the film *Beverly Hills Cop II* in the summer of 1987.

THE POINTER SISTERS

A SIDE/B SIDE	LABEL/CAT NO	DATE
Tulsa Country /		
Don't Try To Take The Fifth	Atln 2845	1971
Send Him Back / Destination		
No More Heartaches	Atln 2893	1972
Yes We Can Can / Jada	Bl Thm 229	1973
Wang Dang Doodle / Cloudburst	Bl Thm 243	1973
Steam Heat / Shaky Flat Blues	Bl Thm 248	1974
Fairytale / Love In Them Thar Hills	Bl Thm 254	1974
Live Your Life Before You Die /		
Shaky Flat Blues	Bl Thm 262	1975
How Long (Betcha' Got A Chick		
On The Side) / Easy Days	Bl Thm 265	1975
Going Down Slowly /		
Sleeping Alone	Bl Thm 268	1975
You Gotta Believe /		
Shaky Flat Blues	Bl Thm 271	1976
Having A Party / Lonely Gal	Bl Thm 275	1976
Fire / Love Is Like A Rolling Stone	Plnt 45901	1978
Happiness / Lay It On The Line	Plnt 45902	1979
Blind Faith / The Shape I'm In	Plnt 45906	1979
He's So Shy	Plnt 47916	1980
I Want To Do It With You /		
American Music	PlntYB13254	6/82
I'm So Excited /		
Nothin' But A Heartache	PlntYB13327	9/82
If You Wanna Get Back Your		
Lady / I'm So Excited	PlntYD13429	2/83
If You Wanna Get Back		
Your Lady / All Of You	PlntYB13430	2/83
I Need You / Operator	PlntYB13639	9/83
Automatic / Nightline	PlntYB13730	1/84
Jump (For My Love) / Heart Beat	PlntYB13780	4/84
I'm So Excited / Dance Electric	PlntTB13857	7/84

A SIDE/B SIDE	LABEL/CAT NO	DATE
Neutron Dance /		
Telegraph Your Love	PlntYB13951	11/84
Baby Come And Get It	Plnt 14041	4/85
Dare Me	RCA 14126	1985
Freedom	RCA 14224	1985
Twist My Arm	RCA 11497	1986
Goldmine	RCA 5062	1986
All I Know Is The Way I Feel	RCA 5112	1987
Mercury Rising	RCA 5230	1987
He Turned Me Out	RCA 6865	1988
I'm In Love	RCA 8378	1988

The Ribitones

Six years before the '80s vocal group ROCKAPELLA achieved a distinctive merging of doo wop, a cappella, and rock, and well before THE NYLONS named their 1989 LP *Rockapella*, there were the Ribitones singing rockapella. Some would later call it "rockabilly doo wop."

Whatever it was called, Freddy (Frogs) Toscano started something different when he formed the group in 1978.

Freddy was a member of the avant-garde baroque & roll pop vocal band the Fourth Dimension ("Land of Make Believe" Columbia, 1967). He played with a variety of fusion bands into the '70s before deciding to return to his rock and roll roots. A club owner he knew named Bill Brienza thought an a cappella night might be a good idea, so Freddy pulled together the voices of his '50s and '60s Brooklyn past, Lou Benevento (lead) and Anthony Carbone (first tenor), along with Carmine De Sena (second tenor) and Fil Spina (baritone) from Queens. When Carmine and Fil moved to Florida they were replaced by Jim Pace (of Bayshore, Long Island) and Frank Russo (Brooklyn), respectively.

Frank had sung with Freddy (bass), Lou, and Tony under the Myrtle Avenue El (elevated railway) in the Bedford-Stuyvesant section of Brooklyn during the doo wop days. After that, he sang in his basement with the group that went on to become the Decades on Avenue D Records (1980). Jim had sung with the Newports on Crystal Ball, and Tony had been with the Jumpin Tones (Raven, 1963).

After a performance at East Rockaway's Crown pub the group felt ready to record, and their first release in 1979 was an a cappella rendering of THE MOONGLOWS' "Most of All" backed by "Crazy Little Mama" (a.k.a. "At My Front Door" by THE EL DOR-ADOS), a song that would soon surface again for the group. That single and the group's standard a cappella versions of oldies like "Your Way" (THE HEARTBEATS) and "Teardrops" (LEE ANDREWS AND THE HEARTS) on their half of the *Patty and the Street-Tones meet the Ribitones* LP in 1980 gave little indication of what was to come. The LP liner notes did give a hint: "They've risen from relative obscurity to being one of the most sought-after acts on the doo wop scene. Using a rhythm guitar in their live act the Ribitones originated the 'rock-apella' sound."

Later in 1979 Freddy started his own label, Off the Wall Records, and produced a version of "Crazy Little Mama" that had a rockabilly rhythm accompanying the Ribitones' harmonies. The record label listed "Freddy Frogs and the BMTs, vocals—The Ribitones." The flip was a rerecorded a cappella version. The side with instrumental backing was a first-of-a-kind merger of two distinctly different forms. Pye Records of England picked up the uniquely conceived master for U.K. distribution and it received extensive airplay.

Fred and company traveled over to England to perform in support of the record. An LP with instrumental accompaniment soon followed, which included some fine versions of "Sincerely" (the Moonglows), "Johnny B. Goode" (Chuck Berry), and the countrified doo wopper "Love Me" (Elvis Presley).

Over the next few years the Ribitones performed their rockapella and rockabilly doo wop at places like Lincoln Center, Studio 54, and Max's Kansas City in New York City, and were heard on various radio stations (WCBS, WPIX, WHBI).

By 1983 the members had decided to go separate ways, with Freddy forming a more traditional a cappella group that included Lou Ligreori (the Riffs, Sunny, 1964), Mike Paquette (the Dedications, Card), and Bill Walsh and Larry Critelli (the Velvet Riffs).

Apart from singing, Freddy ran a contracting company in Ocean Park, New York. Jim Pace worked for Grumman Aircraft and sang with another Long Island group. Frank Russo worked for the Department of Sanitation and also sang with a Long Island group. Lou Benevento worked for Con Edison and sang lead for the Johnny Farina Band (Johnny of Santo and Johnny fame, "Sleepwalk," #1, 1959). Tony Carbone worked for Avis Rent-a-Car. Carmine De Sena was a New York City Policeman before moving to Florida to become a private detective. Fil Spina was a commercial artist.

THE RIBITONES

A SIDE/B SIDE	LABEL/CAT NO	DATE
Most Of All / Crazy Little Mama (a cappella)	Clifton 38	1979
Crazy Little Mama / Crazy Little Mama (a cappella)	OTW SP69	1979
Memories	UGHA	1980
Crazy Little Mama / I Can't Help Falling In Love	OTW	1980

Shalamar

When producer Dick Griffey saw that "Uptown Festival," the Motown disco medley he created with session singers, was taking off in the spring of 1977, he concluded that it might be a good idea to have an actual group so that the name he made up for the label would have an identity. Out of this concept came Shalamar, a trio composed of lead singer Gerald Brown along with Jody Watley and Jeffrey Daniels, both dancers on the "Soul Train" show hosted by Dick's partner, Don Cornelius. After their second charter, "Take It to the Bank" (#79 Pop, #11 R&B, #20 U.K.) on Griffey's new Solar label, Gerald Brown left the group. He was replaced by Howard Hewett, formerly of the gospel family group the Hewett Singers.

In the fall of 1979 the trio had their biggest hit, "The Second Time Around" (#8 Pop, #1 R&B), which sold a million copies and knocked Michael Jackson's "Rock with You" out of the top spot on the R&B chart.

At the height of the group's popularity, Jeff Daniels married *The Wiz* star Stephanie Mills in March 1980. Shalamar continued to have major R&B hits ("Make that Move" [#6, 1981], "A Night to Remember" [#8, 1982], and "Dead Giveaway" [#10, 1983]) and successful LPs, but as big as they were in the U.S. they were even bigger in England. During one period of time in 1982 they had three top 10 U.K. hits ("I Can Make You Feel Good," #7, "A Night to Remember," #5, and "There It Is," #5).

In 1984 Daniels left the act, moving to England to become the host of a newly started "Soul Train"-styled TV show. Watley also departed to start a solo career, and both were replaced by Micki Free and Delisa Davis. The latter was discovered through a nationwide talent hunt, and the former was a guitar player and singer working with Howard.

After 1983 the group became involved in the music of three successful films, charting with "Deadline U.S.A." (#34 R&B, from *D.C. Cab*), "Dancing in the Streets" (#17 Pop, #18 R&B, *Footloose*), and "Don't Get Stopped in Beverly Hills" (#79 R&B, *Beverly Hills Cop*).

In May 1986 Hewett departed for a solo career and ex-Los Angeles Rams football player Sidney Justin took over.

Their last chart record ("Games," #11 R&B, 1987) was their biggest hit in three years, but by then the group had decided to call it quits. Watley went on to great successes with singles like "Looking for a New Love" (#2 Pop, #1 R&B) and "Don't You Want Me" (#6 Pop, #3 R&B), both in 1987. Hewett hit with "I'm for Real" (#90 Pop, #2 R&B) and "Stay" (#8 R&B), both in 1986.

Sha Na Na

The first group to mirror rock and roll of the '50s in the '70s, Sha Na Na was in the forefront of the first rock revival. Denny Green, Johnny Contardo, Scott Powell, Don York, and Richie Jaffe made up the vocal side while Bruce Clark, Elliot Cahn, Henry Gross, Chris Donald, and John Marcelino made up the rhythm section. They all came together at Columbia University in 1969. The vocal group did a local show a cappella, and they were so well-received doing '50s oldies that they decided to add the rhythm section while keeping the oldies concept. Soon after, they touched up their '50s songs with comedy, choreography, and costumes of the period and did a free concert for the school, attracting over 4,000 people.

Inspired by artists like THE FIVE SATINS, THE ORIOLES, Fats Domino, THE DRIFTERS, THE COASTERS, FRANKIE LYMON AND THE TEENAGERS, and Little Richard, the group began playing clubs like the Scene and Fillmore East, where they were accepted as both revivalists and parodists.

Consistent with their theme, they took their name from a line in THE SILHOUETTES' hit "Get a Job."

Sha Na Na's national break came when the group appeared at the Woodstock festival in August 1969, alongside such contemporary rockers as

Jefferson Airplane, the Moody Blues, Blood, Sweat and Tears, the Who, Santana, and CROSBY, STILLS AND NASH.

In 1970 they met Kama Sutra Records executive and producer Artie Ripp and recorded their first LP, which included the single "Rock and Roll Is Here to Stay" (DANNY AND THE JUNIORS).

By now "Screamin'" Scott Simon (vocals and piano), Lenny Baker (sax), and John "Bowzer" Baumann (bass) joined the group while Chris Donald, Don York, and Henry Gross left to pursue other goals. Gross went solo and turned out a 1976 hit called "Shannon" (#6, Lifesong).

Their second single, a medley of "Yakety Yak" (the Coasters)/"Jailhouse Rock" (Elvis Presley), had a B side that was likely their best record while not typical of their '50s style, the ASSOCIATION/ Moody Blues-styled ballad "Only One Song," penned by Scott Simon and produced by Eddie Kramer. Still, it managed to garner some attention as it reached number 110 nationally in the spring of 1971.

The group was not really successful on record (only "Top 40 of the Lord" [#84, 1971] and "Romeo and Juliet" [#55, 1975] charted) since their visual dynamics didn't translate well to vinyl. But they were knockout live performers. Hip musicians like Janis Joplin and Jimi Hendrix would watch their shows from the front rows.

The group performed with a wide range of contemporary talent from THREE DOG NIGHT to Canned Heat and Santana.

In 1977 their unique identity as a '70s group caught in a '50s time warp earned them a syndicated TV series that ran for several successful years.

In 1978 they appeared in the film *Grease* with John Travolta and sang four songs including their last single (which was also their first), "Rock and Roll Is Here to Stay."

SHA NA NA

A SIDE/B SIDE	LABEL/CAT NO	DATE
Pay Day / Rock 'n' Roll Is Here To Stay	KamaS 507	1970
Only One Song / Yakety Yak	KamaS 522	1971
Top Forty / I Wonder Why	KamaS 528	1971
Sea Cruise / The Vote Song	KamaS 2013	1972
Maybe I'm Old Fashioned / Stroll All Night	KamaS 592	1972
In The Still Of The Night*	KamaS 578	1972
Just Like Romeo and Juliet	KamaS 602	1973
Too Chubby To Boogie	KamaS 596	1974
Your The Only Light On My Horizon Now	KamaS 603	1975
Rock 'n' Roll Is Here To Stay / Greased Lightnin'**	RSO 909	1978

* Eddie and the Evergreens
**by John Travolta

The Singers Unlimited

The Singers Unlimited started as an offshoot of the brilliant '50s jazz quartet THE HI-LO'S, but by the '70s they had carved their own well-deserved niche as standard bearers of modern vocal harmony.

When the Hi-Lo's disbanded in 1963 Don Shelton went off to Chicago to do TV commercials. He encouraged Gene Puerling (founder of the Hi-Lo's) to come to the Windy City in 1967 and talk about their futures. With their shared expertise it seemed a logical step to form another vocal group, only this one would work in the lucrative world of commercials.

Don (who had sung with the Js with Jamie) had two associates in the field, Len Dresslar (also with the Js with Jamie) and a female singer who was already known throughout the Chicago commercial community as the first lady of the 30-second song, Bonnie Herman.

With a name that defined rather than boasted of their abilities, the foursome soon became known in commercials for their adventurous harmonies and precision dynamics.

In 1971 when the group had some time left over on a session, they recorded a Gene Puerling arrangement of the Beatles song "Fool on the Hill." The double-tracked a cappella recording found its way to famed jazz pianist Oscar Peterson, who was in Chicago to play the London House. When he heard it he was impressed enough to send a copy to the international record label M.P.S.

Their first LP for M.P.S. was *A Cappella* (1972).

Using their voices like instruments, Singers Unlimited created an LP of songs that included

Lennon/McCartney's "Here, There, and Everywhere," "Michelle," "Fool on the Hill," and Joni Mitchell's "Both Sides Now." In all, the LP beautifully demonstrated the group's ability to walk the tightrope between jazz and pop. It won the German Record Grand Prix of 1973.

Over the years the quartet recorded 10 LPs for M.P.S. including collaborations with Oscar Peterson and Art Van Damme. The group continued to record and do commercials through the '80s.

Sister Sledge

Another in the long line of Philadelphia female groups like the Sapphires, THE ORLONS, Brenda and the Tabulations, the Three Degrees, the Sherrys, and THE BLUE BELLES, Sister Sledge became the City of Brotherly Love's disco queens of the late '70s.

The four Sledge sisters, Kathy, Joni, Kim, and Debbie, grew up under the watchful eye of their opera singing grandmother Viola Williams and in the confines of the Second Macedonia Church of Philadelphia chorus. Originally called Mrs. Williams' Grandchildren at an early age, they evolved into the Brand New Generation, a Group Called Sledge, and later, the Sledge Sisters.

With their mother Flo working several jobs, the girls were often confined to their home so they wouldn't be out on the streets. Singing thus became a regular pastime.

Influenced by acts like GLADYS KNIGHT AND THE PIPS and Aretha Franklin, the group soon played church dances, school functions, and fashion shows, and then graduated to perform in nightclubs. A friend of their older sister Carol was a member of THE STYLISTICS, and he gave the sisters their first taste of a recording studio when he produced their first demo.

They cut the record "Time Will Tell" for the tiny Money Back label in 1971 and were soon doing backup work for Gamble and Huff at Sigma Sound Studios. By then they had changed their name to Sister Sledge.

They came to the attention of Atlantic Records in 1973, but before recording on their own, they sang backup harmony for labelmate Percy Sledge on his summer of 1973 charter "Sunshine" (#89). They then did their first LP, *Circle of Love*, with Bert "Super Charts" De Couteaux (who also arranged) and Tony "Champagne" Sylvester (of THE MAIN INGREDIENT) producing.

Their first LP was issued at the birth of the disco era. On December 28, 1974, the Sister Sledge single "Love Don't You Go Through No Changes on Me" hit the R&B charts and then the Pop charts. "Super Charts" De Couteaux's powerful string and French horn intro and insistent drum rhythm helped define what disco would become over the next few years. With the girls' enthusiastic vocals, they made "Love" Sister Sledge's first chart song, reaching number 31 R&B and number 92 Pop.

The four girls (ranging in age from 15 to 20 in 1974) had three more lower chart singles in 1976 and 1977 and went back to the local club circuit until Atlantic paired them up with Nile Rodgers and Bernard Edwards of Chic. The group now began turning out disco for the masses rather than the dance clubs and the results were hits like "He's the Greatest Dancer" (#9 Pop, #1 R&B, #6 U.K., 1979), "We Are Family" (#2 Pop, #1 R&B, #8 U.K., 1979), "Lost in Music" (#35 R&B, #17 U.K., 1979), "Got to Love Somebody" (#64 Pop, #6 R&B, #34 U.K., 1980), and "All-American Girls" (#3 R&B, #41 U.K., 1981).

The group projected a clean-living, close-family image that endeared them to the public and especially to black audiences. They performed in Europe, where disco was becoming big business, and at Muhammad Ali's championship bout in Zaire, Africa.

If a male group's most common disruption over the decades was the draft, the female version was motherhood. At the time of Sledge's first big tour, Debbie became pregnant with the first of her six children, and sister Carol had to sub for her.

The up-beat enthusiasm and warmth of Sister Sledge came across vividly even in dance tunes, and their signature single "We Are Family" became a rallying cry for numerous causes and was used as the theme song for the 1979 World Champion Pittsburgh Pirates.

In 1982 the group softened the beat to redo Mary Wells's 1964 number one hit "My Guy" (#23 Pop, #14 R&B). By 1983 they were getting more involved in the creation of their own records. Although they produced their next three LPs, *Sisters*, *Betcha You Say That to All the Boys*, and *When the Boys Meet the Girls*, their single "Frankie" (#75 Pop, #32 R&B, 1985) was their last Pop chart entry, and "Dancing on the Jagged Edge" became their last R&B listing at number 71, also in 1985.

By 1989 Kathy had gone on to a solo career. The trio continued to hunt for a niche in the post-disco era, recording an album of dance music in Europe in 1991.

The Starland Vocal Band

Bill Danoff of Springfield, Massachusetts, and Kathleen Nivert of Washington, D.C., were working as a duo in the D.C. area during the late '60s when Bill got a job doing sound and lighting for a club called the Cellar Door. Bill met a number of performers there including the Chad Mitchell Trio, and he became friendly with trio member John Denver (a.k.a. John Deutschendorf).

Bill and Kathleen (she was known as Taffy) became the lead vocalists of Fat City. They issued two folk-classical-rock LPs on Probe-ABC in 1969 and 1971, although neither was successful. There were two more LPs, *Pass It On* and *Aces*, both on RCA, but the group continued to remain anonymous. Bill then wrote a song for John Denver called "I Guess I'd Rather Be in Colorado." When John recorded it, the two began a collaboration which led to the 1971 composition that launched Denver's solo career. The song was "Take Me Home, Country Roads," and it reached number two in the spring and summer.

John Carroll of Washington, D.C., and Margo Chapman of Honolulu, Hawaii, joined Bill and Taffy to form the Starland Vocal Band.

By late 1975 Denver was a top star for RCA. He was granted his own label, Windsong Records, and the first act he signed was the Starland Vocal Band. Bill and Taffy, who were now married, started working on an LP with John and Margo.

One afternoon Bill was having lunch in a Washington restaurant called Clyde's that had a series of "afternoon delights" listed on its menu. That gave him an idea for a song. "Afternoon Delight," with its breezy harmonies and *double entendre* message, charted on May 8, 1976, and reached number one on July 10th.

In an era when having a number one record didn't guarantee a million sales, "Afternoon Delight" sold well over a million, and the group won Grammy awards for Best New Artist and Best Arrangement for Vocals (Duos, Groups, or a Chorus).

Their Starland Vocal Band album sold very well, but follow-up singles failed to match the success of "Delight." The group's last chart effort was in 1980 when "Loving You with My Eyes" hit number 71 in March.

In 1977 the group was given a six-week summer replacement TV show on CBS in the musical variety format. It featured a young comedian named David Letterman. His career outlasted the show and the group.

Starland disbanded in 1980. John Carroll had a hit in 1982 with a song of his, "Get Closer" (Linda Ronstadt, #29), and he later married Margo. Bill and Taffy became separated but reunited as Fat City in Washington during the late '80s.

Stormy Weather

Stormy Weather, a quintet from the Gary-Hammond, Indiana, area, were the chief proponents of the Midwest's revitalized a cappella doo wop sound. The group was the brainchild of Henry Farag, who grew up idolizing local residents THE SPANIELS of "Goodnight, Sweetheart, Goodnight" fame. While establishing a career as a booking agent, Henry kept on forming groups only to have them dissolve because he didn't have the right guys. He came closer to finding the "right guys" in 1969 with the discovery of Nick "Cowboy" Paulitza of Gary. The two then found James "Hambone" Ham and Dave "Iceman" Mitchell, who were singing with an unnamed group in Hammond. The last piece of the puzzle came with the addition of Jimmy "C" Calinski, a lead with the East Chicago, Indiana, Harbor group, the Bonnevilles. By 1974 the lineup of white soul singers included Henry (28, lead through bass), Nick (27, lead, second tenor, and bass), James (28, lead and first tenor), Jimmy (29, lead through baritone), and Dave (30, lead through bass).

The versatile quintet decided on the name Stormy Weather because, as Henry put it, "It was a title of action," not to mention it was the name of one of the Spaniels' most famous recordings. (Other group influences were THE DRIFTERS, THE MARCELS, THE EL DORADOS, and THE DELLS of the '50s and '60s and THE PERSUASIONS of the '70s.)

In the spring of 1975 Stormy Weather took their first foray into recording with the album *No Band*, which was recorded in Henry's living room at his home in Glen Park. The LP's highlights were "Goodnight Sweetheart," "Beauty Is Only Skin Deep," and "When We Get Married," the latter of which would have an impact on one of their releases five years later. Their LP was funded by two local group enthusiasts who formed the Whole Truth Recording Company and issued the 15-cut LP that summer.

For an a cappella album its radio acceptance was terrific, especially in the Chicago area. The unpromoted LP sold over 5,000 units there with another 5,000 in various other areas.

The group's first significant gig was in the summer of 1977 at the Bridge Vu-Theatre in Valparaiso, Indiana, with the Ace Trucking Company, a comedy act that featured Lenny and Squiggy of TV's "Laverne and Shirley" and Fred Willard from "Real People."

The group followed an active performing schedule over the next several years. They appeared in many venues, from Radio City Music Hall in New York City to the Improv in Los Angeles, and made over 30 TV appearances, from NBC's "Today Show" to "Nightlife" with David Brenner.

The quintet built a secondary reputation providing backup vocals on stage for one of the oddest assortments of would-be singers any group's ever been challenged to support. In 1987 they sang behind boxer Ray "Boom Boom" Mancini, disc jockey Casey Kasem, and Gloria Loring on THE FIVE SATINS' "In the Still of the Night" during a telethon. In 1988 they backed WCVB-TV (Boston) host Ilene Prose on "Why Do Fools Fall in Love" during a live telecast. In Los Angeles they backed "Moonlighting" star Bruce Willis on "Oh What a Night" at the Improv, and "Taxi's" Tony Danza on THE CADILLACS' "Gloria."

Easier assignments included vocal support for Chubby Checker on "Goodnight, Sweetheart, Goodnight," Frankie Valli on "Remember Then," Smokey Robinson on "Sunday Kind of Love," Dee Clark on "The Wind," in 1991 Gene Chandler on "The Duke of Earl," and Ronnie Spector on a few street-corner doo woppers like "Why Do Fools Fall in Love" and "ABC's of Love."

Their proudest moment must have been when they backed James "Pookie" Hudson, lead of the revered Spaniels, on "Goodnight, Sweetheart, Goodnight" for a TV pilot titled "Five Plays for a Quarter." On another occasion, Henry sang on a video made in New Orleans with a group that included James "Pookie" Hudson (lead), Eddie Kendricks (first tenor), David Ruffin (falsetto), and Dennis Edwards (bass). The latter three were, of course, from THE TEMPTATIONS.

The group recorded three more LPs (*Dirty City*, *Street Gold*, and *Select-o-Matic*, 1991) plus six singles over the years 1975 to 1991 including 1980's "Christmastime Is Coming," a street carol with a melody that sounded suspiciously similar to that of "When We Get Married." Their 1991 LP *Select-o-Matic* had George Carl and Mike Whitmore replacing long-time regulars Nick Paulitza and Dave Mitchell, though Dave did sing on one cut.

By 1991, James Ham, when not singing, was working at Brumm's Beer Distributor in Hammond. Jimmy Calinski was working for Inland Steel Company. Nick Paulitza was retired from the Lake County Police Department. Dave Mitchell was living in Tucson, Arizona, and was the owner of a beauty salon. Henry Farag was a licensed private investigator.

STORMY WEATHER

A SIDE/B SIDE	LABEL/CAT NO	DATE
Take You Back /		
Java Jive	Canterbury	1976
Middle Class Educated Blues /		
People Get Ready	F.R.A.	3/77
Middle Class Educated Blues /		
People Get Ready	Amerama	10/77
Daddy's Little Boys /		
Daddy's Little Boys		
(instrumental)	Strmy	1/79
Goodnight Sweetheart /		
Bus Fare Home	Canterbury	4/81
Christmastime Is Coming /		
Street Corner Serenade	MgcMo	11/82
'59 Fever / Goodnight Sweetheart	Canterbury	11/83
Christmastime Is Coming /		
Merry Christmas Baby	Canterbury	11/84
The Land Is Wrigley /		
Don't You Just Know It	Canterbury	10/84
You're So Fine /		
Don't You Just Know It	Canterbury	10/84
Monsters Of The Midway /		
Christmastime Is Coming	Canterbury	11/84
For Your Precious Love /		
Ain't No Sunshine	Canterbury	10/86
Cincinatti Reds (Let The Good		
Times Roll)	Strmy	10/90

The Stylistics

The Stylistics recorded some of the finest pop-soul music of the '70s and brought falsetto tenor leads back into vogue. Their collaboration with writer/producers Thom Bell and Linda Creed became one of the most cohesive creative units of the early '70s. The group was formed in 1968, made up of school friends from Benjamin Franklin High School in Philadelphia. Russell Thompkins, Jr. (lead and tenor), Airrion Love (lead, first, and second tenor), and James Smith (bass) sang with the Monarchs while Herbert Murrell (lead and baritone) and James Dunn (baritone) sang with the

Percussions. When the two groups graduated from Ben Franklin, several members of each went on to college while others joined the armed forces. The remaining five (Russell, Airrion, James, Herbert, and James) were encouraged by one of their teachers to join forces and form a new group. Both entities wanted to keep their original name; the stalemate was broken by the group's guitar player, who came up with the name the Stylistics.

The group practiced in basements, recreation centers, and schools until their first break came. Russell was working in a local clothing store when the owner, Henry Hodge, heard him singing. When he learned that Russell had a group, Hodge decided to manage them and took the quintet to Bill Perry and his new Sebring label. "You're a Big Girl Now" was the group's first single, but Sebring had no idea how to promote the record and it disappeared quickly. Hodge then brought the group and the record to Avco Records, where they were signed and introduced to their new producer/writer Thom Bell and his writing partner Linda Creed.

On January 2, 1971, "You're a Big Girl Now," their almost two-year-old single from Sebring, hit the *Billboard* R&B chart on the Avco label and a week later appeared on the Hot 100 chart. It climbed to number 73 (#7 R&B) and stayed on the hit list for almost four months. Russell's immediately identifiable high tenor, James Smith's talking-bass bridge, and the group's harmony and unison vocals in the chorus of this almost nursery-rhyme-styled ballad made "Big Girl" a big favorite with teen buyers.

In the summer of 1971, "Stop, Look, Listen" solidified the group's presence on the airwaves with a number 39 charting (#6 R&B) but it was their Thom Bell/Linda Creed-penned third single, "You Are Everything," that really opened the ears of the pop world to the Philly quintet. An exquisite ballad with a deceptively simple hook, "Everything" reached number nine Pop (#10 R&B) in January 1972 while charting as far away as Australia at number 10 in late spring.

Their next single, "Betcha By Golly, Wow" became a standard of the decade. With its smooth-as-silk vocals and melody line, the ballad became an international best-seller (#3 Pop, #2 R&B, #12 U.K.). Its English debut stood as the first of the Stylistics' 16 runs up the British hit flagpole, putting them in fifth place among American vocal groups for the number of hits on the U.K. charts (ahead of them were THE BEACH BOYS [26], THE FOUR TOPS [25], THE SUPREMES [24], and GLADYS KNIGHT AND THE PIPS [20]).

In 1971 the group began a run of international tours that was continuing more than 20 years later. Their popularity continued to climb with hits like "I'm Stone in Love with You" (#10 Pop, #4 R&B), "Break Up to Make Up" (#5 Pop and R&B), and "Rockin' Roll Baby" (#14 Pop, #3 R&B, #6 U.K.), all written by Bell and Creed.

From January 1971 to the end of 1974 the Stylistics had 12 straight top 10 soul hits, five of which went to the top 10 on the pop charts as well. Only twists of fate can account for the fact that they never had a number one record on either chart.

The peak of their record popularity came in the spring and summer of 1974 when the Bell/Creed-penned "You Make Me Feel Brand New" spent four months on the soul charts (#5) and over six months on the Hot 100 (#2). Europe and Japan loved it also, and "Brand New" reached number two in England and number three in Australia.

Their string of 17 straight Hot 100 singles ended with the 1976 love song "You Are Beautiful" (#79 Pop, #17 R&B), but they continued to release singles and climb the R&B charts. Their number one jinx was broken only in the British Isles, where "Can't Give You Anything (But My Love)" reached the top spot in the summer of 1975 (it hit #18 R&B and only #51 Pop in the U.S.).

In 1981 the James gang—Dunn and Smith that is—retired from the group, leaving Russell, Airrion, and Herbert to carry on. The Jameses were never replaced.

In all, they amassed 30 R&B charters, with their last being 1986's "Let's Go Rockin' Tonight" on Streetwise Records.

THE STYLISTICS

A SIDE/B SIDE	LABEL/CAT NO	DATE
You're A Big Girl Now /		
Let The Junkie Bust The Pusher	Sebr 8370	1970
You're A Big Girl Now /		
Let The Junkie Bust The Pusher	Avco 4555	1970
Stop, Look, Listen / If I Love You	Avco 4572	1971
You Are Everything /		
Country Living	Avco 4581	1971
Betcha By Golly, Wow /		
Ebony Eyes	Avco 4591	1972
People Make The World Go		
Round / People Make		
The World Go Round	Avco 4595	1972
I'm Stone In Love With You /		
Make It Last	Avco 4603	1972
You And Me /		
Break Up To Make Up	Avco 4611	1972

A SIDE/B SIDE	LABEL/CAT NO	DATE
You'll Never Get To Heaven /		
If You Don't Watch Out	Avco 4618	1973
Pieces / Rockin' Roll Baby	Avco 4625	9/73
You Make Me Feel Brand New /		
Only For The Children	Avco 4634	1974
Let's Put It All Together /		
I Take It Out On You	Avco 4640	5/74
Go Now / Heavy Fallin' Out	Avco 4647	1974
Star On A TV Show /		
Hey, Girl Come And Get It	Avco 4649	12/74
Thank You Baby /		
Sing Baby Sing	Avco 4652	3/75
Can't Give You Anything /		
I'd Rather Be Hurt By You	Avco 4656	6/75
Funky Weekend / If You Are There	Avco 4661	1975
Michael Or Me / You Are Beautiful	Avco 4664	1976
Can't Help Falling In Love	H&L 4669	1976
Because I Love You, Girl /		
You Are	H&L 4674	1976
Only You / What Goes		
Around Comes Around	H&L 4676	1976
Shame And Scandal In The Family	H&L 4681	3/77
I'm Coming Home	H&L 4686	6/77
The Lion Sleeps Tonight /		
School For Lovers	Dash 5049	1978
First Impressions	Merc 74006	6/78
Love At First Sight	Merc 74042	1/79
Hurry Up This Way Again /		
It Started Out	TSOP 4789	8/80
And I'll See You No More	TSOP 4798	1/81
What's Your Name?	TSOP 02195	7/81
Give A Little	Strtws 1136	10/84
Some Things Never Change	Strtws 1137	1/85
Special	Strtws 1138	2/86
Let's Go Rocking (Tonight)	Strtws 2241	5/86

The Sylvers

Another family act like THE JACKSON 5 and TAVARES, the Sylvers started out as a brother and sister foursome known as the Little Angels in their hometown of Memphis, Tennessee. Unlike most groups that had to attain success before they could set foot on a national TV show, Leon Frank III, Olympia-Ann, Charmaine, and James Sylvers were performing on TV with Spike Jones, Groucho Marx, and Dinah Shore long before they'd ever been in a recording studio.

Encouraged and trained by their mother Shirley (a former opera singer), the quartet performed at Memphis talent shows before the family moved to Harlem, where the group performed at the Apollo Theatre. When school vacations came for other kids the four sibling Sylvers went on tour throughout

the U.S. and Europe with Ray Charles and, later, Johnny Mathis.

By the early '70s the family was living in the Watts section of Los Angeles under the ever-watchful eye of Mama Shirley. She kept them practicing constantly and developing intricate harmonies with other young members of the family.

By 1971 the group, now calling themselves the Sylvers, was seven strong with the added voices of young Foster, Edmund, and Ricky, and in 1972 they signed with MGM's Pride affiliate.

On September 2, 1972, the family's recording of "Fool's Paradise" hit the *Billboard* R&B charts, reaching number 14 (#94 Pop). "Wish that I Could Talk to You" followed, charting at number 10 R&B and number 77 Pop. Stealing the show at age 11 was Foster, who in mid-1973 had a solo hit called "Misdemeanor" (#22 Pop, #7 R&B). By 1974 the whole family was on the parent label MGM, although they had done better on Pride: only one MGM single, "Through the Love in My Heart" (#50 R&B) reached the charts.

In 1975, Capitol Records' VP Larkin Arnold signed the group and decided to use a tried-and-true formula: get a producer/writer who had worked with other family groups and let him weave a similar '70s magic. The choice was easy: Freddy Perren, the force behind the Jackson 5 and Tavares in the early '70s. With lyricist Keni St. James he created "Boogie Fever," recorded with Edmund on lead. Released on November 10, 1975, "Boogie Fever" was on the *Billboard* black hits list within 19 days. It reached number one on the Hot 100 on May 15, 1976, and also rose to number one R&B.

Although the group never reached the top spot again, they turned out some quality sides that attained a good degree of success. Their follow-up was "Cotton Candy" (#59 Pop, #19 R&B), which in turn was followed by the teen favorite "Hot Line" (#5 Pop, #3 R&B) and more than likely spurred the New Edition's '80s hit "Mr. Telephone Man" (also a Perren production).

"High School Dance" (#17 Pop, #6 R&B) and "Any Way You Want Me" (#72 Pop, #12 R&B) were particularly good, but when records like "New Horizons" (#45 R&B) didn't reach the plateau Capitol hoped for, the group found themselves on Casablanca in 1978 for one chart single, "Don't Stop, Get Off" (#15 R&B).

The group continued with its performance career and in 1984 signed with Geffen Records. The cast now included Foster, Ricky, Angela, Charmaine, James, and Pat Sylvers, but the group's biggest single only reached number 42 ("In One Love and Out the Other").

Tavares

Continuing in the tradition of family groups like the Rocky Fellers, THE JACKSON 5, and THE FIVE STAIRSTEPS, Tavares was an all-male aggregation from New Bedford, Massachusetts, formed around 1959. They practiced doo wop tunes and folk songs of South Atlantic islands such as Cape Verde, where their grandparents were from.

The quartet consisted of Antone "Chubby," Perry Lee "Tiny," Feliciano "Butch," Ralph, and Arthur "Pooch" Tavares.

By 1963 they were performing at clubs and talent shows throughout the New England area under the name Chubby and the Turnpikes. By then their ages were Tiny 9, Butch 10, Chubby 13, Pooch 14, and Ralph 15. In 1973 the group became Tavares and came to the attention of Capitol Records and former Motown producer Johnny Bristol.

Their first single, "Check It Out," charted R&B by August 11th and rose to number five (#35 Pop).

This began a string of nine R&B songs, of which eight crossed over to the Hot 100. "Too Late" (#59 Pop, #19 R&B), "She's Gone" (#50 Pop, #1 R&B, perhaps prompting Atlantic to reissue the Hall and Oates original in 1976 [#7 Pop]), "Remember What I Told You to Forget" (#25 Pop, #4 R&B), and two great disco records produced by Freddie Perren, "It Only Takes a Minute" (#10 Pop, #1 R&B) and "Heaven Must Be Missing an Angel (Part I)" (#15 Pop, #3 R&B), helped solidify their hold on contemporary R&B in the mid-'70s.

"More than a Woman" (#32 Pop, #36 R&B, 1977), another disco gem, found even greater exposure for the group when it was included in the film and on the multimillion-selling soundtrack LP of *Saturday Night Fever*.

The hits continued through the '70s with "Never Had a Love Like This Before" (#5 R&B, 1975) and "Bad Times" (#47 Pop, #10 R&B, 1979–80).

In 1982 the group moved over to RCA and clicked with the Kenny Nolan ballad "A Penny for Your Thoughts" (#33 Pop, #16 R&B), as well as the top 10 hit "Deeper in Love" in 1983.

Their last chart single was "Words and Music" (#29 R&B) in 1983, but the group continued performing through the '80s.

TAVARES

A SIDE/B SIDE	LABEL/CAT NO	DATE
Check It Out / The Judgement Day	Cap 03674	7/73
That's The Sound That		
Lonely Makes / Little Girl	Cap 03794	12/73

A SIDE/B SIDE	LABEL/CAT NO	DATE
Too Late / Leave It		
Up To The Lady	Cap 03882	4/74
She's Gone / To Love You	Cap 03957	9/74
Remember What I Told		
You To Forget / My Ship	Cap 04010	1/75
It Only Takes A Minute /		
I Hope She Chooses Me	Cap 04111	7/75
Free Ride / In The Eyes Of Love	Cap 04184	11/75
The Love I Never Had / In The City	Cap 04221	1/76
Heaven Must Be Missing		
An Angel Part 1 / Part 2	Cap 04270	5/76
Don't Take Away The Music /		
Guiding Star	Cap 04348	10/76
Whodunit / Fool Of The Year	Cap 04398	3/77
Goodnight My Love / Watchin'		
The Women's Movement	Cap 04453	7/77
More Than A Woman /		
Keep In Touch	Cap 04500	10/77
Ghost Of Love Part 1 / Part 2	Cap 04544	1/78
Timber / Feel So Good	Cap 04583	5/78
Never Had A Love Like This		
Before / Positive Forces	Cap 04658	11/78
Straight From The Heart /		
I'm Back For More	Cap 04703	4/79
Let Me Heal The Bruises /		
One Telephone Call Away	Cap 04738	6/79
Bad Times (Theme From		
Defiance) / Got To Have		
Your Love	Cap 04811	12/79
I Can't Go On Living Without You /		
Why Can't We Fall In Love	Cap 04846	3/80
I Don't Want You Anymore /		
Paradise	Cap 04880	6/80
Love Uprising / Hot Love	Cap 04933	9/80
Loneliness / Break Down For Love	Cap 04969	1/81
Turn Out The Nightlight /		
House Of Music	Cap 05019	6/81
Loveline / Right On Time	Cap 05043	9/81
Check It Out / She's Gone	Cap 06243	4/77
Heaven Must Be Missing		
An Angel Part 1 / Part 2	Cap 06253	6/78
More Than A Woman / Whodunit	Cap 06271	10/81
It Only Takes A Minute /		
Remember What I Told		
You To Forget	Cap 06424	4/77
Never Had A Love Like This		
Before / Instrumental	Cap 08505	11/78
A Penny For Your Thoughts	RCA 13292	1982

Three Dog Night

Following the success of the self-contained songwriting/performing Beatles in the mid-'60s, songwriters who were not recording artists found it increasingly difficult to get their works recorded.

Fewer acts were taking songs from others since many felt they could write their own like the Beatles did. A notable exception that became one of the most successful acts of the '70s was Three Dog Night.

Though considered to be a band because of their solid four-piece accompaniment, their vocals and songs are what carried them to popularity.

The group formed in 1968 from Danny Hutton's vision of a pop-rock act of three lead singers with shades of soul. He joined with Cory Wells and Chuck Negron to fulfill that vision along with musicians Jimmy Greenspoon (keyboards), Mike Allsup (guitar), Joe Schermie (bass), and Floyd Sneed (drums).

Hutton, who came from Buncrana, Ireland, did voice-overs for Walt Disney animated shows and then became a studio singer and producer for Hanna-Barbara when they had their own HBR record label in 1965. He hit the charts as an artist with his own "Roses and Rainbows" (#73) in the fall of 1975. After failing in an audition to become one of the Monkees, he decided to form his own act.

Cory Wells of Buffalo, New York, sang with the Enemies, a house band at Los Angeles's famed Whiskey A Go Go.

Negron, from the Bronx, New York, had been singing his soulful style since childhood and was performing at the Apollo in Harlem by 1956 (no ordinary feat for a 14-year-old white singer).

The group's name came from an old Australian expression relating to nighttime temperatures. The colder it was, the more dogs you had sleep beside you to keep warm. A three dog night was the coldest. How three guys from Buncrana, Buffalo, and the Bronx might have picked up on such an expression is anybody's guess.

Late in 1968 they signed to Dunhill Records. From the beginning their choice of material was either new songs by yet-to-be immortalized writers or covers of forgotten or overlooked gems. Their first single, "Nobody," by Dick Cooper, Ernie Shelly, and Beth Beatty, got some airplay. The flip side was a Lennon-McCartney song titled "It's for You."

Their cover of the Otis Redding R&B hit "Try a Little Tenderness" (#4 R&B, 1966) was their first pop charter in February 1969, reaching number 29.

Their follow-up, the Harry Nilsson-penned "One," reached number five in the spring of 1969 and became the first million seller of their career total of nine.

Their LP *Three Dog Night* reached number 11 and was the first of 12 consecutive gold albums they earned in just six years.

They became household names to fans and heroes to the songwriting community, thanks to hits like the Rado/Ragny/McDermott song "Easy to Be Hard" (#4, 1969) from the musical *Hair*, "Eli's Coming" by Laura Nyro (#10, 1969–70), "Celebrate" by Bonner and Gordon (#15, 1970), "Mama Told Me Not to Come" by Randy Newman (#1, 1970, #3 U.K., a song Wells had heard on an Eric Burdon LP), "Out in the Country" by Paul Williams and Roger Nichols (#15, 1970), and "One Man Band" (#19, 1970).

Three Dog Night's opening act on some of their tours was 32-year-old Hoyt Axton. He wrote a song for an animated children's TV series called "The Happy Song" but the show never got off the ground. Axton instead played the piece for the group, and by April 17, 1971, "Joy to the World" was the group's second number one record, their second hit in the U.K. (#24), and their first and only R&B chart single (#46).

With the number one status of "Joy," Hoyt became the second part of the trivia question, "Who were the only mother and son songwriters to have both written number one songs?" His mom, Mae Axton, wrote Elvis Presley's "Heartbreak Hotel," which hit the top in April 1956, 15 years earlier almost to the day.

Three Dog Night continued to blaze trails with Russ Ballard's 1971 "Liar" (#7), "Just an Old-Fashioned Love Song" (#4, 1971), "Never Been to Spain" (#5, 1971), and the Earl Robinson/David Arkin-penned "Black and White" (their third and last number one, 1972). Arkin was the father (now deceased) of actor Alan Arkin, and the song was a 17-year-old celebration of the Supreme Court's 1955 ruling against school segregation. Three Dog Night had heard the Greyhounds' version over Dutch radio while on a European tour.

Hits like "Shambala" (#3, 1973), the Leo Sayer/Dave Courtney song "The Show Must Go On" (#4, 1974), and John Hiatt's "Sure as I'm Sittin' Here" (#16, 1974) gave the group an incredible 18 straight top 20 hits.

In 1973 they appeared on Dick Clark's 20th anniversary TV show with Little Richard.

In 1975 Dunhill Records was dissolved by its parent ABC, and along with it, for the most part, went Three Dog Night's career. Only two more chart singles emerged from the group, "Play Something Sweet" (#33, 1974) and "Till the World Ends" (#32, 1975).

In 1976 Hutton left and was replaced by Jay Gruska, but the group separated soon after. In 1981 the three united to perform but didn't release any new product following their heyday.

THREE DOG NIGHT

A SIDE/B SIDE	LABEL/CAT NO	DATE
Nobody / It's For You	Dnhl 4168	1968
Try A Little Tenderness /		
Bet No One Ever Hurt This Bad	Dnhl 4177	1969
One / Chest Fever	Dnhl 4191	1969
Easy To Be Hard /		
Dreaming Isn't Good For You	Dnhl 4203	1969
Eli's Coming / Circle For A Landing	Dnhl 4215	1969
Celebrate / Feeling Alright	Dnhl 4229	1970
Mama Told Me Not To Come /		
Rock And Roll Widow	Dnhl 4239	1970
Out In The Country /		
Good Time Living	Dnhl 4250	1970
One Man Band / It Ain't Easy	Dnhl 4262	1970
Joy To The World /		
I Can Hear You Calling	Dnhl 4272	1971
Liar / Can't Get Enough Of It	Dnhl 4282	1971
An Old-Fashioned		
Love Song / Jam	Dnhl 4294	1971
Never Been To Spain /		
Peace Of Mind	Dnhl 4299	1971
The Family Of Man /		
Going In Circles	Dnhl 4306	1972
Black And White /		
Freedom For The Stallion	Dnhl 4317	1972
Pieces Of April /		
The Writing's On The Wall	Dnhl 4331	1972
Shambala / Our B Side	Dnhl 4352	1973
Let Me Serenade You /		
Storybook Feeling	Dnhl 4370	1973
The Show Must Go On /		
On The Way Back Home	Dnhl 4382	1973
Sure As I'm Sittin' Here /		
Anytime, Babe	Dnhl 15001	1974
The Show Must Go On /		
On The Way Back Home	Dnhl 15010	1974
Play Something Sweet (Brickyard		
Blues) / I'd Be So Happy	Dnhl 15013	1974
Till The World Ends /		
Ye Te Quiero Hablar	ABC 12114	1975
Everybody Is A Masterpiece /		
Drive On, Ride On	ABC 12192	1975
It's A Jungle Out There /		
Somebody's Gonna Get Hurt	Psprt 7921	

The Village People

When the disco music of the '70s became linked with the American gay social scene, it became inevitable that some clever producer would try to cater to that new market. Jacques Morali, who conceptualized the Village People just for that purpose, went further by using *double entendre* lyrics to cross over to the straight world.

Morali was a French record producer working in the United States in 1977 with his partner Henri Belolo at Can't Stop Productions. One evening while visiting a New York gay bar, he noticed many of the men were dressed up—almost costumed—according to certain archetypal male roles, and Morali found this to be a regular occurrence. He decided to form a vocal group around what a Frenchman perceived these roles to be, including a policeman, a soldier, a construction worker, a cowboy, an Indian, and a biker, but all with a decidedly gay slant. He then hired six actors/singers to flesh out the stereotypes. They were lead singer Victor Willis, Randy Jones, Alex Briley, Felipe Rose, David Hodo, and Glenn Hughes.

The name was created as a reference to New York's Greenwich Village, and the sextet was signed to Neil Bogart's Casablanca label.

Their first single was "San Francisco, You've Got Me" (1977), which charted in the United Kingdom (#45). It was followed by "I Am What I Am," included in both the film *Thank God It's Friday* and its soundtrack LP in 1978.

In the summer of 1978 their campy single "Macho Man" reached number 25 in the U.S. and crossed the million mark. Though the group was not by any stretch of the imagination a traditional or typical vocal group, their singles were slick, professional dance recordings.

Their early 1979 release was the tongue-in-cheek sing-along "Y.M.C.A." (#2).

Their next 45, "In the Navy," also sailed its way to million-plus sales and a number three chart ranking (#2 U.K.), not to mention a top 10 ranking in Paris. The U.S. Navy flirted with the idea of using the song for recruitment drives until they discovered its true intent.

By year's end Willis had left and been replaced by Ray Simpson, Valerie Simpson's brother (of Ashford-Simpson). The group's "Ready for the Eighties" single (#52) became their last chart song in America.

In 1980 the group (which probably had six members just so Morali and Belolo could call them a sextet) co-starred with Valerie Perrine and Bruce Jenner in the movie *Can't Stop the Music*, and the title song sung by the Villagers peaked at number 11 in Britain.

In 1981 the sultans of stereotype changed their image (going romantic) and their label (RCA), and bombed with the LP *Renaissance*.

In 1982 Miles Jay took over for Simpson, but when disco disappeared, so did the Village People. Not, however, before they had sold a reported 18 million LPs worldwide.

The Whispers

The Whispers are a soul group steeped in doo wop tradition whose patience and practice paid off.

Formed in 1962 in the Jordan Downs housing projects located at 103rd and Grape Street in the Watts section of Los Angeles, the group was originally called the Eden Trio. They developed into a quintet consisting of members Walter Scott (lead and tenor), Wallace "Scotty" Scott (lead and tenor and Walter's twin brother), Nicholas Caldwell (tenor), Gordy Harmon (tenor), and Marcus Hutson (baritone). The Jordan High School students practiced day and night, often until 4 in the morning, working on songs by their influences THE FLAMINGOS, THE TEMPTATIONS, THE HI-LO'S, THE FOUR FRESHMEN, Johnny Mathis, and Nat King Cole. They sang everything they could learn, including Hertz car rental commercials.

In 1964 they came to the attention of Lou Bedell and his Vine Street-based Dore Records in Hollywood. He liked their soft sound and renamed them, appropriately, the Whispers. The teenagers recorded five Dore singles, including "It Only Hurts for a Little While," "Never Again," and "As I Sit Here," all worthwhile ballads and all recorded at the legendary Gold Star Studios in Hollywood.

Their first big gig was at the California Club with one of their idols, the Temptations.

In 1969 the group signed with the Fantasy-distributed Soul Clock label and issued a soul harmony ballad called "Great Day." But it was the summer release of their follow-up, "The Time Will Come," with Wallace's wailing lead and the group's weaving, high harmonies, that first put them on national R&B radio. "The Time" charted on August 2, 1969, and rose to number 17.

Their fourth Soul Clock single proved they were on their way as "Seems Like I Gotta Do Wrong" reached number six R&B and number 50 Pop. That success wasn't yet reflected in their life on the road, however; the five-member group and its four-man band often shared one hotel room.

By 1970 they had signed with Janus Records. The single "There's a Love for Everyone" charted the day after Christmas, eventually reaching number 31 R&B and number 116 Pop.

8 of 12 Janus singles charted, and though none made the group household names, they helped the group build a following with songs like "Your Love Is So Doggone Good" (#93 Pop, #19 R&B, 1971) and "I Only Meant to Wet My Feet" (#27 R&B, 1972).

Their only full-time personnel change came in 1971 when Leaveil Degree, who sang for a time with the Friends of Distinction, replaced Gordy Harmon.

By late 1975 the group had moved to the Soul Train label, which gained them some welcome top 10 exposure with "One for the Money (Part I)" (#88 Pop, #10 R&B, 1976) and a rhythmic version of Bread's 1970 hit "Make It with You" (#94 Pop, #10 R&B, 1977).

When Soul Train became Solar Records, the group hit its stride and racked up 22 soul charters from 1978 to 1988 out of only 27 releases. Some of their best included "(Let's Go) All the Way" (#10 R&B, 1978), "And the Beat Goes On" (#19 Pop, #1 R&B, 1980), "Lady" (#28 Pop, #3 R&B, 1980), "It's a Love Thing" (#28 Pop, #2 R&B, 1981), "Tonight" (#84 Pop, #4 R&B, 1983) and the top 10 Pop hit it took them 23 years of recording to get, "Rock Steady" (#7 Pop, #1 R&B).

"Rock Steady" also gave the fledgling writers/producers L. A. and Babyface their first major chart success, as did the group's *Just Gets Better with Time* LP that went double platinum.

After 17 LPs, 38 chart singles, and over 27 years bouncing from the studio to the stage, the title of that 1987 LP pretty much said it all.

THE WHISPERS

A SIDE/B SIDE	LABEL/CAT NO	DATE
It Only Hurts For A Little While /		
The Happy One	Dore 724	1964
Never Again / Slow Jerk	Dore 729	1964
The Dip / It Hurts So Much	Dore 735	1965
As I Sit Here / Shake It Shake It	Dore 740	1965
Doctor Love / Lonely Avenue	Dore 751	1966
Great Day / I Can't See		
Myself Leaving You	Sl Clk 104	1969
The Time Will Come / Flying High	Sl Clk 107	6/69
What Will I Do / Remember	Sl Clk 109	1969
Seems Like I Gotta Do Wrong /		
Needle In A Haystack	Sl Clk 1004	7/70
I'm The One /		
You Must Be Doing All Right	Sl Clk 1005	1970
There's A Love For Everyone /		
It Sure Ain't Pretty	Janus 140	1970
Your Love Is So Doggone Good	Janus 150	1971
Can't Help But Love You	Janus 174	1971
I Only Meant To Wet My Feet /		
You Fill My Life With Music	Janus 184	1972
Can We Love Forever /		
Somebody Loves You	Janus 200	1972
P.O.W.—M.I.A.	Janus 212	1973
Feel Like Comin' Home / I Love		
The Way You Make Me Feel	Janus 222	9/73

A SIDE/B SIDE	LABEL/CAT NO	DATE	A SIDE/B SIDE	LABEL/CAT NO	DATE
A Mother For My Children /			Happy Holidays To You	Solar 11449	12/78
What More Can A Girl Ask For	Janus 231	12/73	Can't Do Without Love	Solar 11590	4/79
Bingo / One More With Feeling	Janus 238	1974	Homemade Lovin'	Solar 11685	7/79
Broken Home /			A Song For Donny	Solar 11739	9/79
What More Can A Girl Ask For	Janus 244	1974	And The Beat Goes On	Solar 11894	12/79
All I Ever Do /			Lady	Solar 11928	2/80
Here Comes Tomorrow	Janus 247	1974	Out Of The Box	Solar 12050	6/80
Give A Little Love	Janus 253	1975	It's A Love Thing	Solar 12154	12/80
In Love Forever / Fairytales	Sl Trn 10430	1975	I Can Make It Better	Solar 12232	4/81
You're A Very Special Part Of Me	Sl Trn 10628	1975	This Kind Of Lovin'	Solar 12295	8/81
One For The Money Part 1 /			I'm The One For You	Solar 13005	11/81
One For The Money Part 2	Sl Trn 10700	1976	In The Raw	Elek 47956	12/81
Living Together In Sin /			Emergency	Elek 48008	4/82
I've Got A Feeling	Sl Trn 10773	1976	Love Is Where You Find It	Elek 69965	8/82
You're Only As Good As You			Tonight	Elek 69842	2/83
Think You Are	Sl Trn 10878	1/77	Keep On Lovin' Me	Elek 69827	4/83
Make It With You	Sl Trn 10996	5/77	Rock Steady	Cap 70006	3/87
I'm Gonna Make You My Wife	Solar 11139	9/77	Just Gets Better With Time	Cap 70012	7/87
(Let's Go) All The Way	Solar 11246	3/78	In The Mood	Cap 70017	11/87
Living Together In Sin	Solar 11328	6/78	No Pain, No Gain	Cap 70020	3/88
(Olivia) Lost And Turned Out	Solar 11353	7/78			

NEW EDITION

THE 1980s

THE BANGLES

EN VOGUE

The 1980s saw a revival of interest in vocal groups, at least in comparison to the '70s. Groups like Wilson Phillips, En Vogue, and the Bangles not only kept vocal acts visible but showed that new female groups were at a more solid parity with their male counterparts.

The most popular American act of the '80s was a vocal group, the megahit quintet New Kids on the Block.

Hip-hop music, a form of urban street dance music combined with doo wop, took hold in the '80s as performed by acts like the Force M.D.'s. New Edition and DeBarge led the way for rhythm and blues acts, and a slew of '60s soul acts re-emerged with hits in the '80s, including Gladys Knight and the Pips, the O'Jays, the Temptations, the Four Tops, the Isley Brothers, the Chi-Lites, and the Dells.

Many older acts resurfaced in the '80s thanks to a renewed interest from a nostalgia-hungry public who had more music to reminisce about than ever before. Even regional nostalgia developed, with the popularity of beach music in the Carolinas and the South. Groups like the Tams, Maurice Williams and the Zodiacs, the Clovers, and many more began selling old recordings that fit the beach music mold.

Gospel groups broadened their appeal in this decade without completely sacrificing their messages; acts like the Winans found themselves high on the charts.

Unfortunately, few pop and pop-rock vocal acts of the past came back to the charts (notable exceptions being the Beach Boys and Crosby, Stills and Nash). However, many did return via the nostalgia tour circuit, and the public thrilled once more to the Tokens, the Mamas and the Papas, Frankie Valli and the Four Seasons, and even early '50s pop stars like the McGuire Sisters.

Organizations honoring and sometimes providing performance opportunities for vocal groups of the past sprang up around the country in the '80s, including the National Music Foundation in Florida, the Doo Wop Hall of Fame in Massachusetts, the Society of Singers in Los Angeles and Las Vegas, the Doo Wop Society of Northern California in San Francisco, the South Florida Group Harmony Association in Miami, the Doo Wop Society of Southern California in Los Angeles, and of course the organization that started it all, the United in Group Harmony Association of Clifton, New Jersey.

Publications that catered to the group sound also came into being, including Bob Belniak's *Echos of the Past* out of Agawam, Massachusetts, Don Mennie's *Record Collectors Monthly* from Mendham, New Jersey, and Greg Milowski's *Cat Tails* in Sterling, Virginia. Also, *DISCovery* magazine and *Goldmine* magazine regularly issued articles on vocal groups.

The U.G.H.A. provided the most excitement of all the oldies organizations, bringing back acts that hadn't performed since the early '50s and '60s: the Chords, the Silhouettes, the Bobbettes, the Bob Knight Four, the Velours, the Mellows, the Dubs, the Wrens, the Swallows, and the Ravens, to mention a few.

In an attempt to reach wider audiences, a cappella groups started to reflect some contemporary influences. Rather than bringing the past to the present, some groups started to bring the present into the past. A cappella acts like Reunion recorded songs of the '70s and '80s in an older vocal group style. Others, like the Bobs, Betty, True Image, Rockapella, and Take 6, began recording everything from avant garde and gospel to novelty songs and parodies—all in an a cappella style. The most successful of these were the Nylons, who used contemporary percussion and old-fashioned four-part harmony to create hits like "Kiss Him Goodbye."

Traditional a cappella groups also maintained an audience, especially in the New York area. New groups like B.Q.E., Yesterday's Memories, the Exquisites, and more sang the standards in standard style. Older a cappella acts swelled the numbers, including the Camelots, Mixed Company, the Emerys, and the Ecstasies, though many groups were informal affairs at best and often broke up after one or two records (or the same number of performances).

Many new vocal groups, along with the known and unknown acts of the '50s, '60s, and '70s, found themselves performing in front of appreciative audiences who often brought their offspring. It was the kind of exposure that ensured the group harmony sound would be carried on into future decades. ■

The Bangles

The Bangles were a female vocal band who, consistent with the "take-charge '80s," became one of the first female vocal bands to record, put out their own record, and then go on to international success.

The original members were Vicki and Debbi Peterson of Northridge, California, Susanna Hoffs of West Los Angeles, and Annette Zalinkas of Los Angeles. They came together from an ad Susanna had put in an L.A. weekly, *The Recycler*, which asked for band members who were into the Beatles, the Byrds, and Buffalo Springfield.

The group practiced in Susanna's garage and called themselves the Colours. THE BEACH BOYS and the Hollies were also influences on the group, so a good deal of time was spent on vocal harmony. Soon after their 1981 formation the Colours became the Supersonic Bangs and then just the Bangs. They wrote their own songs and recorded one, "Getting Out of Hand," on their own Down Kiddie label while they began playing Los Angeles and San Fernando Valley nightspots.

Because their influences were mostly '60s acts, their music positioned them in what became known as the "paisley underground," a collection of folk-rock and neopsychedelic groups. Manager Miles Copeland heard them, signed them up, and sent them on tour with the English Beat and Cyndi Lauper while releasing a five-song EP on his Faulty Products label. When the group was threatened with a potential lawsuit from a pre-existing East Coast Bangs, the girls renamed themselves the Bangles in a Mexican restaurant on the way to Las Vegas.

In 1983 the group signed with Columbia Records. Zalinkas left after not being able to fulfill her desire as lead singer. She was replaced by Michael "Micki" Steele, the original lead singer of the all-girl Runaways.

Their first Columbia LP, *All Over the Place*, did not sell, and it was three more years before the girls hit the charts with "Manic Monday" written by Christopher a.k.a. Roger Nelson a.k.a. Prince. "Manic" reached number two Pop on April 19, 1986, and ironically was kept out of first place by the song "Kiss," written and recorded by Prince and the Revolution. Jules Shear's "If She Knew What She Wants" followed, reaching number 29 and setting the stage for their biggest record, "Walk Like an Egyptian," which was originally turned down by "Mickey" hitmaker Toni Basil. The song, which was submitted to their producer David Kahne by a publisher for songwriter Liam Sternberg, was the third from their double-platinum LP *Different Light*. It reached number one on December 20th and became *Billboard*'s top record of the year. Los Angeles' mayor designated February 23, 1987, as "Bangles Day" in the metropolis.

In late 1987 the Bangles hit again with Simon and Garfunkel's "Hazy Shade of Winter" (#2, February 6, 1988).

The group performed on a sell-out tour and then in 1988 recorded their third and last CBS LP *Everything*, which contained the Fleetwood Mac-styled rocker "In Your Room" (#5, 1988) and the harmony-filled ballad "Eternal Flame" (#1, 1989), with Susanna's fragile voice leading the group through the Billy Steinberg/Tom Kelly-penned composition. Unlike most acts of the '50s and '60s who quit because they could no longer earn a living at what they were doing, the Bangles called it quits while on top; they disbanded in October 1989 to pursue individual goals. Their last chart single was "Be with You" in the spring of 1989 (#30).

Big Daddy

Big Daddy carved its own niche in vocal group history by adhering to a single concept. That concept was the recording and performing of new songs in old rock and roll, doo wop, and country styles.

The quartet (sometimes a quintet) consisted of Marty Kaniger, lead tenor to baritone and falsetto), Bob Wayne (the same), Tom Lee (baritone and bass), David Starns (tenor), and Gary Hoffman (tenor and drummer). Each member sang lead and had worked in groups or bands before Big Daddy became a unit in Los Angeles, circa 1982.

Bob and Marty, old school chums since 1955 (from Brentwood Elementary School to Palisades High School), formed an oldies group in the early '70s called Big Daddy Dipstick and the Lube Jobs, which they eventually shortened to Big Daddy. All the guys were together at Sunburst Studios in Culver City, Los Angeles, in late 1982 when Richard Foos, cofounder of Rhino Records, took their idea of forming an oldies revival group one step further. He suggested they put together a doo wop album of contemporary hits. Big Daddy expanded the concept to include a variety of styles from the '50s and '60s.

Then came the imaginative promo campaign. Their first LP cover was done as a take-off of *The National Enquirer*'s front page (*The Unnatural In-*

quirer) stating, "Big Daddy: What really happened to the band of the fifties?," with a photo of the five greasers and a back cover explaining in tabloid style how the group was on a USO tour of Southeast Asia in 1959 when they were captured by Laotian revolutionaries and forced to perform their repertoire of '50s rock and roll over and over. 24 years after their capture they were freed by a CIA team. Upon returning to the U.S., the group was put in the Camp David Recording Studios and given sheet music to recent hits since the government officials didn't have the stomach to tell them their music was out of date. The resulting recordings (the tabloid went on without cracking a smile) were all done in vintage '50s style, the only rock and roll the group had ever heard. Rhino Records heard of the group's circumstances and after listening to the tapes concluded the songs actually sounded better with '50s arrangements. You can guess the rest.

The LP itself was cut in November and December 1982 and released in early 1983. If the concept was funny, the actual recordings were hilarious. The tracks included Barry Manilow's "I Write the Songs" in a DANNY AND THE JUNIORS "At the Hop" arrangement; Rick James's "Superfreak" as an Everly Brothers-styled song; "Star Wars" sounding like Duane Eddy doing it in a "Telstar" mode; rock doo wop tackles Barbra Streisand's "You Don't Bring Me Flowers"; Bette Midler's "The Rose" done rockabilly; and the Eagles' "Hotel California" as if recorded by Del Shannon.

Big Daddy added John Hatton (bass) after the first LP and went on to take their parody from Los Angeles's Universal Amphitheatre to Lake Tahoe's Caesar's Palace, Chicago's P. J. Flaherty's, and Dingwall's in London, among many other venues.

In 1985 they went back to work figuring there were now enough new mediocre hits to make great with a '50s treatment. So *Meanwhile—Back in the States* was created. The music was once again a series of outrageous pairings: Phil Collins's "Sussudio" done in a DION "Runaround Sue" style; Stevie Wonder's "I Just Called to Say I Love You" to THE DEL-VIKINGS' "Whispering Bells"; Michael Jackson's "Billie Jean" to Gene Vincent's "Be-Bop-A-Lula"; Irene Cara's "Flashdance" to THE DIAMONDS' "Little Darlin'"; Van Halen's "Jump" in an Eddie Cochran "Summertime Blues" interpretation; and Cyndi Lauper's "Girls Just Want to Have Fun" to Gene Chandler and the Dukays' "Duke of Earl."

The second LP did better than the first and continued to widen Daddy's audience. They appealed to the same parody hits market as Weird Al Yankovic.

Around 1986 they backed up Richard Berry for his remake of "Louie Louie" on Rhino's *The Best of Louie Louie* LP.

Over the years they appeared on television in the U.S., England, and Australia. Speaking of England, their version of Bruce Springsteen's "Dancing in the Dark" became a hit on an EP, reaching number 20 on the national charts and selling over 80,000 copies.

In 1986, Don Raymond replaced David Starns. The group continued to perform into the '90s, and in April 1991 their third album for Rhino, *Cutting Their Own Groove*, hit the market and carried on the tradition of the first two LPs.

The Bobs

Taking vocal group harmony to a new level in the '80s, the Bobs became known for their satirical lyrics applied to a cappella arrangements. With original songs like "First I Was a Hippie, Then I Was a Stockbroker, Now I Am a Hippie Again" and "My Husband Was a Weather Man," the group gave notice that no institution would be safe from their biting humor.

They formed in San Francisco in 1982 as the brainchild of Matthew Stull and Gunnar Madsen, two employees of the Western Onion Telegraph Company who performed singing telegrams. After advertising for a bass, they auditioned Richard Green and he got the job. Richard was a former member of the Hoo Doo Rhythm Devils but was perhaps better known for the five notes he sang with his voice descending lower and lower on the words "fall into the Gap" for the Gap clothing store commercials. Although Richard was an excellent bass, he may have gotten the job by default as he was the only one to answer the ad. After adding Jamie Scott, the group came up with the name the Bobs (initials for "best of breed," from dog show terminology) and did their first LP for Kaleidoscope Records in 1983. Stull and Madsen wrote most of the material, with an occasional oldie slipped in ("You Really Got a Hold on Me"). Their second LP came in 1987 on the Great American Music Hall label, entitled *My, I'm Large*, and their third LP, *Songs for Tomorrow Morning*, was released in 1988.

Their LPs contained only a cappella cuts, but their listening and buying audience still seemed to increase with each release. Although their sound was far from the mainstream, the group worked continuously in the U.S. and abroad and performed with such diverse figures as comedian Robin Williams, Frank Zappa, and the Grateful Dead. Their style could be considered new wave doo wop, but their versatility made them as much at home with '40s pop as with a contemporary jazz arrangement. As of 1991 they had never come close to a chart single or LP, but they had built a growing audience and kept a cappella harmony alive.

B.Q.E.

If B.Q.E. had been around in the '60s they might have rivaled doo wop experts THE EARLS. The lineup of a cappella vocalists included four leads, Angelo Termini (tenor), Jason Lemaro (tenor), Luther Rucker (baritone), Jerry Pilgrim (tenor), and a bass, Les Levine. Their mutual vocal group interests brought them together in Glen Oaks, Queens, New York, during the fall of 1985. The name B.Q.E. came about as a choice of five, one submitted by each member on a piece of paper. B.Q.E. stands for Brooklyn Queens Expressway, the motorway connecting the two boroughs the members were from.

Unlike some of the middle-aged amateur a cappella aggregations formed in the '80s, B.Q.E.'s members had all sung and played professionally for years. Angelo, a professional guitarist, sang with JAY AND THE AMERICANS. Jason, formerly of the Performing Arts and Music Department of Queensborough College, was a bass guitarist with the rock group Prophecy. Jerry sang with THE EXCELLENTS and Jay and the Americans. Luther sang with the Celestial Community Choir. Les was with the Arrogants ("Canadian Sunset" on Lute, 1962), backed Richie Cordell and Paul Simon, and worked with Jerry in the Excellents during the '80s.

The group's influences were a cross section of white, black, and racially mixed groups like THE DIAMONDS, THE MARCELS, THE HEARTBEATS, THE MOONGLOWS, and THE SPANIELS.

In 1987 their live performance of THE TOKENS' classic "The Lion Sleeps Tonight" on Don K. Reed's "Doo-Wop Shop" was heard by Starlight Records executive Bob Kretchmar, who called the group and signed them on the basis of that one performance.

In March 1988 B.Q.E. recorded a version of "The Lion Sleeps Tonight" and several other oldies done a cappella.

Their first release was a faithful interpretation of THE COASTERS' "Zing Went the Strings of My Heart,"

featuring bass Les Levine. The flip was a rendition of THE MELLO-KINGS' "Tonight Tonight." Two more adaptations of oldies followed: The previously recorded "The Lion Sleeps Tonight" and Ben E. King's "Stand by Me." "Lion" was featured on Cousin Brucie's "Yesterday and Today" series back-to-back with the Tokens' version.

In September 1988 B.Q.E. made its large-audience debut at the United Nations General Assembly Hall with a potpourri of artists ranging from opera's Roberta Peters to Mongo Santamaria's Latin band.

Their third Starlight single was 1988's "Tonight (Could Be the Night)" (the Velvets, 1961) b/w "I Love You" (THE VOLUMES, 1962). Both were done with high tenor harmony and the trademark bass sound that made Les Levine one of the best bass singers of the last 20 years. Yet as of 1991 the group had not recorded enough music for an LP.

When not singing with B.Q.E., the members were working guys. In 1991 Luther was with the New York Sanitation Department, Jason was a professional musician, Angelo was a professional hair dresser, Jerry was manager for a wire and cable manufacturer, and Les was an independent insurance agent.

B.Q.E. was one of the finest vocal groups, a cappella or not, formed during the '80s.

DeBarge

Another popular rhythm and blues family group, DeBarge started out singing gospel at the Bethel Pentecostal Church in Grand Rapids, Michigan, where two of their uncles were responsible for the choir.

The quintet consisted of Eldra, James, Randy, Mark, and their sister Bunny DeBarge, and it formed in the late '70s starting out doing local gospel shows. Two of the group's brothers (Tommy and Bobby) had migrated to Los Angeles with their band Switch and were signed to Motown, so there were high hopes for the rest of the clan, numbering 10 kids.

The gospel quintet began practicing secular songs and took off for Los Angeles in 1979, where an audition was held for Jermaine Jackson at Motown, arranged by brothers Tommy and Bobby.

Berry Gordy signed the good-looking group with the intent of building another JACKSON 5. The DeBarge LP was issued in 1980 with Eldra singing lead, but it received little response.

▲ THE BOBS

▼ FORCE M.D.'s

▲ DeBARGE

▲ ROCKAPELLA

▲ THE NYLONS   ▼ BIG DADDY

▼ THE WINANS

Two years later they charted with the R&B single "Stop! Don't Tease Me" (#46).

This set the table for their crossover hit, "I Like It" (#31 Pop, #2 R&B), in late 1982. Their *All This Love* LP went gold and the title song followed "I Like It" to number five R&B and number 17 Pop in 1983. That same year their first number one R&B single emerged in the form of "Time Will Reveal" (#18 Pop).

The group was riding high when they went on tour with Luther Vandross in 1984, though Bunny's pregnancy kept her off the road. Their visibility got a major boost when the fivesome appeared in Gordy's *The Last Dragon* that year. Eldra began producing and writing cuts for the next LP, which included the Diane Warren song "Rhythm of the Night" from *The Last Dragon*.

By the summer of 1985 "Rhythm" was a smash hit single (#3 Pop, #1 R&B, #4 U.K.). Their follow-up, the ballad "Who's Holding Donna Now," was also an immense success, reaching number two R&B and number six Pop while the group was on tour in Europe.

Their success appeared to be fleeting when "The Heart Is Not So Smart" became their last Gordy charter (#29 R&B). The label read "El DeBarge with DeBarge."

In early 1986 El opted for a solo career (on Gordy) and younger brother Chico signed with Motown, putting eight family members on the Gordy payroll.

In 1986 El had the solo hit "Who's Johnny" (#3 Pop, #1 R&B) from the film *Shortcircuit*, and in 1987 Bunny went on her own for one charter, "Save the Best for Me" (#18 R&B), but solo activity for Bunny and El meant the demise of the group.

Bobby (of Switch) and James signed to Striped Horse Records under the group name for two final family name chart singles ("Dance All Nite," #33 R&B, and "You Babe," #73) in 1987.

Déjà Vu

Most vocal groups formed while in their teens or 20s, and a good number (especially members of previous groups that couldn't get group singing out of their blood) formed while in their 30s. Rarely, however, have singers in their 40s formed a group from scratch. One vocal act that did was Déjà Vu. In fact, they're probably the oldest working group ever formed and certainly the oldest of the '80s.

The group originated on Staten Island, New York, in January 1982 when four friends who were well on in their respective lives and occupations wanted to have some fun entertaining. Bob Burmeister (43, lead, tenor, and baritone), Frank Pandulo (46, lead and baritone), Pat Moschetto (40, lead to baritone), and Mike Luciano (45, lead and bass) were the mature music lovers. Nine months later the a cappella group picked up relative youngster June DePeppo (34) to alternate on leads.

With influences as varied as DION AND THE BELMONTS, THE DRIFTERS, THE SKYLINERS, THE SHANGRI-LAS, THE FOUR SEASONS, Tony Bennett, and the Monkees (the Monkees?!), they appeared in local night spots on Staten Island and performed on Don K. Reed's "Doo-Wop Shop" radio show on WCBS-FM.

In November 1984 the group recorded for Starlight Records, issuing "Over the Rainbow" in a Demensions/Skyliners style and THE CHANTELS' "Maybe" with June on lead. Both oldies were well done and well received but as of 1991 the group had not recorded again. Instead they formed a band in 1983 to support the vocalists and began performing everywhere from bowling alley dinners and weddings to '50s dances and Vietnam veteran shows.

In 1986 Armando Longobardi replaced the retiring Frank Pandulo. He in turn was replaced in 1987 by Tom Genovese (both were from Yonkers).

Pat Moschetto left in 1988 to go to another group, and Mike Palo arrived. The door kept revolving, with Tom Genovese leaving in 1989 and Bob Curcio stepping in. In 1990 June and Mike were out and Lynn Mikos was in on lead and first tenor. By 1991, Frank Adaro of one of the SALUTATIONS groups had taken over for Lynn. Déjà Vu stayed active. Of the originals, Bob was working at the New York Stock Exchange, Mike was a printer, and Frank was a fire fighter.

En Vogue

En Vogue was the creation of record producers Thomas McElroy (formerly of the Commodores) and Denzil Foster. In 1988 McElroy and Foster held auditions with the goal of putting together a female vocal group for their Atlantic Records concept LP *FM2*. The girls they picked out of hundreds of hopefuls were Dawn Robinson of Connecticut, Maxine Jones of New Jersey, Cindy Herron of San Francisco, and Terry Ellis of Texas. Two of the girls knew two of the others before trying out, though each came in without knowledge of the others' auditioning. Cindy met Terry in Houston while auditioning for Olympic athlete Carl Lewis's band. Maxine met Dawn at her hairdressers' in Oakland, and the two began to harmonize years before they met at the audition.

Their work on the *FM2* project led to the first full En Vogue project, the *Born to Sing* LP in 1989, which had a variety of musical styles from rhythm and blues to hip hop. A standout cut was a reworking of THE ANDREWS SISTERS' "Boogie Woogie Bugle Boy" titled "Hip Hop Bugle Boy."

Their first single was "Hold On," which had an a cappella intro. The single shot to number one R&B in the spring of 1990 and number two Pop, giving the girls national recognition. Their LP went gold and the single sold over a million copies.

Their second single, "Lies," went to number one R&B and number 38 Pop in 1990. "You Don't Have to Worry," their third, also went to number one R&B. The group then took off on a 23-city tour with Freddie Jackson. In all, it was a sensational start for this new generation vocal group.

The Exquisites

The Exquisites came together in 1981 thanks to a swap-and-shop ad that ran on Long Island TV. An enterprising group of singers were looking for a baritone. The wife of former Gino and THE DELLS ("Altar of Love," Golden Crest, 1962) baritone Pete Chacona spotted the solicitation and told her husband. When Pete (40) showed up at the rehearsal, a quick runthrough told him the only member who could really sing was second tenor Bernie Festo (28), so he induced Bernie to join him in locating some others of equal ability.

They put an ad in the Long Island *Newsday* and up popped John O'Keefe (39, first tenor) and Bob Thomas (38, lead, formerly of the Fascinations on Sure, who recorded "At Midnight").

All that was missing was a bass, so Pete called his brother George (32), a former member of the Saints on Clifton. Pete's house at 5 Bear Street in Selden, Long Island, became their rehearsal hall. With idols like THE FLAMINGOS, THE MOONGLOWS, THE TEENAGERS, THE HARPTONES, and THE CADILLACS, there was no doubt about the group's musical direction. With a young sound that belied their age, the Exquisites (named after George's favorite phrase, "That sounds exquisite!") set out to perform in local shows.

In 1983 Mike Paccione took over for first tenor John O'Keefe, who joined the TEENCHORDS.

Their first performance was at a Knights of Columbus night with THE COASTERS, THE EARLS, THE BROOKLYN BRIDGE, and two of their idols, the Harptones and the Cadillacs, on March 11, 1984.

In early 1985 they released "Dedicated to the One I Love" (THE SHIRELLES) on Avenue D Records. The next month Avenue D released another Exquisites 45, "At My Front Door" (THE EL DORADOS). The group's reputation as a white doo wop group with an R&B sound began to spread.

Back in 1984 a tape they sent to Don K. Reed's "Doo-Wop Shop" on WCBS-FM in New York (the number one oldies radio station in America) of a new arrangement of "Walking Along" (THE SOLITAIRES) became a regular opening theme for the show and remained one off and on into the '90s.

In 1987 George Santiago, a latter-day ETERNALS member, joined, and Al Pretea (the Dolphins on Shad and Atlas) came on as Paccione left.

In the summer of 1989 the Exquisites backed Gary U.S. Bonds ("Quarter to Three," #1, 1961) on stage at an outdoor concert. In 1990 an LP project was begun with Avenue D president Catabiani, but since Al's company was more singles oriented he turned the project over to an enthusiastic Ed Engel at Crystal Ball Records. (By then Zeke Suarez was on board and Bernie was out.) The LP contained exciting versions of "Bim Bam Boom" (the El Dorados), "This Magic Moment" (THE DRIFTERS), "Never Never" (THE JIVE FIVE), and a version of "Over the Rainbow."

The LP was released in June 1991, and the group kept at it with the Chacona brothers at the helm. When not creating doo wop George was an auto mechanic and brother Pete was a painting contractor. Zeke was a car salesman, as was former Exquisite Bernie. George Santiago was with the Transit Authority and Al was retired from the same organization. Bob Thomas was self-employed in Ronkonkoma, New York, and John O'Keefe was living in Selden, New York.

The Five Boroughs

When five transplanted New Yorkers decided to carry on the tradition of '50s and '60s vocal group harmony in the '80s, South Florida became the instant beneficiary. Miami, Fort Lauderdale, and Broward County in general experienced a heavy influx of immigrants from the northeastern states during the '70s and '80s. Among those easterners were a group of men who, like many of their transplanted neighbors, were in middle age and had grown up listening to the vocal group sounds played on the radio in New York, Philadelphia, Baltimore, Washington, Pittsburgh, and other cities. Unlike their neighbors, this elite group had sung with professional groups in the '60s and were once again drawn together by their common interest, traceable back to the streets of Brooklyn, Queens, Manhattan, the Bronx, and Staten Island—hence, the Five Boroughs.

One day Frank Iovino called a local oldies radio station looking for other like-minded vocalists and was referred to other former doo woppers living in South Florida. From there, word spread and the group grew to unexpected proportions. By the time they rented a rehearsal studio on Johnson Street in Hollywood, Florida in 1986 there were 11 different singers, of which six had sung in recorded groups.

Tony Passalaqua (the Fascinators, Capitol), Jimmy Gallagher (THE PASSIONS, Audicon), Frank Iovino (THE BOB KNIGHT FOUR, Jubilee), Charlie Notabartolo (the Casual-Aires, Mona Lee), Chuck Epstein (THE EXCELLENTS, Blast), Roy Savigliano (THE CHAPERONES, Josie), and the others called themselves Bits and Pieces. Eventually they pared down to a regular five of Iovino (46, baritone), Notabartolo (47, first tenor), Bruce Goldie (46, lead, THE DREAMERS, Cousins), Dave Strum (46, bass, the Excellents, Blast), and Geno Radicello (40, second tenor, the Bowery Boys, My Gang). Bruce, Frank, and Geno each shared lead vocals, and although the middle-aged music men had wives, families, and full-time jobs, they took their harmonizing very seriously.

They practiced several times a week in a Sunrise, Florida, garage and in June 1986 recorded an EP on Telemedia Records that brought synthesizers and drum machines together with doo wop harmonies. The featured songs were "Gloria," with Tony Passalaqua singing lead (and making the group a temporary sextet) and "Don't Say Goodnight" (THE VALENTINES), with Jimmy Gallagher leading as a guest sixth voice.

The single was a decent oldies market seller, and it launched the group onto the club circuit. In 1987 they recorded two a cappella sides, "Sunday Kind of Love" and a medley of "For Your Precious Love"/"For Your Love" for Avenue D Records. Then they went a cappella again with a terrific version of "See You Next Year" (THE CLEFTONES) for a 1988 single.

Not only were their performance opportunities multiplying, they soon found that their versatile

harmonies were in demand as backup for a myriad of '50s and '60s lead singers coming south to perform, like Dion (THE BELMONTS), Carl Gardner (THE COASTERS), Rudy West (THE FIVE KEYS), Lenny Dean (the Rockin' Chairs), Bill Pinkney (THE DRIFTERS), Carlo (the Belmonts), as well as the aforementioned Tony Passalaqua and Jimmy Gallagher.

As the population of Florida increased, so did the interest in having more and more of the old groups perform, so the Five Boroughs found themselves performing with artists like THE CHANTELS, THE VELOURS, THE ROCKETONES, Joey Dee and the Starlighters, THE IMAGINATIONS, THE DEL-VIKINGS, THE HARPTONES, the Drifters, THE ECHOES, and the Toys.

In May 1990 they became the first non-'50s or '60s group signed to Classic Artists Records and issued the doo wop ballad "Apart" followed by "A Kiss from Your Lips" (THE FLAMINGOS).

In 1991 the members included Iovino, Goldie, Strum, and newcomers Soibhan and Brian Daley (formerly backup for Carlo). When not keeping the vocal group sound alive, Frank Iovino was busy as a Broward Sheriffs Office Detention Division Deputy, Bruce Goldie was a real estate agent, Charlie Notabartolo was a meat manager, Dave Strum was a wallpaper hanger, and Geno Radicello was a bartender.

Force M.D.'s

The Force M.D.'s are a hip-hop vocal group from Staten Island, New York, home of THE ELEGANTS and the '80s a cappella group DÉJÀ VU.

Formed in 1979, they carved a niche by not letting their strong vocals be dominated by the heavy electronic production typical of '80s dance music, even though that music made up most of their recorded output. On ballads, they came across with a Philadelphia DELFONICS style.

Its members were Antoine Maurice "T.C.D." Lundy, Stevie "D" Lundy, Trisco Pearson, Lee Daniels, and Charles Nelson.

They started as an a cappella group practicing on the Staten Island Ferry and local street corners. Originally calling themselves Dr. Rock and the M.C.'s, they often performed in that bastion of personal expression, Greenwich Village.

In the early '80s they met former Elegants lead Vito Picone, who became their manager. With influences ranging from THE PERSUASIONS to THE NEW EDITION, the group built a repertoire of original songs and renamed themselves the Force M.D.'s—Force standing for the struggle they faced growing up in New York City and trying to succeed and M.D. meaning Musical Diversity.

In 1984 they signed with Tommy Silverman's Tommy Boy Records, thanks to a sharp-eared New York disc jockey, Mr. Magic, who heard them and brought them to Silverman's attention.

Their first single, a driving dance track with harmonious vocals called "Let Me Love You," reached number 49 R&B in the spring of 1984. It was followed by the Philadelphia '70s-styled soul ballad "Tears," which became their first top 10 R&B single (#5) and reached *Billboard*'s Bubbling Under at number 102.

In 1985 Tommy Boy became associated with Warner Bros. Records, and the group sang "Tender Love" in the film *Crush Groove*, helping it become their biggest hit (#10 Pop, #4 R&B, 1986).

In 1987 they were honored as Best Vocal Group at the New York Music Awards and were voted Most Promising Group at the R&B Awards. They began tours that encompassed the U.S., Europe, and Japan. The group hit number one R&B in 1987 with their "Love Is a House" and followed with a top 10 R&B single "Touch and Go."

In 1991 the act was still turning out vocal-oriented dance music, a pleasant departure from the synthesizer-heavy dance music of that era.

Mixed Company

Formed in 1981, Mixed Company was an offshoot of a popular Jersey City, New Jersey, a cappella group known as the Street-Tones. The quartet consisted of Joseph Santora (first tenor), Jimmy Woods (second tenor), John "Bull" Zielinski (baritone), and John Romano (bass). Their name came from the acknowledged fact that they spent more time practicing on the street than anywhere else. When John's wife came aboard soon after their 1978 forming, they became Patty and the Street-Tones.

Attracted to that mecca of tri-state group singing the U.G.H.A. (United in Group Harmony Association), the group finished in second place on one of the organization's talent nights and was sufficiently impressive to warrant the recording of a single in 1978 titled "Rendezvous with You" (THE DESIRES) b/w "Oh My Angel" (Bertha Tillman) on U.G.H.A. Records.

In 1979 they switched to the Clifton label for a series of four singles that included the Desires' "Let

It Please Be You" and a doo wop version of "Rudolph the Red-Nosed Reindeer."

By 1980 Jeff Chambers of Bayonne had replaced Joe Santora and David Willis had taken over for John Romano on the Clifton sides. The members, though amateurs, had an endearing enthusiasm that enabled them to perform at a number of charity benefits, political fundraisers, and parties.

In June 1980 Clifton released eight of their a cappella sides on a battle of the groups LP titled *Patty and the Street-Tones Meet the Ribitones* (see THE RIBITONES), with the ubiquitous Ronnie Italiano (head of Clifton) standing in the cover photo trying to keep the menacing-looking groups from clashing with each other. The LP did well as a cappella albums go, but in 1981 the group separated.

Mixed Company was born soon after and consisted of four Street-Tones and bass Charles "Cada" Brooks. The addition of Cada, along with the maturity that comes with experience and time to reflect, made for a much more professional sounding and tighter group. Patty's development was the most pronounced; she went from a pleasant doo wopper in the Street-Tones to a soulful singer with a terrific vocal texture in Mixed Company.

Club dates replaced benefits, and they performed at New York's Studio 54 and the China Club along with various clubs on the Jersey Shore.

In 1986 a cappella benefactor Stan Krause of Catamount Records ran into the talented quintet, resulting in the 45 "Are You Ready." Later that year a 13-song LP was cut for Stan featuring nontraditional songs done in harmony style, including Prince's "Purple Rain" (1984) and Hot's "Angel in Your Arms" (1977). The LP *Buzzin' with Mixed Company* did well for an a cappella release, and later that year they got the chance to go to England to promote the LP. The group did several radio shows over there and performed at a London club, the Fridge.

Today, when not singing those soulful harmonies, Jeff Chambers drives a bus and still lives in Bayonne. Cada Brooks is a painter. Jimmy Woods is a truck driver and still resides in Jersey City. John Zielinski is a Jersey City sanitation engineer, and Patty is the mother of their four children.

MIXED COMPANY

A SIDE/B SIDE	LABEL/CAT NO	DATE
Patty and the Street-Tones		
I'm So In Love /		
Wedding Bells	Clifton 37	1980
Let It Please Be You /		
No, No, No	Clifton 49	10/80

A SIDE/B SIDE	LABEL/CAT NO	DATE
Mommy and Daddy /		
Glory Of Love	Clifton 63	1980
Rudolph The Red-Nosed		
Reindeer	Clifton 66	1988
Mixed Company		
Are You Ready	Catamount	1986

New Edition

Labeled THE JACKSON 5 of the '80s, the quintet of Boston adolescents took their bubblegum funk into the hearts of millions—mostly young girls.

Born in a housing project in the Roxbury section of Boston (the same development that Donna Summer was from), a group of five boys began singing Jackson 5 and TEMPTATIONS songs to impress their friends and hopefully make a few dollars.

Bobby Brown (12), Ricky Bell (14), Michael Bivins (13), Ronald DeVoe (14), and Ralph Tresvant (13) formed their group in 1981.

They entered the "Hollywood Talent Night Contest" hoping to win some money for pizza or a movie. They performed against some 80-plus acts and finished second, doing a medley of (what else?) Jackson 5 songs.

Show sponsor Maurice Starr saw the potential for an '80s Jacksons and took them under his wing, recording the group on "Candy Girl" for the independent Streetwise label. It latched onto the R&B charts on April 2, 1983, reaching number one (number 46 Pop) while ironically pushing Michael Jackson and his "Beat It" out of first place. It also reached number one in England.

Proving that the success was not a fluke, their follow-ups "Is This the End" (#8 R&B) and "Popcorn Girl" (#25 R&B) also sent the girls screaming to the shows and record stores.

As is often the case with rapid success, everyone wanted a piece of the teens, and when the smoke and lawsuits had cleared Starr and Streetwise had lost and conglomerate MCA and New Edition had won.

The group came out smoking on MCA in late 1984 with two number ones, "Cool It Now" and "Mr. Telephone Man," and in early 1985 the group was invited to Michael Jackson's house. He advised them to write songs, and sure enough their next LP included several of their own compositions. The hits kept coming through 1986 with "Count Me Out" (#51 Pop, #2 R&B), "A Little Bit of Love" (#38 Pop, #3 R&B), "With You All the Way" (#51

Pop, #7 R&B), and a remake of the 1955 PENGUINS classic "Earth Angel" (#21 Pop, #3 R&B), which brought the group to the attention of a whole new generation of listeners. Of course, the fact that the song was featured in the film *Karate Kid II* helped a great deal as well.

Producer Freddie Perren (Peaches and Herb) produced "Earth Angel" along with a well-conceived LP of such doo wop standards as THE HEARTBEATS' "A Thousand Miles Away," THE MARCELS' "Blue Moon," and THE SKYLINERS' "Since I Don't Have You." On one cut they backed 47-year-old LITTLE ANTHONY on his and the Imperials' 1958 hit "Tears on My Pillow."

Prior to the "Earth Angel" LP Bobby Brown had gone solo, but the group scored with "Helplessly in Love" (from the film *Dragnet*, #20 R&B) and "If It Isn't Love" (#7 Pop, #2 R&B, 1988).

The quartet once again became a quintet in 1988 with the addition of former Wings of Faith vocalist Johnny Gill ("Perfect Combination," #10 R&B, Cotillion, 1984) on lead.

"Can You Stand the Rain" became their fourth number one R&B hit, but by 1990 New Edition's offshoot combinations were doing more and having more success at it than the combined group ever did. From the New Edition emerged Bell, Biv, Devoe, consisting of Ricky Bell, Michael Bivins, and Ronald DeVoe. Their *Poison* LP went to number one R&B, and Ralph Tresvant had a solo LP that went to number five. Johnny Gill's album topped the R&B charts as well. Even ex-Edition member Bobby Brown was doing better outside than inside the group, having sold over six million copies of his *Don't Be Cruel* LP since late 1988, not to mention his 1988 number one hit "My Prerogative" and the 1990 chart-topper "She Ain't Worth It," accompanying Glenn Medeiros.

In 1990 the members of New Edition carried away five number one R&B hits, more than they tallied as a group. But they continued to record as the New Edition (whenever they could get around to it.)

New Kids on the Block

In a short time the New Kids became the most popular teen group in America and probably the world. Maurice Starr, the producer and writer who discovered and nurtured the NEW EDITION, was combing his hometown of Boston for a white teen group to match the popularity of the black Edition. When he couldn't find a completely formed group

Maurice set about piecing one together. Starr searched through Boston's racially mixed inner city neighborhoods in 1984 for singers and rappers who could dance.

15-year-old Donnie "Cheese" Wahlberg was the first to impress Maurice with his rap spontaneity, and he brought in schoolmates Jordan Knight (14) and Danny Wood (15). Jordan then recruited his brother Jonathan (16), and the last member was 12-year-old Joseph McIntyre. All the boys came from large, middle class families. Donnie's dad was a bus driver, the Knight brothers' dad was a minister, and Dan's father was a mailman. Their musical influences were varied: Joe was into Frank Sinatra, Jordan liked THE STYLISTICS, Danny liked Hall and Oates, and Donnie went for Public Enemy.

Calling the group Nynuk, Starr drilled them on harmony and dance while getting them a few local gigs so they could get the feel of an audience before going for a record deal.

They made their national debut on "Star Search." Maurice, with ex-Motown executive Dick Scott, led the Boston boys to Columbia for a record deal in 1985. The title of their first LP is where they got their new name; *The New Kids on the Block* was issued in 1986 but made little noise.

In the summer of 1988 their hit "Please Don't Go Girl" (#10) culminated in a tour with Tiffany, and the *Hangin' Tough* LP took off.

They became the first teen group in history to have five top 10 singles from one LP. Besides "Please" they had "You Got It" (#3, 1988), "I'll Be Lovin' You Forever" (#1, 1989), "Hangin' Tough" (#1, 1989), and "Cover Girl" (#2, 1989). The flip of "Hangin' Tough," the first LP's first flop single, "Didn't I Blow Your Mind," hit number eight on its new outing. When you're hot you're hot.

Part of what gave them such a lock on the 8-to-18-year-old-girl market was their clean-cut image and the consistent anti-drug message they put forth—in sharp contrast to head bangers like Megadeath and angry rappers. No wonder moms across America were thrilled that there was something "safe" to take their kids to hear. The New Kids style was essentially dance tunes with young love lyrics set in a contemporary Motown rhythm.

Their next LP, *Step by Step*, reached number one in two weeks, lifting the group past the mere popularity stage and placing them in the teen-craze category.

Their later singles, "This One's for the Children" (#7, 1989, from their *Merry Merry Christmas* LP), "Step by Step" (#1, 1990), and "Tonight" (#7, 1990) kept the teen stars under the public microscope.

The youngsters' moms banded together to run the group's fan club. In 1991 it was one of the largest in the world, including over 200,000 members. With all the areas of mass media exploitation available in the '90s their income was staggering—a reported $78 million for 1989 and 1990. Through 1991 they sold over 33 million LPs including 1991's *No More Games*. They had their own hit Saturday morning cartoon show on ABC, their own comic book, their videos (3.3 million sold, outdoing even Michael Jackson), and every conceivable merchandising product from T-shirts to lunch boxes, all displaying their five glowing faces.

Until the music industry creates some competition for the Massachusetts idols, the New Kids are likely to continue receiving 30,000 fan letters a week and adding to their numerous hit records.

The Nylons

Three former actors and one ex-PLATTER were the raw material that made up the Nylons, one of the '80s' pleasant surprises. The unlikely combination was formed in Toronto, Canada, in 1979 and included Paul Cooper, Marc Connors, Claude Morrison, and Arnold Robinson.

Paul, Marc, and Claude were all actors working in Toronto's small but thriving theatre scene. When Arnold Robinson of Wilmington, North Carolina, joined up after spending 1968 through 1972 with Sonny Turner's Platters, later known as Sounds Unlimited, the foursome's philosophy was to harmonize a cappella for enjoyment. They began combining doo wop songs, newer pop covers, and their own material. They started singing together at parties thrown by fellow actors, and at one such bash a guest who owned a nightclub heard them and hired them to perform. They spent six weeks there garnering enthusiastic response and rave reviews. They soon came to the attention of Al Mair, president of Canada's most enlightened indie label, Attic Records, and in 1982 the group began working on its concept of a cappella music done with percussion accompaniment only.

Their first LP, titled *The Nylons*, went gold in Canada in just two months. Their second, *One Size Fits All*, was issued in the United States on Open Air Records and its single, the doo wop, pop-jazz-styled "Silhouettes" (THE RAYS), started getting some American radio attention. The group continued to build a following and on one occasion demonstrated particular polish and skill when they appeared in front of 15,000 people at the Ontario

Palace and the sound system failed. They jumped into THE CHIFFONS' "One Fine Day," and the crowd hushed to the point of hearing a pin drop. When the Nylons finished, the audience exploded into a roaring ovation.

Their next LP, 1986's *Seamless*, contained a reworking of THE TOKENS' classic "The Lion Sleeps Tonight." Then came the *Happy Together* LP in 1987 containing their version of Steam's 1969 number one hit "Na Na Hey Hey (Kiss Him Goodbye)." With an a cappella intro at varying tempos, the Nylons launched into three minutes and 23 seconds of possibly the most exciting power-packed harmony and percussion of any record of the '80s. With chime harmony, a floating and bouncing bass, and wall-to-wall vocalizing, they sounded like the DEL-SATINS of the decade. "Na Na" came out in America in the spring of 1987 and reached number 12 nationally.

A follow-up in the Turtles' "Happy Together" reached number 75 Pop, and soon after, the single "Wildfire" was issued in 1987 from the *Rockapella* LP.

In 1990 Paul left and was replaced by Micah Barner. In 1991 the group's live *Four on the Floor* LP was issued; sadly, Marc Connors died before seeing it hit the marketplace. The group then added Billy Newton-Davis of Cleveland.

In 1991 the Nylons' popularity was still growing. They were one of the few groups to bring dominant vocal harmony to the American charts in the 1980s.

Reunion

A harmony quintet, Reunion took the a cappella '60s doo wop tradition and applied it to a repertoire rarely touched by such groups: '70s solo vocalists' hits. Their a cappella settings of contemporary songs (e.g., Billy Vera's "At This Moment" and Tom Waits's "Heart of Saturday Night") differentiated them from the average oldies-only vocal groups of the '80s.

Formed in 1981, the cast included Steve Schmidt (lead), Lou Spinelli (falsetto tenor), Ron Meyer (tenor), Jack Simcsak (baritone), and Dennis Chervenak (bass). Steve, Ron, and Dennis were all members of a one-shot '60s group, the Chime Times ("What's Your Name, Snowflake"), while Jack and Lou sang with the Memos until the late '70s.

The group hailed from Seaside Heights on the Jersey Shore, forming after Ron and Dennis put an ad in a local paper looking for like-minded vocalists. The first contact they received was from Chime Times veteran Steve Schmidt, whom neither Ron nor Dennis had seen in 10 years. Next came Ed Velasquez, who brought along Lou and Steve D'Onofrio. Ed and Steve had also sung with the central Jersey group the Memos in the '70s. The group started out singing strictly for self-gratification, but after an invitation to perform at a local club, self-gratification turned to self-confidence. Considering that the members had been in previous groups and were, to a degree, reuniting, Reunion seemed an apt name.

At their next club date they were spotted by U.G.H.A. President Ronnie Italiano, who invited Reunion to appear at their September 1982 show. At that time Starlight Records company owner Bob Kretchmer saw the quintet and asked them to record for him. Steve had left just before this appearance.

From the start, Reunion came out of left field with two familiar sides that had never been done a cappella before, the relatively recent '70s songs "Lean on Me" (Bill Withers, 1972) and "Drift Away" (Dobie Gray, 1973). Those two songs were released as their first single in December 1982. It was followed by War's 1972 "Slippin' into Darkness" and the Dion song "Heart of Saturday Night" (1978).

In January 1983 Frank Resola replaced Ed, and the group began to concentrate on personal appearances. They cut a path from Harrah's Casino in Atlantic City to the Westbury Music Fair and performed with THE CADILLACS, THE JIVE FIVE, THE CHANNELS, THE EARLS, THE IMPALAS, THE HARPTONES, and THE TYMES.

In 1987 (with Jack Simcsak now in for Frank) they recorded their third single, the 1980 Little River Band song "Cool Change" along with Eric Clapton's 1978 hit "Wonderful Tonight."

Legendary Philadelphia disc jockey Jerry Blavat called their rendition of "Wonderful" the best a cappella recording he had ever heard.

Following the release of "Cool Change," the group appeared on national TV on "Showtime at the Apollo." One of the best-selling a cappella singles of 1988, "Cool Change" led to a Reunion LP on Clifton.

10 years later Reunion was still recording and performing in the tri-state area. They became the only group ever voted Group of the Year three times by the United in Group Harmony Association membership, which numbers over 15,000 national group enthusiasts.

REUNION

A SIDE/B SIDE	LABEL/CAT NO	DATE
Drift Away / Lean On Me	Strlt SR4517	1982
Heart Of Saturday Night / Slipping Into Darkness	Strlt SR4518	1982
Cool Change / Wonderful Tonight	Clftn 45-79	1987
Always On My Mind / Where Are You Tonight	Clftn 45-91	1991

Rockapella

Rockapella is an energetic vocal group that delivers its music straight, with no instruments.

Formed by Sean Altman (second tenor), Elliott Kerman (baritone), and Steve Keyes (first tenor) in 1986 at Brown University, Juilliard alumnus Barry Carl (bass) joined after a stint with the New York City Opera.

With a polished sound veering between doo wop and barbershop, the "awesome foursome" (as the *New York Post* called them) incorporated Motown, '50s R&B, Elvis, and originals into their stage routine.

Practicing in Sean's East Village apartment and on Columbus Avenue street corners, the quartet added parodies of the stars' deliveries to their repertoire and were soon playing New York dinner parties and corporate affairs for companies like IBM, AT&T, Club Med, and Prudential Bache Securities.

One show brought them to the attention of Comic Strip talent scout Lucien Hold, and soon after they were performing at his club and developing new impressions.

With its members ranging from 26 to 34 years of age, Rockapella is a modern day Sha Na Na in spirit, humor, and vocal ability. With the addition of sound effects and choreography, the group has been able to go from a 1950s "Sixty-Minute Man" to a 1970s "Long Cool Woman" and not lose their audience.

In October 1990 they performed on Spike Lee and Company's "Do It A Cappella" for PBS-TV's Great Performances series with Take 6, THE PERSUASIONS, and True Image, among other vocal-only groups. Later that year they recorded their first CD for Elektra Records, including a single of their original, "Zombie Jamboree." In April 1991 Scott Leonard replaced Steve Keyes.

The Winans

Combining spiritual harmonies and street-wise rhythms, the Winans, became the '80s' foremost exponents of crossover gospel. Formed in 1975 in Detroit the four Winan brothers, Carvin and Marvin (twins) along with Michael and Ronald, started singing in their local church. They originally called themselves the Testimonial Singers and were students at Mumford High School when the professional side of the music bug hit them. The twins were 15, Michael was 14, and Ronald was 17 at the time of the basement rehearsals that led to Motor City talent shows and church performances. Their first big performance was with the Hawkins family at the Ford Auditorium in Detroit.

Their powerful and distinctive sound brought them to the attention of the legendary Andrea Crouch, who arranged a recording contract with the gospel label Light Records.

Their first single, "The Question Is," elicited a good radio response, and a 1983 LP *Long Time Coming* followed.

In 1984 the group was spotted by Quincy Jones, who felt their brand of gospel could and should cross over to a wider rhythm and blues audience.

1985 heralded their *Tomorrow* LP, winning them their first Grammy for Best Soul/Gospel Performance. Their single "Let My People Go (Part I)" indicated crossover acceptance when it hit the R&B charts on November 9, 1985, peaking at number 42. Their 1987 LP *Decisions* also earned them a Grammy as did its single with Anita Baker, "Ain't No Need to Worry" (#15 R&B). Their live LP, recorded at Carnegie Hall in 1988, won them yet another Grammy for Best Soul/Gospel Performance. With Siedah Garrett and the Andrea Crouch Choir they backed up Michael Jackson on his number one blockbuster "Man in the Mirror." They teamed with Thelma Houston on the title song from the film *Lean on Me*. Their success continued with the release of the LP *Return* in 1990, featuring performances by Stevie Wonder and Kenny G.

Windsong

Windsong deserves the Croix de Candlestick (an award for sitting through extra innings at windy Candlestick Park, home of the San Francisco Giants) for maintaining a 20-year career without recording a solitary single.

The members were Henry Richard "Dickie" Harmon (lead, first tenor, and second tenor), Anthony Giusto (first tenor and second tenor), Jordan Montanaro (baritone), and Clinton "Jaki" Davis (bass). The teens originally formed when they were 16 and 17 in Hackensack, New Jersey, and regularly played hops and talent shows, including the Fox Theatre, under the name the Bachelors. They sang together off and on for 20 years but never recorded. In the interim, Dickie and Jaki were part of the '60s groups the Connotations ("Before I Go," Technichord, 1962) and the Notations ("Danny Boy," Relic, 1966).

In 1981 the Bachelors, now all in their 30s, continued their singing for fun when they met Jackie Bland, a smooth female vocalist from Hackensack who added the ingredient that sparked the Bachelors to become Windsong, a contemporary doo wop and R&B group in a RUBY AND THE ROMANTICS style. They practiced songs by their individual influences, ranging from THE FLAMINGOS, LITTLE ANTHONY AND THE IMPERIALS, and THE PERSUASIONS to THE DRAMATICS, Carla Thomas, and of course Ruby and the Romantics.

Dickie, who had sung in 1975 with a group on the brink of success, the soul group Strut (the *Time Moves On* LP, Brunswick), did the musical arranging. The group performed at a U.G.H.A. show later.

Ronnie Italiano liked the smooth and powerful harmony blend and recorded four songs on Windsong during 1981. The four tunes included versions of "Young Wings Can Fly," "Lucky Old Sun," "Imagination," and "Canadian Sunset," and all four sides appeared on their one and only EP issued on Clifton Records soon after. The a cappella disk sold well among the collecting community, but having reached their zenith, the group soon went their separate ways. Dickie Harmon, the most serious singer in Windsong, went on to work as a member of the present-day DEL-VIKINGS.

Yesterday's News

One of the best of the '80s a cappella groups, Yesterday's News was formed in 1979 in the Bronx, New York. The original members were Tony Delvecchio (lead and first tenor), Vinnie Gallo (lead and second tenor), Charlie Valentine (baritone), Vito Ferrante (second tenor), and Dennis Elber (lead and bass). Soon after, Vic Spina replaced Ferrante and also sang lead, as did Valentine's replacement Charlie Rocco. Though all had diverse backgrounds and were in their late 20s and

early 30s, the love of '50s and '60s vocal group harmony was the catalyst that brought the five Italians together, usually to rehearse at Tony's house. Tony and Vinnie had previously been in the Jaynells, who recorded "I'll Be Home" in 1963 on Diamond.

When Charlie Valentine moved to Texas the group disbanded but re-formed in early 1980. They found their name in the *Daily News* while looking for the location of an upcoming audition. After tearing apart the current paper they found the information in . . . yesterday's news.

They started practicing old doo wop standards like "Gloria" and "Traveling Stranger" and by 1979 had found their way to the U.G.H.A. label (United in Group Harmony) in Clifton, New Jersey. The quintet recorded the unlikely debut of "The Mickey Mouse Chant." With their fine-tuned street-corner sound down pat, the Bronx bombers performed at their first big show in 1980 at New York's Beacon Theatre with THE SKYLINERS, THE BOBBETTES, THE CHANTELS, THE FLAMINGOS, THE MONOTONES, and VITO AND THE SALUTATIONS.

Unlike many '80s a cappella groups who performed locally and did occasional oldies shows, Yesterday's News performed all over, from Connecticut to as far west as Dallas, Texas. They played in venues large and small, including the Meadowlands Arena in New Jersey, Grossinger's Hotel in upstate New York, the Bottom Line, Studio 54, Tavern on the Green, the World Trade Center, and Harrah's in Atlantic City.

With '80s oldies radio stations open to live performances right in the studio, Yesterday's News helped pioneer the station visit with impromptu gigs at New York's WCBS, WHBI, WGLI, WGLN, and Cousin Brucie's live WCBS radio show.

Yesterday's News often performed as the backup group behind established lead singers who were no longer with their groups or needed a group on short notice. These included '50s legends like Earl Carroll (THE CADILLACS), Willie Winfield (THE HARPTONES), and Vito Picone (THE ELEGANTS), and '60s stars from Eugene Pitt (THE JIVE FIVE) and Lenny Cocco (THE CHIMES) to Emil Stucchio (THE CLASSICS).

Through the '80s, the Bronx quintet (which included bass Joe Incognoli for a time early in that decade) recorded five singles and two LPs, with a third in the works during 1991.

At that time, when not singing, Vinnie was a credit manager, Dennis was a state worker, Charlie managed a trucking firm, Vic worked for the New York City Transit Authority, and Tony was an electrical inspector, also for the Transit Authority.

The "Acappella" Era

"A cappella," according to *Webster's Dictionary*, is singing "without instrumental accompaniment."

In the 1960s, that style, as applied to popular song, became something of a musical phenomenon. One of the reasons had to do with the method groups used to hone their sound. Almost all who sang harmony started out doing it a cappella, whether they were barbershop quartets, gospel or spiritual groups, rhythm and blues singers, or pop groups. First, it helped them to perfect their harmony without musicians or instruments providing a distraction or covering their efforts. Secondly, instruments and people to play them weren't necessarily available, especially for groups who were just practicing or having an impromptu session.

And a lot of groups were out there practicing. As vocal group harmony made a resurgence in the 1940s after radio killed off barbershop quartets (see the introduction to *The 1940s*), thousands and thousands of aggregations nationwide practiced in every imaginable place, from street corners to police stations, and they did it almost exclusively a cappella. They were practicing for the time when they would record and/or perform with musical accompaniment.

But for some the goal began to change. By the early 1960s, due mainly to the efforts of a few record collectors and a middle-aged New York City record store owner, thousands of groups began practicing a cappella with the intention of recording that way.

The evolution of that new *modus operandi* can be traced to preceding years. As vocal group singing became more and more popular in the late 1940s and early '50s, groups all across the nation found ways to record a cappella demos (demonstration recordings) of their songs and get these musical messages to targeted record companies in hopes of being signed to record. Many groups walked their tapes right into company offices to use as acetate auditions.

In 1955, an extremely talented act did a variety of demos in a church cellar in New Haven, Connecticut. Their name: the Nutmegs (see THE NUTMEGS). They went on to have two hits and many quality releases. But the demos lay somewhere in a studio, lost and forgotten.

In 1960, with the birth of the oldies business, two collectors named Wayne Stierle and Don Fileti, along with record company owner Leo Rogers (the Bruce and Tiptop labels), visited New Haven to buy old master tapes for the purpose of reissuing them. They found some great material, but couldn't arrive at a price, and the projected purchase was aborted. Wayne, who had done various deals with Times Square Records owner Irving "Slim" Rose, soon arranged for Slim to buy the recordings. Among these tapes were the no-instrument sides by the Nutmegs. No one dreamed of releasing a cappella cuts back then, but Wayne felt Nutmegs fans would like them, and the quality of the vocals was top-notch. Slim agreed but wanted to give this type of recording a name (like making it his own brand of music). Thumbing through the dictionary he came upon the entry "a cappella." Perhaps feeling it was too European or too difficult for teen fans to pronounce, he rechristened the music "acapella," pronounced *ack*-apella.

In November 1962, Times Square Records' monthly Top 150 chart of its best-selling oldies read " 'A' oldies expected in soon by Times Square Records, for $1.00, most on Times Square labels (in color)." Among the records on that list were the Crests' "No One to Love," Clyde McPhatter and the Dominoes' "These Foolish Things," the Laddins' "Did It," and five Nutmegs releases, all with the added note "(No Music)." Their records were "Why Must We Go to School," "Down in Mexico," "Let Me Tell You," "Out of My Heart," and "You're Crying."

Slim's December 1962 to January 1963 chart of the Top 150 in sales had the word "acapella" printed for the first time, sitting in parentheses next to the number four seller "Let Me Tell You." Number five was another vocals-only classic Slim had picked up from the Standard label of Connecticut, the legendary Five Satins' "All Mine," recorded around the same time as their hit "In the Still of the Night" in 1954 (it was actually on Slim's best seller list as early as April 1962, but as an oddity).

The Nutmegs' recordings, coupled with their catchy phrase for a cappella music, opened the floodgates. Record stores all over the East Coast started getting orders for the Nutmegs' 45s, and oldies stations started playing them as if they were new releases (which in fact they were, even though they'd been recorded eight years before).

More acapella product was needed to meet the demand. Since unearthing old, unreleased acapella recordings by known groups was extremely difficult, and since it was relatively cheap to record a group in this fashion, the call went out from small labels all over for vocals-only recordings.

Street-corner groups and some better-known entities obliged, and soon acts like the Zircons, the Camelots, the Holidays, the Gents, the Five Sharks, the Velvet Angels (actually the Diablos), and the Five Jades were showing up on labels like Catamount, Dawn, Mellomood, Old Timer, Relic, Yussels, Siamese, and a host of others, all led by Times Square. These recordings were judged by different criteria than the previously accepted competitive standard of top 40 radio and chart success. Since millions of people grew up hearing a cappella music in church, for many this was a return to roots with an even more enjoyable type of music. The key was that if you heard it and liked it, it was because of either the group or the unadorned song. If you didn't, it certainly wasn't because of the arrangement, the position on the charts, or the extensive repeat airplay competitive radio required to sell their acts.

Of course, acapella records could not afford to compete with top 40 radio, so no one tried. The groups recorded what they wanted to sing, giving buyers a vast choice of material. Some recorded old standards or relatively recent oldies. Others cut new originals, or even current hits in a naked harmony arrangement (the Temptations' "My Girl" was a popular acapella hit by the Autumns in 1965).

When acapella albums started surfacing in 1964 and early 1965, the spelling of the word (for some inexplicable reason) showed up as "acappella," and that has remained a popular spelling ever since. (For that reason, "acappella" is the spelling used in this section's singing group profiles.)

The following profiles are of many of the groups who recorded either exclusively or predominantly as acappella acts in the 1960s and in some cases beyond. Little is known about many of them, because their companies rarely kept written records. Most of these groups were unable to make a career of it and disappeared after only a few recordings. Still, the phenomenon became a counterbalance for many who rebelled against the less vocally oriented bands of the British invasion and the psychedelic era and the period's endless list of solo soul singers.

The point here is not how successful the acts were (or in most cases weren't). They were part of a movement that was carrying on the vocal group tradition, and without them there would have been a void in the popular music scene of the mid- to late 1960s. Many acts, like the Persuasions, the Five Jades, the Camelots, and the Chessmen could hold their own against any commercially successful "hit" group. If acappella hadn't become popular in the 1960s, many talented performers might never have had a chance to contribute to vocal group history.

The Atlantics

The Atlantics had a smooth and easygoing sound, and unlike most of the day's acappella groups, they recorded only original songs as opposed to known or obscure oldies. The quintet consisted of Eddy Davenport (lead), Eddy Love (tenor), Charlie Gaston (tenor), John Allen (baritone), and Charlie "Cada" Brooks (bass). They formed in 1964 and were from the Jackson Avenue area of downtown Jersey City, New Jersey. The members were veterans of such groups as the Creators, the Vocal Tones, and the Arabians. They had five recordings on the 1966 *New York to L.A., Acappella All the Way* LP.

The Chessmen

The Chessmen had one of the highest profiles of any of the '60s acappella groups. Their label, Relic Records, filled the market with a steady stream of Chessmen singles, LP compilation cuts, and even their own LP.

The group was a product of the Harlem street corners around 166th Street, and they merged their talents into an acappella attraction in 1963. The quintet of three Puerto Ricans and two blacks included James Meyers (lead), William Ramirez (first tenor), Ted Ziffer (second tenor), Tommy Reyes (baritone), and Arthur Crank (bass).

Eddie Gries of Relic discovered the group in December 1964 and immediately recorded four sides, including "Two Kinds of People" (the Imperials), "For All We Know" (the Flamingos), "All Night Long" (the Du Mauriers), and "Heavenly Father" (a variation of the Castelles' version). All four sides were on Relic's historic 20-cut *Best of Acappella Volume 1* LP in January 1965.

Soon after, an original ballad titled "I Apologize" was released as their first single. By March, the 45 was number five on Times Square's Top 100 Sellers, a list that by this time had become to acappella and doo wop releases what *Billboard*'s Top 100 was to national hits (the Times survey was obviously on a miniscule scale by comparison).

The group, whose sound varied from top amateur to occasionally competent professional, featured James Meyers's straining tenor backed by a prominent bass and a tight trio of harmonizers. Their overall impact was not that of a unique or extremely gifted quintet.

Their second single, the jump side "Ways of Romance," did even better than "I Apologize," making it to number two on Times Square's survey.

One side that should have been a single was their acappella showcase LP cut "I Want to Dance," a ballad/mid-tempo track with lots of falsetto and doo wop to thrill the diehards.

The Chessmen became one of the few strictly acappella acts to appear on the Ted Mack show and at the Apollo Theatre. They also played Town Hall in New York City and the Fox Theatre in Hackensack, New Jersey.

Before 1965 ended the group had released six sides on two more Relic *Best of Acappella* releases (Volumes 2 and 5), two more singles, and their own 20-song showcase LP. But by the time 1966 rolled around the group was gone, decimated by the draft.

The act re-formed in 1974 with original lead James Meyers and four new members: Manny Gizz, Babe Pesante, Tommy Grazione, and Richard Ferrar. To date, this contingent of Chessmen has not had any released records.

The Citadels

A very fine white doo wop group residing just north of New York City, the Citadels sounded like a younger version of the Skyliners. All were 16 to 19 years old and included Dennis Ostrom (18) of Orangeburg, New York, on lead; Steve Paglierani (18) of Tappan, New York; Peter Cacciamani (19) of Nyack, New York; and Jane Eckerson (16) of Nanuet, New York. Jane was reportedly the first female to record with a '60s acappella group and did a fine job on the three sides the group did for New Jersey-based Relic Records' *Best of Acappella*

Volume 2 in June of 1965. Amazingly, the sides "When I Woke Up" (the Bop Chords), "When I Fall in Love" (the Flamingos), and "New Love Tomorrow" (written by Paglierani) were recorded only three weeks after the group formed.

Steve and Dennis formed a new group in 1966 called the Vibraharps and recorded three more sides, "Secret Love" (the Moonglows) and the originals "I Hear Bells" and "A Friend" for Relic's *Best of Acappella Volume 6*.

Dennis went on to record as the Blue Sky Boys in 1972 (doing all the harmony parts on a version of the Mellotones' "I'm Just Another One in Love with You").

The Del-Stars

I n the 1960s, most acappella groups were recording their own versions of well-known oldies, and the Del-Stars were no different. But as it turned out, they became the first to have their B-side originals earn more popularity than their A-side standards. The group was a quintet of Queens lads that formed in late 1963. Ronald Elliott (lead), Marvin Sledge (second tenor), and Noel Bynoe (bass) were all from the Woodside projects while Tony Hackley (first tenor) of Long Island City and Ronnie Walker (lead and baritone, brother of Reggie Walker of the Delroys on Apollo) rounded out the group. Discovered by Mellomood Records' Billy Shibilski, who came from the same Woodside neighborhood, the group recorded its first release in early 1964. The top side was a nicely done version of Ed Townsend's "For Your Love," with a continuous descending line in harmony and a talking bridge, giving the song a feel like that of the Diablos' "The Wind." The flip was an original by Elliott titled "Zop Bop," which utilized enough echo and reverberation to make Phil Spector records sound dry by comparison. "Zop," which sounded like it had been recorded in a six-foot-square subway station, immediately grabbed the attention of local oldies radio and became the preferred side for buyers.

A few months later the Del-Stars recorded the Dells' 1957 ballad "Why Do You Have to Go" in a competent version, but once again the B-side original, this one a Tony Hackley tune titled "Who Said You Wasn't Mine," got all the attention. A grammatical dud title-wise, "Who" was nevertheless a perfect street-corner exercise that belonged in the repertoire of any group trying other up-tempo, nonsense-syllable tunes like "I Wonder Why" or "Little Girl of Mine." WNJR radio's Danny Styles had "Who" at number six on his top 100 in 1964, and "Zop Bop" reached number 29.

Whether the group would have continued to record is not known since Mellomood closed down by early 1965, and the Del-Stars never surfaced on another label.

The Destinations

The best-known white acappella group in Philadelphia, the Destinations formed in January 1966. They were a versatile act consisting of Albert "Froggy" Byer (18, lead), Paul "Pinky" Fiore (18, lead and second tenor), Joe Fiore (17, first tenor), Ken Goodman (19, baritone) and Jerry Utter (18, bass). One of the few acappella acts to record for a mainstream pop label, the quintet from the Frankford-Kensington section of Philadelphia had a 45 out on Cameo Records in June 1966 titled "Tell Her" b/w "I'd Rather Be Hurt."

Performing in such exotic local venues as the Polish-American Club, the Ukrainian Hall, and the Paradise Gardens Club, the group had three sides included on the *Philadelphia's Greatest Acappella* LP in 1967.

The Durhams

The Durhams were a white quintet from Upper Darby, Pennsylvania, near Philadelphia. The group formed in the early '60s at Upper Darby High School with the ever-so-black sounding Walt Taylor on lead. When two members dropped out they were replaced by Phil Carey and Artie Wolf, of a rival school group called the Baroques. By graduation time, the quintet's lineup was Walt on lead, Phil on first tenor, Tony Juliano on second tenor, Artie on baritone, and Jimmy Saltzman on bass.

Walt sent a demo tape to Relic Records, which resulted in a marathon, all-night session yielding about 15 acappella songs. Since Artie was army-bound, he was replaced by former Parktowns baritone Lou Ferri.

The group performed at various ballrooms and hotels, while becoming a favorite of radio personality Jerry Blavit.

In 1965, one of their cuts, an unusually contemporary-sounding up-tempo version of the Moonglows' 1955er "Sincerely," was released by Relic. Soon after, three more Durham sides showed up on the October 1965 LP *Best of Acappella Volume 3*, and one more cut surfaced on Relic *Volume 4* ("Adios," the Five Discs) in 1966.

Meanwhile, the group had moved on to soul music thanks to a personnel realignment partially due to the army: Jimmy was drafted. The quartet signed with Ra-Sel Records, owned by Ray Selden, and recorded an R&B ballad called "Girl of the Night." The group now changed its name to the Uptites and made an appearance on Dick Clark's "American Bandstand" (the same day another white soul group called the Temptones appeared, featuring two newcomers named Daryl Hall and John Oates). The group even managed to attract a fan club whose members, ironically, were mostly young black girls. The Uptites' excitement was short-lived; the army seemed to be forming its own vocal group, soon adding Walt to its membership.

In the late 1960s, Walt, Phil, Artie, and Jean Hillary (of the Magistrates' "Here Comes the Judge" fame; see THE DOVELLS) formed a jazz group called New Process. They recorded several sides that were never released. Tony Juliano became a teacher in the Philadelphia public school system; Phil went on to pursue art; Jimmy Saltzman went to work for Schmidt's Brewery; Artie Wolf settled in Philadelphia; and Walt Taylor eventually ran a collection agency in Upper Darby and sang in a band called Philly Gumbo.

The Five Fashions

The Five Fashions were actually a sextet from Stamford, Connecticut, whose members were Frank Erico, Bruce Burdock, Robert Waters, Richard Melesk, Anthony Motylinsk, and Richard Bour. Solid harmony with a mellow feel was their trademark. Another of the Catamount Records contingent, the group, inspired by the Skyliners, had three singles out between late 1964 and 1965 including "Pennies from Heaven" (the Skyliners) b/w "Ten Commandments of Love" (the Moonglows) (#102), "Solitaire" (the Embers) b/w "Over the Rainbow" (#103), and "My Girl" (the Temptations) b/w "Kiss Kiss Kiss" (#107). They also had five cuts included on the *I Dig Acappella* LP, featuring a beautiful version of the Skyliners' "Comes Love" and another Skyliners gem called "This I Swear."

The Five Jades

The Five Jades were one of the premier acappella groups of the '60s. All the boys had been members of professional acts before they came together in late 1964 in the Bronx. Manager John Solari discovered them and brought the quintet to Fordham University's radio station WFUV, where oldies disc jockeys Joe Marchisani and Tom Luciani were so knocked out by the group's sound that they started their own record label (Your Choice) just to record them.

The Five Jades were Spencer Jackson, lead, along with Ray Goodwin, Manny Hernandez, Junior Romann, and Dennis Cerrato. In early 1965, the Five Jades' first single was a recording of the Larks' 1951 classic "My Reverie" backed with an exceptional rendering of the Five Chimes' "Rosemarie" (Betta). By March both sides were at number 25 on Times Square's Top 100 Sellers list. Their next single was an equally strong up-tempo revision of the Cadillacs' "My Girlfriend." With Tony Moreno replacing Ray Goodwin, a 16-song LP was cut that included superb renditions of "That's My Desire" (the Channels) and "I Was Such a Fool" (the Flamingos).

The end of 1965 saw the group in disarray when Jackson, Moreno, and Romann all joined the service. The Five Jades next surfaced on Relic's *Best of Acappella Volume 6* in 1966 with two sides, a very good interpretation of the Isley Brothers' 1960 classic "Shout" (a difficult song to do without instrumentation and still fill up the space), and their first single's B side, "Rosemarie." Strangely, the group didn't have another single until 1972 with "Out of Sight, Out of Mind" (the Five Keys), although some rumors claim the last single on Mellomood Records in 1965, "Don't Say Goodbye" by the Five Shadows, was in fact the Jades.

In 1980 they recorded a pop harmony LP titled *The Past Is in the Future*. Two years later they did half an album, as indicated by the title *Appearing Tonight: Playground and the Five Jades*. With more recorded output in the 1980s than in the '60s, the group added a concept LP to their catalog in 1986. The group now consisted of Dennis Cerrato, Anthony Hernandez, Frank Izquierdo, Alfred Rivera, and Hector Rosado, Jr., singing the album with the longest title of the year, *Velvet Soul for Lovers Only Volume 2, The 5 Jades in Tribute to the Flamingos*. From "At Night" to "Lovers Never Say Goodbye," it was an elegant effort and a fitting tribute to the best vocal group of them all, the Flamingos. But that should have been expected from probably the best of the acappella groups.

Ginger and the Adorables

If the boys could do it, the girls could, too. So in early 1966 the first female acappella group was formed in West Orange, New Jersey—teased bouffant hairdos and all.

Ginger Scaglione (16) sang lead with Jill Tordell (16, first tenor), Gail Haberman (14, second tenor), and baritones Marlane Esser (14) and Mary Tiffany (16).

Record producer Wayne Stierle heard the group practicing at a candy store in West Orange, New Jersey, and brought them to Relic Records, where they recorded their one and only release, a cover of the Chantels' "He's Gone" on *The Best of Acappella Volume 4* in 1966.

The Holidays

One of the best of the '60s acappella aggregations, the Holidays exhibited street-corner savvy with an exciting white pseudo-soul sound. Part of the group, Michael Wendroff and Steve Baron, started out in the Brooklyn quartet the Night Lords in 1961. Steve then moved to Rockaway and Mike went out to visit on occasion. It was on one of these visits that the boys met three Rockaway High School students who were singing on the boardwalk at 35th Street in the summer of 1964. The five began harmonizing and decided to form a group. The lineup became Mike Wendroff on lead, Dennis Spinelli on first tenor, Steve Baron (of Brooklyn Technical High School) on second tenor, Larry Sorica on baritone, and Dave Rossman on bass.

The quartet ranged from 17 to 19 years of age at the time, and Thomas Jefferson High Schooler Wendroff recalls that it was one of the boys' mothers who came up with the name the Holidays for the group. The boys practiced everywhere, from Larry's house in Far Rockaway to under the 35th Street boardwalk. The resulting acappella sound was so full that instrumental backing was never even considered. They rehearsed songs like "Coney Island Baby" (the Excellents), "Sunday Kind of Love" (the

Harptones), and "Over the Rainbow" (the Del-Vikings), and Michael remembers they were heavily influenced by Little Anthony and the Imperials.

Feeling confident and ready, the group barged into Times Square Records for an impromptu audition for the proprietor, Irving "Slim" Rose. After hearing two songs ("Summertime" from *Porgy and Bess* and an original titled "Chant of the Isles") sung acappella right in the store, Slim pulled a contract out from under the table and signed them on the spot.

The Holidays recorded several sides at Sanders Recording soon after, but strangely, Slim never issued them. When he sold his label masters to Eddie Gries at Relic Records, the Holidays' recordings became part of the package.

In 1965, their first and only single, the standard "Summertime" done in an eerie "So Blue" style (the Vibrations, 1959, and the Vitones, 1965) and backed with an energetic up-tempo version of the Skyliners' "This I Swear," came out on Relic. Soon after, the Holidays had five more of the Slim-produced sides included on Relic's *Best of Acappella Volume 2*, including the beautiful "Chant of the Isles," "Adios" (the Five Discs), and another Skyliners classic, "It Happened Today."

Their vocal arrangements were refreshing and daring, as in their vibrant, up-tempo version of the time-honored standard ballad "Time after Time."

In September 1965, Mike Wendroff went on to Queens College, and with no lead singer, the group soon disbanded.

In 1973, the Holidays' lead recorded a solo single for Buddah Records titled "Only a Fool Fools with Love." In 1978 he recorded the pop-rock Ariola Records LP *Kiss the World Goodbye*, which maybe not so coincidentally contained an original song written by Mendroff titled "Time after Time."

As of this writing Dave still lives in Rockaway, Larry's and Dennis's whereabouts are unknown, Steve is an electrician in Rockaway, and Mike is a cab driver living in Brooklyn with his wife and two children.

Little Joe and the Majestics

A Hispanic group from New York City, Little Joe and company had an excellent feel for Students and Teenagers types of songs, with a high lead tenor and a young teen sound. The members were Little

Joe Rivera (12, lead), Jose Luis Torrez (20, first tenor), Albert Diaz (19, second tenor), Luis Hernandez (19, baritone), and Leoncio Rosado (19, bass).

Their Spanish-language recording of "Ave Maria" on the LP *The Best of Acappella Volume 4* in 1966 was the first known acappella release in a foreign tongue.

They also recorded two more notable sides, "I'm So Young" and "Every Day of the Week" (the Students), for that LP, and "Twilight" (the Paragons) and "This Magic Moment" (the Drifters) for *Volume 5* that same year before passing into unfortunate obscurity.

The Lytations

The Lytations had the distinction of being given a name later in their careers that no disc jockey could legally say on the air, thus killing any chance of their records being exposed. The group formed in Ardmore, Pennsylvania, in 1962 and included Jack Strong (16, lead), Frank Torpey (17, first tenor), Bob Bintliff (19, second tenor), Ken Harper (19, baritone), and Bill Giangiulio (18, bass). Practicing songs like "Just Two Kinds of People" (the Imperials), "Zoom, Zoom, Zoom" (the Collegians), and "Wizard of Love" (the Lydells) on Bill's enclosed porch, the group started out as the Kaptions and recorded their first songs, "Dreaming of You" and "I Know Somewhere," at Sound Plus Studios on Harbison Avenue in northeast Philadelphia during 1962. They took the sides to Ham-Mil Distributors at 1520 North Broad Street in Philadelphia, and owner Bill Hamilton arranged to rerecord the songs for his Ham-Mil label. These sides came out with instrumental backing in early 1963. The Kaptions appeared at Atlantic City's Steel Pier with the Sensations and then went on to make some acappella recordings during 1963-64 with Val Shively, the hippest oldies dealer in the Philadelphia area. The Kaptions renamed themselves after parts of three groups the young quintet admired, the *Ly*dells, the Quo*tations*, and the Imagina*tions*.

In late 1964, their first single, an up-tempo version of "Over the Rainbow," found its way to the marketplace via Time Square Records. Not surprisingly, it charted on Time Square's Top 150 Survey, but surprisingly, it reached number two and stayed around for many months. What set their next record ("Dreaming of You") and its follow-up apart from almost all doo wop group singles then and into the future was the name given to the

Lytations by Shively in an uncontrolled fit of humor. The group was now "The Five Shits (formerly the Miracles)" according to the yellow label that also depicted a dog excreting on top of a lamp post in a not-too-subtly demeaning reference to Philadelphia's Lost Night label (Lost Night had yellow labels and a lamp post logo like the one being defaced). The label's name was Lost Cause, and Shively's lampooning extended beyond the label art; the credits read, "Produced by Elvis Presley, arranged by 'Flush' Boone in part. . . . Recorded at Lefferts Toilet (with the lid up)." Some of the writers he credited on the song (none of whom actually had anything to do with this) were P. Spector, J. Leiber, M. Stoller, L. Silvani, B. Diskin, W. Stierle, E. Gries, C. King, G. Goffin, and R. Nixon. Assuming the first names are Phil, Jerry, Mike, Lou, Bob, Wayne, Eddie, Carole, Gerry, and Richard, it is not likely Mr. Shively endeared himself to those people. In a further slap at conventional form, the publishing credits included "Jobete, Screen Gems, Assorted Music (BMI, ASCAP, SPCA, GEICO, NAACP, WPA)," which translated means, "if anybody sees a cent from this they're lucky." (Try getting your record played on American radio with that as your calling card.)

Their last single, also as the Five Shits on a fake yellow-and-black Chance label (the real Chance Records—a legendary R&B label—had been out of business for years), was a good up-tempo street-corner acappella original called "Stormy Weather."

In 1966, Jack joined the navy and the group disbanded. Jack later became a carpenter, Bill went into renovations, Bob became an accountant, Ken got into the roofing business, and Frank became an auto mechanic. In 1991, Val Shively was still running an oldies emporium, doing mail-order business out of Upper Darby, Pennsylvania, and occasionally even putting his phone on the hook.

The Potentials

Another of Philadelphia's teenage groups, the Potentials didn't really have any, but to leave out a group that was the featured performer at the 1967 Banquet for Commissioner Salvatti, Head of the Fraternal Order of Police, would be criminal. Then again, so were their interpretations of "The Letter" (the Medallions) and "She Cried" (Jay and the Americans) that were included on Pantomime Records' acappella compilation LP in that same year. The group formed in December 1966 and

consisted of Mike Garbesi (20, lead), Rocky Colucci (19, first tenor), Frank Corchetto (21, second tenor), and Paul Galasso (16, bass).

The Potentials were sometimes referred to as the City Hall Singers because of the quartet's penchant for practicing on the 15th Street side of City Hall on Market Street in Philadelphia.

The Regencies

From the Camden, New Jersey, area, this quintet of white teens was good enough to be the only non-Philadelphia group to get on the *Philadelphia's Greatest Acappella* LP in 1967. They formed in January of that year and had the flexibility to go from a Duprees sound on "Bewitched, Bothered, and Bewildered" to an Earls styling on "Don't Stop."

The group attended Trighton Regional High School in Runnemede, New Jersey, and consisted of Pete Carboni (19, lead), Bill Jerome (19, first tenor), Tony Stanza (18, second tenor), John Divetro (18, baritone, lead on their "Bewitched" recording), and Ed Scaduto (18, bass).

The Savoys

A better-than-average group, the five Italian lads known as the Savoys hailed from the Newark, New Jersey, area, on the outskirts of Branch Brook Park at Steven Crane Village. The members were John Faliveno, Joseph Castellano, Angelo Basilone, Joseph Stefanelli, and Sam Monaco.

They performed more than most mid-'60s acappella acts, doing shows at a variety of sites from Fairleigh Dickinson University to the Casino at Seaside on the Jersey Shore.

Their first single was 1964's "Vision of Love," a Duprees-styled 45 with instrumental backing by the Duponts and a rocking version of the Kodaks' "Oh Gee, Oh Gosh" on the flip. Their second single for New Jersey's Catamount label was "Gloria" (the Cadillacs) b/w "The Closer You Are" (the Channels) done acappella. "Gloria" was arranged in a smooth yet powerful Passions style and was one of 1964's best-selling acappella singles, reaching number three on Danny Styles's radio show survey. Their unique up-tempo arrangement of "The Closer You Are," done in a lively "I'm So Happy" vein (the Ducanes), reached number 23 on Times Square's record sales survey in March 1965.

The Savoys became a staple of the Catamount label through 1965 with singles like "If You Were Gone from Me" and "When I Fall in Love." "Gloria" wound up on Relic Records' January 1965 first *Best of Acappella* compilation (a series of seven LPs that would eventually become the dominant contributor to the mid-'60s vocals-only craze). Also in 1965 the Savoys added four sides to the *I Dig Acappella* LP for Cat-Time, including their previous two singles and "A Lovely Way to Spend an Evening" (the Angels) b/w "Zoom, Zoom, Zoom" (the Collegians).

The Versailles

Little is known of this competent group formed sometime in the mid-'60s. Joe, Noar, George, and Harvey Shaplow (he formerly of Ritchie and the Revelations) were from the Marble Hill projects in the Bronx, New York. The white quartet recorded the disc "Little Girl of Mine" (the Cleftones) b/w "Teenager's Dream" (the Kodaks) for Harlequin Records in 1965 and also cut the singles "I'm in the Mood for Love" (the Chimes) b/w "Lorraine" and "Cecelia" for the Old Timer label that same year. Soon after, they recorded "Church Bells May Ring" (the Willows), "One Summer Night" (the Danleers), and "To the Aisle" (the Five Satins) for Stan Krause and Robert Miller's Cat-Time compilation LP *I Dig Acappella*.

The Young Ones

From Brooklyn, New York, the Young Ones were of Hispanic extraction. They managed to sustain enough interest in themselves to wind up on three different predominantly acappella labels in the mid-'60s.

The 1965 lineup featured Eddie Naveraz (18) on lead, Steve Barrientas (18) on first tenor, Edgar Hernandez (20) on second tenor, and Joe Leone (18) on baritone.

Formed in 1963, the quartet recorded three singles that same year for Joe Shulman's Yussels Records of Newark, New Jersey, with "Diamonds and Pearls" (the Paradons) the particular standout. With a style and sound similar to the Passions, the

Young Ones next recorded some sides that wound up on Times Square's label in 1964. Their best-known and most popular singles were "Gloria" (the Cadillacs) and "Sweeter Than" (the Passions).

When Relic Records bought Times Squares' catalog, they chose a few of what they considered to be the best of Times Square's single releases for reissue, and so it was that in 1965 "Gloria" and "Sweeter Than" found their way on to the market again.

The Young Ones also recorded three sides for Relic's *Best of Acappella Volume 2* LP and then faded from the scene.

The Zircons

The Zircons had one of the more interesting ethnic combinations on the acappella scene in 1963, including three Italians, one African American, and a Polish lead singer. The members were Jimmy Gerenetski (lead), Neil Collelo, John Loiacano, Kenneth Pulicino, and Donald Lewis. The quintet was from that predominantly Italian slice of East Harlem between 110th and 120th Streets bounded by First and Second Avenues.

They formed in the fall of 1963, becoming one of the first of the new acappella groups. Record collector Sal Donnarumma discovered the uptown teens and brought their two recordings to associate Billy Shibilski, who was coincidentally about to start his own label named after his favorite group, the Mello-Moods. Gerenetski's vocals were reminiscent of Jimmy Beaumont of the Skyliners, so it's no surprise that one of their two recordings was a beautifully smooth and strong rendition of the Skyliners' "Lonely Way." The flip, a version of the Heartbeats' "Your Way," was backed with music and normally would have been the A side, but "Lonely Way" was so good that tri-state radio began playing it almost exclusively in November 1963 and it became the top-selling acappella single of 1964. An early 1964 "Danny Styles' Kit Kat Club" radio survey (WNJR New Jersey) had it listed as number 18, but it surely went higher on subsequent charts. That makes it all the more surprising that the group, according to Shibilski, never recorded again. (These Zircons, by the way, should not be confused with the same-named Bronx group that recorded for Old Timer records later in 1964 and who were led by Mario Ibanez.)

Photo Credits

COVER (clockwise from top left): The Merry Macs, courtesy of Carolyn McMichael; The Bangles, photo by Randee St. Nicholas, courtesy of Sony Music, Inc. and Stiefel/Phillips Management; The Four Seasons, photo by Maurice Seymour, courtesy of Bob Gaudio and The Four Seasons Partnership; The Hi-Los, courtesy of Gene Puerling; The Hollywood Flames, courtesy of White Castle Productions Inc.; The Pointer Sisters, courtesy of Motown Record Co., L.P. Archives; The Crests, courtesy of Dr. John Stalberg; The Signatures (on back cover), courtesy of Bob Alcivar.

THE 1940s: The Ames Brothers, courtesy of Bernadette Moore, RCA Archives; The Andrews Sisters, courtesy of Maxene Andrews; The Delta Rhythm Boys, photo by James J. Kriegsmann, courtesy of MCA Records; The Four Vagabonds, photo by Mitchell J. Hamilburg, courtesy of Dr. John Stalberg; The Ink Spots, photo by James J. Kriegsmann, courtesy of MCA Records; The Merry Macs, courtesy of Carolyn McMichael; The Mills Brothers, courtesy of MCA Records; The Modernaires, courtesy of Bill Tracy and Paula Kelly, Jr.; The Skylarks, courtesy of Gilda Maiken Anderson; The Soul Stirrers, courtesy of Dr. John Stalberg.

THE 1950s: The Chantels, courtesy of White Castle Productions Inc.; The Chordettes, photo by James J. Kriegsmann, courtesy of Herbie Cox; The Crests, courtesy of Dr. John Stalberg; The Criterions, courtesy of Tim Hauser; The Dells, courtesy of Dr. John Stalberg; The Del-Vikings, courtesy of Dr. John Stalberg; The Dubs, courtesy of Dr. John Stalberg; The Five Keys, courtesy of White Castle Productions Inc.; The Five Satins, photo by James J. Kriegsmann, courtesy of Dr. John Stalberg; The Flamingos, courtesy of Zeke Carey; The Jaguars, courtesy of Val Poliuto; The McGuire Sisters, courtesy of Phyllis McGuire; The Moonglows, photo by Popsie Randolph, courtesy of the Village Music, Inc. Collection; The Paragons, courtesy of Dr. John Stalberg; The Platters, courtesy of the Richard Nader Collection; Maurice Williams and the Gladiolas, courtesy of Maurice Williams.

THE 1960s: The Beach Boys, courtesy of Dr. John Stalberg; The Carolons, courtesy of White Castle Productions Inc.; The Crystals, photo by Bruno of Hollywood, courtesy of Dr. John Stalberg; The Del-Satins, courtesy of Les Cauchi, The Del-Satins; The Demensions, photo by Bruno of Hollywood, courtesy of Lenny Dell; The Belmonts, photo by James J. Kriegsmann, courtesy of Dr. John Stalberg; The Dovells, photo by James J. Kriegsmann, courtesy of Dr. John Stalberg; The Four Seasons, photo by Maurice Seymour, courtesy of Bob Gaudio and The Four Seasons Partnership; The Highwaymen, courtesy of Steve Trott and Ken Greengrass; The Lettermen, photo by Cliff Kalick, courtesy of Tony Butala; The Mamas and the Papas, courtesy of MCA Records; The Marcels, courtesy of Dr. John Stalberg; Martha and the Vandellas, courtesy of Motown Record Co., L.P. Archives; The Miracles, courtesy of Motown Record Co., L.P. Archives; The Orlons, courtesy of Stephen Caldwell, Sr.; Peter, Paul and Mary, courtesy of Martha Hertzberg, Ken Fritz Management; Reparata and the Delrons, courtesy of Reparata Mazzola; The Shirelles, courtesy of Dr. John Stalberg; The Supremes, courtesy of Motown Record Co., L.P. Archives; The Temptations, courtesy of Shelly Berger, Star Directions Inc.; The Tokens, courtesy of Phil Margo.

THE 1970s: Crosby, Stills and Nash, photo by Henry Diltz, courtesy of Larry Richard, Legends Publishing; The Jackson 5, courtesy of Motown Record Co., L.P. Archives; Lady Flash, courtesy of Reparata Mazzola; The Manhattan Transfer, courtesy of Tim Hauser; The Osmonds, courtesy of Olive Osmond; The Persuasions, courtesy of Glen Knight, Headline Talent, Inc.; The Pointer Sisters, courtesy of Motown Record Co., L.P. Archives; Sister Sledge, courtesy of Adam White; The Village People, courtesy of Talent Consultants International Ltd.

THE 1980s: The Bangles, photo by Randee St. Nicholas, courtesy of Sony Music and Stiefel/Phillips Management; Big Daddy, courtesy of Marty Kaniger; The Bobs, courtesy of Scott O'Malley and Associates; DeBarge, courtesy of Motown Record Co., L.P. Archives; En Vogue, photo by Reisig and Taylor, courtesy of Outline; Force M.D.'s, photo by Stephen Aucoin, courtesy of Barbara Frongello; New Edition, courtesy of Ron Shapiro, MCA Records Archives; The Nylons, courtesy of Wayne Thompson; Rockapella, photo by Dan Lenore, courtesy of Sean Altman; The Winans, photo by Mike Jones, courtesy of Carolyn Baker, Warner Brothers Records.

About the Author

Jay Warner was born and raised in Brooklyn, New York. He started playing piano at age seven and guitar in his late teens. Although he was playing concerts by age nine, his classical career (and lessons) came to an abrupt halt at the age of 15, when his mother caught him playing jazz riffs—to "Moonlight Sonata."

While still in his teens, he took on the subject of music history, writing his first work, ambitiously titled *The History of Rock & Roll, 1954–1963* (Crystal Publications).

Jay entered the music business in 1970, joining Record on Film Company, where he learned publishing and administration while working on the development of promotional music clips for record companies (the forerunners of today's music videos).

In 1972 Jay joined Sidney Seidenberg (manager of Gladys Knight and the Pips and B. B. King) as assistant to the president, handling the music catalogs of Neil Diamond, Jeff Berry, Ellie Greenwich, and Gene McDaniels.

By 1973, desirous of a full-time publishing career, Jay convinced Wes Farrell Organization vice president Steve Bedell that he could help their company. He started as a professional manager, and three and a half years later was vice president of Farrell's publishing empire. In 1976 he was relocated to the company's Los Angeles headquarters.

In 1977, on a dare, Jay wrote the definite text on songwriting and music publishing: *How To Have Your Hit Song Published* (Hal Leonard Publications). It was the first in-depth volume ever written, dealing entirely with the publishing and songwriting industry. The best-seller has been in print for 22 years and is in its fifth edition. The same year, Jay became vice president at the Entertainment Company (the forerunner of SBK EMI) and began by organizing and running their West Coast base.

During 1979 Jay was elected to the ASCAP advisory board. He was also the recipient of the American Song Festival's "Ears of the Year" award. Then, in 1980, he received the award for an unprecedented second time!

In 1980 Jay became the founder and president of the Creative Music Group, the worldwide publishing arm of the K-Tel International organization. He established an in-house network of publishing operations in 22 countries, a first for independent publishers. He also developed one of the first internal divisions in America devoted to the full-time pursuit of music coordination of films and music administration for such movies as *Halloween*, *Fade to Black*, and *The Deer Hunter*. When Warner took over the Avco Embassy Pictures catalog, CMG became the first independent music publishing company to administer the music rights for an entire major film operation.

In 1983 Jay put his experience to the test, forming his own company, the Jay Warner Music Group. From the outset it was a chart-topping success, with acquisitions like that of Rick James, Lakeside, and Larry Graham. Continuing his involvement with film, he coordinated the music and administered music for films such as *Inchon* with Sir Lawrence Olivier, *Jimmy the Kid* with Gary Coleman, *Evita Peron*, and *The Mac* with Richard Pryor. Within a year and a half of its establishment, Jay's company racked up 14 hit singles and 7 chart albums. One of his companies was named the number two independent publisher of 1983 by *Billboard* magazine, behind perennial leader Jobete Music.

In mid-1984, Warner merged his company with the Music Group and became president of the combined publishing organization, where he successfully oversees operations to this day.

Through his years as a publisher, Jay has worked with many diverse writers and catalogers, including Barry Manilow, Bruce Springsteen, Rick James, Jimmy Webb, Johnny Rivers, Carol Sager, the Rascals, Bob Gaudio (Four Seasons), Ellie Greenwich, REO Speedwagon, the Commodores, the Emotions, Steppenwolf, Lakeside, Ben Weisman (writer of 57 Elvis Presley songs), Levine and Brown (writers of most of Tony Orlando's hits), Jim Weatherly ("Midnight Train to Georgia"), Scott and Dire ("Sky High"), Bruce Roberts ("Enough Is Enough" by Streisand and Summer), Kenny Nolan ("Lady Marmalade" and "My Eyes Adored You"), Alan Gordon ("Happy Together"), Dobie Gray ("Drift Away"), and many others. He published songs recorded by artists ranging from Elvis and Streisand to Springsteen and Whitney Houston.

Having built a successful career, the six-time Grammy winner with over 120 Top 40 hits (Warner most recently won a Grammy for the number one hit "U Can't Touch This" [Hammer]) decided to expand his musical horizons.

In 1989 Jay wrote, produced, and hosted the uniquely conceptualized "oldies" show *The Time Machine*, which debuted on Los Angeles's major radio station, KGFJ. Its long-running success convinced Jay to write, produce, and host a video version, which began its TV run in 1993 on United Artists Cable. The same year, Warner's epic musical mosaic, *The Billboard Book of American Singing Groups* (Watson-Gutill)—a first-ever history of vocal groups from the 1940s through 1990—was published. During 1996 Jay was elected to the board of the Vocal Group Hall of Fame. In 1997 he wrote another best-seller, *Billboard's American Rock 'n' Roll In Review* (Schirmer/Simon & Schuster), endorsed on the back and inside cover pages by 37 major stars from Neil Diamond to the Beach Boys.

Jay and his wife Jackie reside in Los Angeles, along with their beloved dogs, a cairn terrier named Napoleon, mother-and-son cocker spaniels Cindy and Teddy, and yodeling yorkies Silkie and Sun.